A Dictionary of Archaic and Provincial Words, Obsolete Phrases, Proverbs, and Ancient Customs, from the Fourteenth Century, Volume 2

James Orchard Halliwell-Phillipps

DICTIONARY

OF

ARCHAISMS AND PROVINCIALISMS.

VOL. II.

A

DICTIONARY

OF

𝕬𝖗𝖈𝖍𝖆𝖎𝖈 𝖆𝖓𝖉 𝕻𝖗𝖔𝖛𝖎𝖓𝖈𝖎𝖆𝖑 𝖂𝖔𝖗𝖉𝖘,

OBSOLETE PHRASES, PROVERBS, AND ANCIENT CUSTOMS,

FROM THE FOURTEENTH CENTURY.

BY

JAMES ORCHARD HALLIWELL, ESQ., F.R.S.,

Honorary Member of the Royal Irish Academy; Corresponding Member of the Royal Society of Northern
Antiquaries, of the Society of Antiquaries of Scotland, of the Archæological Society of Stockholm, and the
Reale Academia di Firenze; Honorary Member of the Royal Society of Literature, of the Newcastle
Antiquarian Society, of the Royal Cambrian Institution, of the Ashmolean Society at Oxford, and of the
Society for the Study of Gothic Architecture; Fellow of the Society of Antiquaries; Corresponding
Member of the Comité des Arts et Monuments, &c. &c.

IN TWO VOLUMES.

VOL II. J—Z.

𝕾𝖎𝖝𝖙𝖍 𝕰𝖉𝖎𝖙𝖎𝖔𝖓.

LONDON:

JOHN RUSSELL SMITH, 36, SOHO SQUARE.

MDCCCLXVIII.

DICTIONARY

OF

ARCHAISMS AND PROVINCIALISMS.

JA. A tenon for a mortise. *West.*

JABBER. To talk nonsense. *Var. dial.*

JABELL. A term of contempt, more usually applied to a woman than to a man.

JACE. A kind of fringe. *Devon.*

JACK. (1) A figure outside old public clocks made to strike the bell. It was also called Jack of the Clock, or Clock-house. Till a very recent period, the clock of St. Dunstan's church was furnished with two of these jacks. Dekker gives the phrase to a company of sharpers. See his Lanthorne and Candle-Light, ed. 1620, sig. G. " Strike, like Jack o' th' clock-house, never but in season," Strode's Floating Island, sig. B. ii. *Jacks*, the chimes, Hallamsh. Gloss. p. 53.

(2) A coat of mail; a defensive upper garment quilted with stout leather. The term was more latterly applied to a kind of buff jerkin worn by soldiers; and a sort of jacket, worn by women, was also so termed. See Reliq. Antiq. i. 41 ; Collier's Old Ballads, p. 7. *To be upon their jacks*, i. e. to have the advantage over an enemy.

(3) A whit. *Somerset.*

(4) Half, or a quarter of a pint. *North.* Perhaps from *Black-Jack*, q. v. It also has the same meaning as black-jack, as in the Troubles of Queene Elizabeth, 1639, sig. C. ii.

(5) To beat. *Craven.*

(6) The knave of cards. *North.*

(7) The male of an animal. *West.*

(8) A farthing. An old cant term.

(9) A kind of water-engine, turned by hand, used in mines. *Staff.*

(10) An ape. Hence, a young coxcomb; a sly crafty fellow; a man of any description.

(11) *Jack-at-a-pinch*, a sudden unexpected call to do anything. Also, a poor parson. *Jack-at-warts*, a little conceited fellow. *Jack of the wad*, an ignis fatuus. *Jack in the basket*, a sort of wooden cap or basket on the top of a pole to mark a sand-bank, &c. *Jack in the box*, an irreverent name for the Sacrament. *Jack with the lanthorn*, an ignis fatuus. *Jack of all trades*, one who has a smattering knowledge of all crafts. *Jack by the hedge*, the herb sauce-alone. See Gerard, p. 650. *Jack of long legs*, the summer fly generally called daddy-long-legs. *Every Jack-rag of them*, every person in the party. *Jack in office*, an insolent fellow in authority. *Jack nasty face*, a common sailor. *Jack of Dover*, some article mentioned in the Canterbury Tales as having been sold by the cook, but its precise nature has not been ascertained. *Jack-in-the-green*, a man inside a small house made of flowers and evergreens, who carries it in the procession of the sweeps on May-day morning.

JACK-ADAMS. A fool. *Var. dial.*

JACK-A-DANDY. A pert smart little impertinent fellow. *North.*

JACK-A-LEGS. A large clasp knife. Also, a tall long-legged man. *North.*

JACK-A-LENTS. Stuffed puppets which used to be thrown at during Lent. See Cleaveland's Poems, 1660, p. 64. It is a term of reproach in various instances, as in the Bride, by Nabbes, 4to. Lond. 1640, sig. G. ii. In the West of England the name is still retained for a scarecrow, sometimes called *jaccomite.*

JACK-AN-APES. An ape. See Fletcher's Poems, p. 190. Now used for a coxcomb.

JACK-A-NODS. A simple fellow. *North.*

JACK-BAKER. A kind of owl. *South.*

JACK-BARREL. A minnow. *Warw.*

JACK-BOOTS. Large boots coming above the knees, worn by fishermen. *Var. dial.*

JACK-DRUM. See *Drum* (3), and Topsell's Historie of Serpents, 1608, p. 262.

JACKED. Spavined. A *jacked* horse.

JACKET. A doublet. Sometimes, the upper tunic; any kind of outer coat.

JACKEY. English gin. *Var. dial.*

JACK-HERN. A heron. *I. Wight.*

JACK-IN-BOX. A sharper who cheated tradesmen by substituting empty boxes for similar looking ones full of money. *Dekker.*

JACK-LAG-KNIFE. A clasped knife. *Glouc.*

JACK-MAN. (1) A cream-cheese. *West.*

(2) A person who made counterfeit licenses, &c. Fraternitye of Vacabondes, p. 4.

JACK-NICKER. A goldfinch. *Chesh.*

JACK-PLANE. A coarse plane. *North.*

JACK-PUDDING. A buffoon attendant on a mountebank. See Jones's Elymas, 1682, p. 7; Brand's Pop. Antiq. i. 81.

JACK-ROBINSON. *Before one could say Jack Robinson,* a saying to express a very short time, said to have originated from a very volatile gentleman of that appellation, who would call on his neighbours, and be gone before his name could be announced. The following lines "from an old play" are elsewhere given as the original phrase,—

> A warke It ys as easie to be doone,
> As tys to saye, *Jacke I robys on.*

JACK-ROLL. The roller for winding the rope in a draw-well. *North.*

JACKS. (1) The turnip fly. *Suffolk.*

(2) The servitors of the University.

JACK'S-ALIVE. A game, played by passing round and twirling a match or lighted paper, and he in whose hand it dies, pays a forfeit. Moor mentions it, p. 238.

JACK-SAUCE. An impudent fellow. It occurs in How to Choose a Good Wife, 1634.

JACK-SHARP. A prickleback. Also called *Jack-Sharpling,* and *Jack-Sharpnails.*

JACKSON. A silly fellow. *East.*

JACK-SPRAT. A dwarf. *Var. dial.*

JACK-SQUEALER. The swift. *Salop.*

JACK-STRAW. The black-cap. *Somerset.*

JACK-WEIGHT. A fat man. *Var. dial.*

JACOBIN. A grey friar.

JACOB'S-STAFF. A mathematical instrument used for taking heights and distances.

JACOB'S-STONE. A stone inclosed in the coronation chair, brought from Scotland by Edward I. where it was regarded with superstitious veneration. See Hentzner's Travels, p. 252; Heywood's Royall King, sig. A. iv.

JACOUNCE. A jacinth. Skelton, ii. 18.

JACU. The cry of the pheasant.

JADDER. (1) Shaky; infirm. *East.*

(2) A stone-cutter. *Glouc.*

JADY. A term of reproach. *Shak.*

JAG. (1) To carry hay, &c. *West.* As a subst. a parcel, or load. *Var. dial.*

(2) To trim a hedge, tree, &c. *North.* In old English, to cut or slash. "Jaggede hym thorowe," Morte Arthure, MS. Linc. f. 75.

JAGE. A violent motion. *Craven.*

JAGGEDE. The fashion of jagging garments has already been mentioned, in v. *Dagge.*

> A Jupone of Jerodyne *jaggede* in schredes.
> *Morte Arthure, MS. Lincoln, f. 63.*

JAGGER. One who works draught horses for hire. *North.*

JAGGING-IRON. An instrument with teeth used in fashioning pastry. *Var. dial.*

JAGOUNCE. The garnet stone. (*A.-N.*) See Ashmole's Theat. Chem. Brit. p. 224.

JAGS. Rags and tatters. *North.*

JAGUE. A ditch. *Somerset.*

JAISTER. To swagger. *North.*

JAKES. A privy. The term is applied in Devon to any kind of filth or litter. *Jakes-farmer,* a person who cleaned out jakes.

JALITE. Lively; sprightly. (*A.-N.*)

JALLOWES. Jealousy. *Dekker.*

JAM. To press, or squeeze. *Var. dial.*

JAMB. The upright side of window, door, chimney, &c.; any upright distinct mass of masonry in a building or quarry.

JAMBALLS. Rolls made of sweet bread.

JAMBEUX. Armour for the legs. (*A.-N.*) *Jambler* in Gy of Warwike, p. 325, perhaps an error for *jambier,* which is the Anglo-Norman word. See Roquefort.

JAMBLEUE. Gambolling. (*A.-N.*)

JAMMOCK. A soft pulpy substance. Also, to beat, or squeeze. *East.*

JAMMY. Short for James. *North.*

JAMS. Wire shirt-buttons. *West.*

JAM'S-MASS. St. James's day. *North.*

JAN. John. *Var. dial.*

JANDERS. The jaundice. *West.*

JANE. A coin of Genoa; any small coin. See Tyrwhitt, iv. 284.

JANGELERS. Talkative persons. Sometimes minstrels were so termed. (*A.-N.*) The verb *jangle,* to prate, is still in use.

JANGLE. To rove about idly. *North.*

JANGLESOME. Boisterous; noisy; quarrelsome. *Suffolk.*

JANNAK. Fit; proper; good; fair and honourable; smart, or fine. *North.*

JANNOCKS. Oaten bread made into hard and coarse large loaves. *North.*

JANT. Cheerful; merry. *North.*

> Where were dainty ducks and *jant* ones,
> Wenches that could play the wantons.
> *Barnaby's Journal.*

JANTYL. Gentle; polite. *Lydgate.*

JANUAYS. The Genoese. Horman, 1530.

JANYVERE. January. (*A.-N.*)

> And the fyrste monyth of the yere
> Was clepyd aftur hym *Janyvere.*
> *MS. Cantab. Ff. ii. 38, f. 140.*

JAPE. To jest, mock, or cajole. (*A.-S.*) It is often used in an indelicate sense, similar to *game.* Also a substantive, a jest. *Japer,* a jester, or mocker. *Japerie,* buffoonery.

> Notwithstandyng, she was wrothe, and said to the scnysshalle, *jape* ye with me?   *MS. Digby 185.*
> Bot then in hert full gladde was he,
> And ron up and doun in myrthe and *jape.*
> *Chron. Vilodun. p. 122.*
> Demosthenes his hondis onis putte
> In a wommanis bosum *japyngly.*
> *Occleve, MS. 8vo. Antiq. 134, f. 272.*

JAPE-WORTHY. Ridiculous. *Chaucer.*

JAPING. Copulation. *Palsgrave.*

JAR. (1) Discord; anger. *Var. dial.*

(2) To tick, as a clock. *Shak.*

(3) A jar of oil is a vessel containing twenty gallons of it. *West.*

JARBLE. To wet; to bemire. *North.*

JARCK. A seal. An old cant term, mentioned in Frat. of Vacabondes, 1575. *Jarkemen* are given in a list of vagabonds in Harrison, p. 184; Dekker's Lanthorne and Candle-light.

JARGLE. To make a jarring noise. Not peculiar to Hall's Satires, p. 99, as supposed by the editor. "Jargles now in yonder bush," England's Helicon, p. 46.

JARME. To bawl, or cry. *Yorksh.*

JARROCK. A kind of cork. *Minsheu.*

JARSEY. A kind of wool which is spun into worsted. Also called *jarnsey*; properly, Jersey yarn. Bailey explains *jarsey*, the finest wool, separated from the rest by combing.

ARWORM. An ugly insect peculiar to wet marshy places. *South.*

JASEY. A bobwig. *Var. dial.*

JATTER. To split, or shatter. *Suffolk.*

JAUL. To scold or grumble. *North.*

JAUM. The same as *Jamb*, q. v.

JAUNCE. (1) To ride hard. (*A.-N.*)

(2) A jaunt. Romeo and Jul. ii. 5, 4to. ed.

JAUNDERS. The jaundice. *Var. dial.* Jaunes, Reliq. Antiq. i. 51. *Jaunis*, Brockett.

> Envyus man may lyknyd be
> To the *jaunes*, the whyche ys a pyne
> That men mow se yn mennys yne.
> *MS. Harl.* 1701, f. 27.

JAUP. To splash; to make a splashing noise; to strike; to chip or break by a sudden blow. *North.* See Brockett.

JAUPEN. Large; spacious. *North.*

JAVEL. (1) A gaol, or prison. *North.*

(2) A worthless fellow. "The Lieutenant of the Tower advising Sir Thomas Moor to put on worse cloaths at his execution, gives this reason, because he that is to have them is but a *javel*; to which Sir Thomas replied, shall I count him a *javel* who is to doe me so great a benefit," MS. Lansd. 1033. *Javelyn*, Hall, Henry VI. f. 77. See Digby Mysteries, p. 20.

JAVVER. Idle silly talk. *North.*

JAVVLE. To contend; to wrangle. *Yorksh.*

JAW. (1) A jest. *Lanc.*

(2) Coarse idle language. *Var. dial.*

JAWDEWYNE. A term of reproach, here applied to a Lollard.

> Thow *jawdewyne*, thou Jangeler, how stande this togider?
> By verré contradiccioun thou concludist thisilf.
> *MS. Digby* 41, f. 11.

JAWDIE. The stomach of cattle. *North.*

JAWLED-OUT. Excessively fatigued. *Sussex.*

JAWMERS. Stones used for the jambs or jawms of a window.

JAY. A loose woman. *Shak.*

JAYKLE! An exclamation, or oath. *Devon.*

JAYLARDE. A jailor. Chron. Vilodun. p. 82.

JAYPIE. The jay. *Cornw.*

JAZZUP. A donkey. *Linc.*

JEALOUS. Fearful; suspicious; alarmed. A common sense of the word in old plays, and still in use in some counties. "Before the rain came, I *jealoused* the turnips," i. e. was alarmed for them.

JBAN. Genoa. See Strutt, ii. 71.

JEAUNT. A giant. Other MSS. *journey.*

> What, seyde the erle, yf thys be done,
> Thou getyst anodur *jeaunt* sone.
> *MS. Cantab. Ff. ii.* 38, f. 65.

JED. Dead. *Warw.*

JED-COCK. The jack-snipe. Arch. xiii. 343.

JEE. Crooked; awry. Also, to turn, or move to one side. *North.*

JEEPS. A severe beating. *North.*

JEFFERY'S-DAY. St. Jeffery's day, i. e. never.

JEGGE. A gigot or leg of mutton.

JEGGLE. To be very restless. *North.*

JELIING. Jovial. *Craven.*

JELL. A large quantity. *Warw.*

JELU. Gay. "Be thi winpil nevere so *jelu*," MS. Cott. Cleop. C. vi.

JEMEWDE. Joined with hinges.

JEMMY. A great coat. *Var. dial.*

JEMMY-BURTY. An ignis fatuus. *Cambr.*

JEMMY-JESSAMY. A fop, or dandy.

JENK. To jaunt; to ramble. *North.*

JENKIN. A diminutive of *John*.

JENKIT. A Devonshire dish, made partly of milk and cinnamon.

JENNETS. A species of fur. See Test. Vetust. p. 658; Strutt, ii. 102.

JENNY-BALK. A small beam near the roof of a house. *North.*

JENNY-COAT. A child's bed-gown. *West.*

JENNY-CRONE. A crane. *North.*

JENNY-CRUDLE. A wren. *South.* More commonly called a jenny-wren.

JENNY-HOOKER. An owl. *North.* It is also called a jenny-howlet.

JENNY-QUICK. An Italian iron. *Devon.*

JENNY-TIT. Parus cœruleus. *Suffolk.*

JENTERY. Good breeding; gentility.

> And specyally in youth gentilmen ben tawght
> To swere gret othis, they sey for *jentery*;
> Every boy wenyth it be annext to curtesy.
> *MS. Laud.* 416, f. 39.

JEOBERTIE. Jeopardy. *Harrington.*

JERICHO. A prison. Hence the phrase, to wish a person in Jericho.

JERK. To beat. See Florio, p. 138. *Jerker*, Beaumont and Fletcher, iv. 161. Now pronounced *jerkin*. See Craven Gl. i. 250

JERKIN. (1) A kind of jacket, or upper doublet, with four skirts. A waistcoat is still so called in the North of England.

(2) The male of a gerfalcon. See Gent. Rec.

JEROBOAM. A large goblet. *East.*

JERONIMO. See *Go-by.*

> That he that is this day magnifico,
> To-morrow may *goe by Jeronimo.*
> *Taylor's Workes,* 1630, i. 35.

JEROWNDE. See *Jeryne.*

> Thorowe a *jerownde* schelde he Jogges hym thorowe.
> *Morte Arthure, MS. Lincoln,* f. 84.

JERRYCUMMUMBLE. To shake, or tumble about confusedly. *Var. dial.*

JERYNE. Some part of the armour. See the quotation in v. *Acres.*

JESP. A flaw in cloth. *North.*

JESSE. The Tree of Jesse was a representation of the genealogy of Christ, in the form of a tree. It was formerly a common subject for the professors of the various arts.

JESSERAUNT. A kind of jacket without sleeves, composed of small oblong plates of iron or steel overlapping each other, and sometimes covered with velvet. The term seems also to have been applied to a chain of small gold or silver plates worn round the neck, and likewise to a kind of cuirass.

> Aboven that a *passeraunt* of jentylle maylez.
>
> *Morte Arthure, MS. Lincoln, f. 63.*

JESSES. The short leather straps round a hawk's legs, having little rings to which the falconer's leash was fastened.

JESSUP. Juice; syrop. *Warw.*

JEST. A mask, pageant, or interlude; a tale, or representation of one.

JESTERNES. Part of light armour, mentioned in Holinshed, Hist. Scotland, p. 32.

JET. (1) To jet, according to Cotgrave, "wantonly to goe in and out with the legs." Palsgrave has, "I jette, I make a countenaunce with my legges."

(2) A large water ladle. *East.*

(3) To strut, or walk proudly. Also, to exult, rejoice, or be proud. It seems sometimes to mean, to encroach upon.

(4) To throw, jog, or nudge. *Devon.*

(5) A descent; a declivity. *Heref.*

(6) To turn round, or about. *North.*

(7) To contrive. Hence, a device.

(8) To jet the heck, to put one to the door. Yorkshire Dial. 1697, p. 104.

JETSEN. Goods cast out of a ship, when in danger of foundering. *Blount.*

JETTER. A strutter, or bragger. *Palsgrave.*

JEUPERTYE. Jeopardy. (*A.-N.*)

> His lyf upon so songe a wyzte
> Besette wolde in *jeupertye.*
>
> *Gower, MS. Soc. Antiq. 134, f. 59.*

JEWEL. This term was often used by early writers not merely for a gem or precious stone, but for any piece of jewel-work, or a trinket or ornament worn about the person; sometimes, even, a ring, and constantly a brooch. "A collar, or *jewell,* that women used about their neckes," Baret, 1580, I. 38.

JEWERIE. A district inhabited by Jews.

JEWISE. Judgment; punishment. See Deposition of Richard II. p. 26.

> Avise him if he wolde flitte
> The lawe for the covetise,
> There sawe he redie his *juise.*
>
> *Gower, ed. 1554, f. 153.*

> And every man schalle thanne aryse
> To joye or ellis to *juise,*
> Wher that he schalle for ever dwelle.
>
> *Gower, MS. Soc. Antiq. 134, f. 37.*

> O beste of helle! In what *juise*
> Hast thou deservid for to dye.
>
> *Ibid. MS. Ibid. f. 69*

JEW'S-EARS. A fungus of a beautiful bright red colour, found in old banks adhering to sticks, or trees. See Cotgrave, in v. *Judas, Oreille*; Thomasii Dictionarium, 1644, in v. *Bolus*; Brand's Pop. Antiq. iii. 155.

JEW'S-EYE. Worth a Jew's eye, i. e. a great deal. A very common phrase, and sanctioned by Shakespeare.

JEWS'-MONEY. A name given to old Roman coins, found in some parts of England, mentioned by Harrison, pp. 72, 218.

JEW'S-TRUMP. A Jew's-harp. *Yorksh.* See Kind-Harts Dreame, 4to. Lond. 1592.

JEYANT. A giant. Torrent, p. 18.

JIB. (1) Said of a draught-horse that goes backwards instead of forwards. *Var. dial.*

(2) A stand for beer-barrels. *West.*

(3) The under-lip. Hence *to hang the jib,* to look cross. *Var. dial.*

JIBBER. A horse that jibs. *Var. dial.*

JIBBET. Same as *Spang-whew,* q. v.

JIBBY. A gay frisky girl. *East.* Jibby-horse, one covered with finery.

JIB-JOB-JEREMIAH. A juvenile game mentioned in Moor's Suffolk Words, p. 238.

JICE. A very small quantity. *Essex.*

JICKS. The hiccough. *Cornw.*

JIDDICUMJIDY. A see-saw. *North.*

JIFFLE. To be restless. *Var. dial.*

JIFFY. An instant. *Var. dial.* In a jiffy, a very common phrase. It implies excessive rapidity; momentary action.

JIG. (1) To rove about idly. *North.*

(2) A trick. An old cant term.

(3) Cotgrave, in v. *Farce,* mentions "the jyg at the end of an enterlude, wherein some pretie knaverie is acted." A jig was a ludicrous metrical composition, often in rhyme, which was sung by the clown, who occasionally danced, and was always accompanied by a tabor and pipe. The term is also constantly used for any scene of low buffoonery, and many old ballads are called jigs. *Jigmaker,* a maker of jigs or ballads.

JIGE. To creak. *North.*

JIGGAMAREE. A manœuvre. *Var. dial.*

JIGGER. (1) A swaggerer. *North.*

(2) A vessel of potters' ware used in toasting cheese. *Somerset.*

(3) A cleaner of ores *North.*

(4) A constable. *Hants.*

JIGGER-PUMP. A pump used in breweries to force beer into vats.

JIGGETING. Jolting; shaking; flaunting; going about idly. *Var. dial.*

JIGGIN-SIEVE. A fine cloth which sifts the dust from oats or wheat when they are ground. Salop. Antiq. p. 474.

JIGGS. Dregs; sediment. *Suffolk.*

JIGGUMBOBS. Trinkets; knicknacks.

> Kills monster after monster, takes the puppets
> Prisoners, knocks down the Cyclops, tumbles all
> Our *jiggumbobs* and trinkets to the wall.
>
> *Brome's Antipodes, 1640.*

JIG-PIN. In mining, a pin used to stop a machine when drawing.

JIKE. To creak. *North.*

JILL. A pint of ale, &c. *North.*

JIM. (1) A timber-drag. *East.*

(2) Slender; neat; elegant. *Var. dial.* Spruce, very neat, Tim Bobbin.

JIMCRACKS. Knick-knacks. *Var. dial.*

JIMMERS. Hinges. See *Gimmer.*

JIMMY. The same as *Jim* (2).

JIMP. Slender; indented. *North.*

JINGLE-BRAINS. A wild thoughtless fellow.

JINGLE-CAP. The game of shake-cap. *North.*

JINGLE-JANGLES. Trinkets.

> For I was told ere I came from home,
> You're the goodliest man ere I saw beforne;
> With so many *jingle-jangles* about ones necke,
> As is about yours, I never saw none.
>
> *The King and a poore Northerne Man.*

JINGO. *By-jingo*, a common oath, said to be a corruption of St. Gingoulph.

JINK. (1) To jingle; to ring money. *East.*

(2) To be very gay and thoughtless. *North.*

JINKED. Said of an animal hurt in the loins or back. *East.*

JINNY-SPINNER. The crane-fly. *North.*

JIRBLE. To jumble. *Northumb.*

JITCHY. Such. *Somerset.*

JITTY. A narrow passage. *Linc.*

JOAN. A kind of cap.

JOB. (1) To scold; to reprove. *Cambr.*

(2) Stercus. *Var. dial.*

(3) To strike, hit, or peck. *East.* It occurs in Pr. Parv. p. 36, byllen or jobbyn.

(4) An affair, or business. *Var. dial.*

(5) A small piece of wood. *North.*

JOBARDE. A stupid fellow. (*A.-N.*)

> Tho seyde the emperour Sodenmagard,
> Then was the erle a nyse *jobarde.*
>
> *MS. Cantab. Ff. II. 38, f. 140.*

JOBATION. A scolding. *Var. dial.*

JOBBEL. A small load, generally of hay or straw. *Oxon.* Sometimes called a *jobbet.*

JOBBER. A dealer in cattle. *Var. dial.*

JOBBERHEADED. Dull; stupid. *South.*

JOBBERNOWL. The head. Generally a term of contempt, a blockhead.

JOBBY. (1) Joseph. *Cumb.*

(2) A joist, or beam. *Yorksh.*

JOBLIN. A stupid boy. *Somerset.*

JOBLOCK. A turkey's wattle. *West.*

JOCAUNT. Merry; gay. (*A.-N.*)

JOCE. The deuce. *Warw.*

JOCK. To jolt. *Kent.*

JOCKEY. (1) Gay; very lively. *Suffolk.*

(2) A thin walking-stick. *Devon.*

(3) Rough; uneven. *Kent.*

JOCLET. A small manor, or farm. *Kent.*

JOCONDE. Joyous; pleasant. (*A.-N.*) Jocundnes, gladness, Audelay, p. 26.

JOCOTIOUS. Jocose. *Yorksh.*

JOD. The letter J. *Var. dial.*

JOE. A master; a superior. *North.*

JOE-BEN. The great tit-mouse. *Suffolk.*

JOG. To jog his memory, i. e. to remind him of anything. A common phrase.

JOGELOUR. A minstrel; a jongleur; one who played mountebank tricks. (*A.-N.*)

JOGENNY. A donkey. *Somerset.*

JOGGELY. Unsteady; shaky. *Northumb.*

JOGGER. To shake, or jog. *Suffolk.*

JOGGES. Hits; strikes. See the quotation given under *Jerownde.*

JOGGING. A protuberance on the surface of sawn wood. *East.*

JOGGLE. (1) Same as *Jogger*, q. v.

(2) A mason's term for the fitting of stones together. *Var. dial.*

JOG-TROT. A gentle pace. *Var. dial.*

JOHAN. St. John's wort. Arch. xxx. 409.

JOHN. *Sir John*, an old phrase for a priest. *John Sanderson*, the cushion dance, mentioned under this name in Playford's Dancing Master, 1698. *John in the Wad*, an ignis fatuus. *John's silver pin*, a single article of finery amidst a lot of dirt and sluttery. *John-a-dreams*, a stupid dreaming fellow. *John-among-the-maids*, a man who is always dangling after the ladies. *John-and-Joan*, an hermaphrodite. *John-hold-my-staff*, a parasite. To stay for John Long the carrier, to wait a very long time; to send it by John Long the carrier, i. e. at an indefinite period. See Cotgrave, in v. *Attendre, Borgne, Envoyer.* The phrase occurs in Taylor. *John of Nokes*, a fictitious name formerly used in legal proceedings, similar to John Doe and Richard Roe.

JOHN-APPLE. Same as *Apple-John*, q. v.

JOHN-DORY. A French pirate, whose name seems to have been proverbial. A popular old song or catch so called is frequently referred to. See Nares, in v.

JOHNNY. (1) A jakes. These terms are clearly connected with each other. Also called Mrs. Jones by country people.

(2) A foolish fellow. *Var. dial.* Johnny-Bum, a jackass. *Grose.*

JOHNNY-WOPSTRAW. A farm-labourer.

JOHN-O-LENT. A scarecrow. *South.*

JOIGNE. To enjoin. Rom. Rose, 2355.

JOINANT. Joining. (*A.-N.*)

JOINT. To put a man's nose out of joint, to supplant him in another's affection.

JOINT-GRASS. Yellow bed-straw. *North.*

JOINT-STOOL. A stool framed by joinery work, at first so called in distinction to stools rudely formed from a single block. *Joyned stole*, Unton Inventories, p. 1.

JOIST. To agist cattle. *North.*

JOIT. A sudden stop. *Northumb.*

JOLE. To bump. *Yorksh.*

JOLIF. Jolly; joyful. (*A.-N.*)

JOLIFANT. When two persons ride on one horse, the one on a pillion behind, they are said to ride jolifant. *Devon.*

JOLL. The beak of a bird, or jaw-bone of an animal. Hence, to peck. *Norf.*

JOLLACKS. A clergyman. *Suffolk.*

JOLLE. To beat. *Palsgrave.*

> Ther they *jolledde* Jewes thorow.
>
> *MS. Cott. Calig. A. II. f. 117.*

JOLLIFICATION. A merry feast.

JOLLITRIN. A young gallant. *Minsheu.*

JOLLOP. The cry of a turkey. *Holme.*

JOLLY. Fat; stout; large. *North.* In Devon, pretty. A bitch when *maris appetens* is said to be jolly. *Chesh.*

JOLLY-DOG. A bon vivant. *Var. dial.*

JOLLY-NOB. The head. *Grose.*

JOLTER-HEAD. A stupid fellow. *South.* Properly, thick-headed. *Joulthead*, Cotgrave.

JOLTS. Cabbage plants that in the spring go to seed prematurely. *Warw.*

JOMBRE. To jumble. *Chaucer.*

JONAS. The jaundice. *Yorksh.*

JONATHAN. An instrument used by smokers to light their pipes with. It is a piece of iron, of the size of a short poker, fitted at one end with a handle of wood, and having at the other a protuberance or transverse bar of iron, which is kept heated in the fire for use.

JONGLERIE. Idle talk. *Chaucer.*

JOOK. To crouch suddenly. *North.*

JOOKINGS. Corn which falls from the sheaf in throwing it off the stack. *North.*

JOOPE. A job. *Hampol.*

JOP. To splash in the water. *Yorksh.*

JOPES. Braces in roofs.

JOR. To jostle, or push. *North.*

JORAM. A large dish or jug of any eatables or liquids. *Var. dial.*

JORDAN. A kind of pot or vessel formerly used by physicians and alchemists. It was very much in the form of a modern soda-water bottle, only the neck was larger, not much smaller than the body of the vessel. At a later period the term came to be used for a chamber-pot, having been anciently used occasionally for an urinal.

JORDAN-ALMOND. A kind of large sweet almond, mentioned by Gerard.

JORNAY. A day's journey, or work.

> In this courte thai ar twenty
> At my biddyng to bidde redy
> To do a gode *jornay.*
> *MS. Cantab. Ff. v. 48, f. 53.*

> But if I do Robyn a gode *journé,*
> Ellis mot I hangyt be. *MS. Ibid. f. 54.*

JORNET. A kind of cloak.

JOSEPH. An ancient riding-habit, with buttons down to the skirts.

JOSKIN. A clownish fellow. *Var. dial.*

JOSS. To crowd together. *East.*

JOSSA. Stand still! An address to horses. See Chaucer, Cant. T. 4099. It appears from Moor, p. 188, that *joss* is still in use in the same sense. *Josty,* come to, Tim Bobbin Gl. *Joss-block, jossing-block,* a horse-block.

JOSSEL. A hodge-podge. *North.*

JOSTLE. To cheat. A cant term.

JOSYNG. Rejoicing. Sevyn Sages, 92.

JOT. (1) To touch; to jog, or jolt roughly; to nudge one's elbow. *East.*

(2) Plump; downright. *Suffolk.*

JOT-CART. A cart which has a rough motion, or jolts. *East.*

JOT-GUT. The intestinum rectum. *East.*

JOUDER. To chatter with cold. *Somerset.*

JOUDS. Rags. *Devon.*

JOUISANCE. Enjoyment. Peele, i. 15.

JOUK-COAT. A great coat. *North.*

JOUKE. To sleep. A hawking term.

JOUKERY-PAUKERY. An artifice. *North.*

JOUKES. Rushes. Maundevile, p. 13.

JOUL. A blow. See *Jolle* and *Jowl.*

JOUN. Joined. *Essex.*

JOUNCE. To bounce, or jolt. *East.*

JOURINGS. Scoldings. Devonsh. Dial. 1839, p. 72. It seems to be the same word as that quoted by Nares from Hayman's Quodlibets, 1628, explained *swearings.* Brawlings; quarrellings, *Exmoor.*

JOURMONTE. To vex. (*A.-N.*)

JOURNAL. Daily. *Shak.*

JOURN-CHOPPERS. Regraters of yarn, mentioned in statute 8 Hen. VI. *Blount.*

JOURNEY. The same as *Jornay,* q. v. It is also a day of battle.

JOURS. Cold shiverings. *South.*

JOUSED. Finished; completed. *Worc.*

JOUSTE. A just, or tournament. (*A.-N.*)

JOUSTER. A retailer of fish. *Cornw.*

JOUTE. A battle, or combat. (*A.-N.*)

JOUTES. An ancient dish in cookery so called. See Ord. and Reg. p. 426.

JOVE'S-NUTS. Acorns. *Somerset.*

JOVIAL. Belonging to Jupiter. It occurs in Shakespeare and Heywood.

JOWD. A jelly. *Devon.*

JOWE. A jaw. Maundevile, p. 288.

JOWEL. The space between the piers of a bridge. Also, a sewer.

JOWER. To tire out. *Suffolk.*

JOWL. (1) The same as *Jolle,* q. v.

(2) A large thick dish. *Devon.*

JOWLER. Clumsy; thick. The term is applied to a thick-jawed hound. *North.*

JOWR. To push, or shake. *Cumb.*

JOWS. Juice. Arch. xxx. 409.

JOWYNE. To peck, as birds do. *Pr. Parv.*

JOY. To enjoy. Also, to rejoice, as in the Bride, by Nabbes, 4to. 1640, sig. I. *Joyance,* enjoyment, rejoicing.

JOYFNES. Youth. *Gawayne.*

JOYNE. To enjoin. Apol. Loll. pp. 11, 17.

JOYNETES. Joints. Nominale MS.

> And the *joynetes* of ilk lym and bane,
> And the vaynes ware strydand ilkane.
> *MS. Lincoln A. i. 17, f. 190.*

JOYNTERS. The joints of armour. "Joynter and gemows," MS. Morte Arthure, f. 84.

JUB. A very slow trot. *East.*

JUBALTARE. Gibraltar. *Chaucer.*

JUBARD. The house-leek. (*A.-N.*)

JUBBE. A vessel for ale, or wine.

JUBBIN. A donkey. *Var. dial.*

JUBE. A rood-loft. *Britton.*

JUBERD. To jeopard, or endanger.

JUCK. (1) A yoke; the oil in the fleece of wool. *Cornw.*

(2) The noise made by partridges.

JUDAS-COLOUR. Red. A red beard was called a Judas-coloured beard.

JUDAS-TORCHES. Large torches formerly much used in ceremonial processions.

JUDGESSE. A female judge. See Heywood's Iron Age, 4to. Lond. 1632, sig. C. iv.

JUDICIAL. A "judicial man," a man of judgment. It was reversed with *judicious.*

> I confesse it to me a meer toy, not deserving any *judicial* man's view. *Pierce Penilesse, 1592.*

JUE. To shrink; to flinch. *North.*

JUG. (1) To nestle together. *North.* It occurs in N. Fairfax, Bulk and Selvedge of the World, 8vo. Lond. 1674.

(2) The nickname of Joan.

(3) A common pasture. *West.*

JUGAL. Nuptial. Middleton, iii. 480.

JUGGE. To judge. Also, a judge. (*A.-N.*)

JUGGLE. To jog, or shake. *West.*

JUGGLEMEAR. A swamp, or bog. *Devon.* Also called a *juggle-mire.*

JUGH. A judge. *Hampole.*

JUIL. The month of July. *Chaucer.*

JUISE. The same as *Jewise,* q. v.

JUKE. The neck of a bird. A term in hawking. Gent. Rec. ii. 62.

JULIAN'S-BOWERS. Labyrinths and mazes made of earthwork, the scenes of former rustic amusements.

JULIO. An Italian coin, worth about sixpence. See Webster's Works, i. 70.

JULK. To shake; to splash; to jolt; to give a hard blow. *West.*

JULTY. To jolt. *Devon.*

JUM. (1) The plant darnel. *West.*

(2) A jolt; a concussion; a knock. *Suffolk.*

JUMBLE. Futuo. Florio, p. 75.

JUMBLEMENT. Confusion. *North.*

JUMENTS. Cattle. (*Lat.*)

JUMP. (1) A coffin. *Yorksh.*

(2) A leathern frock; a coat. *North.* "A jump, a half gown or sort of jackett; likewise a sort of boddice used instead of stays," Milles' MS. Holme has the term, 1688. Mr. Hunter explains *jumps,* short stays.

(3) Compact; neat; short. Hence the adverb, nicely, exactly. *North.* " How *jumpe* he hitteth the naile on the head," Stanihurst, p. 34. It is used by Gosson, 1579.

(4) To take an offer eagerly. *Var. dial.* Also, to risk or hazard. *Shak.*

'5) To meet with accidentally. *North.*

(6) *Jump with,* matched. To agree.

And thou to be *jump with* Alexander.
Lyly's Alexander and Campaspe, 1584.

JUMPER. (1) A miner's borer. *North.*

(2) A maggot. *Yorksh.*

(3) The fieldfare? Florio, p. 109.

JUMPING-DICK. A fowl's merry-thought. *North.*

JUMPING-JOAN. A country dance, mentioned in the Bran New Wark, 1785, p. 7.

JUMP-SHORT. Mutton from sheep drowned in the fen ditches. *East.*

JUNAMEY. Land sown with the same grain that it grew the preceding year.

JUNCKER. A contrivance for letting off the superfluous water from a pond or moat. *Suffolk.*

JUNE-BUG. The green beetle. *South.*

JUNIPER. Was formerly burnt to sweeten a chamber. See Ben Jonson, ii. 6.

JUNK. A lump, or piece. *South.*

JUNKET. (1) A sweetmeat; a dainty. See Hollyband's Dictionarie, 1593, in v. *Dragee.*

In Devonshire the term is still used, but restricted to curds and clouted cream.

(2) A long basket for catching fish.

(3) A feast, or merry-making. Also, to gad about, to gossip. *North.* " Junket, or banket," Palsgrave.

JUNO'S-TEARS. The herb vervain.

JUNT. A whore. Middleton, ii. 96.

JUPARTE. To jeopardy. *Palsgrave.*

JUPITER'S-BEARD. Houseleek. *Devon.*

JUPON. The pourpoint, or doublet. It was generally of silk or velvet, and was worn over the armour, being frequently emblazoned with the arms of the owner. In much later times the petticoat seems to have been so called.

Thorz out ys scheld and is haberjone,
Plates, and jakke, and *joupone.*
MS. Ashmole 33, f. 48.

JUR. To hit, strike, or butt. *North.* A corruption of jarr? The noise made by certain birds was termed *jurring.*

JURDECTOUN. Jurisdiction. (*A.-N.*)

And fynally bothe oure liberté
Goeth unto nought of oure *jurdectoun.*
Lydgate, MS. Ashmole 39, f. 23.

JURMUNGLE. A mess; confusion. *Yorksh.*

JURNUT. An earth-nut. *North.*

JUS. Juice. Nominale MS.

Also the *jus* of selyame and powder of brymstone temperyd togedyr al cold is goode therfore.
MS. Med Rec. xv. Cent.

JUSSELL. A dish in ancient cookery, described in Ord. and Reg. p. 462-3. Two receipts for it are given in MS. Sloane 1201, f. 35.

JUSTE. (1) A kind of vessel with a wide body and long straight neck.

(2) To joust, or tilt. (*A.-N.*)

Mekylle was the chevalry,
That then come to Hungary
To go *juste* with ther myghte.
MS. Cantab. Ff. ii. 38, f. 75

JUSTEMENT. Agistment, q. v. See Manners and Household Expences of England, p. 295.

JUSTERS. Horses for tilting. *Weber.*

JUSTICE. To judge. (*A.-N.*) *Justicer,* a judge, a justice of the peace. " A perfect patterne of an upright justicer," Holinshed, Historie of Scotland, p. 63.

JUSTILICHE. Justly; exactly. (*A.-S.*)

JUSTMEN-HOLDERS. Freeholders. *Devon.*

JUST-NOW. Lately; now; presently; immediately. This very common phrase is perhaps most generally used in the Western counties.

JUSTS-OF-PEACE. Peaceable tilts or justs. The method of crying them is given in Arch. xvii. 291. Compare Degrevant, 1261.

JUSTY. The same as *Juste* (2).

Then seyde Befyse to Tarry,
Wyll we to-morowe *justy.*
MS. Cantab. Ff. ii. 38, f. 121.

JUT. (1) To throw; to strike. *South.* " To jut, hit, or run against," Baret, 1580.

(2) A pail with a long handle. *Kent.*

JUTER. The fertile coagulating saltish nature of earth. *More.*

JUTTES. Low persons. (*A.-N.*)

JUTTY. A part of a building which projects beyond the rest. *Shak.*

JU-UM. Empty. *North.*

JUVENAL. A youth. *Shak.*

JUVENTEE. Youth. (*A.-N.*) See Piers Ploughman, p. 402 ; Dial. Creat. Moral. pp. 157, 209.

JUWET. Juditb. *R. de Brunne.*

JYE. To stir ; to turn round. *North.*

JYMIAN. A knick-knack. It occurs in Nash's Pierce Penilesse, 1592, and in the Appendix to Skelton's Works, p. 446. Absurdly spelt *jym jam* in Pr. Parv. p. 257.

KA. (1) Quoth. *Suffolk.* "Ka the cloyster-master," Mar-Prelates Epitome, p. 52.

(2) *Ka me, ka thee,* a proverb implying, if you will do me one favour, I will do you another. See the Merie Tales of Skelton, p. 65.

(3) To look ; to perceive. *East.*

KAAIKE. To stare vacantly. *Cumb.*

KABANE. The cabin of a vessel.

> Mony *kabane* clevede, cabilles destroyede,
> Knyghtes and kene mene killide the braynes.
> *Morte Arthure, MS. Lincoln, f. 91.*

KACHONE. To catch. Const. Freem. 380.

KADES. The dung of sheep. *Linc.*

KAE. (1) A cow. J. de Wageby, p. 8.

(2) An interj. of disbelief, or contempt.

KAF. Chaff. *North.* "Ful of kaff," Apol. Lollards, p. 56.

KAFF. A gardener's hoe. *North.*

KAFFLE. To entangle. *Somerset.*

KAIE. A key. Rom. of the Rose, 2080.

KAIL. Greens; cabbage. *Kail-garth*, a kitchen-garden. *Kail-pot*, a pottage pot, a large metal pot for cooking meat and cabbages together, &c. The term and article are nearly out of use. It is a heavy globular iron vessel, holding three or four gallons, and resting on three little spikes. *Kail-yard*, an orchard.

KAILE. To decline in health. *North.*

KAIN. Rent paid in kind. *East.*

KAIRE. To go ; to proceed ; to depart.

> Comandez the kenely to *kaire* of his landes,
> Ore elles for thy knyghthede encontre hyme ones.
> *Morte Arthure, MS. Lincoln, f. 67.*

KAIRNS. Rude heaps of stones generally found on hills or other conspicuous situations, and supposed to be very ancient funeral monuments. *North.*

KAITE. A dresser of wool.

KAKELE. To cackle. Reliq. Antiq. ii. 80. *Kaklynge* is applied by Chaucer to the noise made by geese, in MS. Cantab. Ff. i. 6, f. 32.

KAL. Hard. A mining term.

KALDE. Cold. Also, cooled, refreshed. It occurs in MS. Cott. Vespas. D. vii.

KALENDAR. A kind of wood, mentioned in Holinshed, Historie of Scotland, p. 59.

KALENDER. A guide, or director. (*Lat.*)

KALTS. Quoits. *Salop.*

KAM. (1) Crooked. *Clean kam*, quite wrong or crooked. "To doe a thing cleane kamme, out of order, the wrong way," Cotgrave.

(2) Came. See Havelok, 863.

KAME. A comb. *North.*

> Me thoghte come to me the speryte of this womane Margarete, the whilke I sawe byfore in payues,

and me thoghte scho was fulle of stronge wondes, als scho hade bene drawene withe *kames.*
> *MS. Lincoln A. i. 17, f. 231.*

KAMPE. Contest ; war. (*A.-S.*)

> Alle the kene mene of *kampe*, knyghtes and other,
> Killyd are colde dede, and castyne over burdes.
> *Morte Arthure, MS. Lincoln, f. 92.*

KANC. A large forest. See Lambarde's Perambulation, ed. 1596, p. 210.

KANDLEGOSTES. Goose-grass. *Gerard.*

KANEL. Collar ; neck. *Gawayne.*

KANGY. Cross ; ill-tempered. *Cumb.*

KANSH. A strain. *Salop.*

KANT. Strong ; courageous.

> He come in at a coste,
> With his brage and his boste,
> With many *kant* knyght.
> *MS. Lincoln A. i. 17, f. 131.*
> The knyghte coueride on his knees with a *kaunt* herte.
> *Morte Arthure, MS. Lincoln, f. 76.*

KANTELED. Different pieces of cloth worked together. See Hall, Henry IV. f. 49.

KAPE. Sleeve of a coat. *Weber.*

KARDEVYLE. Carlile. Launfal, 8.

KARECTIS. Characters ; marks.

> I make a cercle large and round,
> With *karectis* and fygures.
> *MS. Cott. Tiber. A. vii. f. 44.*

KARER. A sieve. *Derbysh.*

KAREYNE. A carcass ; carrion. (*A.-N.*)

KARKE. Care ; anxiety.

> Whene maydens ere maryede, it es thaire maste *karke*
> Lesse thay be maryed to menne that hase bene in the parke.
> *MS. Lincoln A. i. 17, f. 149.*

KARL-HEMP. Late grown hemp. Brockett says, "the largest stalk of hemp."

KARROWS. A set of people formerly in Ireland, who did nothing but gamble. They appear to have been a bad set, and are described by Barnaby Rich as playing away even their clothes. According to Stanihurst, p. 45, "they plaie awaie mantle and all to the bare skin, and then trusse themselves in straw or leaves ; they wait for passengers in the high waie, invite them to game upon the greene, and ask no more but companions to make them sport. For default of other stuffe, they pawne their glibs, the nailes of their fingers and toes, their dimissaries, which they leefe or redeeme at the courtesie of the winner."

KARS. Cresses. Howell, sect. xvi.

KARVE. Sliced ; cut. See *Carf.*

> When hir fadur on slepe was,
> She hyed to hym a gret pas,
> And *karve* his hart in twoo.
> *MS. Cantab. Ff. v. 48, f. 48.*

KAS. A case. Wright's Seven Sages, p. 52.

Kepe the now fro swych a kas,
Ayen God no more to trespas.
MS. Harl. 1701, f. 3.

KASARDLY. Unlucky. *North.*

KASKE. Strong. Havelok, 1841.

KASSYDONYS. The calcedony, which is thus spelt in Emaré, 128.

KATE. To be lecherous. *North.*

KATEREYNIS. Quadrains; farthings.

KAUCE. The same as *Cauci*, q. v.

KAVERSYN. A hypocrite. (*A.-N.*)
Okerers and *kaverayns,*
As wykked they are as Sarasyns.
MS. Harl. 1701, f. 37.

KAW. To gasp for breath. *Devon.*

KAY. Left. *Syr Gawayne.*

KAYLES. The same as *Cailes*, q. v.

KAYN. A nobleman. Havelok, 1327.

KAYNARD. A rascal. (*A.-N.*)
A *kaynard* and a olde folte,
That thryfte hath loste and boghte a bolte.
MS. Harl. 1701, f. 85.

KAYRE. Cairo. Also as *Kaire*, q. v.
Strauʒte unto *Kayre* his wey he fongeth,
Where he the souldan thanne fonde.
Gower, MS. Soc. Antiq. 134, f. 78.

KAYSERE. An emperor. (*A.-S.*)
Es there any kyde knyghte, *kaysere* or other.
Morte Arthure, MS. Lincoln, f. 70.

KAYTEFTEE. Wretchedness. (*A.-N.*)
Thus es ylk mane, als we may see,
Borne in care and *kayteftee,*
And for to dre with dole his dayes,
Als Job sothely hymselfe sayse.
Hampole, MS. Lincoln A. l. 17, f. 277.
Thus es a man, als we may se,
In wrychednes borne and *kaytyftè.*
Ibid. MS. Bowes, p. 27.

KAZZARDLY. Lean; ill-thriven. *North.* Kennett says, "spoke of cattle subject to diseases and death, or other casualties."

KEA. Go! (The imperative.) *North.*

KEACH. To lade out water. *Warw.* "To keach water," Florio, p. 46. *Keach-hole,* a hole in a brook where the cottagers dip for water. *Var. dial.*

KEAK. (1) A sprain. *Yorksh.*
(2) To raise, or prop up, a cart. *North.*

KEAL. A cough; a cold. *Linc.*

KEALER. A small shallow tub used for cooling liquids. *Sussex.*

KEALT. Cowardly. *Lanc.*

KEAME. To comb. See *Kame.*
Thy hands see thou wash,
Thy head likewise *keame,*
And in thine apparell
See torne be no seame.
Schools of Vertue, n. d.

KEAMER. A kind of ferret. *South.*

KEAMY. Covered with a thin white mould, applied to cider. *West.*

KEANE. To scamper. *Cumb.*

KEANS. The scum of ale, &c. *Yorksh.*

KEATCH. To congeal. *Wilts.*

KEATHER. A cradle. *Lanc.*

KEAUSTRIL. Explained by Meriton, "a great boned coarse creature." *Yorksh.*

KEAVE. To plunge; to struggle. *Cumb.*

KEB. (1) A villain. *Yorksh.*
(2) To pant for breath; to sob. *Linc.*

KEBBERS. Refuse sheep taken out of the flock. "Kebbers or cullers, drawne out of a flocke of sheepe," Nomenclator, 1585, p. 50.

KEBBLE. A white opaque spar. *Derb.*

KEBLOCK. The wild turnip. *North.*

KECCHE. To catch. Kyng Horn, 1377.

KECHYNE. A kitchen. Perceval, 455.

KECK. (1) To be pert. *Lanc.*
(2) To lift; to heave. Hence, to reach; to choke. *Var. dial.* It occurs in Gammer Gurton's Needle, meaning the noise made in coughing. See Hawkins, i. 216.

KECKCORN. The windpipe. *West.* More commonly called the *kecker.*

KECKER. (1) Squeamish. *North.*
(2) An overlooker at a coal-mine. *Newc.*

KECK-HANDED. Wrongly. *Oxon.*

KECKLE. (1) Unsteady. *Lanc.*
(2) To laugh violently. *Yorksh.*

KECKLE-MECKLE. Poor ore. *Derb.*

KECKLOCK. Wild mustard. *Leic.*

KECKY. Anything hollow, like a kex. *Linc.*

KEDD. Known; shown. (*A.-S.*)
Wherefore ther passyth here no men
Wyth strenkyth, but they be *kedd.*
MS. Cantab. Ff. il. 38, f. 80.
Tho thai were mounted, y sigge, aplight,
Thai *kedden* her noble might.
Arthour and Merlin, p. 145.

KEDGE. (1) To fill; to stuff. *North.* Hence *kedge-belly,* a glutton.
(2) To adhere; to unite. *Cornw.*
(3) Brisk; active. *East.* It occurs in Prompt. Parv. p. 274, spelt *kygge.*

KEDGER. A fisherman. *Yorksh.*

KEDGY. Pot-bellied. *North.*

KEDLOCK. The charlock. *Salop.*

KEE. Kine; cows. *Devon.*

KEECH. (1) A cake. *Somerset.*
(2) The internal fat of an animal, as rolled up for the tallow-chandler.
(3) To cut grass and weeds on the sides of rivers. *West.* Dean Milles' MS. Glossary.

KEEK. To peep; to look slily. *North.* "Kekyyne, or prively waytyne, *intuor,*" Pr. Parv. p. 269. See Brockett.

KEEL. (1) A strong clumsy boat used by the colliers at Newcastle. "Bottoms or keeles," Harrison, p. 6. A keel of coals, 21 tons, 4 cwt.
(2) To cease; to give over. *Cumb.*
(3) A kiln, as for lime, &c. *South.* "A brick-keele," Florio, p. 304.
(4) To cool anything. "While greasy Joan doth keele the pot;" certainly not to *scum,* as stated by certain editors. See *Kele,* the earlier form.
(5) A ruddle for sheep. *North.*
(6) "To give the keele, to carene, as mariners say," Florio, p. 137.

KEELAGE. Keel dues in port. *North.*

KEEL-ALLEY. A bowling alley. *Devon.*

KEEL-BULLIES. Keel-men. *North.* See the Bishopric Garland, 1792, p. 19.

KEEL-DEETERS. The wives and daughters of keel-men, who sweep and clean the keels. See *Deet* (4).

KEELS. Nine-pins. See *Cailes*.

KEELY-VINE. A black-lead pencil. *North.*

KEEN. Kind. *Yorksh.* A cow, *maris appetens*, is said to be *keen to the bull*.

KEEN-BITTEN. Frost-bitten. Also, keen, hungry, sharp-set. *North.*

KEENDEST. *Any keendest thing*, any kind of thing, ever so much. *Devon.*

KEEP. (1) To dwell; to inhabit. *Var. dial.* It occurs in Pierce Penilesse, 1592.

(2) *To keep one short*, to restrain his liberty. *To keep residence*, to reside. *To keep well*, to live on good terms with any one. *To keep the door*, to be a bawd. *To keep cut with*, to follow the example of. *Keep-and-creak*, a hook and eye. *To keep crows*, to guard newly-sown fields from their ravages. *Keep the pot a boiling*, go on with anything furiously.

(3) Pasture. *Out at keep*, said of animals in hired pastures. *Var. dial.*

(4) To maintain. Also, maintenance.

(5) To keep company with. *Var. dial.*

(6) The chief stronghold of an ancient castle.

(7) A large basket. *Somerset.*

(8) To catch. *Lanc.*

(9) A reservoir for fish by the side of a river.

(10) A safe to preserve meat in summer.

KEEPER. A small clasp. *Suffolk.*

KEEPING. The lair of a hart.

KEEPING-ROOM. The room usually sat in by the family. *East.*

KEEP-TOUCH. To keep faith; to be faithful.

And trust me on my truth,
If thou *keep touch* with me,
My dearest friend, as my own heart
Thou shalt right welcome be.
Songs of the London Prentices, p. 37.

KEER. The mountain ash. *Devon.*

KEEVE. (1) A large tub or vessel used in brewing. *West.*

(2) To heave, or lift up. *North.* Some writers say, to overturn.

KEEVER. A tub. MS. Lansd. 1033.

KEEZER. A sieve. *Devon.*

KEFANS. The same as *Keans*, q. v.

KEFFLE. An inferior horse. *Var. dial.*

So Richard, having no more to say,
Mounted his *keffle* and rode away.
Richard of Dalton Dale, MS.

KEFT. Purchased? Havelok, 2005.

KEGGED. Affronted. *Lanc.*

KEGGY. Soft and pulpy, applied to vegetables when decaying. *Linc.*

KEIED. Locked. Harrison, p. 185.

KEIGHT. Caught. *Spenser.*

KEIK. To stand crooked. *Lanc.*

KEIL. A cock of hay. *North.*

KEILD. A spring. *Grose.*

KEINTLICH. Nicely; curiously. *Pegge.*

KEISTY. Dainty; squeamish. *North.*

KEIVER. A bumper of liquor. *Yorksh.*

KEKE. The cry of the cuckoo.

KEL. A kind of soup.

Thy breakfast thowe gott every day,
Was but pease-bread and *kel* full gray.
MS. Lansdowne 241.

KELCH. A thump. *Linc.*

KELD. (1) The smooth part of a river when the rest of the water is rough. *North.*

(2) A well. *Craven.*

(3) Killed. Octovian, 1063.

(4) To become cold. Reliq. Antiq. ii. 211.

(5) To thump. *Northumb.*

KELE. (1) To cool. *Chaucer.*

And leyde hym flatlyng on the grounde,
To *kele* hys woundys in that stounde.
MS. Cantab. Ff. ii. 38, f. 99.

Bot eftyrwarde when it cesses, and the herte *kelis*
of love of Jhesu, thanne entyrs in vayne glorie.
MS. Lincoln A. i. 17, f. 221.

(2) Time; place; circumstance. *Lanc.*

KELF. (1) A foolish fellow. *West.* Kelfin, a great lubberly fellow, or boy.

One squire Æneas, a great *kelf*,
Some wandering hangman like herself.
Cotton's Works, 1734, p. 85.

(2) To twist; to wrench. *Warw.*

(3) The incision made in a tree by the axe when felling it. *Warw.*

KELIAGE. The herb arsesmart.

KELING. A large kind of cod.

Keling he tok, and tumberel,
Hering, and the makerel.   *Havelok, 757.*

KELK. (1) To groan; to belch. *North.*

(2) To beat severely. *Yorksh.*

(3) The roe or milt of fish. *North.*

(4) A large detached rock. *Cumb.*

KELL. (1) A kiln, as lime-kell, &c. *South.* "A furnace or kell," Cleaveland, p. 40. See also Harrison's England, p. 233.

(2) A child's caul; any thin skin or membrane. Hence, any covering like network; the cell of a small animal. "Rim or *kell* wherein the bowels are lapt," Florio, p. 340. A womans calle (q. v.) was so called. Sir John "rofe my kelle," said a young lady describing the evils attendant on waking the well, MS. Cantab. Ff. v. 48, f. 111.

Sussanne cawghte of her *kelle*,
Butt fele ferles her byfelle.
MS Cott. Calig. A. ii. f 1.

With *kelle* and with corenalle clenliche arrayede.
Morte Arthure, MS. Lincoln, f. 87.

KELLEN. (1) The same as *Keffle*, q. v.

(2) A batch of bricks. *Suffolk.*

KELLICH. To romp. *Sussex.*

KELLOW. Black-lead. *North.*

KELLUS. A white soft stone found in tin-mines in Cornwall. See MS. Lansd. 1033.

KELP. (1) A young crow. *Cumb.*

(2) A crook for a pot or kettle, to hang it over a fire. *North.*

(3) Seaweed burnt to make a cinder or pot-ash for the potters. *Kent.*

KELTER. (1) Rubbish; stupid talk; a confused mass of persons or things. *North.*

(2) Condition; order. *East.* It is occasionally used as a verb.

(3) An awkward fall. *North.*

(4) Money; cash. *Yorksh.*

KEM. Came. Octovian, 1552.

> Whan he to lond *kem*,
> Men tolde the bischop was is em.
> *Beves of Hamtovn*, p. 93.

KEMB. (1) A stronghold. *North.*

(2) To comb. Still in use. *Kemith*, Reliq. Antiq. ii. 176. (*A.-S.*)

KEMBING. A brewing-vessel. *Linc.* Chaucer has *kemelin*, a tub.

KEMBOLL. Arms on kemboll, i. e. a-kimbo.

KEMELING. The same as *Comeling*, q. v.

KEMMET. Foolish; rather silly. *Salop.*

KEMP. (1) A boar. *Suffolk.*

(2) A kind of eel. *Palsgrave.*

(3) To strive for superiority. *North.*

> There es no kyng undire Criste may *kemp* with hym one.   *Morte Arthure, MS. Lincoln,* f. 81.

(4) A knight; a champion. See Perceval, 47, 118, 1004, 1403, 1422. *Kemperye-man*, soldier, warrior. Percy's Reliques, p. 18.

> I slue ten thowsand upon a day
> Of *kempes* in their best aray.
> *Chester Plays,* i. 259.

KEMPS. Hair among wool. *North.* Kempster, a female who cleaned wool. " *Pectrix*, a kempster," Nominale MS.

KEMSE. A light and loose kind of female garment. See R. de Brunne, p. 122.

KEMYN. Came. See Old Christmas Carols, p. 12; Songs and Carols, st. xi.

KEN. (1) A churn. *North.*

(2) A measure of corn. *Yorksh.* It is a hundred-weight of heavier substances.

(3) Kine; oxen. Octovian, 672.

(4) To know; to be acquainted with. Also, to see; a sight. *North.* Sometimes, to teach. (*A.-S.*) Cf. Tundale's Visions, p. 43.

> For the emperyce of ryche Rome
> Fulle welle he hur *kende*.
> *MS. Cantab.* Ff. ii. 38, f. 85.
> Crystofere cristenyde thamme ry'tc' ther,
> And *kend* thamme to leve on Cri .is lare.
> *MS. Lincoln* A. i. 17, f. 128.
> And jyve my body for to brenne,
> Opunly other men to *kenne*.
> *MS. Harl.* 1701, f. 47.

KENCH. A twist, or sprain. *North.* Also the same as *Canch*, q. v.

KENDAL-GREEN. A kind of forester's green cloth, so called from Kendal, co. Westmoreland, which was famous for their manufacture. *Kendal-stockener*, a little thick-set fellow.

KENE. Sharp; earnest; bold. (*A.-S.*)

> He drank, and made the cuppe ful clene,
> And sith he spake wordis *kene*.
> *MS. Cantab.* Ff. v. 48, f. 50.

KENEDE. Kennelled. *Hearne.*

KENET. (1) Ash-colour. *Palsgrave.*

(2) A small hound. See Reliq. Antiq. ii. 7; Wright's Seven Sages, p. 60.

> Fore ferdnesse of hys face, as they fey were,
> Cowchide as *kenetes* before the kyng selvyne.
> *Morte Arthure, MS. Lincoln,* f. 54.

KEN-GOOD. A warning. *North.* Also, a mark or example.

KENLED. Brought forth young. (*A.-S.*)

KENNECIS. Some kind of bird, mentioned in the Archæologia, xiii. 350.

KENNEL. To harbour. A term applied to the fox. See *Hunting.*

KENNELL. A kind of coal. It burns very brilliantly, and is much esteemed.

KENNEN. Half a bushel. *North.*

KENNES. Kind; sort of. *Ritson.*

KENNETS. A coarse Welsh cloth.

KEN-NIFE. A knife. *Cornw.*

KENNING. (1) An inkling. *North.*

(2) The same as *Dalk*, q. v.

(3) The distance a person can see. Also called a *kenny*. See Harrison, p. 60; Hawkins' Engl. Dram. ii. 270; Hall, Henry V. f. 5. "I am within syght, as a shyppe is that cometh within the kennyng, *je blanchis*," Palsgrave, verb. f. 148. See Pr. Parv. p. 272.

KENSBACK. Perverse. *Yorksh.* Sometimes, conspicuous, evident, clear.

KENSILL. To beat. *North.*

KENSPECKLED. Speckled or marked so as to be conspicuous. *North.*

KENT. Was so famous a place for robberies in Elizabeth's time that the name was given to any nest of thieves.

> Some bookes are arrogant and impudent;
> So are most thieves in Cristendome and *Kent*.
> *Taylor's Workes,* 1630, ii. 124.

KENTAL. For quintal, a cwt. (*Fr.*)

KENTE. Taught. Chester Plays, i. 32.

KENTERS. Kentish-men. *Hearne.*

KENYNG. Recognition. Sevyn Sages, 3235.

KEO. A jackdaw. *Prompt. Parv.*

KEOUT. A mongrel cur. *North.*

KEOVERE. To recover; to obtain. (*A.-N.*)

KEP. To reach, or heave. *North.*

KEPE. (1) Care; attention. (*A.-S.*) Also, to take care, to care.

(2) To meet. Towneley Myst. p. 323.

(3) To leave. Nominale MS.

KEPPEN. To hoodwink. *North.*

KEPPING. Lying in wait. *Yorksh*

KEPPY-BALL. The game of hand-ball.

KEPT. (1) Caught. *North.*

(2) Guarded. See Tyrwhitt, iv. 148.

(3) Resided; lived. See *Keep.*

KEPTE. Cared for. See *Kepe* (1).

KER. Occasion; business. (*A.-S.*)

KERCH. A kind of pan. *Devon.*

KERCHE. A head-cloth. (*A.-N.*) "Upon hir hed a *kerché* of Valence," Lydgate's Minor Poems, p. 47.

KERCHEF-OF-PLESAUNCE. An embroidered cloth presented by a lady to her knight to wear for her sake. This he was bound in honour to place on his helmet.

KERCHER. An animal's caul. *Devon.*

KERCHERE. A kerché, q. v. See Cov. Myst. p. 54; *kerchy*, ibid. p. 318. "Kerchew, *ricula*," MS. Arund. 249, f. 88.

KERCHUP. The cry of partridges.

KERE. To recover; to cure. (*A.-S.*)

KERF. (1) An incision. *South.* It occurs in Hampole, cut, carved.

(2) A layer of hay or turf. *West.*

(3) A company of panters. *Coles*

KERL. A loin; a kidney. *West.* Lhuyd's MS. additions to Ray.

KERLEY-MERLEY. A gimcrack. *North.*

KERLOK. The charlock. It is Latinized by *rapistrum* in MS. Sloane 5, f. 9.

KERM. To dig, or hoe. *Somerset.*

KERN. (1) To turn from blossom to fruit, spoken of vegetables. *West.* "To kerne as corne," Florio, p. 217.

(2) To curdle, or turn sour. *West.* Buttermilk is called kern-milk, though perhaps from *kern*, to churn.

(3) To set corn or fruit. *Devon.*

(4) To simmer. *Somerset.*

KERN-BABY. An image dressed up with corn, carried before the reapers to their harvest-home supper, or *kern-supper.* To win the kern, to conclude the reaping.

KERNE. (1) An Irish foot-soldier, of the very lowest and poorest rank. Hence the term was used as one of contempt. Blount says, "we take a *kern* most commonly for a farmer, or countrey-bumkin," and the term occurs in that sense in the King and a poore Northerne Man, 1640.

> Acquainted with rich and eke with poore,
> And kend well every *kerne* whoore.
> *Cobler of Canterburie, 1608.*

(2) To sow with corn. (*A.-S.*)

> Perseyve ꝫc and heere ꝫe my speche, wher he that
> erith schal ere al day for to sowe, and schal he
> *kerne*, and purge his lond. *Wickliffe, MS. Bodl. 277.*

KERNED-BEEF. Salted beef. *Hants.*

KERNEL. (1) A grain. *Var. dial.* See Harrison's Descr. of Britaine, p. 110. Also, the pip of an apple, orange, &c.

(2) The dug of a heifer. *North.*

(3) The bundle of fat before the shoulder; any swelling or knob of flesh. *Var. dial.*

(4) A battlement. (*A.-N.*)

> The cowntas of Crasyne, with hir clere maydyns,
> Knells downe in the *kyrnelles* thare the kyng hovede.
> *Morte Arthure, MS. Lincoln, f. 85.*
> The maydene, whitt als lely-floure,
> Laye in a *kirnelle* of a towre.
> *MS. Lincoln A. 1. 17, f. 107.*

KERNING. Corn-bearing. *Kent.*

KERP. To carp, or scold; to speak affectedly; to tyrannize. *Devon.*

KERRE. Rock. *Gawayne.*

KERRY. (1) A large apron. *West.*

(2) With great and rapid force. *Yorksh.*

KERRY-MERRY-BUFF. A kind of material of which jerkins were formerly sometimes made. The phrase seems to have been proverbial, and is often used jocularly.

KERSE. (1) To cover a wall with tile or slate, especially the latter. MS. Lansd. 1033.

(2) Boldness; courage. *North.*

(3) A water-cress. (*A.-S.*)

> Men witen welle whiche hath the werse,
> And so to me nis worth a *kerse.*
> *Gower, MS. Soc. Antiq. 134, f. 88.*

(4) A crease in linen, &c. *Linc.*

KERSEN. To christen. *North.* See Middleton, i. 429; Beaum. and Flet. iv. 53. *Kersmas,* Christmas, Middleton, v. 139.

KERSOUNS. Water-cresses. *North.*

KERVE. (1) To curdle. See *Carve.*

(2) To cut; to carve. (*A.-S.*) Hence *kervinge,* cutting, sharp.

> So couched them after thei schuld serve,
> Sum for to flee, and sum for to wounde and *kerve.*
> *Chaucer, MS. Cantab. Ff. 1. 6, f. 25*

KESH. A kex, or hollow stem. *North.*

KESLINGS. White bullace. *Devon.*

KESLOP. A stomach used for rennet. *North.*

KESS. A cap. *Devon.*

KESSE. To kiss. (*A.-S.*)

KESSON. A Christian. *Exmoor.*

KEST. (1) To cast. *North.* It has several of the meanings of *Cast,* q. v.

> Sore he spwed, and alle up he *kest*
> That he had rocevyd in his brest.
> *Colyn Blowbol's Testament.*
> So was the mayden feyre and fre,
> That alle hyr love on hym had *keste.*
> *MS. Harl. 2252, f. 92.*
> Into the see he hyt *keste.*   *MS. Ibid. f. 128.*

(2) Twist; knot. (3) Stratagem. *Gawayne.*

KESTER. Christopher. *North.*

KESTERN. Cross; contentious. *North.*

KESTIN. A kind of plum. *Devon.*

KESTRAN. A worthless fellow. Perhaps from kestril, a castrel, q. v.

> I forbud ony *kestran* ou am aw to play boe at my
> buckler.   *MS. Ashmole 826, f. 106*

KET. Carrion; filth. Hence a term of reproach, a slut, an untidy person. *North.*

KETCH. (1) A tub; a barrel. *West.*

(2) To consolidate, as melted wax or tallow when cooling. *West.*

(3) To seize, or catch hold of. *South.* See Doctour Doubble Ale, p. 234.

KETCHER. An animal's caul. *West.*

KET-CRAW. The carrion-crow. *North.*

KETE. Bold? fierce. (*Teut.*)

KETERINS. Irish Scots; marauders who carried off cattle, corn, &c.

KETHE. To make known? (*A.-S.*)

KETLER. Apparently some term of reproach. See Middleton, v. 543. Perhaps from *ket,* q. v.

KETMENT. Filth; rubbish. *North.*

KETTE. To cut. *Lydgate.*

KETTER. (1) Peevish; perverse. *North.*

(2) To diminish in size. *Somerset.*

KETTLE. (1) To tickle. *Northumb.*

(2) A kettle-drum. Hamlet, v. 2.

KETTLE-CASE. The purple orchis. *South.*

KETTLE-HAT. An ancient hat formed of leather. See Pr. Parv. p. 273. "Keste of his ketille-hatte," MS. Morte Arthure, f. 90.

KETTLE-NET. A kind of net used for taking mackerel. *South.*

KETTLE-PINS. Skittles; nine-pins.

KETTLE-SMOCK. A smock-frock. *Somerset.*

KETTY. Nasty; worthless. *North.*

KEVAL. A hard mineral. Also, a coarse sort of spar. *Derb.*

KEVECHER. A head-cloth. *Kevercheffes,* Plumpton Correspondence, p. 202.

KEVEL. (1) A bit for a horse; a gag for the mouth. See Perceval, 424, and my note.

(2) A large hammer. *North.*

KEVERAUNCE. Recovery. (*A.-N.*)

And how of thraldome bi no chaunce
Of his foos mi3t he have *keveraunce*.
Cursor Mundi, MS. Coll. Trin. Cantab. f. 61.

KEVERE. (1) To cover. (*A.-N.*)
'2) To recover. *Chaucer.*

The flesche that fastenyth them amonge,
They *kever* hyt nevyr more.
MS. Cantab. Ff. ii. 38, f. 65.

Whom so thai hitten with ful dent,
Keverd he never verrament.
Arthour and Merlin, p. 303.

(3) To gain ; to arrive ; to accomplish ; to obtain ; to bring ; to descend. *Gawayne.*

KEVIN. Part of a round of beef. *Heref.*

KEVIR. To blubber ; to cry. *Linc.*

KEVISS. To run up and down ; to rollick about ; to beat. *Linc.*

KEVVEL. To walk clumsily. *Cumb.*

KEW-KAW. Awry ; not right. See Depos. Richard II. p. 24. It is spelt *kewwaw* in Taylor's Workes, fol. Lond. 1630, ii. 233.

KEWS. Irons used for the bottoms of shoes. *South.*

KEWTING. Kittening. *Palsgrave.*

KEWTYNE. To mew. Pr. Parv. p. 274.

KEX. A dry hollow stalk of hemlock or similar plant. *Var. dial.* Cotgrave has, " *Canon de suis,* a kex, or elder sticke." It was sometimes used as a substitute for a candle.

KEY. (1) The principal claw in a hawk's foot. *Berners.* Compare the Gent. Rec.

(2) Palsgrave has, " key to knytte walles toguyder, *clef.*" Compare Prompt. Parv. p. 269, " key, or knyttynge of ij. wallys, or trees yn an unstabylle grownde, *loramentum.*"

(3) The fruit of the ash. *Var. dial.* Also called *cats and keys.*

KEY-BEER. Superior ale or beer, kept under lock and key. *East.*

KEY-COLD. As cold as a key. " Key-cold ground," Honest Ghost, 1658, p. 29.

KEYH-WUSS. The left hand. *Lanc.*

KEYS. To wear the keys, i. e. to have the domestic management. *North.*

KEYSAND. Squeamish ; nice. *Cumb.*

KE3TE. Caught. Anturs of Arther, p. 23.

KI. Quoth. *North.*

KIBBAGE. Small refuse ; riff-raff. *East.*

KIBBED. Fenced ; hedged. *Devon.*

KIBBLE. (1) To bruise or grind coarsely, as malt, beans, &c. *Salop.* Also, to clip stones roughly.

'2) The bucket of a draw-well, or of the shaft of a mine. *Devon.*

(3) A stick with a curve or knob at the end, used for several purposes, but generally for playing the game of nurspell, which is somewhat similar to golf, or trap-ball. The game is sometimes called Kibble and Nurspell, or Kibble and Brig.

(4) To walk lamely. *Beds.*

KIBBLE-COBBLE. To crease. *Oxon.*

KIBBLING-AXE. An axe used for cutting kibbles, or fire-wood. *West.*

KIBBO-KIFT. Any proof of great strength or muscular power. *Chesh.*

KIBBY. Sore ; chapped. *Devon.*

KIBE. To jeer, or flout. *Lanc.*

KIBRICK. Sulphur. See Ashmole's Theat. Chem. Brit. 1652, p. 375.

KICHEL. A small cake. (*A.-S.*)

KICK. (1) *To kick the bucket, to kick stiff,* to expire. *To kick the wind,* to be hung. " To die or kicke up ones heeles," Florio, p. 180. *A kick up,* a disturbance. *A kick in one's gallop,* a strange whim.

(2) A novelty ; a dash ; quite the top of the fashion. *Var. dial.*

(3) To sting, as a wasp. *Heref.*

(4) To oppose anything. *Var. dial.*

(5) To stammer. Devonshire Dial. p. 72.

(6) The herb *Palma Christi.*

KICKHAMMER. A stammerer. *Devon.*

KICKING. Smart ; showy ; well-dressed. *West* In some counties, *kicky.*

KICKISH. Irritable. *North.*

KICKLE. Uncertain ; fickle ; unsteady ; tottering. *West.*

KICKS. Breeches. A cant term.

KICKSEE-WINSEE. A strange term, implying restlessness. One of Taylor's pieces, Workes, 1630, ii. 33, is entitled, " The Scourge of Basenesse, or the old lerry, with a new kicksey, and a new-cum twang, with the old winsey." As a substantive it may be explained an unruly jade, and figuratively, a wife. Shakespeare has kicky-wicky in All's Well that Ends Well, ii. 3.

KICKSHAW. A dish in French cookery ; applied metaphorically to a fantastic coxcomb.

KID. (1) Made known ; discovered. (*A.-S.*)

This selkouth mithe nouth ben hyd,
Ful sone it was ful loude *kid.*
Havelok, 1060.

(2) A small tub. *Suffolk.* The term is also applied to a pannier or basket.

(3) A faggot. To bind up faggots. *West.* " Kydde a fagotte," Palsgrave.

(4) The pod of a pea, &c. *Dorset.*

KIDCROW. A calf-crib. *Chesh.*

KIDDAW. " In Cornwal they call the guilliam a kiddaw," Ray, ed. 1674, p. 61.

KIDDIER. A huckster. *East.*

KIDDLE. (1) A dam or open wear in a river, with a loop or narrow cut in it, accommodated for the laying of engines to catch fish. *Blount.*

(2) Saliva ; spittle. *West.*

(3) To embrace ; to cuddle. *East.*

(4) To collect gradually into a heap. The farmer calls a heap of dung collected by small quantities at different times his kiddle-heap.

(5) Unsettled, generally applied to the weather. *Kent.*

KIDDLE-KITTLE. To tickle. *South.*

KIDDON. A loin of meat. *Devon.*

KIDE. A calf-kide, a place made of boughs in the field, or near the cow-house, in which the calf is kept when sucking.

KID-FOX. A young fox. *Shak.*

KIDNEY. Disposition; principles; habits; humour. *Var. dial.*

KIDS. Kidney potatoes. *North.*

KIDWARE. Peas, beans, &c. *Kent.*

KIE. Cows; kine. *North.*

KIEVEL. A lot, or quantity. *Yorksh.*

KIFFE. Kith; kindred. " For kiffe nor for kin," Tusser, p. xxvii.

KIFT. Awkward; clumsy. *West.*

KIHT. Caught; taken away. *Ritson.*

KIKE. To kick. *(A.-S.)*

KILE. An ulcer; a sore. In MS. Med. Linc. f. 283, is a receipt " for *kiles* in the eres."

> Mak it righte hate, and bynd it on a clathe, and
> bynde it to the sare, and it sal do it away or garre it
> togedir to a kile.   *MS. Lincoln. Med.* f. 300.

> Thai fare as dos a rotyn kile,
> That rotys and warkys sore,
> Ay to hit be brokene oute;
> And afterward no more.
>   *MS. Cantab.* Ff. v. 48, f. 85.

KILES. Small leathers used to fasten chains. A mining term.

KILK. Charlock. *Sussex.*

KILL. (1) A kiln. *Var. dial.*

(2) *To kill up,* to kill the remainder where many have been already killed.

KILLAS. A clay slate. *Derb.*

KILL-CLOTH. Some kind of hood.

KILL-COW. A matter of consequence; a terrible fellow. *North.* " You were the onely noted man, th' onely *kill-kow,* th' onely terrible fellow," Cotgrave.

KILLESSE. In architecture, a gutter, grove, or channel. A hipped roof is said to be *kil-lesed,* and a dormer window is sometimes called a killese window. See Oxf. Gl. Arch.

KILLICOUP. A summerset. *North.*

KILLIMORE. An earthnut. *Cornw.*

KILLING-THE-CALF. A kind of droll performance occasionally practised by vagrants in the North of England. It is said to be a very ancient amusement.

KILL-PRIEST. Port wine. *Var. dial.*

KILLRIDGE. The herb arsesmart. *Cotgrave.*

KILPS. Pot-hooks. *North.*

KILSON. The keel of a barge. *West.*

KILT. (1) Small; lean; slender. *Yorksh.*

(2) To tuck up clothes. *North.*

(3) Killed. *Var. dial.* (Spenser.)

KILTER. To dawdle; to gossip. *East.*

KILTERS. Tools; instruments; the component parts of a thing. *Essex.*

KILVER. The same as *Culver,* q. v.

KIMBERLIN. Strangers. *Dorset.*

KIME. A silly fellow. *Kennett.*

KIMED. Cross; ill-tempered; awry; cracked, or silly. *Salop.*

KIM-KAM. Quite wrong; erroneous.

KIMNEL. Any kind of tub for household purposes. See *Kembing.*

KIMY. Fusty; mouldy. *Linc.*

KIN. (1) Kindred. *(A.-S.)*

> That hire kin be ful wei queme.
>   *Havelok,* 393.

(2) To kindle; to light. *Staff.*

(3) A chap, or chilblain. *North.*

KINCH. A small quantity. *Linc.*

KINCHIN-CO. A youth not thoroughly instructed in the art of vagabond knavery. See Dekker's Lanthorne and Candle-Light, 1620, sig. B. iii. *Kinching-morts,* according to Dekker, Belman of London, 1608, are " girles of a yeare or two old, which the morts (their mothers) cary at their backes in their slates; if they have no children of their owne, they will steale them from others, and by some meane disfigure them, that by their parents they shall never be knowne."

KIND. (1) A cricket. *Somerset.*

(2) Intimate. *Not kind,* unfriendly. *North.*

(3) Nature; natural disposition. *Kindly,* naturally. *Var. dial.* A very common archaism.

> He that made kynde may fulfille
> Ajeyn kynde what is His wille.
>   *Cursor Mundi, Coll. Trin. Cantab.* f. 68.

(4) Thriving; prosperous. *West.*

(5) Soft; tender. *North.*

(6) Kindred. Sir Tristrem, p. 145.

> Thys ys the fyrst that y fynde.
> Unbuxumnesse ajens thy kynde.
>   *MS. Harl.* 1701, f. 20.

KINDA. Look yonder. *Suffolk.*

KINDER. Rather. *Var. dial.*

KIND-HART. A jocular term for a toothdrawer. It seems there was an itinerant dentist of this name, or, perhaps, nickname, in Elizabeth's time. He is mentioned in Rowlands' Letting of Humours Blood in the Head Vaine, 1600.

KINDLE. To bring forth young, a term generally applied to rabbits. *North.* Berners calls a litter of cats a kindle.

KINDLESS. Unnatural. *Shak.*

KINDLY. (1) Heartily; well. *Var. dial.*

(2) Natural; native. *(A.-S.)*

> Uche kyng shulde make him boun
> To com to her kyndely toun.
>   *Cursor Mundi, MS. Coll. Trin. Cantab.* f. 70.

KIND-O. In a manner; as it were. *East.*

KINE. (1) A small chink or opening of any kind. *North.*

(2) A weasel. *Sussex.*

KINER. A child's clout. *Suffolk.*

KINES. Kind. *(A.-S.)*

KING. Friday is sometimes called the king of the week. *Devon.*

KING-ARTHUR. A game used at sea, when near the line, or in a hot latitude. It is performed thus:—A man, who is to represent King Arthur, ridiculously dressed, having a large wig made out of oakum, or some old swabs, is seated on the side, or over a large vessel of water. Every person in his turn is to be ceremoniously introduced to him, and to pour a bucket of water over him, crying, Hail, King Arthur! If, during this ceremony, the person introduced laughs or smiles, to which his majesty endeavours to excite him by all sorts of ridiculous gesticulations, he changes place with him, and then becomes King Arthur, till relieved by some brother tar, who has as little command over his muscles as himself.

KING-BY-YOUR-LEAVE. "A playe that children have, where one sytting blyndefolde in the midle, bydeth so tyll the rest have hydden themselves, and then he going to seeke them, if any get his place in the meane space, that same is kynge in his roume," Huloet, 1572. This game is mentioned in Florio, pp. 3, 480; Nomenclator, p. 298.

KINGEUX. The herb crowfoot.

KING-GAME. The pageant of the three kings of Cologne. *Nares.*

KING-GUTTER. A main-drain. *Devon.*

KING-HARRY. King Harry Redcap is the gold-finch, and King Harry Blackap is the blackcap. *King-Harry cut,* a slash over the face.

KING'S-CLOVER. The melilot. It is likewise called the *king's crown.*

KING'S-CUSHION. A temporary seat made by two boys crossing their hands. *North.*

KING'S-PICTURE. Money. *North.*

KINIFE. A knife. *Somerset.*

KINK. (1) To twist; to entangle. Also, a twist in a rope. *North.*

(2) To revive; to recover. *East.*

(3) To laugh loudly. *North.* "With ever-kincking vain," Optick Glasse of Humors, 1639, p. 156. "To lose breath in coughing," Tim Bobbin. "I laghe that I kynke," Towne-ley Mysteries, p. 309.

KINKER. An icicle. *Dorset.*

KINK-HAUST. The chincough. *North.*

KINKLINGS. Periwinkles. *Dorset.*

KINREDE. Kindred. (*A.-S.*)

KINSE. Kind; sort. *Yorksh.*

KINSING. Some operation for the cure of a mad dog. *Hall.*

KINSMAN. A cousin-german. *Norf.* A nephew, in Suffolk.

KIP. The hide of a young or small beast. *Var. dial.* "Kyppe of lambe, a furre," Pals-grave. *Kip-leather,* the tanned hide of a kip.

KIPE. (1) Wrong. *Lanc.*

(2) An osier-basket, broader at top than at bottom, left open at each end, used in Oxford-shire, principally for catching pike.

KIPLIN. The more perishable parts of the cod-fish, cured separately from the body. *East.*

KIPPE. To take up hastily. "Thus y kippe ant cacche," Wright's Political Songs, p. 152.

KIPPER. (1) Amorous. *Lanc.* Also, lively, nimble, gay, light-footed.

(2) A term applied to salmon after their spawning. *North.* Hence, kippered salmon.

KIPPER-NUT. An earth-nut. "Th' earth nut, kipper nut, earth chestnut," Cotgrave.

KIP-TREE. The horizontal roller of a draw-well. Dean Milles' MS. Glossary.

KIRCHER. The midriff. *Somerset.*

KIRK. A church. *North.* Hence *kirk-garth,* a church-yard; *kirk-master,* a churchwarden; *kirk-mass,* a fair.

Kynge Roberd wakenyd, that was in the *kyrke,*
Hys men he thojt woe far to wyrke.
MS. Cantab. Ff. Ii. 38, f. 240

KIRKED. Turning upwards. *Skinner.*

KIRNE. A churn. *North.*

KIROCKS. The same as *Kairns,* q. v.

KIRSOME. Christian. *Nares.*

KIRTLE. A tunic, gown, or jacket. (*A.-S.*) The form of the kirtle underwent various alterations at different times. Palsgrave trans-lates it by *corpset.* It was worn by both sexes. The woman's kirtle of the fourteenth century was a close-fitting dress described in Strutt, ii. 238; and the kirtle is mentioned in Launfal (233) as being laced tightly to the body. It seems to have been a mark of servi-tude or disgrace to appear in a kirtle only. The term is still retained in the provinces in the sense of an outer petticoat. When a long kirtle is spoken of, or when it is implied that the kirtle is long, it must be understood as having a kind of train or petticoat attached to it; and a half-kirtle is either part of this joint article of dress. See Gifford's Ben Jonson, ii. 260. The upper-kirtle was a garment worn over a kirtle.

KIRTYNE. A kind of sauce in ancient cookery. See the Ord. and Reg. p. 460.

KIRVE. To cut coal away at the bottom. A mining term.

KISK. The same as *Kex.* q. v. Hence *kisky,* dry, juiceless, husky.

KISS. *Kiss me at the garden gate,* the garden pansy. *Kiss me ere I rise,* ibid. *To kiss the hare's foot, to kiss the post,* to be too late for any thing. *To kiss the master,* a term at bowls meaning to hit the jack.

KISSES. Small sugar-plums. *Var. dial.*

KISSING-BUNCH. A garment of evergreens ornamented with ribands and oranges, sub-stituted for mistletoe at Christmas, when the latter is not to be obtained.

KISSING-COMFITS. Sugar-plums perfumed, for sweetening the breath.

KISSING-CRUST. That part where the loaves have stuck together in baking. *Var. dial.*

KIST. (1) A chest. *North.*
A *kist* ther wos in that place,
That men put in ther offrande.
MS. Cantab. Ff. v. 48, f. 89.

(2) To cast. *Somerset.*
The grave-lid awey thei *kist,*
And Jhesus loked into the chest.
Cursor Mundi, MS. Coll. Trin. Cantab. f. 89.

(3) Kissed. In the first line it is of course used in the first sense.
Fy on the baggis in the kiste,
I hadde i-nowe, yf I hire *kiste.*
Gower, MS. Soc. Antiq. 134, f. 128.

KISTING. A funeral. *North.*

KISTRESS. A kestrel hawk. *Blome.*

KIT. (1) A smear, or dab. *Cornw.*

(2) Cut off. Batman uppon Bartholome, 1582.

(3) A wooden vessel. *North.*

(4) Brood; family; quantity. *Var. dial.*

(5) Working implements. *North.* Also, the box containing them.

7

(6) An outhouse for cattle. *West.*

(7) A straw or rush basket for herrings or sprats. *East.* Also used for any kind of basket.

(8) A kind of fiddle. " Fidlers kit," Florio, p. 433.

(9) A country clown. *Linc.*

KIT-CAT. A game played by boys in the East of England easier to play than to describe. Three small holes are made in the ground triangularly, about twenty feet apart to mark the position of as many boys, each of whom holds a small stick about two feet long. Three other boys of the adverse side pitch successively a piece of stick, a little bigger than one's thumb, called *cat*, to be struck by those holding the sticks. On its being struck, the boys run from hole to hole, dipping the end of their sticks in as they pass, and counting one, two, three, &c. as they do so, up to thirty-one, which is game, or the greater number of holes gained in the innings may indicate the winners as in cricket.

> Then in his hand he takes a thick bat,
> With which he us'd to play at *kit-cat.*
> *Cotton's Works,* 1734, p. 88.

KIT-CAT-CANNIO. A sedentary game, played by two, with slate and pencil, and decided by the position of certain marks.

KIT-CAT-ROLL. A kind of roller not cylindrical, but somewhat in the form of a double cone meeting in the middle. *East.*

KITCHEN. (1) All sorts of eatables, bread only excepted. *North.* Kitchen-physic, substantial good fare. *Kitchen-stuff,* refuse fat or meat from the kitchen. See the Bride, 1640, sig. C. iii, and Cotgrave.

(2) To be careful, or thrifty. *Linc.*

(3) A tea-urn ; a large kettle. *North.*

KITCHEN-BALL. A woodlouse. *North.*

KITCHINESS-BREAD. Thin soft oat cakes made of thin batter. *Lanc.*

KITE. (1) The belly. *Northumb.*

(2) To strike, beat, or cut. *Glouc.*

(3) A sharper. An old cant term.

(4) To keep ; to preserve. *Somerset.*

KITELLING. A kitten. " *Catalus,* a kytylyng," Nominale MS. *Kitling,* Hollyband's Dictionarie, 4to. Lond. 1593.

KITELLYNGE. Tickling. (*A.-S.*)

> That nowe er deceyved thurgh quayntes of the devel, and *kitellynge* of thaire flesshe.
> *MS. Coll. Eton.* 10, f. 4.

KITH. (1) Kindred: acquaintance. *North.*

(2) Knowledge. *Kyth,* Perceval, 1281.

(3) Country ; region. (*A.-S.*)

KITHE. To show, or make known. (*A.-S.*) Hence, to exhibit in fighting, &c.

> What did ʒe in that place
> Swylk maystris to *kythe.*
> *MS. Lincoln* A. i. 17, f. 131.
> The sothe y wylle the *kythe.*
> *MS. Cantab.* Ff. ii. 38, f. 86.
> For at the justyng wolde y bene,
> To *kythe* me with the knyghtys kene.
> *MS. Ibid.* f. 75.

KITING. A worthless fellow. *North.*

KIT-KARL. Careless. *Suffolk.*

KIT-KEYS. Ash-keys. Bullokar, 1656.

KIT-OF-THE-CANDLESTICK. A vulgar name for the ignis fatuus, mentioned in Aubrey's Wilts, Royal Soc. MS. p. 39. See also R. Scot's Discoverie of Witchcraft, 1584, as quoted in Ritson's Essay on Fairies, p. 45.

KITONE. A kitten. (*A.-N.*)

KIT-PACKS. A kind of buskins. *West.* Spelt *kittibats* by Palmer, p. 59. Dean Milles gives the following enigma:—" Kitteback has what everything has, and everything has what kitteback has," MS. Glossary, p. 160.

KITPAT. The old clogged grease in the stocks of wheels. *Dorset.*

KIT-POLE. A wheel placed horizontally on an upright piece of wood, on which horse-flesh is kept for hounds. *Suffolk.*

KITTEDEN. Cut. (*A.-S.*)

KITTLE. (1) To tickle. *North.* Hence, ticklish, hard, difficult, uncertain, skittish.

(2) To kitten, as cats. *Var. dial.* " *Caller,* to kittle, as a cat," Cotgrave.

(3) *A pretty kittle of fish,* a very bad business, generally meant jocularly. *Kittle-busy,* officious about trifles. *Kittle the chumps,* to stir the fire. *Kittle of hand,* free of hand, apt to strike. *Kittle-pitchering,* a jocular method of effectually interrupting a troublesome teller of long stories by frequent questions.

KITTLE-REAP. Old, young, or unskilful hands, unable to assist in the harvest on equal terms with first-rate workmen, but who help them and do other work at that busy time at higher wages than usual. *Suffolk.*

KITTLE-SMOCK. A smock-frock. *West.*

KITTY. (1) A kit, or company. *West.*

(2) The house of correction. *Newc.*

(3) The bundle of straw by which mines are blasted. *North.*

KITTY-COOT. The water-rail. *West.*

KITTY-KYLOE. A kitten. *Worc.*

KITTY-WITCH. A kind of small crab; a species of sea-fowl ; a female spectre. *East.*

KITTY-WREN. The common wren. *Var. dial.*

KITY. To lade out water. *Beds.*

KIVE. (1) Quoth. *North.* See *Ki.*

(2) The same as *Keeve,* q. v.

KIVER. (1) A cover. *Var. dial.*

(2) A kind of shallow tub. *Sussex.*

KIWING. Carving. Havelok, 1736.

KIX. (1) The same as *Kex,* q. v.

(2) A bullace or wild plum. *South.*

KIZENED. Parched ; husky ; dry. *North.* Also pronounced *kizzard.*

KLEG. A fish, *gadus barbatus.*

KLEMEYN. A claim. See Manners and Household Expences of England, p. 171.

KLEPE. To clip, or embrace. (*A.-S.*)

> Howe *klepet* sche the dede corse, allas !
> *MS. Cantab.* Ff. i. 6, f. 55.

KLEVYS. Rocks ; cliffs. (*A.-S.*)

> Here es a knyghte in theis *klevys* enclesside with hilles,
> That I have cowayte to knawe, because of his wordes.
> *Morte Arthure, MS. Lincoln,* f. 78.

KLICK. (1) A nail, peg, or knob, for hanging articles upon. *North.*

(2) To catch ; to hold ; to seize. *Var. dial.*

KLICK-HOOKS. Large hooks used for catching salmon by day-light. *North.*

KLIKET. A fox. The following lines describe the properties of a good horse.

> Heded of an ox,
> Tayled as fox,
> Comly as a kyng,
> Nekkyd as a dukyng,
> Mouthyd as a *kliket*,
> Witted as a wodkok,
> Wylled as a wedercoke.
> *MS. Cott. Galba E. ix. f. 110.*

KLITE. To take, or pull up. *North.*

KLOTE. The same as *Clote*, q. v.

> Take the rote of the *klote*, and stampe it, and turne it on whyte wyne or ale, and drynk at yeve hoot and at morow kolde. *MS. Med. Rec xv. Cent.*

KLUCKS. Claws; clutches. *North.*

KLUTSEN. To shake. *North.*

KLYNTES. Chasms; crevices. *West.*

> So on rockes and *klyntes* thay runne and dryve,
> That all brekes in pecies and sodenly doith ryve.
> *MS. Lansdowne 208, f. 8.*

KNAA. To know. *North.*

KNAB. To snatch. *To knab the rust*, to get the worst of a bargain. *South.*

KNABBLER. A person who talks much to little purpose. *Sussex.*

KNACK. (1) To gnash the teeth; to snap; to strike; to crack nuts; to clash; to nick; to speak affectedly. *North.* Knack-and-rattle, a noisy and rapid mode of dancing.

(2) A trick; a dexterous exploit. Hence, a joke, a pretty trifle.

(3) A kind of figure made of a small quantity of corn at the end of the harvest, and carried in the harvest-home procession. *Devon.*

KNACKER. (1) A collar and harness-maker, chiefly employed by farmers. *East.* Knacker's-brandy, a sound beating.

(2) A collier's horse. *Glouc.*

KNACKERS. Two pieces of wood struck by moving the hand. A boy's plaything.

KNACK-HARDY. Fool-hardy. *Somerset.*

KNACK-KNEED. Baker-legged, q. v. *Var. dial.*

KNACKS. The game of nine-holes.

KNACKY. Ingenious; handy. *Var. dial.*

KNAD. A knife. Cov. Myst. p. 384.

KNAG. (1) To gnaw. *Linc.*

(2) The rugged top of a hill. *North.*

(3) A wooden peg for clothes. *Devon.* The term occurs in a similar sense in Le Bone Florence of Rome, 1795, and in Syr Gowghter, 194. *Knaged*, nailed, riveted.

(4) The antler of a deer.

KNAGGY. Ill-tempered. *Var. dial.*

KNAMANDEMENT. Commandment. It occurs in Gascoigne's Supposes, 1566.

KNANG. Grumbling; discontent. *North.*

KNAP. (1) The top of a hill. *North.* "A hillocke, or knap of a hill," Cotgrave.

(2) To strike. Also, a blow. "Knap boy on the thumbs," Tusser, p. 261.

(3) To talk short. *North.*

(4) The bud of a flower. *South.*

(5) To break off short; to snap. *Yorksh.*

> *Knap* the thread, and thou art free,
> But 'tis otherwise with me. *Herrick's Works, i. 179.*

KNAPE. A lad; a page. (*A.-S.*)

> Ac right now a litel *knape*
> To Bedingham com with rape.
> *Arthour and Merlin, p. 289.*
> So felle it that this cherlische *knape*
> Hath lad this mayden where he wolde.
> *Gower, MS. Soc. Antiq. 134, f. 238.*

KNAP-KNEES. Knock-knees. *Suffolk.*

KNAPP. To browze. Said of deer.

KNAPPE. A knop; a button. (*A.-S.*)

KNAPPISH. Cross; peevish. "Answering your snappish *quid* with a knappish *quo*," Staniburst's Desc. of Ireland, p. 35.

KNAPPLE. To bite, or nibble. *North.*

KNARLE. A dwarfish fellow. *North.*

KNARLY. Strong; hearty. *Somerset.*

KNARRE. A rock, or cliff. *Gawayne.*

KNARRY. Knotty. *Chaucer.*

KNAST. The snuff of a candle.

KNATCH. To strike, or knock. *Linc.*

KNATTER. To nibble. Metaphorically, to find fault with trifles. *North.*

KNATTLE. The same as *Knatter*, q. v.

KNAVATE. A knave. *Skelton.*

KNAVE. A lad; a servant. (*A.-S.*)

> We ne have to hete, ne we ne have
> Herinne neyther knith ne *knave*. *Havelok, 458.*

KNAVE-CHILD. A boy. (*A.-S.*)

> In holy churche, as clerkes fynde,
> On his douȝtur, agayne kynde,
> Ther he gate a *knave-childe*.
> *MS. Cantab. Ff. v. 48, f. 48.*

KNAWANDE. Gnawing. Arch. xxx. 355, l. 191.

KNAWE. To know. *North.* See Havelok. 2785; Kyng Alisaunder, 724. In some countries we have *knawed*, knew.

KNE. Degree. *Hearne.*

KNEDDE. Kneaded. (*A.-S.*)

KNEE. A bent piece of wood. A term used by carpenters. *North.*

KNEE-HAPSED. Said of wheat, when laid by wind and entangled. *South.*

KNEE-HOLLY. The butcher's broom. *South.*

KNEE-KNAPT. Knock-kneed. *Devon.*

KNEELER. Explained by Holmes, "Stones that stand upright, that makes a square outward above, and inward below."

KNEEN. Knees. (*A.-S.*)

KNEESTEAD. The place of the knee. *Linc.*

KNEESTRADS. Pieces of leather fastened to the knees to protect them from the ladder, worn by thatchers. *Devon.*

KNEP. To bite gently. *North.*

KNEPPARS. Wooden tongs used for pulling up weeds in corn. *Yorksh.*

KNET. Knit; tied. *Weber.*

KNETTAR. A string, or cord. *South.*

KNEW. A knee. (*A.-S.*)

> And sche began mercy to crye,
> Upon hire bare *knew*, and seyde,
> And to hire fadir thus sche seyde.
> *Gower, MS. Soc. Antiq. 134 f. 85.*

KNIBBERS. Young deer when they first begin to have horns; prickers.

32

KNICK-A-KNACKS. Same as *Knackers*, q. v.

KNIFE. Appears sometimes to be used by old writers for a sword or dagger.

KNIFE-GATY. Hospitable. *Linc.*

KNIFE-PLAYING. Tossing up knives and catching them, a sport practised by the ancient jogelours. See Weber, iii. 297.

KNIFLE. To steal; to pilfer. *North.*

KNIGHT. A servant. Generally, a servant in war, a soldier; a knight. (*A.-S.*)

KNIGHTHODE. Valour. *Chaucer.*

KNIGHTLE. Active; skilful. *North.*

KNIGHT-OF-THE-POST. A hired witness; a person hired to give false bail in case of arrest. Hence generally, a cheat or sharper; a robber.

On this account, all those whose fortune's crost,
And want estates, may turn *knights of the post.*
Fletcher's Poems, p. 258.

KNIP. To pinch; to bite. *North.*

KNIPPERDOLLINGS. A sort of heretics, followers of one Knipperdoling, who lived in Germany about the time of the Reformation. Blount's Glossographia, 1681, p. 359.

KNIT. (1) *To knit one up,* to reprove him. *To knit up a matter,* to finish it. See Holinshed, Hist. England, i. 65. *To knit up a man,* to confine him. The phrase occurs in Palsgrave.

(2) Joined; bound; agreed. (*A.-S.*)

(3) To unite; to hang together. *West.* Also, to set, as fruit blossoms.

KNIT-BACK. The herb comfrey.

KNITCH. A bundle. *Somerset.*

KNITS. Small particles of lead ore.

KNITSTER. A female who knits. *Devon.*

KNITTING-CUP. A cup of wine handed round immediately after the marriage ceremony to those who assisted in it.

KNITTING-PINS. Knitting-needles. *East.*

KNITTLE. A string fastened to the mouth of a sack to tie it with. *Sussex.*

KNOB. A round tumour. *South.*

KNOBBED-STICK. A walking-stick, with a knob at the end. *Var. dial.*

KNOBBER. The hart in its second year. See further in v. *Hunting.* Spelt *knobler* in Gent. Rec. ii. 75.

KNOBBLE. To hammer feebly. *West.*

KNOBBLE-TREE. The head. *Suffolk.*

KNOBBLY. (1) Full of knots or lumps. *Var. dial.*
(2) Stylish. *Somerset.*

KNOBLOCKS. Small round coals. *Lanc.*

KNOBS. To make no knobs of a thing, i. e. to make no difficulty about it.

KNOCK. (1) To move about briskly. *East.*

(2) *To knock a man over,* to knock him down. *Knock back ore,* ore mixed with a coarse sort of spar. *Knocked up,* worn out with fatigue. *Knock me down,* strong ale. *To knock at end,* to persevere.

KNOCKING. The cry of hare-hounds.

KNOCKING-MELL. A large wooden hammer used for bruising barley. *Knocking-trough,* a kind of mortar in which that operation was performed.

KNOCKINGS. Native lead ore. *Derb.*

KNOCK-KNOBBLER. The name of the person who perambulates the church during divine service to keep order. *North.*

KNOCKLEDEBOINARD. A term of reproach; a hard-working clown. *Palsgrave.*

KNOCK-SALT. A stupid lout. *Suffolk.*

KNOCKSTONE. A stone used for breaking ore upon. A mining term.

KNODDEN. Kneaded. *North.*

KNOGS. (1) Ninepins. *Yorksh.*
(2) The coarse part of hemp. *West.*

KNOKLED. With craggy projections.

KNOLL. (1) To toll the bell. Still a common word in the provinces.

(2) A little round hill. *Kent.* It occurs in MS. Egerton 614, xiii. Cent.

(3) A turnip. *Kent.* (Kennett, p. 54.)

KNOP. (1) A large tub. *Cumb.*

(2) The bud of a plant. (*A.-S.*) "Out of the knop," Du Bartas, p. 370.

Take half a pound of rede roses floures that be gaderyd erly whyle the dewe lastys, and ben fulle sprad, and pulle of the *knoppes,* and clippe hem with a peyre sherys. *MS. Med. Rec.* xv. Cent.

(3) A knob, or handle; the woollen tuft on the top of a cap.

(4) The knee-cap. Nominale MS.

(5) A button. Rom. of the Rose, 1080.

KNOPPED. A term applied to clothes when partially dried. *Linc.*

KNOPPEDE. (1) Buttoned; fastened. (*A.-S.*)
(2) Full of knops, or knobs. (*A.-S.*)

KNOPPIT. A small lump. *East.*

KNOR. A dwarfish fellow. *North.*

KNORNED. Rugged. *Gawayne.*

KNORRISH. Knottish; full of knots.

KNOT. (1) A rocky summit. *North.*

(2) A boss, a bunch of flowers, &c. An architectural ornament. Oxf. Gl. Arch. p. 221.

(3) *To seek a knot in a rush,* to look for a needle in a bottle of hay. See Elyot, in v. *Scirpus.*

(4) A puzzle. *Var. dial.*

(5) A parterre, or garden plat. *West.*

(6) The key or boss of a vault. It means sometimes a finial.

KNOTCHEL. To cry a woman knotchel is when a man gives public notice he will not pay his wife's debts. *Lanc.*

KNOTLINS. Chitterlins. *Somerset.*

KNOTSTRINGS. Laces. *Devon.*

KNOTTE. A bird, the *Cinclus Bellonii* of Ray. See the Archæologia, xiii. 341. Blount calls it a "delicious sort of small fowl," and says its name is derived from Canute, or Knout, who was said to have been very fond of it.

KNOTTILLES. Knobs. *Somerset.*

He hade a heved lyke a bulle, and *knottilles* in his frount, as thay had bene the bygynnyng of hornes.
MS. Lincoln A. i. 17, f. 1.

KNOTTINGS. Light corn. *Chesh.*

KNOTTLED. Stunted in growth. *South.*

KNOTTY-TOMMY. Oatmeal eaten with boiled milk poured over it. *North.*

KNOULECHE. To acknowledge. (*A.-S.*)

KNOUT. King Canute. (*A.-S.*) *Knoude,* Chronicon Vilodunense, ed. Black, p. 92.

KNOW. (1) Futuo. Still in use.

(2) Knowledge. Also, to acquire knowledge.

KNOWLECHING. Knowledge. (*A.-S.*)

> Of hur for to have a syghte,
> Of hur to have *knowlechyng*.
>> *MS. Cantab. Ff. ii. 38, f. 140.*

> O sothfast Lorde, that haste the *knowlechynge*
> Of every thynge, thorowe thy grete myght.
>> *Lydgate, MS. Ashmole 39, f. 46.*

KNOWLEDGE. *Took his knowledge*, knew him. See Sir Perceval, 1052.

KNOWN. Knew. *Var. dial.*

KNOW-NOTHING. Very ignorant. *East.*

KNOWTH. To know; to acknowledge.

KNOWYNG. Acquaintance. (*A.-S.*)

> That ar aperte of my *knowyng*,
> Thei shalle speke for the to the kyng.
>> *MS Cantab. Ff. v. 48, f. 53.*

KNUBBLE. (1) A small knob. *Suffolk.*

(2) To handle clumsily. *East.*

KNUBLINGS. Small round coals. *Worc.*

KNUCHER. To giggle; to chatter. *Surrey.*

KNUCKER. To neigh. *Kent and Sussex.*

KNUCKLE-DOWN. A phrase at marbles, ordering an antagonist to shoot with his hand on the ground. *Var. dial.* Knuckle-to, to yield or submit. Also, to adhere firmly.

KNUCKLES. The bands of a book.

KNUR. (1) A round hard piece of wood used in the game of knurspell. *North.*

(2) A knot. *Var. dial.* " A bounche or knur in a tree," Elyot, in v. *Bruscum*, ed. 1559.

KNURL. A dwarf. *Northumb.*

KNUTTE. (1) Knights. (2) Knit; tied. *Weber.*

KNYCCHIS. Bundles; sheaves. *Baber.*

KNYLED. Knelt. Percy's Reliques, p. 4.

KNYLLE. To knoll. *North.*

> To wakyne Mildore the bryght,
> With belles for to *knylle*. *MS. Lincoln A. i. 17, f. 136.*

KOCAY. A jakes. *Prompt. Parv.*

KOCOK. A cuckoo. Arch. xxx. 409. It occurs in Nominale MS. spelt *kokoke.*

KOD. Quoth. Robin Hood, i. 92.

KOF. The same as *Cof*, q. v. It means keen, eager, in R. de Brunne, p. 66.

> Allas! queth Beves, whan he doun cam,
> Whilom ichadde an erldam,
> And an hors gode and snel,
> That men clepede Arondel:
> Now ich wolde geve hit *kof*
> For a schiver of a lof. *Beves of Hamtoun*, p. 71.

KOISTER. Ill-tempered. *North.*

KOK. A cook. Havelok, 903.

KOKWOLD. A cuckold.

> And, as I rede in story,
> He was *kokwold* sykerly,
> Forsothe it is no lesyng. *MS. Ashmole 61, f. 59.*

KOLING. The crab-apple. *Salop.*

KOMBIDE. Combed. " Crispid and kombide," Morte Arthure, MS. Lincoln, f. 64.

KONE. To know. (*A.-S.*)

> Thys ensample were gode to *kone*,
> Bothe to the fadyr and eke to the sone.
>> *MS. Harl. 1701, f. 8.*

KONNE. Boldly? (*A.-S.*)

> And alle in fere sey *konne*
> That Degary the pryce hath wonne.
>> *MS. Cantab. Ff. ii. 38, f. 247.*

KONSYONIS. Conscience. *Lydgate.*

KONY. Canny; fine. *North.*

KONYNGESTE. Most learned, or clever.

> The *konyngeste* cardynalle that to the courte lengede
> Knelis to the conquerour, and karpes thire wordes.
>> *Morte Arthure, MS. Lincoln, f 87.*

KOO. A jackdaw. *Palsgrave.*

KOOLESTOCKE. The colewort. Ortus Voc.

KOPPED. Proud; insulting. *North.*

KORBEAU. The miller's thumb. *Kent.*

KOREN. Corn. Havelok, 1879.

KORWE. Sharp. Nominale MS.

KOSTANT. Constantine. *W. Werw.* p. 52.

KOTE. A tunic or coat. (*A.-S.*)

> He dede to make yn the somers tyde
> A *kote* perced queyntly with pryde.
>> *MS. Harl. 1701, f. 23.*

KOTTE. Caught; catched. *Hearne.*

KOTTEDE. Cut. *Lydgate.*

> The *kottede* here forers of ermin,
> The yonge children wende therin.
>> *Beves of Hamtoun, p 136*

KOUP. To bark, or yelp. *Salop.*

KOUS. The same as *Kex*, q. v. *Lanc.*

KOUSLOPPES. Cowslips. Arch. xxx. 409.

KOUTH. Kindred; acquaintance. (*A.-S.*)

> To mi neghburs swithe ma,
> Radnes to mi *kouth* als-swa.
>> *MS. Cott. Vespas.* D. vii. f. 1.

KOVE. *A-kove*, suddenly. (*A.-S.*)

KOWEYNTE. Quaint; cunning.

KOWKE. A cook. Reliq. Antiq. i. 82.

KOWPE. The same as *Chop*, q. v.

KOYCHES? The Cambridge MS. reads *theves*

> Fifteen *koych* com in a stounde
> Al slap, and gaf thay me thys wounde;
> I mun dye tharof, wol I wate,
> Swa icham in ivel state:
> Of myself ne nys me noht,
> On my lemman es al my thoht.
>> *Guy of Warwick, Middlehill MS.*

KRAFTY. Skilfully made. " Fowre crosselettes krafty," MS. Morte Arthure, f. 88.

KRAIM. A booth at a fair. *North.*

KRAKE. To crack; to break. (*A.-S.*)

> With corowns of clere golde that *krakede* in sondire.
>> *Morte Arthure, MS. Lincoln, f. 87.*

KREEKARS. See *Crakers*; Hall, Henry VIII. f. 119; Baker's Chronicle, ed. 1696, p. 272.

KREEL. A worsted ball, the worsted being generally of different colours. *North.*

KRESS-HAWK. A hawk. *Cornw.*

KRESTE. A crest. Nominale MS.

> A *kreste* he beryth in blewe,
> Syr Barnarde then hym knewe.
>> *MS. Cantab. Ff. ii. 38, f. 80*

KREWELLE. Stern; severe.

> With *krewelle* contenance thane the kyng karpis theis wordes,
> I praye the kare noghte, syr knyghte, ne caste you no dredis. *Morte Arthure, MS. Lincoln, f. 95.*

KRIB. A hundred square feet of cut glass. Holme's Academie of Arms, 1688.

KRIKE. A creek. Havelok, 708.

KRINK. A bend, or twist. *East.*

KROCES. Crosses. *Hearne.*

KROUCHEN. Perched. *North.*

KRYE. To cry; to shout.

With knyghttly contenaunce sir Clegis hymselfene
Kryes to the companye, and carpes thees wordes.
Morte Arthure, MS. Lincoln, f. 70.

KRYVE. The grave. Langtoft, p. 91.

KU. A cow. (*A.-S.*)

KUCKUC. A cuckoo. See Mr. Wright's collection of Latin Stories, p. 74.

KUDDE. Showed. (*A.-S.*)
    I·hered be oure Lord Crist
    That here *kudde* his myʒt.
        MS. Coll. Trin. Oxon. 57.

KUKE. A cook. Nominale MS.

KULLACK. An onion. *Devon.*

KULN. A windmill. *North.*

KULPY. Thick-set; stout. *Suffolk.*

KUNDERE. Nearer of kin. (*A.-S.*)

KUNGER. A conger. Reliq. Antiq. ii. 174.

KUNTEYNED. Sat; held himself. *W. Werw.*

KUNTIPUT. A clown. *Somerset.*

KUNY. Coin. *Prompt. Parv.*

KUSSYNYS. Cushions.
    These fresh ladyes and these lordes ben sette
    On *kussynys* of silk togedir to and to.
        MS. Cantab. Ff. i. 6, f. 142.

KUTHTHES. Manners; habits. (*A.-S.*)

KUTTE. To cut. (*A.-S.*)

KUTTER. A swaggerer; a bully. *Kutting,* the adjective, is also found in the same MS.
    I serve the ruffler as the rest,
    And all that brage and swashe;
    The kuttinge *kutters* of Queen hyve.
    And all that revells dashe. *MS. Ashmole* 208.

KYBYTE. A cubit. *Prompt. Parv.*

KYDE. Famous; renowned. (*A.-S.*)
    Thane aftyre at Carlelele a Cr[ ]ynmese he haldes,
    This like *kyde* conquerour, and helde hym for lorde.
        Morte Arthure, MS. Lincoln, f. 53.

KYDEL. A dam in a river for taking fish. See Statute 2 Henry VI. c. 15, quoted in Chitty's Treatise on the Game Laws, 1812, i. 373.
    Fishes love soote smell; also it is trewe
    Thei love not old *kydles* as thei doe the new.
        Ashmole's Theat. Chem. Brit. 1652, p. 71.

KYE. (1) She. *Hearne.*
(2) To cry. Middleton, ii. 485.

KYGHT. Caught. Hartshorne, p. 122.

KYISH. Dirty. *Suffolk.*

KYKE. To look steadfastly. (*A.-S.*)

KYKNYTES. Knights. Cov. Myst. p. 180.

KYLE. A cock of hay. *North.*

KYLOES. Small Highland cattle. *North.*

KYMENT. Stupid. *Heref.*

KYNDE. Begotten. (*A.-S.*)

KYNDONE. A kingdom. (*A.-S.*)
    That my fadres dere chyldren bene
    Into hys blys and *kyndone* withe me.
        MS. Harl. 2260, f. 71

KYNE. Kin; kindred. (*A.-S.*)
    Now hafe I taulde the the *kyne* that I ofe come.
        Morte Arthure, MS. Lincoln, f. 81.

KYNELD. Brought forth young. It occurs in MS. Cott. Vespas. D. vii.

KYNE-MERK. A mark or sign of royalty. *Kyne-yerde,* a sceptre. (*A.-S.*)

KYNG-RYKE. A kingdom. (*A.-S.*)
    I make the kepare, syr knyghte, of *kyng-rykes* manye,
    Wardayne wyrchipfulle to wellde al my landes.
        Morte Arthure, MS. Lincoln, f 60.

KYNLYME. The hearth-stock. *Pr. Parv.*

KYNREDENE. Kindred. (*A.-S.*)
    And here es the *kyredene* that I of come.
        Morte Arthure, MS. Lincoln. f. 81.

KYNTES. Knights. *Hearne.*

KYPE. (1) An ugly grimace. *Chesh.*
(2) A coarse wicker basket, containing nearly a bushel. *Heref.*
(3) To be very stingy. *Linc.*
(4) Heed; care; attention; study. *West.*
(5) To belch; to vomit. *North.*

KYPTE. Caught; drew out. *Hearne.*

KYRED. Changed; altered. (*A.-S.*)

KYRRE. Quarry. A hunting term. (*A.-N.*,) To make the quarry, to cut up the deer, and feed the hounds.
    And after, whenne the hert is splayed and ded,
    he undoeth hym, and maketh his *kyrré*, and en·
    quyrreth or rewardeth his houndes, and so he hath
    gret likynge.   *MS. Bodl. 546.*

KYRST? A wood. *Oxon.*

KYSE. Chester Plays, i. 80. Qu. *byse?*

KYTTED. Caught. *Weber.*

KYX. The bung of a cask. *Prompt. Parv.* Also the same as *Kex,* q. v.

LA. (1) Lo; behold. (Kennett, MS.)
(2) Low. *North.*

LAA. Law. Nominale MS.

LAB. A tittle-tattle; a blab. Also called a lab-o-the-tongue. *West.* It occurs in Chaucer.

LABARDE. A leopard. Isumbras, 189.

LABBER. (1) To bathe. *Northumb.*
(2) To loll out the tongue; to lick up anything. *Somerset.*
(3) To splash; to dirty. *North.*

LABECYDE. Whipped?
    Lett not thy tonge thy evyn-crysten dyspyse,
    Ande than plesyst more myn excellens
    Than yff thu *labecyde* with grett dylygens
    Upon thy nakyde feet and bare,
    Tyll the blode folwude for peyn and vyolens.
        Mind, Will, and Understanding, p. 20.

LABELL. A tassel. *Huloet.* "Labelles hanging·downe on garlands, or crownes," Baret.

LABLYNG. Babbling. See Urry, p. 535.
    He speketh here repreeffe and vylenye,
    As mannys *lablyng* tonge is wont alway.
        Chaucer, MS. Cantab. Ff. i. 6, f. 61

LABONETTA. An old dance, beginning with the pavian. (*Ital.*)

LABOUR. To cultivate the earth. *To labour on the way,* to go onwards.

LABOURSOME. Laborious. *North.*

LABRUN. To labour. Const. Mas. 273.

LACCHESSE. Negligence. (*A.-N.*)
    The firste poynte of slouthe I calle
    Lachesse, and is the chef of alle.
        Gower, MS. Soc. Antiq. 134, f. 103.

LACE. (1) To beat, or thrash. *Var. dial.* The phrase often is, to lace the jacket. *To lace the skin,* to eat enormously, (to tighten it?)
(2) To mix with spirits. *North.* Lac'd coffee, Praise of Yorkshire Ale, 1697, p. 3.

(3) To streak, as with laces on dress; to ornament; to embellish. " What envious streaks do lace the severing clouds," Shakespeare. Compare Macbeth, ii. 3; True Trag. of Richard III. p. 47. Still in use in the North of England. A person splashed with dirt would said to be laced.

(4) A beam. Sharp's Cov. Myst. p. 37.

> Whenne al was purveide in place,
> And bounden togider beem and lace,
> Thei fond greet merryng in her merk.
> *Cursor Mundi, MS. Coll. Trin. Cantab. f. 55.*

(5) To tie; to bind. (*A.-N.*)

LACED-MUTTON. A prostitute. According to Moor and Forby, the term is not yet obsolete. It occurs in Shakespeare.

LACED-TEA. See *Lace* (2).

LACERT. According to Cotgrave, a fleshy muscle, so termed from its having a tail like a lizard. The author of Dial. Creat. Moral. p. 92, compares its shape to that of a crocodile.

LACHE. (1) Sluggish. (*A.-N.*)

(2) A muddy hole; a bog. *Yorksh.*

(3) To catch; to take. (*A.-S.*) " To *lache* fische," Legend of Pope Gregory, p. 17. Hence sometimes, to embrace.

LACHRYMÆ. The title of a musical work by Dowland, frequently alluded to in old plays.

LACK. To blame. *South.* " With-owten lac," without fault, Ywaine and Gawin, 264.

LACKADAISICAL. Very affected, generally applied to young ladies. *Var. dial.*

LACKADAISY. Alack; alas! *Var. dial.*

LACKE. To beat. *Weber.*

LACKEE. To wander from home. *West.*

LACKES. Lackeys; companions. *Hearne.*

LACKEY. To run by the side, like a lackey. Heywood's Edward IV. p. 16.

LACKITS. Odd things; odds and ends; small sums of money. *North.*

LACK-LATIN. A person ignorant of Latin; an uneducated man. " A silly clarke, an informer, a pettiefogger, a promooter, a Sir John Lacke-Latine," Florio, p. 162.

LACKY. To beat severely. *Devon.*

LACKY-BOYS. Very thin soled shoes.

LACTURE. A mixture for salads.

LAD. (1) A man-servant. *North.* In old English, a low common person.

(2) A thong of leather; a shoe-latchet.

LADDE. Led; carried. (*A.-S.*)

LADDERS. The frame-work fixed on the sides of a waggon. *Var. dial.*

LADDY. The diminutive of *lad.*

LADE. (1) To leak or admit water.

> Withynne the ship wiche that Argus made,
> Whiche was so staunche it myȝte no water *lade.*
> *MS. Digby 230.*

(2) Laden. Todd's Gower, p. 215.

(3) To fasten anything with bands of iron. A joiner's term. *North.*

(4) A ditch, or drain. *Norfolk.*

(5) To abuse a person thoroughly.

LADE-GORN. A pail with a long handle to lade water out with. *Derb.* Also called a *lade-pail.* See Jennings, p. 51.

LADES. The same as *Ladders,* q. v. In Somerset they are called *ladeshrides.*

LADE-SADDLE. A saddle for a horse carrying a load or burthen on its back.

LADGE. To lay eggs. *Devon.*

LADGEN. To close the seams of wooden vessels which have opened from drought, so as to make them hold water. *Chesh.*

LADIES-THISTLE. The *Carduus Benedictus,* Lin. See Palmer, p. 59.

LADILY. Ugly; hideous. (*A.-S.*) Brockett has *laidly* in the same sense.

LADLE. To dawdle. *Norfolk.*

LADLICKED. Licked or beaten by a youth or lad. *Salop.*

LADRON. A thief. (*Span.*)

LAD'S-LOVE. Southernwood. *Var. dial.*

LADUN. A burthen. *South.*

LADY. " The ladie of the wicket, a by-word for a midwife," Cotgrave, in v. *Madame.*

LADY-BIRD. A cant term for a whore.

> A cast of lacquyes, and a *lady-bird,*
> An oath in fashion, and a guilded sword.
> *Fletcher's Poems, p. 176 (er. 676.)*

LADY-BUDDICK. An early kind of apple.

LADY-CLOCK. The lady-bird. *Yorksh.*

LADY-OF-THE-LAKE. A cant term for a courtezan, perhaps taken from the well-known character of that name in the Mort d'Arthur.

LADY'S-HOLE. A game at cards.

LADY'S-SMOCK. Canterbury bells. This flower is also called the lady's-nightcap.

LADY'S-TASTE. The same as *Claggum,* q. v.

LAER. A barn. *Yorksh.* (Kennett, MS.)

LAFE. Remainder; remnant. *North.*

LAFF. To laugh. *North.* " Then wold you *laffe,*" Collier's Old Ballads, p. 60.

LAFT. Left; remained. (*A.-S.*) " And laften the gold," Chron. Vilodun. p. 102.

> What foule that sittes or flye,
> Whether it were ferre or nye,
> Sone with hym it *lafte.*
> *MS. Cantab. Ff. v. 48, f. 51*

LAFTER. The number of eggs laid by a hen before she sits. *North.*

LAG. (1) To crack; to split. *West.*

(2) Late; last; slow. *Var. dial.* Also, the last or lowest part. " The weight would *lagge* thee," Heywood's Iron Age, sig. K. iii.

(3) A game at marbles.

(4) The stand for a barrel. Also, the narrow wood or stave. *North*

(5) A law. Kennett, MS. Lansd. 1033.

LAGABAG. A lazy fellow. *Suffolk.* Forby has it, but spelt *lagarag.*

LAGE. To wash. *Lagge,* a bundle of clothes for washing. Old cant terms.

LAGGED. Dirtied; splashed. *Palsgrave.*

LAGGEN. (1) The stave of a cask. *North.*

(2) The angle between the side and bottom of a wooden dish. *Northumb.*

LAGGENE. They lay?

> Thane theire launces they lachene, theis lordlyche byrnez,
> *Laggene* with longe speres one lyarde stedes.
> *Morte Arthure, MS. Lincoln, f. 80*

LAGGER. A green lane; a narrow strip of ground. *West.*

LAGH. Law. (*A.-S.*) It occurs in MS. Cotton. Vespas. D. vii. Ps. 1.

LAGHBERER. A ruler. (*A.-S.*)

LAGHTE. Taken; caught. (*A.-S.*)

And he lordely lyghttes, and *laghts* of his brydille,
And lete his burlyche blonke baite on the flores.
Morte Arthure, MS. Lincoln, f. 81.

LAG-LAST. A loiterer. *North.* "Lastly, *lagly*, behind all," Florio, p. 149. *Lagman*, the last of a company of reapers.

LAG-TEETH. The grinders, so called because the last in growth. See Florio, p. 511.

LAG-WOOD. The larger sticks from the head of an oak tree when felled. *Dorset.*

LAID. (1) Killed; dead. *Suffolk.* The common phrase is, *laid by the wall.*

The kyng of Lebe es laide, and in the felde levyde,
And manye of his lege mene that there to hym langede.
Morte Arthure, MS. Lincoln, f. 73.

(2) Laid down for a nap. *East.*

(3) Just or slightly frozen. *Norf.*

(4) Plotted; designed; contrived. *Shak.*

(5) *Laid out*, bedecked with finery. *Laid up*, confined from sickness. When a coal-pit ceases working, it is said to be *laid in..*

(6) Trimmed, as with lace, &c.

LAIE. A lake. (*A.-S.*)

The blod ran in the valaie,
So water out of a laie. *Arthour and Merlin, p. 197.*

LAIER. Soil; dung. *East.*

LAIGHTON. A garden. *Yorksh.*

LAIN. A layer of anything. The term occurs in Harrison's England, p. 187.

LAINCH. A long stride. *North.*

LAINE. (1) To lay. (*A.-S.*) It is the imperf. pl. in the following example.

And in a chare they hym *layne,*
And ladd hym home into Almayne.
MS. Cantab. Ff. ii. 38, f. 77.

(2) To conceal. (*A.-S.*) "The sothe es noghte to laine," the truth must not be concealed, a very common phrase in old romances.

Sir Degrevaunt, es noghte to *layne,*
His swerd hase he owt-drawene.
MS. Lincoln A. i. 17, f. 137.

(3) Concealment. From the verb.

When Robyn came to Notyngham,
Sertenly withoutene *layne,*
He prayed to God and myld Mary
To bring hym out save agayne.
MS. Cantab. Ff. v. 48, f. 126.

Lady, he sayd, withouten *layne,*
This is Launcelottis sheld de Lake.
MS. Harl. 2252, f. 94.

LAINERS. Straps; thongs. (*A.-N.*)

LAIR. Soil; land. "Layre of a grounde, *terroy*," Palsgrave. Brockett explains it, mire, dirt. "*Laire*, open pasture, common field," Kennett, MS. Lansd. 1033.

Of water his body, is flesshe *laire,*
His heer of fuyr, his honde of ayre.
Cursor Mundi, MS Col. Trin. Cantab. f. 4.

LAIRD. (1) Learned. (*A.-S.*)

Ne riche, ne pour, ne bond, ne fre,
Laird, ne lawed, what sa he be.
John de Wageby, p. 7.

(2) A proprietor of land. *North.* Properly, a lord of the manor.

LAIRIE. An aery of hawks. Florio, p. 129.

LAIRING. Wading through mire, &c. *North.*

LAIRLY. Idle; base, *Cumb.*

LAISTOWE. "The ancient gardens were but dunghils and *laistowes*," Harrison, p. 209. See further in *Lay-stall.*

LAITCH. To be idle and gay; to loiter; to laugh; to titter. *North.*

LAITCHETY. Idle; careless. *South.*

LAITE. To search; to seek for. Still in use in the North of England.

LAITER. The same as *Lafter,* q. v.

LAITH. (1) Loath; loathly. *North.*

(2) To bid, ask, or invite. *Yorksh.*

LAK. Vice; sin; little. *Hearne.*

LAKE. (1) A kind of fine linen. Shirts were formerly made of it. It is mentioned in a laundress's list of articles in MS. Cantab. Ff. i. 6, f. 141, and by Chaucer. The following passage establishes its colour.

The daisé y-corowned white as *lake,*
An vielettis on bankes be bedene.
MS. Cantab. Ff. i. 6, f. 11.

(2) Fault. (*A.-S.*) Octovian, 1394. Kennett explains it, disgrace, scandal.

So ere these bakbytres won,
Thai say the wrast that thai cou,
Ever behynde a manys bake
With ille thai fynde to hym a *lake.*
R. de Brunne, MS. Bowes, p. 31.

For yn the syxte ther y spake,
Y touched of thys yche *lake.*
MS. Harl. 1701, f. 30.

(3) To lap up. *Lanc.*

(4) Any small rivulet. *Devon.*

(5) To be costive. *North.*

(6) To play. Also, a play. *North.* Hence *laker*, a player or actor.

William wel with Meliors his wille than dede,
And *layked* there at lyking al the long daye.
William and the Werwolf, p. 38.

(7) To pour water gently. *North.*

(8) To like; to please. Sevyn Sages, 1212.

(9) A den? See Cov. Myst. p. 387.

(10) Lack of anything. *Palsgrave.*

LAKE-WAKE. The ceremony of watching a corpse previously to burial. It is mentioned by Chaucer, Cant. T. 2960, spelt *liche-wake,* more in accordance with its etymology.

LAKIN. (1) See *Byrlakin.*

(2) A plaything; a toy. *North.* "He putt up in his bosome thes iij. lakayns," Gesta Rom. p. 105. *Lakynes*, Nominale MS.

LAL. A petted, spoilt child. *East.*

LALDRUM. A very great simpleton. *East.*

LALL. (1) Little. *North.*

(2) To lounge, or loiter. *Norfolk.*

LALLOP. To beat, or thrash. *Var. dial.*

LALLOPS. A slattern. *North.*

LAM. To beat soundly. *Var. dial.* "I'le *lambe* your jackett, sirrah," MS. Lansd. 1033, f. 2. Hence *lamb-pie*, a sound beating; and, perhaps, *lamback*, to beat. "*Dob.*, beaten, lammed, bethwacked," Cotgrave.

LAMB-HOGS. Lambs before shearing. *North.*

LAMBOYS. The drapery which came from below the tasses over the thighs, sometimes imitated in steel. See Hall, Henry IV. f. 12.

LAMBREN. Lambs. (*A.-S.*)

LAMBS. Ruffians employed at elections to impress upon the persons and property of the peaceable inhabitants the "physical force" doctrine. Times, Nov. 4th, 1844.

LAMBSKIN. A glutinous substance sometimes found in vinegar. *Linc.*

LAMBSKINES. Strokes. See *Lam.*

> And because therof, I did give her three or four
> *lambskines* with the yerd. Thou servedst her well
> ynough, said he. *MS. Ashmol. 208.*

LAMBSKINET. A juvenile game at cards. *Salop.* From Fr. *Lansquenet.*

LAMB'S-LEG. Nasal dirt. *Var. dial.*

LAMB'S-QUARTERS. The white goose-foot. *Lamb-sucklings,* the flowers of bird's foot clover. *North.*

LAMB-STORMS. Spring storms, often prejudicial to young lambs. *East.*

LAMB'S-TONGUE. Rib-grass. *South.*

LAMB'S-WOOL. Apples roasted, beaten into a pulp, and well mixed with strong ale.

LAMB'S-WOOL-SKY. A collection of white orbicular masses of cloud. *Devon.*

LAMBYKE. An alembic. Arch. xxx. 409.

LAME. (1) Often. (*A.-S.*)

(2) A lamb. "*Agnus,* a lame; *agna,* a new lame," Nominale MS.

(3) Loam; mud; clay. (*A.-S.*)

> Of erthe and *lame* as was Adam
> Makede to noye and nede,
> We er als he maked to be,
> Whilles we this lyfe salle lede.
> *MS. Lincoln A. i. 17, f. 213.*

> Ther is a mon that het Jhesus,
> With *lame* he anoynt myne eyen two.
> *Cursor Mundi, MS. Coll. Trin. Cantab. f. 84.*

(4) A person wounded or injured in any limb was formerly said to be *lame.*

LAMENTABLE. Very. *Var. dial.*

LAMETER. A cripple. *North.* In the West of England a *lamiger.*

LAM-FLOOR. At Wednesbury, co. Staffordshire, the fourth parting or laming in the body of the coal is called the lam-floor.

LAMINGS. The partings of coal. *Staff.*

LAM-LAKENS. See *Bulls-and-Cows.*

LAMM. (1) A plate or scale of metal. An armourer's term. Florio, p. 19.

(2) To catch eels. *Suffolk.*

LAMMEL. Same as *Lambskinet,* q. v.

LAMMING. Huge; great. Formed similarly to *wapping,* &c. from lamming, a beating.

LAMMOCK. To slouch. *Var. dial.*

LAMP. (1) To shine. *Spenser.*

(2) An iron cradle let down with fire into a coal-pit to make a draught of air. *Staff.*

LAMPASS. An excrescence of flesh above the teeth in horses, which prevents their eating. Topsell's Beasts, 1607, p. 362.

LAM-PAY. The same as *Lam,* q. v.

LAMPER-EEL. The lamprey. *East.*

LAMPLOO. An outdoor boy's game.

LAMPORS. A kind of thin silk. (*Dut.*)

LAMPRONS. Lampreys. Ord. and Reg. p. 449.

LAMPSED. Lamed; injured. *West.*

LAMPUS. The same as *Lummox,* q. v.

LAM'S-GRASS. Spring, or early grass. *West.*

LANCASHIRE. "Lancashire law, no stakes, no draw," a saying to avoid payment of a bet when verbally made.

LANCE. Explained by Hearne, "rouse, start, raise, stir up, shoot at." Apparently connected with *Launche,* q. v.

LANCEGAY. A sort of lance. Blount mentions it as prohibited by statute.

> Me thoujte a fyry *lancegay*
> Whilom thorow myn herte he caste.
> *Gower, MS. Soc. Antiq. 134, f. 247.*

LANCE-KNIGHT. A foot-soldier. "*Lasquenet,* a lanceknight, or Germane footman," Cotgrave. "Lansnyght, *lancequenet,*" Palsgrave. These quotations establish the correctness of Gifford's explanation, which is doubted by Nares. "Our lansquenight of Lowe-Germanie," Dekker's Knights Conjuring. p. 59. Blount says, "lance-knights were anciently such horsemen in war as were armed with lances."

LANCELET. A lancet. *Baret.*

LANCEPESADO. "The lowest range and meanest officer in an army is called the *lancepesado,* or *prezado,* who is the leader or governor of half a file," The Soldier's Accidence. The name is variously written.

LAND. (1) That part of ground between the furrows in a ploughed field. *North.*

(2) Freehold, in contradistinction to copyhold. or leasehold. *Devon.*

(3) The same as *Launde,* q. v.

LAND-CRESS. Winter-cress. *South.*

LAND-DAMN. This word is a Shakespearian puzzle. Perhaps the following passage will explain the mystery,—"*Landan, lantan, rantan,* are used by some Glostershire people in the sense of scouring or correcting to some purpose, and also of rattling or rating severely," Dean Milles' MS. Glossary, p. 164.

LAND-DRAKE. The land-rail. *Glouc.*

LANDED. Covered or thickly coated with dirt. *Linc.* It is generally followed by *up.*

LANDER. A man who attends at the mouth of a shaft to receive the kibble, &c.

LANDERER. A person who washed clothes.

LANDERN. A grate. *North.*

LANDFEATHER. A bay of the sea.

LANDLOUPERS. Persons who fly from the country for crime or debt. *North.* Stanihurst, p. 50, has *landleapers,* apparently in the sense of invaders.

LAND-LUBBER. A sailor's term (in ridicule) for any one not a seaman.

LAND-LUNG. The ash-coloured ground liverwort. *Suffolk.*

LANDMALE. A reserved rent, or annual sum of money, charged upon a piece of land by the chief lord of the fee, or a subsequent mesne owner. Finchale Ch.

LAND-MATE. In Herefordshire he that in harvest time reaps on the same ridge of ground or land with another, they call land-mates. Blount, ed. 1681, p. 366.

LAND-MEND. To level ground with a shovel after wheat has been sown. *Glouc.* This is taken from Milles' MS. Glossary.

LANDREN. Ladders. *Hearne.*

LAND-SCORES. Anciently the greatest part of the country lay in common, only some parcels about the villages being enclosed, and a small quantity in *land-scores* allotted out for tillage. Carlisle's Accounts of Charities, p. 295.

LANDSCRAP. A landscape. *Shirley.*

LAND-SHARE. The headland of a field. *Devon.*

LANDSHUT. A land-flood. *Heref.*

LANDSKIP. A landscape. Arch. x. 405.

> Love's like a *landskip*, which doth stand
> Smooth at a distance, rough at hand.
> *Cleaveland's Poems*, 1660, p. 70.

LAND-VINE. A native vine. *Baret.*

LAND-WHIN. The plant rest-harrow. *East.*

LAND-YARDS. Two staves or 18ft. in Cornwall are a land-yard, and 160 land-yards an acre.

LANE. Reward? (*A.-S.*)

> Thorowe Goddis helpe and his knefe,
> Thus hase the geant loste his lyfe;
> Ho loves Gode of his *lane*.
> *MS. Lincoln* A. 1. 17, f. 140.

LANEING. Concealment. *North.*

LANG. Long. *North.* (*A.-S.*)

LANGABERDE. Lombards. *Gawayne.*

LANGAN. The socket of a spade or shovel. *West.* Also called *langit.*

LANGAR. The lash of a whip. *Camb.*

LANG-AVIZED. Long-visaged. *North.*

LANGDEBEF. The herb bugloss.

LANGEE. To long for. *Devon.*

LANGELE. To bind together. *Pr. Parv.* Still in use in the North, to hopple a horse. *Langets*, chains for binding horse's feet. *Langett* occurs in Towneley Myst. p. 26, meaning a strap or thong. " Langot of the shoe, the latchet," Kennett.

LANGELLS. Blankets. Finchale Ch.

LANGET. A strip of ground. *West.* At Islip, co. Oxon, is a field called *Lankot.*

LANGEZ. Belongs ; appertains.

> Thow has clenly the cure that to my coroune *langez,*
> Of alle my werdes wele, and my weyffe eke.
> *Morte Arthure, MS. Lincoln,* f. 60.

LANGHOLDS. Spaniels upon the feet of horses fastened with a horse-lock to keep them from leaping wrong. *North.*

LANGLE. To saunter slowly. *East.*

LANG-LOANING-CAKE. A cake made for schoolboys in the vacation. *North.*

LANGLY. A long time. (*A.-S.*)

> The horse strekede oute his nekke als ferre als he
> myghte, and likked Alexander hand ; and he knelid
> doune on his kneesse, and bihelde Alexander in the
> vessge *langly.* *MS. Lincoln* A. i. 17, f. 1.

LANGOON. A kind of wine, mentioned in the Praise of Yorkshire Ale, 1697, p. 3.

LANGOT. See *Langele.*

LANGOURE. Weakness ; faintness. (*A.-N.*)

LANGREL. Very tall ; long ; lanky. *Linc.*

LANGRETS. False dice, loaded so as to come up *quater or tray* more frequently than the other numbers.

> His *langrets*, with his hie men and his low,
> Are ready what his pleasure is to throw.
> *Rowlands' Humors Ordinarie*, n. d.

LANGSAMENESS. Listlessness. Ellis, iii. 339. *Langsome*, tedious, tiresome.

LANGSYNE. Long ago. *Langsyners*, persons who lived long since. *North.*

LANGTOE.

> Shee added, withall, the report of her better for-
> tunes ; how shee had a swifter and more profitable
> mutation of her ale in former time, how that first
> her ale was ale, and then it was *langtoe,* and then it
> was ale againe. *Rowley's Search for Money,* 1609.

LANGUAGER. A linguist. Thynne. p. 30.

LANGURE. To languish. *Chaucer.*

LANGWORT. The white hellebore.

LANIER. A thong of leather. (*A. N.*) " Lanyer of lether," Palsgrave. The lash of a whip is still so called in Suffolk.

LANK. (1) The groin. *Devon.*

(2) Lean ; miserable. *North.*

LANNARD. The laner hawk. The *lanier* is the male, and the *laneret* the female. See Markham's Countrey Farme, 1616, p. 714.

LANNOCK. A long narrow piece of land. *Wilts.* See *Langet.*

LANSELE. The herb nibwort. (*A.-N.*)

LANT. (1) Urine. *North.* Cotgrave has, " Ecloy, lant, urine."

(2) To beggar, or make poor. *Yorksh.*

(3) Lent. Reliq. Antiq. i. 259.

> In cuntre som tyme was a man
> That *lante* penyes of that he wan.
> *Cursor Mundi, MS. Col . Trin. Cantab.* f. 87.

LANTERED. Hazarded. *Northumb.*

LANTERLOO. A game mentioned in Games Most in Use, 12mo. n. d. The game of *loo* is still termed *lant* in the North.

LANTERN. (1) A lettern. Davies, p. 17.

(2) *Lantern and candle-light*, the old cry of the London belman at night. Its origin is ludicrously accounted for in Hobson's Jests, 1607. One of Dekker's tracts is entitled, " Lanthorne and Candle-Light, or the Bellmans second Nights-walke, in which he brings to light a brood of more strange villanies then ever were till this yeare discovered," 4to. Lond. 1620. (First ed. 1609.)

LANTERN-FISH. The smooth sole. *Cornw.*

LANTERN-LEET. The horn or glass at the sides of a lanthorn. *North.*

LANTERN-PUFF. A hurry. *Warw.*

LANTERN-STAFF. A logger tied to a horse's foot, to enable a person to catch him more easily. *Beds.*

LANTERN-SWASH. A great consternation.

LANTHORN-JAWED. Thin-faced. *Var. dial.*

LANTREE. The bar hooked to a plough or harrow, to which the traces are attached. *Heref.*

LANYELS. Horse-hopples. *Yorksh.*

LAP. (1) To wrap up; to inclose; to cover. Hall, Richard III. f. 3, describing the murder of the infant princes, says, "this Miles Forest and John Dighton about mydnight, the sely children liyng in their beddes, came into the chaumbred and sodenly *lapped* them up amongest the clothes." Still in use.

> They *lapped* hym in on every syde,
> Ther was no bote but to abyde.
> *MS. Cantab.* Ff. ii. 38, f. 78.

> Sewed theme in sendelle sexti faulde aftire,
> *Lappede* them in lede, lesse that they schulde
> Chawnge or chawffe, зif thay myghte eschefle.
> *Morte Arthure, MS. Lincoln,* f. 77.

(2) Leaped; vaulted. *North.*

(3) The end or bottom of a garment; the skirt or lappet. (*A.-S.*)

(4) To flog, or beat. *Somerset.*

(5) To lay anything in a person's lap, i. e. to put it totally in their power. To *lap up*, to relinquish anything; to express in a proper manner.

(6) Porridge. An old cant term. Forby calls it, "thin broth, weak tea," &c.

(7) A covering? See *Lappe*.

> Apes outwardly resemble men very much, and Vesalius saith that their proportion diffreth from mans in moe things then Gallen observeth, as in the muscles of the breast, and those that move the armes, thelbow and the ham, likewise in the inward frame of the hand, in the muscles moving the toes of the feet, and the feet and shoulders, and in the instrument moving the sole of the foot, also in the fundament and messentary, the *lap* of the liver, and the hollow vain holding it up which men have not.
> *Topsell's Four-Footed Beasts,* 1607, p. 3.

LAPARD. The female pudendum. *Devon.*

LAPASSARELLA. The name of an old dance described in Shak. Soc. Papers, i. 27.

LAP-BANDER. Anything that binds two articles more closely together. *North.*

LAP-CLAP. A loud kiss. *Devon.*

LAP-CLOTH. An apron. *Chaucer.*

LAPE. To walk about in the mud; to go slovenly, or untidily. *North.*

LAPISE. Hounds are said to lapise when they open in the string. Gent. Rec. ii. 78.

LAPLOVE. Corn convolvolus. *North.*

LAPPE. Covering. (*A.-S.*)

> And alle ledis me lowttede that lengede in erthe,
> And mowe es lefte me no *lappe* my lygham to hele.
> *Morte Arthure, MS. Lincoln,* f. 83.

LAPPIOR. A dancer. *Cornw.*

LAP-STONE. The stone on which a shoemaker beats his leather. *North.*

LAQUEAR. A ceiling. (Med. Lat.)

LARAS. Any round pieces of wood turned by the turners. *Devon.*

LARD. To baste meat. *North.*

LARDER. Railing; noise. (*A.-N.*)

> Tho was Otuwel fol of mood,
> And faught as he were wood.
> Al the kinges ost anon
> Foleuweden Otuwel echon,
> Roulond and Oliver,
> And maden a foul *larder*.
> *Romance of Otuel,* p. 64.

LARDERY. A larder. See Ord. and Reg. p.

21. "*Lardarium,* a lardyrhows," Nominale MS. Still used in Yorkshire.

LARDING-STICK. An instrument for piercing holes, used in cookery for larding certain fowls, &c.

LARDOSE. A screen behind an altar in a cathedral. *Kennett.*

LARE. (1) A rate or tax. (*A.-S.*)

(2) Learning; lore; doctrine. (*A.-S.*)

> The whilke gladely resayves the *lare* of haly kirke
> thaire moder.   *MS. Coll. Eton.* 10, f. 12.

> Thay lett by thi *lare* lyghte,
> And covetede the golde bryghte.
> *MS. Lincoln* A. i. 17, f. 232.

(3) A quagmire, or bog. *North.*

LAREABELL. The sun-flower. *Linc.*

LARE-FATHER. A schoolmaster. *North.* According to Kennett, an adviser, a counsellor. See MS. Lansd. 1033.

LAREOVERS. When children are over inquisitive as to the meaning or use of any articles, it is sometimes the custom to rebuke them by saying they are *lareovers for meddlers.*

LARGE. (1) *Large and long* were characters in old music. One large contained two longs; one long two breves.

(2) Range. Skelton, ii. 239.

(3) *At my large*, at my liberty.

> I salle at Lammese take leve, and loge at my *large*
> In delitte in his laundes wyth lordes y-nowe.
> *Morte Arthure, MS. Lincoln,* f. 57.

(4) Spacious; free; prodigal. (*A.-N.*)

LARGELY. Fully. *Chaucer.*

LARGENESS. Liberality. (*A.-N.*)

> And that Nature the godesse
> Wylle, off hyre fre *largynesse,*
> With erbys and with flourys bothe
> The feldys and the medwys clothe.
> *MS. Cantab.* Ff. i. 6, f. 1.

LARGESS. A bounty. The reapers in the Eastern counties ask passengers for a largess, and when any money is given to them, all shout together, Largess! Largess! *Largesse* is not uncommon in early English, meaning bounty, liberality. "Crye a larges when a rewarde is geven to workemen, *stipem vociferare*," Huloet, 1552. It was anciently the cry of minstrels at feasts.

LARGYLYCHE. Largely. Rob. Glouc.

LA-RI. An excl. denoting surprise.

LARIOT. The witwal. Florio, pp. 99, 106.

LARK. A wild fellow; a mad prank. Also, to play mad tricks. *Var. dial.*

LARK-HEEL. Long-heeled. *Linc.*

LARKS-LEERS. Arable land not in use; any poor or barren land. *Somerset.*

LARME. An alarum. *Palsgrave.*

LARMY. Sorrowful. *Somerset.*

LARONE. A thief. (*A.-N.*) "Greasie larone," Nabbes' Bride, 1640, sig. F. ii.

LARRICK. Careless. *Yorksh.*

LARRS. Elves, or spirits. *Warner.*

LARRUP. To beat. *Var. dial.*

LARRY. A scolding, or lecture. *West.*

LART. (1) Taught. *Yorksh.*

(2) A wooden floor. *Somerset.*

LARTIN-NAILS. Nails used for fixing laths in floors. *Somerset.*

LARUM. To beat a larum on a woman's stiddy, *rem cum aliqua habere.*

　Tell me, I pray thee, what did he, Tibby ?
　Did he beat a *larum* on thy stiddy?
　　　　　Yorkshire Dialogue, 1697, p. 53.

LARY. Empty. *West.*

LARYDOODLE. The penis. *Devon.*

LAS. A lace ; a snare. (*A.-N.*)

LAS-CHARGEABLE ! Be quiet ! *West.*

LASCHE. In MS. Sloane 1698, f. 9, is a receipt " for to make rede *lasche* or *lether.*"

LASE. Less. Sir Degrevant, 262.

LASER. Leisure. Plumpton Corr. p. 116.

LASH. (1) *To lash out,* to kick ; to be prodigal ; to dilate. *To leave in the lash,* in the dirt, mud, or lurch. *Lash,* extravagant, Holinshed, Conq. of Ireland, p. 30.

(2) To comb the hair. *North.*

(3) A string or cord in which beasts are held ; a snare. See *Las.*

(4) To beat severely. *North.*

(5) Soft ; watery ; insipid. *East.*

LASH-COMB. A wide-toothed comb. *North.*

LASH-EGG. A soft-shelled egg. *Suffolk.*

LASHER. A wear. *Oxon.*

LASHIGILLAVERY. A superfluity, especially applied to articles of food. *North.*

LASHING. Lavish. *Taylor.*

LASHINS. Great quantities. *Northumb.*

LASHNESS. Slackness ; dulness. (*A.-N.*)

LASK. A diarrhœa. See Fletcher's Differences, 1623, p. 33 ; MS. Sloane 1585, f. 121. There is a receipt " to stop a laske" in the same MS. f. 152. It is not quite obsolete.

LASKE. To shorten ; to lessen ; to bring to an end. See Will. Werw. pp. 21, 35.

LASS. Lazy. *I. Wight.*

LASSCHYNGE. Rushing.

　For lyʒte *lasschynge* flame alle the londe over.
　　　　　MS. Cott. Calig. A. ii. f. 111.

LASSE. To lessen, or decrease. (*A.-S.*)

　So that his owen pris he *Lasseth,*
　Whan he suche mesure overpasseth.
　　　　　Gower, MS. Soc. Antiq. 134, f. 54.

　The dayis gon, the moneth passid,
　Hire love encreseth and his *lasseth.*
　　　　　Gower, MS. Ibid. f. 108.

　For schame woche may noʒt be *lassyde*
　Off thyng that was to-fore passyde.
　　　　　MS. Cantab. Ff. i. 6, f. 1.

LAST. (1) The groin. *Suffolk.*

(2) To stretch out ; to extend. *North.*

(3) *On his last legs,* nearly undone. *Of the last edition,* of the newest fashion.

(4) A measure. It is eighty bushels of corn, twelve barrels of fish, fourteen barrels of pitch, tar, or ashes, twelve dozen hides or skins, twenty thousand herrings, twelve sacks of wool, twenty dickers of leather, &c. " White herringes a laste, that is to saye, xij. barrelles," Ord. and Reg. p. 102.

(5) A court held in the marshes of East Kent, consisting of twenty-four jurats, who levy rates for preserving the marshes.

LASTAGE. " Ballesse or lastage for shippes, *saburra,*" Huloet, 1552.

LAST-DAY. Yesterday. *West.*

LASTE. Loss. Reynard the Foxe, p. 85.

LASTENEST. Most lasting. *Var. dial.*

LASTER. The coming-in of the tide. Also the same as *Lafter,* q. v.

LASTREL. Some kind of hawk.

LASTS. The perindum. *Suffolk.*

LASTY. Lasting. *North.*

LAT. (1) A lath. (*A.-S.*) *Lat-river,* a person who makes laths. *North.* " A latt, *asser,*" Nominale MS.

(2) Slow ; tedious. *West.* Lat-a-foot, slow in moving. Wilbraham, p. 53.

(3) To hinder. More usually *let.*

(4) Wet, unseasonable, generally applied to the weather. *North.* See Ray's Words, ed. 1674, p. 29 (wrongly paged 26).

(5) Fashion, or manner. *Scott.*

(6) Leadeth. (*A.-S.*)

　Ac ther the blynde *lat* the blynde,
　In dich thei fallen bothe two.
　　　　　Vernon MS. Bodleian Libr.

LATAND. Letting. (*A.-S.*)

　In that mene tyme Alexander sent a lettre tille Olympyas, his moder, and tille his mayster Arestotle, *latand* thame witte of the batelles and the dyssese that thay suffred.　*MS. Lincoln A. i. 17, f. 46.*

LATBRODS. Lath-nails. Finchale Ch.

LATCH. (1) Fancy ; wish. *Somerset.*

(2) To measure under the surface of a mine to ascertain how much of it has been used. *North.*

(3) To light or fall. *Suffolk.* Kennett gives these meanings as current in Durham.

(4) To support ; to hold. *Var. dial.*

(5) To tarry behind ; to loiter.

(6) To catch. See Macbeth, iv. 3. We have had the older form in v. *Lache.* " *Latching,* catching, infecting," Ray, ed. 1674, p. 29. In the following passage, MS. Bodl. 294 has *lacche,* the best reading.

　How Polyphemus whilom wrought,
　When that he Galathe besought
　Of love, whiche he male not *latche,*
　That made him for to waite and watche.
　　　　　Gower, ed. 1554, f. 27.

(7) A cross-bow. Meyrick, iii. 10.

(8) The same as *Catch* (1).

(9) The same as *Las,* q. v.

(10) *To latch on,* to put water on the mash when the first wort has run off.

LATCH-DRAWER. See *Drawlatch.*

LATCH-PAN. The dripping-pan. *East.* Every cook in Suffolk could settle the dispute on a passage in Mids. Night's Dream, iii. 2. The Athenian's eyes were Puck's *latch-pans.*

LATE. (1) The same as *Laite,* q. v.

(2) An evil, or injury. (*A.-S.*)

　He sal whet his tuskes on Parise ʒates ;
　Almayn sal be ful ferd for his *lates.*
　　　　　Old Prophecies, Cotton MSS.

(3) Feature ; countenance. In the following passage, manner, behaviour.

　Bot thow in this perelle put off the bettire,
　Thow salle be my presonere for alle thy prowde *lates.*
　　　　　Morte Arthure, MS. Lincoln, f. 80.

LATED. Belated. *Shak.*

LATELEST. Most loathly. (*A.-S.*)

LATERED. Delayed. *Chaucer.*

LATESOME. (1) Loathful. It also means, tiresome, tedious. *Warw.*

> But to here of Cristis passioun,
> To many a man it is ful *laytsom.*
>
> *MS. Ashmole 60, f. 5.*

> He es swyft to speke on hys manere,
> And *latsome* and slawe for to here ;
> He prayses awlde men and haldes thalm wyse.
>
> *Hampole, MS. Bowes, p. 35.*

(2) Late ; backward. Plumpton Corr. p. 21. *Lateward.* Cotgrave in v. *Discourtois.*

LATH. (1) An annual court held at Dymchurch, co. Kent. Kennett, MS. Lansd. 1033.

(2) Moveth ; bent down.

(3) To place, or set down. *Linc.*

LATHE. (1) A great part or division of a county, containing three or more hundreds. See Lambarde's Perambulation, ed. 1596, p. 567 ; Harrison, p. 153.

(2) A barn. *North.* An old word. It occurs in Plumpton Correspondence, p. 257.

(3) Hateful ; injured ? Also, injury, harm.

> Sone the erle wexe wrathe,
> And sware many grete athe
> He solde his message be *lathe.*
>
> *MS. Lincoln A. L. 17, f. 131.*

(4) Ease ; rest. *North.*

(5) To ask ; to invite. *Chesh.*

(6) A thistle, or weed of any kind. *Somerset.*

LATHER. (1) Rather. *West.*

(2) Part of a mill. *Var. dial.*

(3) A ladder. See Palsgrave, verb. f. 360; Collier's Old Ballads, pp. 33, 105.

LATHING. An invitation. Kennett says "the use of this word is most proper to Staffordshire." It occurs, however, in Watson, Grose, and Palmer, and is still in use.

LATHY. (1) Strong. *Heref.*

(2) Thin ; slender, like a lath. *Var. dial.*

LATIMER. An interpreter. (*A.-N.*) "Lyare wes mi *latymer*," Wright's Lyric Poetry, p. 49. It is spelt *latyneres* in Maundevile, p. 58, which is the more correct form, *Latin* having been formerly applied to language in general.

LATING. The same as *Lathe* (1).

LATITAT. A noise ; a scolding. *West.*

LATTAGE. An impediment, generally applied to a defect in speech. *West.*

LATTEN. Plate-tin. Palmer says the word is very common in this sense in Devon, and it is also found in the North country glossaries. Shakespeare is said to have given his godson, a child of Ben Jonson, a dozen *latten* spoons, and told the parent he should translate them. The pun is not uncommon in writers of Shakespeare's time, but the old word *latten,* or *latoun,* was not plate-tin, and the provincialism now in use must not mislead us, as it has Brockett, to attribute the same meaning to the archaism. It was a kind of mixed metal, very much resembling brass in its nature and colour. Various articles were made of it, as a cross, Chaucer, Cant. T. 701 : a

basin, Piers Ploughman, p. 462, &c. According to Mr. Hunter, the old brasses in churches are for the most part of latten.

LATTER. To run about idly. *North.* Also the same as *Lafter,* q. v.

LATTER-END. The seat of honour. *South.*

LATTERMATH. See *Aftermath.* "Lateward hay, latermath," Hollyband's Dictionarie, 1593. Still in use.

LATTICE. (1) Plate-tin. *Cornw.*

(2) An ale-house. Many inns formerly had this sign, and the ancient ale-house was generally distinguished by a lattice, not by a glass window, the latter substance being, as Gifford supposes, too fragile for the nature of the customers. See Ben Jonson, i. 96.

LATTING. Late ; backward. *West.*

LAU. (1) Low. (2) A low or flame. (*A.-S.*)

LAUCHAIDS. Terraces, natural or artificial, on the sides of hills. *Devon.*

LAUDATION. Praise. (*Lat.*) It occurs in Hawkins' Engl. Dram. i. 22.

LAUDE. Praise. *Chaucer.*

LAUDES. The service of matins.

LAUGH. To laugh the other side of one's mouth, i. e. to cry. *Var. dial.*

LAUGH-AND-LAY-DOWN. A juvenile game at cards, in which the winner, who holds a certain combination of cards, lays them down upon the table, and laughs at his good success, or, at least, is supposed to do so. Old writers generally call it *laugh and lie down,* as Florio, p. 74. Sometimes the *double entendre* is not of the most delicate description.

> At *laugh and lie downe* if they play,
> What asse against the sport can bray ?
>
> *Lilly's Mother Bombie, ed. 1632, sig. Dd. ii.*

LAUGHE. Taken ; captured.

> Lordes of Lorayne and Lumbardye bothene
> *Laughe* was and lede in with oure lele knyghttes.
>
> *Morte Arthure, MS. Lincoln, f. 85.*

LAUGHT. (1) A loft. *Devon.*

(2) Took ; caught ; received.

> The palem fel ded to grounde,
> His soule *laught* helle hounde.
>
> *Arthour and Merlin, p. 236.*

> Boldely hys swyrde he *laughta,*
> To the gyaunt soche a strok he raghte.
>
> *MS. Cantab. Ff. ii. 38, f. 89.*

(3) The same as *Laughe,* q. v.

> And ther was Lewlyne *laughte,* and Lewlyns brothire,
> With lordes of Lebe, and lede to theire strenghes.
>
> *Morte Arthure, MS. Lincoln, f. 72.*

LAUK. (1) To weed. *Var. dial.*

(2) To strike ; to beat. *North.*

(3) A common exclamation of surprise.

LAUM. To swoon. *Somerset.*

LAUNCE. The sand-eel. *West.*

LAUNCELEY. The herb ribwort. (*A.-N.*)

LAUNCEYNGE. Throwing lances. *Weber.*

LAUNCH. (1) To cry out ; to groan. *Worc.*

(2) To launch leeks is to plant them like celery in trenches. *West.*

(3) A trap used for taking eels, &c.

LAUNCHE. To skip. Forby has it, "to take long strides." It occurs in Sevyn Sages, 1904 meaning, to throw or place.

Who lukes to the lefte syde, whenne his horse launches,
With the lyghte of the sonne men myghte see his lyvere.
Morte Arthure, MS. Lincoln, f. 80.

LAUNDE. A plain place in a wood; an unploughed plain; a park; a lawn. "*Saltus*, a lawnd," Nominale MS.

Now is Gij to a *launde* y-go,
Wher the dragoun duelled tho.
Guy of Warwike, p. 262.

For to hunt at the hartes in thas hye *laundes*
In Glamorgane with glee, thare gladchipe was evere.
Morte Arthure, MS. Lincoln, f. 53.

LAUNDER. (1) Any kind of gutter or channel for conveying water. *Var. dial.*
(2) A washer. Also, to wash. "*Buandière*, launderer." Hollyband's Dictionarie, 1593. *Laundring gold*, washing it.

LAUNDRE. A laundress. *Palsgrave.*

LAUP. To leap. *Yorksh.*

LAUREAT. Crowned with laurel. (*Lat.*) The laureatship at our universities was a degree in grammar, including poetry and rhetoric, so called because the person who graduated was presented with a wreath of laurel.

LAUREOLE. Spurge-laurel. (*A.-N.*)

LAURER. A laurel. *Chaucer.*

LAUS. Loose. (*A.-S.*)

LAUTER. The laurel. (*A.-N.*)

That worthy was the *lauter* to have
Of poetrie, and the palme to atteyne.
Lydgate, MS. Ashmole 39, f. 48.

LAUȝT. Caught; received. (*A.-S.*)

Thenne was Marie Joseph bitauȝt,
And he hir in spousaille lauȝt.
Cursor Mundi, MS. Coll. Trin. Cantab. f. 67.

LAVALTOE. Same as *Lavolta*, q. v.

For lo! the liveless Jacks *lavaltoes* take
At that sweet musick which themselves do make.
Brome's Songs, ed. 1661, p. 133.

LAVANDRE. A laundress. "A tretise for *lavandres*," Reliq. Antiq. i. 26.

LAVANT. A land-spring. *South.*

LAVAS. Lavish. Romeus and Juliet, p. 20.

LAVAST. Uninclosed stubble. *Kent.*

LAVE. (1) The rest; the remainder. *North.*
(2) To lade or draw water. *Chaucer.* Also, to pour, as in Perceval, 2250; to wash, Piers Ploughman, p. 273.
(3) To gutter, as a candle. *Wilts.*
(4) To hang, or flap down. *Hall.*

LAVE-EARED. Long, or flap-eared. See Topsell's Beasts, p. 366; Hawkins, iii. 357; *Lavelugged*, Northumb. Holloway has *lapeared* in use in Sussex and Hants.

LAVEER. To work a ship against the wind. An old sea term.

LAVELL. The flap that covers the top of the windpipe. Still used in Devon.

LAVENDER. *To lay in lavender*, to pawn. This is a very common phrase in old plays. "To lay to pawne, as we say to lay in lavender," Florio, p. 27.

LAVENDREY. Washing. (*A.-N.*)

LAVER. (1) The remainder. *North.*
(2) A cistern, trough, or conduit, to wash in. "*Laver* to washe at, *lavoyr*," Palsgrave. Also, a basin. See Florio, p. 89; Cotgrave, in v.

Esguiere; Leg. Cathol. p. 154; Reliq. Antiq. i. 7; Davies' Ancient Rites, 1672, p. 130.

And fulle glad, certys, thou schalt bee,
Yf that y wylle suffur the
To holde me a *lavour* and bason to my honde.
MS. Cantab. Ff. ii. 38, f. 144.

(3) A dish composed of a kind of sea-weed well washed and boiled. It is also called *laverbread*, Kennett, MS. Lansd. 1033.
(4) *Laver lip*, a hanging lip.

LAVERD. Lord. (*A.-S.*)

That tay after thaym ne went
To du thayr *laverd* comandement.
Guy of Warwick, Middlehill MS.

LAVEROCK. The lark. *North.* See Wright's Lyric Poetry, pp. 26, 40; Reliq. Antiq. i. 86; Wright's Purgatory, p. 55; *laverkes*, Beves of Hamtoun, p. 138.

Sche made many a wondir soune,
Sumtyme liche unto the cok,
Sumtyme unto the *laverok*.
Gower, MS. Soc. Antiq. 134, f. 152.

Tyrlery lorpyn, the *laverocke* songe,
So meryly pypes the sparow;
The cow brake lose, the rope ran home,
Syr, God gyve yow good morow.
Bliss's Bibl. Miscell. p. 54.

LAVISH. Rank, as grass, &c. *West.*

LA-VOLTA. A kind of very active bouncing waltz, formerly much in fashion. The man turned the woman round several times, and then assisted her in making a high spring.

Leave protestations now, and let us hie
To tread *lavolta*, that is women's walk.
Soliman and Perseda, p. 214.

LAVY. Lavish; liberal. *North.*

LAW. (1) To give a hare good law, i. e. a good start before the hounds. It is in very frequent use by boys at play.
(2) A hill, or eminence. *North.*
(3) Custom; manner. See Ellis, ii. 335.
(4) Low. *North.*

He wist not that hym was gode,
But then he putte doune his hode
On knees he fel downe *lawe*.
MS. Cantab. Ff. v. 48, f. 55.

LAWAND. Bowing; humbling.

Anely *lawand* thameselfe to the sacramentes of haly kyrke, thof it be swa that thay hafe bene cumbyrde in syne and with syne alle thaire lyfe tyme.
MS. Lincoln A. i. 17, f. 229.

LAWE. (1) To laugh. Nominale MS.
(2) Rough; violent; brutal. *West.*

LAWED. Ignorant. See *Laird.*

LAWES. The same as *Kairns*, q. v.

LAWESTE. The lowest. *North.*

Lenges all at laysere, and lokes one the wallys
Whare they ware *lawoste* the ledes to assaille.
Morte Arthure, MS. Lincoln, f. 79.

LAWFUL-CASE. An interj. of surprize.

LAWGHE. Low. *Hampole.*

LAWING. (1) Going to law. *Linc.*
(2) Lawing of dogs, i. e. cutting out the balls, or three claws of the fore-feet.

LAWLESS-MAN. An outlaw. (*A.-S.*)

LAWN. The same as *Launde*, q. v.

LAWNDER. The sliding iron in the fore-part of a plough. *Var. dial.*

LAWNGELLE. A blanket. *Prompt. Parv.*

LAWNSETYS. Small javelins. (*A.-N.*)

And also *lawnsetys* wore leyde on hey,
For to schete bothe ferre an ney.

Archæologia, xxi. 52.

LAWRENCE. An imaginary saint or fairy who presides over idleness. *Var. dial.*

LAWRIEN. A kind of oil, formerly used to anoint the ears of deaf people.

LAWSON-EVE. Low Sunday Eve. Hampson, Med. Kalend. ii. 236.

LAW3E. To laugh. (*A.-S.*)

I pray yow alle and warne betyme
That ʒe me calle Joly Robyne,
And ʒe shalle *ldhoʒ* your fille.

MS. Cantab. Ff. v. 48, f. 52.

These *lawʒen* for joye thei ben in lende,
These othere wepen in wo withouten ende.

Cursor Mundi, MS. Coll. Trin. Cantab. f. 141.

LAX. (1) A part. *Somerset.*

(2) Salmon. Wright's Pol. Songs, p. 151.

LAXATIF. A purging medicine. (*A.-N.*)

LAY. (1) A poor·rate. *Linc.*

(2) Law; religious faith. (*A.-S.*)

(3) Summer pasturage for cattle. *North.*

(4) To deliver a woman. *Var. dial.*

(5) A very large pond. *Norf.*

(6) To intend; to lay a plan; to provide; to study; to contrive. *East.*

(7) To lay an edged tool, to re-steel its edge. *Var. dial.*

(8) Belonged. Chron. Vilodun. p. 110.

(9) A wager. See Othello, ii. 3.

(10) Unlearned. *Jonson.*

(11) To lay in wait. It occurs in Shakespeare.

(12) Butter-milk. Dekker's Belman, 1616.

(13) Lay of wind, i. e. a calm.

(14) To strike; to beat. *Somerset.*

(15) Any grass land; a bank. *West.*

(16) A low or flame of fire. *North.* See Kennett, MS. Lansd. 1033.

(17) *To lay in one's dish, or one's light,* to object to a person, to make an accusation against him. *To lay on load,* to strike violently and repeatedly. *To lay down,* to sow ploughed land with grass. *To lay in steep,* to soak. *To lay on,* to fatten; to beat. *To lay the table,* to prepare the table for dinner. *To lay to one's hand,* to help. *To lay an ear,* to listen. *To lay away,* to put out of the way, to lay aside; to break up school. *To lay by,* to cease. *To lay out a corpse,* to prepare it properly for a coffin.

When tablys were *layd* and clothes sprad,
The scheperde into the halle was lad.

MS. Cantab. Ff. v. 48, f. 54.

LAY-BAND. A small roller. *West.* It is explained a *towel* in one MS. glossary.

LAYDLANDS. Untilled lands. *Blount.* "Lay lande, *terre nouvellement, labouree,*" Palsgrave. See Sir Cauline, 107.

LAYEN. A stratum, or layer. *South.*

LAYER. (1) A field of clover or grass; young white thorn; quick. *East.*

(2) A slice of meat. *Var. dial.*

(3) The ordure of cows. *North.*

(4) Land; earth.

Laughte hym upe fulle lovelyly with lordliche knyghttez,
And ledde hyme to the *layere* thare the kyng lyggez

Morte Arthure, MS. Lincoln, f. 77.

LAYERLY. Idle; rascally. *North.*

LAYER-OVER. A whip; a term for any instrument of chastisement. *East.*

LAYERS. The pieces or wood cut and laid in a hedge in spalshing it. *West.*

LAYERY. Earthly.

For it es heghe, and alle that it duellis in it lyftes
abowne *layery* lustes, and vile covaytes.

MS. Lincoln A. L 17, f. 196.

LAY-FEE. The laity. Henry VIII. uses the term in several of his letters.

LAYSERLY. Leisurely. *Laysyr* occurs in Wright's Seven Sages, p. 43.

LAY-STALL. A dunghill. It is spelt *lay-stour* in More's MS. additions to Ray.

LAYTE. Lightning. (*A.-S.*)

And that ys not full moche wonder,
For that day cometh *layte* and thonder.

MS. Cantab. Ff. ii. 38, f. 43.

LAYTH. Lay; faith. Hardyng, f. 88.

LAYTHE. Loathsome; bad. (*A.-S.*)

ʒyf thou herdyst a fals thyng or *layth*,
That were spoke aʒens the feyth.

MS. Harl. 1701, f. 4.

LAYTHELY, Loathly. *Laytheste*, most loathly. "Lucyfere, *lathetheste* in helle," Syr Gawayne, p. 99. Compare Audelay's Poems, p. 32. The editor of Syr Gawayne prints *layeth este.*

We hafe no laysere now these lordys to seke,
For ʒone *laytholy* ladde me lamede so sore.

Morte Arthure, MS. Lincoln, f. 98.

Thase licherouse lurdanes *laytheste* in lede.

MS. Lincoln A. i. 17, f. 232.

LAYVERE. The rest of a spear.

The schafte was strong over alle,
And a welle shaped corynalle,
And was gyrde into the *layvere,*
That he myght not fle ferre nor nere.

MS. Cantab. Ff. ii. 38, f. 247.

LAZAR. A leper. (*A.-N.*)

LAZAROUS-CLAPPER. A door-knocker. This singular phrase occurs in Hollyband, 1593.

LAZE. To be lazy. *East.* "To laze it when he hath most need to looke about him," Cotgrave, in v. *Endormir.*

LAZY. Bad; wicked. *North.* Lazy-weight, a scant, or deficient weight.

LA3. To laugh. See Audelay, p. 49.

A scheperde abides me in halle;
Off hym shalle we laʒ alle.

MS. Cantab. Ff. v. 48, f. 52.

LE. Lie; falsehood. (*A.-S.*)

The kyng that had grete plenté
Off mete and drinke, withoutene *le,*
Long he may dyge and wrote,
Or he have hys fyll of the rote.

MS. Ashmole 61, xv. Cent.

LEA. (1) A scythe. *Yorksh.*

(2) The seventh part of a hank or skein of worsted. *North.*

(3) Meadow; pasture; grass land.

LE-ACH. Hard work, or fatigue. *North.*

LEACH. (1) A lake, or large pool. *Lanc.*

(2) A common way. *Devon.* Leach-road, a road used for funerals.

(3) The leather thong fastened to the jesses of the hawk, by which she is held firmly on the fist. Gent. Rec. ii. 62.

(4) A kind of jelly, made of cream, isinglass, sugar, and almonds, &c. *Holme.*

LEACHMAN. A surgeon. See Nares.

LEACH-TROUGHS. At the salt works in Staffordshire, they take the corned salt from the rest of the brine with a loot or lute, and put it into barrows, the which being set in the *leach-troughs,* the salt drains itself dry, which draining they call *leach-brine,* and preserve it to be boiled again as the best and strongest brine. Kennett, MS. Lansd. 1033.

LEAD. (1) To cart corn. *Var. dial.* Also, to carry trusses on horseback. " Cartyne, or lede wythe a carte," Pr. Parv.

(2) A vat for dying, &c. *North.* A kitchen copper is sometimes so called.

(3) To cover a building with lead.

(4) To chance, or happen. *Devon.*

LEADDEN. A noise, or din. *North.*

LEAD-EATER. Indian rubber. *Yorksh.*

LEADER. (1) A tendon.

(2) A branch of a vein of ore in a mine. *North.*

LEAD-NAILS. Nails used by plumbers in covering the roof of a house with lead.

LEADS. Battlements. *Var. dial.*

LEAD-WALLING. " The brine of twenty-four hours boyling for one house," More's MS. additions to Ray, Mus. Brit.

LEAF. (1) Fat round the kidneys of a pig. *Var. dial.* Also, the kidney itself.

(2) To turn over a new leaf, i. e. to change one's conduct. " To advise the kyng to turne the lefe and to take a better lesson," Hall, 1548.

LEAGUER. A camp. See the Autobiography of Joseph Lister, ed. Wright, p. 25.

LEAK. (1) A gutter. *Durham.*

(2) Mingere. Kennett's MS. Glossary. Also, tap a barrel of beer, &c.

LEAM. (1) To teach. *North.*

(2 A collar for hounds; a leash.

LEAM-HOUND. A kind of hound mentioned in Topsell's Foure-Footed Beasts, 1607, p. 39, the same as *Lyam,* q. v.

LEAN. The same as *Laine,* q. v. " It is not for to leane," Chester Plays, i. 69.

LEAN-BONES. " A dry, a greedie and hungry fellow, a leane bones," Florio, p. 85. Old writers have the phrase, *as lean as a rake.*

LEANING-STONES. Stone seats, such as are sometimes seen in ancient bay windows.

LEAN-TO. A penthouse. *East.*

LEAP. (1) Half a bushel. *Sussex.*

(2) A weel to catch fish. *Lanc.* " Weele or leape," Palsgrave's Acolastus, 1540.

(3) Futuo. The Citye Match, 1639, p. 13.

(4) To leap over the hatch, i. e. to run away.

LEAP-CANDLE. An Oxfordshire game mentioned by Aubrey. Young girls set a candle in the middle of the room, and " draw up their coats in the form of breeches," then dance over the candle backwards and forwards, saying these verses—

The tailor of Bicester he has but one eye,
He cannot cut a pair of green gallicaskins if he were
    to try.

The game is, I believe, obsolete, but the verses are still favourites in the nursery.

LEAPERS. Grey peas. *West.*

LEAPERY. Leprosy. Ryder, 1640.

LEAP-FROG. A boys' game, in which they jump over one another's backs successively.

LEAPING. The operation of lowering tall hedges for the deer to leap over.

LEAPING-BLOCK. A horse-block. *Glouc.* Also called a leaping-stock.

LEAPINGS. Leaps. Florio, p. 97.

LEAPING-THE-WELL. Going through a deep and noisome pool on Alnwick Moor, called the Freemen's Well, a *sine qua non* to the freedom of the borough; a curious custom, well described by Brockett.

LEAR. (1) To learn. *North.*

(2) Hollow; empty. The lear ribs, the hollow under the ribs. *Var. dial.*

(3) Pasture for sheep. *Chesh.* Stubble-land is generally called leers.

LEARN. To teach. *Var. dial.* " Scole to lerne chyldre in, *escole,*" Palsgrave.

LEARNING. Correction; discipline.

LEAR-QUILLS. Very small quills, such as are used to wind yarn on. *Somerset.*

LEARS. The same as *Layers,* q. v.

LEA-SAND. The whetting-stone with which a scythe is sharpened. *North.*

LEASE. A pasture. *Var. dial.* In some places a common is so called.

Brooke lime (Anagallis Aquatica) &c. the bankes enamel'd with it in the *Lease,* cowslip (Arthritica) and primroses (Primula Veris) not inferior to Primrose Hills. *Aubrey's Wilts, Royal Soc. MS. p. 119.*

LEASES. Corbel stones. *Glouc.*

LEASH. A thong or string by which a dog is led. Hence a pack of hounds was formerly called a leash.

Lo ! wher my grayhundes breke ther *leasshe,*
    My raches breke their coupuls in thre ;
Lo ! qwer the dere goos be too and too,
    And holdis over yonde mowntene hye.
        MS. Cantab. Ff. v. 48, f. 121.

LEASING. An armful of hay, or corn, such as is leased or gleaned. *North.*

LEASOW. A pasture-ground. *West.*

LEASTEST. Smallest. *Var. dial.*

LEASTWAYS. At least. *East.* " At the leastwise," Harrison's Britaine, p. 6.

LEASTY. Dull ; wet ; dirty. *East.*

LEAT. (1) To leak ; to pour. *Dorset.*

(2) An artificial brook. *Devon.* Properly one to convey water to or from a mill.

LEATH. (1) Ease or rest. *North.*

(2) Cessation ; intermission. *North.*

(3) Soft ; supple ; limber ; pliant. *Derb.*

(4) Loath ; unwilling. *Yorksh.*

LEATHER. (1) To beat. *Var. dial.*

(2) Skin, not tanned. *North.* To lose leather, to rub the skin off by riding. In hunting,

only to certain integuments. See *Hunting,* art. 5, and the Gent. Rec.

(3) Rather. *Yorksh.* (Kennett MS.)

LEATHER-COAT. The golden russeting. It is mentioned by Shakespeare.

LEATHERHEAD. A blockhead. *North.*

LEATHER-HUNGRY. An inferior sort of cheese made of skimmed milk. *North.*

ATHERING. Huge; large. *Warw.*

ATHERN-BIRD. A bat. *Somerset.* Also called leathern-mouse, leathern-wings.

ATHER-TE-PATCH. A particular kind of step in a dance. *Cumb.*

ATHE-WAKE. Nimber; flexible; pliable. *Yorksh.* " Safe, uncorrupted, flexible, and *leathwake,*" Davies' Ancient Rites, ed. 1672, p. 105. It is given in MS. Lansd. 1033.

LEAUTE. Loyalty. (*A.-N.*)

LEAVANCE. The barm and meal laid together for fermentation ; " to lay the leavance," to put them together for that purpose. *Glouc.* Dean Milles' MS.

LEAVE. (1) To change one's residence ; to give leave, or permit ; to pass over for others. *Leave hold,* let me go ! *Leave tail,* a great demand for anything.

(2) The first offer. *North.*

LEAVEN-KIT. A vessel for preparing the batter for oat-cakes in. *Yorksh.*

LEAVENOR. A luncheon. *Kent.*

LEAVES. Folding-doors, anything shutting or folding up, as the leaves of a table. *North.*

LEAZE. To clean wool. *West.*

LEBARD. A leopard. " Lebarde, a beest, *leopart,*" Palsgrave. " *Leopardus,* a leberde," Nominale MS.

LECH. Liege. Sir Cleges, 409.

LECHE. (1) A physician. *Lechecraft,* the art of healing. (*A.-S.*)

So longe at *leche-crafts* can he dwelle.
MS. Cantab. Ff. ii. 38, f. 68.

(2) To heal. It occurs in Chaucer.

And openly bigan to preche,
And alle that seke were to *leche.*
Cursor Mundi, MS. Coll. Trin. Cantab. f. 2.

(3) A deep rut. *Yorksh.*

(4) To stick, to adhere. *Linc.*

(5) *Leche-lardys,* a dish in ancient cookery, Ord. and Reg. p. 439. *Leche-fryes,* ibid. p. 449. *Leche-Lumbarde,* ibid. p. 472. *Leches* are sometimes cakes or pieces. The term is of constant use in old cookery, meaning generally those dishes which were served up in slices.

LECHOUR. A leacher. (*A.-N.*) It was also applied to a parasite and blockhead.

LECHYDE. Cut into slices.

Scyne bowes of wylde bores, with the braune *lechyde.*
Morte Arthure, MS. Lincoln, f. 55.

LECK. To leak. *To leck on,* to pour on. *To leck off,* to drain off. *North.*

LECKER-COST. Good cheer.

They lyv'd at ease in vile excesse,
They sought for *lecker-cost.*
Riche's Allarme to England, 1578.

LECKS. Droppings. *Yorksh.*

LECTER. A reader. (*Lat.*)

LECTORNE. A reading-desk. (*Lat.*)

Lectornes he saw befor hem stande
Of gold and bokys on hem lyggande.
Visions of Tundale, p. 60.

LECTUARY. An electuary. *Skelton.*

LEDDE. Completely prostrated. (*A.-S.*)

Pers fyl yn a grete syknes,
And as he lay yn hys bedde,
Hym thoghte weyl that he was *ledde.*
MS. Harl. 1701, f. 38.

LEDDER. A ladder. *Ledder-staffs,* the transverse bars or rounds of a ladder.

LEDDY. A lady. *North.*

LEDDYRE. Leather; skin. *R. de Brunne.*

LEDE. (1) People. (2) Land. It sometimes signifies a man, Towneley Myst. p. 21.

That same hoppyng that they fyrst 3ede,
That daunce 3ede they thurghe land and *lede.*
MS. Harl. 1701, f. 61.

In him was al his trust at nede,
And gave him bothe londe and *lede.*
Arthour and Merlin, p. 4.

Herde ever eni of yow telle,
In eni *lede* or eni spelle,
Or in feld, other in toun,
Of a knight Beves of Hamtoun ?
Beves of Hamtoun, p. 83.

Thys tydynges had bothe grete and smalle,
For fayrer fruyt was nevyr in *lede,*
Thorow hys my3t that boght us alle,
Very God in forme of brede.
MS. Cantab. Ff. ii. 38, f. 46.

LEDENE. Speech ; language. (*A.-S.*)

LEDER. Lither ; bad.

Of my kyngdome me grevyth no3t,
Hyt ys for my gylt and *leder* thoghte.
MS. Cantab. Ff. ii. 38, f. 243.

LEDGE. (1) To lay hands on ; to beat ; to lay eggs. *Somerset.*

(2) To allege. *Chaucer.*

Othar dysagrementes thou shalte not read ne se,
Amonge the ancyaunt writers, than ys *ledged* to the.
MS. Lansdowne 208, f. 2.

LEDGER. A horizontal slab of stone, a horizontal bar of a scaffold, &c. A door made of three or four upright boards, fastened by cross-pieces, is called a ledger-door. The bar of a gate, stile, &c. is termed the *ledge.*

LEDGING. Positive. *Leic.*

LEDRON. A leper ; a mean person. (*A.-N.*) See Kyng Alisaunder, 3210.

LED-WILL. A strange phrase, applied to one led away by following false lights, Wills o' the Wisp, &c. *East.*

LEE. (1) Joy ; pleasure ; delight.

(2) A lie. Still in use.

(3) Shelter. See *Lew* and *Loo.*

(4) Urine. Cotgrave, in v. *Escloy.*

(5) Lye of ashes. See Reliq. Antiq. i. 53.

(6) *Lee-lang,* live-long. *Northumb.*

LEECH. A vessel bored with holes at the bottom for making lye. *East.*

LEED-BOWLS. Milk leads. *Yorksh.*

LEEF. Willingly ; equally. *Var. dial.*

LEEFEKYN. A term of endearment, occurring in Palsgrave's Acolastus, 1540.

LEEFEST. Dearest. (*A.-S.*)

Go, soule, and flye unto my *leefest* love,
A fayrer subject then Elysium.
The Woman in the Moone, 1597.

LEEFTAIL. Quick sale. *Cumb.*

LE-EGGING. Waddling. *Somerset.*

LEEMER. Anxious; miserly; keen after money or gain, and not very scrupulous. *North.*

LEEMERS. Ripe nuts. To leem, to shell or drop out of the husk. *Var. dial.*

LEENER. One who lends. (*A.-S.*)

LEENY. Alert; active. *Grose.*

LEER. (1) Leather. *North.*

(2) The same as *Lear,* q. v. Empty. Hence, perhaps, *leer horse,* a horse without a rider. *Leer* is an adjective, meaning uncontrolled. Hence the *leer drunkards* mentioned by Ben Jonson.

(3) To go or sneak away. *North.*

(4) The flank or loin. *Somerset.*

LEERE. Tape. *Kent.* See Nares, p. 281, who was unacquainted with the term.

LEERSPOOLE. A cane or reed.

LEES. A leash for dogs. (*A.-N.*) "The forsaid leese," Arch. xxix. 336, i. e. a pack? See *Leash.* "A brace or leese of bucks," Gent. Rec. ii. 75.

LEESE. The same as *Lese,* q. v.

LEESH. Active. *Northumb.*

LEET. (1) A manor court.

(2) Little. *Leet rather,* a little while ago. *Leet windle,* a small redwing. *Var. dial.*

(3) To pretend; to feign. *Yorksh.*

(4) To happen; to fall out. *North.*

(5) A meeting of cross-roads. *South.*

(6) To alight. " *Leet,* sir, light off your horse," Kennett, MS. Lansd. 1033.

LEETEN. To pretend. See *Leet* (3).

LEETLY. Lightly; little. *Yorksh.*

LEETS. Windows; lights. *North.*

LEEVEN. Believe, pl. Maundevile, p. 108.

LEF. (1) A leaf. W. Mapes, p. 342.

(2) Love; one who is loved.
And scyde how that a-bedde alle warme
Hire *laf* lay nakid in hire arme.
Gower, MS. Soc. Antiq. 134, f. 77.

LEFE. (1) To believe. (*A.-S.*)

(2) Pleasing; dear; agreeable. It sometimes signifies *pleased.* (*A.-S.*)
Be he never so strong a thefe,
Jyf he may jyve he shal be *lefe.*
MS. Harl. 1701, f. 9.

The soule of this synfulle wyjt
Is wonnen into heven bright,
To Jhesu *lefe* and dere.
MS. Cantab. Ff. v. 48, f. 47.

(3) To leave.
Bot if thou come for to feght with us, *feghte* one, for I late the wele witt that oure symplenes wille we on us wyse *lefe.*
MS. Lincoln A. 1. 17, f. 30.

LEFE-LONG. Long; tedious.
She seid, Thomas, thou likes thi play,
What byrde in boure may dwel with the?
Thou marris me here this *lefe-long* day,
I pray the, Thomas, let me be!
True Thomas, MS. Cantab.

LEFMON. Lemman; lover. "Bicom his lefmon," Wright's Anec. Lit. p. 11.

LEF-SILVER. A composition paid in money by the tenants in the wealds of Kent to their lord for leave to plough and sow in time of pannage. Kennett, MS. Lansd. 1033.

LEFSOME. Lovely. *Ritson.*

LEFT. (1) Believed. (2) Remained.

(3) *Left over,* left off. *Over the left shoulder,* entirely wrong. I believe you over the left, i. e. not at all.

LEFTNESS. The state of being left-handed. Metaphorically, wrong, bad.

LEFULL. Lawful. *Chaucer.*

LEG. (1) A bow. It is very often, if not generally, used in a jocular manner. "Make a curtesie instead of a legge," Lilly, ed. 1632, sig. P. xi. Still in use in Craven.

(2) To walk nimbly. *Var. dial.*

(3) *To put the best leg foremost,* to act energetically. *He has broken his leg,* he has had a child sworn to him. *Black leg,* a great rascal. *To give leg bail,* to fly from justice. *Legbanded,* said of cattle when the head and leg are joined by a band or cord to prevent their straying.

(4) At marbles, the boy who commences the game last is called a *leg.*

LEGEANS. Leave; license. (*A.-N.*)
He bethoujt hym and undurstode
In how synfulle life he jede,
His synnes he wolde forsake;
And if he myjt have *legeans*
For his synnes to do penans,
Schrifte he thoujte to take.
MS. Cantab. Ff. v. 48, f. 44.

LEGEM-PONE. A curious old proverbial or cant term for ready money.
There are so manie Danaes now a dayes,
That love for lucre, paine for gaine is sold:
No true affection can their fancie please,
Except it be a Jove, to raine downe gold
Into their laps, which they wyde open hold:
If *legem pone* comes, he is receav'd,
When *Vir haud habeo* is of hope bereav'd.
The Affectionate Shepheard, 1594.

LEGER-BOOK. A monastic cartulary.

LEGESTER. A lawyer. *R. de Brunne.*

LEGGE. (1) To lay; to lay down; to lay, or bet a wager. (*A.-S.*)

(2) To ease. *Chaucer.*

LEGGEREN. A layer. *North.*

LEGGET. A kind of tool used by reed-thatchers. *Norfolk.*

LEGGINGS. Gaiters. *Var. dial.*

LEGHE. To lie; to speak false. It occurs in MS. Cott. Vespas. D. vii.

LEG-RINGS. Fetters. *Marston.*

LEG-TRAPES. A sloven. *Somerset.*

LEIE. To lay. (*A.-S.*)

LEIFER. Rather. *North.* See Topsell's Foure-Footed Beasts, 1607, p. 25.

LEIGER. A resident ambassador at a foreign court. See Arch. xxviii. 121

LEIGHER. A liar. (*A.-S.*)
The messanger was foule y-schent,
And oft y-cleped foule *leigher.*
Arthour and Merlin, p. 95.

LEIK. Body. Havelok, 2793.

LEIKIN. A sweetheart. *North.* From *like.*

LEIL. Faithful; honest. *North.*

LEISER. Leisure; opportunity. (*A.-N.*)

LEISH. Stout; active; alert. *North.*

LEISTER. A kind of trident used in the North of England for striking fish.

LEITE. Light; lightning. (*A.-S.*)

LEITHS. Joints in coal. *Staff.*

LEITS. (1) Meetings appointed for the nomination or election of officers. *North.*

(2) Tracks; footsteps. *North.*

LEKE. (1) Caught; taken. (*A.-S.*)

Then harde he noyse grete
In a valey, and dyntys leke.
MS. Cantab. Ff. ii. 38, f. 246.

(2) A leek. (*A.-S.*) *Not worth a leke*, a common expression in early poetry.

(3) To lock; to shut. *Weber.* Also the part. past, fastened.

(4) To grin frightfully. *Linc.*

LELAND. A cow pasture. *West.*

LELE. Loyal; faithful; true.

Hir love is ever trewe and lele,
Ful swete hit is to monnes hele.
Cursor Mundi, MS. Coll. Trin. Cantab. f. 1.

Bot a clene virgyne that es lele
Has jit more that has the angele.
MS. Harl. 2260, f. 120.

Tho loved Jordaine and sir Bretel
Sir Arthur with hert lel.
Arthour and Merlin, p. 113.

LELELY. Truly; faithfully. The copy in the Cambridge MS. reads *leliche.*

My lufe es lelely lyghte
On a lady wyghte. *MS. Lincoln A. i. 17, f. 132.*

LELEN. To sanction, or authorise. (*A.-N.*)

LELLY. Same as *Lelely*, q. v.

To yelde hym his lufe hafe I na myghte,
Bot lufe hym lelly I sulde tharefore.
MS. Lincoln A. i. 17, f. 219.

They sal thorue holy kyrke rede
Mynystre lely the godes of the dede.
MS. Harl. 2260, f. 50.

That for I trewly many a day
Have lovid lelyest in lond,
Dethe hathe me fette of this world away.
MS. Harl. 2252, f. 101.

LEMANDE. Shining; glittering.

The lawnces with loraynes and lemande scheldes,
Lyghtenande as the levenyng and lemand al over.
Morte Arthure, MS. Lincoln, f. 79.

LEME. (1) Brightness; light. (*A.-S.*) In the North of England, a flame. "The leme of a fyre," Prompt. Parv. p. 38.

The lyght of heven in a leme,
Bryjter than is the sone beme,
Upon that hert gaoe lyght.
MS. Ashmole 61, f. 1.

The sterres, with her lemyng lemen,
Shul sadly falle doun fro heven.
Cursor Mundi, MS. Coll. Trin. Cantab. f. 134.

(2) Limb. Richard Coer de Lion, 3362.

LEMFEG. A doe-fig. *Wilts.*

LEMING-STAR. A comet. From *Leme*, q. v.

LEMMAN. A lover, or gallant; a mistress. (*A.-S.*) See Maundevile's Travels. p. 24; Greene's Works, i. 59; Perceval, 1802. In very early English, the term is sometimes used simply for a dear or beloved person.

Toward the court he can goo,
His doughtur lemman met he thoo,
And alle his cumpanye.
MS. Cantab. Ff. v. 48, f. 51.

He sayse, Lemane, kysse me be-lyve,
Thy lorde me hase the graunte to wyefe,
And Paresche I hafe hym byght;
And I hete the witterly,
The kynges hevede of Fraunce certanely,
To morowe or it be nyghte!
MS. Lincoln A. i. 17, f. 103.

It is a proverbe in England that the men of Tivi-dal, borderers on the English midle marches, have likers, lemmons, and lyerbies.
Melbancke's Philotimus, 1583.

LEMON-TREE. The verbena. *South.*

LEMYERED. Glimmered; shone. (*A.-S.*)

LEMYET. Limit.

A breife of the Bounderes, Wayes and Passages of the Midle Marche, all a longe the Border of Scotland begining at Chiveat Hill, being the lemyet of the Easte Marche, and ending at Kirsop, the Bounder of the Weste Marche of England.
Egerton Papers, p. 278.

LEN. (1) To lend. Still in use.

(2) To lean. *North.*

LENAGE. Lineage; birth. (*A.-N.*)

LENARD. The linnet. *Palsgrave.* Brockett has it, spelt *lennert*, p. 186.

LENCE. A loan. *Dorset.*

LENCH. To stoop in walking. *Linc.*

LENCHEON. A kind of shelf in a shaft. A miner's term.

LENDE. (1) The loin. (*A.-S.*) It occurs in MS. Cotton. Vespas. D. vii. Ps. 37. "Gurdithe youre lendys," Gesta Rom. p. 107.

And a grete gyrdelle of golde, withoute gere more,
He leyde on his lendes with lachettes fulle monye.
MS. Cott. Calig. A. ii. f. 116.

(2) Given. Constit. Freemas. p. 27.

(3) To dwell; to remain; to tarry.

The abbot and the convent with good chere
Worschipeden God al i-feere;
And so do we him that sit above,
That he wolde for that maydenes love
Graunten us hevene withouten eende
With him therin for to leende:
God graunte us grace that hit so be:
Amen! amen! for charité.
Life of St. Euphrosine, Vernon MS.

Thay putt up pavilyons ronde,
And lendid there that nyghte.
MS. Lincoln A. i. 17, f. 131.

(4) To land; to arrive. (*A.-S.*)

LENDY. Limber; pliable. *Devon.*

LENE. To give. Hence our word *lend.* The editor of Havelok absurdly prints *leue.*

To hys lorde he can meene,
And preyed hym that he wolde hym leene
Wepyn, armowre, and stede.
MS. Cantab. Ff. ii. 38, f. 75.

LENGE. To dwell, rest, or remain. (*A.-S.*) Hence, perhaps, our *lounge.*

Lenge at home pur charyté,
Leve soon, y prey the.
MS. Cantab. Ff. ii. 38, f. 150.

I salle at Lammesse take leve to lenge at my large
In Lorayne or Lumberdye, whethire me leve thynkys.
Morte Arthure, MS. Lincoln, f. 57.

LENGER. Longer. *Chaucer.*

LENGTH. Stature. *North.* Speaking of cannon, it means the barrel.

LENGTHE. To lengthen; to prolong.

> Now have we noon wherwith we may
> Lengthe oure lif fro day to day.
> *Cursor Mundi, MS. Coll. Trin. Cantab.* f. 34.

LENKETHE. Length. See the Boke of Curtasye, p. 29; Wright's Seven Sages, p. 91.

> A feyrer chylde nevyr y sye,
> Neyther of lenkyth nor of brede.
> *MS. Cantab.* Ff. ii. 38, f. 96.

LENNOCK. Slender; pliable. *North.*

LENT. (1) A loan. *Somerset.*

(2) Remained; stopped. (*A.-S.*) It has also the meaning of *placed.*

> A doufe was fro heven sent.
> Lijt doun and theronne lent.
> *Cursor Mundi, MS. Coll. Trin. Cantab.* f. 67.
> On a laund are thay lent
> By a forest syd. *MS. Lincoln* A. i. 17, f. 133.

LENT-CROCKING. A custom of boys at Shrove-tide going round in the evening to pelt the doors of the inhabitants with pieces of broken crockery. *West.*

LENTED. Stopped; glanced off. *Lanc.*

LENTEN. (1) A linden tree. (*A.-S.*)

(2) The fare in Lent was not very substantial some centuries ago, and accordingly our ancestors seemed to have used the adjective *Lenten* constantly in a sense of deterioration. " A Lenten lover, a bashfull, modest, or maidenly woer, one thats afraid to touch his mistresse," Cotgrave, in v. *Caresme. Lenten-fig,* a dried fig, a raisin. *Lenton-stuff,* provision for Lent. A ballad by Elderton under this title commences :—

> Lenton Stuff ys cum to the towne,
> The clensynge weeke cums quicklye:
> Yow knowe well inowghe yow must kneele downe,
> Cum on, take asshes trykly,
> That nether are good fleshe nor fyshe,
> But dyp with Judas in the dyshe.
> And keepe a rowte not worthe a ryshe.
> *MS. Ashmole* 48, f. 115.

LENT-EVIL. The ague. MS. Med. Rec.

LENT-GRAIN. The spring crops. *West.*

LENTINER. A hawk taken in Lent.

LENT-ROSE. The daffodil. *Devon.* It is also called the *Lent-lily.*

LENTTE. Given. From *Lene.* (*A.-S.*)

> A fulle harde grace was hir lentte
> Er she owt of this worde wentte.
> *MS. Cantab.* Ff. v. 48, f. 43.

L'ENVOY. A kind of postscript, *sent with* poetical compositions by early authors. It was sometimes used for a conclusion generally. Cotgrave defines it, the " conclusion of a ballet, or sonnet, in a short stanzo by itselfe, and serving, oftentimes, as a dedication of the whole."

LENYT. Leaned. Lydgate, MS. Bodl.

LEO. The lion. (*A.-S.*) " Wildore then the leo," Reliq. Antiq. i. 125. *Leonine,* belonging to a lion.

LEOPART. A leopard. (*A.-N.*)

LEOS. People. *Chaucer.*

LEPANDE. Leaping. (*A.-S.*)

> With lufly launces one lofte they luyschene togedyres
> In Lorayne so lordlye on leppande stedes.
> *Morte Arthure, MS. Lincoln,* f. 68.

LEPE. A large basket, such as is used for carrying seeds, corn, &c. *Var. dial.*

> The spensere selde, methoujte I bere
> A leep, as I was wont do er.
> *Cursor Mundi, MS. Coll. Trin. Cantab.* f. 28.

LEPES. Stories; lies. Ritson, i. 4.

LEPI. Single. See *Anlepi.*

> Wrothlich he seyd to Gii,
> Here is gret scorn sikerly,
> When that o lepi knight
> Schal ous do so michel unright !
> *Gy of Warwike,* p. 78.

> Ne mete ete, ne drank drynke,
> Ne slepte onely a lepy wynke.
> *MS. Harl.* 1701, f. 61.

LEPPIS. Jumps; leaps. (*A.-S.*)

> Here my trouthe i the plyghte,
> He that leppis fulle lyghte
> He salle by it, and I fyghte,
> For alle jour mekille pride.
> *MS. Lincoln* A. j. 17, f. 133.

LEPROSY. The *lues venerea.* This is a very unusual sense of the word. *Shak.*

LERAND. Learning, part. (*A.-S.*)

> Bot it sal be notefulle lerand the way til heven.
> *MS. Coll. Eton.* f. 3.

LERARE. A learner; a teacher. *Pr. Parv.*

LERCH. To cheat or trick. *North.*

LERE. (1) To learn; to teach. (*A.-S.*) Hence, learning, knowledge, precept.

> Then he frayned hym in his ere
> If he wolde passilodion lere.
> *MS. Cantab.* Ff. v. 48, f. 54.

> Bot thai on the erth Cristes wordes here,
> That sal be to thaim withouten ende a lere.
> *MS. Egerton* 927, xv. Cent.

(2) Countenance; complexion. (*A.-S.*)

> For sorow he leste both strength and might,
> The colours changid in his leyre.
> *MS. Harl.* 2252, f. 93.

(3) Shame. Nominale MS.

LERENDE. Learnt. From *Lere* (1).

> So that nother one the see ne on the lande je seke
> na helpe, and that je jeme another manere of doctryne thane we hafe lerende of oure doctours.
> *MS. Lincoln* A. i. 17, f. 32.

LERENESS. Emptiness. Batman, 1582.

LEREP. To trail slovenly. *South.* Also, to limp or walk lamely.

LERRICK. To beat; to chastise. *Devon.*

LERRY. Learning; lesson. Middleton, i. 281.

LES. Lost. *Hearne.*

LESE. (1) To gather; to select. (*A.-S.*) " To leyse, to pick the slain and trucks out of wheat," Hallamsh. Gl. p. 116. In Devon, picking stones from the surface of the fields is called *leasing;* and throughout the Western counties no other word is used for gleaning corn. " To lese here in hervest," Piers Ploughman, p. 121. *Lesinge,* gleaning, Wright's Pol. Songs, p. 149. " To lease straw for thatching, *seligere et componere;* to lease stones, to pick stones in a field," Dean Milles, MS. Glossary, p. 167.

(2) To lose. Still in use. (*A.-S.*)

(3) To deliver ; to release. It occurs in MS. Cotton. Vespas. D. vii. Ps. 7.

(4) Lie ; falsehood. (*A.-S.*)

> At every ende of the deyse
> Sate an erle, withowt *lese*.
>
> *MS. Cantab. Ff. v. 48, f. 54.*

(5) Leash ; band. Octovian, 767.

LESER. Releaser ; deliverer. This occurs several times in MS. Cott. Vespas. D. vii.

LESESE. To lose. See Hycke-Scorner, p. 102. It is perhaps an error of the press.

LESEVE. To pasture, or feed. (*A.-S.*) Drayton has *lessow* in this sense.

LESING. A lie ; a falsehood. (*A.-S.*) *Lesynge berare*, a liar. See Prompt. Parv. p. 298.

> Then shalle I gif the a cote
> Withowt any *lesyng*.
>
> *MS. Cantab. Ff. v. 48, f. 48.*
>
> Lord, he seyd, thou ryche kyng,
> 3It it wer a foulere thing
> To here a *lesyng* of thy mouthe,
> That thou me seyst nowje,
> That I schuld have what I wold,
> Bot nedys a kyng word mot hold.
>
> *MS. Ashmole 61, xv. Cent.*

LESK. The groin or flank. In Lincolnshire the word is in very common use, and frequently implies also the *pudendum*, and is perhaps the only term for that part that could be used without offence in the presence of women.

> The laste was a litylle mane that lnide was benethe,
> His *laskes* laye alle lene and latheliche to schewe.
>
> *Morte Arthure, MS. Lincoln, f. 88.*

LESNESSE. Forgiveness ; absolution. See Rob. Glouc. p. 173 ; Reliq. Antiq. i. 42.

LESSE. (1) *Lesse than*, unless. *Maketh less*, extinguishes. *Weber.* Lesse ne mare, i. e. nothing at all.

(2) To lessen ; to decrease. This occurs in MS. Cotton. Vespas. D. vii. Ps. 11.

LESSES. See *Hunting*, art. 1.

> And 3if men speke and aske hym of the fumes, he shal clepe fumes of an hert croteynge, of a bukke and of the roo-bukke, of the wilde boor, and of blake beestys, and of wolfes, he shal clepe it *lesses*.
>
> *MS. Bodl. 546.*

LESSEST. Least of all. *Var. dial.*

LESSIL. A wanton woman. *Cumb.*

LESSON. To give lessons. *Var. dial.*

LESSOW. The same as *Leseve*, q. v.

LEST. (1) Listen. Imperative, sing.

> *Lest*, my sone, and thou schalt here
> So as it hath bifalle er this.
>
> *Gower, MS. Soc. Antiq. 134, f. 162.*

(2) Inclination ; pleasure. (*A.-S.*)

LESTAL. (1) Saleable, applied to things of good and proper weight. *North.*

(2) A mire ; a jakes. *North.* Urry's MS. additions to Ray. *Leystale* occurs in Ben Jonson, i. 59.

LESTE. To please. *Chaucer.*

LESTEN. Lost. (*A.-S.*)

> Of Grece and Troie the stronge stryve,
> Ther many a thousand *lesten* her lyve.
>
> *MS. Ashmole 60, xv. Cent.*

LESTYGHT. Lasteth. Cov. Myst.

LESUR. A leasow, or pasture. " *Hæc pascua*

pascua est locus herbosus pascendis animalibus aptus, Anglice a lesur," MS. Bibl. Reg. 12 B. i. f. 13.

LET. (1) Leased off. *Linc.*

(2) To leave ; to omit ; to leave, or permit ; to cause ; to hinder. (*A.-S.*) *Let be*, leave off. *To let in*, to cheat. *To let fly at any one*, to abuse him severely. *To let drive*, to attack with violence. *To let light*, to inform, to disclose. *To let wit*. to make known. *Let on*, to light upon. *Let to gate*, went home.

(3) To counterfeit ; to pretend. *North.*

LETCH. (1) A vessel for making lye. *East.*

(2) A wet ditch or gutter. *North.*

(3) An absurd foppish fancy. *Linc.*

LETE. (1) To think, account, or esteem. (*A.-S.*)

(2) Left. See Kyng Alisaunder, 5812. Also, to leave or dismiss any thing.

> Yf thou can a stede welle ryde,
> Wyth me thou schalt be *lete*.
>
> *MS. Cantab. Ff. ii. 38, f. 92.*

(3) To be nearly starved. *Yorksh.*

(4) To look? See Gl. to Syr Gawayne.

> Childre, he selde, 3e luste and *lete*,
> I saw chaf on the watir flete.
>
> *Cursor Mundi, MS. Coll. Trin. Cantab. f. 30.*

LETEWARYE. An electuary. (*A.-N.*)

LETGAME. A hinderer of pleasure.

LETH. Soothing ? See Towneley Myst.

> Thus sal man in heven ay fynd joye and *leth*,
> Above him, withinne him, aboute and beneth.
>
> *MS. Egerton 927.*

LETHAL. Deadly. (*Lat.*) See Fletcher's Differences, 1623, p. 7. It appears from the Nat. Hist. Wilts, Royal Soc. MS. p. 165, that Aubrey considered the bite of newts *lethall.*

LETHE. (1) Death. *Shak.*

(2) Supple ; limber ; pliant. *Palsgrave.*

LETHER. (1) To make a noise, said of horses travelling with great speed. *North.*

(2) Vile ; hateful. *Letherand*, Reliq. Antiq. i. 82 ; *letherly*, MS. Morte Arthure.

> Thou grevyst me, I am not glad,
> To me thou art a *lether* leche.
>
> *MS. Harl. 3054.*
>
> A prowde wrech and a yonge,
> And a *lether* gaddelynge.
>
> *MS. Cantab. Ff. ii. 38, f. 115.*
>
> 3ys, for sothe, a wyle can I,
> To begyle owre *lethur* pye.
>
> *MS. Cantab. Ff. ii. 38, f. 136.*

(3) The skin. Still in use.

> Than wete men never whether ys whether,
> The 3elughe wymple or the *lether*.
>
> *MS. Harl. 1701, f. 23.*

LETHET. Moderated itself.

> Bright and faire the son schone,
> But hit *lethet* sone anon.
>
> *MS. Cantab. Ff. v. 48, f. 36.*

LETHY. (1) Nasty ; filthy. *Cumb.*

(2) Weak ; feeble ; supple. " His ere-lappes waxes *lethy*," Reliq. Antiq. i. 54.

LET-IN. To strike. *South.*

LETTASES. Lattices. Florio, p. 469.

LETTE. Impediment ; hinderance.

> Upon a dey, withouten *lette*,
> The duke with the kyng was sette.
>
> *MS. Ashmole 61, f. 60.*

LETTER. To make an entry in a ledger or book. *Somerset.*

LETTERON. The ancient reading-stand in churches. See Davies, ed. 1672, p. 17.

LETTERS-OF-MART. Letters of marque were formerly so called.

LETTICE. A kind of grey fur. "Lettyce a furre, *letice*," Palsgrave. Whether the *lettice-cap* was a cap in which this fur was introduced I am not certain, but mention is made in an early MS. of " an ermine or lattice bonnet," Planché, p. 262. Nares has fallen into unnecessary conjectures by not understanding this meaning of the term.

LETTIRDE. Lettered; learned. (*A.-N.*)
> And than scho sayd, everylk mane and womane
> that were *lettirde*, that were in any temptacione,
> whilke that I rehersede before, saye he this ympne
> *Veni creator spiritus*, and the devele and the temptacione salle sone voyde fra hym.
>   *MS. Lincoln A. i. 17, f. 257.*

LETTOWE. Lithuania.
> Chases one a coursere, and to a kyng rydys,
> With a launce of *Lettowe* he thrilles his sydes,
> That the lyver and the lungges on the launce lenges.
>   *Morte Arthure, MS. Lincoln, f. 76.*

LETTRURE. Learning; literature.

LEUF. The palm of the hand. *North.*

LEUGH. Laughed. Robin Hood, i. 49.

LEUKE. Luke-warm. Reliq. Antiq. i. 52. It is still in use in Yorkshire.

LEUTERER. A thief; a vagabond.

LEUTH. Shelter. *South.*

LEUWYN. A kind of linen, of which table-cloths were formerly made.

LEUȝE. Laughed. See *Leugh.*
> Than men myght se game i-nowȝe,
> When every cokwold on other *leuȝe.*
>   *MS. Ashmole 61, f. 60.*

LEVABLE. Able to be levied. See the Archæologia, i. 91.

LEVACION. The elevation of the Host, in the Roman Catholic service. See Gesta Rom. p. 266; Ord. and Reg. p. 89.

LEVAND. Living. *Lydgate.*

LEVE. (1) To leave. Also, to believe. Both senses occur in this couplet.
> Tho sayde Maxent to Kateryn,
> *Leve* thy god and *leve* on myn.
>   *MS. Cantab. Ff. ii. 38, f. 38.*

> Sche *levyd* nothyng in the masse,
> That very God was in forme of bredd.
>   *MS. Cantab. Ff. ii. 38, f. 46.*

(2) Leave; permission. (*A.-S.*)

(3) Desire; inclination. (*A.-S.*)

(4) Dear; willing. See *Lefe.*

LEVEL. (1) To assess, or levy. *East.*

(2) A straight ruler. *Palsgrave.*

LEVEL-COIL. A rough game, formerly much in fashion at Christmas, in which one hunted another from his seat. Florio, p. 138, mentions " a Cristmas game called *rise up good fellow*, or *itch buttocke*," which refers to the same amusement. " *Jouèr à cul-leve*, to play at levell-coyle," Cotgrave. Hence the phrase came to be used for any noisy riot. It was also called *level-sice*, and Skelton, ii. 31, spells

it *levell suse.* Blount gives the following very curious explanation, " level-coile is when three play at tables, or other game, by turns, onely two playing at a time, the loser removes his buttock, and sits out ; and therefore called also hitch-buttock," ed. 1681, p. 374.

LEVELLERS. Persons who advocate an equalization of property &c. The term was common during the civil wars, when there were many who professed those opinions.

LEVEN. To alleviate. *Lydgate.*

LEVENE. Lightning. (*A.-S.*)
> The thondir, with his firy *levene*,
> So cruel was upon the hevene.
>   *Gower, MS. Soc. Antiq. 134, f. 191.*

> With sodeyne tempest and with firy *levene*,
> By the goddess sente doun from hevene.
>   *Lydgate, MS. Digby 230.*

> This is the auctor of the hyȝe heven,
> Sette in the sunne clere as any *leven*en.
>   *Lydgate, MS. Soc. Antiq. 134, f. 16.*

LEVENER. The same as *Bever* (1).

LEVER. (1) One of the chief supporters of the roof-timber of a house, being itself not a prop, but a portion of the frame-work. Also, the lower moveable board of a barn-door.

(2) Rather. (*A.-S.*)
> I shalle the whyte, be hode myne,
> How hade I *lever* a conyne.
>   *MS. Cantab. Ff. v. 48, f. 50.*

(3) Better; more agreeable.
> Ther come to hym never a *lever* sonde
> Then the fyscher and the fostere.
>   *MS. Cantab. Ff. ii. 38, f. 141.*

(4) To deliver to. Plumpton Corr. p. 189.

LEVERS. The yellow-flag. *South.*

LEVESELE. A lattice. Chaucer mentions the gay levesele at the tavern as a sign of the wine there sold, and up to a much later period lattices were the distinguishing features of inns. The explanations of this word given in Tyrwhitt, the Oxford Gloss. Architecture, Pr. Parv. p. 300, &c. are certainly erroneous.
> Alle his devocion and hollness
> At taverne is, as for the moste delle,
> To Bachus signe and to the *levesele.*
>   *Occleve, MS. Soc. Antiq. 134, f. 253.*

LEVET. The blast or strong sound of a trumpet. (*Fr.*) It occurs in Hudibras.

LEVETENNANTE. A deputy. *Levetent*, Reliq. Antiq. ii. 22.
> Salle be my *levetennante* with lordchipes y-newe.
>   *Morte Arthure, MS. Lincoln, f. 60.*

LEVEYNE. Leaven.
> He is the *leveyne* of the bred,
> Whiche soureth alle the paste aboute.
>   *Gower, MS. Soc. Antiq. 134, f. 87.*

LEVORE. Lever; mace. *Ritson.*

LEVYNG. Life. Chron. Vilodun. p. 5.

LEVYNGE. Departure; death.
> The aungelle gaf hym in warnynge
> Of the tyme of hys *levynge.*
>   *MS. Cantab. Ff. ii. 38, f. 243.*

LEW. (1) To get into the lew, i. e. into a place sheltered from the wind. *Var. dial.* " Soule-grove sil lew" is an ancient Wiltshire proverb, i. e. February is seldom warm.

(2) Luke-warm. Still in use. *Lewe water*, Ord. and Reg. p. 471.

(3) Weak; faint. Nominale MS.

LEWCOMBE. See *Lucayne*.

LEWD. Ignorant; lay; untaught; useless. (*A.-S.*) In some later writers, vile, base, wicked. In the remote parts of Yorkshire a vicious horse is termed *lewd*.

LEWDSTER. A lewd person. *Shak.* I follow the usual explanation, but should be rather inclined to consider it as meaning a wretch, and perhaps connected with *leuterer*.

LEWESODE. Loosened. "His fedris weron *lewesode* ychon," Chron. Vilodun. p. 125.

LEWINS. A kind of bands put about a hawk. See Florio, p. 289.

LEWIS. A kind of machine used for raising stones. Archæologia, x. 127.

LEWN. A tax, or rate, or lay for church or parish dues. *Chesh.* A benefaction of fourty shillings is payable to the parish of Walsall to ease the poor inhabitants of their *lewnes*. See Carlisle on Charities, p. 296.

LEWSTRY. To work hard. *Devon.*

LEWTE. (1) Loyalty. (*A.-N.*)

(2) A kind of cup or vessel.

(3) The herb restharrow. *Somerset.*

LEWTH. Warmth; shelter. *West.*

LEWYTH. That which is left.

LEWZERNE. A kind of fur.

LEXST. Lyest; speakest false.

> Morgadour answerd anon,
> Stalworth knight as he was on,
> Thi *lexst* amidward thi teth,
> And therfore have thou maugreth.
> *Gy of Warwike*, p. 154.

> Cy, quath the justice, swiche mervalle,
> Thou *lest*, damisel, saun faile.
> *Arthour and Merlin*, p. 35.

LEY. (1) Latitude; room; liberty; leisure; opportunity; law. *North.*

(2) A lea, or pasture. *West.* "One a launde by a ley," Degrevant, 239. *Ley-breck*, sward once ploughed.

(3) Law; faith; religion. (*A.-N.*)

(4) The standard of metals. *Derb.*

(5) To lie. Reliq. Antiq. i. 60.

(6) A flame, or low. (*A.-S.*)

> For y am yn endles peyne,
> Yn fyre and yn *leye* certeyne.
> *MS. Harl.* 1701, f. 44.

(7) A lake. Still in use.

> He made alle a valaye,
> Al so it were a brod *leye*.
> *Arthour and Merlin*, p. 350.

LEYARE. A stonemason. *Pr. Parv.*

LEYCERE. Leisure.

> Now, syres, ye seeyn the lytylle *leycere* here.
> *Chaucer, MS. Cantab.* Ff. 1. 6, f. 30.

LEYD. Laid. See *Feyre*.

LEYGHT. Lyeth. *Lydgate.*

> With harmes to greve in wayte *leyght* shee
> To revene mene of welthe and prosperyté.
> *MS. Cantab.* Ff. 1. 6, f. 157.

LEYNE. Laid; placed. (*A.-S.*)

LEYOND. Laying.

> At the see Jame and Jon he fonde
> As thei were lynes *leyond*.
> *Cursor Mundi, MS. Coll. Trin. Cantab.* f. 82.

LEYTH. Loathly. Audelay, p. 31.

LEY3TLOCURE. More easily. (*A.-S.*)

LHINNE. A lake. Lhuyd's MSS.

LIALE. Loyal. Wright Pol. Songs, p. 303.

LIANCE. An alliance. *Palsgrave.*

LIAR. "Liar, liar, lick dish," a proverbial address to a liar, chiefly used at schools. It is an old saying, being found in the Tragedy of Hoffman, 1631, sig. I. ii.

LIARD. A horse, properly one of a grey colour. Palsgrave mentions a horse called *Lyarde Urbyn.* "One lyarde stedes," Morte Arthure, MS. Lincoln, f. 80.

> Stedis stabillede in stallis,
> *Lyardis* and sore.   *MS. Lincoln* A. 1. 17, f. 130.

LIB. (1) To castrate. *North.* "To capon, to geld, *to lib*, to splaie," Florio, p. 5. See Topsell's Foure-Footed Beasts, 1607, p. 68.

(2) A basket, or leep. *South.*

(3) Half a bushel. Kennett MS.

(4) To lay down. A cant term mentioned in Dekker's Belman of London, 1616.

LIBARDINE. The herb wolfbane. See Topsell's Foure-Footed Beasts, 1607, p. 40. Also called libbard's-bane.

LIBBARD. A leopard. *Skelton.*

> Then owte starte a lumbarte,
> Felle he was as a *lybarte*.
> *MS. Cantab.* Ff. ii. 38, f. 179.

LIBBEGE. A bed. This old cant term is given by Dekker, Lanthorne and Candle-Light, 1620, sig. C. ii.

LIBBEING. Living. (*A.-S.*)

> For to drawen up all thing
> That nede was to her *libbeing*.
> *Arthour and Merlin*, p. 38.

LIBBER. A man who libs or gelds. *North.* "A guelder, a libber," Florio, p. 89.

LIBBET. A billet of wood; a staff, stick, or club. *South.*

LIBBETS. Rags in strips. *West.*

LIBERAL. Licentious; free to excess. It occurs often in this sense in old plays.

LIBERARIE. Learning. *Lydgate.*

LIB-KEN. A house to live in. An old cant term, given by Dekker, Lanthorne and Candle-Light, 1620, sig. C. ii.

LICAME. The body. (*A.-S.*)

> And Jhesus hent up that *licame*
> That lay deed bifore the thronge.
> *Cursor Mundi, MS. Coll. Trin. Cantab.* f. 75.

> That ani man to hir cam
> That ever knewe hir *licham*.
> *Arthour and Merlin*, p. 37.

LICCHORIE. Leachery. *Hearne.*

LICHE. (1) The body. *Weber.* Hence the term liche-wake, or lake-wake, q. v.

(2) Alike. (*A.-S.*)

> In kirtels and in copis riche,
> They weren clothid alle *liche*.
> *Gower, MS. Soc. Antiq.* 134, f. 111.

LICHFOUL. The night-raven. *Rowlands.* Drayton mentions it as the *litch-owl.*

LICH-GATE. The gate through which the

corpse was carried into the church. It had always a roof over it under which the bier was placed, and the bearers rested until the clergyman met the corpse, and read the introductory part of the service as he preceded the train into the church. Several lichgates are still preserved.

LICHWORT. The herb pellitory.

LICIBLE. Pleasant; agreeable.

> Percas as whan the liste what thi wyf pley
> Thi conceyte holdeth it good and *licible*.
> *Occleve, MS. Soc. Antiq.* 134, f. 259.

LICK. To beat, or thrash. Hence, to surpass or excel in anything; to do anything easily. *To lick the eye*, to be well pleased.

LICK-DISH. A term of contempt. See the phrase given in v. *Liar*. A sycophant is still termed a lick-pan. "A lick-sauce, lick-box, *licheron*," Howell.

LICKEN. To compare; to liken. *Craven.*

> These ben the enemyes that fawnyng slays,
> And sleying fawneth, that *lycken* y can
> To Joas, that toke be the chynne Amas.
> *MS. Cantab.* Ff. ii. 38, f. 14.

LICKER. To grease boots or shoes.

LICKLY. Likely. *North.*

LICKOROUS. Dainty; affected. Used also in the sense of lecherous, or voluptuous. "To cocker, to make *likerish*, to pamper," Hollyband's Dictionarie, 1593.

> From women light and *lickorous*
> Good fortune still deliver us.
> *Cotgrave, in v. Femme.*

LICK-POT-FINGER. The fore-finger.

LICKS. A good beating. *North.*

LICKSOME. Pleasant; agreeable. *Chesh.*

LICKSPITTLE. A parasite. *Var. dial.*

LICK-UP. A small pittance. *East.*

LICLIARE. Likelier; more likely.

LID. A coverlet. *Kent.* It is applied to a book-cover in Nomenclator, p. 7, and I find the term so used as late as 1757, in Dr. Free's Poems, p. 47.

LIDDED. The top of the bearing part of a pipe is said to be lidded when its usual space is contracted to a small compass or width. A mining term.

LIDDEN. (1) Long. *Somerset.*

(2) Saying, song, or story. *West.*

LIDDERON. A lazy idle bad fellow. From *lidder*, or *lither*, q. v.

LIDE. (1) Lydia. *Chaucer.*

(2) The month of March. An old provincial term, now obsolete.

LIDGITTS. Some thirty or fourty years ago, when the fields in the Isle of Oxholme were uninhabited, there were gates set up at the end of the villages and elsewhere to prevent the cattle from straying upon the arable lands; these gates were termed lidgitts. *Linc.*

LIDS. (1) Manner; fashion; way; kind; resemblance. *North.*

(2) Transverse bars of wood supporting the roof of a coal-mine.

LIE. (1) To lay down. *Var. dial.*

(2) To subside, as the wind. *Devon.*

(3) *To lie with a latchet*, to tell a monstrous falsehood. *To lie in wait of one's self*, to be very careful. *To lie by the wall, to lie on the cold floor, to lie a bier*, to lie dead before interment.

(4) To reside. Still in use.

(5) The lees of wine. *Pr. Parv.*

LIE-BOX. (1) A great liar. *West.*

(2) A box wherein the lie from wood-ashes is made. *Var. dial.*

LIEF. The same as *Lefe*, q. v.

LIEF-COUP. A sale or market of goods in the place where they stand. *Kent.*

LIEGEMAN. A subject. *Shak.*

LIEGER. An ambassador. See *Leiger*. Spelt *ligier* in Hall, Henry VIII. f. 158.

LIEGES. Subjects. *(A.-N.)*

LIEKD. Loved. *Cumb.*

LIE-LEACH. A box, perforated at bottom, used for straining water for lie. It is also called a lie-latch, lie-dropper, or lie-lip.

LIE-LEY. To lie in grass. *Yorksh.*

LIEN. Lain. *Chaucer.*

LIENDE. Lying. See *Lien.*

> And therto lyounes tweyne *lyende* ther under.
> *MS. Cott. Calig.* A. ii. fol. 111.

LIES. Lees of wine. *(A.-N.)*

LIETON. A church-yard. *Wilts.*

LIEVER. Rather. *Var. dial.*

LIF. Permission. *(A.-S.)*

> For if that we have *lif* therto,
> Ʒoure commaundment shul we do.
> *Cursor Mundi, MS. Coll. Trin. Cantab.* f. 38.

LIFE-DAYS. Life-time. "By his lyfe dayes, de son playn vivant," Palsgrave.

LIFELICHE. Active; piercing. *Liffly*, like the life, Lydgate's Minor Poems, p. 257.

> And that *lifeliche* launce that lepe to his herte
> When he was crucyfiede on crose, and alle the kene naylis,
> Knyghtly he salle conquere to Cristyne men hondes.
> *Morte Arthure, MS. Lincoln*, f. 89
>
> Lyche *lyfly* men among hem day by day.
> *MS. Digby* 232, f. 2.

LIFERS. Leavers; deserters.

LIFFY. In Devon, when a man seduces a girl with strong protestations of honour, and afterwards leaves her to her fate, he is said to *liffy* her, and she is said to be *liffied*.

LIFLODE. Living; state of life. *(A.-S.)*

> Whedir salle we now gaa, or whate partye may we now chese? Whare schalle we now get any helpe tille oure *lyfelade*.
> *MS. Lincoln* A. i. 17, f. 49.

LIFT. (1) The air; the sky. *(A.-S.)*

> Somme in the erthe, somme in the *lift*,
> There thei dreȝe ful harde drift.
> *Cursor Mundi, MS. Coll. Trin. Cantab.* f. 4.
>
> Now at the erthe, now at the *lift*,
> Or however thou wolt the shift.
> *Cursor Mundi, MS. Ibid.* f. 139.

(2) To aid, or assist. *Var. dial.* Perhaps the usual meaning in this passage.

> Son, alle the seyntes that be in heyven,
>   Nor alle the angels undur the Trinité.
> On here-breyde out of this peyne
>   Thei have no pouere to *lift* me.
> *MS. Cantab.* Ff. v. 48, f. 68.

(3) A coarse rough gate without hinges, and moveable. *East.*

(4) A joint of beef. *West.*

(5) To carve up a swan. See the Booke of Hunting, 1586, f. 81.

(6) A trick at whist or other games at cards. To lift for dealing, to draw or cut for the deal.

(7) A falsehood. *Somerset.*

(8) To steal. Still retained in the modern term *shop-lifting.* The lifting law, says Dekker, "teacheth a kind of lifting of goods cleane away." Belman of London, 1608.

(9) A bad character. *Devon.*

LIFTER. A thief. See *Lift* (8).

LIFTERS. An old term for mortises.

LIFTING-MONDAY. Easter Monday, when it was the custom for every couple of men to lift up and kiss each woman they met. Lifting on Easter Tuesday, when the women returned the compliment to the men. This was a common custom in Lancashire about fifty years ago, till the disturbances to which it gave rise called for the interference of the magistrates, and it gradually became obsolete; but it is still retained in some parts of the country.

LIFT-LEG. Strong ale. An old cant term, mentioned in Harrison's England, p. 202.

LIG. The same as *Ligge*, q. v. It is sometimes used for a lie, a falsehood.

LIG-A-LAME. To maim. *North.*

LIGEANCE. Allegiance. *(A.-N.)*

LIGGE. To lie down. *(A.-S.)* Still in common use in the North of England.

> And they here bidden for to slepe,
> *Liggende* upon the bed alofte.
> *Gower, MS. Soc. Antiq.* 134, f. 44.

LIGGEE. A carved coit made of hard wood, used at the game of doddart.

LIGGEMENE. ˙ Subjects.

> Was warre of syr Lucius one launde there he hovys,
> With lordes and *liggemene* that to hymselfe lengede.
> *Morte Arthure, MS. Lincoln,* f. 76.

LIGGER. (1) A plank placed across a ditch for a pathway. *East.*

(2) A line with a float and bait used for catching pike. *East.*

(3) The same as *Ledger*, q. v.

(4) A coverlet for a bed. *Linc.*

LIGGET. A rag or fragment. *West.*

LIGGLE. To lug or carry. *Norfolk.*

LIGGYNG-STEDE. A couch or bed. It occurs in MS. Cott. Vespas. D. vii.

LIGHT. (1) An example. *East.*

(2) To be confined. *Salop.*

> And I shalle say thou was *lyght*
> Of a knave-childe this nyght.
> *Towneley Mysteries,* p. 107.

(3) To descend, or alight. *Var. dial.* "Set a Begger on horsebacke, and they say he will never *light*," Greenes Orpharion, 1599, p. 19. Sometimes *lighten*, as in the English version of the *Te Deum laudamus.*

(4) To enlighten; to make light or pleasant; to grow light. *(A.-S.)*

> The lettres of syr Lucius *lyghttys* myne herte;
> We hafe as losels liffyde many longe daye.
> *Morte Arthure, MS. Lincoln,* f. 56.

(5) *Light timbered,* sickly, weak; also, active, nimble. *To light on,* to meet. *Light day,* clear day, open daylight. *Light-headed,* delirious. *Light-heeled,* active, nimble. *Light-o'-fire,* a term of abuse.

(6) Weak; sickly. *Somerset.*

LIGHTENING. The break of day. *North.*

LIGHTER. (1) A less number. *North.*

(2) The same as *Lafter*, q. v.

LIGHT-HEELED. Loose in character. "She is sure a light heeld wench," the Bride, 1640, sig. G. A light-housewife, a married woman of bad character. "An harlot, a brothel, an hoore, a strompet, a light housewyfe," Elyot, in v. *Meretrix.*

LIGHTING. Light. This occurs in MS. Cotton. Vespas. D. vii. Ps. 26.

LIGHTING-STOCK. A horse-block. *West.*

LIGHTLOKER. More lightly, or easily. *(A.-S.)*

LIGHTLY. (1) Commonly; usually; in ordinary cases. See Tusser, p. 71.

(2) Readily; easily; quickly. *(A.-S.)*

LIGHTMANS. The day. A cant term, given in Dekker's Lanthorne and Candle-Light, 1620, sig. C. ii.

LIGHTNING. *Lightning before death,* a proverbial phrase, alluding to the resuscitation of the spirits which frequently occurs before dissolution.

LIGHT-O'-LOVE. The name of an old dance-tune. It was a kind of proverbial phrase for levity, and a loose woman was frequently so called.

LIGHT-RIPE. Corn has this epithet applied to it, when the stalk or straw appears ripe, and yet the ear contains nothing but a milky juice. *Linc.*

LIGHTS. (1) The lungs. *Var. dial.*

(2) The openings between the divisions of a window, and hence occasionally used by later writers for the windows themselves.

LIGHTSOME. (1) Gay; cheerful. *North.*

(2) Light; full of light. "Lightsome glass-window," Davies, ed. 1672, p. 52.

LIGLY. Likely. *Northumb.*

LIGMANE. Liegeman; subject. *(A.-S.)*

> Gret wele Lucius thi lorde, and layne noghte thise wordes,
> Ife thow be *lygmane* lele, late hyme wiet sone.
> *Morte Arthure, MS. Lincoln,* f. 57.

LIGNE. Lineage; lineal descent. *(A.-N.)*

LIGNE-ALOES. Lignum aloes. *Chaucer.*

LIGNEY. (1) Active; strong; able to bear great fatigue. *Cumb.*

(2) To lighten. Nominale MS.

LIGS. Ulcers on a horse's lips.

LIKE. (1) Likeness.

> That in a mannes *lyke*
> The devel to this mayde com. *MS.Coll. Trin. Oxon.* 57.

(2) To please; to delight; to be pleased.

> What so thai have it may be myne,
> Corne and brede, ale and wyne,
> And alle that may *like* me. *MS.Cantab.* Ff.v.48, f. 50.

(3) In the main. " He is a good sort of man *like*." It is frequently used as a mere expletive. *Like much*, an equal quantity of each. *I am like to do it*, I must do it. *To like oneself*, to like one's situation. This appears to be the second meaning, to please. *To go upon likes*, to go on trial. *To go a liking*, ibid. *And like your majesty*, if it please your majesty. *Like lettuce like lips*, a proverb implying that bad things suit each other. *Good like*, well looking. *Better nor like*, better than was expected. *Life of*, to approve. *Every like*, every now and then.

(4) To grow; to thrive; to agree with one, as food, drink, &c.

(5) To liken; to compare. (*A.-S.*)

(6) Likely; probably. *Var. dial.* " I and my man wer *like* to byn bothe kild by Captin Hammon that was dronke," Forman's Diary, MS. Ashmole, 208.

LIKELY. Suitable; promising; good-looking; resembling. *Likeliness*, resemblance; probability.

LIKEN. Likely. *Suffolk*. I had likened, i. e. I was in danger of.

LIKER. More like. (*A.-S.*)

> His lips wer great, they hanged aside,
> His eies were hollow, his mouth wide.
> He was lothly to looke on ;
> He was *lyker* a devill then a man.
>
> *Bevis of Hampton*, n. d.

LIKES. Likelihood; prospect. *West*. It is sometimes pronounced *likeseunce*.

LIKFULLIST. Most pleasant. (*A.-S.*)

LIKING. (1) Appearance; condition. *North.*

(2) Delight; pleasure. *Chaucer.*

LIKKERWISE. Delightful; pleasant. (*A.-S.*)

LIKNE. To imitate; to mimic; to liken, or make a simile. (*A.-S.*)

LILBURN. A heavy stupid fellow.

LILBYLOW. Perspiration; fever. *Linc.* It is also pronounced *lillipooh.*

LILE. Little. *North.*

> Full *lile* we know his hard griefe of mind,
> And how he did long London to ken ;
> And yet he thought he should finde it at last,
> Because he met so many men.
>
> *The King and a Poore Northerne Man*, 1640.

LILEWORTH. Of little value. *North.*

LILL. (1) To pant; to loll out the tongue. *Wilts.* " I lylle out the tonge as a beest dothe that is chafed," Palsgrave. " To pant and bee out of breath, or *lill* out the tongue, as a dog that is weary," Florio, p. 15.

(2) To assuage pain. *North.*

LILLILO. A bright flame. *North.*

LILLY. The wild convolvulus. Lilly-royal, the herb penny-royal. *South.*

LILLYCONVALLY. The May-lilly.

LILLYWHITECAKE. A short-cake. *South.*

LILLYWUNS. An exclamation of amazement.

LILT. To jerk, or spring; to do anything cleverly or quickly. *North.*

LILTY-PATTEN. A whore. *North.*

LIMAILE. Filings of metal. (*A.-N.*)

LIMATIKE. A crooked person; a cripple.

LIMB. Explained by Forby, " a determined sensualist." The term seems generally to imply deterioration. A limb of Satan, a limb of the law, &c. The first of these phrases is retained from the early English *feendes lyms*. See Hoccleve, p. 29. According to Pegge, a man addicted to anything is called *a limb for it*. Glossary, p. 98.

LIMBECK. An alembic. *Shak.*

LIMBER. Supple; flexible. *Var. dial.* " His eares is *limber* and weake," Topsell's Beasts, 1607, p. 185.

LIMBERS. Thills or shafts. *West.*

LIMB-MEAL. Limb by limb. (*A.-S.*)

LIMBO. Hell. Properly, the *limbus* or place where the righteous were supposed to have been confined before the coming of Christ. " Limbo or hell," Florio, pp. 105, 158. It was also used for a prison, in which sense it is still retained.

> Beholde now what owre Lord Jhesu dide one the Saterday, as sune as he was dede. He went downe to helle to owre holy fadyrs that ware in *lymbo* to tyme of his Resureccione.
>
> *MS. Lincoln* A. i. 17, f. 186.

LIMB-TRIMMER. A tailor. *North.*

LIME. (1) A limb. (*A.-S.*)

> He was a moche man and a longe,
> In every *lym* styff and stronge.
>
> *MS. Cantab.* Ff. ii. 38, f. 75.

(2) To smear, as with bird-lime.

> For who so wol his hondis *lyme*,
> They mosten be the more unclene.
>
> *Gower, MS. Soc. Antiq.* f. 65.

(3) Lime was mixed with wine, sack, &c. to remove the tartness. Egg-shells are now often used for that purpose, and perhaps lime.

(4) Any glutinous substance, as glue, bird-lime, gum, &c. *North.*

(5) Limit; end.

> Ryჳt as we cleye ჳet the same,
> And herrafter shulde withouჳte *lyme*.
>
> *Chron. Vilodun.* p. 4.

(6) A thong. See *Lime-hound.*

LIME-ASH. A composition of sifted ashes and mortar, beaten together, and laid down as a flooring for kitchens and outhouses. *West.*

LIME-BURNER. A dwarfish fellow.

LIMED. Polished; filed. (*A.-N.*)

LIME-HOUND. A common hound or sporting dog, led by a thong called a lime. *Lyne-hounds*, Cotgrave, in v. *Mut.* See Ord. and Reg. p. 325. *Limer*, a blood-hound, Tyrwhitt. " A dogge engendred betwene an hounde and a mastyve, called a *lymmer* or a mungrell," Elyot in v. *Hybris.*

> There ovirtoke I a grete rout
> Of huntirs and of foresters,
> And many relaies and *limers*,
> That hied hem to the forest fast,
> And I with hem, so at the last
> I askid one lad, a *lymere*,
> Say, felowe, who shal huntin here ?
> Quod I, and he answered ayen,
> Sir, the emperour Octovyen,
> Quod he, and he is here faste by.
>
> *The Dreme of Chaucer*, 365.

LIME-ROD. A twig with bird-lime; more

usually called a lime-twig. *Lyme-yerd*, Piers Ploughman, p. 170.

> Ile lend thee *lyme-twigs*, and fine sparrow calls,
> Wherewith the fowler silly birds Inthralls.
> > *The Affectionate Shepheard*, 1594.

LIMIT. A limb. *Shak.*

LIMITATION. A certain precinct allowed to a limitour. (*Lat.*)

LIMITOUR. A begging-friar. Hence in later times, *limit*, to beg.

> The *lymytour* that vesiteth the wleffis,
> I-wys a mane of him ynough may leere,
> To geve pynnys, gerdyllis, and knyeffis,
> > This craft is good. *MS. Cantab. Ff. 1. 6, f. 156.*
> For they go ydelly a *limiting* abrode, living upon the sweat of other mens travels.
> > *Northbrooke's Treatise*, 1577.

LIMITROPHES. Boundaries. This word occurs in the Historie of Palmendos, 1589.

LIM-LIFTER. A term of contempt, perhaps derived from *limitour*. " A scornefull nickname, as we say a lim-lifter," Florio, p. 92.

LIMMER. Mischievous; base; low. Still in use, applied to females.

> Then the *limmer* Scottes hared me, burnt my guddes, and made deadly feede on me, and my barnes. *Bullein's Dialogue*, 1573, p. 3.

LIMMOCK. Very limp. *Var. dial.*

LIMOUS. Sticky; glutinous. *Pr. Parv.*

LIMP. (1) An instrument used for separating lead ore from the stone. Mander explains it, " a small board to skim the sieve with when washing the ore."

(2) Flaccid; limber; supple. *Var. dial.* Also called *limpey.* Stanihurst, p. 11, has *limpeth,* is weak, or unsatisfactory.

(3) Inefficient. *Somerset.*

(4) To chance, or happen.

> The fyfte was Josue. that joly mane of armes,
> That in Jerusalem ofte fulle myche joye *lymppede.*
> > *Morte Arthure, MS. Lincoln, f. 89.*

LIN. (1) Flax; linen. (*A.-S.*) It is sometimes used for female apparel generally. *Lyn*, MS. Med. Rec. Linc. f. 286, xv. Cent. *Lyne-webbers,* Cocke Lorelles Bote, p. 9.

> He dronk never eldre ne wyn,
> Ne never wered clooth of *lyn.*
> > *Cursor Mundi, MS. Coll. Trin. Cantab. f. 79.*
> Bothe pallis, clothes and baudekyn,
> And other of wolle and of *lyn.*
> > *MS. Addit. 10036, fol. 49.*

(2) To cease; to stop. *North.*

> And never did *lin* towring upward, and still upward, for the space, as I might guess, of one whole hour. *The Man in the Moone*, 1657, p. 46.
> Her husband, a recusant, often came,
> To hear mass read, nor would he ever *lin.*
> > *Billingsly's Brachy-Martyrologia*, 1657, p. 200.

(3) A carcase. *Cumb.*

(4) A pool, a cascade, or precipice. " Linnes and huge pooles," Harrison, p. 88. A lake, ibid. p. 130. Still in use in the North.

(5) Lain, or laid. *Sir Tristrem.*

LINAGE. Lineage; family. (*A.-N.*)

LINCELS. Tares in corn.

LINCEUS. Linx-seeing.

> But yet, in the end, their secret driftes are laide

open, and *linceus* eyes, that see through stone walls, have made a passage into the close coverture of their hypocrisie. *Nash's Pierce Pennilesse*, 1592.

LINCH. (1) To beat, or chastise. *North.* Urry's MS. additions to Ray.

(2) A balk of land. *Kent.* Any bank or boundary for the division of land. Also called *lincher* and *linchet.*

(3) A haunch of mutton. *North.*

(4) A hamlet. *Glouc.*

(5) A small step; a narrow steep bank, or footpath. *West.*

(6) A ledge; a rectangular projection.

(7) A small inland cliff, generally one that is wooded. *South.*

(8) To prance about lively. Hollyband mentions a *linching horse* as the translation of *cheval coquelineux*, Dictionarie, 1593.

LINCHPIN. A stag's penis. *Salop.*

LINCOLNSHIRE. A primitive custom in Lincolnshire of washing with the excrement of the pig, and burning dried cow-dung, is memorialized in a proverb occasionally quoted:

> What a wonderful county is Lincolnshire,
> Where pigs [emit] soap and cows [void] fire.

The words between brackets have been changed from the original *causa pudoris*, but put it how you will, the couplet is not very elegant. It is quoted at full by Aubrey, MS. Nat. Hist. Wilts. p. 292.

LINDABRIDES. A mistress. An old term, derived from a character in an early Spanish romance. See Nares.

LINDE. The lime-tree. (*A.-S.*) Sometimes used perhaps for a tree in general.

> As he rood undir a *lynde,*
> Beside a roche, as I the telle.
> > *Gower, MS. Soc. Antiq. 134, f. 53.*
> Than were y gladd and lyȝt as *lynde,*
> Of *parce michi Domine.*
> > *MS. Cantab. Ff. ii. 38, f. 21.*
> A hert he found ther he ley
> Welle feyre under the *lynd.*
> > *MS. Ashmole 61, f. 1.*
> There come a knyght them fulle nere,
> That hyght sir Barnard Messengere,
> Huntyng aftur an hynde,
> And founde that lady lovely of chere,
> And hur sone slepyng in fere,
> Lyeng undur a *lynde.*
> > *MS. Cantab. Ff. ii. 38, f. 74.*

LINE. (1) To beat. *Var. dial.*

(2) To lean; to incline. *Somerset.*

(3) " To line a bitch or cover a mare," Florio, ed. 1611, p. 25. *Lyming*, Topsell's Beasts, 1607, p. 139. Still in use.

(4) *Line of life*, one of the lines in the hand, a term in palmistry.

(5) A place for laying down. *East.*

LINED. Intoxicated. *North.*

LINENER. A linen-draper. See Nares.

LINERS. Bundles. *Devon.*

LINES. *Marriage lines*, a certificate of marriage. *Yorksh.*

LINET. Tinder. *Wilts.*

LINE-WAY. A straight direct path.

LING. Heath; furze. *North.* " Ling or

heath for brushes," Florio, p. 69. *Ling collins,* burnt ling, West. and Cumb. Dial.

> Ther the! beryed hem both
> In nouther moase nor *lyng.*
>
> *MS. Cantab.* Ff. v. 48, f. 129.

LINGE. (1) To work hard. *Yorksh.*

(2) To loll out the tongue. *Oxon.*

LINGEL. A shoemaker's thread. "*Corigea, lyngel,*" MS. Lansd. 560, f. 45. "Lyngell that souters sowe with, *chefyros,*" Palsgrave. "Lynger to sowe with, *poulcier,*" ibid.

> The cobler of Caunterburie, armde with his aul, his *lingel,* and his last, presents himselfe a judiciall censor of other mens writinges.
>
> *The Cobler of Caunterburie,* 1590.

LINGER. To long for anything. *Kent.*

LINGET. A linnet. *Somerset.*

LINGY. (1) Active; strong; tall. *North.*

(2) Idle and loitering. *Kent.*

(3) The same as *Limber,* q. v.

LINHAY. An open shed attached to a farm-yard. *West.* When attached to a barn or house, it is called a hanging-linhay.

LINIATION. Mensuration. (*Lat.*)

LINIEL. The same as *Lingel,* q. v.

LINING. (1) The loins. *Somerset.*

(2) A person who succeeded with a woman was said to get within the lining of her smock.

> But as one of the three chapmen was imploied in his traffike abroad, so the prettie poplet his wife began to be a fresh occupieng giglot at home, and by report fell so farre acquainted with a religious cloisterer of the towne, as that he gat within the *lining* of hir smocke. *Stanihurst's Ireland,* p. 26.

LINK. (1) A sausage. *East.* Hollyband, 1593, explains *lirkes,* "a kinde of meate made of hogges guts kept in brine;" and Holme, 1688, calls them, "a kind of pudding, the skin being filled with pork flesh, and seasoned with diverse spices, minced, and tied up at distances." Howell has, "a link, sausage, or chitterling." Lex. Tet. 1660.

(2) To burn, or give light. (*A.-S.*)

(3) To walk quickly. *North.*

(4) See *Linch* and *Ling.*

LINKERING. Idle. *Salop.*

LINK-PINS. Linch-pins are called *link-pins* and *lin-pins* in the provinces. *Lynpyn* occurs in the Finchale Charters.

LINKS. Sand-hills. *North.*

LINMAN. A flax-seller. *West.*

LINNEN. London. *Devon.*

LINNIT. Lint; tinder. *Dorset.*

LINN-TREE. A lime-tree. *Derb.*

LINNY. The same as *Linhay,* q. v.

LINOLF. Shoemaker's lingel. *Pr. Parv.*

LINSE. To beat severely. *Devon.*

LINSET. The name of the stool on which women sat while spinning.

LIN-SHORDS. To throw lin-shords, i. e. Lent-shords, a custom practised at Ilfracombe, which consists in throwing broken shords into the windows of the houses on one of the days of Lent.

LINSTOCK. A stick with a match or lint at the end used by gunners.

LINT. A halter. *Var. dial.*

LINTEL. When a door or window is square-headed, the upper piece is called a lintel. It is sometimes termed a *lynton* in early writers.

LINTELS. The same as *Lincels,* q. v. Tares are called *lints* in Lincolnshire.

LINTEREL. The same as *Lintel,* q. v.

LINT-WHITE. A lark. *Suffolk.*

LINTY. Idle; lazy; fat. *Var. dial.*

LION. The main beam of a ceiling. *West.* Perhaps from *lie on.*

LIOUR. (1) A mixture. MS. Med. Rec.

(2) The binding or fringe of cloth. "Sett on *lyour,*" Boke of Curtasye, p. 19.

LIP. The same as *Lepe,* q. v.

LIPARY. Wet; rainy. *Somerset.*

LIP-CLIP. A kiss. A cant term. *Lip,* to kiss, Lilly, ed. 1632, sig. Dd. ii.

LIPE. A fragment; a slip, or portion. *Cumb.* "Of every disshe a *lipet* out to take," Lydgate's Minor Poems, p. 52.

LIPIN. To forewarn. *South.*

LIPKEN. A house. See *Lib-ken.*

LIPPED. (1) Laid down. A cant term.

(2) Free; loose; ravelled. *West.* Most probably from *Lipe,* q. v.

LIPPEN. (1) The same as *Lipary,* q. v. *Lippy* is also used in the same sense. *Lipping-time,* a wet season. *Glouc.*

(2) To expect; to rely; to trust to, or place confidence in. *North.*

LIPPER. The spray from small waves, either in fresh or salt water. *North.*

LIPPING-CLOUT. A piece of steel welded to the front of a horse's shoe. *West.*

LIPPIT. Wanton. (*Fr.*)

LIPSEY. To lisp. *Somerset.*

LIP-SHORD. A chip. *Devon.*

LIP-WINGLE. A lapwing. *Beds.*

LIP-WISE. Garrulous. *I. of Wight.*

LIQUIDNESS. Moisture. *Palsgrave.*

LIQUOR. To oil, or anoint. *Glouc.*

LIQUORY-STICK. The plant rest-harrow.

LIRE. (1) Flesh; meat. (*A.-S.*) *Swynes lire,* Ord. and Reg. p. 442. *Lyery,* abounding with lean flesh. *North.*

(2) Face; countenance. (*A.-S.*)

> Hir coloure fulle white it es,
> That lufly in *lyre.*
>
> *MS. Lincoln* A. i. 17, f. 132.

> So bytterly sche wepyd withall,
> By hyre *lyres* the terys gon fall.
>
> *MS. Ashmole* 61, f. 67.

(3) To plait a shirt. *Linc.* Perhaps connected with the old word *lire,* fringe or binding of cloth.

LIRICUMFANCY. The May lily.

LIRIPOOPS. An appendage to the ancient hood, consisting of long tails or tippets, passing round the neck, and hanging down before reaching to the feet, and often jagged. The term is often jocularly used by writers of the sixteenth and seventeenth centuries. "A lirripoop *vel* lerripoop, a silly empty creature, an old dotard," Milles, MS. Devon Gloss. A priest was formerly jocularly termed a *lerry-cum-poop*. It seems to mean a trick or stratagem, in the London Prodigal, p. 111. " And whereas thou takest the matter so farre in snuffe, I will teach thee thy *lyrripups* after another fashion than to be thus malepertlie cocking and billing with me, that am thy governour," Stanihurst, p. 35.

> Theres a girle that knowes her *lerripoope*.
>> *Lilly's Mother Bombie*, 1594.

LIRK. To crease; to rumple. *North.* Perhaps *to jerk* in the following passage. *Lirt*, to toss, West. and Cumb. Dial. p. 368.

> I *lyrks* hyme up with my hond,
> And pray hyme that he wolle stond.
>> *MS. Porkington* 10.

LIRP. (1) To snap the fingers. " A *lirp* or clack with ones fingers ends, as barbers doe give," Florio, p. 199.
(2) To walk lamely. *Somerset.*

LIRRY. A blow on the ear. Also, to reprove, to upbraid. *Kent.*

LIS. (1) To lose. Arch. xiii. 203.
(2) Forgiveness. Kennett, MS. Lansd. 1033.

LISER. The list or fringe of cloth.

LISH. Active; strong. *North.*

LISHEY. Flexible; limber. *Kent.*

LISK. The same as *Lesk*, q. v.

LISSE. (1) To ease, or relieve. (*A.-S.*) See Hardyng, f. 90; Wright's Lyric Poetry, p. 57.

> How that they myȝte wynne a speche,
> Hire wofulle peyne for to *lisse*.
>> *Gower, MS Soc. Antiq.* 134, f. 93.

> That myȝt yow *lysse* owt of thys peyne.
>> *MS. Cantab.* Ff. ii. 38, f. 49.

> I have herde of an erbe to *lys* that peyne,
> Mene seyth it bereth a doubylle floure.
>> *MS. Cantab.* Ff. i. 6, f. 46.

> *Lys* me now in my longoure,
> And gyf me lysens to lyve in ease.
>> *MS. Cantab.* Ff. i. 6.

(2) Joy; happiness; bliss. (*A.-S.*)

LISSEN. A cleft in a rock. *Glouc.* The word is used by Sir Matthew Hale, but spelt by him *lisne*. It is not in common use.

LISSOM. Excessively limber or pliable; light, nimble, or active. *Var. dial.*

LISSUM. A narrow slip of anything. *Somerset.*

LIST. (1) A list house or room, when sounds are heard easily from one room to another. *Kent.*
(2) Cunning; artifice. (*Germ.*) " Tech him alle the listes," Kyng Horn, 239.
(3) " *Le mol de l'oreille*, the lug or *list* of th'eare," Cotgrave, in v. *Mol.*
(4) A boundary line. See Twelfth Night, iii. 1. Topsell, Historie of Serpents, 1608, p. 87, mentions worms " having a black *list* or line running along their backs."
(5) The close dense streak which sometimes appears in heavy bread. *West.*
(6) The flank. *North.* " A list of pork, a bony piece cut from the gammon," Kennett, MS.
(7) The selvage of woollen cloth. It is also called listen. " *Forigo*, a lystynge," Nominale

MS. This is a variation of our fourth meaning. Anything edged or bordered was formerly said to be *listed*. " A targe *listed* with gold" is mentioned in Gy of Warwike, p. 312.

LISTE. To please. (*A.-S.*) Also a substantive, pleasure, inclination. Hence *meat-list*, appetite. *Devon.*

> Ȝe that *liste* has to lyth, or luffes for to here.
>> *Morte Arthure, MS. Lincoln,* f. 53.

LISTEN. To attend to. *Shak.*

LISTLY. Quick of hearing. *East.* Also, easily, distinctly.

LISTOW. Liest thou. *Weber.*

LISTRE. A person who read some part of the church service. (*A.-S.*)

LISTRING. Thickening. *North.*

LISTY Strong; powerful. *North.* " Listy mene and able," Liucoln MS. f. 3.

LIT. To colour, or dye. *North.* " He'll lie all manner of colours but blue, and that is gone to the litting," Upton's MS. additions to Junius.

> We use na clathes that are *littede* of dyverse coloures : oure wiffes ne are noȝte gayly arayed for to plese us.
>> *MS. Lincoln* A. 1. 17, f. 33.

LITANY-STOOL. A small low desk at which the Litany was sung or said.

LITARGE. White lead. (*A.-N.*)

LITE. (1) Few; little. *North.* " Litlum and litlum," by little and little, Piers Ploughman, p. 329, an Anglo-Saxon phrase.
(2) To depend upon, or rely. *Linc.*
(3) Strife. Towneley Mysteries, p. 71.
(4) To hinder, tarry, or delay. (*A.-S.*)

LITEN. A garden. *North.*

LITERATURE. Learning. (*Lat.*)

> Worshypfull maysters, ye shall understand
> Is to you that have no *litterature*.
>> *The Pardoner and the Frere,* 1533.

LITH. (1) A body. (*A.-S.*)
(2) Possessions; property. " Lond ne *lith*," a common phrase in early poetry. See Langtoft, p. 194; Sir Tristrem, p. 220; W. Mapes, p. 341; Havelok, p. 239.
(3) Alighted. Sevyn Sages, 571.

LITHE. (1) To tell; to relate.

> Lystenyth now to my talkynge
> Of whome y wylle yow *lythe*.
>> *MS. Cantab.* Ff. ii. 38, f. 82.

(2) A limb, or joint. (*A.-S.*)

> Fendys bolde, with crokys kene,
> Rente hys body fro *lyth* to *lythe*.
>> *MS. Cantab.* Ff. ii. 38, f. 49.

> Hur sone that than dwellyd hur wyth,
> He was mekylle of boon and *lyth*.
>> *MS. Cantab.* Ff. ii. 38, f. 74.

> Was never arowe that greved hym,
> Ne that hym towched *lythe* nor lyme.
>> *MS. Lincoln* A. 1. 17, f. 128.

(3) Tender; mild; gentle; agreeable; glad. Also, gladly, tenderly. " *Lithe*, calm, quiet," Kennet. It is used in different shades of meaning, implying *softness*. Alleviation, comfort, Havelok, 1338.

> Sche toke up hur sone to hur,
> And lapped hyt fulle *lythe*.
>> *MS. Cantab.* Ff. ii. 38, f. 74.

(4) Supple; pliant. *Var. dial.* " Lythe, delyver, *souple,*" Palsgrave. Also, to soften, to render lithe or supple.

(5) To thicken. Kennett, MS. Broth is said to be *lithened* when mixed with oatmeal.

(6) Obsequious; humble. *North.*

LITHER. (1) Wicked. (*A.-S.*) Still used in the North, meaning *idle, lazy.*

How they whanne wyth were wyrchippis many,
Sloughe Lucyus the *lythyre,* that lorde was of Rome.
Morte Arthure, MS. Lincoln, f. 53.

(2) Supple; limber; pliant. *South.* It is not an uncommon archaism.

LITHERNESS. Idleness. *North.*

Idlenesse, moste delectable to the fleshe, which deliteth above measure in sloth, *lithernesse,* ceasing from occupation. *Northbrooke's Treatise,* 1577.

LITHESOME. Gay; cheerful. *Yorksh.*

LITHEWALE. The herb gromwell.

LITHE-WURT. The plant forget-me-not. The term is still sometimes used.

LITHLICHE. Easily. (*A.-S.*)

LIT-HOUSE. A dyeing house. *North.*

LITHY. (1) Pliant; supple. *South.*

(2) Heavy, warm, applied to the weather.

LITIGIOUS. Injurious. *Var. dial*

LITLING. Very little. *Chaucer.*

LITLUS. The same as *Little-house,* q. v.

LITSTER. A dyer. It is translated by *tinctor* in the Nominale MS. *Lyttesters,* York Records, p. 235.

Tak the greis of the wyne that mene fyndis in the tounnes, that *litsters* and goldsmythes uses.
MS. Linc. Med. f. 313.

LITT. A sheep-cot. *Somerset.*

LITTEN. A church-yard. *South.* Ray has *liten,* a garden, q. v.

LITTER. (1) Nonsense. *Somerset.*

(2) To *litter up,* or *down,* to put bedding under the horses. *West.*

LITTERMAN. A groom. *Warw.*

LITTLE-A-DOW. Worthless. *Northumb.*

LITTLE-EASE. The pillory, stocks, or bilboes. Also, a small apartment in a prison where the inmate could have very little ease. " A streite place in a prisone called littell ease," Elyot, 1559, in v. *Arca.* The *little ease* at Guildhall, where unruly apprentices were confined, is frequently mentioned by our early writers.

LITTLE-FLINT-COAL. A thin measure of coal, the nearest to the surface. *West.*

LITTLE-HOUSE. A privy. *Var. dial.*

LITTLE-MASTER. A schoolmaster. *Baber.*

LITTLE-SILVER. A low price. *East.*

LITTLEST. Least. Common in the provinces, and sanctioned by Shakespeare.

LITTLE-WALE. The herb gromwell.

LITTOCKS. Rags and tatters. *Berks.*

LITTY. Light; active; nimble. *West.*

LIVAND. Living. *Chaucer.*

LIVE. (1) Life. (*A.-S.*) On *live,* alive. *Lives creatures,* living creatures, *lives body,* &c.

So fayre 3it never was figure,
Ry3t as a *lyvis* creature.
Gower, MS. Soc. Antiq. 134, fol. 105.

(2) *To live under,* to be tenant to. *To live upright,* to retire from business.

(3) Fresh, as honey, &c. *Somerset.*

LIVELIHOOD. Liveliness; activity. *Shak.*

LIVELODE. Income; livelihood. Also, a pension, largess, or dole to soldiers.

LIVELY. Fresh; gay; neat. *North.* It is so used in Davies' Rites, 1672, p. 8. Sometimes, living.

LIVER. (1) To deliver. *North.*

And to his men he *liverd* hym hole and feere.
MS. Lansdowne 208, f. 5.

(2) Quick; active; lively. *Palsgrave.*

LIVERANCE. A delivery. *North.*

LIVERED. Heavy, or underbaked. *South.*

LIVEREDE. Red. Rob. Glouc. p. 39.

LIVERING. A kind of pudding made of liver, and rolled up in the form of a sausage. " Two blodynges, I trow, a *leveryng* betwene," Towneley Myst. p. 89. N. Fairfax, Bulk and Selvedge 1674, p. 159, mentions liverings.

LIVERSAD. Caked and matted together, applied to ground. *North.*

LIVERSICK. A hangnail. *South.*

LIVERY. (1) A badge of any kind; the uniform given by a baron or knight to his retainers in battle. Hence the different regiments or parts of an army were termed liveries. " In iche leveré," Morte Arthure, MS. Lincoln, f. 85. The term is used in a variety of senses, and may be generally explained as any grant or allowance at particular seasons. " *Corrodium,* leveraye," Nominale MS. " One that bestowes a livery, or cast of his wit, upon every one he sees," Cotgrave, in v. *Donne-Lardon.*

Ilke nyghte to *lyveré*
Bathe corne and haye.
MS. Lincoln A. i. 17, f. 134.

(2) Delivery. A common law term. *Livery of seisin* is the delivery of property into possession. *To sue one's livery,* to issue the writ which lay for the heir to obtain the seisin of his lands from the King.

(3) Sticky; adhesive. *South.*

LIVERY-CUPBOARD. An open cupboard with shelves, in which the liveries intended for distribution were placed.

LIVING. A farm. *Leic.*

LIVING-DEAR-ENE. An excl. of distress.

LIVISH. Lively.

If there were true and *livish* faith, then would it work love in their hearts.
Becon's Works, 1843, p. 37.

LIXOM. Amiable. *Heref.*

LIZENED. Shrunk, as corn. *Sussex.*

LIZZAH. Anything easily bent. *West.*

LIZZY. Elizabeth. *Var. dial.*

LI3T. Little. See *Lite.*

Felaw, he seid, herkyn a *li3t,*
And on myne errand go thou tyte.
MS. Cantab. Ff. v. 48, f. 52

LO. A large pond. *Yorksh.*

LOACH. A term of contempt for a fool. It occurs in Peele's Jests, p. 26.

LOADED. Bloated. *Devon.*

LOADS. The ditches for draining away the water from the fens. *Load-stone*, a leading-stone for drains.

> It was by a law of sewers decreed that a new drayn or *lode* should be made and maintained from the end of Chauncelors *lode* unto Tylney Smethe.
> *Dugdale's Imbanking*, p. 275.

LOADY. Heavy. *Loady-nut*, a double nut.

LOAK. A small quantity. *North.*

LOAL. To mew like a cat. *Yorksh.*

LOAMY. Damp. *Suffolk.* Loamie, Topsell's Beasts, p. 495, coloured like loam?

LOAN. A lane, or passage. *North.*

LOANING. (1) A lane. (2) A place near a village for milking cows. *North.*

LOAST. A wheel-rut. *Sussex.*

LOB. (1) To throw gently. *Sussex.*
(2) A very large lump. *Linc.*
(3) To kick. *East Anglia.*
(4) To hang down; to droop. Still in use in Somerset, according to Jennings, p. 53. *To lob along*, to walk loungingly.
(5) A clown; a clumsy fellow. "A blunt countrie lob," Stanihurst, p. 17. In Somersetshire, the last person in a race is called the lob.
(6) That part of a tree where it first divides into branches. *Beds.*
(7) To cast or throw. *Durham.*
(8) A very large taw. *Hants.*

LOBBATING. Large; unwieldy. *West.*

LOBBING. Tumult; uproar.

> What a *lobbing* makest thou,
> With a twenty Devill!
> *Mariage of Witt and Wisdome*, 1579.

LOBBS. Irregular veins of ore. Also, stairs under-ground for the miners.

LOBCOCK. A lubber. A very common term of contempt. "*Baligaut*, an unweldie lubber, great lobcocke," Cotgrave. See Jacke of Dover, p. 49; Hawkins, iii. 32; Roister Doister, p. 39; Cotgrave, in v. *Disme.*

> Much better were the *lobcock* lost then wonne,
> Unlesse he knew how to behave himselfe.
> *The Mous-Trap*, 1606.

LOBKIN. A house, or lodging. *Grose.*

LOBLOLLY. Thick spoon meat of any kind. It is thus mentioned by Markham:—"If you rost a goose and stop her belly with whole greets beaten together with egges, and after mixt with the gravy, there cannot be a more better or pleasanter sawce; nay if a man be at sea in any long travel he cannot eat a more pleasant or wholesome meat than these whole *grits* boyled in water till they burst, and then mixt with butter and so eaten with spoons, which though seamen call simply by the name of *loblolly*, yet there is not any meat, however significant the name be, that is more toothsome or wholesome."

LOB'S-COURSE. A dish composed of small lumps of meat mixed up with potatoes and onions, seasoned, and made into a kind of solid stew. It is mentioned in Peregrine Pickle, and is still common.

LOB'S-POUND. An old jocular term for a prison, or any place of confinement. The term is still in use, and is often applied to the juvenile prison made for a child between the feet of a grown-up person.

LOBSTER. The stoat. *East.*

LOBSTERS. Young soles. *Suffolk.*

LOBSTROUS-LOUSE. A wood-louse. *North.*

LOBURYONE. A snail. *Pr. Parv.*

LOBY. A lubber, or looby, q. v.

LOCAL. A local preacher is a dissenting clergyman who preaches at different places.

LOCAND. Looking. *Lydgate.*

LOCH. (1) A lake. *North.*
(2) The rut of a cart-wheel. *Sussex.*
(3) A cavity in a vein. *Derb.*
(4) A place to lay stone in. It is spelt *looch* in Archæologia, x. 72.

LOCK. (1) A lock of hay or wool is a small quantity of it hanging together, a bundle of hay, a fleece of wool. It occurs in Palsgrave, and it is still in use.
(2) To move the fore-wheels of a waggon to and fro. *Devon.* A waggon is said to lock when it is drawn out of its rectilinear motion, so that the fore-wheels make an angle with the hinder ones.
(3) *To be at lock*, to be in a difficulty. *Lock* was any close place of confinement.
(4) A puddle of water. *Heref.*
(5) To grapple. A term in fencing or wrestling, used by Gosson, 1579.

LOCKBANDS. Binding-stones in masonry.

LOCKCHEST. A millepe or wood-louse. I have heard this term in Oxfordshire, and it may probably be used in other counties. "Lokdore, wyrme, or locchester, *multipes*," Pr. Parv. p. 311. [Since writing the above, I have made more particular inquiries, and as I find the word is not in common use, I take the opportunity of substantiating the correctness of my explanation by stating that I am informed by the Rev. Henry Walker of Bletchington, co. Oxon, that a gardener in his employ used to call the wood-louse *lockchester*, which is precisely the term found in the Promptorium.]

LOCKED. (1) Faced, as cards are. *North.*
(2) Caught; fixed; appointed.

LOCKER. (1) A small cupboard or closet; an inner cupboard within a larger one. A drawer under a table or cupboard is still so termed.
(2) Pieces of wood which support the roof of a pit. *Salop.*
(3) To entangle; to mat together. *North.*

LOCKERS. Wooden cells for pigeons fixed to the outer walls of houses. *Oxon.*

LOCKET. The same as *Chape*. (2)

LOCK-FURROW. A furrow ploughed across the balks to let off the water. *South.*

LOCKING. The hip-joint. *Somerset.*

LOCKRAM. A kind of cheap linen, worn chiefly by the lower classes. There was a finer sort, of which shirt-bands, &c. were made.

> A wrought wastcoate on her backe, and a *lockram* smocke worth three pence, as well rent behind as before, I warrant you. *Maroccus Extaticus*, 1595.

LOCKRUM. Gibberish; nonsense. *Beds.*

LOCKS-AND-KEYS. Ash-keys. *West.*

LOCKS-AND-LICE. A kind of cloth.

LOCK-SPIT. A small cut with a spade to show the direction in which a piece of land is to be divided by a new fence.

LOCUSTS. Cockchafers; beetles. *North.*

LOD. Load; cargo. (*A.-S.*)

LODAM. An old game at cards, mentioned in Taylor's Motto, 12mo. Lond. 1622, sig. D. iv; Hawkins, iii. 203; Arch. viii. 149. One way of playing the game was called losing-lodam. "*Coquimbert qui gaigne pert*, a game at cards like our loosing lodam," Cotgrave.

LODDEN.

    But had I thought he'd been so *lodden*
    Of his bak'd, fry'd, boil'd, roast and sodden.
            Cotton's Works, 1734, p. 155.

LODE. (1) A leaning-wall. *Glouc.*

(2) A regular vein of metal ore.

(3) A ford. Dean Milles' MS.

(4) Guidance; behaviour? *Gawayne.*

LODEMANAGE. Pilotage. See Lydgate's Minor Poems, p. 152; Hartshorne, p. 131. Courts of Lodemanage are held at Dover for the appointment of the Cinque Port pilots.

    Mariners that bene discrete and sage,
    And experte bene of here *lodemanage*.
            M.S. Digby, 230.

LODEMEN. Carters; carriers. Nominale MS.

LODE-PLOT. A flat lode. See *Lode* (2).

LODERS. The same as *Lode-men*, q. v.

LODE-SHIP. A kind of fishing-vessel, mentioned in an early statute. See Blount.

LODESMEN. Pilots; guides. (*A.-S.*)

LODESTAR. The pole-star. *Shak.* It is a very common archaism.

LODE-WORKS. Metal works in high places where shafts are sunk very deeply. *Cornw.*

LODEWORT. The plant water-crowfoot.

LODGE. (1) A meeting or convention of the society of freemasons.

(2) To entrap an animal. *Linc.*

(3) A hunting term. See *Hunting*, sect. 3.

LODGED. Said of grass or corn beaten down by wind or rain. *West.*

LODLY. Loathly. See Tundale, p. 24.

    He shal him travaile day and niȝt,
    And *lodly* his body diȝt.
        Cursor Mundi, MS. Coll. Trin. Cantab. f. 46.

LODOLLY. A diminutive girl. *West.*

LOEGRIA. England. This name is sometimes found in old works, and is taken from Geoffrey of Monmouth.

LOENGE. Praising?

    To hewe and brenne in thy service,
    To *loenge* of thy sacrifise.
        Gower, MS. Soc. Antiq. 134, f. 113.

LOERT. (1) Lord; sir, but this title was applied to both sexes. *Derb.*

(2) To travel quickly. *Devon.*

LOFF. (1) Low. *Loffer*, lower. *Var. dial.*

(2) To offer. West. and Cumb. Dial. p. 368.

(3) To laugh. It occurs in the tale of Mother Hubbard, and is a genuine old form.

LOFT. (1) *On loft*, on high, a-loft. (*A.-S.*)

(2) An upper chamber. *North.* "The third loft," Acts, xx. 9.

(3) Lofty. Surrey, quoted by Nares.

(4) The floor of a room. *Spenser.*

LOFTY. Massive; superior. *Derb.*

LOG. (1) To oscillate. *Cornw.*

(2) A perch in measure. *Wilts.*

LOG-BURN. An open drain running from a sink or jakes. *West.*

LOGE. (1) A lodge, or residence. (*A.-N.*)

    He has with hym ȝong men thre,
    Thei be archers of this contré
        The kyng to serve at wille,
    To kepe the dere bothe day and nyȝt;
    And for theire luf a *loge* is diȝt
        Fulle hye upon an hille.
        MS. Cantab. Ff. v. 48, f. 49.

(2) Laughed. Wright's Seven Sages, p. 107.

LOGGATS. An old game forbidden by statute in Henry VIII.'s time. It is thus played, according to Steevens. A stake is fixed in the ground: those who play throw loggats at it, and he that is nearest the stake wins. *Loggats* or *loggets* are also small pieces or logs of wood, such as the country people throw at fruit that cannot otherwise be reached. "*Loggats*, little logs or wooden pins, a play the same with nine-pins, in which boys, however, often made use of bones instead of wooden pins," Dean Milles' MS.

LOGGEN. To lodge, or reside. (*A.-N.*)

LOGGER. (1) The same as *Hobble* (2).

(2) The irregular motion of a wheel round its axle. *Suffolk.*

LOGGERHEAD. (1) The large tiger moth. *North.*

(2) A blockhead. See Florio, p. 69. *To go to loggerheads*, to fight or squabble.

LOGGIN. A bundle, or lock. *North.*

LOGGING. A lodging. *Chaucer.*

LOGGY. Thickset, as cattle. *West.*

LOGH. A lake. See Anturs of Arther, p. 2; Holinshed, Conq. Ireland, p. 23.

LOGHE. Laughed. See *Luyhe.*

    Than sir Degrevant *loghe*
    Ther he stode undir the boghe.
        MS. Lincoln A. i. 17, f. 133.
    Then *logh* oure kyng and smyled stille,
    Thou onswerls me not at my wille.
        MS. Cantab. Ff. v. 48, f. 47.
    There-att alle the kynges *loghe*,
    There was joye and gamene y-noghe
        Amonges thame in the haulle !
    The kynge of Fraunce with hert ful fayne,
    Said, Clement, brynge the mantils agayne,
        For I salle paye for alle.
        Octavian, Lincoln MS.

LOGHER. Lower. *Rob. Glouc.*

LOGHT. Taken away?

    The fierth case es gode or oght,
    That he fro holy kyrk has *loght*.
        Hampole, MS. Bowes, p. 7.

LOINED. Covered. See Harrison, p. 232. This appears to be another form of *line*.

LOITERSACKE. A lazy loitering fellow.

    If the *loitersacke* be gone springing into a taverne,
    Ile fetch him reeling out.
        Lilly's Mother Bombie, 1594.

LOKE. (1) To see; to look upon; to guard, or take care of. (*A.-S.*)

(2) A private road or path. *East.*

(3) Locked; shut up. *Weber.*

(4) The wicket or hatch of a door.

LOKEDES. Ornaments for the head?

> And than the same develle tok wormes, and pykk,
> and tarre, and made *lokedes*, and sett thame appone
> hir hede.   *MS. Lincoln* A. i. 17, f. 253.

LOKER. A carpenter's plane. *Linc.*

LOKINGIS. Looks.

> Forth with his pitous *lokyngis*,
> He wolde make a womman wene
> To gon upon the fayre grene.
>   *Gower, MS. Soc. Antiq.* 134, f. 42.

LOKKEDEN. Locked.

> They wanne with moche woo the walles withinne,
> Mene lepen to anoue and *lokkeden* the jates.
>   *MS. Cott. Calig.* A. ii. f. 115.

LOLL. (1) To fondle; to dandle. *North.*

> He *loll'd* her in his arms,
> He lull'd her on his breast.
>   *North Country Ballad.*

(2) A pet; a spoilt child. *Oxon.*

(3) To box one's ears.

LOLLARDS. Heretics. The followers of Wickliffe were termed Lollards or Lollers, but the term was in use long before the time of that distinguished reformer. It was commonly used as one of reproach for religious hypocrites. A loller is thus described by Audelay,—

> Lef thou me a *loller* his dedis that wyl hym deme,
> Jif he withdraue his deutés from holé cherche away,
> And wyl not worchip the cros, on hym take good eme,
> And here his matyns and his masse upon the haleday,
> And beleevys not in the sacrement, that hit is God
>   veray,
> And wyl not schryve him to a prest on what deth
>   he dye,
> And settis nost be the sacramentis sothly to say,
> Take him fore a *loller* y tel jou treuly,
>   And false in his fay;
> Deme hym after his saw,
> Bot he wyl hym withdrawe,
>   Never fore hym pray.

LOLLIGOES. Idle fellows. *Milles' MS.*

LOLLIKER. The tongue. *Somerset.*

LOLLIPOP. A coarse sweetmeat made of treacle, butter, and flour. *Var. dial.*

LOLLOCK. A lump, or large piece. *North.*

LOLLOP. To lounge, or loll about idly. Hence *lollops*, a slattern. *Var. dial.*

LOLL-POOP. (1) A lazy idle fellow. (2) a coaxing wheedling child. *Suffolk.* Called *lolly-pot* in Somerset.

LOLLY-BANGER. Very thick gingerbread, enriched by raisins. *Somerset.*

LOLLY-COCK. A turkey-cock. *Devon.*

LOLLY-SWEET. Lusciously sweet. *East.*

LOLOKE. To look. Possibly an error of the scribe in MS. Sloane 213 for *loke.*

LOMBARD. A banker. The Italian bankers who settled in this country in the middle-ages gave the name to Lombard-street. See a curious notice of Lombards in Arch. xxix. 286.

LOMBARD-FEVER. A fit of idleness.

LOMBREN. Lambs. Reliq. Antiq. i. 264.

LOME. (1) Frequently. "Oft and lome,"

Octovian, 1944; Ritson's Ancient Songs, i. 72, A common phrase in old English.

> And with his mowthe he cust hit oft and *lome.*
>   *Chron. Vilodun.* p. 96.

(2) A weaver's loom. *Palsgrave.*

(3) An instrument, or weapon; a household utensil. It seems to be some kind of vessel in Holinshed, Hist. England, i. 194; Reliq. Antiq. i. 54. " *Loom*, any utensil, as a tub," Grose. Still in use.

> I se never a wars *lome*
> Stondynge opone mone.   *MS. Porkington* 10.

LOMERE. More frequently. (*A.-S.*)

LOMEY. A spoilt child. *Devon.*

LOMMAKIN. (1) Love-making. *Heref.*

(2) Very large; clumsy. *Var. dial.*

LOMPER. (1) To idle. (2) To walk heavily.

LOMPY. Thick; clumsy; fat. *Kent.*

LONCHE. A loud noise. *Pr. Parv.*

LONCHING. " Quasi *launching*, citato gradu et passibus ingentibus incedens," Milles' MS.

LOND. (1) Land. (*A.-S.*) *In lond*, on the ground. *God of lond*, Lord of the world.

(2) To clog with dirt. *East.*

LONDAGE. Landing. " Awaytynge upon his *londage*," Mort d'Arthur, ii. 433.

LOND-BUGGERE. A buyer of land. (*A.-S.*)

LONDENOYS. A Londoner. *Chaucer.*

LOND-EVIL. The epilepsy. It is misread *loud euel* in the Archæologia, xxx. 410.

LONDON-FLITTING. The removal of parties by stealth before the landlord is paid.

LONDREIS. Londoners. *Hearne.*

LONE. (1) *Lone-woman*, a woman unmarried, or without a male protector. *Lonely woman*, a widow, Hallamsh. Gloss. p. 61. *Lone-man*, a man living unmarried by himself. The first of these phrases is used by Shakespeare.

(2) The palm of the hand.

(3) A lodging-house. *Somerset.*

(4) A supplication for alms. *Devon.*

LONG. (1) Two breves in music.

(2) *Long horned one*, a native or inhabitant of Craven. *A long hundred*, six score. *Long length*, at full length. *Long last*, at length, in the end. *In the long run*, ibid. *Long streaked*, at full length. *A long way*, much. *By long and by late*, after a long time and trouble. *To lie in the long feathers*, to sleep on straw. *For the long lane*, when a thing is borrowed without any intention of repayment. *Long in the mouth*, tough.

(3) Tall. Isumbras, 13, 258.

(4) To belong; to belong to. (*A.-S.*)

(5) To long for; to desire. *Chaucer.*

(6) Great. See Forby, ii. 200. This meaning is also given by Grose.

(7) Tough to the palate. *East.*

(8) To reach; to toss. *Suffolk.*

LONGART. The tail or end-board of a cart or waggon. *Chesh.*

LONG-BOWLING. The game of skittles. It is described by Strutt, p. 269.

LONG-BULLETS. A game played by casting stones in the North of England.

LONG-CRIPPLE. The speckled viper. *Devon.*

LONG-CROWN. A deep fellow. " That caps Long-Crown, and he capped the Devil," A Lincolnshire saying in reference to a great falsehood.

LONG-DOG. A greyhound. *Var. dial.*

LONGE. Lungs.
>   With hys swyrde the bore he stonge
>   Thorow the lyvyr and the *longe*.
>   *MS. Cantab. Ff. ll. 38, f. 100.*

LONGFULL. Long; tedious. *Var. dial.*

LONG-HOME. To go to one's long home, i. e. to depart this life.
>   And thy traveyle shalt thou sone ende,
>   For to thy *long home* sone shalt thou wende.
>   *MS. Harl. 1701, f. 61.*

LONGING-MARKS. The indelible marks on the skins of children. See Digby of Bodies, 1669, p. 425.

LONG-LADY. A farthing-candle. *East.*

LONG-LANE. The throat. *Var. dial.*

LONG-LIFE. The milt of a pig. *Linc.*

LONG-OF. Owing to.
>   Petur, sche seyde, thou myȝt welle see
>   Hyt was *long of* my keyes and not on me.
>   *MS. Cantab. Ff. ll. 38, f. 132.*
>
>   I have spyed the false felone,
>   As he stondes at his masse;
>   Hit is *long of* the, seide the munke,
>   And ever he fro us passe.
>   *MS. Cantab. Ff. v. 48, f. 127.*
>
>   Alasse, why dost thou me suspect
>   Of such a haynous cryme?
>   It was not *long of* me, in faith,
>   That I went at this time.
>   *Gaulfrido and Barnardo, 1570.*

LONG-ONE. A hare. *Var. dial.*

LONG-OYSTER. The sea cray-fish.

LONG-SETTLE. A long wooden seat, with back and arms, somewhat like a sofa. " *Sedile*, a longsetylle," Nominale MS.

LONGSOME. Tedious. *Var. dial.*

LONG-TAILED-CAPON. The long-tailed titmouse. *South.*

LONG-TAILS. An old nick-name for the natives of Kent. See Howell's English Proverbs, p. 21; Musarum Deliciæ, 1656, p. 7. In the library of Dulwich College is a printed broadside, entitled, " Advice to the Kentish *long-tails* by the wise men of Gotham, in answer to their late sawcy petition to the Parliament," fol. 1701.
>   Truly, sir, sayd my hoastesse, I thinke we are called *Longtayles*, by reason our tales are long, that we use to passe the time withall, and make our selves merry. Now, good hoastesse, sayd I, let me entreat from you one of those tales. You shall (sayd shee), and that shall not be a common one neither, for it is a long tale, a merry tale, and a sweete tale; and thus it beginnes.
>   *Robin Goodfellow, his Mad Prankes, 1628.*

LONG-TO. Distant from. *Var. dial.*

LONG-TONGUE. A tale-teller. " A long-tongued knave, one that uttereth all he knowes," Florio, p. 17.

LONGUT. Longed; desired. (*A.-S.*)
>   The kyng red the letturs anon,
>   And seid, So mot I the,
>   Ther was never ȝoman in mery Ingland
>   I *longut* so sore to see. *MS. Cantab. Ff. v. 48, f. 130.*

LONG-WAYS. Lengthways. *South.*

LONGWORT. Pellitory of Spain.

LONIR. A blanket. *Devon.*

LONK. (1) The hip-joint. *Heref.*

(2) A small dingle; a hollow. *West.*

(3) Long; tedious. *North.*

(4) A Lancashire man. A sheep bred in that county is also so called.

LONNING. A lane, or by-road. *North.*

LONT-FIGS. Dried figs. *Somerset.*

LOO. *Under the loo*, the leeward. *To loo*, to shelter from the wind. *Kent.*

LOOBS. Slime containing ore. *Derb.*

LOOBY. A silly awkward fellow. " Long-backt, or ill-shaped, *loobie*," Cotgrave.

LOOED. Supplanted; superseded. *West.*

LOOF. To bring a vessel close to the wind, now pronounced *luff* by seamen. It occurs in Wendover's Chronicle. " *Louffe* you from him," Bourne's Inventions or Devises, 1578.

LOOINDY. Sullen; mischievous. *North.*

LOOK. (1) To weed corn. *Cumb.*

(2) *To look as big as bull beef*, to look very stout and hearty, bull beef having been formerly recommended to those who desired to be so. *You look, you may well look*, you are greatly surprised. *To look at the nose*, to frown, to look out of temper. *Lookee d'ye see*, look ye! do you see? a common phrase for drawing one's attention to any object. *To look on*, to regard with kindness and consideration. *To look sharp*, to be quick, to make haste.

(3) To look for; to expect. *North.*

(4) To behold. Kennett says, " in some parts of England they still say, loke, loke."

LOOK-ABOUT-YE. An old game mentioned in Taylor's Motto, 12mo. Lond. 1622, sig. D. iv.

LOOKER. (1) A weeding-hook. *North.*

(2) A shepherd or herdsman. *South.*

LOOM. (1) To appear larger than in reality, as things often do when at sea.

(2) A chimney. *Durham.*

(3) The track of a fish. *West.*

LOON. An idle fellow; a rascal; a country clown; a low dirty person. *Var. dial.*

LOOP. (1) A length of paling. *East.*

(2) The hinge of a door. *North.*

(3) To melt and run together in a mass, said of iron ore. A mining term.

(4) A gap in the paling of a park made for the convenience of the deer.

(5) A loop-hole; a narrow window.

LOOR. To stoop the head. *North.*

LOOS. Honour; praise. (*A.-S.*)

LOOSE. (1) To discharge an arrow from the string; to let off any projective weapon. It is still in use, according to Salopia Antiq. p. 491. " I spyed hym behynde a tree redy to *lowse* at me with a crosbowe," Palsgrave.

(2) *To be at a loose end*, to be very idle. *Loose-ended*, lewd. *Loose hung*, unsteady. " *Effilé*, weakened or loose-hangled," Cotgrave. *To be loosed*, out of service or apprenticeship. *Loose ladder*, a loop slipped down in a stocking.

(3) Indecent, as language. *Var. dial.*

(4) The privilege of turning out cattle on commons *North.*

LOOT. A thin oblong square board fixed to a staff or handle, used in boiling brine to remove the scum. *Staff.*

LOOTH. The same as *Loo,* q. v.

LOOVER. An opening at the top of a dove-cote. *North.* See *Lover* (2).

LOOVEYD. Praised. *Ritson.*

LOOVEYNG. Praise; honour.

> That was a feyre tokenynge
> Of pees and of *looveyng.*
>> *MS. Cantab.* Ff. ii. 38, f. 162.

LOOZE. A pig-stye. *West.*

LOOȝ. Laughed. "At hym ful fast thei looȝ," MS. Cantab. Ff. v. 48, f. 53.

LOP. (1) A flea. *North.* (*A.-S.*)

> Ys joy y-now so ye your lyggys streyne,
> Ye lade longe-sydyde as a *loppe.*
>> *MS. Fairfax* 16.

(2) To lollop or lounge about. *Kent.*

(3) To hang loosely; to hang down, or droop. *Var. dial.*

(4) The faggot wood of a tree.

LOPE. Leapt. Also, to leap. It seems to be a subst. in the second example.

> As sone as the chylde had spoke,
> The fende ynto hym was *lope.*
>> *MS. Harl.* 1701, f. 40.

> Tyme goth fast, it is full lyght of *lope,*
> And in abydyng men seyn ther lyghte hope.
>> *MS. Rawl. Poet.* 118.

LOP-EARED. Having long pendulous ears like a hound. *Var. dial.*

LOPEN. Leapt. See the Sevyn Sages, 739.

> Whan thy mouthe with shryfte ys opun
> Deth and synne are bothe oute *lopun.*
>> *MS. Harl.* 1701, f. 79.

> The portar set the yatys opon,
> And with that Befyse ys owt *lopon.*
>> *MS. Cantab.* Ff. ii. 38, f. 108.

> Anoon was al that feire gederynge
> *Lopen* undir oure lordes wynge.
>> *Cursor Mundi, MS. Coll. Trin. Cantab.* f. 111.

> Sythen he ys *lopen* on hys stede,
> He with hym Harrawde dud lede.
>> *MS. Cantab.* Ff. ii. 38, f. 154.

LOPE-STAFF. A leaping-staff. "A lope-staffe wherewith men leape ditches," Cotgrave.

LOPIRD. Coagulated. Still in use. See Forby, Brockett, Grose, Kennett, &c.

> Thare he fande none other fode,
> Bot wlatesome glete and *lopird* blode.
>> *MS. Lincoln* A. i. 17, f. 276.

> Thare dwelled a man in a myrke donjowne,
> And in a fowle stede of corrupcyowne,
> Whare he had no fode,
> Bot wlatsome glette and *lopyrd* blode.
>> *Hampole, MS. Bowes,* p. 26.

LOP-LOACH. The leech used by surgeons for drawing blood. *North.*

LOPLOLLY. A lazy fellow. *West.*

LOPPING. Lame. *Dorset.*

LOP-SIDED. One-sided. *Var. dial.*

LOP-START. The stoat. *East.* It is mentioned in Harrison's England, p. 230.

LOPUSTER. A lobster.

LOPWEBBE. A spider's web. (*A.-S.*)
II.

> As a *lopwebbe* fileth fome and gnattis,
> Taken and suffren gret files go.
>> *Occleve, MS. Soc. Antiq.* 134, f. 267.

LOQUINTUE. Eloquent. *Weber.*

LORD. (1) A title of honour given to monks and persons of superior rank. (*A.-S.*)

(2) *Lord have mercy upon us* was formerly the inscription on houses infected with the plague. *Lord have mercy upon me,* a disease thus mentioned in the Nomenclator, "the Illiake passion, or a paine and wringing in the small guts, which the homelier sort of phisicians doe call, *Lorde have mercy upon me.*"

LORDEYN. See *Fever-Lurden.* "The lurgyfever, idleness," Craven Glossary, p. 304.

> I trow he was infecte certeyn
> With the faitour, or the *fever lordeyn.*
>> *MS. Rawl.* C. 86, xv. Cent.

LORD-FEST. Excessively lordly. (*A.-S.*)

LORDINGS. Sirs; masters. (*A.-S.*) It is often used by later writers in contempt.

LORD-OF-MISRULE. The person who presided over the Christmas revels, by no means an unimportant personage in the olden times. He began his rule on All-hallow eve and continued it till Candlemas day. See a list of expences, dated in 1552, in Kempe's Loseley Manuscripts, pp. 44-54. For further information on the subject, see Brand, i. 272; Arch. xviii, 313-335; Hawkins' Engl. Dram. iii. 156; Strutt, ii. 200; Lilly's Sixe Court Comedies. 12mo. 1632, sig. F.

LORDS-AND-LADIES. See *Bulls-and-Cows.*

LORDSHIP. Supreme power. (*A.-S.*)

LORD-SIZE. The judge at the assizes.

LORD'S-ROOM. The stage-box in a theatre was formerly so called. *Jonson.*

LORDSWYK. A traitor. *Ritson.*

LORE. (1) Knowledge; doctrine; advice. (*A.-S.*)

(2) Lost. Still in use in Somerset.

> The kyng seid, Take me thy tayle.
> For my hors I wolde not the fayle,
> A peny that thou *lore.*
>> *MS. Cantab.* Ff. v. 48, f. 51.

LOREFADYR. A teacher. *Loremastir,* Dial. Creat. Moral. p. 243.

> Of al men they do most evyl,
> Here *lorefadyr* ys the devyl. *MS. Harl.* 1701, f. 24.

LOREINE. A rein. See Launfal, 888.

> Hys *loreine* lemyd alle with pride,
> Stede and armure alle was blake.
>> *MS. Harl.* 2252, f. 104.

LOREL. A bad worthless fellow. (*A.-N.*) *Lorels den,* Holinshed, Chron. Ireland, p. 93. *Cocke Lorel* was formerly a generic title for a very great rascal. "Lasy lorrels," Harman, 1567.

LOREMAR. A bit-maker. *Palsgrave.* "Lorimers or bit-makers," Harrison, p. 97.

LORENGE. Iron. (*A.-N.*)

LORER. The laurel-tree. *Chaucer.*

> This Daphne into a *lorer* tre
> Was turnid, whiche is ever grene.
>> *Gower, MS. Soc. Antiq.* 134, f 95.

> And plaunted trees that were to preise,
> Of eldre, palme, and of *lorere.*
>> *Cursor Mundi, MS. Coll. Trin. Cantab.* f. 52.

34

LORESMAN. A teacher. (*A.-S.*)

LORING. Instruction. *Spenser.*

LORNE. Lost; undone; destroyed. Still in use, in the sense of *forsaken.* Also, to lose anything.

> Thys cawse y telle wele for the,
> The ordur of preste he hath lorne.
>   *MS. Cantab.* Ff. ii. 38, f. 48.
> The stewardys lyfe ys lorne,
> There was fewe that rewyd ther on,
> And fewe for hym wepyth.
>   *MS. Cantab.* Ff. ii. 38, f. 74.

LORNYD. Learned.

> I can hit wel and perfitely ;
> Now have I lornyd a play.
>   *MS. Cantab.* Ff. v. 48, f. 54.

LORRE. A dish in ancient cookery. It is described in MS. Sloane 1201, f. 23. See also Reliq. Antiq. i. 81.

LORRIE-UP. A brawl. *Northumb.*

LORRY. A laurel-tree. Arch. xxx. 368.

LORTY. Dirty. *Northumb.*

LOSARD. A coward. *Weber.*

LOSE. (1) Praise ; honour. (2) To praise. (3) Fame ; report. It is used both in a good and bad sense. *Chaucer.*

> There he had grete chyvalry,
> He slewe hys enemyes with grete envy,
> Grete worde of hym aroos :
> In hethennes and yn Spayne,
> In Gaskyn and in Almayne
> Wyt they of hys loos.
>   *MS. Cantab.* Ff. ii. 38, f. 72.

LOSEL. The same as *Lorel,* q. v. Cocke Lorel was also called Cocke Losel.

> I holde you a grota,
> Ye wyll rede by rota,
> That he may wete a cota
> In Cocke Losels bota.
>   *Doctour Doubble Ale,* n. 4.

LOSENJOUR. A flatterer ; a liar. (*A.-N.*)

> What sey men of thes losenjours
> That have here wurdys feyre as flours.
>   *MS. Harl.* 1701, f. 24.

LOSERS. "Such losers may have leave to speak," 2 Henry VI. iii. 1. It has escaped the notice of the commentators that this is a common proverb. See my notes to the First Sketches of Henry VI. p. 93. It occurs in Stephens' Essayes and Characters, 2d ed. 1615, p. 50.

LOSH. To splash in water. *North.*

LOSSE. The lynx. Reynard, p. 146.

LOSSET. A large flat wooden dish used in the North of England.

LOSSUM. Lovesome ; beautiful.

LOSSY-BAG. Lucky-bag. A curious word used by low pedlars and attendant upon fairs, wakes, &c. "Come, put into the lossy-bag, and every time a prize," is the invitation, and the adventurer puts a penny or halfpenny into a bag, and draws out a ticket, which entitles him to a toy or other article of greater or less value than his money. according to his luck.

LOST. (1) Famished. *Heref.* (2) *To be lost,* to forget one's self. *He looks as if he had neither lost nor won,* i. e. stupid, unconcerned. This phrase occurs in Ben Jonson.

Lost and won, a redundant idiom, is found in many early writers.

LOSTELL. The cry of the heralds to the combatants that they should return home.

LOT. (1) To allot. (2) To imagine. *West.* (3) The shoot of a tree. (4) Dues to the lord of the manor for ingress and egress. A miner's term.

LOTCH. To limp; to jump. *Lanc.*

LOTE. (1) A tribute. (*A.-S.*) Ritson, ii. 288, reads *lok,* not explained in glossary.

> In Inglond he arered a lote
> Off iche house that comes smoke.
>   *MS. Cantab.* Ff. v. 48, f. 99.

(2) A loft ; a floor. *South.*

(3) Gesture ; aspect. "With grucchande *lotes,*" Morte Arthure, MS. Linc. f. 68.

LOTEBY. A private companion or bedfellow ; a concubine.

> Now ʒif that a man he wed a wyfe,
> And hym thynke sche plese hym noʒt,
> Anon ther rysis care and stryfe ;
> He wold here selle that he had boʒt,
> And schenchypus here that he hath soʒt,
> And takys to hym a loteby.
> These bargeyn wyl be dere aboʒt,
> Here ore henns he schal aby.
>   *Audelay's Poems,* p. 5.
>
> For almost hyt ys every whore,
> A gentyl man hath a wyfe and a hore ;
> And wyves have now comunly,
> Here husbondys and a ludby.
>   *MS. Harl.* 1701, f. 20.
>
> But there the wyfe haunteth foly
> Undyr here husbunde a ludby.
>   *MS. Harl.* 1701, f. 12.

LOTH. *Loth to depart,* the name of a popular old ballad tune, frequently referred to in old plays.

LOTHE. (1) To offer for sale. Kennett gives this as a Cheshire word. (2) Harm ; hurt ; danger.

> Mete and drynke I ʒaf hem bothe,
> And bad hem kepe hem ay fro lothe.
>   *Cursor Mundi, MS. Coll. Trin. Cantab.* f. 31.
> Why was God moste with hym wrothe,
> For he dyd the pore man luthe.
>   *MS. Harl.* 1701, f. 45.
>
> Hurt twey hostes stoden still and duden no loth.
>   *Chron. Vilodun.* p. 92.

(3) Perverse ; hateful. (*A.-S.*) *Lothes,* that which is hateful.

> We ar neghtburs I and he,
> We were never loth.
>   *MS. Cantab.* Ff. v. 48, f. 52.

LOTHER. (1) More hateful. (*A.-S.*) (2) To splash in water. *North.* (3) Unwilling. *Salop.* (*A.-S.*)

LOTHLY. Loathsome. *Chaucer.*

LOTIEN. To lay in ambush. (*A.-S.*)

LOT-TELLER. A witch. Maunsell, 1595.

LOTTERY. (1) Witchcraft ; divination. (2) A child's picture or print. *Lottery-babs,* juvenile prints. (3) To go to lottery, i. e. to quarrel.

LOTYNGE. Struggling ; striving together.

LOU. Laughed. Reliq. Antiq ii. 275.

LOUCH. To walk slovenly. *West.*

LOUD-AND-STILL. *Bothe loude and stille,* always. This is a very common phrase in old romances.

> Thanne it is guod hothe *loude and stille,*
> For to don al his wille.
>> *MS. Laud.* 108, f. 12.

> Then wende sche sche schulde be schente,
> And me be-het londe and rente,
>> And hyght me to do my wylle,
> But y myselfe wolde noght,
> Ye were evyr in my thoght
>> Bothe *lowde and stylle!*
>> *MS. Cantab.* Ff. ii. 38, f. 72.

LOUGH. (1) See *Lou.* (2) See *Loch.* (3) A cavity in a rock. *Linc.*

LOUK. (1) A blow; a thump. *North.* (2) Coarse grass on the moors. *Linc.* (3) A window lattice. *Suffolk.* (4) To put in place. *Somerset.*

LOUKED. Locked; fastened.

> For thou buriedest Jhesu licame,
> In an hous therfore we *louked* the.
>> *Cursor Mundi, MS. Coll. Trin. Cantab.* f. 108.

LOUKERS. Weeders. *Nor^th,* "Runcator, lowker," *Nominale MS.*

LOUKING. Gawky; awkward. *North.*

LOULE. To carry anything. *Var. dial.*

LOUME. Soft; gentle. *Chesh.*

LOUN. (1) See *Loo.* (2) See *Loon.* (3) To beat; to thrash. *North.* It is also pronounced *lounder.*

LOUNDER. To run or scamper about. *North.*

LOUNDREIS. Londoners. *Hearne.*

LOUNDSING. Lingering. *Camb.*

LOUNER. A large lump of bread. *West.* Brockett has *lounge.*

LOUNT. A small piece of land in a common field. *Chesh.*

LOUP. To leap; to cover. *Loup the long lonnin,* leap-frog. *North.*

LOUPY-DIKE. A term of contempt, applied to an imprudent person. *North.*

LOURAND. Discontented. *Sevyn Sages,* 462.

> Sir Amoraunt withdrough him
> With *lourand* chere wroth and grim.
>> *Gy of Warwike,* p. 320.

LOURDE. Disagreeable. (*A.-N.*)

> And thou3te it was a gret pité
> To see so lusty one as sche
> Be couplid with so *lourde* a wy3te.
>> *Gower, MS. Soc. Antiq.* 134, f. 131.

LOURDY. Sluggish. *Sussex.*

LOURE. To look discontented. (*A.-S.*) *Loury-face,* Lydgate's Minor Poems, p. 52.

> Tydynges of Tryamowre herde he none,
> The kyng began to *loure.*
>> *MS. Cantab.* Ff. ii. 38, f. 78.

LOURY. Threatening rain. *Var. dial.*

LOUSE. (1) To take lice from the person and garments, as beggars do. (2) To think; to consider. *South.*

LOUSE-TRAP. A small tooth-comb.

LOUSH. The same as *Losh,* q. v.

LOUSTER. (1) To make a clumsy rattling noise; to work hard. *South.* (2) To idle and loll about. *Devon.* "Lowtryng and wandryng," Hye Way to the Spyttell Hous, p. 11.

LOUTE. (1) To bend; to bow. (*A.-S.*) "A''s the erthe lowttede," MS. Morte Arthure, f. 41. (2) To lurk. See *Lotien.* "To sneak and creep about," MS. Lansd. 1033. (3) To low, or bellow. (4) To loiter, tarry, or stay. *Hearne.* (5) To neglect. Shakespeare has the word in this sense, incorrectly explained by all his editors. See 1 Henry VI. iv. 3.

> *Louted* and forsaken of theym by whom in tyme he myght have bene ayded and relieved.
>> *Hall, Henry IV.* f. 6.

(6) To milk a cow. *Liddesdale.*

LOVAND. Praising. This occurs in MS. Cotton. Vespas. D. vii. Ps. 17.

LOVE. (1) To praise. See *Lovand. Loveynges,* praises, MS. Cott. Vespas. D. vii.

> For to wynne me *loveyng*
> Bothe of emperowre and of kynge.
>> *MS. Cantab.* Ff. ii. 38, f. 152.

(2) To prefer; to choose. *East.* (3) "*Digitus,* a play used in Italie, where one holds up his finger, and the other, turning away, gives a guesse how many he holds up: it is called here, and in France and Spain, the play of love."—*Thomasii Dictionarium,* 1644. (4) To set a price on anything. *Lovfys,* Townele. Mysteries, p. 177. (5) *To play for love,* without stakes. At whist. a party is *two love, three love,* &c. when their adversaries have marked nothing. *Love in idleness, love and idles,* the herb heart's-ease.

LOVE-ACHE. The herb lovage.

LOVE-BEGOTTEN-CHILD. A bastard. Also called a *love-begot,* a *love-child,* &c.

LOVE-BIND. The herb travellers'-joy.

LOVE-CARTS. Carts lent by one farmer to another. *Oxon.*

LOVE-DAY. A day appointed for the settlement of differences by arbitration. Later writers seem to use the term for any quiet peaceable day.

> But helie is fulle of suche discorde,
> That ther may be no *loveday.*
>> *Gower, MS. Soc. Antiq.* 134, f. 37.

LOVE-DREWRY. Courtship. See *Druery.*

LOVE-ENTANGLE. The nigella. *Cornw.*

LOVE-FEAST. An annual feast celebrated in some parishes on the Thursday next before Easter. See Edwards's Old English Customs, 1842, p. 60.

LOVEL. A common name formerly for a dog. According to Stowe, p. 847, William Collingborne was executed in 1484 for writing the following couplet on the king's ministers:

> The Ratte, the Catte, and *Lovell* our dogge,
> Rule all England under the hogge.

LOVE-LIKINGE. Graciousness; peace. (*A.-S.*)

LOVE-LOCKS. Pendant locks of hair, falling near or over the ears, and cut in a variety of fashions. This ridiculous appendage to the person is often alluded to by the writers previous to the Restoration.

> Why should thy sweete *love-locks* hang dangling downe,
> Kissing thy girdle-stud with falling pride?
> Although thy skin be white, thy haire is browne;
> Oh, let not then thy haire thy beautie hide.
>> *The Affectionate Shepheard,* 1594.

LOVELOKER. More lovely. (*A.-S.*)

LOVE-LONGING. A desire of love. (*A.-S.*)

LOVE-POT. A drunkard. "To gad abrode a gossoping, as a pratling *love-pot* woman," Florio, p. 59.

LOVFR. (1) Rather. (*A.-S.*)

That him was *lover* for to chese
His owen body for to lese,
Than see so gret a mordre wroujte.
Gower, MS. Soc. Antiq. 134, f. 82.

(2) A turret, lantern, or any apparatus on the roof of a building for the escape of smoke, or for other purposes. "*Lover*, a chimney," Hallamsh. Gloss. p. 155. See *Loover*. It means an opening in a chimney in Honoria and Mammon, p. 48. Hall spells it *lovery*. "A loover, or tunnell in the roofe or top of a great hall to avoid smoke," Baret, 1580.

LOVERDINGES. Lords. *Hearne.*

LOVESOME. Lovely. *North.*

Owre emperour hath a sone feyre,
A *lovesome* chylde shalle be hys eyre.
MS. Cantab. Ff. ii. 38, f. 127.

Take thi wyf in thi honde,
Leve je shul this *lufsome* londe.
Cursor Mundi, MS. Coll. Trin. Cantab. f. 6.

LOVIER. A lover. *Var. dial.* Lovien is the old English verb, to love.

LOVING. Praising. MS. Cott. Vesp. D. vii.

LOVING-CUP. The same as *Grace-cup*, q. v.

LOVIS. Loaves.

With *lovis* fyne, thorow his gret foysone,
Fyve thousande y fynde that he dide fede.
Lydgate, MS. Soc. Antiq. 134, f. 26.

LOW. (1) A flame; heat. *North.* It occurs in the first sense in MS. Cotton. Vespas. D. vii. Ps. 28. "Lowe of fyre," Pr. Parv. p. 38. "Rayse a grete lowe," MS. Lincoln A. i. 17, f. 11. *Lowynge*, Degrevant, 1436.

(2) To heap, or pile up. *Devon.*

(3) Low-spirited; melancholy. *Var. dial.*

(4) A small hill or eminence. *North.* "*A low*, a small round hill, a heap of earth or stones ; hence the barrows or congregated hillocks, which remain as sepulchres of the dead, are called loughs," MS. Lansd. 1033. It frequently means a bank or hill in early English, as in Chester Plays, i. 120 ; Reliq. Antiq. i. 120; Kyng Alisaunder, 4348; Sharp's Cov. Myst. p. 89 ; but it should be noticed that the *A.-S.* word is more usually applied to artificial hills, as tumuli, than to natural mounds. The names of many places ending in *low* are thus derived, as Ludlow, &c.; see Mr. Wright's History, p. 13. "A fire on low," Sir Degoré.

He is, he selde, ther he is won
With oure sheep upon the *lowe*.
Cursor Mundi, MS. Coll. Trin. Cantab. f. 46.

(5) Laughed. Reliq. Antiq. i. 60.

LOWANCE. Allowance ; largess. *Var. dial.*

LOWANER. To stint in allowance. *West.*

LOW-BELL. A bell used formerly in bird-batting, q. v. It was rung before the light was exhibited, and while the net was being raised, to prevent the birds from flying out too soon. It is not likely that the unexplained phrase " gentle low-bell" in Beaumont and Fletcher

refers to this. It more probably means *gentle lamb*, or *sheep*, in allusion to the low-bells hung on the necks of those animals. "A low-bell hung about a sheep or goats neck," Howell, Lex. Tet. 1660.

LOWE. (1) Love. Warton, i. 24.

(2) Lied. Amis and Amiloun, 836.

LOWEDE. Lewd ; unlearned. *Weber.*

LOWEN. To fall in price. *East.*

LOWER. (1) To frown, or lour. *West.*

(2) To strike as a clock with a low prolonged sound ; to toll the curfew. *Devon.*

(3) To set up the shoulders. *North.*

(4) A lever. *North.*

(5) Hire ; reward. (*A.-N.*)

Thurch ous thou art in thi power,
Gif ous now our *lower*.
Arthour and Merlin, p. 15.

LOWERST. To exert. *Devon.*

LOW-FORKS. "*Donne toy garde qu'elle ne te pende en ses basse-fourches*, take heede shee hang thee in her *loweforkes*," Hollyband's Dictionarie, 1593.

LOWINGS. The same as *Lunes*, q. v.

LOWL-EARED. Long-eared. *Wilts.*

LOW-LIVED. Low and base. *Var. dial.*

LOWLYHEDE. Meekness. (*A.-S.*)

And whanne the aungelle saw hire *lowlyhede*,
And the hooly rednesse also in hire face.
Lydgate, MS. Soc. Antiq. 134, f. 2.

LOW-MEN. False dice so made as to turn up low numbers. See Taylor's Travels of Twelve-Pence, 1630, p. 73.

LOWNABYLLE. Qu. *lowvabylle ?*

And if thou wille lelely doo this, ferre fra drede,
thou salle be gloryus, and *lownabylle* overcommere.
MS. Lincoln A. i. 17, f. 192.

LOWNE. Loo ; sheltered. *North.* "Still and lowne," Du Bartas, p. 357.

LOWNGES. Lungs. Nominale MS.

LOWRE. Money. A cant term. Dekker's Lanthorne and Candle-Light, 1620, sig. C. ii.

LOW-ROPE. A piece of rope lighted at one end. *North.*

LOWS. Low level land. *Suffolk.*

LOWSEN. To listen. *Dorset.*

LOW-SUNDAY. The first Sunday after Easter. See Cotgrave, in v. *Quasimodo ;* Holinshed. Conq. Ireland, p. 25. It was also called Little-Easter-day.

LOWTHE. (1) Loud. *Ritson.*

(2) Lowness. Becon's Works, p. 272.

LOWTHS. Low-lands. *Yorksh.*

LOWTYN. To be quiet. "*Conquiesco, Anglice,* to lowtyn," MS. Bibl. Reg. 12. B. i. f. 88.

LOWJEN. Laugh, pres. pl.

Aud alle the lordynges in the halle
On the herd thei *lowjen* alle.
MS. Cantab. Ff. v. 48, f. 55.

LOYNE. To carve a sole. This term occurs in the Booke of Hunting, 1586.

LOYOTOUR.

In a surcott of sylke full selkouthely hewede,
Alle with *loyotour* over laide lowe to the hemmes.
Morte Arthure, MS. Lincoln, f. 87.

LOYT. A lute. *Percy.*

LOZENGE. A lollipop. *East.*

LOZIN. A feast or merry-making when a cutler comes of age. *Sheffield.*

LUBBARD. A lubber. *North.* This form occurs in Florio, p. 50.

LUBBER-COCK. A turkey-cock. *Cornw.*

LUBBER-HEAD. A stupid fellow. *Var. dial.*

LUBBER-LAND. See *Cockney.*

LUBBER-WORT. Any food or drink which makes one idle and stupid.

LUBBY. A lubber-head. *Devon.*

LUBRICITY. Incontinency. This word occurs in a rare tract, printed by Pynson, entitled The Churche of yvell Men and Women, n. d., in the Bodleian Library.

LUC. A small pool of water near the sea-shore. *South.*

LUCAYNE. A window in the roof of a house. Moor spells it *lewcome*, p. 212. Still in use.

LUCE. (1) A rut. *South.*

(2) A pike, which was thus called in its stages of life; first a jack, then a pickerel, thirdly a pike, and last of all a luce. "*Luonus*, a lewse," Nominale, MS. "Lucys or pykys," Piers of Fullham, p. 118. Still in use.

LUCENSE. Light. (*A.-N.*)

O lux vera, graunt us jowr *lucense*,
That with the spryte of errour I nat seduct be.
Digby Mysteries, p. 96.

LUCERN. (1) A lamp. *Lydgate.*

(2) A lynx, the fur of which was formerly in great esteem. *Luzardis*, Arch. ix. 245. In a parliamentary scheme, dated 1549, printed in the Egerton Papers, p. 11, it was proposed that no man under the degree of an earl be allowed to wear *luzarnes.*

LUCINA. The moon. *Chaucer.*

LUCK. (1) To make lucky; to be lucky. (2) Chance. *Palsgrave.*

LUCKE. (1) To look. *Hampole.*

(2) To frown; to knit the brows. *North.*

LUCKER. Sort or like. *Devon.*

LUCKING-MILLS. Fulling-mills. *Kent.*

LUCK-PENNY. A small sum of money returned to a purchaser for luck. *North.*

LUCKS. Locks of wool twisted on the finger of a spinner at the distaff. *East.*

LUCKY. (1) *To make one's lucky*, to go away very rapidly. *Var. dial.*

(2) Large; wide; easy. *North.*

LUCKY-BAG. See *Lossy-bag.*

LUDDOKKYS. Loins. Towneley Myst. p. 313.

LUE. To sift. A mining term.

LUEF. Love. *Lufers*, lovers. There are several forms similar to this.

Let be your rule, seid Litull Jon,
For his *luf* that dyed on tre;
je that shulde be dusty mon
Hit is gret shame to se.
MS. Cantab. Ff. v. 48, f. 128.

His verray *lufers* folowes hym fleande honours and lovynges in erthe, and noght lufande vayn glorye. *MS. Coll. Eton.* 10, f. 2.

LUFE. The open hand. *North.* "Towch with my *lufe*," Towneley Myst. p. 32.

LUFES. The ears of a toad. *North.*

LUFF. The wooden case in which the candle is carried in the sport of low-belling.

LUFT. Fellow; person. (*A.-S.*)

LUG. (1) A measure of 16½ ft. It consisted anciently of 20 ft. It is spelt *log* in MS. Gough (Wilts) 5. "*Lug*, a pole in measure," Kennett. Forty-nine square yards of coppice wood make a *lug.*

(2) The ear. *North.* Hence the handle of a pitcher is so called.

If sorrow the tyrant invade thy breast,
Draw out the foul fleud by the *lug*, the *lug*.
Songs of the London Prentices, p. 121.

(3) A pliable rod or twig, such as is used in thatching. *West.* Any rod or pole. *Wilts.*

(4) To pull or drink. *Var. dial.*

(5) A small worm for bait in fishing.

(6) *I cry lug*, I cry sluggard, I am in no hurry. The term *lug* was applied to anything slow in movement.

LUG-AND-A-BITE. A boy flings an apple to some distance. All present race for it. The winner *bites* as fast as he can, his compeers *lugging* at his ears in the mean time, who bears it as long as he can, and then throws down the apple, when the sport is resumed.

LUGDOR. The multipe or woodlouse.

LUGE. A lodge, or hut. Also, to lodge.

And he saw thame ga naked, and duelle in *lugys* and in caves, and thaire wyfes and thaire childre away fra thame. *MS.·Lincoln* A. i. 17, f. 30.

Whenne Darius hadde redde this lettre, ther come another messanger tille hym, and talde hym that Alexander and his oste had *lugede* thame appone the water of Strume. *MS. Lincoln* A. i. 17, f. 9.

LUGEOUS. Heavy; unwieldy. *Devon.*

LUGGARD. A sluggard. From *Lug*, q. v.

LUGGER. A strip of land. *Glouc.*

LUGGIE. A wooden dish. *North.*

LUGGISH. Dull; heavy; stupid. *Luggy* is also heard in the same sense.

LUGHE. Laughed. See *Loghe.*

Yhit lyffed he eftyr fyfteene yheere,
Bot he *lughe* never, ne made blythe chere.
Hampole, MS. Bowes, p. 192.

LUG-LAIN. Full-measure. *Somerset.*

LUG-LOAF. A heavy awkward fellow.

LUGSOME. Heavy; cumbrous. *East.*

LUIK-LAKE. To be playful. *Yorksh.*

LUKE. (1) To protect, or defend. (*A.-S.*)

(2) The leaf of a turnip. *South.*

LUKES. A kind of velvet.

LUKEWARD. A species of cherry which ripens in June, mentioned in MS. Ashmole 1461.

LULLIES. Kidneys. *Chesh.*

LUM. (1) A woody valley. (2) A deep pool. (3) A cottage chimney. *North.*

LUMBARD-PIE. A highly seasoned meat-pie, made either of veal or lamb. The term *Lumbard* was given to several ancient dishes. *Frutour lumbert*, Reliq. Antiq. i. 88.

LUMBER. (1) Harm; mischief. *Var. dial.*

(2) Dirty foolish conversation. *East.*

(3) To stumble. More usually *lumper.*

LUMBISH. Heavy; awkward. *Linc.*

LUMBRIKE. An earth-worm. *Pr. Parv.*

LUMES. Beams. *Ritson.*

LUMMACK. To tumble. *Suffolk.*

LUMMAKIN. Heavy; awkward. *Var. dial.*

LUMMOX. A fat heavy and stupid fellow; an awkward clown. *East.*

LUMP. (1) To beat severely. *Var. dial.*

(2) A kind of fish. See Florio, p. 109; Lilly's Sixe Court Comedies, 1632, sig. D.

(3) To be or look sulky. *Devon.*

LUMPER. The same as *Lumber*, q. v.

LUMPING. Large; heavy. *Var. dial.*

LUMPS. Hard bricks for flooring. *East.*

LUMPY. Heavy; awkward. *South.*

LUM-SWOOPER. A chimney-sweeper. *North.*

LUN. The same as *Loo*, q. v.

LUNARY. The herb moon-wort. This herb was formerly believed to open the locks of horses' feet. See Harrison, p. 131. Some of our early dramatists refer to it as opening locks in a more literal sense.

LUNCH. A thump; a lump. *Var. dial.*

LUNCHEON. A large lump of food. It is spelt *lunshin* in Hallamshire Gl. p. 116.

LUNDGE. To lean or lounge. *Devon.* Batchelor has it *lundy*, Orth. Anal. p. 137.

LUNDY. Heavy; clumsy. *Var. dial.*

LUNES. (1) Lunacy; frenzy. (Fr.)

(2) Long lines to call in hawks. "Lunys aboute her feet," Morte d'Arthur, i. 180.

LUNGE. (1) To beat severely. *East.*

(2) A plunge. (3) To plunge. *Var. dial.* To make a long thrust with the body inclining forward, a term in fencing.

(4) To hide, or skulk. *Northampt.*

(5) To lunge a colt in breaking him in, is to hold him with a long rope, and drive him round in a circle. Still in use.

LUNGEOUS. Awkward; rough; cruel; vindictive; mischievous; quarrelsome; ill-tempered. *Var. dial.* No doubt connected with the older term *lungis*, q. v.

> But somewhere I have had a *lungeous faw,*
> I'm sure o' that, and, master, that's neet uw.
> *Cotton's Works,* 1734, p. 339.

LUNGIS. A heavy awkward fellow. "*Longis,* a lungis, a slimme, slow backe, dreaming luske, drowsie gangrill; a tall and dull slangam, that hath no making to his height, nor wit to his making; also, one that being sent on an errand is long in returning," Cotgrave.

> Let *lungis* lurke and druges worke,
> We doe defie their slaverye;
> He is but a foole that goes to schole,
> All we delight in braverye.
> *Play of Misogonus, circa* 1560.

LUNGS. A fire-blower to a chemist.

LUNGSICKNESS. A disease in cattle. See the Dial. Creat. Moral. p. 57.

LUNGURT. Tied; hoppled. *Lanc.*

LUNT. Short, or surly. *East.*

LUR. Loss; misfortune. *Gawayne.*

LURCH. (1) To lie at lurch, i. e. to lie in wait. To give a lurch, i. e. to tell a falsehood, to deceive, to cheat.

(2) A game at tables.

(3) An easy victory. *Coles.*

LURCHER. (1) A glutton. *Palsgrave.* It is

spelt *lurcare* and *lurcard* in Pr. Parv. p. 317.

(2) A potato left in the ground.

LURCH-LINE. The line by which the fowling-net was pulled over to inclose the birds.

LURDEN. A clown; an ill-bred person; a sluggard. (*A.-N.*) It is still in use in the last sense. See Reliq. Antiq. i. 82, 291; Cov. Myst. pp. 45, 184.

> And seyde, *lurden*, what doyst thou here?
> Thou art a thefe or thefeys fere.
> *MS. Cantab.* Ff. ii. 38, f. 240.

LURDY. Idle; sluggish. *North.*

LURE. (1) A sore on a cow's hoof. *West.*

(2) The palm of the hand. *North.*

(3) A liar. Sir Amadace, lxiv. 11.

(4) A handspike, or lever. *East.*

(5) Is explained by Latham, "that whereto faulconers call their young hawks, by casting it up in the aire, being made of feathers and leather in such wise that in the motion it looks not unlike a fowl."

(6) To cry loudly and shrilly. *East.*

LURGY. The same as *Lurdy*, q. v.

LURKEY-DISH. The herb pennyroyal.

LURRIES. Clothes; garments. *Coles.*

LURRY. (1) To dirt, or daub. *East.*

(2) To lug, or pull. *Northumb.*

(3) A disturbance, or tumult.

> How durst you, rogues, take the opinion
> To vapour here in my dominion,
> Without my leave, and make a *lurry,*
> That men cannot be quiet for ye?
> *Cotton's Works,* 1734, p 13.

(4) To hurry carelessly. *South.*

LUSH. (1) To splash in water. *Cumb.*

(2) A twig for thatching. *Devon.*

(3) Limp. Topsell's Beasts, 1607, p. 343. Ground easily turned is said to be *lush.*

LUSKE. A lazy, idle, good-for-nothing fellow. "Here is a great knave, i. a great lyther *luske,* or a stout ydell lubbar," Palsgrave's Acolastus, 1540. "A sturdie luske," Albion, Knight, p. 61. *Luskyshenesse, luskyshely,* Elyot in v. *Socordia, Socorditer,* ed. 1559. *Lusking,* Mirrour for Magistrates, 1578. *Luskysh,* Hye Way to the Spyttell Hous, p. 10.

LUSKED. Let loose?

> These lions bees *lusked* and lased on sondir,
> And thaire landes shalbe lost for longe tyme.
> *MS. Soc. Antiq.* 101, f. 72.

LUSSHEBURWES. A sort of base coin, resembling and passing for English pennies, strictly prohibited by Statute 25 Edward III. See Blount's Law Dictionary.

LUSSUM. Lovesome; beautiful.

> Therfore he gaf him to bigynne
> A *lussum* lond to dwellen inne,
> A lond of lif joyes and delices
> Whiche men callen Paradis.
> *Cursor Mundi, MS. Coll. Trin. Cantab.* f. 4.

LUSTE. (1) Liked; to like. Also a substantive, liking, desire. *Lustes,* delights, MS. Cotton. Vespas. D. vii. Ps. Antiq.

> And write in suche a maner wise,
> Whiche may be wisdome to the wyse,
> And pley to hem that *luste* to pleye.
> *Gower, MS. Soc. Antiq.* 134, f. 31

In him fonde y none other bote,
For lengir *huste* him nouʒt to dwelle.
Gower, MS. Soc. Antiq. 134, f. 39.

(2) A number, or quantity. *East.*

(3) To bend on one side. *Norf.*

LUSTICK. Healthy; cheerful; pleasant.

LUSTRE. A period of five years. This term occurs in Florio, p. 61.

LUSTREE. To bustle about. *Exmoor.*

LUSTRING. A kind of plain silk.

LUSTY. Pleasant; agreeable; quick; lively; gay in apparel.

Of *lusti* and off swet odoris,
And froit on tre both gret and smale.
MS. Cott. Galba E. ix. f. 2.

LUSTY-GALLANT. A kind of colour in some articles of dress, formerly so called.

LUSTYHEDE. Pleasure; mirth. (*A.-S.*)

LUT. Bowed down. See *Loute.*

On his arsoun dounward he *lut.*
Arthour and Merlin, p. 195.

LUTE. (1) To lie hid. (*A.-S.*) In use in Northumberland, according to Kennett.

It *luteth* in a mannis herte,
But that ne schalle not me asterte.
Gower, MS. Soc. Antiq. 134, f. 51.

(2) Little. See St. Brandan, p. 9.

LUTHER. Bad; wicked. See *Lither.*

LUTHEREN. Leathers; strings. *Hearne.*

LUTHOBUT. But only look! *North.*

LUTTER. To scatter about. *Glouc.*

LUTTER-PUTCH. A slovenly fellow. *Cornw.*

LUXOM. The same as *Lussum,* q. v.

LUXURIE. Lechery. (*A.-N.*) This and *luxurious* are common in early works.

LUYSCHENE. To rush on violently.

With lufty launces one lofte they *luyschene* togedyres.
Morte Arthure, MS. Lincoln, f. 68.

LYAM. A thong or leash. See a curious relation in the Archæologia, xxviii. 97. Hence the lyam, or lime-hound, q. v. Blome makes a distinction between leash and lyam, "the string used to lead a greyhound is called a leese, and for a hound a lyame." See the Gent. Rec. ii. 78.

A youthfull hunter with a chaplet crown'd
In a pyde *lyam* leading foorth his hound.
Drayton's Poems, p. 91.

LYCANTHROPI. Madmen who imagined they were turned into wolves.

LYCCED-TEA. Tea and spirits. *North.*

LYCE. Lies.

If hit be any man so strong,
That come us foure among,
And bryng with hym men of price
To *stale* Jhesu ther he *lyce.*
MS. Cantab. Ff. v. 48, f. 40.

LYCHE. A liege. *Prompt. Parv.*

LYDFORD-LAW. This proverbial phrase, which very significantly explains itself,—

First hang and draw,
Then hear the cause by Lydford law!

is often alluded to in old works. The earliest notice of "the lawe of Lydfford" yet discovered is contained in the curious poem on the Deposition of Richard II. ed. Wright, p. 19.

LYE. (1) Kindred. *Prompt. Parv.*

(2) A flame of fire. Kennett MS.

LYERBY. A kept mistress. It occurs in Melbancke's Philotimus, 4to. 1583.

LYING-DOWN. A woman's accouchement.

LYING-HOUSE. A prison for great offenders. See Davies' Ancient Rites, ed. 1672, p. 138.

LYKUSSE. Likes. See Tundale, p. 21.

LYLSE-WULSE. Linsey-woolsey. *Skelton.*

LYMPHAULT. Lame. *Chaloner.*

LYMPTWIGG. A lapwing. *Exmoor.*

With lowde laghttirs one lofte, for lykyng of byrdes,
Of larkes, of *lynkwhyttes,* that luffyche songene.
Morte Arthure, MS. Lincoln, f. 31.

LYNDECOLE. Charcoal made of the wood of the linden tree. "Half an unce of *lyndecole.*" MS. Soc. Antiq. 101, f. 76.

LYNYE. A line. *Prompt. Parv.*

LYRIBLIRING. Warbling, or singing.

LYTHE. The same as *Lith* (2).

We are comene fro the kyng of this *lythe* ryche,
That knawene es for conquerour corownde in erthe.
Morte Arthure, MS. Lincoln, f. 70.

LYʒET. Lieth.

Now, lord, I pray the
That thou wold ʒiff to me
The feyre lady bryʒt off ble,
That *lyʒet* under this impe tre. *MS. Ashmole* 61.

LYʒTH. Alighted. Degrevant, 1625.

LYʒTHERELY. Badly; wickedly. (*A.-S.*)

M To have an M. under the girdle, i. e. to keep the term *Master* out of sight, to be wanting in proper respect.

MA. (1) To make. Perceval, 1728.

(2) More. See Reliq. Antiq. ii. 281.

His Ave Maria he lerid hym alswa,
And other prayers many *ma.*
MS. Lincoln A. i. 17, f. 142.

MAAK. A maggot. *Yorksh.*

MAAPMENT. A rigmarole. *Cumb.*

MAAT. Mett; measure. *Wickliffe.*

MAB. A slattern. *North.* Also a verb, to dress negligently. Sandys uses the term *mabble.* See Upton on Shakespeare, p. 320.

MABIAR. A young hen. Lhuyd's MS. additions to Ray's Words, 1674.

MACAROON. A fop. *Donne.* This word is still in use, according to Forby.

MACE. (1) A club. (*A.-N.*) *Macer,* one who carries a mace, Piers Ploughman, p. 47.

(2) Masonry. *Weber.*

(3) Makes. Anturs of Arther, p. 19.

MACE-MONDAY. The first Monday after St. Anne's day, so called in some places on account of a ceremony then performed.

MACE-PROOF. Free from arrest.

MACHACHINA. A kind of Italian dance mentioned by Sir John Harrington.

MACHAM. A game at cards, mentioned in the Irish Hudibras, 8vo. Lond. 1689.

MACHE. (1) To match. (2) A match.

Thay hafe bene *machede* to daye with mene of the marches. *Morte Arthure, MS. Lincoln, f.* 69.

MACHINE. To contrive. *Palsgrave.*

MACHOUND. "A *machound*, a bugbeare, a raw-head and bloudie bone," Florio, p. 297. Perhaps Mahound, or Mahomet, a character in old mysteries.

MACILENT. Lean. "Lesse venerous then being macilent," Topsell's Beasts, 1607, p. 231.

MACKE. An ancient game at cards, alluded to in Kind-Harts Dreame, 1592.

MACKEREL. A bawd. *Grose.* Middleton, iv. 497, has *macrio.* It is derived from the A.-N. *maquerel*, and means also a procuress. "Nyghe his hows dwellyd a *maquerel* or bawde," Caxton's Cato Magnus, 1483.

MACKERLY. Shapely; fashionable. *North. Mackish*, smart. *Warw.*

MACKS. Sorts; fashions. *North.*

MACSTAR. A poulterer, or egg-seller.

MACULATION. Spot; stain. (*Lat.*)

MAD. (1) Angry. *Var. dial.*
(2) An earth-worm; a maggot. *North.*
(3) Madness; intoxication. *Glouc.*
(4) A species of nightshade.

MADAM. A title used in the provinces to women under the rank of *Lady*, but moving in respectable society.

MADDE. To madden; to be mad. (*A.-S.*)

MADDER. Pus, or matter. *North.*

MADDERS. The stinking camomile. *West.*

MADDLE. (1) To be fond of. *North.*
(2) To confuse; to be confused; to perplex; to rave, or be delirious. *North.*

MADDOCKS. Maggots. Kennett MS.

MAD-DOG. A cant term for strong ale, mentioned in Harrison's England, p. 202.

MADE. (1) Fastened, as doors. *North.*
(2) *What made you there*, what caused you to be there, what business had you. *You are made for ever*, your fortune is made. See Lilly's Sixe Court Comedies, 1632, sig. Q. ii. A similar phrase occurs in Shakespeare.
(3) Wrote; written. See *Make.*
(4) Made up of different materials. Hence the term made-dish, which was formerly used for any dish containing several meats.

MADER-WORT. The herb mug-wort.

MADE-SURE. Affianced; betrothed.

MADGE. (1) Margaret. *Var. dial.*
(2) An owl. "*Chat huant*, an owle, or madge-howlet," Cotgrave. Some call it the magpie.
(3) The pudendum muliebre. *South.*

MADGETIN. The Margaret apple. *East.*

MADLIN. A bad memory. *Cumb.*

MADNING-MONEY. Old Roman coins, sometimes found about Dunstable, are so called by the country people.

MAD-PASH. A mad fellow. *North.*

MADRILL. Madrid. Middleton, iv. 104.

MÆSTERS. Employment. *Weber.*

MA-FEIE. My faith! (*A.-N.*)

MAFFLARD. A term of contempt, probably the same with *Maffling*, q. v.

MAFFLE. To stammer; to mumble. *North.*

"Somme *mafflid* with the mouth," Depos. Ric. II. p. 29. "To stammer or maffle in speech," Florio, p. 55. The term seems to be applied to any action suffering from impediments. "In such staggering and mafling wise," Holinshed, Chron. Ireland, p. 88. See Stanihurst, p. 13; Cotgrave, in v. *Bredouillard, Bretonnant.*

MAFFLING. A simpleton. *North.*

MAG. (1) To chatter; to scold. *Var. dial.* Sometimes, to tease or vex.
(2) The jack at which coits are thrown.

MAGE. A magician. *Spenser.*

MAGECOLLE. To fortify a town wall with machicolations. (Lydgate.) "Wel matchecold al aboute," Morte d'Arthur, i. 199.

MAGES. The hands. *Northumb.*

MAGGLED. Teazed. *Oxon.*

MAGGOTY. Whimsical; frisky; playful. *Maggots*, whims, fancies. *Var. dial.*

MAGGOTY-PIE. A magpie. Shakespeare has *magot-pie*, and the term occurs under several forms. It is still in use in Herefordshire; and is retained in a well-known nursery song. See Florio, pp. 204, 412; Cotgrave, in v. *Agasse, Dame.* It is given as a Wiltshire word in MS. Lansd. 1033, f. 2. Brockett has *Maggy.*

MAGGY-MANY-FEET. The wood-louse. *West.*

MAGINE. To imagine. *Palsgrave.*

MAGNEL. An ancient military engine used for battering down walls. It threw stones and other missiles, which themselves were also termed *magnels* or *mangonels.* See Kyng Alisaunder, 1593, 3223; Gy of Warwike, p. 86; Langtoft, p. 183.

> With heweing sud with mineinge,
> And with *mangunels* casteinge.
>   *Arthour and Merlin,* p. 91.

MAGNIFICAL. Magnificent; splendid. *Magnificent* is often put for *munificent.*

MAGNIFICATE. To magnify. *Jonson.*

MAGNIFICO. A grandee. (*Ital.*) It is properly applied to a grandee of Venice.

MAGNIFY. To signify. *Devon.*

MAGNOPERATE. To increase greatly. (*Lat.*)

> Some in the affectation of the oeconomicks, some in philosophy, others in poetry, have all brought the depth of their golden studies to bide the touch of your noble allowance; so that after-ages may rightly admire what noble Mecœnas it was that so inchayned the aspiring wits of this understanding age to his only censure, which will not a little *magnoperate* the splendor of your well knowne honour to these succeeding times.
>   *Hopton's Baculum Geodæticum,* 1614.

MAGUDER. The stalk of a plant.

MAHEREME. Wood; timber. (Med. Lat.)

MAHOITRES. Large waddings formerly used for padding out the shoulders. (*Fr.*)

MAHOUN. Mahomet. The term was often used for an idol or pagan deity.

> Hefe uppe your hartis ay to *Mahounde*,
> He will be nere us in oure nede.
>   *York Miracle Plays, Walpole MS.*

MAID. (1) The iron frame which holds the baking-stone. *West.*

(2) A girl. See Warton, iii. 38.

(3) There is a joke of Mrs. Quickly's in the Merry Wives of Windsor, ii. 2, implying she was as much a maid as her mother, which, if I mistake not, alludes to an old saying quoted in the following passages:

If ever Ice doe come heare againe, Ice said,
Chill give thee my mother vor a maid.
MS. Ashm. 36, f. 112.

So smug she was, and so array'd,
He took his mother for a maid.
Cotton's Works, 1734, p. 25.

MAIDEKIN. A little maid. (*A.-S.*)

MAIDEN. A fortress which has never been taken. *Maiden-assize*, a session where no prisoners are capitally convicted. *Maiden-tree*, a tree which has not been lopped. *Maiden-wife-widow*, one who gives herself up to an impotent person, a curious phrase, which occurs in Holme, 1688.

MAIDENHEDE. The state of a maiden.

MAIDEN-RENTS. A noble paid by every tenant in the manor of Builth, co. Radnor, at their marriage, in lieu of the ancient *marchet*.

MAIDENS-HONESTY. The plant honesty.

About Michaelmass all the hedges about Thickwood (in the parish Colerne) are (as it were) hung with *mayden's honesty*, which lookes very fine.
Aubrey's Wilts, MS. Royal Soc. p. 120.

MAID-MARIAN. A popular character in the old morris dance, which was often a man in female clothes, and occasionally a strumpet. Hence the term was sometimes applied with no very flattering intention.

MAIL. (1) To milk a cow but once a day, when near calving. *North.* Maillen, the quantity of milk given at once.

(2) To pinion a hawk. See Gent. Rec.

(3) Rent or annual payment formerly extorted by the border robbers.

(4) That part of a clasp which receives the spring into it.

(5) A defect in vision. *Devon.*

(6) A spot on a hawk. *Mailed*, spotted, Cotgrave, in v. *Goucÿ.* (According to Blome, ii. 62, the mailes are the breast-feathers.) "To *male*, to discolour, to spot, *Northumb.*" Kennett, MS. Lansd. 1033.

MAIN. (1) Very; great. *Var. dial.* Hence, a main man, a violent politician, &c.

(2) The thick part of meat.

(3) A throw at the dice.

(4) The chief or ruler.

(5) To lame. Hallamsh. Gloss. p. 116.

(6)
Observing Dick look'd *main* and blue.
Collins' Miscellanies, 1762, p. 13.

MAIN-HAMPER. A kind of basket used for carrying fruit. *Somerset.*

MAIN-PIN. A pin put through the fore-axle of a waggon for it to turn upon in locking. *Var. dial.*

MAINS. A farm, or fields, near a house, and in the owner's occupation. *North.*

MAINS-FLAID. Much afraid. *Yorksh.*

MAINSWORN. Perjured. *North.*

MAINTAIN. To behave; to conduct. *Maintenance*, behaviour. (*A.-N.*)

MAINTE. To maintain. *Lydgate.*

MAINTENANTLY. Mainly. *North.*

MAIR. A mayor. (*A.-N.*) It occurs in Piers Ploughman, and Archæologia, i. 94.

MAISLIKIN. Foolish. *North.*

MAISON-DEWE. A hospital. (*A.-N.*) Till within the last few years, there was an ancient hospital at Newcastle so called.

Mynsteris and *masondewes* they malle to the erthe.
Morte Arthure, MS. Lincoln, f. 95.

So many *masendewes*, hospytals and spytlle howses,
As your grace hath done yet sens the worlde began.
Bale's Kynge Johan, p. 82.

MAIST. Most; almost. *Var. dial.*

MAISTE. Makest. Chester Plays, i. 49.

MAISTER. A skilful artist; a master. *Maister toun*, a metropolis. *Maister strete*, the chief street. *Maister temple*, the chief temple, &c.

MAISTERFUL. Imperious; headstrong. *North.* It occurs in Lydgate and Chaucer.

MAISTERIE. Skill; power; superiority. *Maistrys*, conflicts, Perceval, 1445.

Who so dose here sich *maistrye*,
Be thou wel sicur he shalle abye.
MS. Cantab. Ff. v. 48, f. 49.

And lytulle *maystyrs* may ye do,
When the grete nede comyth to.
MS. Cantab. Ff. ii. 38, f. 128.

MAISTERLYNG. Master. See Weber, i. 21. *Maisterman*, ruler, governor, husband.

MAISTLINS. Mostly; generally. *North.*

MAISTRESSE. Mistress; governess. (*A.-N.*)

MAISTRISE. Masterly workmanship. (*A.-N.*)

MAKE. (1) *To make a die of it*, to die. *To make bold*, to presume. *To make ready*, to dress provision. Also, to clothe. *To make unready*, to undress. *To make a noise*, to scold. *To make a hand on*, to waste or destroy. *To make on*, or *upon*, to caress, or spoil. Also, to rush on with violence. *To make count*, to reckon, or reckon upon. *To make all split*, a phrase expressing immense violence. *To make danger*, to try, to make experiment. *To make nice*, to scruple or object. *To make fair weather*, to coax a person, to humour him by flattery. *To make forth*, to do. *To make a matter with one*, to pick a quarrel with him. *To make naught*, to corrupt. *To make room*, to give place. *To make sure*, to put in a safe place. *To make to the bow*, to form to one's hand. *To make mouths*, to jeer or grin. *To make up*, to wheedle; to make a reconciliation. Also, to approach. *To make fair*, to bid fair or likely. *To make much of*, to caress or spoil.

(2) An instrument of husbandry, formed with a crooked piece of iron and a long handle, used for pulling up peas. *Suffolk.*

(3) To fasten a door. *Yorksh.* Shakespeare uses the term in this sense.

(4) A mate, or companion. (*A.-S.*) It is applied to either husband or wife.

Rise up, Adam, and awake;
Heare have I formed thee a *make*.
Chester Plays, i. 26.

(5) To compose, or make verses. (*A.-S.*)

(6) To do; to cause. See *Made*.

(7) To dress meat. *Pegge*.

(8) A halfpenny. See Dekker's Lanthorne and Candle-Light, ed. 1620, sig. C. ii. " Brummagem-macks, Birmingham-makes, a term for base and counterfeit copper money in circulation before the great recoinage," Sharp's MS. Warwickshire Gloss.

(9) To prepare, or make ready. Jonson, i. 145.

(10) To assist, or take part in. *Yorksh*.

(11) A sort, kind, or fashion. *North*.

(12) The mass. Sir John Oldcastle, p. 22.

MAKE-BATE. A quarrelsome person. " A *make-bate*, a busie-bodie, a pick-thanke, a seeke-trouble," Florio, p. 89. See also p. 72, and Nares.

MAKE-BEGGAR. The annual pearl-wort.

MAKE-COUNT. A make-weight. *North*.

MAKE-HAWK. An old staunch hawk which will readily instruct a young one.

MAKELES. Without a mate. (*A.-S.*)

MAKELESS. Matchless. *North*.

MAKER. A poet. Jonson, ii. 114.

MAKERLY. Tolerable. *North*.

MAKE-SHIFT. A substitute, generally used contemptuously. It occurs in Halle's Hist. Expostulation, ed. Pettigrew, p. 19.

MAKE-WEIGHT. Some trifle added to make up a proper weight. *Var. dial.*

MAKE-WISE. To pretend. *Somerset*.

MAKRON. A rake for an oven.

MALACK. A great disturbance. *Yorksh*.

MALAHACK. To carve awkwardly. *East*.

MALAKATOONE. A kind of late peach.

MALAN-TREE. The beam in front of or across an open chimney. *East*.

MALARY. Unhappily. (*Fr.*) *Maleuryd*, ill-fortuned, Skelton, ii. 219.

MALCH. Mild. *Craven*.

MALDROP. A ruby. Nominale MS.

MALE. (1) A budget, or portmanteau; a box, or pack. (*A.-N.*)

(2) Evil. Kyng Alisaunder, 1153.

That the dewke in hys perlemeut
Hym forgeve hys *male* entente.
MS. Cantab. Ff. ii. 38, f. 181.

(3) The plant dandelion. *Dorset*.

MALEBOUCHE. Calumny. (*A.-N.*)

And to conferme his accione,
Hee hath withholde *malebouche*.
Gower, MS. Soc. Antiq. 134, f. 63.

MALECOLYE. Melancholy. *Malicholly* occurs in Middleton's play of the Honest Whore.

And prey hym pur charyté
That he wyll forgeve me
Hys yre and hys *malecolye*.
MS. Cantab. Ff. ii. 38, f. 163.

My sone, schryve the now forthi,
Hast thou ben *malencolien*.
Gower, MS. Soc. Antiq. 134, f. 84.

MALEDIȝT. Cursed. (*A.-N.*)

Cometh a childe *malediȝt*
Aȝeyn Jhesu to rise he tiȝt.
Cursor Mundi, MS. Coll. Trin. Cantab. f. 75.

MALEES. Uneasiness. (*Fr.*)

But yn herte y am sory,
For y have nothyng redy,
Whereof the kyng to make at eʋe.
Therfore y am at moche *maiʋes*.
MS. Cantab. Ff. ii. 38, f. 146.

MALEFICE. Enchantment. (*A.-N.*)

MALEK. Salt. Dr. Forman's MSS.

MAL-ENGINE. Wicked artifice. (*A.-N.*) It occurs in Hall, Henry VI. f. 31.

MALE-PILLION. A stuffed leathern cushion behind a servant who attended his master in a journey to carry luggage upon. Also, a male-saddle, or saddle for carrying luggage upon.

MALE-TALENT. Ill-will. (*A.-N.*)

And sire Beves tho veraiment,
Forgaf him alle is *mauntalent*.
Beves of Hamtoun, p. 145.

MALGRACIOUS. Ungracious.

Bothe of visage and of stature
Is lothely and *malgracious*.
Gower, MS. Soc. Antiq. 134, f. 131.

MALGRADO. Maugre; in spite of. (*Ital.*)

MALICE. (1) The marsh-mallow. *Devon*.

(2) Sorcery; witchcraft. See *Malefice*.

(3) To bear malice to. *Linc*. " That hath malic'd thus," Hawkins, ii. 46.

MALICEFUL. Malicious. *North*.

MALICIOUS. Artful. (*A.-N.*)

MALIOTE. A mallet. Nominale MS.

MALISON. Malediction; curse. (*A.-N.*) Still in use, according to Kennett.

MALKIN. (1) A slattern. *Devon*. It was formerly a common diminutive of Mary. Maid Marian was so called. " No one wants Malkin's maidenhead, which has been sold fifteen times," prov. Milles' MS. Chaucer apparently alludes to this phrase. *Malkintrash*, one in a dismal-looking dress.

(2) A scarecrow. *Somerset*.

MALL. (1) A hammer, or club. Also a verb, to knock down with a mall; to beat. " Malle hym to dede," MS. Morte Arthure. " Malled, felled, or knocked downe," Cotgrave.

(2) A plough-share. *Somerset*.

(3) A court or pleading-house.

(4) A kind of game.

But playing with the boy at *mall*,
I rue the time and ever shall,
I struck the ball, I know not how,
For that is not the play, you know,
A pretty height into the air.
Cotton's Works, 1734, p. 221.

MALLANDERS. Sore places on the inside of the fore-legs of horses. " *Mal feru*, a malander in the bought of a horse's knee," Cotgrave.

And some are full of *mallenders* and scratches.
Taylor's Motto, 12mo. Lond. 1622.

MALLERAG. To abuse. See *Ballerag*. *Mallock*, to scandalize. *Linc*.

MALLIGO. Malaga wine. *Nares*.

MALLS. The measles. *Exmoor*.

MALLY. A hare. *North*.

MALSHRAGGES. Caterpillars, palmers, and canker-worms. Also called *mallishags*.

MALSKRID. Wandered. *Will. Werw.*

MALT-BUG. A drunkard. This cant term occurs in Harrison's England, p. 202.

MALT-COMES. The little beards or shoots when malt begins to run. *Yorksh.* Malting-corn, corn beginning to germinate.

MALTE. Melted. (*A.-S.*)

Tille that the sonne his wyngis cauȝte,
Whereof it *malte* and fro the heyȝte,
Withouten helpe of eny sleyȝte,
He felle to his destruccioun.
    Gower, MS. Soc. Antiq. 134, f. 110.

MALTEN-HEARTED. Faint-hearted. *North.*

MALTER. A maltster. *Var. dial.*

MALT-HORSE. A slow dull heavy horse, such as is used by brewers. Hence Shakespeare has it as a term of contempt. See Nares. He would simper and mumpe, as though hee had gone a wooing to a *malt-mare* at Rochester," Lilly, ed. 1632.

MALUE. A mallow. Reliq. Antiq. i. 53.

Take *malues* with alle the rotes, and sethe thame in water, and wasche thi hevede therwith.
    MS. Lincoln A. i 17, f. 282.

MALURE. Misfortune. (*A.-N.*)

MALVESIE. Malmsey wine. See Harrison's England, p. 170; Reliq. Antiq. i. 3; Degrevant, 1415.

Thane spyces unsparyly thay spendyde thereaftyre,
Malvesye and muskadelle, thase mervelyous drynkes.
    Morte Arthure, MS. Lincoln, f. 55.

Ye shall have Spayneshe wyne and Gascoyne,
Rose coloure, whyt, claret, rampyon,
Tyre, caspryck, and *malvesyne*,
Sak, raspyce. alycaunt, rumney,
Greke, ipocrase, new made clary,
Suche as ye never had;
For yf ye drynke a draught or too,
Yt wyll make you or ye thens go
By Goggs body starke madde.
    Interlude of the Four Elements, n. d.

MAM. Mammy; mother. *North.*

MAMBLE. Said of soil when it sticks to agricultural implements. *East.*

MAMELEN. To chatter; to mumble. (*A.-S.*)

MAMERI. A pagan temple.

Aboute the time of mid dai
Out of a *mameri* a sal
Sarasins com gret foisoun,
That hadde anoured here Mahoun.
    Beves of Hamtoun, p. 54.

MAMMER. To hesitate; to mumble; to be perplexed. Still in use. "I stand in doubte, or stande in a *mamorynge* betwene hope and feare," Palsgrave's Acolastus, 1540.

That where before he vaunted
The conquest he hath got,
He sits now in a *mammering*,
As one that mindes it not.
    A Quest of Enquirie, 1595.

MAMMET. A puppet. See *Maumet.*

MAMMOCK. (1) A fragment. *Var. dial.* "Small mammocks of stone," Optick Glasse of Humors, 1639, p. 120. See Florio, pp. 4, 67, 197.

Salt with thy knife, then reach to and take,
Thy bread cut faire and no *mammocks* make.
    The Schoole of Vertue, n. d.

(2) To mumble. *Suffolk.* Moor says, "to cut and hack victuals wastefully." Hence, to maul or mangle; to do any thing very clumsily.

MAMMOTHREPT. A spoilt child.

MAMMY. Mother. *Mammysick,* never easy but when at home with mammy.

MAMPUS. A great number. *Dorset.*

MAM'S-FOOT. A mother's pet-child.

MAM-SWORN. Perjured. *North.*

MAMTAM. A term of endearment.

MAMY. A wife. *Leic.*

MAMYTAW. A donkey. *Devon.*

MAN. (1) Was formerly used with much latitude. Thus the Deity was so called with no irreverent intention. Forby tells us the East Anglians have retained that application of the word.

(2) The small pieces with which backgammon is played are called men. "A queene at chesse or man at tables," Florio, p. 136.

(3) *A man or a mouse,* something or nothing. See Florio, p. 44. *Man alive,* a common and familiar mode of salutation. *Man in the oak,* an ignis fatuus. *Man of war,* a sharp, clever fellow.

(4) To man a hawk, to make her tractable. See Harrison's England, p. 227.

MANACE. To menace, or threaten. Also, anything which threatens. (*A.-N.*)

MANADGE. A box or club formed by small shopkeepers for supplying poor people with goods, the latter paying for them by instalments. *North.*

MANAUNTIE. Maintenance. Langtoft, p. 325

MANCH. To munch; to eat greedily.

MANCHET. The best kind of white-bread. See Hobson's Jests, repr. p. 9.

MANCIPATE. Enslaved. (*Lat.*)

MANCIPLE. An officer who had the care of purchasing provisions for an Inn of Court, a college, &c.

MANCOWE. This term is the translation of *sinozophalus* in Nominale MS.

MAND. A demand; a question.

The emperour, with wordes myld,
Askyd a *mand* of the chyld.
    MS. Ashmole 61, f 87

MANDEMENT. A mandate. (*A.-N.*)

MANDER. To cry. *Suffolk.*

MANDILION. The mandilion or mandevile was a kind of loose garment without sleeves, or if with sleeves, having them hanging at the back. "*Cassacchino,* a mandilion, a jacket, a jerkin," Florio, p. 87. Harrison, p. 172, mentions "the mandilion worne to Collie Weston ward," i. e. awry. This curious early notice of the Colly-Weston proverb was accidentally omitted in its proper place.

French dublet, and the Spanish hose to breech it;
Short cloakes, old *mandilions* (we beseech it).
    Rowlands' Knave of Harts, 1613.

MANDRAKE. The mandragora, Lat. It is often mentioned as a narcotic, and very numerous were the superstitions regarding it. It was said to shriek when torn up. "Mandrakes and night-ravens still shriking in thine eares," Dekker's Knights Conjuring, p. 49.

The male mandrake hath great, broad, long, smooth leaves, of a deepe greene colour, flat spred upon the ground; among which come up the flowers of a pale whitish colour, standing every one upon a single smal and weak footstalk, of a whitish green colour ; in their places grow round apples of a yellowish colour, smooth, soft, and glittering, of a strong smel ; in which are conteined flat and smooth seedes, in fashion of a little kidney, like those of the thorn apple. The roote is long, thick, whitish, divided many times into two or three parts, resembling the legs of a man, with other parts of his bodie adjoining thereto, as the privie parts, as it hath beene reported ; whereas in truth it is no otherwise then in the rootes of carrots, parsneps, and such like, forked or devided into two or more parts which nature taketh no account of. There have been many ridiculous tales brought up of this plant, whether of old wives or some runnagate surgeons or phisickmongers, I know not (a title bad inough for them) but sure some one or moe that sought to make themselves famous in skillfull above others were the first brochers of that errour I spake of. They adde further, that it is never or verie seldome to be founde growing naturally but under a gallows, where the matter that hath fallen from the dead bodie hath given it the shape of a man ; and the matter of a woman, the substaunce of a female plant, with many other such doltish dreames. They fable further and affirm, that he who woulde take up a plant thereof must tie a dogge thereunto to pull it up, which will give a great shrike at the digging up ; otherwise if a man should do it, he should certainly die in short space after ; besides many fables of loving matters, too full of scurrilitie to set foorth in print, which I forbeare to speake of ; all which dreames and old wives tales you shall from hencefoorth cast out of your bookes and memorie, knowing this that they are all and every part of them false and most untrue. For I myselfe and my servaunts also have digged up, planted, and replanted verie many ; and yet never could either perceive shape of man or woman, but sometimes one straight roote, sometimes two, and often sixe or seaven braunches, comming from the maine great roote ; even as nature list to bestowe upon it as to other plants. But the idle drones that have little or nothing to do but eate and drinke, have bestowed some of their time in carving the rootes of Brionie, forming them to the shape of men and women, which falsifying practise hath confirmed the errour amongst the simple and unlearned people, who have taken them upon their report to be the true mandrakes. *Gerard's Herball*, ed. 1597, p. 280.

MANDY. Saucy ; impudent ; frolicsome ; unmanageable. *West.*

MANE. Moan. Reliq. Antiq. i. 60.

MANER. A seat or dwelling. Used in Staffordshire, according to Kennet, MS. Lansd. 1033.

    The kyng soyournyd in that tyde
    At a *maner* there besyde.
           MS. Cantab. Ff. ii. 38, f. 78.

MANERLY. Correctly ; politely.

MANEST. Menaced. Apol. Loll. p. 21.

MANFESOURS. Malefactors. Langtoft, p. 211.

MANG. (1) To mix, or mingle. *West.* Hence, a mash of bran or malt.

(2) To become stupified.
    What say ye, man ? Alas ! for teyn
    I trow ye *mang. Croft's Excerpta Antiqua,* p. 108.

MANGE. To eat. (*A.-N.*)

MANGERING. Perplexing.
    The simple people might be brought in a *mangering* of their faith, and stand in doubt whom they might believe.   *Philpot's Works,* p. 315.

MANGERY. A feast. (*A.-N.*)

There was joye and moche game
At that grete *mangery*. *MS. Cantab. Ff. ii. 38, f. 113.*
    To the kyng he sente them tylle,
    And preyed hym, yf hyt were hys wylle,
    That he faylyd hym not at that tyde,
    But that he wolde come to Hungary
    For to worschyp that *mangery*.
    Ther of he hym besoght.
        MS. Cantab. Ff. ii. 38, f. 81.

MANG-FODDER. Fodder for cows mixed with hay and straw. *Yorksh.*

MANG-HANGLE. Mixed in a wild and confused manner. *Somerset.*

MANGONEL. The same as *Magnel,* q. v.

MANGONIZE. To traffic in slaves. (*Lat.*)

MANHED. Manhood ; race.
    Off women com duke and kyng,
    I jow tell without lesyng,
    Of them com owre *manhed.*
        MS. Ashmole 61, f. 60.

MANICON. A kind of nightshade.
    Bewitch Hermetic men to run
    Stark staring mad with *manicon.*
        Hudibras, III. 1. 324.

MANIE. Madness. (*A.-N.*)

MANIFOLD. To multiply, or increase. It occurs in MS. Cotton. Vespas. D. vii.

MANIPLE. A bundle, or handful. It is also the same with *Fanon,* q. v.

MANK. A trick, or prank. *Yorksh.*

MAN-KEEN. Marriageable. *North.*

MANKIND. Masculine ; furious. A furious beast is still so called. See Craven Gl.

MANKIT. Maimed ; impaired. *Gawayne.*

MANLICH. Humane. (*A.-S.*) It occasionally has the sense of *manfully.*

MANNED. Waited on ; attended.

MANNER. (1) Manure. *Var. dial.*

(2) *To be taken with the manner,* to be caught in a criminal act.

MANNERS-BIT. A portion left in a dish "for the sake of manners." *North.*

MANNIE. A little man. *Linc.*

MANNINGTREE. Formerly a famous place for feasting and sports, and often alluded to by our early writers. "Drink more in two daies then all Maning-tree does at a Whitsunale," Dekker's Knights Conjuring, p. 38.

MANNISH. (1) Manly. It occurs in Palsgrave's Acolastus, 4to. Lond. 1540. *Manny,* to approach to manhood.

(2) Fond of man's flesh. *Palsgrave.*

MAN-QUELLER. A destroyer of men.

MANRED. Vassalage ; dependence. (*A.-S.*)
    Misdoo no messangere for menske of thiselvyne,
    Sen we are in thy *maunrede,* and mercy the beeckes.
        Morte Arthure, MS. Lincoln, f. 54.

MANSBOND. Slaves. Langtoft, p. 115.

MANSCHIPELICHE. Manfully.
    His lord he served treweliche,
    In al thing *manschipeliche.*
        Guy of Warwick, p. 1.

MANSE. (1) A house, or mansion. (*A.-N.*)

(2) To curse, or excommunicate.

MANSHEN. A kind of cake. *Somerset.* Perhaps from the old word *manchet,* q. v.

MANSHIP. Manhood ; courage.

MANSLEARS. Murderers.

> *Mansleas* s they wer had most odious.
>
> *MS. Laud.* 416, f. 50.

MAN'S-MOTHERWORT. The herb *Palma Christi*. It occurs in Gerard.

MANSUETE. Gentle. (*A.-N.*) *Mansuetude*, gentleness. Old Christmas Carols, p. 29.

MAN-SWORE. Forsworn; perjured.

MANT. (1) To stutter. *Cumb.*

(2) Plan; method; trick?

> I have effected my purpose in a great many, some by the aliquote parts, and some by the cubicall *mant*, but this soure crabb I cannot deale with by no method. *Letters on Scientific Subjects*, p. 105.

MANTEL. A term applied to a hawk, when she stretches one wing along after her leg, and then her other wing.

MANTELET. A short mantle. (*A.-N.*)

> That thay be trapped in gete,
> Bathe telere and *mantelets*.
>
> *MS. Lincoln* A. i. 17, f. 134.

MANTEL-TREE. "Mantyl tre of a chymney, *manteau dune cheminee*," Palsgrave. The same writer spells it *mantry*. A strange phrase, "as melancholy as a mantle-tree," occurs in Wily Beguiled, 1623. Mantle-piece for the chimney-piece is very common.

MANTLE. (1) To embrace kindly. *North.*

(2) To ape the fine lady. *Linc.*

(3) To winnow corn. Holme, 1688. Mantle-wind, a winnowing machine.

(4) To rave about angrily. *Linc.*

(5) To froth, as beer does, &c. *Exmoor.*

MANTO. A gown. Properly, a garment made of *manto*, a kind of stuff.

MANUAL. The mass-book. (*Lat.*)

MANURANCE. Cultivation. It occurs in the Triall of Wits, 4to. Lond. 1604, p. 242.

MANUS-CHRISTI. A kind of lozenge.

MANY. (1) A late form of *Meiny*, q. v.

(2) Much. *West.* The A. S. use.

(3) *Many a time and oft*, frequently. *Var. dial.* It occurs in Shakespeare.

MANYEW. The mange in dogs.

> The houndes haveth also another siknesse that is clepid the *manyew*, and that cometh to hem for cause that thei be malencolyous. *MS. Bodl.* 546.

MANY-FOLDS. The intestines. *North.*

MAPPEL. The same as *Maulkin*, q. v.

MAPPEN. Probably; perhaps. *North.*

MAQUERELLE. See *Mackerel.*

MAR. A small lake. *Northumb.*

MARA-BALK. A balk of land. *East.*

MARACOCK. The passion-flower.

MARBLES. The lues venerea. *Greene.*

MARBRE. Marble. (*A.-N.*)

> A tombe riche for the nonis
> Of *marbre* and eek of Jaspre stonis.
>
> *Gower, MS. Soc. Antiq.* 134, f. 127.

MARCH. (1) A land-mark, or boundary. (2) To border on, or be contiguous to. (*A.-N.*) Hence the marches of Wales, &c. "Marches bytwene two landes, *frontieres*," Palsgrave. *Marcher*, a president of the marches. *Marcher-lords*, the petty rulers who lived on the Welsh borders.

MARCHALE. A marshall.

> Of a thousonde men bi tale
> He made him ledere and *marchale*.
>
> *Cursor Mundi, MS. Coll. Trin. Cantab* f. 48.

MARCHALSYE. Horsemanship.

MARCHANDYE. Merchandize.

> Sertanly withowte lye,
> Sum tyme I lyve be *marchandye*,
> And passe welle ofte the see.
>
> *MS. Cantab.* Ff. v. 48, f. 48.

MARCH-BIRD. A frog. *East.*

MARCHE. (1) The herb smallage.

(2) Mercia. Chron. Vilodun. p. 2.

MARCH-HARE. *As mad as a March hare*, a very common phrase. "As mad not as Marche hare, but as a madde dogge," More's Supplycacyon of Soulys, sig. C. ii.

> Than they begyn to swere and to stare,
> And be as braynles as a *Marshe hare*.
>
> *MS. Rawlinson* C. 86.

> As mad as a March hare; where madness compares,
> Are not Midsummer hares as mad as March hares?
>
> *Heywood's Epigrammes*, 1567, n°. 95.

MARCHING-WATCH. A brilliant procession formerly made by the citizens of London at Midsummer. It is fully described by Stowe.

MARCH-LAND. An old name for Mercia.

MARCH-PANE. "Marchpanes are made of verie little flower, but with addition of greater quantitie of filberds, pine nuts, pistaces, almonds, and rosed sugar," Markham's Countrey Farme, 1616, p. 585. According to Forby, ii. 208, the term was retained up to a very recent period. Marchpane was a constant article in the desserts of our ancestors. See Ben Jonson, ii. 295; Topsell's Serpents, p. 165; Warner's Antiq. Culin. p. 103; Harrison's England, p. 167; Florio, p. 134.

> As to surprese by message sad,
> The feast for which they all have had
> their *march-pane* dream so long.
>
> *Songs of the London Prentices*, p. 31.

MARDLE. (1) To gossip. *East.*

(2) A pond for cattle. *Suffolk.*

MARE. (1) An imp, or demon; a hag. "Yond harlot and mare," Towneley Mysteries, p. 198. It was often a term of contempt. See *Meer* in Brockett, p. 201.

> And shame hyt ys aywhare
> To be kalled a prestes *mare*.
>
> *MS. Harl.* 1701, f. 53.

(2) *To win the mare or lose the halter*, to play double or quits.

(3) The sport of *crying the mare* has been already mentioned. It is thus more particularly described in Blount's Glossographia, ed. 1681, p. 398:—"To cry the mare is an ancient custom in Herefordshire, viz. when each husbandman is reaping the last of his corn, the workmen leave a few blades standing, and tye the tops of them together, which is the mare, and then stand at a distance and throw their sickles at it, and he that cuts the knot has the prize; which done, they cry with a loud voice, I have her, I have her, I have her. Others answer, What have you, what have you, what have you? A mare, a mare, a

mare. Whose is she, whose is she, whose is she? J. B. (naming the owner three times). Whither will you send her? To John-a-Nokes, (naming some neighbor who has not all his corn reapt). Then they all shout three times, and so the ceremony ends with good chear. In Yorkshire upon like occasion they have a Harvest Dame, in Bedfordshire a Jack and a Gill."

MAREFART. The herb yellow ragwort.

MAREIS. A marsh. (*A.-N.*) "Maresh grounds," Holinshed, Hist. England, i. 55; *maresse*, Hall, Richard III. f. 33; *mareys*, W. Mapes, p. 351; Maundevile, p. 130; *marise*, Harrison's England, p. 166; Brit. Bibl. iv. 70.

> The mosse and the *marrasse*, the mounttes so hye.
> *Morte Arthure, MS. Lincoln, f. 74.*

MARE'S-FAT. *Inula dysenterica*, Lin.

MARE'S-TAILS. Long, narrow, and irregular clouds, of a dark colour. *Var. dial.*

MARET. Merit; deserving conduct.

> Thaȝ he syng and say no mas the prest unwothelé,
> Both ȝour *maret* and ȝour mede in heven ȝe
> schul have,
> Fore God hath grauntyd of his grace be his auctoreté,
> Be he never so synful ȝoure soulys may he save,
> *Audelay's Poems, p. 44.*

MARGAN. The stinking camomile.

MARGARETTIN. Same as *Madgetin*, q. v.

MARGARITE. A pearl. (*A.-N.*) A "margery perl" is mentioned in Pr. Parv. p. 214.

> No man right honorable, findeth a precious stone, bearing the splendor of any rich *margarite*, but straight hasteth unto the best lapidiste, whose happy allowance thereof begetteth a rare affectation, and inestimable valew of the gem.
> *Hopton's Baculum Geodæticum, 1614.*

MARGARITON. A legendary Trojan hero, frequently alluded to. See Nares.

MARGE. A margin. See Johnson. *Margent*, now a common vulgarism, is sanctioned by our best writers.

MARGERY-HOULET. An owl. Kennett MS.

MARGINAL-FINGER. The index mark.

MARGIT. Margaret. *North.*

MARGTHE. Marrow. Nominale MS. *Marie* is the form used by Chaucer.

MARICHE. A disease of the matrix. A certain receptacle in the matrix is termed *marrys* in MS. Addit. 12195, f. 158.

MARIOLE. Little Mary. *Hearne.*

MARK. (1) A hawk is said *to keep her mark*, when she waits at the place where she lays game, until she be retrieved.

(2) A coin worth thirteen shillings and 4d.

(3) Dark. Tundale's Visions, p. 13.

> The nyght waxed soon black as pycke,
> Then was the miste bothe *marke* and thycke.
> *MS. Cantab. Ff. ii. 38, f. 201.*

(4) A wide gutter. *Devon.*

MARK-BOY. A lad employed by gamblers to mark the scores.

MARKE. Mars. The reading in MS. Douce 291 is "Mars." The whole chapter is omitted in MS. Digby 233.

> Right so thos that bene ordeynyd to the werk of
> *Marke*, that is god of bataile.
> *Vegecius, MS. Laud. 416, f. 241.*

MARKEL. A kind of night-cap.

MARKES. A marquis. Ord. and Reg. p. 12. *Markisesse*, the wife of a marquis.

MARKET-BETER. A swaggerer. See Tyrwhitt's Gl. p. 151. A person in a cozy, comfortable, merry humour, is said in Worcestershire to be *market-peart*. *Market-fresh*, on the verge of intoxication, Salop. Antiq. p. 499. *Market-merry*, tipsy.

MARKET-PLACE. The front teeth. *Linc.*

MARKETS. Marketings; things bought at markets. *Yorksh.*

MARKET-STEDE. A market-place. (*A.-S.*)

MARL. (1) Marvel. See Middleton, iii. 390. Still in use in Exmoor.

> And such am I, I slight your proud commands;
> I *marle* who put a bow into your hands.
> *Randolph's Poems, 1643, p. 19.*

(2) "To dresse any maner of fish with vineger to be eaten colde, which at Southampton they call *marling* of fish," Florio, ed. 1598, p. 3.

(3) To manure with marl. See Florio, p. 114; Lambarde's Perambulation, 1596, p. 445.

(4) To ravel, as silk, &c. *Devon.*

MARLION. The merlin hawk. See Harrison's England, p. 227; Reliq. Antiq. i. 81.

MARLOCK. (1) A fool. *Yorksh.*

(2) A frolic, gambol, or vagary. *North.*

MARM. A jelly. *Kent.*

MARMIT. A pot with hooks at the side.

MARMOL. The same as *Mormal*, q. v.

MARMOSET. A kind of monkey. *Mare mussett*, Chester Plays, i. 244.

MAROT. A nipple. (*A.-N.*)

MARQUESSE. Marchioness. *Shak.*

MARR. To spoil a child; to soil or dirty anything. *Palsgrave.*

MARRAM. The sea reed-grass. *Norf.*

MARRET. A marsh, or bog. *North.*

MARRIABLE. Marriageable. *Palsgrave.*

MARROQUIN. Goat's leather. (*Fr.*)

MARROW. (1) A companion, or friend; a mate or lover. See Ben Jonson, vii. 406. "Pore husbondes that had no *marowes*," Hunttyng of the Hare, 247. "A marrow in Yorkshire a fellow or companion, and the relative term in Paris, as one glove or shoe is or is not marrow to another," MS. Lansd. 1033.

(2) A kind of sausage. *Westm.*

(3) Similar; suitable; uniform. *North.*

MARROW-BONES. The knees. *To bring any one down on his marrow-bones*, to make him beg pardon on his knees. *Marrow-bones and cleavers*, important instruments in rough music, performed by butchers on the occasion of marriages, &c.

MARROWLESS. Matchless. *North.*

MARRUBE. Lavender cotton.

MARRY. An interj. equivalent to, indeed! *Marry on us, marry come up, marry come out*, interjections given by Brockett. *Marry and shall, that I will! Marry come up, my dirty cousin*, a saying addressed to any one who affects excessive delicacy. " *Magnagna*, marry gip sir, true Roger," Cotgrave. Here *marry gip* seems to mean an affirmation, but Gifford says it is a phrase of contempt. See Lilly, ed. 1632, sig. Z. x. " By Mary Gipcy." Skelton, i. 419. " *Marry*, verily, truly," MS. Lansd. 1033. *Marry muff*, nonsense.

MARSHALL. The *marshall of the hall* was the person who, at public festivals, placed every person according to his rank. It was his duty also to preserve peace and order. The *marshall of the field*, one who presided over any out-door game.

MARSHALSEA-MONEY. The county-rate. *East*. It is nearly obsolete.

MARSI. Mercy.

> A man witheout *marsi* no *marsi* shall have,
> In tyme of ned when he dothe it crave,
> But all his lyfve go lick a slave.
> *MS. Ashmole* 46.

MART. (1) Lard. *South*.
(2) Mars. Also, war. *Spenser*.
(3) To sell, or traffic. See Todd. *Martner*, one who marts, Florio, p. 54.
(4) An ox or cow killed at Martinmas, and dried for winter use. *North*. " Biefe salted, dried up in the chimney, Martlemas biefe," Hollyband's Dictionarie, 1593.

MARTE. Wonders; marvels. (*A.-S.*)

MARTEL. To hammer. *Spenser*.

MARTERNS. The fur of a martin. See Test. Vetusta, p. 658. *Marterons tawed*, Booke of Rates, 1545. In an inventory printed in the Archæologia, xxx. 17, mention is made of " an olde cassock of satten, edged with *matrons*."

> Ne *martryn*, ne sabil, y trowe, in god fay,
> Was none founden in hire garnement.
> *Lydgate, MS. Soc. Antiq.* 134, f. 25.

MARTIALIST. A martial man; a soldier. See Dekker's Knight's Conjuring, p. 70.

MARTILL. A marten. Topsell's Beasts, p. 491.

MARTIN. A spayed heifer. MS. Gough (Oxon) 46. See *Free-Martin*.

MARTIN'S-HAMMER. " She has had Martin's-hammer knocking at her wicket," said of a woman who has twins.

MARTIN'S-RINGS. St. Martin's rings were imitation of gold ones, made with copper and gilt. They may have been so called from the makers or venders of them residing within the collegiate church of St. Martin's-le-Grand. See Archæologia, xviii. 55; and Brand's Pop. Antiq. ii. 60.

MARTIRE. To torment. (*A.-N.*) *Martyrd*, spoilt, Erle of Tolous, 1110.

> To mete hym in the mountes, and *martyre* hys knyghtes,
> Stryke theme doune in strates and struye theme fore evere. *Morte Arthure, MS. Lincoln*, f. 59.

MARTLEMAS. Martinmas. *North*.

MARTRONE. The marten. See *Marterns*. Spelt *martryns* in Reliq. Antiq. i. 295.

MARVEDI. A very small Spanish coin, thirty-four to a sixpence.

MARVEL. The herb hoarhound.

MARVELS. Marbles. *Suffolk*.

MARWE. Marrow. Nominale MS. " Mary in a bone, *mouelle*," Palsgrave; *mary-boon*, Lydgate's Minor Poems, p. 165; Collier's Old Ballads, p. 69.

> The grece of the fox and the *mary* be good for the hardynge of the synowes. *MS. Bodl.* 546.

MARY-MAS. The Annunciation B. V.

MARYN. The sea-coast. (*A.-N.*)

MAS. (1) Master.
(2) A mace, or club. (*A.-N.*)
(3) Makes. Perceval, 1086.

> Thou pynnyst hyt on, grete yoye thou *mas*.
> *MS. Cantab. Ff. ii. 38, f. 48.*
> We wol se for what resoun
> That he suche baptisyng *mas*,
> And whether he be Messias.
> *Cursor Mundi, MS. Coll. Trin. Cantab.* f. 79.
> Arghnes also me thinke is harde,
> For that *mase* a man a cowarde.
> *MS. Sloan.* 1785, f. 53.

MASCAL. A caterpillar. *Devon*. " Mascale et maltscale, a palmer-worm," MS. Gloss.

MASCLE. Male. Stanihurst, p. 19.

> Natheles comuneliche hure moste love is the monethe of Janver, and yn that monethe thei renne fastest of eny tyme of the geer bothe *mascle* and femel. *MS. Bodl.* 546.

MASE. (1) To be confounded; to doubt. Still in use, to turn giddy. Also, a substantive, amazement. " A mazed man, an idiot," *Devon*. *Mazy pack*, the parish fool. *Mazelins*, silly persons, *Cumb*. " Maze Jerry Pattick, mad simpleton," Cornwall Gl.

> Here the people are set in a wonderfull *maze* and astonishment, as if witches could plague men in their wrath, by sending their spirits, because they confesse they did it, when their spirits do lye and had no power, but the torments came by naturall causes. *Gifford's Dialogue on Witches*, 1603.

(2) A wild fancy. *Chaucer*.

MASEDERE. More amazed (*A.-N.*)

MASEDNESSE. Astonishment; confusion.

MASELIN. A kind of drinking-cup, sometimes made of maslin or brass, a metal mentioned in Gy of Warwike, p. 421, " bras, *maslyn*, yren and stel."

> Tables, clothes, bred and wine,
> Plater, disse, cop and *maseline*.
> *Arthour and Merlin*, p. 257.
> iiij. c. cuppys of golde fyne,
> And as many of *maskyn*.
> *MS. Cantab. Ff. ii. 38, f. 122.*
> Take a quarte of good wyne, and do it in a clene *mastelyn* panne, and do therto an ownce of salgemme.
> *MS. Med. Rec. xv. Cent.*

MASER. A bowl, or goblet. Tyrwhitt seems to make it synonymous with *maselin*. Cotgrave has, " *Jadeau*, a bowle or mazer." Masers made of hard wood, and richly carved and ornamented, were formerly much esteemed. Randolph, Poems, p. 92, speaks of " carv'd mazers." Davies, Ancient Rites of Durham, ed. 1672, pp. 126-7, mentions several mazers; one " largely and finely edg'd about with silver, and double-gilt with gold;" another, " the outside whereof was of black mazer, and the inside of silver, double-gilt, the edge finely wrought round about with silver, and double-gilt." The maser was generally of a large size. " *Trulla*, a great cuppe, brode and deepe, suche as great masers were wont to bee," Cooper, ed. 1559. " A mazer, or broad piece to drinke in," Baret, 1580. Mazer wood is said to be maple.

> Off lanycolle thou shall prove,
> That is a cuppe to my behove,
> Off *maser* it is ful clene.
> *MS. Cantab. Ff. v. 48, f. 50.*

MASH. (1) A preparation for a horse, generally made of malt and bran. *Var. dial.* " A commixture, a mash," Florio, p. 111.

(2) To act furiously. *Linc.*

(3) A marsh; fen land. *Var. dial.*

MASHELTON. The same as *Maslin*, q. v.

MASHES. A great deal. *Cornw.*

MASH-FAT. The vat which contains the malt in brewing. It is stirred up with a mash-staff, formerly called a mashel or masherel. *Masfattus*, Reliq. Antiq. i. 86. *Maskefatte*, Nominale MS.

MASH-MORTAR. All to pieces. *West.*

MASIDNESSE. Astonishment. *Palsgrave.*

MASK. To infuse. *North.*

MASKEDE. Bewildered. (*A.-S.*) Still in use, spelt *maskerd*, and explained, choked up, stupified, stifled.

MASKEL. A kind of lace. The method of making it is described in a very curious tract on laces of the fifteenth century in MS. Harl. 2320, f. 62.

MASKELIN. A masking, or disguising. *Maskery*, ibid. *Masculer*, a masker.

MASKERD. Decayed. *North.*

MASKIN. An abbreviation of *Mass*. Still in use. See Craven Gl. i. 312. *Matkins*, London Prodigal, p. 18.

MASKS. Mashes; meshes. *Park.*

MASLIN. Mixed corn. *North.* It is generally made of wheat and rye.

> But alleonely of wete,
> The *mastlyone* shul men lete.
> *MS. Harl. 1701, f. 67.*

> I say nor cow, nor wheate, nor *mastlyn*,
> For cow is sorry for her castlyn.
> *Men Miracles, 1656, p. 6.*

MASNEL. A mace, or club.

> With an uge *masnel*
> Beves a hite on the helm of stel,
> That Beves of Hamtoun, veraiment,
> Was astoned of the dent.
> *Beves of Hamtoun, p. 165.*

MASONER. A bricklayer. *Leic.* " A mason-schype, *petronius*," Nominale MS.

MASSELADE. A dish in ancient cookery, described in MS. Sloane 1201, f. 38.

MASSELGEM. The same as *Maslin*, q. v.

MASSER. (1) A mercer. *Lanc.*

(2) A privy, or jakes. *Somerset.*

MASSING. Belonging to the mass. Holinshed, Chron. Ireland, p. 177.

MAST. " Of wax a mast," a tall wax candle.

> And brought with hym of wax a *mast*.
> *Chron. Vilodun. p. 98.*

MASTED. Fattened, as pigs are with mast, &c. See Prompt. Parv. p. 151.

MASTER. (1) Husband. *Var. dial.*

(2) The jack at the game of bowls.

MASTERDOM. Dominion; rule. *Masterful*, imperious, commanding.

MASTER-TAIL. The left handle of a plough.

MASTERY. A masterly operation. So the finding the grand elixir was called.

MASTHEDE. Majesty. This occurs in MS. Cotton. Vespas. D. vii.

MASTICOT. The mastic gum.

MASTY. (1) A mastiff. *North.* " To lead a masty dog," Hobson's Jests, p. 11. *Masty currs*, Du Bartas, p. 46.

(2) Very large and big. *Linc.* Possibly connected with *Masted*, q. v.

MASYE. Confounded; stupified.

> Alas! for syth and sorow sad,
> Mornyng makes me *masye* and mad.
> *Croft's Excerpta Antiqua, p. 107.*

MAT. May. Songs and Carols, xv.

MATACHIN. A dance of fools, or persons fantastically dressed, who performed various movements, having swords and bucklers with which they made a clashing noise.

MATCH. The wick of a candle.

MATCHLY. Exactly alike. Kennett says, " mightily, greatly, extremely." *Norf.* In Lincolnshire, when things are equal or alike, they say they are *matley* or *matler*.

MATE. To stupify, confound, puzzle, defeat, deject, or terrify. " He wase ny mate," i. e. confounded, Torrent, p. 29. *Matesye*, state of confusion, Hardyng, f. 96.

MATERE. The matrix or womb.

MATFELON. The herb knap-weed.

MATH. A mowing. *Somerset.*

MATHEBRU. A kind of wine, mentioned in a list in MS. Rawl. C. 86.

MATHEN.

> Now hadde al tho theves hethen
> Ben to-frust doun to *mathen*.
> *Arthour and Merlin, p. 309.*

> For he lete Cristen wedde hathen,
> And meynt our blod as flesche and *mathen*.
> *Ibid. p. 19.*

MATHER. The great ox-eyed daisy.

MATHUM. A fool or changeling. *Westm.*

MATRES. A kind of rich cloth.

MATRIMONY. A wife. (*Lat.*)

MATTER. (1) To approve of. *North.* Mr. Scatcherd gives exactly the opposite sense.

(2) To burst, as a sore does.

(3) *A matter of*, about. *What is the matter of your age*, how old are you. *No great matters*, no great quantity; not very well.

MATTHEW-GLIN. An old comical term for metheglin, mentioned by Taylor.

MATTRESS. " Mattresse for a crosbowe, *martelas*," Palsgrave.

MATTY. Matted; twisted. *Var. dial.*

MATWOURTH. The herb spragus.

MAUD. A plaid worn by Cheviot shepherds.

MAUDLIN-DRUNK. Said of persons who weep when tipsy. " Some maudlin drunken were, and wept full sore," Yorkshire Ale, 1697, p. 8.

> The fifth is *maudlin drunke;* when a fellowe will weepe for kindnes in the midst of his ale, and kisse you, saying, By God, captaine. I love thee.
> *Nash's Pierce Pennilesse,* 1592.

MAUDLIN-FAIR. A great uproar. *North.*

MAUDRING. Mumbling. *Kent.*

MAUG. A brother-in-law. *North.*

MAUGHT. Might. Gy of Warwike, p. 188.

MAUGRE. In spite of. (*A.-N.*) As a substantive, misfortune. A verb, to defy, Webster's Works, ii. 175.

> That salle he, *maugré* his tethe,
> For alle his gret araye. *MS. Lincoln* A. 1. 17, f. 132.
>   3e, seid the kyng, be my leuté,
> And ellis have I mycul *maugré.*
>   *MS. Cantab.* Ff. v. 48, f. 50.

MAUKY. Maggotty; whimsical. *Mauky-headed,* ibid. *North.*

MAUL. (1) A mallow. (2) A moth. *North.* (3) Clayey, sticky soil. *East.* (4) A hammer or mallet. *Var. dial.*

MAULARD. A drake, or mallard.

> And with a bolt afterward,
> Anon he hitt a *maulard.*
>   *Arthour and Merlin,* p. 154.

MAULES. The measles. *Somerset.*

MAULKIN. A cloth, usually wetted and attached to a pole, to sweep clean a baker's oven. This word occurs in the dictionaries of Hollyband and Miege, and is still in use in the West of England.

MAULMY. Clammy; sticky. *East.* Probably the same as *Maum* (1).

MAUM. (1) Soft; mellow. MS. Lansd. 1033. (2) Sedate; peaceable; quiet. *North.* (3) A soft brittle stone. *Oxon.*

MAUMET. An idol; a puppet. *Maumetrie,* idolatry. From *Mahomet.* Mawments, puppets, trifles. *North.*

MAUNCE. A blunder; a dilemma. *North.*

MAUNCHES. The sleeves of a coat.

MAUND. (1) To command. *Maundement,* a commandment. (*A.-N.*)

> The king *maunded* him her straybht to marry,
> And for killyng her brother he must dye.
>   *2d Part of Promos and Cassandra,* iv. 2.

(2) To beg. An old cant term. *Maunding,* asking, Dekker's Lanthorne and Candle-Light, ed. 1620, sig. C. ii.

(3) A basket. "A maund or hutch," Florio, p. 5. Still in use. Kennett describes it, "a handbasket with two lids or opening covers, chiefly used by market-women to carry butter and eggs; a maund of merchandise in the Book of Rates is a large hamper containing eight bales or two fats."

MAUNDER. (1) A beggar. See *Maund* (2). Still in use, according to Pegge.

> The divill (like a brave *maunder*) was rid a begging himselfe, and wanted money.
>   *Rowley's Search for Money,* 1609.

(2) To mutter, or grumble; to wander about thoughtfully; to wander in talking.

MAUNDREL. A pickaxe sharpened at each end. Howell, 1660, sect. 51.

II.

MAUNDY. Abusive; saucy. *Glouc.*

MAUNDY-THURSDAY. The day of Christ's commandment on instituting the Lord's Supper. See Hampson, ii. 265.

MAUNGE. To gormandize. *Linc.*

MAUNSE. Threatening. Reliq. Antiq. ii. 54.

MAUNT. My aunt! *North.*

MAUP. To mope about stupidly. *Maups,* a silly fellow. *North.*

MAUT. May; can; might. *North.*

MAUTHER. A girl. *East.* The term is used by Ben Jonson, and others.

MAUTHERN. The ox-eyed daisy. *Wilts.*

MAVEIS. Bad; wicked. *Hearne.*

MAVIN. The margin. *Sussex.*

MAVIS. The singing thrush. See Ray's Dict. Tril. p. 29. Still in use.

> Crowes, popingayes, pyes, pekocks, and *mavies.*
>   *Ashmole's Theat. Chem. Brit.* 1652, p. 115.

MAVORTIAL. Martial.

MAW-BOUND. Costive. *Chesh.* Evidently from *maw,* the stomach. (*A.-S.*)

MAWE. An old game at cards. It was played with a piquet pack of thirty-six cards, and any number of persons from two to six formed the party.

MAWKS. A slattern. *Var. dial.*

MAWL. "To make dirty; to cover with dirt, e. g. when persons are walking along a muddy road, they will say, What *mawling* work it is; and when they arrive at their journey's end, their friends are very likely to say of them, that they are quite *mawled* up," MS. Glossary of Lincolnshire Words by the Rev. James Adcock. "Malde up in shame,' covered up in shame, First Sketches of Henry VI. p. 91, where the amended play reads *mayl'd up.* I added in a note, "*from the spelling* of the word in our text, it seems to be a question whether *maul'd* is not the true reading, *at least of the old play.*" Mr. Dyce, in his Remarks, p. 128, chooses to construe this explanation of the older text into an absurd conjectural emendation of my own. *Mailed* is, however, most certainly the correct reading. "Mayling-clothes," cloths for wrappers, Privy Purse Expences of Henry VIII. p. 159.

MAWMENEE. A dish in ancient cookery, described in the Forme of Cury, p. 19; MS. Sloane 1201, f. 24; Warner's Antiq. Culin. p. 76; Ord. and Reg. pp. 430, 455.

MAWN. Peat. *Heref.*

MAWPUSES. Money. *Linc.*

MAWROLL. The white-horehound.

MAWSEY. Soft and tasteless. *Worc.*

MAWSKIN. The stomach of a calf, when prepared for rennet. *Var. dial.*

MAWTH. The herb dog's-fennel.

MAW-WALLOP. Any filthy mess.

MAXEL. A dunghill. *Kent.* Sometimes *maxon,* a form of *mixen.*

MAY. (1) The blossom of the white-thorn. *As welcome as flowers in May,* heartily welcome. "As mery as flowres in May," MS. Cantab. Ff. v. 48, f. 111.

(2) Maid. A common poetical word.

(3) A maze. *Somerset.*

(4) This proverb is still common:

> For who that doth not whenne he *may*,
> Whenne he wolde hit wol be nay.
> *Cursor Mundi, MS. Col. Trin. Cantab. f. 142.*

MAY-BE. Perhaps. *Var. dial.*

MAY-BEETLE. The cockchafer. *Oxon.* It is also called the May-bug.

MAY-BLOSSOMS. The lily of the valley.

MAY-BUSH. The white-thorn. *Var. dial.*

MAY-DAY. The first of May. It was formerly customary to assemble in the fields early on this day, to welcome the return of spring. Many sports were rife on this occasion.

MAYDEWODE. The herb dog's-fennel.

MAY-GAME. A frolic; a trifle, or jest. A may-game person, a trifler, now often corrupted to *make-game.* The expression occurs in Holinshed, Chron. Ireland, p. 79. "A may-game or simpleton," West. and Cumb. Dial. p. 370.

MAYHAP. Perhaps. *Var. dial.*

MAYMOT. Maimed. *(A.-S.)*

> The pore and the *maymot* for to clothe and fede.
> *Chron. Vilodun. p. 31.*

> And crokette and *maymotte* fatton there hurre hele.
> *Ibid. p. 66.*

MAYNE. To manage. *(A.-N.)*

MAYNEFERE. That part of the armour which covered the mane of a horse. It is mentioned in Hall, Henry IV. f. 12, *mainferres.*

MAYNPURNOURE. One who gives bail or mainprise for another person.

> Whan Cryste schall uchewe hys woundys wete,
> Than Marye be oure *maynpurnoure!*
> *MS. Cantab. Ff. ii. 38, f. 5.*

MAY-POLE. An ale-stake. *Coles.*

MAY-WEED. The feverfew. *Var. dial.*

MAZE. A labyrinth cut or trodden on the turf, generally by schoolboys. I have seen one recently on a hill near Winchester, but the practice is nearly obsolete. "The quaint mazes in the wanton green," Shakespeare.

MAZLE. To wander as if stupified. *Cumb.*

MAZZARD. (1) The head. Sometimes corrupted to *mazer.* Still in use.

> Where thou might'st stickle, without hazard
> Of outrage to thy hide and *mazzard.*
> *Hudibras, I. ii. 708.*

(2) A kind of cherry. *Var. dial.* It is in good esteem for making cherry-brandy.

MAZZARDLY. Knotty. *Somerset.*

ME. (1) Men. *Weber.*

(2) Often used redundantly by our old writers. See Johnson and Nares.

MEACOCK. A silly effeminate fellow.

> And shall I then being fed with this hope prove such a *mecocke*, or a milksop, as to be feared with the tempestuous seas of adversitie.
> *Greene's Guydonius, 1593.*

> Having thus a love beside her husband, although hee was a faire man and well featured, yet she found fault with him, because he was a *meacocke* and milksoppe, not daring to drawe his sworde to revenge her wrongs; wherefore she resolved to entertaine some souldier; and so she did; for one Signyor Lamberto, a brave gentleman, but something hard

facde, sought her favour and found it, and him she entertained for her champion.

> *Newes out of Purgatorie, 1590.*

MEADER. A mower. *Cornw.*

MEAD-MONTH. July. So called because it is the season for mowing.

MEADOW. A field shut up for hay, in distinction to a pasture. *Yorksh.*

MEAK. The same as *Make* (2). It is spelt *meak* by Tusser, p. 14; *meek,* Howard, Household Books, p. 113.

MEAKER. The minnow. *Devon.*

MEAKING. Poorly; drooping. *West.*

MEAL. (1) The milk of a cow produced at one and the same milking. *North.*

(2) A sand heap. *Norfolk.*

(3) A speck or spot. *Westm.*

(4) *Meal-bread,* bread made of good wheat, ground and not sifted. *Meal-poke,* a meal-bag, Robin Hood, i. 98. *Meal-kail,* hasty pudding. *Meal-mouthed,* delicate mouthed, using delicate language. *Meal-seeds,* the husks of the oats. *Meal-time,* dinner time.

(5) To melt. *Becon.*

MEAL'S-MEAT. Meat enough for a meal. Forby has *Meal's-victuals.* See, ii. 212.

MEAN. (1) To moan, or lament. *Shak.* Sometimes in a supplicatory manner, as in Chester Plays, i. 209.

(2) To signify, or matter. *Yorksh.*

(3) To beckon or indicate. *West.*

(4) A female who advocates any cause.

(5) A term in music. "Meane a parte of a songe, *moyen,*" Palsgrave. According to Blount, "an inner part between the treble and base." Glossographia, ed. 1681, p. 404.

> Thi organys so hihe begynne to syng ther messe,
> With treble *meene* and tenor discordyng as I gesse.
> *Lydgate's Minor Poems, p. 54.*

(6) To go lamely. *North.*

MEANELICHE. Moderate. *(A.-S.)*

MEANELS. Spots called flea-bites in white-coloured horses. *North.*

MEANEVERS. Meanwhile. *Salop.*

MEANING. An indication, or hint. *East.*

MEAN-WATER. When cattle void blood, they are said to make a mean-water. *Staff.*

MEAR. To measure. *Somerset.*

MEARLEW-MUSE. "*Agios,* blessings and crossings which the papisticall priests doe use in their holy water, to make a *mearlew muse,*"—Hollyband's Dictionarie, 1593.

MEASLED. Diseased, as hogs. *Var. dial.*

MEASLINGS. The measles. *East.* Skinner gives *meslings,* a Lincolnshire word.

MEASURE. (1) A slow solemn dance, suited even to the most grave persons. It is the translation of *bransle* in the French Alphabet, 1615, p. 150.

(2) A Winchester bushel of corn.

(3) A vein or layer of ore. MS. Lansd. 1033.

MEASURING-CAST. A term at the game of bowls, meaning that two bowls are at such equal distances from the mistress that the spaces must be measured in order to determine who is the winner. It is used metaphorically.

MEAT. (1) Food for cattle. (2) To feed. *Meat-ware*, beans, peas, &c. *West.*

MEATCHLEY. Perfectly well. *South.*

MEAT-EARTH. Cultivated land. *Devon.*

MEATH. (1) Metheglin. Ben Jonson, v. 15. (2) " A word frequent in Lincolnshire, as, *I give thee the meath of the buying*, I give you the option, or let you have the refusal," MS. Lansd. 1033.

MEAT-LIST. Appetite. *Devon.* The Craven Glossary gives *meat-haal*, i. 316.

MEATLY. Tolerably. *Leland.*

MEAT-WARD-PEAS. Dry peas that boil tender and soft. Dean Milles' MS.

MEATY. Fleshy, as cattle. *West.*

MEAWT. To think ; to imagine. *Yorksh.*

MEAZE. The form of a hare.

MEAZLE. (1) A sow. *Exmoor.* It is also a common term of contempt.

(2) " A meazell or blister growing on trees," Florio, ed. 1611, p. 97.

MEAZON. Mice. *Suffolk.*

MEBBY-SCALES. To be in the mebby-scales, i. e. to waver between two opinions. The *may-be* scales ?

MEBLES. Moveable goods. (*A.-N.*)

MECHALL. Wicked ; adulterous. Heywood has *michall*, altered by editor to *mickle!* See Nares, in v. *Michall.*

MECHE. A kind of lamp. " *Lichinus*, a meche," Nominale MS.

MECREDE. Reward. (*A.-N.*)
In hope of suche a glad *mecrede*,
Whiche aftir schalle bifalle in dede.
Gower, MS. Soc. Antiq. 134, f. 189.

MED. May. *I. Wight.*

MEDDLE. (1) To mix together. Hence it is occasionally used for *futuo*.
Thus *medlyde* sche with joy wo,
And with hyre sorwe joy alle so.
Gower, MS. Cantab. Ff. 1. 6, f. 2.

(2) *To neither meddle or make*, not to interfere. *To meddle or make*, to interfere, Merry Wives of Windsor, i. 4.

MEDE. (1) A reward. (*A.-S.*) *Medefully*, deservedly, Apol. Loll. p. 25. Palsgrave has *medefulness*.
Sertanly, as I the telle,
He wille take no *mede*.
MS. Cantab. Ff. v. 48, f. 49.

(2) Humble. R. de. Brunne, MS. Bowes.

MEDESTE. Midst. Chester Plays, ii. 36.

MEDETARDE. Mead cress.

MEDING. Meed, or reward. (*A.-S.*)

MEDIN-HILLS. Dunghills.
And like unto great stinkyng mucle *medin-hilles*,
whiche never do pleasure unto the lande or grounde,
untill their heapes are caste abroade to the profites
of many. *Bullein's Dialogue, 1573, p. 7.*

MEDLAY. Multitude. *Weber.*

MEDLE. A medlar ?
A sat and dinede in a wede,
Under a faire *medle* tre.
Bevas of Hamtoun, p. 52.

MEDLEE. Of a mixed stuff, or colour.

MEDRATELE. The herb *germandria.* See a list of plants in MS. Sloane 5, f. 5.

MEDSINE. Medicine. *Lydgate.*

MEDWE. A meadow or lawn.

MED-WURT. The herb *regina.*

MEDYLSOMES. The cords or traces extending from the first to the last of a team of oxen in a plough.

MEDYOXES. Masks divided by the middle, half man half skeleton. (*Lat.*)

MEECH. To creep about softly. *Kent.* Sometimes *meecher.* See *Mich.*

MEEDLES. The wild orach.

MEEDLESS. Unruly ; tiresome. *North.* "Without measure," Hallamsh. Gloss. p. 116.

MEEF. To move. Cov. Myst. p. 243.

MEE-FLOOR. At Wednesbury in Staffordshire in the nether-coal, the second parting or laming is called the mee-floor, one foot thick.

MEEL. To meddle. *Devon.*

MEENE. Poor ; moderate ; middle.

MEENING. A little shivering or imperfect fit of an ague. *Kent.*

MEEON. " Anything enjoyed between two," Hunter's Hallamsh. Gl. p. 155.

MEER. (1) A mare. *North.*

(2) A cooked kidney. *Yorksh.*

(3) *Meer cot*, a country clown. *Meer cit*, a citizen ignorant of rural matters.

(4) A boundary. A balk of land which Kennett terms a *meer walk*, is so called in Gloucestershire. " An auncient meere or bound whereby land from land and house from house have beene divided," Cotgrave in v. *Sangle.* Huloet has *merestafe*, 1552. " *Meer-stakes*, the trees or pollards that stand as marks or boundaries for the division of parts and parcels in coppices or woods," MS. Lansd. 1033. *Mere-stone*, a boundary stone, Stanihurst, p. 48, called a *meer-stang* in Westmoreland. Harrison, p. 234, mentions a kind of stone called *meere-stone.*

(5) " Meer is a measure of 29 yards in the low peak of Darbyshire, and 31 in the high," Blount's Glossographia, ed. 1681, p. 410.

MEESE. A mead, field, or pasture. A certain toft or *meese* place, Carlisle's Accounts of Charities, p. 297.

MEET. Even. See Tarlton's Jests, p. 14 ; Middleton, iii. 262. Still in use. *Meets.* Palmer's Gloss. p. 63. *To meet with*, to be even with, to counteract.

MEETERLY. Tolerably ; handsomely ; modestly ; indifferently. *North.* Meetelie, tolerably, Holinshed, Hist. of England, i. 54.

MEETINER. A dissenter, one who frequents a meeting-house. *East.*

MEET-NOW. Just now. *North.*

MEEVERLY. Easily ; slowly. *Yorksh.*

MEG. The mark pitched at in playing the game of quoits. *West.*

MEGGY-MONNY-LEGS. The millepes. *North.*

MEG-HARRY. A rough hoyden girl. *Lanc.*

MEGIOWLER. A large moth. *Cornw.*

MEGRIMS. Whims ; fancies ; bad spirits. *West.* Perhaps from the disease so called. " *Megre*, a sickenesse, *maigre*," Palsgrave.

And whenne tythynges hereof come to kyng
Philippe, he went to mete hym in the felde with a
few menȝes. *MS. Lincoln A. i. 17, f. 3.*

MEOLLEN. Mills. (*A.-S.*)

MEPHOSTOPHILUS. A well-known character in the old legend of Dr. Faustus. It was
formerly so common as to be used as a term
of jocular reproach.

MER. Mayor. *Hearne.*

MERCENRIKE. The kingdom of Mercia.

MERCERYE. Goods sold by a mercer.

　　　The chapmen of suche *mercerye.*
　　　　Gower, MS. Soc. Antiq. 134, f. 81.

MERCHANT. (1) Formerly a familiar form of
address, equivalent to *chap, fellow.*

(2) A merchant-vessel; a trader.

MERCHANT-VENTURERS. A company of
merchants, who traded with Russia, Turkey,
and other distant parts.

　　Well is he tearmd a *merchant-venturer,*
　　Since he doth venter lands, and goods and all,
　　When he doth travell for his traffique far,
　　Little he knowes what fortune may befall,
　　Or rather, what mis-fortune happen shall:
　　Sometimes he splits his ship against a rocke;
　　Loosing his men, his goods, his wealth, his stocke.
　　　　The Affectionate Shepheard, 1594.

MERCHE. The herb smallage.

MERCIABLE. Merciful. (*A.-N.*)

　　Nowe, lady, sith thou canst and eeke wilt
　　Bee to the stede of Adam *mercyable.*
　　　Romance of the Monk, Sion College MS.

　　That God wol nouȝt be *merciable*
　　So gret a synne to forȝeve.
　　　　Gower, MS. Soc. Antiq. 134, f. 125.

　The height of the heavens is not so present over
the earth, as is his *merciable* goodness over them
that worship him. *Becon's Works,* p. 421.

MERCIEN. To thank. (*A.-N.*)

MERCIFY. To pity. *Spenser.*

MERCURY. (1) The wild orache. *Linc.*

(2) White arsenic. *North.*

MERCY. *I cry you mercy,* an old idiom nearly
equivalent to our *I beg your pardon.*

　　And thi luffsom eyne two
　　Loke on me, as I wer thi fo!
　　God lemane, I cry the *mersye,*
　　Thou late be all this reufull crye,
　　And telle me, lady, fore thi prow,
　　What thing may the helpe now.
　　　　MS. Ashmole 61, xv. Cent.

MERD. Dung, or excrement.

MERE. (1) A lake. Still in use. "A mere, or
water whereunto an arme of the sea floweth,"
Baret, 1580.

(2) Whole; entire; absolute.

(3) A private carriage-road. *North.*

MERECROP. The herb pimpernel.

MERELLE. The world.

　　So that undir the clerkis lawe,
　　Men sen the *merelle* almis drawe.
　　　　Gower, MS. Soc. Antiq. 134, f. 33.

MERELY. Simply; wholly; absolutely. See
Cotgrave, in v. *Nu.*

MERESAUCE. Brine for pickling or soaking
meat in. *Palsgrave.* See the Ordinances
and Reg. pp. 435, 459.

MERESWYNE. A dolphin.

Grassede as a *mereswyne* with corkes fulle huge.
　　　Morte Arthure, MS. Lincoln, f. 65.

MEREWIS. Marrow. *Baber.*

MERGHE. Marrow. "The *merghe* of a fresche
calfe" is mentioned in MS. Med. Linc. f. 283;
"the *merghe* of a gose-wenge." MS. ibid. f.
285. It occurs in Nominale MS.

MERGIN. The mortar or cement found in old
walls. *Norfolk.*

MERGORE. Merrier. *Hearne.*

MERILLS. The game of morris. (*Fr.*)

MERIT. Profit; advantage.

MERITORIE. Meritorious. (*A.-N.*)

　And all thy dedis, though they ben good and
meritorye, thou shalt sette at nought.
　　　Caxton's Divers Fruytful Ghostly Maters.

　　How *meritorye* is thilke dede
　　Of charité to clothe and fede.
　　　　Gower, MS. Soc. Antiq. 134, f. 33.

MERKE. (1) Dark; murky. (*A.-S.*)

　　For he was lefte there allone,
　　And *merké* nyghte felle hym upon.
　　　　MS. Cantab. Ff. ii. 38, f. 240.

(2) A sign, or mark. (*A.-S.*)

(3) To be troubled, or disturbed.

(4) To strike; to cleave in sunder.

MERKIN. False hair, generally explained *pubes
mulieris ascititia.* Jordan tells us that spectators at shows often "screwed" themselves
up in the balconies to avoid the fire-works
which "instantly assaulted the perukes of the
gallants and the *merkins* of the madams."

　　Why dost thou reach thy *merkin,* now half dust?
　　Why dost provoke the ashes of thy lust?
　　　　Fletcher's Poems, p. 95.

　Mirkin rubs of and often spoiles the sport.
　　　　MS. Harl. 7312, p. 124.

MERLE. A blackbird. *Drayton.*

MERLIN. A very small species of hawk. See
Gent. Rec. ii. 30. Chaucer spells it *merlion.*

MERMAID. A cant term for a whore.

MEROWE. Delicate. (*A.-S.*) The copy in
the Auchinleck MS. reads *merugh.*

　　I was so lytull and so *merowe*
　　That every man callyd me dwarowe.
　　　　MS. Cantab. Ff. ii. 38, f. 112.

MERROKES. The fur of the martern?

MERRY. (1) The wild cherry. Aubrey's Wilts,
Royal Soc. MS. p. 136.

(2) Fair, applied to the weather. *Merryweather*
was formerly an idiomatic phrase for joy,
pleasure, or delight. *Mery,* pleasantly, Hartshorne, p. 46.

　　Mery tyme is in aperelle,
　　That mekyll schewys of manys wylle;
　　In feldys and medowys flowyrs spryng,
　　In grovys and wodes foules syng;
　　Than wex ȝong men jolyffe,
　　And than prevyth man and wyffe.
　　　　MS. Ashmole 61, xv. Cent.

　Whi, doith not thi cow make *myry-wedir* in thy dish?
　　　　MS. Digby 41, f. 8.

(3) The following proverb was a great favourite
with our ancestors,—

　　　'Tis merry in hall,
　　　When beards wag all!

MERRYBAUKS. A cold posset. *Derb.* "A
sillibub or merribowke," Cotgrave.

MERRY-BEGOTTEN. Illegitimate. *North.*

MERRY-DANCERS. A name for the Northern lights, or *aurora borealis.*

MERRY-GO-DOWN. An old cant term for strong ale, or huffcap.

MERRY-MAKE. Sport. See Nares.

MERRYNESS. Joy. *Palsgrave.*

MERRY-NIGHT. A rustic ball; a night appropriated to mirth, festivity, and various amusements. *North.*

MERRY-TROTTER. A swing. *North.* The *meritot* is mentioned by Chaucer. "*Merry-trotter*, a rope fastened at each end to a beam or branch of a tree making a curve at the bottom near the floor, or ground, in which a child can sit, and holding fast by each side of the rope is swung backwards and forwards," MS. Yorksh. Gloss.

MERSEMENT. Fine or amercement. See the Gesta Romanorum, p. 288.

MERSHALLE. One who attends to horses; a farrier; a blacksmith.

MERSMALEWE. The marshmallow, mentioned in MS. Sloane 5, f. 2.

MERTH. Greatness; extent. *Cumb.*

MERTILLOGE. A martyrology. It occurs in Nominale MS. xv. Cent.

MERVAILLE. Wonder; marvel. (*A.-N.*)

MERY. Marrow. "The *mery* of a gose," Berners, sig. A. ii. See *Merghe.*

MERYD. (1) Dipped; soaked.

(2) Merit. Audelay's Poems, p. 26.

MESANTER. Misadventure. (*A.-N.*) Still in use, pronounced *mishanter.*

> And ther with ribbes four,
> The palnem starf with *misantour.*
>
> *Arthour and Merlin*, p. 229.

MESCHAUNT. Miserable; wicked.

MESCHEVE. To harm, or hurt. (*A.-N.*)

> For ȝong menne, oftene tymes traystand to mekille
> In thaire awenne doghtynes, thurghe thaire awene
> foly ere mescheved. *MS. Lincoln A. i. 17, f. 3.*

MESE. (1) To soothe. *Northumb.* It occurs in the Towneley Myst. p. 175.

(2) A meal. Perceval, 455, 486.

> By Hym that werede the crowne of thorne,
> In warre tyme blewe he never his horne,
> Ne darrere boghte no *mese.*
>
> *MS. Lincoln A. i. 17, f. 140.*

(3) Moss. *Dorset.*

MESELRYE. The leprosy. (*A.-N.*)

> And sum hadde vysages of *meselrye,*
> And some were lyke foule maumetrye.
>
> *MS. Harl. 1701, f. 68.*

MESEYSE. Trouble. St. Brandan, p. 24.

> Alle the selie men that hy myȝte fynde,
> That povere and feble were,
> In siknesse and in *meseyse,*
> Hy hem broȝte to-gydere there.
>
> *MS. Trin. Coll. Oxon. 57.*

MESH. (1) A marsh. *South.*

(2) A gap in a hedge. *West.*

MESNE. Means.

MESON. The mizen mast. *Palsgrave.*

MESPRISE. To despise, or contemn. (*A.-N.*)

MESS. (1) To muddle. *Var. dial.*

(2) To mess meat, to sort it in messes for the table. A party of four people dining together was called a mess, a term which is still retained in the army for the officers' dinner. *Lower messes*, parties at the lower end of a hall at dinner.

(3) Truly; indeed. *Cumb.* Perhaps from the old oath, By the mass!

(4) To serve cattle with hay. *West.*

(5) A gang, or company. *East.*

MESSAGE. A messenger. (*A.-N.*)

MESSE. (1) The mass. (*A.-S.*)

(2) A messuage or tenement.

(3) The Messiah. Sharp's Cov. Myst. p. 96.

MESSEL. (1) A leper. It is used in old plays as a term of contempt.

> So speketh the gospel of thys vertu
> How a *mesyl* come to Jhesu.
>
> *MS. Harl. 1701, f. 76.*

(2) A table. Nominale MS.

MESSENE. To dazzle the eyes. *Pr. Parv.*

MESSET. A cur. "Dame Julia's messet," Hall's Poems, 1646. Still in use.

MESTE-DEL. The greatest part. (*A.-S.*)

MESTIER. Occupation. (*A.-N.*) See the Boke of Curtasye, p. 15.

MESTORET. Needed. *Ritson.*

MESURABLE. Moderate. (*A.-N.*) *Mesure*, moderation.

MET. (1) A bushel. Some writers say, two bushels. *Met-poke*, a narrow bag to contain a met. See Carlisle on Charities, p. 298.

(2) A limit or boundary. (*Lat.*)

(3) Measured. Also, to measure. A measure of any kind was so called. See Wright's Anec. Lit. pp. 106, 108.

> First forthi shewe we hegh mesure, that es to say
> howe any thynge that has heght may be *met* howe
> hegh it es, and this may be done in many maneres.
>
> *MS. Sloane 213.*

> I knowe the *mett* welle and fyne,
> The lenȝte of a snayle. *MS. Porkington 10.*

(4) Dreamed. (*A.-S.*)

> Also he *met* that a lampe so bryȝt
> Hongede an heyȝe upoun that tre.
>
> *Chron. Vilodun. p. 26*

METAL. Materials for roads. *North.*

METE-FORME. A form or long seat used for sitting on at dinner-time.

> And whenne his swerde brokene was,
> A mete-forme he gatt percas,
> And there-with he ganne hym were.
>
> *MS. Lincoln A. i. 17, f. 106*

METEING. Dreaming. (*A.-S.*)

> In this time Lot the king
> In bed was in gret *meteing.*
>
> *Arthour and Merlin*, p. 141

METELLES. Dreams. (*A.-S.*)

> In thys hest ys forbode alle manere mawmetrye,
> ydolatrye, wychecraft, enchantementes, redyngge of
> *metelles* and alle mysbyleve. *MS. Burney 356, f. 85.*

METELY. Measurely; fitly.

> Of heiȝte he was a *metely* mon,
> Nouther to grete ny to smal.
>
> *Cursor Mundi, MS. Coll. Trin. Cantab. f. 115.*

METER. Fitter. (*A.-S.*)

> In whiche doynge he thought polecie more *meter*
> to be used then force. *Hall's Union, 1548.*

METERER. A poet. *Drayton.*

METE-ROD. A measuring rod. See Withals, ed. 1608, p. 60. *Mete-wand*, Becon's Works, p. 5. "Metwand of gold," Davies' Rites, ed. 1672, p. 159.

METESEL. Dinner-time. (*A.-S.*)

METHE. (1) Courteous. (*A.-S.*)

> Thou was *methe* and meke as maydene for mylde.
> *MS. Lincoln A. L 17, f. 231.*

> Alle that meyné mylde and *moth*
> Went hem into Nazareth.
> *Cursor Mundi, MS. Coll. Trin. Cantab. f. 76.*

(2) Mead; metheglin. See Holinshed, Hist. England, i. 194; W. Mapes, p. 350; Nugæ Poeticæ, p. 10. Metheglin was anciently made of a great variety of materials. See a receipt for it in MS. Sloane 1672, f. 127.

(3) To choke, or breathe hardly. *Cumb.*

METHFUL. Tired; weary. (*A.-S.*)

> I am *methful* for I slepe,
> And I rans for Laverd me kepe.
> *MS. Cotton. Vespas, D. vii. f. 2.*

METHRIDATUM. An antidote against infection, so called from Mithridates, its reputed inventor.

> But what brave spirit could be content to sit in his shop, with a flapet of wood before him, selling *Mathridatum* and dragons water to infected houses.
> *The Knight of the Burning Pestle,* 1635.

METICULOUS. Timorous. It occurs in Topsell's Historie of Serpents, 1608, p. 116.

METRETIS. Measures. *Baber.*

METREZA. A mistress. (*Ital.*)

METRICIENS. Writers in verse.

METROPOLE. A metropolis. It occurs in Holinshed, Conq. Ireland, p. 4.

METTER. A measurer. *North.*

METTES. Manners? *Pleys,* Harl. MS.

> For to reffe hyme wykkydly
> With wrange *mettes* or maystry.
> *R de Brunne, MS. Bowes, p. 10.*

MEVE. To move. (*A.-N.*)

MEVERLY. Bashful; shy; mild. *North.*

MEVY. The thrush. *Browne.*

MEW. (1) Mowed. *Yorksh.*

(2) To moult. Hence, to change the dress. A cage for moulting hawks was called a *mewe.*

> For the better preservation of their health they strowed mint and sage about them; and for the speedier *mewing* of their feathers, they gave them the slough of a snake, or a tortoise out of the shell, or a green lizard cut in pieces.
> *Aubrey's Wilts, MS. Royal Soc. p. 341.*

(3) A stack of corn, or hay. *North.*

MEWET. Mute; dumb. (*A.-N.*)

MEWS. (1) Moss. *Exmoor.*

(2) Public stables. *Var. dial.*

MEWT. The dung of a hawk. It is applied to a dog in Du Bartas, p. 584.

MEYND. Mixed; mingled.

> Off rody colour *meynd* somdelle with rede.
> *MS. Cantab. Ff. i. 6, f. 140.*

> She *meynd* her weeping with his blood, and kissing all his face,
> (Which now became as cold as yse) she cryde in wofull case,
> Alas, what chaunce, my Pyramus, hath parted thee and mee.
> *Golding's Ovid, 1567.*

MEYNE. The company or crew.

> Whanne al was redy, *meyné* and vitaille,
> They bide not but wynde for to saille.
> *MS. Digby 230,* xv. Cent.

MEYRE. A mayor. "*Præses,* a meyre," MS. Egerton 829, f. 78.

MEYTE. Meat; dinner.

> Off hym shalle we laȝ alle
> At the *meyte* when that we bene.
> *MS. Cantab. Ff. v. 48, f. 53.*

MEZZIL-FACED. Red with pimples. *Lanc.* From the old word *mesel?*

MICH. To skulk, or hide secretly; to play truant. "That mite is *miching* in this grove," Lilly, ed. 1632, sig. Aa. ix. Minsheu has, "to miche, or secretly to hide himselfe out of the way, as truants doe from schoole." It is still used in exactly this sense in the provinces. "To miche, to shrug or sneake in some corner, and with pouting lips to shew anger, as an ape being beaten and grinning with his teeth," Florio, p. 6. "*Miche,* to creep softly," MS. Yorksh. Gl. *Micher,* derived from this verb, may be explained, a sly thief, one who steals things of small value, or more usually, a truant or skulking fellow. "*Mecher,* a lytell thefe, *laronceau,*" Palsgrave. It occurs in Rom. of the Rose, 6541, where the A. N. original reads *kierres,* voleur. "Theyves, mychers, and cut-purse," Kennett, p. 105. Grose has, "*Michers,* thieves, pilferers," as a Norfolk word, and it is also given in the same sense in MS. Lansd. 1033. "Thefes and mychers keyn," Towneley Myst. p. 216. "A blackberry moucher, an egregious truant," Dean Milles' MS. p. 180. The application of the word in the sense of truant is often found in later writers, as in Shakespeare, who is well illustrated by the following passage, "in the Forest of Dean to mooche blackberries, or simply to mooch, means to pick blackberries, and blackberries have thus obtained there the name of mooches," Heref. Gl. p. 69. "Fy, fy, it will not besceme us to playe the mychers," Elyot, ed. 1559, in v. *Apage.* "How like a *micher* he standes, as though he had trewanted from honestie," Lilly's Mother Bombie, 1594. "*Circumforanus,* a mycher," Nominale MS. "*Mike,* to idle, loiter," Salop. Antiq. p. 505. It was often used as a term of contempt; Hollyband gives it as the translation of *caignard,* and Cotgrave has, "*Chiche-face,* a chichiface, micher, sneake-bill, wretched fellow."

> Another should have spoke us two betweene,
> But, like a *meacher,* hee's not to be seene,
> Hee's runne away even in the very nick.
> *MS. Poems,* xvii. Cent.

MICHE. (1) Much; great. *Michel,* greatness. *Mychen,* much, Reliq. Antiq. ii. 47.

> Alle the *myche* tresour that traytour had wonnene,
> To commons of the contré, clergye and other.
> *Morte Arthure, MS. Lincoln, f. 66.*

> For hir mi luf is *miche,* I wene.
> *Guy of Warwick,* p. 6.

(2) A kind of rich fur.

(3) A loaf of bread. "With-oute wyn and *miche.*" Reliq. Antiq. ii. 192.

MICHEL. Michaelmas. *Tusser*, p. 19.

MICHELWORT. Elleborus albus. See a list of plants in MS. Sloane 5, f. 5.

MICH-WHAT. Much the same. *North.*

MICKLE. Much; great. *North.* Hence *mickles*, size, greatness.

    Owe he ouȝt *myculle* in the cuntré.
                MS. Cantab. Ff. v. 48, f. 47.

MICKLED. Benumbed. *Exmoor.*

MID. (1) Might. *Somerset.*

(2) The middle; the centre. *Cumb.*

(3) With. *Kyng Alisaunder*, 852.

MID-ALLEY. The nave, or middle aisle.

MIDDEN. A dung-hill. *North.* Ray spells it *midding*, and thinks it is derived from *mud.* It is also a contemptuous name for a very dirty woman. *Midden-crow*, the carrion crow; also called a *midden-daup.*

    A fowler *myddyng* of vyleyn
    Sawyst thou never in londe of peese.
                MS. Cantab. Ff. ii. 38, f. 29.

    A fowler *myddyng* sawe you never none,
    Than a mane es wyth flesche and bone.
           Hampole, MS. Bowes, p. 30.

MIDDES. The middle, or midst. *Middes-part*, the centre of anything.

MIDDLE-BAND. The small piece of pliable leather or skin which passes through the two caps of a flail, joining the hand-staff and swingle. *Var. dial.*

MIDDLE-EARTH. The world. (*A.-S.*)

    And had oon the feyrest orchard
    That was yn alle thys *myddyll-erd.*
              MS. Cantab. Ff. ii. 38, f. 129.

MIDDLE-SPEAR. The upright beam that takes the two leaves of a barn-door. In Yorkshire it is termed a *mid-feather.*

MIDDLE-STEAD. The threshing-floor, which is generally in the middle of a barn. *East.*

MIDDLING. Not in good health. *Worc.* Middling-sharp, tolerably well.

MIDDLING-GOSSIP. A go-between.

MIDGE. A gnat; a very small fly. Hence applied to a dwarf. *North.* "A myge, *sicoma*," Nominale MS.

MIDGEN. The mesentery gland of a pig. Also termed a *midgerim.*

MIDIDONE. Quickly; immediately. It is wrongly explained by Weber, the only glossary in which the word occurs.

    Gii is ogain went ful sone,
    And al his feren *midydone.*
             Gy of Warwike, p. 69.

    The cherl bent his bowe sone,
    And smot a doke *mididone.*
          Arthour and Merlin, p. 154.

MIDJANS. Small pieces; mites. *Cornw.*

MIDLEG. The calf of the leg.

MID-MORN. Nine o'clock, a. m.

MID-OVERNONE. Three o'clock, p. m. It occurs in MS. Cotton. Vespas. D. vii.

MIDREDE. The midriff. "*Diafragma*, a mydrede." Nominale MS.

MIDSUMMER-DOR. The May-bug. *Cambr.*

MIDSUMMER-MOON. It is Midsummer Moon with you, i. e. you are mad.

MIDWARD. Towards the middle. (*A.-S.*)

    The bryght helme was crokea downe
    Unto the *mydward* of hys crowne.
           MS. Cantab. Ff. ii. 38, f. 161.

MID-WINTER. Christmas. (*A.-S.*)

    Whas never syche noblay in no manys tyme
    Mad in *Mydwynter* in tha Weste marchya.
         Morte Arthure, MS. Lincoln, f. 53.

MIE. To pound, or beat. Hence *miere*, a mortar, an instrument for breaking or pounding anything. "*Micatorium*, a myere," Nominale MS. See Ducange, in v. *Micatoria*, which is glossed by A. N. *esmieure.*

MIFF. (1) Displeasure; ill-humour, but generally in a slight degree. *Var. dial.*

    Deal Gainsborough a lash, for pride so stiff,
    Who robs us of such pleasure for a *miff.*
             Peter Pindar, i. 81.

(2) A mow, or rick. *North.*

MIFF-MAFF. Nonsense. *North.*

MIFFY. The devil. *Glouc.*

MIG. Mud. (*A.-S.*)

MIGHELL. Michael. *Palsgrave.* Mihill is very common in old writers.

    The sothfastenes and nothing hele,
    That thou herdest of seynt *Myȝhele.*
       Cursor Mundi, MS. Coll. Trin. Cantab. f. 110.

MIGHTFUL. Full of might; powerful.

MIGHTSOMNES. Power. It occurs in MS. Cotton. Vespas. D. vii.

MIGHTY. Fine; gay. *Somerset.*

MIGNIARD. Tender; delicate. (*Fr.*)

MIGNON. To flatter. (*Fr.*)

MIHTINGE. Power. (*A.-S.*)

    For I knew noht boke writen swa,
    In thi *mihtinges*, Laverd, in sal I ga.
          MS. Egerton 614, f. 47.

MIKELAND. Increasing. It occurs in MS. Cotton. Vespas. D. vii.

MIKELHEDE. Greatness; extent. (*A.-S.*)

MILCE. Mercy; pity. (*A.-S.*)

    Thurch his *milce* was y-bore,
    And bought al that was forlore.
         Arthour and Merlin, p. 26.

MILCH. White. *Hamlet*, ii. 2. Douce has confused this term with *milce*, Illust. ii. 238.

MILCHY. Melted corn. *Cornw.*

MILD. Gentle-flavoured. *Var. dial.*

MILDER. To moulder; to turn to dust. *Linc.*

MILDNESS. Mercy. *Lydgate.*

MILE. Michael. *East.* Jennings has *Milemas*, Michaelmas.

MILES-ENDWAYS. Very long miles. *West.*

MILFOL. Merciful. *Hearne.*

MILGIN. A pumpkin. *Norf.* Pies made in that shape are called *milgin-pies.*

MILK-BROTH. Gruel made with milk. *East.*

MILKEE. To milk a little. *Somerset.*

MILKER. A cow that gives milk.

MILK-FORK. A forked branch of oak used for hanging the milk-pails on.

MILK-LEAD. A cistern lined with lead, used for laying milk in. *West.*

MILKNESS. A dairy. Also, any white dishes made with milk. *North.*

MILK-SELE. A milk-pail. "*Multrale*, a mylksele," Nominale MS.

MILKY. To milk. *Wilts.*

MILL. To rob, or steal. "Mill a ken, rob a house," Dekker's Lanthorne and Candle-Light, ed. 1620, sig. C. ii.

MILLARS-COATS. Brigandines.

MILLED. Tipsy. *Newc.*

MILLED-MONEY. Was first coined in this country in 1561. It is frequently alluded to by our early writers. "Fortie Mark Milsixpences," Citye Match, 1639, p. 14.

MILLER. The large white moth.

MILLERAY. A gold coin worth 14*s.*

MILLER'S-THUMB. The bull-head, a small fish. "No bigger than a miller's thumb," a common simile.

> Therefore as I, who from a groom,
> No bigger than a *miller's thumb.*
>
> *Cotton's Works,* 1734, p. 159.

MILLETS. A disease in the fetlocks of horses. Topsell, 1607, p. 431.

MILL-EYE. The hole through which the grinded corn falls below.

MILL-HOLMS. Watery places about a milldam, MS. Lansd. 1033. *Millums,* Hallamshire Gloss. p. 117.

MILLON. A melon. *Palsgrave.*

MILL-STONE. *To see into a mill-stone,* to fathom a secret. *To weep mill-stones,* not to weep at all.

MILN. A mill. *Milner,* a miller. "*Assitus,* a mylnerpyt," Nominale MS. *Mylnestons,* Reliq. Antiq. i. 81.

> And so fell in the chase of them, that many of them were slayne, and, namely, at a *mylene,* in the medowe fast by the towne, were many drownyd; many rann towards the towne; many to the churche, to the abbey, and els where, as they best myght. *Arrival of King Edward IV,* p. 30.

MILOK. *Hic mello, mellonis,* Anglice, a meloun or mylok, MS. Bib. Reg. 12 B. i. f. 17.

MILSFOLNESSE. Mercy. (*A.-S.*) "Sheu mylsfolnesse," Reliq. Antiq. i. 88.

MILT. (1) The rot in sheep. *West.*

(2) The soft roe of a fish. *Yorksh.*

MILTHE. To pity; to pardon. (*A.-S.*) It occurs in MS. Cotton. Vespas. D. vii. *Mylt,* made merciful, Octovian, 249.

MILWYN. Green fish. *Lanc.*

MIM. Primly silent. *Mimminy primminy* has a similar meaning.

MIMMAM. A bog. *Berks.*

MIMMOCKING. Puny; weakly. *West.*

MIN. (1) The lesser. (*Germ.*)

(2) Man. Used in contempt. *West.*

MINATING. Threatening. (*Lat.*) See Hayward's Queen Elizabeth, p. 58.

MINCE. To walk in an affected manner. "To jump about," MS. Devon Gloss. *Don't mince the matter,* do not conceal or soften anything in it.

MINCH. A nun. *Mynchys,* Wright's Monastic Letters, p. 228. The nunnery at Littlemore is still called the minchery. "This house of mynchyn," MS. Cantab. Dd. viii. 2.

> There was a *mynchun* withinne that abbay tho,
> The wheche was come off heyse lynage.
>
> *Chron. Vilodun.* p. 110.

MIND. (1) To remember; to observe; to notice particularly. *Var. dial.*

(2) To watch; to take care of. *West.*

(3) *Took in mind,* was offended.

(4) To intend. Middleton, i. 179.

MINDE. Remembrance. (*A.-S.*)

MINDING. Recollection. *West.*

MINE. (1) To penetrate. (*A.-N.*)

(2) To long for. *Devon.*

(3) Mien; countenance. *Shak.*

(4) Any kind of mineral. *Kent.*

(5) Was formerly a familiar adjunct, sister-mine, brother-mine, &c. "Mam, *mother-mine,* or mammie, as children first call their mothers," Florio, p. 297. *Mother of mee,* Hoffman, 1631.

MINE-EARTH. A white earth near the surface of the ground, a certain sign or indication of iron ore or iron stone. *Staff.*

MINEVER. The fur of the ermine mixed with that of the small weasel. The white stoat is called a *minifer* in Norfolk.

MING. (1) To mind or observe. To ming at one, to mention. *North.* To ming the miller's eye out, i. e. to begin more than your materials suffer you to complete.

(2) To mix or mingle. To ming bread, to knead it. *East.*

> Hys sorow *myngyd* alle hys mode,
> Whan the corps in armys he hente.
>
> *MS. Harl. 2252, f. 133.*

MINGE. To mention. Still in use. *Mingd,* Batchelor's Orthoep. Anal. p. 138.

MINGINATER. "One that makes fret-work; it is a rustick word used in some prat [part] of Yorkshire," Ray ed. 1674, p. 33.

MINGING. The same as *Meening,* q. v.

MINGLE. (1) A contr. for *mine ingle.*

(2) A mixture. *Mingle-cum-por, mingle-mangle,* a confused mixture of anything. "A mingle mangle of manie matters in one booke," Nomenclator, 1585, p. 5. "Such a confused mingle mangle, and varietie of apish toyes in apparrell," Wright's Summons for Sleepers, 1589. See Florio, pp. 93, 404.

MING-WORT. Wormwood. *North.*

MINIFER-PIN. The smallest sized pin of the common sort. *East.*

MINIKE. Trifling; cheating.

MINIKIN. (1) Small; delicate; elegant. "To *minikin* Nan," Tusser, p. xxv. "A minikin, a fine mincing lass," Kennett, MS. "A minikin wench, a smirking lasse," Florio, p. 315. Still in use in Devon.

(2) A lute-string. It was properly the treble-string of a lute or fiddle. Nares's explanation is wrong, and the quotations given by Mr. Dyce, Middleton, ii. 127, do not establish his definition. "Leute stringes called mynikins," Brit. Bibl. ii. 407.

MINIM. (1) The minnow. *Somerset.*

(2) A kind of brown tawny colour.

MINION. (1) A kind of gun. "Minions all," Gaulfrido and Barnardo, 1570. Bourne, Inventions or Devises, 1578, mentions it as requiring shot three inches in diameter.

(2) Pleasant; agreeable. (*Fr.*)

> The straunge pagiauntes, the behavior of the lordes, the beautie of the ladies, the sumptuous feast, the delicate viander, the marciall justes, the fierce turnals, the lustie daunces, and the *minion* songes.
> *Hall, Henry VI. f. 66.*

MINISH. To diminish.

> Wherfore to abbridge his power, and to *minishe* his authoritie, they determined to bryng hym into the hatred of the people, and into the disdain of the nobilitie.
> *Hall, Henry VI. f. 81.*

MINISTERS. Minstrels. *Chaucer.*

MINISTRES. Officers of justice. (*A.-N.*)

MINK. To attempt; to aim at. *East.*

MINK-MEAT. Mixed food for fowls, &c. *East.*

MINKS. A kind of fur. (*Fr.*)

MINNE. To think; to remember. (*A.-S.*)

> Man, my mercy yf thou hyt *mynned*,
> I have the yt shewyd on many wyse,
> Sythen the tyme that thou fyrste synned
> Aȝenste my heest in paradyse.
> *MS. Cantab. Ff. ii. 38, f. 17.*

> The clowdys ovyr-caste, all lyȝt was leste,
> Hys myȝt was more then ye myȝt *mynne*.
> *MS. Cantab. Ff. ii. 38, f. 47.*

> Syr of one thinge I wolle you *mynne*,
> And beseche you for to spede.
> *MS. Harl. 2252, f. 88.*

MINNETS. Small pebbles, &c. *Var. dial.* Small particles of anything are called *minnetsons*, or *minittoons*.

> And alle the *mynyssionys* of that nayle,
> That weron fyled of that nayle with the file.
> *Chron. Vilodun. p. 41.*

MINNIN-ON.. A luncheon. *Yorksh.*

MINNOK. One who affects much delicacy. *East.* This is the reading of the 4to. ed. in Mids. Night's Dream, iii. 2. Forby considers it the right reading, but the folio *mimick*, an actor, is no doubt correct.

MINNY. Mother. *North.*

MINNYNG-DAY. The anniversary festival in which prayers were offered up for the souls of the deceased. (*A.-S.*)

> A solempne feste make and holde
> On hys wyvys *mynnyng-day*.
> *MS. Cantab. Ff. ii. 38, f. 244.*

MINORESSE. A nun under the rule of St. Clare. *Chaucer.*

MINOUR. A miner; an excavator.

> *Mynurs* they make yn hyllys holes,
> As yn the West cuntré men seke coles.
> *MS. Harl. 1701, f. 71.*

MINTE. (1) To intend. Also, intended. Still used in Lincolnshire, to endeavour.

> To bere hym downe he had *mynte*,
> In hys schylde he sye the dynte.
> *MS. Cantab. Ff. ii. 38, f. 247*

(2) To aim; to strike, or beat.

> Tryamowre at hym come *mynte*,
> Hys swerde felle fro hym at that dynte,
> To the grownde can hyt goo!
> Then was Burlonde fulle gladd,
> And that lady was sore adradd;
> Knyghtys were fulle woo!
> *MS. Cantab. Ff. ii. 38, f. 81.*

> Wyth grete wrath he can *mynte*,
> But he fayled of hys dynte.
> *MS. Cantab. Ff. ii. 38, f. 189.*

(3) To resemble. *Somerset.*

(4) A mite. *Minty*, mity. *West.*

(5) Gold. See Brit. Bibl. ii. 521.

(6) To invent, or feign. *North.*

> Many times pretending an indisposition of health, or some other *minted* excuse, to prevent her journey, by remaining there where shee had planted her fancy.
> *The Two Lancashire Lovers*, 1640, p. 60

MINUTE. A mite. "*To a minute*, accurately, not only as to time, but also as to knowledge," Heref. Gloss. p. 67.

MIP. A nymph.

MIPLIN. A delicate feeder. *Derb.*

MIR. A marsh, or bog. (*A.-S.*)

MIRCHIVOUS. Mischievous. *Devon.*

MIRE-BANK. A separation. *Norf.*

MIRE-DRUM. A bittern. "A myrdrumnyll or a buture," Ortus Vocab. *North.*

MIRGURRE. Merrier; more pleasant.

> That hee had delyveryd hym ouȝt of his peynne,
> And brouȝt hym into a *mirgurre* plase.
> *Chron. Vilodun. p. 125.*

MIRI. Merry; pleasant. (*A.-S.*)

> Floures schewen her forjoun,
> *Miri* it is in feld and toun.
> *Arthour and Merlin, p 65.*

MIRKE. (1) To darken. *Palsgrave.* (2) Dark, Holinshed, Hist. Scot. p. 51. (3) Darkness.

> Ȝyf thou brake ever any kyrke,
> On day or yn nyȝt, yn *myrke*,
> Thou art acursed, thou woste weyl.
> *MS. Harl. 1701, f. 15.*

MIRKSHUT. Twilight. *Glouc.*

MIRKSOME. Dark. *Spenser.*

MIRL. To pine; to grieve. *North.*

MIRSHTY. Mischief. *Somerset.*

MIRTHE. To rejoice. It occurs in MS. Cotton. Vespas. D. vii. (*A.-S.*) *Mirthes*, tunes, Tristrem, p. 204.

MIRTLE. To crumble, as ground, &c. *North.*

MISAGAFT. Mistaken; misgiven. *Sussex.*

MISAGREE. To disagree. (*A.-N.*)

MIS-BEDEN. To injure. (*A.-S.*)

MISBEHOLDEN. Disobliging. *North.*

MIS-BEYETE. A bastard. (*A.-S.*)

MIS-BORNE. Ill-behaved. *Chaucer.*

MIS-CALL. To abuse. *North.*

MIS-CAS. Misfortune. See Isumbras, 784. *Miscasualty*, an unlucky accident. *East.*

MISCHEFE. (1) Misfortune. (*A.-N.*) It is in very common use for *injury*. To hurt, or injure, Robinson Crusoe, p. 177. Sometimes, to destroy, to kill.

> Kyng Ardus of Arragone
> Come rydyng to the towne,
> And sawe them fyght in fere;
> Hyt dud the kyng mekylle grefe,
> When he sawe the chylde at *myschefe*,
> That was hym leve and dere!
> *MS. Cantab. Ff. ii. 38, f. 77.*

(2) The devil. *Somerset.*

MISCHIEF-NIGHT. May-eve. *Yorksh.*

MISCOMFORTUNE. Misfortune. *Miscomhap*, mishap. *Suffolk.*

MISCONSTER. To misconstrue.

> Theodorus, the atheist, complayned that his schollers were woont, how plaine soever hee spake,

to *misconster* him, how righte soever hee wrote, to wrest him.   *Gosson's Schoole of Abuse,* 1579.

MISCONTENT. To discontent. (*A.-N.*)

MISCOUNSEL. To counsel wrongly. (*A.-N.*)

MISCREAUNTES. Infidels. (*Lat.*)

MISCREDENT. A miscreant. *Devon.*

MISCREED. Discovered; detected; decried; depreciated. *North.*

MISDELE. Qu. an error for *mildele?*

When the fynd so hard drou,
Saynt Austyn stod and low,
Saynt Gregoré con grame.
Never the lesse for grame he get,
Sone after masse the Austyn he met,
And *mysdele* mad his mone.
    Legend, MS. Douce 302.

MISDOUBT. To doubt, or suspect.

MISEISIORE. More troubled. (*A.-N.*)

A *miseisiore* man than he thoujte,
No man ne mijte i-seo.
    MS. Laud. 108, f. 117.

MISENTREAT. To treat one badly.

MISER. A miserable person.

But without any watch comest to sleep like a
miser and wretch.   *Becon's Works,* p. 172.

MISERERE. A lamentation. (*Lat.*)

MISERICORD. A thin-bladed dagger.

MISERICORDE. Compassion; pity. (*A.-N.*)

For here byforne ful oft in many a wyse
Hastowe to *mysericorde* resceyved me.
    Romance of the Monk, Sion College MS.

And in this wise they acorde,
The cause was *misericorde.*
    Gower, MS. Soc. Antiq. 134, f. 102.

MISEROUS. Miserable. *Palsgrave.*

MISERY. Constant bodily pain. *East.*

MISEYSETE. Diseased. *Baber.*

MISFARE. Misfortune. (*A.-S.*)

MISPEET. Ill deed; wrong. (*A.-N.*)

MISFORTUNATE. Unfortunate. *Palsgrave.*

MISGEE. To be doubtful. *South.*

MIS-GIED. Misguided. *Chaucer.*

MIS-GONE. Gone wrong. Lydgate MS.

MISH-MASH. A confused mass. "A chaos, a confused lump, a formelesse masse, a mish-mash," Florio, p. 95. "A confused or dis-ordered heape of all things together, a mish-mash," Nomenclator, p. 362. Brockett has mixty-maxty, and mixy-maxy.

MISHTERFULL. Mischievous. *East.*

MIS-KEN. To be ignorant of. *North.*

MISKIN. (1) A little bag-pipe.

(2) A dunghill. See *Mixen.*

MISKIN-FRO. A sluttish maid-servant, used in contempt. From *Miskin* (2).

MISLEST. To molest. *Var. dial.*

MISLIKE. To dislike. *Misliken,* to disap-point. *Yorksh.*

MISLIKING. Indignation. *Palsgrave.*

MISLIN-BUSH. The mistletoe. *East.*

MISLIPPEN. To disappoint. *North.*

MISMANNERED. Unbecoming. *Cumb.*

MIS-MOVE. To teaze; to trouble. *North.*

MISNARE. To incommode. *Cumb.*

MISPROUD. Arrogant. 3 Henry VI. ii. 6.

MISS. Wicked; wrong.

MISSAKE. To renounce or forsake.

MIS-SATE. Misbecame. *Chaucer.*

MISSAY. To revile, or abuse. (*A.-S.*)

Also thai sal ilkone othyr werye,
And *myssay* and sclander Godd Almyghty.
    Hampole, MS. Bowes, p. 241

MISSEL. A cow-house. *Yorksh.*

MISSELDEN. Mistletoe. "An eater of mis-selden," Elyot in v. *Turdus.* Tusser has *mistle,* p. 79.

MISSENS. Anything missing. *North.*

MISSET.

Hee would • supply the place well enough of a ser-vile usher, with an affected grace to carry her *misset,*
open her pue.
    The Two Lancashire Lovers, 1640, p. 21.

MISSOMER. Midsummer. *West.*

At *Missomer* on an nyght,
The mone schane fulle bright.
    MS. Lincoln A. i. 17, f. 136.

MISTAKE. To transgress; to take away wrong-fully or by mistake.

MISTECH. A bad habit. *North.*

MISTER. (1) Kind; species; trade; occupa-tion; manner of life. (*A.-N.*) Hence *mis-tery,* an art or trade, a company or guild of traders.

(2) Need; necessity.

Kyng Ardus seyde then,
Y have *myster* of soche a man,
God hath hym hedur broght!
Fulle welle y am be-gone,
Y trowe God hath me sent wone,
That shalle Moradas bryng to noght!
    MS. Cantab. Ff. ii. 38, f. 76

Seynt Jhonne commaunded hys aumenere
To jyve hym outher syxe, for he had *mystere.*
    MS. Harl. 1701, f. 46

MISTIHEDE. Darkness. *Chaucer.*

MIS-TREE. Dim-sighted. *Devon.*

MISTRESS. (1) Wife. *Var. dial.*

(2) The jack at bowls. "The mistris or block at bowles," Florio, p. 279.

MISTRY. To deceive. *Devon.* A mistry man, a very deceitful fellow.

MISTURE. Misfortune.

Bonâ fide, it is a great *misture* that we have not men swine as well as beasts, for then we should have porke that hath no more bones than a pudding, and a side of bacon that you might lay under your head in stead of a bolster. *Nash's Pierce Pennilesse,* 1592.

MISWENT. Gone wrongly. (*A.-S.*)

But felle alle hoot to hire assente,
And thus the whel is alle *miswent.*
    Gower, MS. Soc. Antiq. 134, f. 55.

MISWONTED. Tender. *North.*

MISWROUGHT. Done amiss.

Schryfte of the byschop the lady besoght,
I have grevyd my God in worde and dede:
The byschop seydd, Thou haste *mywrought*
Ageyne thy God in forme of brede.
    MS. Cantab. Ff. ii. 38, f. 47.

MIT. To commit. *South.*

MITAINE. A glove. (*A.-N.*) The term was not restricted to gloves without fingers. Ray inserts *mittens* in his list of South and East Country Words, with the following explana-tion, "gloves made of linnen or woollen, whether knit or stitched: sometimes also they

call so gloves made of leather without fingers."
" *Mencus*, a meteyne," Nominale MS.

Take the porter thi staffe to halde,
And thi *mytens* also.

MS. Cantab. Ff. v. 48, f. 52.

MITE. A small worm. (*A.-S.*)

MITH. Might. Still in use. *Mythy*, mighty,
Archæologia, xxx. 365.

MITHE. To conceal; to hide. (*A.-S.*)

MITHER. To muffle up; to smother; to encumber. *Northampt.* Hence, occasionally,
to perplex.

MITHERS. To be in the mithers, i. e. quite intoxicated. *Linc.*

MITS. (1) Even. (2) Mittens. *Var. dial.*

MITTING. Darling. A term of endearment.
See Chester Plays, i. 124.

MIVER. A mortar. *Somerset.*

MIVEYS. Marbles. *Var. dial.*

MIX. (1) To clean out. *West.*

(2) Wretch. Hence *mixed*, vile, bad.

MIXEN. A dunghill. Ray says, " I find that
this word is of general use all over England."
The mixen cart, Mirr. Mag. p. 89. " A dunghill, a mizen," Stanihurst, p. 11. Grose has
Mixhill. Still in use.

MIX-PLENTON. The herb less-morel.

MIXTELYN. Rye and wheat ground together,
of which the inferior brown bread was made.
See the Archæologia, xxv. 425. See *Maslin.*

MIXTION. A mixture. *Palsgrave.*

MIZ-MAZE. Confusion. Also as *Maze*, q. v.

MIZZICK. A boggy place. *North.*

MIZZLE. (1) To rain softly. *Var. dial.*

(2) To go; to run; to sneak off; to succumb, or
yield. Sometimes, to get tipsy.

Then their bodies being satisfied, and their heades
prettily *mizzeled* with wine, they walke abroad for a
time, or els conferre with their familiars.

Stubs' Anatomie of Abuses, 1595, p. 57.

MIZZY. A quagmire. *North.*

MO. (1) To make. Perceval, 1900.

(2) More. Adv. and adj. (*A.-S.*)

To them I wyshe even thus, and to no *mo*,
That as they have hys judgement and hys yeares,
Even so I would they had hys fayre long eares

Old Ballad, Bibl. Soc. Antiq.

Sexty knyȝtes and ȝit *mo*,
And also fele ladys ther-to,
Hastely to the quene thei come,
And in ther armys thei hyr name,
And brouȝt hyre to bed in haste,
And kepyd hyre both feyre and faste.

MS. Ashmole 61, xv. Cent.

Al fort our Dright seyd ho,
So thai blleved ever *mo*.

Arthour and Merlin, p. 25.

MOAK. Hazy; dark. *Linc.*

MOAM. Mellow. *North.*

MOANT. Might not. *Yorksh.*

MOATS. To play the moats, i. e. to be angry.

MOB. (1) To scold. *Suffolk.*

(2) To dress awkwardly. *Yorksh.* " Mobb'd
up, dresst in a coarse clownish manner,"
Kennett, MS. Lansd. 1033. This is, perhaps,
connected with *mobled* in Hamlet, ii. 2.

MOB-CAP. A cap tying under a woman's chin

by an excessively broad band, generally made
of the same material as the cap itself.

MOBILE. The mob. (*Lat.*)

MOBLES. Goods; moveables. (*A.-N.*)

To mynystre my *mobles*, fore mede of my saule,
To mendynnantes and mysese in myschefe fallene.

Morte Arthure, MS. Lincoln, f. 60.

MOCCINIGO. A small Venetian coin, worth
about ninepence.

MOCHA. A term applied to a cat of a black
colour intermixed with brown. From the
mocha pebble. *East.*

MOCHE. Great. (*A.-S.*)

She ledde hym to a *moche* felde,
So grete one never he behelde.

MS. Harl. 1701, f. 22.

When he was armed on a stede,
He was a mykelle man of brede
And also *moche* man of myght.

MS. Cantab. Ff. ii. 38, f. 76.

In Parys a monyth the oost lay,
For they had takyn a day
With the Sowdon, *moche* of myghte.

MS. Cantab. Ff. ii. 38, f. 87.

MOCK. (1) Ground fruit. *Devon.*

(2) *To mock the Church*, not to marry after the
banns have been published.

(3) A root or stump; a large stick; a tuft of
sedge. *Dorset.*

(4) The pomage.

MOCKADO. A kind of woollen stuff, made in
imitation of velvet, and sometimes called
mock-velvet.

My dream of being naked and my skyn all over-
wrowght with work like some kinde of tuft *mockado*,
with crosses blew and red. *Dr. Dee's Diary. p. 6.*

MOCKAGE. Mocking. See Collier's Old Ballads, p. 48; Harrison, p. 235.

MOCKBEGGAR. " A bug-beare, a scarcrow,
a mockbegger, a toy to mocke an ape," Florio,
p. 58. Mocke-clowne, ibid. p. 253. Forby
has mock-beggar-hall, a house looking well
outside, but having a poor interior. There is
a house so called at Claydon.

MOCKET. A napkin. Cotgrave, in v. *Emba-
veté.* Mocketer, ib. in v. *Baverette.*

For eyen and nose the nedethe a *mokadour*.

Lydgate's Minor Poems, p. 30.

MOCKET-HEAD. See *Ancony.*

MOCKS. Trifles. *Somerset.*

MOCK-SHADOW. Twilight. *Heref.* Blount
has *mock-shade*, p. 180, ed. 1681.

MODDER. " Lasse, girle, modder," Cotgrave,
in v. *Putre.* See *Mauther.*

MODE. (1) Anger; passion. (*A.-S.*)

To turne aweye from hem, Fadyr, thy *mode*,
But whether nat evyl be ȝulde for gode.

MS. Harl. 1701, f. 86.

(2) Mind. Perceval, 589, 1327, 1695.

MODER. To regulate, especially the temper or
disposition. " I moder or temper myselfe
whan I am provoked to any passyon," Palsgrave. *Modyr*, Ord. and Reg. p. 61.

MODERN. Trivial. *Shak.*

MODER-NAKED. Quite naked.

Sey that I bydde hem by redy, byschop and alle,
To-morwe or the n.ydday alle *moder-naked*.

MS. Cott. Calig. A, ii. f. 112.

MODGE. To crush, or bruise. *Warw.*

MODI. Brave; high-minded.

Hof on ich herde sale,
Ful *modi* mon and proud. *MS. Digby 86, f. 165.*

MODIR. Mother. (*A.-S.*)

MOFFLE. To do anything badly or ineffectually. *Var. dial.*

MOG. (1) To move away. *West.*

(2) To enjoy one's self in a quiet easy comfortable manner.

Wit hung her blob, ev'n Humour seem'd to mourn,
And sullenly sat *mogging* o'er his urn.
Collins' Miscellanies, 1762, p. 122.

MOGGHETIS. The paunch.

MOGHTYS. Moths.

The *moghtys* that thy clothes ete.
MS. Cantab. Ff. ii. 38, f. 16.

MOG-SHADE. The shadow of trees.

MOGWED. Mugwort. See an early list of plants in MS. Sloane 5, f. 2.

MOIDER. To distract, or bewilder. Also, to labour very hard. *North.*

MOIL. (1) To become dirty. *West.*

(2) To toil or labour very hard. Generally coupled with *toil.* See Forby, ii. 218.

I hath bin told, ben told, in proverbs old,
That souldiares suffer both hunger and cold,
That souldiares suffer both hunger and cold;
And this sing we, and this sing we,
We live by spoyle, by spoyle, we *moyle* and toyle;
Thus Snach and Catch doth keepe a coyle!
And thus live we, and thus live we,
By snatchin a catchin thus live we.
Mariage of Witt and Wisdome, 1579.

(3) A mule. Still in use.

I geve to everyche of the cheefest men of lawe a *moyle* to brynge hym to hell, and two right handes to helpe himselfe withall to take money of bothe parties. *The Wyll of the Devill, n. d.*
They drewe owt of dromondaries dyverse lordes,
Moylles mylke whitte, and mervaillous bestes.
Morte Arthure, MS. Lincoln, f. 77.

(4) A sort of high shoe.

MOILY. Having no horns. *North.*

MOINE. A dunghill. *Berks.*

MOISE. (1) To mend; to improve. *East.*

(2) A kind of pancake.

(3) Cider. See *Apple-moise.*

MOISON. Harvest; growth. (*A.-N.*)

MOIST. (1) New, applied to liquors.

(2) Warm and *moist* were the appropriate terms in the time of Shakespeare for what we should now call an *aired* and a *damp* shirt. See Whiter's Specimen of a Commentary on Shakespeare, 1794, p. 82; and the French Schoole Maister, 1631, p. 39.

(2) To moisten. *Somerset.*

MOITHERED. Tired out. *Glouc.*

MOKE. (1) The mesh of a net. *South.* Hence applied to any wicker-work.

(2) "*Tinia*, a moke," Nominale MS.

MOKERAD. A deceiver. (*A.-N.*)

Avaryce, ryche and harde,
Ys a thefe, a *mokerad. MS. Harl. 1701, f. 41.*

MOKY. Misty. *Linc.*

MOLD. (1) Earth; ground. It is constantly applied to the ground in works of art. See Degrevant, 1039.

(2) Hermodactili. See a list of plants in MS. Sloane 5, f. 5.

(3) A model used as a guide by masons when doing ornamental work.

(4) To disarrange; to crumple. *North.*

(5) The suture of the skull. Left unexplained in Archæologia, xxx. 410.

(6) Form; fashion; appearance.

MOLDALE. Spiced or mulled ale.

MOLD-BOARD-CLOUTS. Plates of iron which protect the mold-board, or projecting side, of the plough, from the wear and tear of the earth and stones it meets with.

MOLDEN. A mole. *Warw.*

MOLD-STONE. The jamb of a window.

MOLDWARP. A mole. Also pronounced *moodiwart.* It is still in use, and means sometimes the mole-hill.

Tak a *moldwarppe,* and sethe it wele in wax, and wryng it thorowe a clathe, and do it in boystes.
MS. Linc. Med. f. 306.

That king Henry was the *moldwarpe,* cursed of Goddes owne mouth, and that they thre were the dragon, the lion, and the wolffe, whiche shoulde devide this realme betwene theim.
Hall's Union, 1548, Hen. IV. f. 90.

And for to set us hereon more agog,
A prophet came (a vengeance take them all)
Affirming Henry to be Gogmagog,
Whom Merlin doth a *mold-warpe* ever call,
Accurst of God, that must be brought in thrall
By a wolfe, a dragon, and a lion strong,
Which should divide his kingdome them among.
Phaer, quoted in Notes to Henry IV.

MOLE. (1) Form. Topsell's Beasts, p. 194.

(2) A stain in linen cloth, spelt *muyle* in Urry's MS. additions to Ray in Bodleian library. *Moled,* spotted, stained. *A.-N.*)

(3) To speak. "Moles to hir mildly," Morte Arthure, MS. Lincoln, f. 85.

(4) To destroy moles. *North.*

MOLEDAY. A day of burial. *West.*

MOLEINE. Scabs; swellings; cracks.

MOLE-SHAG. A caterpillar. *Glouc.*

MOLESTIE. Trouble. (*A.-N.*)

MOLHERN. A female heron. *Warw.*

MOLKIT. An effeminate boy. *West.*

MOLL. (1) A measure of wood containing one cubic metre. (*A.-N.*)

(2) A whore. An old cant term.

(3) The familiar name of *Mary.*

MOLL-ANDREW. A merry-Andrew. *South.*

MOLLART. A maulkin, q. v. *Lanc.*

MOLLED. Mouldy?

Thy drynkes sowren thy *mollyd* mete,
Where with the feble myghte wel fare.
MS. Cantab. Ff. ii. 38, f. 16.

MOLLEWELLE. The sea-calf. This term occurs in the Nominale MS. xv. Cent.

MOLLICRUSH. To beat severely. *West.*

MOLLIFY. To sooth. *Var. dial.*

MOLL-WASHER. The water-wagtail. *South.*

MOLLYCODDLE. An effeminate person. A term of contempt. *Var. dial.*

MOLLYPEART. Frisky; lively. *Oxon.*

MOLOUR. A grinding-stone.

MOLT. To perspire. *East.* Possibly connected with *molte*, melted. A very hot day is often termed *a melting day*. Molt-water, clear perspiration.

MOLTER. The toll to the miller for grinding corn. *North.*

MOLTLING. The same as *Angle-berry*, q. v.

MOM. A mum, or soft sound. (*A.-S.*)

MOMBLEMENT. Confusion; disorder. *West.*

MOME. (1) Soft; smooth. *North.*

(2) A blockhead. "A gull, a ninny, a *mome*, a sot," Florio, p. 81.

> Words are but wind, but blowes come home,
> A stout tongu'd lawyer's but a *mome*.
> *Brome's Songs*, 1661, p. 105.

(3) An aunt. Nominale MS.

MOMELLYNGE. Mumbling. (*A.-S.*)

> These makes hippynge, homerynge,
> Of medles *momellynge*.
> *MS. Lincoln* A. 1. 17, f. 206.

MOMENTANY. Lasting for a moment. It occurs in Cornwallyes' Essayes, 1632, e. 5.

MOMMERED. Worried. *Oxon.*

MOMMICK. (1) A scarecrow. *Somerset.*

(2) To cut anything awkwardly. *South.*

MON-AMY. A dish composed chiefly of cream, curds, and butter. (*A.-N.*)

MONANDAY. Monday. *Westm.* (*A.-S.*)

MONCE. Mischance. *Yorksh.*

MONCHELET. A dish in old cookery described in the Forme of Cury, p. 17.

MONCORN. "Beere corne, barley bygge, or moncorne," Huloet, 1552.

MONE. Many. Still in use.

> Of Frawnce he mad him anon regent,
> And wedid Kateren in his present;
> Into Englond anon he went,
> And cround our quene in ryal aray.
> Of quen Kateryn our kyng was borne,
> To save our ryzt that was fore-lorne,
> Oure faders in Frawns had won beforne,
> Thai han hit hold *mone* a day.
> *MS. Douce* 302, f. 29.

(2) Money.

> Forthe thei went alle thre
> To pay the scheperde his *mone*.
> *MS. Cantab.* Ff. v. 48, f. 53.

MONE. (1) To advise; to explain; to tell; to relate; to admonish. Also a substantive, mind, opinion. (*A.-S.*)

> What may this *mene*, quod these *mene*;
> *Mone* it us mare. *MS. Lincoln* A. 1. 17, f. 233.
> By a tale y shal zou *mone*,
> That fyl betwyx the fadyr and the sone.
> *MS. Harl.* 1701, f. 8.

(2) Must. MS. Cotton. Vespas. D. vii.

> A-lake for low mey leyfe ys lorne,
> Yn betture balys here *mone* I be,
> Fore one of the breyteyst that ever was borne,
> With-yowtyne speyre hat wondyd me.
> *Manners and Household Expenses of England*, p. 620.

(3) A month.

> And so bifelle upon a day,
> And that was in the *mone* of May.
> *Gower, MS. Soc. Antiq.* 134, f. 51.

MONEKENE. Monkish. *Hearne.*

MONELICH. Meanly. (*A.-N.*) Explained *moneylesse* in Rob. Glouc. p. 647.

MONE-PINS. Teeth. "Thy mone-pynnes bene lyche old yvory," Lydgate's Minor

Poems. p. 30. *Mompyns*, Towneley Myst. p. 89. Still in occasional use.

MONESTE. To admonish. (*A.-N.*)

MONEY. Silver. *North.*

MONEY-MAKERS. Counterfeiters of coin.

MONEY-SPIDER. The *aranea scenica*. It is likewise called a money-spinner.

MONGE. To eat; to munch. *West.*

MONGER. A merchant, or trader. Now only used in composition. Also, a small kind of merchant vessel. From this latter meaning, which is given by Blount, may be derived *monkey*, explained by an uneducated man "a barge wot's covered over."

MONIAL. (1) A mullion. "Postes or mony-elles," Hall, Henry VIII. f. 73.

(2) A nun. Archæologia, xxii. 280.

MONIOURS. Coiners. (*A.-N.*)

MONISH. To admonish. *Monition*, admonition, Davies, ed. 1672, p. 107. "The wordes of *monisshone* of oure Lord Jhesu Crist," MS. Ashmole 59, f. 67.

MONK'S-CLOTH. A kind of worsted.

MONMOUTH-CAP. A kind of flat cap formerly worn by the common people.

MONNYLICHE. Manly. Kyng Alis. 3569.

MONRADE. Homage. (*A.-S*)

> Whose buyth any thyng,
> Hit is hys ant hys ofspryng
> Adam hungry com me to,—
> *Munrade* dude y him me do,
> For on appel ich zef hym,
> He is myn ant al hys kun.
> *Harrowing of Hell*, p. 19.

MONSLAZT. Murder; manslaughter.

> The syn of sodomi to heven
> Hit crysen on God Almyzt;
> And *monslazt* with a rewful steven
> Hit askys vengans day and nyzt.
> *Audelay's Poems*, p. 2.

MONSOPE. The herb orobus.

MONSTRE. (1) To exhibit; to show. (*A.-N.*)

(2) A pattern. *Chaucer.*

MONTANTO. An old fencing term.

MONTEM. An annual custom at Eton, fully described by Brand, i. 237. An account of the procession *ad montem* occurs in MS. Sloane 4839, f. 85.

MONTENANCE. Amount; extent.

> And ilk a nyghte take the *montenance* of a fiche, and do it in thyne eghne byfore thou laye the doune, and it salle mend the.
> *MS. Lincoln Med.* f. 283.
> They had not ridden but a while,
> Not the *mountenance* of a mile,
> But they met with a giaunt,
> With a full sory semblant.
> *Beves of Hamtoun*, n. d.

MONTERO. "A montero, or close hood wherewith travellers preserve their faces and heads from frost-biting, and weather-beating in winter," Cotgrave.

MONTETH. A kind of vessel used for cooling wine-glasses in.

MONTHLY. Madly. Middleton, ii. 552.

MONTHLY-NURSE. A nurse who attends the month of a woman's confinement.

MONTH-MINDS. Monthly remembrances of the departed.

> And that no *month-minds* or yearly commemorations of the dead, nor any other superstitious ceremonies, be observed or used.
> *Grindal's Remains*, p. 136.

MONTH'S-MIND. To have a month's mind, i. e. a strong inclination. A common phrase in our early dramatists, and still in use.

MONTURE. A riding or saddle horse. A French word used by Spenser. It may have also some reference to the Latin word *ascensorium*, Englished by Maundevile as *mountour*, and explained by Ducange to be "quo quis in equum ascendit, tollitur," Glossarium, ed. 1772, i. 405.

MOO. (1) To low as a cow. *North.*
(2) To mock. *Palsgrave.* (Tempest, ii. 2.)

MOOD. (1) A sweetbread. *Devon.*
(2) The mother of vinegar. *Somerset.*
(3) Crowded; crammed. *Yorksh.*

MOODLE. To fold up. *North.*

MOODY. Angry. "Mody angerfull, *ireux, attayneux*," Palsgrave.

MOODY-HEARTED. Melancholy. *West.*

MOOIL. Mould, or earth. *Yorksh.*

MOOL. To rumple; to disorder. *North.*

MOON. (1) *To level at the moon, to cast beyond the moon,* to be very ambitious, to calculate deeply, to make an extravagant conjecture.
(2) Moan; grief. Also, to moan.

> For thy love hym to schende
> Wyth lytulle *moon.*
> *M. Cantab.* Ff. ii. 38, f. 95.

> Then were y schente, what shall y doo,
> I have no man to *moone* me too.
> *MS. Cantab.* Ff. ii. 38, f. 171.

(3) Wicked creature? (*A.-S.*)

> He sende up for the lady soone,
> And forth sche cam, that olde *moone.*
> *Gower, MS. Soc. Antiq.* 134, f. 49.

MOON-CALF. "A moonecalfe, a hard swelling or shapelesse peece of flesh in the wombe, which makes women beleeve they are with child when they are not," Cotgrave. The term was often applied to a monster, or a fool. In Somerset, a crying child is so called.

MOONER. A kind of dog, mentioned in Topsell's Beasts, 1607, p. 175.

MOONGE. The bellowing of cattle. *Cumb.*

MOONLIGHT-FLITTING. The same as *London-flitting*, q. v.

MOONLING. A fool; a lunatic.

MOON-MEN. Thieves; robbers.

MOON-SHINE. (1) An illusive shadow.
(2) A dish composed partly of eggs.
(3) Smuggled or illicit spirits. *South.*

MOOR. (1) To void blood. *Yorksh.*
(2) A heath, common, or waste land. In Suffolk, any uninclosed ground.
(3) A bailiff of a farm. *North.*

MOOR-COOT. A moor-hen. *Somerset.*

MOOR-GOLLOP. A sudden squall across the moors. *Devon.*

MOORISH. Wishing for more. *South.*

MOOR-MASTER. The same as *Barmaster*, q. v.

MOOR-PALM. The flower of the dock.

MOOR-POOT. A young moorgame. Metaphorically, an ignorant fellow. *North.*

MOORS. Turnips. *Devon.*

MOOR-STONE. A kind of granite found on the moors. *Devon.* It is fully described in Brome's Travels, ed. 1700, p. 242.

MOOSLE. To muzzle. *Somerset.*

MOOT. (1) To discuss a point of law in an Inn of Court. Hence, contention.

> The rollyng fordothe croppe and rote,
> And ryʒt of tho that wulde the *mote.*
> *MS. Harl.* 1701, f. 65.

(2) The stump of a tree. *West.*
(3) A note on a horn. (*A.-N.*)

MOOT-END. The backside. *South.*

MOOT-HALL. The hall of assembly. (*A.-S.*) A town-hall is still so called in the North of England.

MOOTING-AXE. A grubbing-axe. *West.*

MOOYSEN. To wonder. *Yorksh.*

MOOZLES. A stupid sloven. *Linc.*

MOP. (1) To drink greedily. *Var. dial.*
(2) A meeting or fair where servants are hired. *West.*
(3) The young whiting. The young of any animal was so called, and the term was even applied to a girl.
(4) A tuft of grass. *West.*
(5) To muffle up. See *Mob.*
(6) A grimace, or contemptuous grin.
(7) A fool. See Sevyn Sages, 1414. *Moppis.* Depos. Rich. II. p. 24. A doll was so called.
(8) *All mops and brooms*, half-seas over, intoxicated. *In the mops*, sulky.
(9) A napkin. *Glouc.*
(10) To fidget about. *North.*

MOPAN-HEEDY. Hide-and-seek. *Devon.*

MOP-EYED. Short-sighted. See the Muses Looking Glass, 1643, p. 58.

MOPO. A nickname given by Chettle, in his Kind-harts Dreame, 1592, to some ballad vender of the sixteenth century. Who he was, does not appear to be known.

MOPPER. A muffler. *Somerset.*

MOPPET. A term of endearment to a young girl. See *Mop* (3).

MOPPIL. A blunder; a mistake. *Yorksh.*

MOPSEY. A slovenly untidy woman. Also the same as *Moppet*, q. v.

MOPSICAL. Low-spirited. *Suffolk.*

MOPT. Deceived; fooled. *Devon.*

MOR. A mayor. *Hearne.*

MORAL. (1) Model; likeness. *Var. dial.*
(2) Meaning. Much ado about Nothing, iii. 4.

MORCROP. The herb pimpernell.

MORDYDY. Morrowtide; early part of the morning. (*A.-S.*)

> This was in the *mordydy* after that that sonne
> shone bryʒt. *Chron. Vilodun.* p. 88.

MORE. (1) A root. *West.* Morede, rooted up, Rob. Glouc. p. 499.

> In our Western language *squat* is a bruise, and a route we call a *more.*
> *Aubrey's Wilts, Royal Soc. MS.* p. 127.

(2) Greater. King John, ii. 1.
(3) A hill. *North*

(4) Delay. (*Lat.*)

> That gan to hem clerly certifye,
> Withoute more, the childis dwellynge place.
>
> *Lydgate, MS. Soc. Antiq. 134, f. 24.*

(5) To increase. See Lydgate, p. 243.

MORE-HERBYW. The herb devil's-bit.

MOREL. (1) The wood night-shade.

> Tak moreoles, and the rute of everferne that waxes
> on the ake, and stamp it wele, and temper it with
> mylk, and anoynte the scabbes therwith.
>
> *MS. Linc. Med. f. 295.*

(2) The morris. (*Fr.*)

> That can set his throe along in a row,
> And that is fippeny morrell I trow.
>
> *Apollo Shroving, 1627, p. 49.*

(3) A name for a horse, properly a dark-coloured one. See Towneley Myst. p. 9.

> Have gode, now, my gode morel,
> On many a stour thou hast served me wel.
>
> *MS. Ashmole 33, f. 49.*

(4) A fungus. *North.*

MOREN. The morning. (*A.-S.*)

MOREOVER. *Moreover than that*, besides, over and above that. *East.*

MORE-SACKS-TO-THE-MILL. A very rough game, mentioned in Dean Milles' MS. p. 180.

MORE-SMEREWORT. The herb mercury.

MOREYNE. A murrain.

> Yn Rome fyl a grete moreyne,
> A pestilens of men, a venjaunce to pyne.
>
> *MS. Harl. 1701, f. 10.*

MORFOND. A disease in a horse occasioned by its taking cold.

MORGAN. Tares in corn. *South.*

MORGIVE. A marriage gift. (*A.-S.*)

MORGLAY. A sword. Beves of Hampton had a celebrated sword so termed, and hence the name. It is alluded to in the Worke for Cutlers, 4to. Lond. 1615. "A trusty *morglay* in a rusty sheath," Cleaveland Revived, 1660, p. 15. See also Greene's Works, ii. 131.

MORGLE. To maul; to beat. *Beds.*

MORIEN. A blackamoor; a negro.

MORIGEROUS. Dutiful; obedient. This word is not of very usual occurrence.

> But they would honor his wife as the princesse of
> the world, and be morigerous to him as the com-
> mander of their soules. *History of Patient Grisel, p. 6.*
>
> The resigned will of a morigerous patient makes
> that cure easie, which to a perverse patient would
> become desperate.
>
> *Brathwait's Arcadian Princesse, 1635, i. 247.*

MORINE. Dead.

MORION. A conical skull-cap, with a rim round it.

> To Diprant my small coat of mail, the piece of
> plate which my Lord the Prince gave me, called
> breast-plate, the pance which belonged to my lord
> my father, whom God pardon, my housell, and my
> iron morion. *Test. Vetust. p. 189.*

MORISCO. See *Morris-dance.*

MORKIN. A beast, the produce of an abortive birth. According to some, one that dies by disease or accident.

MORK-SHRIEK. A mockery. *East.*

MORLATION. A large quantity. *Yorksh.*

MORLING. The wool taken off the skin of a dead sheep. *Blount.*

II.

MORMAL. A cancer, or gangrene. "*Luxiria* ys a lyther mormale," MS. Cantab. Ff. i. 6, xv. Cent. Compare Tyrwhitt, iv. 157.

MORME. The short point at the end of a spear to prevent injury.

MORMERACYONE. Murmur. Arch. xxi. 66.

MORMO. A spectre.

> One would think by this play the devils were
> mere mormos and bugbears, fit only to fright children
> and fools.
>
> *Collier's Short View of the English Stage, 1698, p. 192.*

MORN-DRINK. Morning draught.

> The bore come fro the see,
> Hys morne-drynke he had tan.
>
> *MS. Cantab. Ff. ii. 38, f. 65.*

MORNIFLE. "Mornyfle a maner of play, mornifle," Palsgrave.

MOROSOPH. A learned fool. (*Gr.*)

MORPHEW. A leprous eruption on the face. "A morpheu or staynyng of the skynne," Elyot, in v. *Alphos*, ed. 1559.

MORPION. A kind of louse. (*Fr.*)

MORRIS. See *Five-penny-Morris.*

MORRIS-DANCE. A very ancient dance, in which the performers were accustomed to be dressed in grotesque costume, with bells, &c. The dance is still common in many parts of the country. In Oxfordshire, a few ribands generally constitute the sole addition to the ordinary costume. The following curious notice is taken from the original accounts of St. Giles', Cripplegate, 1571, preserved in MS. Addit. 12222, f. 5,—"Item, paide in charges by the appointment of the parisshioners, for the setting forth of a gyaunt morres daunsers with vj. calyvers, and iij. boies on horsback, to go in the watche befoore the Lorde Maiore uppon Midsomer even, as may appere by particulers for the furnishinge of the same, vj. li. ix. s. ix. d."

> In Fleet strete then I heard a shoote :
> I putt my hatt, and I made no staye,
> And when I came unto the rowte,
> Good Lord ! I heard a taber playe,
> For so, God save mee ! a morrys-daunce.
> Oh ther was sport alone for mee,
> To see the hobby-horse how he did praunce
> Among the gingling company.
> I proffer'd them money for their coats,
> But my conscience had remorse,
> For my father had no oates,
> And I must have had the hobbie-horse.
>
> *MS. Harl. 3910, xvii. Cent.*

MORRIS-PIKE. A large pike. It is translated by *picque* in Palsgrave.

> The Frenchemen with quarelles, morispikes,
> slynges, and other engynes, began to assaut the
> walles. *Hall, Henry VI. f. 73.*
>
> The fourth shilde blewe, betokenyng the assaulte,
> with such wepons as the capitain of the castle shal
> occupie, that is Morrice pike, sworde, target, the
> poynt and edge abated. *Hall, Henry VIII. f. 133.*

MORT. (1) A great quantity. *Var. dial.*

> He gave her a mort of good things at the same
> time, and bid her wear them in remembrance of her
> good friend, my lady, his mother. *Pamela.*

(2) Death. *Northumb.* It occurs in Reliu. Antiq. i. 27. The notes formerly blown on

36

the horn at the death of the deer was called the mort.

(3) A female. A cant term. "A doxie, morte," Cotgrave in v. *Belistresse*.

(4) Hog's-lard. *Devon.*

MORTACIOUS. Mortal; very. *North.*

MORTAGON. *Herba martina.* Arch. xxx. 410.

MORTAISE. To give land in mortmain.

MORTAL. Very; great. *Var. dial.*

MORTALNESS. Mortality. *Palsgrave.*

MORTAR. A kind of wax-candle. "Morter of wax," Ord. and Reg. p. 341; Boke of Curtasye, p. 33.

MORTASSE. A mortise.

> For they reysede the crosse with thi body,
> And fychede it in a tre *mortasse* vyolenttly,
> In wilke the crosse swilke a jage tuke
> That thi body thurghe weghte al to-schoke.
> *MS. Lincoln* A. i. 17, f. 190.

> Into a *mortaps* withouten more
> The cros was bore up, and he
> Thai lete doun dasshe, alas! therfore
> Ho can not wepe come lerne at me.
> *MS. Bodl.* 423, f. 198.

> Then up thai lyft that hevé tro,
> And gurdid into a *mortes* of stoo. *MS. Douce* 302, f. 15.

MORTEAULX. A game resembling bowls.

MORTIFIE. To render quicksilver in a fit state for medicine. (*Fr.*)

MORTIFY. To teaze. *West.*

MORTLIN. The same as *Morkin,* q. v. The skin is called a *mort.*

MORTREWES. A dish in ancient cookery, very frequently mentioned in early works. See Reliq. Antiq. i. 81, 85, 86; Pr. Parv. pp. 13, 70; Ord. and Reg. pp. 438, 454.

MORUB. The periscaria.

MORWE. Morning; morrow. (*A.-S.*) *Morwening* is also often met with. *Morwhen* occurs in MS. Cott. Vesp. D. vii.

MOSARE. An earthen pickle-jar. *West.*

MOSCHE. Much.

> Of onest merth sche cowde rith *mosche,*
> Too daunce and synge and othre suche.
> *Gower, MS. Cantab.* Ff. i. 6, f. 43.

MOSE. (1) A disorder in the chine of horses was formerly so called.

(2) A smoulder of wood. *West.*

MOSELEY'S DOLE. An annual payment so called at Walsall, Staffordshire, which the corporation are accustomed to make of a penny apiece to all the inhabitants of the parish of Walsall, and of the adjoining parish of Rushall. See Edwards's Old English Customs. 1842, p. 55.

MOSES. Grose says, "a man is said to stand Moses when he has another man's bastard child fathered upon him, and he is obliged by the parish to maintain it." This may perhaps be connected with a phrase given by Cotgrave, "Holie Moyses, whose ordinarie counterfeit having on either side of the head an eminence, or luster, arising somewhat in the forme of a horne, hath imboldened a prophane author to stile cuckolds *parents de Moyse.*" He here apparently alludes to the character of Moses in the old miracle-plays.

MOSEY. Mealy. *Glouc.* Rough; hairy. *Suffolk.* "*Incipiens barba,* a younge *moocie* bearde," Elyot, ed. 1559.

MOSKER. To rot; to decay. *North.*

MOSKYLLADE. A dish made of muscles, &c. See MS. Sloane 1201, f. 52.

MOSS. A morass. *North.* I can make moss nor sand of him, i. e. nothing of him.

MOSS-BEGROWN. Long out of use.

MOSS-CROP. Cotton grass. *North.*

MOSSE. "Napping, as Mosse tooke his mare," Cotgrave, in v. *Desprouveu.* This proverb is still current in Cheshire, according to Mr. Wilbraham. Mosse took his mare napping because he could not catch her when awake.

MOSSELL. A morcel.

> He let serve them full tyte,
> Or he wolde any *mossell* byte.
> *MS. Cantab.* Ff. ii. 38, f. 160.

MOSS-WOOD. Trunks and stumps of trees frequently found in morasses.

MOST-AN-END. Continually; perpetually; mostly; generally. The phrase occurs in Fairfax, Bulk and Selvedge, 1674. *Most in deal* is a similar phrase.

> He that with other mens trades will be medling,
> Doth *most-an-end* lose the fruit of his pedling.
> *Cotgrave, in v. Vache.*

MOSTE. Greatest. (*A.-S.*)

> But the *moste* fynger of myn hande,
> Thorow my sonys fete y may put here.
> *MS. Cantab.* Ff. ii. 38, f. 48.

MOSTLY. Usually; generally. *Var. dial.*

MOSTRE. Appearance. (*A.-N.*)

MOST-WHAT. For the most part.

MOSY. A dish in cookery, described in the Ord. and Reg. p. 460.

MOT. (1) May; must. Perceval, 287, 333, &c.

> Pray the porter, as he is fre,
> That he let the speke with me,
> Soo faire hym *mot* be-falle.
> *MS. Cantab.* Ff. v. 48, f. 48.

> They byed on hym and can hym wrye,
> In helle *mote* they long lye!
> *MS. Cantab.* Ff. ii. 38, f. 103.

(2) A mark for players at quoits.

(3) A moat. *Var. dial.*

(4) A motto. Ben Jonson, i. 103. It occurs also in Hawkins, ii. 205.

MOTE. (1) A mite; a small piece. *South.*

(2) The large white moth. *West.*

(3) To discuss. See *Moot.*

> What schalle we more of hym *mote?*
> *MS. Cantab.* Ff. ii. 38, f. 80.

(4) The stalk of a plant. *Devon.*

(5) Assemblage; meeting. *Gawayne.*

MOTERE. To mutter. Pr. Parv. p. 30.

MOTH. A mote, or atom. It occurs in Florio, ed. 1598, p. 130, col. 1.

MOTHER. Phlegm. *Bacon.*

(2) Hysterical passion. Middleton, i. 186.

(3) A round piece of leather on the bladder inside a foot-ball. *West.*

MOTHERING. A custom still prevalent in the West of England of going to visit parents on Mid-lent Sunday, and making them a present of money, trinkets, or some nice eatable.

Why, rot the, Dick! see Dundry's Peak
Lucks like a shuggard *Motherin-cake*.

Collins' Miscellanies, 1762, p. 114.

MOTHERISH. Mammy-sick. *Oxon.*

MOTHER-LAW. A mother-in-law. *West.*

MOTHER-OF-THE-MAIDS. The chief of the ladies of honour was so called. Grose has the term for a bawd.

MOTHER'S-SON. A man. This quaint phrase was formerly in common use.

Thryes thorow at them he ran
Then for sothe, as I yow sey,
And woundyt many a *moder sone*,
And xij. he slew that day.

MS. Cantab. Ff. v. 48, f. 127.

The yṣꝛ brake als sone als Darius was paste over, and alle that ware on the yṣꝛ ware perischte iik a *moder sone*, and drownede in the water.

MS. Lincoln A. i. 17, f. 19.

MOTHER-WIT. No wit at all. An old writer gives the following as an example of mother-wit—" like that which was in a certaine country gentleman, whom the Queene of Arabia meeting, and knowing him to be a man of no great wisedome, demaunded of him when his wife should be brought to bed: who answered, Even when your highnesse shall command."

A grave discreet gentleman having a comely wife, whose beauty and free behaviour did draw her honesty into suspition, by whom hee had a sonne almost at mans estate, of very dissolute and wanton carriage. I muse, said one, that a man of such stayd and moderate gravity should have a sonne of such a contrary and froward disposition. Sir, reply'd another, the reason is that his pate is stuffed with his *Mothers wit*, that there is no roome for any of his father's wisedome: besides, the lightnesse of her heeles is gotten into her sonnes braines.

Taylor's Wit and Mirth, 1630, p. 185.

MOTHWOCK. Moderately flexible.

MOTION. A puppet. Also, a puppet-show. It is of very common occurrence, especially in old plays.

MOTIVE. Motion. *Lydgate.*

MOTLADO. A kind of mottled cloth.

MOTLEY. The dress of the domestic fool. Hence *men of motley*, fools.

MOTON. (1) In armour, a plate put on the right shoulder. Arch. xvii. 292.

(2) A small French gold coin, which bore the stamp of a lamb or sheep.

MOTONE. A sheep. (*Fr.*)

The hynde in pees with the lyone,
The wolfe in pees with the *motone*.

Gower, MS. Soc. Antiq. 134, f. 37.

MOTONER. A wencher. Lydgate, p. 168.

MOTTEY. (1) The mark aimed at in the game of pitch-and-toss. *North.* Also the same as *Mot*, q. v.

(2) Talk; speech; opinion. *Lanc.* This seems to be derived from the French.

MOTTOWS. The rent of a piece of meadow ground, in two parcels or *mottows*, is to be appropriated to the poor of Bradley, in the county of Stafford. See Carlisle's Account of Charities, p. 298.

MOU. Mowing. *Hearne.*

MOUCE. Mischance. *Yorksh.*

MOUCH. (1) To eat greedily. *Linc.*

(2) To stroke down gently. *West.*

MOUCHATS. A moustachio.

MOUCHING. Shy. *Linc.*

MOUDY. A mole-catcher. *Moudy-rat*, a mole. *Moudy-hill*, a mole-hill.

MOUGHT. (1) Might; must.

(2) A moth. Palsgrave, 1530. It also occurs in Lydgate's Minor Poems, p. 58.

MOUK-CORN. The same as *Maslin*, q. v.

MOUL. (1) Mould. Still in use.

(2) To pull or tumble about. *West.*

MOULDER. Mould; clay.

Not that we are privy to the eternall counsel of God, but for that by sense of our ayrie bodies we have a more refined faculty of foreseeiug, than men possibly can have that are chained to such heavie earthly *moulder*.   *Nash's Pierce Pennilesse*, p. 85.

MOULDY-PUDDING. A slattern. *Yorksh.*

MOULE. To grow mouldy. (*A.-S.*) " Moul-lyde brede," Reliq. Antiq. i. 85.

MOULING. Digging. *Devon.*

MOUN. May; must. (*A.-S.*)

MOUNCH-PRESENT. " Mounch Present is he that is a great gentleman, for when his mayster sendeth him with a present, he wil take a tast thereof by the waye. This is a bold knave, that sometyme will eate the best and leave the worst for his mayster," Fraternitye of Vacabondes, 1575. The term occurs ir Palsgrave, meaning a glutton.

MOUND. A fence or hedge. *East.*

MOUNDE. (1) A helmet. *Weber.*

(2) Size. Gy of Warwike, p. 3.

Fourti thousand men thai founde,
To batalle men of grete mounae.

Arthour and Merlin, p. 138.

MOUNGE. To whine; to low. *North.*

MOUNT. (1) A horse-block. *Var. dial.*

(2) To equip. *Northamptonsh.*

(3) Futuo, said of beasts. *Var. dial.*

MOUNTABAN. A kind of hat.

MOUNTAIN-OF-PIETY. A society for granting loans at reasonable interest.

MOUNTANCE. Amount; quantity. (*A.-N.*)

MOUNT-CENT. Same as *Cent*, q. v.

MOUNTEE. In hawking, the act of rising up to the prey.

MOUNTFAULCON. The female pudendum. Apparently from the Italian. It occurs in Florio, and is still in use.

MOUNTOUNS. Amount.

And withholde therof no thyng
The *mountouns* of a ferthyng.

MS. Harl. 1701, f. 38.

MOUNTOUR. Throne. " And in the myddes of this palays is the *mountour* for the grete Cane that is alle wrought of gold and of. precyous stones and grete perles," Sir J. Maundevile's Travels, ed. 1839, p. 217. In the Latin version we find the word *ascensorium*

MOUNT-ROSE. A kind of wine. See the Squyr of Lowe Degré, 755.

MOURDANT. The tongue of a buckle. (*A.-N.*)

MOURE. A turkey. *Somerset*

MOURNIVAL. A term at the game of gleek, meaning four of a sort. Hence applied to any set of four.

> It can be no treason,
> To drink and to sing
> A *mournival* of healths to our new-crown'd king.
> *Brome's Songs*, 1661, p. 56.

MOUSE. (1) A piece of beef. It is the part below the round.

(2) Mouth. See Tusser, p. 114.

(3) As drunk as a mouse was formerly a very common simile.

> Then seke another house,
> This is not worth a louse;
> As dronken as a *mouse.*
> *Doctour Doubble Ale*, n. d.

(4) A term of endearment. Alleyn, the actor, terms his wife " my good sweete mouse." See Collier's Memoirs, p. 25.

MOUSE-FOOT. An oath.

> I know a man that will never swear but by cock and pye, or *mouse-foot.* I hope you will not say these be oaths. *Dent's Pathway*, p. 142.

MOUSE-HOUND. A weasel. *East.* Not connected with Shakespeare's *mouse-hunt.*

MOUSELL. A muzzle. " Mousell of a beest, groing, moe ; mousell for a beare or a dogge, *mouseau*," Palsgrave.

MOUSEL-SCAB. A distemper in sheep.

MOUSER. A cat. *Var. dial.*

MOUSE-SNAP. A mouse-trap. *Somerset.*

MOUSFICHE.

> Gyff thame at drynk therof arely at the morne, and late at evene, of the grettnes of a *mousfiche.*
> *MS. Lincoln A. i. 17, f. 308.*

MOUSPECE. Same as *Mousell*, q. v.

MOUSTER. (1) To moulder. *West.* Perhaps more usually pronounced *mouter.*

(2) To stir ; to be moving. *Somerset.*

MOUT. To moult. *Var. dial.*

> When fethurs of charyté begynnen to *mowte,*
> Than all the preyers turne to synne.
> *MS. Cantab. Ff. ii. 38, f. 25.*

MOUTCH. On the *moutch*, shuffling. *Wilts.*

MOUTH. " Down i' the mouth" is an old English proverbial saying, for a person who is dejected and disheartened.

MOUTH-HOD. Food for cattle. *North.*

MOUTH-MAUL. To talk very badly ; to sing quite out of tune. *West.*

MOUTH-SPEECH. Speech. *Devon.*

MOVE-ALL. A juvenile game.

MOVED. Angry. *Palsgrave.*

MOW. (1) May. (*A.-S.*)

> Hym semys a felow for to be;
> Moo bourdis yet *mow* we se.
> *MS. Cantab. Ff. v. 48, f. 52.*

(2) A mock ; a scornful grin.

> Unto his mother they complain'd,
> which grieved her to heare,
> And for these pranks she threatned him
> he should have whipping cheare,
> If that he did not leave his tricks,
> his jeering mocks and *mowes;*
> Quoth she, thou vile, untutor'd youth,
> these pranks no breeding shewes.
> *The Merry Puck*, n. d.

(3) Futuo. *North.*

(4) A stack of corn, &c. *Var. dial.*

(5) A sister-in-law.

(6) The sea-mew, a well-known bird.

MOW-BURNT-HAY. Hay which has fermented in the stack. *Yorksh.*

MOWCHE. To spy, or eaves-drop.

MOWEL. The fish mullet.

MOWER. A mocker ; a scorner. *Palsgrave.*

MOWHAY. A barton or inclosure for ricks of hay or corn. *Devon.*

MOWING. Ability. *Chaucer.*

MOWL. (1) Mould. *Kent.*

(2) To knead. *Yorksh.*

MOW-LAND. Meadow land. " And allso to have as much *mow land* for rent, as myght pleasure me sufficiently," Dr. Dee's Diary, p. 38.

MOWROUN. Morrow. Degrevant, 937.

MOWSEPEASE. The herb orobus.

MOW-STEADS. Staddles. *Devon.*

MOWSTRYDE. Mustered. Arch. xxi. 50.

MOWTHE. To speak, or explain. (*A.-S.*)

MOY. Muggy ; close. *North.*

MOYENAUNT. By means of. (*Fr.*)

> Suche, namely, as many dayes had bene lad to great inconveniences, and mischevs-doynge, *moyenaunt* the false, faynyd fables, and disclandars.
> *Arrival of King Edward IV.* p. 21.

MOYNES. Moans ; lamentations.

> Nathelesse dayly came certayne personns on the sayde Erls behalve to the kinge, and made greate *moynes*, and desired him to treat withe hym, for some gode and expedient appoyntment.
> *Arrival of King Edward IV.* p. 9.

MOYRED. Stuck in the mire.

MOZIL. A stirrup-cup. *Devon.*

MO3TE. Might. (*A.-S.*)

MUBBLE-FUBBLES. To be in the mubble-fubbles, to be depressed in spirits without any serious cause. A cant term.

MUCH. (1) A term or expression of contempt common in old plays, and generally meaning *little or none, far from it, by no means.* It is similarly used as an adjective, in all cases inferring denial.

(2) To make much of; to coax ; to stroke gently. *West.*

(3) A wonder ; a marvel. *Chesh.*

(4) Great ; numerous. (*A.-S.*) Hence the adjective *muchly.*

> The Ladie Cantabrigia speedelie,
> And all her learn'd with greate solemnitie,
> Went gravelie dight to entertaine the dame,
> They *muchlie* lov'd, and honor'd in her name.
> *MS. Bibl. Reg. 17 B. xv*

MUCH-HOW. Indeed ! *Devon.*

MUCHNESS. Similarity. *Var. dial.*

MUCH-ONE. Much the same. *South.*

MUCH-WHAT. For the most part. See Holinshed, Hist. Scotland, pp. 44, 94.

MUCK. (1) To manure land. *Var. dial.* Also, to clear of dung. It is a term of reproach.

(2) Moist; damp; wet. *Lanc.*

(3) To run a muck, i. e. to go out of one's mind. *Devon.*

(4) To labour very hard. *Kent.*

(5) *Muck-cheap*, very cheap. *Muck-heap*, a

dirty untidy person. *Muck-grubber*, a miser. *Muckhill*, a dunghill.

MUCKER. To be dirty. *West.*

MUCKETTY. Dirty; untidy. *Suffolk.*

MUCK-FORK. A dung-fork; a fork with crooked prongs to distribute manure. *Mocke-forccus*, Reliq. Antiq. i. 86; *mokeforke*, Lydgate's Minor Poems, p. 189; *mokhak*, Finchale Ch. It is also called a mud-croom, and used for other purposes.

MUCK-HILL. A dunghill. *Var. dial.* "A muckelle, *funarium*," Nominale MS.

MUCKINDER. A handkerchief. Also called a *muckinger* or a *muckiter*. The term is still in use, but generally applied to a dirtied handkerchief.

MUCKLE. To disarrange, or disorder. *East.*

MUCKLE-DOWN. To stoop. *Devon.*

MUCKLETON. An old male rat.

MUCK-OF-SWEAT. Excessive perspiration.
One of them, I thought, expressed her sentiments upon this occasion in a very coarse manner, when she observed that, by the living jingo, she was all of a *muck-of-sweat*. *Vicar of Wakefield.*

MUCKRE. To heap. *(A.-S.)*

MUCKSCUTCHEON. A dirty person. *Linc.*

MUCKSEN. Dirty. *Muckson up to the huckson*, dirty up to the knuckles. *Muck-spout*, a foul-mouthed person. *Muck-suckle*, a filthy or very untidy woman.

MUCKSHADE. Twilight. *North.* Grose has *muckshut*, p. 109.

MUCK-WEED. The goose-foot. *Norf.*

MUCK-WET. Very wet or sloppy. "*Enfondu*, mucke-wet," Cotgrave.

MUCK-WORM. A miser. Also, an upstart.

MUCKY. Dirty. *Mucky-white*, said of a sallow complexion. *North.*

MUD. (1) Must; might. *North.*
(2) A small nail or spike used by cobblers. *North.*
(3) To bring up. *Wilts.*
(4) A stupid fellow. *I. Wight.* Muddy, confused, muddled.

MUDDLE. To confuse; to perplex. *East.*

MUDDLY. Thick; foggy. *North.*

MUDGE. Mud; dirt. *Derbysh.*

MUDGELLY. Squashed; trampled on as straw is by cattle. *South.*

MUDGIN. A kind of chalky clay used for daubing. *Norf.* Soft stone turning into and mixing with mud is called mud-stone.

MUD-LAMB. A pet-lamb. *South.*

MUD-PATTENS. Wide flat pieces of board which are strapped on the feet, and used to walk over the soft mud deposited in harbours by the sea. *Hants.*

MUD-SHEEP. Sheep of the large old Teeswater breed. *North.*

MUE. To change. *(A.-N.)*

MUET. Dumb; mute. *(A.-N.)*

MUFF. (1) To speak indistinctly. *Muffle* is more commonly used.
(2) A stupid fellow. *Var. dial.*

MUFF-COATED-DUCKS. Muscovy ducks.

MUFFETEE. A small muff worn over the wrist. *Var. dial.*

MUFFLED-MAN. A man in disguise.

MUFFLER. A kind of wide band or wrapper, chiefly covering the chin and throat, but sometimes nearly all the face, worn formerly by ladies. "A kerchiefe or like thing that men and women used to weare about their necke and cheekes, it may be used for a muffler," Baret, 1580.

MUFFS. Mittens. *Yorksh.*

MUG. (1) A fog or mist. *North.*
(2) The mouth. Also, the face. *Var. dial.*
(3) A pot; an earthern bowl. *North.* A hawker of pots is a *mugger.*
(4) A sheep without horns. *Yorksh.*
(5) The rump of an animal. *Devon.*

MUGED. Stirred; hovered. *Gawayne.*

MUGEROM. The caul or fat in the inwards of a hog. *North.*

MUGGARD. Sullen; displeased. *Exmoor.*

MUGGETS. Chitterlings. Hence applied to a crispy ruffled shirt. *West.* Mugilty-pie, Archæologia, xiii. 388.

MUGGLE. (1) To be restless. *Devon.*
(2) To drizzle with rain. *Yorksh.*

MUGGLETONIANS. "A new blasphemous sect, which began about the year 1657 when Lodowic Muggleton, a journey man taylor, and one Reeves, declared themselves the two last witnesses of God that ever should be upon earth, and that they had absolute power to save and damn whom they pleased; to which end one called himself the blessing, the other the cursing prophet. Reeves dyed unpunish'd, but Muggleton was sentenc'd at the Old Baily, Jan. 1676, to stand on the pillory, was fined 500£, and to lye in prison till he paid it," Blount, p. 426.

MUGGLETONY. A mongrel. *South.*

MUGGY. (1) Close and damp, generally applied to the weather. *Var. dial.*
(2) The white-throat. *North.*
(3) Half-intoxicated. *Essex.*

MUG-HOUSE. A pottery. *West.*

MUGIARD. A miserly person.

MUGLE. The mullet. Gratarolus, Direction for Health, 1574.

MUGWORT. Wormwood. *North.*

MULBREDE. To break; to crumble.

MULCH. Straw half-rotten, saturated for manure. *East.*

MULCKT. A blemish or defect.

MULERE. A weasel. *Somerset.*

MULET. A mule. *Yorksh.*

MULFER. (1) To stifle up. (2) To moulder.

MULHARDE. A keeper of mules. It occurs in the Nominale MS. *Mulett*, Archæologia, xxviii. 98.

MULIERE. A wife; a woman. *(A.-N.)* *Mulierlieborne*, legitimately, Holinshed, Chron. Ireland, p. 113.

MULITER. A muleteer. *Shak.*

MULL. (1)
And there they fonde the cofre ful,
Sperd wyth the devylys *mul*.
MS. Harl. 1701, f. 41

(2) A throw of a peg-top which fails to spin. Hence *mulled*, sleepy, inactive.

(3) Dust; dirt; rubbish. *North.*

> That other cofre of straw and *mulle*,
> With stonis meynde he filde also.
> *Gower, MS. Soc. Antiq.* 134, f. 141.

(4) To pull, or tumble about. *West.* Also, to break into small pieces.

(5) Soft, breaking soil. *Norf.*

(6) To boil or stew.

(7) To rub, squeeze, or bruise. *West.*

(8) To rain softly. *Nominale MS.*

(9) A blunder, mess, or failure. *South.*

MULLETS. (1) Spurs. (*A.-N.*)

> The brydylle reynys were of sylke,
> The *molettys* gylte they were.
> *MS. Cantab.* Ff. ii. 38, f. 87.

(2) Small pincers for curling the hair.

MULLEY. A cow. *Suffolk.*

MULL-HEAD. A stupid fellow. *West.*

MULLIGRUB-GURGIN. A grub which feeds exclusively on gurgin meal.

MULLIGRUBS. To have the mulligrubs, i. e. to be ill-tempered and grumbling.

MULLIN. Metheglin. *Somerset.*

MULLING. A term of endearment applied to a little boy.

MULLOCK. (1) A mess; a blunder; a dilemma; an ill-managed affair.

(2) Dirt; refuse; rubbish. Still in use in the North of England.

(3) The stump of a tree. *West.*

MULLS. The name by which milkmaids call their cows. *Northamptonsh.*

MULL-WINE. A corruption of *mulled wine.*

MULLY. To bellow. A farmer told a person who was afraid to pass through the field where his bull was, on account of the noise he made, "Don't fear, a woll *mully, mully, mully,* but a 'ont run." *Suffolk.*

MULNE. A mill. Still in use.

MULP. To pout; to be sulky. *East.*

MULSE. Sweet wine.

MULSY. Dirt; rubbish. *Beds.*

MULTIPLICATION. The art of making gold and silver. (*A.-N.*)

MULTIPLYING-GLASS. A magnifying-glass. See the Bride, 1640, sig. F. ii.

MULTON. A sheep. (*Fr.*)

MULVELL. The haddock? Translated by *mulvellus* in Nominale MS.

MUM. (1) A beetle. *South.*

(2) Silent, secret anger. *Essex.*

MUMBLE. To stick together. *Suffolk.* Sticky soil is said to be *mumbly.*

MUMBLE-A-SPARROW. A cruel sport practised at wakes and fairs, in the following manner: A cock sparrow whose wings are clipped, is put into the crown of a hat; a man having his arms tied behind him, attempts to bite off the sparrow's head, but is generally obliged to desist, by the many pecks and pinches he receives from the enraged bird.

MUMBLE-MATINS. A Popish priest.

MUM-BUDGET. A cant word implying silence. "*Avoir le bec gelé*, to play mumbudget, to be

tongue-tyed, to say never a word," Cotgrave. "To play at mumbudget, *demurer court ne sonner mot,*" Howell.

> In the city of Glocester M. Bird of the chappell met with Tarlton, who, joyfull to regreet other, went to visit his friends; amongst the rest, M. Bird, of the queenes chappell, visited M. Woodcock of the colledge, when meeting, many friendly speeches past, amongst which, M. Woodcock challenged M. Bird of him, who mused that hee was of his affinity and hee never knew it. Yes, sayes M. Woodcock, every woodcock is a bird, therefore it must needs be so. Lord, sir, sayes Tarlton, you are wide, for though every woodcock be a bird, yet every bird is not a woodcock. So Master Woodcock like a woodcock bit his lip, and *mumbudget* was silent.
> *Tarlton's Jests,* 4to. Lond. 1611.

MUMCHANCE. An old game, mentioned in Cotgrave, in v. *Chance*; Apollo Shroving, 1627, p. 49; Taylor's Motto, 1622, sig. D. iv. According to some writers, silence was an indispensable requisite to this game, and in Devon a silent stupid person is called a mumchance, Milles' MS. Gloss.

MUMMER. A masker. The term *mummers* is now applied to the youths fantastically dressed who dance about at Christmas, and sometimes act a dramatic piece.

> *A-mumming,* quoth you; why, there can be nothing worse then for a man to goe *a-mummings* when he hath no mony in his purse.
> *Marriage of Witt and Wisdome,* 1579.

MUMMY. (1) To beat any one to a mummy, i. e. very severely.

(2) Topsell, p. 83, mentions a herb so called. Egyptian mummy, or rather a substitute for it, was formerly used in medicine. "To make *mummee* of her grease," Fletcher's Poems, p. 256. Blount describes mummy, "A thing like pitch sold by apothecaries; it is hot in the second degree, and good against all bruisings, spitting of bloud, and divers other diseases. There are two kinds of it, the one is digged out of the graves in Arabia and Syria of those bodies that were embalmed, and is called *Arabian Mummy.* The second kind is onely an equal mixture of the Jews lime and Bitumen."

MUMP. (1) To beat; to bruise. *North.*

(2) To beg; to cheat; to intrude. *West.*

(3) To make grimaces. "Simper and *mumpe,*" Lilly, ed. 1632, sig. Cc. x.

(4) A protuberance; a lump. *Somerset.* Florio mentions "swellings in the necke called the *mumps,*" p. 425.

(5) To be sulky. *Suffolk.*

(6) Any great knotty piece of wood; a root. *Glouc.*

MUMPER. A beggar. *Var. dial.*

MUMPING-DAY. The twenty-first of December, when the poor go about the country, begging corn, &c. *Herefordsh.* See Dunkin's History of Bicester, p. 270, ed. 1816.

MUMPOKER. A word used to frighten naughty children. "I will send the *mumpoker* after you." *I. of Wight.*

MUMPSIMUS. An old error, in which men obstinately persevere; taken from a tale of an ignorant monk, who in his breviary had always said *mumpsimus* instead of *sumpsimus*, and being told of his mistake, said, " I will not change my old *mumpsimus* for your new *sumpsimus*." Bentley has made good use of this tale in his Epistles on Phalaris.

> Some be to stiffe in their old *mumpsimus*, other be to busy and curious in their newe sumpsimus.
> *Hall, Henry VIII f. 261.*

MUM-RUFFIN. The long-tailed tit. *Worc.*

MUN. (1) Must. *Var. dial.*

(2) The mouth. A common cry at Coventry on Good Friday is—

One a penny, two a penny, hot cross buns,
Butter them and sugar them and put them in your *muns.*

(3) *Mun fish*, rotten fish used in Cornwall for manure.

(4) A low familiar mode of address, said to be a corruption of *man*, but applied to both sexes.

MUNCH. Something to eat.

MUNCHATOES. Moustachios.

> Now in my two *munchatoes* for a need,
> Wanting a rope, I could well hang myselfe.
> *How to Choose a Good Wife, 1634.*

MUNCH-PRESENT. One who takes bribes. " Maunche present, *briffault*," Palsgrave.

MUNCORN. Mixed corn. *North.* In Herefordshire a muncorn team means a team of horses and oxen mixed.

MUNDAINE. Worldly possessions.

MUNDEFIE. To clear; to make clean. See Topsell's Beasts, p. 343; Serpents, p. 76.

MUNDICK. " A yellow ore mixd with tinn in the stannaries of Cornwall, which is wrought into true copper, and thereby affords a great advantage," Kennett.

MUNDLE. A slice or stick used in making puddings, &c. *North.*

MUNG. (1) Food for chickens, because usually of a mixed nature.

(2) A crowd of people. *Chesh.*

MUNGE. To munch. *Var. dial.*

MUNGER. (1) To mutter; to grumble. *North.*

(2) A horse collar made of straw.

MUNGY. Sultry; hot. *West.*

MUNITE. To strengthen; to fortify.

> Their realmes and countries are fortified and *munited* wyth a double power, that is to say, with their owne strength and the ayde of their frendes.
> *Hall, Richard III. f. 18.*

MUNNION. A mullion. *Moxon.* Still in use, Barnes' Dorset Glossary, p. 329.

MUNSWORN. Forsworn. *Yorksh.*

MUNT. To hint. *North.*

MUNTE. (1) To give; to measure out mede.

(2) Went. Piers Ploughman, p. 461.

MUNTELATE. A dish in ancient cookery described in Ord. and Reg. p. 429.

MUNTINS. The intermediate upright bars of framing. A joiner's term.

MUR. (1) A mouse. *Devon.*

(2) A severe cold with hoarseness.

> Deafe eares, blind eyes, the palsie, goute and *mur*,
> And cold would kill thee, but for fire and fur.
> *Rowland's More Knaves Yet, 1612.*

MURAY. A wall. (*A.-N.*)

MURCH. A diminutive man.

MURCHY. Mischief. *Devon.* The old-murchy, a term for the devil.

MURDERER. A very destructive piece of ordnance. It is called a murdering piece by Shakespeare.

MURDERING-PIE. The butcher-bird.

MURDLI. Joyful; pleasant. (*A.-S.*)

MURE. (1) A wall. (*Lat.*) Also a verb, as in Harrison's England, p. 216.

(2) Husks or chaff of fruit after it has been pressed. *North.*

(3) Soft; meek; demure. *East.*

(3) To squeeze. *Cornw.*

MURELY. Nigh; almost. *Cornw.*

MURENGER. A superintendent of the walls of a town or city. *Chesh.*

MURFLES. Freckles; pimples. *Devon.*

MURGE. To joy; to gladden. (*A.-N.*) *Murgost*, merriest, Rob. Glouc. p. 349.

MURGIN. A bog; a quagmire. *Chesh.*

MURKINS. In the dark. *North.*

MURL. To crumble. *North.* .

MURNE. Sorrowful. (*A.-S.*)

> Ther lete we hem sojurne,
> And speke we of chaunces hard and *murne*.
> *Arthour and Merlin, p. 308.*

MURRAIN-BERRIES. The berries of the black briony are so called in the Isle of Wight.

MURRE. An old dish in cookery, described in Warner's Antiq. Culin. p. 83.

MURREY. A dark red colour.

MURRLE. To muse attentively. *Cumb.*

MURTH. Plenty; abundance. *North.*

MURUNS. The herb chickweed.

MUS. Muzzle; mouth. Spelt *mux* in Tim Bobbin, Gl. ed. 1806.

MUSARD. (1) A wretch, or vagabond.

> Ich wene thou art a fole *musard*
> When thou of love me hast bisaught.
> *Gy of Warwike, p. 10.*

(2) A foolish fellow. *Devon.*

MUSCADINE. A rich sweet-smelling wine. Also called the *muscadel.*

> And I will have also wyne de Ryne,
> With new maid Clarye, that is good and fyne,
> *Muscadell*, terantyne, and bastard,
> With Ypocras and Pyment comyng afterwarde.
> *MS. Rawl. C. 86.*

MUSCET. A muscle. Nominale MS.

MUSCLE-PLUM. A dark purple plum.

MUSCOVY-GLASS. Talc.

MUSCULL. A pustule.

MUSE. (1) To wonder. *Shak.*

(2) A hole in a hedge through which game passes. Also called *muset.*

> But the good and aproved hounds on the contrary, when they have found the hare, make shew therof to the hunter, by running more speedily, and with gesture of head, eyes, ears, and taile, winding to the hares *muse*, never give over prosecution with a gallant noise, no not returning to their leaders, least they loose advantage.
> *Topsell's Four-Footed Beasts, 1607, p. 182.*

> Or with hare-pypes set in a *muset* hole,
> Wilt thou deceave the deep-earth-delving coney.
> *The Affectionate Shepheard. 1594.*

(3) To gaze. (*A.-N.*)

MUSH. (1) Dust; dusty refuse. *North.*

(2) Guardedly silent. *East.*

(3) Anything mashed. *Lanc.*

(4) To break a child's spirit by unnecessary harshness. *Warw.*

(5) The best kind of iron ore.

MUSHERON. A mushroom; toadstool. It occurs in Palsgrave, 1530. *Mushrump*, another form, is found in Marlowe, and Shakespeare, Tempest, ed. 1623, p. 16, col. 2.

MUSHROOM-HITCHES. Inequalities in the floor of a coal mine, occasioned by the projection of basaltic or other stony substances. *North.*

MUSIKER. A musician.

MUSK. The herb cranes-bill.

MUSKEL. A caterpillar. *Devon.*

MUSKET. The male sparrow-hawk. See Harrison, p. 227. It is the translation of *capus* in MS. Addit. 11579.

MUSKIN. "A proper visage," Palsgrave.

MUSROLL. The nose-band of a horse's bridle. (*Fr.*) Still in use.

MUSS. (1) A mouse. Jonson, i. 49.

(2) A scramble. There was a scrambling game amongst children so called. "Striving as children play at musse," Florio, p. 38.

(3) The mouth. *North.*

MUSSELL. A lump of bread, &c.

MUST. (1) Ground apples. *West.*

(2) New wine. A very common term in old authors.

(3) *Well must ye*, an elliptical phrase for wishing good luck to any one.

(4) To turn mouldy. *Palsgrave.*

MUSTILER. Armour for the body.

MUSTIR. To talk together privately.

MUSTREDEVILLIARS. A kind of mixed grey woollen cloth, which continued in use up to Elizabeth's reign. It is sometimes spelt *mustard-villars.*

MUT. Must; might. *North.* This form occurs in Torrent, p. 61.

MUTE. (1) A mule of the male kind out of a she-ass by a horse, though some will have it that a mule so bred is termed a *mute* without reference to sex. *Linc.*

(2) The dung of hawks.

One used an improper tearme to a falconer, saying that his hauke dung'd. The falconer told him that he should have said *muted*. Anon after this fellow stumbled, and fel into a cowshare, and the falconer asking him how hee came so beray'd, he answered, In a cow mute

Wits, Fittes, and Fancies, 1595, p. 178.

(3) To mew; to moult.

(4) A pack of hounds. Sometimes, the cry of hounds. Gent. Rec.

MUTESSE. The same as *Mute* (2).

MUTHE. An army. (*A.-N.*)

MUTIN. Mutinous. *Shak.*

MUTTING. Sulky; glumping. *Cornw.* Muttinge, muttering, Chester Plays, i. 132.

MUTTON. A prostitute. *Mutton-monger*, a man addicted to muttons. Both terms are still in common use. "A noteable smel-

smocke, or muttonmunger, a cunning solicitor of a wench," Cotgrave.

MUTTON-TOPS. The young tops or shoots of the goose-foot.

MUTTY-CALF. A very young calf. Also, a simpleton. *Yorksh.*

MUTUATE. Borrowed. (*Lat.*)

Whiche for to set themselfes and their band the more gorgeously forward had *mutuate* and borowed dyverse and sondry summes of money.

Hall, Henry VII. f. 27

MUWEN. May. (*A.-S.*)

MUX. Muck; dirt. Hence *muxen*, a dunghill. *West.* Lye has *muxy*, a Devonshire word.

MUZWEB. A cobweb. *North.*

MUZZLE. (1) The face. *Var. dial.*

(2) To drink excessively. *Linc.*

(3) To trifle; to skulk. *Yorksh.* It seems to occur in a similar sense in Florio, ed. 1611, p. 25.

(4) To grub up with the snout, as swine do. *Devon.*

MUZZY. Half drunk. *Var. dial.*

MYCULLE. Much; great.

Now alle wymmen that has your wytte,
And sees my childe on my knees ded,
Wepe not for yours, but wepe for hit,
And ȝe shalle have ful *myculle* mede.
He wolde agayne for your luf blede,
Rather or that ȝe damned were;
I pray yow alle to hym take hede :
For now liggus ded my dere son dere.

MS. Cantab. Ff v. 48. f. 73.

MYDDYNG-PYTTE. Dunghill-pit. See *Midden.*

That contré es so fayre on to loke,
And so bryght and brade, als says the buke,
That alle this world thare we wonne yhitte,
War noght bot als a *myddyng-pytte*
To regarde of that contré so brade.

Hampole, MS. Bowes, p. 223.

MY-EYE. A very common low exclamation of astonishment.

MY-HEN-HATH-LAID. A kind of game mentioned by Florio, p. 474.

MY-LADY'S-HOLE. A game at cards.

MYLATE. A dish in ancient cookery, described in Forme of Cury, p. 69.

MYR. Pleasant. (*A.-S.*) *Myrré*, merry, Torrent of Portugal, p. 13.

Quy shuld thou leve so *myr* a thyng,
That is likand and swete. *MS. Cantab. Ff. v. 48, f. 82.*

MYSBREYDE. Evil birth. (*A.-S.*)

For thys skyle hyt may be seyde,
Handlyng synne for oure *mysbreyde.*

MS. Harl. 1701, f. 1.

MYSE. To mince, or cut in small pieces.

MYSELL. Myself. *North.* I have also heard *mysen* in the same sense.

MYSELVENE. Myself. (*A.-S.*)

MYSFARYNGE. Hurt; injured.

He sawe a knyghte rydynge,
Hys ryght arme was *mysfarynge.*

MS. Cantab. Ff. ii. 38, f. 154.

MY-SOW-PIGGED. An old game mentioned in Taylor's Motto, 12mo. 1622, sig. D. iv.

MYSPAYRE. Evil?

Syr, he seyde, the kyng Edgare
Dryveth the to grete *myspayre.*

MS. Cantab. Ff. ii. 38. f. 123.

MYSSE. To fail. (*A.-N.*)

He shal have warryng for blysse,
And of blessyng shall he *mysse*
MS. Harl. 1701, f. 9.

MYSTHROWE. To mistrust. (*A.-S.*)

But our Lady was evyr stedfast in the feith,
And *mystrowid* not of his resureccion.
MS. Laud. 416, f. 42.

Tel me, therfore, if it be so,
Haatow thin yhe ought *mysthrowe ?*
Gower, MS. Bodl. 294, f. 11.

And be no morre so *mystroward,*
But trow trewly.
Croft's Excerpta Antiqua, p. 110.

MYSTYMED. Skinner explains this, *male tempus in hoc mundo impendit.*

And as he hath the world *mystymed.*
Gower, MS. Bodl. 294.

MYS3. Mice.

After this, ther come oute of the redes a grete multitude of *mys3,* als grete als foxes, and ete up the dede bodys. *MS. Lincoln* A. i. 17, f. 28.

MYTHE. Mild.

O Judas, sore ashamed thou be may
So meke and so *mythe* a mayster to tray.
MS. Harl. 1701, f. 85.

MY3TVOL. Powerful. Rob. Glouc.

NA. No. *North.* It is even a mark of North country dialect in some MSS.

NAB. (1) A cant term for the head. See a list in Brit. Bibl. ii. 521.

(2) The summit of an eminence. *North.*

(3) To catch; to seize; to overtake a person unexpectedly. *Var. dial.* To nab the rust, i. e. to receive punishment unexpectedly.

(4) Kennett has, " nab of a bolt, the sholder of iron sticking out about the middle of the bolt in a lock, the use of which is to receive the bottom of the bit of the key, when, in turning it about, it shoots the bolt backwards and forwards."

NABALL. A fool. One of Rowlands' epigrams, in his More Knaves Yet, 1612, is addressed " to all London's *naballs.*"

NABBITY. Dwarfish. *East.*

NABCHET. A hat or cap. An old cant term, given by Harman, 1567. *Nabcher,* Earle, p. 253. Grose has nab-cheat.

NAB-NANNY. A louse. *East.*

NA-BUT. Only. *North.*

NACKENDOLE. Eight pounds of meal. *Lanc.* It is supposed to be a kneading-dole, the quantity usually taken for kneading at one time. Often pronounced *aghendole.* It occurs in Prompt. Parv. under the form *eytendele.*

NACKER. (1) A young colt. *Devon.*

(2) To snap the fingers. *Wilts.*

NACKING. A handkerchief. *Cornw.*

NADDE. For *ne hadde,* had not. (*A.-S.*)

NADDLING. Nodding. *Devon.*

NÆVE. A spot; a fault. (*Lat.*)

NAF. The pudendum muliebre. *North.*

NAFFING. Grumbling; haggling. *North.*

NAG. To nick, chip, or slit. *Linc.*

NAGE. The backside. (*A.-N.*)

NAGGING-PAIN. A slight but constant pain, as the toothache. *West.*

NAGGLE. (1) To gnaw. *North.*

(2) To toss the head in a stiff and affected manner. *East.*

NAGGLED. Tired. *Oxon.*

NAGGY. Touchy; irritable. *North.*

NAGRE. A miserly person. *North.*

NAID. Denied. Skelton, ii. 197.

NAIF. A term applied by jewellers to a stone of true natural lustre.

NAIL. (1) Eight pounds, generally applied to articles of food. *South.*

(2) To prick a horse in shoeing.

NAIL-BIT. A gimlet. *Heref.*

NAILBURN. A kind of temporary brook or intermittent land-spring, very irregular in its visitation and duration. There are several nailburns in Kent. One may be mentioned below Barham Downs, which sometimes ceases to flow for two or three years, and then breaks out very copiously, and runs into the lesser Stour at Bridge. Warkworth, Chronicle, p. 24, gives a very curious account of these singular streams, and mentions one " byside Canturbury called Naylborne," which seems to be that above alluded to.

NAILED. Caught; secured; fixed. It occurs in the Pickwick Papers, p. 429, as a slang term, but may possibly be genuine from A.-S. nealæcean.

NAILER. A person who sells nails.

NAIL-PASSER. A gimlet. *West.* Kennett has *nailsin* in the same sense.

NAIL-SPRING. A hang-nail. *Devon.*

NAITINE. To deny. *Prompt. Parv.*

NAKAR. A naked person. Nominale MS.

NAKE. To make naked. (*A.-S.*)

NAKED-BED. A person undressed and in bed was formerly said to be in naked-bed, and, according to Brockett, the phrase is still in use applied to any one entirely naked. The term was probably derived from the ancient custom of sleeping without night linen, which was most common in this country during the thirteenth, fourteenth, and fifteenth centuries. The Danes and Saxons appear to have been far more civilized in this respect. In Isumbras, 102, a mother and her children are described as escaping from a fire " alle als nakede als thay were borne;" but it would seem from a passage in Piers Ploughman, p. 273, that the practice was not quite universal. See Mr. Wright's notes, p. 557; Ritson's Anc. Pop. Poet. p. 49. Compare also Armin's Nest of Ninnies, p. 24, " Jemy ever used to lye naked, as is the use of a number." Two very curious anecdotes in Hall, Henry VII. ff. 20, 53, may also be consulted. " In naked bedde, *au lict couché tout nud ;* in naked bedde, *couchez nud a nud*, or *on les trouva coucher ensemble nud a nud*," Palsgrave.

Ne be thi winpil nevere so jelu ne so stroutende,
Ne thi faire tail so long ne so trailende,
That tu ne schalt at evin al kuttid bilevin,
And tou schalt to bedde gon so nakid as tou were
[borin].   *Reliq. Antiq.* ii. 15.

A noysom worm, or coverlid,
Or side-piece of thy *naked* bod.
     Fletcher's Poems, p. 105.

At twelve aclock at night,
It flowde with such a hed,
Yea, many a woful wight
Did swim in *naked* bed.
     Ballad by Tarlton, 1570.

NAKED-GULL. An unfledged bird. This term is still used in Cheshire.

NAKED-LADIES. The plant saffron.

NAKER. (1) Mother of pearl. (*Fr.*)

(2) A kind of drum. A kettle-drum, according to Warton, i. 169. " Pipes, trompes, and nakers," Minot, p. 63. Ducange describes it to have been a kind of brazen drum used in the cavalry, and Maundevile, p. 281, mentions it as a high-sounding instrument.

With trompis and with *nakerers*,
And with the schalmous fulle clere.
     MS. Lincoln A. i. 17, f. 134.

NAKETTE. A sort of precious stone, mentioned in Emaré, 94, 142.

NAKID. Empty ; unrigged.

And hath ordeyned, as sche thou3te,
A *nakid* schip withoute stere.
     Gower, MS. Soc. Antiq. 134, f. 65.

NAKINS. No kind of. (*A.-S.*) *Nakyn,* Ywaine and Gawin, 897.

NAKKE. The neck. Perceval, 692.

NAKNED. Made naked ; nakened. (*A.-S.*)

NALE. Ale ; ale-house. *Atte nale,* a corruption of A.-S. æt þan ale, is common. See Piers Ploughman, p. 531 ; Skelton, ii. 117 ; Tyrwhitt's Glossary, p. 165 ; Thynne's Debate, p. 53 ; and example in v. *Atte.*

While men loveden meri song, gamen and feire tale,
Nou hem is wel levere gon to the *nale*,
Ucchen out the gurdel and rume the wombe,
Comen erliche thider and sitte ther ful longe.
     MS. Bodl. 652, f. 1.

NALL. An awl. See Tusser, p. 10. *Naule,* Topsell's Beasts, 1607, p. 183.

NALTERJACK. A toad. *Suffolk.*

NAM. For *ne am*, am not. (*A.-S.*)

NAME. Took. (*A.-S.*)

The kyng had a crounne on hys hede,
It was no sylver ne gold rede,
It was all off presyous stone,
Als bry3t as any sone it schone !
Also sone as he to me come,
Whether I wold ore not up he me *name*.
     MS. Ashmole 61, xv. Cent.

On a day the erle to hur came,
And yn hys armys he hur *name*.
     MS. Cantab. Ff. ii. 38, f. 117.

Goddes aungeles the soule *nam*,
And bare hyt ynto the bosum of Abraham.
     MS. Harl. 1701, f. 44.

Downe be an hylle the wey she *name*,
And to the firekeysoh see sche came.
     MS. Cantab. Ff. ii. 38, f. 84.

NAMELESS. Anonymous. Reginald Scot, in his Discoverie of Witchcraft, 4to. Lond. 1584, quotes " T. R. a *nameles* author." It occurs in Two Gent. of Verona, ii. 1.

NAMELY. Especially.

NAMMET. A luncheon. *South.*

NAMMORE. No more. (*A.-S.*)

He segh the child so queinte of lore,
He wolde techen him *nammore*.
     The Sevyn Sages, 1018

NAN. (1) Used for *Anan*, q. v.

(2) A small earthern jar. *Devon.*

(3) None. Still in common use.

In al Rom that riche stede,'
Suche ne was ther *nan*.
     Legend of St. Alexander, MS.

NANCY. (1) A small lobster. *East.*

(2) *Miss Nancy,* an effeminate man. '

NANG. To insult. *West.*

NANGATIS. In no manner. (*A.-S.*)

NANGNAIL. A hangnail. *Var. dial.*

NANKINS. No kind of. (*A.-S.*)

NANNACKS. Valueless trifles. *East.*

NANNLE-BERRIES. See *Anberry.*

NANNY. A goat. Hence, a kept woman or whore. *Nanny-house,* a brothel.

NANNY-HEN. As nice as a nanny hen, i. e. very affected or delicate. Cotgrave has the phrase, " as nice as a nunnes henne."

Women, women, love of women
Make bare purs with some men.
Some be nyse as a *nanne hene*,
3It al thei be nat so ;
Some be lewde, some all be shreude,
Go schrewes wher thei goo.
     MS. Lambeth 306, f. 135.

NAN-PIE. A magpie. *North.*

NANTERSCASE. In case that. *North.*

NANTHING. Nothing. (*A.-S.*)

NANTLE. To fondle ; to trifle. *North.*

NAP. (1) Expert. *Yorksh.*

(2) A stroke ; a blow. *Devon.* " I nawpe one in the necke," Palsgrave.

(3) A small rising ; a hillock. *West.*

(4) To cheat at dice. *Grose.*

(5) To seize ; to grasp. *North.*

NAP-AT-NOON. The purple goat's beard.

NAPE. (1) A piece of wood used to support the fore-part of a loaded waggon. *North.* See Kennett, p. 77.

(2) A hole, or fracture. *Devon.*

(3) To behead ; to kill by a stroke in the neck. Nominale MS.

NAPERY. Linen. Generally table linen. "Naprie store of lynen, *linge*," Palsgrave. The term is still in use, and any kind of light ornamental ware is called *napery-ware* in the North of England. *Napré,* MS. Cantab. Ff. i. 6, f. 58.

NAPET. A napkin ; a handkerchief.

NAPIER'S-BONES. An instrument consisting of small rods, much used in the seventeenth century to expedite arithmetical calculations so called from its inventor, Lord Napier, who published an account of it under the title of *Rabdologiæ, seu numerationis per virgulas,* *libr: Juo*, 8vo. Edinb. 1617. See a notice of Napier's bones in Cleaveland Revived, 1660, p. 32, in a poem by Hall.

> A moon dial, with *Napier's bones*,
> And several constellation stones.
> *Hudibras*, II. iii. 1095.

NAPKIN. A pocket-handkerchief. Ray says, "so called about Sheffield in Yorkshire." It is frequently found in old plays, and is not yet obsolete.

NAPPE. To sleep. (*A.-S.*)

NAPPER. The head. *Var. dial.*

NAPPERN. An apron. *North.* We have *naprun* in Pr. Parv. p. 25.

NAPPERS. The knees. *Linc.*

NAPPING. Taken napping, i. e. taken in the fact, especially in adultery. "To take napping with rem in re," Florio, p. 126.

NAPPY. Strong, as ale, &c. "Noppy as ale is, *vigoreux*," Palsgrave.

NAR. Near; nearer. *North.*

> So longe we may goo seke
> For that which is not farre,
> Till ended be the week,
> And we never the *narre*. *MS. Cotton. Vesp.* A. xxv.

NARD. (1) Odoriferous.

> To my smell
> *Nard* sents of rue, and wormwood.
> *The Muses Looking Glass*, 1643, p. 27.

(2) The herb pepperwort.

NARE. (1) A nose. (*Lat.*)

(2) Never. *Devon.* Also as *Nar*, q. v.

NARES. The nostrils of a hawk.

NARGWE. Narrow. *Narger*, narrower, is still used in Somerset.

> Make a pipe with a brod end on the stone and the *nargwe* end on the sore tothe, so that the smok may come thorw the pype to the tothe.
> *MS. Med. Rec.* xv. Cent.

NARLE. A hard swelling on the neck, arising from a cold. *Glouc.* Also, a knot in a tree; a knot in thread, &c.

NARN. Never a one. *West.*

NARREL. A nostril. "A haukes *narell*, one of the little holes whereat she drawes in, and lets out, her breath," Cotgrave.

NARROW-DALE-NOON. One o'clock. The top of Narrowdale Hills in Staffordshire is so high that the inhabitants under it for one quarter of the year never see the sun, and when it appears again they see it not till one by the clock, which they call thereabout the *narrow-dale-noon*, using it proverbially when they would express a thing done late at noon.

NARROW-SOULED. Very stingy. *North.*

NARROW-WRIGGLE. An earwig. *East.*

NARRY. Not either; none. *West.*

NAR-SIN. Never since. *North.*

NARWE. Close; narrow. (*A.-S.*)

NAS. Was not. (*A.-S.*)

> Our princes speken wordes falle,
> And seyd that her king
> *Nas* bot a bretheling.
> *Arthour and Merlin*, p. 7.

NASH. (1) Chilly. *Wilts.*

(2) Firm; stiff; hard. *Derb.*

NASK. A prison. An old cant term.

NAST. (1) Dirt; nastiness. *West.*

(2) For *ne hast*, hast thou not?

NASTEN. To render nasty. *Somerset.*

NASTIC. Short-breathed. *Devon.*

NASTY. Ill-tempered. *Var. dial.*

NASTY-OFF. In a bad plight; awkwardly situated. *Somerset.*

NAT. A mat. *Palsgrave.* "A natt, *scorium*," Nominale MS. [Storea.]

NATAL. Presiding over nativity.

NATCHES. The notches or battlements of a church-tower. *Kent.*

NATE. (1) Naught; bad. *Kent.*

(2) To use; to make use of. *Northumb.*

NATELIE. Neatly; in order. (*A.-S.*)

NATHE. The nave. "Nathe stocke of a whele," Palsgrave. Still in use.

NATHELESSE. Nevertheless. (*A.-S.*)

NATHEMORE. Not the more. *Spenser.*

NATION. (1) A family. (*A.-N.*)

(2) Very; excessive. *Var. dial.* Said to be a corruption of *damnation*.

NATIVE. Native place. *Var. dial.*

NATIVITY-PIE. A Christmas-pie.

NATLINGS. Chitterlings. *Devon.*

NATRELLE. The crown of the head. "*Vertex*, a natrelle," Nominale MS.

NATTERED. Ill-tempered. *North.*

NATTLE. (1) To strike; to knock. *North.*

(2) To be busy about trifles. *East.*

NATTY. Neat; spruce. *Var. dial.*

NATTY-BOXES. The contribution paid periodically by the workmen in various branches of trade to the trade union to which they belong. *York.*

NATTY-LADS. Young pickpockets.

NATURABLE. (1) Natural. (2) Kind.

NATURAL. (1) Native disposition.

(2) An idiot. Still in use.

(3) Legitimate. Constantly used in this sense by early writers.

(4) Quite. *Dorset.*

(5) Kind; charitable. *Linc.* Sir Thomas More apparently uses the word in this sense in the Supplycacyon of Soulys, sig. I iii. Shakespeare has *nature* for *good feeling, natural affection*. In Devonshire, simplicity is often denominated *good nature*.

(6) A term at vingt-un, a game at cards, meaning a tenth card and an ace, or the whole number of twenty-one realized at once with two cards.

NATURELIKE. Natural. *Palsgrave.*

NATY. Fat and lean, in good order for eating. *Devon.*

NAUFRAGIATE. To shipwreck. It occurs in Lithgow's Pilgrimes Farewell, 1618.

NAUGHT. Bad; naughty. *Be naught awhile*, an oath or execration. *To be naught with*, to be adulterous. *To call one to naught*, to abuse excessively.

NAUGHTY-PACK. An old phrase of abuse. Still in use, but generally applied to children in a softer manner.

NAUN. Nothing. *Suffolk.*

NAUNTLE. To elevate gently. *North.*

NAUP. The same as *Nap* (2).

NAUR. Nowhere. *Hearne.*

NAVE. (1) Have not. (*A.-S.*)

> That I *nave* childe reweth me sore ;
> If I miʒte have lever me wore.
> *Cursor Mundi, MS. Coll. Trin. Cantab.* f. 64.

(2) A wooden instrument on which the straw is laid in thatching. *Oxon.*

NAVEGOR. An auger, a carpenter's tool. This word occurs in an inventory dated A. D. 1301, and in Nominale MS.

NAVEL-HOLE. The hole in a millstone for receiving the grain.

NAVET. Rape-seed. (*Fr.*) It is more generally spelt *navew.*

> If he eate spiders he instantly dyeth thereof, except he eate also wilde ivy or sea-crabs. Likewise *navew-gentill* and oleander, kill the hart.
> *Topsell's Four-Footed Beasts,* 1607, p. 130.

NAVIES. Excavators. *Var. dial.*

NAVY. A canal *North.*

NAWDER. Neither. Still in use.

NAWEN. Own. Lydgate, p. 110. Still in use. Craven Gl. ii. 5.

NAWL. The navel. *Somerset.* It is an archaism. See Pr. Parv. p. 296.

NAWT. Nought.

> In wordely muk ys here conscidence,
> For they sette at *nawt* clene consciennce.
> *MS. Cantab.* Ff. i. 6, f. 139.

NAWTH. Poor ; destitute.

NAWT-HEAD. A blockhead ; a coward. *North.*

NAXTY. Nasty ; filthy.

NAY. To deny. Also, denial, as in Sir Eglamour, 1130. *It is no nay,* it is not to be denied.

> The cardinall, then beyng Bishop of Winchester, toke upon hym the state of cardinall, whiche was *nayed* and denayed hym by the kyng of moste noble memory. *Hall, Henry VI.* f. 61.

NAYE. An egg.

> The two eyne of the byeryne was brighttere thane silver,
> The tother was ʒalowere thenne the ʒolke of a *naye.*
> *Morte Arthure, MS. Lincoln,* f. 88.

NAYNSTE. The nonce. Nominale MS.

NAY-SAY. A refusal. *North.*

NAY-THEN. A phrase implying doubt, disappointment, or wonder.

NAY-WORD. A watch-word. Also, a proverb, a bye-word. *Shak.*

NAZART. A mean person ; an ass. *Derb.* Sometimes *nazzle,* in the same sense. " Some selfe-conceited *nazold,*" Optick Glasse of Humors, 1639, p. 160. Mr. Scatcherd has, " *nazzald,* an insignificant lad."

NAZE. The same as *Bevel* (1).

NAZY. Intoxicated. *North.*

NAZZLES. Ill-tempered. *Yorksh.*

NE. Not ; nor. (*A.-S.*)

> Bi Appolyn, that sitteth on hie !
> A fairer childe never I *ne* sye,
> Neither of lengthe *ne* of brede,
> *Ne* so feire lemys hede. *Bones of Hamtoun, MS.*

NEAGER. A term of reproach. *North.*

NEA-MAKINS. No matter. *Yorksh.*

NEAMEL. Nimble. *Yorksh.*

NEANY. None.

NEAP. A turnip. *Cornw.*

NEAPENS. Both hands full. *North.*

NEAR. (1) Empty. *South.*

(2) Close ; penurious. *Var. dial.*

(3) The kidney. Forby says it is the fat of the kidney. " Neare of a beest, *roignon,*" Palsgrave. " *Ren,* a nere," Nominale MS.

(4) The left side of a horse is usually termed the *near side.*

(5) Nearer. See *Nar.*

(6) Neither. *Linc.* See Skinner.

NEAR-HAND. Almost. Also, probably. *Nerehande,* near, Perceval, 496.

> Madam, it is *ner-hand* passyd prime,
> And me behoves al for to dyne,
> Bothe wyn and ale to drynke ;
> Whenne I have dynyd thenne wole I fare,
> God may covere hem off here care,
> Or that I slepe a wynke.
> *Romance of Athelston,* p. 92.

NEARING-CLOTHES. The garments or linen worn next the skin.

NEAR-NOW. Not long since. *Norf.*

NEAR-SIGHTED. Short-sighted. *Var. dial.*

NEART. Night. *Devon.*

NEAT. Horned oxen. *Neat-house,* a cow-house, is still in use. *Neat-foot-oil,* oil or grease extracted from cows' feet.

NEATRESS. A female keeper of herds.

NEB. (1) The nose. Also, a bill or beak. Hence, to kiss. *North.* It sometimes means *the face* in early English, as in Reliq. Antiq. i. 124 ; Gy of Warwike, p. 303.

> Hir gray eyghen, hir *nebbis* schene.
> *Guy of Warwick,* p. 6.

> Fram the cheke the *neb* he bar,
> The scheld fram the schulder thar.
> *Arthour and Merlin,* p. 229.

> Josep cam into halle and sauʒ his brethren wipe ;
> He kisseth Benjamin, anon his *neb* he gan wipe.
> *MS. Bodl.* 652, f. 10.

> Into his bour he is come,
> And stant bifore hire bed,
> And find thar twa *neb* to *neb,*
> *Neb* to *neb,* an mouth to mouth ;
> Wele sone was that sorwe couth !
> *Florice and Blanchefloour,* 618.

(2) The pole of an ox-cart. *South.*

(3) The handle of a scythe. *North.*

NEBBOR. A neighbour. *North.*

NEBLE. A woman's nipple. *Palsgrave.*

NECANTUR. The book of accounts of the slaughter-house. (*Lat.*)

NECE. A niece ; a cousin. (*A.-N.*)

NECESSAIRE. Necessary. (*A.-N.*)

NECESSITY. Bad illicit spirit. *Devon.* See Marshall's West of England, i. 232.

NECK. (1) *To come in the neck,* to follow immediately afterwards. *Neck and crop,* completely.

(2) The turning up, or plait, of a cap, was formerly called its *neck.*

NECKABOUT. Any linen or garment about a woman's neck. *Sheffield.*

NECK-BAND. A gorget. *Palsgrave.*

NECK-BARROW. A shrine on which relics or images were carried in processions.

NECK-BREAK. Complete ruin. *East.*

NECK-COLLAR. A gorget. *Palsgrave.*

NECKED. When the ears of corn are bent down and broken off by wind, &c., the corn is said to be necked. *North.*

NECKING. A neck-handkerchief. *East.* Also called a *neck-tye.*

NECK-OF-THE-FOOT. The instep.

NECK-PIT. The bend at the back of the neck. *Neckepyt*, Archæologia, xxx. 411.

NECK-ROPE. A wooden bow to come round the neck of a bullock, and fastened above to a small transverse beam, by which bullocks are fastened with a cord.

NECK-TOWEL. A small towel used for wiping delicate crockery, &c. *Linc.*

NECKUM. The three draughts into which a jug of beer is divided are called *neckum, sinkum, swankum.*

NECK-VERSE. The beginning of the 51st psalm, read formerly by criminals claiming the benefit of clergy.

> And it behoves me to be secret, or else my *necke-verse* cun :
> Well, now to pack my dead man hence it is hye tyme
> I run. *1st Part of Promos and Cassandra*, iv. 4.
> At this assizes fear not to appear ;
> The judge will read thy *neck-verse* for thee here.
> *Clobery's Divine Glimpses*, 1659, p. 119.

NECK-WEED. Hemp. *Var. dial.*

NED-CAKE. A rich girdle cake. *North.*

NEDDER. (1) An adder. *North.* It occurs in the Boke of Curtasye, p. 9. " *Serpens*, alle maner nedris," Nominale MS.

(2) Lower; inferior. *North.*

NEDDY. A jackass. *Var. dial.*

NEDE. (1) To force ; to compel. (*A.-S.*)

(2) We should probably read " ende" in the following passage :

> A rugged taile so a fende,
> And an heved at the *nede.*
> *Arthour and Merlin*, p. 57.

NEDEFUL. Distressed ; indigent. (*A.-S.*)

NEDELLER. A maker of needles.

NEDELY. Necessarily. (*A.-S.*) *Nedelinges* is also used in the same sense.

> Sithe it *nedelyngis* shall be so.
> *MS. Harl.* 2252, f. 97.

> And thay went thurghe a dry cuntree, sandye and withowttene water, and *nedlynges* thame byhoved wende armede, ther was so grete plentee of neddirs and cruelle wylde bestes.
> *MS. Lincoln* A. 1. 17, f. 27.

NEDINGE. Need ; trouble.

NEDIRCOP. A spider. Nominale MS.

NEE. Nigh. Wright's Seven Sages, p. 48.

NEED-FIRE. Ignition produced by rubbing wood together. *North.*

NEEDHAM'S-SHORE. An indigent situation. This proverb is given by Ray. See Tusser, ed. 1812, p. 284.

NEEDLE. (1) To nestle ; to lodge.

(2) A piece of wood put by the side of a post to strengthen it. *East.*

(3) *To hit the needle*, to strike the centre of the mark. A term in archery, often used metaphorically.

NEEDLE-HOUSE. A small case for needles.

" *Acuare*, a nedylhowu," Nominale MS. xv. Cent. It occurs in Lydgate.

NEEDLE-POINT. A sharper. *Needler*, a keen active man ; a niggard.

NEEDLE-WEED. The plant shepherd's needle.

NEEDLE-WORK. The curious frame-work of timber and plaster with which many old houses are constructed.

NEEDMENTS. Necessaries.

> Her wit a commonwealth containes
> Of *needments* for her houshold store.
> *Deloney's Strange Historie*, 1607.

NEEDS. (1) Necessities. (2) Of necessity. (3) Forsooth ; indeed. *Somerset.*

NEELE. A needle. Also *neeld.* It is an archaism, and is still in use.

NEEN. The eyes. *Yorksh.*

NEEP. Draught-tree of a waggon.

NEESE. To sneeze. *North.* This form of the word occurs in Welde's Janua Linguarum, 1615, Index in v. *sternuto.*

NEEST. Nighest ; next. *North.*

NEET. Night. *North.*

NEEVEYE. Descendants.

NEEZLE. To nestle. *Var. dial.* Bird's-nesting is often called *birds'-neezing.*

NEGH. Almost ; nearly. (*A.-S.*)

NEGHE. To near ; to approach. (*A.-S.*)

> For night *neghed* and that had nede,
> Bot of herber might thai noght spede.
> *MS. Harl.* 4196, f. 13.

NEGHEN. Nine. See *Defauteles.*

NEGHST. Nighest ; nearest. *Hampole.*

NEGLECTION. Neglect. *Glouc.*

NEGLIGENT. Reckless. This stronger meaning than is usually assigned to the word is used by Shakespeare.

NEGON. A niggard ; a miser. Wrongly explained in Gl. Towneley Myst. p. 320.

> Covaytice of wylle is os a bayt ;
> Avaryce is a *negon* haldyng strayt.
> *R. de Brunne, MS. Bowes,* p. 89.
> And thus men schall teche odur by the,
> Of mete and drynke no *negyn* to bee.
> *MS. Cantab.* Ff. ii. 38, f. 109
> What seye ȝe by these streyte *negons*,
> That se al day Goddes personee.
> *MS. Harl.* 1701, f. 40.
> To ȝow therof am I no *nigon.*
> *Occleve, MS. Soc. Antiq.* 134, f. 262.

NEGROES-HEADS. Brown loaves delivered to the ships in ordinary.

NEIF. Fist, or hand. *North.*

> Alle lyardes menne, I warne ȝowe byfore,
> Bete the cownte with ȝour *neffes*, whene ȝe may do no more.
> Thus endis lyarde, at the laste worde,
> Yf a manne thynke mekille, kepe somewhate in horde.
> *MS. Lincoln* A. 1. 17, f. 149.

NEIGHBOUR. There is a game called " Neighbour, I torment thee," played in Staffordshire, " with two hands and two feet and a bob, and a nod as I do."

NEIGHBOURING. Gossiping. *Yorksh.*

NEIL. Never.

> Whos kyngdome ever schalle laste and *neil* fyne.
> *Lydgate, MS. Soc. Antiq.* 134, f. 2.

NEIST. Near ; next to. *Devon.*

NEITHER-OF-BOTH. Neither. *East.*

NEIVEL. To give a blow with the neive or fist. *Cumb.*

NEKED. Little or nothing. *Gawayne.*

NEKIST. Nearest; next. (*A.-S.*)

NELE. Evil; cowardly.

NELL-KNEED. Knock-kneed. *North.*

NELSON'S-BALLS. A globular confection, in great esteem with boys.

NEMBROT. Nimrod.

> And over that thorow synne it come,
> That *Nembrot* suche emprise nom.
> *Gower, MS. Soc. Antiq.* 134, f. 37.

NEME. Uncle. " *Neme*, neam, gossip, (Warw.)," Kennett, MS. Lansd. 1033.

> Ther undur sate a creature,
> As briȝt as any son-beme,
> And angels did hym gret honoure,
> Lo! childe, he seid, this is thy *neme*.
> *MS. Cantab.* Ff. v. 48, f. 69.

> In evyll tyme thou dedyst hym wronge;
> He ys my *neme*, y schall the honge.
> *MS. Cantab.* Ff. ii. 38, f. 151.

NEMEL. Capable. *Lydgate.*

NEMELINE. To name; to call.

NEMLY. Quickly; sharply.

NEMPNE. To name; to call. (*A.-S.*) *Nempt*, Holinshed, Hist. England, i. 81.

NENE. Neither. (*A.-S.*) It occurs in MS. Cotton. Vespas. D. vii.

NENEEVEN. Temperance. See Batman uppon Bartholome, 1582.

NENET. Will not. (*A.-S.*)

NENTE. The ninth.

> Of this *nente* make we ende,
> And begyne of the tende.
> *R. de Brunne, MS. Bowes,* p. 11.

NEOPHYTE. A novice. (*Gr.*)

NEP. (1) A turnip. *North.*

(2) The herb cat-mint. *Palsgrave.* Spelt *nept* in MS. Lincoln, f. 292.

NEPHEW. Grandson; descendant.

NEPKIN. A nectarine. *Somerset.*

NEPPERED. Cross; peevish. *Yorksh.*

NER. Never. (*A. S.*)

> As I stod on a day, me self under a tre,
> I met in a morveninge a may, in a medwe;
> A semilier to min sithe saw I *ner* non,
> Of a blak bornet al wos hir wede,
> Purfiled with pellour doun to the teon.
> *MS. Arundel. Coll. Arm.* 27, f. 130.

NERANE. A spider. Nominale MS.

NERE. (1) Nigher; nearer. (*A.-S.*)

(2) For *ne were*, were not. (*A.-S.*)

(3) The ear. MS. Cott. Vesp. D. vii.

NERFE. Nerve; sinew. (*A.-N.*)

NERLED. Badly treated. *North.*

NERVALLE. The following receipt is from an early MS. in my possession—

> For to make a noyntement callyd *nervalle;* It is gode for senowys. Take wylde sage, amerose, camemylle, betayne, sage, mynte, heyhove, horehownde, red-nettylle, lorel-levys, walworte, of eche halfe a quartone; and than wesche them, and stampe them with a *lt.* of May buttur, and than put to a quarton of oyle olyf, and medylle them well together, and than put it in a erthyn pott, and cover it welle, and than sett it in a moyste place ix. dayys,

and than take and fry hit welle, and store it welle for bornyng to the botome; and than take and streyne it into a vessele, and when it ys streynyd, set the lekur on the fyur ayene; and than put therto halfe a quarton wex, and a quarton of wedurse talow that is fayer moltyn, and a quarton frankensens, and than store it welle together tylle it be welle medelyd; and than take it downe, and streyne it, and let it kele; and than take and kut it thyn, and let owt the watur therof, and clense it clene on the other syde, and than set it over the fyur ayenne tyl it be moltyn, and than with a feyr skome it clene, and than put it in boxus, and this ys kyndle made *nervalle.*

NESCOCK. An unfledged bird. *North.* Figuratively applied to youth. " A nesslecock, or youth o' th' towne," Bride, 1640, sig. A. iv.

NESEN. Nests. *Suffolk.*

NESETHRULLUS. Nostrils. This form occurs in the Nominale MS. " *Narus*, a nestthyrylle," MS. ibid.

NESH. (1) Tender; soft; delicate; weak; poor-spirited. *North.*

> Take the rute of horsehelme, and sethe it lange in water, and thanne tak the *neschette* therof, and stamp it with alde gres. *MS. Lincoln* A. i. 17, f. 295.

(2) Hungry. *Suffolk.*

NESHIN. To make tender. *Chesh.*

NESP. To peck; to bite. *Linc.*

NESPITE. The herb calamint.

NESS. A promontory of land. (*A.-S.*)

NESSE. Soft. Here used for good fortune.

> In *nesse*, in hard, y pray the nowe,
> In al stedes thou him avowe.
> *Arthour and Merlin,* p. 116.

NESSES. Nests. *West.* Another form, *nestis*, is common everywhere.

NESSLE. To trifle. *Sussex.*

NESSLETRIPE. The youngest or most weakly of a brood or litter. *West.* Also called a *nestle-draft*, and *nestling.*

NEST. (1) The socket of the eye.

(2) A quantity or collection of articles together. " A nest of shelves" is in common use. " A bowle for wine, if not an whole neast," Harrison's England, p. 189. Mr. Dyce tells us that a nest of goblets is a large goblet containing many smaller ones of gradually diminishing sizes, which fit into each other, and fill it up.

NESTARME. An intestine.

NEST-EGG. An egg left in the nest to induce the hen or other bird to lay more in the same. *Var. dial.* Metaphorically a fund laid up against adversity.

NESTLE. To fidget about. *North.*

NET. To wash clothes. *Yorksh.*

NETHEBOUR. A neighbour.

NETHELESSE. Nevertheless. (*A.-S.*)

NETHER. (1) An adder. (2) Lower. (*A.-S.*)

(3) To starve with cold. *North.*

NETHERSTOCKS. Stockings. It is the translation of *un bas de chausses* in Hollyband's Dictionarie, 1593. Kennett calls them, "boots, buskins." MS. Lansd. 1033.

NETT. Eat not. (*A.-S.*)

> His lif him thoughte al to long,
> Thre daies after he *nett* ne drong.
> *Beves of Hamtoun,* p. 65.

NETTING. Urine. *North.*

NETTLED. Out of temper; provoked. An ill-tempered person was said to have [watered] on a nettle.

NETTLE-HOUSE. A jakes. *North.*

NETTLE-SPRINGE. The nettle-rash. *East.*

NETT-UP. Exhausted with cold. *Sussex.*

NEUP. A blaze. *Devon.*

NEULTIES. Novelties; dainties. *Oxon.*

NEUME. Modulation of the voice in singing. Nominale MS.

NEVE. A nephew. Also, a spendthrift, corresponding to the Latin terms.

NEVEDE. Had not. (*A.-S.*)

NEVELINGE. Snivelling. (*A.-S.*)

NEVENE. To name; to speak. (*A.-S.*)

Not fulle sele that men coude *nevyne.*
MS. *Harl.* 2252, f. 117.

The kyng callyd knyghtys fyve,
And bad them go belyve
And fynde hym at hys play;
No evylle worde to hym ye *nevyn,*
But sey to hym with mylde stevyn,
He wylle not sey yow nay!
MS. *Cantab.* Ff. ii. 38, f. 78.

That the crowne in the wynters nyght
Of Adrian ne of the sterres seven,
To hir fayrenesse ne be not for to *neven.*
Lydgate, *MS Ashmole* 39, f. 8.

NEVER-A-DELE. Not a bit.

NEVER-THE-LATTERE. Nevertheless.

Never-the-lattere whenne thei that were in the castelle beseged saw that the sege was withedraw for fere, and the Scottes host afferde, also thei came oute of the castelle and lefte them opene &c.
Warkworth's Chronicle, p. 2.

NEVER-THE-NERE. Never the nearer; to no purpose; uselessly.

NEVER-WHERE. Nowhere. (*A.-S.*)

NEVIN. A kind of rich fur.

NEVY. Nephew. *Var. dial.*

NEW-AND-NEW. Freshly; with renovated beauty or vigour; again and again. It occurs in Chaucer.

NEW-BEAR. A term applied to a cow that has very lately calved. *Linc.* Brockett terms it *newcal-cow.*

NEWCASTLE-HOSPITALITY. Roasting a friend to death. *North.*

NEW-COMES. Strangers newly arrived. See Holinshed, Conq. Ireland, p. 55. The time when any fruit comes in season is called a *new-come.*

NEW-CUT. A game at cards. It is mentioned in an epigram in MS. Egerton 923; Taylor's Motto, 1622, sig. D. iv. Jennings, p. 57, mentions a game called *new coat and jerkin.*

Cast up the cardes, the trickes together put,
And leaving Ruffe, lets fall upon *New Cut.*
Machivells Dogge, 1617.

NEWDICLE. A novelty. *East.*

NEWE. (1) Newly. *All newe, of newe,* newly, lately, anew, afresh.

(2) Fretted. Holme, 1688.

(3) To renew. It occurs in MS. Cotton. Vespas. D. vii. (*A.-S.*)

Now me *neweth* al my wo.
Cursor Mundi, MS. Coll. Trin. Cantab. f. 124.

Then beganne hur sorowe to *nett a.*
MS. *Cantab.* Ff ii. 38, f. 186

NEWEFANGELNESSE. Inconstancy.

NEWEL. "A pillar of stone or wood, where the steps terminate in a winding staircase," Kennett, MS. Lansd. 1033.

NEWELTIE. Novelty. *Palsgrave.*

NEWEYNGE. A new-year's gift.

NEWGATE. Nash, in his Pierce Penilesse, says that Newgate is "a common name for al prisons, as *homo* is a common name for a man or a woman."

NEWING. Yeast; barm. *Essex.*

NEW-LAND. Land newly broken up and ploughed. *Kent.*

NEWSED. Reported; published. *East.*

NEWST-ONE. Much the same. *South.*

NEXING. Very near. *Next kin* is a very common phrase in this sense, and *next door* is also used.

NEXT-DAY. The day after to morrow. *Sussex.*

NEXTE. Nighest. *Chaucer.* Fairfax has *nextly,* nearest to, Bulk and Selvedge of the World, 1674, ded.

NEXT-WAYS. Directly. *Var. dial.*

NEYDUR. Neither. Eglamour, 883.

NEYE. (1) To neigh.

He *neyed* and made grete solas
Wondurly yn that place.
MS. *Cantab.* Ff. ii. 38, f. 111.

(2) Near; nigh.

That birde bad on hir boke evere as he yede,
Was non with hir but hir selve a-lon;
With a cri gan sche me sey,
Sche wold a-wrenchin awey,
But for I was so *neye.*
MS. *Arundel. Coll. Arm.* 27, f. 130.

NEYTENE. Sickness; disease.

NI. (1) A brood of pheasants. "A *ny* of feysands, covey of partridges," MS. Porkington 10. Still in common use.

(2) An exclamation of amazement.

NIAISE. A simple witless gull. (*Fr.*) Forby has *nisy,* Vocab. ii. 233.

NIAS. A young hawk. "*Niard,* a nias faulcon," Cotgrave. See *Eyas.*

NIB. (1) The handle of a scythe. *Derb.*

(2) To cut up into small fragments. *Linc.*

(3) The shaft of a waggon. *South.*

NIBBLE. To fidget the fingers about. "His fingers began to *nibble,*" Stanihurst, Descr. Ireland, p. 26. "To nibble with the fingers, as unmannerly boies do with their points when they are spoken to," Baret, 1580.

NICE. (1) Foolish; stupid; dull; strange. It occurs in Shakespeare.

The eld man seyd anon,
Ye be *nice,* everichon.
Arthour and Merlin, p. 73.

He toke the wyne, and laft the spice,
Then wist thei wel that he was *nyce.*
MS. *Cantab.* Ff. v. 48, f. 55.

(2) Clever; fine; good. *North.*

(3) Fastidious; fantastic. Still in use.

NICED. A breast-cloth; a light wrapper for the bosom, or neck.

NICELY. Well in health. *North.*

NICET. Agreeable. *Yorksh.*

NICETEE. Folly. (*A.-N.*)

NICH. To stir a fire slightly. *North.*

NICHIL. (1) To castrate. *Yorksh.*

(2) A person who pays nothing. *West.*

NICHOLAS. The patron saint of boys. In boys' games, the cry of *Nicholas* entitles the speaker to a temporary suspension of the amusement. *St. Nicholas's clerks,* a cant term for thieves. "One of saint Nicholas clerks, or an arrant theefe," Cotgrave, in v. *Compter.* Grose has this phrase.

NICK. (1) Used in the proverbial expression "to knock a *nick* in the post," i. e., to make a record of any remarkable event. This is evidently an ancient method of recording. Similarly we have "cut your stick," in which the reference is clearly to the ancient tallies; it is equivalent to "make your mark and pass on." Hence also, "in the *nick* of time," i. e., just as the notch was being cut. *In the nick,* exactly. *North.*

(2) *To nick with nay,* to deny, a very common phrase in early English.

> On her knees they kneleden adoun,
> And prayden hym off hys benysoun;
> He nykkyd hem with nay;
> Neyther of cros ueyther off ryng,
> Hadde they non kyns wetyng,
> And thanne a knyȝt gan say.
> *Romance of Athelstone.*

(3) To deceive; to cheat. *Var. dial.*

(4) To cut vertical sections in a mine from the roof. *North.*

(5) A wink. *North.* (Teut.)

(6) To win at dice. *Grose.* "To tye or nicke a cast at dice," Florio, p. 280.

(7) *To nick the nick,* to hit exactly the critical moment or time.

(8) A raised or indented bottom in a beer-can, formerly a great grievance with the consumer. A similar contrivance in a wine-bottle is called the *kick.* Grose has *neck-stamper,* the boys who collect the pots belonging to an ale-house sent out with beer to private houses.

> There was a tapster, that with his pots smalnesse, and with frothing of his drinke, had got a good summe of money together. This *nicking* of the pots he would never leave, yet divers times he had been under the hand of authority, but what money soever hee had [to pay] for his abuses, hee would be sure (as they all doe) to get it out of the poore mans pot againe.
> *Life of Robin Goodfellow,* 1628.
> From the *nick* and froth of a penny pot-house,
> From the fidle and cross, and a great Scotch-louse,
> From committees that chop up a man like a mouse,
> *Fletcher's Poems,* p. 133.
> Our pots were full quarted,
> We were not thus thwarted
> With froth-canne and *nick-pot,*
> And such nimble quick shot.
> *Elynour Rummynge,* ed. 1624.

(9) To catch in the act. *Var. dial.*

NICKER. (1) To neigh. *North.*

(2) A little ball of clay or earth baked hard and oiled over for boys to play at *nickers.*

NICKER-PECKER. A woodpecker. *North.*

NICKET. A small short faggot. *West.*

NICKIN. A soft simple fellow.

NICKING. Convenient. *Somerset.*

NICKLE. To move hastily along in an awkward manner. *West.*

NICKLED. Beaten down and entangled, as grass by the wind. *East.*

NICK-NINNY. A simpleton. *South.*

NICKOPIT. A bog; a quagmire. *Kent.*

NICK-STICK. A tally, or stick notched for reckoning. *North.*

NICKY. A faggot of wood. *West.*

NICOTIUM. Tobacco.

NIDDE. To compel. (*A.-S.*)

NIDDERED. Cold and hungry. *North.*

NIDDICK. The nape of the neck. *West.*

NIDDICOCK. A foolish fellow. Polwhele has *nicky-cox* as a Devonshire word. "They were never such fond *niddicockes,*" Holinshed, Conq. Ireland, p. 94.

NIDDY. A fool. *Devon.*

NIDDY-NODDY. A child's game.

NIDERLING. A mean inhospitable fellow. This word is not in frequent use, but may be heard occasionally. *Linc.*

NIDES. Needs; necessarily.

> Thus athe sche fullyche overcome
> My ydeinys tylle y sterve,
> So that y mote *nydes* serve.
> *MS. Cantab.* Ff. i. 6, f. 4.

NIDGERIES. Trifles. *Skinner.*

NIDGET. (1) To assist a woman in her labour or travail. *East.*

(2) Part of a plough. *Kent.*

(3) A fool. "*Nigaud,* a fop, nidget, ideot, a doult, lobcocke," Cotgrave.

NIDING. A coward; a wretch. (*A.-S.*)

NIE. Nigh; near. (*A.-S.*)

NIECE. A relative in general, not confined to our meaning. *Shak.*

NIEGHEND. The ninth. *Hampole.*

NIF. If. *Somerset.*

NIFF. To quarrel; to be offended. *West.*

NIFFLE. (1) A spur for a horse. *East.*

(2) To steal; to pilfer. *North.*

(3) To whine; to sniffle. *Suffolk.* It occurs in Reliq. Antiq. ii. 211.

(4) To eat hastily. *Beds.*

NIFF-NAFFS. Trifles; knick-knacks. *Niffy-naffy,* a trifling fellow. *North.*

NIFLE. A trifle. "I weigh them not a *nifle,*" Optick Glasse of Humors, 1639, p. 161. "Nyfles in a bagge, *de tout nifles,*" Palsgrave. "Trash, rags, *nifles,* trifles," Cotgrave.

NIFLES. Glandules. *Yorksh.*

NIG. To clip money. *Grose.*

NIGARDIE. Stinginess. (*A.-N.*)

NIGG. A small piece. *Essex.*

NIGGED-ASHLAR. Stone hewn with a pointed hammer. *Oxf. Gloss. Arch.*

NIGGER. A fire-dog. *North.*

NIGGLE. (1) Futuo. Dekker, 1616.

(2) To deceive; to draw out surreptitiously; to steal. Still in use.

(3) To play with; to trifle. Hence, to walk mincingly. *North.*

(4) To eke out with extreme care. *East.*

(5) To complain of trifles from ill temper. *Dorset.*

(6) To nibble; to eat or do anything mincingly. *West.*

NIGGLING. Contemptible; mean. *West.*

NIGHE. To approach. See *Neghe.*

> The batayle lasted wondur longe,
> They seyde, Be Burlonde never so stronge,
>   He hath fonde hys pere.
> Wyth swerdys scharpe the faght faste,
> At ylke stroke the fyre owt raste,
>   They *nyghed* wondur nere.
> *MS. Cantab.* Ff. ii. 38, f. 81.

NIGHEST-ABOUT. The nearest way. *North.*

NIGH-HAND. Probably. *Leic.*

NIGHT-BAT. A ghost. *North.*

NIGHT-COURTSHIP. This custom, which appears to be now falling into disuse, is thus described in a note to Anderson's Ballads:—

> A Cumbrian peasant pays his addresses to his sweetheart during the silence and solemnity of midnight, when every bosom is at rest, except that of love and sorrow. Anticipating her kindness, he will travel ten or twelve miles over hills, bogs, moors, and mosses, undiscouraged by the length of the road, the darkness of the night, or the intemperature of the weather; on reaching her habitation, he gives a gentle tap at the window of her chamber, at which signal she immediately rises, dresses herself, and proceeds with all possible silence to the door, which she gently opens, lest a creaking hinge or a barking dog should awaken the family. On his entrance into the kitchen, the luxuries of a Cumbrian cottage—cream and sugared curds—are placed before him by the fair hand of his *Dulcinea*; next, the courtship commences, previously to which, the fire is darkened or extinguished, lest its light should guide to the window some idle or licentious eye; in this dark and uncomfortable situation (at least uncomfortable to all but lovers), they remain till the advance of day, depositing in each other's bosoms the secrets of love, and making vows of unalterable affection.

NIGHT-CROW. A well-known bird, otherwise called the night-jar. "*Nicticorax*, a nyght-craw" Nominale MS. Palsgrave translates it by *cresserelle.*

NIGHTERTALE. Night-time. (*A.-S.*)

> His men coom bi *nyytertale*,
> With hem awey his body stale.
> *Cursor Mundi, MS. Coll. Trin. Cantab.* f. 49.
> By *nyytertale* he was slayne be kynge Darie.
> *Occleve, MS. Soc. Antiq.* 134, f. 272.

NIGHTGALE. The nightingale.

> Wyth alkyne gladchipe thay gladdene themeselvene,
> Of the *nyghtgale* notes the noises was swette.
> *Morte Arthure, MS. Lincoln,* f. 63.

NIGHT-KERT-CHEF. A lady's neck handkerchief. It is the translation of *collerette* in Hollyband's Dictionarie, 1593.

NIGHT-MAGISTRATE. A constable.

NIGHT-MARE. The charm for the night-mare mentioned in the following curious passage is quoted in Beaumont and Fletcher, and other early writers:

> If this disease chancing often to a man, be not

ri.

cured in time, it may perhaps grow to a worse mischiefe, as to the faling evil, madnesse, or apopelexy. But I could never learne that horses were subject to this disease, neither by relation, nor yet by reading, but only in an old English writer, who sheweth neither cause nor signes how to know when a horse hath it, but onely teacheth how to cure it with a fond foolish charme, which because it may perhaps make you, gentle reader, to laugh, as wel as it did me, for recreation sake I will heere rehearse it. Take a flint stone that hath a hole of his owne kinde, and hang it over him, and write in a bill,

> In nomine Patris. &c.
> Saint George our Ladies knight,
> He walked day, so did he night,
> Untill he her found,
> He her beate, and he her bound,
> Till truely her troath she him plight,
> That she would not come within the night,
> There as saint George our Ladies knight,
> Named was three times, saint George.

And hang this scripture over him, and let him alone: with such proper charmes as this is, the false friers in times past were wont to charme the mony out of plaine folks purses. *Topsell's Beasts,* 1607, p. 363.

NIGHT-RAIL. A sort of vail or covering for the head, often worn by women at night. See Middleton's Works, i. 164. Mr. Dyce absurdly explains it night-gown, which makes nonsense in the passage referred to. Howell has, "a night-rail for a woman, *toca de muger de nochez.*"

NIGHT-RAVEN. The bittern. "*Niticorax*, a nyte-rawyn," Nominale MS.

NIGHT-SHADE. A prostitute.

NIGHT-SNAP. A night-robber.

NIGHT-SNEAKERS. "Wanton or effeminate lads, night-sneakers," Florio, p. 105.

NIGHT-SPELL. A spell or charm against the night-mare.

NIGHTWARD. The night-watch.

NIGHTY. Dark. *Oxon.*

NIGIT. A coward; a dastard.

> This cleane *nigit* was a foole,
> Shapt in meane of all.
> *Armin's Nest of Ninnies,* 1608.

NIGMENOG. A very silly fellow.

NIGROST. Negroes. *Hall.*

NIGRUM. Dark; black. (*Lat.*)

NIKIR. A sea monster. (*A.-S.*)

NIKLE. An icicle. Pr. Parv. p. 259.

NILE. The upper portion of a thresher's flail. *Salop.*

NILL. (1) A nail. *Somerset.*

> Thorow my lyfte honde a *nyl* was dryve!
> Thenke thou theron, yf thou wolte lyve.
> *MS. Cantab.* Ff. ii. 38, f. 6.

(2) Will not. (*A.-S.*) *Will he nill he,* whether he will or not. Hence, to be unwilling.

> *Nylling* to dwell where syn is wrought.
> *Ashmole's Theat. Chem. Brit.* 1652, p. 117.

(3) A needle. Still in use.

NIM. (1) To take. Also, to steal. Hence the character Corporal Nym.

> *Nym*, he seyde, this theof
> Faste in alle wyse,
> And wyn of him the tresour,
> And make him do sacrifyse.
> *MS. Trin. Coll. Oxon.* 57

37

Then boldly blow the prize thereat,
Your play for to *nime* or ye come in.
The Books of Hunting, 1586.

(2) To walk with short quick steps. *North.*

(3) To take heed; to take care.

NIMBER. Active.

The boy beinge but a xj. yers old juste at the death of his father, yet having reasonable wit and discretion, and being *nymber* sprited and apte to anythinge. *MS. Ashmol.* 208.

NIMGIMMER. A surgeon.

NIMIETY. Satiety. (Lat.)

NIMIL. Large; capacious.

NIMMEL. Nimble. *North.*   " Lyght and nymel," Morte d'Arthur, i. 285.

NIN. (1) None. *North.*

(2) A child's term for liquor. " The word that children call their drinke by, as our children say *ninne* or bibbe," Florio, p. 64.

NINCUMPOOP. A person nine times worse than a fool. See Grose.

NIND. Needs must. *Linc.*

NINE-EYED. A term of reproach.

NINE-EYES. A kind of small eel.

NINE-HOLES. A game differently described by various writers. According to Forby, nine round holes are made in the ground, and a ball aimed at them from a certain distance; or the holes are made in a board with a number over each, through one of which the ball is to pass. Nares thinks it is the same game with *nine-men's morris*, called in some places *ninepenny-marl.*

NINE-MURDER. A kind of hawk. See Florio, p. 205. Cotgrave apparently mentions two birds so called, in v. *Escriere, Soucie.*

NINE-MUSES. An old dance, mentioned in MS. Rawl. Poet. 108.

NINE-PINS. A game somewhat similar to skittles. It is mentioned by Florio, ed. 1611, p. 15, and is still in use.

NINETED. Wicked; perverse. *South.*

NINETING. A severe beating. *West.*

NINGLE. A contracted form of *mine ingle*, common in old plays.

NINNY-NONNY. Uncertain. *Linc.*

NINNYVERS. The white water-lily.

NINNYWATCH. A vain hope; a silly or foolish expectation. *Devon.*

NINT. To beat; to anoint. *Var. dial.*

NIP. (1) A satirical taunt. Also a verb, to taunt satirically. " *S'entrepicquer*, to pricke, nip, taunt, quip, cut, each other," Cotgrave. " A dry-bob, jeast, or nip," ibid.

(2) A thief. An old cant term. " To nyp a bong," to cut a purse, Harman's Caveat, 1567.

(3) Cut. Robin Hood, i. 100.

(4) To snatch up hastily. *Yorksh.*

(5) A short steep ascent. *North.* Occasionally, a hill or mountain.

(6) To pinch closely. Hence applied to a parsimonious person. *Var. dial.*

(7) A turnip. *Suffolk.*

NIP-CHEESE. A miserly person. *Var. dial.* Sometimes called a *nip-squeeze*, or a *nip-farthing.*

NIP-NOSE. A phrase applied to a person whose nose is bitten by frost.

NIPPER. A cut-purse. *Dekker.* Also termed a *nipping-Christian.*

NIPPERKIN. A small measure of beer.

NIPPET. A small quantity. *Essex.*

NIPPITATO. Strong liquor, chiefly applied to ale. A cant term.

NIPPLE. " A little cocke, end, or nipple perced, or that hath an hole after the maner of a breast, which is put at the end of the chanels of a fountaine, wherthrough the water runneth forth," Baret, 1580.

NIPPY. (1) Hungry. *Dorset.*

(2) A child's term for the penis.

NIPTE. A niece; a grand-daughter.

NIRE. Nigher; nearer. *West.*

NIRRUP. A donkey. *Dorset.*

NIRT. Cut; hurt. *Gawayne.*

NIRVIL. A diminutive person.

NIS. Is not. (*A.-S.*)

NISGAL. The smallest of a brood or litter. *Salop.*

NISOT. A lazy jade. *Skelton.*

NISSE. Navy; ships. *Hearne.*

NIST. (1) Nigh; near. *Somerset.*

(2) Nice; pleasant; agreeable. *Linc.*

NISTE. Knew not. (*A.-S.*)

And hou Fortiger him wold have nome,
Ac he *nist* where he was bicome.
Arthour and Merlin, p. 72

That was eclipcid fer oute of my syste,
That for derkenesse y *niste* what to done.
Lydgate, MS. Soc. Antiq. 134, f. 6

NIT. Not yet. *West.*

NITAMOST. Nothing like it. *South.*

NITCH. (1) Neat. *Dorset.*

(2) A small bundle. *Var. dial.*

(3) Got a nitch, i. e. tipsy.

NITHE. Wickedness.

But in pride and treachery,
In *nythe* and onde and lecchery.
Cursor Mundi, MS. Coll. Trin. Cantab. f. 138.

NITHER. A grimace. *Worc.*

NITHING. A wicked man. *Nythying*, Audelay, p. 16. Also, sparing, parsimonious, wicked, mean.

NITLE. Neat; handsome. *Var. dial.*

NITOUR. Brightness.

The amber that is in common use groweth rough, rude, impolished, and without cleareness, but after that it is sod in the greace of a sow that giveth sucke, it getteth that *nitour* and shining beauty, which we find to be in it. Topsell's Beasts, 1607, p. 681.

NITTICAL. Nitty; lousy. *Nitty* is not an uncommon word.

NITTLE. " A childish word for *little*," Urry MS. Adds. to Ray.

NIX. (1) Nothing. A cant term.

(2) To impose upon. See *Nick.*

NO. (1) Often used ironically by our early dramatists to express excess, e. g. Here's no rascal, implying a very great rascal.

(2) Nor; not. Still in use.

Tho were thai wounded so strong,
That thai *no* might doure long.
Arthour and Merlin, p. 208.

The clfre in the ritht side was first wryte, and jit be tokeneth nothinge, no the secunde, no the thridde, but thei maken that figure of 1 the more signyficatyf that comith after hem.

Rare Mathematica, p. 29.

NOAH'S-ARKS. Clouds in the forms of arks, indicating rain. *Suffolk.*

NOB. (1) To beat; to strike. *North.*

(2) The head. *Var. dial.* Hence, a person in a superior station of life.

(3) A young colt. *Heref.*

NOBBLE. (1) To beat; to rub. *North.*

(2) A lump of anything. *East.*

NOBBLE-TREE. The head. *Suffolk.*

NOBBLY. Round, as pebbles, &c. *Var. dial.*

NOBBY. (1) A fool. *East.*

(2) Fine; fashionable. *Var. dial.*

NOBBY-COLT. A young colt. *Glouc.*

NOBILE. Grandeur; magnificence.

Sothly by Arthurys day
Was Bretayne yn grete *nobyls*,
For yn hys tyme a grete whyle
He sojourned at Carlile.

MS. Rawlinson C. 86.

NOBILLARY. Nobleness; nobility.

NOBLE. (1) The navel. *East.*

(2) A gold coin worth 6s. 8d.

NOBLESSE. Dignity; splendour. *(A.-N.)* *Nobley* has the same meanings.

Of what richesse, of what *nobley*,
These bokis telle, and thus they say.

Gower, MS. Soc. Antiq. 134, f. 197.

And so they mett betwixt both hostes, where was right kynde and lovynge langwage betwixt them twoo, with parfite accord knyt togethars for evar here aftar, with as hartyly lovynge chere and countenaunce, as might be betwix two bretherne of so grete *nobley* and astate.

Arrival of King Edward IV. p. 11.

Ilkone be worscheped in hys degré
With grete *nobelay* and seere honowres.

Hampole, MS. Bowes, p. 222.

NOBSON. A blow; a stroke. *North.*

NOB-THATCHER. A peruke-maker.

NO-BUT. Only; except. *North.*

NOCENT. A wicked man. *(Lat.)*

An innocent with a *nocent*, a man ungylty with a gylty, was pondered in an egall balaunce.

Hall, 1548, Hen. IV. f. 14.

NOCK. (1) A notch, generally applied to the notch of an arrow or a bow. It is the translation of *coche* in Hollyband's Dictionarie, 1593. To nock, to set the arrow on the string. See Drayton's Poems, p. 80. *Beyond the nock*, out of reason.

(2) To tip or finish off an article with something of a different material.

(3) The posteriors. More usually called *nock-andro.* Cotgrave has, " *Cul*, tayle, *nockandroe*, fundament." (4) Florio, " *Cunno*, a womans nocke; *cunnúta*, a woman well nocked."

NOCKLE. A beetle, or mallet. *Norf.*

NOCKY-BOY. A dull simple fellow.

NOD. He's gone to the land of Nod, i. e. he's gone to bed.

NODCOCK. A simpleton. *Somerset.*

NODDY. (1) A fool. *Minsheu.*

(2) An old game at cards, conjectured to be the same as cribbage. It appears from the Complete Gamester, 1682, p. 76, that *Knave Noddy* was the designation of the knave of trumps in playing that game. The game is by no means obsolete. Carr mentions *noddy-fifteen* in his Craven Gl. Noddy is now played as follows: Any number can play—the cards are all dealt out—the elder hand plays one, (of which he hath a pair or a *prial* if a good player)—saying or singing " there's a good card for thee," passing it to his right hand neighbour—the person next in succession who holds its pair covers it, saying " there's a still better than he;" and passes both onward—the person holding the third of the sort (ace, six, queen, or what not) puts it on with " there's the best of all three:" and the holder of the fourth crowns all with the emphatic—"And there is *Niddy-Noddeee*." —He wins the tack, turns it down, and begins again. He who is first *out* receives from his adversaries a fish (or a bean, as the case may be) for each unplayed card. This game is mentioned in Arch. viii. 149; Taylor's Motto, 1622, sig. D. iv.

NODDY-HEADED. Tipsy. *Oxon.*

NODDY-POLL. A simpleton. *Noddy-pate* is also used, and Florio, p. 214, has *noddy-peake.* " *Benet*, a simple, plaine, doltish fellow, a noddipeake, a ninnyhammer, a pea-goose, a coxe, a sillie companion," Cotgrave.

NODILE. The noddle or head. " *Occiput*, a nodyle," Nominale MS.

NODOCK. The nape of the neck. " His forehead very plaine, and his *nodocke* flat,' Triall of Wits, 1604, p. 25.

NOE. To know. Nominale MS.

I *noe* none that is with me,
Never jit sent after the ;
Never seth that my reyne begane,
Fond I never none so herdy mane,
That hyder durst to us wend,
Bot iff I wold after hym send.

MS. Ashmole 61, xv. Cent.

NO-FAR. Near; not far. *North.*

NOG. (1) A sort of strong ale.

(2) To jog; to move on. *North.*

(3) A square piece of wood supporting the roof of a mine. *Derb.*

NOGGED. Strong limbed. *North.*

NOGGEN. Made of nogs, or hemp. Hence, thick, clumsy, rough. *West.*

NOGGERHEAD. A blockhead. *Dorset.*

NOGGIN. "A mug or pot of earth with a large belly and narrower mouth; in Cheshire, a wooden kit or piggin is called a noggin," Kennet, MS. Lansd. 1033.

NOGGING. The filling up of the interstices in a building composed partly of wood.

NOGGLE. To walk awkwardly. *North.* Hence *noggler*, a bungling person.

NOGGS. The handle of a scythe. *Chesh.*

NOGGY. Tipsy; intoxicated. *North.*

NO-GO. Impracticable. *Var. dial.*

NOGS. (1) Hemp. *Salop.*

(2) The shank-bones. *Yorksh.*

NO-HOW. Not at all. *East.*

NOHT. Nought; nothing. (*A.-S.*)

NOIE. To hurt; to trouble. Also a substantive. Palsgrave has *noieing*, a nuisance.

NOILS. Coarse locks of wool. *East.* By a statute of James I. no one was permitted to put *noyles* into woollen cloth.

NOINT. To beat severely. *Var. dial.*

NOISE. (1) *To make a noise at one*, to scold. *To noise one*, to report or tell tales of. *Noise in the head*, a scolding.

(2) A company of musicians. "Those terrible *noyses*, with thredbare cloakes," Dekker's Belman of London, 1608.

(3) Tumult; dispute. *Weber.*

(4) To make a noise. (*A.-N.*)

NOISFLODE. *Cataclismus*, Nominale MS.

NOK. A notch in a bow.

NOKE. (1) A nook, or corner.

He coverde the childe with his mantille *noke*,
And over the water the way he tuke.
MS. Lincoln A. i. 17, f. 125.

(2) An oak. Nominale MS.

Ther may no man stonde hys stroke,
Thogh he were as stronge as an *noke*.
MS. Cantab. Ff. ii. 38, f. 166.

NOKES. A ninny; a simpleton.

NOKETT. A nook of ground. *Warw.*

NOLDE. Would not. (*A.-S.*)

And *nolde* calle hirselfe none other name
But Goddis handmayde in fulle lowe maner.
Lydgate, MS. Soc. Antiq. 134, f. 2.

Forsothe harme *nold* he do nonne,
Bot he wold do meche gode.
Chron. Vilodun. p. 5.

NOLE. A head. It is sometimes applied to a simpleton, as in Mirr. Mag. p. 222.

NOLT. Black cattle. *North.*

NO-MATTERS. Not well. *Suffolk.*

NOMBRE. Number. (*A.-N.*)

NOME. (1) Took; held. (*A.-S.*)

Ete ne drynke wold he never,
But wepyng and sorowyng evir:
Syrea, sare sorow hath he *nome*,
He wold hys endyng day wer come,
That he myght ought of lif goo
MS. Rawlinson C. 86.

Aftur thys the day was *nomyn*,
That the batelle on schulde comyn.
MS. Cantab. Ff. ii. 38, f. 93.

Thow ert *nome* thef y-wis !
Whar stele thow stede Trenchesis,
That thow ridest upon here ?
Bevea of Hamtoun, p. 73.

And grethur credence to hym he there *nome*
Then he dudde ony tyme therby fore.
Chron. Vilodun. p. 71.

(2) Numb. *Somerset.*

(3) A name. Nominale MS.

Her jongest brother thei lefte at home,
Benjamin was his *nome*.
Cursor Mundi, MS. Coll. Trin. Cantab. f. 30.

NOMELICHE. Namely. (*A.-S.*)

NOMINE. A long speech. *North.*

NOMMER. To number. (*A.-N.*)

For I do the wele to wiete thou myghte nerehand alsonne *nommer* the sternes of hevene, as the folke of the empire of Perse. *MS. Lincoln A. i. 17, f. 7.*

NOMPERE. An arbitrator. *Chaucer.*

And nempned hym for a *nounpere*,
That no debat nere. *Piers Ploughman, p. 97*

NOMPION. One who is possessed of more knowledge than the common people. *Lanc*

NON. Not one; none; not.

NONATION. Wild; incoherent. *West.*

NONCE. Purpose; intent; design; occasion. This word is not yet entirely obsolete. It is derived, as Price observes, from the A.-S. *for than anes.*

I have a slyng for the *nonce*,
That is made for gret stonys.
MS. Cantab. Ff. v. 48, f. 50.

For the *nonest*, I forbare to allege the learneder sort, lest the unlearned should say they could no skill on such books, nor knew not whether they were truly brought in. *Pilkington's Works, p. 644.*

Bot jif thowe wolde alle my steryne stroye fore the *nonys*. *Morte Arthure, MS. Lincoln, f. 73.*

NONE. (1) No time. *West.*

(2) Not at all. *Var. dial.*

(3) The hour of two or three in the afternoon. (*A.-N.*)

NONEARE. Now; just now. *Norf.*

NONE-OR-BOTH. Neither. *Essex.*

NONE-SO-PRETTY. London-pride. *East.*

NONE-SUCH. Black *nonsuch* is trefoil-seed, and white non-such is rye-grass-seed. *Norf.*

NONINO. A burden to a ballad. Shakespeare has it, *hey, nonny, nonny*. The term *nonny-nonny* was applied to the female pudendum, and hence many indelicate allusions. "Nony-nony or pallace of pleasure," Florio, p. 194.

NONKYNS. No kind of. (*A.-S.*)

The lady lay in hir bede and slepe ;
Of tresone tuke sche *nonkyns* kepe,
For therof wyste sche noghte.
MS. Lincoln A. i. 17, f. 119.

NONNE. A nun. (*A.-S.*)

NONNOCK. To trifle; to idle away the time. *Nonnocks*, whims. *East.* Some use *nonny* in the same sense.

NON-PLUNGE. Nonplus. *Nonpower* is also used. *Var. dial.*

NONSICAL. Nonsensical. *West.*

NONSKAITH. A wishing, or longing. *Cumb.*

NONUNIA. A quick time in music, containing nine crotchets between the bars.

NOODLE. A blockhead. *Var. dial.*

NOOK. The quarter of a yard-land, which varies according to the place from 15 to 40 acres. See Carlisle's Account of Charities, p. 298. Still in use.

NOOKED-END. The very farthest extremity of a corner. *Var. dial.*

NOOK-SHOTTEN. Having or possessing nooks and corners. Pegge says, "spoken of a wall in a bevil, and not at right-angles with another wall." The term is still in use, and metaphorically means *disappointed, mistaken.*

NOOLED. Curbed; broken spirited. *North.*

NOON. None. (*A.-S.*)

NOONING. A repast taken by harvest-labourers about noon. *Var. dial.* Pegge has *noonscape*, the time when labourers rest after dinner. *Nooiningscaup*, Hallamsh. Gl. p. 156.

NOONSHUN. A luncheon. *Browne.*

NOONSTEAD. The period of noon.

NOORY. A young boy. (*Fr.*)

NOOZLE. To nestle. *Somerset.*

NOPE. A bullfinch. *Var. dial.*

NOR. Than. Very common.

NORATION. Rumour; speech. *Var. dial.*

NORCHE. To nourish. Cov. Myst. p. 208.

NORFOLK-CAPON. A red-herring.

NORFOLK-DUMPLING. A small globular pudding, made merely with dough and yeast, and boiled for twenty minutes, according to the approved receipt of that county.

> Well, nothing was undone that might be done to make Jemy Camber a tall, little, slender man, when yet he lookt like a *Norfolke dumpling*, thicke and short. *Armin's Nest of Ninnies*, 1608.

NORGANE. Norwegian.

NORI. A foster-child. (*A.-N.*)

> For mj lordes douhter sche is,
> And ich his *nori* forsothe ywis. *Gy of Warwike*, p. 7.
> Fye on thee, feature, fie on thee !
> The devilles owine *nurrye. Chester Plays*. ii. 162.

NORICE. A nurse. (*A.-N.*) " *Nutrix*, norysche," Nominale MS.

NORIE. To nourish. Gesta Rom. p. 215.

NORISTRY. A nursery.

NORLOGE. A clock. Nominale MS.

NORN. Neither; nothing. *West.*

NORRA-ONE. Never-a-one. *Devon.*

NORREL-WARE. A bit-maker, or lorimer.

NORRID. Northward. *Var. dial.*

NORSTHING. Nourishment.

NORSTHYD. Nourished; taught; educated.

NORT. Nothing. *Somerset.*

NORTELRIE. Nurture; education.

NORTH. The following proverb is given by Aubrey in his MS. Collections for Wiltshire in the Ashmolean Museum.

> " The *North* for largeness,
> The East for health !
> The South for buildings,
> The West for wealth."

NORTHERING. Wild; incoherent. *West.* A silly person is called a *northern*, and some of our old dramatists use the latter word in the sense of *clownish*, or *silly*.

NORTH-EYE. To squint. *Suffolk.*

NORTHUMBERLAND. Lord Northumberland's arms, i. e. a black eye.

NORWAIS. Norwegians. *Hearne.*

NORWAY. A whetstone. *Devon.*

NORWAY-NECKCLOTH. A pillory.

NOSE. (1) *To pay through the nose*, to give an extravagant credit price. *Nose of wax*, a proverbial phrase for anything very pliable. *To follow one's nose*, to go straightforward. *To measure noses*, to meet. *To have one's nose on the grindstone*, to be depressed. *As plain as the nose on one's face*, quite evident. *Led by the nose*, governed. *To put one's nose out of joint*, to rival one in the favour of another. *To make a bridge of any one's nose*, to pass by him in drinking. *He cut off his nose to be revenged of his face*, he has revenged his neighbour at the expense of injuring himself. *To make a person's nose swell*, to make him jealous of a rival. *To play with a person's nose*, to ridicule him.

(2) To smell. *Var. dial.* Hence, metaphorically, to pry into anything.

(3) A neck of land. *South.*

(4) To be tyrannical. *Oxon.*

NOSE-BAG. A bag of provender fastened to a horse's head.

NOSEBLEDE. The plant milfoil. *Millifolium*, MS. Sloane 5, f. 6.

NOSE-FLY. A small fly very troublesome to the noses of horses.

NOSEGENT. A nun. An old cant term, given in Brit. Bibl. ii. 521.

NOSE-GIG. A toe-piece to a shoe. *West.*

NOSELING. On the nose. "Felle doune *noselynge*," Morte d'Arthur, ii. 286.

NO-SENSE. A phrase implying worthlessness or impropriety. *West.*

NOSETHIRLES. The nostrils. (*A.-S.*) Spelt *neyse-thrilles* in Reliq. Antiq. i. 54.

NOSIL. (1) To encourage or embolden an animal to fight; to set on.

(2) To grub in the earth.

NOSING. The exterior projecting edge of the tread of a stair.

NOSLE. The handle of a cup, &c. The nosle of a candlestick is that part which holds the end of a candle.

NOSSEN. Noise; rumour; report.

NOSSET. (1) A dainty dish. *Somerset.*

(2) To carouse secretly. *Devon.*

NOST. Knowest not. (*A.-S.*)

NOST-COCKLE. The last hatched bird; the youngest of a brood.

NOSYLLE. A blackbird. *Merula*, MS. Arundel 249, f. 90. It occurs in Nominale MS.

NOT. (1) Know not. (*A.-S.*)

> For whane men thenken to debate,
> I *not* what other thynge is good
> *Gower, MS. Soc. Antiq.* 134, f. 38.

(2) Smooth; without horns. *Var. dial.* Hence, to shear, or poll. *Not-head*, a craven crown.

(3) Not only. 1 Thess. iv. 8.

(4) A game like bandy. *Glouc.*

(5) Well tilled, as a field. *Essex.*

NOTABILITEE. A thing worthy of observation. *Chaucer.*

NOTCH. (1) The female pudendum.

(2) *Out of all notch*, out of all bounds. Lilly, ed. 1632, sig. Aa. xi.

NOTCHET. A notable feat. *East.*

NOTE. (1) Use; business; employment. To use, or enjoy. *Lanc.*

> But thefte serveth of wykked *note*,
> Hyt hangeth hys mayster by the throte.
> *MS. Harl.* 1701, f. 14.

(2) A nut. Maundevile, p. 158.

(3) To push, strike, or gore with the horns, as a bull. *North.*

(4) The time during which a cow is in milk. *North.* Kennett has, " *noyt*, a cow's milk for one year." MS. Lansd. 1033.

(5) To contend with; to fight.

(6) To eat. *Durham.* (Island.)

(7) Neat or cattle. *North.*

NOTELESS. Stupefied. *Essex.*

NOTEMUGE. Nutmeg. *Chaucer.*

NOTERER. A notary.

NOTE-SCHALE. A nutshell.

But alle nis worth a *note-schale.*
    Gower, MS. Soc. Antiq. 134, f. 107.

NOTFULHEDE. Profit; gain; utility. It occurs in MS. Cotton. Vespas. D. vii, and is connected with A.-S. nytlicnys.

NOTHAG. The jay. "Nothagge, a byrde, jaye," Palsgrave. Spelt *nothak* in Nominale MS. f. 6. "*Ficedula*, a nuthage," Vocab. Rawl. MS. "The nuthake with her notes newe," Squyr of Lowe Degré, 55.

NOT-HALF-SAVED. Foolish. *West.*

NOTHELES. Nevertheless. (*A.-S.*)

Notheles yn here dedys,
Se was chaste as Menerhedys. *MS. Harl.* 1701, f. 11.

NOTHER. Otherwise; nor; neither; other; another. (*A.-S.*)

NOTHING. Not; not at all. (*A.-S.*)

His hatte was bonde undur his chyn,
He did hit *nothyng* of to hym,
He thoçt hit was no tyme. *MS. Cantab.* Ff. v. 48, f. 48.

NOTORIE. Notorious. *Lydgate.*

NOTTLE. Foolish; trifling; absurd; wanton. Milles' MS. Glossary.

NOTWITHUNDERSTANDING. Notwithstanding. A curious corruption, sometimes heard, and perhaps the longest word ever used by a rustic. *Isle of Wight.*

NOUCHE. A jewel; a necklace. Oftener spelt *ouche*, as in Nominale MS.

To my Lord and nephew the king the best *nouche* which I have on the day of my death.
    Test. Vetust. p. 141.

Whan thou hast taken eny thynge
Of lovis çifte, or *nouche* or rynge.
    Gower, MS. Soc. Antiq. 134, f. 54.

NOUGHT-A-DOW. Worthless. *North.*

NOUGHT-MERCHANTABLE. Not well. *Devon.*

NOUGHTY. Possessed of nothing. (*A.-S.*)

NOUMBRED. A number; the sum total.

NOUN. No. (*A.-N.*)

NOUSE. Sense; knowledge. *Var. dial.* Apparently from the Greek νους.

Oh I said, as lofty Homer says, my *nouse*
To sing sublime the Monarch and the Louse.
    Peter Pindar, i. 229.

NOUSLE. To nestle; to cherish; to wrap up. Also spelt *nozzle.* "See with what erroneous trumperies antiquitie hath bene *nozzeled*," Batman's Golden Booke, 1577, ded. *Nuzzeled*, brought up in youth, Holinshed, Hist. Engl. i. 108; nursed, habituated, Holinshed, Conq. Ireland, pp. 46, 78.

And *nusled* once in wicked deedes I feard not to offende,
From bad, to worse and worst I fell, I would at leysure mende.
    1st *Part of Promos and Cassandra,* ii. 6.

NOUSTY. Peevish. *North.*

NOUT-GELD. Cornage rent, originally paid in neat or cattle. *North.*

NOUTHE. (1) Now. (*A.-S.*)

(2) Nought; nothing. Hence, *nouthe-con*, to know nothing. (*A.-S.*)

(3) To set at nought; to defy.

NOVELLIS. News. (*A.-N.*)

NOVELRYE. Novelty. (*A.-N.*)

Ther was a knyçt that loved *novelrye*,
As many one haunte now that folye.
    MS. Harl. 1701, f. 23

NOVER. High land above a precipitous bank *Sussex.*

NOVUM. A game at dice played by five or six persons. It is mentioned in Florio, p. 210 Taylor's Motto, 1622, sig. D. iv.

NOW-AND-NOW. Once and again. *Now and then,* occasionally.

NO-WAY-BUT-ONE. A phrase implying an inevitable certainty.

NO-WAYS. Not at all. *Var. dial.*

NOWEL. A cry of joy, properly that at Christmas of joy for the birth of the Saviour. (*Lat.*) It signified originally the feast of Christmas, and is often found in that sense. A political song, in a MS. of Henry VI.'s time, in my possession, concludes as follows,—

Tyll home Sulle Wylekyne,
    This joly gentylle sayle,
Alle to my lorde Fueryn,
    That never dyd fayle.
Therfore let us alle syng nowelle;
Nowelle! Nowelle! Nowelle!
And Cryst save mery Ynglond and sped yt welle.

NOWELE. The navel. Arch. xxx. 354.

NOWIE. Horned cattle. *North.*

NOWITE. Foolish; witless; weak.

NOWLE. The noddle or head. "The *nowle* refine," Lilly, ed. 1632, sig. Aa. viij.

NOWMER. Number. *Prompt. Parv.*

NOW-NOW. Old Anthony Now-now, an itinerant fiddler frequently mentioned by our old writers. Anthony Munday is supposed to be ridiculed under this name, in Chettle's Kindhart's Dreame, 1592.

NOWP. A knock on the head. *Linc.*

NOWRE. Nowhere. Isumbras, 544. *Nowrewhare* occurs in Hampole.

NOW-RIGHT. Just now. *Exmoor.*

NOWSE. Nothing. *North.*

NOWUNDER. Surely; certainly.

NOY. To annoy; to hurt. *North.*

Corporal meat, when it findeth a belly occupied with adverse and corrupt humours, doth both hurt the more, *noy* the more, and helpeth nothing at all.
    Becon's Works, p. 117.

Of wilke some are *noyeand* tille us kyndly,
And some are profytable and esye.
    MS. Lincoln A. i. 17, f. 189.

Thus do ye recken; but I feare ye come of clerus,
A very *noyfull* worme, as Aristotle sheweth us.
    Bale's Kynge Johan, p. 116.

NOYNTE. To anoint. *West.*

I axst a mayster of fysyke lore,
    What wold hyme drye and dryve away;
Elymosina ys an erbe ther-fore,
    Oon of the best that ever I say.
Noynte heme therwyth ay whenne thow may,
    Thingk that Requiem shalle in the rente and sese,
And sone after, within a nyght and a day,
    Thou shalt have lycens to lyve in ease.
    MS. Cantab. Ff. i. 6, f. 47.

NOYSAUNCE. Offence; trespass. (*A.-N.*)

NOZZLE. The nose. *Var. dial.*

NOST. Not. Perceval, 98, 143, 515, &c.

> The lordis seid to hym anon,
> Joly Robyn let hym *nost* gon
> Tille that he have etyn.
> *MS. Cantab. Ff. v. 48, f. 52.*

NUB. (1) To push; to beckon. *North.*

(2) The nape of the neck. *East.*

(3) A husband. A cant term.

NUBBLE. To bruise with the fist.

NUBBLINGS. Small coal. *Worc.*

NUBILATED. Clouded. (*Lat.*)

> About the beginning of March, 1660, I bought accidentally a Turkey-stone ring; it was then wholly serene; toward the end of the moneth it began to be *nubilated*. *Aubrey's Wills, MS. Royal Soc. p. 100.*

NUCH. To tremble. *Northumb.*

NUCKLE. Trifling work; uncertain and unprofitable employment. *North.*

NUDDLE. (1) The nape of the neck. *East.*

(2) To stoop in walking. *Var. dial.*

NUDGE. A gentle push. It is also a verb, to strike gently, to give a person a hint or signal by a private touch with the hand, elbow, or foot. *Var. dial.*

NUFFEN. Cooked sufficiently. *Linc.*

NUG. (1) A rude unshapen piece of timber; a block. *Somerset.*

(2) A knob, or protuberance. *Devon.*

(3) A term of endearment.

NUGGING-HOUSE. A brothel.

NUG-HEAD. A blockhead. *Somerset.* Carr has *num-head,* Craven Gl.

NULL. To beat severely.

NUM. Dull; stupid. *East.* Also a verb, to benumb or stupefy. "Nums all the currents that should comfort life," Tragedy of Hoffman, 1631, sig. K. iii.

NUMBLES. The entrails, or part of the inwards of a deer.

> Brede and wyne they had ynough,
> And *nombles* of the dere.   *Robin Hood, i. 8.*

NUMPOST. An imposthume. *East.*

NUMPS. A fool. *Devon.*

NUN. "A litle titmouse, called a *nunne,* because his heade is filletted as it were nunlike," Nomenclator, p. 60.

NUNC. A large lump or thick piece of anything. *South.*

NUNCH. A luncheon. *Var. dial.*

NUNCHEON. A lump of food sufficient for a luncheon. *Kent.*

NUNCLE. (1) An uncle. Still in use.

(2) To cheat; to deceive. *North.*

NUNMETE. A luncheon. *Pr. Parv.*

NUNNERY. A brothel. A cant term.

NUNQUAM. One who never returns from an errand. (*Lat.*)

NUNRYE. A nunnery. Isumbras, 485.

NUNT. To make an effort. *North.*

NUNTING. Awkward looking. *Sussex.*

NUNTY. Stiff; formal; old-fashioned; shabby; mean; fussy. *Var. dial.*

NUP. A fool. *Nupson* occurs in this sense in Ben Jonson, and Grose has it in C. D. V. T.

NUR. The head. *Warw.*

NURCHY. To nourish. "*Nutrio,* to nurchy," Vocab. MS. xv. Cent. f. 72, in my possession. Said to be in use in Devon.

NURLY. Lumpy; knotty. Hence, metaphorically, ill-tempered. *North.*

NURPIN. A little person. *Heref.* Possibly connected with *nyrvyl* in Pr. Parv.

NURSE. To cheat. A cant term.

NURSE-CHILD. A child before weaning. "A nource childe, or babe that sucketh," Withals. ed. 1608, p. 271.

NURSE-GARDEN. (1) The crab-apple tree.

(2) A nursery-garden. "Settes of young trees, or nursegardaynes," Cooper, ed. 1559, in v. *Semen.* Still in use.

NURSES-VAILS. The nurse's clothes when penetrated by nepial indiscretions. *Oxon.*

NURSPELL. A boy's game in Lincolnshire, somewhat similar to trap-ball. It is played with a *kibble,* a *nur,* and a *spell.* By striking the end of the spell with the kibble, the nur of course rises into the air, and the art of the game is to strike it with the kibble before it reaches the ground. He who drives it to the greatest distance, wins the game.

NURT. To nurture; to bring up.

NUSENESS. A nuisance. *East.*

NUSHED. Starved; ill-fed. *East.*

NUT. (1) Sweet-bread. *East.*

(2) The stock of a wheel. *Var. dial.*

(3) The lump of fat called the pope's-eye. "*Muguette de mouton,* the nut of a leg of mutton," Cotgrave.

(4) A silly fellow. *Yorksh.* This word is not applied to an idiot, but to one who has been doing a foolish action.

(5) A kind of small urn.

> Also oon littel standyng peece, with a gilt kover, which hath at the foote a crown, and another on the kover, weying 22 ounces, also a standyng gilt *nutt,* and the best dosein of the second sort of my spones.
> *Test. Vetust. p. 365.*

NUTCRACKERS. The pillory.

NUT-CRACK-NIGHT. All Hallows' eve, when it is customary to crack nuts in large quantities. *North.*

NUTCROME. A crooked stick, used for lowering branches of hazels, in order to reach the fruit. *East.*

NUT-HOLE. The notch in a bow to receive the arrow.

NUT-HOOK. A bailiff.

NUTMEGS. The testes. *Var. dial.*

> My precious *nutmegs* doe not wound,
> For fear I should not live;
> I'll pay thee downe one hundred pound,
> If thou wilt me forgive.
> *History of Jack Horner, ed. 1697, p 18.*

NUTRE. A kind of worm.

NUTRITIVE. That which has nourished.

> Yf ever God gave victorye to men fyghtinge in a juste quarell, or yf he ever ayded such as made warre for the wealthe and tuicion of their owne natural and *nutritive* countery.
> *Hall, Richard III. f. 31.*

NUTTEN. A donkey. *I. Wight.*

NUT-TOPPER. The bird nut-pecker. Withals' Dictionarie, ed. 1608, p. 21.

NUVITOUS. Nutritious. *Salop.*

NUY. Annoyance; injury.

> An·l thare was so grete habundance of nedders and other venymous bestez, that thame byhoved nedez travelle armed, and that was a grete *nuy* to thame, and an heghe discse.
> *MS. Lincoln A. i. 17, f. 27.*

NUZZLE. To loiter; to idle. *North.*

NYE. (1) An eye. Nominale MS.

> Fro nyse japys and ribadry
> Awey thou muste turne thi *nye*;
> Turne thi *nye*, that thou not se
> This wyccud worldis vanyté.
> *MS. Cantab. Ff. v. 48, f. 1.*

(2) Annoyance; injury; trouble.

> The patryark sawe hys grete *nye*,
> For Befyse he wepyd, so thoyt hym rewly.
> *MS. Cantab. Ff. ii. 38, f. 109.*

(3) To neigh. *Palsgrave.*

NYME. To name.

> For every creature of God that man can *nyme*,
> Is good of hymself after his first creacion.
> *MS. Digby 181.*

NYMPHAL. A short poem relating to nympha. *Drayton.*

NYMPHS. Young female bees.

NYMYOS. Excessive.

> Now, gracyous Lord, of your *nymyos* charyté,
> With hombyll harts to thi presens complayne.
> *Digby Mysteries, p. 115.*

NYNON. Eyes.

> And wash thou thi *nynon* with that water.
> *Chron. Vilodun. p. 77.*

NYTE. To deny. See *Nick.* Qu. nycyde?

> Trewly in his entent,
> In batelle ne in tournament
> He *nytyde* us never with naye.
> *MS. Lincoln A. i. 17, f. 139.*

NYTTE. To require; to use. (*A.-S.*)

NY3E. Nigh; near. (*A.-S.*)

> Fore thofe thou wyrke bothe dey [and] nyght,
> He wyll not the, I sey the ryght;
> He wones to *ny3e* the ale-wyffe,
> And he thouht ever fore to thryffe.
> *MS. Ashmole 61, xv. Cent.*

O. (1) Of. Still in use.

> A! perles pryns, to the we pray,
> Save our kyng both nyyt and day!
> Fore he is ful jong, tender of age,
> Semelé to se, o bold corage,
> Lovelé and lofté of his lenage,
> Both perles prince and kyng veray.
> *MS. Douce 302, f. 29.*
> The wrang to here o right is lath,
> And pride wyt buxumnes is wrath.
> *MS. Cotton. Vespas. A. iii. f. 2.*

(2) One. Also, on. *Chaucer.*

> Be-teche tham the proveste, in presens of lordez,
> O payne and o pelle that pendes there-too.
> *Morte Arthure, MS. Lincoln, f. 70.*
> Where that Merlin dede him se
> In o day in thre ble.
> *Arthour and Merlin, p. 74.*

(3) Anything circular; an heraldic term for a kind of spangle. Shakespeare terms the stars "those fiery o's."

(4) A lamentation. *Shak.*

(5) The arithmetical cypher.

(6) All. Bran New Wark, 1785.

(7) The woof in weaving.

OAF. A fool. Still in use.

OAK. (1) *To sport the oak*, to close the outer door, a phrase used at Cambridge.

(2) The club at cards. *West.*

OAKEN-APPLE-DAY. The 29th of May, on which boys wear oaken apples in their hats in commemoration of King Charles's adventure in the oak tree. The apple, and a leaf or two, are sometimes gilt and exhibited for a week or more on the chimney piece, or in the window. This rustic commemoration is, however, getting into disuse. Sectarians have left it off, and in a few years it will probably be seldom seen. I can recollect when not a boy in a whole village let the day pass unobserv-

ant of the oaken apple. Fears were sometimes entertained in a backward season that the apples would not be forward enough for our loyal purpose. Moor's Suffolk MS.

OAK-WEB. The cockchafer. *West.*

OAMY. Light, porous, generally spoken of ploughed land. *Norf.*

OAR. "A busie-body, medler in others matters, one that hath an oare in others boates," Florio, p. 37.

OARS. Watermen.

> Tarlton being one Sunday at court all day, caused a paire of *oares* to tend him, who at night called on him to be gone. Tarlton, being a carousing, drunk so long to the watermen, that one of them was bumpsie; and so, indeede, were all three for the most part. *Tarlton's Jests, 1611.*

OAST. (1) Curd for cheese. *North.*

(2) A kiln for malt or hops. *Kent.*

OAT-FLIGHT. The chaff of oats. *East.*

OATMEALS. One of the many terms for the roaring-boys.

OATS. (1) To sow one's wild oats, i. e. to leave off wild habits.

(2) In the south of England, when a horse falls upon his back, and rolls from one side to the other, he is said to earn a gallon of oats.

OAVIS. The eaves of a house. *Essex.*

OBADE. To abide. Tristrem, p. 178.

OBARNI. A preparation of mead.

OBEED. A hairy caterpillar. *Derb.*

OBEISSANT. Obedient. *Palsgrave.*

> That were *obeissant* to his heste.
> *Gower, MS. Soc. Antiq. 134, f. 54.*

OBESSE. "Play at *obesse*, at billors, and at cards," Archæologia, xiv. 253.

OBFUSCATE. Obscured. (*Lat.*)

> Whereby the fame of all our estimacion shall now bee *obfuscate*, utterly extinguyshed, and nothyng set by. *Hall, Edward IV. f. 10.*

OBIT. A funeral celebration.

These *obets* once past o're, which we desire,
Those eyes that now shed water shall speake fire.
Heywood's Iron Age, 1632, sig. H. iv.

OBITCH'S-COLT. "Forty as one like Obitch's cowt," a Shropshire phrase.

OBITERS. Small ornaments.

OBJECTION. A subject or argument.

OBLATRATION. A barking-at. (Lat.)

OBLAUNCHERE. Fine white meal?

With *oblaunchere* or outher floure,
To make hem whytter of coloure.
MS. Harl. 1701, f. 22.

OBLE. A kind of wafer cake, often sweetened with honey, and generally made of the finest wheaten bread. The consecrated wafer distributed to communicants at mass was so termed. "*Oblata*, oble," MS. Lansd. 560, f. 45. *Oblete*, a thin cake. (Teut.) "*Nebula*, oblys," Nominale MS.

Mak paste, and bake it in *oble-pryns*, and ett growelle of porke, and after ete the *oblates*, and thou sal have deliverance bathe abowne and bynethe.
MS. Lincoln A. i. 17, f. 291.

Ne Jhesu was nat the *oble*
That reysed was at the sacre.
MS. Harl. 1701, f. 66.

OBLIGATE. To oblige. *Var. dial.*

OBLOCUTION. Interruption. (Lat.)

OBLYSCHED. Obliged; compelled.

It helpyth to paye owre dettes for synne,
In whych to God *oblysched* ben wee.
MS. Cantab. Ff. ii. 38, f. 14.

Thei ben *oblisched* and thei felle, but we roos, and we ben righted. *MS. Tanner* 16, p. 51.

The whole felowship, marchauntes, burgesses, and commonaltye of the same towne, to be bounde and *oblysched* by ther presentes unto the most excellent and most mighty prince Edward.
Hall, Edward IV. f. 57.

OBRAID. To upbraid. *Somerset.*

Now, thus accoutred and attended to,
In Court and citie there's no small adoe
With this young stripling, that *obraids* the gods,
And thinkes, 'twixt them and him, there is no ods.
Young Gallants Whirligig, 1629.

OBRUTED. Overthrown. (Lat.)

Verily, if ye seriously consider the misery wherewith ye were *obruted* and overwhelmed before, ye shall easily perceive that ye have an earnest cause to rejoice. *Bacon's Works*, p. 57.

OBS-AND-SOLS. The words *objectiones et solutiones* were frequently so contracted in the marginal notes to controversial divinity, and hence the phrase was jocularly used by more lively writers.

OBSCENOUS. Obscene; indecent.

OBSCURED. Disguised. *Shak.*

OBSECRATIONS. Entreaties. (Lat.)

Let us fly to God at all times with humble *obsecrations* and hearty requests.
Bacon's Works, p. 187.

OBSEQUIOUS. Funereal. *Shak.*

OBSEQUY. Obsequiousness. *Jonson.*

OBSERVANCE. Respect. *(A.-N.)*

OBSERVE. To obey; to respect; to crouch.

OBSESSION. A besieging. (Lat.)

OBSTACLE. Obstinate. A provincial word, very common in Shakespeare's time. It is ex-

plained "stubborne or wilfull" in Batman uppon Bartholome, 1582.

OBSTINATION. Obstinacy. *Palsgrave.*

OBSTRICT. Bounden. (Lat.)

To whom he recogniseth hymself to be so moche indebted and *obstricte*, that non of thise your difficulties shalbe the stop or let of this desired conjunccion. *State Papers*, i. 252.

OBSTROPOLOUS. Obstreperous. A very common vulgarism. " I was going my rounds, and found this here gemman very *obstropolous*, whereof I comprehended him as an auspicious parson." This is genuine London dialect.

OBTRECT. To slander. (Lat.)

OC. But. *(A.-S.)*

Oc thourgh the grace of God almight,
With the tronsoun that he to prisoun tok
A slough hem alle, so saith the bok.
Bevea of Hamtoun, p. 61

OCAPYE. To occupy; to employ.

Tho seyde Gye, so schalt thou no3t,
In ydull thou *ocapyest* thy tho3t.
MS. Cantab. Ff. ii. 38, f. 211.

OCCAMY. A compound metal, meant to imitate silver, a corruption of the word alchemy. See Nares.

OCCASIONS. Necessities of nature.

OCCIDENT. The West. *(A.-N.)*

Of Inglande, of Irelande, and alle thir owtt illes,
That Arthure in the *occedente* ocupyes att ones.
Morte Arthure, MS. Lincoln, f. 78.

OCCUPANT. A prostitute. From the old word *occupy*, futuo. "A bawdy, or occupying-house," Florio, p. 194.

I can swive four times in a night: but thee
Once in four years I cannot *occupie*.
Fletcher's Poems, p. 110.

OCCUPY. To use. *Occupier*, a tradesman.

OCCUR. Ochre. *Palsgrave.*

OCCURRE. To go to. (Lat.)

Secondarely yf he should reyse an army so sodainly, he knewe not where to *occurre* and mete his enemies, or whether too go or where to tary.
Hall, Richard III. f. 14.

OCCURRENTS. Incidents; qualities. Meetings, Optick Glasse of Humors, 1639, p. 139.

Julius Cæsar himselfe for his pleasure became an actor, being in shape, state, voyce, judgement, and all other *occurrents*, exterior and interior, excellent.
Heywood's Apology for Actors, 1612.

OCCYAN. The ocean.

In verré soth, as y remembre can,
A certeyne kynrede towarde the *occyan*.
Lydgate, MS. Soc. Antiq. 134, f. 22.

OCEAN-SEA. This phrase is often used by Sir Thomas More. "The greate brode botomlesse ocean-see," Supplycacyon of Soulys, sig. C. ii. It occurs likewise in Hall.

OCHEN. To break; to destroy. *(A.-N.)*

OCIVITY. Sloth. *Hooper.*

OCKSECROTIA. Tipsy. A cant term.

OCUB. The cockchafer. *Somerset.*

OCY. The nightingale's note.

ODAME. A brother-in-law. (Germ.)

O-DAWE. Down. See *Adawe* (2).

Loke 3e blenke for no bronde, ne for no bryghte wapyne,
Bot beris downe of the beste, and bryng theme *o-dawe*
Morte Arthure, MS. Lincoln, f. 93

ODD. (1) Only; single; alone. (2) Lonely; out of the way. *Linc.*

(3) *Odd and even*, a game at marbles. *Odd come shortly*, a chance time, not far off. *Odd-come-shorts*, odds and ends, fragments.

ODD-FISH. A strange fellow. *Var. dial.*

ODD-MARK. That portion of the arable land of a farm which, in the customary cultivation of the farm, is applied to a particular crop. *Heref.*

ODDMENTS. Trifles; remnants. *North.*

ODDS. (1) To fit; to make even. Also, occasionally, to alter. *West.*

(2) Consequence; difference. *Var. dial.*

ODDY. (1) A snail. *Oxon.*

(2) Active; brisk. Generally applied to old people. *Oxon.*

ODDY-DODDY. A river-snail. *Oxon.*

ODE. Woad for dyeing.

ODER. Other. Still in use.
> And beryd the cors with bothe her rede,
> As she sodenly hade be ded,
> That no man *odur* wiste.
> *MS. Cantab. Ff. v. 48, f. 44.*

ODERWORT. The herb dragance.

ODIBLE. Hateful. (Lat.)
> And thou shalt be maister of that worme *odible*,
> And oppresse hym in his owne stalle.
> *MS. Laud. 416, f. 56.*

> All suche othis be to our Lord *odible*
> That be made and promysid to an evill entencion.
> *MS. Laud. 416, f. 69.*

ODIFFERAUNT. Odoriferous.

ODIOUS. Ill-tasted; ill-scented. *East.*

ODORAUNT. Sweet-smelling. (*A.-N.*)
> The thrid day next my sone went doune
> To erthe, whiche was disposed plentuously
> Of aungels bright and hevenly soune
> With *odoraunt* odoure ful copiously.
> *MS. Bodl. 423, f. 204.*

ODSNIGGERS. An exclamation of rebuke. An immense number of oaths and exclamations may be found commencing with *ods*, a corruption of *God's*.

OEN. Owe; are indebted.
> I telle it the in priveté,
> The kynges men *oen* to me
> A m¹. pounde and mare.
> *MS. Cantab. Ff. v. 48, f. 47.*

O'ERLAY. A girth; a cloak. *North.*

OERTH-IVI. The *hedera nigra.*

OERTS. In comparison of. *West.*

OES. Eyes. Nominale MS.
> And notwithstondinge your manly hart,
> Frome your *oes* the teres wald starte
> To shew your hevynesse.
> Com hithere Josephe and stande ner this rood,
> Loo, this lame spared not to shedd his blude,
> With most paynfulle distresse.
> *MS. Bodl. e Mus. 160.*

OF. In; out of; from; at; on; off; by. Many of these meanings are still current in the provinces.

OFCORN. Offal corn. Finchale Chart. The term occurs in Tusser. *East.*

OF-DAWE. To recover. *Weber.*

OF-DRAD. Afraid; frightened. (*A.-S.*)

O-FERRE. Afar off.

> Beholde also how his modire and alle his frendes
> stand alle *o-ferre* lokande and folowande theme
> withe mekylle murnyng and hertly sorowe.
> *MS. Lincoln A. i. 17, f. 181.*

OFF. (1) Upon; out of. *Off at hooks*, out of temper, or unwell. *Off and on*, changeable. *Off nor on*, neither one thing nor another.

(2) The line from which boys shoot in commencing a game of marbles.

(3) Provided; furnished. *Var. dial.*

OFF-AT-SIDE. Mad. *North.*

OFFENCIOUS. Offensive. Marlowe, ii. 305.

OFFENDED. Hurt. *Chaucer.*

OFFENSIOUN. Office; damage. (*A.-N.*)

OFF-HAND. A man holding a second farm on which he does not reside is said to farm it *off-hand. Suffolk.*

OFFICE. The eaves of a house. *West.*

OFFICES. The rooms in a large house, appropriated to the use of the upper servants. The term is still in common use, applied to the menial apartments generally.

OFFRENDE. An offering. (*A.-N.*)
> And sche bigan to bidde and prey
> Upon the bare grounde knelende,
> And aftir that made hir *offrende*.
> *Gower, MS. Soc. Antiq. 134, f. 44.*

OFF-SPRING. Origin. *Fairfax.*

OFF-TOOK. Took by aim; hit.

OF-LONG. For a long period.

OF-SIGH. Saw; perceived. (*A.-S.*)

OF-TAKE. Taken. St. Brandan, p. 19.

OFTER. Oftener. *North.*
> *Ofter* bryngeth on day,
> That alle the ȝere not may.
> *MS. Douce 52, f. 13.*

OFTE-SITHES. Often-times. (*A.-S.*)
> For thou and other that leve your thyng,
> Wel *ofte-sithes* ye banne the kyng.
> *MS. Cantab. Ff. v. 48, f. 48.*

OF-WALKED. Fatigued with walking. (*A.-S.*)

OGAIN. Again. Still in use.
> Fortiger nam gode coure
> That he no might *ogain* hem doure.
> *Arthour and Merlin, p. 16.*

> And dede hem *ogain* thre thousinde,
> And acontred that carroy.
> *Arthour and Merlin, p. 178.*

OGAINSAGHES. Contradictions. It occurs in MS. Cotton. Vespas. D. vii.

OGE. Again. "Come now son ogé," Gy of Warwike, p. 110.

OGHE. Ought. *Gawayne.*

OGLES. Eyes. A cant term.

OGNE. Own.
> And thoght ther was resone yune,
> And ȝyh hys *ogne* lyf to wynne.
> *Gower, MS. Cantab. Ff. i. 6, f. 38.*

OGOS. Caves along the shore. *Cornw.*

OIL. To oil his old wig, i. e. to make him tipsy. *North.*

OIL-OF-BARLEY. Strong beer.

OIL-OF-HAZEL. A severe beating.

OILY. Smooth; adulatory. *Var. dial.*

OINEMENT. Ointment. (*A.-N.*)
> Now of the seventhe sacrament,
> These clerkys kalle hyt *oynament*.
> *MS. Harl. 1701, f. 74.*

OINT. To anoint. *Palsgrave.*

OKE. Aked. Pret. pl. (*A.-S.*)

OKE-CORNE. An acorn. *Ortus Voc.*

OKERE. To put money out to usury. Also, usury. *Okerer,* an usurer.

> Anyʒt, when men hadde here rest,
> He okered pens yn hys cheste.
> > *MS. Harl. 1701, f. 18.*

> Okur hyt ys for the outrage
> To take thy catel and have avauntage.
> > *MS. Harl. 1701, f. 16.*

> One nyʒte qwene mene had ryste,
> He skyrryde penyes unto hys kyste.
> > *Robert de Brunne, MS. Bowes, p. 5.*

> An okerer, or elles a lechoure, sayd Robyn,
> With wronge hast thou lede thy lyfe.
> > *Robin Hood, I. 10.*

OKERS. "Bootes for ploughmen called *okers*," Huloet, 1552. "*Carpatinæ,* plowmens bootes made of untanned leather, they may be called *okers*," Elyot, ed. 1559.

OKY. Moist; sappy. *North.*

OLD. (1) Famous; great; abundant. *Warw.* Shakespeare uses the word in this sense. "There will be an *old* abusing of God's patience, and the king's English." It sometimes is used to denote approbation, fondness, or endearment; as, in Virginia and Maryland, the most endearing appellation by which a fond husband could address a beloved wife, used to be his calling her *dear old woman.*

> On Sunday, at masse, there was *olds* ringing of bels, and old and yong came to church to see the new roode, which was so ill favourde, that al the parish misllkt It, and the children they cryed, and were afraid of it. *Tarlton's Newes out of Purgatorie,* 1590.

(2) Cross; angry. *Suffolk.*

(3) *Old Bendy, Old Harry, Old Scratch,* terms for the devil. *Old Christmas,* Christmas reckoned by the old style. *Old coat and jerkin,* a game at cards. *Old dog, old hand,* a knowing or expert person. *Old stager,* one well initiated in anything. *Old lad,* a sturdy old fellow. *Old stick,* a complimentary mode of address to an old man, signifying he is a capital fellow. *Old file,* an old miser.

OLDHAMES. A kind of cloth.

OLD-HOB. A Cheshire custom. It consists of a man carrying a dead horse's head, covered with a sheet, to frighten people.

OLD-KILLED. Squeamish and listless. *North.*

OLD-LAND. Ground that has been untilled a long while, and is newly broken up. *Essex.*

OLD-LING. Urine. *Yorksh.*

OLD-MAID. The lapwing. *Worc.*

OLD-MAN. Southernwood. *Var. dial.*

OLD-MAN'S-GAME. The game of astragals. MS. Ashmole 788, f. 162.

OLD-MILK. Skimmed milk. *North.*

OLD-SARAH. A hare. *Suffolk.*

OLD-SHEWE. A game mentioned in the Nomenclator, p. 298. It is apparently the same as King-by-your-Leave, q. v.

OLD-SHOCK. A goblin said to appear in the shape of a great dog or calf. *East.*

OLD-SONG. A trifle. *Var. dial.*

OLD-SOW. A wood-louse. *East.*

OLD-TROT. An old woman who is greatly addicted to gossiping.

OLD-WITCH. The cockchafer. *East.*

OLD-WIVES-TALE. "This is an *old wives tale,* or a fashion of speech cleane out of fashion," Cotgrave, in v. *Langage.*

OLIFAUNT. An elephant. (*A.-N.*)

> Felled was king Rion standard,
> And the four *olyfaunce* y-slawe.
> > *Arthour and Merlin,* p. 344.

> The scarlet cloth doth make the bull to feare;
> The cullour white the *ollivant* doth shunne.
> > *Deloney's Strange Histories,* 1607.

OLIVER. (1) A young eel. *Devon.*

(2) To give a Rowland for an Oliver, a phrase still in use, derived from two well-known characters in ancient romance.

> Soche strokys were never seen yn londe,
> Syth *Olyvere* dyed and Rowlonde.
> > *MS. Cantab. Ff. ii. 38, f. 108.*

OLIVERE. The olive-tree. (*A.-N.*)

OLIVER'S-SCULL. A chamber-pot.

OLLET. Fuel. Ray inserts this in his South and East-Country Words. Aubrey, in his MS. Nat. Hist. of Wilts, tells us that cow dung and straw was used for fuel at Highworth, and called by that name.

OLODDE.

> For-thi thou gyffe, whils thou may lyfe,
> Or alle gase that thou may gete,
> Thi gaste fra Godd, thi gudes *oludde,*
> Thi flesche foldes undir fete.
> With I. and E. fulle sekire thou be,
> That thynne executurs
> Of the ne wille rekke, bot skikk and skekke
> Fulle baldely in thi boures.
> > *MS. Lincoln A. i. 17, f. 212.*

O-LONKE. Along. MS. Harl. 2253.

OLY. Oil. Nominale MS.

OLYET. A little hole in anything, such as cloth, &c. Forby has *oylet-hole,* a perforation in a garment to admit a lace. The small openings in ancient fortifications were called *olyets,* or oylets. "Oyliet hole, *oillet.*" Palsgrave.

OLYPRAUNCE. Gaiety? Holloway has, "*Olyprance,* rude, boisterous merriment, a romping match, *Northampton.*"

> Of rich atire es ther avaunce,
> Prikkand ther hors with *olypraunce.*
> > *R. de Brunne, MS. Bowes, p. 64.*

OLYTE.

> For whan thou doust yn longe respyte
> Hyt ys forʒete that long ys *olyte.*
> > *MS. Harl. 1701, f. 75.*

OMAN. A woman. *Var. dial.*

OMAST. Almost. *Cumb.* Several of the glossaries have *ommost.*

OMBER. (1) The shade. *Lanc.* Kennett has *oumer,* MS. Lansd. 1033.

(2) A hammer. Salop. Antiq. p. 523.

OMBRE. A game at cards, of Spanish origin. It appears to be merely an alteration or improvement of primero. It is thus described in the Compleat Gamester, ed. 1721, p. 12— "There are several sorts of this game called L'Ombre, but that which is the chief is called Renegado, at which three only can play, to whom are dealt nine cards apiece; so that discarding the eights, nines and tens, there will remain thirteen cards in the stock; there is no trump but what the player pleases; the first hand has always the liberty to play or pass, after him the second, &c."

OME. The steam or vapour arising from hot liquids. *Dunelm.*

OMELL. Among; between. See Ywaine and Gawin, 119; and *Amell* (2).

OMFRY-FLOOR. At Wednesbury, co. Staff., in the nether coal, as it lies in the mine, the fourth parting or laming is called the omfry-floor, two feet and a half thick. Kennett, MS.

OMNIUM-GATHERUM. A miscellaneous collection of persons or things.

OMPURLODY. To contradict. *Beds.*

ON. (1) In. It is a prefix to verbs, similar to *a.* " The kinge of Israell on-huntynge wente," MS. Douce 261, f. 40.

(2) One. *After on,* alike. *At on,* agreed. *Ever in on,* continually. *I mine on,* I singly, I by myself. *On ane,* together, MS. Cotton. Vespas. D. vii. of the thirteenth century.

(3) Of; onwards. *Var. dial.* To be a little *on,* i. e. to be approaching intoxication. A female of any kind, when *maris* appetens, is said to be *on.* It is sometimes an expletive, as *cheated on,* cheated, &c.

ONANE. Anon. *Ritson.*
> Hys hors fet wald he noht spare,
> To he cam thar the robbour ware;
> He yed unto thayr loge onans.
>   *Gy of Warwike, Middlehill MS.*

ONARMED. Took off his armour.
> Tryamowre wened to have had pese,
> And onarmed hym also tyte.
>   *MS. Cantab. Ff. ii. 38, f. 76.*

ONBEAR. To uncover, applied to the opening of a quarry. *West.*

ON-BOLDE. Cowardly; not fierce.
> A man oon he ys holde,
> Febulle he wexeth and on-bolde.
>   *MS. Cantab. Ff. ii. 38, f. 95.*

ONBRAID. To upbraid; to reproach. *Palsgrave.*

ONCE. Once for all. A common sense of the word in old plays.

ONDE. (1) Zeal; envy; malice; hate; hatred; breath. (*A.-S.*)
> Aschamid with a pitous onde,
> Sche tolde unto hire husbonde
> The sothe of alle the hole tale.
>   *Gower, MS. Soc. Antiq. 134, f. 44.*

(2) Ordained. *Yorksh.*

ONDEDELY. Immortal. (*A.-S.*)

ONDINE. To breathe. *Prompt. Parv.*

ONDOAR. One who expounds.

ON-DREGHE. Back; at a distance.

ONE. (1) A; an individual; a person. *Var. dial.*

(2) Singular. *Leic.*

(3) Alone; singly. (*A.-S.*) " By youreselfe one," MS. Morte Arthure, f. 62.
> And ther y gan my woo compleyne,
> Wisschyng and wepynge alle myn oone.
>   *Gower, MS. Soc. Antiq. 134, f. 39.*

ONE-AND-THIRTY. An ancient and very favourite game at cards, much resembling vingt-un. It could be played by two persons,

as appears from Taylor's Workes, 1630, ii. 181. It is mentioned in the Interlude of Youth, ap. Collier, ii. 314; Earle's Microcosmography, p. 62; Taylor's Motto, 1622, sig. D. iv; Florio, p. 578; Upton's MS. Adds. to Junius.

ONED. (1) Made one; united. (*A.-S.*)

(2) Dwelt; remained.
> Than axed anon sir Gii,
> To the barouns that oned him bi.
>   *Gy of Warwike, p. 27.*

ONEDER. Behind. *Chesh.* According to Ray, this is the Cheshire pronunciation of *aunder,* the afternoon.

ONEHEEDE. Unity. (*A.-S.*)
> For Gode walde ay with the Fader and the Sonne,
> And wythe the Holy Gost in oneheede wonne.
>   *Hampole, MS. Bowes, p. 13.*

> And stere them all that ever they may,
> To oonhedd and to charyté.
>   *MS. Cantab. Ff. ii. 38, f. 3.*

ONELOTE. An oblation.

ONEMENTE. A reconciliation. (*A.-S.*)
> Bot onemente thar hym nevyr wene,
> Or eyther other herte have sought.
>   *MS. Harl. 2252, f. 115.*

ONENCE. Against. Sevyn Sages, 2872.

ONE-O'CLOCK. Like one-o'clock, i. e. very rapidly, said of a horse's movement, &c.

ONE-OF-US. A whore.

ONE-PENNY. " *Basilinda,* the playe called, one penie, one penie, come after me," Nomenclator, p. 298.

ONERATE. To load. (*Lat.*)

ONERLY. Lonely; solitary. *North.*

ONES. Once. (*A.-S.*)
> Evyr on hys maystyrs grave he lay,
> Ther myght no man gete hym away
> For oght that they cowde do,
> But yf hyt were onys on the day,
> He wolde forthe to gete hys praye,
> And sythen ageyne he wolde goo.
>   *MS. Cantab. Ff. ii. 38, f. 74.*

ONE-SHEAR-SHEEP. A sheep between one and two years old. *Var. dial.*

ONFANG. Received. (*A.-S.*)

ON-FERROME. Afar off. (*A.-S.*)
> Bot Alexander went bi hym ane uppone an heghe cragge, whare he myghte see on-ferrome fra hym, and thane he saw this pestellenclus beste the basilisc.
>   *MS. Lincoln A. i. 17, f. 38.*

ONGOINGS. Proceedings; goings on. *North.*

ONHANDE. In the hand; to the will. It occurs in MS. Cott. Vespas. D. vii, the Egerton MS. reading *wiht wille.*

ON-HELD. Bowed down.

ON-HENELY. Ungently; uncourteously.

ONICLE. The onyx. *Onycle,* Wright's Lyric Poetry, p. 25. (*A.-N.*)

ONID. Mixed and joined. Batman uppon Bartholome, 1582.

ONIMENT. Ointment. Vocab. MS.

ONING. The only one. (*A.-S.*)
> And in the tenthe men myhte se
> The oonyng and the unyté.
>   *MS. Cott. Vitell. C. xiii. f. 38.*

ONION-PENNIES. " At Silchester in Hampshire they find great plenty of Roman coins, which they call *onion-pennies* from one Onion, whom they foolishly fancy to have been a giant, and an inhabitant of this city," Kennett, MS. Lansd. 1033.

ON-LENTHE. Afar. *Gawayne.*

ONLEPI. The same as *Anlepi*, q. v. *Onlepiliche* occurs in MS. Arund. 57, f. 28.

> Ich leve ine God, Vader Almiȝti, makere of hevene and of erthe ; and ine Jesu Crist, his sone *onlepi*, oure Lord.   *MS. Arundel. 57, f. 94.*

ONLIEST. Only. *Chesh.* It is singularly used as a superlative.

ONLIGHT. To alight, or get down. *West.*

ONLIKE. Alone ; only. (*A.-S.*)

> Blissed Laverd God of Israel
> That dos wondres *onlike* wele.
>   *MS. Egerton 614, f. 48.*
> Of thi baptesme and of thi dedes,
> Of *onlych* lif that thou here ledes.
>   *Cursor Mundi, MS. Coll. Trin. Cantab. f. 79.*

ON-LOFT. Aloft.

> And gat up into the tre esely and soft,
> And hyng hymself upon a bowgh *on-loft.*
>   *MS. Laud. 416, f. 61.*

ONNETHE. Scarcely. (*A.-S.*)

> Him thouȝte that he was *onnethe* alive,
> For he was al overcome.
>   *MS. Laud. 108, f. 117.*

ONNISH. Somewhat tipsy. *North.*

ONONE. Anon ; immediately. (*A.-S.*)

> And as [they] satt at the supere, they knewe hym in brekyng of brede, and *onone* He vanyste awaye fro hem.   *MS. Lincoln A. i. 17, f. 186.*

ON-O-NENA. Always. *Lanc.*

ON-RYGHTE. Wrong.

> Hys own lyfe for hur he lees
> Wyth mekulle *on-ryghte.*
>   *MS. Cantab. Ff. ii. 38, f. 95.*

ONSAY. An onset.

ONSET. A dwelling-house and out-buildings. *North.* A single farmhouse is called an *onstead.*

ONSETTEN. Small ; dwarfish. *North.*

ON-STAND. The rent paid by the out-going to the in-going tenant of a farm for such land as the other has rightfully cropped before leaving it. *North.*

ONSTE. Once. Chester Plays, ii. 100.

ON-STRAYE. Apart.

> The stede strak over the force,
> And strayed *on-straye.*
>   *MS. Lincoln A. i. 17, f. 137.*

ONSWERID. Answered.

> Kyng Edwart *onswerid* agayne,
> I wil go to these erles twane.
>   *MS. Cantab. Ff. v. 48, f. 53.*

ONT. Will not ; w'ont. *West.*

ON-THENDE. Abject ; out-cast.

ONTHER. Under. Octovian, 609.

ON-TYE. To untie.

> And yede Arondell all to nye,
> And wolde have hym *on-tye.*
>   *MS. Cantab. Ff. ii. 38, f. 120.*

ONWILLI. Unwillingly. *Pr. Parv.*

ONYOLBUN. A herb mentioned in MS. Bibl. Reg. 12 B. i. f. 14.

OO. (1) One. See *O.*

> And at oo worde sche platly gan him telle
> The childis myte his power dide eccelle.
>   *Lydgate, MS. Soc. Antiq. 134, f. 16.*

(2) Aye ; ever. Tundale's Visions, p. 48.

OOBIT. The larvæ of the tiger-moth.

OON. An oven. *North.*

OONABLE. Awkward ; unwieldly.

OONE. Alone. only. (*A.-S.*)

> Alle makid but here achertis *oone*,
> They wepte and made moche mona.
>   *Gower, MS. Soc. Antiq. 134, f. 32.*

OON-EGG. A soft-egg, one laid before the shell is formed. *West.*

OONRYGHTTWYSLYE. Unrighteously.

> He was in Tuskayne that tyme, and tuke of oure knyghttes,
> Areste theme *oonryghttwyslye*, and raunsound thame aftyre.   *Morte Arthure, MS. Lincoln, f. 56.*

OONT. A want, or mole. *West.*

OONTY. Empty. *Devon.*

OOR. Hoary ; aged.

OOSER. A mask with opening jaws along with a cow's skin, put on for frightening people. *Dorset.*

OOST. An host, or army. (*A.-N.*)

OOTH. Wood ; mad. *Pr. Parv.*

OOZLING. Hairy. *North.*

OP. To get up. *Somerset.* Also *oppy.*

OPE. An opening. *West.*

OPE-LAND. Land in constant till, ploughed up every year. *Suffolk.*

OPEN. (1) A large cavern. When a vein is worked open to the day, it is said to be *opencast.* A miner's term.

(2) Not spayed, said of a sow, &c. *East.*

(3) Mild, said of the weather. *Var. dial.*

OPEN-ERS. The medlar. (*A.-S.*) "Oponhers, medler," MS. Sloane 5, f. 6 ; *openarces*, MS. Bodl. 30. Palsgrave has *opynars.*

OPEN-HEDED. Bare-headed. *Chaucer.*

OPEN-HOUSE. To keep open-house, i. e. to be exceedingly hospitable.

OPEN-TIDE. The time between Epiphany and Ash-Wednesday, wherein marriages were publicly solemnized, was on that account formerly called open-tide ; but now in Oxfordshire and several other parts, the time after harvest, while the common fields are free and open to all manner of stock, is called open-tide. Kennett, MS. Lansd. 1033.

OPER. A bumper of wine. *North.*

OPERANCE. Operation ; effect.

OPERANT. Operative ; fit for action. Heywood's Royall King, sig. A. iv.

OPIE. Opium. (*A.-N.*)

OPINION. (1) Credit ; reputation.

(2) To opine ; to think. *Suffolk.*

OPPILATIONS. Obstructions. (*Lat.*)

> This Crocus is used very successfully for the green-sickness stopping of the Terms, Dropsy and other diseases, that proceed from *Oppilations ;* the Dose is from 15 grains to a Drachm.
>   *Aubrey's Wilts, MS. Royal Soc. p. 111.*

OPPORTUNITY. Character ; habit.

OPPOSE. To question ; to argue with.

> Problemes and demandes eke
> Hys wysdom was to finde and seke,
> Wherof he wolde in sondry wyse
> *Opposen* hem that weren wyse.
>   *Gower, MS. Cantab. Ff. i. 6, f. 30.*

OPPRESSE. To ravish. (*A.-N.*) Hence *oppression*, rape.

OPTIC. A magnifying-glass. " Not legible but through an optick," Nabbes' Bride, 1640, sig. G. i. Coles has the term.

OPUNCTLY. Opportunely. *Greene.*

OQWERE. Anywhere ?

> If his howsholde be *oqwere*,
> Thi parishen is he there.
> > *MS. Cantab.* Ff. v. 48, f. 5.

OR. (1) Ere ; before. *North.*

> Punysche paciently the transgressones
> Of mene disreuled redressing thaire errour.
> Mercy preferryng *or* thou do rigour.
> > *MS. Cantab.* Ff. i. 6, f. 129.

(2) Lest. Perceval, 911.

(3) Than. " Rather or that," an idiom still current in the midland counties.

> He wolde ageyn for youre love blede
> Rather *or* that ye dampned were.
> > *MS. Cantab.* Ff. ii. 38, f. 48.

(4) Their. Wright's Seven Sages, p. 47.

ORANGE-TAWNEY. A dull orange colour.

OR-A-ONE. Ever a one. *South.*

ORATION. Noise ; uproar. *Var. dial.*

ORATORIE. A private chapel ; a closet for the purposes of prayer. (*A.-N.*)

ORBELL.

> In the lowest border of the garden, I might see a curious *orbell*, all of touch, wherein the Syracusan tyrants were no lesse artfully portrayed, than their severall cruelties to life displayed.
> > *Braithwait's Arcadian Princesse*, 1635. ii. 148.

ORBS. Panels. Nominale MS.

ORCEL. A small vase. (*A.-N.*)

ORD. A point, or edge. (*A.-S.*) *Ord and ende*, the beginning and end, Gy of Warwike, p. 33, a common phrase. In Suffolk, a promontory is called an *ord*.

> And touchede him with the speres *ord*,
> That nevere eft he ne spak word.
> > *Romance of Otuel*, p. 74.
> He hit him with the speres *ord*,
> Thurch and thurch scheldes bord.
> > *Arthour and Merlin*, p. 276.
> Saul himself drowʒe his sword,
> And ran even upon the *ord*.
> > *Cursor Mundi, MS. Coll. Trin. Cantab.* f. 49.

ORDAIN. To order ; to intend. *Devon.*

ORDENARIE. An ordinance. (*A.-N.*)

ORDER. Disorder ; riot. *West.*

ORDERED. Ordained ; in holy orders.

ORDERS. A North-country custom at schools. In September or October the master is locked out of the school by the scholars, who, previous to his admittance, give an account of the different holidays for the ensuing year, which he promises to observe, and signs his name to the *orders*, as they are called, with two bondsmen. The return of these *signed orders* is the signal of capitulation ; the doors are immediately opened ; beef, beer, and wine deck the festive board ; and the day is spent in mirth.

ORDERS-FOUR. The four orders of mendicant friars. *Chaucer.*

ORDINAL. The ritual.

ORDINANCE. (1) Fate. *Shak.*

(2) Orderly disposition. (*A.-N.*)

(3) Apparel. Palsgrave, 1530.

ORDINATE. Regular ; orderly. (*Lat.*)

> For he that stondeth clere and *ordinate*,
> And proude happis suffreth underslide.
> > *Boetius, MS. Soc. Antiq.* 134, f. 296.

ORDONING. Ordinance. *Palsgrave.*

ORE. (1) Over. *Var. dial.*

(2) Grace ; favour ; mercy. (*A.-S.*)

> Syr, he seyde, for Crystys *ore*,
> Leve, and bete me no more.
> > *MS. Cantab.* Ff. ii. 38, f. 86.

(3) Sea-weed, used for manure. *South.* Holinshed, Chron. Ireland, p. 183, mentions *orewads*.

(4) A kind of fine wool.

ORF. Cattle. (*A.-S.*)

> Into the breris they forth kacche
> Here *orf*, for that they wolden lacche.
> > *Gower, MS. Soc. Antiq.* 134, f. 33.

ORFRAYS. Embroidery. (*A.-N.*) The term is perhaps most generally applied to the borders of embroidery or needle-work, down the cope on each side in front. See Cotgrave. " Orphrey of red velvet," Dugdale's Monast. iii. 283. It occurs in Chaucer.

> Fretene of *orfrayes* feste appone scheldez.
> > *Morte Arthure, MS. Lincoln*, f. 76.

ORGAMENT. Wild marjorum.

> The blood of harts burned together with herbedragon, orchanes, *orgament*, and mastick have the same power to draw serpents out of their holes, which the harts have being alive.
> > *Topsell's Four Footed Beasts*, 1607, p. 150.

ORGAN. The herb pennyroyal.

ORGANAL. An organ of the body.

ORGLES. Organs. *Weber.*

> Oure gentyl ser Jone, joy hym mot betyde,
> He is a meré mon of mony among cumpané,
> He con harpe, he con syng, his *orgius* ben herd ful wyd,
> He wyl noʒt spare his prese to spund his selaré.
> > *MS. Douce* 302, f. 3.

ORGULOUS. Proud. (*A.-N.*) *Orgulist*, proudest, Morte d'Arthure, ii. 432. *Orgulyte*, pride, ibid. ii. 111.

ORIEL. This term is stated by Mr. Hamper to have been formerly used in various senses, viz. a penthouse ; a porch attached to any edifice ; a detached gate-house ; an upperstory ; a loft ; a gallery for minstrels. See a long dissertation in the Archæologia, xxiii. 106-116. Perhaps, however, authority for an interpretation may be found which will compress these meanings, few words having really so comprehensive and varied an use. It may generally be described as a recess within a building. Blount has *oriol*, "the little waste room next the hall in some houses and monasteries, where particular persons dined ;" and this is clearly an authorised and correct explanation. *Nisi in refectorio vel oriolo pranderet*, Mat. Paris ; *in introitu, quod porticus vel oriolum appellatur*, ibid. The oriel was sometimes of considerable dimensions See a note in Warton, i. 176.

ORIENT. The east. (*A.-N.*)

ORIGINAL. Dear ; beloved. *Linc.*

ORISE. To plane, or make smooth. *West.*

ORISON. A prayer.

> When thai hade made theire *aryson*,
> A voyce came fro heven down,
> That alle men myȝt here ;
> And seid, The soule uf this synfulle wyȝt
> Is wonnen into heven bright,
> To Jhesu lafe and dere.
>> *MS. Cantab. Ff. v. 48, f. 47.*

ORISONT. The horizon. (*A.-N.*)

ORISSE. To prepare, or make ready.

ORL. The alder-tree. *West.*

ORLIAUNCE. Orleans. (*A.-N.*)

> Rede wyn, the claret, and the white,
> With Teynt and Alycaunt, in whom I delite ;
> Wyn ryvers and wyn sake also,
> Wyne of Langdoke and of *Orliaunce* therto,
> Sengle bere, and othir that is dwobile,
> Which causith the brayn of man to trouble.
>> *MS. Rawl. C. 86.*

ORLING. An ill-grown child. *North.*

ORLINGS. The teeth of a comb.

ORLOGE. A clock, or dial. (*A.-N.*)

> Gelosye salle kepe the *orloge*, and salle wakkyne
> the other ladyse, and make thame arely to ryse and
> go the wyllylyere to thaire servysse.
>> *MS. Lincoln A. 1. 17, f. 175.*

ORLOGER. A man who keeps clocks.

ORN. (1) Either. *Somerset.*

(2) To run ; to flow. (*A.-S.*)

> He *orn* aȝein him with grete joie,
> And biclupte him and custe.
>> *MS. Laud. 108, f. 2.*

ORNACY. Cultivated language.

ORNARY. Ordinary. *Var. dial.*

ORNATE. Adorned. (*Lat.*)

> The milke white swannes then strain'd in stile
> sublime,
> Of *ornate* verse, rich prose, and nervous rime.
> In short, to tellen all, doth not behove,
> Wheare wellcome, sat weare powr'd in cuppe of love.
>> *MS. Bibl. Reg. 17. B. xv.*

ORNATELY. Regularly ; orderly.

ORNDERN. Same as *Aandorn*, q. v.

ORNIFIED. Adorned. *Oxon.*

ORPED. Bold ; stout. The term is used by late writers. It occurs in Golding's Ovid, and in the Herrings Tale, 1598.

> Houndes ther be the whiche beth bolde and
> *orpede*, and beth cleped bolde, for thei be bolde and
> goode for the hert. *MS. Bodl. 546.*

> Orpedlich thou the bistere, -
> And thi lond thou fond to were.
>> *Arthour and Merlin, p. 65.*

> Doukes, kinges and barouns,
> Orped squiers and garsouns.
>> *Arthour and Merlin, p. 81.*

> That they wolle gete of here acorde
> Sum orpid knyȝte to sle this lorde.
>> *Gower, MS. Soc. Antiq. 134, f. 55.*

ORPHARION. A kind of musical instrument in the form of a lute.

ORPINE. Yellow arsenic. "Orpine or arsenike," Hollyband's Dict. 1593.

ORR. A globular piece of wood used in playing at doddart.

ORRI. A name for a dog. See MS. Bibl. Reg. 7 E. iv. f. 163.

ORROWER. Horror. *Pr. Parv.*

ORSADY. Tinsel. See *Arsedine.*

ORTS. Scraps ; fragments. *Var. dial.* It is a common archaism.

ORUALE. The herb orpin.

ORUL. To have a longing for. *West.*

ORYBULLY. Terribly.

> He apperyd fulle *orybully*, but not as he dud before.
>> *MS. Cantab. Ff. ii. 38, f. 52.*

ORYELLE. The alder-tree. *Pr. Parv.*

ORYNALLE. An urinal.

> Anon he askud an *orynalle* schene,
> And sawe theryn of kyng and quene.
>> *MS. Cantab. Ff. ii. 38, f. 133.*

ORYONS. The orient, or east.

> Stonys of *oryons* gret plenté,
> Hir here aboute hir hed hit hong ;
> She rode out over that lovely le,
> A-while she blew, a-while she song.
>> *MS. Cantab. Ff. v. 48, f. 116.*

ORYTHE. Aright. Arch. xxx. 357.

OSCHIVES. Bone-handled knives.

OSEY. A kind of wine, mentioned in the Squyr of Lowe Degré, 762 ; Harrison. p. 167 ; Nugæ Poeticæ, p. 10 ; MS. Morte Arthure, f. 55.

> Her land hath wine, *osey*, waxe, and graine,
> Figges, reysins, hony and cordoweyne.
>> *Hakluyt's Navigations, 1599, i. 189.*

OSIARD. An osier-bed. *Palsgrave.*

OSKIN. An oxgang of land, which varies in quantity in different places.

O-SLANTE. Aslant ; slanting.

> His hand sleppid and slode *o-slante* one the mayler.
>> *Morte Arthure, MS. Lincoln, f. 93.*

OSMOND. A kind of iron. Manners and Household Expences, p. 301.

OSNY. To forbode ; to predict. *West.*

OSPREY. The sea-eagle. Palsgrave calls it the *ospring.*

OSPRYNG. Offspring.

> I wolde that Bradmonde the kyng
> Were here with all his *ospryng*.
>> *MS. Cantab. Ff. ii. 38, f. 109.*

OSS. To offer, begin, attempt, or set about anything ; to be setting out ; to recommend a person to assist you. *Chesh.* Ray gives the Cheshire proverb, " ossing comes to bossing." Edgeworth, temp. Hen. VIII., uses to *oss* for to *prophesy.*

OSSELL. Perhaps. *Yorksh.*

OSTAYLE. An inn, or lodging.

> And in her place he toke his *ostayle*,
> Supposyng a lytill while ther to duelle.
>> *MS. Laud. 416, f. 59.*

> Men taghte hym sone to hem weyl,
> He come and toke ther hys *osteyl.*
>> *MS. Harl. 1701, f. 13*

O-STEDE. Instead.

> The whyche, as the custum was,
> Songe a balad *o-stede* of the masse.
>> *MS. Cantab. Ff. i. 6, f. 42.*

OSTENTS. Appearances ; prodigies.

> When ambitious Pyles, th' *ostents* of pride
> To dust shall fall, and in their ruins hide.
>> *Randolph's Poems, 1643.*

OSTERY. An inn. This word occurs in MS. Addit. 11812, f. 12. The term *osthouse* is used in Yorkshire. Palsgrave has *ostry.*

OSTILLER. An ostler. Vocab. MS.

OSTRECE. Austria. *Hearne.*

OSTREGIER. A falconer. This term was generally limited to a keeper of goshawks and tercels. *Ostringer* occurs in Blount's Gloss. p. 459, and Shakespeare has *astringer.*

OSTRICH-BORDE. Wainscoting.

OSTYLMENT. Furniture. *Quilibet utensile in domo, Anglice,* ostylment of howse, MS. Bibl. Reg. 12 B. i, f. 13.

OSTYRE. An oyster. Nominale MS.

OTE. Knows. (*A.-S.*)

OTEN. Often. *Somerset.*

OTHE. To swear. Still in use, according to Moor's Suffolk Words, p. 258. "*Adjurare,* to othe," MS. Egerton 829, f. 17.

OTHER. Or; either; or else. (*A.-S.*)

OTHER-GATES. Otherways. *North.*

OTHER-SOME. Some other. A quaint but pretty phrase of frequent occurrence. *Otherwhere,* in some other place.

Some blasfemede hym and said, fy one hym that
distroyes; and *othersome* saide, othire mene saved
be, bot hymselfe he may nott helpe.
MS. Lincoln A. i. 17, f. 183.

How she doth play the wether-cocke,
That turne with every winde;
To some she will be foolishe stout,
To *othersome* as kinde.
Gaulfrido and Barnardo, 1570.

OTHER-WHILE. Sometimes. *Var. dial.*

Than dwellyd they togedur same,
Wyth mekylle yoye and game,
Therof they wantyd ryght noght:
They went on hawkyng be the rever,
And *other-whyle* to take the dere,
Where that they gode thoght.
MS. Cantab. Ff. ii. 38, f. 80.

OTTOMITES. The Ottomans. *Shak.*

OTTRE. To utter. Lydgate, p. 150.

OTWO. In two; asunder. (*A.-S.*)

Al hem thoghte they wulde here slo,
For they clove here mouthe evyn *otwo.*
MS. Harl. 1701, f. 11.

OTYRE. An otter. It is the translation of *lutricius* in Nominale MS.

OU. How. MS. Digby 86.

OUCH. A jewel. "Ouche a jowell, *bague,*" Palsgrave; "ouche for a bonnet, *afficquet, affichet,*" ibid. The term seems to have been sometimes applied to various ornaments.

Of gyrdils and browchis, of *ouchis* and rynggis,
Pottys and pens and bollis for the fest of Nowell.
MS. Laud. 416, f. 97.

OUGHEN. To owe; to possess, or own. (*A.-S.*)

A certain king, which, when he called his servants to accompts, had one brought to him which *ought* him ten thousand talents.
Becon's Works, p. 154.

Amaris he hight, that many a toune *ought,*
Prince was of Portingall, proudest in thought.
Roland, MS. Lansd. 388, f. 388.

OUGHT. Something suitable. *Sussex.*

OULE.

But *oule* on stok and stok on *oule,*
The more that a man defoule.
Gower, MS. Soc. Antiq. 134, f. 88.

OUMER. The grayling fish. *North.*

OUNDE. (1) A kind of lace. (2) A curl. *Oundy,* waving, curly, said of hair laid in rolls. (*A.-N.*)

Cloth of gold of tissue entered *ounde* the one with the other, the *ounde* is warke wavynge up and doune, and all the borders as well trapper as other was garded with letters of fine golde.
Hall, Henry VIII. f. 79.

The hynder of hym was lyk purpure, and the tayle was *ounded* overthwert with a colour reede as rose.
MS. Lincoln A. i. 17, f. 30.

OUNFERD. Displeasure?

To thi neзbour fore love of me,
To make debate ny dyscorde,
And thou dust me more *ounferd,*
Then thaз thou wentust barefote in the strete.
MS. Douce 302, xv. Cent.

OUNGOD. Bad; wicked. (*A.-S.*)

OUNIN. A weak spoilt boy. *North.*

OUNSEL. The devil. From the old word *ounseli,* wicked. "Ich were ounseli," MS. Digby 86. (*A.-S.*)

OUPH. A fairy, or sprite. *Shak.*

OUR. (1) Hour. Still in use.

There may areste me no pleasaunce,
And *our* be *our* I fele grevaunce.
MS. Cantab. Ff. i. 6, f. 117.

(2) Anywhere. *Weber.*

(3) Over. Still in use. This would generally be printed *ovre.*

Hit was leid *oure* a broke,
Therto no man hede toke;
Oure a streme of watur clene,
Hit servyd as a brygge I wene.
MS. Cantab. Ff. v. 48, f. 30.

(4) A term implying relationship. *Our Thomas,* Thomas belonging to our family. *Var. dial.*

OURN. Ours. *Var. dial.*

OURY. Dirty; ill-looking; untidy. *Linc.*

OUSE. The liquor in a tanner's vat.

OUSEL. The blackbird.

House-doves are white, and *ousels* blackebirds bee,
Yet what a difference in the taste we see?
The Affectionate Shepheard, 1594.

OUSEN. Oxen. *North.*

OUSET. A few small cottages together, like a Highland clachan. The word is originally oustead, one-stead, i. e. one farmhouse and its appurtenances standing *solus,* all alone by itself, and no other one near it. *North.*

OUST. To turn out. *Var. dial.*

OUT. (1) Away! It is often an exclamation of disappointment. (*A.-S.*) *Out, alas!* occurs in Shakespeare.

The gentill prynce and his pepull to London did passe,
Into the cite he enteryd with a company of men and trew,
For the wiche his enmys cryed, *Oute* and alas!
Thayre red colowrus chaungid to pale hewe;
Thanne the nobyll prynce began werkys new,
He toke prisoners a kyng and a clerke, loo,
How the will of God in every thynge is doo!
MS. Bibl. Reg. 17 D. xv.

(2) Full; completely. Tempest, i. 2. Still in use, Heref. Gl. p. 76.

(3) An excursion of pleasure.

(4) *Out o'cry,* out of measure. See the Comedy of Patient Grissel, p. 20. *Out of heart,* worn out, applied to land; down-hearted, to a man,

Out at heels, out at the elbows, very shabbily dressed. *Out at ley*, said of cattle feeding in hired pastures. *Out of hand*, immediately, without delay. *Out of temper*, too hot or too cold. *Out of the way*, extravagant, uncommon. *To be at outs*, to quarrel. *To make no outs of a person*, not to understand him.

OUTAMY. To injure, or hurt?

> Ae the helm was so hard y-wrost,
> That he mist *outamy* him nost
> Wyth no dynt of swerde.
> > *MS. Ashmole*, 33, f. 49.

OUT-AND-OUT. Throughout; entirely; completely. *Out-and-outer*, a slang phrase implying anything supremely excellent.

> The kyng was good alle aboute,
> And she was wyckyd *oute and oute*,
> For she was of suche comforte,
> She lovyd mene ondir her lorde.
> > *MS. Rawlinson* C. 86.

OUTAS. (1) The octaves of a feast.

(2) A tumult, or uproar. *Nominale MS.*

OUT-ASKED. On the third time of publication, the couple are said to be out-asked, that is, the asking is out or over. Used in the South-East of England.

OUT-BEAR. To bear one out; to support one in anything. *Palsgrave.*

OUT-BORN. Removed. (*A.-S.*)

OUT-BY. A short distance from home.

OUT-CAST. The refuse of corn. *Pr. Parv.* It is explained in Salop. Antiq. p. 524, "the overplus gained by maltsters between a bushel of barley, and the same when converted into malt."

OUT-CATCH. To overtake. *North.*

OUT-CEPT. To except. *Palsgrave.*

OUTCOME. A going out. It occurs in MS. Cotton. Vespas. D. vii.

OUT-COMLING. A stranger. *Lanc.*

OUT-CORNER. A secret or obscure corner. "An *out-nooke* in a towne where poore folkes dwell," Florio, p. 97. *Out-place*, Palsgrave.

OUT-CRY. An auction. An auctioneer was called an *out-crier*.

OUT-DONE. Undone.

> A supper was drest, the king was a guest,
> But he thought 'twould have *outdone* him.
> > *Robin Hood*, ii. 169.

OUT-DOOR-WORK. Field-work. *West.* Also called *outen-work*.

OUTELICHE. Utterly; entirely.

OUTEN. Strange; foreign. *Outener*, a non-resident, a foreigner. *Linc.*

OUTENIME. To deliver. (*A.-S.*)

OUT-FALL. A quarrel. *North.*

OUT-FARING. Lying without. *Somerset.*

OUTGANG. A road. *North.*

OUT-GO. To go faster, or beat any one in walking or riding.

OUT-HAWL. To clean out. *Suffolk.*

OUTHEES. Outcry. (*Med. Lat.*)

OUTHER. Either. Still in use.

> And syf y were de yn *outher* werlde,
> Hys preyer shulde for me be herde.
> > *MS. Harl.* 1701, f. 70.

> For *outher* it wille falle on the umbre toward or on the umbre froward. *MS. Sloane* 213.

OUTHOLD. To hold out; to resist.

OUT-HORNE. An outlaw.

OUTING. (1) A feast given to his friends by an apprentice, at the end of his apprenticeship: when he is *out* of his time. In some parts of the kingdom, this ceremony is termed by an apprentice and his friends burying his wife. *Linc.*

(2) An airing. *Var. dial.*

(3) An evacuation, or letting-out. *North.*

OUTLAY. Expenditure. *Var. dial.*

OUTLER. An animal not housed. *North.*

OUTLERS. Out-standing debts. *Yorksh.*

OUT-LESE. The privilege of turning cattle out to feed on commons. *North.*

OUT-LESS. Unless. *Yorksh.*

OUTNER. A stranger. *North.*

OUT-OF. Without.

> Neither can anything please God that we do, if it be done *out-of* charity. *Bacon's Works*, p. 184.

OUTPARTERS. Thieves.

OUT-PUT. To cast out. (*A.-S.*)

OUTRAGE. Violence. (*A.-N.*)

OUTRAIE. To injure; to ruin; to destroy. (*A.-N.*) Palsgrave explains it, to "do some outrage or extreme hurt."

> Sir Arthure, thyne enmy, has *outrayede* thi lordes,
> That rode for the rescowe of sone riche knyghttes
> > *Morte Arthure, MS. Lincoln*, f. 74.

OUTRAKE. An out-ride or expedition. To raik, in Scottish, is to go fast. Outrake is a common term among shepherds. When their sheep have a free passage from inclosed pastures into open and airy grounds they call it a good outrake. *Percy.*

OUTRANCE. Confusion. (*A.-N.*)

OUTRE-CUIDANCE. Pride. (*Fr.*)

OUT-REDE. To surpass in counsel. (*A.-S.*)

OUTRELY. Utterly. (*A.-N.*)

OUT-RIDERS. (1) Bailiffs errant, employed by the sheriffs to summon persons to the courts. See Blount's Law Dictionary, in v.

(2) Highwaymen. *Somerset.*

OUT-ROP. A public auction. *North.* "An out-cry or outrope," Howell, 1660.

OUTSCHETHE. To draw out a sword.

OUTSCHONNE. To pluck out. (*A.-S.*)

OUTSETTER. An emigrant. *Yorksh.*

OUT-SHIFTS. The outskirts. *East.*

> And poore schollers and souldiers wander in backe lanes, and the *out-shiftes* of the citie, with never a rag to their backes. *Nash's Pierce Pennilesse*, 1592.

OUTSHOT. A projection of the upper stories in an old house. *North.* Hence *outshot-window*.

OUTSIDE. (1) At the most. *Var. dial.*

(2) Lonely; solitary; retired. *North.* In Dorsetshire it is *outstep*.

OUTSTEP. Unless.

> My son's in Dybell here, in Caperdochy, i'tha gaol, for peeping into another man's purse; and, *outstep* the king be miserable, he's like to totter.
> > *Heywood's Edward IV.* p. 78.

OUT-TAKE. To deliver (*A.-S.*)

OUT-TAKEN. Taken out; excepted. *Out-take*, except, is also common. It occurs several times in Lydgate.

> Bot he my₃te no₃te wynne over, the water was so depe and so brade, bot if it had bene in the monethe of July and Auguste; and also it was fulle of ypo-taynes and scorpyones, and cocadrilles, *out-takene* in the forsaid monethes. *MS. Lincoln A. i. 17, f. 31.*

> Alle that y have y graunt the
> Owttake my wyfe.
> *MS. Cantab. Ff. ii. 38, f. 96.*

OUTWALE. Refuse. *North.*

OUTWARD. An outside. *Shak.*

OUTWERINGNES. Abuse. (*A.-S.*)

OUT-WINDERS. Bow-windows. *South.*

OUT-WRIGHE. To discover. (*A.-S.*)

OUZE. Mud. Still in use.

> To voyage his large empire, as secure
> As in the safest ouse, where they assure
> Themselves at rest.
> *Heywood's Marriage Triumphe, 1613.*

OU₃TE. Aught; anything.

> But that thynge may y not embrace
> For ou₃te that y can speke or doo.
> *Gower, MS. Soc. Antiq. 134, f. 46.*

> Hou faryth that noble clerk,
> That mekyl can on Goddys werk,
> Knowest thou ou₃t hys state?
> And come thou ou₃t be the eerl off Stane,
> That wurthy lord in hys wane,
> Wente thou ou₃t that gate?
> *Romance of Athelston.*

OVEN. (1) The following proverb is given by Ray, and is still in use.

> A suspicious ill liver, for the wife would never have sought her daughter in the oven unlesse she herselfe had beene there in former times.
> *The Man in the Moone, 1609, sig. F. iii.*

(2) A great mouth. *Var. dial.*

OVEN-BIRD. The long-tailed titmouse. It's nest is called an *oven's-nest.*

OVENED. Sickly; shrivelled. *Linc.*

OVEN-RUBBER. A pole used for stirring the fire in a large oven.

OVER. (1) Compared with. *West.*

(2) Upper. Still in use.

(3) Above; besides; beyond. (*A.-S.*)

(4) To recover; to get over. *North.*

(5) Important; material. *Exmoor.*

(6) Too. Sir Perceval, 1956.

(7) *To put one over the door,* to turn him out. *Over the left,* disappointed.

OVERAIGNES. Gutters.

OVER-ALL. Everywhere.

OVERANENT. Opposite. *Var. dial.*

OVERBLOW. To blow hard. *Chesh.*

OVERBOD. Remained or lived after. (*A.-S.*)

OVER-BODIED. When a new upper part is put to an old gown. *Lanc.*

OVER-BUY. To give more for anything than it is really worth.

OVER-CLOVER. A boy's game, so called in Oxfordshire, the same as *Warner,* q. v. They have a song used in the game, commencing,

> " Over clover,
> Nine times over."

OVER-CRAPPID. Surfeited. *Devon.*

OVERCROW. To triumph over; to sustain.

> " Laboured with tooth and naile to *overcrow* "
> Holinshed, Chron. Ireland, p. 82.

OVER-DREEP. To overshadow.

> The aspiring nettles, with their shadie tops, shall no longer *over-dreep* the best hearbs, or keep them from the smiling aspect of the sunne, that live and thrive by comfortable beames.
> *Nash's Pierce Pennilesse, 1592.*

OVERE. Shore. (*A.-S.*) Jennings has *overs,* the perpendicular edge, usually covered with grass, on the sides of salt-water rivers.

> For michulle hongur, I undurstonde,
> She come out of Sexlonde,
> And rived here at Dovere,
> That stondes upon the sees *overe.*
> *MS. Cantab. Ff. v. 48, f. 96.*

OVERESTE. Uppermost. (*A.-S.*)

> An appille *overeste* lay on lofte,
> There the poyson was in dighte.
> *MS. Harl. 2252, f. 96.*

OVERFACE. To cheat. *Somerset.*

OVER-FARE. To go over. It occurs in MS. Cotton. Vespas. D. vii.

OVER-FLOWN. Intoxicated.

OVER-FLUSH. An overplus. *East.*

OVER-FRET. Made into fretwork.

> Scho come in a velvet,
> With white perle *overfret.*
> *MS. Lincoln A. i. 17, f. 133.*

OVERGANGER. One who escapes.

> By Jacob in haly writt es undirstande ane *over-ganger* of synnes. *MS. Lincoln A. i. 17, f. 224.*

OVERGET. To overtake. *Var. dial.* It occurs in Palsgrave, 1530.

OVERGETH. Passed over.

> The tyme of ₃eris *overgeth*
> That he was a man of brede and lengthe.
> *Gower, MS. Soc. Antiq. 134, f. 97.*

OVERGIVE. (1) To ferment. (2) To thaw. *East.*

OVER-GO. To pass over. (*A.-S.*) It is here used for the part. pa.

> As I went this undyre tyde,
> To pley me be myn orcherd syde,
> I fell on slepe all-be-dene,
> Under an ympe upone the grene;
> My meydens durst me not wake,
> Bot lete me ly₃e and slepe take,
> Tyll that the tyme over-passyd so,
> That the undryne was *over-go.*
> *MS. Ashmole 61, xv. Cent.*

OVER-HAND. The upper-hand. *North.*

> Thurghe the helpe of our goddis, he schalle hafe the *over-hande* of alle ₃oure neghtebours, and ₃our name schalle spred over alle the werlde.
> *MS. Lincoln A. i. 17, f. 3.*

> He sent us never no schame ne schenchipe in erthe,
> Bot ever ₃it the *over-hands* of alle other kynges.
> *Morte Arthure, MS. Lincoln, f. 98.*

OVERHED. A cut given over the head in fencing. Kyng Alisaunder, 7396.

OVERHERRE. Superior. (*A.-S.*)

> Spaynardis also that withoute doute bothe in nombre of peple and strengthe of bodies of olde tyme have ben oure *overherrs.*
> *Vegecius, MS. Douce 291, f. 5.*

OVERHEW. To overgrow and overpower, as strong plants do weak ones. *East.*

OVER-HIE. To overtake. *North.*

OVER-HILT. Covered over. (*A.-S.*)

OVER-HIP. To hop, or pass over.

OVER-HOPE. Sanguineness. (*A.-S.*)

On ys presumpcion of herte bold,
That ys *overhope* on Ynglische told.
MS. Bodl. 48, f. 123.

OVER-HOUSE-MEN. Small wire drawers.

OVERING. Passing over. *Var. dial.*

OVERIST-WERKE. The clerestory.

He beheld the werke full wele,
The *overyst-werke* above the walle
Gane schyne as doth the crystalle.
A hundreth tyretes he saw full stout,
So godly thei wer bateyled aboute.
MS. Ashmole 61, xv. Cent.

OVER-KEEP. Good living. *Var. dial.*

OVERLAND. A roofless tenement. *Overland-farm*, a parcel of land without a house to it. *Devon.*

OVERLAYER. A piece of wood used to place the sieve on, after washing the ore in a vat. *Derb.* A mining term.

OVER-LEDE. To oppress. *Lydgate.*

OVERLIGHT. To alight, or descend. *West.*

OVERLING. Ruler; master.

I have made a kepare, a knyghte of thyn awene,
Overlyng of Ynglande undyre thyselvene.
Morte Arthure, MS. Lincoln, f. 60.

OVER-LIVE. To outlive. (*A.-S.*)

OVERLOOKED. Bewitched. *West.* The term occurs in Shakespeare.

OVERLY. (1) Slight; superficial. Sometimes an adverb. "I will doe it, but it shal be *overly* done, or to be ridden of it," Hollyband's Dictionarie, 1593. "Thou doest this *overlie*, or onely for an outward shewe," Baret, 1580.

He prayeth but with an *overly* desire, and not from the deep of his heart, that will not bend his endeavours withal to obtain what he desireth: or rather indeed he prayeth not at all.
Sanderson's Sermons, 1689, p. 51.

(2) To oppress. *Overlie*, oppressively, Stanihurst's Ireland, p. 22.

OVERMASTE. Overgreat. (*A.-S.*)

Gye was oon of the twelve,
Overmaste he sate be hymselve.
MS. Cantab. Ff. ii. 38, f. 215.

OVERMASTER. To overcome one.

OVER-MEASURE. One in twenty given over and above in the sale of corn.

OVERNOME. Overtaken. (*A.-S.*)

OVER-PEER. To overhang. *Shak.* It occurs in Cotgrave, in v. *Nageoire.*

OVER-QUALLE. Be destroyed. (*A.-S.*)

That jere whete shalbe over alle;
Ther shalle mony childur *over-qualle*.
MS. Cantab. Ff. v. 48, f. 77.

OVER-RINNE. To overtake. (*A.-S.*)

OVER-RUN. To leave unfinished. *West.*

OVER-SAIL. To project over, a term used by bricklayers. *North.* "Ere I my malice cloake or *oversile*," Du Bartas, p. 357, which seems to be used in a similar sense.

OVERSCAPE. To escape.

Whiche for to counte is but a jape,
As thynge whiche thou myjte *overscape*.
Gower, MS. Soc. Antiq. 134, f. 53.

OVER - SCUTCHED - HUSWIVES. Whores.

Shak. "An overswitcht houswife, a loose wanton slut, a whore," Kennett, MS.

OVERSE. To overlook. *Palsgrave.*

That he should rule, *oversé*, and correct the maners and condicions of the people.
Hall, 1548, *Hen. V.* f. 1.

OVERSEEN. (1) Mistaken; deceived. *West.* It occurs in Palsgrave.

(2) Tipsy. "Well nigh whittled, almost drunke, somewhat *overseene*," Cotgrave. See Thoms' Anecd. and Trad. p. 54.

OVERSEER. (1) An overlooker frequently appointed in old wills. Sometimes the executor was so called. According to MS. Harl. 3038, "too secuturs and an overseere make thre theves."

(2) A man in the pillory.

OVERSET. To overcome. Still in use.

OVERSHOOT. To get intoxicated.

OVERSLEY. The lintel of a door.

OVER-STOCKS. Upper-stockings. *Baret.*

OVER-STORY. The clerestory.

OVERTAKE.

Summe of hem began to strife,
Gret *overtake* for to dryfe.
MS. Cantab. Ff. v. 48, f. 13.

OVERTAKEN. Intoxicated.

OVERTE. Open. (*A.-N.*)

OVERTHROWE. To fall down. (*A.-S.*)

OVERTHWART. Across; over against. (*A-S.*) As an adjective, cross, contrary, contradictory, perverse, opposite. It is sometimes a verb, to wrangle.

That strekes the nekes out als the hert,
And als ane hors of prys that lokes *overwhert*.
MS. Harl. 2260.

He thawght his hart so *overthwart*,
His wysdom was so suer-a,
That nature could not frame by art
A bewty hym to lure-a. *MS. Ashmole* 48, f. 120.

OVER-TIMELICHE. Too early. (*A.-S.*)

OVER-WELTED. Overturned. *North.* We have *over-walt*, overcome, in Syr Gawayne.

OVERWEMBLE. To overturn. *Beds.*

OVER-WHILE. Sometimes; at length.

OVER-WORN. Quite worn out. *East.*

OVER-YEAR. Bullocks which are not finished at three years old, if home-breds, or the first winter after buying, if purchased, but are kept through the ensuing summer to be fatted the next winter, are said to be kept *over-year*, and are termed *over-year* bullocks. *Norfolk.*

OVVIS. The eaves of a house. *Devon.*

OW. You. Still in use in Yorkshire.

OWE. To own; to possess.

Ah, good young daughter, I may call thee so,
For thou art like a daughter I did *owe*.
Chron. Hist. of King Leir, 1605.

When Charles the fifth went with his armye into Affrique and arived at Larghera, a noble citty of Sardinia, there happened an exceeding great wonder, for an oxe brought forth a calfe with two heades, and the woman that did *owe* the oxe, presented the calfe to the Emperor.
Topsell's Four-Footed Beasts, 1607, p. 99.

OWENNE. Own. (*A.-S.*)

To lese myne *owenne* lyfe therfore.
MS. Lincoln A. i. 17, f. 116.

OWERE. An ewer. " Basyne and *owere*,"
MS. Lincoln A. i. 17, f. 135.

OWHERE. Anywhere. (*A.-S.*)

> The heȝest hille that was *owhore*,
> The flood overpassed seven ellen and more.
> *Cur or Mundi, MS. Coll. Trin. Cantab. f. 12.*
>
> Aȝen langoure the beste medicyne
> In alle this world that *owhere* may be founde.
> *Lydgate, MS. Soc. Antiq. 134, f. 21.*
>
> For thogh y be bryghte of blee,
> The fayrest man that ys *oughtwhare*.
> *MS. Cantab. Ff. ii. 38, f. 19.*
>
> Wist ich *owhar* ani bacheler,
> Vigrous and of might cler.
> *Arthour and Merlin, p. 244.*

OWL. (1) A moth. *Sussex.*

(2) *To take owl*, to be offended, to take amiss.
*I live too near a wood to be frightened by an
owl*, I understand matters too well to be
alarmed by you. *To walk by owl-light*, to skulk
for fear of being arrested.

(3) A kind of game so called is mentioned by
Howell, Lex. Tet. 1660, sect. 28.

(4) Wool. *North.*

(5) To go prying about. *West.*

OWLER. (1) The alder-tree. *North.*

(2) A smuggler. *South.* Kennett says, " those
who transport wool into France contrary to
the prohibition are called *owlers.*"

OWLERT. An owl. *Salop.*

OWLGULLER. To pry about. *Suffolk.*

OWLISTHEDE. Idleness.

OWL'S-CROWN. Wood cudweed. *Norf.*

OWLY. Half stupid ; tired. *Suffolk.*

OWMAWTINE. To swoon.

OWMLIS. The umbles of a deer. This occurs
in Nominale MS.

OWN. To acknowledge. *Var. dial.*

OWRE. An hour. *North.*

> Aftur mete a longe *owre*
> Gye went with the emperowre.
> *MS. Cantab. Ff. ii. 38, f. 173.*

OWRISH. Soft ; wet ; marshy. *Linc.*

OWSE. Anything. *North.*

OWTED. Put away.

> Thee night with brightnes is *owted*.
> *Stanyhurst's Virgil, 1583, p. 90.*

OWTTANE. Taken out. (*A.-S.*)

> Sex cases thare are *owttane*,
> That nane assoyles bot the pape allane.
> *Hampole, MS. Bowes, p. 5.*

OWT-ȝETTEDE. Scattered out. " Oyle owt-
ȝettede es thi name," MS. Lincoln A. i. 17,
f. 192. (*A.-S.*)

OWUNE. An oven. *Devon.*

> Tak the a hate lafe as it comes owt of the *owune*,
> and mak soppes of the crommes in gude rede wyne.
> *MS. Lincoln A. i. 17, f. 292.*

OWYTH. Ought. (*A.-S.*)

> He was bothe meke and mylde, as a gode chylde
> *owyth* to ben. *MS. Cantab. Ff. ii. 38, f. 51.*

OX-BOW. The bow of wood that goes around
the neck of an ox. Still in use.

OXENFORDE. Oxford.

> Away rode the abbot all sad at that word,
> And he rode to Cambridge, and *Oxenford*;
> But never a doctor there was so wise,
> That could with his learning an answer devise.
> *King John and the Abbot of Canterbury.*

OXEY. Of mature age. *Glouc.*

OX-EYE. The larger titmouse. *North.*

OX-FEET, (in a horse) is when the horn of the
hind-foot cleaves just in the very middle of
the fore part of the hoof from the coronet to
the shoe : they are not common, but very
troublesome, and often make a horse halt.

OX-HOUSE. An ox-stall. *Exmoor.* It occurs
in Nominale MS.

OXLIP. The greater cowslip. *Var. dial.*

OX-SKIN. A hide of land.

> Fabian, a chronogapher, writing of the Con-
> querour, sets downe in the history thereof another
> kinde of measure, very necessary for all men to un-
> derstand ; foure akers (saith he) make a yard of
> land, five yards of land contain a hide, and 8 hides
> make a knights fee, which by his conjecture is so
> much as one plough can well till in a yeare ; in
> Yorkeshire and other countries they call a hide an
> *oxe-skinne*. Hopton's Baculum Geodæticum, 4to. 1614.

OXT. Perplexed. *Warw.*

OXTER. The armpit. *North.*

OXY. Wet ; soft ; spungy. It is generally ap
plied to land. *South.*

OYAN. Again. (*A.-S.*)

> Thai seghen all the wonded man,
> And leved hem wel, and went *oyan*.
> *The Sevyn Sages, 2348.*

OYE. A grandchild. *North.*

O-YES. For *oyez*, the usual exclamation of a
crier. *Shak.*

OYINGE. Yawning ; gaping. *Weber.*

OYNEȝONES. Onions. This occurs in a receipt
in MS. Lincoln A. i. 17, f. 295. *Oynone.*
Nominale MS.

OYS. Use ; nature.

> Alswa here es forbodene alle maner of wilfulle
> pollusyone procurede one any maner agaynes
> kyndly *oys*, or other gates.
> *MS. Lincoln A. i. 17, f. 196.*

OYSE. To use.

> For a man excuses noght hys unconnyng,
> That hys wytte *oyses* noght in leerenyng.
> *Hampole, MS. Bowes, p. 16.*
>
> And therefore, sene Godd hymselfe made it, than
> awe it maste of alle othire orysones to be *oysede* in
> alle haly kyrke. *MS. Lincoln A. i. 17, f. 209.*

OYSTER. An oyster of veal is the blade-bone
dressed with the meat on.

OYSTERLY. A kind of green plum, ripening
in August. MS. Ashmole 1461.

OȝT. Out ; completely.

> And when the halle was rayed *oȝt*,
> The scheperde lokid al aboute.
> *MS. Cantab. Ff. v. 48, f. 54.*

P To mind one's P's and Q's, i. e. to be very careful in behaviour.

PACADILE. A kind of collar put about a man or woman's neck to support and bear up the band or gorget. See *Piccadel*.

PACE. (1) To parse verbs. *Lilly*.

(2) A herd or company of asses.

(3) To pass away; to surpass. (*A.-N.*)

(4) In architecture, a broad step or any slightly raised stone above a level. See Britton.

PACE-EGGS. Eggs boiled hard and dyed or stained various colours, given to children about the time of Easter. A custom of great antiquity among various nations, and still in vogue in the North of England.

PACEGARDES. Part of ancient armour, mentioned in Hall's Union, 1548, Hen. IV. f. 12.

PACEMENT. Peace; quietness.

PACK. (1) A dairy of cows. *Chesh*. Properly, a flock of any animals.

(2) A heap, or quantity. *Var. dial.*

> He lefte slayne in a slake
> Tene score in a *pakke*.
> *MS. Lincoln* A. i. 17, f. 131.

(3) A term of reproach, generally applied to a woman. " A whore, queane, punke, drab, flurt, strumpet, harlot, cockatrice, naughty *pack*, light huswife, common hackney," Cotgrave. See *Naughty-pack*.

(4) A measure of coals, containing about three Winchester bushels.

(5) A pedlar's bundle. *Var. dial.*

(6) To collect together, to combine, especially for an unlawful or seditious purpose. *Packs*, agreements, combinations, Harrison's England, p. 246.

(7) *Pack and Penny Day*, the last day of a fair, when bargains are usually sold.

(8) To truss, or fill up. *North*.

PACKERS. Persons employed in barrelling or packing up herrings.

PACKET. (1) A false report. *Var. dial.*

(2) Any horse-pannel to carry packs or bundles upon. *Chesh*.

PACK-GATE. A gate on a *pack-way*, q. v.

PACKING. *To go packing*, to go away about one's business. *Var. dial.* " Make speede to flee, be packing and awaie," Baret's Alvearie, 1580.

PACKING-WHITES. A kind of cloth.

PACKMAN. A pedlar. *Var. dial.*

PACK-MONDAY. The first Monday after the 10th of October.

PACK-PAPER. Paper used for packing tradesmen's wares in, &c.

PACK-RAG-DAY. Old May-day: so called because servants being hired in this county from Old May-day to Old May-day, pack up their rags or clothes on this day preparatory to leaving their then servitudes for home or fresh places. *Linc.* Forby gives the term to Old Michaelmas-day.

PACK-STAFF. A pedlar's staff, on which he carried his pack. " As plain as a *pack-staff*" was a proverbial simile. We now say *pike-*staff. It was also a term of contempt. Thus *aerumna* is translated " a *pack-staff* misery" in Welde's Janua Linguarum, 1615.

PACK-THREAD. *To talk pack-thread*, to use indecent language well wrapped up.

PACK-THREAD-GANG. A gang that would not hold long together, some of whom might be induced by a reward to split upon the others. *Linc.*

PACK-WAY. A narrow way by which goods could be conveyed only on pack-horses. *East.*

PACKY. Heavy with clouds packed together: thus they say before a thunderstorm, " It looks *packy*." *Linc.*

PACOBI. A kind of wine, so called from some sort of Brazilian fruit.

PACOLET'S-HORSE. An enchanted steed belonging to Pacolet, in the old romance of Valentine and Orson. He is frequently alluded to by early writers.

PACTION. Combination; contract.

> Since with the soule we in soft *paction* bee,
> These sounds, sights, smels, or tastes, can nere please mee;
> My soule is fled, no more in me't can move,
> Alas! my soule is only where I love.
> *Tyrocinium Poeseos, Rawl. MS.*

PAD. (1) A path. *Linc.* In canting language, the highway was and is so called.

(2) A quire of blotting-paper, used in offices for clerks to write on. *Var. dial.*

(3) A pannier. *Norf.*

(4) *A pad in the straw*, something wrong, a screw loose. " Here lyes in dede the padde within the strawe," Collier's Old Ballads, p. 108. Still in use.

(5) A kind of brewing tub. *Devon*.

(6) To make a path by walking on an untracked surface. *East.*

(7) To go; to walk. *Var. dial.* Especially spoken of a child's toddling.

(8) The foot of a fox. *Var. dial.*

(9) A sort of saddle on which country-market women commonly ride, different both from the pack-saddle and side-saddle, of a clumsy make, and as it were padded and quilted; used likewise by millers and maltsters.

(10) "A burthen fit either for a person on foot, or to carry behind upon a pad-nag; item a pad of yarn, a certain quantity of skains made in a bundle; a pad of wool, a small pack such as clothiers and serge-makers carry to a spinning-house," MS. Devon Gl.

PADDER. A footpad.

PADDINGTON-FAIR. An execution. Tyburn is in the parish of Paddington.

PADDLE. (1) A small spade to clean a plough with. *West.*

(2) To lead a child. *North.*

(3) To abuse any one. *Exmoor.*

(4) To toddle; to trample. *East.*

(5) " *To paddle*, proprie aquam manibus pedibusque agitare, metaphorice adbibere plus paulo; *to have paddled*, to have made a little too free with strong liquor; *to paddle* etiam designat molliter manibus tractare aliquid et

agitare, as to paddle in a ladies neck or bosom," MS. Devon Glossary.

PADDLE-STAFF. A long staff, with an iron spike at the end of it, like a small spade, much used by mole-catchers.

PADDLING-STRINGS. Leading strings. *North.*

PADDOCK. A toad. In the provinces the term is also applied to a frog. " In Kent we say to a child, your hands are as cold as a paddock," MS. Lansd. 1033. To bring haddock to paddock, i. e. to outrun one's expenses. It is used as a term of contempt in the following passage:

Boys now blaberyn bostynge of a baron bad,
    In Bedlem is born be bestys, suche bost is blowe;
I xal prune that *padduk* and prevyn hym as a pad,
    Scheldys and sperys shalle I there sowe.
                    Coventry Mysteries, p. 164.

PADDOCK-CHESE. The asparagus. This name occurs in an ancient list of plants in MS. Bib. Soc. Antiq. 101, f. 89.

PADDOCK-RUD. The spawn of frogs. *Cumb.*

PADDOCK-STOOL. A toadstool. *North.*

PADDY. Wormeaten. *Kent.*

PADDY-NODDY. Embarrassment. *North.*

PAD-FOOIT. A kind of goblin. *Yorksh.*

PAD-LAND. A parish pound. *Devon.*

PAD-NAG. " I immediately form'd a resolution of following the fashion of taking the air early next morning; and fix'd upon this young ass for a *pad-nag*," Life of Mrs. Charke.

PADOWE. Padua. Warkworth, p. 5.

He set hym up and sawe their biside
A sad man, in whom is no pride,
Right a discrete confessour, as I trow,
His name was called sir John Doclow;
He had commensed in many a worthier place
Then ever was Padow, or Boleyn de Grace.
                    MS. Rawl. C. 86.

PADSTOOL. A toadstool. *North.*

Hermolaus also writeth this of the Lycurium, that it groweth in a certaine stone, and that it is a kind of mushrom, or *padstoole*, which is cut off yearely, and that another groweth in the roome of it, a part of the roote or foot being left in the stone, groweth as hard as a flint, and thus doth the stone encrease with a naturall fecundity; which admirable thing (saith he) I could never be brought to beleeve, untill I did eate thereof in myne owne house. *Topsell's Beasts*, 1607, p. 494.

PAD-THE-HOOF. To walk. *North.*

PAE. A peacock. *Ritson.*

PAFFELDEN. Baggage. *Cumb.*

PAFFLING. Trifling; idle; silly. *North.*

PAG. To carry pick-a-back. *Linc.*

PAGAMENT. A kind of frieze cloth.

PAGE. The common and almost only name of a shepherd's servant, whether boy or man. It is, I believe, extensively used through Suffolk, and probably farther. As an appendage of royalty or nobility, a page is now chiefly known to us. In old English, the term is applied to a boy-child, or boy-servant.

PAGENCY. A scaffold. The term pageant was originally so used, and metaphorically applied to a part in the stage of life. *Pagion*, a pageant, Misfortunes of Arthur, p. 61.

PAGETEPOOS. Efts; lizards; frogs. *Cornw.*

PAGYIN. Writing?

This boke of alle haly writes es mast usede in haly kirke servyse, forthi that it es perfeccioun of divyne *pagyin*. *MS. Coll. Eton.* 10, f. 1.

PAID. (1) A sore. *Staff.*

(2) Drunk; intoxicated.

PAIDE. Pleased; satisfied. (*A.-N.*)

So excusyd he hym tho,
The lady wende hyt had byn soo
    As Syr Marrokk sayde.
He goth forthe and holdyth hys pese,
More he thenkyth then he says,
    He was fulle evylle *payde*.
                    MS. Cantab. Ff. ii. 38, f. 72.

PAIGLE. The cowslip. *East.*

The yellow marigold, the sunnes owne flower,
Pugle, and pinke, that decke faire Floraes bower.
                Heywood's Marriage Triumphe, 1613.

PAIK. To beat severely. *North.*

PAILLET. A couch. (*A.-N.*)

PAIL-STAKE. A bough with branches, fixed in the ground in the dairy-yard for hanging pails on. *Glouc.*

PAIN-BALK. An instrument of torture, probably the same as the *brake.*

PAINCHES. Tripe. *North.*

PAINCHES-WAGGON. A north-country phrase implying incessant labour.

PAINE-MAINE. A fine bread. " Payne mayne, *payn de bouche*," Palsgrave.

Paynedomaynes prevaly
Scho fett fra the pantry. *MS. Lincoln* A. i. 17, f. 136.

PAINFULLY. Laboriously. The French Alphabet, 8vo. Lond. 1615, was, as we are told on the title-page, "*painfully* gathered and set in order."

Most happy we were, during our continuance here, in the weekly sermons and almost frequent converse of Mr. Edward Calamie, that was the preacher of that parish; and this indeed was one of the chief motives that drew us thither to partake of his *painful* and pious preaching. *MS. Harl.* 646.

PAINING. Pain; torture. (*A.-S.*)

Ther he saw many a sore torment,
How sowlis were put in gret *paynyng;*
He saw his fadur how he brent,
And be the memburs how he hyng.
                    MS. Cantab. Ff. v. 48, f. 67.

PAINT. To blush.

PAINTED-CLOTH. Cloth or canvass painted in oil, a cheap substitute for tapestry. It was frequently the receptacle of verses or mottos.

PAINTER. The rope that lies in the ship's longboat or barge, always ready to fasten her or hale her on the shore. Whence we have the sea-proverb, *I'll cut your painter*, meaning I will prevent your doing me any hurt, injury, or mischief. See Grose, in v.

PAINTICE. Penthouse. The shed where blacksmiths shoe horses. *Derby.*

PAIR. (1) A number. *Cornw.*

(2) A pack of cards.

(3) To grow mouldy, as cheese. *West.*

(4) Only a pair of shears between them, i. e. little or no difference.

And some report that both these fowles have seene
Their like, that's but a *payre* of sheeres betweene.
                    Taylor's Workes, 1630, i. 108.

PAIRE. To impair. (*A.-N.*)

Hit was wel i-wroughte and faire,
Non egge-tol mighte it nought *peire*.
Bevea of Hampton, p. 40.

PAIRING. The name of a marriage feast in Devon, when the friends of the happy couple present them with various things, and sometimes money. MS. Devon Glossary, p. 172. It is now obsolete.

PAIR-OF-STAIRS. A flight of stairs.

PAIR-OF-WINGS. Oars. *Grose.*

PAIR-OF-WOOD. Timber supporting the broken roof of a mine.

PAIR-ROYAL. A term at cards, meaning three of a sort. See *Prial.*

PAISE. (1) To weigh. (*A.-N.*)

Paise thy materes or thou derne or decerne,
Let ryght in causes holde thy lanterne.
MS. Canteb. Ff. l. 6, f. 129.

(2) To open a bolt or lock by shoving as with a knife point. *Northumb.*

PAISFULIK. Peacefully. It occurs in MS. Cotton. Vespas. D. vii. Ps. 34.

PAISTER. " I comber, I payster with over many clothes wearyng aboute one, *jemmougle*," Palsgrave. Pester ?

PAIT. The rut of a wheeL " *Orbita, Anglice* a paytt," Nominale MS.

PAITRICK. A partridge. *North.*

PAITRURE. Part of a horse's armour, for defending the neck.

PAIWURT. The herb saxifrage.

PAJOCK. This word occurs in Hamlet, iii. 2, altered by modern editors to peacock, a substitution by no means satisfactory, nor are far-fetched etymological conjectures more so. The nearest approach to the term I have met with in old English is to be found in the word *paphawkes* in the Coventry Mysteries, p. 179. Both are used as terms of contempt.

PAKE. To peep at. " What are you *paking* at ?" Perhaps it would be better spelt peak. *Suffolk.*

PALABRAS. Words. (*Span.*)

PALACE. A storehouse. *Devon.* " At Dartmouth I am told there are some of these storehouses called palaces cut out of the rock still retaining the name," MS. Devon Gloss.

PALASINS. Belonging to the court.

PALATE. A thin oval plate or board with a hole at one end for admittance of the thumb, which a painter holds to spread and mix his colours while he is drawing.

PALAVER. To flatter. *Var. dial.*

PALCH. To walk slowly. *Devon.*

PALCHIN. This word is of very unusual occurrence. It seems to mean a kind of short spear such as is used for spearing large fish. " Pawlchyne for fyssche, lunchus," Nominale MS. Ducange explains *lunchus* as *lancea, hasta*, from the Greek λογχος. It does not occur in the Prompt. Parv. nor in the Medulla.

PALCHING. Mending clothes. *Exmoor.*

PALE. (1) To beat barley. *Chesh.*

(2) To ornament ; to stripe.

Palaises proudliche pyghte, that *palyd* ware ryche
Of palle and of purpure, wyth precyous stones.
Morte Arthure, MS. Lincoln, f. 67.

(3) A ditch, or trench. (*A.-S.*) It occurs in MS. Egerton 829, f. 5.

(4) A small fortress.

(5) An inclosure for cattle. *Linc.*

(6) A stripe in heraldry.

(7) To make pale. (*A.-N.*)

(8) A limit or boundary. *Shak.*

(9) To leap the pale, i. e. to be extravagant, to exceed one's expenses.

If you proceede as you have begunne, your full feeding wil make you leane, your drinking too many healthes will take all health from you, your *leaping the pale* will cause you looke pale, your too close following the fashion will bring you out of all forme and fashion.
The Man in the Moone, 1609, sig. C. iv.

PALEIS. A palace. (*A.-N.*)

PALERON. Part of the armour. " A pece of harnesse, *espalleron*," Palsgrave.

PALESTRALL. Athletic. It occurs in Chaucer's Troilus and Creseide, v. 304.

PALET. Scull ; head. " Knok thi palet," Minot's Poems, p. 31. There was a kind of armour for the head also so called, as appears from Pr. Parv., probably lined with fur.

PALEW. Pale. It occurs in the Optick Glasse of Humours, 1639, p. 108.

It is somewhat fatty, in colour *palew*, reddish, high coloured, and without other signes of concoction.
Fletcher's Differences, 1623.

PALFREIS. Saddle-horses. *Chaucer.*

And wel a *palefrey* bistride,
And wel upon a stede ride. *Havelok*, 2060.

PALING. Imitating pales. (*A.-N.*)

PALINGMAN. A fishmonger. *Skinner.*

PALL. " I palle as drinke or bloode dothe by longe standyng in a thynge, *je appallys*," Palsgrave. Still in use.

PALLADE. Palle, or rich cloth. " He dyd of his surcote of pallade," Isenbras, 124.

PALL-COAT. A short garment, somewhat like a short cloak with sleeves.

PALLE. A kind of fine cloth. It was used at a very early period to cover corpses, and the term is still retained for the cloth which covers the coffin ; but this was by no means its most general use, for the robes of persons of rank are constantly mentioned as made of " purpure palle ;" and in a passage in Launfal tapestry of that material is mentioned. An archbishop's pall is thus described by Stanihurst, p. 31—" A pall is an indowment appropriated to archbishops, made of white silke the breadth of a stole, but it is of another fashion." Descr. of Ireland, 1586.

So fere he went I sey i-wys,
That he wyst not where he was.
He that sate in boure and halle,
And on hym were the purpull *palle*,
Now in herd beth he lyset,
With levys and gresse his body l.ydyth.
MS. Ashmole 61, xv. Cent.

For also wel to him hit falles
As a dongehulle sprad with *palles*.
MS. Addit. 10036, f. 31.

This twayle y-bordryd abousgt was
With *palle*, the mountenesse of han hondbrede
Chron. Vilodun. p. 64.

PALLED. (1) Turned pale. *Devon.*

(2) Senseless, death-like, as one is from excessive drinking. In use in Yorkshire.

PALLEE. Broad; used only in conjunction with another word, as *pallee-foot*, a large broad foot, *pullee-paw*, a large broad hand. *Somerset.*

PALLEN. To knock. (*A.-S.*)

PALLESTRE. A child's ball. (*A.-N.*)

PALL-HORSE. A horse bearing a pannier. "*Sagmarius*, *Anglice* a palhors," Nominale MS. f. 4. Ducange explains *sagmarius* by *equus clitellarius.*

PALLIAMENT. A robe; the white gown of a Roman candidate. *Shak.*

PALLIARD. A born beggar. According to the Fraternitye of Vacabondes, 1575, " is he that goeth in a patched cloke, and hys doxy goeth in like apparell." *Paliardize*, dirtiness and shabbiness, Hamblet, 1608, p. 181; Downfall of Robert, Earl of Huntington, p. 36. The following account of them is given by a writer of the last century :—A cant name for a wretched set of men and women, whose whole delight is to live by begging, thieving, &c. or any thing but honest industry, and who to move compassion in the spectators, the women go about with one, two, or more small children, in a dirty, ragged condition, who are continually crying or making wry faces, as though starved with hunger, and the women making a lamentable cry, or doleful tale, of being a distressed widow, and almost starved, &c. at the same time her male companion lies begging in the fields, streets, &c. with cleymes or artificial sores, made with spearwort or arsenick, which draws them into blisters, or by unslacked lime and soap, tempered with the rust of old iron, which being spread upon leather, and bound very hard to the leg, presently so frets the skin, that the flesh appears raw, and shocking to the sight; the impostor at the same time making a hideous noise, and pretending great pain, deceives the compassionate, charitable, and well-disposed passengers, whom, when opportunity presents, he can recover his limbs to rob, and even murder, if resisted.

PALLING. Languishing; turning pale.

PALLIONES. Tents. *Northumb.*

PALL-MALL. A game, thus described by Cotgrave, "A game wherein a round box bowle is with a mallet strucke through a high arch of vron (standing at either end of an ally one) which he that can do at the fewest blowes, or at the number agreed on, winnes." See *Mall* (4). James I. mentions *palle maillé* among the exercises to be used *moderately* by Prince Henry. " *Pale maille* a game wherein a round bowle is with a mallet struck through a high arch of iron, standing at either end of an alley, which he that can do at the fewest blows, or at the number agreed on, wins. This game is used at the long alley near St. James's, and vulgarly called Pell-Mell," Blount's Gloss. ed. 1681, p. 463.

PALL-WORK. Rich or fine cloth, work made of *palle*, q. v. See Degrevant, 629.

PALM. (1) Properly exotic trees of the tribe *palmacea*; but among our rustics, it means the catkins of a delicate species of willow gathered by them on Palm Sunday. "Palme, the yelowe that groweth on wyllowes, *chatton*," Palsgrave, 1530.

(2) The broad part of a deer's horn, when full grown. (Gent. Rec.) *Palmed-deer*, a stag of full growth.

PALM-BARLEY. A kind of barley fuller and broader than common barley.

PALMER. (1) Properly, a pilgrim who had visited the Holy Land, from the palm or cross which he bore as a sign of such visitation; but Chaucer seems to consider all pilgrims to foreign parts as palmers, and the distinction was never much attended to in this country.

> Says John, if I must a begging go,
> I will have a *palmer's* weed,
> With a staff and a coat, and bage of all sort,
> The better then I may speed.
> *Robin Hood*, ii. 129.

(2) A wood-louse. "A worme having a great many feete," Hollyband's Dictionarie, 1593.

(3) A stick or rod.

PALMING-DICE. A method of cheating at dice, formerly in vogue, by secreting one of the dice in the palm of the hand instead of putting in the box, and then causing it to fall with the other, the number of the former of course being guided by the hand. Hence the expression to palm anything upon one.

PALM-PLAY. Tennis. (*Fr.*)

PALPABLE. "Apte or mete to be felte, *palpable*," Palsgrave. See Macbeth, ii. 1.

PALPED. Obscured; darkened.

PALSTER. A pilgrim's staff.

PALTER. To hesitate; to prevaricate. *Linc.* " To haggle, hucke, dodge, or *paulter* long in the buying of a commoditie," Cotgrave. "Most of them are fixed, and *palter* not their place of standing," Harrison's England, p. 182.

PALTERLY. Paltry. *North.*

PALTOCK. A kind of doublet or cloak which descended to the middle of the thigh. (*A.-N.*) Cotgrave explains *palletoc*, " a long and thicke pelt or cassocke; a garment like a short cloake with sleeves, or such a one as the most of our moderne pages are attired in." The paltock was worn by priests, Piers Ploughman, p. 438; and in the Morte d'Arthur, i. 149, Gawayne says he attended Arthur " to poynte his *paltockes* that longen to hymself." Palsgrave has, " paltocke of lether, *pellice*; paltocke a garment, *halcret*; paltocke a patche, *palleteau*." The second meaning apparently refers to some defensive garment. Paltock seems also to have been applied to some ornament or ornamental cap worn on the head of a person high in authority.

PALTRING. A worthless trifle. " Triflinga, *paltrings* not worth an old shoe," Florio, p. 100. Forby has *paltry*, rubbish, refuse.

PALVEISE. A shield. See Florio, p. 353.

PALY. A roll of bran such as is given to hounds. " Paly of bryn, *cantabrum*," Pr. Parv. " *Cantabrum*, furfur caninum, quo canes pascuntur," Papias. See Ducange.

PALYNGE. Turning pale. (*A.-N.*)

> For in here face alwey was the blode,
> Withoute *palynge* or eny drawynge doune.
> > *Lydgate, MS Ashmole* 39, f. 47.
> For in hire face alwey was the blode,
> Withoute *palynge* or any drawynge doun.
> > *Ibid. MS. Soc. Antiq.* 134, f. 8.

PAM. The knave of clubs.

PAME. (1) The mantle thrown over an infant who is going to be christened. *West.*
(2) The palm of the hand. *West.*

PAMENT. A pavement. *Palsgrave.* Square paving bricks are called *pamments* in Norf.

PAMFILET. A pamphlet. (*A.-N.*)

PAMMY. Thick and gummy; applied to the legs of such individuals as are at times said to have beef down to the hocks. *Linc.*

PAMPE. To pamper; to coddle.

PAMPERING. " The craft of pampering or setting out saleable things," Howell, 1660.

PAMPESTRIE. Palmistry.

PAMPILION. A coat of different colours, formerly worn by servants. It occurs with this explanation in Hollyband's Dictionarie, 1593. There was a kind of fur so called.

PAMPINATION. Pulling leaves that grow too thick. List of old words prefixed to Batman uppon Bartholome, 1582.

PAMPLE. (1) To indulge. *North.*
(2) To toddle, or pad about. *East.*

PAMPRED. Pampered; made plump.

PAN. (1) To unite; to fit; to agree. *North.* Douce gives the following proverb in his MS. Additions to Ray—

> Weal and women cannot *pan*,
> But wo and women can.

(2) Hard earth, because, like a pan, it holds water and prevents it from sinking deeper. *East.* Is this the meaning in Ben Jonson, v. 43?
(3) The skull; the head. (*A.-S.*)

> That he ne smot his hed of thanne,
> Whereof he tok awey the *panne*.
> > *Gower, MS. Soc. Antiq.* 134, f. 54.

(4) In houses, the pan is that piece of timber which lies upon the top of the posts, and upon which the beams rest.
(5) Money. A cant term.
(6) A tadpole, or frog. *Somerset.*

PANABLE. Likely to agree. *North.*

PANACHE. The plume of feathers on the top of a helmet. (*A.-N.*)

PANADE. A kind of two-edged knife. (*A.-N.*) Misread *pavade* by Tyrwhitt. See Wright's Anecdota Literaria, p. 24.

PANADO. A caudle of bread, Florio, p. 353. Currants, mace, cinnamon, sack, and sugar, with eggs, were added to complete the caudle. There were different ways of making it.

> *To make a Ponado.*
> The quantity you will make set on in a posnet of fair water; when it boils put a mace in and a little piece of cinnamon, and a handful of currans, and so much bread as you think meet; so boil it,

and season it with salt, sugar and rose-water, and so serve it.

> *A True Gentlewomans Delight,* 1676, p. 74.

Another receipt, which differs somewhat from this, may be worth giving.

> *To make Panado after the best fashion.*
> Take a quart of spring-water, which, being hot on the fire, put into it slices of fine bread, as thin as may be; then add half a pound of currans, a quarter of an ounce of mace; boil them well, and then season them with rose-water and fine sugar, and serve them up.
> > *The Accomplished Ladies Rich Closet,* 1706, p. 74.

PANARY. A storehouse for bread.

PANCAKE-TUESDAY. Shrove-Tuesday, which is a pancake feast day in all England. At Islip, co. Oxon, the children of the cottagers go round the village on that day to the different houses to collect pence, singing these lines—

> Pit-a-pat, the pan is hot,
> We are come a-Shroving.
> A little bit of bread and cheese
> Is better than nothing.
> The pan is hot, the pan is cold!
> Is the fat in the pan nine days old?

PANCHEON. A large broad pan. *East.*

PANCRIDGE. A common corruption of St. Pancras. *Pancridge parson,* a term of contempt, Woman is a Weathercock, p. 30.

> Great Jacke-a-Lent, clad in a robe of ayre,
> Threw mountaines higher then Alcides beard;
> Whilst *Pancradge* church, arm'd with a samphier blade,
> Began to reason of the businesse thus.
> > *Taylor's Workes,* 1630, i. 190.

PANCROCK. An earthen pan. *Devon.*

PANDEL. A shrimp. *Kent.*

PANDEWAFF. Water and oatmeal boiled together, sometimes with fat. *North.*

PANDORE. A kind of lute. It is probably the same as *Bandore,* q. v.

PANDOULDE. A custard. *Somerset.*

PANE. (1) A division; a side; a piece. " A pane, piece, or pannell of a wall, of wainscot, or a glasse window," Cotgrave. " Pane of a wall, *pan de mur,*" Palsgrave. The term is still in use, applied to a division in husbandry work.

> In the West part of the same gate and the way into the college, on the North *pane* eight chambers for the poore men, and in the West *pane* 6 chambers.
> > *Nichols' Royal Wills,* p. 300.

(2) A hide or side of fur; fur. (*A.-N.*) " Pane of furre, *panne*; pane of gray furre, *panne de gris,*" Palsgrave. " A pane of ermines," Ord. and Reg. p. 122. See Eglamour, 858; Gy of Warwike, p. 421. *Pane* has our first meaning in a pane or piece of cloth. " A pane of cloth, *panniculus,*" Baret, 1580, an insertion of a coloured cloth in a garment. It seems to mean the skirt of a garment in Ywaine and Gawin, 204, and also in the following passage:

> She drouze his mantel bi the *pane*.
> > *Cursor Mundi, MS. Coll. Trin. Cantab.* f. 28.
> Saying, him whom I last left, all repute,
> For his device, in handsoming a suit,
> To judge of lace, pink, *panes,* print, cut, and pleit,
> Of all the court to have the best conceit.
> > *Donne's Poems,* p. 121.

PANED-HOSE. Breeches formed of stripes, with small panes or squares of silk or velvet,

Paned, striped, Thynne's Debate, p. 10. Forby, ii. 243, mentions *paned curtains*, made of long and narrow stripes of different patterns or colours sewed together.

PANEL. An immodest woman. *Linc.*

> Panels march by two and three,
> Saying, Sweetheart, come with me.
>
> *Old Lincolnshire Ballad.*

PANES. Parsnips. *Cornw.*

PANG. To fill; to stuff. *North.*

PANHIN. A small pan. *East.*

PANICK. A kind of coarse grain like millet. Kennett, MS. Lansd. 1033.

PANK. To pant. *Devon.*

PANNAGE. The mast of the oak and beech which swine feed on in the woods.

> Besides that a man shall read in the hystories of Canterburie and Rochester, sundrie donations, in which there is mention onely of *pannage* for hogges in Andred, and of none other thing.
>
> *Lambarde's Perambulation*, 1596, p. 211.

PANNAM. Bread. A cant term. The following is a curious old canting song:

> The ruffin cly the nab of the harman-beck,
> If we mawned *pannam*, lap or ruff-peck,
> Or poplars of yarum; he cuts bing to the ruffmans,
> Or els he sweares by the light-mans
> To put our stamps in the harmans.
> The ruffian cly the ghost of the harman-beck,
> If we heave a booth, we cly the jerke.
>
> *Dekker's Lanthorne and Candle-Light*, 1630.

PANNEL. The treeless pad, or pallet, without cantle, with which an ass is usually rode. "Pannell to ryde on, *batz, panneau*," Palsgrave. See Tusser, p. 11.

PANNICLE. A membrane. (*Lat.*)

> The headeach either commeth of some inward causes, as of some cholerick humor, bred in the *pannicles* of the braine, or else of som outward cause, as of extream heat or cold, of some blow, or of some violent savour. Eumelus saith, that it commeth of raw digestion; but Martin saith most commonly of cold. *Topsell's Beasts*, 1607, p. 348.

PANNIER-MAN. A servant belonging to an inn of court, whose office is to announce the dinner. See Grose.

PANNIERS. To fill a woman's panniers, i. e. to get her with child. "*Emplir une femelle*, to fill her panniers, get her with yong." Cotgrave. The phrase is still in use.

PANNIKELL. The skull, or brain-pan. *Spenser.*

PANNIKIN. Fretting; *taking on*, as a sickly or wearisome child. *Suffolk.*

PANNY. A house. A cant term.

PAN-PUDDING. A mention of the *pan puddings* of Shropshire occurs in Taylor's Workes, 1630, i. 146.

PANSHARD. A piece or fragment of a broken pan. *Dorset.*

PANSHON. An earthenware vessel, wider at the top than at the bottom, used for milk when it has to be skimmed; also for other purposes. *Linc.*

PANSY. The heartsease. *Var. dial.*

PANT. (1) A public fountain; a cistern; a reservoir. *North.*

(2) A hollow declivity. *West.*

PANTABLES. Slippers. "To stand upon one's pantables," to stand upon one's honour. Baret, 1580, spells it *pantapple*.

> Is now, forsooth, so proud, what else!
> And stands so on her *pantables*.
>
> *Cotton's Works*, 1734, p. 85.

> Plutarche with a caveat keepeth them out, not so muche as admitting the litle crackhalter that carrieth his master's *pantables*, to set foote within those doores. *Gosson's Schoole of Abuse*, 1579.

> Hee standeth upon his *pantables*, and regardeth greatly his reputation.
>
> *Saker's Narbonus*, 1580, 2d part, p. 99.

PANTALONE. A zany, or fool. (*Ital.*) In early plays, he generally appeared as a lean old man wearing spectacles. "A pantaloon or Venetian magnifico," Howell, 1660.

PANTALOONS. Garments made for merry-andrews, &c., that have the breeches and stockings of the same stuff, and joined together as one garment.

> Bring out his mallard, and eft-soons
> Beshake his shaggy *pantaloons*.
>
> *Cotton's Works*, 1734, p. 13.

PANTAS. A dangerous disease in hawks, whereof few escape that are afflicted therewith; it proceeds from the lungs being, as it were, baked by excessive heat, that the hawk cannot draw his breath, and when drawn cannot emit it again; and you may judge of the beginning of this evil by the hawk's labouring much in the pannel, moving her train often up and down at each motion of her pannel, and many times she cannot mute nor slice off; if she does, she drops it fast by her. The same distemper is also perceived by the hawk's frequent opening her clap and beak. *Markham.*

PANTER. A net, or snare. (*A.-N.*) "Panter, snare for byrdys," Pr. Parv. "The birdd was trapped and kaute with a pantere," Lydgate, p. 182. See Ashmole's Theat. Chem. Brit. 1652, p. 215; Apol. Loll. p. 93; Hartshorne's Anc. Met. Tales, pp. 122, 123, 124, 126. "Panther to catche byrdes with, *panneau*," Palsgrave.

PANTERER. The keeper of the pantry. Grose has *pantler*; a butler.

> Panterer yche the prey, quod the kyng.
>
> *Chron. Vilodun.* p. 15.

PANTILE-SHOP. A meeting-house. *Var. dial.*

PANTO. To set seriously about any business or undertaking. *North.*

PANTOFLE. A slipper, or patten. "A wooden pantofle or patin," Florio, p. 71. "*Se tenir sur le haut bout*, to stand upon his pantofles, or on high tearmes," Cotgrave, in v. *Bout.* See *Pantables.* "The papall panton heele," Lithgow's Pilgrimes Farewell, 1618.

PANTON. An idle fellow. *Somerset.*

PANTON-GATES. "As old as Panton Gates," a very common proverb. There is a gate called Pandon Gate at Newcastle-on-Tyne.

PANTRON. A small earthen pan. *Linc.*

PANYM. A heathen. *Palsgrave.* Hardyng, f. 91, has *panymerye*, idolatry.

PAP. "To give pap with a hatchet," a proverbial phrase, meaning to do any kind action in an unkind manner.

PAPALIN. A papist.

PAPAT. The papacy. (*A.-N.*)

A cardinalle was thilke tide,
Whiche the *papat* longe hath desirid.
Gower, MS. Soc. Antiq. 134, f. 79.

PAPDELE. A kind of sauce. " Hares in pap-dele," Forme of Cury, p. 21.

PAPELARD. A hypocrite. (*A.-N.*) In the following passage, subtle, cunning.

I se the aungels bere the soule of that womane to hevyne, the which so longe I have kepte in synne. He, this *papelarde* preste, hathe herde oure cownsaylle, ande hathe delyverede here frome synne, ande alle oure powere.   *Gesta Romanorum, p. 455.*

PAPELOTE. A kind of caudle.

PAPER. To set down in a paper, or list. See an obscure passage in Henry VIII. i. 1.

PAPERN. Made of paper. *West.*

PAPER-SKULLED. Silly; foolish. *Var. dial.*

PAPER-WHITE. White as paper.

PAPEY. A fraternity of priests in Aldgate ward, suppressed by Edward VI.

PAP-HEAD. A woman's nipple. *Palsgrave.*

PAPISHES. Papists. *Devon.*

PAPLER. Milk-pottage. *Somerset.*

PAP-METE. Pappy food such as is given to children. *Pr. Parv.*

PAPMOUTH. An effeminate man. *North.*

PAPPE. (1) The female breast. (*Lat.*)

O woman, loke to me agayn,
That playes and kisses your childre *pappys*;
To se my son I have gret payn,
In his brest so gret gapis,
And on his body so many swappys.
MS. Cantab. Ff. v. 48, f. 72.

(2) To pamper; to coddle.

PAP-WORT. The herb mercury.

PAPYNES. A dish in cookery, described in MS. Sloane 1201, f. 50.

PAPYNGAY. A parrot. Maundevile, p. 238.

PAR. (1) A young salmon; also, the young coalfish. *North.*

(2) A pen for animals. *East.*

PARABOLES. Parables; proverbs. (*A.-N.*)

PARADISE. A garden, library, or study. See Britton's Arch. Dict. in v.

PARADISE-APPLE. " Is a curious fruit, produced by grafting a permain on a quince," Worlidge's Treatise of Cider, 1678, p. 207.

PARAFFYS. Paragraphs. " Paraffys grete and stoute," Reliq. Antiq. i. 63. It occurs in Pr. Parv. and Nominale MS.

PARAGE. Parentage; kindred. (*A.-N.*) See Lydgate's Minor Poems, p. 26.

Persones grete, and of his *parage*.
Lydgate, Rawlinson MS.

PARAGON. To excel greatly. *Shak.*

PARAILLE. (1) Apparel; arms. (2) Nobility; men of rank. (*A.-N.*)

PARAMARROW. A sow-gelder. *North.*

PARAMENTS. Furniture; ornaments; hangings of a room. (*A.-N.*)

PAR-AMOUR. Love; gallantry. (*A.-N.*)

PARAMOUR. A lover of either sex. (*A.-N.*)

PARAQUITO. A paroquet. (*Ital.*) Sometimes used as a term of endearment.

PARASANGUE. A measure of the roads among the ancient Persians, varying from thirty to sixty furlongs, according to time and place.

Whatever instructions he might have [had] from his master Johnson, he certainly by his own natural parts improved to a great heighth, and at last became not many *parasangues* inferior to him in fame by divers noted comedies.
Phillips Theatrum Poetarum, ed. 1675, ii. 157.

PARAVANT. Beforehand; first. (*Fr.*)

PARAVENTURE. Haply; by chance. (*A.-N.*)

PARAYS. Paradise. (*A.-N.*)

Blessed be thou, levedy, ful of heovene blisse,
Suete flur of *paraye*, moder of mildenesse.
MS. Harl. 2253, f. 81.

PARBREAK. To vomit.

Oh, said Scogin's wife, my husband *parbreaked* two crows. Jesus, said the woman, I never heard of such a thing.   *Scogin's Jests.*

PARBREAKING. Fretful. *Exmoor.*

PARCAS. Perhaps. MS. Sloane 213.

PARCEIT. Perception. (*A.-N.*)

PARCEL. (1) Much; a great deal. *Devon.*

(2) Part, or portion. *Parcel-gilt*, partly gilt, Dugdale's Monast. ii. 207.

Thou wilt not leave me in the middle street,
Though some more spruce companion thou dost meet,
Not though a captain do come in thy way,
Bright *parcell guilt*, with forty dead mens pay:
Not though a brisk perfum'd pert courtier
Deign with a nod thy curtesie to answer.
Donne's Poems, p. 118.

(3) Parsley. *North.*

PARCEL-MAKERS. Two officers in the Exchequer, who make out the parcels of escheators' accounts, and deliver them to one of the auditors of that court.

PARCEL-MELE. By parcels, or parts. (*A.-S.*)

PARCENER. One who has an equal share in the inheritance of an ancestor, as a daughter or sister.

So nevertheles that the yongest make reasonable amends to his *parceners* for the part which to them belongeth, by the award of good men.
Lambarde's Perambulation, 1596, p. 575.

PARCHEMINE. Parchment. (*Fr.*)

By a charter to have and to hold,
Under my seale of lede made the mold,
And writen in the skyne of swyne,
What that it is made in *parchemyn*,
Because it shuld perpetually endure,
And unto them be both stable and sure.
MS. Rawl. C. 86.

PARCHMENT. A kind of lace.

PARCHMENTER. A parchment-maker.

PARCLOSE. A parlour. In earlier writers, the term is applied to a kind of screen or railing. " Parclos to parte two roumes, *separation*," Palsgrave. See the Oxf. Gloss. Arch.

I pray you, what is there written upon your *parclose* door?   *Bacon's Works, p. 63.*

The fader loggid hem of sly purpos
In a chambre nexte to his joynynge,
For bitwixe hem nas but a *perclos*.
Occleve, MS. Soc. Antiq. 134, f. 275.

That the roof of that chapel be raised, the walls enhanced, the windows made with strong iron work, with a quire and *perclose*, and two altars without the quire.   *Test. Vetust. p 335.*

PARCYAND. The character &.   *North.*

PARDAL. A leopard.

> The souldiors of the moores weare garments made of lyons, *pardals*, and beares skinnes, and sleepe uppon them; and so is it reported of Herodotus Megarensis the musitian, who in the day-time wore a lyons skin, and in the night lay in a beares skin.
> *Topsell's Beasts*, 1607, p. 39.

PARDE. *Par Dieu*, a common oath.   *Pardy* is used by Elizabethan writers.

> And for that licour is so presious,
> That oft hath made[me] dfonke as any mous,
> Therfor I will that ther it beryd be
> My wrecchid body afore this god *pardé*,
> Mighti Bachus that is myn owen lorde,
> Without variaunce to serve hym or discorde.
> *MS. Rawl. C. 86.*

PARDONER. A dealer or seller of pardons and indulgences. *(A.-N.)*

PARDURABLE. Everlasting. *(A.-N.)*

> But th' Erle, whether he in maner dispaired of any good *pardurable* continuaunce of good accord betwixt the Kynge and hym, for tyme to come, consyderinge so great attemptes by hym comytted agaynst the Kynge.   *Arrival of King Edward IV.* p. 12.

PARE. To injure; to impair.

PARELE. To apparel.   *Lydgate.*

> But I am a lady of another cuntré,
> If I be *parellid* moost of price,
> I ride aftur the wilde fee,
> My raches rannen at my devyse.
> *MS. Cantab. Ff. v. 48, f. 117.*

PARELL. Whites of eggs, bay salt, milk, and pump water, beat together, and poured into a vessel of wine to prevent its fretting.

PARELS. Perilous.   *Parell*, peril.

> He knewe the markys of that place,
> Then he was in a *parels* case.
> *MS. Cantab. Ff. ii. 38, f. 291.*

> How mervelous to man, how dowtfull to drede,
> How fer paste mannys reson and mynde hath it bee!
> The comyng of Kynge Edwarde and his good spede,
> Owte of Dochelonde into Englonde over the salte see.
> In what *parell* and trowbill, in what payne was hee,
> Whanne the salte watur and tempest wrought hym gret woo,
> But in adversitee and ever, Lorde, thy wille be doo!
> *MS. Bibl. Reg.* 17 D. xv.

PAREMENTS. (1) Pavements.   *North.*
(2) Ornamental furniture, or clothes.
(3) The skin of deer, &c.

PARENTELE. Kindred. *(A.-N.)*

PARENTRELYNARIE. Interlineal. *(A.-N.)*

PARFAITNESS. Perfection; integrity.   *Parfit*, perfect, is common both as an archaism and provincialism. *(A.-N.)*

PARFOURME. To perform. *(A.-N.)*

PARFURNISH. To furnish properly.

PARGARNWYNE. A reel for winding yarn.

PARGET. To roughcast a wall. It is the translation of *crépir* in Hollyband's Dictionarie, 1593, and is explained in Mr. Norris's MS. Glossary, "to plaster the inside of a chimney with mortar made of cow dung and lime." Ben Jonson uses the term metaphorically. It is also a substantive, as in Harrison's England, p. 187; *parjetings*, ib. p. 236.

> Thus having where they stood in vaine compizized of their wo,
> When night drew neare they bad adue, and ech gave kisses sweete
> Unto the *parget* on their side, the which did never meete.   *Golding's Ovid*, 1567.

> To the Trinity Gild of Linton, for the mending of the cawsy, and *pergetyng* of the Gild Hall, xj. s. viij. d.   *Test. Vetust.* p 618.

PARIETARY. The herb called pellitory. This form of the word occurs in Hollyband's Dictionarie, 1593.

PARINGAL. Equal. *(A.-N.)*

> For he wolde not ȝe were
> *Paringal* to him nor pere.
> *Cursor Mundi, MS. Coll. Trin. Cantab. f. 5.*

PARING-AND-BURNING. Burnbeating; denshering; sodburning.   *Yorksh.*

PARING-IRON. An iron to pare a horse's hoofs with.   *Palsgrave.*

PARING-SPADE. A breast-plough.   *Yorksh.*

PARIS-BALL. "Lytell Pares balle, *esteuf*," Palsgrave.

PARIS-CANDLE. A large wax candle.   *Periscandelle*, Wardrobe Acc. Edw. IV. p. 121.

PARIS-GARDEN. "Paris Garden is the place on the Thames bank-side at London, where the bears are kept and baited; and was anciently so called from Robert de Paris, who had a house and garden there in Richard the Second's time; who by proclamation ordained that the butchers of London should buy that garden for receipt of their garbage and entrails of beasts; to the end the city might not be annoyed thereby," Blount's Glossographia, 1681, p. 473. Paris Garden seems to have been first employed as a place for baiting wild beasts as early as Henry VIII.'s time. See Collier's Annals of the Stage, i. 251. A dreadful accident which occurred there on January 13th, 1582-3, by the fall of some scaffolding, is alluded to by several contemporary writers. Dr. Dee, Diary, p. 18, thus mentions it,—"On Sonday the stage at Paris Garden fell down all at ones, being full of people beholding the bearbayting, many being killed thereby, more hart, and all amased. The godly expownd it as a due plage of God for the wickednes ther usid, and the Sabath day so profanely spent." Allusions to Paris Garden are very common; to its loud drum, to the apes, &c.

PARISHENS. Parishioners. *(A.-N.)*

> The furst princypale parte lungus to ȝour levyng:
> The ij. part to holé church to hold his honesté;
> The iij. part to ȝour *parechyngs* that al to ȝoue bryng,
> To hom that faylun the fode, and fallun in poverté.
> *Blind Audelay's Poems*, p. 33.

> The prest wote never what he menes
> That for lytyl curseth hys *paryshenes*.
> *MS. Harl.* 1701, f. 72.

PARISHING. A hamlet or small village adjoining and belonging to a parish.

PARISH-LANTERN. The moon.

PARISH-TOP. A large top formerly kept in a village for the amusement of the inhabitants. *Shak.*

PARIS-WORK. A kind of jewellery.

PARITOR. An apparitor.   *Hall.*

PARK. (1) A farm, field, or close. *Devon.*

(2) Slang term for a prison. *York.*

(3) A kind of fishing net. This word occurs in Hollyband's Dictionarie, 1593.

PARKEN. A cake made chiefly of treacle and oatmeal. *North.*

PARKER. "Parcar, *verdier*," Palsgrave.

PARKLEWYS. The herb *agnus castris.*

PARLE. To speak; to confer with. (*A.-N.*)
A president that any man, being a member therof, might without cause be excluded, and so letted to *parle* theare his mynd in publique matters for the wealth of the realme, and such other private causes as doo occur. *Egerton Papers*, p. 96.

PARLEMENT. A consultation; an assembly for consultation. (*A.-N.*)

PARLEY. To argue. *Yorksh.*

PARLISH. Perilous; dangerous. Also, clever, acute, shrewd. *North. Parlous* is very common in old plays. In MS. Ashmole 59, f. 132, is a receipt "for heme that hath a *parelles* coche," i. e. perilous cough.
Beshrew you for it, you have put it in me:
The *parlossst* old men that ere I heard.
Chron. Hist. of King Leir, 1605.

PARLOUR. In the cottages of poor people, if there are two rooms on the ground floor, the best room they live in is called the house; the other is called a *parlour*, though used as a bedroom. *Linc.* In ancient times, the parlour was a room for private conversation or retirement. Kennett explains it, "the common-room in religious houses into which after dinner the religious withdrew for discourse and conversation."

PARMACITY. Spermaceti. *Shak.* Still in use, according to Craven GL ii. 32.

PARMASENT. Parmesan cheese. It would seem from Dekker that there was a liquor so called, but see Ford, i. 148.

PAROCH. A parish. *Leland.*

PAROCK. "When the bayliff or beadle of the Lord held a meeting to take an account of rents and pannage in the weilds of Kent, such meeting was calld a *parock*," Kennett, MS.

PARODE. An adage, or proverb. (*Gr.*)

PAROLIST. A person given to talking much or bombastically. See Wright's Passions of the Minde, 1621, p. 112.

PAROS. A parish. *Pr. Parv.*

PAROSYNNE. Gum. MS. Med. Rec.

PAROW. The rind of fruit.

PARPLICT. Perplexity.

PARRE. (1) To inclose. (*A.-S.*) "Ful straitly *parred*," Ywaine and Gawin, 3228. Forby has *par*, an inclosed place for domestic animals.
Bot als-swa say ȝe are *parred* in, and na ferrere may passe; therfore ȝe magnyfye ȝour manere of lyffynge, and supposes that ȝe are blyssed because that ȝe er so spered in. *MS. Lincoln* A. i. 17, f. 37.

(2) A young leveret. *Devon.*

PARRELL. A chimney-piece. (*A.-N.*)

PARRICK. "Parrocke a lytell parke, *parquet*," Palsgrave. Still in use. *Parroken*, to inclose or thrust in, occurs in Piers Ploughman, and Pr. Parv. The term was also applied to a cattle-stall.

PARROT'S-BILL. A surgeon's pincers.

PARSAGE. An old game at cards, mentioned in "Games most in Use," 12mo. Lond. n. d.

PARSE. To pierce. Pilkington's Works, p. 273.

PARSEN. Personal charms. *Cumb.*

PARSEYVE. To perceive.
Thoghe a man *parseyve* hyt noghte,
Thou stelyst hyt and thefte hast wroghte.
MS. Harl. 1701, f. 16.

PARSIL. Parsley. *North.*

PART. (1) Some; little. *North.*

(2) To partake; to share. (*A.-N.*)

(3) "I dye, I parte my lyfe," Palsgrave. "Timely-parted ghost," Shakespeare.

PARTABLE. Partaker. Lydgate, p. 86.
Thoghe hyt were outher mennys synne,
Ȝyt art thou *partable* therynne.
MS. Harl. 1701, f. 90.

PARTAKER. An assistant.
Yet thou must have more *partakers* in store,
Before thou make me to stand.
Robin Hood, II 31.

PARTED. Endowed with abilities.

PARTEL. A part, or portion.
So this pleyinge hath thre *partelis*, the firste is that we beholden in how many thingis God hath ȝyven us his grace passynge oure neȝtheboris, and in so myche more thanke we hym, fulfillyng his wil, and more tristyng in hym aȝen alle maner reprovyng of owre enmys. *Reliq. Antiq.* ii. 57.

PARTENELLE. Partner; partaker. MS. Harl. 1701 reads *partable*.
Yf it were other mens syne,
Ȝit ert thou *partenelle* therin.
Robert de Brunne, MS. Bowes, p. 13.

PARTIAL. Impartial. See Nares.

PARTICULARS. Great friends. *North.*

PARTIE. (1) A part. (2) A party. (*A.-N.*)

PARTISAN. A kind of short pike. See Harrison's Britaine, p. 2. It was used in places where the long pike would have been inconvenient. "A partison, a javeline to skirmish with," Baret, 1580.

PARTISE. Parts; bits. (*A.-N.*)
And as clerkes say that are wise,
He wrouȝte hit not bi *partise*.
Cursor Mundi, MS. Coll. Trin. Cantab. f. 3.

PARTLESS. In part; partly. *East.* In Durham, *partlings* is similarly used.

PARTLET. A ruff or band formerly much worn about the neck by both sexes, but more latterly it seems to have been worn exclusively by women. "A maydens neckerchefe or lynnen parlette," Elyot, ed. 1559, in v. *Strophium.* The term was sometimes applied to the habit-shirt. "Wyth gay gownys and gay kyrtels, and mych waste in apparell, rynges, and owchis, wyth partelettes and pastis garneshed wyth perle," More's Supplycacyon of Soulys, sig. L. ii. "A neckerchiefe or partlet," Baret, 1580.

PARTNERS. The two thick pieces of wood at the bottom of a mast.

PARTNIT. "Partnyt that bredeth under ones arme, *mort pou*," Palsgrave.

PARTOURIE. Portion.

PARTRICH. A partridge. *Jonson.*

PARTURB. To pervert, or confound.

> Mary, therfore, the more knave art thou, I say,
> That *parturbest* the worde of God, I say.
> > *The Pardoner and the Frere*, 1533.

PARTY-CLOTH. Cloth made of different colours. *Pr. Parv.* Shakespeare has *party-coated* and *party-coloured*.

> Whose *party-coloured* garment Nature dy'd
> In more eye-pleasing hewes with richer graine
> Then Iris bow attending Aprils raine.
> > *Browne's Britannia's Pastorals*, p. 115.

PARTY-FELLOW. A copartner. *Palsgrave.*

PARURES. Ornaments. " Parowr of a vestiment, *parure*," Pr. Parv. Ducange has *parare*, *ornare*.

> I bequethe to the said chirche ane hole sute of vestmytes of russet velvet. One coope, chesible diacones, for decones; with the awbes and *parures*.
> > *Test. Vetust.* p. 267.

PARVENKE. A pink. (*A.-N.*)

> Hire rode is ase rose that red is on rys;
> With lilyewhite leres lossum he is.
> The primerole he passeth, the *parvenke* of pris,
> With alisaundre thare-to, ache and anys.
> > *MS. Harl.* 2253, f. 63.

PARVIS. A church porch. The parvis at London was the portico of St. Paul's, where the lawyers met for consultation.

> And at the *parvyse* I wyll be
> A Powlys betwyn ij. ande iij.
> > *Mind, Will, and Understanding*, p. 8.

PARWHOBBLE. To talk quickly. *West.* "A parwhobble, a parley or conference between two or three persons," MS. Devon. Gloss.

PARYARD. The farmyard. *Suffolk.*

PARYLE. Peril. (*A.-N.*)

> That he wolde wende in exsyle,
> And put hym in soche *paryle*.
> > *MS. Cantab.* Ff. ii. 38, f. 194.

PARYST. Perished.

> So that no hare sall wante in no stede,
> For thare sall no hare be *paryst*.
> > *Hampole, MS. Bowes*, p. 149.

PAS. A foot-pace. (*A.-N.*)

> He thost more then he seyde,
> Towarde the court he gaf a brayde,
> And sede a welle gode *pas*.
> > *MS. Cantab.* Ff. v. 48, f. 51.

> I stalked be the strems, be the strond,
> For I be the flod fond
> A bot doun be a lond,
> So passed I the *pas*.
> > *Reliq. Antiq.* ii. 7.

PASCHAL. A large candlestick used by the Roman Catholics at Easter.

PASCH-EGGS. See *Pace-Eggs*.

PASE. (1) To ooze out. *Dorset.*

(2) To raise; to lift up. *North.*

PASE-DAY. Easter-day. The following proverbial lines refer to the Sundays in Lent:

> Tid, mid, misera.
> Carl, Paum, good *Pase-day*.

PASH. (1) To strike with violence so as to break to pieces. *Palsgrave.*

> Comming to the bridge, I found it built of glasse so cunningly and so curiously, as if nature herself had sought to purchase credit by framing so curious a peece of workmanship; but yet so slenderly, as the least waight was able to *pash* it into innumerable peeces.
> > *Greene's Gwydonius*, 1593.

> Shall *pash* his cox-combe such a knocke,
> As that his soule his course shall take.
> > *How to Choose a Good Wife*, 1634.

(2) A heavy fall of rain or snow.

(3) Anything decayed. *North.*

(4) A great number. *North.*

PASKE. The passover; Easter. (*A.-S.*)

> To Moyses oure Lorde tho tolde
> What wise thei shulde *Paske* holde.
> > *Cursor Mundi, MS. Coll. Trin. Cantab.* f. 39.

PASKEY. Short-breathed; asthmatic. *West.*

PASMETS. Parsnips. *Wilts.*

PASS. (1) A whipping or beating. *Cornw.*

(2) To die. *Palsgrave.*

(3) To surpass; to excel. (*A.-N.*) Hence, to be very extraordinary.

(4) To judge; to pass sentence. (*A. N.*)

(5) To report; to tell. *Devon.*

(6) To care for, or regard. *Shak.*

(7) A frame on which stones pass or rest in forming an arch.

(8) To toll the bell for the purpose of announcing a death. In general use.

(9) To go. Also, let it go, or pass. It was also a term used at primero and other games.

> The knyght *passyd* as he come.
> > *MS. Cantab.* Ff. ii. 38, f. 244.

(10) *Well to pass*, well off, rich; equivalent to *well to do*, which is in very common use.

> His mothers husband, who reputed was
> His father, being rich and *well to passe*,
> A wealthy merchant and an alderman,
> On forraigne shores did travell now and than.
> > *Scot's Philomythie*, 1616.

PASSADO. A term in fencing, meaning a pass or motion forwards.

PASSAGE. (1) A ferry. *Devon.*

(2) An old game at dice, thus described in the Compleat Gamester, ed. 1721, p. 67 :—"Passage is a game at dice to be play'd at but by two, and it is performed with three dice. The caster throws continually till he has thrown doublets under ten, and then he is out and loses, or doublets above ten, and then he passes and wins; high runners are most requisite for this game, such as will rarely run any other chance than four, five, or six, by which means, if the caster throws doublets, be scarcely can throw out."

PASSAMEN. A kind of lace. (*Fr.*) In a parliamentary scheme, dated 1549, printed in the Egerton Papers, p. 11, it was proposed than no man under the degree of an earl be allowed to wear *passamen* lace.

PASSAMEZZO. A slow dance, very often corrupted to passa-measure, or passing-measure, and by Shakespeare to passy-measure. The long-disputed phrase *passy-measures pavin* has thus been explained, but it is in fact the name of an ancient dance, thus described in a MS. quoted by Mr. Collier in the Shak. Soc. Papers, i. 25, " two singles and a double forward, and two singles syde, reprynce back." It is only necessary to read this, and have seen a drunken man, to be well aware why Dick is called a " passy-measures pavin."

PASSANCE. A journey.

Thus passed they their *passance*, and wore out the weerie way with these pleasant discourses and prettie posies.

Saker's Narbonus, 1st part, 1580, p. 131.

PASS-BANK. The bank or fund at the old game of passage. See Grose, in v.

PASSE. Extent; district.

All the *passe* of Lancashyre,
He went both ferre and nere. *Robin Hood*, i. 63.

PASSEL. Parcel; a great quantity.

PASSEN. Surpass; exceed.

Hys toschys *passen* a fote longe.
MS. Cantab. Ff. ii. 38, f. 65.

PASSENGER. A passage-boat.

PASSER. A gimlet. *Leic.*

PASSING. Exceeding; excessive.

In sooth, he tould a *passing, passing* jest.
How to Choose a Good Wife, 1634.

An elder brother was commending his younger brother's green cloak which he wore, and said it became him *passing* well. Faith, brother, says he, but a black mourning cloak from you will become me better. *Oxford Jests*, 1706, p. 83.

PASSING-MEASURE. An outrage.

PASSION. Sorrow; emotion.

PASSIONAR. A book containing the lives and martyrdoms of saints. (*Lat.*) It occurs in the Nominale MS. in my possession.

PASSIONATE. Pathetic; sorrowful. Also a verb to express passion, or sorrow.

PASS-ON. To adjudicate. *Shak.*

PAST-ALL. Uncontrollable. *Var. dial.*

PASTANCE. Pastime. It occurs in Holinshed, Chron. Ireland, p. 19.

Thowgh I sumtyme be in England for my *pastaunce*,
Yet was I neyther borne here, in Spayne, nor in Fraunce. *Bale's Kynge Johan*, p. 8.

PASTE. A term in old confectionary for hard preserves of fruit.

PASTEIIS. Pasties. (*A.-N.*)

Ther is a wel fair abbei
Of white monkes and of grei.
Ther beth bowris and halles;
Al of *pasteiis* beth the walles.
Cocaigne, ap. Wright's Purgatory, p. 58.

PASTELER. A maker of pastry. See Rutland Papers, p. 42. More usually *pasterer*. Palsgrave has *pastler*.

PASTE-ROYAL. Is mentioned in Ord. and Reg. p. 455. The ancient manner of making paste-royal is thus described:

How to make Paste-royal in Sauces.

Take sugar, the quantity of four ounces, very finely beaten and searced, and put it into an ounce of cinnamon and ginger, and a grain of musk, and so beat it into paste with a little gum-dragou steep'd in rose-water; and when you have beaten it into paste in a stone mortar, then roul it thin, and print it with your moulders; then dry it before the fire, and when it is dry, box it up and keep it all the year. *True Gentlewomans Delight*, 1676, pp. 53-54.

PASTETHE. A perfuming-ball.

PASTICUMP. A shoemaker's ball. *Linc.*

PASTOREL. A shepherd. (*A.-N.*)

Poveralle and *pastorelles* passede one aftyre
With porkes to pasture at the price yates.
Morte Arthure, MS. Lincoln, f. 86.

PASTRON. Fetters for unruly horses, affixed to that part of the animal's leg called the pastern. See Archæologia, xxvi. 401. "Pastron of an horse, *pasturon*," Palsgrave.

PASTS. "Payre of pastes, *unes pases*," Palsgrave. See *Partlet*.

PASTURE. To feed. Gesta Rom. p. 85.

PAT. (1) Pert; brisk; lively. *Yorksh.*

(2) A hog-trough. *Sussex.*

PATACOON. A Spanish coin, worth 4s. 8d.

PATAND. The lowest sill of timber in a partition. (*A.-N.*)

PAT-BALL. To play at ball. *Oxon.*

PATCH. (1) A fool. The domestic fool was formerly so called.

Why doating *patch*, didst thou not come with me this morning from the ship? *Menœchmi*, 1595.

(2) A cherry-stone. *Devon.*

(3) A child's clout. *West.*

(4) *To patch upon*, to blame. *East.*

PATCHES. Black patches were formerly worn on the face, and considered ornamental. This curious fashion is alluded to in a rare work entitled Several Discourses and Characters, 8vo. 1689, p. 175.

PATCH-PANNEL. Shabby; worn out.

PATE. (1) A badger. *North.*

(2) Weak and sickly. *Exmoor.*

PATENE-CUT. Tobacco cut up and tied, prepared for smoking. *North.*

PATEREROS. Chambered pieces of ordnance. See the Archæologia, xxviii. 376.

PATERONE. A workman's model, a pattern. More usually spelt *patron*.

Disfigurid *pateronys* and quaynte,
And as a dede kyng thay weren paynte.
Archæologia, xxii. 381.

PATES. Boats; vessels. *Weber.*

PATH. To go in a path; to trace or follow in a path. *Shak.*

PATHERISH. Silly, applied to sheep that have the disease called "water on the brain." *Sussex.*

PATHETICAL. Affected. *Shak.*

PATIENATE. Patient. *West.*

PATIENCE-DOCK. Snakeweed. *North.*

PATIENT. To tranquillize. *Shak.*

PATIENTABLE. Patient. *Devon.*

PATINE. The cover of a chalice.

PATISING. (1) "Patisyng, a treatie of peace, as frontier townes take one of another, *pastisaige*," Palsgrave. "I patyse as one frontyer towne dothe with another in tyme of warre to save them bothe harmlesse, *je patyse*," ib.

(2) Splashing in water. *Devon.*

PATLET. The same as *Partlet*, q. v.

PATREN. To pray; properly, to repeat the paternoster; to mutter. *Chaucer.*

PATRICK'S-PURGATORY. A celebrated cavern in Ireland, an eminent object of pilgrimages and superstitions. Its entire history is to be found in Mr. Wright's work so called, 8vo. 1844.

They that repaire to this place for devotion his sake use to continue therein foure and twentie houres, which dooing otherwhile with ghostlie me-

ditations, and otherwhile a dread for the conscience of their deserts, they saie they see a plaine resemblance of their owne faults and vertues, with the horror and comfort thereunto belonging, the one so terrible, the other so joious, that they verelie deeme themselves for the time to have sight of hell and heaven. The revelations of men that went thither (S. Patrike yet living) are kept written within the abbeie there adjoining. When anie person is disposed to enter (for the doore is ever spard) he repaireth first for devise to the archbishop, who casteth all pericles and dissuadeth the pilgrime from the attempt bicause it is knowen that diverse entering into that cave, never were seene to turne backe againe. But if the partie be fullie resolved, he recommendeth him to the prior, who in like maner favourablie exhorteth him to choose some other kind of penance and not to hasard such a danger. If notwithstanding he find the partie fullie bent, he conducteth him to the church, injoineth him to begin with praier and fast of fifteene daies, so long togither as in discretion can be indured. This time expired, if yet he persevere in his former purpose the whole convent accompanieth him with solemne procession and benediction to the mouth of the cave, where they let him in, and so bar up the doore untill the next morning. And then with like ceremonies they await his returne and reduce him to the church. If he be seene no more they fast and praie fifteene daies after. Touching the credit of these matters, I see no cause, but a Christian being persuaded that there is both hell and heaven, may without vanitie upon sufficient information be resolved, that it might please God, at sometime, for considerations to His wisdome knowen, to reveale by miracle the vision of joies and paines eternall. But that altogither in such sort and by such maner, and so ordinarilie, and to such persons, as the common fame dooth utter, I neither beleeve nor wish to be regarded. I have conferd with diverse that had gone this pilgrimage, who affirmed the order of the premisses to be true; but that they saw no sight, save onelie fearefull dreames when they chanced to nod, and those they said were exceeding horrible. Further they added, that the fast is rated more or lesse, according to the qualitie of the penitent.
Stanihurst's Description of Ireland, ed. 1586, pp. 28-29.

PATRICO. A cant term among beggars for their orator or hedge priest. This character is termed *patriarke-co* in the Fraternitye of Vacabondes, 1575, " a patriarke-co doth make marriages, and that is untill death depart the married folke, which is after this sort : when they come to a dead horse or any dead catell, then they shake hands, and so depart every one of them a severall way."

PATRON. A sea-captain. " Patrone of a gally, *patron de galee*," Palsgrave. Generally, any superior person, and sometimes a king.

PATTEN. A plaister. This is given as a Wiltshire word in MS. Lansd. 1033, f. 2.

PATTENS. Stilts. *Norf.*

PATTER. To mutter. *Palsgrave.*

His herte was full of payne and wo,
To kepe theyr names and shewe them ryght,
That he rested but lytell that nyght.
Ever he *patred* on theyr names faste ;
Than he had them in ordre at the laste.
How the Ploughman learned his Paternoster.

PATTERN. A pittance. *North.*

PATTICK. A simpleton ; a fool, one that talks nonsense ; a little jug. *West.*

PAUK. To pant for breath. *West.*

PAUKY. Sly ; mischievous ; pettish ; proud ; insolent. *North.*

PAUKY-BAG. A bag for collecting fragments from a wreck. *Norf.*

PAUL. To puzzle. *North.*

PAULING. A covering for a cart or waggon. *Linc.* Qu. from *palle ?*

PAUL'S. As old as St. Paul's, a common proverbial saying in Devon, and is found in old writers. The weathercock of Paul's is frequently referred to in early books. " I am as very a turncoté as the wethercoke of Poles," Mariage of Witt and Wisdome, p. 24. A chronicle in MS. Vespas. A. xxv. under the reign of Henry VII. thus mentions it—

M. Knelsworth, mayir. Then came in dewke Phillip, of Burgon, agaynst his wille with tempast of wethir, as he was goyng into Spayn, whiche afterward was kyng of Castelle. Then was Polles wethir-cok blown doun.

Old St. Paul's was in former times a favorite resort for purposes of business, amusement, lounging, or assignations ; bills were fixed up there, servants hired, and a variety of matters performed wholly inconsistent with the sacred nature of the edifice. " A poore siquis, such as forlorne forreiners use to have in Pauls Church," Hopton's Baculum Geodæticum, 4to. Lond. 1614.

In *Powls* hee walketh like a gallant courtier, where if hee meet some rich chuffes worth the gulling, at every word he speaketh hee makes a mouse of an elephant ; he telleth them of wonders done in Spaine by his ancestors ; where, if the matter were well examined, his father was but swabber in the ship where Civill oranges were the best merchandize : draw him into the line of history, you shall heare as many lies at a breath as would breed scruple in a good conscience for an age. *Wits Miserie*, 1596.

PAULTRING. Pilfering stranded ships. *Kent.*

PAUL-WINDLAS. A small windlass used for raising or lowering the mast of a vessel.

PAUME. (1) The palm of the hand. (*A.-N.*)
With everyche a pawe as a poste, and *paumes* fulle huge.
Morte Arthure, MS. Arthure, f. 61.
A bryd whynged merveyllousely,
With *pawmes* streynynge mortally.
MS. Cott. Tiber. A. vii. f. 77.
His smale *pawmis* on thy chekis leyne.
MS. Cantab. Ff. ii. 38, f. 19.

(2) A ball. (*A.-N.*) " Paume to play at tenys with, *paulme*," Palsgrave.

PAUMISH. Handling anything in an awkward manner, like one who has no fingers and is obliged to do everything with his palms, or hands. *Somerset.*

PAUNCE. (1) The viola tricolor.
The purple violet, *paunce*, and heart's-ease,
And every flower that smell or sight can please.
Heywood's Marriage Triumphe, 1613.

(2) A coat of mail.
Thurghe *pawnce* and plates he percede the maylez,
That the prowde penselle in his *pawnche* lengez.
Morte Arthure, MS. Lincoln, f. 78.

PAUNCH. To wound a man in the paunch. Also, to gut an animal. *Palsgrave.*

PAUNCH-CLOUT. (1) Tripe. (2) A belly-band.

PAUNCH-GUTS. A person with a large stomach. *South.*

PAUNED. Striped; ornamented.

> After the banket ended with noise of minstrelles, entered into the chamber eight maskers with white berdes, and long and large garmentes of blewe satyn pauned with sipres. *Hall, Henry VIII. f. 69.*

PAUNSONE. A coat of mail?

> A pesane and a paunsone, and a pris girdille. *Morte Arthure, MS. Lincoln, f. 80.*

PAUP. To walk awkwardly. *North.*

PAUPUSSES. Paupers. *Suffolk.*

PAUSATION. A pause. *Devon.*

PAUSE. To kick. *North.*

PAUSER. Calmer; more temperate.

> The expedition of my violent love
> Outran the pauser reason. *Macbeth, ii. 3.*

PAUT. To paw; to walk heavily; to kick; to beat. *North.* Cotgrave has *Espautrer*, to paut, pelt, thrash, beat, &c.

PAUTCH. To walk in deep mud. *Somerset.* "Sossing and poessing in the durt," Gammer Gurton, p. 178.

PAVAGE. A toll or duty payable for the liberty of passing over the soil or territory of another.

> All thes thre yer, and mor, potter, he seyde,
> Thow hast hantyd thes wey,
> Yet wer tow never so cortys a man
> One peney of pavage to pay. *Robin Hood, i. 83.*

PAVED. Turned hard. *Suffolk.*

PAVELOUNS. Pavilions; tents. *(A.-N.)*

PAVES. The stall of a shop.

PAVIN. A grave and stately dance.

PAVISE. A large kind of shield.

> And at the nether ende of the pavise he gart nayle a burde, the lenthe of a cubit, for to covere with his legges and his fete, so that no party of hym myȝte be sene. *MS. Lincoln A. i. 17, f. 38.*

> And after that the shotte was done, whiche they defended wyth pavishes, thei came to handestrokes, and were encontred severally, as you shall here. *Hall, Henry VIII. f. 42.*

> Them to help and to avanc,
> With many a prowd pavys. *Reliq. Antiq. ii. 22.*

PAVISER. A soldier armed with a pavise, or buckler. *(A.-N.)*

> Theire prayes and theire presoneres passes one aftyre,
> With pylours and pavysers and pryse men of armes.
> *Morte Arthure, MS. Lincoln, f. 85.*

PAVONE. A peacock. *Spenser.*

PAVY. The hard peach.

PAVYLERS. Pavilioners; the men who pitched the tents. *(A.-N.)*

PAWK. To throw about awkwardly. *Suff.* Hence *pawky*, an awkward fellow.

PAWMENT. A pavement. *Pr. Parv.*

PAWN. (1) A peacock. *Drayton.*

(2) The palm of the hand.

PAWNCOCK. A scarecrow. *Somerset.*

PAWN-GROPER. A dirty miserly fellow.

PAW-PAW. Naughty. *Var. dial.*

PAWT. A similar word to *potter.* A servant is said to *pawt* about when she does her work in an idle slovenly way, when she makes a

II.

show only of working, putting out her hands and doing in fact nothing. *Linc.*

PAWTENERE. (1) A purse; a net-bag. "*Mercipium*, a pawtnere," Nominale MS. probably for *marsupium.* Palsgrave has "pautner, *malette.*" "Pence in thy pauwkner," Ashmole's Theat. Chem. Brit. 1652, p. 192:

> I toke hyt owt and have hyt here,
> Lo! hyt ys here in my pawtenere.
> *MS. Cantab. Ff. ii. 38, f. 244.*

> Clement xl. pownde can telle
> Into a pawtenere. *MS. Cantab. Ff. ii. 38, f. 87.*

> Alas he ner a parsun or a vecory,
> Be Jhesu! he is a gentylmou and jolyle arayd;
> His gurdlis harneschit with silver, his baslard hongus bye,
> Apon his parté pautener uche mon ys apayd.
> *MS. Douce 302, f. 3.*

(2) Wickedness. *(A.-N.)*

> Then answeryd the messengere,
> Fulle false was hys pawtenere,
> And to that lady seyde;
> Madame, yf y ever dyskever the,
> I graunt that ye take me,
> And smyte of my hedd.
> *MS. Cantab. Ff. ii. 38, f. 95.*

(3) A vagabond; a libertine. *(A.-N.)*

> For themperour me seyd tho,
> And trewelich me bihete therto,
> That he me wold gret worthschipe,
> And now he me wil sle with schenschipe,
> For the speche of a losanger,
> And of a feloun pautener. *Gy of Warwike, p. 113.*

(4) Cruel? Ellis, i. 197, has *partener* in the following passage, where the editor (Mr. Turnbull) reads *pantever*!

> Gode knight hardi, and pautener,
> Y nam noither your douke no king.
> *Arthour and Merlin, p. 8.*

PAX-BREAD. A small tablet with a representation of the crucifixion upon it, presented in the ceremony of the mass to be kissed by the faithful. Coles erroneously explains it by *panis osculatorius.* "Paxe to kysse, paix," Palsgrave, 1530.

PAX-WAX. See *Faxwax.* This term occurs in the Prompt. Parv.

PAY. (1) To beat. Still in use.

> If they uncase a sloven and not unty their points,
> I so pay their armes that they cannot sometimes untye them, if they would. *Robin Goodfellow, 1620.*

> When he had well din'd and had filled his panch,
> Then to the winecellar they had him straight way,
> Where they with brave claret and brave old Canary,
> They with a foxe tale him soundly did pay.
> *The King and a poore Northerne Man, 1640.*

(2) To make amends. Also a substantive, satisfaction. *(A.-S.)*

> Than can the maydyn up-stande,
> And askyd watur to hur hande;
> The maydenys wysche withowten lett,
> And to ther mete they ben sett.
> Gye entendyd alle that daye
> To serve that lady to hur paye.
> *MS. Cantab. Ff. ii. 38, f. 148.*

(3) To please; to satisfy. *(A.-N.)*

PAYEN. A pagan, or heathen. *(A.-N.)*

> The painems and king Saphiran
> Defolled our Cristen men.
> *Arthour and Merlin, p. 139.*

And this was the furst passage,
That the apostlis in party
Made among folke that were *poeny*.
    Cursor Mundi, MS. Coll. Trin. Cantab. f. 122.

PAYL. (1) To beat, or thrash. *Salop.*
(2) The band of a tub or barrel.

PAYLOUNS. Pavilions; tents. *Weber.*

PAYMAN. A kind of cheese-cake.

PAYMENT. (1) Impairment. They say, "He'll take no *payment*," meaning, He'll take no injury, he'll be none the worse. *Linc.*
(2) To give a woman her payment, i, e. to get her with child.

PAYNE. (1) A coat of mail.
    The knyght rase, and his *paynes* sett.
        MS. Lincoln A. i. 17, f. 143.
(2) Bread. Piers Ploughman, p. 529.
(3) Field; plain. "I salle dy in the *payne*," MS. Lincoln A. i. 17, f. 132.

PAYNES. Pence. R. de Brunne, MS.

PAYS. (1) Country. (2) Pitch. (*A.-N.*)

PAYSAUNCE. Pausing or stopping. *Chauc.*

PAY-THE-PEPPERIDGE. A schoolboy having on a new suit of clothes is subjected to have a button pulled off unless he "pay the pepperidge," by giving a douceur to his playfellows. *Suffolk.*

PEA. (1) A peahen. See Nares.
(2) To look with one eye. *North.*
(3) A weight used in weighing anything with the steelyard. *South.*

PEA-BLUFF. A tube, one, two, or three feet long, usually of tin, through which boys blow a pea with considerable force and precision. *Suffolk.*

PEACH. To tell, or inform against. *Var. dial.*

PEA-ESH. Pease-stubble. *West.*

PEA-GOOSE. A silly fellow. Perhaps more properly peak-goose. Cotgrave has the term, in v. *Benet, Niais.* Forby explains it, "one who has an aspect both sickly and silly."

PEA-JACKET. A loose rough coat, with conical buttons of a small size. *North.*

PEAK. Lace. *Var. dial.*

PEAKISH. Simple; rude.
    Once hunted he untill the chace,
    Long fasting, and the heat
    Did house him in a *peakish* graunge
    Within a forest great. *Warner's Albions England.*

PEAKRELS. A name given to the inhabitants of the Peak in Derbyshire.

PEAL. (1) A noise, or uproar. *North.*
(2) To pour out a liquid. *Glouc.*
(3) A batch of bread. *Devon.*

PEALE. To cool. *Yorksh.*

PEALING. A lasting apple that makes admirable cider, and agrees well with this climate, the tree being a good bearer.

PEA-MAKE. See *Make* (2).

PEAN. To strike or beat. *Cumb.*

PEAR-COLOURED. Red.

PEARK. To peep. *Var. dial.*

PEARL. (1) This term was metaphorically applied to anything exceedingly valuable.
(2) White spots in the eyes were called pearls. See Harrison's England, p. 234. According

to the Dictionarium Rusticum, pearl, pin, and web, or any unnatural spot or thick film over a horse's eye, comes from some stroke or blow given him, or from descent of the sire, or dam; the pearl being known by a little round, thick, white spot, like a pearl, from which it had its name, growing on the sight of the eye. Among hunters, pearl is that part of a deer's horn which is about the burr.

PEARL-COATED. A sheep with a curled fleece is said to be pearl-coated. *North.*

PEARLINS. Coarse bone-lace.

PEART. Brisk; lively. *Var. dial.*
    Give your play-gull a stoole, and my lady her foole,
    And her usher potatoes and marrow,
    But your poet were he dead, set a pot on his head,
    And he rises as *peart* as a sparrow.
        Brit. Bibl. ii. 167.

Then, as a nimble squirrill from the wood,
Ranging the hedges for his filberd food,
Sits *peartly* on a bough his browne nuts cracking.
    Browne's Britannia's Pastorals, p. 135.

PEAS-AND-SPORT. See *Scadding-of-Peas.*

PEAS-BLOSSOM-DAMP. A damp in coal-pits less noisome than ordinary damps.

PEASCOD. "I remember the wooing of a *peascod* instead of her," &c. Shakespeare. "The efficacy of *peascods* in the affairs of sweethearts is not yet forgotten among our rustic vulgar. The kitchen maid, when she shells green pease, never omits, if she finds one having *nine* pease, to lay it on the lintel of the kitchen door, and the first clown who enters it, is infallibly to be her husband, or at least her sweetheart," Mr. Davy's MS. Suffolk Gloss. Anderson mentions a custom in the North, of a nature somewhat similar. A Cumbrian girl, when her lover proves unfaithful to her, is, by way of consolation, rubbed with pease-straw by the neighbouring lads; and when a Cumbrian youth loses his sweetheart, by her marriage with a rival, the same sort of comfort is administered to him by the lasses of the village. "Winter time for shoeing, peas-cod time for wooing," old proverb in MS. Devon Gl. The divination by peascods alluded to by Mr. Davy is thus mentioned by Gay,—
    As peascods once I pluck'd, I chanc'd to see
    One that was closely fill'd with three times three;
    Which, when I cropp'd, I safely home convey'd,
    And o'er the door the spell in secret laid;
    The latch mov'd up, when who should first come in,
    But, in his proper person,—Lubberkin!
But perhaps the allusion in Shakespeare is best illustrated by the following passage, which seems to have escaped the notice of all writers on this subject,—
    The peascod greene oft with no little toyle
    Hee'd seeke for in the fattest fertil'st soile,
    And rend it from the stalke to bring it to her,
    And in her bosome for acceptance wooe her.
        Browne's Britannia's Pastorals, p. 71.

PEASE. (1) To issue from a puncture in globules resembling peas. *Somerset.*
(2) To appease.
    The ten commandments bring no man to perfec-

tion, and are nothing less than able to *pease* the divine wrath. *Becon's Works*, p. 49.

(3) A single pea. *Spenser.*

PEASE-BOLT. Pease-straw. *East.* It occurs in Tusser, ed. 1812, p. 28.

PEASE-BRUSH. Pease-stubble. *Heref.*

PEASE-PORRIDGE-TAWNY. A dingy yellow.

PEASHAM. Pea-straw. *South.*

PEASIPOUSE. Peas and beans grown together as a crop. *Glouc.*

PEA-SWAD. A peascod. *North.*

PEAT. A delicate person.

> A citizen and his wife the other day
> Both riding on one horse, upon the way
> I overtook, the wench a pretty *peat*,
> And (by her eye) well fitting for the seat.
> *Donne's Poems,* p. 90.

PEAWCH-WAL. A sort of coal, which reflects various colours. *Staff.*

PEBBLE-BOSTER. A stone-breaker; a man who breaks stones for mending the roads. *Staff.*

PECCAVI. A familiar use of this Latin phrase is common among schoolboys, equivalent to a confession of being in the wrong. It occurs in the Historie of Promos and Cassandra, p. 32, and in Hall.

PECE. A drinking-cup. *Palsgrave.* "Cateria, Anglice a pese," Nominale MS.

> They toke away th.. s lver vessell,
> And all that they myght get,
> *Peces,* masars, and spones,
> Wolde they non forgete.
> *Robin Hood,* l. 32.

PECH. To pant; to breathe heavily. *Cumb.*

PECK. (1) Meat; victuals. Dekker uses it in this sense. *Linc.* To eat. *Oxon.* "We must scrat before we peck."

(2) A pickaxe. *West.*

(3) *To peck upon,* to domineer over.

(4) To stumble. *Yorksh.*

(5) A large quantity. *Var. dial.*

(6) To pitch. Still in use.

PECKHAM. "It's all holiday at Peckham with me," i. e. it is all up with me.

PECKISH. Hungry. *Var. dial.*

PECKLED. Speckled. Still in use.

PECTOLL.

> Beholde the rolled hodes stuffed with flockes,
> The newe broched doublettes open at the brestes,
> Stuffed with *pectoll* of theyr loves smockes.
> *A Treatyse of a Galaunt,* n. d.

PECTORAL. Armour for the breast. The term was also applied to a priest's stole. The second meaning of *pectorale* given by Ducange is *rationale,* stola pontificalis.

PECULIAR. A mistress. *Grose.*

PECUNIALL. Belonging to money.

> It came into hys hed that the Englyshmen did litle passe upon the observacion and kepynge of penall lawes or *pecuniall* statutes, made and enacted for the preservacion of the commen utilytee and wealthe. *Hall, Henry VII. f. 57.*

PECUNIOUS. Money-loving.

PECURIOUS. Very precise. *East.*

PED. A species of hamper without a lid, in which mackerel are hawked about the streets.

East. Moor tells us, in Norwich an assemblage whither women bring their small wares of eggs, chickens, &c. to sell, is called the *Ped-market.* Ray says, "Dorsers are *peds* or panniers carried on the backs of horses, on which higglers used to ride and carry their commodities. It seems this homely but most useful instrument was either first found out, or is the most generally used, in this county (Dorset), where fish-jobbers bring up their fish in such contrivances, above an hundred miles, from Lime to London." In his North-country words he has "a whisket, a basket, a skuttle, or shallow *ped.*" Tusser uses *ped,* ed. 1812, p. 11. Holme, 1688, has explained it an angler's basket.

PEDAILE. Footmen. *Hearne.*

PEDANT. A teacher of languages.

PED-BELLY. A round protuberant belly, like a ped, q. v. *East.*

PEDDER. (1) A pedlar. *Var. dial.* Forby explains it, one who carries wares in a ped, pitches it in open market, and sells from it. (2) A basket. Nominale MS.

PEDDLE. Employment. *North.*

PEDDLE-BACKED. Said of a man carrying a ped or pack like a pedlar.

PEDDLING. Trifling; worthless.

PEDELION. Helleborus niger. *Gerard.*

PEDER. A small farmer. *Linc.*

PEDESAY. A kind of cloth.

PEDISSEQUANTS. Followers. (*Lat.*)

> Yet still he striveth untill wearied and breathlesse, he be forced to offer up his blood and flesh to the rage of al the observant *pedissequants* of the hunting goddesse Diana.
> *Topsell's Four-Footed Beasts,* 1607, p. 136.

PEDLAR'S-BASKET. Ivy-leaved snap-dragon.

PEDLAR'S-FRENCH. The cant language. The term was also applied to any unintelligible jargon. Still in use.

PEDLAR'S-PAD. A walking-stick. *North.*

PEDNAMENE. Head to feet; as in many Cornish huts large families lie, husband, wife, and children (even grown up) of both sexes, all in one bed. *Pohwhele.*

PEDNPALY. A tomtit. *Cornw.*

PEED. Half-blind. See *Pea.*

PEE-DEE. A young lad in a keel, who takes charge of the rudder. *North.*

PEEK. A grudge. *Simultas,* Upton's MS additions to Junius.

PEEKED. Thin. *Dorset.*

PEEKING. "A peeking fellow, one that carries favour by low flattery and carrying tales, and picks holes in the character of others by lies or ill-natur'd stories," MS. Devon Gl.

PEEL. (1) A pillow; a bolster; a cushion for lace-making. *West.*

(2) A square tower; a fortress. *North.*

(3) Stir; noise; uproar. *Yorksh.*

(4) To peel ground, i. e. to impoverish it, Kennett, MS. Lansd. 1033.

(5) To strip. *Var. dial.* Peel'd priest, stripped or bald priest. There is an early receipt for "a man *pelyd* or scallyd," in Lincoln MS.

(6) The long-handled shovel with which bread, &c. is thrust into a hot oven, or taken out. "Also put into an oven with a *peele*," Florio, p. 237. "Pele for an ovyn, *pelle a four*," Palsgrave. "Pele, *pala*," Nominale MS. Thus described by an anonymous lexicographer : a wooden instrument of about a yard and a half long, and three quarters broad, on which pastry-cooks put many pies and tarts, &c. at once, either to carry them from gentlemen's houses to be baked, or from the oven to where they are to be used at feasts or great entertainments ; also the name of the instrument that bakers, &c. use to put into the oven to draw their bread, pies, &c. with ; also an instrument that printers hang up their sheets with, upon lines or wooden rails, as they come from the press, that they may dry.

PEEL-BEARS. Pillow-cases. *Devon.*

PEEL-CLOTH. A pillow-case. *Devon.*

PEELER. An iron crow-bar. *Kent.*

PEELING. A paring. *Var. dial.*

PEENGING. Fretful ; whining. *North.*

PEEP. (1) An eye. *Somerset.* Grose has *peepers*, eyes, Class. Dict. Vulg. Tong.

(2) A flock of chickens. Also, to chirp. " *Pipio*, to peepe like a chicke," Elyot.

PEEP-BO. A nursery pastime, in which a child is amused by the alternate hiding and exposure of the face ; "suiting the word to the action." The term is extended to the occasional obscuration of a debtor, or of one accused of anything rendering his visibility inconvenient.

PEEPER. An egg-pie. *Devon.*

PEEPING-TOM. A nickname for a curious prying fellow, derived from an old legendary tale, told of a tailor of Coventry, who, when Godiva Countess of Chester, rode at noon quite naked through that town, in order to procure certain immunities for the inhabitants (notwithstanding the rest of the people shut up their houses) slily peeped out of his window, for which he was miraculously struck blind. His figure, peeping out of a window, is still kept up in remembrance of the transaction, and there is an annual procession yet held at Coventry, in which the feat of Lady Godiva is attempted to be represented, without violating the principles of public decency. A newspaper of last year tells us that,—

> The Godiva procession at Coventry was celebrated with much pomp last week. The lady selected for the occasion (who was a handsome-looking woman, and conducted herself with great propriety) was very differently habited from the great original she personated, being clad, from shoulder to feet, in close-fitting woven silk tights. Over this was placed an elegant pointed satin tunic, fastened by an ornamental girdle. Two handsome lace scarfs formed the body, and was fastened underneath each arm to a blonde Polka edged with gold. A zephyr's wing, in folds, descended from the shoulders, and was fastened on the bosom by a rich brooch, attached to which was a white cord and gold tassels. The head gear consisted of a pearl coronet, surmounted by a

large plume of white ostrich feathers.—The procession was obliged, by a heavy shower of rain, to beat a premature retreat.

PEEPY. Sleepy ; drowsy. Go to peepy-by, i. e. to sleep. *Var. dial.*

PEER. (1) To peep. *Shak.*

(2) To pour out liquid. *Oxon.*

(3) Tender ; thin ; delicate. *Linc.*

(4) The minnow. *Somerset.*

PEERELLE. A pearl. See *Abounde.*

PEERK. To walk consequentially. *North.*

PEERY. Inquisitive ; suspicious. It occurs in ' A Narrative of the Life of Mrs. Charlotte Charke,' 8vo. 1755, p. 155.

PEES. Peace. (*A.-N.*)
> Wyth grete honowre under hys honde
> He made *pees* as he wolde.
> > *MS. Cantab.* Ff. ii. 38, f. 147.

> Gladys-more that gladis us alle,
> This is begynyng of oure gle,
> Gret sorow then shalle falle,
> Wher rest and *pees* were wont to be.
> > *MS. Cantab.* Ff. v. 48, f. 123.

PEESE. To ooze out. *South.*

PEET. A pit. *Somerset.*
> And bad with that goo make a *peet*,
> Whereinne he hath his douŷter set.
> > *Gower, MS. Soc. Antiq.* 134, f. 169.

PEEVISH. (1) Piercing cold. *North.*

(2) Foolish ; trifling ; silly. Ray gives it the meanings, witty, subtle.

PEE-WEE. To peak ; to whine. *East.*

PEE-WIT. The lapwing. *Var. dial.*

PEFF. To cough faintly. *North.* In Lincolnshire, a short, dry, hacking cough is often called a peffling cough.

PEG. (1) To move briskly. *Var. dial.* To peg away, to do anything very quickly.

(2) To beat. To take down a peg or two, i. e. to humble a person.

(3) A diminutive of Margaret.

(4) A leg, or foot. (5) A tooth.

PEG-FICHED. A West country game. The performers in this game are each furnished with a sharp-pointed stake. One of them then strikes it into the ground, and the others throwing theirs across it endeavour to dislodge it. When a stick falls, the owner has to run to a prescribed distance and back, while the rest, placing the stick upright, endeavour to beat it into the ground up to the very top.

PEGGY. A sort of slender poker, with a small portion of the end bent at right angles for the purpose of raking the fire together. Davy's MS. Suffolk Gl.

PEG-IN-THE-RING. At top, is to spin the top within a certain circle marked out, and in which the top is to exhaust itself, without once overstepping the bounds prescribed.

PEGNIS. Machines ; erections. (*Lat.*)

PEGO. The penis. *Grose.*

PEGS. Small pieces of dough rolled up, and crammed down the throats of young ducks and geese.

PEG-TRANTUM. A wild romping girl. *East.* Gone to Peg Trantum's, i. e. dead.

PEIGH. To pant; to breathe hardly.

PEINE. Penalty; grief; torment; labour. Also, to put to pain. (*A.-N.*)

PEIREN. To diminish, injure. (*A.-N.*)

PEISE. A weight. (*Fr.*)

PEITRELL. The breastplate; the strap that crosses the breast of a horse. This word occurs in Chaucer, and in an old vocabulary in MS. Jes. Coll. Oxon. 28.

> In the sacrifices of the goddesse Vacuna, an asse was feasted with bread, and crowned with flowers, hung with rich jewels and *peytrels*, because (as they saye) when Priapus would have ravished Vesta being asleepe, she was suddenly awaked by the braying of an asse, and so escaped that infamie: and the Lampsaceni in the disgrace of Priapus did offer him an asse. *Topsell's Beasts*, 1607, p. 23.

> Hir *paytrelle* was of a rialle fyne,
> Hir cropur was of arafe,
> Hir bridulle was of golde fyne,
> On every side hong bellis thre.
> *MS. Cantab.* Ff. v. 48, f. 116.

PEIZE. To weigh down; to oppress.

PEJON. A pigeon. *Lydgate.*

PEKE. To pry about. *Palsgrave.* Also, to peep, to jut or project out.

PEKISH. Ignorant; silly.

PEKKE. Pack. Reliq. Antiq. i. 84.

PEL. A kind of post, at which a knight would exercise for jousting.

PELCH. Weak; faint; exhausted. *North.*

PELDER. To encumber. *Cumb.*

PELE. (1) A paling; a rail.

> Ryghte as he thoghte he ded eche dele,
> He jede and clambe upp on a *pele.*
> *MS. Harl.* 1701, f. 14.

(2) To pillage; to rob.

> Namly pore men for to *pele,*
> Or robbe or bete withoute skyle.
> *MS. Harl.* 1701, f. 16.

PELER. A pillar.

> To a *peler* y was bownden all the nyght,
> Scorged and betyd tyl hyt was day lyght.
> *MS. Cantab.* Ff. ii. 38, f. 40.

PELETIR. The pellitory. *Palsgrave.*

PELF. Rubbish, refuse. *Warw.* Money is rubbish, and hence the term. "Pelfe, trash, *id est*, mony," Florio, p. 63. "Who steals my purse steals trash," Shakespeare. *Pelfish*, silly, trifling, Holinshed, Chron. Ireland, p. 80. Ill-gotten gains are called *pelfry.*

PELFIR. Spoil; booty; pillage.

PELK. To beat; to thrash. *North.*

PELL. (1) A hole of water, generally very deep, beneath an abrupt waterfall. To pell, is to wash into pells or pools, as water does when it flows very violently. To pell away, is to wash away the ground by the force of water. *Sussex.*

(2) A heavy shower. *North.*

(3) To drive forth. "Shal ich forth pelle," Havelok, 810.

(4) Fur; a skin of an animal. "Arayd with pellys aftyr the old gyse," Cov. Myst. p. 246. (*A.-N.*) It occurs in Lydgate.

(5) An earthen vessel. *Devon.*

PELLER. A peg, or pin.

PELLERE. A loose outer covering of fur for the upper part of the body. Any fur garment was so called. *Pelury*, rich fur, Hardyng, f. 72. Hall has *pellerie.*

> And furryd them with armyne,
> Ther was never jyt *pellere* half so fyne.
> *MS. Cantab.* Ff. ii. 38, f. 242.

PELLES. A kind of oats. *Cornw.*

PELLET. (1) Sheep's dung. *Palsgrave.*

(2) A shot, or bullet. See Holinshed, Chronicles of Ireland, p. 132.

PELLET-GUNS. "Two little cannons called *pellet-guns*, namely, one of iron and the other of brass, fitted with wood," MSS. in Winchester Archives, dated 1435.

PELL-WOOL. An inferior wool; wool cut off after a sheep's death.

PELOTE. A pellet; a small round piece of anything, not necessarily globular.

> Of picche sche tok him a *pelote,*
> The whiche he schulde into the throte
> Of Minotaure caste ryst.
> *Gower, MS. Soc. Antiq.* 134, f. 160.

PELOWARE. A pillar. Vocab. MS.

PELRINE. A poor pilgrim. (*A.-N.*)

PELSE. (1) Rain; sleet. *North.*

(2) Trash; refuse; vile stuff.

PELSEY. (1) Obstinate; cross; mischievous; bad; wicked; evil. *North.*

(2) A stroke or blow. *Beds.*

PELT. (1) The skin, applied chiefly to the skin of a sheep, hence a "sheep's *pelt*;" and a man stripped is in his pelt. *North.*

(2) Put. See Sevyn Sages, 751.

> Thurch chaunce, and eke thurch gras,
> In hir for sothe *pelt* y was.
> *Arthour and Merlin*, p. 40.

(3) A miserly stingy fellow. "A pelt or pinchbecke," Huloet, 1552.

(4) In falconry, the dead body of a fowl killed by a hawk. See Gent. Rec.

(5) Rage; passion. *Var. dial.* It occurs as a verb in Shakespeare.

(6) To yield; to submit.

(7) A blow; a stroke. *East.* It is a verb in the following passage:

> Wherefore, seyd the belte,
> With grete strokes I schalle hym *pelte;*
> My mayster schall full welle thene,
> Both to clothe [and] fede his men.
> *MS. Ashmole* 61.

(8) A kind of game, similar to whist, played by three people.

PELTER. (1) Anything large. *Cumb.*

(2) To patter; to beat. *North.*

PELTING. (1) Angry. See *Pelt* (5)

> At which, Mistres Minerva beeing netled, and taking the matter in dudgeon thus to be provoked, and withall reprehending the mayde very sharply for her saucines, in a *pelting* chafe she brake all to peeces the wenches imagery worke, that was so curiously woven, and so full of varietie, with her shittle. The mayde heereat beeing sore greeved, halfe in despayre not knowing what to doe, yeelding to passion, would needes hang herselfe.
> *Topsell's Serpents*, 1608, p. 259.

(2) Trifling; paltry; contemptible.

That Wednesday I a weary way did passe,
Raine, wind, stones, dirt, and dabbling dewie grasse,
With here and there a *pelting* scatter'd village,
Which yeelded me no charity or pillage.
Taylor's Workes, i. 124.

PELT-ROT. A disease that kills sheep, arising from ill-feeding. *North.*

PELTRY. Skins. *Var. dial.*

PEN. (1) A place in which sheep are inclosed at a fair or market. *Var. dial.*
(2) To shut up, to confine. *Heref.*
(3) A spigot. *Somerset.*
(4) The root of a feather. The feather itself is also so called. *Pennes*, quills, Maundevile, p. 269.
(5) A sow's pudendum. *North.*
(6) A dam or pond-head to keep the water before a mill. In common use.
(7) A prison. A cant term.
(8) A barrel kept for making vinegar.

PENAKULL. (1) An isolated rock?
He ys yn a castelle styffe and gode,
Closyd with the salte flode,
In a *penakull* of the see.
MS. Cantab. Ff. ii. 38, f. 104.
(2) A pinnacle.
He ledd hym forth upon the playne,
He was war of a *penakulle* pyghte.
MS. Cantab. Ff. ii. 38, f. 49.

PENANCE. Repentance. (*A.-N.*)
PENANCE-BOARD. The pillory.
PENANT. A person doing penance.
PEN-BAUK. A beggar's can.
PENCI. Thought. (*A.-N.*)
PENCILED. Painted.
PEND. (1) To distress, or to be in need. Also, a case of necessity. *East.*
(2) To depend. *I. of Wight.*
(3) A roof vaulted with masonry, but not joined.
(4) Pressure; strain; force. *Suff.* Also, to incline or lean.
PENDALL. The keystone of an arch.
PENDANT. A carpenter's level.
PENDANT-FEATHERS. The feathers at the joints of a hawk's knee. *Berners.*
PENDANTS. Hanging ornaments.
PENDICE. A penthouse. Strutt, ii. 131.
PENDICLES. Lice. MS. Devon. Gl.
PENDID. Belonged. Perceval, 1936.
PENDIL. A pendulum. *North.*
PENDLE. Suddenly. *Heref.* "He came *pendle* over the hill upon him."
PENDLE-ROCK. The top stratum in the stone-quarry at Islip, co. Oxon, is called the *pendle-rock.* There is a mountain called Pendle Hill, and the word seems genuine, though it is singular how it could have found its way there. The word *pen* is said to be of Phœnician extraction, and signifies *head* or *eminence.* It was first introduced into Cornwall, where the Phœnicians had a colony who worked the tin mines. Hence we have many names in Cornwall which begin with *pen.*
PENDOLLY. A child's doll. *Linc.*
PENDUGAM. The penguin. Skelton, ii. 344.
PENELLES. Strong wooden boards.

PENEST. Punished; pained.
PENFEATHERED. Shabby. *Linc.* A horse, whose hair is rough, is so called.
PENIBLE. Industrious; painstaking.
That wyl serve the to pay,
Payneble al that he may
MS. Harl. 1701, f. 39.
With many woundys ful terryble,
And rebukys ful *penyble.*
MS. Cott. Vitell. C. xlii. f. 98.

PENITENCER. A priest who enjoins penance in extraordinary cases. (*A.-N.*)
PENMAN. A person who writes.
PENNER. A pen-case. "*Pennare*, a pener," Nominale MS. inter nomina rerum pertinentium clerico. It is the translation of *calamar* in Hollyband's Dictionarie, 1593.
PENNET. An occasional pen used for sheep, or cows. *Somerset.* Jennings has *pennin* in the same sense.
PENNE-VAIR. A kind of fur.
PENNILESS. To sit on the penniless bench, i. e. to be very poor. There was a public seat at Oxford so called. See Brand, i. 240.
PENNING-TIME. Bedtime. *Oxon.*
PENNITAUNCER. The priest who enjoins penances. "Penytauncer, *penitancier*," Palsgrave. It occurs in Nominale MS.
PENNOCK. A little bridge over a water-course. *Sussex.*
PENNY. *Penny wise pound foolish*, careful in small matters and extravagant in great ones. *Clean as a penny*, very clean, completely. *Head penny*, a penny formerly paid to a curate at a burial by poor people. *Penny hop*, a country club of dancers, where each person pays a penny to the fiddler on every night they meet to improve themselves in dancing. In London, a private ball of the lower gentry, admission one penny, is so called. *Penny-lattice-house*, a very low ale-house. *Penny-pots*, pimples on the face of a drunken person. *Penny-worth*, a small quantity, an equivalent. *A good penny-worth*, a cheap bargain.
PENNYD. Winged. *Palsgrave.*
PENNY-FATHER. A penurious person. "Hee (good old *penny-father*) was glad of his liquor, and beganne to drinke againe," Pasquil's Jests, 1629. It occurs in Palsgrave.
Ranck *peny-fathers* scud, with their halfe hammes
Shadowing their calves, to save their silver dammes.
Morgan's Phœnix Britannicus, p. 33.

Againe, the great men, the rich mysers and *penny-fathers*, following the example of their princes and governours, they in like sort sent packing out of their doores the schoole-mistresse of all labour, diligence and vertue, and will not permit a webbe, the very patterne, index, and anathema of supernaturall wisedome, to remaine untouched.
Topsell's Beasts, 1607, p. 262.

PENNY-MEASURE. A clay lying above the penny-stone, of which coarse earthenware is made.
PENNY-PRICK. "A game consisting of casting oblong pieces of iron at a mark," Hunter's

Hallamsh. Gl. p. 71. Grose explains it, "throwing at halfpence placed on sticks which are called hobs."

Their idle houres, (I meane all houres beside
Their houres to eate, to drinke, drab, sleepe and ride)
They spend at shove-board, or at *penny-pricks.*
Scot's Philomythie, 1616.

PENNY-STONE. (1) A kind of coarse woollen cloth. "Transforme thy plush to pennystone and scarlet," Citye Match, 1639, p. 5. It was in common use for linings.

(2) The game of quoits, played with stones or horseshoes. *Kennett.*

(3) The best iron ore. *Salop.*

PENNY-WAGTAIL. The water-wagtail. *East.*

PENNYWEED. The plant rattle.

PENNY-WHIP. Very small beer. *Lanc.*

PENNY-WINKLE. The periwinkle. *Var. dial.*

PENONCEAL. A banner. (*A.-N.*)
Endelonge the schippis borde to schewe
Of *penonceals* a riche rewe.
Gower, MS. Soc. Antiq. 134, f. 235.

PENS. Pence. (*A.-S.*) *Pens-lac,* lack of pence, or money.

PENSE. To be fretful. *East.* Hence *pensey,* fretful, complaining, dull.

PENSELL. A small banner. *Palsgrave.*

PENSIFEHED. Pensiveness. *Chaucer.*

PENSIL. A large blister. *Somerset.*

PENSION. "That assembly or convention which in the two Temples is called a Parliament, in Lincoln's Inn a Council, is in Gray's Inn called a Pension," Kennett.

PEN-STOCK. A floodgate erected to keep in or let out water from a millpond as occasion may require. *South.*

PENSY. The pansy. *Palsgrave.*

PENT. Pended, or appended.

PENTACLE. The figure of three triangles, intersected and made of five lines, was so called, and was formerly worn as a preservative against demons. When it was delineated in the body of a man, it was supposed to touch and point out the five places wherein our Saviour was wounded. "Their lights and pentacles," Ben Jonson.

PENTAUNCER. A penitent.

PENTECOSTAL. An offering made at Whitsuntide by the churches and parishes in each diocese to the cathedral.

PENTED. Belonged; pertained.

PENT-HOUSE-NAB. A broad-brimmed hat.

PENTICE. The part of a roof that projects over the outer wall of a house, and sometimes sufficiently wide to walk uuder; an open shed or projection over a door; a moveable canvass blind to keep the sun and rain from stores outside a door. It is the translation of *auvens* in Hollyband's Dictionarie, 1593. "Pentes or paves, *estal, soubtil,*" Palsgrave. "Pentys over a stall, *auvent,*" ibid.

PENTICLE. A covering. *Fairfax.*

PENULE. The scrotum. (*Lat.*)

PEOLOUR. A furred robe. (*A.-N.*)

PEON. A barbed javelin.

PEOREN. Equals; companions. (*A.-N.*)

PEPILLES. The water purslain.

PEPINE. A kernel. This word occurs in Hollyband's Dictionarie, 1593.

PEPINNERY. That part of an orchard where fruit-stones are set for growing.

PEPLE. People. (*A.-N.*)

PEPLISH. (1) To fill with people. *Palsgrave.*

(2) Vulgar. Troilus and Creis. iv. 1677.

PEPPER. (1) To overreach. *Linc.*

(2) To rate, or scold. *Var. dial.*

(3) To beat; to thrash. *East.*

(4) To take pepper in the nose, i. e. to be angry, to take offence. To suspect, or mistrust, Florio, p. 11.

Myles, hearing him name the baker, took straight *pepper* in the nose, and, starting up, threw of his cardinals roabes, standing in his dustye cassocke, swore I by cockesbread, the baker; and he that sales to the contrary, heere stand I, Myles, the bakers man, to have the proudest cardinall of you all by the eares. *Tarlton's Newes out of Purgatorie,* 1590.

Pepper ye come to a marvelus pryce,
Som say, thys Lenton season;
And every body that ys wyse
May soone perceve the reson:
For every man takes *pepper i' the nose*
For the waggynge of a strawe, God knowse,
With every waverynge wynd that blowese.
Elderton's Lenton Stuffe, 1570.

(5) To rain quickly. *Var. dial.*

PEPPERED. Infected with *lues venerea.*

PEPPERERS. Grocers. *Stowe.*

PEPPERGATE. There is a Cheshire proverb, "When the daughter is stolen, shut the *peppergate.*" This is founded on the fact, that the mayor of Chester had his daughter stolen as she was playing at ball with other maidens in Pepper-street; the young man who carried her off came through the Pepper-gate, and the mayor wisely ordered the gate to be shut up; agreeable to the old saying, "When the steed is stolen shut the stable door."

PEPPERIDGE. The barberry. *East.*

PEPPERNEL. A lump, or swelling.

PEPPERQUERN. A pepper-mill. *Palsgrave.*

PEPPER-SQUATTER. A pair of snuffers.

PEPPERY. Warm; passionate.

PEPS. To throw at. *West.*

PER. Liquid *pers* when it falls connected like a string. *Lanc.*

PERADVENTURE. Without all peradventure, i. e. without all doubt.

PERAGE. Rank. (*A.-N.*)

PERAUNTER. Perchance. (*A.-N.*)
For in some houre, softhly this no fable,
Unto some man she graunteth his desyres,
That will not after in a thousande yeares
Peraunter ones condescende
Unto his will nor his lust him sende.
Lydgate's Troye, 1555, sig. P. iii.
I dar the hete a foule or twoo,
Perauntur with a conyne.
MS. Cantab. Ff. v. 48, f. 51.

PERCASE. Perchance. *Palsgrave.*

PERCEIVANCE. Perception. *East.* It occurs in Palsgrave's Acolastus, 1540. *Perceiverance.* Middleton, iii. 388.

PERCEIVE. To understand. *Palsgrave.*

PERCEL. A parcel, or part. (*A.-N.*)

PERCELEY. Parsley. *Palsgrave.*

PERCEL-MELE. Piecemeal. (*A.-N.*)

PERCER. A rapier; a short sword. "Percer blade, *estoc*," Palsgrave.

PERCH. A measuring-rod.

PERCHE. (1) To pierce; to prick.

This ilke beste myȝte thay on na wyse *perche* with thaire speres, bot with mellis of yrene thay slew it.
MS. Lincoln A. i. 17, f. 30.

(2) To perish, or destroy.

And ȝif it the woman in drynkynge,
And sche schal be dilyverd withoute *perchyng.*
MS. Harl. 2869, f. 96.

PERCHEMEAR. A parchment-maker.

PERCHER. A large wax candle, generally used for the altar. MS. Sloane 1986.

The Maister of the Roles dyd present her torches and *perchers* of wax, a good nombre.
State Papers, i. 583.

PERCILE. Parsley. (*A.-N*)

PERCLOSE. A conclusion.

But looke for smoother matter in the middest, and most smooth in the *perclose* and wind-up of all.
Dent's Pathway, epist.

PERCOCK. A kind of early apple.

PERCULLIS. A portcullis. *Hall.*

PERDE. *Par Dieu,* verily. (*A.-N.*)

Hitt were peté
Butt they shold be
Begelid, *perdé!*
Withowtyne grase.
MS. Cantab. Ff. i. 6, f. 45.

PERDICLE. The eagle-stone.

PERDU. A soldier sent on a forlorn hope; any person in a desperate state. (*Fr.*) It sometimes means, in ambush.

PERDURABLE. Everlasting.

But gain is not alwayes *perdurable*, nor losse alwayes continuall.
Hall, Henry VI. f. 59.

PERDURE. To endure; to last.

PERDY. Same as *Perde*, q. v. It seems sometimes to mean, perchance.

Perdy, seid the scheperde, nowe
Hit shalbe thouȝt if that I mow.
MS. Cantab. Ff. v. 48, f. 54.

This is their practise, if *perdy* they cannot at the first time smelling, find out the way which the deede doores tooke to escape. So at length get they that by art, cunning, and diligent indevour, which by fortune and lucke they cannot otherwise overcome.
Topsell's Beasts, 1607, p. 166.

PERE. (1) To appear. (*A.-N.*)

The xiiij. nyghte was come to ende, the gostȝ muste *pere* ageyne. *MS. Cantab. Ff. ii. 38, f. 52.*

To a bisschop that heȝt Aubert
Saynt Myghell *perw'* be nyȝt.
MS. Cantab. Ff. v. 48, f. 79.

(2) A peer; an equal. (*A.-N.*)

That on was ffyfftene wyntyr old,
That other thryttene, as men me told,
In the world was non her *pere;*
Also whyt so lylye flour,
Red as rose off here colour,
As bryȝt as blosme on brere.
Romance of Athelston.

Then was ther a bachylere,
A prowde prynce withowtyn *pere*,
Syr James he hyght.
MS. Cantab. Ff. ii. 38, f. 76.

(3) To strive to be equal.

In hevene on the hyghest stage
He wolde have *peeryd* with God of blys.
MS. Cantab. Ff. ii. 38, f. 13.

PEREGALL. Equal. *Chaucer.*

Everyche other through great vyolence
By very force bare other unto grounde,
As full ofte it happeth and is founde,
Whan stronge doth mete with his *peregall.*
Lydgate's Troye, 1555, sig. P. v

ȝit ther were any of power more than hee,
Or *peregalle* unto his degré.
Lydgate, MS. Soc. Antiq. 134, f. 16.

PEREGRINE. A kind of falcon.

Brave birds they were, whose quick self-less-ning kin
Still won the girlonds from the *peregrin.*
Browne's Britannia's Pastorals, ii. 23.

PERESINE. Gum.

PERFECT. Certain; sure. *Shak.*

PERFITE. Perfect; skilful.

Were thou as *perfite* in a bowe,
Thou shulde have moo dere I trowe.
MS. Cantab. Ff. v. 48, f. 30.

PERFIXT. Predetermined.

PERFORCE. To force or compel. *Palsgrave.* As an adverb, of necessity. *Force perforce,* absolute necessity. *Patience perforce,* a phrase when some evil must be endured which cannot by any means be remedied.

PERFORMED. Complete. *Devon.* To perform up a sum, i. e. to make it up, occurs in several old writers.

PERFORMENTS. Performances.

PERFOURNE. To finish, complete, furnish.

PERGE. To go on. (*Lat.*)

PERHAPPOUS. Perhaps. Lydgate, p. 35.

PERIAGUA. A boat, or canoe. A term familiar to readers of Robinson Crusoe.

PERIAPT. A magical bandage.

PERICLES. Dangers. (*Lat.*)

PERIHERMENIALL. *Perihermeniall principles*, principles of interpretation. *Skelton.*

PERILLE. A pearl. "*Margarita, Anglice* a *perylle*," Nominale MS. f. 8.

PERILLOUSLI. Dangerously; rudely.

PERIOD. To put a stop to; to cease.

PERIS. Persia.

Inde and *Peris* and Arabie,
Babilone, Juda, and Sulie.
Cursor Mundi, MS. Coll. Trin. Cantab. f. 14.

PERISH. (1) To destroy. *Shak.* Wilbraham has *perished,* starved with cold.

(2) To injure; to pain. *Essex.*

PERITE. Skilful. (*Lat.*)

No decree could demonstrate unto them anything sufficient to respect a more civill and *perite* life.
Kenelworth Parks, 1594, p. 10.

PERIWINKE. A periwig. *Hall.*

PERJENETE. A young pear. (*A.-N.*)

Ac pescoddes and *perejonettes,*
Plombes and cheries.
Piers Ploughman, Rawl. MS

PERK. (1) A park. *Yorksh.*

Hawkis of nobille ayere
On his *perke* gunne repayre.
MS. Lincoln A. i. 17, f. 130.

(2) To examine thoroughly. *North.*

(3) Proud; peart; elated. Still in use, Craven

GL. ii. 38 ; Wilbraham, p. 107 ; Forby, ii. 249. *To perk one's self up*, to adorn. *To perk up again*, to recover from sickness.

(4) A perch. *Suffolk.* "Ovyr the perke to pryk," Skelton, i. 124. It also occurs in Reliq. Antiq. i. 294.

(5) A wooden frame against which sawn timber is set up to dry. *East.*

PERKERS. Young rooks. *North.*

PERKIN. Water cyder.

PERKY. Saucy ; obstinate. *West.*

PERLATANE.

The haulle also of this palace was sett fulle of ymages of golde, and bitwix thame stode *perlatanes* of golde, in the branches of whilke ther were many maners of fewles. *MS. Lincoln A. i. 17, f. 25.*

PERLESY. A pleurisy.

And smyttis hym als it were with a *perlesy*, that alle his lymes dryes, that he may na gud do als he sulde. *MS. Lincoln A. i. 17, f. 246.*

PERLID. Ornamented with pearls ; studded with any ornaments.

And many a *perlid* garnement
Embroudid was ajen the day.
Gower, MS. Soc. Antiq. 134, f. 54.

PERLIN. The piece of timber which runs along under the middle part of the spars or bearers of a roof, to give such bearers additional strength.

PERLOWES. Perilous. *Palsgrave.*

PERMAFAY. By my faith. (*A.-N.*)

PERMANSIE. Magic ; necromancy.

PERN. (1) To prosper. *Somerset.*

(2) To pick and dress birds, particularly applied to dressing the heron.

PERNASO. Mount Parnassus.

PERNEL. The pimpernel, a flower that always shuts up its blossoms before rain.

But these tender *pernels* must have one gown for the day, another for the night.
Pilkington's Works, p. 56.

PERPEND. To consider attentively.

You'll quickly know, if you do well *perpend*,
And observe rightly what's the proper end.
Brome's Songs, 1661, p. 182.

PERPENDICLE. The plumb line of a quadrant. This word occurs in an old treatise on mensuration, in MS. Sloane 213.

PERPENTINE. A porcupine. "Perpoynt, *kystrix*," Pr. Parv. The form *perpentine* occurs in Shakespeare, most incorrectly altered to *porcupine* by modern editors. It is the genuine old word.

PERPENT-STONE. A large stone reaching through a wall so as to appear on both sides of it. Oxf. Gl. Arch. p. 280. In the North of England, a thin wall, the stones of which are built on the edge, is called a *perpent*.

PERPETUANA. A kind of glossy cloth, generally called *everlasting*.

PERPLANTED. Planted securely.

Requirynge theim as his especiall truste and confidence was *perplanted* in the hope of their fidelité, that they would occurre and mete hym by the waye with all diligent preparacion.
Hall, Richard III. f. 27.

PERQUIRE. To search into. Clobery's Divine Glimpses, 1659, p. 73.

PERR. (1) Perry. (2) A pearl.

PERRE. A dish in old cookery, made chiefly of peas, onions, and spices.

PERRIER. A kind of short mortar, formerly much used for stone shot.

PERRIWINKLE. A periwig. *Stubbe.*

PERRONENDERE. A pardoner. *Hearne.*

PERRY-DANCERS. The aurora borealis. *East.*

PERRYE. (1) A squall.

It happened Harold his sonne to arrive at Pountiou against his will, by occasion of a sudden perry, or contrarie winde, that arose while he was on seaboorde. *Lambarde's Perambulation, 1596, p. 357.*

(2) A little cur dog. *North.*

(3) Precious stones ; jewels. (*A.-N.*)

And alle was set with *perrye*,
Ther was never no better in Crystyanté.
MS. Cantab. Ff. ii. 38, f. 242.

PERS. (1) Persia.

We woot bothe bi story and vers
That the kyndam of Grace and *Pers*
Were hede kyngus in forme tide.
Cursor Mundi, MS. Coll. Trin. Cantab. f. 139.

(2) Company.

Al we wite it thi defaut,
So siggeth al our *pers*.
Arthour and Merlin, p. 9.

(3) Sky, or blueish gray colour. There was a kind of cloth so called.

PERSAUNT. Piercing. (*A.-N.*)

That of the stremis every maner wyjte
Astonied was, they weren so bryjte and shene,
Ant to the ye for *persaunt* for to sene.
Lydgate, MS. Soc. Antiq. 134, f. 23.

For thy *perseynt* charité.
Gower, MS. Soc. Antiq. 134, f. 109.

PERSCRUTE. To search through. (*Lat.*) Used by Andrew Borde, Brit. Bibl. iv. 24.

PERSE. Equality. (*A.-N.*)

PERSEL. Parsley. *Pegge.*

PERSEVER. To persevere. *Shak.*

Whether a daw sit, or whether a daw fly,
Whether a daw stand, or whether a daw lye,
Whether a daw creepe, or whether a daw cry,
In what case soever a daw *persever*,
A daw is a daw, and a daw shall be ever.
Tarlton's Jests, 1611.

PERSIAN-WHEEL. An engine invented to raise a quantity of water sufficient for overflowing lands, that border in the banks of rivers, where the streams lie so low, as to be incapable of doing it.

PERSON. A mask, or actor. (*Lat.*)

PERSONABLE. Personally visible.

My saied lorde of Winchester saied unto the kyng that the kyng his father, so visited with sicknesse, was not *personable*. *Hall, Henry VI. f. 13.*

PERSONE. A man. Generally, a man of dignity, a parson or rector of a church.

PERSORE. A piercing-iron.

Je, je, seyd the *persore*,
That at I sey it shall be sure ;
Whi chyd je iche one with other ?
Wote je wele I ame jour brother !
Therefore none contrary me,
Yore as I sey so schall it be. *MS. Ashmole 61.*

PERSPECTIVE. A reflecting-glass.

PERSPICIL. An optic-glass. It occurs in Albumazar, 1634, sig. B. iv.

PERSTAND. To understand. *Peele.*

PERSUADE. Persuasion.

PERSUADERS. Spurs. Also, pistols.

PERSWAY. To mitigate. Ben Jonson, iv. 428.

PERT. Beautifully delicate. It is the translation of *subtilis* in Gesta Rom. p. 142.

> For hete her clothes down sche dede
> Almest to her gerdyl stede,
>   Than lay sche uncovert ;
> Sche was as whyt as lylye yn May,
> Or snow that sneweth yn wynterys day,
>   He seygh never non so *pert*.
>   *Illustrations of Fairy Mythology*, p. 1̄.

PERTE. (1) To part. Still in use.

> Then Thomas a sory man was he,
> The terys ran out of his een gray ;
> Luffy lady, 3et tell thou me
> If we shalle *porte* for ever and ay.
>   *MS. Cantab.* Ff. v. 48, f. 125.

(2) Of good appearance.

> Ther was no man in the kynges lande
> More *porte* then was he.
>   *MS. Cantab.* Ff. ii. 38, f. 244.

PERTELICHE. Openly. (*A.-N.*)

> Than syr Priamous the prynce in presens of lordes
> Preses to his penowne, and *pertly* it hentes.
>   *Morte Arthure, MS. Lincoln,* f. 84.

PERTELOTE. The name of a hen.

PERTENERE. A partner.

> God graunt us mekenesse in angurs here,
> And grace to lede owre lyfe here soo,
> That may aftur be *pertenere*
> Of hevene, whan we hens schall goo.
>   *MS. Cantab.* Ff. ii. 38, f. 14.

PERTRYCHE. A partridge.

> Ryght as the *pertryche* is constreyned undir the
> claues and nayles of the hauke, is as halfe deed for
> drede.   *Caxton's Divers Fruytful Ghostly Maters.*

PERTURBE. To trouble. *Palsgrave.*

PERTY. Part. *Lydgate.*

> God that sittis in Trinité,
> Gyffe thaym grace wel to the,
>   That lystyns me a whyle ;
> Alle that lovys of melody,
> Off hevon blisse God graunte tham *perty*,
>   Theyrr soules shelde fro peryle.
>   *MS. Cantab.* Ff. v. 48, f. 47.

PERUR. A kind of cup.

PERUSE. To examine, or survey.

> Monsieur Soubies having *perused* the fleet, returned to the king, and told him there was nothing ready ; and that the mariners and souldiers would not yeeld to goe the voyage till they were paid their arrears.   *MS. Harl.* 383.

PERVEY. To provide. (*A.-N.*)

PERVINKE. The herb periwinkle. (*A.-S.*)

PERYE. A pear-tree. (*A.-N.*)

> But for hur lorde sche durste not done,
> That sate benethe and pleyed hym merye,
> Before the towre undur a *perye*.
>   *MS. Cantab.* Ff. ii. 38, f. 141.

PERYSSE. Pears. (*A.-N.*)

> Then was the tre ful of ripe *perysse*,
> And began down to falle.
>   *MS. Cantab.* Ff. v. 48, f. 114.

PESANE. A gorget of mail or plate attached to the helmet. " A *pesane* and a paunsone," MS. Morte Arthure, f. 89.

PESATE. Is when a managed horse rises handsomely before and upon his haunches, and at the same time bends his fore-legs up to his body.

PESE. (1) Peace. Perceval 980, 981.

(2) To sooth ; to appease.

> Tylle y be sewre of youre hartys ese,
> Nothing but hit may my grevys *pese*.
>   *MS. Cantab.* Ff. i. 6, f. 132.

PESEN. Peas. This is the common early form of the word, and occurs in Chaucer, Legende of Good Women, 648. Holloway gives the following couplet, as seen lately on a board in a pea-field in Berkshire—

> Shut the gate after you, I'll tell you the reason,
> Because the pigs shouldn't get into the *peason*.

Ben Jonson has made the same words rhyme in his 133d epigram.

> As for his sallets, better never was
> Then acute sorrell, and sweet three-leav'd grasse,
> And for a sawce he seldome is at charges,
> For every crab-tree doth affoord him vergis ;
> His banket sometimes is greene beanes and *peason*,
> Nuts, peares, plumbes, apples, as they are in season.
>   *Taylor's Workes*, 1630, i. 97.

PESIBLE. Peaceable. (*A.-N.*)

PESIBLETE. A calm. (*A.-N.*)

PESK. A peach. Nominale MS.

PESON. An instrument in the form of a staff, with balls or crockets, used for weighing before scales were employed.

PESS. A hassock. *Suffolk.*

PESSCOD-SCALDING. A kind of merry-making in summer evenings ; the treat, green field peas boiled in the shells. *Yorksh.*

PESSIPE. A kind of cup.

PESTERED. Crowded. Peele, ii. 235.

PESTERMENT. Embarrassment. *North.*

PESTLE. (1) A leg of an animal, generally of a pig. A pestle of pork is still in common use. " Pestels of venison," Warner's Antiq. Culin. p. 98. " Pestell of flesshe, *jambon*," Palsgrave. A pestle-pie is a large standing pie which contains a whole gammon, and sometimes a couple of fowls and a neat's tongue, a favorite dish at country fairs, and at Christmas feasts.

(2) A constable's staff.

PESTLE-HEAD. A blockhead.

PETE. Pity. See Cov. Myst.

> Long lay the kyng, there away wolde not hee ;
> Dayly he propherid batayle : the enmys durst not fyghte
> Lacke of logynge and vitayle it was grett *peté*,
> Causid the gentill prynce to remeve, siche was Goddes
>   my3te !
> Lowe, how the good Lorde his owne gentill kny3te,
> Because he shulde remembir hym in wele and in woo,
> Thus in every thyng, Lorde, thy wille be doo !
>   *MS. Bibl. Reg.* 17 D. xv.

PETEOSE. Merciful ; compassionate.

> Many men spekes of lamentacioun,
> Off moders and of their gret desolatioun,
>   Which that thay did indure
> When that their childer dy and passe,
> But of his *peteose* tender moder, alasse !
>   I am verray sure,
> The wo and payn passis alle othere.
>   *MS. Bodl. e Mus.* 160.

PETER. (1) An oath. Similar to Mary! See MS. Lincoln, Pf. 140, 144, 146, and Weber's Gl. It is very common.

(2) To go through St. Peter's needle, i. e. to be subjected to severe discipline, applied to children. "To rob Peter to pay Paul," to take from one to give to another.

(3) Cowslips. Arch. xxx. 411.

(4) A portmanteau, or cloak bag.

(5) A kind of wine, one of the richest and most delicate of the Malaga wines, generally termed *Peter-see-me*, a corruption of Pedro-Ximenes.

> I am mightie melancholy,
> And a quart of sacke will cure me ;
> I am cholericke as any,
> Quart of claret will secure me ;
> I am phlegmaticke as may be,
> *Peter-see-me* must inure me ;
> I am sanguine for a ladle,
> And coole Rhenish shall conjure me.
> *Braithwait's Law of Drinking*, 1617, p. 80.

(6) Some kind of cosmetic.

> Then her boxes of *peeter*, and patches, and all her ornamental knacks and dresses she was wont every day to wast so much time about.
> *Several Discourses and Characters*, 1689, p. 175.

PETER-BOAT. A boat which is built sharp at each end, and can therefore be moved either way. *Suffolk.*

PETER-GUNNER. A nickname for a gunner or sportsman. "Peter Gunner will kill all the birds that died last summer."

PETERMAN. A fisherman. *East.*

PETER'S-STAFF. Tapsus barbacus. *Gerard.*

PETER-WAGGY. A harlequin toy.

PETH. (1) A well, a pump. *West.*

(2) A road up a steep hill. *North.*

(3) A crumb of bread. *Heref.*

PETHUR. To run; to ram; to do anything quickly or in a hurry. *North.*

PETIT. Little. (*A.-N.*)

PETITION. An adjuration. *East.*

PETITORY. Petitionary.

PET-LIP. A hanging-lip. *North.*

PETMAN. The smallest pig in a litter. *East.*

PETREL. A breast-plate. *Kennett.*

PETROLL. A kind of chalky clay, mentioned in Florio, ed. 1611, p. 327.

PETRONEL. A kind of blunderbuss, or horse-pistol. *Sir Petronel Flash*, a boasting fellow, a braggadocio, Florio, p. 585.

> Give your scholler degrees, and your lawyer his fees,
> And some dice for *Sir Petronell Flash* :
> Give your courtier grace, and your knight a new case,
> And empty their purses of cash. *Brit. Bibl.* ii. 167.

PETTED. Indulged; spoilt. *Var. dial.*

PETTICOAT-HOLE. A small piece of ground in the parish of Stockton-in-the-Forest, co. York. It is subject to an ancient custom of providing a petticoat yearly for a poor woman of Stockton, selected by the owner of the land. See Reports on Charities, viii. 720.

PETTICOAT-PENSIONER. One kept by a woman for secret services or intrigues.

PETTIES. Low or mean grammar scholars.

PETTIGREW. A pedigree. "Petygrewe, genealogie," Palsgrave.

PETTISH. Passionate. *Var. dial.*

PETTLE. (1) To trifle. (2) Pettish; cross; peevish. *North.*

PETTOUNE. A spittoon.

> Tobacco by the fire was there caroused,
> With large *pettounes* in plase perfum'de and soused.
> *Scot's Certaine Pieces, &c.* 1616.

PETTYCOAT. A waistcoat. *Kent.*

PETTY-LASSERY. Petty larceny.

PETTY-SESSIONS. A kind of court held in some places at which servants are hired, and the engagements registered. *Norf.*

PETTY-SINGLES. The toes of a hawk.

PETUYSLY. Piteously; compassionately.

> Thai schul be schewed ful *petuysly*
> At domysday at Cristis cumyng,
> Ther God and mon present schal be,
> And al the world on fuyre brennyng.
> *MS. Douce 302, f. 1.*

PEUST. Snug; comfortable. *North.*

PEVRATE. A kind of sauce, formerly eaten with venison, veal, &c.

PEW. A cow's udder. *Glouc.*

PEW-FELLOW. A companion; one who sits in the same pew.

PEWKE. Puce colour. *Palsgrave.*

PEWTNER. A pewterer. *West.*

PEYL. (1) To weary. (2) To beat. *North.*

PEYNE. A plain or common.

> Upon a *peyne* befounde in the cité,
> Where he was borne withoute more delay.
> *Lydgate, MS. Ashm. 39, f. 49.*

PHÆBE. The name of a dance mentioned in an old nursery rhyme. A correspondent gives me the following lines of a very old song, the only ones he can recollect :

> Cannot you dance the Phæbe ?
> Don't you see what pains I take ;
> Don't you see how my shoulders shake ?
> Cannot you dance the Phæbe ?

PHANTASIED. Fancied.

> This wydow founde suche grace in the kynges eyes that he not only favoured her suyte, but muche more *phantasied* her person. *Hall, Edward IV. f. 5.*

PHARISEES. Fairies. *Sussex.*

PHAROAH. Strong ale. "Old Pharoh" is mentioned in the praise of Yorkshire Ale, 1697, p. 3.

PHAROS. A watch-tower. (*Gr.*) See Dekker's Knight's Conjuring, repr. p. 30.

PHASMATION. An apparition. (*Lat.*)

PHEERE. Companion. See *Fere* (1).

PHEEZE. To beat; to chastise; to humble. *West.* It occurs in Shakespeare and Ben Jonson. Forby has *pheezy*, fretful, irritable, which he supposes to be connected with this word. "To phease, i. e. to pay a person off for an injury," MS. Devon Gl.

PHETHELE. A girdle, or belt. (*A.-S.*)

> Off oon as I koude understonde,
> That bare a *phethele* in his hand.
> *MS. Cott. Tiber. A. vii. f 77.*

PHILANDERING. Making love.

PHILIP. The common hedge-sparrow, still termed. It occurs in Middleton's Works, iii.

PHILIP-AND-CHENEY. A kind of stuff, merly much esteemed. See Nares.

Alason, what would our silken mercers be ?
What could they doe, sweet hempseed, but for thee ?
Rash, taffata, paropa, and novato,
Shagge, fillisetta, damaske, and mockado,
No velvets piles, two piles, pile and halfe pile,
No plush or grograines could adorne this ile,
No cloth of silver, gold, or tisue here ;
Philip and Cheiny never would appeare.

Taylor's Workes, 1630, iii. 64.

PHILISTINES. A cant term applied to bailiffs, sheriffs' officers, and drunkards.

PHILOSOPHER'S-EGG. The name of a medicine for the pestilence, described in MS. Sloane 1592, f. 151.

PHILOSOPHER'S-GAME. An intricate game, played with men of three different forms, round, triangular, and square, on a board resembling two chess-boards united. See Strutt, pp. 314, 315.

PHIP. (1) A sparrow. The noise made by a sparrow, Lilly, ed. 1632, sig. Bb. x.

(2) To snap the fingers.

PHISNOMY. Physiognomy. *Palsgrave.*

PHITONESSE. A witch. (*Lat. Med.*)

PHIZ-GIG. A wizened old woman dressed extravagantly, or as they say here an old yow (i. e. ewe) dressed lamb-fashion. *Linc.*

PHRASE. " I shall soon larn the *phrases* of the house ;" that is, the habits of the family. *Cornw.*

PHUNKY. Land completely saturated by rain is said to be phunky. *Warw.*

PHY. (1)
The wyche my specyall Lord hath be,
And I his love and cause wyll *phy.*

Digby Mysteries, p. 113.

(2) An exclamation of disgust.

PIACLE. A heavy crime. (*Lat.*)

PIANOT. A magpie. *North.*

PICARO. A rogue. (*Span.*) *Picaroon* is, perhaps, the more usual form.

PICCADEL. Is thus described by Blount, " the round hem or the several divisions set together about the skirt of a garment or other thing ; also, a kind of stiff collar, made in fashion of a band. That famous ordinary near St. James's called *Pickadilly* took denomination from this, that one Higgins a taylor, who built it, got most of his estate by piccadilles, which in the last age were much in fashion," Glossographia, ed. 1681, p. 495. Minshen describes it as " a peece fastened about the top of the coller of a doublet," ed. 1627, p. 546, and Cotgrave, " the severall divisions or peeces fastened together about the brimme of the collar of a doublet." In Middleton, v. 171, the term is apparently to the implement used by the tailor in the making of the *piccadel.* See Mr. Cunningham's notes to Rich's Honestie of this Age, p. 74. The piccadel was made so that it could be taken off at the pleasure of the wearer.

And in her fashion she is likewise thus,
In every thing she must be monstrous ;
Her *picadell* above her crowne up beares,
Her fardingale is set above her eares.

Drayton's Poems, p. 235.

PICCHE. (1) To pick. (*A.-S.*)

(2) A pike. Nominale MS. f. 6.

(3) A bee-hive. *North.*

PICCHETTO. A game at cards.

PICHE. Pitch. Nominale MS.

He was black as any *pyche* and lothely on to loke,
All for-faren wyth the fyre stynk, and all of smoke.
Allas, gode fadur, seyde Wyllyam, be ye not amendyd 3yt ?
To see yow come in thys degré, nere-hande y lese my wytt.

MS. Cantab. Ff. ii. 38.

PICHED. Fastened ; situated. *Gawayne.*

PICIERE. A breast-piece for a horse.

PICK. (1) A pitchfork. *North.*

(2) To play at pitch-and-toss. *Linc.*

(3) To go forth from a place. *To pick a matter*, to pick a quarrel with any one. *Pick a thank*, to crouch for a favour. *Picks and hearts*, red spots on the body. *To turn a pick-pie*, to make a summerset.

(4) To fling or pitch ; to throw. " I holde a grote I pycke as farre with an arowe as you." Palsgrave. Compare Coriolanus, i. 1. In Lincolnshire, an animal that casts her young untimely is said to pick it.

(5) A spike ; the sharp point fixed in the centre of a buckler. " The pickes of painfull woe," Mirr. Mag. p. 74.

(6) A fork.

(7) To worm out a secret. *West.*

(8) To glean corn. *West.*

(9) An emetic. *North.* We have *pyke* in the same sense in Nominale MS. " Pykyd, or purgyd from fylth, or other thyng grevous," Pr. Parv. MS. Harl. 221.

(10) A diamond at cards. Grose says it means a spade.

(11) Thin ; delicate. *Linc.*

(12) A basket used for drawing coals up out of a pit. *Chesh.*

(13) To dress out finely.

(14) To pick up, i. e. to improve gradually in health. *Var. dial.*

PICK-A-BACK. To ride pick-a-back is to ride on the back and shoulders of another. *Var. dial.*

PICKATREE. The woodpecker. *North.*

PICK-CHEESE. The titmouse. *East.*

PICK-DARK. Quite, or pitch-dark. *North.*

PICKEARER. One who robs. (*Span.*)
The club *pickearer*, the robust churchwarden,
Of Lincolne's Inn back corner, where he angles
For cloaks and hats, and the smale game entangles.

Fletcher's Poems, p. 190.

PICKED. Finically smart in dress.

PICKEDEVANT. A beard cut to a sharp point in the middle under the chin.
Boy, oh ! disgrace to my person ! Sounes, boy,
Of your face ! You have many boyes with such
Pickadevaunts I am sure. *Taming of a Shrew*, p. 184.

PICKEER. To rob, or pillage. (*Span.*) Properly, to skirmish before a battle begins.
Ye. garrison wth some commons and the scotch horse *picquoring* a while close by the walls on the east, drew off, after they had failed in snapping Col. Graye's small regement of hors at Stanwick, with much ado gott into the towne without losse.

Tullie's Narrative of the Siege of Carlisle, p. 6.

PICKING-HOLE. A hole in a barn to receive sheaves of corn. *North.*

PICKLE. (1) To pick. *Var. dial.*

(2) To soak wheat. *West.*

(3) A small quantity. *North.*

(4) A mess; a confusion. Harrison seems to use the word in a like sense in his Desc. of of Britaine, p. 111. *To have a rod in pickle,* to have one ready for correcting a boy with.

(5) A mischievous boy. *Devon.*

(6) To glean a field. *East.*

(7) A hayfork. *Somerset.*

(8) To provide. *North.*

(9) To eat mincingly, or squeamishly.

PICKLE-HERRING. A merry-andrew.

PICKLING. (1) Providing. *North.*

(2) A sort of fine canvass used for sieves or covering safes. *Linc.*

PICK-NIGHT. Dismal; murky. *North.*

PICK-POINT. A children's game.

PICK-PURSE. Common spurrey. *Norf.*

PICKRELL. A small or young pike, properly the fish between a jack and a pike. It is the translation of *brocheton* in Hollyband's Dictionarie, 1593.

PICKSOME. Hungry; peckish. *Sussex.*

PICK-THANK. A flatterer. Still in use. The term was often applied to a talebearer.

The *pick-thank's* bannish'd the Ausonian gate ;
The lifes of princes from their gifts take date.
Fletcher's Poems, p. 127.

The *pickethanke,* a ship of great imployment, that commonly sayles out of sight or hearing, her lading being for the most part, private complaintes, whispering intelligences, and secret informations.
Taylor's Workes, 1630, i. 86.

PICK-TOOTH. A toothpick. This once fashionable instrument is said by Nares to have been sometimes carried in the hat.

A curious parke pal'd round about with *pick-tooth.*
Randolph's Amyntas, ii. 6.

PICK-UP. To vomit. *Yorksh.*

PICOISE. A kind of pick-axe. (*A.-N.*)

With *picoises,* mattoke, many a knyʒt
Felde the walles to grounde riʒt. *MS. Addit.*10036, f. 50.

PICT-HATCH. A notorious haunt of prostitutes in Clerkenwell.

Borrow'd and brought from loose Venetians,
Becoms *Pickt-hatch* and Shoreditch courtizans.
Du Bartas, p. 576.

These be your *Picke-hatch* curtezan wits that merit (as one jeasts upon them) after their decease to bee carted in Charles waine.
Optick Glasse of Humors, 1639, p. 89.

PICTREES. Ghosts. *North.*

PICTURE. Figure; a perfect pattern of a thing; e. g. " It's a *picter* of a horse," i. e. an excellent one; also used ironically, as " you are a pretty *picter,*" i. e. a strange figure.

PIDDLE. (1) To pick straws or do any light work. *Glouc.*

(2) To go about pretending to work, but doing little or nothing, as after illness; a man is said to go *piddling* about, though as yet unable to do much. *Suffolk.*

(3) Mingere. *Var. dial.*

(4) To eat mincingly or daintily.

PIE. (1) A receptacle for rape-seed. *Yorksh.*

(2) When potatoes are taken up out of the ground wherein they have grown, they are put, for the purpose of preserving them, into a pit or grave, and covered over with earth; they are then said to be in *pie* and to be *pied.* *Linc.*

(3) The Popish ordinal. See Blount, who was puzzled with the term.

(4) *To make a pie,* to combine in order to make money. *North.*

(5) A magpie. (*A.-N.*) Hence, a prating gossip, or telltale. *Wily pie,* a sly knave. " Howbeit in the English pale to this day they use to tearme a slie cousener a *wilie pie,*" Stanihurst's Descr. of Ireland, p. 13.

Then Pandare, lyke a wyly *pye,*
That cowld the matter handell,
Stept to the tabell by and by,
And forthe he blewe the candell.
Ballad of Troilus, c. 1580

I wylbe advysyd, he sayde,
The wynde ys wast that thow doyst blowe ;
I have anoder that most be payde,
Therfore the *pye* hathe pecked yow.
MS. Rawl. C. 258.

(6) The sum total; the entire quantity. Ord. and Reg. p. 227. Also, a list or roll. A " pye" of the names of bailiffs, 1 Edward VI. is preserved among the miscellaneous documents at the Rolls House, i. 140.

(7) The beam or pole that is erected to support the gin for loading and unloading timber. It is also called the *pie-tree.*

PIECE. (1) A cask, or vessel of wine.

(2) A whore. " This lewde crack'd abominable *peice,*" Strode's Floating Island, sig. E. i, meaning that she had the *lues venerea.*

(3) A little while. *North.*

(4) A field, or inclosure. *West.*

(5) *To fall in pieces,* parturio.

(6) The piece or double sovereign was worth twenty-two shillings.

(7) When potters sell their goods to the poor crate men they reckon them by the piece, i. e. quart or hollow ware, so that six pottle or three gallon bottles make a dozen or 12 pieces, and so more or less as of greater or less contents. The flat wares are also reckoned by pieces and dozens, but not (as the hollow) according to their contents, but their different breadths. *Staff.*

PIECE-OF-ENTIRE. A jolly fellow.

PIEFINCH. A chaffinch. *North.*

PIELES. Pills ?

Likewise if a man be sicke of the collicke, and drink three *pieles* thereof in sweet wine, it procureth him much ease; being decocted with hony and eaten every day, the quantity of a beane in desperate cases, mendeth ruptures in the bowels.
Topsell's Beasts, 1607, p. 276.

PIEPICKED. Piebald. *Devon.*

PIE-POUDRE-COURT. A summary court of justice formerly held at fairs.

PIERS. Handrails of a foot-bridge.

PIEUST. Comfortable. *Northumb.*

PIE-WIPE. The lapwing. *East.*

PIF. Pith. Nominale MS.

PIFLE. To steal, or pilfer. *North.* Also, to be squeamish or delicate.

PIG. (1) A woodlouse. *Var. dial.*

(2) Sixpence. A cant term.

(3) *To pig together*, to lie or sleep together two or more in a bed. *To buy a pig in a poke*, to purchase anything without seeing it. *Pig eyes*, very small eyes. *He can have boiled pig at home*, he is master of his own house. *Brandy is Latin for pig and goose*, an apology for drinking a dram after either. *To please the pigs*, (see *Pix.*) *To bring one's pigs to a fine market*, to be very unsuccessful. *He's like a pig, he'll do no good alive*, said of a selfish covetous man. *As happy as a pig in muck*, said of a contented person dirty in habit.

PIGACE. The meaning of the last line of the following passage may be best interpreted as a phrase implying superior excellence. I know not whether it has any connexion with the ordinary meaning of *pigace*, an ornament worn on the sleeve of a robe.

> If thou gafe Jogyllours of thi thinge,
> For to be in thaire prayssynge,
> Or thou made wrystlyng in place,
> That none ware haldyne to thi *pygace*.
>
> *R. de Brunne, MS. Bowes,* p. 36.

PIG-ALL. The whitethorn berry. *West.*

PIG-CHEER. All such edibles as are principally composed of pork ; such as raised pork-pies, sausages, spareribs, &c. These are sent as presents to friends and neighbours about Christmas time, when it is usual in this county to kill pigs by wholesale. *Linc.*

PIG-COTE. A pigsty. *West.*

PIG-EATER. A term of endearment.

PIGEON-HOLES. A game like our modern *bagatelle*, where there was a machine with arches for the balls to run through, resembling the cavities made for pigeons in a dove-house.

> Three-pence I lost at nine-pins ; but I got
> Six tokens towards that at *pigeon-holes.*
>
> *The Antipodes*, 1638.

> Ox roasted whole, horse-racing, *pigin-holes*,
> Great football matches, and a game at bowls.
>
> *Ballads on Frost Fair*, 1684, p. 29.

PIGEON-PAIR. Twins, when a boy and girl. It is believed by some that pigeons and doves always sit on two eggs, which produce a male and female chick, which live and love together their lives through.

PIGEONS. Sharpers who, during the drawing of the lottery, wait ready mounted near Guild-hall, and as soon as the first two or three numbers are drawn, which they receive from a confederate on a card, ride with them full speed to some distant insurance office, before fixed on, where there is another of the gang, commonly a decent-looking woman, who takes care to be at the office before the hour of drawing ; to her he secretly gives the number, which she insures for a considerable sum. *Grose.*

PIGEON'S-MILK. A scarce article, in search of which April fools are despatched.

PIGER. A pitcher. *Somerset.*

PIGGATORY. Great trouble. *Essex.*

PIGGINS. (1) Small wooden vessels made in the manner of half-barrels, and having one stave longer than the rest for a handle.

(2) The joists to which the flooring is fixed ; but more properly the pieces on which the boards of the lower floor are fixed. *Devon.*

PIGGLE. To root up potatoes with the hand. *Northamptonsh.*

PIGGY-WHIDDEN. The little white pig, the smallest of the veers. One is generally smaller than the rest, weak and white ; its whiteness denoting imbecility.

PIGHT. (1) Strength ; pith.

(2) The shoulder *pight* in horses is well described in Topsell's Four-Footed Beasts, 1607, p. 399, and in Dict. Rust.

(3) Placed ; pitched ; fixed.

> Sche had a lorde, a gentyll knyght,
> That loved wele hys God, the sothe to say ;
> The lady was in sorowe *pyght* ;
> Sche grevyd God, false was hur lay.
>
> *MS. Cantab.* Ff. ii. 38, f. 46.

> The king being therof advertised, with great diligence brought his army to Blacke Heath, and there *pight* his tentes. *Hall, Henry VI.* f. 81.

> At Covyntre that gentill prynce was trowblid mervelously,
> Wyth the scourge of God thus betyn was hee :
> Mete, dryncke, and logynge his pepull lackyd certaynly,
> Yett he *pight* his felde in placis thre
> To fyght with Warwicke and all his meny ;
> But he was affrayed, and his people also,
> In every thynge, Lorde, thy wille be doo !
>
> *MS. Bibl. Reg.* 17 D. xv.

PIGHTLE. A small meadow ; any small enclosed piece of land. *East.*

> Also I will that my feoffees in those my said lands, tenements, rents, services, wards, marriages, reliefs, escheats, *pighyts*, meadows, &c.
>
> *Test. Vetust.* p. 572.

PIG-HULL. A pigsty. *North.*

PIG-IRON. A flat piece of iron, which the cook interposes between the fire and meat roasting, when she wants to retard, or *put back* that operation. It is hung on the bars by a hook.

PIGLE. The herb shortwort.

PIG-LEAVES. The cotton thistle. *North.*

PIGLING. Trifling ; insignificant.

PIGNOLL. The pine-apple. *(Fr.)*

PIGNUTS. Earth-nuts. *North.*

PIG-POKER. A pig-driver. *Var. dial.*

PIG-RUNNING. A piece of game frequently practised at fairs, wakes, &c. A large pig, whose tail is cut short, and both soaped and greased, being turned out, is hunted by the young men and boys, and becomes the property of him who can catch and hold him by the tail, above the height of his head.

PIG-SCONCE. A dull heavy fellow.

PIGS-CROW. A pigsty. *Devon.*

PIGS-LOOSE. A pigsty. *West.*

PIGS-LOUSE. A woodlouse. *Somerset.*

PIGSNIE. A term of endearment, generally to a young girl. See the Tales of the Mad Men of Gotham, p. 19.

And here you may see I have
Even such an other,
Squeaking, gibbering, of everie degree.
The player fooles deare darling *pigenie*
He calles himselfe his brother,
Come of the verie same familie.
Tarlton's Horse-loads of Fooles.

PIGS-PARSNIP. Cow parsnip. *West.*

PIGS-SNOUT. A kind of caterpillar.
There is yct another catter-piller of yellow-blackish colour, called Porcellus, we may in English call it *pigges-snoute*, in respect of the fashion of the head, especially the greater sort of these, for the lesser have round white specks upon their sides, and these live and are altogether to be found amongst the leaves of the Marsh Trifolie, which they consume and devoure with an incredible celeritie.
Topsell's Serpents, 1608, p. 104.

PIGS-WHISPER. A very low whisper.

PIG-TAIL. The least candle, put in to make up weight. *Yorksh.*

PIG-TREE. A pigsty. *North.*

PIGWIGGEN. A dwarf. Drayton gives this name to one of his fairies.
What such a nazardly *pigwiggen*,
A little hand-strings, in a biggin.
Cotton's Works, 1734, p. 197.

PIHER. A gipsey; a tramp. *Sussex.*

PIK. Pitch. *North.*
Y se men come to shryfte so thykke
Of some here soules as blak as *pykke.*
MS. Harl. 1701, f. 83.

PIKAR. A little thief. *Prompt. Parv.*

PIK-AXE. The ace of spades. *West.*

PIKE. (1) A hayfork, especially a pitching-fork. *Glouc.* In Salop, a pickaxe is so called.
(2) The top of a hill.
Not far from Warminster is Clay-hill, and Corrip about a quarter of a mile there; they are *pikes* or vulcanos. *Aubrey's Wilts, Royal Soc. MS.* p. 71.
(3) To steal. (4) To peep. *Chaucer.*
(5) A large cock of hay. *North.*
(6) The crackowe or long-pointed shoe, which was introduced into England about 1384. See Vita Ricardi II. ed. Hearne, 1729, pp. 53, 126. "Pyke of a shoo," Pr. Parv.
(7) To pick. Nominale MS.
But ever, alas! I make my mone,
To se my sonnys hed as hit is here;
I *pyke* owt thornys be on and on,
For now liggus ded my dere son dere.
MS. Cantab. Ff. v. 48, f. 72.
Y *pyke* owt thornys by oon and oon.
MS. Cantab. Ff. ii. 38, f. 47.
(8) To run away. *Grose.*
(9) A staff. See Isumbras, 497.
Both *pyke* and palme, alles pilgram hym scholde.
Morte Arthure, MS. Lincoln, f. 90.
(10) To mark? (*A.-S.*)
And now y syng, and now y syke,
And thus my contynaunce y *pyke.*
Gower, MS. Cantab. Ff. i. 6, f. 4.
With the upcaste on hire he siketh,
And many a continaunce he *piketh.*
Gower, MS. Soc. Antiq. 134, f. 43.
For alle men on hym can *pyke,*
For he rode no nodur lyke.
MS. Cantab. Ff. ii. 38, f. 242.
(11) A turnpike. *Var. dial.*
(12) To cleanse. See *Pick* (9).

PIKED. Pointed. Thynne, p. 19.

PIKE-HARNEYS. Plunderers. (*A.-N.*)

PIKEL. A pitchfork; a hayfork. *North.*

PIKELED. Fine and small. *Hearne.*

PIKELET. A kind of crumpet; a thin circular tea-cake. *Var. dial.*

PIKE-OFF. Be gone! *East.*

PIKE-PENNY. A miser. *Prompt. Parv.*

PIKER. (1) A tramp. *East Sussex.*
(2) A small vessel, or fishing boat.

PIKES. Short butts which fill up the irregularity caused by hedges not running parallel.

PIKE-WALL. A wall built in a manner diverging to a point at its summit. *West.*
"Pykewall, *murus pyramidalis*," Pr. Parv.

PIK-IRON. The pointed end of an anvil.

PIKY. A gipsey. *Kent.*

PIL. A heavy club. *North.*

PILCH. An outer garment, generally worn in cold weather, and made of skins of fur. "*Pelicium*, a pylche," Nominale MS. The term is still retained in connected senses in our dialects. "A piece of flannel or other woollen put under a child next the clout is in Kent called a pilch; a coarse shagged piece of rug laid over a saddle for ease of a rider is in our midland parts called a pilch," MS. Lansd. 1033. "Warme *pilche* and warme shon," MS. Digby 86. In our old dramatists, the term is applied to a buff or leather jerkin, and Shakespeare has *pilcher* for the sheath of a sword.
Wha so may noghte do his dede, he salle to park,
Barefote withowttene schone, and ga with lyarde.
Take hym unto his *pilche,* and to his pater noster,
And pray for hym that may do, for he es bot a wastur.
MS. Lincoln A. i. 17, f. 148.
Thy vesture that thou shalt use ben these, a warme *pylche* for wynter, and oo kirtel, and oo cote for somer. *MS. Bodl.* 423, f. 182.

PILCROW. The mark ☞. "Pylcrafte yn a booke," Prompt. Parv. MS. Harl. 221.

PILE. (1) An arrow.
Thus he arrives unto these heroes sight,
His vesture pierc'd with *piles*, as oft in fight
He did such glorious markes receive from foes.
Howard's Brittish Princes, 1669, p. 11.
(2) Deeply involved. "In a *pile* of wrangle," i. e. deeply involved in the dispute.
(3) The side of a coin having no cross. See *Cross-and-Pile.*
(4) The head of an arrow.
(5) A small tower. *North.* See Harrison's Descr. of Britaine, p. 38.
(6) To break off the awns of barley with an iron. *Var. dial.*
(7) A blade of grass. *North.*
(8) A weight of anything.
(9) A kind of poker, with a large flat handle, used by bakers. A drawing of one is given in my copy of the Nominale MS. f. 21.
(10) To welt a coat. *Somerset.*

PILE-MOW. A wooden hammer used in fencing. *Lanc.*

PILF. Light grass and roots, raked together to be burnt. *Cornw.*

PILGER. A fish-spear. *East.* Most probably connected with *algere*, q. v.

PILGRIM-SALVE. An old ointment, made chiefly of swine's grease and isinglass.

PILIERS. Places on the downs interrupting their equable smooth surface, tufts of long grass, rushes, short furze, heath, &c. often matted together and often forming good cover for hares. *Cornw.*

PILIOL. Wild thyme. It is mentioned in a receipt in MS. Lincoln A. i. 17, f. 286.

PILL. (1) To steal; to spoil.

> Thou sal noght be tyrant til thaim, to *pills* thaime, and spoyle thaim, als the wicked princes dus.
> *MS. Coll. Eton.* 10, f. 5.

> Item he assembled certain Lancashire and Cheshire men to the entent to make warre on the foresaid lordes, and suffered them to robbe and *pill* without correction or reprefe. *Hall, Henry IV. f.7.*

(2) To peel. Dent's Pathway to Heaven, p. 20.

(3) The kernel of a nut; the rind green shell of fruit. "The huske or *pill* of a greene nut which blacketh ones fingers and hands," Hollyband's Dictionarie, 1593. "Pyll of hempe, *til*," Palsgrave.

(4) The refuse of a hawk's prey.

(5) A kind of pitcher. *South.*

(6) A small creek. *Heref.* "S. Caracs pill or creeke," Harrison, p. 61. The channels through which the drainings of the marshes enter the river are termed *pills.*

> From S. Juste *pills* or creke to S. Manditus creeke, is a mile dim.
> *Leland's Itinerary,* 1769, iii. 29.

(7) A rock. *Somerset.*

PILLAW. A sea dish, mentioned in the novel of Peregrine Pickle, cap. 9.

PILL-COAL. A kind of peat. *West.*

PILLED. Bald. "Pylled as one that wanteth heare, *pelks*," Palsgrave. A bad head when the hair comes off was also so called.

> The Sphinx or Sphinga is of the kinde of apes, having his body rough like apes, but his breast up to his necke, *pilde* and smooth without hayre: the face is very round yet sharp and piked, having the breasts of women, and their favor or visage much like them: in that part of their body which is bare without haire, there is a certaine red thing rising in a round circle like millet seed, which giveth great grace and comelinesse to their coulour, which in the middle parte is humaine. *Topsell's Beasts,* 1607.

> He behelde the body on grownde,
> Hyt stanke as a *pyllyd* hownde.
> *MS. Cantab. Ff. ii. 38, f. 192.*

PILLER. A robber. *Palsgrave.* One who committed depredations without indulging in a criminal act was also so called; a person who imposed, as an overcharging innkeeper.

PILLERDS. Barley. *Cornw.*

PILLET. A skin or hide. *Pr. Parv.*

PILLEWORTHIS. Pillows.

PILLIARD. A kind of cloak. (*A.-N.*)

PILLICOCK. The penis. It occurs very frequently in Florio, pp. 159, 382, 385, 409, 449, 454, &c. A man complaining of old age, in a poem of the beginning of the thirteenth century, says,—

> Y ne mai no more of love done,
> Mi *pilkoc* pisseth on mi schone.
> *Reliq. Antiq.* ii. 211.

The word also occurs in some lines in King Lear, iii. 4, which are still favorites in the nursery under a slightly varied form. See Collier's Shakespeare, vii. 427. It was likewise a term of endearment. "A prime-cocke, a *pillicocke*, a darlin, a beloved lad," Florio, p. 382. See also ibid. p. 554; Cotgrave, in v. *Turelureau, Vitault.*

PILLION. The head-dress of a priest or graduate. "Hic pilleus est ornamentum capitis sacerdotis vel graduati, Anglice a hure or a pyllyon," MS. Bibl. Reg. 12 B. i. f. 12. In the MS. Morte Arthure, f. 89, a king is represented as wearing a "pillione hatt."

PILLOWBERE. A pillow-case. "vij. pylloberys," inventory, MS. Cantab. Ff. i. 6, f. 58. Also called a *pillow-slip* or *pillow-tie.*

PILL-PATES. Shaven heads; friars.

PILM. Dust. *Devon.* Grose has *pillum.* Hence *pilmy,* dusty.

PILMER. Fine small rain. *Devon.*

PILRAG. A fallow field. *Sussex.*

PILT. Put; placed. (*A.-S.*)

> Now am y of my lande *pylte,*
> And that ye ryght that y so bee.
> *MS. Cantab. Ff. ii. 38, f. 242.*

> And ho so curseth withoutyn gylt,
> Hyt shal on hys hede be *pylt.*
> *MS. Harl. 1701, f. 9.*

PILWE. A pillow. (*A.-S.*) "Pulvinar, pylwe," MS. Lansd. 560, f. 45.

PIME. To peep about; to pry. *North.*

PIMENT. A favorite drink with our ancestors. The manner of making it is thus described in a MS. of the fifteenth century in Mr. Pettigrew's possession, "Take clowis, quibibus, maces, canel, galyngale, and make powdir therof, tempryng it with good wyne, and the thrid party hony, and clense hem thorow a clene klothe; also thou mayest make it with good ale."

> Ther was *piment* and claré,
> To heighe lordinges and to meyné.
> *Arthour and Merlin,* p. 116.

> Hyt was y-do without lette,
> The cloth was spred, the bord was sette,
> They wente to hare sopere.
> Mete and drynk they hadde afyn,
> *Pyement,* claré, and Reynysch wyn,
> And elles greet wondyr hyt wer.
> *Illustrations of Fairy Mythology,* p. 13.

> And saf him souke of the *pyment* soote.
> *Lydgate, MS. Soc. Antiq.* 134, f. 9.

> And yafe hym sauke of the *pyment* sote,
> That sponge and grewe oute of the holy rote.
> *Lydgate, MS. Ashmole* 39, f. 53.

> Malmasyes, Tires, and Rumneys,
> With Caperikis, Campletes, and Osneys,
> Vernuge, Cute, and Raspays also,
> Whippet and Pyngmedo, that ben lawyers therto;
> And I will have also wyne de Ryne,
> With new maid Clarye, that is good and fyne,
> Muscadell, Terantyne, and Bastard,
> With Ypocras and *Pyment* comyng afterwarde.
> *MS. Rawl. C. 86.*

PIMENTARIE. Balm. *Gerard.*

PIMGENET. A small red pimple. "Nine *pimgenets* make a pock royal," Old Saying.

PIMPING. Little ; pitiful. *West.*

PIMPLE. The head. *Var. dial.*

PIN. (1) A disease in hawks.

(2) The hip. *Somerset.*

(3) *On the pin*, on the *qui vive.* In a merry pin, i. e. a merry humour, half intoxicated.

(4) A small peg of wood.

> Hit was so clene y-take away withinne on nyȝt,
> That there was never a *pynne* stondyng ther.
> *Chron. Vilodun.* p. 117.

(5) To do a thing in haste. *Lanc.*

PIN-AND-WEB. A kind of excrescence in the ball of the eye.

> Untill some quack-salver or other can picke out that *pin and webbe* which is stucke into both his eyes. *A Knight's Conjuring,* 1607.

> For a *pin or web* in the eye. Take two or three lice out of ones head, and put them alive into the eye that is grieved, and so close it up, and most assuredly the lice will suck out the web in the eye, and will cure it, and come forth without any hurt. *The Countess of Kent's Choice Manual,* ed. 1676, p. 75.

PINAUNTE. A penitent. (*A.-N.*)

> Thys maketh me to drowpe and dare,
> That y am lyke a pore *pynaunte.*
> *MS. Cantab.* Ff. ii. 38, f. 21.

PIN-BASKET. The youngest child of a family ; often the weakest and smallest.

PIN-BONE. The hip-bone. *West.*

PINBOUK. A jar, or earthen vessel.

PIN-CASE. A pincushion. *North.*

PINCH. (1) To be niggardly. *Var. dial.*

(2) To plait linen.

> Thus leud men that can sey,
> He is an honest prest in good faye,
> ȝif his goune be *pynchit* gay.
> *MS. Douce* 302, f. 5.

(3) The game of pitch-halfpenny, or pitch-and-hustle. *North.*

(4) "I pynche courtaysye as one doth that is nyce of condyscions, *je fays le nyce,*" Palsgrave.

PINCH-BECK. A miserly fellow. Huloet, 1552. *Pinchvart,* Devon. Gloss. *Pinch-gut* is very common, and *pinch-penny* occurs in Hollyband's Dictionarie, 1593, as the translation of *chiche.*

PINCHEM. A tom-tit. *Beds.*

PINCHER. A niggard. Still in use.

PINCHERWIG. An earwig. *South.*

PIN-CLOTH. A pinafore. *Somerset.*

PINCOD. A pincushion. *North.*

PINCURTLE. A pinafore. *Devon.*

PINCUSHION. The sweet scabious. *East.*

PIND. (1) To impound an animal.

> Weddes to take and bestes to *pynd,*
> That was hym not commyn of kynd.
> *MS. Ashmole* 61, f. 3.

(2) Tainted, mouldy, said of meat. A saw which has lost its pliancy from being over-bent is said to be pind, or pinny. *West.*

PINDER. The petty officer of a manor whose duty it was to impound all strange cattle straying upon the common. "*Inclusor,* a pynder," Nominale MS.

> In Wakefield there lives a jolly *pinder,*
> In Wakefield all on a green. *Robin Hood,* ii. 16

PINE. (1) Pain ; grief. (*A.-S.*) Still in use, according to MS. Lansd. 1033.

> But sone aftur come tythynges,
> Marrok mett hys lorde kynge,
> And faste he can hym frayne.
> Syr, he seyde, for Goddys *pyne,*
> Of a thyng that now ys ynne
> Whareof be ye so fayne ?
> *MS. Cantab.* Ff. ii. 38, f. 72.

> Thei goo aboute be viij. or nyne,
> And done the husbondes myculle *pyne.*
> *MS. Cantab.* Ff. v. 48, f. 48.

> Hwo haveth helle dure unloke,
> That thu art of *pyne* i-broke.
> *MS. Coll. Jes. Oxon.* I. 29.

(2) To torment ; to torture. (*A.-S.*) In use in the provinces in the sense to starve with cold or hunger. *Pined,* reduced by hunger.

(3) The end. *Somerset.*

(4) Difficult ; hard. *North.*

(5) To inclose, or shut up.

> Moné men of holé cherche thai ben al to lewd,
> I lekyn ham to a bred is *pynud* in a cage ;
> When he hath shertly hymselfe al be-scherewd,
> Then he begynnys to daunce, to harpe, and to rage.
> *MS. Douce* 302, f. 5.

PINER. A pioneer. (*Fr.*)

PINFALLOW. Winter fallow. *North.*

PINFOLDS. Pounds for cattle. Palsgrave has this word, " I pounde I put horse or beestes in the pynfolde." *Inclusorium,* a pynfold. Nominale MS.

PING. (1) To push. *West.*

(2) A kind of sweet wine.

PINGE. To prick. See *Ping* (1).

> He *pingde* his stede with spores kene,
> And smot a strok that was sene.
> *Romance of Otuel,* p. 55.

PINGLE. (1) A small inclosure, generally one long and narrow. *North.*

(2) To eat with very little appetite. Sharp's MS. Warw. Gl. Nash uses the word.

(3) To labour very hard, without a corresponding progress. *North.*

PINGLER. Generally from *Pingle* (2), as in the following passage. It was also a term of contempt, applied to any small inferior person or animal.

> For this little beast is not afraide to leape into the hunters face, although it can doe no great harme, either with teeth or nailes. It is an argument that it is exceeding hot, because it is so bold and eager. In the uppermost chap, it hath long and sharp teeth, growing two by two. It hath large and wide cheekes, which they alwaies fill, both carrying in, and carrying out, they eate with both, whereupon a devouring fellow, such a one as Stasimus a servant to Plautus was, is called Crycetus, a hamster, because he filleth his mouth well, and if no *pingler* at his meate.
> *Topsell's Beasts,* 1607, p 536

PINGMEDO. A kind of wine.

PINGOT. A small croft. *Lanc.*

PINGSWIG. A scarecrow. *Yorksh.*

PIN-HEAD. Not worth a pin-head, i. e. of very little value indeed.

PINIKIN. Delicate. *West.*

PINING-STOOL. A stool of punishment; a cucking-stool. (*A.-S.*)

PINION. The skirt of a gown.

PINIONS. Refuse wool. *Somerset.*

PINIOUS. Of a weak appetite. *North.*

PINK. (1) To dye a pink colour.

(2) A kind of linnet. *Linc.* In some counties, the chaffinch is so termed.

(3) A stab. Also, to stab. *Grose.*

(4) A minnow. Still in use.

(5) A kind of small vessel. It occurs in the Merry Wives of Windsor, ii. 2. *Pinksterm*, a very narrow boat used on the Severn.

(6) Small. *Pinky, pinky-winky*, very small, excessively small; also, peeping with small pink eyes. *North.*

(7) To peep slily. *North.* Hence *pinker*, to half shut the eyes. *Pinking*, winking, Harrison's England, p. 170.

(8) A game at cards, the same as Post and Pair. See MS. Egerton 923, f. 49; Collier's Hist. Dram. Poet. ii. 315.

(9) A pinch. "Aye pynckes is your paye," Chester Plays, i. 126. *North.*

(10) To deck; to adorn. *Somerset.*

PINKER. A robber, or ruffian; a cutter. "So many pinkers," Collier's Old Ballads, p. 6. It is left unexplained in Skelton, ii. 203. "*Eschiffeur*, a cutter or pinker," Cotgrave.

PINK-EYED. Small eyed. *Pinkany*, pink-eye, which is often a term of endearment, as in the Two Angrie Women of Abington, p. 68. Pinckan-ey'd, Soliman and Perseda, p. 274.

PINKING. Poorly; unwell. *Dorset.*

PINKNEEDLE. The herb shepherd's-bodkin.

PINNACE. A small vessel. Shakespeare apparently applies the term to a person of bad character, a panderer, or go-between, several instances of which use may be supplied, though not noticed by the commentators.

Hold, sirrah, bear you these letters tightly;
Sail like my *pinnace* to these golden shores.
Merry Wives of Windsor, i. 3.

For when all the gallants are gone out o' th' town,
O then these fine *pinaces* lack their due lading.
Songs of the London Prentices, p. 66.

PINNE. To bolt a door. (*A.-S.*)

PINNER. A narrow piece of cloth which went round a woman's gown at the top near the neck. "Pinners, the upper parts of a lady's head-dress were in fashion," MS. Devon Glossary.

PINNING. The low masonry which supports a frame of stud-work. Ground pinning or under-pinning is the masonry which supports the wooden frame-work of a building, and keeps it above the ground.

PINNOCK. (1) The hedge-sparrow. "A pinnocke or hedge sparrowe which bringeth up the cuckoes birds insteed of her owne," Withals' Dictionarie, ed. 1608, p. 22.

Thus in the *pinnick's* nest the cuckoo lays,
Then, easy as a Frenchman, takes her flight.
Peter Pindar, i. 416.

(2) *To bring pinnock to pannock*, to bring something to nothing, to destroy. ' Brynge somethynge to nothynge, as the vulgare speache is, to brynge pynnock to pannock," Huloet, 1552.

(3) A brick or wooden tunnel placed under a road to carry off the water. *Sussex.*

PINNOCKS. Fine clothes. *Salop.*

PINNOLD. A small bridge. *Sussex.*

PINNONADE. A confection made chiefly of almonds and pines, and hence the name. See the Forme of Cury, p. 31.

PINNOTE-TREE. The round-leaved vine. (*A.-N.*) *Pynote*, MS. Bibl. Reg. 12 B. i.

PIN-OF-THE-THROAT. The uvula.

PIN-PANNIERLY-FELLOW. A covetous fellow. "A pin-pennieble fellow, a covetous miser that pins up his baskets or panniers, or that thinks the loss of a pin to be a pain and trouble to him," Kennett, MS.

PIN-PATCHES. Periwinkles. *East.*

PIN-PILLOW. A pincushion. *Palsgrave.* Cotgrave has, "*Espinglier*, a *pin-pillow* or cushinet to sticke pinnes on."

PINS. Legs. *Var. dial.*

PINSONS. (1) A pair of pincers. *Palsgrave.* Still in use in the Western counties.

And this Pliny affirmeth to be proper to this insect, to have a sting in the tayle and to have armes; for by armes hee meaneth the two crosse forkes or tonges which come from it one both sides, in the toppes whereof are little thinges like *pynsons*, to detaine and hold fast, that which it apprehendeth, whiles it woundeth with the sting in the tayle.
Topsell's Historie of Serpents, 1608, p. 224.

(2) Thin-soled shoes. "*Calceolus*, pinsone," Nominale MS. Compare MS. Arundel 249, f. 88. "Pynson sho, *caffignon*," Palsgrave. The copy of Palsgrave belonging to the Cambridge public library has " or socke" written by a contemporary hand. "*Soccatus*, that weareth stertups or pinsons," Elyot, ed. 1559. See Ord. and Reg. p. 124.

PINSWEAL. A boil. *Dorset.*

PINT. To drink a pint of ale.

PINTLE. Mentula. There is a receipt " for bolnyng of *pyntelys*" in MS. Sloane 2584, p. 50.

For sore *pyntulles*. Take lynschede, and stampe smale, and than temper it with swete mylke, and than sethe theme together, and than therof make a plaster, and ley to, and anoynte it with the joste of morell til he be whole. *MS. Med. Rec.* xv. Cent.

PINTLEDY-PANTLEDY. Pit-a-pat. *Linc.*

PIN-WING. The pinion of a fowl.

PINY. The piony. *Var. dial.*

Using such cunning as they did dispose
The ruddy *piny* with the lighter rose.
Browne's Britannia's Pastorals, ii. 82.

PIOL. A kind of lace. The method of making it is described in a very curious tract on laces of the fifteenth century, MS. Harl. 2320, f. 59.

PIONES. The seeds of the piony, which were formerly used as a spice. (*A.-N.*)

PIOT. A magpie. *North.*

PIOTTY. Variously coloured. *Yorksh.*

PIP. (1) A single blossom. *Warw.* Also, a small seed, any diminutive object.

(2) The lues venerea. *South.*

(3) Anger; offence. *Exmoor.*

PIPE. (1) A beer cask. *North.* Pipe-staves, staves for a cask, Florio, p. 159.

(2) A charge of powder, or shot, which was formerly measured in the bowl of a pipe.

(3) A small ravine or dingle breaking out from a larger one. *Chesh.*

(4) A large round cell in a beehive used by the queen bee. *West.*

(5) To cry. A cant term. From *pipe*, the throat, or voice; the windpipe. *Piping*, wheezing, Exmoor Dial. p. 7.

PIPE-DRINK. Sparkling weak ale, in great estimation by pipe-smokers. *West.*

PIPER. An innkeeper. *Devon.*

PIPERE. The lilac tree. Urry, p. 415, l. 178.

The boxtre, *pipere*, holye for whippes to lasche.
MS. Cantab. Ff. i. 6, f. 25.

PIPE-STOPPEL. A tobacco-stopper. *North.*

PIPIN. The windpipe. Nominale MS.

PIPING. (1) The noise made by bees preparatory to swarming. *North.*

(2) The cry of young birds. Hence, metaphorically, said of anything innocent or harmless.

PIPING-HOT. Very hot. *Palsgrave.*

Piping hot, smoking hot !
What have I got ?
You have not ;
Hot grey pease, hot ! hot ! hot ! London Cries, p. 12.

PIPION. A young crane. " Cranes whyche be yonge called pipions," Huloet, 1552.

PIPLE. To pipe. *Skelton.*

PIPLIN. A poplar tree. *Somerset.* Called a *pipple* in some counties.

PIPPERIDGE. The barberry tree. *East.*

PIPPIN. A pipkin. *Linc.*

PIRAMIS. A pyramid. *Drayton.*

PIRE. A pear tree. (*A.-N.*)

Of good *piré* com gode perus,
Werse tre wers fruyt berus.
Cursor Mundi, MS. Coll. Trin. Cantab. f. 1

PIRIE. A storm of wind. *Palsgrave.*

For sodainly there rose a straunge storme and a quicke *pirie*, so mischevous and so pernicious, that nothinge more execrable, or more to be abhorred, could happen in any Christian region.
Hall, Henry VI. f. 55.

PIRL. To spin as a top; to wind wire of gold or silver. *West.* Pirling-wheel, a spinning-wheel in a clock.

PIRLE. A brook, or stream.

A broket or *pirle* of water renning out of an hille nere the toun and cumming thorough a peace of the toun withyn the walle.
Leland's Itinerary, 1769, iii. 132.

PIRLED. Flat. *Devon.*

PIRLY. Small and round. *Northumb.*

PIRN. A piece of wood turned to wind thread on. A stick with a loop of cord for twisting on the nose of refractory horses. *North.* " Pyrne or webstars lome, *mestier à tisser,*" Palsgrave, 1530.

PIRNED. Dried up; pined. *Cumb.*

PIROPES. A stone of a red colour.

PIRTLE. To slaver at the mouth.

Now I *pirtle*, I pofte, I poute,
I snurpe, I snobbe, I snelpe on snoute.
Reliq. Antiq. ii. 211.

PIRTY. Pretty. *Var. dial.*

PISCINE. A shallow stone basin generally placed in a niche in old churches and furnished with an outlet for the water in which the priest washed his hands, &c.

PISHTY. A call used to a dog.

PISNET. A pump or slipper. *Holme.*

PISPER. To make mischief. *Devon.*

PISSABED. The dandelion.

PISSANNAT. The common ant. *Salop.*

PISSING-CANDLE. The least candle in a pound, put in to make up weight.

PISSING-CONDUIT. The name of a small conduit situated near the Royal Exchange, and said to have been so termed from its running a small stream.

PISSING-WHILE. " But a pyssynge whyle, *tant quon auroyt pissé*, or *ce pendent,*" Palsgrave. The phrase occurs in Shakespeare.

PISSMOTE. Ants, or pismires. *West.*

PIST. Hist ! An exclamation.

PISTEL. A wild disorderly fellow.

PISTELL. An epistle. (*Lat.*) *Pisteller*, one who reads or sings the epistle. Palsgrave, however, has, " pysteller that syngeth the masse." It occurs in Nominale MS.

PISTER. To whisper. *Exmoor.*

PISTOL. A swaggering fellow. Perhaps from *pistolfo*, explained by Florio, " a roguing begger, a cantler, an upright man that liveth by cosenage." Hence Shakespeare's character of that name.

PISTOLET. Meant both a Spanish pistole, and a small pistol.

One would move love by rythmes ; but witchcrafts charms,
Bring not now their old fears, nor their old harms.
Rams and slings now are silly battery,
Pistolets are the best artillery. *Donne's Poems*, p. 122.

PISTURE.

My fires have driven, thine have drawn it hence ;
And I am rob'd of *pisture*, heart, and sense.
Dwells with me still mine irksome memory,
Which both to keep and lose grieves equally.
Donne's Poems, p. 196.

PIT. (1) A spot, or mark. (2) To match.

PITAILE. Foot-soldiers. (*A.-N.*)

PITANCE. A mess of victuals. (*A.-N.*) *Pitancer*, one who gave out provisions.

PITCH. (1) A skin of fur.

(2) Weight or momentum. *Var. dial.* It occurs in Holinshed, Conq. Ireland, p. 60.

(3) The height to which a hawk soars before stooping on its prey.

(4) The quantity taken up at one time on a hay-fork. *West.* Also, to load hay or straw.

(5) To sit down. *Var. dial.*

(6) An iron crow-bar with a thick square point for making holes in the ground. Hence to pitch, to make holes in the ground for hurdles, &c.

(7) *Pitch and pay*, throw down your money at once, pay ready money.

(8) To pave roughly. *South.*

(9) *Pitch in*, to set to work ; to beat or thrash a person.

(10) The point of the shoulder.

This is when the shoulder point or *pitch* of the shoulder is displaced, which *griefe* is called of the Italians *spallato*, and it cometh by reason of some great fal forward rush or straine. The signes be these. That shoulder point wil sticke out further then his fellow, and the horse will halt right downe. *Topsell's Four-Footed Beasts*, 1607.

(11) To fall away, or decline, as to lose flesh in sickness. *Somerset.* A liquid is said to *pitch* when it stands, and a sediment takes place at the bottom of the vessel.

PITCH-AND-HUSTLE. Chuck-farthing. The game of *pitch-and-toss* is very common, being merely the throwing up of halfpence, the result depending on a guess of heads or tails.

PITCHATS. Broken glass, china, &c.

PITCHED-AWAY. Emaciated. *Devon.*

PITCHED-MARKET. One in which corn is brought and sold by the sack, not by the sample.

PITCHER. (1) A pollard willow. *West.*

(2) The man who lifts or pitches the reaped corn or hay up on to the waggon. His work is of course called *pitchen*, his implement a *pitch-fork*. Those who unload the waggons on to the stack, or goof, are called *impitchers*.

(3) A fierce mastiff. *Yorksh.*

PITCHING. Precipitation. It is used in its chemical sense. *West.*

PITCHING-AXE. A large axe used chiefly in felling timber. *Salop.*

PITCHING-NET. A large triangular net attached to two poles, and used with a boat chiefly for the purpose of catching salmon.

PITCHING-PENCE. Pence formerly paid in fairs and markets for every bag of corn. Brand, ii. 271.

PITCHING-PRONG. A pitchfork. *South.*

PITCHING-STONES. Round stones used instead of paving. *I. of Wight.*

PITCH-POLE. To make a thing pitch-pole is to make it fetch double what you gave for it. *Oxon.*

PITCH-UP. To stop. *I. of Wight.*

PIT-COUNTER. A game played by boys, who roll counters in a small hole. The exact description I have not the means of giving.

PIT-FALL. A peculiar kind of trap set in the ground for catching small birds.

PITH. (1) A crumb of bread. *Devon.*

(2) Force; strength; might. (*A.-S.*) Still in use, according to Moor. " Pyththy, of great substance, *substancieux* ; pyththy, stronge, *puissant*," Palsgrave.

Thay called Percevelle the wight,
The kyng doubbed hym to knyghte ;
Thofe he couthe littille in sighte,
The childe was of *pith*. *Percevael*, 1640.

PITHER. To dig lightly; to throw earth up very gently. *Kent.*

PITHEST. Pitiful. *Devon.*

PIT-HOLE. A grave. *Var. dial.*

PITISANQUINT. Pretty well. *Somerset.*

PITMAN'S-PINK. The single pink. *Newc.*

PITOUS. Merciful; compassionate; exciting compassion. *Chaucer.*

PIT-SAW. A large saw used in pits for cutting a tree into planks. *Var. dial.*

PIT-STEAD. A place where there has been a pit. *Chesh.*

PITTER. (1) To grieve. (2) To squeak. *East.* The second meaning is an archaism.

PITTER-PATTER. To go pit-a-pat ; to beat incessantly ; to palpitate. *North.*

PITTHER. To fidget about. *West.*

PITY. " It were pity on my life," it would indeed be a pity.

For if I should as lion come in strife
Into this place, 'twere *pity on my life*. *A Mids. Night's Dream*, v. 1

And should I not pay your civility
To th' utmost of my poor ability,
Who art groat Jove's sister and wife,
It were e'en *pity of my life*.
Cotton's Poetical Works, 1734, p. 7

PITYFULL. Compassionate. *Palsgrave.*

PIX. (1) To glean orchards. *West.*

(2) The box or shrine in which the consecrated wafers were kept. Hence is said to be derived the phrase *please the pigs*.

(3) A name given to the custom of the goldsmiths of London making a trial of the public coin by weighing it before the privy council. See a long paper by Mr. Black in the Journal of the British Archæological Association, i. 128, and Blount's Gloss.

PIXLIQUID. A kind of oil.

PIXY. A fairy. The term is not obsolete, and like *fairy*, is common in composition. *Pixy-puff*, a broad species of fungus. *Pixy-rings*, the fairy circles. *Pixy-seats*, the entangled knots in horses' manes. *Pixy-stool*, the toadstool. " Pyxie-led, to be in a maze, to be bewilder'd, as if led out of the way by hobgoblin, or puck, or one of the fairies ; the cure is to turn one of your garments the inside outward, which gives a person time to recollect himself : the way to prevent it, some say, is for a woman to turn her cap inside outward, that the pyxies may have no power over her, and for a man to do the same with some of his clothes," MS. Devon Gl.

Thee *pixie-led* in Popish piety,
Who mak'st thyself the triple crowns base drudge.
Clobery's Divine Glimpses, 1659, p. 73.

PIZE. (1) Fretful; peevish. *West.*

(2) A kind of oath. " What the pize ails them," Whiter's Specimen, 1794, p. 19.

PIȜT. Placed; reared.

He led hym forth upon that pleyne,
He was war of a pynapulle *piȝt* :
Sechan had he never seyne,
Off clothes of gold burnysshed briȝt.
MS. Cantab. Ff. v. 48, f. 69.

PLACARD. (1) A man's stomacher, which was frequently adorned with jewels ; a kind of breast-plate.

Some had the helme, the visere, the two baviers and the two *plackardes* of the same curiously graven and conningly costed.
Hall, Henry IV. f. 12.

(2) A printed sheet, folded so as to form a little quarto book.

PLACE. (1) A house, or residence. (2) A barton. (3) A jakes. *Var. dial.*

(4) The pitch of a hawk or other bird of prey. See Macbeth, ii. 4.

PLACEAN. Places. *Leic.*

PLACEBO. To sing placebo, i. e. to endeavour to curry favour.

PLACIDIOUS. Gentle; placid.

> There was never any thing more strange in the nature of dogs, then that which hapned at Rhodes besieged by the Turke, for the dogges did there descerne betwixt Christians and Turkes; for toward the Turkes they were most eager, furious, and unappeasable, but towards Christians, although unknowne, most easie, peaceable, and *placidious.*
>
> *Topsell's Four-Footed Beasts,* 1607, p. 158.

PLACINACION. Satisfaction; atonement. This word occurs in a curious macaronic poem, of which there are copies in MSS. Harl. 536 and 941, and a fragment in MS. Harl. 218, f. 32. (*Lat. Med.*)

PLACING. Going out to service. *North.*

PLACK. (1) A piece of money. *Cumb.*

(2) A portion or piece of anything, a piece of ground, a portion of labour, &c. *West.*

PLACKET. A woman's pocket. Still used in this sense, according to Forby, ii. 255. It was metaphorically applied to the female pudendum; and the penis was termed the *placket-racket.* This word has been so much misunderstood that I am compelled to be somewhat plain in defining it. Grose has *placket-hole,* a pocket-hole. Nares, Dyce, and other writers, tell us a *placket* generally signifies a petticoat, but their quotations do not bear out this opinion. According to Moor, the term is in some places applied to a shift.

> Deliro playing at a game of racket,
> Far put his hand into Florinda's *placket;*
> Keep hold, said shee, nor any further go,
> Said he, just so, the *placket* well will do.
>
> *Select Collection of Epigrams,* 1663.

PLAD. Played. *Somerset.*

PLADDE. Pleaded.

> And long for hit forsothe he *pladde.*
>
> *Chron. Vilodun.* p. 108.

PLAGES. The divisions of the globe.

PLAGGIS. Cowslips. Arch. xxx. 411.

PLAGUY. Very. *Var. dial.*

PLAIFAIER. A playfellow.

> In so muche that for imprisonmente of one of his wanton mates and unthriftie *plaifaiers* he strake the chiefe justice with his fiste on the face.
>
> *Hall's Union, Henry V.* f. 1.
>
> He left the conseyle of theise olde wyse menys, and dede after the consel of chyldrin that weryn his *pleyforyn.*
>
> *Wimbolton's Sermon,* 1388, *MS. Hatton,* 57, p. 11.

PLAIN. (1) Middling. *Dorset.* "How's your wife to day." "Oh, very *plain,* thankee, sir."

(2) To complain. *North.*

(3) An open space surrounded by houses nearly answering to the Italian Piazza. In the city of Norwich there are several: as St. Mary's *Plain,* the Theatre *Plain,* &c.

(4) A field. *Palsgrave.*

(5) Simple; clear. Also, clearly.

> Lorde, the unkyndnes was shewld to kynge Edward that day,
> At his londyng in Holdyrnes he had grett payne;
> His subjectes and people wolde not hym obey.
> Off hym and his people thay had grett disdayn;
> There schewed hym unkyndnes and answerid hym *playne,*
> As for kynge he shulde not londe there for wele ne woo;
> Yett londid that gentill prynce, the will of God was soo!
>
> *MS. Bibl. Reg.* 17 D. xv.

(6) Play; sport. *Weber.*

(7) A kind of flannel.

PLAIN-DEALING. A game at cards.

PLAIN-SONG. Simple melody.

> Our life is a *plain-song* with cunning pen'd,
> Whose highest pitch in lowest base doth end.
>
> *The Return from Parnassus,* p. 277.

PLAINT. A complaint.

> How miserable's he who in his mind
> A mutiny against himself must find!
> Justly this Spirit doth our *plaints* provoke,
> So insupportable that makes our yoak;
> That presseth our assent above the skie,
> Though we are made of earth, and cannot flie.
>
> *MS. Poems,* xvii. Cent.
>
> From the zeale of old Harry lock'd up with a whore,
> From waiting with *plaints* at the Parliament dore,
> From the death of a King without why or wherefore.
>
> *Fletcher's Poems,* p. 134.

PLAISE-MOUTHED. Small mouthed, like a plaice; and hence metaphorically used for primness or affectation.

PLAIT. A kind of small ship. Blount calls it "a hoy or water vessel."

PLANCH. To plash hedges. *Staff.*

PLANCHED. Boarded. *Dorset.* It is also an archaism. *Planchen,* boards. *Devon.* "Plancher made of bordes, *planché,*" Palsgrave. Forby has *plancher,* a boarded floor; and Palmer gives *planches,* the planks of a flooring.

> The goodwife, that before had provided for afterclaps, had found out a privie place between two seelings of a *plauncher,* and there she thrust Lionello, and her husband came sweting. What news, quoth shee, drives you home againe so soone, husband? Marrye, sweet wife, quoth he, a fearfull dreame that I had this night, which came to my remembrance.
>
> *Tarlton's Newes out of Purgatorie,* p. 100.

PLANCHER. A plate. *Norf.*

PLANE. The shaft of a crossbow.

PLANET. Climate. *North.*

PLANETS. Rain falls *in planets,* when it falls partially and with violence. *North.* Forby has the phrase *by planets,* capriciously, irregularly, changeably.

PLANET-STRUCK. Paralytic. *Linc.* This phrase appears to have been formerly in use for any sudden and violent attack not known by a familiar appellation. "A blasting or planetstreeking," Florio, p. 44. According to Markham, horses are said to be planet-struck when there is a deprivation of feeling or motion, not stirring any of the members, but that they remain in the same form as when the beast was first struck. It comes to a horse sometimes by choler and phlegm superabundantly mixed together; sometimes from melancholy blood, being a cold and dry humour, which annoys the hinder part of the brain; sometimes of extraordinary heat or cold, or raw digestion striking into the veins suddenly; or lastly, from extreme hunger, occasioned by long fasting.

PLANISH. To cover anything, as a table, room, &c. with all sorts of articles untidily placed; as, when children have been playing together and a room is heaped up with their playthings. (Qu. from Plenish for Replenish?) *Linc.*

PLANT. (1) An aim. *Middx.*

(2) A club, or cudgel. *Var. dial.*

(3) The foot. See Jonson, vii. 194. *To water one's plants,* to shed tears.

PLANTING. A plantation. *East.*

PLASAD. In a fine condition. *Exmoor.*

PLASE. A palace. *Spenser.*

Ho ys more worthy wlthyn my *plase* ?
Mystryst the never, man, for thy mysdede.
Pieces of Ancient Poetry, p. 43.

PLASH. (1) To lower and narrow a broad-spread hedge by partially cutting off the branches, and entwining them with those left upright. A rod cut half through, and bent down, is termed a plash.

(2) A pool of water; a large puddle, " *Lacuna,* a playche of water," Nominale MS.

Betwyx a *plasche* and a flode appone a flate lawnde.
Morte Arthurs, MS. Lincoln, f. 83.
Roares, rages, foames, against a mountaine dashes,
And in recoile makes meadowes standing *plashes.*
Browne's Britannia's Pastorals, p. 53.
If thu drynke the halfe, thu shalt fynde it no scoff:
Of terryble deathe thu wylt stacker in the *plashes.*
Bale's Kynge Johan, p. 78.
At length, comming to a broad *plash* of water and mud, which could not be avoyded, I fetcht a rise, yet fell in over the anckles at the further end.
Kemp's Nine Daies Wonder, 1600.

PLASHY. " Plashy waies, wet under foot; to plash in the dirt, all plash'd, made wet and dirty; to plash a traveller, to dash or strike up the dirt upon him," MS. Lansd. 1033. " A wet or a plashie ground," Nomenclator, 1585, p. 382.

PLAT. (1) Plaited straw, of which bonnets are made. *Linc.*

(2) The mould-board of a plough. *Norf.*

(3) " I platte with claye, *iardille,*" Palsgrave. " He platteth his butter upon his breed w'. his thombe as it were a lytell claye," ibid.

(4) Place; situation. *North.*

(5) A small bridge. *Chesh.*

(6) A round of cow-dung. *North.*

(7) The flat of a sword. *(A.-N.)*

(8) Anything flat or horizontal, as a piece of timber so laid in building, &c.

(9) A map, or plan.

PLAT-BLIND. Entirely blind.

PLATE. (1) Illegal silver money, but often applied to money generally. *(Span.)*

(2) To clinch; to rivet. *North.*

(3) A flat piece of metal, a term used in ancient armoury; an iron glove. " Plate of a fyyr herth" is mentioned in the Pr. Parv. and explained by Ducange, in v. *Retrofocilium,*

" illud quod tegit ignem in nocte, vel quod retro ponitur."

PLAT-FOOTED. Splay-footed. *Devon.*

PLAT-FORM. A ground-plan, or design; the list of divisions in a play, &c.

PLATLY. Plainly; perfectly.

For she here crafte *platly* and her konnyng
Spente upon him only in wirkyng.
MS. Digby 230.
And resoun also *platly* can y none,
How a mayde with childe schulde gone,
And floure forth in hire virginité.
Lydgate, MS. Soc. Antiq. 134, f. 5.
Whereof *platly* I am nothynge in doute.
Lydgate, MS. Ashm. 39, f. 55

PLATNESS. Flatness. *Palsgrave.*

PLATNORE. A species of clay. *South.*

PLATTE. To throw down flat. *(A.-N.)*

PLATTER-FACE. A very broad face.

PLATTINDE. Journeying forth.

Of hem ne wolde nevere on dwelle,
That he ne come sone *plattinde,*
Hwo hors ne havede, com gangande.
Havelok, 2282.

PLATTY. Uneven, having bare spots, as corn-fields sometimes have. *Sussex.*

PLAUSIVE. Plausible. *Shak.*

The Earl again is chosen, his title is sent him. and he, in requital, sends many flattering and *plausive* letters, and, that they might be the more acceptable, being sent unto scholars, wrote to them in Latin. It is intolerable the flattery that he used.
MS. Harl. 4888.

PLAW. To parboil. *East.* " And *plawe* is togedyr wel and fyne," Arch. xxx. 352. *Playing-hot,* boiling hot. " Bollynge owere as pottys plawyn," Pr. Parv. p. 43.

PLAY. (1) Sport; pleasure. *(A.-S.)*

(2) A country wake. *Somerset.*

PLAY-DAY. A holiday. *Var. dial.*

PLAY-FERE. A playfellow. *Palsgrave.*

He sayd, How I hase thou here
Fondene now thi *playfere* ?
Ʒe schalle haby it fulle dere
Er that I hethene go! *Perceval,* 1902.

PLAY-IN. To begin at once. *South.*

PLAY-LOME. A weapon. *(A.-S.)*

Go reche me my *playlome,*
And I salle go to hym sone;
Hym were better hafe bene at Rome,
So ever mote I thryfe!
Perceval, 2013.

PLAYNESS. The plain fact.

PLAY-PEEP. To offer the least opposition.

PLAY-SHARP. Be quick. *Var. dial.*

PLAYTOUR. A pleader. *(A.-N.)*

Thyr was a man that byghte Valentyne,
Playtour he was and ryche man fyne.
MS. Harl. 1701, f. 58.

PLAY-UP. To commence playing upon a musical instrument. *Var. dial.*

PLAZEN. Places. *Somerset.*

PLEACH. To intertwine. This term is still current in the word *plash,* q. v.

PLEAN. A tell-tale, or gossip. *North.*

PLEASANT. Merry. *Var. dial.* " Pleasante, propre, *galliarde,*" Palsgrave.

PLEASAUNCE. Pleasure; delight. *(A.-N.)*

PLEASAUNTES. A kind of lawn or gauze. It is mentioned in MS. Cantab. Ff. i. 6, f. 141.

Over their garmentes were vochettes of *pleasauntes*, rouled with crymosyne velvet, and set with letters of gold like carettes, their heades rouled in *pleasauntes* and typpers lyke the Egipcians.
Hall. Henry VIII. f. 7.

On every side of her stoode a countesse holding a clothe of *pleasaunce* when she list to drinke.
Hardyng, Suppl. f. 78.

PLEASE. To satisfy. *North.*

PLEASURE. To please. Still in use.

PLEASURE-LADY. A whore. See the Bride, by Thomas Nabbes, 4to. 1640, sig. E.

PLEASURES. Ornaments for dress.

PLEBE. The populace.

Which, borne out as well by the wisedome of the poet, as supported by the worth of the actors, wrought such impression in the hearts of the *plebe*, that in short space they excelled in civility and government. *Heywood's Apology for Actors*, 1612.

PLECK. (1) A place. *North.*

(2) A plat of ground; a small inclosure; a field. *Warw.*

PLECKS. A term in haymaking, applied to the square beds of dried grass. *Chesh.*

PLECTRE. A quill. (*Lat.*)

PLEDGE. To become a surety for another; to redeem one. *Palsgrave.*

PLEDGET. A small plug; a piece of lint, by which the nostrils are plugged when excessive bleeding takes place. *Linc.*

PLEE. Pleading; discord?

Plenté maketh pride,
Pride maketh *plee.*
MS. Soc. Antiq. 134, f. 30.

PLEEK. A parcel, or small packet.

PLEENPIE. A talebearer. *North.*

PLEIGHTTE. Plucked. *Weber.*

PLEIGNEN. To complain. *Gower.*

Luke it be done and delte to my dere pople,
That none *playne* of theire parte o peyne of your lyfez.
Morte Arthure, MS. Lincoln, f. 66.

PLEIR. A player. Nominale MS.

PLEK. A place, or plot. (*A.-S.*)

Thenne loke where a smothe *plek* of grene is, and theder bere al this upon the skyn with as muche blood as may be saved, and there lay it, and sprede the skyn therupon the heer syde upward.
MS. Bodl. 546.

PLENE. To fill. (*A.-N.*)

Thai grone and *plene* thaire stomake,
For thaim bus nede ille fare.
MS. Cantab. Ff. v. 48, f. 84.

PLENER. Completely; fully. (*A.-N.*)

He lokede yn hys alner,
That fond hym spendyng alle *plener*,
Whan that he hadde nede,
And ther nas noon, for soth to say,
And Gyfre was y-ryde away
Up Blaunchard hys stede.
Illustrations of Fairy Mythology, p. 25.

PLENERLICHE. Fully. (*A.-N.*)

Not only upon ten ne twelve,
But *plenerliche* upon us alle.
Gower, MS. Soc. Antiq. 134, f. 34.

PLENNY. To complain fretfully. *East.*

PLENTETHE. Plenty.

Thonour in Marche syguyfyes that seme *scry* grett wyndes, *plentethe* off cornes, and grette stryff amanges the peple.
MS. Lincoln A. i. 17, f. 50.

PLENTEVOUSNESS. Plentifulness.

Now, God, that art ful of al *plentevousnesse*,
Of al vertuys, grace, and charyté.
MS. Cantab. Ff. i. 6, f. 137.

PLENY-TIDES. Full tides. *Greene.*

PLES. Palace. Thornton Rom. p. 194.

PLESERY. A flower garden. *Linc.*

PLESINGES. Pleasures. *Chaucer.*

PLETE. To plead. (*A.-N.*)

Thou schalt be an apersey, my sone, in mylys ij. or thre,
Y wolde thou had some fayre syens to amende wyth thy degree;
I wolde thou were a man of lawe, to holde togedur my londe,
Thou schalt be *pletyd* with, when y am gon, fulle wele y undurstonde. *MS. Cantab. Ff. ii. 38, f. 51.*
Who shall than *plete* for the erly or late,
For all thy synnys thou stondist dissolate.
MS. Laud. 416, f. 41.

PLETHAN. To braid; to plait. *Cornw.*

PLETTE. To strike. (*A.-S.*)

He bounden him so fele sore,
That he gan crien Godes ore,
That he sholde of his hende *plette*
Havelok, 2444.

PLEVINE. Warranty; assurance. (*A.-N.*)

PLEW. A plough. *North.*

PLEX. A shield. (*Lat. Med.*)

PLEYT. Playeth. (*A.-N.*)

Fortunes whele so felly wyth me *pleyt*,
Of my desire that I may se ryghte noghte.
MS. Cantab. Ff. i. 6, f. 12.

PLEYTES. The threads or plats of a cord.

This corde is costome, that is of thre *pleytes*, that is of ydul thout, unoneste speche and wyckyd dede.
Wimbelton's Sermon, 1388, MS. Hatton 57, p. 23.

PLIERS. A kind of tongs used by smokers for taking up a lighted wood coal. *Glouc.*

PLIF. A plough. *Yorksh.*

PLIGHTE. (1) To engage; to promise. (*A.-S.*)

His staffe was a yong oake,
He would give a great stroke.
Bevis wondrod, I you *plight*,
And asked him what he hight;
My name, sayd he, is Ascapart,
Sir Grassy sent me hetherward.
Bevis of Hampton, n. d.

The shype ax seyd unto the wryght,
Mete and drynke I schall the *plyght*,
Clene hose and clene schone,
Gete them wer as ever thou kane.
MS. Ashmole 61, f. 23.

(2) A measure or piece of lawn. See Blount, in v. *Plite.* Spenser uses it for a fold or pleat.

(3) To twist, or braid. Greene, ii. 227.

The auncient horsse-men of the Romaines had no brest-plates, (as Polibius affirmeth,) and therefore they were naked in their fore parts, providing for the daunger that was behind them, and defending their breasts by their owne celerity: their shieldes were made of oxe-skinnes *plighted* and pasted togither, being a little round in compasse like the fashion of a man's belly.
Topsell's Four-Footed Beasts, 607, p. 318.

(4) Pulled; plucked. (*A.-S.*)

(5) In plyght, i. e. on a promise to fight again in the morning.

> Thus they justyd tylle hyt was nyght,
> Then they departyd in *plyght*,
>   They had nede to reste ;
> Sone on the morne when hyt was day,
> The knyghtes gysed them fulle gay,
> And proved them fulla preste.
>   *MS. Cantab. Ff. ii. 38, f. 76.*

PLIM. (1) Pliable. *Heref.*

(2) To fill ; to swell. *Var. dial.* As an adjective, stout and fat.

(3) Perpendicular. *Warw.* A plummet is sometimes called a plim. *Plom* occurs in Towneley Mysteries, p. 33.

(4) To pounce down on prey.

PLISH. To excoriate. *North.*

PLITH. Harm. *(A.-S.)*

> He [hath] mi lond with mikel onrith,
> With michel wrong, with mikel *plith*,
> For I ne misdede him nevere nouth,
> And havede me to sorwe brouth. *Havelok,* 1370.
>   The kynge upon this wrongful *plit.*
>   *Gower, MS. Soc. Antiq.* 134, f. 80.

PLIȜT. Same as *Plighte* (1). *I pliȝt,* I promise you, a kind of expletive.

> Then he tolde hym alle the case
> Off passilodion what it was,
> And berafrynde, I *plyȝt. MS. Cantab. Ff. v. 48, f. 54.*

PLOAT. To pull feathers ; to tear off the garments. *Northumb.*

PLOCK. (1) A small field. *Heref.*

(2) A block for chopping wood on. *West.*

PLODGE. To walk in mud or water ; to plunge. *Northumb.*

PLOG. To clog, or hinder. *Sussex.*

PLOGHE. Sport ; pleasure.

> He askede tham mete for charyté,
> And thay bade hym swynke, and swa do we,
> Hafe we none other *ploghe.*   *Isumbras,* 397.

PLOKE. To pluck, or pull.

> Whan ichave thin hed of-take,
> Be the berd y schel him schake,
>   That him schel smerte sore :
> So y schel him therbi *ploke,*
> That al is teth schel roke,
>   That sitteth in is heved. *Romance of Rembrun,* p. 474.

PLOLL-CAT. A whore.

PLOMAILE. Plumage ; feathers. *(A.-N.)*

PLOME. A plummet. *Palsgrave.*

PLOOD. Ploughed. *Northumb.*

PLOOKY. Pimpled. *North.*

PLOSHETT. A swampy meadow. *Devon.*

PLOT. A patch. *(A.-N.)*

PLOTE. To scald a pig. *North.*

PLOUCHS. Pimples. Kennett, MS.

PLOUGH. (1) Used for oxen kept to draw the plough, not for horses. (2) A wheel carriage drawn by oxen and horses.

PLOUGH-HALE. The handle of a plough.

PLOUGHING. The depth of a furrow.

PLOUGH-IRON. A ploughshare. *Var. dial.*

PLOUGHJAGS. Labourers begging on the first Monday after Twelfth-day, generally called Plough Monday. *Linc.*

PLOUGH-JOGGER. A ploughman. *Norf.*

> On a Sunday, Tarlton rode to Ilford, where his father kept ; and, dining with them at his sisters,

there came in divers of the countrey to see him, amongst whom was one plaine countrey *plough-jogger*, who said hee was of Tarlton's kin, and so called him cousin.   *Tarlton's Jests,* 1611.

PLOUGH-LAND. As much land as one plough will till in a year. *Pr. Parv.*

PLOUGH-MONDAY. "The Monday next after Twelfth-day, on which day, in the North of England, the plowmen themselves draw a plough from door to door, and beg plow-money to drink, which, having obtained, they plow two furrows across in the base court, or other place near the houses. In other parts of England, if any of the plowmen, after their days work on that day, come to the kitchin-hatch with his goad or whip, and cry *Cock in the pot* before the maids say *Cock on the dunghill,* then they gain a cock for Shrove-Tuesday," Blount's Glossographia, ed. 1681, p. 501. Tusser thus alludes to this singular custom,—

> Plough Munday, next after that Twelf-tide is past,
> Bids out with the plough, the worst husband
>   is last :
> If plowman get hatchet, or whip to the skreene,
> Maids loseth their cocke, if no water be seen.

PLOUGH-PADDLE. A small plate or paddle used for cleansing the plough. *Var. dial.*

PLOUGH-SOCK. A ploughshare. *North.*

PLOUGH-START. A plough handle. *Palsgrave.*

PLOUGH-STOTS. The procession of the plough-stots still continues in Yorkshire on the second Monday in the year, when a plough is drawn along without the share, preceded by a number of rustics decorated with ribands, and blowing a cow's horn.

PLOUNCE. To flounce about ; to plunge in with a loud noise. *Var. dial.*

PLOUT. (1) A plant. *Somerset.*

(2) A long walking-stick carried by foot-hunters. *North.*

PLOUTER. To wade through anything ; to be busied in dirty work. *North.* Grose has *plowding,* wading, p. 120.

PLOVER. A whore. An old cant term.

PLOW. A ploughed field. *Suffolk.*

PLOWDEN. "The case is altered, quoth Plowden," a very favourite old proverbial phrase. Plowden was an eminent lawyer in Queen Mary's time, who being asked what legal remedy there was against some hogs that trespassed on the complainant's ground, he answered, he might have very good remedy; but the other telling him they were his hogs, "Nay, then, the case is altered," quoth Plowden.

> There *Ployden* in his laced ruff starch'd on edg
> Peeps like an adder through a quickset hedg,
> And brings his stale demur to stop the course
> Of her proceedings with her yoak of horse ;
> Then fals to handling of the case, and so
> Shews her the posture of her over-throw,
> But yet for all his law and double fees
> Shee'le bring him to joyn issue on his knees,
> And make him pay for expedition too :
> Thus the gray fox acts his green sins anew.
>   *Fletcher's Poems,* p. 192.

PLOWEFERE. Companion in play. (*A.-S.*)

PLOWKKY. Covered with pimples.

> For hyme that is smetyne with his awenne blode,
> and spredis over alle his lymmes, and waxes *plowckky*,
> and brekes owte.   *MS. Lincoln Med.* f. 294.

PLOW-LODE. "*Caracuta*, plow lode," Nominale MS. It seems to be the same as *Plough-land*, q. v.

PLOWMELL. A small wooden hammer occasionally fixed to the plough, still used in the North; in the Midland counties in its stead is used a plough-hatchet.

PLOWRING. Weeping. *Prompt. Parv.*

PLOWSHO. A ploughshare. *Kennett.*

PLOY. A merry-meeting. *North.*

PLOYE. A plough. Nominale MS.

PLUCK. (1) Courage. *Var. dial.* "To pluck up one's heart," to be bold, to rejoice. Against the pluck, i. e. against the inclination.

(2) To pluck a crow or goose with any one, i. e. to quarrel with him.

(3) To pluck a rose, i. e. to go to the jakes, said of women. Middleton, iv. 222.

(4) A dry pluck, i. e. a severe stroke.

> This same is kind cuckolds luck :
> These fellowes have given me a drie *pluck*,
> Now I have never a crose to blesse me.
>   *Mariage of Witt and Wisdome*, 1579.

(5)
> Our kynge and Robyn rode togyder,
> Forsoth as I you say,
> And they shote *plucks* buffet,
> As they went by the way. *Robin Hood*, i. 75.

(6) Same as (1)?
> ———— I had the luck
> To seè, and drink a little *pluck*.
>   *Brome's Songs*, 1661, p. 167.

(7) A student who fails in an university examination is said to be *plucked*.

PLUCKING. The worsted plucked from the machine while the wheel is turning. *North.*

PLUERE. Weeping. (*A.-N.*)

PLUF. A tube of tin through which boys blow peas. *Linc.* Also called a *pluffer*.

PLUFE. A plough. *Yorksh.*

PLUFFY. Spongy; porous. *Devon.* It is sometimes explained, soft, plump.

PLUG. A dwarfish fellow. *East.*

PLUM. (1) Light; soft. *West.*

(2) Sensible; honest. *North.*

(3) Very; exceedingly. *Kent.*

(4) Straight; upright; perpendicular. *Plum downe*, Cotgrave in v. *Escarpé.*

(5) *Plum round*, quite round. "Make their attire to sit *plum round*," Harrison, p. 172. *Plum fat*, Florio, p. 33.

PLUMAKIN. The magnum-bonum plum.

PLUME. To pick or pluck the feathers off a hawk or other bird.

PLUMED-SWAN. A white colour. One of the terms of ancient alchemy.

PLUMMY. Soft; wet; mouldy. *Devon.*

PLUMP. (1) Dry; hard. *Kent.*

(2) A clump of trees. *North.*

(3) A crowd of people; a mass of anything. It is sometimes a verb, to collect together.

> "Assemble theymselfes in plumpes," More's Supplycacyon of Soulys, sig. F. ii.
> Rydes into rowte his dede to revenge,
> Presede into the *plumpe* and with a prynce metes.
>   *Morte Arthure, MS. Lincoln,* f. 76.
> When kynge Richard perceved that the people by *plumpes* fled from hym to Duke Henry.
>   *Hall's Union,* 1548.

(4) A pump; a draw-well. *Cornw.*

(5) A hard blow. *Var. dial.*

(6) Directly; exactly. *Var. dial.* Forby has *plumpendicular*, perpendicular.

PLUM-PORRIDGE. Porridge with plums in it, a favourite dish at Christmas in some parts of the country. It is mentioned as part of Christmas fare in the Humourist, ed. 1724, p. 22, and by Addison.

PLUMP-PATE. A thick-headed fellow.

PLUMPY. To churn. *Cornw.*

PLUMTEN. Plunged. *Weber.*

PLUM-TREE. The female pudendum. *Have at the plum tree* seems to have been either the burden of a song or a proverbial phrase. It occurs in Middleton, although Mr. Dyce does not seem to be acquainted with the meaning of the term itself, which may be gathered from Cotgrave, in v. *Hoche-prunier*, and the Mariage of Witt and Wisdome, p. 16.

PLUNGE. (1) A deep pool. *Somerset.*

(2) A strait or difficulty. *Greene.*

PLUNGY. Wet; rainy. (*A.-N.*)

PLUNKET. A coarse woollen cloth.

PLUNKY. Short; thick; heavy. *East.*

PLUNT. A walking-stick, generally one which has a large knob. *Glouc.*

PLURISY. Superabundance. *Shak.*

PLUSHES. The thin hoops which hold a besom together. *West.*

PLY. To bend; to consent, or comply. Still in use in Dorset, Barnes's Gl.

PLYER. A very common bawd.

PLYMOUTH-CLOAK. A cane, or stick. So called, says Ray, "because we use a staff *in cuerpo*, but not when we wear a cloak."

PO. A peacock. (*A.-S.*)

> A pruest proud ase a *po*,
> Seththe weddeth us bo.
>   *Wright's Political Songs*, p. 159.

POACHED. Land is said to be *poached* when it is trodden with holes by heavy cattle. *Var.dia.*

POACHING. Swampy. *Devon.*

POAD-MILK. The first milk given by cows after calving. *Sussex.*

POARE-BLIND. Dim-sighted. The word occurs in Hollyband's Dictionarie, 1593.

POAT. To kick. *Devon.*

POBS. Porridge. *Craven.*

POCHE. A pocket. (*A.-N.*)

> Unto another she dyde as moche ;
> For they love none but for theyr *poche*.
>   *The Complaynte of them that ben to late Maryed.*

POCHEE. A dish in ancient cookery consisting principally of poached eggs. *Pegge.*

POCHERS. Potters ?

POCHIN. A hedgehog. *Somerset.*

POCHIT. A pollard tree. *Linc.*

POCK. To push. *Somerset.*

POCK-ARR. A pock mark. *North.*

POCKET. (1) A lump of bread.

(2) A measure of hops. *Kent.* Half a sack of wool is called a pocket.

POCKET-CLOCK. A watch.

> Though as small *pocket-clocks*, whose every wheel
> Doth each mis-motion and distemper feel,
> Whose hands gets shaking palsies, and whose string
> His sinews slackens, and whose soul, the spring,
> Expires, or languishes ; whose pulse, the flee,
> Either beats not, or beats unevenly.
> *Donne's Poems,* p. 247.

POCK-FREDDEN. Marked with the smallpox.

POD. (1) A foot. *North.* Generally a child's foot, and hence the verb *pod*, to toddle.

(2) To put down awkwardly. *North.*

(3) A large protuberant belly. Hence applied to the body of a cart. *South.*

(4) A young jack, nearly full grown.

PODAGER. Gout in the feet. Berners mentions this disease in hawks as the *podagre.*

PODART. A young sheep. *Linc.*

PODDEL. A puddle. *Palsgrave.*

> The porter and hys men in haste
> Kynge Roberd in a *poddelle* caste ;
> Unsemely was hys body than,
> That he was lyke non odur man.
> *MS. Cantab.* Ff. ii. 38, f. 241.

PODDER. (1) Beans, peas, tares, or vetches, or such ware as have pods. *Kent.* Also, a gatherer or seller of peas, one who takes them to market for sale.

(2) "A weed called *podder*, winding about hempe or other like," Hollyband's Dictionarie, 4to. Lond. 1593.

PODDER-GRATTEN. Podder stubble. The following sentence was used by the gardener of a gentleman living in Kent, describing a feat of his own. "I took up a libbet that lay by the sole, and hove it at a haggister that sat in the *podder-gratten.*"

PODDISH. Porridge. *Craven.*

PODDY. Round and stout in the belly.

PODE. A tadpole. "Irannys, or podys, or vermyn." Arch. xxx. 353. Mr. Dyce, Skelton, ii. 104, conjectures it to mean *a toad ;* but Grose has *pohead* in the sense we have given.

PODECHE. Pottage. Nominale MS. *Podish* occurs in the West. and Cumb. Dial. p. 379.

PODGE. (1) Porridge. Still in use.

> A! sirra, my masters, how saist thou, Hodge?
> What, art thou hungrie? wilt thou eat my *podge?*
> *Mariage of Witt and Wisdome,* 1579.

(2) To stir and mix together. *East.*

(3) A pit, or hole ; a cesspool. *Kent.*

PODGER. A platter, or dish. *West.*

PODING. A pudding. *Palsgrave.*

POD-WARE. Pulse growing in pods or cods. *Kent.* See *Podder.*

POE. A turkey. *North.*

POFF. To run very fast. *Linc.*

POG. A push, or blow. *Somerset.*

POGH. (1) A poke ; a sack. "When me profereth the pigge, opon the *poghe*," MS. Douce 52, xv. Cent.

(2) An interjection of contempt. See Stani-

hurst's Description of Ireland, p. 13. Still in very common use.

POGRIM. A religious fanatic. *East.*

POGY. Intoxicated. *Var. dial.*

POHEADS. Musical notes. So called perhaps from their resemblance to tadpoles. *North.*

POHEN. A peahen. *Skelton.*

POICH. A hive to take bees in after they have swarmed. *Yorksh.*

POIGNIET. A wristband. (*Fr.*) "Poygniet for ones sleeves, *poignet*," Palsgrave.

POILE. Apulia. *Lydgate.*

POINADO. A dagger, or poniard. See Heywood's Royall King, 4to. 1637, sig. I.

POINAUNT. Sharp ; cutting. (*A.-N.*)

POINE. (1).

> I *poyne* alle his pavelyones that to hymselfe pendes,
> Dyghttes his dowblettes for dukes and erles.
> *Morte Arthure, MS.* Lincoln, f. 81.

(2) A little fellow, or dwarf.

> Michel wonder had Leodegan,
> That swiche a litel *poine* of man
> So fele in so litel thrawe
> So manliche had y-slawe.
> *Arthour and Merlin,* p. 219.

POINT. (1) To show, or explain ; to point out ; to declare ; to write.

(2) The principal business. (*A.-N.*)

(3) A tagged lace, used in ancient dress. *To truss a point,* to tie the laces which held the breeches, and hence *to untruss a point,* to untie them, a delicate mode of expressing *alvum exonerare.*

(4) To fill up the open interstices of a wall with mortar. *Var. dial.*

(5) *To point the earth,* to put down one's foot to the ground. *North.*

(6) To appoint, or equip.

(7) *In good point,* in good condition. This phrase occurs in Holinshed's Engl. i. 162.

(8) A deed, or martial exploit.

> Yf thow durst, par ma fay,
> A *poynt* of armys undyrtake,
> Thow broke her wille fore ay.
> *Torrent of Portugal,* p. 36.

(9) To paint, or portray.

POINT-DEVICE. With the greatest exactness ; excessively exact. Chaucer, Cant. T. 3689.

> The wenche she was full proper and nyce,
> Amonge all other she bare great price,
> For sche coude tricke it *point device,*
> But fewe like her in that countree.
> *The Miller of Abington,* n. d.

POINTEL. (1) A style, or pencil, for writing. (*A.-N.*) "*Stilus,* a poyntyle," Nominale MS. *Nomina rerum pertinencium clerico.* "Poyntell or caracte, *esplingue de fer,*" Palsgrave.

> And be assayed with thilk doctrine which the secretaries of God hath set in *pointell.*
> *Philpot's Works,* p. 376.

> Thenne loked aftir Sir Zakary
> Tables and *poyntel* tyte.
> *Cursor Mundi, MS. Coll. Trin. Cantab.* f. 68.

(2) Chequer work in paving floors.

POINTEN. To prick with a pointed instrument or with anything pointed. (*A.-N.*)

POINTING-STOCK. A laughing-stock ; a person so silly as to be pointed at in ridicule.

POINTLET. A small promontory.

POINTMENT. An appointment.

The Sairsins be set the *poyntment* to hold,
And to God they be gevyn the bodys bold.
Rowland, MS. Lansd. 388, f. 396.

POINTOURE. A painter, or artist.

POINTS. The divisions in the side of a quadrant. MS. Sloane 213.

POISE. Weight.

We been informed how ye have laboured, contrary to natural kindness and duty of legiance, divers matters of great *poise ;* and also how proclamations have been made in your name and our cousin's of Warwick, to assemble our liege people, no mention made of us. *MS. Harl.* 543.

As for his corporature, I suppose verily that if we had him here in this world to be weighed in the ballance, the *poyse* of his body would shew itself more ponderous than five and twenty, peradventure thirty of ours. *The Man in the Moone*, 1657, p. 74.

POIT. (1) To push, or kick. *North.*

(2) A poker for a fire. *Yorksh.*

(3) Impertinent; very forward. *East.*

POKE. (1) A bag, or sack. *North.*

(2) A cesspool. *Kent.*

(3) To thrust the head forward; to stoop in walking. *West.*

(4) A large wide long sleeve, very much worn about the year 1400, and shortly before that period.

An hool cloth of scarlet may not make a gowne,
The *pokes* of purchace hangen to the erthe.
MS. Digby 41, f. 7.

(5) Scurf in the head. *Linc.*

(6) A finger-stall. *Craven.*

(7) To project, or lean forward. *Var. dial.*

(8) A cock of hay. *Devon.*

(9) To gore, as a bull does. *West.*

(10) To give an offence. *North.*

POKE-CART. A miller's cart, filled with sacks or pokes of meal. *East.*

POKE-DAY. The day on which the allowance of corn is made to labourers, who, in some places, receive a part of their wages in that form. *Suffolk.*

POKE-MANTLE. A portmanteau. *North.*

POKE-PUDDING. (1) A long round pudding.

(2) The long-tailed titmouse. *Glouc.*

POKER. (1) A single-barrelled gun.

(2) The same as *Poking-stick*, q. v.

POKE-SHAKKINS. The youngest pig of a litter. *North.*

POKEY. (1) Saucy. *Cumb.*

(2) Miserably small. *Var. dial.*

POKING-STICK. An instrument for putting the plaits of a ruff in a proper form. It was originally made of wood or bone; afterwards of steel, in order that it might be used hot.

A ruffe about his neck, not like a ruffian but inch broad, with small sets, as if a peece of a tobacco-pipe had beene his *poking-stick ;* his gloves are thrust under his girdle that you may see how he rings his fingers.
The Man in the Moone, 1609, sig. D. iv.

POKOK. A peacock.

A fair *pokok* of pris men palen to Juno.
MS. Bodl. 264, f. 213.

POLACK. A Polander. *Shak.*

POLANS. Knee-pieces in armour.

POLAYL. Poultry. (*A.-N.*) *Polayl briddis,* domestic poultry, barn-door fowls.

POLBER. A kind of early barley.

POLCHER. A poacher. *Northampt.*

POLDER. A boggy marshy soil. *Kent.*

POLE. Some kind of fish mentioned in MS. Bibl. Coll. S. Johan. Cantab. B. vi.

POLEAPS. A leather strap belonging to some part of cart harness. *Var. dial.*

POLE-HEAD. A tadpole. Palsgrave has *polet,* which is still in use. See *Pode.*

POLEIN. (1) A sharp or picked top set in the fore-part of the shoe or boot. *Blount.*

(2) A pulley. Nominale MS.

POLE-PIECE. A woman's caul. *Devon.*

POLER. A barber. *Chesh.*

POL-EVIL. A kind of eruption on the neck and ears of horses. *West.*

POLE-WORK. A long tedious business.

POL-GARMENTS. Cloth for garments, smooth on one side and rough on the other, as velvet, and similar materials.

POLICE. Policy. *Nabbes.*

POLIFF. A pulley.

Than be-spake the *polyff,*
With gret strong wordes and styffe,
How, ser twyvel, me thinke you grevyd !
What devylle who hath you thus mevyd ?
MS. Ashmole 61.

POLIMITE. Many coloured ?

Of yonge Josephe the cote *pollimité,*
Wrouyte by the power of alle the Trinité.
Lydgate, MS. Soc. Antiq. 134, f. 13.

POLING. A plank of wood used in mines to prevent earth or stone from falling. *Derb.*

POLIPRAGMAN. A busy meddler.

POLISSER. A smock-frock. *Devon.*

POLK. (1) Bulk. *Hearne.*

(2) A pool. "Her hors a polk stap in," Sir Tristrem, p. 284. It seems to mean an eddy or whirlpool in Pr. Parv.

Ther was swilk dreping of the folk,
That on the feld was nevere a *polk,*
That it ne stod of blod so ful,
That the strem ran intil the hul.
Havelok, 9685.

POLKE. To place or put.

POLL. (1) To rob; to cheat. "Pilling and polling" was a very common phrase.

And have wynked at the *pollyng* and extorcion of hys unmeasurable officiers. *Hall's Union,* 1548.

(2) To cut the hair.

(3) The head. *Var. dial.* Hence the phrase *poll by poll,* head by head, one by one.

POLLAGE. A head-tax.

POLLARD. (1) Coarse flour; bran. The coarsest bran, according to Harrison, p. 168.

(2) A clipped coin. See Blount.

(3) A stag without horns.

POLLAX. A heavy halberd. (*A.-S.*) This term is still used by butchers.

POLLDAVY. A coarse cloth or canvas.

Your deligence knaves, or I shall canvase your *poledavyes ;* deafen not a gallant with your anon, anon, sir, to make him stop his eares at an over-reckoning. *The Bride,* 1640, sig. C. iii.

POLLE. To cut down or lop a wood.

And dystroye my castels and my townes,
Bothe be dales and be downes,
The *polle* my wodeys and forestes downe.
MS. Cantab. Ff. ii. 38, f. 211.

So may thy pastures with their flowery feasts,
As suddenly as lard, fat thy lean beasts;
So may thy woods oft *poll'd*, yet ever wear
A green, and (when she list) a golden hair.
Donne's Poems, p. 175.

POLLED-COW. One without horns. *North.*

POLLED-OFF. Intoxicated. *Var. dial.*

POLLENGER. A pollard tree.

POLLEPIT. A pulpit. Nominale MS.

POLLER. (1) A hen-roost. *Norf.*

(2) To beat in the water with a pole. Figuratively, to labour without effect.

(3) A robber; an extortioner.

(4) A kind of dart. Nominale MS.

POLLETTES. Pieces of armour for the shoulders, mentioned in Hall, Henry IV. f. 12.

POLLING. Retaliation. *Var. dial.*

POLLRUMPTIOUS. Restive; unruly; foolishly confident. *Var. dial.*

POLLYWIGS. Tadpoles. "Tadpoles, polewigges, yongue frogs," Florio, p. 212. "Polwygle wurm" occurs in the Prompt. Parv.

Dame, what ails your ducks to die?
Eating o' *pollywigs*, eating o' *pollywigs*.
Whiter's Specimen, 1794. p. 19.

POLMAD. In a rage for fighting.

POLRON. That part of the armour which covered the neck and shoulders. "Avant bras d'un harnois, the *poldern* of an armoure," Hollyband's Dictionarie, 1593. It is mentioned in Hall, Henry IV. f. 12.

And some only but a sure gepon,
Over his *polrynges* reaching to the kne.
Clariodes MS.

POLSHEN. To polish. (*A.-N.*)

POLSHRED. To lop a tree. *Palsgrave.*

POLT. (1) A thump or blow. *Var. dial.*

(2) A rat-trap that falls down. *Kent.*

(3) Saucy; audacious. *Kent.*

(4) To cut, or shave. *Somerset.*

POLTATE. A potato. *Cornw.*

POLT-FOOT. A club foot. Ben Jonson terms Vulcan "this polt-footed philosopher."

POLTING-LUG. A long thin rod used for beating apples off the trees. *Glouc.*

POMAGE. (1) Cyder. Harrison, p. 170.

Where of late dales they used much *pomage*, or cider for want of barley, now that lacke is more commonly supplied with oates.
Lambard's Perambulation, 1596, p. 10.

(2) A pumice-stone. It is the translation of *pumex* in the Nominale MS. xv. Cent.

POMANDER. A kind of perfume, generally made in the form of a ball, and worn about the person. Sometimes the case for holding pomanders was so termed. Receipts for making this perfume differ considerably from each other. Perhaps the following will suffice.

Take pyppyns or other lyke melowe apples, and laye them upon a tyle for to bake in an oven; than take out the core and the kernels, and make theym cleane wythin, brayenge and breakynge the reste, and strayne it thoroughe a fyne canvesse or straynour.

Thys done, take as muche fat or grease of a kydde as you have apples, and strayne it lykewyse, boylinge it all together in a newe vessell well leaded, untyli the rose water bee consumed; then adde to it muske, cloves, nutmegges, and such lyke substances of a reasonable quantitye according to your discretion; provided alwayes that they be well brayed and broken in pyeces as is above sayed; and boyle them in the like maner aforesayed; then straine them and kepe them. *The Secretes of Mayster Alexis,* 1559, p. 57.

To make pomanders.

Take two penny-worth of labdanum, two penny-worth of storax liquid, one penny-worth of calamus aromaticus, as much balm, half a quarter of a pound of fine wax, of cloves and mace two penny-worth, of liquid aloes three penny-worth, of nutmegs eight penny-worth, and of musk four grains: beat all these exceedingly together till they come to a perfect substance, then mould it in any fashion you please, and dry it. *Markham's English House-Wife,* ed. 1675, p. 109.

POME. (1) To pelt continuously. *North.*

(2) To pummel with the fist. *Cornw.*

(3) A young rabbit. *Devon.*

POME-GARNADE. A pomegranate. (*A.-N.*)

POMEL. A ball, or knob; a globular ornament, or anything globular. (*A.-N.*) It means sometimes the top of the head. Is *pomet touris* in Lybeaus Disconus, 1295, an error for *pomel touris*, round towers? I have not met with the phrase elsewhere.

She saughe there many comly telde
Wythe *pomelles* bryghte as goldis beghe.
MS. Harl. 2252, f. 118.

On the *pomelle* yt wase wret,
Fro a prynce yt wase get,
Mownpolyardus he hyght.
Torrent of Portugal, p. 31.

POMELEE. Spotted. *Maundevile.*

POME-WATER. A kind of apple. See Lydgate's Minor Poems, p. 15. In the Widow of Watling Street, p. 15, the apple of the eye is termed a *pomwater.*

POMICE. The residue of apples after the juice has been extracted. *West.*

POMMADO. Vaulting on a horse, without the aid of stirrups, by resting one hand on the saddle-bow. The pommado reversa was vaulting off again.

POMON. Lungs. (*A.-N.*)

POMPAL. Proud; pompous.

Thy elder sisters loves are more
Than well I can demand,
To whom I equally bestow
My kingdome and my land,
My *pompal* state and all my goods,
That lovingly I may
With those thy sisters be maintain'd
Until my dying day.
Ballad of King Leir, n. d.

POMPED. Pampered. *Hawes.*

POMPILLION. An ointment made of black poplar buds. See Cotgrave, in v. *Populeon.* A more complete account of it will be found under *popilion.*

POMPION. A pumpkin. (*Fr.*) It is the translation of *citrouille* in Hollyband's Dictionarie, 4to. Lond. 1593.

POMPIRE. Melagium. A kind of apple mentioned in Rider's Dictionarie, 1640. "Poumper, frute," *Palsgrave.*

POMPLE. To hobble?

I lench, I len, on lyme I lasse,
I poke, I pomple, I palle, I passe. *Reliq. Antiq.* ii. 211.

POMSTER. To doctor or play the quack with salves and slops; to apply a medicament to a wound or contusion, or to administer medicine internally. *West.*

PON. A pond. *Drayton.*

PONCHONG. A puncheon of iron, used in making holes in iron or steel.

PONENT. Western. (*Ital.*)

PONGE. A pound. Const. Freem. p. 20.

PONIAUNT. Poignant; acute. (*A.-N.*)

PONICHE. To punish. *Lydgate.*

Maryes sone, most of honoure,
  That ryche and pore may *ponyche* and please,
Lys me now in my longoure,
  And gyf me lysens to lyve in ease.
             MS. Cantab. Ff. i. 6.

PONIET. A wristband.

PONTED. (1) Bruised; indented. *West.*

(2) Tainted; not fresh. *Dorset.*

POO. To pull. *North.*

POOCH. (1) A pot; a jug. *South.*

(2) To thrust out the lips in a sullen discontented manner. *West.* Grose and Polwhele have *poochee,* to make mouths at a person, screwing up the mouth like a pouch. *Grose.*

POODLE. The English Channel. *Cornw.*

POODLER. The young coalfish. *North.*

POOK. (1) To kick. *Devon.*

(2) A calf's stomach for rennet. *West.*

(3) A cock of hay. *Somerset.* To pook hay or barley, to make it up into cocks.

(4) The belly; the stomach. *West.*

POOK-NEEDLE. The cockle in corn. *Sussex.*

POOLE. A measure of work in slating, or covering houses with slate, where every *poole* of work is either six feet broad and fourteen feet upon both sides, or 168 feet in length and one in breadth.

POOLINGS. The fat which is stripped off from the intestines of an animal. *North.*

POOLS. The spaces on each side of the threshing-floor of a barn. *Devon.*

POOL-SPEARE. A reed. *South.*

POOLY. Mictura. *West.*

POOMER. Anything very large. *North.*

POON. To kick. *North.*

POOP. (1) A puppy. *Somerset.*

(2) A gulp in drinking. *North.*

(3) To cheat; to deceive; to cozen.

POOP-NODDY. The game of love.

POOR. Lean, out of condition; applied to live stock. *Var. dial.*

POOR-AND-RICH. An old game, mentioned in Taylor's Motto, 12mo. Lond. 1622, sig. D. iv.

POOR-BODY. A very common expression of pity or sympathy for an unfortunate person.

POOR-JOHN. A kind of fish, salted and dried. It was cheap and coarse.

POORLY. Somewhat unwell. *Var. dial.*

POOT. (1) A chicken, or pullet. *Chesh.*

(2) To cry, or blubber. *Somerset.*

(3) A lake, or pool of water.

POOTY. A snail-shell. *Northampt.*

POP. (1) Ginger-beer. *Var. dial.*

(2) A short space. *Lanc.*

POP-GLOVE. The foxglove. *Cornw.*

POPE. (1) A term of contempt. "What a *pope* of a thing." *Dorset.*

He, having no answere, began to curse and ban, bidding a *pope* on all women.
            Westward for Smelts, 1620.

(2) "I know no more than the Pope of Rome," a very common simile.

A simple fellow being arraign'd at the bar, the judge was so favourable to him as to give him his book, and they bid him read. Read! truly, my Lord, says he, I can read no more than the Pope of Rome.   *Oxford Jests,* 1706, p. 93.

POPE-JULIUS. An old game, possibly similar to the modern game of Pope Joan.

POPELER. A kind of bird, explained by *populus* in the Prompt. Parv.

POPELOT. A deceiver. (*A.-N.*)

POPERIN. A kind of pear. There were two sorts, the summer-poperin, and the winter-poperin.

POPES. Weevils. Urry gives this as a Hampshire word, in his MS. adds. to Ray.

POPES-HEAD. A broom with a very long handle for sweeping ceilings and high places.

POPET. A puppet. (*A.-N.*)

POP-GUN. Elder-wine. *South.*

POP-HOLY. Hypocrisy. Lydgate, p. 46.

POPILION. The following receipt *for to make popylyone* is from a MS. in my possession.

Take liij. *ll.* of popelere levys, and iij. *ll.* of erbe watur, and a pownde of henbane, and a *ll.* of pete morell, a *ll.* of orpyn, a *ll.* of syngrene, halfe a *ll.* of weybrod, halfe a *ll.* of endyve, halfe a *ll.* of vyolettes, halfe a *ll.* of welle cressyn, and then wese them clene, and stampe them; and than put to them ij. *ll.* and a half of moltyn barowse grese, and medylle them welle togethur; and than put them in a close pott ix. dayys, and than take and worche it up.

POPILLE. Tares. Nominale MS. *Popple* occurs in the provincial glossaries.

POPINJAY. A parrot. (*A.-N.*) *Popingaye blue,* a kind of coloured cloth.

And pyping still he spent the day,
  So merry as the *popingay:*
    Which liked Dowsabel:
That would she ought, or would she nought,
  This lad would never from her thought;
    She in love-longing fell. *Drayton's Pastorals.*

POPLAIN. The poplar tree. *West.*

POPLE. To stalk about; to hobble; to go prying and poking about. *Exmoor.*

POPLER. (1) Pottage. Dekker, 1616.

(2) A sea-gull. Nominale MS.

POPLET. A term of endearment, generally applied to a young girl. *Poppet* is still in common use.

POPPED. Nicely dressed. *Chaucer.* Still in use in Leicestershire.

POPPER. A dagger. *Chaucer.*

POPPET. An idol, or puppet.

Wyth lyeng and sweryng by no *poppets,*
But teryng God in a thowsand gobbets.
    Play of Wit and Science, Bright's MS.

POPPILARY. The poplar tree. *Chesh.*

POPPIN. A puppet. *East.* " Moppe or popyne," Prompt. Parv.

POPPING. Blabbing; chattering. *West.*

> For a suretie this felowe waxeth all folyshe, l. doth utterly or all togyther dote, or is a very *popyng* foole.   *Acolastus,* 1540.

POPPLE. (1) The poplar tree. *East.* " *Populus,* a popyltre," Nominale MS.

(2) A bubble. (3) To bubble up. Still in use in the North of England.

(4) A pebble. *Var. dial.* (*A.-S.*)

(5) A cockle. *North.*

(6) To tumble about. *Suffolk.*

POPPY-PILL. Opium. *North.*

POPULAR. Common; vulgar.

POR. A poker. *North.* " A porr of iron," Arch. xi. 438. See also ibid. 437.

PORAILLE. The poor people. (*A.-N.*)

PORBEAGLE. A kind of shark.

PORCELLYS. Young pigs. (*Lat.*)

PORCHIANS.

> For the better knowledge, salf and sure kepinge together of the premisses, and of every parte therof, lest some lewde persons mighte or woulde imbesill, the same with the detriment of the *porchians.*   *Egerton Papers,* p. 14.

PORC-PISCE. A porpoise. *Jonson.*

PORCUPIG. A porcupine.

> Had you but seen him in this dress,
> How fierce he look'd and how big,
> You would have thought him for to be
> Some Egyptian *porcupig.* *The Dragon of Wantley.*

PORE. (1) Power.

> To sawe a saule everlastyngly
> I have ful *pore* and mastry.
>   *Pieces of Ancient Poetry,* p. 43.

(2) To look earnestly.

(3) To supply plentifully. *Glouc.*

PORE-COTE. A coat of coarse cloth.

PORED-MILK. Any milk that turns or curdles in the boiling is in Kent called *pored milk,* especially the first milk of a cow when she has calved.

PORET. A young onion. *Porrectes,* Forme of Cury, p. 41. (*A.-N.*)

PORISHLY. Weak-sighted. *Palsgrave.*

PORISME. A corollary. (*Gr.*)

PORKER. A young hog fatted for the purpose of being eaten fresh. *Var. dial.*

PORKLING. A small pig. *East.*

PORKPOINT. A porcupine.

PORKY. Fat; plump. *North.*

PORPENTINE. A porcupine. *Shak.*

> Gallus, that greatest roost-cock in the rout,
> Swelleth as big as Bacchus did with wine:
> Like to a hulke he beares himselfe about,
> And bristels as a boare or *porpentine.*
>   *The Mous-Trap,* 1606.

PORPIN. A hedgehog. *Somerset.*

PORR. (1) A plumber, or glazier. *North.*

(2) To push, or thrust. *Cornw.* This word occurs in Baret's Alvearie, 1580, P. 579.

(3) To stuff with food. *Somerset.*

PORRA. A kind of pottage.

PORRINGER. A vessel for porridge.

PORRIWIGGLES. Tadpoles. *North.*

PORRON.

> I charge and pray mine executors and feoffees, to perform my will that ensueth touching these manors, advowsons, and *porrons,* chauntries, lands and tenements, abovesaid.   *Test. Vetust.* p. 260.

PORT. (1) Carriage; behaviour. (*A.-N.*)

> And then y am so symple off *port,*
> That for to fayn sum dysport,
> Y play with here lytylle hounde,
> Now on the bedde, now on the grounde.
>   *Gower, MS. Cantab.* Ff. i. 6, f. 4.
> Ther ben loveris of suche a sorte,
> That faynen an umble *porte.*
>   *Gower, MS. Soc. Antiq.* 134, f.42.

(2) A piece of iron, somewhat in the shape of a horseshoe, fixed to the saddle or stirrup, and made to carry the lance when held upright. It is mentioned in Hall, Henry IV. f. 12.

(3) State; attendance; company of retainers. *Shak.* " As lyberall a howse, and as greate a porte," Arch. xxviii. 108.

PORTAGE. A port, or porthole.

PORTAGUE. A Portuguese gold coin, worth about three pounds twelve shillings. " The portigue, a peece verie solemnelie kept of diverse, and yet ofttimes abased with washing, or absolutelie counterfeited," Harrison's England, p. 219.

> Ten thousand *portagues,* besides great pearls,
> Rich costly jewels and stones infinite.
>   *The Jew of Malta,* i. 2.

PORTANCE. Manner; deportment. *Shak.*

PORTASSE. A breviary.

> The pawment of the chyrche the aunchent faders tredes,
> Sum tyme with a *portas,* sumtyme with a payre oc bedes.   *Bale's Kynge Johan,* p. 27.
> And also we thank your noblesse and good fatherhood of our green gowns, now sent unto us to our great comfort, beseeching your good lordship to remember our *porteus,* and that we might have some fine bonnets sent unto us by the next sure messenger for necessity so requireth.
>   *MS. Cotton. Vespas.* F. iii

PORT-CANNONS. See *Canions.*

PORTCULLIS. A coin struck in Elizabeth's reign with a portcullis stamped on the reverse.

PORTECOLISE. A portcullis. (*A.-N.*)

PORTE-HOIS. A portasse, or breviary.

PORTER. To portray anything. *Palsgrave.*

PORTER'S-KNOT. A peculiar kind of knot, particularly strong and effective.

PORTER'S-LODGE. The usual place of chastisement for the menials and humbler retainers of great families. Our old dramatists constantly refer to it.

PORTE-SALE. An open sale of wares.

PORTINGALL. A Portuguese.

PORTLET. A small port. Harrison, p. 60.

PORTMANTLE. A portmanteau, of which the ancient form was sometimes port-mantua. " A port-mantua or a cloke-bagge," The Man in the Moone, 1609, sig. D.

PORTNANES. Appurtenances. " Men have a jerd with other *portnanes,*" MS. Addit. 12195.

PORTPANE. A cloth used for carrying bread from the pantry to the dinner-table.

PORTRAITURE. Portrait; likeness.

> I will that my executors provide and ordain a marble stone, with an image and *portraiture* of our Saviour Jhesu and of a priest kneeling, with a cedule in his hand, to the foot of the said image of Jhesu.
> *Test. Vetust.* p. 495.

PORTREVE. The chief magistrate of a town. See a brief dissertation on the origin of the portreeve of Gravesend in Lambard's Perambulation, 1596, p. 483.

PORTSALUT. Safe port. (*A.-N.*)

PORTURE. Carriage; behaviour. (*A.-N.*)

POS. A deposit, or pledge. (*A.-N.*)

POSE. (1) A hoard of money. *North.*

(2) To suppose; to place, or put as a supposition. (*A.-N.*) It occurs in Lydgate.

(3) A cold, a rheum in the head.

> His eare erect, his cleanely nose,
> That ne're was troubled with a *pose*.
> *Mon Miracles,* 1656, p. 33.

POSER. The bishop's examining chaplain. See Harrison's England, p. 139. The term is still retained at Eton for the examiner for the King's College fellowships. No doubt from *posen*, which is explained by *examino* in Prompt. Parv. p. 144. In cant language, a *poser* is an unanswerable question or argument.

POSH. A great quantity. *West.*

POSNET. A little pot. *Palsgrave.* "Urciolus, a posnet," Nominale MS. f. 8.

> Then skellets, pans, and *posnets* put on,
> To make them porridge without mutton.
> *Cotton's Works,* 1734, p. 17.

> And that is this, the cunning man biddeth set on a *posnet,* or some pan with nayles, and seeth them, and the witch shal come in while they be in seething. and within a fewe daies after her face will be all bescratched with the nayles.
> *Gifford's Dialogue on Witches,* 1603.

POSS. (1) To dash about. *North.* Pegge explains it, to punch or kick, and *posse*, to push, occurs in Chaucer.

> And therin thay keste hir, and *possede* hir up and downe, and sayd, take the this bathe for thi slewthe and thi glotonye. *MS. Lincoln* A. i. 17, f. 253.

(2) A waterfall. *Yorksh.*

POSSE. A number of people; no doubt derived from the sheriff's *posse comitatus.*

POSSEDE. To possess. *Palsgrave.*

> A ! lady myn, how God hath made the riche,
> Thysilfe allone alle richesse to *possede.*
> *Lydgate, MS. Soc. Antiq.* 134, f. 19.

POSSESS. To inform; to persuade; to convince. Still in use. See Craven Gl.

POSSESSIONERS. An invidious name for those religious communities which were endowed with lands. (*Lat.*)

POSSET. A drink of wine or treacle boiled with milk. "Quoddam genus cibi, *a posete,*" Ortus Vocabulorum, 1500. Junius, in the MS. notes in his copy of the book in the Bodleian, says "hodiernis in Anglis dicitur *posset.*" A posset was usually taken before retiring to rest. See Merry Wives of Windsor, v. 5.

> It is his mornings draught when he riseth, his conserves or cates when he hath well dined, his afternoones nunclons, and when he goeth to bedde his *posset* smoaking hote.
> *The Man in the Moone,* 1609, sig. C. 1.

POSSIBILITIES. This word means *possessions* in the Merry Wives of Windsor, i. 1, in reference to the property of Anne Page, which is well illustrated by a MS. letter dated about 1610, in the library of Dulwich College, being a letter from a suitor to a father for his permission to woo the daughter, in which he says, "I ryette to you first this cisone, as Londone fashen is, to intrete you that I may have your good will and your wiefs, for if we geete the fathers good will first, then may wee bolder spake to the datter, for my *possebeletis* is abel to mantayne her."

> My *possibilities* may raise his hopes
> To their first height.
> *Heywood's Royall King,* 1637.

POSSONE. To drive away.

POSSY. Thick, short, and fat. *North.*

POST. (1) A prop, or support. (*A.-S.*)

(2) "Knock your head up against a post," an address to a blockhead.

(3) *Post alone,* quite alone. *Devon.*

(4) The stakes at cards or dice.

(5) Haste; speed. The expression *post-haste* is still in common use.

(6) A courier, or special messenger.

> One night a drunken fellow josled against a post, but the fellow thought somebody had josled him, and fell a beating the post till his fingers were broken. Says one to him, Fie! what do you do to fight with a post? Is it a post? Why did he not blow his horn, then. *Oxford Jests,* 1706, p. 101.

> What though such *post* cannot ride post
> Twixt Exceter and this
> In two months space, yet careless they
> Those ten whole months to mis.
> *Ballads, MS. temp. James I.*

POST-AND-PAIR. An old game at cards, mentioned in Florio, p. 210; Taylor's Motto, 1622, sig. D. iv. A game called *pops and pairs* is mentioned in the West. and Cumb. Dial. p. 379.

POST-AND-PAN-HOUSE. A house formed of uprights and cross pieces of timber, which are not plastered over, but generally blackened, as many old cottages are in various parts of England.

POST-BIRD. The gray birdcatcher. *Kent.*

POSTIK. A pestle for a mortar.

POSTIME. An imposthume.

POSTISIS. Posts. *Var. dial.*

POSTISSER. Pots. *Berks.*

POSTLE. (1) An Apostle.

> Like a *postle* I am,
> For I preche to man.
> *Armonye of Byrdes,* p. 7.

(2) A comment, or short gloss.

POSTOLICON. A white ointment.

POST-PAST. A kind of dessert.

POST-PIN. A very small pin. It is the translation of *camion* in Hollyband's Dictionarie, 4to. Lond. 1593.

POSTURE. To strut. *I. of Wight.*

POSTOURE. A pastor.

> The chapitre of a chirche cathedral,
> Whan they han chosen here heed or *postoure.*
> *Occleve, MS. Soc. Antiq.* 134, f. 267.

POST-POSED. Put back. (*Fr.*)

POT. (1) A hollow vessel made of twigs with which they take fish. *South.*

(2) A stick with a hemisphere of wicker-work on it, used as a shield in cudgel-playing.

(3) A helmet, or head-piece. The scull was so called. Parts of " the potte of the hede" are mentioned in MS. Sloane 965, f. 44.

(4) *Gone to pot*, ruined.

(5) To deceive. To make a pot at one, to make a grimace or mow. To pot verses, to cap them.

(6) To drink. Still in use.

(7) " The pot is a hog's black-pudding made with the blood and grits unground stuffed into pigs' guts or chitterlings, otherwise *blackpot*; the *pudding* is more of the sausage kind, and has no blood in it, but minced pork, and sometimes raisins and currants and spice to season it, and many other rich materials, stuffed commonly into the larger guts," MS. Devon. Gl.

POTAGRE. The gout. (*Gr.*)

> Somme schul have in lymes aboute
> For slouthe a *potagre* and a goute.
> *MS. Ashmole* 41, f. 37.

POTATOE-BOGLE. A scarecrow.

POT-BOILER. A housekeeper. *East.*

POT-CAKE. A light Norfolk dumpling.

POTCH. To poke; to thrust at; to push, or pierce. Still in use.

POT-CLAME. A pot-hook. *Pot-clep*, Kennett, MS. Lansd. 1033.

POT-CRATE. A large open basket to carry earthenware in. *Lanc.*

POT-DAY. A cooking-day. *Norf.*

POT-DUNG. Farmyard dung. *Berks.*

POTE. (1) To push, or kick. *North.*

(2) A broad piece of wood used by thatchers to open the old thatch and thrust in the new straw. *Oxon.*

(3) To creep about moodily.

POTECARY. An apothecary. *West.*

> This ressayt is bought of no *poticarye*.
> *Lydgate's Minor Poems*, p. 69.

POTED. Plaited.

> He keepes a starcht gate, weares a formall ruffe.
> A nosegay, set face, and a *poted* cuffe.
> *Heywood's Troia Britanica*, 1609, p. 89.

POTE-HOLE. A small hole through which anything is pushed; a confined place. *West.*

POTENT. (1) A potentate. *Shak.*

(2) A club, staff, or crutch. (*A.-N.*) Stilts are called *pottens* in Norfolk.

> Loke sone after a *potent* and spectacle,
> Be not ashamed to take hem to thyn ease.
> *Lydgate's Minor Poems*, p. 30.

POTENTIAL. Strong; powerful. (*A.-N.*)

POTERNER. A pocket, or pouch.

> He plucked out of his *poterner*,
> And longer wold not dwell,
> He pulled forth a pretty mantle,
> Betweene two nut-shells.
> *The Boy and the Mantel.*

POTESTAT. A chief magistrate. (*A.-N.*)

POTEWS. A dish in ancient cookery, described in the Forme of Cury, p. 80.

POT-GUN. A pop-gun; a mock gun, or plaything for schoolboys; consisting of a wooden tube turned somewhat like the cylindrical part of a cannon, or the barrel of a common handgun, open at both ends, one of which being stuffed or stopped up with a pellet of tow, &c. another of the same kind is violently thrust into the other end by a rammer made on purpose, which so compresses the air between the two pellets, that the first flies out with a considerable force and noise. There was a kind of small cannon so called. " And yet will winke for to discharge a *potgun*," Tell-Tale, Dulwich College MS.

POT-HANGLES. Pot-hooks. *North.*

POTHELL-SLOTH. A puddle of water.

POTHELONE. To dig, or grub in the earth.

POTHER. To shake; to poke. *West.*

POTHERY. Hot; close; muggy. *West.*

POT-HOOKS-AND-HANGERS. The rude strokes of a boy beginning to write.

POT-KNIGHT. A drunken fellow.

POT-LADLES. Tadpoles. *East.*

POT-LUCK. To take pot-luck, i. e. to partake of a family dinner without previous invitation.

POT-PUDDING. " A white-pot, or pot-pudding," Florio, p. 99. Markham says blackpuddings are called *pots* in Devon.

POTS. The panniers of a packsaddle. *West.*

POT-SHARE. A potsherd, or piece of broken pottery. Also called a pot-scar.

POT-SICK. Tipsy. Florio, p. 68.

POT-SITTEN. Ingrimed. *Yorksh.*

POT-STICK. " *Contus*, potstyk," MS. Lansd. 560, f. 45. " Potstycke, *batton*," Palsgrave.

POT-SURE. Perfectly confident.

> When these rough gods beheld him thus secure,
> And arm'd against them like a man *pot-sure*,
> They stint vain storms: and so Monstrifera
> (So hight the ship) touch'd about Florida.
> *Legend of Captain Jones*, 1659.

POTTENGER. A porringer. *Palsgrave.* " A potenger or a little dish with eares," Baret, 1580. Still in use in Devon.

POTTER. (1) To go about doing nothing; to saunter idly; to work badly; to do anything inefficiently. *Var. dial.*

(2) To stir; to poke. *North.*

(3) To hobble, as a horse. *Warw.*

(4) To confuse, or disturb. *Yorksh.*

POTTERY-WARE. Earthenware. *West.*

POTTLE. A measure of two quarts.

POTTLE-BELLIED. Pot-bellied. *West.*

POTTLE-DRAUGHT. The taking a pottle of liquor at one draught.

POT-WABBLERS. Persons entitled to vote for members of parliament in certain boroughs from having boiled their pots therein. " Tanodunii in agro Somersetensi vocantur *pot-walliners*," Upton's MS. additions to Junius, in Bodleian Library.

POT-WATER. Water used for household purposes, for cooking, &c. *Devon.*

POTY. Confined; crammed; close. *West.*

POU. (1) To pull. *North.*

(2) A pan, or platter. *Lanc.*

POUCE. (1) A pulse. (*A.-N.*) " Pouce of the arme, *pouce* " Palsgrave.

(2\ Nastiuess. *North.* Hence, *poucy*, dirty, untidy, in a litter.

POUCH. (1) A pocket. (*A.-N.*)

(2) To poke, or push. *West.*

POUD. A boil, or ulcer. *Sussex.*

POUDERED. Interspersed. " A garment *poudered* with purple studdes," Hollyband's Dictionarie, 1593.

POUDERING TUB. The tub used for salting meat. It is the translation of *charnier* in Hollyband's Dictionarie, 1593. It was also a nickname for the cradle or bed in which a person was laid who was affected with the *lues venerea.*

POUDER-MARCHANT. Pulverized spices.

POUDRE. (1) To salt or spice meat.

(2) Dust. Kyng Alisaunder, 2180.

> For the *poudre* of this charging,
> No might men se sonne schining.
> > *Arthour and Merlin*, p. 176.

> Lo ! In *powdur* y schall slepe,
> For owt of *powdur* fyrst y came.
> > *MS. Cantab.* Ff. ii. 38, f. 19.

POUKE. (1) A devil ; a spirit. Hence the term Puck, applied to Robin Goodfellow, as in Shakespeare, and other writers.

> The heved fleighe fram the bouke,
> The soule nam the helle *pouke.*
> > *Arthour and Merlin*, p. 266.

(2) A pimple, or blister. *North.* Cotgrave has *ampoulé*, " full of water-poukes or wheales."

POUL. St. Paul. (*A.-N.*)

POULAINS. Pointed shoes. (*A.-N.*)

POULDER. Powder. (*A.-N.*)

POULDERING. An Oxford student in his second year. See the Christmas Prince, ed. 1816, p. 1.

POULT. To kill poultry. An old hawking term. See Gent. Rec. ii. 34, 62.

POULTER. A poulterer. This form of the word occurs in Hollyband's Dictionarie, 1593.

POUMYSSHE. Pounce for writing. *Palsgrave.*

POUN. A pond. *Northumb.*

POUNCE. (1) A thump, or blow. *East.*

(2) A puncheon of iron.

(3) A pulse. Gesta Rom. p. 318.

(4) To cut glass or metal for cups, &c. ; to perforate or prick anything ; to ornament by cutting. A pounced decanter would be what we now term a cut decanter. See Arch. xxix. 55. " *Bulino,* a kind of *pouncer* that gravers use," Florio, p. 71.

POUNCES. The claws of a hawk.

POUNCET-BOX. A box perforated with holes used for carrying perfumes. *Shak.*

POUNCINGS. Holes stamped in garments, formerly made by way of ornament.

POUND. (1) A cyder mill. *Devon.*

(2) A head of water. *Var. dial.*

(3) To beat, or knock. *Glouc.*

POUNDER. Same as *Auncel*, q. v.

POUND-MELE. By the pound. (*A.-S.*)

POUND-NEEDLE. The herb *acus demenys.*

POUNDREL. The head. (*A.-S.*)

> So nimbly flew away these scoundrels,
> Glad they had 'scap'd, and sav'd their *poundrels.*
> > *Cotton's Works*, 1734, p. 14.

POUND-STAKLE. The floodgates of a pond.

POUNSONE. To punch a hole. (*A.-N.*)

POUNT-TOURNIS. A point or place to behold the tournament. (*A.-N.*)

POUPE. (1) A puppet. *Palsgrave.*

(2) To make a noise with a horn.

POURCHACE. To buy ; to provide. (*A.-N.*)

POURD-MILK. Beastlings. *Sussex.*

POURE. Poor. (*A.-N.*)

POURETT. Garlick. *Herefordsh.*

POURISH. To impoverish. (*A.-N.*) See Palsgrave, in v. *Make bare.*

POURIWINKLE. A periwinkle. *Palsgrave.*

POURTRAITURE. A picture, or drawing. *Pourtraiour,* a drawer of pictures. (*A.-N.*)

POUSE. Hazy atmosphere. *Lanc.*

POUSED. Pushed. Tryamoure, 1202.

POUSEMENT. Dirt ; refuse. *North.*

POUSTEE. Power. (*A.-N.*)

> In Alisaundre that grete citee
> Ther was a mon of muche *pousté ;*
> Pathmicius forsothe he hiht,
> He kepte wel the heste of God almiht.
> > *Vernon MS. Bodl. Lib.* f. 103.

> Erle he was of grete *pousté,*
> And lorde ovyr that cuntré.
> > *MS. Cantab.* Ff. ii. 38, f. 147.

POUT. A young bird. " *Fasanello,* a phesant pout," a young pheasant, Florio, p. 181.

POUTCH. To pout. *Poutle* is also used.

POVERLY. Poorly. (*A.-N.*)

> Yf hyt so *poverly* myghte sprede.
> > *MS. Cantab.* Ff. ii. 38, f. 93.

POVERT. Poverty. (*A.-N.*)

> Plee maketh *povert,*
> *Povert* maketh pees.
> > *MS. Soc. Antiq.* 134, f. 59.

> He beheld hyr and sche hym eke,
> And never a word to other thei speke,
> Fore the *poverte* that sche on hym se,
> That had bene so rych and hyge,
> The terys rane doune by hyr eyge !
> > *MS. Ashmole* 61, xv. Cent.

POVERTY-WEED. Purple cow-wheat. A weed growing in corn, having a fine large flower, yellow, pale red, and purple ; it is very injurious, and betokens a poor, light, stony, soil. Its popular name is peculiar to the Isle of Wight.

POVEY. An owl. *Glouc.* " Worse and worse, like Povey's foot," a West country proverb.

POVICE. A mushroom ; a fungus. *North.*

POW. (1) The poll, or head. *North.*

(2) The pricklebat. *Somerset.*

POWCHE. The crop of a fish.

POWDER. (1) Bustle ; haste. *Cumb.*

(2) To sprinkle ; to lay over lightly.

> And sythene sche broght in haste
> Plovers *powdird* in paste.
> > *MS. Lincoln* A. 1. 17, f. 136

POWDERINGS. Small pieces of fur powdered or sprinkled on others, resembling the spots on ermine.

POW-DIKE. A dike made in the fens for carrying off the waters.

POWE. A claw or finger. (*A.-N.*)
> Everich *powe* a span long,
> The fer out of his mothe sprong.
> *Arthour and Merlin*, p. 57.

POWER. (1) A large number. *Var. dial.*
> M. Gotes, mayir. Then came into Inglond kynge Jamys of Skotland, with a *pouar* of men, after Alhalow tide, and one John a Musgrave, with his company, met with hym, and in that skyrmysche the kyng was hurte or drounde.
> *MS. Cotton. Vespas.* A. xxv.

(2) Poor. (*A.-N.*)
> Thes *power* folk somtyme they bene ful wyse.
> *MS. Cantab.* Ff. i. 6, f. 159.

(3) The fish *gadus minutus.*

POWERATION. A great quantity. *West.*

POWLER. A barber. See the first part of Promos and Cassandra. v. 5, and Nares.

POWS. A pulse. See *Pouce* (1).
> Thurgh certeyne tokenes in *pows* and brethe,
> That bifalleth whenne he is nye the dethe.
> *Archæologia*, xix. 322.

POWSE. Pulse, beans, peas, &c. *Heref.*

POWSELS. Dirty scraps and rags. *Chesh.*

POWSE-MENT. One who does what is not right; but this name is generally given to those who are mischievous. *Lanc.*

POWSEY. Fat; decent-looking. *North.*

POWSH. A blister. Huloet, 1552.

POWSODDY. A Yorkshire pudding.

POWT. (1) To stir up. *North.*

(2) A cock of hay or straw. *Kent.*

POWTIL. To work feebly. *Northumb.*

POWTLE. To come forth out of the earth as moles do from their holes. *North.*

POW-WOW. Flat on one's back.

POX. The smallpox. This word was formerly a common and not indelicate imprecation.

POX-STONE. A very hard stone of a gray colour found in some of the Staffordshire mines. Kennett, MS. Lansd. 1033.

POY. A long boat-hook by which barges are propelled against the stream. *Linc.*

POYNET. A small bodkin.

POYSES. Posies.
> On every dore wer set whit crosses and ragged staves, with rimes and *poyses.*
> *Hall, Edward IV.* f. 23.

PRAALING. Tying a clog or canister to the tail of a dog. *Cornw.*

PRACTICE. Artifice; treachery. *Practisants*, associates in treachery.

PRACTICK. Practice. (*A.-N.*)

PRAISE. (1) Opinion. This word was formerly used in a more general sense than it now is. "Laus, Anglice, good preys; vel vituperum, Anglice, bad preys," MS. Bib. Reg. 12 B. i. f. 16.

(2) To show a sense of pain. *Dorset.*

(3) *Praise at parting*, a very common proverbial phrase in old writers, implying good wishes. It occurs in Towneley Myst. p. 320, the earliest instance of it I have met with.

PRANE. A prawn. *Palsgrave.*

PRANK. (1) To adorn; to decorate. It is the translation of *orner* in Hollyband's Dictionarie, 1593. In the same work we have, "*fame*

bien attintée, a woman *pranked* up," which phrase also occurs in the Winter's Tale, iv. 3. Palsgrave has, "I pranke ones gowne, I set the plyghtes in order."
> Fourthlye, that they be not *pranked* and decked up in gorgious and sumptious apparell in their play.
> *Northbrooke's Treatise*, 1577.

(2) To be crafty or subtle. *Palsgrave.*

PRANKLE. (1) To prance.

(2) A prawn. *I. of Wight.*

PRAPS. Perhaps. *Var. dial.*

PRASE. A small common. *Cornw.*

PRAT. A buttock. Dekker's Lanthorne and Candle-light, 1620, sig. C. ii.

PRATE-APACE. A forward child. *South.* In old writers, a talkative person.
> Prince of passions, *prate-apaces*, and pickl'd lovers; duke of disasters, dissemblers, and drown'd eyes; marquis of melancholy and mad folks; grand signior of griefs and groans; lord of lamentations, hero of heighhos! admiral of ay-mes! and monsieur of mutton laced. *Heywood's Love's Mistress*, p. 26.

PRATT. The following rhyme is still common, *Jack Spratt* being generally substituted.
> Archdeacon Pratt would eat no fatt,
> His wife would eat no lean;
> Twixt Archdeacon Pratt and Joan his wife,
> The meat was eat up clean.
> *Howell's English Proverbs*, p. 20.

> They fared somewhat like old Bishop Pratt and his wife, and were fain to consume even the very dreggs of the little which chance had set before them.
> *A Voice from Sion*, 1679, p. 3.

PRATTILY. Softly. *North.*

PRATTLE-BASKET. A prattling child.

PRAVANT. For *provant*, occurs in A Welch Bayte to spare Provender, 4to. Lond. 1603.

PRAVE. Depraved; bad. *Pravities*, depravities, Harrison's Britaine, p. 26.

PRAY: (1) To rid a moor of all stock, which is generally done twice a year (at Lady Day, and at Michaelmas), with a view to ascertain whether any person has put stock there without a right to do it. The unclaimed stock is then pounded till claimed by the owner, who is usually obliged to pay for trespassing. *West.*

(2) To lift anything up. *Suffolk.*

(3) Press; crowd. *Weber.*

PRAYD. Invited. *Weber.*

PRAYED-FOR. Churched. *North.*

PRAYELL. A little meadow. (*A.-N.*) *Prayere* occurs in Syr Gawayne.

PREACE. A press, or crowd. *Shak.*

PREACHMENT. A sermon.
> They'l make a man sleep till a *preachment* be spent,
> But we neither can warm our blood nor our wit in't.
> *Brome's Songs*, 1661, p. 72.

PREAMBULATION. A preamble. (*A.-N.*)

PREASER. Rennet. *Yorksh.*

PREAST. Praised. *Lanc.*

PREAZ. To try; to endeavour; to press forward. *Yorksh.*

PRECACIONS. Invocations. (*Lat.*)
> Beside our daily praiers and continual *precacions* to God and his saintes for prosperus successe to ensue in your merciall exployte and royall passage.
> *Hall, Henry V.* f. 5.

PRECE. To proceed. *Gawayne.*

PRECEDENT. Prognostic; indication. (2) A rough draft of writing. *Shak.*

PRECELLE. To excel. *Palsgrave.* See Lydgate's Minor Poems, p. 12.

· PRECEPT. A magistrate's warrant.

PRECESSIONERS. Candles used in procession at Candlemas Day. "For 2 *preshessiners* of 2ⁱⁱ redy made against Candlemas Day, 14ᵈ.," Merton College MSS.

PRECIE. Delicate; excellent. (*A.-N.*)

PRECIOUS. (1) Great; extraordinary. *Essex.* Often used ironically, implying worthlessness. (2) Over-nice. (*A.-N.*)

PRECISIAN. A serious person; a Puritan.
> I hope too the graver gentlemen, the *precisians* will not be scandaliz'd at my zeal for the promotion of poetry. *Gildon's Miscellaneous Letters and Essays*, 8vo. Lond. 1694, pref.

PRECONTRACT. A previous contract.

PREDE. Spoil; booty. Also, to spoil. See Stanihurst's Ireland, pp. 29, 45.

PREDESTINE. Predestination. (*A.-N.*)

PREDIAL-LANDS. Farm-lands.

PREDICATION. Preaching; a sermon. (*A.-N.*)
> He gaf me many a good certacion,
> With right and holsom *predicacion*,
> That he had laboured in Venus secrete cell,
> And me exponyd many a good gossepell,
> And many a right swete epistell eke,
> In hem perfite and not for to seke. *MS. Rawl.C. 86.*
> So befelle, thorow Goddis sonde,
> The bisshop that was of that londe
> Prechid in that cité;
> Alle gode men of that towne
> Come to his *predicacion*,
> Hym to herkyn and se.
> *MS. Cantab.* Ff. v. 48, f. 45.

PREEDY. With ease. "That lock goes mighty *preedy*," i. e. that lock goes well or with ease. *Cornw.*

PREEN. To prime, or trim up trees.

PREEZE. Mingere. *North.*

PREFE. Proof. Also, to prove. See the Sacrifice of Abraham, p. 15.
> And that ys ever my beleff,
> The trewth indede hytselff welle *preff*.
> *MS. Cantab* Ff. i. 6, f. 123.

PREFECT. The chief magistrate. (*Lat.*)

PREFIX. To fix or appoint a time for anything. "The prefixed hour," Shak.

PREGNANCY. Readiness of wit. From *pregnant*, intelligent, shrewd, artful.

PREIERE. A prayer. (*A.-N.*)

PREISABLE. Commendable; laudable.

PREISE. To appraise, or value. (*A.-N.*)

PREKE. (1) Prick, a piece of wood in the centre of the target.
> All they schot abowthe agen,
> The screffes men and he,
> Off the marke he welde not fayle,
> He cleffed the *preke* on thre. *Robin Hood*, i. 91.
(2) To ride quickly.
> Tryamowre rode forthe in haste,
> And *prekyd* among the oost
> Upon the tother syde ;
> The fyrste that rode to hym thon
> Was the kynge of Arragon,
> He kepeyd hym in that tyde.
> *MS. Cantab.* Ff. ii. 38, f. 76.

> The dewke of Lythyr sir Tyrré,
> He *prekyd* forthe fulle pertly.
> *MS. Cantab.* Ff. ii. 38, f. 76.
> The kyng come, with mony a man,
> *Prekyng* owt of the towne.
> *MS. Cantab.* Ff. ii. 38, f. 247.

PRELACIONE. Preference.
> Thorow oute the trompe into his ere,
> To sowne of suche *prelacione*.
> *Gower, MS. Soc. Antiq.* 134, f. 80.

PREME. Fierce; strong.
> Ther was no man yn hethyn londe
> Myght sytte a dynte of hys honde,
> The traytour was so *preme*.
> *MS. Cantab.* Ff. ii. 38, f. 89.

PREMEDIATE. To advocate one's cause.

PREMYE.
> The cytle of London, through his mere grauht and *premye*,
> Was first privyleged to have both mayer and shryve,
> Where before hys tyme it had but baylyves onlye.
> *Bale's Kynge Johan*, p. 85.

PRENDID. Pricked.

PRENE. An iron pan. *Somerset.*

PRENT. Chiefly; in the first place.

PRENTIS. An apprentice. "*Apprenticius*, a prentys," Nominale MS. A barrister was called a prentice, or prentice-of-law.

PREOVEST. Most approved. (*A.-S.*)

PREPARAT. Prepared. (*Lat.*)

PREPARE. Preparation. *Shak.*

PREPOSITION. " Prayse made before a great man, or preposition, *harengue*," Palsgrave.

PREPOSITOUR. A scholar appointed by the master to overlook the rest. Hormann, 1530.

PREPOSTERATE. To make preposterous.

PREPUCIE. Circumcision. (*Lat.*)

PRESANDE. A present. (*A.-N.*)
> I ete thaim not myself alon,
> I send *presandes* mony on,
> And fryndes make 1 me.
> *MS. Cantab.* Ff. v. 48, f. 50.

PRESBYTERIAN-TRICK. A dishonest bargain; a knavish trick. *Essex.*

PRESCIT. Reprobate. (*Lat.*)

PRESCRIPT. Order in writing. (*Lat.*)

PRESE. (1) A press, or crowd. (*A.-N.*)
> In he rydes one a rase,
> Or that he wiste where he was,
> In-to the thikkeste of the *prese*.
> *Perceval*, 1147.
(2) To crowd. Sometimes, to hasten.
> Of alle this yonge lusty route,
> Whiche al day *presen* hire aboute.
> *Gower, MS. Soc. Antiq.* 134, f. 64.

PRESEANCE. Priority of place.

PRESENCE. (1) A presence-chamber. *Shak.*
(2) Aspect; outward appearance. *East.*

PRESENT. (1) Immediate. (*Lat.*)
(2) A white spot on the finger-nail, supposed to augur good fortune. *West.*
(3) " At this present" means *now*, at this present time. The phrase occurs in our Prayer Book, and in Rider's Dictionarie, 1640.

PRESENTARIE. Present. (*Lat.*)

PRESENTERER. A prostitute. (*A.-N.*)

PRESENTLY. At this present time.
> Compiled and put in this forme suinge, by a servaunt of the Kyngs, that *presently* saw in effect a

great parte of his exploytes, and the resydewe knewe by true relation of them that were present at every tyme.   *Arrival of King Edward IV.* p. 1.

PRESEPE. A precept or order.

As wyfes makis bargans, a horse for a mare,
Thay lefe ther the febille and brynges ham the freche ware,
Clense wele jour eghne, and standis on bakke,
For here es comene a *presepe*, swykke menne to take.
    MS. Lincoln A. i. 17, f. 148.

PRESOMSEON. Presumption.

Corsid covetyse hit is the cause, prid, *presomseon*,
Je beth ungroundid in grace, jour God ye con not knowe,
Jour dedus demeys joue dredles, devocioun hit is withdraw,
Je han chasid away charité and the reule of relegyon.
    MS. Douce 302, f. 4.

PRESSING-IRON. An iron for smoothing linen. *Presser*, one who irons linen, caps, &c.

PRESTE. (1) Ready. (*A.-N.*)

The tother knyghtys, the boke says,
Prekyd to the palays,
   The lady for to here ;
Knyghtys apperyd to hur *preste*,
Then myght sche chose of the beste,
   Whych that hur wylie were.
    MS. Cantab. Ff. ii. 38, f. 77.

Whan they had fared of the best,
   With bred and ale and weyne,
To the bottys they made them *prest*,
   With bowes and boltys foll feyne.
    Robin Hood, i. 89.

And, therfore, *pristly* I jow praye
That je wille of joure talkyng blyne.
    MS. Lincoln A. i. 17, f. 149.

(2) A loan ; money paid before due ; earnest money given to a soldier at impressment. In *prest*, in advance, Ord. and Reg. p. 12. *Prest-money*, ibid. p. 309.

(3) Neat ; tight ; proper.

(4) A barrow or tumulus. *Yorksh.*

PRESTER-JOHN. The name of a fabulous Christian King of India. See Maundevile, ed. 1839.

Mount now to Gallo-belgicus ; appear
As deep a statesman as a garretteir.
Homely and familiarly, when thou com'st back,
Talk of Will. Conquerour, and *Prester Jack*.
    Donne's Poems, p. 261.

PRESTIGIATE. To deceive.

Even as a craftie juggler doth so *prestigiate* and blinde mens outward senses by the delusions of Sathan.   *Dent's Pathway to Heaven*, p. 10.

PRETENCE. Intent ; design. *Shak.*

PRETEND. (1) To intend. *Shak.*

(2) To lay claim to. (*A.-N.*)

(3) To portend ; to forebode.

PRETENSED. Intended ; designed. The word is used several times by Hall, and also occurs in Sir John Oldcastle, ii. 3. See *Incepted.*

They can never be clerely extirpate or digged out of their rotten hartes, but that they wille with hande and fote, toothe and nayle, further if they can their *pretensed* enterprice.   *Hall, Henry VII.* f. 6.

It is *pretensed* mynde and purpose set,
That bindes the bargain sure.
    Turbevile's Ovid, 1567, fol. 144.

Requiring you to joine with us and we with you in advauncing forward this our incepted purpose, and *pretensed* enterprice.   *Hall, Henry IV.* f. 5.

PRETERIT. Passed. (*A.-N.*)

PRETERMYT. To omit.

I *pretermyt* also the ryche apparell of the pryncesse, the straunge fasshion of the Spanyshe nacion, the beautie of the Englishe ladyes.
    Hall, Henry VII. f. 53.

PRETOES. Loans ?

Our great landlords bespake him with lofty rents, with fines, and *pretoes*, and I know not what.
    Rowley's Search for Money, 1609.

PRETORY. The high court. (*Lat.*)

Pilate up ros, and forth he jede
Out of the *pretory*.
    Cursor Mundi, MS. Coll. Trin.Cantab. f. 101.

PRETTY. (1) Neat ; fine. (2) Crafty.

PRETTY-FETE. A moderate quantity. *Berks.*

PREVALY. Privily ; secretly.

The golde unto his chambir he bare,
And hyd it fulle *prevaly* thare.
    Isumbras, 641.

Then longed he at home to bene
And for to speke with hys quene,
   That hys thoght was ever upon,
And he gate schyppys *prevay*,
And to the schypp on a day
He thoght that he flewe anon.
    MS. Cantab. Ff. ii. 38, f. 72.

PREVE. (1) To prove. (2) A proof.

Thou most have fayth, hope, and charyté,
This is the ground of thi beleve,
Ellys i-savyd thou mat nojt be,
Thus Poul in his pystyl he doth *preve*.
    MS. Douce 302, f. 2.

Preves i-now ther ben of youre peté.
    MS. Cantab. Ff. i. 6, f. 134.

PREVELACHE. Privilege.

I say the, broder Salamon, tel in thi talkyng,
Furst of the frerys thus meve thou may,
Of here *prevelache*, and of here prayrys, and here preching,
And of here clergé and clannes and onest aray.
    MS. Douce 302, f. 4.

PREVELYKE. Privily. See *Prevaly.*

And thoghte yn hys herte *prevelyke*,
That many a woman ys odur y-lyke.
    MS. Cantab. Ff. ii. 38, f. 143.

PREVENT. To go before ; to precede ; to anticipate. (*Lat.*)

PREVENTION. Jurisdiction. (*Lat.*)

Your sayd Grace, by verteu off your legantine prerogative and *prevention*, conferr to hys chapleyn, Mr. Wilson, the vicarege of Thackstedd.
    State Papers, i. 311.

PREW.

They helde hym vyler than a Jew,
For no man wulde hys *prew*.
    MS. Harl. 1701, f. 18.

PRIAL. Three cards of a sort, at the game of commerce particularly : a corruption, probably, of *pair-royal.* Under the latter term, Nares confirms this derivation, and gives many quotations in illustration of the word. Moor's Suffolk Words.

PRICE. Estimation ; value. *To bere the pryce,* to win the prize, to excel.

The Kyng jorneyd in Tracyens,
That is a cyté off grete defence,
And with hym hys quene off *price*,
That was callyd dame Meroudys;
A feyrere lady than sche was one,
Was never made off flessch ne bone;
Sche was full off lufe and godnes,
Ne may no mane telle hyre feyrnes.

       MS. Ashmole 61, xv. Cent.

Then the qwene was fulle gladd,
That sche soche a lorde hadd,
     Ye wott, wythowtyn lees.
Sche seyde, Y have welle sped
That soche a lorde hath me wedd,
     That beryth the *pryce* in prees.

       MS. Cantab. Ff. ii. 38, f. 82.

PRICER. A person whose duty it was to regulate the prices of a market.

PRICH. Thin weak liquor. *North.*

PRICHELL. A brake; an instrument for dressing hemp or flax. It is the translation of *brosse* in Hollyband's Dictionarie, 1593.

PRICK. (1) The same as *Preke* (1). Hence *prick and praise*, the praise of excellence.

And therfore every man judged as he thought,
and named a sicknes that he knew, shothing not
nere the *pricke*, nor understanding the nature of the
disease.   *Hall, Henry V.* f. 50.

    Then leave off these thy burning rays,
    And give to Pan the *prick* and praise;
    Thy colour change, look pale and wan,
    In honour of the great god Pan.

       Heywood's Love's Mistress, p. 42.

Now Tarlton's dead, the consort lacks a vice,
For knave and fool thou must bear *pricke* and price.

       A Whip for an Ape, 1589.

(2) A term of endearment. It occurs in Palsgrave's Acolastus, 1540.

(3) A point; a dot.

Like to a packe without a *pricke*,
Or o-per-se in arithmeticke.

       MS. Egerton 923, f. 3.

(4) A skewer.

I geve to the butchers *prickes* inoughe to sette up
their thinne meat that it may appeare thicke and
well fedde.   *The Wyll of the Devill*, n. d.

(5) A goad for oxen; a pointed weapon of almost any kind. (*A.-S.*) In the provinces, a pointed stick is still so called.

(6) To wound; to spur a horse; to ride hard. See *Preke* (2).

(7) To trace a hare's footsteps.

(8) To germinate. Still in use.

(9) A period of time.

(10) To turn sour. *Somerset.*

(11) To decorate. "I *pricke* a cuppe or suche lyke thynge full of floures, *je enfleure*," Palsgrave. "I *pricke* full of bowes as we do a place or a horse whan we go a mayeng, *je rame*," ibid. In Lincolnshire, the slips of evergreens with which the churches are decorated from Christmas eve to the eve of Candlemas day are termed *prickings*.

PRICKASOUR. A hard rider. (*A.-S.*)

PRICKER. (1) Any sharp-pointed instrument. "*Punctorium*, a prykker," Nominale MS.

(2) A light horseman. There was formerly a cavalry regiment termed the *prickers*.

PRICKET. (1) A wax taper.

(2) The buck in his second year.

If thou wilt come and dwell with me at home.
My sheepcote shall be strowed with new greene
    rushes;
Weele haunt the trembling *prickets* as they rome
    About the fields, along the hanthorne bushes;
I have a pie-bald curre to hunt the hare,
So we will live with daintie forrest fare.

       The Affectionate Shepheard, 1594.

PRICKING-KNIFE.

Than bespake the *prykyng-knyfe*,
   He duellys to nyje the ale-wyfe;
Sche makes oft tyme his purse full thynne,
No peny some tyme sche levys therin;
Tho thou gete more than other thre,
Thryfty man he canne not be.   *MS. Ashmole* 61.

PRICKINGS. The footsteps of a hare.

Unto these also you may adde, those which cannot discerne the footings or *prickings* of the hare, yet will they runne speedily when they see her, or else at the beginning set forth very hot, and afterward tyre, and give over lazily; all these are not to be admitted into the kennell of good hounds.

       Topsell's Four-Footed Beasts, 1607, p. 152.

PRICKLE. (1) To prick. *North.*

(2) A wicker basket. *Var. dial.*

PRICK-LOUSE. A nickname for a tailor.

She would in brave termes abuse him, and cal'
him rascall, and slave, but above all *pricklouc:*
which he could not abide: wherefore having often
forbad her, and seeing she would take no warning,
on a day tooke heart at grasse, and belaboured her
well in a cudgel: but all would not suffice; the more
he beat her, the more she calde him *pricklouse*.

       Tarlton's Newes out of Purgatorie, 1590.

PRICK-LUGGED. Having erect ears.

PRICKMEDENTY. A finical person.

PRICK-POST. A timber framed into the principal beam of a floor. Pricke-posts are mentioned in Harrison's England, p. 187.

PRICKS. A game like bowls.

PRICKSONG. Music pricked or noted down, full of flourish and variety.

So that at her next voyage to our Lady of Court
of Strete, she entred the chappell with "Ave Regina
Coelorum" in *pricksong*, accompanied with these
commissioners, many ladies, gentlemen, and gentlewomen of the best degree.

       Lambarde's Perambulation of Kent, 1596, p. 192.

My *prick-songs* alwayes full of largues and longs,
Prick-song (indeed) because it pricks my hart;
And song, because sometimes I ease my smart.

       The Affectionate Shepheard, 1594.

And all for this pevysh *pryk-song* not worth to
   strawes
That we poore sylye boyes abyde much woe.

       Ballad by Redford, Bright MS.

PRICK-WAND. A wand set up for a mark to shoot arrows at. *Percy.*

PRIDE. (1) A mud lamprey. *Wes'.* "Lumbrici are littell fyshes taken in small ryvers, whiche are lyke to lampurnes, but they be muche lesse, and somewhat yeolowe, and are called in Wilshyre *prides*," Llyotes Dictionarie, fol. Lond. 1559.

(2) "*Pryde* goyth byfore, and shame comyth after," MS. Douce, 52. The same proverb occurs in Wyntown's Chronykil, and Nash's Pierce Penilesse, 1592.

For if she sons tume and be variable,
And put the drede of God out of mynd,
Pride gothe byfor and shame comyth behynd.
MS. Laud. 416, f. 57.

(3) In good flesh and heart, in good condition. An old hawking term.

(4) Fineness; splendour. *North.*

(5) Lameness; impediment. *Chesh.*

PRIDELES. Without pride. (*A-S.*)

PRIDY. Proud. *Cornw.*

PRIE. The plant privet.

PRIEST-ILL. The ague. *Devon.*

PRIEST'S CROWN. "Prestes crowne that flyeth about in somer, *barbedieu*," Palsgrave. See Cotgrave, in v. *Dent.*

PRIG. (1) A small pitcher. *South.*

(2) To higgle in price. *North.*

(3) A small brass skellet. *Yorksh.*

(4) To steal. *Var. dial.* Prygman, a thief, Fraternitye of Vacabondes, 1575.

(5) An old coxcomb. *Devon.*

(6) To ride. A cant term. Dekker's Lanthorne and Candle-light, sig. C. ii.

PRIGGISH. Conceited; affected. *North.*

PRIG-NAPPER. A horse-stealer.

PRIJEL. An iron tool for forcing nails out of wood, otherwise perhaps called a monkey. Moor's Suffolk MS.

PRIKELLE. To drive, or push. *Hearne.*

PRIKERE. A rider. *Lydgate.*

PRILL. (1) To turn sour. *Devon.*

(2) A small stream of water. *West.*

(3) A child's whirligig toy.

PRIM. (1) The fry of smelts. *East.*

(2) A neat pretty girl. *Yorksh.*

(3) The plant privet. *Tusser.*

PRIMAL. Original; first. *Shak.*

PRIMA-VISTA. Primero. "The game at cardes called primero or prima vista," Florio, p. 400. It is called *primefisto* in a list of games in Taylor's Motto, 12mo. 1622, sig. D. iv.

PRIME. (1) To trim trees. *East.*

(2) Good; excellent. *Var. dial.*

(3) The hour of six o'clock, a. m.

Thou wotte welle that hit is soo,
And other gatis hit shalle goo
Er to morne at *prime*;
Thou hast me brou3t into this ille,
And I shalle ful wele have my wille
When I se my tyme.
MS. Cantab. Ff. v. 48, f. 44.

(4) First. *Prime temps*, first time.

(5) A term at primero.

(6) Eager; maris appetens. *Shak.*

(7) The footstep of a deer.

(8)

For (as a thrifty wench scrapes kitching-stuff,
And barrilling the droppings, and the snuffe
Of wasting candles, which in thirty year
(Reliquely kept) perchance buyes wedding chear)
Piecemeal he gets lands, and spends as much time
Wringing each acre, as maids *pulling prime*.
Donne's Poems, p. 124.

PRIME-COCK-BOY. "A prime-cock-boy, a freshman, a novice, a milke-sop, a boy new come into the world," Florio, p. 227.

PRIMED. (1) Intoxicated. *North.*

(2) Spotted from disease. *Suffolk.*

PRIME-GOOD. Excellent. *North.*

PRIMELY. Capitally. *North.*

PRIMER. First; primary.

He who from lusts vile bondage would be freed,
Its *primier* flames to suffocate must heed.
Sin is a plant, which if not from the root
Soon pluckt, will soon to spreading mischief shoot:
Which if it does, its venom soon we find
Infecting all our blood, and all our mind.
History of Joseph, 1691.

Forasmuch as it hath pleased our Lorde God for to suffer and graunte me grace for the *primer* notable workes purposed by me.
Nichols' Royal Wills, p. 293.

PRIMERO. A game at cards. According to the Compleat Gamester, ed. 1721, p. 49, it went rapidly out of fashion after the introduction of the game of ombre. The same authority informs us that primero was played with six cards, and was similar to the latter game. See Ben Jonson, ii. 31; Florio, pp. 71, 400, 410.

PRIMEROLE. A primrose. (*A.-N.*)

The honysoucle, the froishe *prymerollys*,
Ther levys splaye at Phebus up-rysyng.
Lydgate's Minor Poems, p. 242.

PRIMETEMPS. Spring. (*A.-N.*) Some Elizabethan poets have *prime-tide.*

PRIMINERY. A difficulty. *North.*

PRIMORDIAL. Original; earliest.

PRIMOSITY. Prudery. A word used by Pitt and Lady Stanhope. Memoirs of Lady Hester Stanhope, 8vo. 1845.

PRIMP. To be very formal. *Cumb.*

PRIM-PRINT. The plant privet.

The most excellent is the greene coloured catterpiller, which is found uppon that great bushy plant, usually termed privet, or *primprint,* which hath a circle enclosing round both his eyes and all his feete, having also a crooked horne in his tayle: these catterpillers are blackish-redde, with spots or streakes going overthwart theyr sides, beeing halfe white and halfe purpelish, the little pricks in these spots are inclining to redde: the rest of theyr body is altogether greene.
Topsell's Historie of Serpents, p. 103.

PRIMY. Early. *Shak.*

PRIN. (1) A pin. *North.*

(2) Prim; affectedly neat.

Hee looks as gaunt and *prin,* as he that spent
A tedious twelve years in an eager Lent.
Or bodyes at the Resurection are
On wing, just rarifying into ayre.
Fletcher's Poems, p. 140.

PRINADO. A sharper.

PRINCHE. To be niggardly?

Ther was with him non other fare
But for to *prinche* and for to spare,
Of worldis muk to gete encres.
Gower, MS. Soc. Antiq. 134, f. 157.

PRINCIPAL. (1) A heirloom. Sometimes the mortuary, the principal or best horse led before the corpse of the deceased.

And also that my best horse shall be my *principal,* without any armour or man armed, according to the custom of mean people. *Test. Vetust.* p. 75.

(2) The corner posts of a house, tenoned into

the ground plates below, and into the beams of the roof.

PRINCOCK. A pert saucy youth. Brockett has *princox* as still in use, and *princy-cock* is given by Carr, ii. 58.

If hee bee a little bookish, let him write but the commendation of a flea, straight begs he the coppie, kissing, hugging, grinning, and smiling, till hee make the yong *princocks* as proud as a pecocke.
Lodge's Wits Miserie, 1596.

PRINCOD. A pincushion. *North.* Figuratively, a short thickset woman.

PRINGLE. A little silver Scotch coin, about the value of a penny, current in the north parts of England. Kennett, MS.

PRINIT. Take it. *Wilts.*

PRINK. (1) To adorn; to dress wel; to be smart and gay. "To be prinkt up, to be drest up fine or finical like children or vain women," MS. Lansd. 1033.

(2) To look at; to gaze upon. *West.*
(3) To be pert or forward. *North.*

PRINSEDE. A principality. It is t e translation of *principatus* in Nominale MS.

PRINT. (1) An imprint, or impression; an effigy, or image; the imprint of money.

(2) A mould for coin, &c.
(3) *In print*, with great exactness. Still in use, according to Palmer and Forb.
(4) Clear and bright. *Kent.*
(5) A newspaper. *Var. dial.*

PRIOR. The cross-bar to which the doors of a barn are fastened, and which prevents them from being blown open.

PRISE. (1) A lever. *Var. dial.*
(2) The note of the horn blown on the death of a deer in hunting.

Syr Eglamour hase done to dede
A grete herte, and tane the hede;
The *pryse* he blewe fulle schille.
MS. Lincoln A. i. 17, f. 140.

(3) Fine; good; prized.

PRISED. Overturned; destroyed.

PRISON. A prisoner. (*A.-N.*)

PRISONER'S-BARS. A game. See *Base* (4).

PRISTE. A priest.

The kynge his false goddis alle forsuke,
And Crystyndome of *priste* he tuke.
MS. Lincoln A. i. 17, f 129.

PRISTINATE. Former; pristine.

I thynke, yea and doubt not but your line shalbe again restored to the *pristinate* estate and degree.
Hall, Richard III. f. 13.

PRITCH. (1) To check, or withstand. *West.*
(2) Any sharp-pointed instrument. Hence, to pierce or make holes. *East.*

PRITCHEL. An iron share fixed on a thick staff for making holes in the ground. *Kent.*

PRITTLE. To chatter. "You *prittle* and prattle nothing but leasings and untruths," Heywood's Royall King, 1637, sig. B. *Prittle-prattle*, childish talk.

PRIVADO. A private friend. (*Span.*)

And here Franklin, a kind of physician, Weston, a servant to Sir Thomas, and Sir Jervace Yelvis, who is (as you shall hereafter hear) *privado* to the Earl and Viscount, and the Countess and Mrs.

Turner, are made instruments to kill and dispatch Sir Thomas Overbury. *MS. Harl.* 4888.

PRIVATE. Interest; safety; privacy.

PRIVE. Private; secret. (*A.-N.*) Also a verb, to keep or be secret.

Til gentilmen and yomanry,
Thei have thaim alle thei ar worthy,
Those that are *privé*.
MS. Cantab. Ff. v. 48, f. 50.

PRIVETEE. Private business.

PRIVY-COAT. A light coat or defence of mail concealed under the ordinary habit.

PRIVY-EVIL. According to Markham, is in hawks "a secret heart-sickness procured either by overflying corrupt food, cold, or other disorderly keeping, but most especially for want of stones or casting in the due season: the signs are heaviness of head and countenance, evil enduring of her meat, and fowl black mutings," Cheap and Good Husbandry, ed. 1676, p. 133.

PRIZALL. A prize. *D ntel.*

PRIZE. (1) "A *prize* of that," meaning I don't mind it; "a pish for it." Do they not mean a *pize* or *pish* for it: as if they should say, it's but a trifle and not to be cared about, therefore a pize of it. *Linc.*

(2) To favour an affected limb, as a horse does. *Dorset.*

PROANDER. Peradventure. *Cornw.*

PROBABLE. Proveable.

PROBAL. Probable. *Shak.*

PROCEED. To take a degree. This term is still used at the Universities.

PROCERE. Large.

Be it never so strong, vallant fair, goodly, plaant
In aspect, *procere*, and tall. *Becon's Works*, p. 204.

PROCES. Story; relation; progress.

PROCKESY. A proxy. *Palsgrave.*

PROCLIVE. To be prone to.

PROCT. A large prop of wood. *Linc.*

PROCTOR. One who collected alms for lepers, or other persons unable to do it themselves. According to Kennett, beggars of any kind were called *proctors*. The Fraternitye of Vacabondes, 1575, has the following notice:—

"Proctour is he that wil tary long, and bring a lye, when his maister sendeth him on his errand." Forby has *proctor*, to hector, swagger, or bully, which he considers derived from the older word.

PROD. A goad for oxen; any sharp-pointed instrument. Also a verb, to prick or goad; to thrust. *North.* We have also *proddle* used in the same sense.

PRODIGAL. Proud. *Heref.*

PRODIGIOUS. Portentous; horrible.

PROFACE. An exclamation equivalent to "Much good may it do you." See the Downfall of Robert, Earl of Huntington, p. 57.

PROFER. A rabbit burrow.

PROFESSIOUN. The monastic profession.

PROFETS. Buskins. *Exmoor.*

PROFFER. To dodge any one. *Devon.*

PROFLIGATE. To drive off.

With how fervent heart should we *profligate* and chase away sin. *Becon's Works*, p 66 'n the which I doubt not but God will rather aid us ; yea, (and fight for us) than see us vanquished and *profligated*, by such as neither fear Him nor His laws, nor yet regard justice or honesty.

Hall's Union, 1548.

PROFUND. To lavish. (*Lat.*)

For the exchewing of grete expences, whiche shuld be *profunded* and consumed in the said interview, wherof ther is no node here, considering the grete sommes of money that promptely be to be payde.

State Papers, i. 251.

PROG. (1) Food. *Var. dial.*

(2) The same as *Prod*, q. v.

PROGRESS. The travelling of the sovereign and court to various parts of the kingdom.

PROHEME. A preface.

PROIGNE. To prune. Here it means to pick out damaged feathers, as birds do. According to Markham, "a hawk *proines* when she fetches oil with her beak over her tail."

For joye they *proigne* hem evyry mornynge.

MS. Ashmole 59, f. 20.

PROINER. A pruner. *Somerset.*

PROINING. Prying. *Linc.*

PROJECTION. An operation in alchemy ; the moment of transmutation.

He revealed to one Roger Cooke the great secret of the elixar, as he called it, of the salt of metalls, the *projection* whereof was one upon an hundred.

MS. Ashmole 1788, f. 147.

PROKE. To entreat, or insist upon. Also, to stir, or poke about. Hence perhaps *proking-spit*, a kind of rapier, mentioned in Hall's Satires, p. 99.

PROKETOWR. A proctor. *Pr. Parv.*

PROKING-ABOUT. A familiar term applied to a person who is busily looking for something, and examining, as we say, " every hole and corner." Sharp's MS. Warw. Gloss.

PROLIXIOUS. Prolix ; causing delay.

PROLLE. To search, or prowl about ; to rob, poll, or steal ; to plunder.

PROLONGER. A mathematical instrument, mentioned in Trenchfield's Cap of Gray Hairs for a Green Head, 12mo. Lond. 1688, p. 153.

PROMESSE. To promise. (*A.-N.*)

Thou knowyst my ryȝte, Lorde, and other men also ;
As it is my ryȝte, Lorde, so thou me defende :
And the quarell that is wronge, it may be overthrow,
And to ryght parte the victory thou sende.
And I *promesse* the, good Lorde, my lyffe to amende,
I knoleye me a synner wrappid in woo,
And all said with one voyse, Lorde, thy will be doo !

MS. Bibl. Reg. 17 D. xv.

PROMISCUOUSLY. Accidentally ; by chance.

PROMISE. To assure. *Var. dial.*

PROMITTED. Disclosed. (*Lat.*)

Promisinge to theim franke and free pardone of all offences and commes [crimes ?] *promitted*, and promocious and rewardes, for obeynge to the kynges request. *Hall, Henry VII.* f. 33.

PROMONT. A promontory.

PROMOTER. An informer.

PROMOVE. To promote, or patronize.

PRONE. Changeable. *Shak.*

PRONG. (1) A point. *North.*

(2) A hayfork. *Prong steel*, the handle of a hayfork. *South.*

PRONOTORY. A chief notary.

PROOF. Land is said to be *proof*, when it is of an excellent quality. *Warw.*

PROOFY. Nutritious. *South.*

PROP. To help, or assist. *North.*

PROPER. (1) Very ; exceeding. *Var. dial.*

(2) Handsome ; witty. Still in use in Cornwall, according to Polwhele.

(3) *To make proper*, to adorn.

(4) To appropriate. *Palsgrave.*

(5) Becoming ; deserved. *East.*

PROPERTIES. Dresses of actors ; articles and machinery necessary for the stage.

PROPERTY. A cloak, or disguise.

PROPHACION. Profanation. *Hall.*

PROPICE. Convenient ; propitious. (*Lat.*)

Wherfore he edified bulwarkes, and buylded fortresses on every syde and parte of his realme, where might be any place *propice* and mete for an armie to arrive or take lande. *Hall, Edward IV.* f. 3.

PROPINE. To drink healths. (*Lat.*)

PROPONED. Proposed. (*Lat.*)

Denlyng fiersly, al the other new invencions alleged and *proponed* to his charge.

Hall's Union, 1548.

Which being *proponed* and declared to the said emperor, and that in the final determination of our said cause, and all the whole circumference thereof, we have, according to our most bounden duty, nothing else studied. *MS. Cotton. Nero*, B. vi.

PROPOS. A proposition.

PROPOUNDERS. Monopolists. *Blount.*

PROPRIS. Possessions ; property.

PROPS. Legs. *Var. dial.*

PROPULSE. To repulse. (*Lat.*)

By whiche craftie ymagined invencion they might either cloke or *propulse* from them al suspicion of their purposed untruthe and shamefull disloyaltie.

Hall, Henry VII. f. 19.

Perceavyng that all succours were clerely estopped and *propulsed* from them, and so brought into utter despaire of aide or comfort. *Hall, Henry VII.* f. 23.

PROSCRIBE. To prescribe. " I *proscrybe* (Lydgate) for I prescrybe," Palsgrave.

PROSPECTIVE. A perspective glass.

PROSPERATION. Prosperity.

PROSS. (1) Talk ; conversation. *North.*

(2)

They have onely three speers or *prosses*, the two lower turne awry, but the uppermost groweth upright to heaven, yet sometimes it falleth out (as the keepers of the saide beast affirmed) that either by sicknes or else through want of food, the left horn hath but two branches ; in length they are one Roman foot and a halfe, and one finger and a halfe in bredth, at the roote two Roman palmes.

Topsell's Four-Footed Beasts, p. 327.

PROTENSE. Extension ; drawing out.

PROTER. A poker. *Suffolk.*

PROTHODAWE.

An arche foole cannot forge a lye for his pleasure, but a *prothodawe* wyll faine a glose to mainteine his folish fantasie. *Hall, Henry V.* f. 41

PROTRACT. Delay. (*Lat.*)

PROTRITE. Beaten up. (*Lat.*)

The fourth most *protrite* and manifest unto the world is their inconstancie.

Wright's Passions of the Minde, 1621, p. 40.

.PROU. An interjection used in driving cattle when they loiter.

PROUD. (1) Luxuriant. *North.*

(2) Full; high; swelled. *Linc.* Pegge explains it *large*, ed. 1839, p. 123.

(3) Swelling; having a sore inflammation, as flesh has. *West.*

(4) To be maris appetens. *North.*

> Yong man wereth jolif,
> And than *proudeth* man and wilf.
>
> *Arthour and Merlin*, p. 11.

PROUD-PEAR. A kind of pear. It is mentioned in Florio, ed. 1611, p. 182.

PROUD-TAILOR. A goldfinch. *Var. dial.*

PROULER. A cozener, or thief.

PROVAND. Provender; provision.

> Whilles that lyarde myght drawe, the whilles was he luffed,
> Thay putt hym to *provande*, and therwyth he provede;
> Now he may noghte do his dede, as he myght by-forn,
> Thay lyg by-fore hym pese-straa, and beris away the corn.   *MS. Lincoln A. i. 17, f. 143.*

> And though it were as good, it would not convert clubs and clouted shoone from the flesh-pots of Egipt, to the *provant* of the Low-countreyes.
>
> *Nash's Pierce Pennilesse*, 1592.

> These sea-sick soldiers rang hills, woods, and vallies,
> Seeking *provant* to fill their empty bellies;
> Jones goes alone, where Fate prepar'd to meet him
> With such a prey as did unfriendly greet him.
>
> *Legend of Captain Jones*, 1659.

PROVANG. A whalebone instrument used for cleansing the stomach. See Aubrey's Wilts, Royal Soc. MS. p. 191.

PROVANT-MASTER. A person who provided apparel for soldiers. See B. Riche's Fruites of Long Experience, 1604, p. 19. In Webster's Works, ii. 152, we have *provant apparel*, apparel furnished to soldiers. *Provant-breeches*, Middleton, iv. 489.

PROVE. (1) To thrive; to be with young, generally said of cattle.

(2) *To prove masteries*, to make trial of skill, to try who does the best.

PROVENDE. A prebend; a daily or annual allowance or stipend. (*A.-N.*)

> Ne çit a lettre for to sende,
> For dignité ne for *provende*.
>
> *Gower, MS. Soc. Antiq.* 134, f. 32.

PROVIAUNCE. Provision. (*A.-N.*)

PROVISOUR. A purveyor, or provider.

PROVOKEMENT. Provocation. *Spenser.*

PROVOSTRY. The office of provost.

PROVULGE. To publish. (*Lat.*)

> Considering that the king hath alredy, and also before any censures *provulged*, bothe provoked and appeled.   *State Papers*, i. 413.

PROW. A small boat attendant on a larger vessel. Kennett, MS. Lansd. 1033.

PROWE. Honour; profit; advantage.

> In long abydyng is ful lytyl *prowe*.
>
> *MS. Rawl. Poet.* 118.

> Yif any man wil say now,
> That I not deyde for mannys *prow*,
> Rather thanne he schulde be forlorne,
> Yet I wolde eft be al to-torne.
>
> *MS. Coll. Cati Cantab.*

PROWESSE. Integrity. (*A.-N.*)

PROWEST. Most valiant. *Spenser.*

PROWOR. A priest. (*A.-N.*)

PROWSE. Prowess. *Warner.*

PRU. The same as *Prowe*, q. v.

> Do nat as the Pharysee
> Preyde God açens hys *pru*.
>
> *MS. Harl.* 1701, f. 77

> Ne more hyt ys lore the vertu
> Of the messe, but mannys *pru*.
>
> *MS. Harl.* 1701, f. 16.

PRUCE. Prussia.

> And I bequeth, yef that I dey shall,
> For to hold my fest funeral,
> An hundreth marke of *pruce* money fyne,
> For to bistow upon bred and wyne,
> With other drynkys that dilicious be,
> Whiche in ordre herafter ye shall se.
>
> *MS. Rawl.* C. 86.

PRUDGAN. Pert; brisk; proud. *Prud*, proud, occurs in Havelok, 302.

PRUGGE. A partner, or doxy.

PRUMOROLE. A primrose. (*A.-N.*)

> He shal ben lyk the lytel bee,
> That seketh the biosme on the tre,
> And souketh on the *prumorole*.
>
> *MS. Addit.* 11307, f. 67.

PRUNE. The same as *Proigne*, q. v.

PRUNES. It appears from passages in Maroccus Extaticus, 1595, and other works, that stewed prunes were commonly placed in the windows of houses of disreputable character.

PRUT. An exclamation of contempt.

> And setteth hym ryçt at the lefte,
> And seyth *prut* for thy cursyng prest.
>
> *MS. Harl.* 1701, f. 90

PRUTE. To wander about like a child.

PRUTTEN. To be proud; to hold up the head with pride and disdain. *North.* *Prute*, proud, occurs in Wright's Pol. Songs, p. 203.

PRYNE. Chief; first? (*A.-N.*)

> Be hyt wyth ryghte or wyth synne,
> Hym wyl he holde moste *pryne*.
>
> *MS. Harl.* 1701, f. 30.

PRYOWRE. The first; the chief.

> Sche seyde thou semyste a man of honour,
> And therfore thou schalt be *pryowre*.
>
> *MS. Cantab. Ff. ii. 38, f. 110.*

PRYVATED. Deprived.

> They woulde not onelye lese their wordely substaunce, but also be *pryvated* of their lives and worldly felycytie, rather then to suffre Kynge Rycharde, that tyraunt, lenger to rule and reygne over them.   *Hall, Richard III.* f. 17.

PSALL. A soul. *Percy.*

PUANT. Stinking. *Skelton.*

PUB. The poop of a vessel.

PUBBLE. Plump; full. *North.* Kennett applies it to corn, MS. Lansd. 1033.

> Thou shalt me fynde fat and well fed,
> As *pubble* as may be;
> And, when thou wilt, a merie mate
> To laughe and chat with thee.
>
> *Drant, ap. Warton*, iii. 346.

PUBLE. A pebble. *Palsgrave.*

PUBLIC. An inn, or alehouse. *Var. dial.*

PUCELLE. A virgin; a girl. (*Fr.*)

PUCK. (1) Picked. *Warw.*

(2) A fiend. Robin Goodfellow was often so

called. The term is still retained in the Western counties in the phrase *puck-ledden*, bewitched, fairy led, strangely and unaccountably confused.

PUCKER. Confusion; bother; perplexity; fright; bustle. *Var. dial.*

PUCKETS. Nests of caterpillars. *Sussex.* Moor says it is used in Suffolk.

PUCK-FIST. The common puff-ball, or fungus. It was frequently used by early writers as a term of contempt; an empty, insignificant, boasting fellow.

> Old father *pukfist* knits his arteries,
> First strikes, then rails on Riot's villanies.
> *Middleton's Epigrams*, 1608.

> If with these honors vertue he embrace,
> Then love him : else his *puckfoist* pompe abhorre.
> Sunshine or dung-hils makes them stinke the more,
> And honor shewes all that was hid before.
> *Taylor's Workes*, 1630, I. 3.

PUCKLE. (1) A pimple. *Salop.*

(2) A spirit, or ghost ; a puck.

PUCKRELS. A small fiend or puck.

> And I thinke he told me, that he shewed him her in a glasse, and told him she had three or foure impes, some call them *puckrels*, one like a grey cat, another like a weasel, another like a mouse, a vengeance take them, it is a great pitie the country is not rid of them, and told him also what he should do ; it is half a yeare ago, and he never had any hurt since. *Gifford's Dialogue on Witches*, 1603.

PUCKSY. A quagmire. *West.* Possibly from *Puck*, who led night-wanderers into bogs, &c. Hence the phrase, " he got out of the muxy and fell into the pucksy"—

> Incidit in Scyllam cupiens vitare Charybdini.

PUD. (1) Budded. *Weber.*

(2) The hand, or fist. *West.*

PUDDER. Confusion ; bother.

> Upon which my Lorde Willoughbie's counsell, though to little purpose, made a great deale of *pudder*, for all the acts of parliament from E. 3 time till R. 2 are enroled in French. *MS. Harl.* 388.

PUDDERING-POLE. A stirring-pole ?

> So long as he who has but a teeming brain may have leave to lay his eggs in his own nest, which is built beyond the reach of every man's *puddering-pole*. *N. Fairfax, Bulk and Selvedge*, 1674.

PUDDING. A stuffed cushion put upon a child's forehead when it is first trusted to walk alone.

PUDDING-BAG. A bird of the pea-eater kind, so called from its nest being in the form of a long pudding-bag, with a hole in the middle.

PUDDING-DIP. Sauce. *Yorksh.*

PUDDING-GRASS. The herb pennyroyal.

PUDDING-HEADED. Thick-headed ; stupid.

PUDDING-HOSE. Large wide breeches.

PUDDING-PIE. A piece of meat plunged in batter and baked in a deep dish, thus partaking of the nature of both pudding and pie. *East.* It is sometimes called a *pudding-pie-doll*, and in Oxfordshire the like name is given to batter pudding baked in a hard crust. A mention of *pudding-pyes* occurs in Taylor's Workes, 1630, i. 146.

> Did ever John of Leyden prophecy
> Of such an Antichrist as *pudding-pye*.
> *Fletcher's Poems*, p. 155.

> A quarter of fat lambe and three-score eggs have beene but an easie colation, and three well larded *pudding-pyes* he hath at one time put to foyle.
> *The Great Eater of Kent*, 1630.

PUDDING-POKE. The long-tailed titmouse.

PUDDING-PRICK. The skewer which fastened the pudding-bag. "For this I care not a *puddyng-prycke*," Shak. Soc. Papers, i. 63. Ray gives the proverb, " he hath thwitten a mill-post into a pudding-prick." See his English Words, ed. 1674, p. 49. This phrase was applied to a spendthrift.

> Or that I fear thee any whit
> For thy curn nips of sticks,
> I know no use for them so meet
> As to be *puding-pricks*. *Robin Hood*, i.).

PUDDING-ROPE. A cresset-light.

PUDDINGS. The intestines. *North.* An untidy slovenly person is said to have his puddings about his heels.

PUDDING-TIME. In pudding-time, in the nick of time, at the commencement of dinner ; it having formerly been usual to begin with pudding, a custom which still continues in humble life. " I came in season, as they say, in pudding-time," Withal's Dictionarie, 1608. p. 3. Said to be still in use.

> But Mars, who still protects the stout
> In *pudding-time* came to his aid.
> *Hudibras*, I. ii. 865.

PUDDING-TOBACCO. A kind of tobacco, perhaps made up into a roll like a pudding.

PUDDINING. The ancient offering of an egg, a handful of salt, and a bunch of matches, on the first visit of a young child to the house of a neighbour, is still very prevalent in many parts of the North of England at the present time. In the neighbourhood of Leeds the ceremony is termed *puddining*, and the recipient is then said to be *puddined*.

PUDDLE. (1) To tipple. *Devon.*

(2) Short and fat. *Yorksh.* "A fat body," Hallamshire Gloss. p. 120.

PUDDLE-DOCK. An ancient pool from the river in Thames-street, not of the cleanest appearance. An affected woman was sometimes termed Duchess of Puddle-dock.

PUD-DUD. To pad about. *Oxon.*

PUDGE. (1) An owl. *Leic.*

(2) A ditch, or grip. *Linc.*

PUE. (1) Pity. Test. Vetust. p. 380.

(2) An animal's udder. *West.*

(3) To chirp as birds do.

PUET. The peewit. *Markham.*

PUFF. A puff-ball. *Somerset.*

PUFFIN. Malum pulmoneum. A kind of apple mentioned in Rider's Dictionarie, 1640.

PUFF-LOAF. A kind of light bread.

PUFF-THE-DART. A game played with a long needle, inserted in some worsted, and blown at a target through a tin tube.

PUFF-WINGS. That part of the dress which sprung from the shoulders, and had the appearance of an inflated or blown-up wing.

PUG. (1) To sweat. *Warw.*

(2) A kind of loam. *Sussex.*

(3) A thrust. (4) To strike. *West.* Λ.so, to pluck out, to pull.

(5) In large families, the under-servants call the upper ones *pugs*, and the housekeeper's room is known as *pugs'-hole*.

(6) A third-year salmon.

(7) A monkey. " Monkies, apes, *pugs*," Florio, p 63. It was also a familiar and intimate mode of address. " My pretty pug, *ma belle, m'amie*," Howell, 1660. (8) To eat. *Wilts.*

PUG-DRINK. Water cyder. *West.*

PUGGARD. A thief. *Pugging* in Shakespeare is said to mean *thieving.*

PUGGEN. The gable-end. *Devon.*

PUGGINS. Refuse wheat. *Warw.*

PUGGLE. To stir the fire. *Essex.*

PUGGY. Damp; moist; foggy. *Var. dial.*

PUG-MIRE. A quagmire. *Derb.*

PUG-TOOTH. The eye-tooth. *Devon.* Possibly the same as *pugging-tooth* in Shakespeare.

PUG-TOP. A spinning-top. *West.*

PUISNE. A small creature. (*Fr.*)

PUISSANCE. Might; power.

 King Edwarde beeyng nothyng abashed of thys small chaunce, sente good wordes to the Erle of Penbroke, animatyng and byddyng hym to bee of a good courage, promysyng hym not alonely ayde in shorte tyme, but also he hymself in persone royall would folowe hym with all hys *puyssaunce* and power. *Hall, Edward IV.* f. 19.

PUKE. Explained by Baret, a colour between russet and black. " *Chiáro scúro*, a darke puke colour," Florio, p. 97.

 That a camell is so ingendred sometimes, the roughnes of his haire like a boares or swines, and the strength of his body, are sufficient evidences ; and these are worthily called Bactrians because they were first of all conceived among them, having two bunches on their backes ; whereas the Arabian hath but one. The colour of this camell is for the most part browne, or *puke*, yet there are heards of white ones in India. *Topsell's Four-Footed Beasts,* 1607.

PULCHE. To polish. (*A.-N.*)

PULCHER. St. Sepulchre.

 Consider this, and every day conjecture
That *Pulcher's* bell doth toll to Tyburn Lecture.
  Satire against Laud, 1641.

Then shall great volumes with thy travels swell,
And Fame ring lowder then Saint *Pulcher's* bell.
  Taylor's Workes, ii. 81.

 The said lord Dakars above saide was beryid in *Snynt Powlkurs* Churche, and the said lord Dakars was hanggid for robbré of the kyngges deer, and murther of the kepars. *MS. Cotton. Vespas.* A. xxv.

PULCHRITUDE. Beauty. (*Lat.*)

PULDRONS. Armour for the shoulder and the upper part of the arm.

PULE. (1) A pew. *Lanc.*

(2) To cry; to blubber. *Yorksh.*

PULER. A puling person, one who is weak, who eats without appetite.

 If she be pale of complexion, she will prove but a *puler* ; is she high coloured, an ill cognizance.
  The Man in the Moone, 1609, sig. G.

PULETTE. A chicken. (*A.-N.*)

PULFIN. A large fat boy. *West.*

PULID. A kite; a glead. *Linc.*

PULK. (1) A coward. *Linc.*

(2) A pool; a puddle. *Var. dial.*

(3) A short fat person. *East.*

PULL. To pull down a side, i. e. to injure or damage a cause.

PULLAILE. Poultry. (*A.-N.*) *Pullain* and *pullen* is found in several early plays. " *Poullailler*, a poulter or keeper of pullaine," Cotgrave.

 The sixt house denoteth servants, sicknesse, wild beasts, ryding, hunting of and by dogs, sheepe and muttons, goates and *pulleine*, and hath some signification over prisons, unjustice, and false accusations, and is called, The house cadant of the fourth, and otherwise ill fortune, and hath government over the belly and bowels.
  Judgements of the Starres, 1595.

PULLE. Pool. (*A.-S.*)

 Tho hi migten drinke that hi weren fulle,
Hi floten swithe rived bi dich and bi *pulle.*
  MS. Bodl. 652, f. 1.

PULLEN. The small crab used for baiting sea-fishing-hooks. *North.*

PULLER. A loft for poultry. *Norf.*

PULLEY-PIECES. Armour for the knees.

PULL-FACES. To make grimaces.

PULLING-TIME. The evening of a fair-day, when the wenches are pulled about. *East.*

PULLISH. To polish. *Palsgrave.*

PULL-OVER. A carriage-way over the banks of the sea. *Linc.*

PULL-REED. A long reed used for ceilings instead of laths *Somerset.*

PULLS. The chaff of pulse. *North.*

PULL-TOW-KNOTS. The coarse and knotty parts of the tow. *East.*

PULLY-HAWLY. (1) To pull stoutly.

(2) To romp about. *Var. dial.*

PULLY-PIECES. The poleins, or armour for the knees. See Howell, in v.

PULMENT. A kind of pottage. " *Pulmentorium*, a pulment," Nominale MS.

PULPATOONS. Confections.

PULPIT-CUFFER. A violent preacher.

PULSE. Pottage. *Somerset.*

PULSEY. A poultice. *North.*

PULSIDGE. Pulse. *Shak.*

PULT. *Out pult*, put out.

 Ave excludit penalitatem, ave ys out *pult* al hardnesse. *MS. Burney* 356, p. 83.

PULTER. A poulterer. *Palsgrave.* Also, the royal officer who had charge of the poultry.

PULTERS. The men in mines who convey the coal from the hewers. *North.*

PULVERING-DAYS. Any days when the community assemble to let to farm the town lands ; but the contract was always confirmed on a particular day, as at Southwold, on the 6th of December.

PULVER-WEDNESDAY. Ash-Wednesday.

PULWERE. A pillow. (*A.-N.*)

PUM. To beat, or thump. *North.*

PUMMEL. To beat soundly. *Var. dial.*

PUMMEL-FOOTED. Club-footed. *West.* Some of the glossaries have *pumple-footed.*

PUMMEL-TREE. A whippletree for horses.

PUMMER. Big ; large. *North.*

PUMMY. Soft; pulpy. *Var. dial.*

PUMPET-BALL. The ball with which a printer lays ink on the forms.

PUM-PUM. A ludicrous term, applied by Marston to a fiddler.

PUN. (1) To pound, or beat. *West.* "To stampe or *punne* in a morter," Florio, p. 6.

(2) A child's pinafore. *Devon.*

(3) A small iron skillet. *Linc.*

PUNAY. A small fellow; a dwarf.
> Arthour, with a litel *punay*,
> Hadde y-driven hem oway.
> *Arthour and Merlin*, p. 121.

PUNCCION. A puncture. (*Lat.*)
> But I thinke thys was no dreame, but a *punccion*
> and pricke of his synfull conscience, for the con-
> science is so muche more charged and aggravate, as
> the offence is great and more heynous in degre.
> *Hall, Richard III.* f. 29.

PUNCH. (1) A hard blow. *Var. dial.*

(2) To kick. *Yorksh.*

(3) A kind of horse. *Suffolk.*

(4) Short; fat. *North.* A pot-bellied man is said to be *punchy.*

(5) To work very hard. *Oxon.*

PUNCH-AND-JUDY. A kind of dramatic exhibition with puppets, still very popular.

PUNCH-CLOD. A clodhopper. *North.*

PUNCHION. (1) A bodkin. *North.*

(2) An upright piece of stout timber in a wooden partition. "*Asser*, a punchion or joyst," Elyot, ed. 1559.

PUNCHITH. To punish. (*A.-N.*)

PUNCTED. Punctured. (*Lat.*)
> And after that she came to her memory, and was
> revyved agayne, she wept and sobbyd, and with pite-
> full scriches she replenesshyd the hole mancion, her
> breste she *puncted*, her fayre here she tare.
> *Hall, Richard III.* f. 4.

PUND. A pound. *North.*

PUNDER. (1) To puzzle. *Westm.*

(2) To balance evenly. *East.*

(3) A mortar. *Yorksh.*

PUNEAR. To peruse a book. *South.*

PUNG. (1) A purse.

(2) Pushed. *Exmoor.*

PUNGAR. A crab. *Kent.*

PUNGEDE. Pricked.
> Behalde his bludy flesche,
> His helde *pungede* with thorne.
> *MS. Lincoln* A. l. 17, f. 222.

PUNGER. To spunge upon. *West.*

PUNGLED. Shrivelled; tough. *East.*

PUNICE. To punish. (*A.-N.*)

PUNIES. (1) Small creatures. (*Fr.*) Freshmen at Oxford were called *punies of the first year.*

(2) Lice or insects. *Hall.*

PUNISHMENT. Pain. *West.*

PUNK. (1) Touch-wood. *North.*

(2) A prostitute. "Seated cheek by jowle with a punke," Dekker's Knight's Conjuring, p. 20, Percy Society repr.
> His pimpship with his *punke*, despight the horne,
> Eate gosling giblets in a fort of corne.
> *Taylor's Workes*, 1630, i. 110.

PUNKY. (1) Dirty. *Derb.*

(2) A chimney-sweeper. *Yorksh.*

PUNSE. To punch, or beat. *North.*

PUNTO. A term in fencing; *punto dritta*, a direct stroke; *punto riversa*, a back-handed stroke. See Rom. and Jul. ii. 4.

PUOY. A long pole with spikes at the end, used in propelling barges or keels. *North.*

PUPPY. A puppet. *East.*

PUR. (1) The poker. *Linc.*

(2) A one year old male sheep.

(3) To whine, as a cat. *Var. dial.*

(4) *Pur, pur-chops, pur-dogs, pur-ceit,* &c. terms at the old game of Post-and-Pair.

(5) To kick. *North.*

(6) A boy. *Dorset.*

PURCHASE. The booty of thieves. A very common term in old plays.

PURDY. (1) Proud; surly; rude. *East.*

(2) A little thickset fellow. *North.*

PURE. (1) Mere; very. Still in use. A countryman shown Morland's picture of pigs feeding, corrected the artist, by exclaiming, "They be *pure* loike surelye, but whoever seed three pigs a-feeding without one o' em having his foot in the trough?"

(2) Poor. R. de Brunne, Bowes MS.
> Now wate I wele you covaytes to wyte whilke
> are verray *pure*, and whilke noghte.
> *MS. Lincoln* A. i. 17, f. 202.

(3) In good health. *Var. dial.*

(4) To purify. Maundevile, p. 286.

(5) A prostitute. A cant term.

PURED. Furred. *Ritson.*

PURELY. (1) Prettily; nicely. *East.*
> Ortolan, a delicate bird, of the bigness of a lark.
> It sings *purely*, and is good to eat.
> *Miege's Great French Dictionary*, 1688.

(2) The same as *Pure* (3).

PURFLE. The hem of a gown. Also, to ornament with trimmings, edgings, or embroidery. "A blac lamb furre without *purfile* of sable," Lydgate's Minor Poems, p. 57.
> To the Lady Beaumont, my daughter, a *purfle* of
> sable, my best feather-bed, and other furniture.
> *Test. Vetust.* p. 471.

PURGATORY. The pit grate of a kitchen fire-place. *West.*

PURGY. Proud; conceited. *North.*

PURITAN. A whore. A cant term.

PURKEY. A species of wheat.

PURL. (1) Border; hem; fringe; stitch-work; a twist of gold or silver.

(2) To turn swiftly round; to curl or run in circles; to eddy, as a stream.

(3) Guard; watch. *Cornw.*

(4) A term in knitting. It means an inversion of the stitches, which gives to the work, in those parts in which it is used, a different appearance from the general surface. The seams of stockings, the alternate ribs, and what are called the clocks, are *purled.*

PURLE. To prowl about for prey.

PURLEY. Weak-sighted. *Wilts.*

PURLICUE. A flourish in writing.

PURLINS. Those pieces of timber that lie across the rafters on the inside, to preserve them from sinking in the middle of their length.

PURL-ROYAL. A liquor made with sack mixed with various spices.

PURN. An instrument for holding a vicious horse by the nose whilst the blacksmith is shoeing him.

PURPAIN. A napkin. The counterpane of a bed was called the *purpain* or *purpoint*.

PURPLES. A species of orchis.

PURPOOLE. Gray's-inn, so called from the ancient name of its manor or estate.

PURPOSES. A kind of game. "The prettie game which we call *purposes*," Cotgrave, in v. *Opinion*.

PURPRESTURE. An encroachment on anything that belongs to the king or the public.

    A brief discoverie of the great *purpresture* of newe buyldinges nere to the cittie, with the meanes howe to restraine the same.
                        Archæologia, xxiii. 121.

PURPRISE. An inclosure. (*A.-N.*)

PURPURING. Having a purple colour.

PURR-BARLEY. Wild barley.

PURREL. A list ordained to be made at the end of kersies to prevent deceit in diminishing their length. See Blount.

PURSE. To steal, or take purses.

PURSE-NET. A net, the ends of which are drawn together with a string, like a purse.

    For thinke yee to catch fishe with an unbaited hooke, or take a whale with a *pursenet*, then may yee retuourne with a bare hooke, and an emptie purse.
         Rowley's Search for Money, 1609.

PURSEWEND. Suitable; pursuant. (*A.-N.*)

PURSLEN. Porcelain.

PURST. Lost; gone away.

PURT. To pout; to take a dislike; to be sullen, or sulky. *West.*

PURTE. Purity.

PURTENANCE. (1) That which belongs. *Appurtenance* is still in use as a law term.

    Alle the londys and passessions
    That I have lying within the bowns
    Of Southwerke and of the stwes syde,
    As wynde-melles ande water-milles eke,
    With alle their *purtenaunces* lying on every syde,
    That be there redy and ar not for to seke.
                 MS. Rawl. C. 86.

    And to alle that clerkys avaunce
    To holy cherches *portynaunce*.
                 MS. Harl. 1701, f. 72.

(2) An animal's intestines. *Palsgrave.*

PURTING-GLUMPOT. A sulky fellow. *Devon.*

PURTRED. Portrayed. (*A.-N.*)

    There was *purtred* in ston
    The fylesoferus everychon,
    The story of Absolon.   *Sir Degrevant*, 1449.

PURVEY. To provide. (*A.-N.*) It is a substantive in our second example.

    Yf he wyste that hyt wolde gayne,
    He wolde *purvey* hym fulle fayne
        That lady for to wynne;
    He had nothyr hors nor spere,
    Nor no wepyn hym with to were,
        That brake hys herte withynne.
            MS. Cantab. Ff. ii. 38, f. 76.
    The which, when they hear of the arrival and

purvey that ye, and other of our subjects make at home in help of us, shall give them great courage to haste their coming unto us much the rather, and not fail; as we trust fully. *Letter of Henry V.* 1419.

PURVEYANCE. (1) Providence; foresight. (2) Provision. (*A.-N.*)

    Body and sowle so they may hem lede
    Into blysse of eternalle *purvyaunce*.
            MS. Cantab. Ff. i. 6, f. 137.

    Was never slylke a *purvesunce*
    Made in Yngland ne in France.
            MS. Lincoln A. i. 17, f. 138.

PURVIDE. To provide. *East.*

PURVIL. To gain one's livelihood by artful and cunning means. *North.*

PURWATTLE. A splashed hedge. *Devon.*

PUR-WIGGY. A tadpole. *Suffolk.*

PURYE. A kind of pottage.

PUSAYLE. A guard, or archer. (*A.-N.*)

    Scarsly couthe I chare away the kite,
    That me bireve wolde my *pusayle*.
         Occleve, MS. Soc. Antiq. 134, f. 255.

PUSESOUN. Poison. (*A.-N.*)

    Mani taketh therof *pusesoun*,
    And dyeth in michel wo.
        Rouland and Vernagu, p. 11.

PUSH. (1) An exclamation, as Pish!

(2) A boil. *East.* "Red pimples or *pushes* in mens faces," Florio, p. 69. "A little swelling, like a bladder or *push*, that riseth in bread when it is baked," Baret, 1580.

PUSH-PIN. A child's play, in which pins are pushed with an endeavour to cross them. So explained by Ash, but it would seem from Beaumont and Fletcher, vii. 25, that the game was played by aiming pins at some object.

    To see the sonne you would admire,
    Goe play at *push-pin* with his sire.
           Men Miracles, 1656, p. 15.

    Love and myselfe, beleeve me, on a day,
    At childish *push-pin*, for our sport, did play.
           Herrick's Works, i. 22.

PUSH-PLOUGH. A breast-plough. *Staff.*

PUSKILE. A pustule.

PUSKITCHIN. A tale-teller. *West.*

PUSKY. Wheezy. *Somerset.*

PUSS. (1) A hare. *Var. dial.*

(2) A woman, in contempt.

PUSSOMED. Poisoned. *Yorksh.*

PUSSY-CATS. Catkins. *South.*

PUSTLE. A pustule. Florio, p. 64.

PUT. (1) An attempt. *Warw.*

(2) *To put a girdle round anything*, to travel or go round it. *To put to business*, to vex or trouble. *To put about*, to teaze or worry. *To put on*, to subsist; to impose upon. *To put the miller's eye out*, to make pudding or broth too thin. *To put the stone*, to throw the stone above hand, from the uplifted hand, for trial of strength. *Put to it*, at a loss for an expedient. *To put forth*, to begin to bud. *To put off*, to delay. *Put out*, annoyed, vexed.

(3) To push, or propel. *North.* It occurs in Pr. Parv. and Havelok.

(4) A two-wheeled cart used in husbandry, and so constructed as to be turned up at the axle to discharge the load.

(5) To stumble. *Norf.*

(6) A mole-hill. *Suffolk.*

(7) A pit, or cave. (*A.-S.*)

(8) A game at cards.

> There are some playing at back-gammon, some at trick-track, some at picket, some at cribidge, and, perhaps, at a by-table in a corner, four or five harmless fellows at *put*, and all-foures.
> *Country Gentleman's Vade Mecum,* 1699, p. 75.

(9) In coal mines, to bring the coals from the workings to the crane or shaft.

(10) A stinking fellow. *Devon.*

PUTAYLE. The populace. (*A.-N.*)

PUTAYN. A whore. (*A.-N.*) *Fiz à putain*, son of a whore, a common term of reproach, misprinted in Gy of Warwike, p. 295.

PUT-CASE. Suppose a case, i. e. take an example from an imaginary case.

PUTCH. A pit, hole, or puddle. *Kent.*

PUTCHKIN. A wicker bottle. *West.*

PUTE. To impute. Still in use.

PUTERIE. Whoredom. (*A.-N.*)

> And bygan ful stille to spye,
> And herde of hyre *putrye.*
> *Wright's Seven Sages,* p. 47.

PUTHE. Pitch. *Hearne.*

PUTHER. (1) Pewter. *North.*

(2) The same as *Pudder*, q. v.

PUTHERY. Said of a sheep which has water on the brain. *Sussex.*

PUTLOGS. The cross horizontal pieces of a scaffold in building a house.

PUT-ON. (1) To be depressed, or sad.

(2) Put your hat on; be covered. This phrase occurs in Massinger and Middleton.

(3) To excite, or stir up; to go fast.

PUTOUR. A whoremonger. (*A.-N.*)

PUT-OVER. (1) A hawk was said to *put over* when she removed her meat from the gorge into the stomach.

(2) To recover from an illness.

PUT-PIN. The game of *pushpin*, q. v. There is an allusion to it under this name in Nash's Apologie, 1593.

> That can lay downe maidens bedds,
> And that can hold ther sickly heds:
> That can play at *put-pin*,
> Blowe-poynte, and near lin.
> *Play of Misogonus,* MS.

PUTRE. To cry. *North.*

PUTTER. A lever. *Suffolk.*

PUTTER-OUT. (1) A distributor.

(2) One who deposited money with a party on going abroad, on condition of receiving a great interest for it on his return, proportionable to the dangers of the journey, and the chances of his arrival to claim it. This custom was very common in Shakespeare's time, and is alluded to in the Tempest, iii. 3.

PUTTICE. A stoat, or weasel. *Kent.*

PUTTOCK. (1) A common prostitute.

(2) A kite. The term was metaphorically applied to a greedy ravenous fellow.

> Who sees a hefer dead and bleeding fresh,
> And sees hard-by a butcher with an axe,
> But wil suspect twas he that made the slaughter?
> Who findes the partridge in the *puttocks* neast,
> But will imagine how the bird came there.
> *First Part of the Contention,* 1600.

> I am a greate travelir.
> I lite on the dunghill like a *puttock!*
> Nay, take me with a lye,
> And cut out the brane of my buttock.
> *Mariage of Witt and Wisdome,* 1579

PUTTOCK-CANDLE. The least candle in a pound, put in to make up weight. *Kent.*

PUT-UP. (1) To sheath one's sword.

(2) To tolerate; to bear with. Also, to take up residence at an inn. *Var. dial.*

PUZZEL. A filthy drab.

PUZZLE-HEADED-SPOONS. Apostle-headed-spoons; each with the figure of an apostle, his head forming the top of the spoon. They may be seen at several places in Cornwall and Devon. See *Apostle-spoons.*

PUZZUM. Spite; malice. *North.*

PYE. *Father of the Pye*, the chairman of a convivial meeting. *Devon.*

PYKE. To move or go off.

PYONINGS. Works of pioneers; military works of strength. *Spenser.*

PYRAMIDES. Spires of churches.

PYTE. Mercy; pity. (*A.-S.*)

> Fro dalis deep to the I cryde,
> Lord, thow listyn the voys of me!
> This deep presoun that I in byde,
> Brek it up Lord for thin *pyté.*
> Be thow myn governowr and myn gyde,
> Myn gostly foode, that I nou3t fle,
> And let out of thin herte glyde,
> That I have trespasyd a3ens the.
> *Hampole's Paraphrase of the Psalms,* MS.

Q. The same as *Cue* (1). "Go for a q," Lilly's Mother Bombie, ap. Nares.

QD. Contr. for *quod* or *quoth.*

QHYP. A whip. *Prompt. Parv.*

QRUS. Wrathful. See *Crous* (1).

QUA. Who.

> Qua herd ever a warr auntur,
> That he that noght hadd bot of him,
> Agayn him suld becum 'sua grim.
> *MS. Cott. Vespas.* A. iii. f. 4.

QUAB. An unfledged bird. Hence, anything in an imperfect, unfinished state.

QUABBE. A bog, or quagmire.

QUACK. To be noisy. *West.* The term is applied to any croaking noise.

QUACKING-CHEAT. A duck. An old cant term, given by Dekker, 1616.

QUACKLE. To choke, or suffocate. *East.*

QUACKSALVER. A cheat or quack.

> But the juglers or *quacksalvers* take them by another course, for they have a staffe slit at one end like a payre of tongs, those stand open by a pinne; now, when they see a serpent, viper, adder or snake, they set them uppon the necke neere the head, and pulling foorth the pinne, the serpent is inevitably taken, and by them loosed into a prepared vessell, in which they keepe her, and give her meate.
> *Topsell's Historie of Serpents,* 1608, p. 49

QUAD. Bad; evil. *Chaucer.*

QUADDLE. To dry, or shrivel up. *West.*

QUADDY. Broad; short and thick. *East.*

QUADE. To spoil, or destroy.

QUADRAT. Arranged in squares.

And they followed in a *quadrat* array to the entent to destroy kyng Henry.

Hall's Union, 1548. Hen IV. f. 13.

QUADRELLS. Four square pieces of peat or turf made into that fashion by the spade that cuts them. *Staff.*

QUADRILLE. A game at cards, very similar to *Ombre*, q. v.

QUADRILOGE. A work compiled from four authors. A Life of Thomas Becket was so called.

The very authours of the *quadriloge* itselfe, or song of foure parts, for they yeeld a concert, though it be without harmonie, doe all, with one pen and mouth, acknowledge the same.

Lambarde's Perambulation, 1596, p. 515.

QUADRIVIUM. The seven arts or sciences were formerly divided into the *quadrivium*, or fourfold way to knowledge; and the *trivium*, or threefold way to eloquence. The former comprised arithmetic, geometry, music, and astronomy; the latter, grammar, rhetoric, and logic.

QUAER. Where.

That I mit becum hir man, I began to crave,
For nothing in hirde fondin wold I let;
Sche bar me fast on hond, that I began to rave,
And bad me fond ferther, a fol for to feche.
Quaer gospellis al thi speche?
Thu findis hir noht hire the sot that thu seche.

MS. Arundel 27, f. 130.

QUAG. A bog, or quagmire. *Var. dial.* Hence *quaggy*, soft and tremulous.

QUAGGLE. A tremulous motion. *South.*

QUAIL. (1) To go wrong.

(2) To shrink, flinch, or yield. To soften or decrease, Holinshed, Conq. Ireland, p. 21. Sometimes, to faint, to droop, to fall sick.

(3) To curdle. *East.* "I quayle as mylke dothe, *ie quaillebotte*; this mylke is quayled, eate none of it," Palsgrave. "The cream is said to be *quailed* when the butter begins to appear in the process of churning," Batchelor's Orthoep. Anal. p. 140.

(4) A whore. An old cant term.

(5) To overpower, or intimidate.

QUAIL-MUTTON. Diseased mutton. *Linc.*

QUAIL-PIPE. A pipe used to call quails. *Quail-pipe boots*, boots resembling a quail-pipe, from the number of plaits or wrinkles.

QUAINT. Elegant; neat; ingenious. Occasionally, prudent. *Quaintness*, beauty, elegance. Now obsolete in these senses.

QUAINTE. To acquaint; inform.

There if he travaile and *quainte* him well,
The Treasure of Knowledges is his eche deale.

Recorde's Castle of Knowledge, 1556.

QUAIRE. A quire, pamphlet, or book.

Thow litell *quayer*, how darst thow shew thy face,
Or com yn presence of men of honesté?
Sith thow ard rude and folowist not the trace
Of faire langage, nor haiste no bewté;
Wherefore of wysedom thus I councell the,
To draw the bake fer out of their sight,
Lest thow be had in reproef and dispite.

MS. Rawl. C. 86.

QUAISY. (1)

Hit most be a curet, a crouned wyght,
That knowth that *quaysy* frome ben and pese,
Or ellys theyre medsyns they have no myght
To geve a mane lysens to lyve in ease.

MS. Cantab. Ff. i. 6

(2) Indigestible; tough. *North.*

QUAKE. (1) To shake. *Shak.*

(2) Fear, trembling. (*A.-S.*)

Thou shal bye thi breed ful dere,
Til thou turne ajeyn in *quake*
To that erthe thou were of-take.

Cursor Mundi, MS. Coll. Trin. Cantab. f. 6.

QUAKER-GRASS. The shaking grass. *Worc.*

QUAKING-CHEAT. A calf, or sheep.

QUALE. To kill, or destroy. (*A.-S.*)

QUALESTER. "*Chorista*, a qwalester," Nominale MS. of the fifteenth century.

QUALIFY. To soothe, or appease.

QUALITY. Profession; occupation.

QUALITY-MAKE. The gentry. *North.*

QUALLE. A whale.

The lady whyte als *qwallis* bane,
Alle falowed hir hewe.

MS. Lincoln A. i. 17, f. 143.

QUALME. (1) Sickness; pestilence. (*A.-S.*)

(2) The noise made by a raven.

QUAMP. Still; quiet. *West.*

QUANDORUM. A polite speech. *South.*

QUANK. To overpower. *West.*

QUANT. A pole used by the bargemen on the Waveney between Yarmouth and Bungay, for pushing on their craft in adverse or scanty winds. It has a round cap or cot at the immerged end to prevent its sticking in the mud. Some of the *quants* are nearly thirty feet long. The term occurs in Pr. Parv.

QUANTO-DISPAINE. An ancient dance described in MS. Rawl. Poet. 108.

QUAPPE. To quake; to tremble.

QUAR. (1) A quarry. *West.*

When temples lye like batter'd *quarrs*,
Rich in their ruin'd sepulchers,
When saints forsake their painted glass
To meet their worship as they pass.

Fletcher's Poems, p. 136.

(2) To coagulate, applied to milk in the female breast. *Somerset.*

QUARE. To cut into pieces.

QUAREL. A stone quarry. "*Saxifragium*, a qwaryle," Nominale MS.

QUARELLES. Arrows. (*A.-N.*)

Qwarelles qwayntly swappez thorowe knyghtes
With iryne so wekyrly, that wynche they never.

Morte Arthure, MS. Lincoln, f. 75.

QUARIER. A wax-candle, consisting of a square lump of wax with a wick in the centre. It was also called a *quarion*, and is frequently mentioned in old inventories. "All the endes of quarriers and prickets," Ord. and Reg. p. 295.

QUARKEN. To suffocate; to strangle.

With greatte dyfficultie I fynde it out I have a throte-bolle almoste strangled i. snarled or *quarkennyd* with extreme hunger.

Palsgrave's Acolastus, 1540.

QUARL. To quarrel. *Somerset.* "Quarled

poison," quotation in Nares. Should we read " *gnarled* poison ?"

QUAROF. Whereof.
> With Litylmon, the lest fynger,
> He begynnes to hoke,
> And sayes, *quarof* ard thou so ferd ?
> Hit is a litil synne.
> *MS. Cantab.* Ff. v. 48, f. 82.

QUARRE. Square.
> *Quarré* scheld, gode swerd of steil,
> And launce stef, biteand wel.
> *Arthour and Merlin,* p. 111.

QUARREL. (1) A square of window glass, properly one placed diagonally. Anciently, a diamond-shaped pane of glass. Hence the cant term *quarrel-picker,* a glazier. The word was applied to several articles of a square shape, and is still in use.

(2) A duel, or private combat.

QUARRELOUS. Quarrelsome. *Shak.*

QUARRIER. A worker at a quarry.

QUARROMES. The body. A cant term. See a list in Dekker's Lanthorne and Candle-light, 4to. Lond. 1620, sig. C. ii.

QUARRY. (1) Fat; corpulent. " A quarry, fat man, *obesus,*" Coles' Lat. Dict.

(2) See *Quarier* and *Quarrell.*

(3) Prey, or game. *Quarry-hawk,* an old entered and reclaimed hawk.

(4) An arrow. Drayton, p. 29.

QUART. (1) A quarter. *Spenser.*

(2) Three pounds of butter. *Leic.*

QUARTER. (1) An upright piece of timber in a partition. *Somerset.*

(2) A noise; a disturbance.
> Sing, hi ho, Sir Arthur, no more in the house you
> shall prate ;
> For all you kept such a *quarter,* you are out of the
> councell of state.
> *Wright's Political Ballads,* p. 154.

(3) A square panel. *Britton.*

QUARTERAGE. A quarter's wages.

QUARTERER. A lodger. *Devon.*

QUARTER-EVIL. A disease in sheep, arising from corruption of the blood. *South.*

QUARTER-FACE. A countenance three parts averted. *Jonson.*

QUARTEROUN. A quarter.
> And there is not the mone seyn in alle the luna-
> cioun, saf only the seconde *quarteroun.*
> *Maundeville's Travels,* p. 301.

QUARTER-SLINGS. A kind of ropes or chains used on board a ship.
> Thy roaring cannons and thy chens
> Be layde on every side ;
> Yea bases, foulers, *quarter-slings,*
> Which often hath been tride.
> *Gaulfrido and Barnardo,* 1570.

QUARTLE. A fourth part, or quarter.

QUASH. A pompion.

QUASS. To quaff, or drink. Some suppose this to be a corruption of *quaff.*

QUASTE. Quashed; smashed.
> Abowte scho whirles the whele and whirles me
> undire,
> Tille alle my qwarters yt whille whare *quaste* al to
> peces. *Morte Arthure, MS. Lincoln,* f. 89.

QUASY. Same as *Queasy ?*

> I have passed full many *quasy* dayes,
> That now unto good I cannot mate,
> For mary I dyde myselfe to late.
> *The Complaynte of them that ben to late maryed.*

QUAT. (1) To squat down. *Dorset.* To go to quat, i. e. alvum levare.

(2) Full; satiated. *Somerset.* " Quatted with other daintier fare," Philotimus, 1583.

(3) A pimple, or spot. Hence, metaphorically, a diminutive person.

(4) To flatter. *Devon.*

QUATCH. (1) To betray; to tell; to peach. A woman speaking of a person to whom she had confided a confidential secret, said, " I am certain he won't *quatch.*" *Oxf.*

(2) A word. *Berks.*

(3) Squat, or flat. *Shak.*

QUATE. Thought.
> To blide he hade gode *quate,*
> At London he made a gate.
> *MS. Cantab.* Ff. v. 48, f. 94.

QUATER-JACKS. The quarters or divisions of the hour struck by the clock. *Linc.*

QUATHE. Said ?
> The king it al hem graunted rathe,
> And hye him al merci *quathe.*
> *Arthour and Merlin,* p. 60.

QUATHING. In good condition.

QUATRON. A quartern. (*A.-N.*)

QUAUGHT. To drink deeply.

QUAVE. To shake, or vibrate. *Derb.* " Al the world quaved," Piers Ploughman, p. 373.

QUAVE-MIRE. A bog, or quagmire. *Palsgrave.* It is spelt *quakemire* in Stanihurst's Description of Ireland, p. 20. " A verie *quave mire* on the side of an hill," Harrison, p. 61. Cf. Holinshed, Chron. Scot. p. 48.

QUAVERY-MAVERY. Undecided. *East.*

QUAVIN-GOG. A quagmire. *Wilts.*

QUAWKING. Croaking; cawing. *Var. dial.*

QUAY. " *Quay* or sower mylke," MS. note by Junius, in his copy of the Ortus Vocab. in the Bodleian Library.

QUAYED. Quailed; subdued. *Spenser.*

QUAYT. A gnat. Nominale MS.

QUE. A cow. *Linc.*

QUEACH. (1) A thicket. *Coles.*

(2) A plat of ground left unploughed on account of queaches or thickets. *East.*

QUEACHY. Wet; saturated; quashy; swampy; marshy. Sometimes, running like a torrent of water. " *Torrens,* quechi," MS. Lansd. 560, f. 45, a vocabulary of the fifteenth century, written in Lancashire.

QUEAL. To faint away. *Devon.*

QUEAN. A slut; a drab; a whore; a scold. The term is not necessarily in a bad sense in some writers. " *Anus,* a old quene," MS. Bibl. Reg. 12 B. i. f. 40.

QUEASY. (1) Squeamish; nice; delicate. Still in use, meaning *sickish.* It sometimes signifies *mad.*

(2) Short; brief. *Devon.*

QUEATCHE.
> For they that lacke customers all the weeke,
> either because their haunt is unknowen, or the coa-

stables and officers of their parish watch them so narrowly that they dare not *queatche*, to celebrate the Sabboth, flocke too theaters, and there keepe a generall market of bawdrie.

Gosson's Schoole of Abuse, 1579.

QUEATE. Peace; quietness.

QUECK. A blow?

But what and the ladder slyppe,
Than I am deceyved yet;
And yf I fall I catche a *quecke*,
I may fortune to breke my necke,
And that joynt is yll to set.
Nay, nay, not so! *Enterlude of Youth*, n. d.

QUECORD. A game prohibited by an ancient statute, and supposed by Blount to be similar to shovel-board.

QUED. A shrew; an evil person.

Namly an eyre that ys a *qued*,
That desyreth hys fadrys ded.
MS. Harl. 1701, f. 42.

QUEDE. (1) Harm; evil. Also, the devil.

As he stode stylle and bode the *quede*,
One com with an asse charged with brede.
MS. Harl. 1701, f. 37.

(2) A bequest. (*A.-S.*)

QUEDER. To shake, or shiver.

QUEDNES. Iniquity. This word occurs in MS. Cotton. Vespas. D. vii. Ps. 10.

QUEDUR. Whether.

She seid; Alas! how shuld I lyfe,
Er thus my life to lede in lond;
Fro dale to downe I am dryfe,
I wot not *quedur* I may sit or stond.
MS. Cantab. Ff. v. 48, f. 109.

QUEE. A female calf. *North.*

QUEED. The cud. " To chamme the *queed.*" This is given as a Wiltshire word in MS. Lansd. 1033, fol. 2.

QUEEK. To press or squeeze down; to pinch. *Heref.*

QUEEL. To grow flabby. *Devon.*

QUEEN-DICK. That happened in the reign of Queen Dick, i. e. never.

QUEEN-OF-HEARTS. An old country dance, mentioned in the Bran New Wark, 1785, p. 7.

QUEEN'S-GAME. A game at tables.

QUEEN'S-STICK. A stately person. *Linc.*

QUEER. (1) To puzzle. *Var. dial.*

(2) Bad; counterfeit. A cant term.

QUEERQUIST. A quiz. *Heref.*

QUEER-STRET. A phrase thus generally used: " Well! that have put me in *queer-stret*," meaning, puzzled me queerly or strangely. *Suffolk.*

QUEER-WEDGES. Large buckles. *Grose.*

QUEEST. A wood-pigeon. *West.* Spelt *queeze* in Wilbraham's Gloss. p. 108. The ringdove, Ray's Catalogue of English Birds, 1674, p. 85. " A ringdove, a stockdove, a quoist," Florio, p. 109.

QUEEVE. To vibrate. *Beds.*

QUEINT. The pudendum muliebre.

QUEINTANCE. Acquaintance.

But folke that beon fallen in poverté,
No man desirethe to have theire *queyntance.*
MS. Ashmole 59, f. 35.

QUEINTE. (1) Quenched. (*A.-S.*)

II.

Whan hit hathe *quaynt* his brendis bright,
Than efte ayen hit yevyth hym a newe light.
Lydgate, MS. Ashmole 39, f. 32.

(2) Strange; curious; cunning; artful; trim; neat; elegant. (*A.-N.*)

QUEINTISE. Neatness; cunning.

To go aboute the boke seise,
And al bi the devells *quayntise.*
MS. Ashmole 41, f. 55.

QUEITE. Crept. *Will. Werw.*

QUEK. To quack; to make a noise like a goose or duck. Urry, p. 417.

He toke a gose fast by the nek,
And the goose thoo begann to *quek.*
Reliq. Antiq. i. 4.

QUEKED. Sodden, as wine is.

QUELCH. A blow, or bang.

QUELE. A wheel. *Prompt. Parv.* " Qwel, *rota*," MS. Lansd. 560, f. 45.

QUELLE. To kill. (*A.-S.*)

QUELLIO. A ruff for the neck. (*Span.*)

QUELME. To kill; to destroy. (*A.-S.*) It occurs in MS. Cotton. Vespas. D. vii.

QUELTRING. Sultry; sweltering. *West.*

QUEME. (1) To please. (*A.-S.*)

Of all vertues yeve me eke largesse
To be acceptid the to *queme* and serve,
To fyne onely thy grace I may deserve.
Lydgate, MS. Ashmole 39, f. 12.

(2) To bequeath; to leave by legacy.

(3) The same as *queint*, q. v. " I tell you, Hodge, in sooth it was not cleane, it was as black as ever was Malkin's queme," Tumult, play dated 1613, Rawl. MS. Grose has *quim*, which he derives from the Spanish *quemar*, to burn. It is, perhaps, connected with the old word *queint*, which, as I am informed by a correspondent at Newcastle, is still used in the North of England by the colliers and common people.

QUENCH. To lay or place in water, without reference to extinguishing. See Harrison's England, p. 130.

QUENE. When.

Quene that the kyng Arthur by conqueste hade wonnyne
Castelles and kyngdoms and contrees many.
Morte Arthure, MS. Lincoln, f. 53.

QUENINGES. Quinces. (*A.-N.*)

QUENTLY. Easily. *Gawayne.*

QUEQUER. A quiver.

To a *quequer* Roben went. *Robin Hood*, i. 90.

QUERDLING. A kind of apple, perhaps the original of what we call *codlin*.

QUERELE. A complaint.

Thou lyf, thou luste, thou mannis bele,
Biholde my cause and my *querele.*
Gower, MS. Soc. Antiq. 134, f. 39.

That all ministers, now to be deprived in this *querele* of rites, may be pardoned of all the payments of first-fruits due after deprivation.
Grindal's Remains, 1843, p. 289.

QUERESTAR. A chorister. *Palsgrave.*

Thy harp to Pan's pipe, yield, god Phœbus,
For 'tis not now as in diebus
Illis; Pan all the year we follow,
But semel in anno ridet Apollo;
Thy *quirister* cannot come near
The voice of this our chanticleer.
Heywood's Love's Mistress, p. 43.

QUERK. (1) To grunt; to moan. *West.*

(2) A moulding in joinery. *North.*

QUERKEN. To stifle, or choke. *North.* "Chekenyd or qwerkenyd," Pr. Parv.

It wil grow in the ventricle to such a masse that it wil at the receit of any hot moisture send up such an ascending fome that it wil be ready to *quirken* and stifie us. *Optick Glasse of Humors*, 1639, p. 124.

QUERN. (1) Corn. *Salop.*

(2) A mill. This word is generally applied to a hand-mill. (*A.-S.*) "*Mola*, a qwernstone," Nominale MS.

Having therefore groond eight bushels of good malt upon our *querne*, where the toll is saved, she addeth unto it halfe a bushell of wheat meale. *Harrison's Description of England*, p. 169.

QUERPO. Same as *Cuerpo*, q. v. "Me must den valke in *quirpo*," Nabbes' Bride, 4to. Lond. 1640, sig. F. iv.

A batt, who nigh in *querpo* sat,
Lay snug, and heard the whole debate. *Collins' Miscellanies*, 1762, p. 132.

QUERROUR. A worker in a quarry.

QUERT. Joyful. Also, joy. *In quert*, joyful, in good spirits. See Lydgate, pp. 32, 38; Ritson's Met. Rom. iii. 408-9.

Remembyr thy God while thou art *quert*. *MS. Laud.* 416, f. 76.

And that hym byhoveth leve hyt in *querte*,
And be overcomen and caste to helle pytt. *MS. Cantab.* Ff. ii. 38, f. 14.

But thouȝe that Noe was in *quert*,
He was not al in ese of hert. *Cursor Mundi*, *MS. Coll. Trin. Cantab.* f. 12.

QUEST. (1) The sides of an oven. Pies are said to be *quested* when their sides have been crushed by each other, or so joined to them as thence to be less baked. *North.*

(2) To give tongue as hounds do on trail. "To bay or *quest* as a dog," Florio, p. 1. Still in use. See Forby, ii. 268.

Kenettes *questede* to quelle,
Al so breme so any belle,
The deer daunteden in the delle,
That al the downe denede. *Reliq. Antiq.* ii. 7.

(3) An inquest. *Var. dial.* Both words are used by Hall, Henry VIII. ff. 50, 53.

QUESTANT. A candidate; one who is seeking for some object. *Shak.*

QUESTE. A prayer, or demand. (*A.-N.*)

QUESTEROUN. Cooks, or scullions.

QUEST-HOUSE. The chief watch-house of a parish, generally adjoining a church, where sometimes quests concerning misdemeanours and annoyances were held. The *quest-house* is frequently mentioned in the accounts of St. Giles, Cripplegate, 1571, MS. Addit. 12222.

QUESTMEN. "Those that are yearly chosen, according to the custom of a parish, to assist the churchwardens in the enquiry, and presenting such offenders to the ordinary as are punishable in the court-christian," Blount's Glossographia, ed. 1681, p. 594.

QUESTMONGER. A juryman.

Awake, awake, ye *questmongers*, and take heed you give a true, just, and right verdict. *Becon's Works*, p. 370.

QUESTUARY. Profitable.

QUETE. Wheat. It is the translation of *frumentum* in MS. Lansd. 560, f. 45.

That ȝere shalbe litulle *qwete*,
And plenté shalbe of appul ȝrete. *MS. Cantab.* Ff. v. 48, f. 75.

QUETHE. (1) Harm; mischief. (*A.-S.*)

(2) To say; to declare. (*A.-S.*)

(3) To bequeath. *Lydgate.*

Hous and rente and outher thyng
Mow they *quethe* at here endyng. *MS. Harl.* 1701, f. 42.

(4) Cry; clamour. *Gawayne.*

QUETHING. Saying, crying?

Being alive and seinge I peryshe, i. beinge quycke and *quethyng* I am undone. *Palsgrave's Acolastus*, 1540.

QUETHUN. Whence. *Robson.*

QUETOURE. A scab, or swelling.

QUEVER. Gay; lively. *West.*

QUEW. Cold.

QUEZZEN. To suffocate. *East.*

QUHILLES. Whilst.

Quhylles he es qwykke and in qwerte unquellyde with handis,
Be he never mo savede ne socourede with Cryste. *Morte Arthure*, MS. Lincoln, f. 93.

QUIB. A taunt, or mock. *Coles.*

QUIBIBES. Cubebs. "*Quiperium*, a quybybe," Nominale MS.

QUIBLIN. An attempt to deceive.

QUICE. A wood-pigeon. *Glouc.*

QUICHE. To move.

QUICK. (1) Alive; living.

In thilke time men bem tok
With juggement withouten les,
And also *quic* dolven hes. *Arthour and Merlin*, p. 98.

Sir, he seid, assay of this,
Thei were ȝisturday *qwyk* i-wysse. *MS. Cantab.* Ff. v. 48, f. 50.

Quyk? ye, forsothe, *qwyk* it was,
As wel I may tel you all the case. *The Sacrifice of Abraham*, p. 18.

(2) The growing plants which are reared or set for a hedge. *Var. dial.*

(3) Sharp; piercing. *Devon.*

QUICK-DEER. Deer with young.

QUICKEN. (1) Couch grass. *North.*

(2) To work with yeast. *Quickening-dish*, the yeast or balm that is put to new drink to make it work. *North.*

(3) To revive. Still in use.

(4) To conceive with child.

QUICKER. A quickset hedge. *West.*

QUICKLINGS. Young insects. *East.*

QUICKMIRE. A quagmire. *Devon.*

QUICKWOOD. Thorns. *Yorksh.*

QUID. (1) The cud. *Var. dial.* Hence, generally, to suck one's tongue.

(2) A mouthful of tobacco. *Var. dial.*

QUIDDITY. A subtlety; a subtle quirk or pretence. *Quiddit* was also used.

QUIERIE. A royal stable.

QUIET. Gentlemanly. *West.*

QUIETUS. The official discharge of an account. (*Lat.*) It is chiefly used metaphorically, and it means in slang language a severe blow, in other words a *settler*.

QUIFTING-POTS. Small drinking pots holding half a gill. *Lanc.*

QUIL. The reed on which the weavers wind their heads for the shuttle. See Robin Goodfellow, p. 24.

QUILE. A pile, heap, large cock, or cop of hay put together ready for carrying, and to secure it from rain; a heap of anything.

QUILKIN. A frog. *Cornw.*

QUILL. (1) The stalk of a cane or reed; the faucet of a barrel. Hence, to tap liquor. *Devon.*

(2) The fold of a ruff. Also to plait linen in small round folds. " After all your starching, *quilling*, turning, seeking, pinning," Strode's Floating Island, sig. C.

(3) *In the quill*, written. *Shak.*

QUILLER. An unfledged bird.

QUILLET. (1) A furrow. *North.*

(2) A croft or grassyard. *Devon.*

(3) A little quibble. *Shak.*

> So you, only by conceit, thinke richly of the operation of your Indian pudding, having contrarie qualities in it, a thing repugnant to philosophy, and working miraculous matters, a *quillit* above nature.
> *The Man in the Moone*, 1609, sig. C. ii.

QUILL-TURN. The machine or instrument in which a weaver's quill is turned.

QUILLY. To harden; to dry. *Devon.*

QUILT. (1) To beat. *Var. dial.*

(2) To swallow. *West.*

(3) Almost worn out. *I. Wight.*

(4) To be very fidgety. *South.*

QUILTED-CALVES. Sham calves for the legs made of quilted cloth.

QUIN. A kind of spikenard.

QUINCE. The king's-evil.

> For the *quynce*. Take horehownde and columbyne, and sethe it in wyne or ale, and so therof let hym dryncke fyrste and laste. *MS. Rec. Med.*

QUINCE-CREAM. Is thus described.

> Take the quinces and put them into boiling water unpared; then let them boil very fast uncovered that they may not colour; and when they are very tender, take them off and peel them, and best the pap very small with sugar; and then take raw cream, and mix with it till it be of fit thickness to eat like a cream. *True Gentlewoman's Delight*, 1676, p. 5.

QUINCH. (1) To make a noise.

(2) To stir, or move. Sometimes a substantive, a twitch, or jerk.

QUINE. Whence.

> Fro *quyne* come yon kene mane, quod the kynge thanne,
> That knawes kynge Arthure and his knyghttes also.
> *Morte Arthure, MS. Lincoln, f.* 90.

> Bethynke the welle *quyne* thou came,
> Ilkone we ere of Adam.
> *R. de Brunne, MS. Bowes,* p. 15.

QUINET. A wedge. *Glouc.*

QUINNY. Not quite; not just yet. *East.*

QUINOLA. A term in the game of primero, signifying the chief card.

QUINRE. Some poisonous animal.

QUINSE. To carve a plover, spelt *cuinse* in the

Booke of Hunting, 1586. It occurs in Hall's Satires, p. 82.

QUINTAIN. " A game or sport in request at marriages in some parts of this nation, specially in Shropshire; the manner now corruptly thus, A quintin, buttress, or thick plank of wood is set fast in the ground of the highway where the bride and bridegroom are to pass, and poles are provided with which the young men run a tilt on horse-back; and he that breaks most poles, and shews most activity, wins the garland," Blount, ed. 1681, p. 535. The quintain was often gaily painted.

> Thy wakes, thy *quintels*, here thou hast,
> Thy May-poles too with garlands grac't.
> *Herrick's Poems*, ii. 44.

QUINTASENCIA. Some preparation for converting the baser metals into gold.

QUINTER. A two-year-old sheep.

QUINTURE. Delivery; cure. *Hearne.*

QUIP. A sharp retort. " Merrie quipps or tauntes wittily spoken," Baret.

> Tarlton meeting with a wily country wench, who gave him *quip* for *quip*. *Tarlton's Jests*, 1611.

QUIRBOILE. A peculiar preparation of leather, by boiling it to a condition in which it could be moulded to any shape, and then giving it, by an artificial process, any degree of requisite hardness.

> Whyppes of *quyrboyle* by-wente his white sides.
> *MS. Laud.* 656, f. 1.

QUIRE-BIRD. One who has lately come out of prison, and seeks for a place.

QUIRE-CUFFIN. A churl. *Dekker.*

QUIRISON. A complaint. (*A.-N.*)

QUIRK. (1) To emit the breath forcibly after retaining it in violent exertion. *West.*

(2) To grunt; to complain. *Devon.*

(3) The clock of a stocking. *Devon.* The term occurs in Stubbe, 1595.

(4) A pane of glass cut at the sides and top in the form of a rhomb.

QUIRKY. Merry; sportive. *Linc.*

QUIRLEWIND. A whirlwind. It is translated by *turbo* in MS. Egerton 829, f. 14.

QUISERS. Christmas mummers. *Derb.*

QUISES. Cushions for the thighs, a term in ancient armour. *Hall.*

QUISEY. Confounded; dejected. *North.*

QUISHIN. A cushion. *Palsgrave.*

> Swythe chayers thay fett,
> *Quyssyns* of velvett.
> *MS. Lincoln* A. i. 17, f. 135.

QUISIBLE.

> For all this to prouffyt is no more possyble
> Than for to drynke in a *quysyble*.
> *Early Interlude in Bibl. Lambeth.*

QUISSONDAY. Pentecost; Whit-Sunday.

QUISTER. A bleacher. Nominale MS.

QUIT. (1) To remove by force.

(2) To be even, or equal with. The modern phrase is *to be quits*.

(3) Acquitted. See *Quite* (3).

QUITCH. To flinch. Also as *quinch*, to stir or move, to make a noise.

QUITE. (1) Free; quiet. (*A.-N.*)

(2) To pay off; to requite. (*A.-N.*)

> Os hyt ys in the story tolde,
> xl^{tl}. Syr Roger downe can folde,
> So *qwyt* he them ther mede;
> Had he bene armyd y-wys,
> Alle the maystry had byn hys;
> Allas! why wantyd he hys wede?
> *MS. Cantab.* Ff. ii. 38, f. 7ᴿ

> Syr Roger smote them on the hede,
> That to the gyrdylle the swerde yede,
> Of hym were they *qwyte* :
> They hewe on hym faste as they were wode,
> On eche syde then sprong the blode,
> So sore on hym they dud smyte.
> *MS. Cantab.* Ff. ii. 38, f. 73.

(3) To acquit. Sometimes acquitted.

> *Quyte* the weyl oute of borghegang,
> That thou ne have for hyt no wrang.
> *MS. Harl.* 1701, f. 63.

> Herof they *quyttene* hyme as treue mene,
> And sith spake they farder thenne,
> That yf he myght hys lemane bryng
> Of whome he maide knolishyng.
> *MS. Rawlinson* C. 86.

(4) White. (*A.-S.*)

> The childe, that was so nobulle and wyse,
> Stode at his fadurs grafe at eve;
> Ther cam on in a *qwyte* surplisse,
> And pryvely toke him be the slefe.
> *MS. Cantab.* Ff. v. 48, f. 67.

QUITE-BETTER. Entirely recovered.

QUITECLAYM. Free from claim.

> Fram henne to Ynde that cité
> *Quiteclaym* thai schul go fre.
> *Gy of Warwike*, p. 310.

QUITELICH. Freely; at liberty. (*A.-S.*) It is wrongly explained by Ellis, ii. 77.

QUITEMENT. Completely; entirely.

QUITTER. (1) Thin nasty matter or filth that runs from a wound. "Qwytur or rotunnes, *putredo*," Nominale MS.

(2) Whiter; more delicate. See the example in v. *Blaunchette*.

QUIVER. Nimble; active. In use in Suffolk, according to Moor. "*Agilis*, nimble, light, lieger, *quiver*," Elyot, ed. 1559. *Quivery*, shaky, nervous.

> They bothe swetely played;
> A sergeaunt them afrayed,
> And sayd they were full *quaver*.
> *Boke of Mayd Emlyn*, p. 27.

QUIZZLE. To suffocate. *Norf.*

QUO. Contraction of *quoth*.

QUOB. A quicksand, or bog. *West.* We have *quobmire* in Salop. Antiq. p. 539.

QUOCKEN. To vomit. *North.*

QUOD. (1) To fish for eels with worms tied on worsted. *Hants.*

(2) A prison. *Var. dial.*

(3) Quoth; says. (*A.-S.*)

> Avaunce baner! *quod* the kyng, passe forthe anone,
> In the name of the Trynyté and oure Lady bryghte,
> Seynt Edward, Seynt Anne and swete seynt John,
> And in the name of Seynt George, oure landis knyzte!
> This day shew thy grett power and thy gret myzte,

> And brynge thy trew subjectes owte of payn and woo,
> And as thy wille is, Lorde, thys jorney be doo.
> *MS. Bibl. Reg.* 17 D. xv.

QUODLING. This disputed term occurs in Ben Jonson. It may be a cant term for a fool. "The codled fool," Cap of Gray Hairs, 1688, p. 169. It is probably derived from the apple so called. "A quodling, *pomum coctile*," Coles' Lat. Dict.

QUOIF. A cap. Florio, p. 123.

QUOIL. A noise, or tumult.

> But disturbs not his sleep,
> At the *quoil* that they keep.
> *Brome's Songs*, 1661, p. 78.

QUOK. Quaked for fear.

> This scharpe swerde to hire he tok,
> Whereof that alle hire body *quok*.
> *Gower, MS. Soc. Antiq.* 134, f. 86.

> And whan he did with his honde embrace
> His yerde ayen fulle debonaire of loke,
> For innocence of humble drede he *quoke*.
> *Lydgate, MS. Ashmole* 39, f. 16.

QUOME. A man. R. de Brunne, MS.

QUONDAM. A person formerly in office. Still in use as an adjective. (*Lat.*)

QUONIAN. A drinking-cup.

QUONS. A hand-mill for grinding mustard-seed. *East.* Forby seems to consider it a mere corruption of *quern*, q. v.

QUOP. To throb. *West.*

> But zealous sir, what say to a touch at praier?
> How *quops* the spirit? In what garb or ayre.
> *Fletcher's Poems*, p. 203.

QUORLE. A revolving spindle.

> *Qworle* in tho qwew go lyghtly,
> Qwene I was a zong man so dyd I.
> Gira in algore leniter,
> Quum fui juvenis ita feci.
> *Reliq. Antiq.* ii. 40.

QUOST. A coast. See Eliotes Dictionarie, fol. Lond. 1559, in v. *Jacto*.

QUOT. Quiet. *Oxon.*

QUOTE. To notice; to write down. This sense is used by Shakespeare, Jonson, &c.

QUOYNTE. Cunning. (*A.-N.*)

> Sende me hidere, zif that ich mizhte
> Ani *quoynte* carpenter finde.
> *MS. Laud.* 108, f. 161.

QUY. A calf, or young cow. "*Juvenca*, a qwye; *vitula*, a qwye calffe," Nominale MS.

QUYCE. The furze. *Pr. Parv.*

QWESEYNS. Cushions.

> Deliveryd on Monday next after blak Monday, a bote with a payr of orys, a russet mantyll, a payr of *qweseyns*, a tapet of red say, unlynyd, with a bar hed.
> *MS. Bodl. e Mus.* 229.

QWHICHE. Which.

> And so kynge Edward was possessed of alle Englonde, excepte a castelle in Northe Wales called Harlake, whiche Sere Richard Tunstall kepte, the *qwhiche* was gotene afterwarde by the Lord Harberde.
> *Warkworth's Chronicle*, p. 3.

RA. A roe-deer. (*A.-S.*) It occurs in Chaucer, Cant. T. 4084.

RAAF. Ralph. *Pr. Parv.*

RAAS. To tear away. See *Race* (1).

And *raas* it frome his riche mene and ryste it in sondyre. *Morte Arthure, MS. Lincoln, f. 57.*

RAASTY. Restive. *East.*

RAATH. In good condition. *North.*

RAB. (1) A kind of loam ; a coarse hard substance for mending roads. *Cornw.*

(2) A wooden beater to bruise and incorporate the ingredients of mortar.

RABATE. Said of a hawk that recovers the fist after the hand has been lowered.

'RABBATE. To abate. *Palsgrave.*

RABBEN. Turnips. (*A.-N.*)

RABBETING. When two boards cut on the edges with a rabbet plane are lapped with the edges one over another, this lapping over is called *rabbeting*. Kennett, MS. The groove in the stone-work of a window to admit the glass was also so called.

In each of these rulers must be two hollow chanels, *rabboth*, or transumes, as carpenters call them ; they must be under hollowed dovetaile wise, so that the two hollowed sides beeing turned together, there may be a concavity or hollownesse of a quarter of an inch square, representing this figure.
Hapton's Baculum Geodeticum, 1614.

RABBISH. Foolhardy ; grasping ; given to extortion, theft, or rapine.

RABBIT-SUCKER. A sucking rabbit.

RABBLE. (1) A kind of rake.

(2) To speak confusedly. *North.*

Let thy tunge serve thyn hert in skylle,
And *rable* not wordes recheles owt of reson.
MS. Cantab. Ff. ii. 38, f. 94.

RABBLEMENT. (1) A crowd, or mob.

(2) Idle silly talk. *North.*

(3) Refuse ; dregs. *Somerset.*

RABBLE-ROTE. A repetition of a long rigmarole roundabout story. *West.*

RABBLING. Winding ; rambling. *North.*

RABIN. A raven. Nominale MS.

RABINE. Rapine ; plunder.

RABIT. A wooden drinking-can.

Strong beer in *rabits* and cheating penny cans,
Three pipes for two-pence and such like trepans.
Praise of Yorkshire Ale, 1697, p. 1.

RABITE. A war-horse.

Then came the dewke Segwyne.ryght,
Armed on a *rabett* wyght.
MS. Cantab. Ff. ii. 38, f. 161.

Syr Gye bestrode a *rabyghte*,
That was moche and lyghte.
MS. Cantab. Ff. ii. 38, f. 124.

RABONE. A radish.

RABSHAKLE. An idle profligate.

RABUKE. A she-goat ? It is the translation of *capra* in Nominale MS.

RACE. (1) To pull away ; to erase.

Swownyng yn hur chaumbur she felle,
Hur heere of can sche *race*.
MS. Cantab. Ff. ii. 38, f. 94.

(2) The meeting of two tides, often over an uneven bottom running together, producing a great and sometimes dangerous sea. The *Race* of Alderney, Portland *Race*, &c.

(3) A string. *Devon.*

(4) The liver and lungs of a calf.

(5) A succession ; a great number.

(6) Rennet for cheese. *North.*

(7) The peculiar flavour or taste of anything the original disposition.

(8) A small stream. *Yorksh.*

(9) A thrust with a dagger.

(10) To rake up old tales. *South.*

(11) To prick, mark, or note.

(12) A course in building.

RACEN. A pothanger. *Yorksh.*

RACERS. A variety of tares. *Var. dial.*

RACH. Rushes for thatching.

RACHE. (1) To stretch out ; to catch. *Palsgrave.* From the first meaning comes *rack* in Much Ado about Nothing, iv. 1.

(2) A scenting hound. (*A.-S.*)

Denede dale and downe, for dryft of the deer in drede,
For meche murthe of mouth the murie moeth made ;
I ros, and romede, and sey roon *raches* to jede,
They stalke under schawe, schatereden in schade.
Reliq. Antiq. ii. 7.

For we wylle honte at the herte the hethes abowte,
With *racches* amonge hem in the rowe bankes.
MS. Cott. Calig. A. ii. f. 118.

Thre grehoundes he ledde on hond,
And thre *raches* in on bond.
Arthour and Merlin, p. 179.

She was as feyre and as gode,
And as riche on hir palfray ;
Hir greyhoundis fillid with the dere blode,
Hir *rachis* coupuld, be my fay.
MS. Cantab. Ff. v. 48, f. 119.

RACINE. A root. (*A.-N.*)

RACK. (1) Light, thin, vapoury clouds ; the clouds generally. Still in use in the Northern counties, and sometimes there applied to a mist. See the Archæologia, xxii. 373. " As the sunne shines through the *rack*," Du Bartas, p. 616. In some instances it appears to imply *the motion of the clouds*, and is so explained by Chapman in his translation of Homer. A disputed passage in which this word occurs, in the Tempest, iv. 1, " leave not a *rack* behind," merits special consideration. Our choice lays between considering it to mean *a single fleeting cloud*, or as a form of *wrack* or *wreck*. Mr. Hunter has expressed his belief that *rack* in the first sense is never used with the indefinite article, and unless the passage now given from Lydgate tends to lighten the objection, it seems to me to be absolutely fatal to the adopted reading. On the other hand, we have *rack* in the old folios of Beaumont and Fletcher, where the sense requires *wreck*. See Mr. Dyce's edition, vii. 137. On the whole, then, unless *rack* can elsewhere be found with the indefinite article, it appears safer to adopt *wreck*, which certainly agrees better with the context. Upton, Critical Observations, ed. 1748, p. 213, supposes it to mean a track or path, in which sense it is still used in the North. See our second meaning, and Brockett, who adopts Upton's explanation of the Shakespearian passage; but there is no good authority for anything of the kind, although Brockett is as decisive as if he had possessed the reading and knowledge of Gifford.

As Phebus doeth at mydday in the southe,
Whan every *rak* and every cloudy sky
Is voide ciene, so hir face uncouth
Shall shewe in open and fully be unwry.
Lydgate, MS. Ashmole 39, f. 51.

Treulé ʒif ʒe wil haloue this holeday,
The *rakkis* of heven I wil opyn.
MS. Douce 302, f. 16.

Now we may calculate by the welkins *racks*,
Æolus hath chaste the clouds that were so blacke.
Heywood's Marriage Triumphe, 1613.

(2) A rude narrow path like the track of a small animal. *West.* Brockett explains it, a track, a trace.

(3) To pour off liquor; to subject it to a fermentive process.

(4) *To work by rack of eye*, to be guided in working by the eye. *In a high rack*, in a high position.

(5) To care; to heed. *North.*

(6) A rut in a road. *East.*

(7) The neck of mutton, or pork. Kennett, MS. Lansd. 1033.

(8) That part of a cross-bow in which the gaffle moved.

(9) A liquor made chiefly of brandy, sugar, lemons, and spices.

(10) A trout. *Northumb.*

(11) Weeds; refuse. *Suffolk.*

(12) *Rack and ruin*, destruction.

(13) That pace of a horse which is between a trot and an amble.

(14)
Some thinke the putride backe-bone in the grave rack'd,
Or marrow chang'd, the shape of snakes to take.
Topsell's Historie of Serpents, p. 6.

(15) To exaggerate. See *Rache* (1).

(16) The cob-iron of a grate.

(17) To relate or tell anything.

RACK-AND-MANGER. A man's *rack and manger* was his housekeeping. To be at rack and manger, to live at reckless expense.

When Vertue was a country maide,
And had no skill to set up trade,
She came up with a carriers jade,
And lay *at racke and manger*
She whift her pipe, she drunke her can,
The pot was nere out of her span;
She married a tobacco man,
A stranger, a stranger.
Life of Robin Goodfellow, 1628.

RACKAPELT. An idle rascal. *Linc.*

RACKET. (1) A hard blow. *East.* Perhaps from the instrument with which the ball was struck at tennis.

(2) A kind of net.

(3) A struggle. *North.*

RACK-HURRY. The track or railway on which waggons run in unloading coals at a hurry; that is, at a staith or wharf.

RACKING. Torture. Still in common use as an adjective, agonizing.

RACKING-CROOK A pot-hook. *Northumb.*

RACKLE. (1) Noisy talk. *West.* Also to rattle, of which it may be a form.

(2) Rude; unruly. *North.* It is an archaism meaning *rash.*

And than to wyving be thou nat *racle*,
Beware of hast thouhe she behest to please.
Lydgate's Minor Poems, p. 30.

RACKLE-DEED. Loose conduct. *Cumb.*

RACKLING. A very small pig. *Suffolk.*

RACKRIDER. A small trout. *North.*

RACKS. (1) The sides of a waggon. This word occurs in Hollyband's Dictionarie, 1593.

(2) Range; kitchen fire-place. *Essex.*

RACK-STAFF. A kind of pole or staff used for adjusting the mill-stones.

RACK-UP. To supply horses with their food for the night. *South.*

RACK-VINTAGE. A voyage made by merchants into France for racked wines procured what was called the rack-vintage.

RACK-YARD. The farmyard, where beasts are kept: from the racks used there.

RAD. (1) Afraid. Apol. Loll. p. 27.
Thow wold holde me drade,
And for the erle fulle *rade.*
MS. Lincoln A. i. 17, f. 132.

(2) Advised; explained. (*A.-S.*)
In the castelle had sche hyt hyght,
To defende hur with alle hur myghte,
So as her counsayle *radd.*
MS. Cantab. Ff. ii. 38, f. 80.

Now with the messanger was no badde,
He took his hors as the bysschop *radde.*
Reliq. Antiq. ii. 101.

RADCOLE. A radish.

RADDLE. (1) To weave. *North.*

(2) The side of a cart.

(3) To do anything to excess. *Linc.*

(4) A hurdle. *South.* Kennett has *raddles*, small wood or sticks split like laths to bind a wall for the plastering it over with loam or mortar. "In old time," says Harrison, p. 187, "the houses of the Britons were slightlie set up with a few posts and many *radels*, with stable and all offices under one roofe." In Sussex the term is applied to long pieces of supple underwood twisted between upright stakes to form a fence, or to slight strips of wood which are employed in thatching barns or outhouses. Also called *raddlings.*

(5) To banter. *North.*

RADDLINGS. (1) Windings of a wall. *North.*

(2) Bribery money at elections. *West.*

RADE. An animal's maw. *Linc.*

RADEGUNDE. A disease, apparently a sort of boil. Piers Ploughman, p. 430.

RADELICHE. Readily; speedily. (*A.-S.*)
In slepyng that blessud virgyn apperede hym to,
And badde hym arys *radeliche* and blyve.
Chron. Vilodun. p. 126.

RADES. The rails of a waggon.

RADEVQRE. Tapestry.

RADIK. A radish. It occurs in an early collection of receipts in MS. Lincoln f. 290, and is the A.-S. form.

RADLY. Quickly; speedily. (*A.-S.*)

Up then rose this prowd schereff,
And *radly* made hym jare ;
Many was the modur son
To the kyrk with hym can fare.
MS. Cantab. Ff. v. 48, f. 127.

Thomas *radly* up he rase,
And ran over that mounteyne hye,
And certanly, as the story sayes,
He hir mette at eldryne tre.
MS. Cantab. Ff. v. 48, f. 116.

RADNESSE. Fear. See *Rad* (1).

He said, I make myne avowe verreilly to Cryste,
And to the haly vernacle, that voide schalle I nevere,
For *radnesse* of na Romayne that regnes in erthe.
Morte Arthure, MS. Lincoln, f. 56.

RAERS. The rails of a cart. *North.*

RAFE. (1) Tore. (*A.-S.*)

Hir clothes ther scho *rafe* hir fro,
And to the wodd gane scho go.
Percevat, 2157.

(2) Weak ; silly ; foolish. *Suffolk.*

RAFF. (1) Scum ; refuse. Formerly applied to persons of low condition. Now *riff-raff.*

And maken of the rym and *raf*
Suche gylours for pompe and pride.
Appendix to W. Mapes, p. 340.

(2) A raft of timber. *North.*

(3) Abundance ; affluence. *North.* In old English, a confused heap.

(4) Spoil ; plunder. *Kent.*

Ilk a manne agayne his gud he gaffe,
That he had tane with ryfe and *raffe.*
MS. Lincoln A. i. 17, f. 148.

(5) In *raff*, speedily. (*A.-S.*)

(6) Idle ; dissolute. *North.*

RAFFERTORY. Masterful. *Linc.*

RAFFLE. (1) To stir the blazing faggots, &c. in an oven. The wooden instrument with which this is done is called the *rafflen pole.* Brushing off ripe walnuts is also called *rafflen 'em.*

(2) To live disorderly. *North.* Hence *raffle-coppin*, a wild fellow.

(3) A kind of fishing-net.

(4) To move, or fidget about. *Linc.*

RAFFS. (1) The students of Oxford are so called by the town's people.

(2) Long coarse straws. *Northumb.*

RAFFYOLYS. A dish in ancient cookery described in Warner's Ant. Cul. p. 65.

RAFLES. Plays with dice. (*A.-N.*)

RAFORT. A radish.

RAFT. (1) To irritate. *Dorset.*

(2) A damp fusty smell. *East.*

RAFTE. Seized, or taken away. (*A.-S.*)

Rafte awey forsothe is he ;
How, thei selde, may this be ?
Cursor Mundi, MS. Coll. Trin. Cantab. f. 108.

My chylde ys thus *rafte* me froo.
MS. Cantab. Ff. ii. 38, f. 68.

Be God, quod Adam, here is a stun,
It shalle be his bane anon !
Thus sone his life was *rafte.*
MS. Cantab. Ff. v. 48, f. 51.

RAFTER-RIDGING. A particular kind of ploughing used in Hampshire, so called from each ridge being separated by a furrow. Balk-ploughing. *Hants.*

RAFTY. (1) Rancid ; fusty. *Var. dial.*

(2) Wet ; foggy cold. *Suffolk.*

(3) Violent in temper. *South.*

RAG. (1) To scold, or abuse. *Var. dial.*

(2) A kind of basalt. *Warw.*

(3) The catkins of the hazel. *Yorksh.*

(4) A mist, or drizzling rain. *North.*

(5) A shabby looking fellow. " Tag and rag,' the riff-raff, Harrison, p. 215.

(6) A farthing. A cant term.

(7) A herd of young colts.

RAGABRASH. Low idle people. *Cumb.* Nares has *raggabash* in the singular.

RAGAMUFFIN. A person in rags. Perhaps derived from *ragomofin*, the name of a demon in some of the old mysteries.

RAGE. (1) Madness ; rashness. (*A.-N.*)

(2) To romp, or play wantonly. (*A.-N.*)

When sche seyth galantys revell yn hall,
Yn here hert she thynkys owtrage,
Desyrynge with them to pley and *rage*,
And stelyth fro yow full prevely.
Reliq. Antiq. i. 29.

(3) A broken pan. *Somerset.*

RAGEOUS. Violent ; furious. *North.* It occurs in Gascoigne.

RAGERIE. Wantonness. (*A.-N.*)

RAGGALY. Villanous. *Yorksh.*

RAGGED. (1) A term applied to fruit trees, when they have a good crop. Thus they say, " How full of fruit that tree is ! it's as *ragged* as it can hing." In some parts of Yorkshire the catkins of the hazel are called *rag*, and perhaps this word has some connexion therewith. *Linc.*

(2) Hawks were called *ragged* when their feathers were broken. Gent. Rec.

RAGGED-ROBINS. The keepers' followers in the New Forest.

RAGGULED. Sawed off. *Devon.*

RAGHTE. Reached. (*A.-S.*)

The kyng of Egypt hath take a schafte,
The chylde satt and nere hym *raghte.*
MS. Cantab. Ff. ii. 38, f. 79.

RAGINGUES. Ragings ; rompings.

Leisingue and pleizes and *raginguee,*
He bliefte also. *MS. Laud. 108, f. 111.*

RAGLER. An officer in South Wales who collected fines, &c.

RAGMAN. (1) The charter by which the Scots acknowledged their dependence on the English crown under Edward I. was popularly called a *ragman roll;* and hence the term, with or without the last word, came to be applied to several kinds of written rolls and documents, especially if of any length. Thus a papal bull with many seals is termed a *rageman* in Piers Ploughman, p. 5 ; and the list of names in Fame's book is called *ragman roll* in Skelton, i. 420. See also Plumpton Corr. p. 168. In a letter of Henry IV. dated 1399, printed in Rymer, mention is made of *literas patentes vocata raggemans sive blank chartres.* In Piers Ploughman, p. 461, it seems to mean a person who made a list or ragman.

Rede on this *ragmon*, and rewle yow theraftur.
MS. Cantab. Ff. v. 48, f. 1.

Mayster parson, I marvayll ye wyll gyve lycence
To this false knave in this audience
To publish his *ragman rolles* with lyes.
The Pardoner and the Frere, 1533.

(2) An ancient game at which persons drew by chance poetical descriptions of their characters, the amusement consisting, as at modern games of a similar kind, in the peculiar application or misapplication of the verses so selected as hazard by the drawers. This meaning of the term was first developed by Mr. Wright in his Anecdota Literaria, 8vo. 1844, where he has printed two collections of ancient verses used in the game of ragman. Mr. Wright conjectures that the stanzas were written one after another on a roll of parchment, that to each stanza a string was attached at the side, with a seal or piece of metal or wood at the end, and that, when used, the parchment was rolled up with all the strings and their seals hanging together, so that the drawer had no reason for choosing one more than another, but drew one of the strings by mere chance, on which the roll was opened to see on what stanza he had fallen: if such were the form of the game, we can very easily imagine why the name was applied to a charter with an unusual number of seals attached to it, which when rolled up would present exactly the same appearance. Mr. Wright is borne out in his opinion by an English poem termed *Ragmane roelle*, printed from MS. Fairfax 16:

My ladyes and my maistresses echone,
Lyke hit unto your humbyble wommanhede,
Resave in gré of my sympill persone
This rolle, which withouten any drede
Kynge Ragman me bad me sowe in brede,
And cristyned yt the merour of your chaunce;
Drawith a strynge, and that shal streight yow leyde
Unto the verry path of your governaunce.

That the verses were generally written in a roll may perhaps be gathered from a passage in Douglas's Virgil,—

With that he raucht me ane roll: to rede I begane,
The royetest ane ragment with mony ratt rime.

Where the explanation given by Jamieson seems to be quite erroneous.

Venus, whiche stant withoute lawe,
In non certeyne, but as men drawe
Of *Ragemon* upon the chaunce,
Sche leyeth no peys in the balaunce
Gower, MS. Soc. Antiq. 134, f. 244.

(3) The term *rageman* is applied to the devil in Piers Ploughman, p. 335.

RAGOUNCE. The jacinth stone.

RAG-PIECE. A large net.

RAG-RIME. Hoar frost. *Linc.*

RAGROWTERING. Playing at romps. *Exm.*

RAGS-AND-JAGS. Tatters; fragments; rags.

RAG-TOBACCO. The tobacco leaf cut into small shreds. *North.*

RAGWEED. The herb ragwort.

RAGYD. Ragged.

Som were *ragyd* and long tayled,
Scharpe clawyd and long nayled.
MS. Ashmole 61, f. 65.

RAID. (1) Early. *Kent.* From *rathe.*

(2) A hostile incursion. *North.*

(3) Dressed; arrayed; furnished.

RAIKE. To go, rush, or proceed.

And thane he *raykes* to the rowte, and ruysches one helmys;
Riche hawberkes he rente, and rasede schyldes.
Morte Arthure, MS. Lincoln, f. 85.

RAIL. (1) To stray abroad. Perhaps from the older word *reile*, to roll.

(2) A revel, a country wake. *West.*

(3) A garment of fine linen formerly worn by women round the neck. "Rayle for a womans necke, *crevechief, en quartire doubles,*" Palsgrave. "Anything worne about the throate or necke, as a neck-kercher, a partlet, a *raile*," Florio, p. 216. The night-rail seems to have been of a different kind, and to have partially covered the head; it was a gathered linen cloth.

And then a good grey frocke,
A kercheffe and a *raile*.
Friar Bacons Prophesie, 1604.

(4) To talk over anything. *Devon.*

(5) To teaze, or provoke a person to anger. *Norfolk.*

RAILED. (1) Set; placed. See Minot, p. 16. *Raylide*, MS. Morte Arthure, f. 87.

(2) Covered with net-work.

RAIME. To rule oppressively.

RAIN. A ridge. *North.*

RAIN-BIRD. The woodpecker. *North.* "Reyne, fowle bryde, *gaulus, picus, meropes,*" Prompt. Parv.

RAINES. Rennes, in Bretagne, much esteemed for its manufacture of fine cloth.

RAINY-DAY. A day of misfortune.

RAISE. (1) A cairn of stones. *North.* Anciently, any raised mound, or eminence.

In the parishes of Edenhall and Laxonby, in Cumberland, there are yet some considerable remains of stones which still go by the name of *raises*, though many of them have been carried away, and all of them thrown out of their ancient form and order.
Hutchinson's History of Cumberland.

(2) To expectorate badly. *Suffolk.*

(3) To make additional loops in a stocking in order to fit it to the leg.

(4) A robbery. *North.*

RAISE-MOUNTAIN. A braggadocio.

RAISER. In carpentry, is the front board that stands upon the edge to support the board, flat board, or step; in the game of cricket, the name of a small stick that is put aslant into the hole with a ball upon it, which being struck upon the end, causes a ball to fly or jump up, in order to be struck with a stick, ready in the hand of him that did the former act. *Dyche.*

RAISINS. Pieces that lie under the end of a beam in a wall. Harrison, p. 187.

RAIT. To dissipate the sap of vegetables, by exposing them abroad to the weather. Hay is said to be *raited* when it has been much exposed to an alternancy of wet and dry weather. *Yorksh.*

RAITCH. A line or list of white down the face of a horse. *Yorksh.*

RAITH. Weeds, stick, straw, or other rubbish, in a pool of water. *West.*

RAKE. (1) To rouse up. *Somerset.*

(2) To cover anything in the fire with ashes. This explanation is given by Palsgrave, 1530. It is used metaphorically by Shakespeare. To rake is still in use, meaning to cover up a fire to keep it alive.

(3) A term applied to a hawk when she flew wide of the game.

(4) To walk or move about. *North.* Forby says, to gad or ramble idly.

> Now pass we to the bold beggar,
> That *raked* o'er the hill.
> *Robin Hood,* l. 105.

(5) To start up suddenly. *West.*

(6) To reach. Sir Tristrem, p. 292.

(7) To repeat a tale. *Durham.*

(8) The inclination of the mast of a vessel from the perpendicular.

(9) The sea *rakes* when it breaks on the shore with a long grating sound.

(10) A rut, crack, or crevice. *North.*

(11) A mine, or quarry.

(12) Course; road. *Gawayne.*

RAKEHELL. A wild dissolute fellow.

> With a handfull of *rakehelles* which he had scummed together in this our shire, whilest the king was in his returne from Tewxbury.
> *Lambarde's Perambulation,* 1596, p. 478.

RAKEL. Hasty; rash. *Chaucer.*

> The sowden sayd it is not soo;
> For your prestes, that auld tech vertus trace,
> They ryn *rakyll* out of gud race,
> Gyffe ylle ensampille and lyese in synne.
> *MS. Bodl. e Mus.* 160.

RAKENE. To reckon.

RAKENTEIS. A horse's manger.

> Whan that hors herde nevene
> His kende lordes stevene,
> His *rakenteis* he al te-rof,
> And wente into the kourt wel kof.
> *Beves of Hamtoun,* p. 84.

RAKER. A person who raked and removed the filth from the streets, generally termed *Jack Raker.*

> So on a time, when the cart came, he asked the *raker* why he did his businesse so slacklye: Sir, said he, my fore horse was in the fault, who, being let bloud and drencht yesterday, I durst not labour him.
> *Tarlton's Jests,* 1611.

RAKES-AND-ROANS. A boy's game, in which the younger ones are chased by the larger boys, and when caught, carried home pick-a-back.

RAKE-STELE. The handle of a rake.

RAKET. To racket, or rove about. *To play raket,* to be inconstant.

RAKE-TEETH. Teeth wide apart, similar to those of a rake. *North.*

RAKETYNE. A chain. *Hearne.*

RAKING. Violent. Ortus Vocab.

RAKKE. A manger.

> Of all that ylke vij. yere,
> At the *rakke* he stode tyed.
> *MS. Cantab.* Ff. ii. 38, f. 107.

RAKS-JAKES. Wild pranks.

RALLY. (1) A projecting ledge in a wall built

thicker below than above, serving the purpose of a shelf.

(2) A coarse sieve. *East.*

(3) A crowd, or multitude. *Devon.*

RALPH. The name of a spirit supposed to haunt printing-houses. See Dr. Franklin's Works, 1819, p. 56.

RALPH-SPOONER. A fool. *South.*

RAM. (1) Acrid; fetid. *North.*

(2) To lose anything by flinging it out of reach. *Somerset.*

RAMAGE. Wild. (*A.-N.*) The term was very often applied to an untaught hawk.

> Yet if she were so tickle, as ye would take no stand, so *ramage* as she would be reclaimed with no leave. *Greene's Gwydonius,* 1593.

RAM-ALLEY. A passage leading from Fleet-street to the Temple, famous for cooks, victuallers, sharpers, and whores. It is constantly mentioned in old plays.

RAMAST. Gathered together. (*Fr.*)

> And when they have *ramast* many of several kindes and tastes, according to the appetite of those they treat, they open one vessel, and then another.
> *A Comical History of the World in the Moon,* 1659.

RAMBERGE. A kind of ship. (*Fr.*)

RAMBLE. To reel, or stagger. *West.*

RAMBUZE. "A compound drink at Cambridge, and is commonly made of eggs, ale, wine, and sugar; but in summer, of milk, wine, sugar, and rose-water," Blount's Gloss. p. 538.

RAMBY. Prancing?

> I salle be at journee with gentille knyghtes
> On a *ramby* stede fulle jolyly graythide.
> *Morte Arthure, MS. Lincoln,* f. 57.

RAMCAGED. Withered, said of trees.

RAME. (1) To cry aloud; to sob; to ask for anything repeatedly. *North.* Rayme, to cry out against, Erle of Tolous, 431.

(2) To reach, or stretch after. "To rame, *pandiculor,*" Coles' Dict.

(3) To rove, or ramble. *Yorksh.*

(4) To pull up. *North.*

(5) To rob, or plunder. *Linc.*

RAMEL. Rubbish, especially bricklayer's rubbish, or stony fragments. Also a verb. "To rammell or moulder in pieces, as sometimes mud walles or great masses of stones will doe of themselves," Florio, p. 195. The prior of St. Mary's of Coventry, in 1480, complained sadly of "the pepull of the said cité carrying their donge, *ramel,* and swepinge of their houses" to some place objectionable to him.

RAMELL-WOOD. Natural copse-wood.

> There growyth many allers and other *ramell-wood,* which servethe muche for the buyldinge of suche small houses. *MS. Cotton. Calig.* B. viii.

RAMES. The dried stalks of beans, peas, potatoes, &c. *Devon.* Also, the relics of a branch after the leaves are off.

RAM-HEADED. Made a cuckold.

RAMJOLLOCK. To shuffle the cards.

RAMMAKING. Behaving riotously and wantonly; tearing about, as they say, like a ram. *Linc.*

RAMMED. Excessive. *Kent.*

RAMMEL-CHEESE. Raw meal. *I. Wight.*

RAMMILY. Tall; rank. *Var. dial.*

RAMMISH. (1) Rank; pungent. *North.*

(2) Violent; untamed; ramage.

It is good (saith hee) to apply to sinnewes that are dissected, the powder of earth-wormes mixed and wrought up with old *rammish*, and unsavery barrowes grease, to be put into the griefe.

Topsell's Historie of Serpents, p. 311.

RAMP. (1) To be rampant.

(2) *To ramp up*, to exalt. This is the meaning in Ben Jonson, ii. 518. The illustration quoted by Gifford is irrelevant, and is used in Forby's sense, to grow rapidly and luxuriantly.

(3) *To ramp and reave*, to get anything by fair means or foul.

(4) An ascent in the coping of a wall.

(5) Bending a piece of iron upwards to adapt it to wood-work, of a gate, &c. is called ramping it.

(6) A highwayman, or robber.

RAMPADGEON. A furious, boisterous, or quarrelsome fellow. *North.*

RAMPAGE. To be riotous; to scour up and down. *Rampaging* and *rampageous*, as adjectives, are riotous, ill-disposed.

RAMPALLION. A term of reproach, corresponding to our *rapscallion.*

RAMPANTUS. Overbearing. *Linc.*

RAMPE. (1) To climb. (*A.-N.*)

(2) A coarse woman, a severe term of reproach. Hall, describing Joan of Arc, says she was "a *rampe* of suche boldnesse, that she would course horses and ride theim to water, and do thynges that other yong maidens bothe abhorred and wer ashamed to do." *Hall, Henry VI.* f. 25.

(3) To rush. (*A.-S.*)

He *rawmpyde* so ruydly that alle the erthe ryfes.

Morte Arthure, MS. Lincoln, f. 61.

RAMPER. i. e. Rampire, generally applied to any turnpike road: more particularly however to such highways as are on the site of the old Roman roads. *Linc.*

RAMPICK. According to Wilbraham, a *rampicked* tree is a stag-headed tree, i. e. like an old overgrown oak, having the stumps of boughs standing out of its top.

Thus doth he keepe them still in awfull feare,

And yet allowes them liberty hough;

So deare to him their welfare doth appeare,

That when their fleeces gin to waxen rough,

He combs and trims them with a *rampicke* bough.

Washing them in the streames of silver Ladon,

To cleanse their skinnes from all corruption.

The Affectionate Shepheard, 1594.

RAMPIRE. A rampart.

RAMPISH. Rampant. *Palsgrave.*

RAMPSE. To climb. *Somerset.* Hence *rampsing*, tall, high.

RAMRACKETING. A country rout, where there are many noisy amusements. *Devon.*

RAM-RAISE. A running a little backward in order to take a good leap. *North.*

RAMS. Wild garlic. *Var. dial.*

RAMS-CLAWS. Crowfoot. *Somerset.* Ramsfoot is the water crowfoot.

RAMSHACKLE. (1) Loose; out of repair; ungainly; disjointed. *Var. dial.*

(2) To search or ransack. *North.*

RAM'S-HORN. A winding-net supported by stakes, to inclose fish that come in with the tide. *Somerset.*

RAMSONS. A species of garlic.

Ramsons tast like garlick: they grow much in Cranbourn-chase: a proverb,

Eate leekes in Lide, and *ramsins* in May,

And all the yeare after physicians may play.

Aubrey's Wilts, MS. Royal Soc. p. 184.

RAM-STAG. A gelded ram. *South.*

RAMSTAM. Thoughtless. *North.*

RAN. (1) Force; violence. *North.*

(2) The hank of a string. *West.*

(3) A saying. Sevyn Sages, 2723.

(4) Open robbery and rapine.

RANCE. A kind of fine stone. It is mentioned in Archæologia, x. 423.

With ivorie pillars mixt with jett and *rance*,

Rarer and richer then th'old Carian's was.

Works of Du Bartas, p. 245.

RANCH. A deep scratch. *East.* "A ranche or clinch with a beasts paw," Cotgrave in v. *Griffade.*

RANCHET. A kind of bread.

RANCON. A weapon like a bill.

RAND. (1) A long and fleshy piece of beef cut from the part between the flank and buttock. "Rande of befe, *giste de beuf*," Palsgrave.

(2) A hank of line or twine; a strip of leather. *East.*

(3) Rushes on the borders and edges of land near a river. *Norf.* In old English, the margin or border of anything.

(4) To canvass for votes. *West.*

RANDALL. Random. *Coles.*

RANDAN. (1) The produce of a second sifting of meal. *East.*

(2) A noise, or uproar. *Glouc.*

RANDEM-TANDEM. A tandem with three horses, sometimes driven by University men, and so called at Oxford.

RANDIES. Itinerant beggars, and balladsingers. *Yorksh.*

RANDING. Piecemeal. *Berks.*

RANDLE. To punish a schoolboy for an indelicate but harmless offence.

RANDLE-BALK. In Yorkshire, the cross piece of wood in a chimney, upon which the pothooks are hung, is called the *randle-balk* or *rendle-balk.* Kennett's MS. Glossary.

RANDOM. A straight line. *North.*

RANDONE. A long speech. "Randone or long reuge of wurds, *haringa*," Pr. Parv.

RANDOUM. Force; rapidity. (*A.-N.*)

He rod to him with gret *randoum*,

And with Morgelai is fauchoun

The prince a felde in the feld.

Beves of Hamtoun, p. 139.

They saylyd ovyr the (?) *randown*,

And londed at Sowth-hampton.

MS. Cantab. Ff. ii. 38, f. 123.

Then rode he este with grete *randowne*,

And thoght to bere hym adowne.

MS. Cantab. Ff. ii. 38, f. 247.

RANDY. (1) Boisterous; noisy; obstreperous; also, maris appetens. *North.*

(2) A spree; they say, " Such a one is on the *randy*," meaning thereby, that he is spending his time in a continued round of drunkenness and debauchery.

RANDY-BEGGAR. A tinker. *North.*

RANDY-DANDY. A violent and vulgar quarrelsome woman. *North.*

RANDYROW. A disturbance. *West.*

RANE. Coarse, as linen, &c. *West.*

RANES. The carcase or skeleton of a fowl or bird. *Devon.*

RANG. Rebellious. (*A.-S.*)

> And yif that ani were so *rang*,
> That he thanne ne come anon,
> He swor bi Crist and seint Johan,
> That he sholde maken him thral,
> And al his ofspring forth withal.
> *Havelok*, 2561.

RANGE. (1) A sieve. *Somerset.* Elyot has, " *Sisacthea*, a rangeyng sieve;" and Huloet, " bult, raunge, or syeve meale." The second best wheaten bread was called range-bread.

(2) To cleanse by washing. *North.*

(3) The shaft of a coach. *Devon.*

(4) To take a range in firing.

> Their shot replies, but they were *rank'd* too high
> To touch the pinnace, which bears up so nigh
> And plays so hot, that her opponents think
> Some devil is grand captain of the Pink.
> *Legend of Captain Jones*, 1659.

RANGER. A chimney rack. *North.*

RANGLE. (1) To range about in an irregular and sinuous manner. *West.*

(2) Is when a hawk has gravel given her to bring her to a stomach. Blome, ii. 63.

RANISH. Ravenous. *Devon.*

RANK. (1) In a passion. *Chesh.*

(2) Thick; full; abundant. *Rankness*, abundance, fertility.

(3) A row of beans, &c. *I. Wight.*

(4) Very; excessive. *Var. dial.*

(5) Strong. See Isumbras, 200.

> He ryfes the *raunke* stele, he ryghttes theire brenez,
> And reste theme the ryche mane, and rade to his strenghes.
> *Morte Arthure, MS. Lincoln*, f. 69.

(6) Wrong. *Lanc.*

RANK-RIPE. Quite ripe. *Chesh.*

RANNACK. A worthless fellow. *Rannigal* is also used. *North.*

RANNEL. (1) A whore. A cant term.

(2) To ruffle the hair. *Yorksh.*

RANNILY. Fluently; readily; without hesitation. *Norfolk.*

RANNY. A shrew-mouse. *Suffolk.* Browne has the term in his ' Vulgar Errors.'

RANPIKE. Same as *Rampick*, q. v.

RANSCUMSCOUR. Fuss; ado. *Devon.* Also, a passionate person.

RANT. To drink, or riot. *North.*

> Mistake me not, custom, I mean not tho,
> Of excessive drinking, as great *ranters* do.
> *Praise of Yorkshire Ale*, 1697, p. 5.

RANTAN. To beat soundly. *Glouc.* It apparently alludes to a tinker's constant hammering in the following passage :

> There is *ran-tan* Tom Tinker and his Tib,
> And there's a Jugler with his fingers glib.
> *Taylor's Workes*, 1630, l. 110.

RANTER. (1) A large beer-jug. Hence, to pour liquor from a large into a smaller vessel.

(2) To mend or patch a rent in a garment very neatly. *Suffolk.*

RANTIPIKE. An ass. *Dorset.*

RANTIPOLE. A rude romping child. *West.*

RANTREE. The mountain ash. *North.*

RANTY. Wild; frisky; riotous. *Ranty-tanty*, in a great passion. *North.*

RAP. (1) To seize; to ravish.

(2) To exchange, or swap. *Var. dial.*

(3) To risk, or hazard. *North.*

(4) To brag, or boast. *Devon.*

(5) *Rap and rend*, to seize hold of everything one can. The phrase occurs in Palsgrave, and is still in use. Compare Florio, p. 20. " To get all one can rap and run," Coles's Lat. Dict. " To rape and renne," to seize and plunder, Chaucer.

RAPE. (1) Haste. (*A.-S.*) Its meaning in the third example appears more doubtful.

> And commaunded alle yn *rape*
> Awey that wrytyng for to skrape.
> *MS. Harl.* 1701, f. 47.

> Ne was ther non that mighte ascape,
> So Beves slough hem in a *rape*.
> *Beves of Hamtoun*, p. 27.

> A thefe to hys thefte hath *rape*,
> For he weneth evermore for to skape.
> *MS. Harl.* 1701, f. 15.

(2) To steal; to plunder.

> Ravenows fisches han sum mesure; whanne thei hungren thei *rapyn* ; whanne thei ben ful they sparyn.
> *Wimbelton's Sermon*, 1388, *MS. Hatton* 57, p. 16.

(3) A division of a county, comprising several hundreds.

(4) To scratch. *Somerset.*

(5) To take captive. (*A.-S.*)

(6) To bind or lace tightly. *Devon.*

(7) To prepare. (*A.-S.*)

(8) A heap of corn.

(9) A turnip. Ord. and Reg. p. 426.

RAPER. A rope-maker.

RAPEY. A dish in ancient cookery, described in MS. Sloane 1201, f. 46.

RAPID. Gay. *Var. dial.*

RAPIER-DANCE. This is nearly the same as the sword-dance among the ancient Scandinavians, or as that described by Tacitus among the Germans. The performers are usually dressed in a white frock, or covered with a shirt, to which as also to their hats, or paper helmets, are appended long black ribands. They frequently go from house to house, about Christmas, and are treated with ale after their military exercise. At merry-nights, and on other festive occasions, they are introduced one after another by the names and titles of heroes, from Hector and Paris, princes of Troy, down to Guy of Warwick. A spokesman then repeats some verses in praise of each, and they begin to flourish the rapier. On a signal given, all the weapons are united, or interlaced, but soon withdrawn again, and brandished by the heroes, who exhibit a great variety of evolutions, being usually accompanied by slow music. In the last scene, the rapiers are united round the neck of a person kneeling in the centre, and when they are suddenly withdrawn, the victim falls to the ground; he is afterwards carried out, and a mock funeral is performed with pomp, and solemn strains. *Willan's Yorksh.*

RAPLY. Quickly; speedily. (*A.-S.*)
  So *raply* thay ryde thare that alle the rowte rynges.
  Morte Arthure, MS. Lincoln, f. 72.

RAPPE. To hasten. (*A.-S.*)
  Loke ye *rappe* yow not up to ryde.
  MS. Harl. 2252, f. 129.

RAPPER. A great or extravagant falsehood; a vehement oath. *West.*

RAPPER-DANDIES. Red barberries. *North.*

RAPPING. Large. *Var. dial.*

RAPPIS. A dissolute person. *Cumb.*

RAPPLE. A ravelled thread. *North.*

RAPS. (1) News. *Yorksh.*

(2) Games; sports. *Salop.*

(3) A disorderly fellow. *Yorksh.*

RAPSCALLION. A low vagabond.

RAPTE. Ravished; enraptured.
  Whose amyable salutes flewe with suche myght,
  That Locryne was *rapte* at the fyrst syght.
  MS. Lansd. 208, f. 22.

RARE. (1) Fine; great. *South.*

(2) To roar. *North.* "Rare or grete, *vagire,*" MS. Dictionary, 1540.
  Lowde he gane bothe rowte and *rare :*
  Allas! he sayde, for sorowe and Care.
  MS. Lincoln A. i. 17, f. 126.

(3) Underdone; raw. *Var. dial.*

(4) Early. *Devon.*

(5) Ready; prepared. *Somerset.*

RARELY. Quite well in health.

RARNING. Thin, as cloth is. *West.*

RAS. Space; time. *Hearne.*

RASALGER. The fume of minerals. So explained in A New Light of Alchemy, 1674.
  Alume, atriment, alle I suspende,
  Rasalger and arsnick I defende,
  Ashmole's Theat. Chem. Brit. 1652, p. 271.

RASARDE. A hypocrite?
  Out on thee, *rasarde,* with thy wiles,
  For falslye my people thou begyles,
  I shall thee hastelye honge;
  And that lurden that standes thee by,
  He puttes my folke in greate anoye
  With his false flatteringe tonge.
  Chester Plays, ii. 163.

RASCAL. A lean animal, one fit to neither hunt nor kill. "Rascall, refuse beest, *refus,*" Palsgrave, 1530.

RASCALL. Common; low. It is the translation of *commune* in Hollyband's Dictionarie, 1593. The word also occurs in this sense in The First Part of the Contention, ed. 1843, p. 31. *Rascalye,* low people, refuse of anything.

RASCOT. A knave, or rascal. *Cumb.*

RASE. (1) To scratch. *Suffolk.* "Rased their hardened hides," Harrison, p. 188.

(2) To erase. (3) An erasure.

(4) A channel of the sea. (*A.-N.*)
  Felowes, they shall never more us withstonde,
  For I se them all drowned in the *rase* of Irlonde.
  Hycke-Scorner, ap. Hawkins, i. 89.

(5) Rage; anger. (*A.-S.*) *Rase-brained,* violent, Wilbraham, p. 67.

(6) A swift pace. Perceval, 1145.

(7) To snarl, as dogs do.

RASEN. In timber buildings, that piece of timber to which the bottoms of the rafters are fastened.

RASER-HOUSE. A barber's shop.

RASH. (1) To snatch, or seize; to tear, or rend. Gifford explains it, "to strike obliquely with violence, as a wild boar does with his tusk."
  They buckled then together so,
    Like unto wild boares *rashing ;*
  And with their swords and shields they ran
    At one another slashing.
      Sir Lancelot du Lake.

(2) Brittle. *Cornw.*

(3) Said of corn in the straw which is so dry that it easily falls out of the straw with handling of it. *North.*

(4) Sudden; hasty. *Shak.*

(5) A kind of inferior silk. It is mentioned by Harrison, p. 163.

RASHED. Burnt in cooking, by being too hastily dressed. "How sadly this pudding has been *rashed* in the oven." "The beef would have been very good if it had not been *rashed* in the roasting." Rasher, as applied to bacon, probably partakes of this derivation. *Wilts.*

RASHER. (1) A rush. *North.*

(2) A box on the ears. *Glouc.*

RASING. A blubbering noise. *North.*

RASINGES. Shavings; slips.

RASKAILE. A pack of rascals.

RASKE. To puff, or blow.
  Than begynneth he to klawe and to *raske,*
  And yyveth Terlyncel hys taske.
  MS. Harl. 1701, f. 29.

RASOUR. The sword-fish.

RASP. (1) To belch. *East.*

(2) A raspberry. *Var. dial.*

(3) The steel of a tinder-box

RASPIS. The raspberry. A wine so termed is mentioned by Harrison, p. 167.

RASSE. Rose; ascended.
  He *rasse* agayne thurghe his godhede.
  MS. Lincoln A. i. 17, f. 212.

RASSELS. The land-whin. *Suffolk.*

RASSLE. To stir the embers in an oven with a long pole. *East.*

RASTER. A kind of cloth.

RASTIR. A shaving-razor.

RASURE. A scratch. (*A.-N.*)

RAT. (1) An old contemptuous nickname for a clergyman.

(2) Reads. Wright's Pol. Songs, p. 327.

RATCH. (1) A straight line. *North.*

(2) To stretch; to pull asunder. *Cumb.*

(3) A subsoil of stone and gravel, mixed with clay. *Heref.*

(4) To spot, or streak. *North.*

(5) To tell great falsehoods. *Linc.*

RATCHEL. Gravelly stone. *Derb.*

RATCHER. A rock. *Lanc.*

RATE. (1) To expose to air. *North.*

(2) To become rotten. *Cumb.*

(3) To call away or off. *Kent.*

(4) Ratified; valid.

RATHE. (1) Soon; early. *Var. dial.* In the second example, eager, anxious. *Rathlike,* speedily, MS. Cotton. Vespas. D. vii.

> He did it up, the sothe to say,
> But sum therof he toke away
> In his hand ful *rathe.*
>> *MS. Cantab.* Ff. v. 48, f. 53.

> Now than are thay leveande bathe,
> Was no3te the rede knyghte so *rathe*
> For to wayte hym with skathe.
>> *Sir Perceval,* 98.

> And it arose ester and ester, tille it aroose fulle este; and *rather,* and *rather.*
>> *Warkworth's Chronicle,* p. 22.

(2) Savage; hasty. *Robson.*

(3) To rede, or advise. Havelok, 1335.

RATHELED. Fixed; rooted. *Gawayne.*

RATHER. (1) *Rather of the ratherest,* said of underdone meat. *Norf.*

(2) *Rather-n'else,* rather than not.

RATHERLINGS. For the most part. *North.*

RATHERLY. Rather. *Yorksh.*

RATHES. Only used in the plural; a frame extending beyond the body and wheels of a cart or waggon to enable farmers to carry hay, straw, &c. *Craven.*

RATION. Reasoning. *(Lat.)*

RATON. A rat. *(A.-N.)* "*Sorex,* a raton," Nominale MS. For the following lines compare King Lear, iii. 4. *Ratten,* Hunter's Hallamsh. Gl. p. 75.

> *Ratons* and myse and soche smale dere,
> That was hys mete that vij. yere.
>> *MS. Cantab.* Ff. ii. 38, f. 106.

RATONER. A rat-catcher. *(A.-N.)*

RATS. Pieces; shreds; fragments. *North.*

RATTEEN. A kind of cloth.

RATTEN. To destroy or take away a workman's tools, or otherwise incapacitate him from working, for not paying his *natty* to the fund, or for having offended the Union in any matter. *York.*

RATTEN-CROOK. A long crook reaching from the rannel-balk to the fire.

RATTLE. (1) To beat, or thrash. *North.*

(2) To stutter, or speak with difficulty. It is now used in exactly the opposite sense, and so it was by Shakespeare, Mids. N. D. v. 1. It also meant to revile. "Extreamely reviled, cruelly *ratled,* horribly railed on," Cotgrave.

RATTLE-BABY. A chattering child.

> That's strange, for all are up to th' ears in love:
> Boys without beards get boys, and girls bear girls;
> Fine little *rattle-babies,* scarce thus high,
> Are now call'd wives: if long this hot world stand,
> We shall have all the earth turn Pigmy-Land.
>> *Heywood's Love's Mistress,* p. 9.

RATTLE-BONE. Worn out; crazy. *Sussex.*

RATTLE-MOUSE. A bat.

RATTLEPATE. A giddy chattering person.

RATTLER. A great falsehood. *Var. dial.*

RATTLES. The alarming rattle in the throat preceding death. *Var. dial.*

RATTLETRAPS. Small knickknacks.

RATTOCK. A great noise. *East.*

RATY. Cold and stormy. *North.*

RAUGH. A tortuous course. *West.*

RAUGHT. (1) Reached. *West.* In later writers sometimes, snatched away.

> Unto the cheftane he chese,
> And *raughte* hym a strake,
>> *MS. Lincoln* A. L 17, f. 134.

(2) Cared; recked. *(A.-S.)*

> Thanne the kyng hys hand up rau3te,
> That ffalse man his trowthe be-tau3te,
> He was a devyl off helle.
>> *Romance of Athelston.*

RAUGHTER. A rafter. *Lilly.*

RAUHEDE. Rawness; crudity.

RAUK. (1) Smoke. *Sussex.*

(2) To mark, or scratch. *North.*

RAUL. To pull about roughly; to entangle thread, &c. *West.*

RAUM. (1) To retch. *Yorksh.*

(2) To sprawl. *Suffolk.*

(3) To shout, or cry. *Linc.*

RAUMER. A kind of fighting-cock.

RAUN. The roe of salmon prepared in a particular manner, and used as a bait to fish with. *North.* "A rawne of fysche, *lactis,*" MS. Dictionary, dated 1540.

RAUNCH. (1) To wrench, or pull out.

(2) To gnaw, or craunch. *Devon.*

RAUNING-KNIFE. A cleaver. *West.*

RAUNSON. A ransom. *(A.-N.)*

> For with oure Lord is gret mercy,
> And *raunsun* ek gret plenté;
> He payed for us his owyn body,
> This aughte be takyn in gret deuté;
> His blood he schad also largely,
> To make us and oure fadris fre,
> And alle oure *raunsouns* by and by
> He qwit hymself and non but he.
>> *Hampole's Paraphrase of the Psalms,* MS.

RAUT. To low, as a cow. *North.*

RAUX. To stretch. *Northumb.*

RAVAYNE. Theft. *Palsgrave.*

> The thrydde branche es *ravayne,*
> That es calde a gret synne.
>> *MS. Harl.* 2260, f. 50.

> Thou schalt not stele thy neghbours thyng
> Be gyle ne *raveyne* ne wrong withholdyng.
>> *MS. Cantab.* Ff. ii. 38, f. 5.

RAVE. To tear up. *Linc.* It is also used as a substantive in a cognate sense. "It's dangerous to make a *rave* in an old building, so do not attempt any alterations." *Cumb.*

> Ande he worowede him, and slowhe him; ande thanne he ranne to the false emperes, ande *ravide* hir evine to the bone, but more harme dide he not to no mane. *Gesta Romanorum,* p. 202.

RAVEL. To talk idly. *North.*

RAVEL-BREAD. Whity-brown bread. *Kent.* According to Harrison, p. 168, "the raveled is a kind of cheat bread, but it reteineth more of the grosse and lesse of the pure substance of the wheat."

RAVELLED. Confused; mixed together.

REBEN. A kind of fine cloth.

REBESK. Arabesque. *Coles.*

REBOKE. To belch, or cast up.

REBONE.

Thow false lordeyn, I xal fell the flatt !
Who made the so hardy to make swych *rebone.*
Digby Mysteries, p. 131.

REBOUND. To take an offer at rebound, i. e. at once, without consideration.

RECCHE. To reck, or care for. (*A.-S.*)

Ne may non me worse do,
Then ich have had hiderto.
Ich have had so muche wo,
That y ne *recche* whyder y go.
Harrowing of Hell, p. 21.

The stiwarde therof I ne *reche,*
I-wisse I have therto no meche.
MS. Cantab. Ff. v. 48, f. 53.

RECEITE. A receptacle. *Lydgate.*

RECEIVE. *To receive the canvas,* an old phrase for being dismissed.

RECEST. Withdrawn.

And he imagining with hisself that he had the 12. of July deserved my great displeasure, and finding himself barred from vew of my philosophicall dealing with Mr. Henrik, thowght that he was utterly *recest* from intended goodnes toward him.
Dr. Dee's Diary, p. 13.

RECETTE. To receive, or harbour. (*A.-N.*)

My lorde hym *recetted* in hys castell
For the dewkys dethe Oton.
MS. Cantab. Ff. ii. 38, f. 290.

RECHASE. Properly, to call the hounds back from a wrong scent, but often used for calling them under any circumstances. " Seven score raches at his rechase," i. e. at his call, Squyr of Lowe Degré, 772. A *recheat* is explained by Blome, " a farewell at parting." In Dorset, sheep are said to be *rechased* when they are driven from one pasture to another.

RECHAUSED. Heated again. *Warw.*

RECHEN. To reach ; to stretch out. (*A.-S.*)

Pestilence es an yvel *rechande* on lenthe and on brede. *MS. Coll. Eton.* 10, f. 2.

RECHES. Costly things. (*A.-S.*)

RECK. A hand-basket. *Somerset.*

RECKAN. A hook for pots. *North.*

RECKEY. A child's long coat. *Yorksh.*

RECKLING. The smallest and weakest in a brood of animals. *North.*

RECKON. To think, or guess. *Var. dial.*

RECKON-CREEAK. A crook suspended from a beam within the chimney to hang pots and pans on. *Yorksh.*

RECK-STAVEL. A staddle for corn.

RECLAIM. (1) To reclaim a hawk, to make her gentle and familiar, to bring her to the wrist by a certain call. It is often used metaphorically, to tame.

(2) To proclaim. *Hall.*

RECLINATORYE. A resting-place.

And therinne sette his *reclynatorye.*
Lydgate, MS. Soc. Antiq. 134, f. 3.

RECLINE. To incline towards.

RECLUSE. To shut up. (*Lat. Med.*)

RECOLAGE. Wantonness.

And sytte up thare wyth *recolage,*
And jyt do moche more outrage.
MS. Harl. 1701, f. 48.

RECOLDE. To recollect. (*A.-N.*)

RE-COLLECTED. Collected again in his mind or spirits.

RECOMFORTE. (1) Comfort. (*A.-N.*)

In *recomforte* of his inwarde smerte.
Lydgate, MS. Soc. Antiq. 134, f. 5.

(2) To encourage. (*A.-N.*)

RECONUSAUNCE. Acknowledgment.

RECORD. (1) Witness ; testimony. (*A.-N.*)

(2) To chatter as birds do before they can sing. Hence, to practise singing, to sing ; to repeat lessons. It occurs in Palsgrave.

RECORDE. To remember. (*A.-N.*)

RECORDER. A kind of flageolet. The following story is very common in old jest books, and told of various persons.

A merrie recorder of London mistaking the name of one Pepper, call'd him Piper : whereunto the partie excepting, and saying, Sir, you mistake, my name is Pepper, not Piper ; hee answered, Why, what difference is there, I pray thee, between Piper in Latin and Pepper in English ? is it not all one ? No, Sir, reply'd the other, there is even as much difference betweene them as is between a Pipe and a Recorder.

RECORTE. To record. (*A.-N.*)

The day i-sett come one hynge,
His borowys hyme brought before the kyng ;
The kyng lett *recorte* tho
The sewt and the answer also.
MS. Rawlinson C. 86.

RECOUR. To recover.

But she said he should *recour* of it, and so he said hee did within some teune daies.
Gifford's Dialogue on Witches, 1603.

RECOURSE. A repetition. *Shak.*

RECOVER. In hunting, to start a hare from her cover or form.

RECRAYED. Recreant. (*A.-N.*) *Recray-handes* is the substantive pl.

With his craftes ganne he calle,
And callede thame *recrayhandes* alle,
Kynge, knyghtes in-with walle. *Perceval* 610.

RECREANDISE. Fear ; cowardice. (*A.-N.*)

RECTE. To impute ; to ascribe.

RECULE. (1) A collection of writings, but used for any book or pamphlet. (*Fr.*)

(2) To go back ; to retreat. (*A.-N.*)

RECULES. Reckless.

As for the tyme y am but *recules,*
Lyke to a fygure wyche that ys hertlees.
MS. Cantab. Ff. i. 6, f. 14.

RECURATIVE. A remedy. (*Lat.*) Gratarolus, Direction for Health, 1574.

RECURE. To recover ; to get again. (*A.-N.*) Also a substantive, recovery.

Willing straunglers for to *recure,*
And in Engeland to have the domynacion.
MS. Soc. Antiq. 101, f. 98.

But Hector fyrst, of strength most assured,
His stede agayne hath anone *recured.*
Lydgate's Troye, 1555, sig. P. v.

RECURELESS. Irrecoverable.

Ye are to blame to sette yowre hert so sore,
Sethyn that ye wote that hyt [ys] *rekeurles.*
MS. Cantab. Ff. i. 6, f. 14

READ. (1) Rennet. *North.*

(2) *To read the inwards,* to strip the fat from the intestines ; also to vomit.

(3) To comb the hair. *North.*

READEPT. To recover.

> The which Duchie, if he might by their meanes *readept* and recover, he would never let passe out of hys memorie so great a benifite, and so frendly a gratuitie to hym exhibited. *Hall, Edward IV. f. 25.*

READSHIP. Confidence ; rule. *West.*

READY. (1) Rid. *Essex.*

(2) To get ready, i. e. to dress. *Ready,* dressed, occurs in old plays.

(3) To forward, or assist. *North.*

(4) Done, as meat, &c. *Wilts.*

(5) To prepare, or make ready.

READY-POLE. A piece of iron across a chimney supporting the pot-hook. It was formerly made of wood, and that material may still be occasionally seen used for the same purpose. *Var. dial.*

REAF. To unravel, or untwist. *Devon.*

REAFE. To anticipate pleasure in, or long for the accomplishment of a thing ; to speak continually on the same subject. *Sussex.*

REAKS. Pranks. "To revell it, or play *reakes,*" Cotgrave in v. *Degonder.*

REAL. (1) Royal. *(A.-N.)*

(2) A Spanish sixpence. *Rider.*

REALTEE. Royalty. *(A.-N.)*

REAM. (1) Cream. *North.* "Mylke reme" is mentioned in a receipt in MS. Lincoln, f. 285.

> That on is white so milkes *rem,*
> That other is red, so fer is lem.
> *Arthour and Merlin,* p. 55.
> Methenke this pain es swetter
> Than ani milkes *rem.*
> *Legendæ Catholicæ,* p. 88.

(2) To hold out the hand for taking or receiving. *North.*

(3) To stretch out ; to bear stretching or drawing out ; to draw out into thongs, threads, or filaments. Also to widen a hole, especially in metal.

(4) Bread is said to *ream,* when made of heated or melted corn.

REAMER. An instrument used to make a hole larger. *Somerset.*

REAM-KIT. The cream-pot. *Yorksh.* Pegge has *ream-mug,* p. 128.

REAM-PENNY. (i. e. Rome-penny). Peterpence. He reckons up his ream-pennies ; that is, he tells all his faults. *North.*

REAN. (1) To eat greedily. *West.*

(2) To droop the head. *Suffolk.*

(3) The furrow between the ridges of ploughed land to take off the water ; any gutter ; a water-course, or small stream. *Var. dial.*

> Therfore of cornes fayer and cleane,
> That growes one rigges out of the *reian,*
> Cayme, thou shalt offer, as I meane,
> To God in magistie. *Chester Plays,* l. 36.
> And thilke that beth maidenes clene,
> That mai hem wassche of the *rene.*
> *Florice and Blauncheflour,* 307.

REAP. A bundle of corn. *North.* "As mych as oone reepe," Townley Myst. p. 13.

REAP-HOOK. A sickle. *Var dial.*

REAR. (1) To mock, or gibe. *Devon.*

(2) Underdone ; nearly raw. *North.* "Reere as an egge is, *mol,*" Palsgrave.

> If a man sicke of the bloody-flixe drinke therof in a *reere* egge two scruples for three daies together fasting, it will procure him remedy.
> *Topsell's Beasts,* 1607, p. 275.

(3) To raise, especially applied to raising the wood-work of a roof. Also, to rise up before the plough, as the furrows sometimes do in ploughing.

(4) To carve a goose.

REARING-BONE. The hip-bone of a hog.

REARING-FEAST. A supper, or feast, given to the workmen when the roof is *reared,* or put on the house. *Linc.*

REARING-MINE. A vein of coal which descends perpendicularly in the mine.

REARLY. Early. Still in use.

REART. To right, or mend. *West.*

REARWARD. The rear. *Shak.*

REASE. Thing ; circumstance.

> Hys emels wyffe wolde he wedde,
> That many a man rewyd that *rease.*
> *MS. Harl. 2252, f. 122.*

REASON. A motto.

REAST. To take offence. *Linc.*

REASTED. Tired ; weary. *North.*

REASTY. (1) Restive. *East.*

(2) Rancid. *Var. dial.* "Restie or rustie bacon," Nomenclator, 1585, p. 86. "Tak rest bacon," Reliq. Antiq. i. 53. *Reez'd bacon,* Hall's Satires, p. 81.

REAVE. To unroof a house. *Norf.*

REAWNT. Did whisper. *Lanc.*

REAWP. A hoarse cold. *Lanc.*

REAWT. Out of doors. *Lanc.*

REBALLING. The catching of eels with earthworms attached to a ball of lead, suspended by a string from a pole.

REBANDED. Adorned with bands.

> They toke ladies and daunsed, and sodainly entered eight other maskers, apparelled in rych tinsel, matched wyth clothe of golde, and on that Turkey clokes, *rebanded* with nettes of silver.
> *Hall's Chronicle,* 1550.

REBARD. Rhubarb. *Heywood.*

REBATE. To blunt metal. It is metaphorically used in Stanihurst, p. 24.

REBATO. A kind of plaited ruff which turned back and lay on the shoulders.

> I pray you, sir, what say you to these great ruff.s, which are borne up with supporters and *rebators,* as it were with poste and raile ?
> *Dent's Pathway,* p. 42.

REBAWDE. A ribald, or scamp.

> Siche a *rebawde* as yowe rebuke any lordes,
> Wyth theire retenux arrayede fulle realle and noble.
> *Morte Arthure, MS. Lincoln,* f. 67

REBBIT. To clinch, or rivet. *Yorksh.*

REBECK. A kind of violin. *(A.-N.)*

REBEKKE. Rebecca. *Chaucer.*

REBEL. (1) To revel. *Heref.*

(2) Disinclined ; unwilling.

REBELLING. The ravelines. *Heywood.*

REBELLNESS. Rebellion.

REDLES. Without advice; helpless. (*A.-S.*)

Hys wyffe *redles*, chyldren gydles, servauntes
withdraw hym fro. *Reliq. Antiq.* i. 270.

REDLID. Twisted; woven.

RED-MAD. Quite mad. *Durham.*

RED-MAILKES. The corn-poppy.

REDOUTED. Dreaded; feared. (*A.-N.*)

REDOUTING. Reverence. *Chaucer.*

REDRESSE. To relieve, or remedy; to make
amends for; to recover. (*A.-N.*)

Or any mane that wist,
Alle wranges ware *redrischt.*
MS. Lincoln A. i. 17, f. 138.

RED-ROW. When the grains of ripening barley
are streaked with red, the crop is said to be
in the *red-row. Norf.*

REDS. Red tints; blushes. *West.*

RED-SEAR. When, in forging, the iron breaks
or cracks under the hammer while it is working between hot and cold, it is said to *red-sear.*
There was a species of iron ore so called on
account of its liability to red-sear.

RED-SHANKS. (1) The arsesmart. *North.*

(2) A contemptuous appellation for Scottish
Highlanders, and native Irish. See Harrison's
England, p. 6.

REDSTREAK. Cider made of a kind of apple
so called, and much esteemed.

Back-recruiting chocolet for the consumptive
gallant, Herefordshire *redstreak* made of rotten
apples at the Three Cranes, true Brunswick Mum
brew'd at S. Katherines, and ale in penny mugs not
so big as a taylor's thimble.
Character of a Coffee-house, 1673, p. 3.

RED-TAIL. The redstart.

REDUBBE. To remedy; to redress. (*Fr.*)

If he shulde, before the same were put in good
ordre, leve those matiers unperfited, it shulde be
long bifore he coude *redubbe* or conduce them to
good effect. *State Papers,* i. 193.

I doubte not by Goddes grace so honestly to *redubbe* all thynges that have been amys.
Ellis's Literary Letters, p. 4.

REDUBBORS. Those that buy stolen cloth
and disguise it by dyeing. *Blount.*

REDUCE. To bring back. (*Lat.*)

REDUCEMENT. Reduction. (*Lat.*)

After a little *reducement* of his passion, and that
time and further meditation had disposed his senses
to their perfect estate.
History of Patient Grisel, p. 40.

REDUCTED. Led back. (*Lat.*)

Onely for the cause of Maximilian newly elected
king of Romanes, should be *reducted* and brought
again into their pristine estate and consuete fami-
liaritee. *Hall, Henry VII.* f. 27.

RED-WATER. Same as *Blend-water,* q. v.

RED-WEED. The common poppy. *East.*

RED-WHOOP. The bullfinch. *Somerset.*

RED-WINDS. Those winds which blast fruit
or corn are so called.

REDYN. Sailed; moved.

So on a day, hys fadur and hee
Redyn yn a schyppe yn the see.
MS. Cantab. Ff. ii. 38, f. 144.

REE. (1) To shake corn in a sieve, so that the
chaff collects to one place. *South*

) A disease in hawks.

(3) An imperative, commanding the leading horse
of a team to turn or bear to the right. *Heit*
and *Camether,* turn or incline to the left.
" Riddle me, riddle me *ree*" is therefore, Riddle me *right.*

A base borne issue of a baser syer,
Bred in a cottage, wandring in the myer,
With nailed shooes and whipstaffe in his hand,
Who with a hey and *ree* the beasts command.
Micro-Cynicon, 1599.

REEANGED. Discoloured; in stripes.

REECE. A piece of wood fixed to the side of
the chep. *Kent.*

REECH. Smoke. *Reechy,* Shakespeare.

The world is wors then men neven,
The *reech* recheth into Heven.
Cursor Mundi, MS. Coll. Trin. Cantab. f. 18.

REED. (1) Unbruised straw. *West.* Hence,
to reed or thatch a house.

(2) The fundament of a cow. *Derb.*

(3) Angry; ill-tempered. *Yorksh.*

(4) A very small wood. *East.*

REED-BILLY. A bundle of reed. *West.*

REEDHOLDER. A thatcher's bow fastened to
the roof to hold the straw. *West.*

REEDIFICATION. Rebuilding. (*Lat.*)

The toun was compelld to help to the *reedification*
of it. *Leland's Itinerary,* 1769, iii. 125.

REED-MOTE. Same as *Feasetraw,* q. v.

REED-PIT. A fen. *Pr. Parv.*

REED-RONDS. Plots, or beds of reed; or,
the swamps which reeds grow in. *Norf.*
Forby has *reed-roll.*

REED-STAKE. An upright stake to which an
ox is tied in the shippen. *Durh.*

REEF. The itch. *North.* According to some,
any eruptive disorder.

REEK. (1) Smoke or vapour. *North.* Perhaps
for *incense* in the following passage, but glossed
by *fumus* in the original.

Reke, that is a gretyngful prayer of men that
dus penance. *MS. Coll. Eton.* 10, f. 25.

(2) To reach. Still in use.

(3) A rick. Nominale MS. *Reek-time,* the
time of making, or stacking hay.

(4) Money. A cant term.

(5) To wear away; to waste. *North.*

(6) Family; lineage. *Yorksh.*

(7) Windy; stormy. *North.*

REEKING-CROOK. A pothook. *North.*

REEK-STAVAL. A rick-staddle.

REEM. (1) To cry, or moan. *North.*

(2) To tie fast. *Somerset.*

(3) The hoar, or white frost.

REEOK. A shriek. *Lanc.*

REEP. To trail in the dirt. *West.*

REEPLE. A beam lying horizontally in the
roof of a coal-mine. *West.*

REES.

Her olyves with her wyn trees,
These foxes brent with her *rees.*
Cursor Mundi, MS. Coll. Trin. Cantab. f. 45.

REESES. Waves of the sea.

REESOME. To ted pease; that is, to put them
into little heaps. *Linc.*

REET. (1) Right. *Var. dial.*

(2) To smooth, or put in order; to comb the hair. *North.*

REETLE. To repair. *North.*

REEVE. (1) To wrinkle. *West.*

(2) To separate corn that has been winnowed from the small seeds which are among it. This is done with what they call the reeving-sieve. *Var. dial.*

(3) The female of the ruff.

REEZED. See *Reasty* (2).

REF. Plunder. (*A.-S.*)

REFECT. Recovered. (*Lat.*)

REFEDE. Deprived; taken away.

> Many lede with his launce the liffe has he *refede.*
> *Morte Arthure, MS. Lincoln, f. 72.*

REFEERE. To revert. *Hoccleve.*

REFELL. To refute. (*Lat.*)

> Which I thinke your clemencie will not reject nor *refell.*
> *Hall's Union, 1548, Hen. IV. f. 28.*

REFFERTORY. Refractory. *Linc.*

REFFICS. Remnants; relics. *North*

REFICTE. Shelter; refuge.

REFLAIRE. Odour. (*A.-N.*)

> We hafe lykyng also for to bihalde faire feldes al over floresched with flores, of the whilke a swete *reflaire* enters intille oure noses, in the whilke a sensible saule hase maste delite.
> *MS. Lincoln A. i. 17, f. 33.*

REFOCILLATION. Restoration of strength by refreshment. (*Lat.*)

REFORM. To repair. *Stowe.*

REFORMADO. A disbanded soldier.

REFORME. To inform.

REFOURME. To renew, or remake. *Gawayne.*

REFRAIN. (1) To restrain.

(2) The burden of a song. (*A.-N.*) *Refraide* and *refret* are also used.

> Here nowe folowethe a balade ryal made by Lydgate affter his resorte to his religyoun, with the *refrayde* howe everything drawethe to his semblable.
> *MS. Ashmole 59, f. 18.*

REFREIDE. To cool. (*A.-N.*)

REFRET. The burden of a song.

> This was the *refret* of that caroull, y wene,
> The wheche Gerlen and this mayden song byfore.
> *Chron. Vilodun. p. 115.*

REFRINGE. To infringe upon. *Palsgrave.*

REFTE. (1) Bereaved; took away.

> 3yf thou ever yn any tyme
> *Rafte* any man hys lyme.
> *MS. Harl. 1701, f. 9.*

> Alle thyng that men withholde,
> Stole or *refte*, 3yve or solde.
> *MS. Harl. 1701, f. 57.*

(2) A chink or crevice. (*A.-S.*)

REFUGE. Refuse. Still in use.

REFUSE. (1) To deny. (2) Refusal.

> But they of the suggestione
> Ne couthen nou3te a worde *refuse.*
> *Gower, MS. Soc. Antiq. 134, f. 44.*

> And it was the custum and use,
> Amonges hem was no *refuse.*
> *Gower, MS. Soc. Antiq. 134, f. 233.*

REFUYT. Refuge. (*A.-N.*)

> But thoroughe thee have wee grace as wee desyre,
> Ever hathe myne hope of *refuyt* ben in thee.
> *Romance of the Monk, Sion College MS.*

REGAL. A groove in timber. *West.*

REGALOS. Choice sweetmeats.

REGALS. A musical instrument, made with pipes and bellows like an organ, but small and portable. There was till lately an officer in the King's Chapel at St. James's called "Tuner of the Regals," with a salary of £56.

> Praise him upon the claricoales.
> The lute and simfonie:
> With dulcemers and the *regalls*,
> Sweete sittrons melody.
> *Leighton's Teares or Lamentations, 1613.*

REGALYE. Rule; royalty. (*A.-N.*)

> Of heven and erthe that hath the *regalye*,
> And schalle distroye alle fals mawmetrye.
> *Lydgate, MS. Soc. Antiq. 134, f. 16.*

REGENERATE. Degenerate. *Nares.*

REGHTE. Right; quickly. (*A.-S.*)

> Whenne he was dighte in his atire,
> He tase the knyghte bi the swire,
> Keste hym *reghte* in the fyre.   *Perceval, 791.*

REGIMENT. Government. (*Lat.*)

> I have obteined and possessed the rule and *regiment* of this famous realme of England.
> *Hall's Union, 1548.*

REGLE. A rule; a regulation.

REGNE. To reign. (*A.-N.*)

REGNIS. Kingdoms. (*Lat.*)

> And the pepils and *regnis* everichone
> Stoden unto him undir lowe servage.
> *Lydgate, MS. Soc. Antiq. 134, f. 16.*

REGRACES. Thanks. "With dew regraces." Plumpton Correspondence, p. 5.

REGRATE. To retail wares. (*A.-N.*)

REGREDIENCE. A returning. (*Lat.*)

> No man comes late into that place, from whence
> Never man yet had a *regredience.*
> *Herrick's Works, ii. 40.*

REGREET. To greet again.

REGREWARDE. The rearward.

> The *regrewarde* it tok awey,
> Cam none of hem to londe dreye.
> *Gower, MS. Soc. Antiq. 134, f. 7½.*

REGUERDON. A reward. (*A.-N.*)

REHETE. (1) To revive; to cheer; to encourage. (*A.-N.*) "Him would I comforte and rehete," Rom. Rose, 6509.

> Thane the conquerour kyndly carpede to those lordes,
> *Rehetede* the Romaynes with realle speche.
> *Morte Arthure, MS. Lincoln, f. 55.*

(2) To persecute. (*A.-S.*)

REHETING. Burning; smarting. (*A.-S.*)

REIDE. Arrayed.

> Thane the eorle was payd,
> Sone his batelle was *rayde*,
> He was nothyng afreyd
> Off that feris knyght.   *Sir Degrevant, 200.*

REIGH. The ray fish.

REIKE. (1) To walk about idly. *Reawk*, to idle in neighbour's houses, Tim Bobbin Gloss. appears to be the same word.

(2) A chaffinch. Nominale MS.

(3) To reach or fetch anything. *North.*

REILE. To roll. *Chaucer.*

REIMBASK. A term in hunting, to return to the lair or form.

REIN. To droop the head; to bear it in a stiff and constrained posture. *East.*

REP. (1) Reaped. *Essex.*

(2) A jade, or lean horse.

REPAIRE. To return ; to resort. A substantive, resort, in the following passage :

> Whiche is my Sone and myn owen eyre,
> That in hire breste schalle have his *repayre.*
> *Lydgate, MS. Soc. Antiq.* 134, f. 1.

REPAISE. To appease one. (*A.-N.*)

REPARE. The haunt of a hare.

REPAREL. Apparel ; clothing.

> Within hymselfe, by hys deligent travel,
> To aray hys garden with notabil *reparel.*
> *Ashmole's Theat. Chem. Brit.* 1652, p. 214.

REPARELLE. To repair.

> He that schalle bygge this citee agayne salle hafe
> thre victories, and whenne he hase getene thre victories, he salle onane come and *reparelle* this citee,
> and bigge it agayne also wele als ever it was.
> *MS. Lincoln* A. i. 17, f. 11).

REPASSE. A common term used by jugglers, alluded to in Kind-Hart's Dreame, 1592.

REPAYRE. A carrier of sea-fish.

REPE. A handful, as of corn, &c.

REPEAL. To recall. *Shak.* "Repell callyng agayne, *repel,*" Palsgrave.

REPENDE.

> Thane riche stedes *rependes,* and rasches one armes.
> *Morte Arthure, MS. Lincoln,* f. 75.

REPILLE-STOCK. A kind of rod or staff used for beating flax.

REPLENISH. To revive. *Palsgrave.*

REPLET. Repletion. *Chaucer.*

REPOLONE. Said of a horse that gallops straight forwards and back again.

REPON. Moving force ; momentum.

REPOSANCE. Repose. *Hall.*

REPPLE. A long walking staff as tall or taller than the bearer. *Chesh.*

REPRESSE. Suppression ; repressing.

REPREVE. To reprove. (*A.-N.*)

> Cokwoldes no mour I wyll *repreve,*
> For I ame aue, and aske no leve.
> *MS. Ashmole* 61, f. 61.

REPREVINGE. A reproof.

> And there it lykede him to suffre many *reprevinges* and scornes for us.
> *Maundevile's Travels,* p. 1.

REPRIME. To grumble at anything.

REPRISE. (1) A right of relief.

(2) Blame ; reproach. (*A.-N.*)

> That alle the world ne may suffise
> To staunche of pride the *reprise.*
> *Gower, MS. Soc. Antiq.* 134, f. 60.

REPROOF. Confutation. *Shak.*

REPRY. To reprieve. *Huloet.*

REPUGN. To fight against. (*Lat.*)

REPULDE. Ripped up ?

> And smote Gye wyth envye,
> And *repulde* hys face and hys chynne,
> And of hys cheke all the skynne.
> *MS. Cantab.* Ff. ii. 38, f. 209.

REPUNGE. To vex, or goad. (*Lat.*)

> I am the king of Persia,
> A large and fertil soil :
> The Egiptians against us *repunge,*
> As verlets slave and vile.
> *King Cambises,* p. 254.

REPURVEAUNCE. Provision.

> The good knyȝt syre Degrivaunce,
> He had y-made *repurveaunce*
> For al hys retenaunce.   *Degrevant,* 1146.

RERAGE. Arrears, or debt. (*A.-N.*)

> That alle the ryche salle repente that to Rome langes
> Or the *rereage* be requit of rentes that he claymes.
> *Morte Arthure, MS. Lincoln,* f. 71.

RERD. Roaring ; noise. "He him kneu wel by his *rerde,*" Reliq. Antiq. ii. 274.

RERE. (1) To raise. (*A.-S.*)

(2) Moderately flexible ; firm, but not too hard, as applied to meat, &c.

RERE-BANKET. A second course of sweets or desserts after dinner. *Palsgrave.* It is made synonymous with rere-supper in Leigh's Romane Emperours, 1637, p. 92.

REREBRACE. Armour for the back of the arm. (*A.-N.*)

> Bristes the *rerebrace* with the bronde ryche.
> *Morte Arthure, MS. Lincoln,* f. 80.

REREBRAKE. Probably the projection put on the crupper to prevent the horseman being pushed over the horse's tail by the thrust of a lance, as was often the case in a tournament. *Meyrick.*

REREDEMAIN. A back-handed stroke.

> I shall with a *reredemayns* so make them rebounde to our commen enemye that calleth hymselfe kynge, that the beste stopper that he hath at tenyce shal not well stoppe without a faulte.
> *Hall, Richard III.* f. 11.

RERE-DORS. Some part of armour.

> Ane hole brest-plate, with a *rere-dore*
> Behynde shet, or elles on the syde.
> *Clariodes, MS.*

RERE-DORTOUR. A jakes.

> If any suster in the *rere-dortour,* otherwyse callyd the house of esemente, behave her unwomanly or unreligiously, schewynge any parte bare that nedeth not, whyle they stonde or sytte there.
> *MS. Arundel,* 146.

REREDOSSE. (1) An open fire-hearth. Harrison says, p. 212, "now have we manie chimnies, and yet our tenderlings complaine of rheumes, catarbs, and poses ; then had we none but *reredosses,* and our heads did never ake."

(2) This word in general signifies the screen of stone or wood at an altar, but it is occasionally applied to the tapestry hanging at the back of it.

RERE-MOUSE. A bat. *West.* "*Vespertilio,* a reremouse or batte," Elyot, ed. 1559.

RERE-SUPPER. A late supper after the ordinary meal so called, taken "generallie when it was time to go to rest," Harrison, p. 170. Palsgrave mentions "the rere-supper, or banket where men syt downe to drynke and eate agayne after their meate," Acolastus, 1540. Pegge gives *re-supper,* a second supper. *Lanc.*

> My stomak accordeth to every meete,
> Save *reresoupers* I refuse lest I sorfette.
> *Piers of Fullham,* p. 196.

> Than is he redy in the wey
> My *rere-soper* for to make.
> *Gower, MS. Soc. Antiq.* 134, f. 182.

RES. Violence; impetus; quick pace.

> That I ful ofte, in suche a *res*,
> Am werye of myn owen lyf.
> > *Gower, MS. Soc. Antiq. 134, f. 92.*

> He wolle rape hym on a *resse*
> Myldely to the holy londe.
> > *MS. Harl. 2252, f. 118.*

> Whenne thei were war of Moises,
> Thei fleyge away al in a *res*.
> > *Cursor Mundi, MS. Coll. Trin. Cantab. f. 41.*

RESALGAR. Ratsbane.

> Notwithstanding, I must needs say that our chirurgions and also ferrers do find both arsenicke and *resalgar* to be so sharpe, hotte, and burning things, as when they minister the same to any part of the body, they are forced to alay the sharpenesse thereof.
> > *Topsell's Beasts, 1607, p. 429.*

RESAYVE. To receive. (*A.-N.*)

> To Westmynstur the kyng be water did glide,
> Worshypfully *resayvid* with procession in frett,
> *Resayvid* with reverence, his dewté not denye,
> The cardinall uppon his hede the crowne did sett;
> The septure in his honde withowte interrupcione or lett,
> Thenne to Seyn Edwardes shryne the prynce did goo,
> Thus in every thyng the wille of God is doo!
> > *MS. Bibl. Reg. 17 D. xv.*

> Mekille comforthe it *reschayves* of oure Lorde nojte anely inwardly in his prevé substance be the vertu of the anehede to oure Lorde.
> > *MS. Lincoln A. i. 17, f. 220.*

RESCEN. Rushes. *Exmoor.*

RESCHOWE. To rescue. (*A.-N.*)

RESCOUS. Rescue. (*A.-N.*)

RESE. (1) A boast. *R. de Brunne.*

(2) To raise, or stir up.

RESELL. To put away; to refute. (*A.-N.*)

RESEMBLABLE. Like.

> For man of soule resonabille,
> Is to an aungelle *resemblable*.
> > *Gower, MS. Soc. Antiq. 134, f. 37.*

RESENT. To smell of. *Drayton.*

RESET. To receive.

> And je hit make, and that me greves,
> A den to *reset* inne theves.
> > *Cursor Mundi, MS. Coll. Trin. Cantab. f. 91.*

RESH. Fresh; recent. *East.*

RESHES. Wire-rush, a weed. *Yorksh.*

RESIANS. Inhabitants; residents.

RESIGNE. A deer was called a *hert-resigne* when he had quite left off growing.

RESILE. To spring back. (*Lat.*)

> If the Quene wold herafter *resile* and goo back from that, she semeth nowe to be contented with, it shuld not be in her power soo to doo.
> > *State Papers, i. 343.*

RESILVATION. A retrogression. (*Lat.*)

> There is, as phisicians saye, and as we also fynd, double the perell in the *resilvacion* that was in the fyrste sycknes.
> > *Hall, Edward V. f. 11.*

RESIN-BEAM. A beam in a roof.

RESINING. Resignation.

RESNABYL. Reasonable.

> Ellys a mon he were unabille,
> As a best ys of kynd;
> Better mon ys made *resnabyl*,
> Good and evyl to have in his mynd.
> > *MS. Douce 302, f. 2.*

RESOLUTION. Conviction; assurance.

RESOLVE. (1) To dissolve, or melt.

> Take aqua vite, gomme of Arabik, and vernesse, of iche iliche meche, and let him stonde tyl the gomme be *resolvyd*.
> > *MS. in Mr. Pettigrew's possession, xv. Cent.*

(2) To convince; to assure; to satisfy. Very common in old plays. "Resolve the princesse we must speake with her," Troubles of Queene Elizabeth, 1639, sig. B. i.

RESON. Arose.

> He blewe hys horne in that tyde,
> Hertys *reson* on eche a syde.
> > *MS. Cantab. Ff. ii. 38, f. 64.*

RESOUN. Speech; discourse. (*A.-N.*)

> Then seid the kyng in his *resoun*,
> Who so were in a gode town
> This wold ha costed dere.
> > *MS. Cantab. Ff. v. 48, f. 50.*

RESPASSE. The raspberry. *Herrick.* Tusser has *respe*, p. 4, ed. 1812.

RESPECT. To postpone. (*Lat.*)

> As touching the musters of all the soldiours upon the shore, we have *respected* the same tyll this tyme for lacke of money. *State Papers,* i. 832.

RESPECTIVE. Respectful. It has sometimes the meaning of *respectable.*

> The same day, at night, my servant returned from Clare, and brought me word of the fair and *respective* receipt, both of my lines and the carcanet, and how bountifully himself had been rewarded before his departure thence. *MS. Harl.* 646.

RESPECTLESS. Careless; regardless.

RESPICE. (1) Respect. (*A.-N.*) Chaucer has *respite*, perhaps for *respice.*

(2) A wine. Ritson, iii. 176.

RESPITEN. To excuse. (*A.-N.*)

RESPLENDE. To shine. *Lydgate.*

RESPONDE. (1) An answer. (*A.-N.*)

(2) "A half pillar or pier, in middle-age architecture, attached to a wall to support an arch," Oxf. Gloss. Arch. p. 306. "*Responsorium*, Anglice a responde," Nominale MS.

RESSAUNT. An ogee-moulding.

RESSE. Qu. *On* his resse. See *Res.*

> The hundis at the dere gunne baye;
> That herde the geant ther he laye,
> And repid hym of his *resse*.
> > *MS. Lincoln A. i. 17, f. 140.*

RESSET. A place of refuge; an abode. (*A.-N.*) In hunting, a resting place for those who followed the chase on foot.

> I shal jou aske sum *resset*,
> Wel I woot I shal jou get.
> > *Cursor Mundi, MS. Coll. Trin. Cantab. f. 33.*

REST. (1) To conclude upon anything. At primero, to set up rest meant to stand up upon one's cards. Nares thinks our first meaning metaphorical from the second, but I much question it.

(2) To roast. *Somerset.*

(3) A wrest by which the strings of harps and instruments are drawn up.

(4) A support for the ancient musket. It consisted of a pole of tough wood, with an iron spike at the end to fix it in the ground, and a semicircular piece of iron at the top to rest the musket on. The soldier carried it by strings fastened over the shoulder.

(5) To arrest. *Palsgrave.*

(6) The wood on which the coulter of a plough is fixed. MS. Lansd. 560, f. 45.

RESTAR. One who arrests.

RESTAYED. Stopped ; driven back.

RESTITUE. To restore, or, restitute.

RESULTANCE. Rebound. (*Lat.*)

> For I confesse that power which works in me
> Is but a weak *resultance* took from thee.
> *Randolph's Poems,* 1643.

RESVERIE. Madness.

> In those times to have had an inventive and enquiring witt was acounted *resverie :* which censure the famous Dr. William Harvey could not escape for his admirable discovery of the circulation of the blood : he told me himself that upon his publishing that booke, he fell in his practise extremely.
> *Aubrey's Wiltshire, Royal Soc. MS. p. 5.*

RESYN. Arose.

> The knyghtes *resyn* on every syde,
> Bothe more and lasse.
> *MS. Cantub. Ff. ii. 38, f. 98.*

RET. To soak in water, as in seasoning timber, hemp, &c. *East.* It occurs in Pr. Parv. of the fifteenth century.

RETALIATION. Return. (*Lat.*)

> First, I will shew you the antiquity of these manors. Secondly, I will a little discuss the ancient honour of this manor of Lavenham. Thirdly, I will give you a touch what respects you are likely to find from me ; and fourthly, what *retaliation* I expect again from you. *MS. Harl. 646.*

RETAUNT. Repetition of a taunt.

> He dyd not onelye fyrste delaye me, and afterwarde denay me, but gave me suche unkynde woordes, wyth suche tauntes and *retauntes,* ye, in maner checke and checke mate to the uttermooste profe of my pacience. *Hall, Richard III. f. 10.*

RETCH. To stretch, or reach. *Var. dial.* "I retche with a weapon or with my hande, *je attains,*" Palsgrave.

RETCHLESS. Reckless. *Skelton.*

RETCHUP. Truth. *Somerset.*

RETEN. Garrison ; followers. (*A.-N.*)

> Syre Degrivaunt ys whom went,
> And aftyr hys *reten* sent. *Sir Degrevant,* 910.

RETENAUNCE. Retinue.

> That he with alle his *retenaunce,*
> He myzte nouzt defende his lyf.
> *Gower, MS. Soc. Antiq. 131, f. 71.*

RETHERNE-TOUNGE. The herb buglos. See a list in MS. Sloane 5, f. 3.

RETHOR. A rhetorician. (*A.-N.*)

RETIRE. A retreat in war. *Shak.*

RETOUR. Retire. (*A.-N.*)

> Scho ladde fram bour to bour,
> And dede here mené make *retour.*
> *The Sevyn Sages,* 436.

RETOURTE. To return.

> Zif they *retourte* azen by Jerusalem.
> *Lydgate, MS. Soc. Antiq. 134, f. 24.*

RETRICLE.

> Othersome againe hold the contrary, assuring us upon their owne experience, that not exceeding their due quantity, they may be taken with other correctories, to serve as a *retricle* to transport them to the place affected, so that you see either side hath his strength and reasons.
> *Topsell's Serpents,* 1608, p. 98.

RETRIEVE. To recover game after it has been once sprung. *Blome.*

RETTE. To impute ; to ascribe,

RETURNS. The terminations of the dripstone of a window or door. *Oxf. Gl. Arch.*

REUELICH. Sorrowful. (*A.-S.*)

> For to hem com a messanger,
> And gret hem with *reuelich* chere.
> *Arthour and Merlin,* p. 158.

REUL. To be unruly. *North.*

REUME. The tide. Nominale MS.

REUMED. Spoken of. (*A.-S.*)

REURTHE. Pity. (*A.-S.*)

REUZE. To extol highly. *North.*

REVAIDE.

> By that the messe was sayde,
> The haulle was ryally arrayed ;
> The erle thane had *revayde,*
> And in hert was lyghte.
> *MS. Lincoln A. i. 17, f. 133.*

REVE. (1) A bailiff.

> In auncient time, almost every manor had his *reve,* whose authoritie was, not only to levie the lords-rents, to set to worke his servaunts, and to husband his demeasnes to his best profit and commoditie ; but also to governe his tenants in peace, and to leade them foorth to war, when necessitie so required. *Lambarde's Perambulation,* 1596, p. 484.

(2) To pull or tear the thatch or covering from a house. *Westm.*

(3) To bereave ; to take by force.

> Where we shall robbe, where we shall *reve,*
> Where we shall bete and bynde.
> *Robin Hood,* l. 4.

REVEL. An anniversary festival to commemorate the dedication of a church ; a wake.

REVELLE. A rivulet.

> In that depe valay ware treesse growand, of whilks the fruyte and the lefes ware wonder savory in the tastynge, and *revelles* of water faire and clere.
> *MS. Lincoln A. i. 17, f. 38.*

REVEL-MEDE. A meadow between Bicester and Wendlebury, at the mowing of which different kinds of rural sports were formerly practised, and a kind of fair held. See Dunkin's History of Bicester, 1816, p. 269.

REVELOUR. A reveller.

REVELRIE. Pleasure. *Chaucer.*

REVEL-ROUT. A roaring revel. (*Fr.*)

REVELS. The broken threads cast away by women at their needlework.

REVEL-TWINE. A fine twine. *West.*

REVENGEMENT. Revenge. *Shak.*

REVENYS. Ravens. Holme, 1688.

REVERB. To reverberate. *Shak.*

REVERE. A river. (*A.-S.*)

REVERENCE. A native woman of Devon in describing something not peculiarly delicate, apologized with the phrase, " saving your reverence." This is not uncommon in the country, " saving your presence" being sometimes substituted. It occurs in Shakespeare, Romeo and Juliet, i. 4, and is of great antiquity as an apologetic expression, being found in Maundevile's Travels, p. 185.

REVERS. Contrary. (*A.-N.*)

REVERSE. (1) To overturn. (*A.-N.*)

(2) The burden of a song. *West.*

REVERSION. What is left at table.

REVERSUT. Trimmed. *Robson.*

REVERT. To turn back. (*A.-N.*)

REVERYSE. Robbery ; plunder.

> Bot I lett for my gentryse
> To do swylke *reveryse.*
> > *MS. Lincoln* A. i. 17, f. 132.

REVESCHYD. Clothed.

> The byschop *reveschyd* hym in holynes,
> And bare that blessyd body to an autere.
> > *MS. Cantab.* Ff. ii. 38, f. 47.
> He *revested* him on his manere,
> And so went to the autere.
> > *Cursor Mundi, MS. Coll. Trin. Cantab.* f. 68.
> Twey prestes weron *revysshnde* at hurr byddyng.
> > *Chron. Vilodun.* p. 131.

REVESTRY. A vestibule or apartment in a church where the priest revested himself, i. e. put on the sacred garments. Hence the term *vestry.*

REVETTE. To strike back or again.

REVIE. At cards, to vie (q. v.) again.

> Hee swore, as before hee had done, that there he left him, and saw him not since : she vied and *revied* othes to the contrary that it was not so.
> > *Rowley's Search for Money,* 1609.

REW. (1) To regret, or abie anything.

> Robyn, he seid, thou art trwe,
> I-wis it shalle the never *rew,*
> Thou shalt have thy mede.
> > *MS. Cantab.* Ff. v. 48, f. 52.

(2) The shady side of a street. *Devon.*

REWALL. To govern. *Lydgate.*

REWALT. To give up, or surrender.

REWARD. (1) Regard ; respect. (*A.-N.*)

> 3if thou wil asaie hit, gif it an hownde that is besie abowte a bycche of sawte, and anon he wil leve her, and take no more *rewarde* than he were splayed ; and if thou geve it to the bicche, it is wondure but sche wex wood.
> > *MS. in Mr. Pettigrew's possession,* xv. Cent.

(2) To stand to one's reward, i. e. to be dependent upon him, or his reward or countenance. *North.*

(3) " A reward or good reward, a good colour or ruddiness in the face, used about Sheffield in Yorksh." Ray's English Words, 1674, p. 38. The word seems to be no longer known.

(4) A dessert, or course of fruit or pastry after the meats are removed. It seems, however, to be applied to a course of roast meat in the Ord. and Reg. p. 55.

REWDEN-HAT. A straw hat. *West.*

REWE. (1) To pity, or regret. (*A.-S.*)

> The stewardys lyfe ys lorne,
> There was fewe that *rewyd* theron.
> > *MS. Cantab.* Ff. ii. 38, f. 74.

(2) Row ; order ; rule.

> And so he goth bi *rewe* and kusseth hem everrich on,
> Seththe he cam into Egypte nas he so blithe man.
> > *MS. Bodl.* 652, f. 10.

REWEL. (1) Rule. (*A.-S.*)

(2) Pitiful ; compassionate.

REWIN. A raven. Nominale MS.

REWING. Pity. (*A.-S.*) It occurs in MS. Cotton. Vespas. D. vii. Ps. Antiq.

REWLE. To rule, or command. (*A.-S.*)

> *Rewlys* before the ryche of the rounde table,
> Assignes ilke a contree to certayne lordes.
> > *Morte Arthure, MS.* Lincoln, f. 61.

REWLY. Tranquil ; quiet.

REX. To play rex, i. e. to handle roughly, to overthrow, to act despotically.

REXEN. (1) Rushes. *West.*

(2) To infect, as with itch, smallpox, or any infectious disorder. *Kent.*

REY. To dress, or clean. *Var. dial.*

REYES. Dances. *Chaucer.*

REYF. Robbery.

> For maisterfull and violent thefte or *reyf* by night or daie, and for secret stealing, wherewith is joyned eyther bodillie hurt of men, women, or children.   *Egerton Papers,* p. 233.

REYKED. Cracked.

> Ropes fulle redyly then *reyked* in sunder.
> > *MS. Cott. Calig.* A. ii. f. 109.

REYN. The river Rhine.

REYNE. Ran.

> And from his eysen the salte teris *reyne,*
> Liche as hee wolde drowne himselfe of newe.
> > *Lydgate, MS. Soc. Antiq.* 134, f. 5.

REYNGENED. Reined up.

> At the haulle-dore he *reyngened* his stede,
> And one fote in he 3ede.
> > *MS. Lincoln* A. i. 17, f. 106.

REZZLE. To wheeze. *North.*

RE3TE. Right.

> Fals wreche, quod he, that presumes to telle thyng of that ere to come, *re3te* als thou were a prophete, and knewe the prevatés of hevene.
> > *MS. Lincoln* A. i. 17, f. 1.

RHE. The course of water, and the overflowing of it. "Even to this daie in Essex," observes Harrison, p. 46, "I have oft observed that when the lower grounds by rage of water have beene overflowen, the people beholding the same have said, *All is on a rhe,* as if they should have said, All is now a river." This observation is copied by Stowe.

RHENOISTER. A rhinoceros.

RHEUM. Spleen ; caprice. Hence *rheumatic,* choleric, splenetic.

RHEUMATIZ. Rheumatism. *Var. dial.*

RHIME. To talk nonsense. *Devon.*

RHIME-ROYAL. A peculiar sort of verse consisting of ten lines.

RHODOSTAUROTIC. Rosicrucian.

RIAL. An English gold coin, worth about fifteen shillings.

RIALLE. (1) Royal ; noble.

> A *ryalle* feste the knyghte let make,
> So worschypfully on Crystymas day,
> Of lordys and ladyes that wolde hyt take,
> And knyghtys that were of gode array.
> > *MS. Cantab.* Ff. ii. 38, f. 46.

(2) The mother of liquor.

RIALTE. Royalty ; noble conduct.

> Therfore that lady feyre and gente,
> Wyth them wolde sche assente
> A justyng for to crye ;
> And at that justyng schalle hyt bee,
> Whoso evyr wynneth the gree
> Schalle wedde hur wyth *ryalté.*
> > *MS. Cantab.* Ff. ii. 38, f. 75

RIAME. A framework, or skeleton; the ligament of anything. *West.*

RIB. (1) A wife. *North.*

(2) The bar of a fire-grate. *North.*

(3) The common water-cress. *East.*

(4) An instrument for dressing flax.

(5) A scraper or rasp for bread.

RIBAUD. A profligate low person. (*A.-N.*) The word was properly applied to a particular class in society, the lowest sort of retainers of the nobility, who were employed in all kinds of disgraceful actions. See Wright's Political Songs, p. 369. Hence *ribaudrie*, low profligate talk; *ribaudour*, a teller of low tales. Shakespeare has *ribaudred*, obscene, filthy.

> The Brytans, as the boke seys,
> Off diverse thinges thei made ther leys;
> Som thei made of herpynges,
> And some of other diverse thinges;
> Some of werre and some off wo,
> Some of myrthys and joy also,
> Some of trechery and some off gyle,
> Some of happys that felle some whyle,
> And some be of *rybawdry*,
> And many there ben off fary.
> *MS. Ashmole* 61, xv. Cent.

RIB-BASTE. To beat severely.

RIBBINS. Carriage reins. *Midx.*

RIBBLE-RABBLE. Base disorderly people; also, idle indecent talk. *North.*

RIBBLE-ROW. A list of rabble.

> This witch a *ribble-row* rehearses,
> Of scurvy names in scurvy verses.
> *Cotton's Works*, 1734, p. 119.

RIBE. To rend; to tear. *North.*

RIBIBE. A kind of fiddle. "*Vitula*, a rybybe," Nominale MS. "Tho ratton rybybyd," i. e. played on the ribibe, Reliq. Antiq. i. 81. *Vitula* may have interchanged with *vetula*, and hence we have the term applied to an old woman, as in Chaucer, Skelton, and Ben Jonson.

> Harpe and fidul both thei fande,
> The getorn and also the sautry,
> The lute and the *ribybe* both gangand,
> And alle maner of mynstralcy.
> *MS. Cantab.* Ff. v. 48, f. 119.

RIBIBLE. A small ribibe. "Rote, ribible," Squyr of Lowe Degré, 1071.

RIBINET. A chaffinch.

RIB-LINE. To coast along.

RIBROAST. A sound beating.

> Such a peece of filching is as punishable with *ribroast* among the turne-spits at Pie Corner.
> *Maroccus Estaticus*, 1595.

RIBS. Bindings in hedges. *Kent.*

RIBSKIN. "Theyr rybskyn and theyr spyndell," Skelton, i. 104. The term probably means some piece of leather used or worn in flax-dressing. Palsgrave mentions a *rib* for flax. "*Pellicula*, Anglice a rybschyn; *nebryda*, idem est," Nominale MS.

RIC. A call to pigs. *West.*

RICE. (1) A turning-wheel for yarn. "A rice to winde yarn on," Howell.

(2) Small wood, or the tops of trees; brushwood. This appears to be a corruption of the old word *rise*, q. v., and not the modern term, as Holloway has it.

RICE-BALKING. A mode of ploughing.

RICH. To enrich. *Shak.*

RICHARD-SWARY. A dictionary. So Taylor has it in his Motto, 12mo. 1622, introd. *Richard-Snary* is a commom jocular term. A country lad, having been reproved for calling persons by their nicknames, being sent to borrow a dictionary, asked for a *Richard-Snary*.

RICHE. (1) A kingdom. (*A.-S.*) "Cominde thi *riche*," Reliq. Antiq. i. 42.

(2) To go; to prepare; to dress; to march. Gloss. to Syr Gawayne.

RICHELLE. Incense. *Pr. Parv.*

RICHELY. Nobly. (*A.-S.*)

RICHEN. To become rich. (*A.-N.*)

RICHESSE. Wealth; riches. (*A.-N.*)

RICK. (1) An ankle. *South.* Occasionally a verb, to sprain the ankle.

(2) A stack of hay, &c. *Var. dial.*

(3) To scold; to make a noise. *Lanc.*

RICK-CLOTH. A large canvas sheet put over an unfinished stack.

RICKLE. (1) A heap, or bundle. *North.*

(2) To make a rattling noise.

RICKNEST. A rickyard. *South.*

RICKY. Masterly. *East.*

RID. (1) To get rid of. *Var. dial.* "Willingness rids way," Shakespeare. *It rids well*, it goes on fast, a North country phrase. Shakespeare also has *rid*, destroyed, got rid of.

(2) To finish, or complete.

(3) To clear anything of litter; to remove, or take away. *Var. dial.* To rid the stomach, to vomit, a North country phrase.

(4) To empty, or clear ground.

(5) To part, or interpose. *Lanc.*

(6) A hollow place where anything is secreted. *North.*

RIDDE. To release; to rescue.

RIDDELED. Plaited. *Tyrwhitt.* "Rydelid gownes and rokettis," Reliq. Antiq. i. 41.

RIDDELS. Curtains; bed-curtains.

> That was a mervelle thynge
> To se the *riddels* hynge
> With many red golde rynge
> That thame up bare.
> *MS. Lincoln* A. 1. 17, f. 136.
>
> Was there no pride of coverlite,
> Curteyn, *riddelles* ny tapite.
> *Cursor Mundi, MS. Coll. Trin. Cantab.* f. 70.

RIDDENER. To chatter. *Linc.*

RIDDER. A large sieve used for sifting wheat in a barn. *Oxon.*

RIDDLE. (1) To riddle, or darn a hole in linen or woollen, to fill it up by working it cross and cross. This meaning of the word is given by Urry, in his MS. notes to Ray.

(2) A coarse wire sieve. *Var. dial.* "Rydel of corn clensyng," Pr. Parv. "Go and tell your granny to turn her milk through a *riddle*, and not schede it."

(3) To perforate with shot, so as to resemble a sieve, or riddle.

(4) The ring to which the neck-rope of an animal in a stable is fastened.

RIDDLE-CAKES. Thick, sour, oaten cakes, which differ little from that which is called hand-hoven-bread, having but little leaven, and being kneaded stiffer. *North.*

RIDDLED. Wrinkled. (*A.-N.*)

RIDDLER. A dealer in wool. *Linc.*

RIDDLE-WALL. A wall made up with split sticks worked across each other. *Kent.*

RIDE. (1) A saddle-horse. *Norf.*
(2) To rob; to ride out on horseback for the purpose of robbing. *North.*
(3) *To ride grub*, to be out of humour, to sulk and pout.
(4) A little stream. *Hants.*
(5) Futuo. An old cant term.
(6) To be made angry. *West.*
(7) To move, rive, or part asunder.
(8) To be carted for a bawd. "I can but ride," Massinger, iv. 54.
(9) To proceed. *Gawayne.*
(10) A hazle-rod.

RIDEABLE. Passable with horses.
For at this very time there was a man that used to trade to Hartlepool weekly, and who had many years known when the water was *rideable*, and yet he ventured in as I did, and he and his horse were both drowned at the very time when I lay sick.
Lister's Autobiography, p. 45.

RIDER. (1) A moss-trooper. *North.*
(2) A rock protruding into a vein.
(3) Eight sheaves of corn put up together to defend them from the weather. *Chesh.*
(4) A Dutch coin, worth about twenty-seven shillings, so called because it had the figure of a man on horseback on one of its sides.

RIDES. The iron hinges fixed on a gate, by means of which the gate is hung on the hooks in the post, and which enable it to swing or ride. *Sussex.*

RIDGE-BAND. That part of the harness which goes over the saddle on a horse's *rig* or back, and being fastened on both sides, supports the shafts of the cart. It is sometimes called a *ridger*, and occasionally *ridge-stay.* Cotgrave has, "*Surselle*, a broad and great band or thong of strong leather, &c. fastened on either side of a thill, and bearing upon the pad or saddle of the thill-horse: about London it is called the *ridge-rope.*" Kennett has it *ridge-with*, as a Cheshire word.

RIDGIL-BACK. A high back; a back having a rise or ridge in the middle.

RIDGLING. A refuse sheep; one selected out of a flock on account of disease, &c.

RID-HOUSE. To remove all the furniture from a house. *Var. dial.*

RIDICULOUS. This is used in a very different sense in some counties from its original meaning. Something very indecent and improper is understood by it; as, any violent attack upon a woman's chastity is called "very *ridiculous* behaviour:" a very disorderly, and ill-conducted house, is also called a "*ridiculous* one."

RIDING. (1) A third part of a county, a division peculiar to Yorkshire.
(2) A road cut in a wood. *North.*
(3) An encounter. *Robson.*
(4) *Riding of the witch*, a popular phrase for the nightmare, still in use.
(5) A royal procession into the city of London. Chaucer, Cant. T. 4375.

RIDING-HAG. The nightmare.

RIDING-KNOT. A running knot.
Then anon Jocyan, yn hyeng,
Made on hur gyrdull a *knott-rydyng*.
MS. Cantab. Ff. ii. 38, f. 117.

RIDING-RHYMES. Couplet rhymes.

RIDING-ROD. A riding-stick.

RIDING-SPEAR. A javelin. *Palsgrave.*

RIDING-STOCKINGS. Large worsted stockings without feet, used instead of gaiters.

RIDING-THE-FAIR. The steward of a court baron attended by the tenants through the town, proclaiming a fair.

RIDING-TIME. See *Ride* (5).
The hares haveth no season of hure love, that as I sayde is clepid *rydyng-tyme*, for in every moneth of the jeer ne shal not be that some ne be with kyndle.
MS. Bodl. 546.

RIDLESS. Unavailing. *Skelton.*

RIDLING. A riddle.

RIDLINGLY. With riddles?
Though poetry, indeed, be such a sin,
As, I think, that brings dearth, and Spaniards in ;
Though like the pestilence, and old fashion'd love,
Ridlingly it catch men, and doth remove
Never, till it be starv'd out, yet their state
Is poor, disarm'd, like Papists, not worth hate.
Donne's Poems, p. 121.

RIDMAS. Holy-cross day. *Devon.*

RIDOUR. Great hardness, as of iron.

RIDS. The *rids* are out, i. e. the sky is very bright at sunrise, or sunset. *Dorset.*

RIE. (1) Fun; merriment.
(2) The raised border on the top of a stocking.
(3) To sieve corn. *North.*

RIFE. (1) Plundering. *Lydgate.*
(2) To thrust through. (*A.-S.*)
(3) Abounding; prevalent. *North.* It is a common archaism. Its original proper meaning is, openly known, manifest, common.
There is a brief how many sports are *rife*,
Make choice of which your highness will see first.
A Mids. Night's Dream, v. 1, fol. edit.
(4) Ready; quick to learn. *Cumb.*
(5) A salt-water pond. *South.*
(6) Infectious. *North.*

RIFF. (1) The belly; the bowels. (*A.-S.*)
Then came his good sword forth to act his part,
Which pierc'd skin, ribs, and *riffe*, and rove her heart.
The head (his trophy) from the trunk he cuts,
And with it back unto the shore he struts.
Legend of Captain Jones.
(2) Speedily. Cov. Myst. p. 4.
(3) A garment. (*A.-S.*) "I have neither *ryff* nor ruff," Sharp's Cov. Myst. p. 224.

RIFFE. To cut down?
Than the renkes renownd of the rownd table
Ruffes and ruysaches downe renayede wreches.
Morte Arthure, MS. Lincoln, f. 84.

RIFF-RAFF. (1) Sport; fun.

(2) Rubbish; refuse. It is commonly applied to a low crowd, or mob.

It is not Ciceroes tongue that can peerce their armour to wound the body, nor Archimedes prickes, and lines, and circles, and triangles, and rhombus, and *riffe-raffe*, that hath any force to drive them backe. *Gosson's Schoole of Abuse*, 1579.

RIFLE. (1) A bent stick standing on the but of the handle of a scythe.

(2) To raffle. See Brand, i. 160. "A rifling, or a kind of game wherein he that in casting doth throw most on the dyce takes up all the mouye that is layd downe," Nomenclator, 1585, p. 293.

RIFLER. A hawk that seizes the feathers of a bird instead of the body.

RIFLOWR. A robber, or plunderer.

Riche mannis *riflowr*,
Povere mannis purveyowr,
Old mannis somenowr,
Prowd mannis mirowr.
Reliq. Antiq. ii. 121.

RIFLY. Especially?

With kenettes kene, that wel couthe cries conne,
I hiede to holte, with honteres hende;
So *ryfly* on rugge roon and raches ronne,
That in launde under lynde me leste to lende.
Reliq. Antiq. ii. 7.

RIFT. (1) To belch. *Var. dial.*

(2) To cleave ground; to plough. When mould turns up in lumps, it is said in Lincolnshire to rift.

The scytall like the double-head thou shalt in feature find,
Yet is it fatter, and tayle that hath no end much thicker is,
As bigge as crooked hand is wonted for to wind
The haft and helve of digging-spade the earth that *rifts*. *Topsell's Historie of Serpents*, p. 233.

(3) A cleft, or crack. *West.* "Clyft or ryfte," Pr. Parv. p. 81.

(4) A pole, or staff.

RIFTER. (1) A blow on the ribs.

(2) Rotten wood powdered. *Devon.*

RIG. (1) A ridge or elevated part in a ploughed field, upon which the sheaves of corn are arranged after being cut and bound up in harvest. *North and East.* See Warton's Hist. Eng. Poet. ed. 1840, ii. 484; and Sherwen's Introduction to an Examination, 1809, p. 11. A pair of ribbed stockings are yet said to be knit or woven in *rigs* and furrows. The most elevated piece of timber in the angle or roof of a house is called the rigging-tree in the North of England.

They toke ther stedys with ther spurres,
They prekyd over *rugges* and forows.
MS. Cantab. Ff. ii. 38, f. 179.

(2) A wanton. *North.* "Foolish harlots, broad hipt rigs," Florio, p. 97.

Wantonis is a drab!
For the nonce she is an old *rig*;
But as for me, my fingers are as good as a live twig
Mariage of Witt and Wisdome, 1579.

(3) The back. *North.* The printed edition reads *ridge-bone* in the following passage:

And selde to the peple whanne thei comyn afew,
my lefte fyngyr is gretter than my fadrys *rygge*.
Wimbelton's Sermon, 1388, *MS. Hatton* 57, p. 11.

The stede *rigge* undyr hym braste,
That he to grounde felle that tyde.
MS. Harl. 2252, f. 113.

Some he breketh ther neck anon,
And of some the *rygboon*.
MS. Cantab. Ff. ii. 38, f. 246.

A knight he toke with the egge,
That him clef heved and *rigge*.
Arthour and Merlin, p. 122.

(4) A frolic. *Var. dial.*

(5) To get over or through the fence of a field. *South.*

(6) To ruck, or rumple. *Oxon.*

(7) A rib in a stocking. *East.*

(8) *To rig out*, to dress. *Var. dial.* To run a rig, to banter any one.

(9) A tub for new cider.

(10) To make free with.

(11) To ride pick-a-back. *North.*

(12) To run and tumble about.

(13) A strong blast of wind. *Chesh.*

RIGADOON. A French dance.

Whose dancing dogs, in *rigadoons* excel;
And whose the puppet-shew, that bears the bell.
Peter Pindar, i. 317.

RIGATT. A small channel out of a stream made by the rain. *North.* Perhaps from *riget*, a groove in a mullion for the glass.

RIGENALE. Original.

RIGGED. (1) Sour; musty. *Dorset.*

(2) Said of a sheep when laid upon its rig or back. *North.*

RIGGEN. The ridge of a house. Sometimes, the thatch. *North.* To ride the riggen, to be very intimate.

RIGGER. Lead half melted. *Salop.*

RIGGING-STONES. Slates. *North.*

RIGGING-TREE. See *Rig* (1).

RIGGISH. Wanton. *Shak.*

RIGGOT. An imperfect ram, or any other animal half castrated. *North.* "Ridgil is the male of any beast who has been but half gelt, that is, only one stone taken away; others add that also to be a ridgil, whose stones never came down, but lie in his reins," Blount.

RIGHT. (1) *To do right*, see *Do* (4).

(2) *Has a right*, ought. *By good rights*, it ought to be so. *Var. dial.*

(3) To put in order. *East.*

(4) Rightly; exactly; completely.

(5) Good; true. Sir Perceval, 5.

(6) The following curious example is given by Urry, in his MS. notes to Ray:—"Pray Mr. *Wright*, take care and *write* me these thre words distinguishably *right*, that I or some other Northern man doe not mistake them all for *rite*."

RIGHT-DOWN. Downright. *Hall.*

RIGHTE. To tear, or cut. *Robson.*

RIGHT-FORTH. Direct; straight.

RIGHTFUL. Just; true. (*A.-S.*)

RIGHTLE. To set to rights; to put things in their proper places. *Linc.*

RIGHT-NAUGHT-WORTH. Worthless.

RIGHT-ON. Downright; violently; entirely; positively; straight forward. *Right-out*, directly, uninterruptedly, completely.

RIGHT-SHARP. In one's senses. *Linc.*

RIGHT-SIDE. To *right-side* a matter, often means to set it right, whether it be a matter of account or otherwise.

RIGHT-UP. (1) "He makes too many *right-ups*," said of a labourer, who, from laziness, makes too many rests by standing upright.

(2) Tetchy, easily offended. *East.*

RIGHT-UP-AND-DOWN. In a dead calm the wind is said to be "*right-up-and-down*," that is, no way at all. *I. of Wight.*

RIGHTWISE. Righteous.

> And the form of his *rightwise* making is present with their childer'r children. *Becon's Works*, p. 421.
>
> 3if thow take hede to al wickidnesse,
> Lord, who schal it susteyne?
> For be the lawe of *ryżtwisnesse*,
> Endeles thanne were al oure peyne;
> But evere we hope to thin goodnese,
> That whanne thou schalt this werde afreyne,
> With mercy and with myldenesse
> Thin ryżtful thow schalt refreyne.
> *Hampole's Paraphrase of Psalms, MS.*

RIGHTWISHED. Made righteous. (*A.-S.*)

RIGLETS. Flat, thin, square pieces of wood, as the pieces that are intended to make the frames for small pictures before they are moulded are called riglets. "A riglet, *assula plana et quadra*," Coles.

RIGMAROLE. A continued, confused, unconnected discourse or recital of circumstances; a long unmeaning list of anything.

RIGMUTTON. A wanton wench. *Devon.*

RIGOL. A circle. (*Ital.*)

RIGOLAGE. Wantonness; extravagance.

> In ryot and in *rigolage*
> Spende mony her zouthe and her age.
> *Cursor Mundi, MS. Coll. Trin. Cantab. f. 1.*

RIG-RUFF. A thick dead skin covering over a scab or ulcer. *North.*

RIGSBY. A wanton. *North.*

RIGWELTED. Same as *Rigged* (2).

RIKE. (1) Rich. Sir Tristrem, p. 203.

> And than thou may be sekur to spede,
> To wynne that place that ys so *ryke*.
> *MS. Cantab. Ff. ii. 38, f. 31.*

(2) A kingdom. (*A.-S.*)

> Loverd God! zef us leve,
> Adam ant me ys wyf Eve,
> To faren of this lothe wyke,
> To the blisse of hevene *ryke*.
> *Harrowing of Hell*, p. 25.

(3) To govern; to rule. (*A.-S.*)

RIKILS. Incense.

> And thay ware lyke lorers or olyve treeses, and out of thame thare rane *rykyls* and fyne bawme.
> *MS. Lincoln A. i. 17, f. 39.*

RILE. To disturb; to vex. *East.*

RILLE. A woman's *rail*, q. v.

RILLET. A small stream or rivulet. See Harrison's England, p. 54.

RILTS. The barberry fruit.

RIM. (1) To remove. *Glouc.*

(2) The membrane inclosing the intestines. Still in use.

(3) A rabble, or crowd. (*A.-S.*)

RIME. (1) A margin, or edge. (*A.-S.*)

> God yeve hur gode tyme
> Undur the wode *ryme*.
> *MS. Cantab. Ff. ii. 38, f. 120*

(2) A hoar-frost. *Var. dial.*

> Fro Heven fel so greet plenté,
> As a *ryme-frost* on to se.
> *Cursor Mundi, MS. Coll. Trin. Cantab. f. 41*

RIMER. A tool used for enlarging screw-holes in metal.

RIME-STOCK. A wooden calendar.

RIMEYED. Composed in rhyme.

RIMOURES. Rhymers; poets. They are mentioned as unfit to be chosen knights in Vegecius, MS. Douce 291, f. 10.

RIMPLE. A wrinkle. *East.* It occurs in Chaucer and Lydgate.

RIMS. The steps of a ladder. *North.*

RIMTHE. Space; room; leisure.

RIN. (1) Brine. *Norf.*

(2) To run. Reliq. Antiq. i. 74.

(3) A small stream. (*A.-S.*)

> Out of the south-est parte of the said mountayne springeth and descendeth a lytle *ryn*.
> *MS. Cotton. Calig. B. viii.*

RIND. (1) Frozen to death. *North.*

(2) To melt tallow or fat. *Linc.*

RINDE. (1) To destroy.

(2) A thicket; a small wood.

RINDEL. (1) A rivulet. (*A.-S.*) A gutter is still so called in Lancashire.

(2) A sieve for corn. *North.*

RIND-SPINDLE. The mill rynd is a strong piece of iron inserted in the hole in the centre of the upper and moving mill-stone. The spindle which passes through the nether mill-stone being moved by the machinery, and being itself, where it enters the driver, of a square form, and fitted to a cavity of the same shape, the upper mill-stone, the rynd, and the driver, all move round with the spindle.

RINE. (1) Rind, or bark.

> He lykkyd hym tylle he stanke,
> Than he began and konne hym thanke
> To make a pytt of ston,
> And to berye hym was hys purpos,
> And scraped on hym bothe *ryne* and mosse,
> And fro hym nevyr wolde gone.
> *MS. Cantab. Ff. ii. 38, f. 73*

(2) To touch, or feel. *North.*

(3) The skin of a person. *Linc.*

RINER. A toucher. It is used at the game of quoits. A riner is when the quoit touches the peg or mark. A whaver is when it rests upon the peg and hangs over, and consequently wins the cast. "To shed riners with a whaver" is a proverbial expression in Ray, and means, to surpass anything skilful or adroit by something still more so. *Wilbraham.*

RING. (1) To sound. (*A.-S.*)

(2) A row. *Kent.*

(3) That part which encircles the mouth of a cannon. *Howell.*

(4) To surround. *Somerset.* It occurs in Dekker's Knights Conjuring, p. 49.

Let us alle abowte hym *rynge*,
And harde strokys on hym dynge.
MS. Cantab. Ff. ii. 38, f. 99.

(5) A circular parterre. *Linc.*

RINGE. (1) The border, or trimming of any article of female dress. *East.*

(2) A tub for carrying water. *Kent.*

(3) A large heap of underwood.

RINGEINS. Coarse flour. *East.*

RING-FENCE. A property situated compactly together is said to be in a ring-fence.

RING-FINGER. The finger on which the ring is placed in marriage. The Romish Church encouraged the notion of immediate intercourse between the heart and the *ring-finger*. In the Hereford, York, and Salisbury Missals, the mystical ring is directed first to be put on the thumb, then upon the first, then upon the second, and lastly, on the third finger, where it is to remain, *quia in illo digito est quædam vena procedens usque ad cor.*

As for the ring-finger, which is so called, because commonly a ring is worn on it, especially on the left hand, the physitians and anatomists give the reason of it, because in the finger there is a sinew very tender and small that reaches to the heart; wherefore it ought to wear a ring as a crown for its dignity. But besides observe, that in the ceremonies of marriage, they first put the matrimonial ring on the thumb, whence they take it, and put it on every one till they come to this, where it is left. Whence some who stood (as Durand in his Rational of Divine Offices) to discourse on these ceremonies, say it is done because that finger answers to the heart, which is the seat of love and the affections. Others say, because it is dedicated to the sun, and that most rings are of gold, a mettal which is also dedicated to it : so that by this sympathy it rejoyces the heart.
Sanders' Chiromancy, 1652.

RING-HEAD. An engine used in stretching woollen cloth. *Blount.*

RINGLE. A little ring. *East.* Tusser has it as a verb, ed. 1812, p. 22, to put ringles into the snouts of hogs. *Ringled*, made of small rings.

RINGLEADER. The person who opens a ball. The word occurs in this sense in Hollyband's Dictionarie, 1593.

RINGLED. Married. *Suffolk.*

RINGMAN. The third finger of the left hand, on which the marriage ring is placed, and is vulgarly believed to communicate by a nerve directly with the heart.

RINGS. Women's pattens. *North.*

RING-TAW. A game at marbles. A ring is made into which each boy puts a certain number of marbles. The taw is then thrown in by each in turn, who wins as many as he can strike out, a fine being made on those who leave the taw in the ring.

RING-THE-JACK. See *Collar* (4).

RING-WALK. The track of a stag.

RINISH. Wild; unruly; rude. *North.*

RINK. (1) A ring, or circle. *Derb.*

(2) A man. Reliq. Antiq. i. 78.

RINKIN. A fox. *Suffolk.*

RINNARS. Runners; frequenters.

And fle farre from besy tungges as bytter as gall,
And *rynnars* to howsis wher good ale is.
MS. Laud. 416, f. 39.

RINT. To rinse clothes. *North.*

RIOTE. (1) A rabbit.

What rache that renneth to a conyng yn any tyme,
hym aughte to be ascryed, saynge to hym loude,
War, *ryote*, war! for noon other wylde beest yn
Ingelonde is called *ryote* saf the conyng alonly.
MS. Bodl. 546.

(2) A company or body of men.

And I may se the Romaynes that are so ryche haldene,
Arayede in theire *riotes* on a rounde felde.
Morte Arthure, MS. Lincoln, f. 57.

RIP. (1) Mr. Jennings explains it " a vulgar, old, unchaste woman," and adds, " hence most probably the origin of Demirep." But the word *rip* is applied to men and boys, and even to animals, if they appear to be lean half-starved, or otherwise ill-conditioned; *demirep* is a contraction of demi-repute, and means a female who has only a sort of half reputation; not however a vulgar, or an old woman, but generally a young and fashionable demirep, a demirep of quality. *Wilts.*

(2) An oval flat piece of wicker-work on which the lines are coiled. *Hartlepool.*

(3) To reap. *Kent.*

(4) To be very violent. *East.*

(5) *To rip up*, to bring old grievances to recollection. *Var. dial.*

(6) To rate, or chide. *West.*

(7) To rob; to plunder. *North.*

(8) News; a fresh report. *Cumb.*

(9) A whetstone for a scythe. *Linc.* " Ripe, riffle, vel ripple, a short wooden dagger with which the mowers smooth their scythes after they have used the coarse whetstone," MS. Devon Glossary.

(10) A pannier, or basket used for carrying fish. Hence *rippers*.

A stirte til him with his *rippe*,
And bigan the fish to kippe. *Havelok*, 893.

RIPE. (1) To cleanse. *North.*

The young men answered never a word,
They were dum as a stane ;
In the thick wood the beggar fled,
E'er they *riped* their een.
Robin Hood, i. 112.

(2) To examine strictly. (*A.-S.*)

His Highnes delyvered me the boke of his said
wil in many pointes refourmed, wherin His Grace
riped me. *State Papers,* i. 295.

(3) A bank. See Harrison, p. 240. Still in use in Kent and Sussex.

Whereof the principall is within a butt sboote of
the right *ripe* of the river that there cometh downe.
Leland's Itinerary, 1769, iv. 110.

(4) *To ripe up*, to destroy.

(5) Prevalent; abounding. *North.* Ready, Piers Ploughman, p. 100.

(6) To ripen. Still in use.

(7) To grow old; to have one's manners habituated by age.

(8) To ask, or inquire after. *North.*

(9) Learned; clever. *Devon.*

(10) To break up rough ground. *North.*

(11) To investigate thoroughly. *Yorksh.*

RIPE-MEN. Harvest-men; reapers.

RIPIER. A robber. *Durham.*

RIPING. *Riping and tearing,* going on in a dissolute way. *North.*

RIPLE. To tell falsehoods. *Durham.*

RIPPERS. Persons who carried fish from the coast to inland towns. See Brome's Travels, ed. 1700, p. 274.

RIPPING. Great. *Somerset.*

RIPPLE. (1) To clean flax. *Var. dial.* It occurs in Howell, 1660, sect. 50.

(2) A small coppice. *Heref.*

(3) To scratch slightly. *North.*

RIPPLES. The rails of a waggon.

RIQUILANT. Nimble: quick.

RIS. Arise! *Imperat.* (*A.-S.*)

RISE. (1) A twig, or branch. (*A.-S.*) Still found in some dialects. *Rise-wood,* small wood cut for hedging. *Rise-dike,* a hedge made of boughs and twigs.

> Anone he lokyd hym besyde,
> And say syxty ladés on palferays ryde,
> Gentyll and gay as bryd on *ryse,*
> Not a man among them i-wyse,
> Bot every lady a faukon bere,
> And rydene on huntyng be a ryvere.
> *MS. Ashmole* 61, xv. Cent.

> Heyle, roose on *ryse!* heyle, lyllye!
> Heyle, semelyest and swettest savour.
> *MS. Cantab.* Ff. ii. 38, f. 4.

(2) To raise. *Var. dial.*

(3) *Rise up, good fellow,* a term for the game of level-coil.

(4) Reggio, in Calabria.

RISER. (1) A pea-stick. *Warw.*

(2) One who creates rebellion.

RISH. (1) Swiftly; directly. *South.*

(2) A rush. Also, to gather rushes.

> Thouȝ it avayle hem nouȝt a *risshe.*
> *Gower, MS. Soc. Antiq.* 134, f. 61.

(3) A sickle. Nominale MS.

RISING. (1) A man working above his head in the roof is said to be rising.

(2) A small abscess, or boil. *West.*

(3) Yeast. *Suffolk.* It occurs in Lilly's Mother Bombie, ed. 1632, sig. A. vii.

RISP. (1) The green straw of growing peas or potatoes. *Suffolk.*

(2) To make a noise. *North.*

(3) A bush, or branch; a twig.

RISSE. Risen. Of constant occurrence in our old dramatists. *Riz* is still a common vulgarism, very much used in London.

RISTE. (1) To tear; to rend.

(2) To rest. *Lydgate.*

> Regne in my realtee, and *ryste* whenne me lykes,
> By the reyvere of Reone halde my rounde table.
> *Morte Arthure, MS. Lincoln,* f. 57.

(3) Fierce; furious. *Yorksh.*

(4) Any kind of rise. *East.*

(5) Arose; risen. (*A.-S.*)

(6) Rust. Nominale MS.

RIT. (1) Rideth. (*A.-S.*)

> Beves an hakenai bestrit,
> And in his wei forth a *rit.*
> *Beves of Hamtoun,* p. 51.

> Styfly to the kynge he *ryt.*
> *MS. Cantab.* Ff. ii. 38, f. 247.

(2) To swallow greedily. *North.*

(3) To dry hemp or flax. *Kent.*

RITHE. A small stream, usually one occasioned by heavy rain. *South.*

RITHENE. Frankincense.

RITHES. Stalks of potatoes. *North.*

RITLING. The least or youngest of a litter of pigs. *Var. dial.*

RITTE. To tear; to break.

> And when that lady gane hyr wake,
> Sche cryed and grete noys gane make,
> And wrong ther hondes with drery mode,
> And crachyd hyr vysage all on blode;
> Hyre ryche robys sche all *to-rytte,*
> And was ravysed out of hyr wytte.
> *MS. Ashmole* 61, xv. Cent.

> Thus thas renkes in rewthe *rittis* theire brenyes.
> *Morte Arthure, MS. Lincoln,* f. 92.

RITTLE. To snore; to wheeze. *Exmoor.*

RIVAGE. Shore, or border.

> Jhon Vicount Narbon, Vice-admirall of Fraunce, had brought the whole navy to the *rivage* and shore adjoynyng to the toune. *Hall, Henry V.* f. 21.

RIVAILE. A harbour. (*A.-N.*)

> And they in sothe comen to the *ryvaille*
> At Suncourt, an havene of gret renoun.
> *MS. Digby* 230.

RIVAL. An associate. *Shak.*

RIVAYE.

> Bot now hym lyste noght playe,
> To hunt ne to *ryvaye;*
> For Maydyne Myldor, that may,
> His carls are calde.
> *MS. Lincoln* A. i. 17, f. 139.

> I salle never *ryvaye,* ne racches un-cowpylle,
> At roo ne rayne dere that rynnes appone erthe.
> *Morte Arthure, MS. Lincoln,* f. 95.

RIVE. (1) A rake. Nominale MS.

(2) To belch. *Linc.*

(3) Amorous. *I. Wight.*

(4) To split; to fall asunder. (*A.-S.*)

(5) To eat ravenously. *North.*

(6) The sea-shore. (*Lat.*)

(7) To arrive at; to land.

> That iche, lef and dere,
> On londe am *rived* here.
> *MS. Laud.* 108, f. 220.

> Forweried moche aftir here travaille,
> They caste to *rive* ȝif it wolde availle,
> Hem to refreisshe and disporte in joye
> Upon the boundes of the londe of Troye.
> *MS. Digby* 230

> Yn Egypt forthe sche *ryvythe.*
> *MS. Cantab.* Ff. ii. 38, f. 68.

RIVELIN. Wrinkled. (*A.-S.*)

> Hire chekis ben with teris wet,
> And *ryvelyn* as an empty skyn,
> Hengande doun unto the chyn.
> *Gower, MS. Soc. Antiq.* 134, f. 46.

RIVELING. A rough shoe formerly worn by the Scots, and hence the term was jocularly applied to them.

RIVELY. Especially?

> Ȝit may we noghte be assoylede of the trespas bot of oure beschope, or of hym that hase his powere, for swylke caas es *ryvely* reservede tille hyme-selvene.
> *MS. Lincoln* A. i. 17, f. 216.

RIVEN. Very bad tempered. *Linc.*

RIVERET. A small river. " Brookes and riverets," Harrison's Britaine, p. 54.

RIVERING. Hawking by the river side ; flying the hawks at river-fowl.

RIVET. The roe of a fish.

RIVETS. Bearded wheat. *East.*

RIVINGS. Refuse of corn.

RIVO. An exclamation used by bacchanalians at their revels.

RIX. A reed. *Exmoor.*

RIXY. Quarrelsome. *Devon.*

RIZOME. The head of the oat. *Chesh.* " A plume, or bell, or bunch of oats, and such other corn as does not grow in an ear," Kennett, MS. Lansd. 1033.

RIZZERS. Small poles for confining faggots when used for inclosing yards, and also being split for securing splints in daubing. *East.*

RIZZLE. (1) To creep, as ivy, &c. *Glouc.*

(2) To warm ; to roast imperfectly. *Cumb.*

RIЗT. Addressed ; prepared. *Gawayne.*

RIЗTLECHE. To govern. *Will. Werw.*

RO. Peace ; quietness.

> There had he nouther *roo* ne *reste,*
> But forthe he went evyn Weste.
>   *MS. Harl.* 2252, f. 129.

> The chylde had nodur reste ne *ro,*
> For thoght how he myзt come hur to.
>   *MS. Cantab.* Ff. ii. 38, f. 90.

ROACH. A rash, or thick scorbutic eruption on the skin. *Cornw.*

ROAD. (1) An inroad.

(2) To jostle one off the road by riding against him. *East.*

(3) Same as *Cockshut,* q. v.

ROADING. The act of running races on the road with teams. *Norf.*

ROADLING. Delirious. *Cornw.*

ROADSTER. A horse fitted for the road.

ROAKY. (1) Hazy ; misty. *Linc.* It occurs twice in this sense in Pr. Parv. " *Roky* or mysty, *nebulosus ;*" and previously, " Mysty or *rooky* as the eyre." Grose also has it, spelt *rooky,* and Shakespeare uses the term in a fine passage in Macbeth, iii. 2. " *Rook,* a steam or vapour ; *rooky,* misty or dark with steam and vapour," Kennett's Glossary, MS. Lansd. 1033.

(2) Hoarse. *North.*

ROAN. (1) The town of Rouen.

(2) A clump of whins. *Northumb.*

ROAPY. Viscous ; glutinous. *South.*

ROARER. A broken-winded horse.

ROARING. Fast ; quick. *Var. dial.*

ROARING-BOYS. The riotous blades of Ben Jonson's time, who took delight in annoying quiet people. At one period, their pranks in London were carried to an alarming extent. They were sometimes called *roarers.*

> England salutes him with the general joys
> Of court and country ; knights, squires, fools,
>   and boys
> In every town rejoice at his arrival,
> The townsmen where he comes their wives do
>   swive all,

> And bid them think on Jones amidst this gloe,
> In hope to get such *roaring boys* as he.
>   *Legend of Captain Jones,* 1659

ROARING-MEG. A kind of humming-top.

ROAST. (1) To *rule the roast,* a phrase meaning, to take the lead.

> Jhon, duke of Burgoyn, which *ruled the rost,* and governed both kyng Charles the Frenche kyng, and his whole realme.
>   *Hall's Union,* 1548. *Hen. IV.* f. 30

(2) To ridicule any one severely.

ROATING. Coarse, rank, as grass.

ROB. Jam ; fruit jelly. *East.*

ROBA. Wanton ; whore ; bona roba.

ROBBLE. An instrument used for stirring dough in an oven. *West.*

ROBBLY. Faulty. A mining term.

ROBBRESS. A female robber.

ROB-DAVY. Metheglin.

ROBERD. A chaffinch.

ROBERDSMEN. A gang of lawless vagabonds, rife in the fourteenth century. They are mentioned in Piers Ploughman, there called *Roberdes knaves.*

ROBERT. The herb stork-bill.

ROBERYCH. Rubric. Cov. Myst. p. 277.

ROBIN. *Robin-run-in-the-hedge,* bindweed. *Robin Hood's hatband,* the common club moss. *Robin in the hose,* lychnis sylvestris.

ROBINET. The cock of a cistern.

ROBIN-GOOD-FELLOW. A kind of merry sprite, whose character and achievements are recorded in the well-known ballad " From Oberon in Fairy Land." The earliest mention of him occurs in a MS. tale of the thirteenth century, printed in Wright's Latin Stories, p. 38. Reginald Scot, who published his ' Discoverie of Witchcraft' in 1584, has several curious notices of Robin Goodfellow. " There go as manie tales," says he, " upon Hudgin in some parts of Germanie, *as there did in England of Robin Goodfellove.*" Elsewhere he says, " and know you this by the waie, that *heretofore* Robin Goodfellow and Hobgobblin were as terrible, and also as credible to the people, as hags and witches be now ; and, in truth, they that mainteine walking spirits have no reason to deníe Robin Goodfellow, *upon whom there hath gone as manie and as credible tales as upon witches,* saving that it hath not pleased the translators of the Bible to call spirits by the name of Robin Goodfellow." The cheslip or woodlouse was called *Robin Goodfellow's louse.* " Cheeselyppworme, otherwyse called Robyngodfelowe his lowse, *tylus,*" Huloet, 1552.

ROBIN-GRAY. A bonnet. *North.*

ROBINHOOD. The red campion. *West.*

ROBIN-HOOD. " Many talk of Robin Hood, that never shot in his bow," an old proverb found in Walker's Proverbs, 1672, p. 56. " To sell Robin Hood's pennyworths," is spoken of things sold under half their value. See Ritson's Introd. to Robin Hood, p. xc. The number of extravagant tales about this celebrated archer was so great, that his name became proverbial for any improbable story. See Florio, p. 70 ; Holinshed's England, p. 69.

> Many man spekyth wyth wondreng
> Of Robyn Hode, and of his bow,
> Whych never shot therin I trow.
> *Ashmole's Theat. Chem. Brit.* 1652, p. 175.

ROBIN-RUDDOCK. A redbreast. *West.*

ROBLET. A large chicken. *East.*

ROBRISH. (1) A rubric. (2) Rubbish. "Robrisshe of a boke, *rubriche*," Palsgrave. "Robrisshe of stones, *plastras, fourniture*," ibid. It occurs in Hawes.

ROCCILLO. A cloak. *North.*

ROCHE. (1) A rock. *Palsgrave.* Refuse gritty stone is still so called.

> This schip whiche wende his helpe a croche,
> Drof alle to pecis on the *roche.*
> *Gower, MS. Soc. Antiq.* 134, f. 91.

(2) A kind of wine, perhaps Rochelle. "Rynische wyne and Rochelle," Morte Arthure, MS. Lincoln, f. 55.

> And ever scho drewe thame the wyne,
> Bathe the *Roche* and the Ryne.
> *MS. Lincoln* A. i. 17, f. 136.

ROCHERE. A rock.

> He wolde not forgete in no manere
> The tresure in the hye *rochere*,
> That they fonde betwene them twoo.
> *MS. Cantab.* Ff. ii. 38, f. 210.

ROCHESTER-EARTH. A name for saltpetre.

ROCHET. (1) A little blue cloth cloak. *Devon.* Perhaps the same as the following :—"*Superior vestis mulierum*, Anglice a rochet," MS. Bibl. Reg. 12 B. i. f. 12. "Instita, a rochyt," Nominale MS. The bishop's rochet is a linen vest worn under a satin robe. "Rochet a surplys, *rochet*," Palsgrave.

(2) The piper fish. Nominale MS.

ROCHLIS. The rattle. *Heref.*

ROCK. (1) A kind of very hard cheese made from skimmed milk, and used in Hampshire. In satirical allusion to its hardness, it is said to be used to make pins to fasten gates.

(2) A distaff held in the hand from which the thread was spun by twirling a ball below.

> In the old time, sc. Edw. 6, &c. they used to spinn with *rocks :* in Staffordshire, &c. they use them still. *Aubrey's Wilts, Royal Soc. MS.* p. 268.
> What, shall a woman with a *rokke* drive thee away ?
> Fye on thee, traitor, now I tremble for tene.
> *Digby Mysteries,* p. 11.

(3) A young hedgehog. *Somerset.*

ROCKED. Bad; false; impure. "That rocked reball," Chester Plays, i. 161.

ROCKEL. A woman's cloak. *Devon.*

ROCKER. (1) A nurse.

(2) The long handle of the bellows in a smith's forge, which is drawn down to raise the moving-board of the bellows. The cross staff upon which it is fastened is called the rockstaff. *Var. dial.*

(3) A long wicker sieve used in dressing beans, &c. *Beds.*

ROCKET. (1) A cloak without a cape, the same as *Rochet*, q. v. Mr. Fairholt describes it "a close upper garment," London Pageants, p. 207. It occurs in Palsgrave.

(2) A portion. *Suffolk.*

ROCKING. Walking with alternate sideway motion. *Northamptonsh.*

ROCKING-PAN. In the allom works at Whitby in Yorkshire, the allom, after it is shotten and crystallized on the sides of the cooler, is scraped and washed, and put into the *rockingpan*, and there melted. Kennett, MS.

ROCKLED. Rash and forward. *North.*

ROCKLEY. "Prove at the partynge, quod Rockley," Palsgrave.

ROCKY. Tipsy. *Var. dial.*

RODE. (1) To spawn. *Suffolk.*

(2) A company of horsemen.

(3) Complexion. (*A.-S.*)

(4) A harbour for ships.

(5) *To go to rode* means, late at night or early in the morning, to go out to shoot wild-fowl which pass over head on the wing.

RODED. Lean mingled with fat. *West.*

RODEDE. Rotted. *Hearne.*

RODE-LAND. Land which has been cleared or grubbed up; land lately reclaimed and brought into cultivation.

RODE-NET. A sort of bird-net.

RODOK. A chaffinch. *Frigella*, Nominale MS. Or is it the redbreast ?

RODOMONT. A boaster. This term is derived from the name of a famous hero in Ariosto so called. Hence *Rhodomontade.*

RODS-GOLD. The marygold.

RODY. Ruddy ; red. (*A.-S.*)

> That chylde was fulle welle dyghte,
> Gentylle of body and of *rody* bryghte.
> *MS. Cantab.* Ff. ii. 38, f. 144.

ROE-DOE. A young female hind.

ROENDE. Round. Reliq. Antiq. ii. 109.

ROET. Pasture ground. *Berks.*

ROFE. Tore. (*A.-S.*)

> Hyre surkotte sleve he *rofe* of thenne,
> And sayde, by this ȝe salle me kenne,
> Whenne ȝe se me by syghte.
> *MS. Lincoln* A. i 17, f. 104.

ROFFE. A roof. See *Aboffe.*

ROFOAM. The waist. *Devon.*

ROGE. (1)

> Fye, harlote ! fye, hounde !
> Fye on thee, thou taynted doge !
> What ! laye thou still in that stonde,
> And let that losinger go on the *roge ?*
> *Chester Plays,* ii. 94.

(2) To tramp, as beggars, &c.

ROGER. (1) The ram is so called by the shepherds in most parts of England. See Collins' Miscellanies, 1742, p. 116.

(2) A rogue. A cant term.

(3) *Roger of the buttery*, a goose.

ROGERIAN. A wig. *Hall.*

ROGER'S-BLAST. A sudden and local motion of the air, no otherwise perceptible but by its whirling up the dust on a dry road in perfectly calm weather, somewhat in the manner of a water-spout. *Forby.*

ROGGAN. A rocking-stone. *North.*

ROGGE. To shake. (*A.-S.*) Brockett has *roggle* in this sense.

He romede, he rarede, that raggede alle the erthe,
So ruydly he rappyd at to ryot hymselvene.
> *Morte Arthure, MS. Lincoln, f. 61.*

So hard Rofyn rogud his roll,
That he smot with his choule,
Azayns the marbystone.
Of that dynt thai had gret doute,
Al that setyn ther aboute,
Fore thai herd hit echon.
> *MS. Douce 302, xv. Cent.*

The croice, the crownne, the spere bese bowne
That Jhesu raggede and rente,
The nayles ruyde salle the conclude
With thyne awene argument !
> *MS. Lincoln A. i. 17, f. 213.*

ROGHE. Rough.
Roghe he was as a schepe.
> *MS. Cantab. Ff. ii. 38, f. 101.*

ROGHTE. Recked ; cared. *(A.-S.)*
He roghte not what woman he toke,
So lytylle he sett by hys spouse-hede.
> *MS. Cantab. Ff. ii. 38, f. 48.*

Syr Befyse was so wery for-faghte,
That of hys lyfe roghte he noghte.
> *MS. Cantab. Ff. ii. 38, f. 106.*

ROGHTLESSE. Reckless ; careless.
Dreding ye were of my woos roghtlesse
That was to me a grevous hevinesse.
> *MS. Cantab. Ff. i. 6, f. 116.*

ROGLRE. Rough.

ROGUE. A professed beggar. Also as *Roge* (2). " Raunging, roguing about," Cotgrave in v. *Divague.*

ROGUE-HOUSE. A prison. *North.*

ROIGNOUS. Scabby ; rough. *(A.-N.)*

ROIL. (1) A Flemish horse. Mr. Dyce seems at fault in Skelton, ii. 379.

(2) To romp ; to disturb ; to trouble ; to vex ; to perplex, or fatigue. *North.* " Were woont to rome and *roile* in clusters," Stanihurst's Ireland, p. 21, where it means to rove about, as in Reliq. Antiq. ii. 175.

(3) A great awkward hoyden. " A big ungainly slammakin," MS. Devon GL.

ROILY. To traduce ; to backbite. *West.*

ROIST. To bully ; to riot. " They ruffle and *roist* it out," Harrison's England, p. 149. " *Roister*, to be rude, to ramp about," MS. Lansd. 1033. *Roisterer*, a swaggerer, is still in use in the North of England.

ROISTON-CROW. A species of crow, called by Ray *cornix cinerea frugilega*, ed. 1674, p. 83. It is mentioned by Cotgrave.

ROIT. To walk about idly.

ROKE. (1) Mist ; steam. *Var. dial.*

(2) To shake ; to roll. Still in use, to shake or stir liquids. Also, to cleanse armour by rolling it in a barrel of sand.
Were thay wighte, were thay woke,
Alle that he tille stroke,
He made thaire bodies to roke.
> *Perceval, 1375.*

(3) A scratch. *Yorksh.*

(4) A vein of ore. *North.*

(5) The rook at chess.
After chee for the roke ware fore the mate,
For jif the fondment be false, the werke most nede falle.
> *MS. Douce 302, f. 4.*

ROKY. The same as *Roaky*, q. v.

ROLL. A large heavy wooden roller for breaking clods. *North.*

ROLLE. (1) To enrol. *(A.-N.)*

(2) " *Antiæ*, the heare of a woman that is layed over hir forheade ; gentilwomen dyd lately call them their *rolles*," Elyot, ed. 1559. At one time they were much worn in Ireland. See Holinshed, Chron. Ireland, p. 134.

ROLLEKY. Rough ; uneven. *East.*

ROLLER. A bundle of reed. Used proverbially, e. g. as weak as a *rawler*, or as easily thrown down as a bundle of reed set on an end.

ROLLEY. A large kind of sledge drawn by a horse, used in coal mines. *North.*

ROLLICK. To romp about recklessly ; to gad idly ; to roll. *Var. dial.*

ROLLIPOKE. Coarse hempen cloth. *East.*

ROLLOP. This word was heard between Ipswich and Bury in the phrase, " There they come *rolloppin* along," and was applied to the hasty, noisy approach of horsemen, compounded perhaps of *romp* and *gallop.*

ROLLS. *Books in rolls*, those which have a row of gold on the edges of the cover.

ROLY-POLY. (1) A pudding made in round layers, with preserves or treacle between. *Var. dial.* Taylor mentions it.

(2) A low, vulgar person. *Linc.*

(3) A game played with a certain number of pins and a ball, resembling half a cricket ball. It is played thus. One pin is placed in the centre, the rest (with the exception of one called the *jack*) are placed in a circle round it ; the jack is placed about a foot or so from the circle, in a line with one in the circle and the one in the centre. The centre one is called the king, the one between that and jack the queen. The king counts for three, queen two, and each of the other pins for one each, except jack. The art of the game lies in bowling down all the pins except jack, for if jack is bowled down, the player has just so many deducted from his former score as would have been added if he had not struck the jack. Holloway, pp. 142-3. This game was formerly called half-bowl, and was prohibited by a statute of Edward IV.

ROMAGE. To set a ship to rights ; to clear the hold of goods ; to remove things in it from one place to another.

ROMANCE. (1) The French language.

(2) To lie. *Var. dial.*

ROMASING. Wonderful ; romantic. *West.*

ROMAUNT. A romance. *(A.-N.)* Still in use in Suffolk as a verb, to exaggerate or exceed the truth.

ROMB. To shiver with cold.

ROMBEL. A rumbling noise ; a rumour.

ROM-BOUSE. Wine. A cant term, given in Dekker's Belman, 1616.

ROME. (1) The expression of " the Boke of *Rome*," sometimes found in old romances, is a travesty of the old phrase *the Roman*, which was applied to signify the French language, in which most of the old romances were originally written.

> He that schalle wend soche a wey,
> Yt were nede for hym to pray
>   That Jeshu hym schuld save.
> Yt ys in *the boke of Rome*,
> Ther was no knyght of Kyrstendome
>   That jorney durst crave. *Torrent of Portugal*, p. 6.

(2) " Rome was not built in a day," is a proverb in common use to excite perseverance. It is found in the French Alphabet, 1615.

(3) To growl; to roar.

> He comanded that thay sulde take a yonge dameselle, and nakkene hir, and sett hir bifore hym, and thay did soo; and onane he ranne apone hir *romyand*, as he hadd bene wodd. *MS. Lincoln* A. i. 17, f. 37.

(4) Place; situation; office.

(5) Broad; spacious. (*A.-S.*)

> Jhesu that made the planettes vij,
> And all the worlde undur hevyn,
> And made thys worlde wyde and *rome*.
>   *MS. Cantab.* Ff. ii. 38, f. 105.

(6) To walk about. (*A.-S.*) Hence, sometimes, to depart from.

> As he *romeyd* all abowte,
> He lokyd on a towre withowte.
>   *MS. Cantab.* Ff. ii. 38, f. 148.

(7) A space. (*A.-S.*)

> That tho Sarsyns yn a *rome*
> At that tyme were overcome.
>   *MS. Cantab.* Ff. ii. 38, f. 101.

(8) In space or length?

> The geaunt was wonder strong,
> *Rome* thretti fote long. *Beves of Hamtoun*, p. 73.

ROME-BOWSE. Wine. *Dekker.*

ROME-MORT. A queen. A cant term.

ROMKIN. A drinking-cup.

ROMMLE. To speak low or secretly.

ROMMOCK. To romp boisterously.

ROMNAY. A kind of Spanish wine.

> Larkys in hot schow, ladys for to pyk,
> Good drynk therto, lycyus and fyne,
> Blwet of allmayne, *romnay* and wyin.
>   *Reliq. Antiq.* ii. 30.

ROMPSTAL. A rude girl. *West.*

ROMULIK. Abundantly; plentifully.

ROMVILE. London. Dekker, 1616.

RON. Conversation; treatise. (*A.-S.*)

> The laste resun of alle this *ron*
> Sal be of hir concepcion.
>   *MS. Cotton. Vespas.* A. iii. f. 2.

RONCE. To romp about. *North.*

RONCLED. Wrinkled. (*A.-S.*)

> Whoso that yow beholdyth well, and seyth
> Your *roncled* face and your rawe eyen tweyne,
> Your shrunkyn lyppis and your gowuldyn tethe,
> How may he lyve fro dystresse and payne?
>   *MS. Fairfax* 16.

ROND. The same as *Foolen*, q. v.

RONDURE. Roundness. (*Fr.*)

RONE. (1) Rained. (*A.-S.*)

(2) To protect; to comfort.

(3) Rouen in Normandy.

(4) The roe of a fish. *North.* " The roan of fish, *piscium ova*," Coles.

RONETTE. Round; circular.

RONEZ. Thickets; brushwood. *Gawayne.*

RONG. The step of a ladder. *Var. dial.* " A

ronge of a tre or ledder, *scalare*," MS. Dict A. D. 1540.

RONGE. To bite; to gnaw. *West.*

RONGENE. Rung. (*A.-S.*)

> He hade morthirede this mylde be myddaye war *rongene*,
> Withowttyne mercy one molde, not watte it ment.
>   *Morte Arthure, MS. Lincoln*, f. 63.

RONK-RIPE. Quite ripe. *Chesh.*

RONNER. A sort of coarse cloth.

RONNING. Rennet. " Ronnyng of chese, *maisgue*," Palsgrave.

RONT.

> But downe they burst the windows for ayre, and there was no little boot to bid *ront*; shee was nine or ten dayes ere she recovered that fit on my knowledge. *Armin's Nest of Ninnies*, 1608.

RONYON. A mangy animal. (*Fr.*)

ROO. Rough. *Devon.*

ROOD. The cross, or crucifix. (*A.-S.*) *Rood-beam*, the beam supporting the rood. *Rood-door*, a door leading out of the church near the altar.

> On Saynt Mathies day thapostulle, the xxiiij. day of February, Sonday, did the bisshop of Rochester preche at Polles Cros, and had standyng afore hym alle his sermon tyme the pictur of the *roode of grace* in Kent, that had byn many yeris in the abbey of Boxley in Kent, and was gretely sought with pilgryms, and when he had made an ende of his sermon, the pictor was toorn alle to peces.
>   *MS. Cotton. Vespas.* A. xxv.

ROOD-LOFT. A gallery, or platform, over the screen, at the entrance of the chancel, upon which was the *rood* or cross, with images. See Grindal's Remains, p. 154.

ROODY. Rank in growth. *North.*

ROOFE. Split.

> So harde togedur they drofe,
> That Ser Befyse schylde *roofe*.
>   *MS. Cantab.* Ff. ii. 38, f. 124.

ROOFING. The ridge-cap of thatched roofs. *Norf.*

ROOK. (1) To huddle together. *West.*

(2) A crow-bar. *Salop.*

(3) A cheat, or sharper. *Rookery*, a place of resort for sharpers.

> Gramercies watt mets mesters and the rest,
> His smock-stain'd dames will ha a game at chest,
> And sweare to me thi knights be not turned knaves,
> Thy *rookes* turne flesh-crowes or devouring slaves.
>   *MS. Poems in Dr. Bliss's Possession*, xvii. Cent.
> Your city blades are cunning *rookes*,
> How rarely you collogue him!
>   *Songs of the London Prentices*, p. 91.

(4) To thrust the fingers in the mouth, said of children. *Oxon.*

ROOKERY. A disturbance; a scolding.

ROOKY. Same as *Roaky*, q. v.

ROOL. To ruffle; to rumple. *North.*

ROOM. (1) Dandruff. *Somerset.*

(2) Place. In such phrases as, " *Room* for my Lord," it is equivalent to give place to, make way for.

ROOMER. To go or put roomer, to tack about before the wind. An old sea term, very incorrectly explained " a very large ship" by Ash and others. It occurs in Bourne's Inventions

or Devises, 1578 ; Harrington's Nugæ Antiquæ, ii. 233 ; Apolonius and Silla, ap. Collier's Shak. Lib. p. 32 ; Taylor, quoted in Hunter on the Tempest, p. 46.

> Yet did the master by all meanes assay,
> To steare out *roomer*, or to keepe aloofe.
> *Harrington's tr. of Orlando Furioso,* 1591, p. 343.

> Hereupon she discharged herself from the Towne of Taryffa, and when wether served agreyng with the maister for her passage, herself with her daughter repaired aborde the barke, which beyng put to sea, was forced by the extremitie of a contrary winde, to put themselves *romer* for the safetie of their lives, to a cleane contrary place. *Riche's Farewell,* 1581.

> Rowse, quoth the ship against the rocks ; *roomer* cry I in the cocke; my Lord wept for the company, I laught to comfort him. *Tragedy of Hoffman,* 1631.

ROOMTH. Room. *Drayton.*

ROONE. Vermilion. This term has been wrongly explained by all the glossarists.

> Y schalle yeve the a nobylle stede,
> Also redd as ony *roone.*
>   *MS. Cantab.* Ff. ii. 38, f. 66.

ROORT. Roared. *Lanc.*

ROOP. (1) A halloa. *Var. dial.*

(2) A hoarseness. *North.* A sort of hoarseness in fowls is so called.

ROOSELING. Sloping down. *Exmoor.*

ROOST. To drive. *Devon.*

ROOST-COCK. The common cock. *Devon.* See the example under *Porpentine.*

ROOT. (1) A rut. *Glouc.*

(2) To turn up the ground, as hogs do with their noses. *Lanc.*

(3) Gross amount ; sum total.

(4) To rot. *Somerset.*

> I *root*, he seyde, fro the boon,
> Jhesu Cryste, what schall y done ?
>   *MS. Cantab.* Ff. ii. 38, f. 114.

ROOTAGE. Extirpation.

ROOTER. A rough attack. *North.*

ROOTLE. To root up, as swine. *Beds.*

ROOTY. Rank, as grass. *Yorksh.*

ROOVE. To dry meat in a chimney, or over a kiln. *Glouc.*

ROOZE. To shed ; to scatter. *Cornw.*

ROP. Reaped. (*A.-S.*)

ROPE. (1) A word formerly taught to parrots. *A rope for a parrot* was a common proverbial expression.

(2) A dwarf. *Somerset.*

(3) To tether, as a horse. *Norf.*

(4) A measure of twenty feet. *Devon.*

(5) A bundle of twigs laid over a gutter instead of a plank. *Devon.*

ROPE-PULLING. The ancient custom of *rope-pulling* is always strictly observed in Ludlow on Shrove Tuesday. At about four o'clock in the afternoon the rope is given out from the Town-hall by the Mayor, on whom this important duty by right devolves. Immediately on the rope being let down from a window, an indescribable struggle and trial of strength commences between the denizens of the different wards, which is not concluded without an obstinate contention. There are afterwards

ordinaries at the various inns, and pleasure and conviviality are the order of the day.

ROPER. (1) A rope-maker.

(2) A crafty fellow ; a rogue.

ROPE-RIPE. Fit for hanging, a phrase applied to anything very wicked. " A rope-ripe-rogue ripe for the rope, or deserving the rope ' " Howell's Lex. Tet. 1660.

ROPERY. Roguery. *Shak.*

ROPES. The entrails. *West.* " The ropes in the small guttes," Palsgrave. " Almost confined at present to the guts of woodcocks, which are often dressed with the ropes in them," MS. Devon Gl.

ROPY. Wine or other liquor is said to be *ropy*, when thick and coagulated. *Linc.* Bread is said to be *ropy* when in warm close weather a sort of second fermentation takes place after baking. *Var. dial.*

RORDE. Sound ; noise ; roar.

RORE. (1) Dew. (*Lat.*) *Rorid,* dewy, Marlowe, iii. 364 ; Hawkins, iii. 151.

(2) Trouble ; stir ; noise. Hence, perhaps, the name of *roaring-boys.*

(3) To barter, or exchange merchandize. " Rooryne or chaungyne on chaffare for another," Pr. Parv. p. 71.

RORY-TORY. Having a mixture of gay colours ; showy ; dashing. *Devon.*

ROSARY. A rose-bush. *Skelton.*

ROSE. (1) The rose was a symbol of secrecy among the ancients, and from hence is said to be derived the adage " under the rose " when a secret is to be kept, and used with great propriety on privy seals, which came into use about the middle of the twelfth century. Snelling's Coins, p. 2.

(2) When the upper part of a quarry or well falls in, it is said *to rose in.*

(3) To drop, or fall, said of seed or corn when over-ripe. *Somerset.*

(4) The erysipelas.

(5) A knot of ribands, frequently worn in the ear, on the shoe, &c.

(6) To praise. Still in use.

(7) The top of the spout of a watering-pot, perforated for the purpose of distributing the water ; the top of a leaden pipe, perforated in a similar manner, to prevent leaves or rubbish from entering a water-butt.

ROSEE. An ancient confection, composed chiefly of milk, dates, spices, &c.

ROSEMARYNE. Rosemary.

> Tak of rewe a grete qwantite, and sawge halfe als mekille, and *rosemaryne* the same quantitee.
>   *MS. Linc. Med.* f. 283.

ROSEMARY-STONES. Friable stones of a deep yellow colour found amongst the fattest marles about Audley, co. Staff. and used by the painters. Kennett, MS.

ROSE-NOBLE. A gold coin, stamped with a rose, worth sixteen shillings.

ROSER. A rose-bush. (*A.-N.*)

ROSE-RYAL. A gold coin formerly worth thirty shillings, but it rose three shillings in value in the reign of James I. See Snelling's Coins, p. 24.

ROSE-YARD. A place where roses grow. *Palsgrave.*

ROSIAR. A rose-tree. (*A.-N.*)

> The knyghte and his sqwyere
> Risted undir a *rosere*
> Tille the day wex clere,
> Undrone and mare. *MS. Lincoln* A. i. 17, f. 133.

ROSIL. Rosin. *East.* "*Rosina*, rosyle," Nominale MS. xv. Cent.

ROSILLY. Said of sandy and gritty soil, like rosin. *East.* Harrison, p. 111, mentions *rosellie* mould.

ROSIN-END. A shoemaker's thread. *North.*

ROSINNED. Tipsy. *Craven.*

ROS-LAND. Heathy land. *East.*

ROSPE. To belch.

ROSS. (1) The refuse of plants.
(2) A morass. *Heref.*

ROSSEL. (1) To heat; to roast. *North.*
(2) To kick severely. *Salop.*

ROSELLED. (1) Decayed. *North.*
(2)

> Throwe a rownnde rede schelde he ruschede hym sone,
> That the *rosselde* spere to his herte rynnes.
> *Morte Arthure, MS. Lincoln,* f. 83.

ROSSHETON. Rushed.

> They *rossheton* aȝeynne the wall of ston.
> *Chron. Vilodun.* p. 123.

ROST. To turn boast to rost, i. e. to turn from swaggering to humility.

ROSTER. A rost-iron, an iron grate used in roasting; a gridiron. Nominale MS. "Lay hom on a rostynge yrne, and roste hom," Ord. and Regulations, p. 451.

ROSTLE. To ripen. *Lanc.*

ROSY. Healthy. Hens, when they commence laying, and their combs look red and healthy, are said to be rosy.

ROT. (1) Great nonsense. *West.*
(2) A body of six soldiers.

ROTA-MEN. A name given to certain politicians during the Commonwealth, who suggested that a third part of the parliament should go out by rotation.

ROTE. (1) A kind of cymbal, said to be the same as the hurdy-gurdy. "Dulcimers or dowble harpe called a roote, *barbitos*," Huloet, 1552.

> He tauȝte hire til sche was certen
> Of harpe, of citole, and of *rote.*
> *Gower, MS. Soc. Antiq.* 134, f. 234.

> Wele to playe one a *rotte,*
> To syng many newe note,
> And of harpyng, wele I wote,
> He wane the pryse aye. *MS. Lincoln* A. i. 17, f. 130.

(2) A root. (*A.-S.*)
(3) Practice. (*A.-N.*) Also a verb, to practise, to repeat by rote.
(4) Writing; record.

> Men say yn olde *rote,*
> A womans bolt ys sone schote.
> *MS. Cantab.* Ff. ii. 38, f. 103.

ROTEN. Rotten. *Chaucer.*

> Myn sowle hath suffrid in his word,
> In God myn goost hath had his trust,
> For synne is scharp as knyvis ord,
> It makith hem lame that levyn in lust.

Therfore, Jhesu, myn lovely Lord,
> When I am *rotyn,* rub of the rust,
> Er I be brouȝt withinne schippys bord,
> To sayle into the dale of dust.
> *Hampole's Paraphrase of the Psalms, MS.*

ROT-GUT. Bad small beer.

> Beer-a-bumble—
> 'Twool bust yar guts, afore t'al make ye tumble.

ROTHER. (1) The rudder of a ship. (*A.-S.*)

> And thus putte every man out other,
> The schip of love hath loste his *rother.*
> *Gower, MS. Soc. Antiq.* 134, f. 77

> Alle ys the toon with the touther,
> As a shyppe that ys turned with the *rother.*
> *MS. Harl.* 1701, f. 31.

(2) A horned beast. "In Herefordshire the dung of such beasts is still called *rother soyl,*" Kennett, MS. Lansd. 1033. According to Sharp's MS. Glossary, the word is current in Warwickshire, and he adds that the beast-market at Stratford-on-Avon is called the *rother market.* "It is the pasture lards the rother's sides," Shakespeare; the old editions reading *brother's.* For this emendation we are indebted to Mr. Singer, and is exceedingly ingenious, although it must at the same time be admitted that sense can be made of it as it stands in the original. "*Bucerum pœcus,* an hearde of *rother* beastes," Elyot, ed. 1559.

(3) Name of a river?

> Drof of hors and gyl of fisch.
> So hat my lemman war ȝe ys;
> Water of *rother* and Taymys brother,
> So hat my lemman in non other.
> *MS. Douce* 257, f. 77.

(4) A sailor. Nominale MS.

ROTOURE. A player on the rote.

> Ȝyf thou ever with jogeloure,
> With hasadoure or with *rotoure,*
> Hauntyst taverne. *MS. Harl.* 1701, f. 7.

> He is a persone, she thynkethe, of fair figure,
> A yong *rotour,* redy to hir plesder.
> *Lydgate's Minor Poems,* p. 35.

ROTTLE-PENNY. The herb yellow-rattle.

ROTYNG. Root.

> Jessé, he selde, of his *rotyng*
> Certeynly a ȝerde shal spring.
> *Cursor Mundi, MS. Coll. Trin. Cantab.* f. 58.

ROU. Cold; bleak; damp. *North.*

ROUCHED. (1) Wrinkled. *Northumb.*
(2) Beer is said to be *rouched* when it acquires a tartness. MS. Devon Gl.

ROUDGE. A rough coarse cloth.

ROUGE. To gnaw; to devour. *Somerset.*

ROUGH. (1) To make rough, applied to horses' shoes when they are made rough to prevent them slipping in frosty weather.
(2) A wood, or copse. *Sa'op.*
(3) Luxuriant, as grass. *North.*
(4)

> Up she rose ageyn the *roughe,*
> With sorefulle hert and care inoughe,
> Carefulle of blood and bone;
> She sye it myght no better be,
> She knelid down uppon her kne,
> And thankid God and Seynt John.
> *Torrent of Portugal,* p. 79.

(5) To trump one's adversary's card at the game of whist.

ROUGH-CANDLE. A torch, or link.

ROUGH-CAST. A composition of sand, grit, and mortar, used for walls. &c.

ROUGHED. Streaked; speckled. *Devon.*

ROUGH-LEAF. The true leaf of a plant, in distinction from its seed leaves. *West.*

ROUGH-MUSIC. A discordant din of sticks, pans, and a heterogeneous collection of instruments, a species of entertainment which takes place when a woman has been beaten by her husband. It is got up principally by boys, who parade the village accompanied by the musical band, in which nearly all take a part, and the performance concludes with burning the effigy of the offender, which has been carried in procession. A curious notion is universally prevalent, that if the rough music is not continued for three successive nights, all the boys participating in these means of passing a public censure can be banished from the village for a limited period by the *homo delinquens.*

ROUGHNESS. Plenty; store. *Cumb.*

ROUGH-RIDER. One who breaks in horses.

ROUGH-SETTER. A mason who only did rough coarse work, as walls, &c.

ROUGH-SPUN. Rude; unpolished; blunt.

ROUGHT.

> Invidia the therd wound ys,
> A wyckkyd gnawer or venym or gowt,
> He ys a wyckyd wound I gess,
> Ther he hath power to reyne or *rought.*
> *MS. Cantab.* Ff. i. 6.

ROUK. (1) A large number. *North.*

(2) To wander. (3) To be restless.

ROUKE. To lie close. *(A.-S.)*

> Thei shul for thurst the hedes souke
> Of adders that doth aboute hem *roukn,*
> As childe that sittith in moders lappe,
> And soukith whan him likith the pappe.
> *MS. Addit.* 11305, f. 97.

ROULE. To roll; to run easily.

ROUMER. Wider. *Chaucer.*

ROUNCEVAL. Large; strong. Coles makes mention of *Rounceval pease;* and he has also, " a rounsival, *virago.*"

ROUNCIE. (1) A common hackney horse. Sometimes, a horse of any kind.

> Befyse sadelyd hys *rounsy,*
> The bore he thoght to hunty
> *MS. Cantab.* Ff. ii. 38, f. 100.

> Syr Befyse lepyd on hys *rownsy,*
> And wyth hym hys cosyn ser Tarry.
> *MS. Cantab.* Ff. ii. 38, f. 120.

(2) A vulgar coarse woman.

ROUND. (1) A turret or tower of a circular form; a room or closet within such a turret. *Willson.*

(2) To counsel secretly; to rowne, or whisper. It is of common occurrence under this form.

(3) A kind of dance. " The round danse, or the dansing of the rounds," Nomenclator, 1585, p. 299. There was a sort of song or ballad also so called.

(4) *To round the head,* to cut the hair round. *Round dealing,* plain honest dealing. *Round*

sum, a considerable sum. *Round and square,* everywhere.

(5) A toast at a drinking revel; a health to pass round.

(6) Full; large. *North.*

(7) Certain soldiers, whose office it was *to go round* and inspect the sentinels, watches, and advanced guard, were called *gentlemen of the round.*

(8) Plain in speaking. *Oxon.* " A round answer," Holinshed's England, i. 10.

(9) A regiment, or troop.

(10) A globular pebble. *Devon.*

(11) An animal's rump. *Var. dial.*

(12) A kind of target.

ROUND-DOCK. The common mallow.

ROUNDEL. (1) Anything round, as a circle, a trencher, &c. " A roundell to set dishes on for soiling the tablecloth," Baret, 1580.

(2) The midriff. *Somerset.*

(3) A roundelay, or catch.

ROUNDELET. A rundlet for wine.

ROUNDERS. A boy's game at balls.

ROUND-FROCK. A gaberdine, or upper garment, worn by the rustics. *Var. dial.*

ROUNDGE. A great noise; a violent push or stroke. *Northumb.*

ROUNDHEAD. A puritan, so called because the hair was cut in a close circular fashion.

> And ere their butter 'gan to coddle,
> A bullet churnd i'th *Roundheads* noddle.
> *Men Miracles,* 1656, p. 43.

ROUNDLY. Plainly; evidently; vehemently; quickly. Also, severely. " Ile make them come off and on *roundly,*" Nabbes' Bride, 1640, sig. G. ii.

ROUND-ROBIN. A small pancake. *Devon.*

ROUNDS. Fragment of statues in paintings were termed *rounds.*

ROUND-SHAVING. A reprimand. *West.*

ROUND-TAG. A children's game, at which they all stand in a ring. *Devon.*

ROUND-TILTH. Sowing a *round-tilth* is sowing land continuously without any fallow. *Kent.*

ROUNE. To whisper. Sometimes for speech or song in general. *(A.-S.)* It is occasionally used in its primitive sense, to counsel or consult.

> Somer is comen with love to toune,
> With blostme and with brides roune.
> *Relig. Antiq.* i. 241.
> Lenten ys come with love to toune,
> With blosmen ant with briddes *roune.*
> *Ritson's Ancient Songs,* ed. 1829, i. 63.
> On hys knees he sette hym downe
> With the prest for to *roune.*
> *MS. Harl.* 1701, f. 83.

ROUNGE. (1) A wheelbarrow.

(2) To nip, or cut. *(A.-N.)*

> For ever on hem y *rounge* and gnawe,
> And hindir hem alle that ever y may.
> *Gower, MS. Soc. Antiq.* 134, f. 64.

ROUNSEPICK. Same as *Rampick,* q. v.

ROUN-TREE. The mountain-ash. *North.*

ROUP. A filthy boil on the rumps of fowls. *Bailey.*

ROUPE. Outcry; lamentation.

ROUS. Boasting. *North.*

> Ne be nat proude, thoghe thou weyl dous,
> Yn thyn herte to make a rous.
>> *MS. Harl.* 1701, f. 34.

> Thou mayst nat excuse the with rous,
> And sey al the worlde so dous.
>> *MS. Harl.* 1701, f. 16.

ROUS-ABOUT. Big; unwieldy. *West.* Also, a restless fidgetty person.

ROUSE. (1) To shake and flutter. A term in ancient hawking.

(2) To turn out. *Var. dial.*

(3) A full glass; a bumper. Very common in old plays.

(4) Noise; intemperate mirth. *Devon.*

ROUSEN. A report. *Devon.*

ROUSER. A great falsehood. *A rousing lie,* from *rousing,* great, excessive. "A rousing lye, *mendacium magnificum,*" Coles.

ROUSING. Rough; shaggy. *Devon.*

ROUST. To rouse, or disturb. *Glouc.*

ROUTE. (1) A company. *North.* Also a verb, to assemble in a company.

> Is this flowre a monkes weed?
> A faire lilly for so fowle a *rowte.*
>> *MS. Coll. S. Johan. Cantab.* G. 14.

> When hur fadur was dede,
> Moche warre began to sprede
> Yn hur lande alle abowte;
> Therfore sche ys gevyn to rede,
> To take a lorde to rewle and to lede
> Hur londe wyth hys *rowte.*
>> *MS. Cantab.* Ff. ii. 38, f. 75.

(2) Recked; cared. (*A.-S.*)

> The wolf in the putte stod,
> Afingret so that he ves wod;
> I-nou he cursede that thider him broute;
> The vox ther of luitle *route.*
>> *Reliq. Antiq.* ii. 277.

(3)

> And Eagelle alle bryghte schalle fly alle abowyte,
> And helpe the frome there handes, that er so hygthe
> of *routs.*   *Reliq. Antiq.* ii. 12.

(4) To snore. "*Dormendo sonare,* Anglice to rowtyn," *MS. Bibl. Reg.* 12 B. i. f. 88. Also, to roar or bellow, as animals; to hollow.

(5) Great or violent stir. *Devon.*

> To make *rowtte* into Rome with ryotous knyghtes
> Within a sevenyghte daye with sex score helmes.
>> *Morte Arthure, MS. Lincoln,* f. 57.

(6) Coarse grass. *East.*

(7) To belch. Palsgrave, 1530.

(8) Crepo; pedo. Coles' Lat. Dict.

ROUTED. If an animal strays and is pounded, it remains, when unclaimed, three sunsets and three sunrisings in the pound or pinfold, afterwards it is taken to the *rout* (or green) yard, till the owner can be found, and is then said to be *routed.* This term is used in the neighbourhood of Horncastle more particularly than elsewhere, and it is no uncommon thing to see in the provincial papers advertisements beginning thus, *routed* at—2 pigs, &c. *Linc.*

ROUTH. (1) Plenty; abundance. *North.*

(2) Rough, as shaggy hair, &c.

ROUTHE. Compassion; pity. (*A.-S.*)

> But sche hadde o defaute of slouthe
> Towardis love, and that was *routhe.*
>> *Gower, MS. Soc. Antiq.* 134, f. 111.

> O, blisfulle Lorde, have on this mater *routhe!*
>> *Lydgate, MS. Soc. Antiq.* 134, f. 5.

ROUTOUS. Riotous; noisy. *North.*

ROUT-OUT. (1) A Saturday pie. *Cornw.*

(2) To seek or hunt very narrowly for any person or thing. *Var. dial.*

ROVE. (1) A scab. *Suffolk.*

(2) To shoot an arrow with an elevation, not point blank.

(3) A mode of ploughing. *East.*

(4) To shrug; to stir up.

> With his scholder he gan *rove.*
>> *Arthour and Merlin,* p. 73.

(5) To cleave, or cut.

> His brand and his brade schelde al blody be *rovene;*
> Was never oure semliche kynge so sorowfulle in herte.
>> *Morte Arthure, MS. Lincoln,* f. 94.

ROVER. An archer. *Jonson.*

ROVERS. Arrows shot with a certain degree of elevation, generally at 45°. There were marks on the target also so called. "Shooting still at rovers," Clobery's Divine Glimpses, 1659, p. 4. *Running at rovers,* having too much liberty.

ROVERTED. Returned to life. (*Lat.*)

ROW. (1) A hedge. *Var. dial.*

(2) To look for. *Heref.*

(3) A riot; a disturbance. *Var. dial.*

(4) To rake, or stir about. *North.*

ROW-CLOTH. A folding cloak, made of a kind of warm but coarse cloth completely dressed after weaving.

ROWD. The finscale fist. *Suffolk.*

ROWDLE. To move gently. *Oxon.*

ROWE. (1) Rushed.

> Upon agen the nadder *rowe,*
> And breide awei his right browe.
>> *Beves of Hamtoun,* p. 61.

(2) Rough. Rough-cast is still called *row-cast* in many places.

> He was wonderliche strong,
> Rome thretté fete long:
> His berd was bothe gret and *rowe,*
> A space of a fot betwene is browe!
>> *Beves of Hamtoun,* p 91.

> I had better bee hanged in a withie, or in a cowtaile, then be a *rowfooted* Scot, for thei are ever fare and fase.   *Bullein's Dialogue,* 1573, p. 3.

> Bot it was blacker
> Than another, and wel *rower.Arthour and Merlin,* p.38.

(3) A red ray of light. "The *rowis* red of Phebus light," Chaucer.

ROWELL. The circular wheel of a spur; a spur; anything circular. (*A.-N.*)

> The *rowelle* whas rede golde with ryalle stonys,
> Raylide with reched and rubyes i-newe.
>> *Morte Arthure, MS. Lincoln,* f. 87.

ROWENS. After-grass. *Suffolk.*

ROWET. Old withered grass. *South.*

ROWL. A wake, or fair. *Exmoor.*

ROWLAND. See *Oliver* (2).

> But to have a *Rowland* to resist an Oliver, he sent solempne ambassadors to the kyng of Englande, offeryng hym hys doughter in mariage.
>> *Hall, Henry VI.* f. 84.

ROWLAND-HO. A Christmas game.

ROWNEY. Thin, uneven, as cloth; having some threads stouter than others. *East.* "Rowy or stricky, as some stuffs are," Howell.

ROWORGIN. An organ. *Northumb.*

ROWS. The galleries, ranges, or walking places, raised and covered over, having shops on both sides, along the public streets in Chester. Kennett, MS. Lansd. 1033.

ROWTH. A root. *Yorksh.*

ROWTY. Rank, said of grass. It occurs in Harrison's Britaine, pp. 110, 221.

ROW-UP. To devour. *Cumb.*

ROWƷE. Rough. (*A.-S.*)

Hys body is awey dwyned,
And fore grete cold al to-schend.
Hys berd was both blake and *rowƷe*,
And to hys gyrdell sted it drewƷe;
He cane telle off grete care
The suffyre x. wynter and more.
MS. Ashmole 61, xv. Cent.

He shal do the see be *rowƷe*,
And also to be smethe i-nowƷe.
Cursor Mundi, MS. Coll. Trin. Cantab. f. 132.

ROXALL. To wrestle. *I. of Wight.*

ROXT. Rotten; decayed; applied to apples and pears. *West.*

ROY. (1) A king. (*A.-N.*)

In the kalendes of Maye this caas es befallene
The *roy* ryalle renownde with his rownde table.
Morte Arthure, MS. Lincoln, f. 78.

(2) To swagger; to boast; to indulge in convivial mirth. *North.*

ROYAL-MERCHANT. In the thirteenth century the Venetians were masters of the sea; the Sanudos, the Justiniani, the Grimaldi, &c. all merchants, erected principalities in several places of the Archipelago, which their descendants enjoyed for many generations, and thereby became truly and properly *royal merchants;* which, indeed, was the title generally given them all over Europe. *Warburton.* The phrase occurs in old plays.

ROYALS. (1) Taxes. *South.*

(2) Gold pieces worth fifteen shillings.

ROYATOUR. A dissipated sharper.

ROYNISH. Mangy; scabby. (*Fr.*) Metaphorically, mean, low, base. "The sloven and the careless man, the *roynish* nothing nice," Tusser, p. 289. "The roynish clown," the base clown, Shakespeare. "Such a *roinish* rannel," Harvey, 1593. Mr. Hunter imagines it to mean *obtrusive, troublesome,* in Shakespeare, on a misinterpretation of a single passage. Parkinson, speaking of plants suitable for borders for flower-beds, says of the germander, that on account of its disposition to spread itself, it must be taken up and new set once in three or four years, "or else it will grow too *roynish* and troublesome." *Roynish* here means *coarse;* and *troublesome* is used in a somewhat peculiar sense.

ROYSTER. An inventory. *Yorksh.*

ROYTHER. The same as *Roister,* to behave turbulently; to make noise and confusion. *Yorksh.* See *Roist.*

ROZIM. A quaint saying. *West.*

RUB. (1) Any unevenness of surface. Metaphorically, an imperfection. The term was much used at bowls. "Like a bowle that runneth in a smooth allie without anie *rub,*" Stanihurst, p. 18. To rub, to touch another ball or the jack.

(2) A sand-stone for a scythe. "The rub or brickle stone which husbandmen doo occupie in the whetting of their sithes," Harrison, p. 235. Still in use.

(3) To do work hastily.

(4) A slight reproof. *Var. dial.*

RUBBACROCK. A filthy slattern. *West.*

RUBBAGE. Rubbish. *Var. dial.*

RUBBELL. Refuse of mason's work, broken stones, &c. "*Cæmentitius,* made of masons woorke, or of morter, or of *rubbell* and broken stones," Elyot, ed. 1559. "Cary away *rubbell* or brokell of olde decayed houses," Huloet, 1552. It is explained in the Herefordshire Glossary, p. 88, "a mixture of stones and earth in a quarry;" and the term is now applied to various sorts of gritty rubbish. "Rubble, as morter and broken stones of old buildings," Baret, 1580.

RUBBER. (1) Same as *Rub* (2).

(2) An instrument used for cleaning various parts of the dress.

(3) A limited series of games by which the stakes are reckoned. "Rubbers at bowls," Poor Robin's Visions, 1677, p. 132.

RUBBERS. At bowls, are two bowls that rub or touch each other.

RUBIFY. To make red. It occurs in Ashmole's Theat. Chem. Brit. 1652, p. 188. Shakespeare has *rubious,* red.

RUBINS. Rubies. (*A.-N.*)

RUBOWRE. Redness. (*A.-N.*)

RUBRICK. Red ochre.

The same in sheeps milke with *rubricke* and soft pitch, drunke every day or eaten to your meate, helpeth the ptisicke, and obstructions. Anatolius approved beane meale sifted and sod with harts marrow to be given to a horse which stalleth blood for three daies together.
Topsell's Beasts, 1607, p. 132.

RUCK. (1) To repent. *Linc.*

(2) A heap. Also a verb, to gather together in heaps. *Var. dial.* "There in another *rucke,*" Drayton's Poems, p. 5.

(3) To crease linen. Also a substantive, a fold, plait, or crease. *Var. dial.*

(4) To go about gossiping. *Linc.*

(5) A rut in a road. *Heref.*

(6) A small heifer. *Somerset.*

(7) To huddle together. *Chesh.*

(8) A gigantic bird, the same with the *rock* of the Arabian tales.

(9) To squat, or crouch down. *North.* Palmer has *ruckee,* to cower, to stoop, to squat.

But now they *rucken* in hire neste,
And resten as hem liken beste.
Gower, MS. Soc. Antiq. 134, f. 114.

Thai sal for thryste the hefed sowke
Of the neddyr that on thaime sal *rowke.*
Hampole, MS. Bowes, p. 198.

RUCKET. To rattle. *Oxon.*

RUCKING. A hen is called a *rucking* hen, when she wants to sit, probably from the noise she makes at that time. *Linc.*

RUCKLE. (1) To rumple. See *Ruck* (3).

(2) A struggle. *Kent.*

RUCKLING. The least of a brood.

RUCKSES. Racks. *North.*

RUCKSTIR. To stir about; to make a great stir or fuss. *Warw.*

RUCTION. An uproar. *Westm.*

RUD. (1) Ruddle for sheep. *North.*

(2) A reed. *Somerset.*

(3) A material for garters.

(4) To rub; to polish. *Devon.*

RUDDE. Complexion. (*A.-S.*)

RUDDER. (1) A sieve. *Dorset.*

(2) Copulation. *Somerset.*

RUDDERISH. Passionate; hasty. *West.*

RUDDLE. (1) Red. The red ochre with which sheep are marked is called *ruddle.*

His skin, like blushes which adorn
The bosom of the rising morn,
All over *ruddle* is, and from
His flaming eyes quick glances come.
Baker's Poems, 1697, p. 11.

(2) To make a fence of split sticks plaited across one another. *Kent.*

RUDDLE-WATTLE. A hurdle made of small hazle rods, interwoven. *Kent.*

RUDDOCK. (1) The redbreast. (*A.-S.*) See a list in Harrison's England, p. 223.

(2) *Red ruddocks,* gold coin.

(3) A kind of apple. *Howell.*

RUDDOCKS. The fibrous parts of tallow which will not melt. *North.*

RUDESBY. A rude person. *Shak.*

RUDGE. A partridge. *Cornw.*

RUDGE-TIE. A chain lying over the ridge-tree to hold up the shafts of a waggon or cart. *Dorset.*

RUDGE-WASH. Kersey cloth made of fleece-wool, worked as it comes from the sheep's back, and not cleansed after it is shorn.

RUDLE. (1) A riddle. *Yorksh.*

(2) A beverage composed of warm beer and gin, sugar, and lemon peel.

RUD-STAKE. The piece of wood to which an ox in his stall is tied. *Durham.*

RUDY. Rude. *Sussex.*

RUE. (1) To sieve corn. *Devon.*

(2) A young goat. *Somerset.*

RUE-BARGAIN. A bad bargain. When a man withdraws his banns of marriage, he considers it a *rue-bargain. North.*

RUEL-BONE. Is mentioned by Chaucer, and in the following passage, as the material of a saddle. It is not, of course, to be thence supposed that ruel-bone was commonly or even actually used for that purpose, both instances occurring in romance poems. In the Turnament of Tottenham, Tibbe's garland is described as "fulle of ruelle bones," which another copy alters to *rounde bonys.* In the romance of Rembrun, p. 458, the coping of a wall is mentioned as made "of fin *ruwal,* that schon swithe brighte."

Hir sadille was of *rewylle bone,*
Semely was that sight to se,
Stifly sette with precious stone,
Compaste aboute with crapoté.
MS. Cantab. Ff. v. 48, f. 116.

RUELLES. Wrinkles.

RUFF. (1) A roof. *Var. dial.*

(2) Said when a hawk hits her prey, but does not fix it.

(3) An old game at cards. "At trump or ruff," Florio, p. 39. These were not, however, the same game. At ruff "the greatest sorte of the sute carrieth away the game," Peele, i. 211, note. *Ruff* was also a term for a court-card. To ruff, to trump at cards, Florio, p. 452, in v. *Ronfàre.*

(4) A kind of frill, formerly much worn by both sexes. The hand-ruff as a ruff adjoined to the wristband of the shirt.

(5) The height, or extremity.

(6) Rough. *Palsgrave.*

And when th'art wearie of thy keeping sheepe,
Upon a lovely downe, to please thy minde,
Ile give thee fine *ruffe-footed* doves to keepe,
And pretie pidgeons of another kinde.
The Affectionate Shepheard, 1504.

RUFFATORY. A rude boisterous boy, fond of horse-play, knocking and shoving his play-fellows about at all risks.

RUFFET. Furze. *Dorset.*

RUFFIAN. The devil. A cant term.

RUFFIAN'S-HALL. "So that part of Smithfield was antiently called, which is now the horse-market, where tryals of skill were plaid by ordinary ruffianly people with sword and buckler," Blount, p. 562.

RUFFINER. A ruffian. *North.*

RUFFLE. (1) To draw into plaits. The ruffle of a boot was the top when turned down and scalloped, or in a manner plaited.

His crisping and frizling irons must be used; his bald head with a *ruffling* periwig furnished.
The two Lancashire Lovers, 1640, p. 263.

(2) To swagger, or bully. Hence *ruffler,* a swaggerer, in reality a coward.

Are yea billing? what, my man Lob
Is become a jolly *ruffler?*
You are billing. you! I must be faine
To be a snuffler.
Mariage of Witt and Wisdome, 1579.

(3) A tumult; a bustle; discord.

RUFFMANS. Woods, or bushes. A cant term, occurring in Dekker's Belman, 1616.

RUFF-PECK. Bacon. A cant term.

RUFF-TREE. The roof-beam of a house.

RUFO. Rueful. *Lanc.*

RUFTER-HOOD. Among falconers, a plain leather hood, large and open behind, to be worn by a hawk when she is first drawn.

RUFULLICHE. Ruefully. (*A.-S.*)

RUG. (1) Same as *Rogge,* q. v.

(2) Snug; warm. *Devon.*

RUGE. (1) To wrinkle. *Somerset.*

(2) To slide down a declivity; to sweep away quickly. *Devon.*

RUGGE. The back. See *Rig*.

> To bere ane bok at heore *rugges*,
> And ane staf in heore hond.
> > *MS. Laud.* 108, f. 125.

> The knyght to the bore ys gon,
> And clevyth hym be the *rugge-bone*.
> > *MS. Cantab.* Ff. ii. 38, f. 66.

RUGGLE. (1) " To *ruggle* about," a term used in Kent by old people and invalids, and appears to imply walking and getting about; a lame person would say, " I'm troubled to *ruggle* about." *Kent*.

(2) To play the hurdy-gurdy.

(3) A child's rattle. *Devon*.

RUGGY. Rough. *Chaucer*.

RUID. Strong; violent.

> *Ruyd* armes as an ake with rusclede sydes.
> > *Morte Arthure, MS. Lincoln*, f. 65.

RUIN. A woodman's term, signifying a pole of four falls standing. At the first fall, it is a plant or wicket; at the second, a white pole; at the third, a black pole; and at the fourth, a *ruin*.

RUINATED. Reduced to ruin. *Var. dial.* It is also an archaism.

RUISE. To drive away. *Devon*.

RULE. (1) Tumultuous frolicsome conduct; a rough or lively sport. " Now I will go see what rule they keep, *nunc in tumultum ibo*," Coles. The primitive meaning is *behaviour*.

(2) To fall out, said of corn or any grain over-ripe. *Somerset*.

(3) To swap, or barter. *Devon*.

(4) To sit in strange postures. *West*.

RULE-STONE.

> ȝe, than seyd the *rewle-stone*,
> Mayster hath many fone;
> And ȝe wold helpe at his nede,
> My mayster schuld the better spede,
> Bot whatsoever ȝe brage our boste,
> My mayster ȝet shall reule the roste.
> > *MS. Ashmole* 61.

RULY. Rueful. (*A.-N.*)

> Whe[n] I gan my-selve awake,
> *Ruly* chere I gane to make,
> Fore I saw a sembly syȝt;
> To-werd me come a gentyll knyȝt,
> Wele i-armyd at all ryȝht,
> And bad I schuld upon hyȝeng,
> Come speke with hys lord the kyng.
> > *MS. Ashmole* 61, xv. Cent.

RUM. (1) Odd; queer. *Var. dial.*

(2) Old-fashioned rubbish. *Devon*.

RUM-BARGE. Warm drink. *Yorksh*. Probably corrupted from *Rambuze*, q. v.

RUMBELOW. A very favorite burden to an ancient sea-song. The burden of the Cornwall furry-day song is, " With halantow rum-below."

RUMBULLION. A great tumult. *Devon*.

RUMBUR. A run before leaping. *Cumb*.

RUMBUSTICAL. Boisterous. *Rumgumptious* is also used. *Var. dial.*

RUM-DUKE. An odd grotesque figure.

RUM-KIN. A tailless fowl.

RUMMAGE. Lumber; rubbish. *West*.

RUMMEL-GUMSHON. Wit; sense.

RUMMEN. To move or tumble any things out of their place. *Yorksh*.

RUMMET. Dandruff. *Cornw*.

RUMMLE. To rumble. *North*.

RUMMUETON. To whisper; to mutter.

RUMNEY. Budge fur. (*A.-N.*)

RUMP. To turn the back to one.

RUMP-AND-STUMP. Entirely; completely. *Linc*.

RUMPED. Acrid; rancid. *Devon*.

RUMPLE. A large debt, contracted by little and little. 'Twill come to a rumple, or breaking, at last. *Somerset*.

RUMPLED-SKEIN. Anything which is in great confusion. *West*.

RUMPUS. A noise; an uproar. *Var. dial.*

RUMSTICH. The game of mawe. (*Germ*.)

RUN. (1) To sew slightly. *Var. dial.* To run stockings, to darn or mend them.

(2) *To run a rig*, to play a trick. *To run together*, to grow like one another. *To run upon one*, to assail him. *To run against*, to calumniate. *To give one the run of his teeth*, to maintain him. *To run counter*, to go contrary to our wishes, a phrase borrowed from the chase. *To run down*, to abuse, to depreciate. *To run on the hirl*, to run about idly. *To run thin*, to go from a bargain.

(3) To guess; to suppose. *North*.

(4) To hazard; to run a hazard.

RUNAGATE. A runaway. *Kent*.

RUNAWAY-CROP. A thin or bad crop of corn or turnips. *I. of Wight*.

RUNCH. Wild mustard, or radish. *Runch-balls*, dried charlock. *Cumb*.

RUNDEL. (1) A moat with water in it. Sometimes, a small stream.

(2) A hollow pollard tree. *West*. It here seems to mean a young tree.

> The little *rundles* in shrowdes, which are come to their full growth (which will be about eighteen yeares.)   *Aubrey's Wilts, MS. Royal Soc.*

RUNE. A water-course. *Somerset*.

RUNG. (1) A staff. *North*.

(2) Ringed, as sows are.

(3) To run or go?

> As for salt water to become fresh by percolation through sand, 'tis a vain and frivolous opinion now exploded, for the dissolved salt being incorporated with the water, will *rung* along with it, and pass thorough as well as fresh water.
> > *Aubrey's Wilts, MS. Royal Soc.* p. 107.

RUNGE. A long tub. *Lanc*. Ray explains it a flasket.

RUNISH. Violent; fierce; rough.

RUNKLE. To crease; to wrinkle. *North*. *Runkylle* occurs in Nominale MS.

RUNNABLY. Currently; smoothly. *East*.

RUNNEL. Same as *Rundel*, q. v.

RUNNER. An upper millstone.

> And somtimes whirling, on an open hill,
> The round-flat *runner* in a roaring mill.
> > *Du Bartas*, p. 14.

RUNNING. (1) Rennet. *Devon*.

(2) Consecutively. *Var. dial.*

(3) Moveable. "A running campe," Stanihurst's Ireland, p. 56.

RUNNING-BOYS. Jockeys; boys who rode the king's racing horses.

RUNNING-BULL. A string of iron, an inch or more in diameter, fixed on a cross-bar in the front of the harrow, reaching almost, but not quite, from side to side.

RUNNING-FITTER. A fitter's deputy.

RUNNING-LEATHER. His shoes are made of running leather, i. e. he is given to rambling about. A very common phrase.

RUNNING-POITRAL. A breast leather.

RUNNING-SHOES. Pumps.

RUNNULUS. Rennet. *Heref.*

RUN-OUT. To grow, or sprout. *Devon.*

RUNT. (1) The rump. *North.*

(2) An ox. "A yongue *runt*, steere, or heafer," Florio, p. 63. The term is applied in contempt to an old woman, and was formerly said of a rough rude person of either sex. Brockett calls it, a jocular designation for a person of strong though low stature. "A dwarf," Tim Bobbin Gl. " An old runt, *vetula*," Coles.

(3) The stump of underwood. Also, the dead stump of a tree. *Var. dial.* Also, the stem of a plant.

RUN-TO-SEED. Enceinte. *Var. dial.*

RUNTY. (1) Surly; rude. *East.*

(2) Dwarfish; little. *Yorksh.*

RURD. Noise; clamour. *Gawayne.*

RURFIN. A ringleader. *Somerset.*

RUSCHE. To dash or throw down.

> And seyne ryde in by Rone, that rynnes so faire,
> And of alle his ryche castelles *rusche* doune the walles. *Morte Arthure, MS. Lincoln, f. 67.*

RUSE. (1) To slide down a declivity with a rustling noise. *Devon.*

(2) To extol. See *Ruysand.*

RUSH. (1) A small patch of underwood; a disease in cattle. *Northumb.*

(2) A feast, or merry-making. *North.*

(3) "The rush, weeke, or match, that mainteineth the light in the lampe," Baret's Alvearie, fol. Lond. 1580, R. 481.

RUSH-BEARING. The wake or day of a church's dedication is, in the West Riding of Yorkshire, called a rush-bearing, from the circumstance of carrying rushes to adorn the church. Kennett, MS.

RUSH-BUCKLER. A swash-buckler.

RUSHIN. A tub of butter.

RUSHING. A refreshment. *North.*

RUSH-RING. A custom extremely hurtful to the interests of morality appears anciently to have prevailed, both in England and other countries, of marrying with a rush ring; chiefly practised, however, by designing men, for the purpose of debauching their mistresses, who sometimes were so infatuated as to believe that this mock ceremony was a real marriage. *Brand.*

RUSINGES. Boastings.

> And of this false grounde sprynges errours and

herysyes, false prophecyes, presumpcyons, and false *rusynges*, blasfemyes and sclandirynges.
MS. Lincoln A. i. 17, f. 221.

RUSKES. Roots. *Robson.*

RUSPICE. A kind of red wine.

RUSSE. A Russian.

RUSSEL. A kind of satin.

RUSSETING. Coarse cloth of a dingy brown colour. Hence the term was applied to a clownish person, one clothed in russet.

> He must chaunge his *russetting*
> For satin and silke,
> And he must weare no linnen shirt
> That is not white as milke,
> To come of a well borne familie.
> *Tarlton's Horse-loads of Fooles.*

RUST. (1) To roost. *Palsgrave.*

(2) The mildew of wheat. *Devon.*

RUST-BALLS. Yellow lumps of iron ore found among chalk near Foulmire, in Cambridgeshire.

RUST-BURN. The plant restharrow. *North.*

RUSTICOAT. A countrified person.

RUSTILER. A raft. (*A.-N.*)

RUSTY. (1) Filthy. *Rustynes*, filthiness, occurs in Cov. Myst. p. 47.

(2) Restive; unruly. *Var. dial.*

RUSTY-FUSTY-DUSTY. Excessively dirty; begrimed with dust and filth.

> Then from the butchers we bought lamb and sheep,
> Beere from the ale-house, and a broome to sweepe
> Our cottage, that for want of use was musty,
> And most extremely *rusty-fusty-dusty.*
> *Taylor's Workes, 1630, ii. 24.*

RUT. (1) To be maris appetens.

> Thei sleeth and hurteth and fighteth with ayther other, whan thei beth in *rutte*, that is to say, in hure love. *MS. Bodl. 546.*

(2) To keep a rut; i. e. to be meddling and doing mischief. *Kent.*

(3) The dashing of the waves. *Chesh.*

(4) To throw; to project; to cast.

RUTE. "He *rutes* it, *Chesh.*, spoken of a child, he cries fiercely, i. e. he rowts it, he bellows," Ray's English Words, 1674, p. 39. The word appears to be now obsolete.

RUTHE. Pity; compassion. (*A.-S.*)

RUTSELE. To slip, or slide. (*Dut.*)

RUTTEN. (1) To snore. (*A.-S.*)

(2) A stick used in beating up porridge or batter. *Yorksh.*

RUTTER. (1) A directory to show the proper course of a vessel.

> I, Mr. Awdrian Gilbert, and John Davis, went by appointment to Mr. Secretary to Mr. Beale his howse, where onely we foure were secret, and we made Mr. Secretarie privie of the N. W. passage, and all charts and *rutters* were agreed uppon in generall. *Dr. Dee's Diary, p. 18.*

(2) Properly, a rider or trooper, from the German; but the term was usually applied to a fine, dashing, boasting gallant; one so fashionable as to speak much in foreign languages.

> Some authors have compared it to a *rutter's* codpiece, but I like not the allusion so well, by reason the tyings have no correspondence; his mouth is allwaies mumbling, as if hee were at his mattens; and his beard is bristled here and there like a sow.
> *Lodge's Wit's Miserie, 1596.*

RUTTING-TIME. Time of copulation.

> They have but one braunch growing out of the stem of their horne, which is not bigger then a mans finger, and for this cause, in the *rutting-time*, when they joyne with their females, they easily overcome the vulgar hart, with his branched and forked hornes. *Topsell's Four-Footed Beasts*, 1607, p. 122.

RUTTLE. To rattle. *Var. dial.*

> Then was *rutlynge* in Rome, and rubbynge of helmes. *MS. Cott. Calig.* A. ii. f. 111.

RUTTLING. A ruttling in the throat is the gurgling sound occasioned by difficulty in respiration. *South.*

RUWET. A small trumpet. " Ruet, *cornu*," MS. Dictionary, dated 1540.

RUYSAND. Exulting; boasting. *North.*

> Connynge es that makes a man of gude noghte *ruysand* hyme of his reghtewysnes, bot sorowand of his synnys. *MS. Lincoln* A. i. 17, f. 196.

RUZURE. The sliding down of a hedge, mound of earth, bank, or building. *Devon.*

RUZZOM. An ear of corn. *Yorksh.*

RUƷE. Rye. Wright's Pol. Songs, p. 152.

RYE. A disease in hawks which causes the head to swell.

RYNGSED. Cleansed; renovated. This occurs in MS. Bib. Reg. 12 B. i. f. 75.

RYNT. " *Rynt ye*, by your leave, stand handsomly; as, rynt you, witch, quoth Besse Locket to her mother," Ray's Words, ed. 1674, p. 39. The older form of this word is *aroint* (q. v.) and its proper explanation is of so much importance, that I am tempted to give the following extract from a MS. communication transmitted to me by a native of Lancashire. " The word *roint* is, or was thirty years ago, a common Lancashire provincialism. I have heard it used, scores and scores of times, in a sense I will presently state. But first as to its orthography; if I had never seen the word, and been asked to spell it from hearing it pronounced, I should certainly have written *roynt*, for though to a southern the sound would be much more like *rynt*, yet one accustomed to the dialect would know that the *o* was not altogether lost, any more than it is in *royal, loyal, boy*, which are pronounced in a somewhat similar way; the lost *o* to me has no difficulty in being distinguished as incorporated in the force given to the pronunciation of the *r*. Now as to the sense in which the word is applied, I must premise that in the part of the country in which I was born, it is usual (except in the summer season) to milk the cows in what is called a shippon; these shippons have what are called *boosts* (stalls similar to those in a stable, only wider, and the sides are lower); each boost accommodates *two* cows. When the milkmaid comes with her pail and stool, it frequently happens that the cow is standing close to the right hand division or partition of the boost, so that no space is left for her to plant her milking stool; sometimes the cow obstinately resists gentle means used to induce her to move aside towards the left, when the milkmaid, losing her temper, uses the expression *roynt ta*, accompanied with a push against the side of the cow's rump, to force her to make the movement required. When used as a ' household' word, which it sometimes, though seldom, is, it denotes an angry and insulting mode of saying, ' stand aside, get out of my way,' or rather ' out of my gait.' This is the sense in which the proverb above given includes the expression."

Boucher, in v. *Aroint*, asserts that he has heard the word in Cheshire, but it was not always confined to that county. In Thoresby's letter to Ray, 1703, I find " *Ryndta*, used to cows to make them give way and stand in their stalls or booyses." This sufficiently confirms the explanation above given.

SA. (1) A large tub, or soe. " A saa or tebbe, *tina*," MS. Dict. A. D. 1540.

(2) A term in fencing?

> And as for single rapier, he values Monsieur with his *sa, sa*, as little as jack-pudding does a custard. *Poor Robin's Visions*, 1677, p. 15.

SAAG. Urine. *Dorset.*

SABATINES. Steel coverings for the feet; sometimes, slippers or clogs.

SABBED. Wet; saturated. *Sussex.*

SABRAS. Salve; plaster.

SAC-FRIARS. A fraternity of friars; the *fratres saccati.* Arch. iii. 129. They wore a coarse upper garment called *saccus.*

SACHELLES. Small sacks. (*A.-N.*)

SACHEVEREL. The iron door or blower to the mouth of a stove.

SACK. (1) *To get the sack*, to be turned off, or dismissed, a common expression with servants. *Sack and seam road*, a horse road.

(2) Sherry. The term was also given to any Spanish white wine. " Spanish wines, called *sacke*," Ord. and Reg. p. 300. A Malaga sweet wine was termed *Canary sack*. The term must not be confused with what is now termed *sack*, an entirely different wine.

(3) A loose upper garment; a kind of surtout. See *Sac-friars*. It was generally made of coarse materials, but Ben Jonson, ii. 465, mentions " the finest loose sacks the ladies use to be put in." Compare Peele, iii. 88, " Frumpton's wench in the frieze *sacke*," misprinted *seake*. " A sack, in Yorkshire, a shirt," Kennett, MS. Lansd. 1033.

SACK-BUT. A bass trumpet.

SACK-CIDER. A drink composed partly of sack and partly of cider.

SACKERSON. A famous bear kept at Paris Garden in Shakespeare's time. It is frequently mentioned by writers of that period.

SACKLE. To saunter about. *Linc.*

SACKLESS. Innocent; faultless; weak; simple; foolish. *North.*

SACK-POSSET. Was formerly eaten on the evening of the wedding-day, just before the company retired.

> And then they did foot it and toss it,
> Till the cook brought in the *sack-posset*,
> The bride-pye was brought forth,
> A thing of mickle worth,
> And so all, at the bed-side,
> Took leave of Arthur and his bride.
> *Song of Arthur of Bradley.*

To make a sack-posset.

Take two quarts of pure good cream, a quarter of a pound of the best almonds, stamp them in the cream and boil amber and musk therein; then take a pint of sack in a bason, and set it on a chafing-dish till it be blood warm; then take the yolks of twelve eggs, with four whites, and beat them very well together; and so put the eggs into the sack, and make it good and hot; let the cream cool a little before you put it into the sack; then stir all together over the coals, till it be as thick as you would have it; if you take some amber and musk, and grind it small with sugar, and strew it on the top of the posset, it will give it a most delicate and pleasant tast.
A True Gentlewoman's Delight, 1676, p. 10.

SACK-WHEY. Wine-whey. *Devon.*

SACRAMENT. An oath. (*Lat.*)

SACRARYE. A sacred place. (*A.-N.*)

> God ches thy wombe for his habitacle,
> And halowid it so clene in every coste,
> To make it *sacrarye* for his owen goost.
> *Lydgate, MS. Soc. Antiq.* 134, f. 27.

SACRE. (1) To consecrate. (*A.-N.*)

(2) A sacred solemnity. *Chaucer.*

SACREAR. A receptacle for relics.

SACRETTES. Small hawks? A kind of birds mentioned in Maundevile's Travels, 1839, p. 238. See *Saker* (1).

SACRING. "Sacryng of the masse, *sacrement*," Palsgrave. *Sacring-bell*, the small bell rung at different parts of the service during mass.

SAD. (1) Serious; discreet; sober.

> He set hym up and sawe their blside
> A *sad* man, in whom is no pride,
> Right a discrete confessour, as I trow,
> His name was called Sir John Doclow.
> *MS. Rawl.* C. 86.

(2) Heavy; applied to bread when the dough, through bad yeast or from not having been well kneaded, does not rise properly. *North.* "Sad bread, *panis gravis*," Coles.

(3) A deep dark colour. *North.* "Sadde colour" occurs in Palsgrave.

(4) Heavy, solid, close, firm, said of iron, stone, &c. *North.* "Sad or hard, *solidus*," Pr. Parv. MS. Harl. 221.

SAD-BAD. Very ill. *Var. dial.*

SADDEN. To harden; e. g. when, after a long frost, the roads by the thaw become very soft and miry, and, subsequently, drier and harder, they are said in the latter case to sadden, or to be *saddened*. *Linc.*

SADDER. "Fagot of *sadder* and rounde ctyckes, *cottret*," Palsgrave.

SADDLE. To impute to. *Var. dial.*

SADDLE-BACKED. Low backed. *South.*

SADDLE-TREE. The arson of a saddle.

SADDUED. Settled; made firm, as some timber is by standing.

SADE. To satiate. *West.* "To sade, cloy *satio*," Coles' Lat. Dict. in v.

SAD-IRONS. Smoothing-irons. *Staff.*

SADNESS. Gravity; seriousness.

SAFE. (1) Sure; certain. *Var. dial.*

(2) To secure; to make safe. *Shak.*

(3) To assuage; to alleviate. *Gawayne.*

SAFE-CONDUCT. A security or protection given by the prince under the broad seal, or by any other person in authority, most commonly for a stranger's quiet coming in and passing out of the realm. *Blount.*

SAFE-GUARD. A riding skirt; a large outer petticoat worn by females when riding to protect them from the dirt. *Var. dial.* "A kind of aray or attire reaching from the navill downe to the feete, like a womans *safegard*, or a bakers," Nomenclator, 1585, p. 167.

SAFFI. A catchpole. (*Ital.*)

SAFFLE. Dull; sad; melancholy. *Linc.*

SAFFRON. To tinge with saffron.

SAFT. Safety. *North.*

SAG. (1) To hang down heavily, as oppressed by weight. *North.*

> Sir Rowland Russet-coat, their dad, goes *sagging* everie day in his round gascoynes of white cotton.
> *Pierce Pennilesse*, 1592.

(2) To subside, as water. *Kent.*

(3) To decline in health. *East.*

(4) To crease, or wrinkle.

(5) A kind of reed. *Somerset.*

SAGE. A saw. *North.*

SAGE-CHEESE. A cheese provided at an accouchement. *Warw.*

SAGER. A lawyer. *Yorksh.*

SAGGARD. The rough vessel in which all crockery, fine or coarse, is placed when taken to the oven for firing. *Staff.*

SAGH. Saw. *Yorksh.*

SAGHE. Language; speech. It occurs in MS. Cotton. Vespas. D. vii.

SAGHETYLLE. To be reconciled. (*A.-S.*)

> I salle hym surelye ensure that *saghetylle* salle we never,
> Are we sadlye assemble by oureselfene ones.
> *Morte Arthure, MS. Lincoln*, f. 56.

> Alle the werld travelles to brynge thame to hande alle that thame nedis, so that thay may with more ryst better serve Godde, and with thaire haly dedis *saughetelynge* make bytwyx God and mane.
> *MS. Lincoln* A. L. 17, f. 239.

> What maner and with what thing
> May I gete thi *sauztelyng*.
> *Cursor Mundi, MS. Coll. Trin. Cantab.* f. 6.

SAGINATION. Fattening. (*Lat.*)

There remaine yet of this discourse of oxen two other necessary tractats, the one naturall and the other morral. That which is natural contayns the several uses of their particular parts: and first for their flesh, which is held singular for norishment, for which cause, after their labour which bringeth leannesse, they use to put them by for *sagination*, or [as it is sayd] in English for feeding, which in all countries hath a severall manner or custom.
Topsell's Four-Footed Beasts. p. 81.

SAG-LEDGE. A cross-bar to a gate. *East.*

SAID. Wearied; tired; quieted. *North.*

SAID-SAW. A proverb. *Palsgrave.*

SAIE. Saw. *Chaucer.*

SAILE. To assail. (*A.-N.*)

SAILING-WARE. Canvass cloth.

SAILLE. To leap. (*A.-N.*) Hence *sailours*, leapers, dancers.

SAILS. The wings of a hawk.

SAIL-WOUND. Twisted in the manner of windmill sails. *Beds.*

SAIM. (1) Lard; fat. *Var. dial.*

Tak the rute of horslue, and stamp it, and fry it in a panne with swyne *ssyme*, and wryng it owte, and do it in boistes. *MS. Linc. Med. f. 295.*

For rankelyng. Take the marow and the gresse of a male swyne, that is for to say the *sayme*, and fry et togedur, and lay therto, and it schal be hole. *MS. in Mr. Pettigrew's possession, xv Cent. f. 11.*

Sate barrelling up the droppings of her nose, in steed of oyle, to *sayme* wool withall, and would not adventure to spit without halfe a dosen of porrengers at her elbow. *Nash's Pierce Pennilesse, 1592.*

(2) A crack in crockery. *Linc.*

SAIN. Said. Still in use.

SAIND. A message. *North.*

SAINE. (1) Seen. *Chaucer.*

(2) To bless; to sanctify.

Smale stanes of the see *saynede* thou thare, And thay warre saphiri for sothe was nane swylke sene. *MS. Lincoln A. i. 17, f. 232.*

SAINT. (1) Cent, a game at cards. Lord North, in 1578, notes losing fifteen shillings "at *saint*," Archæologia, xix. 297.

Tut, he hath cards for any kind of game, Primero, *saunt*, or whatsoever name. *Rowlands' Humors Ordinarie, n. d.*

At what game shall we play, at *sant*, at primero, at trumpe? *The French Alphabet, 1615, p. 148.*

(2) A cincture, or girdle.

(3) *Saint Cuthbert's duck*, the eider duck. *Saint John's nut*, a double nut. *Saint Mary's nut*, a triple nut.

(4) Same as *Samite*, q. v.

SAINT-JOHN. See *Borowe.*

Stones brosten, the erth schoke, and dede folk ganne awake; That this is soth in holy boke, *Seynt Jone* to borow I take. With an O and an I. *Seynt Jone* I take *to borw*. Marie and Cristes passione us help a sorow. Amen. *MS. Ashmole 41, f. 134.*

SAINT-MONDAY. Monday is so called by some of the London mechanics, who often make that day a holiday.

SAINTOUR. A centaur? See p. 335, col. 1.

SAINT'S-BELL. The small bell of a church which called to prayer and other offices.

Her tongue is the clapper of the devil's *saints-bell*, that rings all into confusion; it runs round like a wheel, one spoak after another, and makes more noise and jangling than country steeples on the fifth of November. *Poor Robin's True Character of a Scold, 1678, p. 4.*

SAIR-TEMS. Hard labour attended with discouraging circumstances. *Northumb.* Corrupted from *sore times?*

SAIRY. Poor; helpless. *North.*

SAKE. (1) A land-spring. *West.*

(2) Strife; contention. (*A.-S.*)

Nai, queth Josian, at that *sake* Never eft ne schel his heved ake. *Beves of Hamtoun, p. 118.*

(3) Reason; cause. *Devon.*

(4) Guilt; sin. (*A.-S.*)

Synne and *sake*, shame and strif, That now over al the world is rif *Cursor Mundi, MS. Coll. Trin. Cantab. f. 8.* Forȝyve me that I dud ȝou take Into bondes withouten *sake*. *Cursor Mundi, MS. Coll. Trin. Cantab. f. 32.*

(5) To forsake. Still in use.

For sche *sakyth* owre lay. *MS. Cantab. Ff. ii. 38 f. 38.*

(6) To kill. (*A.-S.*)

SAKELET. A little sack, or bag.

SAKER. (1) The peregrine hawk. "Sacre a hauke, *sacre*," Palsgrave.

(2) A piece of ordnance of three inches and a half bore, weight of shot five pounds and a half. According to Harrison, p. 198, the weight of the saker was 1500 lbs.

We cam to Netley by the Gallion, whom we hayled with half a dosen *sacres*, and she us with as many. *MS. Addit. 5008.*

The cannon, blunderbuss, and *saker*, He was th' inventor of and maker. *Hudibras, I. ii. 355.*

SAKERINGE. The sacrament.

SALAMANDER. A large poker; a circular iron plate used for culinary purposes.

SALAMON. The mass. Dekker's Lanthorne and Candle-Light, 1620, sig. C. iii.

SALANDINE. The calcedony. (*A.-N.*)

SALD. Given; sold. (*A.-S.*)

SALE. (1) Hall.

Sone thay sembled in *sale*, Bathe kyuges and cardenale. *MS. Lincoln A. i. 17, f. 138.* When he had tolde this tale To that semely in *sale*, He hade wordis at wale. *Perceval, 1586.*

(2) To glad; to content. (*A.-N.*)

And as the snowe from Jubiter doeth falle Thorowe the force of Sagittarius bowe, And Zepherus doeth the floures *sale* On white blossomes when she doeth blowe. *Lydgate, MS. Ashmole 39, f. 35.*

(3) To sell. Octovian, 1909.

(4) The iron or wooden part of the collar of a cart-horse. *East.*

(5) *To set to sale*, to offer to any one. True Tragedy of Richard III. p. 23. "To set to sale, *venalem habere*," Coles.

Fayre lordings, if you list to heere A mery jest your mindes to cheere, Then harken to this mery tale, Was never meryer *set to sale*. *The Milner of Abington, n. d.*

SALERE. (1) A salt-seller. *Pr. Parv.*

(2) A solere or upper chamber.

They toke a basyn with watur clere, And they went up ynto a *salere*, And sett up a candulle bryghte Ovyr the pyes cage fulle ryghte. *MS. Cantab. Ff. ii. 38, f. 148.*

SALES. The upright stakes of a hurdle.

SALET. A light helmet. (A.-N.) "Salet of harnesse, *salade*," Palsgrave.

There was shotyng of gonnys and arows plenté,
There was showtyng and crying that the erthe did quake;
There was hewyng of harnes, peté, was to see,
For fere of that fray many man did shake!
There was tremelyng and turnyng, thayre woo did wake;
There was hewyng of helmettes and *salettes* also,
Hit pleisd God that season it shulde be soo.
MS. Bibl. Reg. 17 D. xv.

He never tawght his to weare nowther sword ne *sallett*,
But to preche abrode withowt staffe, scrypp, or walett.
Bale's Kynge Johan, p. 52.

SALEWE. To salute. (A.-N.)

Wiche on hir fete gunnen streit to goon
To Thessalie, and *salewe* there the kyng.
MS. Digby 230.

SALE-WORTH. Ready for sale.

SALFE. To save.

Thou *salfe* thi saules sare.
MS. Lincoln A. I. 17, f. 222.

SALGHE. A sallow, or willow. "A salghe or saly, *salix*," MS. Dict. A. D. 1540.

SALIED. Danced. Becon, p. 373.

SALISBURY-PLAIN. Aubrey, Royal Soc. MS. p. 173, gives the following Wiltshire proverb:

Salisbury Plain,
Never without a thief or twain.

SALK. The swipple or shorter part of a thrashing flail. *Yorksh.*

SALLE. (1) Soul. Nominale MS

To thi awyn *salle* be never on-kynd.
MS. Lincoln A. I. 17, f. 52.

(2) Shall. Still in common use. Brockett calls it a vulgarism.

That he scholde qwyte hym that dynt,
That he of his handes hynte;
Salle never this travelle be tynt. *Perceval*, 91.

SALLET. A salad. *Hall.*

SALLIS. Hog's-lard. *Glouc.*

SALLOT. Shall not. *North.*

SALLY. (1) A sallow, or willow. *West.*

Who that byldeth his howse all of *salos*,
And prikketh a blynde horsse over the folowes,
And suffereth his wif to seke many halos,
God sende hym the blisse of everlasting galos.
Reliq. Antiq. i. 233.

(2) To move, or run from side to side; to pitch forward. *Var. dial.*

(3) A tottering situation. *Sussex.*

(4) The serving, or pluffy part of a bell-rope. Batchelor, p. 142.

SALLY-WITHY. A willow. *Wilts.*

SALME. To sing psalms. It occurs in MS. Cotton. Vespas. D. vii.

SALMON-GUNDY. Apples, onions, veal, or chicken, and pickled herrings, minced fine, and eaten with oil and vinegar. Hence a nickname for a cook.

SALMON-SPRINT. A young salmon. *North.* Minsheu and Coles have *salmon-pele.*

SALSE. Sauce; seasoning.

SALSER. A salt-cellar. (*Lat.*)

SALSTER. A dealer in salt.

SALSUTTER. A kind of small fish, like a roach, but stouter in the body. *West.*

SALT. (1) Maris appetens. Also, a leap in a similar sense. *North.*

Then they grow *salt* and begin to be proud; yet in ancient time, for the more ennobling of their race of dogges, they did not suffer them to engender till the male were foure yeare old, and the female three: for then would the whelpes proove more stronge and lively. *Topsell's Beasts*, 1607, p. 139.

(2) At the ancient long dinner-table a large salt was placed in the middle, those sitting at the upper end being *above the salt*, and were the superior guests; the others were *below the salt*. This custom is often metaphorically referred to.

There is another sort worse then these, that never utter anything of their owne, but get jests by heart, and rob bookes and men of prettie tales, and yet hope for this to have a roome *above the salt*.
Essayes by Cornwallyes, 1632, no. 13.

(3) A salt-cellar. *Var. dial.* "Salts of pure beaten gold," Middleton, v. 491.

(4) Pointed language. "She speaks with salt," Citye Match, 1639, p. 15. "Salt, a pleasaunt and merrie word that maketh folks to laugh, and sometime pricketh," Baret, 1580.

SALT-CAT. Same as *Cat* (1).

SALT-COTE. A salt-pit. Nominale MS. See Harrison's England, p. 240.

SALT-EEL. A game something like hide and find. The name of *Salt eel* may have been given it from one of the points of the game, which is to baste the runaway individual whom you may overtake all the way home with your handkerchief twisted hard for that purpose. *Salt-eel* implies, on board ship, a rope's ending, and on shore, an equivalent process. "Yeow shall have *salt eel* for supper," is an emphatic threat, referring to the back rather than to to the belly. *Moor.*

SALT-GEM. A kind of crystal salt.

SALTIMBANCO. A mountebank.

SALT-KIT. A salt-box. *North.*

SALT-PIE. (1) A box for salt. (2) A building of that form. *North.*

SALTS. Marshes near the sea flooded by the tides. *Sussex.*

SALT-STOLE. Some kind of dish. "*Ferculum*, a salt stole," Nominale MS.

SALT-WAJER. A salvager; one employed on the sea coast by the lord of a manor to see to his rights of salvage, wreck, or waif. *Suff.*

SALT-WEED. Toad-rush. *Suffolk.*

SALUE. To salute, or greet. (A.-N.)

Launcelott forth wendys he
Unto the chambyr to the quene,
And sette hym downe upon his kne,
And *salues* there that lady shene.
MS. Harl. 2252, f. 87.

Heyle, *saluyng* of seyntys in hevene.
MS. Cantab. Ff. ii. 38, f. 5.

SALUST. Saluted. *Gawayne.*

SALUTARY.

Mervel ȝe not of this makyng,
I me excuse, hit ys not y,
Hit ys Goddus worde and his techyng,
That he taȝt a *salutary.*
MS. Douce 302, xv. Cent.

SALUTE. According to Hall, fol. 43, Henry V.

in his eighth year, " caused a new coyne to be made called the *salute*, wherin wer the armes of Fraunce, and the armes of England and Fraunce quarterly."

SALVAGE. Savage; cruel.

And yf ȝe wiste what I am,
And oute of what linage I cam,
Ȝe wolde not be so *salvage*.
    Gower, MS. Soc. Antiq. 134, f. 240.

SALVE. To save. It occurs in the Triall of Wits, 4to. 1604, p. 217.

It myghte *salve* hyme of sore that sounde was nevere.
    Morte Arthure, MS. Lincoln, f. 63.

SAM. (1) To skim. *North.*
(2) To curdle milk. *North.*
(3) To put things in order. *Lanc.*
(4) To collect together. *North.* It is an archaism. See *Samned.*
(5) To stand *sam* for one, is to be answerable for him, to be his surety.

SAMARE. The skirt of a mantua.

SAMBUKE. A kind of harp. (*Lat.*)

SAMBUS. A saddle cloth. *Warton.*

Saumbues of the same threde,
That wroght was in the heythen thede.
    MS. Harl. 2252, f. 115.

SAMCAST. Two ridges ploughed together. *Cumb.*

SAMCLOTH. A sampler. There was also a sort of jacket so called.

SAME. (1) In *same*, together. (*A.-S.*)

They seyde, " God be at yowre game !"
He seyde, " Welcome alle *same* !"
He lete hymselfe then be gylyd.
They seyde, " Syr, ys hyt thy wylle
To come and speke owre kyng tylle,
Wyth wordys meke and mylde ?"
    MS. Cantab. Ff. ii. 38, f. 78.

That they myghte bothe in *same*
Wende to ther brodur, the Pope of Rome.
    MS. Cantab. Ff. ii. 38, f. 242.

Whan these oates gan *samen* glyde,
Withe vois and hydous hornys sownc.
    MS. Harl. 2252, f. 113.

(2) Shame ; wickedness. (*A.-S.*)

And thau thou saie me ani *same*,
Ne shal I the nouȝt blame.   *MS. Digby* 86.

SAMEKILL. So much ; as long as.

SAMEL. Gritty ; sandy. *North.*

SAMELIKE. Similarly. *North.*

And darkeden there in that den al that day longe,
Slepten wel swetly *samll* togadere.
    William and the Werwolf, p. 67.

SAMENAND. Gathering together. It occurs in MS. Cotton. Vespas. D. vii.

SAMI. Watery ; soft. *Beds.*

SAMITE. A very rich silk, sometimes interwoven with gold or silver thread.

Or was ther any velvet cremesyn ?
Or was ther any *samite* or satin ?
    Lydgate, MS. Soc. Antiq. 134, f. 25.

The mayden is redy for to ryde
In a fulle ryche aparaylmente
Off *samytte* grene with mykylle pryde,
That wroght was in the oryente,
    MS. Harl. 2252, f. 111.

SAMMARON-CLOTH. A cloth between flaxen and hempen, finer than one, and coarser than the other.

SAMMEN-BRICKS. Half-burnt bricks. *East*

SAMMODITHU. Tell me how you do. *Norf*

" The form of greeting or saluting among the common people in Norfolk and Suffolk, and seems to signifie as much as, So maist thou thrive," Kennett, MS.

SAMMY. (1) A fool. *Var. dial.*
(2) A short stride, giving an unfair advantage in the game of leap-frog.
(3) Close ; clammy ; heavy ; generally said of bread. *Salop.*

SAMNED. Assembled together.

Erles, kinges, lasse and more,
And fiftene kinges wer *samned* thore.
    Beves of Hamtoun, p. 67.

Alle were they *sampneds* appone a daye,
With grete solace and mekille playe.
    MS. Lincoln A. i. 17, f. 100.

SAM-OPE. Half open. *Devon.*

SAMPERE. Samphire. Elyot, 1559.

SAMPLARIE. Type ; first copy. (*A.-N.*)

SAMPLARS. Young trees left for standers upon the cutting down of under-wood. *Oxon.*

SAMPLETH. A sampler. *North.*

SAMPSON. A drink made of brandy, cider, sugar, and a little water. *Cornw.*

SAMPSON'S-POSTS. A mouse-trap, so formed that the little animal when caught is crushed to death. The name is also given to a kind of notched post. See Harrison, p. 185.

SAM-SODDEN. Sodden, or coddled, applied to meat not dressed enough. *Dorset.*

SAM-SODE. Half sewed, speaking of an ignorant person, half witted, stupid.

SANAPPUS. Hand-napkins. " *Manutergium, a sanope,*" Nominale MS.

Towellus of Eylyssham,
Whyȝth as the seeys fame,
Sanappus of the same,
Thus servyd thei ware.
    Sir Degrevant, 1387.

SANCEBELL. A Saint's-bell, q. v.

And with a trice trusse up thy life in the string of thy *sancebell.*   *Nash's Pierce Pennilesse,* 1592.

SANCITED. Ordained ; ratified.

SANCOME. A quagmire. *Yorksh.*

SANCTIMONY. Holiness. (*Lat.*)

SAND. Sound. *North.*

SAND-BLIND. Nearly blind. It is the translation of *berlue* in Hollyband's Dictionarie, 4to. 1593. Still in use.

SANDED. Short-sighted. *North.*

SANDENER. Red ochre.

Take powder of coperose, and of *sandener*, of eyther y-liche moche be weyȝt, and medle hem welle tcgedyr, and do hem in the wounde.
    MS. Med. Rec. xv. Cent.

SANDERS. Sandal wood.

SAND-GALLS. Same as *Galls,* q. v.

SANDGATE-RATTLE. A quick and violent stamping in vulgar dancing. *North.*

SANDISMENE. Messengers. (*A.-S.*)

Thou sees that the emperour es angerde a lyttille,
Yt semes be his *sandismene* that he es sore grevede.
    Morte Arthure, MS. Lincoln, f. 56.

SAND-TOT. A sand-hill. *Somerset.*

SANDWEED. Common spurrey. *Norf.*

SANDY-BREAD. Gritty bread; bread made of meal insufficiently sifted.

SANE. A medical composition, described in MS Linc. Med. f. 308.

SANG. (1) *By my sang*, a North country exclamation of revenge, or defiance. From *par la sangue Dieu*. *Sang is it*, indeed it is.

(2) A handful of corn. *Devon.*

(3) A song. *North.*

> Sangis faire of selouth ryme,
> Englisch, Frensch, and Latyne.
> *MS. Ashmole 60, f. 5.*

SANGAREE. Rack punch. Hence it is used as a term for a drunken bout.

SANGINARIE. The herb milfoil.

SANGING-EATHER. The large dragon-fly.

SANGLANT. Sanguinary. (*Fr.*)

SANGRAYLE. The holy vessel out of which the last Passover was eaten.

> The knightis of the table round,
> The *sangrayle* whan they had sought.
> *MS. Harl. 2252, f. 86.*

SANGRE. Singing.

SANGRONIE. Blood-red colour. *Sangwene*, a person of that colour. " Sanguine in grain," Harrison's England, p. 160.

> Off the *sangwene* also it is a synge,
> To be demuer, ryght curtes, and benigne.
> *MS. Cantab. Ff. i. 6, f. 140.*

SANK. (1) A great quantity. *Cumb.*

(2) Blood. (*A.-N.*)

SANNOCK. To cry bitterly. *Sanny* is also in use. *East.*

SANS. Without. (*Fr.*)

SANT. Providence. (*A.-S.*)

> Thay thanked God of his *sant*,
> Alle the tother syde.
> *MS. Lincoln A. i. 17, f. 134.*

SANZACK. The governor of a city.

SAP. (1) Ale. *Sheff.*

(2) To drench. *Yorksh.* Sappy drinking, protracted and excessive drinking.

(3) To put a sop or toast into liquor. Kennett, MS. Lansd. 1033.

SAPE. Soap. Nominale MS.

SAP-HEAD. A blockhead. *Craven.* Several glossaries have *sapscull.*

SAP-WHISTLE. A whistle made of a twig in sap, when the bark will peel off.

SAPY. (1) Moist; sodden. *West.*

(2) Sickly. (3) Foolish. *Var. dial.*

SAR. To serve; to earn. *West.*

SARADYN. The sardine stone.

> Some were of safewrs and some of *saradyn*,
> And some were emrodys fyne.
> *MS. Cantab. Ff. ii. 38, f. 221.*

SARCE. (1) Vegetables. *Essex.*

(2) A small hair sieve. " Sarce for spyce, *sas*," Palsgrave.

SARCELS. The extreme pinion feathers in a hawk's wing. *Holme.*

SARD. Futuo. " Go teach your grandam to *sard*, a Nottingham proverb," Howell, p. 17.

SARE. Withered; dry. In old writers it is *sear*. It is well though not generally known, that ash when green makes good firewood;

II.

and, contrary to all other perhaps, is bad for that purpose when dry. This is kept in mind by the following verse:

> Burn ash-wood green, 'tis a fire for a queen;
> Burn ash-wood sere, 'twool make a man sware.

(2) Tender; rotten. *Kent.*

(3) Much; very; greatly. *North.*

(4) Melancholy; bad; severe. *North.*

SARE-BANED. Stingy; unkind. *Yorksh.*

SARESBURY. Salisbury. (*Lat.*)

SAREY. Poor; pitiable. *Cumb.*

SARFIT. A table-cloth. *Devon.*

SARGENT. A sergeant. *Lydgate.*

SARGON. The fish gilthead.

SARK. (1) A shirt, or shift. *North.* It occurs in Nominale MS. xv. Cent.

(2) A porridge-pot. *Yorksh.*

SARKLE. To harrow, or rake. " To sarkle, *sarrire*, *sarculare*," Coles. " To sarkle, to harrow, or rake over againe," Florio, p. 444.

SARLINISH. A kind of silk. *Skinner.*

SARMONDE. A sermon. *Var. dial.*

> Your Lordships poore orator was commyng from the cathedrall church of Sarum, about the houer of aleaven of the clocke in the foore nowne, from the *sarmonde*. *Chancery Bills, Ff. 10, No. 53.*

SARN. A sort of oath. *Salop.*

SARNICK. (1) Inanimate. *East.*

(2) A small quantity. *Suffolk.*

SARPE. A girdle. " With a riche *sarpe* and garter," Rutland Papers, p. 4. " *Sarpys* of gold about their quarters," Morte d'Arthur, ii. 414. It also occurs in Hall.

SARPELERE. (1) A coarse packcloth made of hemp. *Glouc.* See Lydgate, p. 204, and Tyrwhitt's Gloss. in v. " *Segestre*, a sarplar or canvas to wrap up wares," Coles.

(2) " A sarplar of wool, a pocket or half a sack of wool; in Scotland a *serpliath*, which contains eighty stone," Kennett MS.

SARRA. To serve. *North.*

SARRAD. Sewed. *Yorksh.*

SARRANT. A servant. *Somerset.*

SARRE. Sorer; more sore. (*A.-S.*)

SARRELICHE. Closely. (*Fr.*)

> The knave taught her way sikerliche,
> Thai riden wel *sarreliche*.
> *Arthour and Merlin, p. 290.*

> It was nede for Cleodalis
> Stode on fot, and mani of his
> Aboute him stode *sarreliche*.
> *Arthour and Merlin, p. 224.*

SARS-A-MINE. A moderated and good-humoured sort of imprecation. *East.*

SARSENS. Round bolder stones. *Wilts.*

SARSIN. A Saracen. *Palsgrave.*

SARSNET. A thin slight kind of silk. " *Sarsenet* sylke, *taffetas*," Palsgrave.

> But, quoth he, there is no reason why Maries smocke shoulde be of *sarsnet*, seeing Joseph's breeches were not of silke.
> *Mar-Prelate's Epistle, p. 62.*

SART. Soft; softly. *Devon.*

SARTIES. Certainly; indeed. *North.* Apparently a corruption of the old word *certes*.

SARTIN. Certain. *Var. dial.*

45

SARTRIN. A kind of hoe.

SARVER. A scuttle for a stable.

SARY-MAN. An expression of pity.

SASARARA. A corruption of *certiorari*, a kind of legal writ. *Var. dial.*

SASIN. A reaping-hook. *Devon.*

SASSE. A lock in a river.

SASSIFAX. The meadow saxifrage.

SASSLE. Sleepy; drowsy. *Somerset.*

SAT. (1) Became. (*A.-N.*)

> Chosyn of God for to stynte oure stryfe
> Of all wommen by hirselfe allone,
> Wherfore it *sat* not hir to crie and grone.
> *Lydgate, MS. Ashmole 39, f. 52.*

(2) Opposed. (*A.-S.*)

SATE. Soft. *Dorset.* Hence *satepoll*, a soft-head, or silly fellow.

SATER. Saturday.

SATES. Quickset. *Salop.*

SATISFYINGLY. Contentedly.

> A long time before this, my wife and myself were admitted into the church at Kipping, with which we walked *satisfyingly* many years.
> *Lister's Autobiography, p. 50.*

SATLE. To fall; to hang down; to subside; to sag. *Yorksh.*

SATLED. Shackled; embarrassed.

SATTEN. The name of a dog.

SATTET. Quiet; settled. *Lanc.*

SATTIE. Matted together. *Northumb.*

SATTLE. To settle. *North.*

> Wharefore hafand reward and compassione of oure disesse, we beseke yow that ye late oure prayeres *sattelle* in your hert, and helpe for to succour us now at oure nede. *MS. Lincoln A. i. 17, f. 20.*

SATTY. A kind of frigate.

SATURDAY-STOP. A space of time in which of old it was not lawful to take salmons in Scotland and the North of England; that is, from evensong on Saturday till sun-rising on Monday. *Blount.*

SAUCE. (1) Impertinence. *Var. dial.* Also a verb, to be saucy, to abuse.

(2) To box the ears. *Yorksh.*

(3) To garnish; to adorn. *Devon.*

(4) To serve the same sauce, i. e. to treat in the same fashion.

> After him another came unto her, and served her with the same *sauce*: then a third: at last she began to wax warie.
> *The Man in the Moone telling Strange Fortunes, 1609.*

SAUCE-BOX. A saucy fellow. *Var. dial.* In old English we have *sauceling*.

SAUCE-JACK. An impudent fellow. Gifford apparently was unacquainted with the term. See Massinger, ii. 182.

> Nor Jacke of Dover, that grand-jury Jacke;
> Nor *Jacke Sawce*, the worst knave amongst the pack.
> But of the Jacke of Jackes, great Jacke a Lent,
> To write his worthy acts is my intent.
> *Taylor's Workes, 1630, i. 113.*

SAUCE-MADAME. A dish in ancient cookery, described in the Ord. and Reg. p. 432.

SAUCEPAN. To have the saucepan on the fire, i. e. to be ready to scold.

SAUCER-EYES. Large prominent eyes.

SAUCY. Dirty; untidy. *West.*

SAUF. (1) Safe. (*A.-N.*)

> The schelde of Pallas gan embrace,
> With whiche he covereth *sauf* his face.
> *Gower, MS. Soc. Antiq. 134, f. 41.*

(2) To save. MS. Cott. Vesp. D. vii.

(3) The willow, or sallow. *Yorksh.*

SAUFY. Wet, as land is. *North.*

SAUGH. The sallow willow. *North.*

SAUGHTE. Peace; quietness.

> They send it hyme sothely for *saughte* of the pople,
> Sekerly at that sesone with certayne knyghtez.
> *Morte Arthure, MS. Lincoln, f. 64.*

SAUL. (1) To beat. *Yorksh.*

(2) The solid substance in the inside of a covered button. *North.*

(3) A kind of moth. *North.*

SAULCERY. The department in the royal household which provided the sauces.

SAULT. To assault; to attack. *Palsgrave.*

SAUM. To walk lazily; to go dreaming on; to repeat anything too often. *Var. dial.*

SAUMBER. A covering for the arm.

> Helme, and brim, and hauberjoun,
> *Saumbers*, quissers, and aketoun.
> *Arthour and Merlin, p. 111.*

SAUMPLE. An example.

> By alle gode *saumple* men may see
> That very God ys in forme of brede.
> *MS. Cantab. Ff. ii. 38, f. 47.*

SAUNCE-BELL. A sacring-bell. See *Sacring*.

> Now what is love I will the tell.
> It is the fountaine and the well,
> Where pleasure and repentance dwell;
> It is perhaps, the *sancing-bell*,
> That rings all into heaven or hell.
> And this is love, as I heare tell.
> *Heywood's Rape of Lucrece, i. 3.*

SAUNDRES. Sandal wood. *Sandali, albi, et rubei, et citrini*, MS. Sloane 5, f. 10.

SAUNDRIS. Slanders.

> I may stonde in thilke rowe,
> Amonge hem that *saundris* use.
> *Gower, MS. Soc. Antiq. 134, f. 74.*

SAUN-FAIL. Without fail. (*A.-N.*)

> And went to Londen *saun fail*,
> Where the king, Sir Arthour,
> Was afong with gre[t] honour.
> *Arthour and Merlin, p. 126.*

SAUNT. To disappear; to vanish. *North.*

SAUNTER-WHEEL. A wheel which works facewise from a spur-wheel. *West.*

SAUR. Urine from the cow-house. *North.* Hence *saur-pool*, a stinking puddle. "Saur-pool, *graveolens*," Coles.

SAURIN. Vinegar. *Cumb.*

SAUSEFLEMED. Having red spots or scabs on the face. A medicine that "helith *sawse-flemed* vysagyes" is mentioned in a MS. of the xv. Cent. in Mr. Pettigrew's possession. It would appear from Arch. xxx. 412, to have sometimes engendered scabs.

SAUT. At peace; at friendship?

> Help, dame Sirith, if thou maut,
> To make me with the sueting *saut*,
> And ich wille geve the gift ful stark,
> Moni a pound and moni a marke.
> *Wright's Anec. Lit. p. 8.*

SAUTE. (1) To jump. (*A.-N.*)

(2) To assault. (3) An assault.

> Johne and Moch and Wylle Scathlok,
> For sothe as I yow say,
> Thir slew oure men upon oure wallis,
> And *sautene* us every day.
> *MS. Cantab.* Ff. v. 48, f. 130.

> For ofte tymys men talken of here travayle,
> Bothe of *sautys* and also of batayle.
> *Archæologia*, xxi. 48.

SAUTER. The Psalter. (*A.-N.*)

SAU3T. Peace. (*A.-S.*)

> Thei shul him take and deme to de3e
> Withouten any *sau3t*.
> *Cursor Mundi, MS. Coll. Trin. Cantab.* f. 93.

SAVE. (1) The herb sage. (*Lat.*)

(2) To house hay or corn. *Devon.*

SAVE-ALL. (1) A kind of candlestick formerly used for burning the ends of candles. " A sort of candlestick contrived to make the ends of candles useful; metaphorice, a very stingy fellow," MS. Devon Gl.

(2) A child's pinafore. *Cornw.*

SAVEGUARD. A wardrobe. *Devon.*

SAVELICK. The excrescence on the briar, so called because it is supposed by boys when worn about the arm to be an effectual charm against flogging.

SAVELOYS. Large sausages.

SAVEMENT. Safety; protection. (*A.-N.*)

> Save him fram cumberment,
> And him ogain bring in *savement*.
> *Gy of Warwike*, p. 134.

SAVERE. Saviour.

> This like mayden good and mylde
> Modir shal ben of a childe,
> Of hir shal com monnes *Savere*.
> *Cursor Mundi, MS. Coll. Trin. Cantab.* f. 66.

SAVERLY. By saving. *Tusser.*

SAVERS. The boys' cry of *halves!*

SAVERTH. Savoureth.

> Tharfore hys wysdom hys owne rede
> *Saverth* byt yn wyne and brede.
> *MS. Harl.* 1701, f. 66.

SAVETE. Safety. (*A.-N.*)

SAVIARDE. A kind of jacket, worn towards the end of the seventeenth century.

SAVOREN. To savour; to taste. (*A.-N.*)

SAVOUR. Knowledge. (*A.-N.*)

SAVOUROUS. Sweet; pleasant.

SAWCE. To make salt.

SAWCISTRE. A kind of sausage. " Lynke or sawcistre," Pr. Parv. p. 306. " A sawsyrlyng," Nominale MS.

SAWDE. Hire; pay. (*A.-N.*)

> I wolle ordeyn that everyche of you schalle have thirty m¹. men of armes for the whiche I schal paye their *sawde* for thre yere. *MS. Digby*, 185.

SAWDERS. Soldiers.

> They sayled over the salt see with *sawders* manye.
> *MS. Cott. Calig.* A. ii. f. 111.

SAWE. Speech; discourse. (*A.-S.*)

> Then was that herd a carful man,
> And never so sory as he was than,
> When he herd that *sawe*.
> *MS. Cantab.* Ff. v. 48, f. 55.

SAWL. Drink; liquor. *North.*

SAWNDER. Alexander.

SAWNDEVERE. Sandever.

> Anoynt the heved therwith ylk daye til he be hale, bot schafe the hede at the begynnynge, and gare it blede, and powdere the scalles with *sawndevere*. *MS. Lincoln* A. i. 17, f. 282.

SAWNEY. (1) Liquor. *Yorksh.*

(2) A silly fellow. *Var. dial.*

(3) Lucky; fortunate. *North.*

SAWSE. To carve a tench.

SAWSTIRE. A sausage. Nominale MS.

SAWTER-CRAWN. A silly fellow.

SAX. (1) A knife. *Linc.* " Nymeth 3oure saxes," Robert Glouc. Chron. p. 125.

(2) A satchel; a small sack.

SAY. (1) Saw. (*A.-S.*)

> To a clyfe of ston than rydyth hee,
> And *say* the bore come fro the see.
> *MS. Cantab.* Ff. ii. 38, f. 65.

> Thenne thei *say* that bare thei were,
> In welthe and joye that were clad ere.
> *Cursor Mundi, MS. Coll. Trin. Cantab.* f. 5.

(2) The same as *Assay* (4).

> I bequeth mi body to the colde seler,
> I wolde that a lady toke the *say* of me.
> *Wyl Bucks*, p. 4.

(3) A delicate serge, or woollen cloth. " Saye clothe, *serge*," Palsgrave.

(4) To try; to try on; to assay. As a substantive, a trial, a taste, a sample.

(5) An opinion. *Var. dial.*

(6) Give us something to say, i. e. give us a toast. *Kent.*

(7) Influence; sway. *North.*

(8) To say nay, i. e. to deny. Forby explains it, to refuse, to forbid.

(9) Song; speech. *Palsgrave.*

(10) *Say of it*, fast of it. *Suffolk.*

(11) Saint. *Gawayne.*

SAYMENT.

> Torrent sayd, so mot I the,
> And other *sayment* wolle I bee
> Ore I take ordor of knyght.
> *Torrent of Portugal*, p. 3.

SAY-NAY. A lamprey. *Lanc.*

SAYNE. Saint. " Sayne Johan the Evaungelist," MS. Lincoln A. i. 17, f. 231.

SAYSLANG. A long pole; a stang. It occurs in Hollyband's Dictionarie, 1593. Also spelt *saystang*, which is perhaps the correct form

SAY-SO. A mere nominal advantage.

SAYSTE. Sawest. (*A.-S.*)

> Ther dwellyth a yeaunt in a foreste,
> Soche oon thou nevyr *sayste* are.
> *MS. Cantab.* Ff. ii. 38, f. 64.

SAY3ERDE. A sail-yard. Translated by *antenna* in MS. Dictionary, A.D. 1540.

SCAB. An ape; a baboon. Metaphorically, a poor worthless fellow.

> This kinde of flatt'ry makes a whore take state,
> Growes pocky pround, and in such port doth beare her,
> That such poore *scabs* as I must not come neere her.
> *Taylor's Workes*, 1630, ii. 111.

SCABBARD. A mangy scabby person.

SCABLINES. Chippings of stone. *North.*

SCABRIDGE. The plant scabious.

SCABY. Stingy; shabby. *North.*

SCACE. Scarce. *Lydgate.*

SCAD. (1) Shed. MS. Devon Gloss.

And sayeth to day is venim sched
In holy chirche of temporalie,
Whiche medeleth with the spiritalie.
Gower, MS. Soc. Antiq. 134, f. 84.

(2) A carcase ; a dead body.

(3) The wild black plum. Sussex.

SCADDING-OF-PEAS. A custom in the North of boiling the common gray peas in the shell, and eating them with butter and salt, first shelling them ; a bean, shell and all, is put into one of the pea-pods ; whosoever gets this bean is to be first married. Generally called a Scalding of Peas. The company usually pelt each other with the pods. It is therefore called in the South Peas and Sport.

SCADDLE. (1) Thievish, generally in a petty way only ; used in contempt. Kent.

(2) Confusion ; mischief. North.

(3) Timid ; bashful ; shy. Yorksh.

SCADE. Severed. Gawayne.

SCADWYS. Shadows ; shady places. Loca umbrosa in silvis, Anglice schadwys, MS. Bib. Reg. 12 B. i. f. 18.

SCAFE. To run up and down ; to wander ; to lead a scampish vagabondly life : thus they say, "An't ye ashamed of yesen, scafing up and down about the country." Linc.

SCAFFEL. A small spade or skuppet used in draining, and in out-hawling or feying narrow bottomed ditches. It differs from a spade in not tapering toward the edge, and in having its sides slightly turned up. It has a cot for the handle like a scuppit. I never heard the word but in Suffolk, nor saw it but in Tusser. Moor's Suffolk Words, p. 352.

SCAFFERON. Part of the ancient caparisonment of a horse, mentioned in Hall's Union, 1548, Hen. IV. f. 12.

SCAFFLE. To scramble. Somerset.

SCAFFLING. An eel. Chesh.

SCAGE. To throw a stick. Yorksh.

SCAGGLE. Fearful ; timid. North.

SCAGGY. Rough ; shaggy. Glouc.

SCAIT. To have a diarrhœa. Devon.

SCAITHFUL. Given to breaking pasture. Also, liable to be run over by stock ; as open fields, &c. Norfolk.

SCALADO. A scaling of walls.

Yet all their talke is bastinado,
Strong armado, hot scalado.
Taylor's Dogge of Warre, p. 229.

SCALBEGRES. Herba Cristofori. List of plants in MS. Sloane 5, f. 5.

SCALD. (1) Scabby, particularly in the head. Hence used for mean, shabby, disgusting. A person infected with lues venerea was said to be scalded.

Other news I am advertised of, that a scald trivial lying pamphlet is given out to be of my doing.
Pierce Penilesse, 1592.

(2) A multitude. East.

(3) A patch in a barley field scorched and withered up. East.

(4) To scorch. Norf.

SCALD-CREAM. Cream raised by heat. West.

SCALDING. Partial. Oxon.

SCALDRAG. One who boils rags.

For to be a laundres imports onely to wash or dresse lawne, which is as much impeachment as to cal a justice of the peace, a beadle ; a dyer, a scald-ragge ; or a fishmonger, a seller of gubbins.
Taylor, ed. 1630, ii. 165.

SCALE. (1) To spread ; to disperse abroad. North. The term is an archaism. It is found in Hall, Richard III. f. 15, "sodenly scaled and departed." The word occurs in Coriolanus, i. 1, but is there a misprint for stale, as distinctly proved by Gifford, and still more elaborately in Dyce's Remarks, p. 158. The observations of Brockett on this passage, which he quite misunderstands, lead me to observe that, with a few trifling exceptions, the very worst annotations on Shakespeare have proceeded from the compilers of provincial glossaries, to whom the philological student would be more deeply indebted if they would confine themselves to the correct explanation of words in actual use, without entering into subjects that require a distinct range of reading and study.

(2) To weigh as in scales. "A scal'd pottle," a pottle of the right measure.

Plague, not for a scal'd pottle of wine.
The Honest Whore, I. 1.

(3) To throw at fruit on trees, as apples, walnuts, &c. South.

(4) To change. Dorset.

(5) A very steep hill. North.

(6) To beat. Yorksh.

(7) To stir the fire. North.

(8) A drinking-cup. Somerset.

SCALE-DISH. A milk-skimmer. North.

SCALE-IN. To plough in with a shallow furrow. Norf.

SCALES. The outermost cuts of a piece of timber with the bark on, not thick enough to be called planks. Devon.

SCALIS-MALIS. Cadiz. Skelton, ii. 195.

SCALL. A scale, or scab. (A.-S.)

SCALLAGE. A lich-gate. West.

SCALLARD. A scald-head.

SCALLEWORT. Centrum galli. List of herbs in MS. Sloane 5, f. 4.

SCALLIONS. A good beating. North.

SCALLOPS. An awkward girl.

SCALOUN. A shilling. Octovian, 1313.

SCALY. Mean ; stingy. Var. dial. In some places it means mischievous, thievishly inclined.

SCAM. A spot, or stain. North.

SCAMBLE. To scramble ; to shift. "Scamblingly, catch that catch may," Cotgrave.

Thus sithe I have in my voyage suffred wracke with Ulisses, and wringing-wett scambled with life to the shore, stand from moe, Nausicaa, with all thy traine, till I wipe the blot from my forhead, and with sweete springs wash away the salt froth that cleaves to my soule. Gosson's Schoole of Abuse, 1579.

SCAMBLED. Defeated ; balked. West.

SCAMBLING. Sprawling. Heref.

SCAMBLING-DAYS. Days in Lent, when no regular meals were provided, but every one scrambled and shifted for himself as he could.

SCAME. To hurt, or injure.

SCAMELS. This word, which occurs in the Tempest, and is most probably a misprint, has baffled all annotators on Shakespeare. *Sea-mell* is the generally received reading, but cannot be correct on account of the quantity of the first syllable. Mr. Dyce conjectures *staniels*, but surely a trisyllable cannot be right. Read *stannels*, and we may perhaps have the true word. "A stannel, *tinnunculus*," Coles. If I recollect rightly, this was one of the conjectures proposed by Theobald.

SCAMINE. The scammony.

SCAMP. A great rascal. *Var. dial.*

SCAN. To scoff; to scold. *Devon.*

SCANDAL-BROTH. Tea. *Var. dial.*

SCANDRET. A drunkard. *Worc.* I give this word on the authority of an anonymous correspondent.

SCANT. Scarce; insufficient. Also an adverb, as in the following passage:

And whan thei wil fighte, thei wille schokken hem togidre in a plomp; that ʒif there be 20,000 men, men schalle not wenen that there be *scant* 10,000. *Maundevile's Travels, p. 252.*

For mine owne part, I live not in such want
But that I eate and sleepe, though coyne be *scant*.
Taylor's Workes, 1630, ii. 112.

SCANTELOUN. A carpenter's measure. See Romaunt of the Rose, 7114.

Do we wel and make a tour
With squyre and *scanteloun* so even.
Cursor Mundi, MS. Coll. Trin. Cantab. f. 14.

Soft, ser, seyd the *skantylʒon*,
I trow ʒour thryft be wele ny done;
Ever to crewyll thou arte in word,
And ʒet thou arte not worth a tord:
Fore all the gode that thou gete myght,
He wyll spend it on a nyght.
MS. Ashmole 61, xv. Cent.

SCANTISH. Scarce. *North.*

SCANTITY. Insufficiency. *East.*

SCANTLE. To become scanty.

The chines of beefe in great houses are *scantled* to buie chains of gold; and the almes that was wont to releeve the poore, is husbanded better to buy new rebatoes. *Lodge's Wit's Miserie, 1596.*

SCANTLING. A portion of anything, generally meant as a specimen. "Scantlon of a clothe," Palsgrave. The size to which joiners intend to cut their stuff is called the *scantling.*

SCAPE. (1) A misdemeanour.

(2) To escape. (*A.-S.*)

Johan toke the munkes horse be the hed,
For sothe as I yow say;
So did Much, the litulle page,
For he shulde not *scape* away.
MS. Cantab. Ff. v. 48, f. 129.

xl. he had chaunged for oon,
Ther *skaped* but two away.
MS. Cantab. Ff. ii. 38, f. 74.

(3) A trick, shift, or evasion.

SCAPE-GALLOWS. A bad fellow, one who has narrowly escaped the gallows. *Scape-grace.* a hair-brained fellow. *Scape-thrift*, a thriftless fellow.

Off fidlers, pedlers, fayle scape slaves,
Of tinckers, turnecoates, tospot knaves,
Of theifes and *scapethrifts* many a one,
With bounsing Besse and jolly Joane,
Of idle boyes and journeymen,
And vagrants that the country runn.
MS. Harl. 1221, f. 99.

SCAPELLAR. A narrow piece of cloth worn by monks over the rest of their dress, reaching almost to the feet. "Skapplers and cootes," Skelton's Works, ii. 420.

SCAPLOREY. A scapulary.

SCAPPLE. To rough-hew, generally applied to stones. See Craven Gl. ii. 101.

SCAR. (1) Exposed to. *Sussex.*

(2) To scare, or frighten. *Linc.*

(3) A scarecrow. *Palsgrave.*

(4) A bare and broken place on the side of a mountain, or in the high bank of a river. *North.* Ray explains it " the cliff of a rock, or a naked rock on the dry land," and thinks it is the origin of the name of Scarborough The definitions here given do not, however quite convey the ancient meaning of *scar*, which must be interpreted a *precipice.* "Verie deepe *scarrie* rockes," Harrison's Britaine, p. 93. *Scarry*, full of precipices, Craven Glossary, ii. 102. "A scar, cliff, *mons præ-ruptus*," Coles. The passage in Shakespeare, "men make ropes in such a scarre," is difficult of explanation; but the old text, obscure as it is, is certainly to be preferred to any emendation yet proposed. Mr. Knight's explanation is nearly as difficult as the text, and although, as he remarks, Shakespeare is accustomed to the use of strong metaphorical expressions, yet we may fairly doubt whether, in the whole range of his plays, such an unnatural and forced construction is adopted as in the passage printed with Mr. Knight's punctuation. Looking fully at the context, I would explain it thus. Diana, at the moment of uttering this speech, is on the point of pretending to yield to Bertram's wishes; she has combated his assurances of sincerity in the vows of love, but apparently struck with the urgency of his arguments, she says, *I see that men make ropes in such a scarre, that we'll forsake ourselves;* I see that men make reasons to assist their views even in such a barren difficult subject, that we will desert ourselves, and yield to them. Then comes the result, "Give me that ring;" and no further solicitation is necessary on Bertram's part, who wins "a heaven on earth," by producing arguments for a course which no proper reasons could justify, in short, by making "ropes in such a scarre."

He loked abowte; thanne was he warre
Of an ermytage undir a *skerre.*
MS. Lincoln A. i. 17, f. 123.

Marry, even heaved over the *scarr*, and sent a-swimming toward Burtholme, his old habitation, if it bee not intercepted by some seale, sharke, sturgeon, or such like. *Hoffman, 1631.*

(5) A shred, or piece. *North.*

SCARAB. A beetle. (*Lat.*)

With secret contemplation doth contemne the base minds of such as, with the *scarab* flye, delighteth only to live in dung and mire.
Greene's Planetomachia, 1585, f. 1.

SCARAMOUCH. The name of a famous Italian posture-master, who in the year 1673 came to act here in England, from whom all those persons that perform feats of agility, and are dressed in particular Spanish habits, bear that as a common name. *Dyche.*

SCARBABE. A scarecrow. "And, like a *scarbabe*, make him take his legs," Wily Beguiled, ap. Hawkins, iii. 329.

SCARBOROUGH. *Scarborough leisure*, no leisure at all, Stanihurst's Ireland, p. 23. *Scarborough warning*, no warning, or a very brief one.

SCARBOT. A kind of beetle.

SCAR-BUGGE. A bugbear.

For sinne is no *scar-bugge*, and wee shall one day finde it so. *Dent's Pathway*, p. 345.

SCARCE. (1) To sieve. Also, a sieve.

Tak hert-horne, and brynne it, and bete it to powdir, and *scarce* it thorow a *scarce*, and use it ilk daye to thou be hale. *MS. Lincoln A. i. 17, f. 292.*

(2) Sparing; stingy. (*A.-N.*)

(3) To make one's self scarce, i. e. to go away. A common phrase.

SCARD. A shard, or fragment. *Yorksh.*

SCARE. (1) To spend; to consume. *Suffolk.*

(2) Lean; scraggy; scanty. *East.*

(3) A cur to drive away pigs, &c.

(4) "I've got the *scare* of him," I have frightened him so as to force him to do or prevent his doing anything. We also say, "I have put the *scare* upon him." *East.*

(5) Wild; timid; shy. *North.*

SCARE-A-JOB. A phrase implying that the job will be nearly finished, and tantamount to the expression "making it look foolish." *Essex.*

SCARE-BRAKE. A stick from a hedge? Thoms' Anecdotes and Trad. p. 27.

SCARET-ROOT. The herb skirwort.

SCARF. A silken ornament hung loosely upon any part of a lady's dress, tied on by a knight, and worn as a mark of her favour. *To scarf*, to wear loose, like a scarf; to cover or bandage up.

SCAR-FIRE. An alarm of fire.

SCARIFIED. Frightened. *Var. dial.*

SCARIOT. Judas Iscariot.

SCARL. A scarecrow, or bugbear.

SCARMISHE. A skirmish; a battle. (*A.-N.*)

SCARMONY. A kind of spice.

SCARN. Dung of cattle. *North.*

SCARN-BEE. A dung-bee. *Westm.*

SCARNY-HOUGHS. A dirty drab. *Westm.*

SCARPED. Dried up, or parched, as when in fever the skin becomes dry and hard, it is said to be *scarped*. Qu. a corruption of *scarfed*, scarf being the outer skin. *Linc.*

SCARPIN. A scorpion. "*Scorpio*, Anglice a scarpyn," Nominale MS. f. 7.

SCARSE. To go away; to disperse.

The wyndy storme began to *scarse*,
The sonne ariste, the wedir clereth.
Gower, MS. Soc. Antiq. 134, f. 236.

SCARSTEE. Scarcity. (*A.-N.*)

And eke to me it is a grete penaunce,
Syth ryme in Englyssh hath such *scarstee*.
MS. Cantab. Ff. i. 6, f. 57

And of grace lete be no *skarstė*,
Good lady, that arte of grace welle.
Lydgate, MS. Soc. Antiq. 134, f. 19.

SCART. To scratch. *North.*

SCARTERS. The dugs of a cow. *Linc.*

SCARTOCCIOS. Covers; folds of paper.

SCARVE. A contrivance for taking fish.

SCARVISH. Bright; clear. *Devon.*

SCARYWHIFF. Askew. *Somerset.*

SCASSENES. Scarcity. *Pr. Parv.*

SCAT. (1) A passing shower. *Devon.*

When Haldon hath a hat,
Let Kenton beware of a *skat*.
Old Devonshire Proverb.

(2) To dash; to burst; to slap. *West.* Also a substantive, a blow.

(3) Scared. *Essex.*

(4) Broken; ruined. *Cornw.*

(5) A continuance. *West.*

(6) Go away! Get along! *North.*

SCATCH. (1) A horse's bit. (*Fr.*)

(2) A hedge of dry branches.

SCATCH-PAWED. Left-handed. *Essex.*

SCATE. (1) Diminution; injury.

Make hit long and large y-now, withoute ony *scate*.
Chron. Vilodun. p. 98.

(2) A light-heeled wench. *North.*

(3) To have a diarrhœa. *Glouc.*

SCATHE. Harm; loss; damage. (*A.-S.*) "One doth the scathe and another hath the scorn," North Country proverb.

That, god Wilekin, me reweth thi *scathe*,
Houre Loverd sende the help rathe!
MS. Digby 86.

I hist the sisturday seven shyllyng,
Have brok it wel to thi clothyng,
Hit wil do the no *skathe*.
MS. Cantab. Ff. v. 48, f. 53.

SCATHEFUL. Destructive; pernicious.

SCATHERED. Said of feet ingrimed by water and small coals getting into the shoes. *Northumb.*

SCATLOE. Loss; harm; prejudice. *North.*

SCATTE. (1) Money. (2) Tax. (*A.-S.*)

SCATTERBRAINED. Giddy. *North.*

SCATTY. Showery. *South.*

SCAU. A fig. *Northumb.*

SCAUMY. Clear; bright; glossy. *North.* This differs from the meaning given by Kennett, who says "any imperfect disagreeable colour is said to be scawmy, or of a scawmey colour."

SCAUP. (1) A bare thin soil. *Yorksh.* Also, a lean scraggy person.

(2) Head; skull; scalp. *Yorksh.*

SCAUT. (1) To push violently. *West.*

(2) The pole attached to the axle of a waggon, and let down to prevent its running back while ascending a hill.

SCAVEL. Voracious; greedy. *North.* "Scavel, *avidus, vorax*," Coles.

SCAVEL-AN-GOW. Confused talking. *Cornw.*

SCAVERNICK. A hare. *Cornw.*

SCAVILONES. Drawers; pantaloons. *Strutt.*

SCAW. The elder tree. *Cornw.*

SCAWBERK. A scabbard.

> In the mydde off a book sche heelde a swerd,
> Other *scawberk* hadde sche noou.
>
> *MS. Cott. Tiber. A. vii. f. 49.*
>
> Biside that tresour lay a dragoun,
> And theron lay a swerd broun,
> The *sckauberk* comly corn. *Gy of Warwike*, p. 348.

SCED. The parting of the hair on a person's head. Nominale MS. xv. Cent.

SCEDE. To spill. *Lanc.*

SCELEROUS. Wicked. (*Lat.*)

> Kynge Richard by this abominable and *scelerous* act, thinkyng hymselfe well relevyd bothe of feare and thought, woulde not have it kept counsaill.
>
> *Hall, Richard III. f. 4.*

SCELLUM. A thief. A cant term.

> But if a drunkard be unpledg'd a kan,
> Drawes out his knife, and basely stabs a man,
> To runne away the rascall shall have scope;
> None holds him, but all cry, Lope, *scellum*, lope!
>
> *Taylor's Workes*, 1630, ii. 123.

SCENT. A descent. *South.*

SCH. For many or most words beginning with *sch*, see under *sh*.

SCHADONS. Young bees. *North.*

SCHALE. A scale; a ladder.

> Sithen thou of Jacob arte the ryɜte *schale*,
> The wey of lyf, the laddir of holynesse.
>
> *Lydgate, MS. Soc. Antiq. 134, f. 26.*

SCHAMELLE. A camel. " *Camelus*, Anglice a schamelle," Nominale MS.

SCHEFT. The auncel-weight.

SCHEKINE. A chicken. " *Pullus*, Anglice a schekyne," Nominale MS.

SCHELL. To overturn. *Linc.*

SCHEME. A party of pleasure.

SCHERCHE. Church. Sevyn Sages, 1823.

SCHESELLE. A chisel. Nominale MS.

SCHISMS. Frivolous excuses. *East.*

SCHISM-SHOP. A dissenting chapel.

SCHOAT. A kneading trough. *Kent.*

SCHOCHE. To suspect. *Will. Werw.*

SCHOOL. (1) To put back the ears, as a horse when provoked. *Var. dial.*

(2) A shoal of fish, probably a corruption of the word shoal. *Linc.*

SCHOOLING. Education. *Var. dial.*

SCHOOL-STREET. The university. *Oxon.*

SCHOUR. Battle; conflict.

> The good Duc of Gloucestrie in the seson
> Of the parlement at Bury beyng,
> Was put to deth; and ay sith gret mornyng
> Hath ben in Ingeland with many a scharp *schour*.
>
> *MS. Bibl. Soc. Antiq. 101, f. 98.*

SCHREWARD. A ribald; a rascal.

SCHROUGE. To press; to rub. *West.*

SCHYE. The sky.

> I woowld I had the nymbell wynges
> Of mylk-whyte dove that clyps in *schye*.
>
> *MS. Ashmole 48.*

SCHYLDEN. To bring forth a child. This occurs in MS. Bib. Reg. 12 B. i. f. 60. " *Puer*, Anglice a schyle.' Nominale MS.

SCIENT. Learned. *Lydgate.*

SCIMMINGER. A piece of counterfeit money of base metal rubbed over or cased with silver. *Kent.*

SCIND. To wash. *Durham.*

SCINDARIZE. To break to pieces. Ashmole's Theat. Chem. Brit. 1652, p. 415.

SCINK. A newt; a lizard.

SCIRTLE. Hasty; wild; changeable.

SCITTLE. Skittish. *Kent.*

SCITTURN. A shrewd turn. *Hants.*

SCL. For many words commencing with *scl*, see under *sl*.

SCLATYRE. To be negligent.

> *Sclatyr* thy clothys bothe schort and syde,
> Passyng all mennes syse.
>
> *MS. Cantab. Ff. ii. 38, f. 15*

SCLAU. To scratch, or claw. *Cornw.*

SCLAUNDRE. Slander. (*A.-N.*)

SCLEEZY. Said of cloth, when the threads are irregular and uneven. *Devon.*

SCLENT. Glided?

> A fote ynto the erthe hyt *sclente*.
>
> *MS. Cantab. Ff. ii. 38, f. 113*

SCLIɜE. Discreet; cunning.

> The knyghtes rydyn on horsys hye,
> With wordes myld, feyre, and *sclyɜe*.
>
> *MS. Ashmole 61, f. 3.*

SCLOWED. Scratched. *Devon.*

SCOAD. To scatter, or throw abroad any loose earth, as mole-hills, &c. *Devon.*

SCOANES. Stones; pavement. *Cornw.*

SCOBY. A chaffinch. *Yorksh.*

SCOCHONS. Scutcheons. (*A.-N.*) "Schochen a badge, *escuisson*," Palsgrave.

> The *scochenus* of many knyɜt
> Of gold and cyprus was i-dyɜt,
> Brode besauntus and bryɜt. *Degrevant*, 1481.

SCOCKERD. Sappy, as timber. *East.*

SCODE. To scatter. *Cornw.*

SCODIRDE. Whizzed along?

> The schafte *scodyrde* and schott in the schire byerne
> And soughte thorowowte the schelde, and in the
> schalke rystes. *Morte Arthure, MS. Lincoln, f. 76.*

SCOG. To brag; to boast. *West.*

SCOIL. Rubbish; the head of a quarry before the strata appear. *Devon.*

SCOLAIE. To attend school; to study.

SCOLDING-STOOL. A cucking-stool. Mr. Wright discovered the following entries in a MS. register at Southampton, dated 1540:

> Costes doon in makyng of the *scooldyngstoole*:
> Furste, paid for j. pece tymbre boughte of Robert Orchiere for the same stole, xd.
> For carriage of the same fro Hille to the west holle, iijd.
> Item, for sawing of the same piece in iij. peces, viijd.
> Item, for iij. boltes and ij. pinnes of iron for the same stoole, vid.
> Item, for the wheeles to convey the said stole by commandement of the meyre, iijs. iiijd.
> Item, paid to Robert Orcherd for the makyng of the said stoole and wheells, for iij. days laboure to him and his man, xd. the day, summa ijs. vjd.
> Summa xs. viijd. ob.

SCOLE. A weighing-scale. *Pr. Parv.*

SCOLLOP. To notch; to indent. *West.*

SCOLOPENDRA. A venomous serpent. Metaphorically used for a courtesan.

SCOMBRE. Stercoro.

> Also whan thei may noht *scombre*, then taketh the rote of a cawlworte, and putte it yn oylle d'olyf, and put it yn his foundement.   *MS. Bodl. 546.*

SCOME. To skim. *Skomyne*, Pr. Parv.

> And do hit thane ageyne overe the fyre, and *scome* hit welle thane, and do hit in boxun.
> *MS. Med. Rec.* xv. Cent.

SCOMERFARE.

> Ana with this noyse, and with this crie,
> Out of a barge faste by,
> Whiche hid was there on *scomerfare*,
> Men sterten out.   *Gower*, ed. 1554, f. 181.

SCOMFETE. To discomfit.

> The Almayns be *scowmfett*
> Wythowte any more lett.
>   *MS. Cantab.* Ff. ii. 38, f. 157.
> And yf yowre knyght happyn soo
> To be *scowmfetyd* or be sloo,
> Os hyt wylle be may,
> He wylle put hym yn yowre wylle,
> To make yowre pees, as hyt ys skylle,
> Wythowtyn more delay.
>   *MS. Cantab.* Ff. ii. 38, f. 77.
> And spedde ryʒt well all his journay,
> And *scomfede* his enmyes and droff hem ouʒt.
>   *Chron. Vilodun.* p. 96.
> After this bataile and *scumfite*.
>   *Arthour and Merlin*, p. 239.
> And when the deevel herd hym thus say,
> Als *scomfet* he vanysschet away.
>   *Hampole, MS. Bowes.* p. 73.
> And ʒif tu goiste to batayl this orisone say,
> And thow ne schalt noʒt be *scoufityd* that day.
>   *MS. Harl.* 2989, f. 96.

SCOMFISH. To discomfit; to oppress with heat; to stifle. *North.* Apparently connected with *scomfete.*

SCOMOWR. A cook's skimmer.

SCOMTHER. To scorch severely. *Cumb.*

SCONCE. (1) A blockhouse; a small fort.

> Except thy head, which, like a *skonce* or fort,
> Is barracado'd strong, lest wits resort.
> *Taylor's Workes*, 1630, ii. 75.

(2) The pavement. *Cornw.*

(3) A lantern; originally a light used for sacred purposes. "A sconse, or little lanterne," Baret, 1580. In the North of England the term is given to a kind of candlestick, with a tin back, hung against the wall.

(4) To conduct a jocular warfare of words; to carry on good-humoured raillery. *North.*

(5) The head. A cant term. "A head, a pate, a nole, a *skonce*," Florio, p. 82.

(6) A screen. *Cumb.* Brockett says, "a seat at one side of the fire-place in the old large open chimney; a short partition near the fire upon which all the bright utensils in a cottage are suspended." In Beaumont and Fletcher, iii. 102, it seems to mean some sort of stall on which switches were to be displayed.

(7) "To sconce, to eat more than another, *Winton*; to sconce, to impose a pecuniary mulct, *Oxon*," Kennett, MS. To sconce at Oxford, was to put a person's name in the College buttery books by way of fine.

SCONFIT. Discomfiture?

> Josian lai in a castel
> And segh that *scorfit* everich del.
>   *Beves of Hamtoun*, p. 37.

SCONS. Cakes of barley-meal. *Cumb.*

SCOOP. (1) A shovel used by maltsters. The term is generally applied to an instrument used for scooping out anything.

(2) The neck and breast of mutton cut as one joint. *Devon.*

SCOOSE. To discourse with. *Somerset.*

SCOOT. An angle, or corner, generally a cornered portion of a field. *Var. dial.*

SCOOTER. A syringe, or squirt. To go like scooter, i. e. very quick. *East.*

SCOP. The scalp; the head.

> If I get a knop upon the bare *scop*,
> Thou canst as well shite as shoote.
>   *Robin Hood*, ii. 32.

SCOPE. A kind of basin with a handle used for lading water. *Lanc.*

SCOPE-LAW. A space given to one in running a race. *Dorset.*

SCOPIOUS. Spacious; ample.

SCOPPE. Scoop; leap. *(A.-S.)*

SCOPPERIL. A plaything with children, being a mould button with a hole in it, through which a piece of wood or quill is put for the purpose of spinning like a tetotum. *Linc.* Metaphorically, a nimble child. Kennett has, "a scoppering or scopperell, a little sort of spinning top for boys to set up between the middle finger and thumb." The term occurs in a MS. Dictionary dated 1540.

SCORE. (1) Twenty yards. This was a common term in ancient archery and gunnery.

(2) Twenty pounds weight. *West.*

(3) The core of an apple. *Glouc.*

(4) A mark, or notch. *Var. dial.*

> And for the hire of two horses to Weybridge, to survey the timber, 12d.; and 12d. paid divers men, for raising and turning the timber there to see the *scores*; and 12d. for the expenses of the accomptant and his servant, and their two horses there.
>   *Archæologia*, xxiv. 304.

(5) To beat so as to mark the skin, a common term in Devon.

> Of the yeerde somtyme I stood in awe,
> To be *scooryd*, that was al my dreede.
>   *Lydgate's Minor Poems*, p. 235.

SCOREL. A squirrel. *Pr. Parv.*

SCORER. A scout; a scourer.

> The kynge, beinge at Notyngham, and or he came there, sent the *scorers* al abowte the contries adjoynynge, to aspie and serche yf any gaderyngs were in any place agaynst hym.
>   *Arrival of King Edward IV.* p. 7.

SCORING. According to Marshall, the Norfolk ploughmen have a singular expedient to prevent the soil when moist from turning up in whole glossy furrows, which they term *scoring*; for which purpose they tie a piece of strong rope-yarn round the plate or mould-board, which, by this means, is prevented from acting as a trowel upon the soil. See his Rural Economy of Norfolk, i. 139

SCORK. The core of an apple. *Salop.*

SCORSE. To exchange. It is the translation

of changer in Hollyband's Dictionarie, 1593, and is still in use.

SCORT-ABOUT. To disturb ; to injure. *Warw.*

SCORTE. Scorn ; derision.

SCOTCH. (1) To stop the wheel of a coach or waggon with a stone; &c. *Var. dial.*

(2) To cut slightly ; to mince. Hence, metaphorically, to spare, to refrain.

> For when they come to giving unto holy and necessarie uses, then they will sticke at a pennie, and scotch at a groat, and every thing is too much.
> *Dent's Pathway,* p. 74.

(3) *Out of all scotch*, excessively.

(4) To amerce ; the same as to dock in other counties ; thus, when a labourer has not done work in quantity or quality to satisfy his master, the latter will say, " I'll *scotch* you for this." *Linc.*

SCOTCH-AND-ENGLISH. In Cumberland the game of *prisoner's base* is sometimes so called, in allusion probably to the border wars.

SCOTCH-FIDDLE. A fiddle thus played :— the fore-finger is the fiddlestick, which plays between the thumb and fingers of the other hand. *North.*

SCOTCH-FOG. A kind of misty rain. There is an old saying that " a *Scotch-fog* will wet an Englishman through."

SCOTCH-HOP. The game of hop-scotch. It is mentioned in Clarke's Phraseologia Puerilis, 1655, p. 322. Moor calls it *Scotch-hob.*

SCOTE. (1, A prop. *I. Wight.*

(2) A dragstaff. *Glouc.*

(3) To plough up. *Heref.*

SCOTH. To clothe, or cover up.

SCOTOMY. A dizziness in the head.

SCOTS. Scotch cattle. *North.*

SCOTTERING. A custom among boys of burning a bundle of pease-straw at the end of harvest. " In Herefordshire, boys at the latter end of harvest use to burn a wad of pease in the straw, which they call a *scottering*, and eat the pease being so parched," Blount.

SCOTTLE. To cut badly, raggedly. " How you have *scottled* that leather ;" " the beef was *scottled* shamefully." *Wilts.*

SCOTTLES. An amusement with boys, who pelt each other with the stubble of wheat pulled up with the earth about the roots. This is called " playing at *scottles.*" *Suffolk.*

SCOUB. A rod sharpened at both ends used in thatching. *Northumb.*

SCOUL. To burn fiercely ; to look red, generally said of the sky. *Devon.*

SCOUP. To leap at prey. *Palsgrave.*

SCOUR. (1) To scour a hedge, to deepen the ditch, and to breast up the hedge with the soil taken out. *North.*

(2) A shallow, gravelly part of a river. *Warw.*

(3) To clean out ponds, &c. *East.*

(4) A scourging, or beating.

(5) A noise; a tumult. *Somerset.*

SCOURGE. To sweep with a besom. *Kent.*

SCOURGE-METTLE. The instrument with which a boy whips his top. " Every night I

dream I am a town-top, and that I am whipt up and down with the *scourge* stick of love, and the *metal* of affection," Grim the Collier of Croydon, ap. Dodsley, xi. 206.

SCOURING. (1) A beating. *North.* It occurs in Nabbes' Bride, 1640, sig. H. iv, and earlier in the Prompt. Parv.

(2) A difficult affair. *Yorksh.*

(3) A diarrhœa. *Var. dial.*

SCOURING-STICK. A stick used in cleaning the barrel of a gun.

SCOUT. (1) A high rock. *Lanc.*

(2) A college errand boy. *Oxon.*

(3) A watchman. A cant term. Tusser has *scoutwatch*, ed. 1812, p. xxv.

(4) A small division of land. *West.*

SCOUTH.

> And he get scouth to wield his tree,
> I fear you'll both be paid. *Robin Hood,* i. 106.

SCOUTHER. An uproar ; a confusion. *North.*

SCOUT-WATCH. A spy. See *Scout* (3).

SCOVE. To run fast. *East.*

SCOVEL. A baker's maulkin.

SCOVEN. The neck of lamb. *Somerset.*

SCOVING. " Scoving is shoving the barley forward in order for binding," MS. Devon. Gl.

SCOVY. Uneven. *Devon.* " Scovy wool, wool of various colours not duely mixt in combing or scribbling, but streaky," MS. Devonshire Glossary.

SCOWDER. A bustle; a confusion. *North.*

SCOWULE. A showl, or shovel.

SCOY. Thin, poor, generally applied to silks or stuffs. *Cornw.*

SCO3IES. Scourges.

> The her of his hed is al to-drawe,
> The body with sco3ies al to-flawe.
> *MS. Addit.* 11307, f. 49.

SCRAB. (1) The crab-apple. *North.*

(2) To scratch, or claw. *East.*

SCRABBED-EGGS. A lenten dish, composed of eggs boiled hard, chopped and mixed with a seasoning of butter, salt, and pepper.

SCRABBLE. (1) To scramble. *Somerset.*

(2) To scratch with the nails. *Linc.*

SCRADGE. To dress and trim a fen-bank, in order to prepare it the better to resist an apprehended overflow. All loose materials within reach are raked together; and such additions as are to be had are procured, and so applied, as to heighten and strengthen the upper part on the side next to the flood. Forby's East Anglia, ii. 290.

SCRAFFISCH. The cray-fish.

SCRAFFLE. To scramble ; to struggle ; also, to wrangle or quarrel.

SCRAG. (1) A ghost. *North.*

(2) Offal ; remnants. *Yorksh.*

(3) A crooked forked branch. *West.*

(4) A lean, thin person. *Devon.* The adjective *scraggy* is common everywhere.

SCRAGGED. Hanged. A cant term.

SCRAGGLE. To scramble. *Dorset.*

SCRAM. Distorted ; awkward. Also, benumbed with cold. *West.*

SCRAMB. To pull, or rake together with the hands. *Yorksh.*

SCRAMBED. Deprived of the use of some limb by a nervous contraction of the muscles. *Somerset.*

SCRAMMISHES. Scratches. *West.*

SCRAMP. To catch at ; to snatch. *North.*

SCRAN. (1) A bag. *Wilts.*

(2) Victuals ; food. *North.*

SCRANCH. To scratch. *East.*

SCRANCHUM. Crisp gingerbread. *North.*

SCRANNEL. A lean person. *Lanc.*

SCRANNY. Thin ; meagre. *Var. dial.*

SCRANS. Scraps ; refuse. *Dorset.*

SCRANT. To scorch. *Somerset.*

SCRAP. (1) To scratch. *East.* " To scrappe as a henne dose," MS. Dictionary, 1540.

(2) A plan, or scheme.

SCRAPE. (1) To shave badly. *Var. dial.*

(2) To bow, or make obeisance.

SCRAPE-GOOD. A miserly fellow.

SCRAPER. A bad fiddler. *Var. dial.*

SCRAPPLE. To grub about. *Oxon.*

SCRAPS. As well as in the common sense, this word is in Suffolk particularly descriptive of the small pieces of fat pork remaining after the operation of boiling, for the purpose of extracting the lard for store for domestic use. Moor's Suffolk Words, p. 334.

SCRAPT. Slightly frozen. *Devon.*

SCRAT. (1) To scratch. (2) Scratched. *West.*

> On the sege then sate y,
> And he *scrattud* me fulle vylenaly.
> > *MS. Cantab. Ff. ii 38, f. 152.*
> And ylkane *skratte* othyr in the face,
> And thaire awen flesche of ryve and race.
> > *Hampole, MS. Bowes, p. 215.*
> And *scratted* hur vysage alle with blood,
> And cryed owt as sche were wode.
> > *MS. Cantab. Ff. ii. 38, f. 129.*

(3) A swaggerer ; a bully.

(4) The itch. *Salop.*

(5) A miserly fellow. *West.*

(6) An hermaphrodite. *North.* " A scrat, *hermaphroditus*," Coles.

(7) Nearly worn out. *North.*

(8) A rack for pigs. *Beds.*

SCRATCH. The stone which forms the stratum immediately under the soil. *Linc.*

SCRATCH-CRADLE. A game played by crossing thread or string between the two hands in a peculiar manner.

SCRATCHED. Slightly frozen. *Devon.*

SCRATCHINGS. The remainder of the fat, after it has been melted down into lard. *Worc.*

SCRATE. An old woman.

SCRATTLE. To scratch. *Var. dial.*

SCRAUK. To scratch. *Yorksh.*

SCRAWF. Refuse. *West.*

SCRAWL. (1) To crawl. *West.* " To scrall, stir, *motito*," Coles' Lat. Dict.

(2) The young of the dog-crab, or a bastard sort of crab itself. *Linc.*

(3) Any things which have been thrown about in a disorderly confused manner are said in Hampshire to be *scrawled*

SCRAWLING. Slight ; mean. *Heref.*

SCRAWLY. Thin, as corn. *Derb.*

SCRAWMY. Awkwardly tall ; thin and ungainly ; said of one, who is all legs and wings like a giblet pie. *Linc.*

SCRAWN. To clamber up. *North.*

SCREAK. To creak, as a door, &c.

SCREDE. Shroud ; dress. *Weber.*

SCREE. (1) A coarse sieve. *North.*

(2) A precipice ; a scar. *Cumb.*

(3) To hollow out loudly. *Linc.*

SCREECH. (1) The swift. *West.*

(2) The missel thrush. *Var. dial.* The term was anciently applied to the screech-owl. " *Strix*, Anglice a schrych," Nominale MS.

SCREECH-OWL. The swift. *I. Wight.*

SCREECHY. i. e. Scratchy, applied to land, when the *scratch* or rock is covered with a very thin layer of earth. *Linc.*

SCREED. (1) Avoided. *Dorset.*

(2) A narrow slip of land. *Linc.*

(3) The border of a cap. *Var. dial.*

(4) Scrip. *Devon.*

(5) A rent, shred, or fragment. *North.*

SCREEDLE. To scrune over the embers, to hover over them, covering them with one's coats as with a screen. *Devon.*

SCREENED. Sifted. *North.* A *screen* is a high standing sieve for cleansing corn.

SCREES. Small stones or pebbles. *North.*

SCREET. (1) Half a quarter of a sheet of paper. *East.*

(2) Flexible ; supple.

SCREEVE. To run with corrupt matter, as a wound, a corpse, &c. *Lanc.*

SCREFFE. The sheriff.

> Whan Roben ynto the hall cam,
> The *screffe* sone he met,
> The potter cowed of corteysscy,
> And sone the *screffe* he gret.
> > *Robin Hood, i. 88.*

SCREIK. (1) To shriek ; to scream. *Yorksh.*

(2) The peep of day. *North.*

SCRETE. Slight ; supple ; limber.

SCREW. (1) A miser. *Var. dial.*

(2) To have the stomach-ache.

(3) A courtesan. A cant term.

SCREW-BOX. A kind of shell-fish.

SCREWDY. To crowd. *Beds.*

SCRIBBLE. To card wool. *Devon.*

SCRIBBLE-SCROBBLE. Scribbling. *North.*

SCRIBE. To write ; to make marks with instruments, as carpenters. *North.*

SCRIDE. To stride. *Somerset.*

SCRIGG'D. Forced ; squeezed out. *Northamptonsh.*

SCRIGGINS. Apples left on a tree after the ingathering. *Glouc.*

SCRIGGLE. To writhe ; to struggle. *East.*

SCRIKE. A scream. *North.* Also a verb, to shriek ; to scream.

> Which lye in torments, yet die not,
> With manie wofull *scrikes*. *MS. Ashmole 208.*
> The deevels ay amang on thaime sal stryke,
> And the synful tharewith ay crye and *skryke*.
> > *Hampole, MS. Bowes, p. 214.*

SCRIM. To crush; to bruise. *I. of Wight.*

SCRIMED. Shrivelled up. *Devon.*

SCRIMER. A fencer. *(Fr.)*

SCRIMMAGE. (1) A skirmish; but now used for a general row. *Var. dial.*

> Prynce Ouffur at this *skrymage* for all his pryde
> Fled full fast, and sowght no gyde.
> *MS. Lansdowne 208, f. 10.*

(2) A mean dwarfish person. *West.*

SCRIMMITY. Stingy; close. *West.*

SCRIMP. To spare; to pinch. *Var. dial.* Hence *scrimption*, a small pittance.

SCRIN. A small vein of ore. *Derb.*

SCRINGE. To shrink; to cringe. *Var. dial.*

SCRINKT. Screwed. *Cornw.*

SCRINT. To scorch or singe, applied generally to those substances that shrink together a good deal in burning, as leather, parchment, silk, woollen, the hair, &c. *Somerset.*

SCRIP. A list; a slip of writing; a writing. *Script* occurs in Chaucer.

SCRIPTURES. Writings; books. *(A.-N.)*

SCRIT. A writing; a deed.

> A *scrit* of covenaunt l-mad ther was
> Bytwene me and Sathanas. *MS. Addit. 11307, f. 95.*
> He dyde on hys clothys astyte,
> And to Seynt Jhone he wrote a *skryte.*
> *MS. Harl. 1701, f. 46.*

SCRITCH. To shriek. *Devon.* The thrush is called a *scritch* from its noise.

SCRITHE. To writhe about.

SCRITTICK. A mite of money. *South.*

SCRIVE. (1) To describe. *Palsgrave.*

(2) To shriek; to scream. *North.*

SCRIVENER. A writing-master. *Scriveines,* writers, transcribers. *(A.-N.)*

SCRIVING-IRON. An instrument used for numbering trees for sale.

SCROBBLE. To scramble. *West.*

SCROFF. Refuse of wood. *Dorset.*

SCROG. A stunted bush. *North. Scroggy,* abounding in underwood. "The wey toward the cité was stony, thorny, and *scroggy,*" Gesta Romanorum, p. 18. "*Scrogs,* blackthorn," Kennett, MS. Lansd. 1033.

SCROGGLINGS. The small worthless apples which are left hanging on the trees after the crop has been gathered. *Worc.*

SCROGGY. Twisted; stunted. *East.*

SCROG-LEGS. Bandy legs. *Norf.*

SCROME. To walk awkwardly. *North.*

SCROOBY-GRASS. Scurvy-grass. *North.*

SCROODGE. A crush. *North.*

SCROOF. Dry scales, or scabs. *Lanc.*

SCROOP. To creak. *West.*

SCROUGE. To crowd; to squeeze. *Var. dial.*

SCROW. (1) To work hard. *North.*

(2) Uproar; confusion. *Yorksh.*

(3) Cross; angry; surly. *Wilts.* Ray gives it as a Sussex word. At Winchester I heard an ugly woman described as looking *scrow,* apparently without any reference to the temper.

(4) A roll, or scroll. *Palsgrave.*

> He is so pullid that he may not grow,
> Countyrfetid in a figur and payntid in a *scrow.*
> *MS. Laud. 416, f. 53.*

SCROWL. To broil, or roast. *Devon*

SCROW-ROW. An uproar. *North.*

SCROYLE. A mangy fellow. A term of contempt used by Shakespeare and Jonson.

> Then upon Sabbath dayes the *scroyle* beginnes,
> With most unhallowed hands, to weed up sinnes.
> *Taylor's Workes, 1630, iii. 11.*

SCRUB. A mean fellow. *Var. dial.*

SCRUBB. To get rid of. *Devon.*

SCRUBBADO. The itch. A cant term.

SCRUBBED. Squalid; mean; shabby.

SCRUCE. A truce at play. *East.*

SCRUDDY. Short; dwarfish. *North.*

SCRUDE. To rub.

SCRUDGE. A courtesan. *Devon.*

SCRUFF. "A kind of fuel which poor people, when firing is dear, gather up at ebbing water in the bottom of the Thames about London, and consists of coal, little sticks, cockle-shels, and the like," Blount.

SCRUGGLE. To struggle. *Palsgrave.*

SCRUMP. (1) Crisp. *South.*

(2) To craunch. *Somerset.*

(3) To double up. *Devon.*

SCRUMSHUS. Stingy. *Suffolk.*

SCRUNCH. To craunch. *Var. dial.*

SCRUNCHLIN. A small green shrivelled apple stunted in its growth. *West.*

SCRUNT. An overworn wig, besom, &c.

SCRUNTY. Short; stunted. *North.*

SCRUPULOUS. Doubtful.

SCRUSE. A truce. *Suffolk.*

SCRUSH. A bandy, or club. *Devon.*

SCRUTCHELL. Refuse of wood. *Sussex.*

SCRUTHING-BAG. A coarse bag through which cider is strained. *West.*

SCRY. A flock of wild fowl.

SCRYE. To descry. *North.*

> I knewe never mane so wys,
> That couth telle the servise,
> Ne *scrye* the metys of prys
> Was servyd in that sale. *Degrevant, 1860.*

SCRYLE. Couch-grass. *West.*

SCRYVED. Emitted purulent matter. Still in use in Lancashire. See *Screeve.*

> His woundis *scryved* and stille he lay.
> *MS. Harl. 2259, f. 91.*

SCUCH. A hanging-shelf. See Withals' Dictionarie, ed. 1608, p. 136.

SCUD. (1) To spill. *Devon.*

(2) To clean with saliva. *Yorksh.*

(3) A slight rapid shower. *Var. dial.*

(4) A scab. *Devon.*

(5) A scud of larks is a small number, less than a flock. *Oxon.*

SCUDDER-OF-FLAME. Same as *Scud* (3).

SCUDDICK. Anything of very small value; of the smallest worth. *North.*

SCUE. Shade; shadow. *Dunelm.*

SCUFF. (1) Or *scruff* of the neck, is the back part of the neck; it is generally used when a person seizes another by that part. *North.*

(2) To shuffle in walking. *West.*

SCUFFIN. Same as *Fruggan* (1).

SCUFFLE. (1) A linen garment worn by children to keep their clothes clean; a pinafore;

a coarse apron worn by servants when doing dirty work. *Sussex.*

(2) A garden hoe. *Salop.*

(3) To scuffle out one's shoes, to kick them out as if always at football. *West.*

SCUFFLER. A sort of plough, with a share somewhat like an arrow-head, drawn by a horse betwixt the ridges where turnips have been drilled, to root out the weeds; thus acting like a Dutch hoe, but on a larger scale. *Linc.*

SCUFFLINGS. Refuse of wood. *East.*

SCUFTER. To bustle; to hurry. *Cumb.*

SCUG. (1) To hide; to take shelter. *North.* As a substantive, a place of shelter.

(2) The declivity of a hill. *Yorksh.*

(3) A squirrel. *Hampsh.*

SCUGGERY. Secrecy. *Yorksh.*

SCULK. (1) An impure person. *(A.-S.)*

(2) A company of foxes.

SCULL. (1) A shoal. Generally of fishes, but Lilly mentions " a scul of pheasants," ed. 1632, sig. X. xii. " Skulles of herrings," Holinshed, Hist. Scot. p. 139.

> Into ye town of Rochell, they say, God hath sent a *skull* of fish for their relief, as he did miraculously when H. ye 3d besieged it. *MS. Harl.* 388.

(2) To scold. *Devon.*

SCULSH. Rubbish, but most generally used with reference to the unwholesome things children delight to eat, lollipop, &c. *Kent.*

SCULVERING. Low; sculking. *Linc.*

SCUM. (1) To mow. *Suffolk.*

(2) To strike any one on the mouth.

SCUMBER. To dung. A hunting term, applied properly to foxes. It is frequently written *scummer*, as in Florio, p. 72.

> But he that gaines the glory here,
> Must *scumber* furthest,.... most clear.
> *Musarum Deliciæ,* 1656, p. 6.

SCUM-FELLOW. A very low person.

SCUMMER. (1) Wonder. *Somerset.*

(2) To daub, or smear. *West.* Also, ventrem exonerare. " A skummering of a dog," Florio, p. 475, in v. *Schinchimurra.*

(3) A fire-shovel. *Yorksh.*

SCUN. (1) To reproach in a public manner, with a view of exposing to contempt or shame. *Somerset.*

(2) To throw a stone. *North.*

(3) To shun; to avoid. *Devon.*

SCUNNER. (1) To loathe; to shun. *North.*

(2) To notice; to observe. *Northumb.*

SCUNNING. A disease of the heart.

SCUPPER'D. Spoken of leaves of trees that are turned black, and crumpled up with frost or blight. A Herefordshire word, according to Urry's MS. additions to Ray.

SCUPPIT. A shovel, or spade, of uniform width, the sides turned a little inward. A spade tapers toward the cutting edge. The tiller handles too differ, the scuppit having merely a cot on the top of the tiller, and the spade having the top of its tiller perforated, which is called an eye tiller. The scuppit is sometimes used for digging as well as the spade, but is not so suitable for flag or strong land. *Moor.*

SCUR. To move hastily. *Yorksh.*

SCURE. To secure. *South.*

SCUREL. A rabbit. " *Sirogrillus, scurellus,* scurelle," Nominale MS.

SCURGE. A whip for a top.

SCURRAN-TOP. A peculiar kind of top formerly used at a game called scurran-meggy, which was much in vogue in Cumberland during the last century. MS. Glossary in my possession.

SCURRICK. A small piece. *Yorksh. West.* Sometimes *scuddick*, and perhaps more generally *scrittick*, an atom.

SCURRIFUNGE. To lash tightly. Also, coire carnaliter. *Devon.*

SCURRY. (1) To scour in pursuit. *East.*

(2) To hasten away. *Var. dial.*

SCURVY-ALE.

> But to conclude this drinking alye tale,
> We had a sort of ale called *scurvy ale.*
> *Taylor's Workes,* 1630, l. 126.

SCUSE. To excuse. *Var. dial.*

SCUT. (1) The tail of a hare or rabbit. The hare itself was also so called. Also, to dock an animal's tail. Still in use.

(2) Short, as a garment, &c.

SCUTCH. (1) Couch grass. *West.*

(2) To strike or beat slightly. *Yorksh.* Pegge has *scutch'd*, whipped.

(3) To cleanse flax. *Worc.*

SCUTCHELL. A long dark passage. *Linc.*

SCUTCHEON. A key-stone. " A *scutcheon* in the middest of a vaute, where all the course of the carved stones or timber doth resort," Hollyband's Dictionarie, 1593.

SCUTE. (1) A scute was declared to be worth half a noble by a proclamation of Henry V., printed in Hall, f. 37. " *Scute*, a present of money," Devonshire Glossary.

(2) A reward; a gift. *Dorset.*

SCUTLIN. A small apple pasty; a taffata tart. *Winton.*

SCUTTER. To have a diarrhœa. *North.*

SCUTTLE. (1) To walk fast. *Linc.*

(2) A small piece of wood, pointed at both ends, used at a game like trap-ball. *Chesh.*

(3) A shallow basket or wicker bowl, much in use in the barn, and in other departments of husbandry. " A *scuttle*, dosser, basket to carrie on the backe," Cotgrave in v. *Hotte.*

(4) A dish, or wooden platter.

SCUTTLES. The hatches of a ship at which the goods are let down.

SCUTTY. Short in stature. *Yorksh.*

SCUTTY-WREN. The wren. *West.*

SCWON. Shone; glittered.

> In a cloud off blewe,
> Hyt did never remewe
> The spere;
> But evere in one
> Bryght hyt *scwon*
> Stremeyt clere. *MS. Cantab.* Ff. 1. 6.

SCY. A scythe. *Cumb.*

SE. A seat; a kingdom. *(A.-N.)*

> And ryȝte forthwith the aungelle tarieth nouȝt,
> But helde his wey from the *see* of glorye.
> *Lydgate, MS. Soc. Antiq.* 134, p. 1.

Undir the foot of mount Mambré,
There he chees to sette his ee.
Cursor Mundi, MS. Coll. Trin. Cantab. f. 16.

SEA. A large number or quantity of anything. *Sussex.*

SEA-ADDER. The pipe-fish. *Cornw.*

SEA-BEANS. Small black pebbles. *Devon.*

SEABLE. Visible; to be seen.

SEA-BOTTLE. Many of the species of the sea-wrack, or *fucus*, are called *sea-bottles*, in consequence of the stalks having round or oval vesicles or pods in them; the pod itself.

SEA-CROW. A cormorant. *South.*

SEAKY. Boggy; wet. *Salop.*

SEAL. Part of horse armour.

SEALE. (1) The sallow. *Yorksh.*

(2) A furnace for boiling salt.

SEALED-DOVE. A dove with the eyelids sown up, in which state she rises perpendicularly till her strength is quite exhausted, and then falls down lifeless.

Thy windows all are shut in this dark cave:
Thy eyes clos'd up; and when, like *sealed dove*,
Thou fain wouldst flutter upward, light to have,
This flesh to thee united will not move,
But draws thee back, and clips thy soaring wings,
Or at thy lofti'st pitch thee downward flings.
Clobery's Divine Glimpses, 1659, p. 78.

SEAM. (1) A horse-load of wood. Ray gives this as a Sussex word, but it seems to have fallen out of use in that county. See, however, Marshall's Rural Economy of the West of England, i. 398, who gives it as a West Devonshire word.

(2) A strata of coal. *North.*

(3) Lard. *North.* "Cold meat fryed with hogs *seame*," Cotgrave in v. *Gramouse.* "Seme for to frye with, *seyn de pourreau*," Palsgrave.

(4) A quarter of an acre. Also, a quarter of corn. *South and East.*

(5) A horse-load. *Cornw.*

SEA-MALL. A bird thus described by Holme, "The bill white, but yellow towards the tip, bending towards the point; the feet of a pale green, claws black."

SEAM-RENT. Ragged; very shabby. As a verb, to unsew or make ragged.

SEAMS. The marks of the smallpox.

SEAM-SET. A shoemaker's instrument for smoothing the seams of boots and shoes.

SEAN. (1) A sort of net. *Linc.* Polwhele describes it a pilchard net, and a very large net used in Hampshire for catching mackerel and herrings is so called. "Sean, or seyn, a great and very long fish net," Howell.

(2) Soon. *North.*

SEA-NAG. A ship. *Westm.*

SEA-PINK. The plant thrift. *Yorksh.*

SEA-PYE. The oyster catcher. *Drayton.*

SEAR. (1) The yellow betwixt the beak and the eyes of a hawk. *Berners.*

(2) Dry; withered. "Seare and saplesse leaves," Dekker's Knight's Conjuring. p. 53.

Whereas her fresh flourishing prime would brook
ill to be imbraced by thy *seere* and saplesse armes.
The Two Lancashire Lovers, 1640, p. 26.

(3) The touchhole of a pistol. Hence used metaphorically for the pudendum muliebre. *Light of the seare* is, of course, equivalent to light-heeled, loose in character. *Tickle of the sear*, wanton, immodest. The commentators have never yet satisfactorily explained a passage in Hamlet, ii. 2, "the clown shall make those laugh, whose lungs are *tickled o' the sere*," i. e., those whose lungs are wanton, or excited to laughter by coarse ribaldry. That this is the correct explanation there cannot, I imagine, be the slightest doubt. "Discovering the moods and humors of the vulgar sort to be so loose and *tickle of the seare*," Howard's Defensative, 1620, ap. Douce, ii. 230. These senses of the word have never before been developed.

Even as a pistole that is ready charged and bent,
will flie off by and by, if a man do but touch the
seare. *Lambarde's Perambulation, 1596, p. 452.*

She that is fayre, lusty, and yonge,
And can comon in termes wyth fyled tonge,
And wyll abyde whysperynge in the eare,
Thynke ye her tayle is not *lyght of the seare*.
Commune Secretary and Jalousye, n.d.

SEARCER. A fine sieve; a strainer.

SEARCH. (1) A tent, or probe.

(2) To penetrate. *Var. dial.*

SEARCHERS. Persons appointed to examine corpses, and report the cause of death.

SEARCHING. Keen; piercing. *Var. dial.*

SEARSINGS. Siftings; cleansings.

When your three *searsings* be done after my lore,
Then breake the stone as you did before.
Ashmole's Theat. Chem. Brit. 1652, p. 408.

SEARY. Thin, or worn. *Devon.*

SEASON. (1) To seize or pounce on anything as a hawk does.

(2) "*Admissura*, seasoning of a cow, and coverynge of a mare," Eliote's Dictionarie, 1559.

SEAT. (1) The summit of a mountain.

(2) A number or nest of eggs; on which they *set* poultry. Thus they say: "I'll give you a *seat* of eggs." "I found in the stable, &c., a *seat* of eggs I did not expect." *Linc.*

SEATER. A piece of cloth worn so thin, as to be almost in a hole, is said to be "all in a *seater*." *North.*

SEAT-RODS. Hazel twigs. *Salop.*

SEAU. A water-pail. *North.*

SEAVE. A gown. *Somerset.*

SEA-VELE. A seal.

The sea calfe, in like manner, which our countrymen for brevity sake cal a seele, other more largely name a *sea vele*, maketh a spoile of fishes betweene rockes and banckes, but it is not accounted in the catalogue or number of our English dogs, notwithstanding we call it by the name of a sea dog or a sea-calfe. *Topsell's Four-Footed Beasts, 1607, p. 171.*

SEAVES. Rushes. *Var. dial.* "A seave, a rush that is drawn thro' in dripping or other grease, which in ordinary houses in the North they light up and burn instead of a candle," Kennett, MS. Lansd. 1033.

SEA-WARE. Sea-weed. *Northumb.*

SEAWL. Wet stuff. *Lanc.*

SEAWSE. To strike a person over the face. *Lanc.*

SEAWTERYED. A stupid fellow. *Lanc.*

SECATOUR. An executor.

> Then is he a traytour,
> Fore he trustys to his *secatour*,
> He schuld his soule socour. *MS. Douce 302, f. 2.*
> Wyse mon if thou art, of thi god
> Take part or thou hense wynde;
> For if thou leve thi part in thi *secature* ward,
> Thi part non part at last end. *Reliq.Antiq.* i.314.

SECCLELED. Sickened. *Will. Werw.*

SECHAN. Such a one. (*A.-S.*)

SECHE. To seek. (*A.-S.*)

> By dereworthy God, sayd Robyn,
> To *seche* all Englond thorowe,
> Yet founde I never to my pay,
> A moch better borowe." *Robin Hood, i.13.*

SECHETH. Visits. *Weber.*

SECK. (1) Such. *North.*

(2) A sack. Still in use.

(3) To seek. *Yorksh.*

SECKERLY. As usual. *North.*

SECKET. A term of contempt, addressed generally to a child. *Linc.*

SECKING. Canvas for sacks. *North.*

SECONDS. Second-rate flour. *Var. dial.*

SECREE. Secret. (*A.-N.*)

SECRET-HOUSE. A country-seat.

SECT. (1) Sex. Very common.

(2) A suit. (*A.-N.*)

(3) A small hammer, sharp on one end of the iron part, used in chipping large stones, &c.

SECTURE. An executor. *Palsgrave.*

> That that comed in the *sectures* hondes.
> *MS. Rawl.* xv. Cent.

SECURRE. Sure; certain; positive.

SEDE. To produce seed. (*A.-S.*)

SEDEKINE. A sub-dean.

SEDGELY-CURSE. A horrible imprecation, thus given by Howell,—"the devil run through thee booted and spurred with a scythe on his back."

SEDIKE. A sea-ditch, or sea-water creek.

SEDLED. Lulled to sleep.

SEDOCKE. The herb brank-ursine.

SEDOW. The fish aurata. "*Aurata*, Anglice a sedow," Nominale MS.

SEDULL. A schedule.

> Yea, if I should gather up all inconveniences in heape, I should not be satisfied with a *sedull*, but write a whole volume. *Don Simonides, 2d Part, 1584.*

SEDYR. Cider. *Prompt. Parv.*

SEE. (1) Saw. Isumbras, 604.

> The nativity according to our modern authors, is one of the best that ever I *see*, but according to our method it is a very evil one, and yet I do beleive there is not one artist in 40 can give any reason for his death at that time, or why he should dye of a consumption, seeing the ascendent is no ways afflicted. *Bishop's Marrow of Astrology, p. 64.*

(2) The sea. (*A.-S.*)

(3) To make a see of it, i. e., to be able to see. *Oxon.*

(4) To look on; to protect.

> Now God you save, our queen, madam,
> And Christ you *save and see*:
> Here you have chosen a new true love,
> And you will have none of me.
> *Ballad of Sir Aldingar.*

(5) *To see the devil*, to get tipsy. *To see the back of anything*, to get rid of it.

SEECH. A land-spring. *Chesh.*

SEED. Saw. *Var. dial.*

SEED-BIRD. The water-wagtail. *North.*

SEED-COD. A seed-lip, or basket out of which seed-corn is sown. *Var. dial.* "*Saticulum*, a sedelyppe," Nominale MS.

SEEDNESS. Seed-time. *Yorksh.* Called *seedny* in Herefordshire.

SEEDS. Young grasses; land newly laid to grass. *Staff.*

SEEDSMAN. A foreman on a farm, whose duty it is to sow the corn. *South.*

SEEDY. Poor and miserable-looking. The term is used by Goldsmith.

SEEING-GLASS. A looking-glass. *North.*

SEEK. (1) To seek, i. e., at a loss.

(2) To starch clothes. *Somerset.*

SEEKING-RAKE. A small-toothed rake.

SEEL. (1) See *Sealed-Dove.*

(2) Good fortune; happiness. (*A.-S.*)

> Now doghty, now in dowte,
> Now in sorow, now in *seels.*
> *MS. Cantab. Ff. ii. 38, f. 25.*

(3) To wainscot. Harrison, p. 187.

(4) A sieve. *Lanc.*

SEELEN. Seldom. *Lanc.*

SEELS. The wooden exterior of the collar of a cart-harness. *East.*

SEELY. Simple; silly; harmless. (*A.-S.*)

SEEM. To think, suppose, imagine. "I *seem* 'tis a terrable longsome time." *Devon.*

SEEMEY. Seemly. *Coles.*

SEEN. (1) A cow's teat. *Kent.*

(2) Experienced; skilled. "Excellentlie *seene* in the Greeke and Latine toongs," Harrison's Britaine, p. 23.

SEER. (1) Sure. *North.*

(2) An overlooker. *Somerset.*

SEERGYNG. A searching; an examination.

SEE-SAW. A kind of swing, formed of a plank on a fulcrum.

SEEST. *Seest thou me* is apparently a game at the dice or tables.

> Wonder it is to see how the Frenchmen juggle with this phantasticall lawe, folowyng the crafty hasarders, which use a play called *seest thou me*, or *seest thou me not.* *Hall, Henry V. f. 4.*

SEE-TRE. Cloth worn till it is threadbare, i.e., see-through. *North.*

SEEVY-CAP. A cap made of rushes.

SEFYNT. Seventh. (*A.-S.*)

> The *sefynt* heven, as sey the story,
> Is paradys after purgatory.
> *MS. Ashmole 61, f. 83.*

SEG. (1) A castrated bull. *North.*

(2) To totter; to give way. See *Sag.*

SEGE. (1) A seat. (*A.-S.*)

> One softe *seges* was he sett,
> Amonge grete lordes at the mete,
> And servède of many riche brede.
> The chylde was sett with grete honowre
> Bytwixe the kynge and the emperoure,
> His mete thay gane hym schrede.
> *Octavian, Lincoln MS.*

A *sege* was ordeyned for hem thre
To beholde alle the pryvyté
Of that holy Sacrament.
MS. Harl. 1701, f. 66.

On softe *seges* was sche sett.
MS. Cantab. Ff. ii. 38, f. 89.

(2) A jakes. MS. Arund. 249, f. 88. It was used for *stool* in all senses of that word, even the dirtiest, as in the Tempest, ii. 2. "*Latrina*, a siege or jakes," Elyot, ed. 1559.

(3) A man; a knight. (*A.-S.*)
And whan the batelle enjoined,
With speres ferisly they foynede,
There myght no *sege* be ensoynd,
That faught in the ffeld. *Degrevant*, 275.

To the senatour Petyr a sandesmane es commyne,
And saide, syr, sekyrly your *segges* are suppryside.
Morte Arthure, MS. Lincoln, f. 68.

(4) To besiege. R. de Brunne MS.
SEGET. A subject. (*A.-N.*)
SEGGE. (1) The sedge. It occurs in a list of plants in MS. Sloane 5, f. 2.
(2) The hedge-sparrow. *Devon.*
SEGGON. A poor labourer, in contempt. Tusser, p. 260. *Segger* occurs as a term of reproach in Chester Plays, ii. 51. *Seg-head*, a blockhead, Craven Gloss. *Segkite*, a term applied to a young person who is overgrown and greedy.
SEGGRUMS. Ragwort. *Yorksh.*
SEGGY. Hard, as skin is. *Cumb.* "A wound with a callous skin over it is said to be segg'd," Kennett, MS.
SEGHE. Saw. Isumbras, 17, 259.
SEGREGATE. To separate. (*Lat.*)
Such never came at all forward to better themselves, neither by reputations for vertues which they were carelesse to possesse, nor for desire they had to purge or *segregate* themselves from the soft vices they were first infected withall.
Kenelworth Parke, 1594, p. 10.

SEGS. Sedges. See *Segge* (1).
SEHID. Said?
Maister, shall I tellen more?
3e, quad the vox, al thou most sugge,
Other elles-wer thou most abugge.
Gossip, quod the wolf, for3ef hit me,
Ich habbe ofte *sehid* qued bi the.
Men seide, that thou on thine live
Misferdest mild mine wive.
Reliq. Antiq. ii. 276.

SEIE. (1) To tell. (*A.-S.*)
Go *sei* thi fadur he is to blame,
That he for gode dose me schame.
MS. Cantab. Ff. v. 48, f. 54.

(2) To go; to arrive.
SEIFE. A reed, or bush.
SEIGH. (1) A sieve. *Lanc.*
(2) To sag down heavily. *North.*
SEIGN. Seven. *Lanc.*
SEIGNORIE. Power; dominion. (*A.-S.*)
SEILINGE. Assault; attack.
And in the first of that *scylinge*
Thai slowen michel hethen genge.
Arthour and Merlin, p. 305.

SEINDE. Singed. (*A.-S.*)
SEINE. To sign. *Lydgate.*
SEINT. (1) A saint. (*A.-N.*)

That prynce it perceyvid and he let it passe and goo,
That was to Cryst his creature he did call,
To oure Lady and to Saynt *George*, and other *seyntes* moo;
Then sodenly uppone his knes the prynce did fall,
Besechyng the good Lorde and his *seyntes* alle
His ryght hym to sende and defende hym of his foo,
And said, ever, good Lorde, thy wille be doo!
MS. Bibl. Reg. 17 D. xv.

(2) A girdle. (*A.-N.*) "Seynt of a gyrdell, *tissu*," Palsgrave.
A *seynt* of silke whiche sche ther hadde
Sche knitte, and so hireselfe sche ladde.
Gower, MS. Soc. Antiq. 134, f. 108.

SEINTUARIE. A sanctuary. (*A.-N.*)
SEINURYE. Lordship.
Thogh God have 3eve hym the *seynurye*,
He 3af hym no leve to do robborye.
MS. Harl. 1701, f. 18.

SEITE. Sight. See *Gewyt.*
SEIT-HOUSE. A dwelling-house.
SEIVE. A dwarf-rush. *Cumb.*
SEIZIN. Possession. Still in common use as a law term, applied to property.
Hit is the calsere shal be thin,
Of him shal thou soone have *seisyn.*
Cursor Mundi, MS. Coll. Trin. Cantab. f. 21.

SEIZLING. A young carp.
SEK. (1) A sack. (2) Sackcloth.
(3) A second. Batchelor, p. 144.
SEKE. Sick; ill. (*A.-S.*)
SEKERE. Secure; certain.
As *sekere* as bred ys made of floure,
Smelle theme in sesyne with thy nese,
The swetnes of that savoure
Shalle geve the lysens to lyve in ease.
MS. Cantab. Ff. i. 6.

Or we wyll the walles kepe,
The *sekyrlyar* may we slepe.
MS. Cantab. Ff. ii. 38, f. 161.

SEKERINGE. A securing.
That thay shalle make me a *sekerynge*
A trews to holde us bytwene.
MS. Harl. 2252, f. 114.

SEKERSTEINE. A sacristan.
SEKESTE. Most ill or sick.
Of povre mene that myghte ille goo,
Thay tuke inne welle a sexty or moo,
Of thame that *sekeste* were.
Isumbras, 560.

SEKILMAN. An invalid.
SEKKE. "Fyl the bag," marg. gloss.
The whyles the executours *sekke*,
Of the soule they ne rekke.
MS. Harl. 1701, f. 41.

SEKUR. Certain.
He seyde, Befyse, thou schalt dye anon,
For *sekur* we schall the sloon.
MS. Cantab. Ff. ii. 38, f. 124.

SEL. Self. *North.*
SELADYNES. Chalcedonies. *Gawayne.*
SELCOUTH. Strange; wonderful; uncommon. (*A.-S.*) *Selkouthede;* wonderful, MS. Cotton. Vespas. D. vii. "Selkow or seeldam seyne," Pr. Parv. MS. Harl. 221.
SELDE. Seldom. (*A.-S.*)
Yet ever in on my dwellynge is with thee,
For *selde* or never I parte oute of thy sight.
Lydgate, MS. Ashmole 39, f 22.

SELDEN. Seldom. " *Selden* i-seize is sone forȝete" is the burden of a song in the Vernon MS. corresponding to the well-known proverb, " out of sight, out of mind." The following stanza in a copy of the Cuckowe and the Nightingale appears not to have been printed. It follows l. 200 of Urry, p. 545.

Wyth swiche a lord wille I never be,
For he ys blynde and may nothyng see,
And whome he hit he not or whome he failith,
And in hys courte ful *selden* trouth avaylyth,
So dyverse and so wilful ys he.
MS. Cantab. Ff. i. 6, f. 19.

SELE. (1) A yoke for cattle.
(2) Fortunate? (*A.-S.*)
(3) Season; time. (*A.-S.*) Still in use in the Eastern counties.

A servant letting himself, asked his master " if he would stand *seels* and *meals*," it was, perhaps, for harvest, and I understand the question to mean, would he promise the usual time for rest and refreshment, as well as for the commencement and cessation of daily labour. The *seels* referring, perhaps, more especially, to the leveners and forses. If the query was to a tradesman, say a bricklayer, it would probably refer to what is usually allowed in the way of rest and food. " I dont know much of her, only just to give her the *seel* of the day." That is, " good morning" or " good evening."
Moor's Suffolk MS.

Lorde, thoght the clerk, now whom
Myst y fynde thys yche *sele*
To whom y myȝt selle Pers wele-
MS. Harl. 1701, f. 38.

SELEN. To seal. (*A.-S.*)
SELERE. A cellar.

There was his food and his norischynge pure
Sothfast *selers* of his sustinaunce.
MS. Cantab. Ff. ii. 38, f. 19.

SELERELLE. A visor, or mask.
SELF. Self; same. (*A.-S.*) This is the objective case. *Selves*, plur.
SELF-BLACK. The natural colour, not dyed.
SELF-HEAL. The herb pimpernel.
SELFISH. Self-conceited. *Heref.*
SELF-UNED. United to itself.
SELF-WILDNESS. Obstinacy.
SELION. A short piece of land in arable ridges and furrows, of uncertain quantity. It is sometimes defined to be a ridge of land lying between two furrows. See Carlisle's Account of Charities, p. 305. " A selion, ridge of land, *porca*," Coles.
SELK. Such. (*A.-S.*)

For al the world ne woldi nout
That ich were to chapitre i-brout,
For none *selke* werkes. *MS. Digby* 86.
That ne shal nevere be,
That I shal don *selk* falseté,
On bedde ne on flore. *MS. Digby* 86.

SELL. (1) A saddle. (*Fr.*)

And turning to that place, in which whyleare
He left his loftie steed with golden *sell*,
And goodly gorgeous barbes, him found not theare.
Spenser's Faerie Queene, II. ii. 11.

(2) A porpoise. *Northumb.*
(3) An unexpected failure. *Var. dial.*
(4) A cell. *Chaucer.*
SELLED. Sold. *Linc.*

SELLENGER'S-ROUND. St. Leger's round, a favorite old country dance.
SELLICH. Sweet; mild. (*A.-S.*)

Love is les, love is lef, love is longinge;
Love is fol, love is fast, love is frowringe;
Love is *sellich* an thing, wose shal soth singe.
Love is wele, love is wo, love is geddede;
Love is lif, love is deth, love may hous fede.
Wright's Anecdota Literaria, p. 96.

SELLING. " *Chytrinda*, the play called selling of peares, or how many plums for a penie," Nomenclator, 1585, p. 298.
SELLY. Wonderfully. (*A.-S.*)

Sikurly I telle the here,
Thou shal hit bye ful *selly* dere.
Cursor Mundi, MS. Coll. Trin. Cantab. f. 8.

SELMS. Gate rails. *Northumb.*
SELN. Self. *Linc.*
SELOURE. The canopy of a bed.

Hir bed was of asure,
With a chekir *seloure*.
MS. Lincoln A. i. 17, f. 136.

SELT. (1) Sold. *North.*
(2) Chance; uncertainty. *Chesh.* " Selt, *casus ;* it's but a selt whether, *forte fortuna accidit*," Coles' Latin Dict.
SELTHE. Advantage; benefit. (*A.-S.*)

Nim in with the to Denemark bathe,
And do thou nouth onfrost this fare,
Lith and *selthe* felawes are. *Havelok*, 1338.

SEL-TIMES. Seldom. *Somerset.*
SELVYN. Self; same. (*A.-S.*)

Netheles the *selvyn* messe
Ys nother the wurse ne the lesse.
MS. Harl. 1701, f. 16.

SELWYLLY. Self-willed. *Pr. Parv.*
SELY. " Sely or fearfull, *paoureux*," Palsgrave. " Sely wretched, *meschant*," Ibid.
SELYBLE. Easy; comfortable.
SELYNES. Happiness. (*A.-S.*)

We wrecches willefuly forsake
The *selynes* that never shal slake.
Cursor Mundi, MS. Coll. Trin. Cantab. f. 141.

SEM. (1) Needlework.
(2) To think. *Devon.*
SEMANT. Slender. *North.*
SEMANZE. Glue; mortar. *North.*
SEMBLABLE. Likeness. (*A.-N.*)

Thus every thing drawethe to his *semblable*.
Lydgate, MS. Ashmole 59, f. 18.

SEMBLABLY. Similarly.

Semblably cold is that love, yea, rather it is no love, which containeth not in it the virtue and strength of working. *Becon's Works*, p. 39.

SEMBLANDE. (1) Appearance. (*A.-N.*)

And yef her may devyse bryght and shyne
Werne fairer thane the quene,
In maykyng, *semblaunt* and hewe,
They wold quyte hyme gode and true.
MS. Rawl. C. 86.

(2) Behaviour. (*A.-N.*)

The kynge behelde the quene mylde,
And sawe that sche was wyth chylde,
Then made he glad *semland.*
Twenty tymys he dud hur kysse,
Then made they game and blysse,
And he toke hur be the hande.
MS. Cantab. Ff. ii. 38, f. 72.

SEMELAND. Appearance. (*A.-N.*)

Hys body, hys vysage, ych ways
Of semeland, he semyd curtays.
MS. Cantab. Ff. ii. 38, f. 244.

SEMELE. Comely. [Assembled?]
Here comyth the kyng of Yraelle
Wyth mony a man semelé.
MS. Cantab. Ff. ii. 38, f. 69.

SEMELEDE. Assembled. (*A.-S.*)
Thane the semelede the sale,
Kyng and cardynale,
And the emperoure ryale. *Sir Degrevant*, 1841.

SEMELICHE. Seemly; comely. (*A.-S.*)

SEMEN. To seem; to appear; to resemble.
Occasionally, to look. (*A.-S.*)

SEMENAUNT. Comeliness. (*A.-N.*)
Semenaunt is a wonder thing,
It begylyt bothe knyʒt and kyng,
And makit maydenys of love longyng;
I warne ʒou of that gyle. *Reliq. Antiq.* ii. 166.

SEMENDE. Seemingly.
So that semende of lyʒte they werke
The dedis, whiche were inwarde derke.
Gower, MS. Soc. Antiq. 134, f. 42.

SEMENE. Chance. (*A.-S.*)
Thuse whelpus that burken on the so snelle,
Withinne hur moder body by semene.
Chron. Vilodun. p. 26.

SEMICOPE. A half cloak. *Chaucer.*

SEMINARY. A seminary priest; an English popish priest educated abroad.

SEMINGE. Resembling. (*A.-S.*)

SEMISOUN. A low or broken tone.

SEMLY. An assembly; a crowd.

SEMMENT. Soft; silky. *North.*

SEMMIT. Limber; supple. *North.*

SEMOTED. Separated; removed.
Is it enough if I pray with my mind, the heart being semoted from mundane affairs and worldly businesses. *Becon's Works,* p. 136.

SEMPLE. Common; low. *North.*

SEMPSTER. A sempstress. *Hall.*

SEMY. Brisk; active.

SEMY-VIF. Half alive, i. e. half dead. (*A.-N.*)

SEN. (1) Since. *North.*
And after nobull kyng Arthour
Lyved and dyʒed with honour,
As many hath don senne.
MS. Ashmole 61, f. 62.

(2) To say. *Salop.*

(3) Self, as mysen, &c. *North.*

SENAS. Senate. *Kyng Alisaunder,* 1477.

SENBY. Sign; likelihood; appearance.

SENCE. Properly. *South.*

SENCERE. A censer.
And with encence caste in the sencere,
He dede worschipe unto the autere.
Lydgate, MS. Soc. Antiq. 134, f. 16.

SENCHE. To offer or place before.
And sett hir bi him on the benche,
Win and piment he dede senche.
Arthour and Merlin, p. 87.

SENCION. The common groundsel.
For to take fysche with thy handys.—Take groundis walle that ys senchion, and hold yt yn thi handes, yn the water, and alle fysche wylle gaddar thereteo.
Reliq. Antiq. i. 324.

SEND. To go to send, to accompany any one on the road. To come send, to go to meet. *Heref.*

II.

SENDALL. Same as *Cendal,* q. v.
And the duke of Surrey that daie high marshall of England entred into the listes with a great company of men apareled in silke sendall embrodered with silver both richely and curiously.
Hall's Union, 1548.

SENE. (1) To see. *Isumbras,* 749.
He is cum to aske iiij. pounde;
Goo and fech it in a stounde,
The sothe that I may sene.
MS. Cantab. Ff. v. 48, f. 53.

(2) An assembly of scholars.

SENEK. Seneca. *Chaucer.*

SENENE. Seen. (*A.-S.*)
The pament was as clene as hit byfore was,
And no thyng senene that there was do.
Chron. Vilodun. p. 74.

SENEVE. To change, said of a corpse; to warp, said of wood. *Chesh.*

SENFY. Sign; appearance. *North.*

SENG. Shelter; shade. *Yorksh.*

SENGILLY. Continually.
Bot I am sengilly here with sex sum of knyghtes;
I beseke ʒow, syr, that we may sounde passe.
Morte Arthure, MS. Lincoln, f. 58.

SENGLES. The claws of a hawk.

SEN-GREEN. The house-leek. "Howsleke herbe, or sengrene," Prompt. Parv. p. 251.

SENNE. Sin. (*A.-S.*)
Her havest thou, sone, mikel senne.
Loverd, for his mete nome,
Lete the therfore haven no shome!
MS. Digby 86.

SENNET. (1) A particular set of notes on the trumpet or cornet.

(2) Seven-night, or week. *North.*

SENNETH. Mustard-seed. *Baber.*

SENOWRYE. A senate. *Pr. Parv.*

SENOYS. The people of Sienna.

SENSE. (1) To understand. *West.*

(2) No sense, poor, not good. *East.*

SENSEN. To incense. See Maundevile's Travels, p. 174; and Hollyband's Dictionarie, 1593, in v. *Encenser.*

SENSINE. Since then. *Cumb.*

SENSTERE. A sempstress.

SENT. (1) Assent; agreement.
Many armys were tynt,
That were never at the sent
To come to that tournament,
To do swylke dedis.
MS. Lincoln A. i. 17, f. 134.

(2) Commanded.

SENTAWSTEN. St. Austin.
Thurrow Goddes helpe and Sentawsten,
The spere anon he toke to hym.
Torrent of Portugal, p. 4s

SENTENCE. Meaning.

SENTHURY.
I wil grant hym blethely
Of al my landes the senthury.
Guy of Warwick, Middlehill MS.

SENTINE. A kennel. (*Lat.*)

SENYES. Signs, referring to the system the monks had of talking with their fingers.
Dedyst thu never know the maner of owr senyes?
Bale's Kynge Johan, p. 9

SENʒE. Synod.

46

SEP. Sheep. (*A.-S.*)

Have her twenti shilling,
This ich jeve the to meding,
To buggen the *sep* and swin.   *MS. Digby* 86.

SEPT. A railing. *Britton.*

SEPULTURE. A grave. (*A.-N.*)

SEQUACIS. Followers.

They abuse theymeself, and also othir thire *se-quacis*, gheving credence to such as wrigten of affec-clon, leving the trouth that was in deede.
Hearne's Fragment, p. 296.

SEQUENCE. Regular order; succession. *Sequent*, following; a follower.

SEQUESTER. Separation. *Shak.*

SER. Sure. Const. Freemas. 602.

SERE. (1) The same as *Sear*, q. v.

(2) Several; many; each. It is still in use in the Northern counties.

Hys handys he suffurd, for thy sake,
Thus to be bored with nayles *sere*.
MS. Cantab. Ff. ii. 38, f, 48.

Hem is levere for to here
Romaunces, many and *sere*.
MS. Ashmole 60, f. 4.

To gayr yow kene and knaw me clere,
I shall yow schew insampylles *sere*.
Croft's Excerpta Antiqua, p. 107.

Bot also in many other comforthes and savours,
swettnes, and wondirfulle felynges one *sere* maners.
MS. Lincoln A. i. 17, f. 220.

Now hafe je here a graythe lessowne,
Of *seere* maters that je solde leere.
Hampole, MS. Bowes, p. 3.

(3) Safe?

And thankyd God ofte-aythe
That sche sawe hur lorde so dere
Comyn home bothe hoole and *sere*.
MS. Cantab. Ff. ii. 38, f. 222.

(4) The claw of a bird of prey.

SERELOPES. Severally; by themselves. (*A.-S.*) It occurs in Piers Ploughman.

SERE-MONTH. August. *Aubrey.*

SERENE. The unwholesome air or damp of the evening. (*Fr.*)

SEREPE. Sirop. Nominale MS.

SEREW. A disease in a horse thus described by Topsell, 1607, p. 431:

A *serew* is a foule sorance; it is like a splent, but it is a little longer, and is most commonly on the outside of the forelegge, as the splint is on the in-side. The cure is thus. Take two spoonefuls of strong wine-vinegar, and one spoonefull of good sallet-oyle, mingle them together, and every morn-ing bestow one houre in rubbing the sorance with it altogether downeward til it be gone, which will not be long in going.

SEREWE. Sorrow. (*A.-S.*)

Bote if hoe wende hire mod,
For *serewe* mon ich wakese wod.
MS. Digby 86.

SERF-BORW. Surety; pledge. (*A.-S.*)

Sithe fey that y owe to the,
Therof shal I me *serf-borw* be.
Havelok, 1667.

SERFULLICHE. Sorrowfully. *Lydgate.*

SERGE. (1) To search.

(2) A sieve, or colander.

(3) A wax taper.

And swithe feire also je singe,
With *serges* and with candels brijt.
Cursor Mundi. MS. Coll. Trin. Cantab. f. 126.

SERGEANT. (1) A sheriff's officer.

The *serjeant* I before the jaylor name,
Because he is the dog that hunts the game:
He worries it and brings it to the toyle,
And then the jaylor lives upon the spoyle.
Taylor's Workes, 1630, iii. 10.

(2) A soldier; a squire, an attendant on a person of rank; a royal servant. (*A.-N.*)

Be sekere of this *sergeaunt*, he has me sore grevede;
I faghte noghte wyth syche a freke this fystene wyntyrs.
Morte Arthure, MS. Lincoln, f. 65.

SERICON. The flowers of zinc.

Mr. E. K. at nine of the clok afternoone sent for me to his laboratory over the gate to se how he dis-tilled *sericon*, according as in tyme past and of late he hard of me out of Riplay. *Dr. Dee's Diary*, p. 26.

SERIE. A series. (*A.-N.*)

SERIOUSLY. Seriatim.

Thus proceding to the letters, to shewe your Grace summarily, for rehersing everything *seri-ously*, I shal over long moleste your Grace.
State Papers, i. 299.

SERIS. The skin about the legs and feet of a hawk. *Berners.*

SERJOUR. A searcher; one who searches.

SERKIN.

Storis also of *serkyn* thyngis,
Of prince, prelatis, and of kyngis;
Sangis faire of selcouth ryme,
Englisch, Frensch, and Latyne.
MS. Ashmole 61, f. 5

SERKYLL. A circle.

A *serkyll* of golde that wolde noghte
With an o. pownde of golde be boghte.
MS. Cantab. Ff. ii. 38, f. 170.

SERMUN. To speak; to discourse.

Seynt Jhone to Troyle bygan to *sermun*,
Wyth ensamples of gode resun.
MS. Harl. 1701, f. 46.

SERONE. A barrel or package of soap.

SERPELL. Wild thyme.

SERPENTARY. A kind of still.

Do therto a galun of good reed wyne, and let hym stonde so al nyjt, and stepe tyl the morow, and thanne distille him thorow a *serpentarie*.
MS. in Mr. Pettigrew's possession, xv. Cent

SERPENTINE. (1) A kind of cannon.

As the *serpentine* pouder is quickly kindled, and quickly out, so the salamander stone once set on fire can never be quenched.
Greene's Gwydonius, 1593.

(2) Pertaining to the serpent.

The bytter galle pleynly to enchace
Of the venym callid *serpentyne*.
Lydgate, MS. Ashmole 39, f. 6.

SERPET. A wicker or rush basket. "A serpet, *corbis scirpeus*," Coles.

SERPIGO. A kind of tetter, or dry eruption on the skin. *Shak.*

SERRE. To join closely. (*Fr.*)

SERRY. Idiotic; mean. *Linc.*

SERTAN. Certain; certainly.

The porter rose anon *sertan*
As sone as he herd Johne calle;
Litul Johne was redy with a swerd,
And bare hym to the walle.
MS. Cantab. Ff. v. 48, f. 131.

Thus *seys* the boke *serteynlye*,
God, that is both gode and hend,
Gyff you grace that ye may mend,
And bryng us alle unto his blysse,
That never fro us schall mysse ! *MS. Ashmole* 61.

SERTE.
We hafe bene thy sowdeours this sex yere and more ;
We forsake the to daye be *serte* of owre lorde.
Morte Arthure, MS. Lincoln, f. 84.

SERTLE. To surprise ; to startle. *Essex.*

SERTTES. Certainly ; surely.
Serttes, yf I hym slepyng slone,
Manfulle ded were yt none.
Torrent of Portugal, p. 7.

SERUNDEL. The eaves of a house.

SERVAGE. Bondage ; slavery. (*A.-N.*)
The othere he putte in presoun, and solde hem to
servage, 30 for o peny. *Maundevile's Travels*, p. 83.

SERVANT. A lover. The corresponding term
mistress is still retained.

SERVE. (1) To earn. *West.*

(2) To impregnate. *Berks.*

(3) To relieve a beggar. *Derb.*

(4) To feed animals. *Var. dial.*
A lady of the West country gave a great entertainment to most of the gentlemen thereabout, and
among others to Sir Walter Raleigh. This lady,
though otherwise a stately dame, was a notable
housewife, and in the morning early she called to
one of her maids, and asked her if the pigs were
served. Sir Walter Raleigh's chamber joined the
lady's, so that he heard her. A little before breakfast, the lady coming down in great state into a
room full of gentlemen, as soon as Sir Walter
Raleigh set his eyes upon her, he said, Madam, are
the pigs *served ?* The lady answered, You know
best whether or no you have had your breakfast.
The Witty Alarum, n. d.

(5) To deserve. *Gawayne.*
Jis, quod syr Gawayne, so me God helpe,
I gyfe the grace and graunt, thofe thou hafe grefe
servede. *Morte Arthure, MS. Lincoln*, f. 80.

SERVEE. Service.
And make youre self sogettys to be
To hem that owyn yow *servee*.
MS. Harl. 1701, f. 8.

SERVELLE.
Tille a clyffe the sqwyere come sone,
A sees a knyghte hewand hym one,
And with swerde *servelle*.
MS. Lincoln A. i. 17, f. 141.

SERVICE. (1) Allowance of food.
Now the best time to feede them in the winter is
about the cock-crowing, and afterward in the morning twy-light, and soone after that let them drinke :
in the summer let them have their first meate in the
morning, and their second *service* at noone, and then
drinke after that second meate or eating, and their
third meate before evening againe, and so let them
drinke the second time. *Topsell's Beasts*, 1607, p. 81.

(2) The first stroke of a ball at the game of
tennis.

SERVICES. Bold and daring actions, an ancient military term.

SERVIOUS. Obsequious. *Pr. Parv.*

SERVOILE. The wild honeysuckle.

SES. Cessation.
Of swiche bataile nas no *ses*
To the night fram arnemorwe.
Arthour and Merlin, p. 339.

SESE. (1) To cease ; to make to cease.
Mesagers to him send in hast,
Fore wele he west hit was bot wast
Hem to withstond in hone way ;
And prayd hym to *sese* of his outrage,
And take Kateryn to mareage,
Al Frawnce to him schuld do homage,
And croune him kyng afftyr his day.
MS. Douce 302, f. 29.
They *seayd* not tylle hyt was nyghte.
MS. Cantab. Ff. ii. 38, f. 76.

(2) To give seizin to.
I gyf the my doghtur be the hande,
And *sese* the in alle my lande.
MS. Cantab. Ff. ii. 38, f. 247.

(3) To seat, or place.
In Tyberyus tyme, the trewe emperour,
Syr Sesar hymself *sesed* in Rome.
MS. Cott. Calig. A. ii. f. 109.

(4) To seize.
Thow sulde his ceptre have *seseds*, and syttyne
aboune,
Fore reverence and realtee of Rome the noble.
Morte Arthure, MS. Lincoln, f. 58.

SESKAR. A small Scotch coin.

SESOURS. Scissors ; candle-nippers.

SESS. Invitation to a dog to eat something,
perhaps smell to it first. *Dorset.*

SESSING. An assessment. *Palsgrave.*

SESSIONS. (1) A difficult job. *North.*

(2) Possessions ; property.

SESSLE. To change seats very often.

SESS-POOL. A receptacle for filth ; a kind of
reservoir for drains.

SESSY. Cease. (*Fr.*) The word *sest* is used
by Marston apparently in the same sense.

SESTIANS. Sestiana mala. A kind of apple
mentioned in Rider's Dictionarie, 1640.

SE-STOERRE. Sea-star. (*A.-S.*)
Heyl, levedy, *se-stoerre* bryht,
Godes moder, edy wyht,
Mayden ever vurst and late.
Reliq. Antiq. ii. 228.

SESTRON. A cistern. *Percy.*

SET. (1) To hire ; to let. *Var. dial.* Also a
substantive, a lease or grant.
For to save hym in his ryght
My goodes beth *sette* and solde.
Robin Hood, i. 11.

(2) A game, as at whist, &c. Also a verb, to
win the game. *East.*

(3) Astounded. *East.*

(4) *To set by*, to treat with consideration. "For
connynge they set not by," Interlude of the
iiij. Elements, n. d. *To set store by*, to set
value upon. *A set-down*, a rebuke. *To set
at*, to put a price on anything. *To set up a
side*, to become partners in a game at cards.
A set-to, an attack, or onset. *Hard set*, in a
difficulty. *To set on*, to put yeast to wort. *A
dead set*, a combined scheme against any one.
Set fast, confined. *Set off*, to go. *Set out*, a
commencement or beginning. *To set up*, to
be refractory ; to oppose ; to be raised above
one's merits. *To set off*, to reduce a reckoning by striking off too heavy charges.

(5) Disposal. *North.*

(6) To push ; to propel. *Newc.*

(7) To protect; to accompany. *Yorksh.*

(8) A young plant; a shoot.

(9) Set the hare's head to the goose-giblet, i. e., tit for tat.

(10) A gambrel. *Yorksh.*

(11) To settle; to bind. *Var. dial.*

(12) To place to account. (*A.-S.*)

(13) The Deity is mentioned in the Towneley Mysteries, pp. 97, 118, as He that " sett alle on seven," i. e., set or appointed everything in seven days. A similar phrase at p. 85 is not so evident. It is explained in the glossary, " to set things in, to put them in order," but it evidently implies in some cases an exactly opposite meaning, to set in confusion, to rush to battle, as in the following examples. " *To set the sleven,* to agree upon the time and place of meeting previous to some expedition," West. and Cumb. Dial. p. 390. These phrases may be connected with each other. Be this as it may, hence is certainly derived the phrase *to be at sixes and sevens,* to be in great confusion. Herod, in his anger at the Wise Men, says,—

Bot he thay past me by, by Mahowne in heven,
I shalle, and that in hy, *set alle on ses and seven ;*
Trow ye a kyng as I wyll suffre thaym to neven
Any to have mastry bot myself fulle even.
            Towneley Mysteries, p. 143.

Thus he *settes on sevene* with his sekyre knyghttez.
            Morte Arthure, MS. Lincoln, f. 76.

The duk swore by gret God of hevene,
Wold my hors so evene,
Зet wold *I sett all one seven*
ffor Myldor the swet !
            Degrevant, 1279.

Old Odcombs odnesse makes not thee uneven,
Nor carelesly set all *at six and seven.*
            Taylor's Workes, 1630, ii. 71.

SETE. A city. (*A.-S.*)

There ys a gyant of gret renowne,
He dystrowythe bothe *seté* and towyn.
            Torrent of Portugal, p. 39.

SETEWALE. The herb valerian.

Fykes, reisyn, dates,
Almaund rys, pomme-garnates,
Kanel and *setewale.*
            Gy of Warwike, p. 421.

SETH. (1) Since. (*A.-S.*)

Never *seth* we wedyd ware,
Therefore I make full mekyll care ;
Bot now we must per[t]e a-two,
Do thou the best, fore I must go.
            MS. Ashmole 61, xv. Cent.

(2) A scythe. Nominale MS.

SETHE. To boil. (*A.-S.*)

SET-HEDGE. A quickset hedge. *East.*

SETILLE. Seat. (*A.-S.*)

Fowles of heven er prowde inow that wald heghe
thaire *setills* aboven alle other sesshe of the se.
            MS. Coll. Eton. 10, f. 13.

Apon the *setyl* of hys majesté
That day sal alle men before hym be.
            Hampole, MS. Bowes, p. 180.

SETLINGS. Saplings.

For such as be yet infirm and weak, and newly
planted in the religion of Christ, and have taken no
sure root in the same, are easily moved as young
setlings.   *Becon's Works,* p. 18.

SETNESSE. A decree. *Hearne.*

SET-OPE. Anything by means of which a gate or door is set or kept open.

SETS. The plaits of ruffs.

SET-SPEECH. A speech carefully prepared and studied before it is delivered in public.

SETTE. Ruled. *Scott.*

SETTEN-ON. Short in growth. *North.*

SETTER. (1) To cut the dew-lap of an ox or cow, into which helleboraster, called setter-work, being put, an issue is made for ill-humours to vent themselves. *North.*

(2) An accuser. *Coles.*

SETTER-GRASS. The herb bear's-foot. *Yorksh.* Spelt *setyrgrise* in Nominale MS.

SETTER-OUT. An editor, or author.

SETTING. The west, so called because the quarter of the setting sun.

SETTING-DOWN. Said of a hawk when put into the mew. Gent. Rec. ii. 63.

SETTING-PIN. A dibble. *Glouc.* " Debbyll or settyng stycke," Huloet, 1552.

SETTING-STICK. A stick used for making the plaits or sets of ruffs.

SETTLE. (1) To fall in price. *Linc.*

(2) A long seat, generally one with a long back to it. *North.* It is an archaism. See *Setille.*

SETTLE-BED. A folding bed.

SETTLE-STONES. Stones at the edge of a gutter in a cow-house. *North.*

SEU. Suit. *Hearne.*

SEUGH. A wet ditch; a drain. *North.* " The towne sinke, the common sew," Nomenclator, 1585, p. 391.

SEUNE. Seven. *Cumb.*

SEUREMENT. Security, generally used in the legal sense. (*A.-N.*)

SEURETEE. Certainty. (*A.-N.*)

SEVEN-NIGHT. A week. This word occurs in The French Alphabet, 1615, p. 18.

He levyth not oon *sevenyghts.*
            MS. Cantab. Ff. ii. 38, f. 68.

SEVEN-YEAR. " Has been a vile thief this seven year," Shakespeare. It was a proverbial expression for *a long time.*

O, the body of a Gorge,
I wold I had them heare ;
In faith, I wold chope them,
Thay ware not so hack this *seven yeere !*
            Mariage of Witt and Wisdome, 1579.

I can then thanke Sensuall Apetyte :
That is the best daunce without a pype
That I saw this *seven yere.*
            Interlude of the Four Elements, n. d.

SEVERALS. Portions of common assigned for a term to a particular proprietor, the other commoners waiving for the time their right of common over them. See Hunter on Shakespeare, i. 267.

SEVERY. A division or compartment of a vaulted ceiling. " Severous of a howse," MS. Dictionary, 1540.

SEW. (1) Same as *Assue,* q. v.

(2) Sowed. *Linc.*

(3) To wipe the beak, a term in ancient hawking given by Berners.

(4) A kind of pottage. "Sadduleres in sew,"
Reliq. Antiq. i. 81.

> The flosche, whan it was so to-hewe,
> Sehe taketh and maketh therof a *sewe*.
>
> *Gower, MS. Soc. Antiq.* 134, f. 164.

(5) To ooze out. *Suffolk.*

(6) To drain land. A covered drain or wet
ditch is called a sew. *Var. dial.*

(7) To mourn; to lament. *Kennett.*

SEWANT. The plaice. *Northumb.*

SEWE. (1) To assay meat at table. " I sewe
at meate, *je taste*," Palsgrave.

(2) To follow. (*A.-S.*)

> In wyntur, in the depe snowe,
> On every side the wil me trace ;
> Be my steppys they wil me knowe,
> And *seuen* me fro place to place.
>
> *MS. Cantab.* Ff. v. 48, f. 110.
>
> Syr, he seyde, y come ryghte nowe,
> Go before, y wylle *sewe* yow.
>
> *MS. Cantab.* Ff. ii. 38, f. 154.

(3) To make suit for a thing.

SEWELL. A scarecrow, which generally consisted of feathers tied to a string to prevent
deer from breaking ground, by frightening
them. The term is metaphorically used in a
passage quoted by Nares, in v. *Shewelles*,
who entirely misunderstands it.

SEWENT. Even; regular. *West.* Coles has
it in the sense of convenient, fit.

SEWER. The officer who set and removed the
dishes, tasted them, &c.

SEWSTER. A sempstress. *Somerset.* The
term occurs in the Pr. Parv.

SEXESTEN. A sexton.

> The *sexesten* went wolle than,
> That he had be a wode man.
>
> *MS. Cantab.* Ff. ii. 38, f. 240.

SEXTARY. A pint and a half. It varied in
measure in different countries.

> Then must the quantity be two drams of cas-
> toreum, one *sextary* of honey and oyle, and the like
> quantity of water, but in the fit it helpeth with
> vineger by smelling to it. It helpeth the palsie,
> taken with rew or wine, sod in rew, so also all heart
> trembling, ache in the stomack, and quaking of the
> sinewes. *Topsell's Beasts,* 1607, p 49.

SEXTE. Sixth. Perceval, 248.

SEXTIPARTITE. In six parts.

> They not onely made an indenture *sextipartite*
> sealed wyth their seales and signed with their handes.
>
> *Hall's Union,* 1548.

SEXTRY. A sacristy, or vestry.

SEY. A skimming dish. *West.*

SEYLENDE. Sailing.

> And thus by schip forth *seylende*,
> Hire and hire childe to Rome he brou3te.
>
> *Gower, MS. Soc. Antiq.* 134, f. 69.

SEYNE. Sodden, or boiled.

SEYNOWRES. Noblemen. (*A.-N.*)

> Salle he never sownde see his *seynowres* in Rome,
> Ne sitt in the assemblé in syghte wyth his feris.
>
> *Morte Arthure, MS. Lincoln,* f. 70.

SEYNTWARE. A sanctuary.

> And uche wonde that thei there bare,
> He spered hem in her *seyntware*.
>
> *Cursor Mundi, MS. Coll. Trin. Cantab.* f. 43.
>
> And intrede into Seynt Edes *seyntwarye*.
>
> *Chron. Vilodun.* p. 82.

SEYPER. A drunkard. *Cumb.*

SHAAD. A meadow.

SHAB. The itch in animals. *West.* In old
English, a scab. " He shrapeth on is shabbes,'
Wright's Pol. Songs, p. 239. *Shabby*, mangy,
itchy, Palmer, p. 80.

> Alle that ben sore and *shabbid* eke with synne,
> Rather with pité thanne with reddure wynne.
>
> *Lydgate, MS. Soc. Antiq.* 134, f. 22.

SHABBAROON. A mean shabby fellow.

SHAB-OFF. To abscond. *North.*

SHAB-RAG. A mean beggarly person.

SHAB-WATER. A water generally prepared
with tobacco, and sometimes with the addition
of some mercurial, to cure the *shab.*

SHACK. (1) To rove about. As a substantive,
an idle worthless vagabond. *Var. dial.*

(2) In Norfolk and Suffolk, liberty of winter
pasturage, the lords of manors having the
privilege to feed their sheep at pleasure upon
their tenants' lands during the six winter
months. Also a custom in Norfolk to have
common for hogs, from the end of harvest till
seed-time, in all men's grounds; whence *to
go at shack* in that county signifies as much
as to go at large. *Dict. Rust.*

(3) The grain left after harvest and gleaning ;
fallen mast or acorns. *East.* Tusser has the
phrase *shack-time.*

(4) To shed, or shake out. *Var. dial.*

SHACK-A-BACK. An idle vagabond.

SHACKATORY. A hound.

> No *shackatory* comes neere him : if hee once get
> the start, hee's gone, and you gone too.
>
> *The Wandering Jew.*

SHACKED. Rough ; shaggy. *West.* "Their
haire is *shacked*," Harrison, p. 41.

SHACKELY. To shake out, or scatter, as hay
from a waggon. " How ut do *schakely*
about !" *Devon.*

SHACKET. A small cart-load. *North.*

SHACK-FORK. A wooden fork for shaking
straw off the barn floor. *Yorksh.* " A schak-
forke, *pastinatum*," MS. Dict. 1540. For
pastinum? Kennett explains it, " a fork of
wood which threshers use to shake up the
straw withall that all the corn may fall out
from amongst it."

SHACK-HOLE. A hollow in the ground which
receives the surface water. Craven Gl. ii. 111.

SHACKLE. (1) The wrist. *North.*

(2) A twisted band, generally made of rushes or
straw. *Somerset.*

(3) An iron loop moving on a bolt.

(4) Stubble. *Heref.*

> The cure is thus : let him blood of his two
> breast vaines, of his two *shackle* vains, and of his
> two vaines above the cronets of his hinder hooves ;
> if the vaines wil bleed, take from them three pints
> at least, if they wil not bleed, then open his neck
> vain and take so much from thence. Save the
> blood, and let one stand by and stir it as he bleeds,
> lest it grow into lumps.
>
> *Topsell's Beasts,* 1607, p. 400.

SHACKLE-HAMMED. Bow-legged.

SHACKLE-NET. The flue net. *North.*

SHACKLES. Cow-chains. *North.*

SHACKLING. Idle; loitering. *Var. dial.*

SHACKLOCKS. Locks for fetters.

And bids his man bring out the five-fold twist,
His shackles, *shacklocks*, hampers, gyves, and chaines.
Browne's Britannia's Pastorals, i. 129.

SHAD. (1) Overdid; excelled. *Lanc.*

(2) Separated; shaded. *Hearne.*

SHADANDE. Shedding; scattering.

The schafte schoderede and schotte in the schire beryne,
That the *schadande* blode over his schanke rynnys.
Morte Arthure, MS. Lincoln, f. 93.

SHADBRID. A minnow.

SHADE. (1) A sheath. *Suffolk.*

(2) The same as *Shard,* q. v.

(3) A shed. (4) To shed. *North.*

(5) " *Discrimen,* the schade of the hede," Nominale MS. inter membra humani corporis. It means the parting of the hair on the head.

(6) Shed; flowed. *Gawayne.*

SHADEL. A water-gate; a gate for stopping water used in mill-streams.

SHADOW. (1) Same as *Bone-grace,* q. v.

(2) An uninvited guest. (*Lat.*)

SHAFF. (1) Chaff. (*A.-S.*)

(2) Nonsense; stupid talk. *North.*

SHAFFERONS. Chaffrons, or champfrains.

SHAFFLES. A bungler. *Yorksh.*

SHAFFLING. (1) Indolent. (2) An awkward and insignificant person. *North.*

SHAFT. (1) The handle of anything. A broomstick is a *besom shaft,* and the use of the word is extended to the handle of a spoon or fork, &c. *Linc.*

(2) Creature. (*A.-S.*) The copy in MS. Vespas. A. iii, f. 4, reads " wit tuin maner o *scaft.*"

For he wolde be that Kyng of craft,
Worscheped with two maner *shaft.*
Cursor Mundi, MS. Coll. Trin. Cantab. f. 3.

(3) An arrow; a spear. *Palsgrave.*

(4) A maypole.

(5) A lead-mine, or coal-pit. *North.*

(6) A net for catching birds.

SHAFTED. Set; sank. *Gawayne.*

SHAFTMAN. A measure taken from the top of the extended thumb to the utmost part of the palm, and generally considered as half a foot. (*A.-S.*) " A shafman, shafmet, or shaftment, the measure of the fist with the thumb set up," Ray's English words, ed. 1674, p. 40. Florio, p. 414, gives it a particular meaning, " a certaine rate of cloth that is given above measure, which drapers call a handfull or *shaft-man.*"

The cantelle of the clere schelde he kerfes in sondyre,
Into the schuldyre of the sch ilke a *schaftmonde* large.
Morte Arthure, MS. Lincoln, f. 97.

SHAG. (1) Rough hair. *Devon.*

(2) A slice of bread. *Cumb.*

(3) A kind of cloth, used for lining of cloaks, church hassocks, &c. *Silk shag* is occasionally mentioned.

(4) To shake, or jog.

(5) The same as *Shack,* q. v.

(6) A cormorant. *South.* Hence the phrase, as wet as a shag.

(7) To slink away. *Glouc.*

SHAGAPENTER. A shoulder of pork roasted, with the blade-bone cut into it. *Devon.*

SHAGEBUSH. (1) A sackbut.

(2) A harquebuss, or hand-gun. " Schagbusshe a gonne, *hacquebutte,*" Palsgrave.

SHAG-FOAL. A sort of ghost or spectre, which under this appearance is thought to haunt different parts of the county. *Linc.*

SHAG-HAT. A sort of hat made very long in the down. *North.*

SHAG-RAG. A mean beggarly fellow. " *Guerluset,* somewhat like our *shagrag,* a by-word for a beggerlie souldior," Cotgrave.

A scurvie *shagragge* gentleman new come out of the North, a punie, a freshman, come up hither to learne fashions and seeke to expell me.
Exchange Ware at the Second Hand, 1615.

For plainnesse is despisde, and honestie
Is fellow *shagrag* with simplicitie.
Scot's Certaine Pieces of this Age, 1616.

The *shak-rag* shag-haird crue, whose boundles minds
Must be supplide with shifting or by stealth.
Taylor's Urania, ed. 1630, p. 7.

SHAIL. To walk crookedly. " I shayle with the fete, *jentretaille des pieds,*" Palsgrave. Still in use, Forby, 294. *Shailer,* a cripple. See further in *Shale* (4).

SHAKE. (1) To dance. Originally, to go at a great rate, to move rapidly. (*A.-S.*)

(2) *To shake the elbow,* to play at dice. *To shake a fall,* to wrestle. *No great shakes,* nothing extraordinary.

(3) A crack in wood. *North.* Hence *shaky,* full of cracks.

(4) A fissure in the earth. *Derb.*

(5) Futuo. This seems to be the ancient form of *shag,* given by Grose. " *Lascivus,* Anglice a schakere," Nominale MS.

(6) To brag, or boast.

SHAKE-BAG. A large game-cock.

SHAKEBUCKLER. A swashbuckler; a bully.

SHAKE-CAP. A North country game.

SHAKEN. Paltry; mean; poor. *Shaken-brained,* disordered in mind. *North.*

SHAKES. (1) A bad character. *North.*

(2) Applied sometimes to quick action. " I'll do it in a brace of *shakes.*" *East.* " Thei wente a nobull schakke," at a great rate, Hunttyng of the Hare, 96. " Schokkes in with a schakke," Morte Arthure, MS. Lincoln, f. 72.

SHAKING. (1) The ague. *North.*

As to the nature of our Wiltshire sheep, negatively they are not subject to the *shaking,* which the Dorsetshire sheep are.
Aubrey's Wilts, MS. Royal Soc. p. 309.

(2) *Shaking of the sheets,* an old country dance, frequently mentioned with a double entendre by our old dramatists.

Besides, there are many pretty provocatory dances, as the kissing dance, the cushin dance, the *shaking of the sheets,* and such like, which are important instrumentall causes whereby the skilfull hath both clyents and custome.
Taylor's Workes, 1630, ii. 96.

SHAKING-NAUGHT. Worthless.

SHAKY. Feeble; weak. *Var. dial.*

SHALDER. (1) A kind of slate.

(2) To give way; to tumble down.

(3) A broad flat rush.

SHALE. (1) A husk. " The *shailes* or stalkes of hempe," Hollyband's Dictionarie, 1593. Also a verb, to husk or shell, as peas, &c.

And mony *shalus* he syʒe falle from hurr heyʒe tho.
Chron. Vilodun. p. 123.

His coloure kepynge ever in oone by kynde.
And doth his pipines in the *schalls* bynde.
Lydgate, MS. Soc. Antiq. 134, f. 13.

(2) An earthen pan. *Somerset.*

(3) Loose ore or substance from a mine or quarry; alum ore. *North.*

(4) " Proper to the feet, in with the heels and out with the toes," Hallamsh. Gl. p. 121. " *Esgrailler*, to shale, or straddle with the feet or legs," Cotgrave. See *Shail.* " To drag the feet heavily,". Craven Gl.

(5) To give way, or slide down.

SHALKE. (1) Chalk.

Thurghe a faire champayne undyr *schalke* hyllis,
The kyng fraystes a-furth over the fresche strandes.
Morte Arthure, MS. Lincoln, f. 66.

(2) A man; a soldier. *(A.-S.)*

Thane the *schalkes* scharpelye scheftys theire horses,
To schewen them semly in theire scheene wedes.
Morte Arthure, MS. Lincoln, f. 79.

(3) Armour for the shoulder?

Sembles one the sowdeours, and settys theire dyntys,
Thourghe the scheldys so schene *schalkes* they towche.
Morte Arthure, MS. Lincoln, f. 92.

SHALL. A shoal. *Devon.*

SHALLIGO. Scanty, thin, applied to dress. *Dorset.*

SHALLOP. A two-masted vessel.

The very flower and prime of the Spanish army, in fourscore ponts or long-bottomed boats and *shallops,* before Stavenisse, a little island in Zealand, some of the *shallops* then running on ground, and the fleet of the United Provinces setting upon them, divers endeavoured to escape, who were slain or drowned. *MS. Harl.* 646.

SHALLOW. The finscale fish. *East.*

SHALLY-WALLY. A term of contempt. *North.*

SHALM. (1) To shriek. *Suffolk.*

(2) The tapestry of a bed.

SHALMIE. A psaltery. *Chaucer.*

SHAM. (1) Shame; bad conduct. *Sham-a-sterne,* not one. *North.*

(2) To blush with shame.

SHAMBLE. (1) To disperse. *East.*

(2) To walk awkwardly. Metaphorically, to be unsteady in conduct. *Var. dial.*

SHAMBLES. The frame of wood that hangs over a shaft-horse in a cart. *Oxon.*

SHAMEFAST. Modest. *Palsgrave.*

SHAMERAGS. Shamrocks.

Whilst all the Hibernian kernes, in multitudes,
Did feast with *shamerags* stew'd in usquebagh.
Taylor's Workes, 1630, ii. 4.

SHAMES. A mode of exclamation. What the shames! i. e. are you not ashamed?

SHAMES-DEDE. A death of shame.

Therefore at hym thay hade envy;
A tornament than did thay crye,
Thay thoghte to do hym quede,
And *schames-dede* with-alle. *Isumbras,* 612.

SHAMEW. Same as *Chammer,* q. v.

SHAMMING-ABRAHAM. An odd phrase, common among soldiers and sailors, used when they counterfeit sickness or infirmity. It was probably derived from the Abraham men of Shakespeare's time, described in King Lear. See *Abraham-Men.*

SHAMMOCKS. A bad going horse.

SHAMNEL. A masculine woman. *Glouc.*

SHAMS. Gaiters. *Linc.*

SHAN. (1) Bashful; confused. *North.* " Shan, pudor, verecundia," Coles.

(2) To turn out the toes. *Yorksh.*

(3) Wild; said of cattle when inclined to run; sometimes also, I believe, of a profligate spendthrift. *Linc.*

SHANDERY-DAN. A kind of small cart or trap, generally without springs.

SHANDLICHE. Vileness; baseness. *(A.-S.)*

No for Merlin the gode clerk,
That can so michel *schandliche* werk.
Arthour and Merlin, p. 159.

SHANDY. (1) Shabby; untidy. *Dorset.*

(2) Mild; gentle. *North.*

(3) Wild; unsteady. *Yorksh.*

SHANGY. A riot, or row. *North.*

SHANK. (1) The projecting point of a hill, joining it with the plain. *North.*

(2) The spoke of a wheel. *Devon.*

(3) Dusk; twilight. *Yorksh.*

(4) The upright part of a candlestick. " The shanke of a candlesticke betweene the nose and the foote," Baret, 1580.

(5) The tunnel of a chimney.

SHANKS. (1) Slates. *Durham.*

(2) Fur from the legs of animals. " Schanke of bouge, *fourrure de cuissettes,*" Palsgrave.

Also at the goynge up of Master Chaunceller into the Lollars tower, we have good proofe that there laye on the stockes a gowne eyther of murrey or crimosyn in grayn furred with *shankes.*
Hall, Henry VIII. f. 51.

SHANK'S-NAG. On foot. *Var. dial.*

SHANNA. Shall not. *North.*

SHANNY. Wild; foolish. *East.*

SHANTEGOS. Half-bricks. *Var. dial.*

SHANTY. Smart; gay; showy. *Var. dial.*

SHAPE. (1) To begin; to commence. *North.* Also, to tell a tale.

(2) A mess; a litter. *Devon.*

(3) A dress of disguise. A very common term in old plays.

(4) The A.-S. gesceapu, *verenda, pudenda.* "Count, a womans shappe, *con,*" Palsgrave. Still in common use in Lincolnshire, used especially in the case of infants and children. " The shape of a mare," Elyot in v. *Hippomanes.* See Chester Plays, i. 29.

Bochas rehersith of wyfis many oone,
Which to her husbondis were contrarious;
Among alle other he wrytyth of oone,
Semeramis hir name, of levyng vicious,
Quene of Assirie, he callyth hir thus:
Which wold no man in eny wyse donye,
But wyth her crokid *shap* encrece and multeply.
Reliq. Antiq. ii. 23

(5) A portrait, or picture. *Devon.*

6) Formed; figured. (*A.-S.*)

> Thy councellere schalle be an ape,
> And in a clothyng ye schalle be *schape.*
> > *MS. Cantab. Ff. ii. 38, f. 241.*

SHAPES. A tight-laced girl.

SHAPING-KNIFE. A shoemaker's paring-knife. *Palsgrave.*

SHAPLY. Fit; comely. (*A.-S.*)

> Constant in vertu, flemer of malyce,
> Trew of your worde, of wordys mesurable,
> Benigne and gracius, al voyd of vyce,
> Humbil of speryt, discreyt and honourable,
> *Shaply* and fayre, jocunde and ameabille.
> > *MS. Fairfax 16.*

> He is noust *schaply* for to wyve
> In erthe amonge the wymmen here.
> > *Gower, MS. Soc. Antiq. 134, f. 81.*

SHAPPEROON.

> Her *shapperoones,* her perriwigs and tires,
> Are reliques which this flatt'ry much admires;
> Rebatoes, maske, her busk and busk-point too,
> As things to which mad men must homage doe.
> > *Taylor's Workes, 1630, ii. 111.*

SHAPPERS. Makers; creators.

> But she kunne the poyntes of crystenyng,
> Ne beleveth nat on these *shappers.*
> > *MS. Harl. 1701, f. 64.*

SHAPS. Oats without the grain. *North.*

SHARCHE. To search. "*Rimor,* to be scharchyd," Vocabulary, MS. xv. Cent.

SHARD. (1) A piece of broken pottery; a fragment of stone or any brittle substance. *Var. dial.* "Shardes of marble wherewith they used to playster theyr walles," Elyot in v. *Crusta.*

(2) An opening in a wood. *Yorksh.*

(3) The shell or hard outward covering of insects. *North.* The scales of an animal. "The shard-borne beetle," the beetle borne on by its shard, Shakespeare. Some are of opinion that Shakespeare here means shard-born, born in a shard, or dung, and Harrison, p. 229, calls the beetle the *turdbug.*

> For longe tyme it so befelle,
> That with his swerd, and with his spere,
> He might not the serpent dere;
> He was so *sherded* all aboute,
> It held all edge toole withoute.
> > *Gower, ed. 1554, f. 103.*

(4) A notch. *Var. dial.*

(5) Cow dung. *North.* "Sharde and dunge," Elyot in v. *Bonasus,* ed. 1559.

(6) A gap in a fence. *Var. dial.* According to Stanihurst, p. 11, it was so called in his time by the inhabitants of Fingal. "Nethe style ne sherd," Lydgate, p. 114.

(7) To take a shard, i. e. to take a cup too much, to get tipsy. *Devon.*

SHARE. (1) To cut. (*A.-S.*)

> The beste stedes that thei hade
> By the scholders he them *scharde,*
> He was never so hard y-stade
> > ffor wele ne for wo! *Degrevant 1630.*

> As the prest hyt brak, the aungel hyt *share.*
> > *MS. Harl. 1701, f. 66.*

> Hur skarlet sleve he *schare* of then,
> He seyde, lady, be thys ye schalle me ken.
> > *MS. Cantab. Ff. ii. 38, f. 89.*

(2) A crop of grass. *Somerset.*

(3) The sycamore tree. *West.*

(4) A vile woman. *Devon.*

(5) To ridicule any one. *Linc.*

(6) The pubes of a man. (*A.-S.*)

> Sychone se I never ere
> Stondynge opone *schare.*
> > *MS. Porkington 10.*

SHAREVIL. A garden fork. *Salop.*

SHARGE. Futuo. *North.*

SHARHOG. A yearling sheep. *North.*

SHARK. (1) To swindle; to defraud. *Shak.* Also a substantive, a thief, or swindler. Grose gives it as an Exmoor word. *Shark-gull, sharker,* one who preys on simpletons.

> These thieves doe rob us with our owne good will,
> And have dame Nature's warrant for it still;
> Sometimes these *sharks* doe worke each others wrack,
> The ravening belly often robs the backe.
> > *Taylor's Workes, ii. 117.*

> The owle-eyd *sharkers* spied him how he felt
> To finde a post; his meaning soone they smelt.
> > *Scot's Philomythie, 1616.*

(2) A notch. *Glouc.*

SHARM. To make a confused chattering noise. *Sharming,* a confused noise, a din, a buzzing, such as is made by chattering or unruly children, Moor's Suffolk Words, p. 339.

> And though thei *sharme* and crye, I care not a mygh,
> But with my sharpe sworde ther ribbes I shall strake.
> > *Digby Mysteries, p. 10.*

SHARN. Cow dung. *North.* A cockchafer is called a *sharn-bug* in Sussex.

SHARNEBUDE. A beetle. Kennett gives it as a Kent word for a black beetle.

> Lyke to the *sharnebudes* kynde,
> Of whose nature this I fynde,
> That in the hotest of the day,
> Whan comen is the mery May,
> He spret his wynge, and up he fleeth.
> > *Gower, MS. Bodl. 294, f. 29.*

SHARP. (1) Cold; frosty. *Var. dial.*

(2) The shaft of a cart. *West.*

(3) Pungent in taste. (*A.-S.*)

(4) Quick; active. *Var. dial.* It occurs in Pr. Parv. MS. Harl. 221.

(5) A sword.

> I desire that a chalice be made of my great *sharpe,* and offered to our Lady in the Lady Chapel at Tewksbury. *Test. Vetust. p. 240.*

SHARPING-CORN. "Is a customary gift of corn, which, at every Christmas, the farmers in some parts of England give to their smith for sharping their plough-irons, harrow-tines, and such like, and exceeds not half a bushel for a plough-land," Blount.

SHARPLYNGS. Nails. "Item, for *sharplyngs* for nalyng of gressys, j. d." Croft's Excerpta Antiqua, p. 19.

SHARPS. The refuse of flour; sometimes, an inferior sort of flour.

SHARPSET. Very hungry. *Var. dial.*

> And so I thinke that if anie were so *sharpe set* as to eat fried flies, butterd bees, stued snailes, either on Fridaie or Sundaie, he could not be therefore indicted of haulte treason.
> > *Stanihurst's Ireland, 1586, p. 19.*

SHARTHE.

> Thane warme it hate in a *scharthe*, and anoynte
> the gowte bi the fire, and do so ofte, and it wille see
> inekille. *MS. Lincoln. Med. f. 306.*

SHASHOONS. A sort of stiff leathers tied round the small of the leg to make the boots look smooth and in shape. *Glouc.*

SHASOR. A wine-cooler.

SHATERANDE. Dashing. *Gawayne.*

SHATTED. Bespattered. *Devon.*

SHATTER. (1) To sprinkle. *Kent.*

(2) A number, or quantity. *South.*

(3) Harebrained; giddy. *North.*

(4) To scatter about. *Dorset.* Hence *shattery*, loose, not compact.

SHATTER-PATE. A giddy, weak fellow.

SHATY. To chastise. *R. de Brunne.*

SHAUL. (1) Shallow. *Var. dial.*

(2) A small washing-tub, made hollow, and without staves. *Kent.*

(3) To cast the first teeth. *West.*

(4) A wooden shovel without a handle, used for the purpose of putting corn into a winnowing machine. *Sussex.*

(5) Salve for bruises. *Devon.*

(6) To dispute; to wrangle. *Linc.*

SHAVE. A small coppice. *Kent.*

SHAVELDER. A fellow who goes wandering idly about like a vagabond.

SHAVELING. A friar, in contempt.

> John preached to al men repentance of former
> misdoing, and Becket proclaimed to his *shavelinge*
> immunitie of condigne punishment, even in a case
> of most wicked murthering.
> *Lambarde's Perambulation, 1596, p. 438.*

SHAVER. *A cunning shaver*, a subtle fellow; *a young shaver*, a boy.

SHAVES. Shafts. *West.*

SHAVING. Anything very small.

SHAW. (1) To scold sharply. *West.*

(2) A thicket. This word is often explained a small wood, and in the glossary to Syr Gawayne, a grove, or wood. In early English writers it has usually the meaning I have assigned to it, but the other senses are also employed. "Under the shawe of the wood," Morte d'Arthur, i. 374. Still in use in the provinces.

> He that come forthermast es slayne
> In that *schawe* schene.
> *MS. Lincoln A. 1. 17, f. 137.*
> That range in the sesone in the schene *schawes*
> So lawe in the lawndes so lykand notes.
> *Morte Arthure, MS. Lincoln, f. 81.*
> It thouзte hire fayre and seyde, here
> I wol abide undir the *schawe.*
> *Gower, MS. Soc. Antiq. 134, f. 111.*
> In somer when the *shawes* be sheyne,
> And leves be large and long,
> Hit is fulle mery in feyre foreste
> To here the foulys song.
> *MS. Cantab. Ff. v. 48, f. 125.*
> Levere is the wrenne,
> Abouten the *schowe* renne,
> Than the fithel draut,
> Other the floute craf.
> *Reliq. Antiq. ii. 107.*

(3) To rub the skin off by friction. Still in use. (Swed.)

SHAWE. To show.

> We have зou tolde the sothe sawe
> Of al that we have leve to *shawe.*
> *Cursor Mundi, MS. Coll. Trin. Cantab. f. 113.*

SHAW-FOWL. An artificial bird, made for fowlers to shoot at. *Dict. Rust.*

SHAWM. A shalm; a sort of pipe resembling a hautboy. Arch. xxiii. 44.

SHAWNTY. Showy; flashy. *Norf.*

SHAWS. The tops of turnips, &c. *Lanc.*

SHAY. (1) A chaise. *Shay-lad*, a post-boy.

(2) A light colour. *Kent.*

SHAZZAASING. An awkward person. *Devon.*

SHE. Her. *West.*

SHEAD. (1) To slope regularly. *Chesh.*

(2) A rough pole of wood. *Kent.* Harrison, p. 193, mentions "sheads for poles." *Sheed-wood*, rough poles.

SHEAF. A bundle of arrows. Drayton, p. 29, mentions "a sheafe arrow."

SHEAL. (1) To shell peas, &c.

(2) A temporary summer hut.

SHEAR. (1) To gnaw, or eat off; to tear with the teeth. See Palsgrave, and Thoms' Anecd. and Traditions, p. 27.

> But this must be wrought under the earth in the
> caves, dennes, or furrowes, made of purpose, which
> is to be performed two manner of waies, one by pla-
> cing the gin in some perch of wood, so as that assoone
> as the beast is taken by the necke, it may presently
> fly up and hang him, for otherwise with his teeth
> hee will *sheare* it asunder and escape away alive.
> *Topsell's Beasts, 1607, p. 225.*

(2) A sheath for scissors. *West.*

(3) To reap. *Var. dial.*

(4) A crop of grass, &c. *Devon.*

SHEAR-GRASS. A species of sedge.

SHEAR-HOG. A ram or wether after the first shearing is so called. *Midl. C.*

SHEARING. A sheep only once shorn.

SHEARING-KNIFE. A thatcher's tool used for shearing the roof. *Yorksh.*

SHEARMAN. "Scherman, *tondeur*," Palsgrave. "Schermannes poole, *preche a draps*," Ibid. "*Tondeur de draps*, a shearman or cloth-worker," Cotgrave.

SHEAT. A young hog. *South.* "*Gorret*, a little sheat," Cotgrave.

SHEATH. (1) The prepuce of an animal.

(2) The piece of timber which holds the beam and throck together.

(3) A fountain of salt water.

SHEAVE. To bind corn. *Midl. C.*

SHED. (1) The parting of the hair. "*La greve de moun cheef*, the schod of my eved," MS. Arund. 220, f. 297. "*Discrimen*, the sced of the hede," Nominale MS. "The deviding or *shedding* of a womans haire of hir head," Florio, p. 483. Still used in the North, to divide, to separate. Compare Kyng Alisaunder, 48, *shedynges*, Bodl. MS.

> In heed he had a *sheed* biforn,
> As Nazarenus han there thei are born.
> *Cursor Mundi, MS. Coll. Trin. Cantab. f. 116.*

(2) Mingere. *Devon.*

(3) Difference. *Lanc.*

(4) To spill. Still in use. *Schedez*, pours, occurs in Syr Gawayne.

(5) The handle of a pail. *Devon.*

(6) To surpass; to excel. *Lanc.*

(7) Surprised. *Yorksh.*

(8) The sheath of a knife. *East.* It occurs as a verb in the Pr. Parv.

(9) The slope of a hill. " Schedde of an hyll, *tertre*," Palsgrave.

(10) A tub for cream. *Linc.*

SHEDELE. A channel of water.

SHEDER. A female sheep. *Linc.*

SHEEDINGS. The seventeen kirks or parishes in the Isle of Man are divided into six parts, which are there call'd *sheedings*, every sheeding comprehending three kirks or parishes, except one which has only two. Kennett, MS.

SHEELY. The chaffinch. *North.*

SHEEN-NET. A large drag-net.

SHEENSTRADS. Spatterdashes. *Devon.*

SHEEP-BITER. A thief. A cant term. The word is played upon in the following passage:

A sepulchre to seafish and others in ponds, moates, and rivers; a sharp *sheepe-biter*, and a marvellous mutton-monger, a gorbelly glutton.

Man in the Moone, 1609.

SHEEP-CRATCH. A frame of wood on which sheep are laid. *North.*

SHEEP-GATE. (1) A right of stray for one sheep. Craven Gloss. ii. 117.

(2) A hurdle with bars. *Kent.*

SHEEP-KILLING. The herb pennywort.

SHEEP-RAIK. A sheep-walk. *North.*

SHEEP'S-EYE. A wanton look. *Var. dial.*
"Affectionate winke, a sheepes eye," Cotgrave.

SHEEP'S-FOOT. A kind of hammer, the handle of which is made of iron, and has a claw at the end. Hence its name.

SHEEP'S-SLITE. Sheep's pasture, or walk. *Dorset.*

SHEEP-WASH. A festival in the North. See Brand's Pop. Antiq. ed. 1841, ii. 20.

A seed-cake at fastens; and a lusty cheese-cake at our *sheepe-wush*.

The Two Lancashire Lovers, 1640, p. 19.

SHEER. (1) Sharp; cold. *Glouc.*

(2) Clear; transparent; pure. The more ancient form is *shere*. Forby has it, " bright red, shining with inflammation."

(3) Absolute; mere; pure. *Var. dial.*

(4) Brittle. *East.*

(5) Quick; at once. *Var. dial.*

(6) A fishing spear. *Sussex.*

(7) Odd; singular. *North.*

SHEER-THURSDAY. Maundy Thursday.

SHEESENS. Hers. *Dorset.*

SHEET. To shoot down, as water.

SHEETED-COW. A cow having a white band like a sheet round her body.

SHEEVE. A pulley, a small wheel driven by a belt or rope. *Northumb.*

SHE-FAMILIAR. A kept mistress.

SHEFE. A shive of bread. This form of the word occurs in Nominale MS.

SHEFFE. Thirty gads of steel.

SHEFTE. To shift about.

Thus they *schaften* fore schotys one thas schire strandys.

Morte Arthure, MS. Lincoln, f. 91.

SHEIT. To shoot.

The bisshop, for his absolucyon;
The priste, the clerk, for her syngyng swete:
Knyghtis and squyers, for armys and renoun;
Yomen and grome, for thay styfly *sheyt*.

MS. Fairfax 16.

SHEKILS. Ague, or trembling. " He is in the *shekyls*," Towneley Myst. p. 99.

SHEKIR. The game of chess.

SHELD. (1) A shield. (*A.-S.*)

(2) Shallow. Still in use.

Wade thei muste, the water was *scheld*
By every syde the wyld feld.

MS. Ashmole 61, f. 2.

(3) Spotted; variegated. *Coles.*

(4) Shoal; coast. *Weber.*

SHELDAPPLE. The chaffinch. " A chaffinch, a sheld appel," Nomenclator, 1585, p. 58.

SHELDER. Shovelling earth downwards to give a bank or elevation a greater slope is called *sheldering* it. *Suff.*

SHELF. *On the shelf*, said of ladies when too old to get married.

SHELL. (1) An inner coffin. *Var. dial.*

(2) The hard horny part of the neck of a hog, kept for the purpose of being manufactured into brawn. It is when so manufactured called the " horny part" by the partakers of that edible. *East.*

SHELLED. Piebald. *East.*

SHELLET. A sort of imperfect or rotten slate. *Devon.*

SHELL-FIRE. The phosphorescence sometimes exhibited in farm-yards, &c., from decayed straw, &c. or touchwood. *Kent.*

SHELLS. Money. A cant term.

SHELLY. An ait in a river. *West.*

SHELTROUNE. A regiment of soldiers.

Thane schotte owtte of the schawe *schiltrounis* many,
With scharpe wapynes of ware schotande at ones.

Morte Arthure, MS. Lincoln, f. 72.

How he schal have for knowynge and wys insyyt
of all perellis and harmes that listliche mowe bifalle
in *scheltromes* or batailes.

Vegecius, MS. Douce 291, f. 5.

Aforcynge hem by *sheltroun* in batayle,
By felle malice this fayre lambe to assayle.

Lydgate, MS. Soc. Antiq. 134, f. 14.

Heyle, *scheltrun* schouris to shelde!
Heyle, bryghtnes evyr schynyng!

MS. Cantab. Ff. li. 38, f. 4.

SHELTY. A Shetland pony. *North.*

SHELVE. (1) To turn manure, &c., from a cart, by raising its front part and causing it to lie obliquely. *Sussex.*

(2) To remove the surface of land with a shovel. *Suffolk.*

SHELVINGS. The rails of a waggon.

SHELVING-STONE. A blue tile or slate for covering the roofs of houses, so called from the position in which it hangs.

SHEMERING. A glimmering. (*A.-S.*)

SHEMEW. Same as *Chammer*, q. v.

The admyrall was in a goune of cloth of silver raysed, furred with ryche sables, and al his company almost were in a new fassion garment, called a *shemew*, which was in effect a goune cut in the middle. *Hall, Henry VIII. f. 65.*

SHENCHE. To pour out ; to drink.

And halt taverne for to *schenche*
That dryoke, whiche maketh the herte brenne.
Gower, MS. Soc. Antiq. 134, f. 81.

SHENDE. (1) To mar, or destroy. (*A.-S.*)

Thre synns princypaly a man doth mare,
Murthyr, theft, and avoutré ;
Thai wyl 3ou *schend* ore 3e be ware,
Be thai done never so prevely.
MS. Douce 302, f. 1.

(2) To defend. Browne uses it in this sense, and it occurs in Palsgrave. " And sing his praise that *shendeth* David's fame," Peele, ii. 33.

(3) To forbid. (4) To punish.

(5) To dirty one's clothes.

SHENDSHIP. Ruin ; punishment.

SHENE. Bright ; shining. (*A.-S.*)

SHENK. A dish used for taking the cream off milk. *Yorksh.*

SHENKE. Same as *Shenche*, q. v.

SHENLON. Glossed by *puer*.

Al thus eld me for-dede,
Thus he toggith ute mi ted,
And drawith ham on rewe :
Y ne mai no more of love done,
Mi pilkoc pisseth on mi schone,
Uch *schenlon* me bischrewe.
Reliq. Antiq. ii. 211.

SHENT. (1) Abashed ; confounded.

Sorely *shent* wi' this rebuke,
Sorely *shent* was the heire of Linne ;
His heart, I wis, was near to brast
With guilt and sorrowe, shame and sinne.
The Heir of Linne.

(2) " I shent one, I blame hym for a faulte," Palsgrave, 1530.

The tender girle, spoil'd of her virgin shame,
Yet for that sinne no ravisher was *shent* ;
Blacke is my inke, more blacke was her defame,
None to revenge, scarce any to lament.
Drayton's Poems. p. 93.

SHEPEN. Same as *Shippen*, q. v.

SHEPHERD. The long-legged spider.

SHEPHERD'S-POUCHES. Clover broom-rape.

SHEPHERD'S-SUN-DIAL. The scarlet pimpernel. *Suffolk.*

SHEPPECK. A hay-fork. *Glouc.*

SHEPSTER. A sheep-shearer. *Palsgrave.*

SHEPSTERT. A starling. *North.*

SHERDEL. Skinned ; scaled.

He was so *scherdel* alle aboute,
It helde alle egge-tool withoute.
Gower, MS. Soc. Antiq. 134, f. 150.

SHERE. (1) To run aground, as a ship does. An ancient sea term.

(2) To cut ; to slash ; to carve.

Him thou3te his fadir her corn *shere*,
There his elleven bretheren were.
Cursor Mundi, MS. Coll. Trin. Cantab. f. 26.
Thorowe scheldys they schotte, and *scherds* thorowe males ,
Both *eschers* thorowe schoulders a schaft-monde large.
Morte Arthure, MS. Lincoln, f. 80.
The 3ong knyghte ser Antore,
That byfore hir did *schere*.
MS. Lincoln A. i. 17, f. 120.

Sharpe *schudering* of schote, *shering* of mailes.
MS. Ashmole 44, f. 45.

(3) Countenance ; mien. *Gawayne.*

SHERE-GRASS. A kind of sedge.

SHERENKENE. Shrank.

So they *scharenkene* fore schotte of the scharppe arowes,
That all the scheltrone schoute and schoderide at ones.
Morte Arthure, MS. Lincoln, f. 75.

SHEREWARDE. Shrew. *Hearne.*

SHEREWDHED. Cursedness. (*A.-S.*)

And for his *scherewdhed*, Sir Berard,
Themperour hath made him his steward.
Gy of Warwike, p. 340.

SHEREWE. A sheriff. *Lydgate.*

SHERIFFED. When in an evening there is an unusual blush of red or yellow in the clouds they say, " How *sheriffed* the sky is to night : we shall have wind, &c." Has this any allusion to the battle of Sheriffmuir, just before which the old folks will tell you there were such appearances in the heavens ? *Linc.*

SHERIFF'S-MAN. The seven-coloured linnet.

SHERIFF'S-POSTS. Posts were usually set up at the doors of sheriffs on which the royal proclamations were fixed. It was usual to remain uncovered while reading them.

SHERK. (1) To shrug. (2) To cheat. *North.*

SHERN. A vessel into which the cream is taken up from the milkpans before it is made butter. *Devon.*

SHERRY. To sculk away. *Var. dial.*

SHERRY-MOOR. A fright. *North.* From the battle of Sheriffe-muir, where all was blood, uproar, and confusion.

SHESELL. Gravel. Nominale MS.

SHET. (1) Running water. *Devon.*

(2) Shall. *Somerset.*

(3) Slipped down.

Burlond to fyghte was bowne,
Hys fote *schett* and he felle downe.
MS. Cantab. Ff. ii. 38, f. 81.

(4) Shut ; closed.

Here slouthe brou3te it so aboute,
Fro him that they ben *schet* withoute.
Gower, MS. Soc. Antiq. 134, f. 104.

SHETAR. An archer. *Prompt. Parv.*

SHETE. (1) To shoot. (*A.-S.*)

I durst mete hym with a stone,
And gif hym leve to *schete*.
MS. Cantab. Ff. v. 48, f. 48.

(2) To fling down. *Devon.*

SHETH. A partition of a field.

SHEU. Nonsense ! An interjection.

SHEUD. Showed. (*A.-S.*)

As the prynce passid to Londone, God shewid ryghte
Secrett thyng to hym, tokyne of victory,
In presence of the same prynce, by Goddus power and my3te,
And ymage wiche was closid, brake opyn sodenly t
God *scheud* hym this comforte in the Abbey of Deyntré,
Because he schulde be stidfast in wele and in woo ;
The ymage was of Saynte Anne, God wolde it shulde be so. *MS. Bibl. Reg. 17 D. xv.*

SHEVERIDE. Shivered ; splintered.

Thourghe the scheldys so schene schalkes they towche,
With schaftes *scheveride* schorte of thas schene launces.
Morte Arthure, MS. Lincoln, f. 93.

SHEWDS. Husks of oats. *North.*

SHEWER. (1) An example. (2) A witness.

SHEWING. A warning; a prophecy.

SHIBBANDS. Shoestrings. *Yorksh.*

SHICKLE. Fickle?

> Pardon to crave of sottish multitude,
> That saucie giddie-headed monster rude,
> Who knowes not when ought well is, or amis,
> Of shallowe *shickle* braine a token is.
> *Honours Academie,* fol. Lond. 1610.

SHICK-SHACK-DAY. A term for the 29th of May, or Royal Oak Day. *Surrey.*

SHIDE. (1) A billet of wood; a thin board; a block of wood. Still in use. " *Tedula,* schyde of wode," Nominale MS. " Schyde of wode, *buche, moule de buches,*" Palsgrave.

> And made upon the derke nyʒte,
> Of gret *schidis* and of blokkis,
> Gret fyre aʒen the grete rockis.
> *Gower, MS. Soc. Antiq.* 134, f. 91.
>
> Hewen *schides* and corven ston,
> And laiden foundament anon.
> *Arthour and Merlin,* p. 21.

(2) To shell peas, beans, &c.

SHIDER. (1) A shiver. Also, to shiver.

> And hewen on with gret powers,
> On *schider* so doth this carpenters.
> *Arthour and Merlin,* p. 224.
>
> Faste they smote then togedur,
> That ther sperys can to *schyder.*
> *MS. Cantab.* Ff. ii. 38, f. 156.

(2) A shrew; a scold.

SHIEL. A shepherd's cottage or hut. Connected with *shield,* shelter.

SHIELD-BOARD. Part of a plough, somewhat resembling a shield. *West.*

SHIELD-BONES. Blade-bones. *North.*

> Some of his bones in Warwicke yett
> Within the castle there doe lye:
> One of his *sheeld-bones* to this day
> Hangs in the citye of Coventrye.
> *The Legend of Sir Guy.*

SHIFE. The wheel of a pulley.

SHIFT. (1) To divide. *Sussex.* A division of land among co-heirs is called a *shifting.* It is an archaism, and occurs in Chaucer. Hence, to deal the cards.

(2) To chance; to risk. *Linc.*

(3) To remove one's dwelling. *Var. dial.*

(4) To be changeable. *North.*

(5) *To shift himself,* to change his dress. *To shift for himself,* to provide for himself.

(6) A change of linen. *Var. dial.*

SHIFTE. To move about. *(A.-S.)*

> And so they *schyfte* and schove; he schotte to the erthe.
> *Morte Arthure, MS.* Lincoln, f. 93.

SHIFTEN. (1) To change linen. *East.*

(2) To shift stitches from one pin to another in knitting. *East.*

SHIFTENING. A change of linen.

SHIFTER. (1) A cozener. " A shifter whome they call a cunny-catcher," Withals, ed. 1608, p. 263. *Shifty,* cunning, artful, Craven Gl. ii. 117. In use in the North.

> And let those *shifters* their owne judges be
> If they have not bin arrant thieves to me.
> *Taylor's Workes,* 1630, ii. 122.

(2) A superintendent. *North.*

SHIFTS. Parts of a farm allotted for the reception of stock or crops. *Norf.*

SHIGGED. Ruined; beggared. *North.*

SHIGING. Flinging; shaking; dashing.

> He come *schygynge* ayene,
> And of hys folk was fyene,
> And fond nevere one slayne,
> Ne worse be a pere. *Degrevant,* 345.

SHILBOARDS. The boards or external radii fixed to the rim of an undershot water-wheel, the projecting levers by means of which the water turns the wheel. Their length corresponds with the breadth of the wheel-rim, and they are in general about a foot long.

SHILDE. To shield. *God shilde,* God shield, or forbid! *(A.-S.) Schilder,* protector, MS. Cotton. Vespas. D. vii.

SHILDER. The shoulder. *Lanc.*

SHILL. (1) To shell. *North.* " Crakkyne, or schyllen nothys," Pr. Parv. p. 100.

(2) Shrill in sound. Not an error, as asserted by Conybeare. It is a verb in Sevyn Sages, 1380. See Thornton Rom. p. 311.

> Then had syr Egyllamowre don to dedd
> A grete herte, and tan the hedd,
> The pryce he blcwe fulle *schylle* !
> *Eglamour,* 390.
>
> The kyng come to the chamber to the quene,
> And before hym knyʒtes tenne,
> And wepte and seyd with grete pyté,
> My leffe wyff, what ayles the ?
> Thou that hast be so stylle,
> Why cryest thou wonder *schylle ?*
> *MS. Ashmole* 61, xv. Cent.

SHILLA. A stony beach. *Cumb.*

SHILLARD. A shilling's worth. *Devon.* In some counties, a *shillincher.*

SHILLIN. Shelled oats. *Craven.*

SHILLY-SHALLY. Irresolute. *Var. dial.* This phrase was originally *Shall I? Shall I?*

> There's no delay, they ne're stand *shall I shall I,*
> Hermogenes with Dallila doth dally.
> *Taylor's Workes,* 1630, iii. 3.

SHILSTONES. Slates for roofing. *Devon.* They are called also *shilling-stones.*

SHILT. Beaten down?

> Al his folk so was *schilt,*
> And never on ther nas spilt.
> *Arthour and Merlin,* p. 76.

SHIM. (1) A horse-hoe for cleaning the ground between rows of beans or of hops. *Sussex.*

(2) It seems. *Wilts.*

(2) The *shimm,* or rase downe the face of a horse, or strake down the face. More's MS. Additions to Ray's North Country Words.

(4) Appearance. *West.*

(5) A clear bright white. *Chesh.*

SHIMBLE. Loose; unconnected. *West.*

SHIMMER. To glitter; to shine. *Var. dial.* Ray spells it *shimper,* ed. 1674, p. 76.

> The little windowe dim and darke
> Was hung with ivy, brere, and yewe;
> No *shimmering* sunn here ever shone;
> No halesome breeze here ever blew.
> *The Heir of Linne.*

SHIMPER. (1) To simmer. *East.*

(2) A small shelf of sand, or other rising bank in the channel of a river. *Surr.*

SHIN. (1) To carve a chevin.

(2) To trump at cards. *North.*

(3) Shall. *Shinna,* shall not. *West.*

SHINBAWDE. Armour for the shins?

That the schadande blode over his schanke rynnys,
And schewede one his *schynbawde* that was schire bur-
neste. *Morte Arthure, MS. Lincoln, f. 93.*

SHINDER. To shiver in pieces.

SHINDLE. The thin cleft stone out of which they cut slates.

SHINDY. A disturbance. *Var. dial.* A *shine* is also frequently used.

SHINE. (1) *Every shine,* every one. *West.*

(2) Entirely; utterly. *Somerset.*

(3) Light; brightness; lustre.

I to my chimney's *shine*
Brought him, as love professes,
And chaf'd his hands with mine,
And dry'd his droping tresses.
Herrick's Works, l. 35.

SHINER. (1) A clever fellow. *North.*

(2) A guinea. A cant term.

SHIN-FEAST. A good fire. *North.*

SHINGLE. To hammer iron. *West.* "At the iron works they roll a sow into the fire, and melt off a piece call'd a loop, which they take out with their shingling tongues, and beating it first with iron sledges, hammer it gently till the cinder and dross is beat off, and then they hammer it thicker and stronger till they bring it to a bloom, which is a four square mass of about three foot long; this operation they call shingling the loop," Kennett, MS. Lansd. 1033, f. 363.

SHINGLES. Wooden tiles made of oak, used for roofs, steeples, &c. and still used in some counties. There are several church steeples in Sussex covered with shingles. "Shyngles, hyllyng of an house," Palsgrave. "Shyngled ship," ship made of planks, Piers Ploughman, p. 168. It occurs in Nominale MS.

Flureu cakes beth the *schingles* alle,
Of cherche, cloister, boure, and halle.
Cocaygne, ap. Warton, i. 8.

SHINGLY. Abounding in loose gravel, as the beach on the sea-shore. *Sussex.*

SHINK. A skimming-dish. *Derb.*

SHINLOCK. The herb rocket.

SHINNER. "Neather stockins or *shinners,*" Florio, p. 74. "An hose, a nether stocke, a *shinner,*" Nomenclator, 1585, p. 167.

SHINNEY. A boy's game played with knobbed sticks and a knur, called also Bandy and Hocky. The object of the contending parties is to drive the knur over a line and within a certain marked out space called the goal. If the knur is driven over the line or rather side of the inclosed space, it is called a bye. *North.*

SHINS. *Against the shins,* unwillingly. *To break one's shins,* to be in a hurry.

SHIN-SPLINTS. Pieces of wood placed on the legs of persons who break stones for roads.

SHIP. (1) Sheep. *West.*

(2) A censer. "*Acerra,* a schyp for censse," Nominale MS. xv. Cent. "A ship, such as

was used in the church to put frankincense in." Baret, 1580.

(3) At Namptwych, Droitwych, &c. the vessel whereinto the brine is by troughs convey'd from the brine pit is called the *ship,* Kennett, MS. Lansd. 1033, f. 363.

SHIPE. A shovel for cutting turf.

SHIPLET. A small ship. Harrison, p. 65.

SHIP-LORD. The owner of a ship.

SHIPMAN. A mariner; the master of a barge. (*A.-S.*)

SHIPMAN'S-CARD. "Shypmans carde, *carte,*" Palsgrave. See Macbeth, i. 3.

SHIPPEN. A stall, stable, or shed. (*A.-S.*) A cow-house is still so called. *North.*

Whi is not thi table sett in thi cow-stalle,
And whi etist thou not in thi *shipun* as wele as in
thin halle? *MS. Digby 41, f. 8.*

SHIP-SPY. A telescope used on the coast.

SHIR. The cherry-tree. *North.*

SHIRE. (1) Thin; scanty. *Northumb.* "Shyrenesse, thynnesse, *delievre,*" Palsgrave; "shyre nat thycke, *delie,*" ibid.

(2) Clear; bright; shining.

Had lifte awey the grave stone,
That clothed was as snow *shire.*
Cursor Mundi, MS. Coll. Trin. Cantab. f 106.
Thou seest stykkes that are smale,
They brenne fyrst feyre and *shyre.*
MS. Harl. 1701, f. 89.
The bordoure of his bacenett be bristes in sondire,
That the *schire* rede blode over his brene rynnys.
Morte Arthure, MS. Lincoln, f. 97.
Yhit moght it noght slecken it ne abate,
No mare than a droope of watyr *schyre,*
Yf alle Rome brynned, moght slecken that fyre.
Hampole, MS. Bowes, p. 194.

(3) An egg that has not a tread in it is called a *shire,* a clear egg. *Linc.*

(4) To pour off a liquor so as to leave the sediment. *Northumb.*

(5) Direct; immediately. *North.*

SHIRE-MAN. Any man who had not the good fortune to be born in one of the sister counties, or in Essex. He is a sort of foreigner to us; and to our ears, which are acutely sensible of any violation of the beauty of our phraseology, and the music of our pronunciation, his speech soon bewrays him. "Aye, I knew he must be a *shere-man* by his tongue," Forby, p. 296.

SHIRE-WAY. A bridle-way. *South.*

SHIRK. To slink from anything. Hence *shirky,* deceitful. *South.*

SHIRL. (1) Shrill. *Palsgrave.* Still in use, according to Moor, p. 515. "Shryked shyrly," Morte d'Arthur, ii. 350.

(2) To slide. *Northumb.*

(3) To cut with shears. *Yorksh.*

(4) To romp about rudely. *Devon.*

SHIRL-COCK. The missel-thrush. According to Lower, the Derbyshire pronunciation is *shrill-cock.*

SHIRPING. "*Buffa,* the dispisyng blaste of the mouthe that we call *shirpyng,*" Thomas's Italian Dictionarie.

SHIRREVE. A sheriff.

> Erles of Ynglande with archers y-newe ;
> *Schirreves* scharply schiftys the comouns.
> *Morte Arthure, MS. Lincoln, f. 61.*

SHIRT. The inmost of the three membranes which enwrap a womb-lodged infant. See Cotgrave, in v. *Agneliere.*

SHIRT-BAND. The wristband of a shirt.

SHIRY. Sharp and cutting ; applied to grass, which is consequently not good herbage. A plantation in the parish of Nettleham is so called, because the herbage of the adjoining field is of that kind. *Linc.*

SHIT. Shut up; inclosed.

> And alle the richesse of spirituelle science
> In hire were *schit* and closid eke also.
> *Lydgate, MS. Soc. Antiq. 134, f. 3.*

SHITABED. The dandelion. *Wilts.*

SHITESTICKS. A mean miserly fellow. Also called *shiterags.* See Florio, p. 72.

SHITFIRE. A hector, or bully.

SHITSAC. An oak-apple. *Wilts.*

SHITTELNESS. " Shyttelnesse, *variableté,*" Palsgrave. " Shyttell nat constant, *variable,*" ibid. " The vaine shittlenesse of an unconstant head," Baret, 1580.

SHITTER. To have the diarrhœa. *North.*

SHITTILWIKE. A shuttlecock. It occurs in Honour in his Perfection, 4to. 1624.

SHITTLE. The bar of a door.

SHITTLE-BRAINED. Giddy ; thoughtless.

SHITTLE-COME-SHAW. A North country exclamation, expressing contempt. Brockett has *shittletidee!*

SHITTLECOMESHITES. Idle stories ; trifles. It occurs in Coles, translated by *affaniæ.*

SHITTLES. Buns such as are given to school children on certain days. *Rutland.*

SHIVE. (1) A small iron wedge, which fastens the bolt of a window-shutter. *East.*

(2) A slice of any edible, generally said of bread. *Var. dial.* " Take shives of bred tosted," Warner, p. 85. To cut a shive out of a person's loaf, i. e. to follow his example. *Shiver* is also common for a small slice, slip, &c.

> Russius saith that tho rootes of reed, being stampt and mingled with hony, will draw out any thorne, or *shiver ;* and so will snailes, as he saith, being stampt and wrought with fresh butter ; and if the place be swollen, he saith it is good to mollifie it with hogs grease and hony, which wil asswage any new swelling that commeth by stripe or otherwise.
> *Topsell's Beasts, 1607, p. 421.*
> A man shall not find a *sheve* of it to fetch fire in, or to take water out of the pit.
> *Becon's Works, p. 469.*

(3) A thin wooden bung used by brewers to stop their casks very close with.

SHIVER. The wheel of a pulley.

SHIVES. The refuse of flax or hemp.

SHOAD. Loose stones of tin mixed with the earth, indicating a mine. *Cornw.*

SHOAD-STONE. A small stone or fragment of ore made smooth by the action of the water passing over it.

SHOARD. To take a shoard, i. e. to drink a cup too much. *Exmoor.*

SHOARS. Stakes set at a distance to shoar or bear up toils or nets in hunting.

SHOAT. A young pig. *Chesh.* It is a term of contempt said of a young person.

SHOBIL. A shovel. Nominale MS.

SHOCK. (1) To sponge. *Norf.*

(2) Twelve sheaves of corn. *North.*

(3) To butt, as rams do.

(4) A rough-coated dog. " My little shock," Nabbes' Bride, 1640, sig. H.

SHOCKER. A bad character.

SHOD. (1) Shed, or spilt. *Devon.*

(2) Covered ; overwhelmed. (*A.-S.*)

SHODE. (1) To divide the hair.

> But with no crafte of combis brode,
> They myȝte hire hore lokkis *schode.*
> *Gower, MS. Soc. Antiq. 134, f. 49.*

(2) Shod ; having shoes on. (*A.-S.*)

> Hosyd and *schode* he was ryghte,
> He semyd wele to be a knyghte.
> *MS. Cantab. Ff. ii. 38, f. 174.*

(3)

> Hem bituen a gret *schode,*
> Of gravel and erthe al so.
> *Arthour and Merlin, p. 56.*

SHODEREDE. Quivered.

> The schafte *schoderede* and schotte in the schire beryne.
> *Morte Arthure, MS. Lincoln, f. 93.*

SHOD-SHOVEL. A wooden shovel, shod at its extremity with iron.

SHOE. (1) *To tread the shoes straight,* to be upright in conduct. *To tread the shoe awry,* to fall away from the paths of virtue. " A woman to play false, enter a man more then she ought, or tread her shooe awry," Cotgrave. Compare Heywood's Edward IV. p. 148. *To shoe the cobler,* to give a quick and peculiar movement with the fore-foot when sliding on the ice. *Shoemaker's pride,* the creaking of shoes. *To shoe the goose,* to be tipsy.

(2) She. *North.*

(3) *Over shews over butes,* equivalent to, " one may as well be hanged for a sheep as for a lamb," implying that the speaker has made up his mind to sit a little later, partaker in another bottle or bowl, &c.

> Ev'n so seem'd I amidst the guarded troope
> Of gold-lac'd actors, yet all could not droope
> My fixed mind, for where true courage roots,
> The proverb sayes, *Once over shooes, o'r boots.*
> *Taylor's Workes, 1630, ii. 145.*

SHOEING-HORN. Metaphorically, anything which helps to draw something on ; an inducement.

SHOEING-THE-COLT. A quaint phrase for the social exaction of a fine, on the introduction of an associate to any new office. If he meet his companions at a periodical dinner, a bottle of wine, or a bowl of punch, in a certain rank of life, is a common fine on the *colt's* health being drank. " Paing his footen" is an equivalent phrase and practice. *Moor.*

SHOEMAKERS'-STOCKS. Tight shoes.

SHOE-THE-MARE. A Christmas sport.

> Of blind-man-buffe, and of the care
> That young men have to *shoe the mare.*
> *Herrick's Works, i. 171.*

SHOFE. (1) Pushed. (*A.-S.*)

(2) Shaved. *Shope*, pr. edit.

> I *schofe* Syr Gandere a crowne,
> When we mette laste yn batayle.
> *MS. Cantab. Ff. ii. 38, f. 109.*

SHOG. (1) To shake; to jog. *Palsgrave.* "To rocke, shake, *shog*, wag up and downe," Cotgrave. "The see was *schoggid* with wawis," Wiclif, p. 18. Brockett has *shoggle*.

(2) To slink away. *West.*

SHOKE. Shook. (*A.-S.*)

> For the dynt that he tuke,
> Oute of sadille he *schoke*,
> Who so the sothe wille luke. *Perceval, 694.*

SHOKKE. To rush; to snatch up.

> He schodirde and schrenkys, and schoutes bott lyttille,
> Bott *schokkes* in scharpely in his schene wedys.
> *Morte Arthure, MS. Lincoln, f. 97.*

SHOLD. Shallow. *Prompt. Parv.*

SHOLDRON. Shoulders. *Weber.*

SHOLE. Shallow. This word is given by Urry, in his MS. additions to Ray.

SHOLT. An Iceland shaggy dog. *East.*

> Besides these also we have *sholts* or curs dailie brought out of Iseland, and much made of among us bicause of their sawcinesse and quarrelling.
> *Harrison's England, p. 231.*

SHOME. Confusion. (*A.-S.*)

> Whenne he to his lorde come,
> The lettre sone he hym nome,
> And sayde, Alle gose to *schome*!
> And went on his way. *MS. Lincoln A. L 17, f. 130.*

SHOMGNES. Shame. (*A.-S.*)

SHOMMAKY. Slovenly; dirty.

SHOMMOCKS. Shoes. *Warw.*

SHOMORE. A skimmer. "*Spumatorium*, Anglice a schomore," Nominale MS.

SHONDE. Dishonour. (*A.-S.*)

> The to sle with schame and *schonde*,
> And for to wynne agayn hys londe.
> *MS. Cantab. Ff. ii. 38, f. 116.*

SHONDEN. To shun. (*A.-S.*)

> Al dai thou mijt understonden,
> And thi mirour bi-foren the sen,
> Wat is to don, wat is to *shonden*,
> And wat to holden, and wat to flen.
> *MS. Digby 86.*

SHONE. (1) Shoes. A knight who conquered in combat was said to *winne his shone*.

> Owthyr schalle he sle me sone,
> Or on hym y schalle *wynne my schone*.
> *MS. Cantab. Ff. ii. 38, f. 79.*

> Tryamowre sparyd hym noght,
> But evyr in hys hert he thoght,
> To day was y maked knyght!
> Owthyr schalle he sle me sone,
> Or on hym y schalle *wynne my schone*,
> Thorow the grace of God Almyght!
> *MS. Cantab. Ff. ii. 38, f. 79.*

> It es an harde thyng for to saye
> Of doghety dedis that hase bene done,
> Of felle feghtynges and batelles sere,
> And how that thir knyghtis hase *wone thair schone*.
> *MS. Lincoln A. i. 17, f. 149.*

(2) To shun, or escape.

> For the drede that ys to come
> Of the dome, that no man may *schone*.
> *MS. Cantab. Ff. ii. 38, f. 43.*

SHONED. Ashamed. It occurs in MS. Cotton. Vespas. D. vii, *schoned*.

SHONK. Hearty; healthy. *West.*

SHONTE. Remained; delayed?

> Qwene alle was schyppede that scholde, they *schounte* no lengere,
> Bot ventelde theme tyte as the tyde rynnes.
> *Morte Arthure, MS. Lincoln, f. 61.*

SHONTO. A donkey. *I. Wight.*

SHOO. (1) A shovel; a spade. *Lanc.*

(2) A word used for driving away poultry. "To cry *shooe, shooe*, as women do to their hens," Florio, p. 477. Forby has *shoo*, to scare birds.

SHOODS. Hulls of oats. *North.*

SHOOFEDDE. Shoved. (*A.-S.*)

> Brennynge brymstone and lede many a barelle fulle,
> They *shoofedde* hit downne ryyte as shyre watur.
> *MS. Cott. Calig. A. ii. f. 115.*

SHOOF-FORK. A fork with two long tines and a long stale for pitching shooves of corn into the loading waggon at harvest, or off it into the stack. It is the same or nearly the same as pitchfork. *Suffolk.*

SHOOK. (1) To shrug. *Yorksh.*

(2) Split, as wood is by shrinking.

SHOOL. (1) A shovel. *North.* "Shoole for shoovell," Stanihurst's Ireland, ed. 1586, p. 9.

(2) To saunter about. *East.*

(3) To beg. *Var. dial.*

SHOOLER. An idle, lazy fellow. *Sussex.*

SHOORT. To shift for a living. *Exm.*

SHOOT. (1) To have a diarrhœa.

(2) To select out the worst cattle to prevent them from injuring the drove.

(3) *To shoot the bridge*, a phrase formerly used by watermen to signify going through London-bridge at the turning of the tide. *To shoot compass*, to shoot wide of the mark.

(4) The game of shovel-board.

(5) The crick in the neck.

(6) A narrow steep lane. *I. Wight.*

(7) The woof in weaving. *Devon.*

(8) A spout for rain-water. *South.*

SHOOTHRED. A shoemaker's thread. It is the translation of *chegros* in Hollyband's Dictionarie, 1593.

SHOOTY. Coming up regularly in the rows, as potatoes, &c. *Salop.*

SHOOVEN. A calf or colt is said to be shoovin, when parting with its early teeth; trees putting forth their leaves are also *shooven*.

SHOPE. Made; created; shaped. (*A-S.*)

> Al that ever God *shope* to be,
> Shal come and fyзt aзens the.
> *MS. Harl. 1701, f. 25.*

> He *schop* his regne to divyde
> To knyзtes, whiche him hadde servid.
> *Gower, MS. Soc. Antiq. 134, f. 35.*

> Nay, by Hym that me made,
> And *shope* both sonne and mone,
> Fynde a better borowe, sayd Robyn,
> Or mony getest thou none. *Robin Hood, i. 13.*

SHORE. (1) A post used with hurdles in folding sheep. *Dorset.*

(2) To threaten. *North.*

(3)

> He thoghte to wyrke by the lawe,
> And by no nother *schore*.
> *MS. Lincoln A. i. 17, f. 139.*

(4) Sheared; cut. (*A.-S.*) Still in use in Suffolk, according to Moor, p. 345. " His scarlet mantell than *shore* he," Syr Isenbras, 127. See Chaucer, Cant. T. 13958.

(5) A sewer. Still in use in Devon.

> She in plaine termes unto the world doth tell,
> Whores are the hackneys which men ride to hell,
> And by comparisons she truely makes
> A whore worse then a common *shore* or jakes.
> *Taylor's Workes*, 1630, il. 106.

SHOREDITCH. The most successful of the London archers was called the *Duke of Shoreditch*, a mock title, frequently said in ridicule. The sixteenth article in the Poore Man's Peticion to the Kinge, 1603, is, " Good king, make not good Lord of Lincoln Duke of Shorditche, for he is a &c."

SHORE-POST. A buttress.

SHORER. The share, or male pubes.

SHORING. Awry; aslant. *East.*

SHORLING. A shaveling, or priest.

SHORRY. A large stick on which hedgers carry faggots. *Oxon.*

SHORT. (1) Wide of the mark, a technical phrase in archery. Still in use.

(2) Light and crisp. Cakes and biscuits are said to eat *short*.

(3) Peevish; angry. *Var. dial.*

(4) The short and long of it, i. e. the absolute truth in few words.

> The *short* and the long of't is, she's an ugly creature, make of her what thou can'st.
> *Heywood's Love's Mistress*, p. 63.
>
> Yf ye will nedys know *at short and longe*,
> It is evyn a womans tounge,
> For that is ever sterynge.
> *Interlude of the Four Elements*, n. d.

(5) Small; portable. *Somerset.*

SHORT-CAKES. Rich sweet cakes which break *short*, such as the Cumbrian peasants present to their sweethearts at fairs. *Westm. and Cumb. Dial.* " Alice Shortcake," Shakespeare, Merry Wives, i. 1.

SHORTENING. Anything put into flour to make the cakes short. A man who is easily put in a passion is said to have had too much *shortening* put into him.

SHORT-HEELED. Unchaste.

SHORTLY. Quickly; peevishly.

> A ferly strife fel them betwene,
> As they went bi the wey;
> Litulle Johne seid he had won v. s.
> And Robyn Hode seld *schortly* nay.
> *MS. Cantab.* Ff. v. 48, f. 126.

SHORT-OF-PUFF. Short-winded. *Linc.*

SHORTS. Coarse flour. The term is also applied to the refuse of corn. *Var. dial.*

SHORT-START. A kind of apple, mentioned by Cotgrave in v. *Carpendu.*

SHORT-WAISTED. Angry; tetchy. A stage-coachman (a Suffolk man) lost a passenger by misconduct, and was at odds with himself; another (a countryman) said, " he is very *short-waisted*, when anything puts him out."

SHOSHINGS. Aslant; sloping. *East.*

SHOST. Shouldest?

> Hire lord she wile theder *sende*,
> For the love for to schende
> With lite melni ;
> Tharaboute thow *schoot* be souse,
> And thow schelt after wedde to spouse
> To thin amy. *Beves of Hamtoun*, p. 7.

SHOT. (1) A kind of trout. *West.*

(2) Turned out rapidly, now especially applied to *shooting* out a waggon load by tilting it. " Rubbish may be shot here," is a very common notice in plots of ground where the owner requires rubble for any purpose.

> Percevelle sayde hafe it he wolde,
> And *schott* owtt alle the golde;
> Righte there appone the faire molde
> The ryng owte glade. *Perceval*, 2114.

(3) A foot-soldier who carried fire-arms. The term is still applied to a shooter. He is a good shot, i. e. a good marksman.

(4) A reckoning at an inn. This word must now be considered a provincialism, although lately in good use.

(5) Firm; stable; secure.

(6) A young pig. *Var. dial.*

(7) A handful of hemp. *Kent.*

SHOT-CLOG. A simple foolish person, a clog on the company, but who was tolerated because he paid the shot or reckoning for the whole of the company. Ben Jonson uses the term.

> Drawer, take your plate. For the reckoning there's some of their cloaks : I will be no *shot-log* to such.
> *Amends for Ladies*, p. 51.

SHOTER. (1) The yew-tree. (*A.-S.*)

(2) A little bark, or pinnace.

SHOT-FLAGON. The host's pot, given where the guests have drank above a shilling's worth of ale. *Derb.*

SHOT-ICE. A sheet of ice. *North.*

SHOT-NET. A mackerel net. *Kent.*

SHOT-POT. A fellow that spends so much in an ale-house that he is entitled to the landlord's pot or shot-flagon. *Glouc.*

SHOTS. The refuse of cattle taken out of a drove. *Craven.*

SHOTSHIPE. An assembly of persons who pay pecuniary contributions. (*A.-S.*)

> Deus ! quoth Ubbe, hwat may this be ?
> Betere is I go miself, and se :
> Hwether he sitten nou and wesseylen,
> Or of ani *shotshipe* to-deyle. *Havelok*, 2099.

SHOTT. (1) A stitch in the side.

(2) A nook, an angle, a field, a plot of land. See Carlisle's Account of Charities, p. 305.

SHOTTEN. (1) Shall not. *West.*

(2) Sour, curdled, as milk.

SHOTTEN-HERRING. A gutted herring, dried for keeping. Metaphorically, a lean meagre fellow, a term of contempt. " Thou art a *shotten-herring* Jackalent Spanyard," Nabbes' Bride, 1640, sig. G. ii.

> This man is as wise as a wood-cock, his wit's in a consumption, his conceit is as lanck as a *shotten-herring*. *Optick Glasse of Humors*, 1639, p. 27.
> Though they, like *shotten herrings* are to see,
> Yet such tall souldiers of their teeth they be,
> That two of them, like greedie cormorants,
> Devoures more then sixe honest protestants.
> *Taylor's Workes*, 1630, iii. A

SHOTTES. Arrows; darts; any missiles hurled with a projective power. (*A.-S.*)

SHOTTLES. Quasi *shutholes?* Bars or rails which passing through morticed holes in posts may be removed at pleasure. *Linc.*

SHOT-WINDOW. Explained by Ritson, a window that opens and shuts.

Alyce opened a *shot wyndow,*
And loked all about,
She was ware of the justice and shirife bothe,
Wyth a full great route. *Ancient Popular Poetry,* p. 8.

SHOUFFED. Shoved; pushed.

And whenne the Macedyns and the Grekes sawe Alexander entir into the citee, they *schouffed* to the walles all at anes, and clambe over
MS. Lincoln A. i. 17, f. 6.

SHOUGH. A shock-dog; a shog.

SHOULDER. A young lady who has unfortunately listened to the persuasions of the other sex, is said to have a *slip of the shoulder.*

SHOULDER-CLAPPER. A bailiff.

A back-friend, a *shoulder-clapper,* one that countermands
The passages of alleys, creeks, and narrow lands.
Comedy of Errors, iv. 2.

SHOULDER-SPIKE. A long iron spike used for supporting shelves against a wall. *West.*

SHOULERE. The bird shoveller.

SHOUPE. Shaped; prepared.

Within fyftene dayes his flete es assemblede,
And thane he *schoupe* hym to chippe, and schownes no lengere. *Morte Arthure, MS. Lincoln, f. 91.*

SHOUPS. The hips. *North.*

SHOURE. (1) To scour; to ride quick. *Weber.*
(2) A conflict.

For now is he holden nouȝt in *shourts,*
But he con love paramouris.
Cursor Mundi, MS. Coll. Trin. Cantab. f. 1.

SHOUT. (1) A hill. *Yorksh.*
(2) A small boat, nearly flat-bottomed and very light, used for passing over the drains in various parts of the county : when broader and larger it is used for shooting wild ducks in the marshes, and is then called a gunning *shout. Linc.* The term *shoutemen* has some connexion with this, although the boats used for carrying timber could not have been very light.

Out of which 74s. 6d. paid to divers mariners, called *shoutemen,* for the carriage of 74 loads of timber from the wood of Wildwode, carried from Weybridge to the manor of the Savoye, by the river Thames, carriage at 12d. a load. *Archæologia,* xxiv. 304.

And from two boats forfeited anew in this year, of which one dung-boat, called a *showte,* nothing here, because not yet appraised, but remaining in the custody of the accomptant of waifs and estrays.
Archæologia, xxiv. 303.

SHOUTHER. The shoulder. *Shouther-fellow,* a companion in any manual labour requiring more than one person's exertions.

SHOVE. (1) To germinate; to shoot. Also, to cast the first teeth. *East.*
(2) To put the loose corn into heaps for the convenience of being taken up. *Sussex.*

SHOVELARDE. A shovel.

SHOVEL-BOARD. A trivial game very common in former days, and not yet laid aside. A shilling or other smooth coin was placed on the extreme edge of the shovel-board, and propelled towards a mark by a smart stroke with the palm of the hand. It is mentioned under various names, according to the coin employed, as shove-groat, &c. The game of shove-halfpenny is mentioned in the Times of April 25th, 1845, as then played by the lower orders. It is called *shooyts* in the Hallamshire Glossary, p. 121.

Bowles, *shove-groats,* tennis, no game comes amis,
His purse a nurse for anybody is.
Taylor's Motto, 12mo. Lond. 1622.

Taylor, the water-poet, says that " Edw. shillings for the most part are used at shoveboord," and he thus describes the complaint of one of them :

You see my face is beardlesse, smooth, and plaine,
Because my soveraigne was a child, 'tis knowne,
Whenas he did put on the English crowne.
But had my stamp beene bearded, as with haire.
Long before this it had beene worne out bare ;
For why ? With me the unthrifts every day
With my face downwards do at *shove-boord* play :
That had I had a beard, you may suppose
Th' had worne it off, as they have done my nose.
Taylor's Workes, ed. 1630, i. 68

SHOVELL. The bird shoveller, mentioned in Hollyband's Dictionarie, 1593, where it is the translation of *un cueillier.* Perhaps *shovellefotede* is having feet like shovells.

Schovelle-fotede was that schalke, and schaylande hyme semyde,
With schankes unschaply schowande togedyrs.
Morte Arthure, MS. Lincoln, f. 65.

SHOW. (1) To push, or shove. *East.*
(2) To show a fair pair of heels, i. e. to run away very quickly. *Var. dial.*

SHOWEL. A blind for a cow's eye, made of wood. *South.*

SHOWER. Used in the I. of Wight for rain, though it may last many hours, or even a whole day.

SHOW-FIGHT. To be willing to fight.

SHOW-HACKLE. To be willing to fight. *I. of Wight.*

SHOWHE. A jackdaw. *Prompt. Parv.*

SHOWL. A shovel. *Var. dial.* " *Tribula,* Anglice a schowle," Nominale MS.

Who'll dig his grave ?
I, said the owl, with my spade and *showl,*
And I'll dig his grave. *The Death of Cock Robin.*

SHOW-OFF. To commence. Also, to exhibit finely before others. *Var. dial.*

SHOWRLY. Surely. See Middleton, iii. 636. Jennings has *shower,* sure.

SHOWS. Prints; pictures. *Devon.*

SHRADDES. Shards, or coppices.

Whan shaws beene sheene, and *shraddes* full fayre,
And leaves both large and longe. *Robin Hood,* L. 115.

SHRAF-TIDE. Shrovetide. *Palsgrave.*

SHRAGERS. Coarse metal pots made of marl, in which wares are baked. *Staff.*

SHRAGGES. Rags; patches; slips. Our second example refers to a jagged hood.

With flatte ferthynges the freke was floreschede alle over ;
Many schredys and *schragges* at his skyrttes hynges.
Morte Arthure, MS. Lincoln, f. 98.

A red hod on hir heved, *shragid* al of shridis,
With a riche riban gold be-gon.
        MS. Arund. Coll. Arm. 27, f. 130.

SHRAGS. The ends of sticks, of the birchen twigs in a broom ; or of whins or furze. " Yar brum owt ta ha' fine shrags." This was said to a man about to dress recently thrashed barley for market. The clippings of live fences. *Moor.* " Hoke to hev wyth woode, or *schraggynge*," Pr. Parv. p. 242. " To shrag trees, *arbores putare*," Baret, 1580.

SHRAIL. A light rail, or any very slight fence, more to warn persons from breaking through it than for real protection. *East.*

SHRAMMED. Benumbed with cold. *West.*

SHRANK. Sunk ; pierced. *Gawayne.*

SHRAP. (1) A thicket. *Devon.*
(2) A snare for birds ; a place prepared and baited with corn or chaff for the purpose of catching birds.
    He busies himselfe in setting silver lime twigs to entangle young gentlemen, and casting foorth silken *shraps* to catch woodcocks.
        Nash's Pierce Pennilesse, 1592.

SHRAPE. (1) To scrape. (*A.-S.*)
    Herly in the morowe to *shrapyn* in the vale,
    To fynde my dyner amonge the wormes smale.
        Lydgate's Minor Poems, p. 184.
(2) To scold. *Sussex.*

SHRAVEL. Dry faggot wood. *Suffolk.*

SHRAVEY. A loose subsoil, something between clay and sand. *Sussex.*

SHRED. (1) To cut off the smaller branches of a tree ; to cut the twigs from a pole when cut down. *East.* It occurs in the Pr. Parv.
(2) To cut into shreds. *West.* " To morsell, to mince, or *shred* in peeces," Florio, p. 2. Metaphorically, to ruin or plunder any one.
(3) To spread manure. *South.*
(4) A tailor. A cant term.

SHREDE. (1) Clothed. Also, to clothe. (*A.-S.*)
    Beves of is palfrei alighte,
    And *schrede* the palmer as a knighte.
        Beves of Hamtoun, p. 80.
    In a kirtel of silk he gan him *schrede*,
    Into chaumber wel sone he ȝede.
        Gy of Warwike, p. 4.
(2) To cut through. (*A.-S.*)
    Thoffe my schouldire be *schrede*, and my schelde thyrllede,
    And the wielde of myne arme werkkes a littille.
        Morte Arthure, MS. Lincoln, f. 81.
(3) Covered up. (*A.-S.*)
    It ware worthy to be *schrede* and schrynede in golde,
    For it es sakles of synne, sa helpe me oure Lorde.
        Morte Arthure, MS. Lincoln, f. 95.
    Schyre scheldus they *schrede*,
    Many dowghty was dede,
    Ryche maylus wexen rede.
        Degrevant, 293.

SHRED-PIES. Mince-pies. Tusser, p. 73.

SHREFE. A sheriff. *Palsgrave.*
    The proverbe saies, hee that will sweare will lie,
    He that will lie will steale by consequency :
    Swearers are lyers, lyers most are thieves,
    Or God helpe jaylors and true *under-shrieves*.
        Taylor's Wit and Mirth, p. 189.

SHREG. To lop trees. *Somerset.*

SHRENKEDE. Pierced through.

Schalkes he schrede thurghe, and *schrenkede* mayles .
Baneres he bare downe, bryttenede scheldes.
        Morte Arthure, MS. Lincoln, f. 76.

SHREW. (1) A screw. *Somerset.*
(2) A scold. In earlier writers it often signified a wicked person of either sex, one malicious or badly disposed.
(3) To curse. (*A.-S.*)
(4) The field mouse. *North.*

SHREWD. Malicious ; badly-disposed.

SHRICHE. To shriek. (*A.-S.*)
    And the maid, al for-drede,
    Bigan to *schrichen* an to grede.
        Florice and Blancheflour, 454.

SHRICK. To shriek, a term formerly applied to the badger's noise at rutting time.

SHRIDE. To hew or lop wood. Jennings has *shride*, to cut off wood from the sides of trees, to cut off wood from trees generally. " Hooke to hewe wode, or schrydynge," Pr. Parv. p. 242.

SHRIEVY. Having threads withdrawn. *Sussex.*

SHRIFT. Confession. (*A.-S.*) *Shrifte-fader,* a father confessor.

SHRIGHT. Shrieked. (*A.-S.*)
    It was the tyme when soyle
    With foggie deaw was dight,
    But lately faine ; and shrowded foule
    In shadie bushes *shright*.
        Turbevile's Ovid, 1567, f. 60.
    Thou schalt be mordrid in this stede !
    This mayden tho for fere *schrihte*.
        Gower, MS. Soc. Antiq. 134, f. 238.

SHRIKE. (1) The lesser butcher-bird, so called by Turner, according to Ray, ed. 1674, p. 83.
(2) To shriek. *Palsgrave.*

SHRIMMED. Chilled. *Cornw.*

SHRINE. A charnel-house. This sense of the word occurs in Hollyband's Dictionarie, 1593, as well as the ordinary meaning.

SHRIP. To rate, or chide. *Kent.*

SHRITE. The missel-thrush. *South.*

SHRIVE. (1) To confess. (*A.-S.*)
(2) To regard ; to praise.
(3) To prune trees. *Kent.*

SHROCKLED. Withered. *Kent.*

SHROCROP. The shrew-mouse. *Dorset.*

SHROE. A shrew. Peele, i. 49.

SHROF. Shrived. See *Cof.*

SHROGGS. Shrubs ; thorns ; briars.
    They cutt them down two summer *shroggs*,
    That grew both under a breere.
        Robin Hood, i. 120.

SHROMP. A black worm, common in horse-dung. *Var. dial.*

SHROOD. To trim or lop trees. *Glouc.*
    A fellow in North Wales, *shrowding* of a tree, fell down on his head, and his braine fractured, and lay for dead.   *Aubrey's Wiltshire, MS. Ashmole.*

SHROUD. To gather together, as beasts do for warmth. *Palsgrave.*

SHROUDED. Concealed, covered, screened, sheltered, overgrown, shaded. " In the two latter senses I lately heard this speech, enforcing the argument for the thickly planting of apple trees.—See how the cottagers trees are *shrouded*, and what crops they always bear," Moor's Suff. MS. Chaucer uses the verb *shroude*, to hide.

SHROUDES. Clothes. (*A.-S.*)

SHROVE. To be merry ; probably derived from the sports and amusements of Shrovetide. "One that loveth to *shrove* ever and make good cheere," Florio, p. 59. *Shrove-Prentices*, a phrase which has never been correctly explained, was a name given to a set of ruffianly fellows, who took upon them at Shrovetide the name of London Prentices, and in that character invaded houses of ill-fame.

> More cruell then *shrove-prentices*, when they,
> Drunk in a brothell house, are bid to pay.
> *Davenant's Madagascar*, 1648, p. 28.

SHROVE-CAKES. Small cakes made to give children on Shrovetide.

SHROVERS. Children who go from house to house at Shrovetide singing for cakes.

SHROVE-TUESDAY. Perhaps the following account of Shrove-Tuesday by Taylor, the Water Poet, is one of the most curious and illustrative that could be produced in explanation of the numerous allusions in early writers to the feasting and sports in vogue on that day. "Welcome merry Shrovetide," Shakespeare, 2 Henry IV. v. 3.

Alwayes before Lent there comes wadling a fat grosse bursten-gutted groome, called Shrove-Tuesday, one whose manners shewes that he is better fed then taught : and indeed he is the onely monster for feeding amongst all the dayes of the yeere, for he devoures more flesh in foureteene houres, then this whole kingdome doth (or at the least should doe) in sixe weekes after: such boyling and broyling, such roasting and toasting, such stewing and brewing, such baking, frying, mincing, cutting, carving, devouring, and gorbellyed gurmondizing, that a man would thinke people did take in two months provision at once into their paunches, or that they did ballast their bellies with meate for a voyage to Constantinople or to the West Indies. Moreover, it is a goodly sight to see how the cookes in great men's kitchins doe fry in their masters suet, and sweat in their owne grease, that if ever a cooke be worth the eating it is when Shrove-Tuesday is in towne, for he is so stued and larded, roasted, basted, and almost over roasted, that a man may eate the rawest bit of him and never take a surfet. In a word, they are that day extreme cholericke, and too hot for any man to meddle with, being monarchs of the marow-bones, marquesses of the mutton, lords high regents of the spit and the kettle, barons of the gridiron, and sole commanders of the fryingpan. And all this hurly burly is for no other purpose but to stop the mouth of this land-wheale Shrove-Tuesday. At whose entrance in the morning all the whole kingdome is in quiet, but by that time the clocke strikes eleven, which (by the helpe of a knavish sexton) is commonly before nine, then there is a bell rung, cald The Pancake Bell, the sound whereof makes thousands of people distracted, and forgetfull either of manner or humanitie : Then there is a thing cald wheaten flowre which the sulphory necromanticke cookes doe mingle with water, egges, spice, and other tragicall magicall inchantments, and then they put it by little and little into a frying-pan of boyling suet, where it makes a confused dismall hissing (like the Learnean snakes in the reeds of Acheron, Stix or Phlegetôn) untill at last by the skill of the cooke, it is trans-

form'd into the forme of a flap-jack, which in our translation is cald a pancake, which ominous incantation the ignorant people doe devoure very greedily (having for the most part well dined before :) but they have no sooner swallowed that sweet candyed baite, but straight their wits forsake them, and they runne starke mad, assembling in routs and throngs numberlesse of ungoverned numbers, with uncivill civill commotions. Then Tim Tatters (a most valiant villaine) with an ensigne made of a piece of a bakers mawkin fixt upon a broome-staffe, he displaies his dreadfull colours, and calling the ragged regiment together, makes an illiterate oration, stuft with most plentifull want of discretion : the conclusion whereof is, that somewhat they will doe, but what they know not. Untill at last comes marching up another troope of tatterdemalians proclayming wars against no matter who, so they may be doing. Then these youths arm'd with cudgels, stones, hammers, rules, trowels, and hand-sawes, put playhouses to the sacke, and bawdy houses to the spoyle, in the quarrell breaking a thousand quarrels (of glasse I meane) making ambitious brickbats breake their neckes, tumbling from the tops of lofty chimnies, terribly untyling houses, ripping up the bowels of feather-beds, to the inriching of upholsters, the profit of plaisterers, and dirt-dawbers, the gaine of glasiers, joyners, carpenters, tylers, and bricklayers. And which is worse, to the contempt of justice for what availes it for a constable with an army of reverend rusty bill-men to command peace to these beasts, for they with their pockets instead of pistols, well char'd with stone-shot, discharge against the image of authority whole volleyes as thicke as hayle, which robustious repulse puts the better sort to the worser part, making the band of unscowred halberdiers retyre faster then ever they came on, and shew exceeding discretion in proving tall men of their heeles. Thus by the unmanerly maners of Shrove-Tuesday constables are baffled, bawds are bang'd, punckes are pillag'd, panders are plagued, and the chiefe commanders of these valourous villiacoes, for their reward for all this confusion, doe in conclusion purchase the inheritance of a jayle, to the commodity of jaylors, and discommodity to themselves, with a fearefull expectation that Tiburne shall stoppe their throats, and the hangman take possession of their coates, or that some beadle in bloudy characters shall imprint their faults on their shoulders. So much for Shrove-Tuesday, Jacke-a-Lents Gentleman Usher, these have beene his humours in former times, but I have some better hope of reformation in him hereafter, and indeed I wrote this before his comming this yeere 1617. not knowing how hee would behave himselfe ; but tottering betwixt despaire and hope, I leave him.

Taylor's Workes, 1630, i. 114-5.

SHROVY. Shabby. *Var. dial.*

SHROWDS. Places under ground, as the burrows of animals, vaults, &c. "Into the walks and *shrowds* of wild beasts," Harrison, p. 205. "A shrowdes or lyke buildinge under the grounde," Elyot, in v. *Apogæum*, ed. 1559. The crypt of a church was sometimes so called. *Shrowed*, sheltered, Arch. xi. 224.

> To schewe his lyyte in every *shrowed* and shade.
> *Lydgate, MS. Soc. Antiq.* 134, f. 23.

SHRUB. To reduce to poverty by winning a person's whole stock, a term used at play. *Somerset.*

SHRUCK. Shrieked. *Suffolk.*

SHRUDDE. Clothed. (*A.-S.*)

Ich the vedde wel and *shrudde* the;
And thou wyth eysyl drinkest to me,
And wyth spere styngest me. *Reliq. Antiq.* ii. 296.

SHRUFF. Light rubbish wood; any short dry stuff used for fuel. *Var. dial.* The term *schroff* in Depos. Ric. II. p. 13, may perhaps be connected with this.

SHRUMP. To shrug; to shrink. *West.*

SHRUMPSED. Beaten, in games. *Devon.*

SHRUMP - SHOULDERED. Hump-backed. *West.* Also used in Surrey.

SHRUPE. To hem in; to inclose.

SHUCK. (1) To shake. *Sussex.*

(2) A call to pigs. *Dorset.*

(3) A shell, or covering; a husk, or pod. *Var. dial.*

SHUCKEN. To shuffle. *Devon.*

SHUCKISH. Unpleasant; unsettled; showery, generally applied to the weather. *Sussex.*

SHUCKLE. To chuckle. It occurs several times in Florio, pp. 109, 215, 441.

SHUCKLED. Growing beans are said to be *shuckl'd* when beaten down by hail or wind.

SHUCK-TROT. A slow jog-trot. *East.*

SHUCKY. Deceitful. *Linc.*

SHUDDE. (1) To shed; to fall.

(2) A hut, shed, or hovel.

SHUDDER. To shiver. *Var. dial.*

SHUF. To shy, as horses do. *Oxon.*

SHUG. (1) Menacing. *Devon.*

(2) To writhe the body forward and backward, or from side to side, so as to produce friction against one's clothes, as those who have the itch. *Somerset.* Palsgrave has it, to jog or shake.

(3) To shrug; to scratch. *South.*

(4) A slow shaking trot. *Norf.*

SHUGGY-SHOW. A swing. *North.*

SHULDEN. Should. (*A.-S.*)

What is the cause, allas! quod sche,
My fadir that I ee *schulden* be
Bed and destroyed in suche a wise?
Gower, MS. Soc. Antiq. 134, f. 59.

SHULDERE. Rocky; craggy.

SHULDIR. A shoulder. (*A.-S.*)

He was mekille mane and lange,
With *schuldirs* brode and armes strange.
Isumbras, 14.

SHULL. A spade, or shovel. *North.*

SHULL-BANE. The shoulder-bone. *North.*

SHULVE. A shovel. *East.*

SHUN. To push; to shove. *South.* "Go shun, as they say in Sussex, *trudo*," Coles.

SHUNCH. The same as *Shun,* q. v.

SHUNDER. Slander; scandal.

SHUNNISH. To treat unkindly, often applied to the improper treatment of children. *Sussex.*

SHUNTE. (1) To delay; to put off.

Schape us an ansuere, and *schunte* yow no nengere,
That we may schifte at the schorte, and schewe to my lorde. *Morte Arthure, MS. Lincoln,* f. 67.

(2) To shun; to move from. *North.*

Then I drew me down into a dale, whereas the dumb deer
Did shiver for a shower; but I *shunted* from a freyke:
For I would no wight in this world wist who I were,
But little John Nobody, that dare not once speake.
Little John Nobody, c. 1550.

(3) To shy, or start. *Warw.*

(4) To slip down, as earth. *North.*

SHUPPARE. Maker; creator. (*A.-S.*)

SHUPPICK. A hay-fork. *West.*

SHURDE. Dressed. *Gawayne.*

SHURET. A shift. *Devon.*

SHURL. To trim the ends of the neck-feathers of a fighting-cock. *North.*

SHURNE. Cacare. This is given as a Wiltshire word in MS. Lansd. 1033, f. 2.

SHURTY. To bustle about. *Devon.*

SHUT. (1) To weld iron. *West.*

(2) A riddance. *To get shut,* to get rid of anything. *Var. dial.*

(3) A narrow street. *West.*

(4) An accession of water in a river, as from rain, floods, &c. *West.*

(5) To do; to manage. *Kent.*

(6) To join; to agree. *Dorset.*

(7) *To shut up,* to stop. *Var. dial.*

(8) To be extravagant. *North.*

SHUTFUL. Extravagant. *North.*

SHUTHER. To shiver with cold. *Linc.*

SHUT-OUT. To leave off ploughing, to unhook the horses. *Beds.*

SHUTS. Stout wooden poles. *Warw.*

SHUTTANCE. Riddance. *North.*

SHUTTEN-SATURDAY. The Saturday in Passion Week, the day on which our Saviour's body lay inclosed in the tomb.

SHUTTER. Same as *Shunte,* q. v.

SHUTTING. Covering up, applied to a table quite covered with dishes or eatables, &c.

SHUTTING-IN. The evening. *East.*

SHUTTLE. Slippery; sliding. *West.*

But nowe the fletynge fancyes fonde,
And eke the *shuttle* wyttes;
The mad desyres of women now,
Theyr rage in folysh fyts.
Hermaphroditus and Salmacis, 1565.

SHUTTLEBAG. When a man is husky from phlegm in his throat, he is said to have "swallowed a *shuttlebag.*"

SHUTTLE-BOARD. A shuttlecock. *North.*

SHUTTLE-HEADED. Foolish; rude.

Nor can you deeme them *shuttle-headed* fellowes,
Who for the Lord are so exceeding zealous.
MS. Poems, temp. Charles I.

SHY. (1) To fling. *Var. dial.*

(2) To start, said of a horse.

(3) The same as *Shrail,* q. v.

(4) Keen; piercing; bold; sharp. *North.*

(5) To avoid a person. *South.*

SIB. Relation; companion. (*A.-S.*) Still in use in Lincolnshire. He is *sib* to us, i. e., he is my cousin. "Sib'd, a-kin; no sole sib'd, nothing a-kin: no more sib'd then sieve and riddle, that grew both in a wood together. *Prov. Chesh.* Syb, or sybbe is an ancient Saxon word, signifying kindred, alliance, affinity," Ray's Words, ed. 1674, p. 40.

I sett yow here a soveraynge, ascente yif yowe lykys,
That es me sybb, my syster sone, sir Mordrede hym-selvene. *Morte Arthure, MS. Lincoln,* f. 60.

SIBBE. Related; allied. (*A.-S.*)

t hat in that wrye a gode frende,
Thou3 e were ri3t sibbe of my kynde,
He were worthy gret shame.
MS. Cantab. Ff. v. 48, f. 50.

' seeke 3ow, syr, as my sybbe lorde,
'. hat 3e wille for charyté cheese 3ow another.
Morte Arthure, MS. Lincoln, f. 60.

SIBBERIDGE. The banns of matrimony. It is often called *sibrit*, which would lead us to suppose it was connected with *sibrede*, q. v., and the latter was the more ancient and correct form. " Sybrede, *banna*," Pr. Parv. This word has been for a length of time peculiar to the Eastern counties, more especially Suffolk. Sir Thomas Browne refers it to Norfolk, and Ray to Suffolk. Major Moor derives it from the beginning of the banns as they used to be published in Latin, *si quis sciveret*. Ray's derivation from A.-S. *sib* appears to me to be much more probable.

SIBILACIONS. Hissings; growlings. (*Lat.*)

SIBILE-SAGE. The Queen of Sheba.
Sone after that verrayment
Tho *Sibile Sage* to Jerusalem went
To heren of Salamones wit.
MS. Trin. Coll. Oxon. 57, art. 2.

SIBLATOUR. One who hisses. (*Lat.*) " An hisser, or a *siblatour*," Gesta Romanorum, p. 116. It occurs in Lydgate.

SIBMAN. A relative. (*A.-S.*) It is the translation of *affinis* in Nominale MS. *Sibnesse*, relationship.
David thou were bore of my kyn,
For thi godnesse art thou myn,
More for thi godnesse
Then for eny *sibnesse*.
Harrowing of Hell, p. 27.

SIBREDE. Relationship; kindred. It is sometimes a substantive. (*A.-S.*)
Jhesu brother called was he,
For *sibrede*, worshepe and beauté.
Cursor Mundi, MS. Coll. Trin. Cantab. f. 79.
For every man it schulde drede,
And nameliche in his *sibrede*.
Gower, MS. Soc. Antiq. 134, f. 230.
Bot I forsake this gate, so me Gode helpe !
And sothely alle *sybredyne* bot thyselfe one.
Morte Arthure, MS. Lincoln, f. 96.

SIC. A call to pigs. *North.*

SICATE. Dry. (*Lat.*)
Reade not in spight, but take delight
In this, whiche once was prose ;
Whose watered plants scarse *sicate* were,
Till he this same did close.
Gaulfrido and Barnardo, 1570.

SICE. (1) Sixpence. A cant term.
(2) A gutter, or drain. *Somerset.* Grose has *sick*, a small stream or rill. It is from the A.-S. *sich.*

SICH. (1) Such. *Var. dial.*
And in the courte I have *sich* a frende,
I shalbe servyd or I wende,
Withowt any delay.
MS. Cantab. Ff. v. 48, f. 48.
Scho that was his lady
Mighte be fulle sary,
That lorne hade *siche* a body.
Percevall, 159.
(2) A wicked fellow. *Devon.*

SICK. In travail. *North.*

SICKER. The same as *Siker*, q. v.

SICK-FEATHERS. The young ungrown feathers at the time of moulting. *Devon.*

SICKINGE. Sighing ; lamenting.

SICKNESS. The plague was formerly termed for distinction's sake *the sickness.*

SICLATOUN. A kind of rich stuff.
There was mony gonfanoun,
Of gold, sendel, and *siclatoun*.
Kyng Alisaunder, 1964.

SICLE. A shekel. " A sicle, being an olde Persian coyne, and seemeth to be ninepense in value of our monie," Nomenclator, 1585, p. 330. It occurs also in Howell.

SICUR. Secure ; certain.
With me thei lefte alle theire thyng,
That I am *sicur* of theire comyng.
MS. Cantab. Ff. v. 48, f. 48.

SID. Saw. *West.*

SIDDER. Wider. (*A.-S.*)

SIDDOW. Vulgarly *siddow*. Peas which become soft by boiling are said to be *siddow.* *Glouc.*

SIDE. (1) Long ; trailing. *North.* " Used as in Skinner's time, e. g. " I do not like *side* frocks for little girls." I had thought this word obsolete, till two or three months ago I heard it used by an old lady, who numbers between 70 or 80 years," MS. Glossary of Lincolnshire Words, by the Rev. J. Adcock.
His berde was *side* with myche hare,
On his heede his hatt he bare.
Cursor Mundi, MS. Coll. Trin. Cantab. f. 33.
Hevedys tyfed wyth grete pryde,
With heer and hornes *syde*.
MS. Harl. 1701, f. 22.
(2) To carve a haddock.
(3) To take the part of another.
(4) To equal ; to stand in equal place.
(5) To decide ; to settle ; to coincide ; to set things aside, or out of the way. *North.*
(6) Rough ; rude. *Devon.*

SIDE-BOARDS. The rails of a cart.

SIDE-BOX. A seed-lepe. *South.*

SIDE-COATS. The long trailing coats or frocks worn by young children.

SIDE-LANDS. The outside parts of a ploughed field, adjoining the hedges, running parallel with the lands or ridges. *South.*

SIDE-LANIELS. Hopples for horses.

SIDE-LAY. In hunting, a fresh set of hound to be laid in on the scent.

SIDE-LIKE. Such like. *North.*

SIDELINE. Evenly in rows. *Devon.* Its correct and ancient meaning is *slanting.*

SIDELING. The slope of a hill. *South.*

SIDELINGS. Aslant ; sideways. *East.*
And *sydlynges* of the segge the syghte had he rechide.
Morte Arthure, MS. Lincoln, f. 64

SIDELONG. To fetter as a preventive from straying, or breaking pasture, by chaining a fore and a hind foot of the same side together. *Yorksh.*

SIDEMEN. Assistants to the churchwarden. See Harrison's England, p. 163. The same as *Questmen*, q. v.

SIDENANDIS. Aslant; on one side.

SIDENESS. Length. *Palsgrave.*

SIDER. An orderly person. *Lanc.*

SIDERE.

> For hit was brijt and ful fayre tre,
> Men myjt hit fulle fere se;
> That stode in erth was *sydere* gode,
> For hit shulde not rote as hit stode.
> *MS. Cantab. Ff. v. 48, f. 31.*

SIDE-SHEAR. On all sides. *Percy.*

SIDE-WAVERS. The beams in the roof of a house which form the angle of the roof. See Thoresby's Letter to Ray, 1703, in v. *Bawks.*

SIDE-WIPE. An indirect censure.

SIDE-WISE. Breadthwise. *North.*

SIDGOREN. This term was given to a part of the dress about the bosom.

SIDITHERUM. A creeping, slow-motioned person. *Linc.*

SIDLE. (1) To go sideways; to saunter idly about in no particular direction. *Var. dial.*
(2) To sit down gently. *Devon.*

SIDNESS. Seed-time. *West.*

SIDRON. A citron.

SIDY. Surly; moody. *Sussex.* This word was given by Ray in 1674, but I do not know whether it be still in use.

SIE. (1) A drop. Also, to drop. *North.*
(2) To pull, or stretch. *Yorksh.*
(3) Saw. *Chaucer.*
(4) To strain milk. *Palsgrave.* It is still in use in Derbyshire.

> Sometime itt was of cloth in graine,
> 'Tis now but a *sigh-clout* as you may see,
> It will neither hold out winde nor raine;
> And Ile have a new cloake about mee.
> *Percy's Reliques,* p. 52.

SIEGE. (1) A company of herons.
(2) The same as *Sege,* q. v.

SIELE. To vault. *Elyot, 1559.*

SIENE. Since.

> I salle jow telle als trewe a tale
> Als ever was herde by nyghte or daye;
> And the maste mervelle, for-owttyne naye,
> That ever was herde by-fore or *ayene.*
> *MS. Lincoln A. i. 17, f. 149.*

SIESIN. Yeast; barm. *Kent.*

SIESTA. The rest usually taken about noon in hot countries, as in Spain.

SIETHES. A kind of chives.

SIEVER. All the fish caught in one tide. *East Sussex.*

SIEVES. Chives; a small kind of onion. It is so spelt in Hollyband's Dictionarie, 1593.

SIFE. To sigh. *Somerset.* Carr has *siff* in the Craven Glossary, ii. 124.

SIFFLEMENT. Whistling.

SIG. Urine. *South.*

SIGALDRY. (1) Deceit; trick. (2) To deceive; to act by a stratagem, or unlawfully.

> Josephe, take hym then to thee,
> And burye hym wher thy wil be.
> But look thou make no *sigaldry,*
> To rayse him up agayne. *Chester Plays,* ii. 69.
> There was a wycche and made a bagge,
> A bely of lethyr, a grete swagge;
> She *sygaldryd* so thys bagge bely,
> That hyt jede and soke mennys ky. *MS. Harl.* 1701, f. 4.

SIGGER. To leak. *Cornw.*

SIGGETH. Says. *(A.-S.)*

> And *siggeth* Merlin wil hem abide
> In the forest here bside.
> *Arthour and Merlin,* p. 73.

SIGH. To become larger. *North.*

SIGHT. (1) A great quantity. *Var. dial.*

> Where is so great a strength of money, i. where is so huge a *syght* of mony.
> *Palsgrave's Acolastus,* 1540.

(2) The perforation in a helmet through which the wearer looked.
(3) Sighed. *Spenser.*

> Than syr Degrevraunt *syght,*
> And byheld the hevene up-an hyght,
> Jhesus, save me in my ryght,
> And Maré me spede! *Sir Degrevant,* 209.

(4) To cite; to quote.

SIGHTLESS. (1) Invisible. (2) Unsightly.

SIGHTS. (1) Eyes. *Somerset.*
(2) Spectacles. *Var. dial.*

SIGHTSOME. Sightly. *More.*

SIGHTY. Glittering; shining.

SIGINNES.

> Let them learne, let them learn, simple *siginnes* as they are, that the Apostle speaketh in this place of ecclesiasticall functions.
> *Mar-Prelate's Epitome,* p. 43.

SIGN. To intend; to design. *South.*

SIGNE. To appoint. *(A.-N.)*

SIGN-HILL. A slight eminence on the sea bank, on which a tall pole is set up for the purpose of making signs to vessels out at sea. *Linc.*

SIGNIFER. The zodiac. *(Lat.)*

SIGNIFIAUNCE. Signification. *(A.-N.)*

SIGNIFICATION. Importance. *Var. dial.*

SIGNIORIZE. To govern, or bear rule.

SIGNIORY. Government; dominion; domain, or lordship; seniority.

SIGN-TREE. A beam in the roof of a house. See Thoresby's Letter to Ray, 1703, in v. *Bawks.* Still in use.

SIGNWYNARYE. A blood-stone.

> I will to my eldest son and heir, Edward Montagu, my great ring with a *signwynarye* in it, which my father gave me, that remaineth in my study at Brigstock. *Test. Vetust.* p. 743.

SIGOLLE. The cycle.

> As for divers other purposes, to caste therin in metalle the *sigolle* of any plannet, when he is stronge in the heavens. *MS. Ashmole* 240.

SIGRIM. (1) The herb segrum.

> Tak *sygryme,* waybrede, columbyne, and sile thamme thorow a clathe, and qwete flour, and temper tille it be thikke. *MS. Lincoln A. i. 17, f.* 290

(2) A name for the fox.

> For he thoute mid soumme ginne,
> Him self houp bringe, thene wolf therinne.
> Quod the vox, Wo is nou there?
> Ich wene hit is *sigrim* that ich here.
> *Reliq. Antiq.* ii. 274.

SIH. Saw. See *Ogne.*

SIKE. (1) Such. *North.*

> Hir palfray was of dappulle gray,
> *Sike* on se I never non,
> As dose the sune on somers day
> The cumly lady hirselfe schone.
> *MS. Cantab. Ff. v. 48, f. 116*

(2) To sigh. Still in use.

> Yf that the feende hymself wolde have a make,
> Ys none to hym so lyke as ye allone.
> He that yow seith, and *sykyth* for your sake,
> I pray to God that evere he *syke* and grone.
>> *MS. Fairfax* 16.

> The lady *sykyd* and sayde, allas !
> Into the worlde that sche was wroght.
>> *MS. Cantab. Ff. ii. 38, f. 46.*

(3) A sick person. *North.*

(4) A gutter; a stream. *North.*

SIKER. Secure; safe. *North.*

> I am *siker* and I bileve
> That none yvel schal thi fadre greve.
>> *MS. Addit. 10036, f. 2.*

> Ac arst ye schul me make *siker*,
> With me held in everi biker.
>> *Arthour and Merlin, p. 206.*

> That schip had a ful *siker* mast,
> And a sayl strong and large. *Vernon MS.*

SIKERDE. Assured. (*A.-S.*)

SIKERLYE. Certainly; surely.

> Thou arte here, *sykerlye*,
> Thys churche to robbe with felonye.
>> *MS. Cantab. Ff. ii. 38, f. 240.*

SIKERNESSE. Security. (*A.-S.*)

SIKIS. A scythe. Nominale MS.

SILD. Seldom. For *Selde.*

SILDE. A shed. *Stowe.*

SILE. (1) To strain; to skim. *North.*

> Take a handeful of sauge, and stampe it, and temper it with hate ale, and sythene *syle* it thorowe a hate clathe. *MS. Lincoln A. i. 17, f. 281.*
> Do therto gud wyne, and stepe alle togidre, and drinke the licoure *siled* thorgh a clothe v. dayes morne and evene.
>> *MS. in Mr. Pettigrew's possession*, xv. Cent.

(2) To sink; to drop; to make to sink, or settle; to flow; to rain. *North.*

> Many balde garte he *syle*
> With the dynt of his spere.
>> *MS. Lincoln A. i. 17, f. 131.*

> And thane syghande he saide with *sylande* terys,
> We are with Sarazenes besett appone sere halfes.
>> *Morte Arthure, MS. Lincoln, f. 93.*

(3) Filth; sediment. *North.*

(4) To boil gently; to simmer. *North.*

SILED. Canopied.

> AH the tente within was *syled* wyth clothe of golde and blewe velvet, and all the blewe velvet was embrowdered with H. K. of fyne golde.
>> *Hall, Henry VIII. f. 32.*

SILENCED. Ministers prohibited from preaching were said to be *silenced.*

SILERIC. Adorned with carving.

SILGREEN. The houseleek. *West.*

SILING-DISH. A milk-strainer. *North.*

SILKER. A court-card. *Somerset.*

SILK-SHAG. A fine kind of shag cloth.

> Flower-poudred mantles, and embroidered gowns
> Of grass-green *silk-shag*, and the gawdie pride
> Of all her jewels and her Jems beside.
>> *Du Bartas, p. 641.*

SILL. (1) A step. *Oxon.*

(2) The young of a herring. *North.*

(3) A seat, or throne.

> The precyouse stones semly to see appone *sylle.*
>> *MS. Lincoln A. i. 17, f. 232.*

(4) The shaft of a vehicle. *North.* Sill-horse, the shaft horse.

(5) A stratum of coal. *Staff.*

(6) To swell, or puff up.

SILLER. (1) Silver. *North.*

(2) A covering of tapestry, in the form of a canopy for a bed, altar, &c.

> The kynge hymeselfene es sette and certayne lordes
> Undyre a *sylure* of sylke, sawghte at the burdes.
>> *Morte Arthure, MS. Lincoln, f. 87.*

SILLY. Sickly; weakly. *North.*

SILLYBAUK. A sillabub. *Linc.*

SILLY-BOLD. Impertinently forward.

SILLY-CORNES.

> And I will looke babbies in your eyes, and picke *silly-cornes* out of your toes.
>> *The Two Lancashire Lovers*, 1640, p. 19.

SILLY-HEW. A child's caul. *Durham.*

SILT. Sediment; ooze. *East.*

> I suppose it to be the *silt* of the water, which the wind and the water brought together.
>> *Aubrey's Wilts, Royal Soc. MS. p. 262.*

SILT-UP. To obstruct the course of a stream, or the free passage of boats upon it, by a large accumulation of sand.

SILVER-CHAIN. The white laburnum.

SILVERLINGS. Coins; pieces of money.

SILVER-SPOON. To be born with a silver spoon in one's mouth, i. e. to be very rich.

SILYNG. Tapestry.

> The Frenche kyng caused the lorde of Countay to stande secretly behynde a *silyng* or a hangyng in his chamber. *Hall, Edward IV. f. 43.*

SIM. To seem; to think. *West.*

SIMATHIN. Liking; partiality. *Devon.* "A simmathing, something of an inclination, some tenderey towards love, a sneaking kindness," MS. Devon Gloss.

SIMBLING-CAKES. Currant cakes eaten in Lancashire on Midlent Sunday.

SIME. A frame of straw used for setting pans on. *North.*

SIMEN. A salmon. *North.*

SIMILLITT. A likeness. *Hall.*

SIMINACION. Breeding. (*Lat.*)

> Thus thay enduring in lust and delyte,
> The sprectes of tham gat that were gyauntes tyte,
> With the nature of themeselves and *syminacion*,
> Thay wer brought forthe by there ymaginacion.
>> *MS. Lansdowne 208, f. 2.*

SIMKIN. A silly fellow. *South.*

SIMLIN. A kind of fine cake intended for toasts. *Somerset.*

SIMMIT. Smooth. *North.*

SIMNEL. A kind of rich cake, generally made in a three-cornered form. The term is applied in Salop to a plum-cake with a raised crust.

SIMPER. To simmer. *East.* "The creame of simpering milke," Florio, p. 189.

SIMPER-DE-COCKET. An affected mealy-mouthed girl. *Cotgrave.* "A simper-de-cocket, *coquine, fantastica*," Howell, 1660.

SIMPHANGLE. A musical instrument.

> Yn harpe, yn thabour and *symphangie*,
> Wurschepe God yn troumpes and sautre.
>> *MS. Harl. 1701, f. 32.*

SIMPHONER. A musician.

SIMPLE. (1) Weak; infirm, applied to the old and sickly. *Salop.*

(2) Of little value ; mean.

SIMPLES. He wants cutting for the simples, said of one doing a foolish action. "He must go to Battersea, to be cut for the simples," Old Proverb.

SIMPLE-SIMON. An idiot. " Simon Suck-egg sold his wife for an addle duck-egg."

SIMPLESSE. Simplicity. (A.-N.)

SIMPSON. Groundsel. East.

SIMULACRE. An image. (Lat.)

SIMULAR. Counterfeited. Shak.

SIN. (1) To stand. East.

(2) Since. Still in use.

SINALD. A signal. Greene.

SINAMONE. Cinnamon. (A.-N.)

SINCANTER. An old worn-out person.

SIND. To wash down ; to rinse ; to empty out ; to quench thirst. North.

SINDER. To settle or separate the lees or dregs. Kent.

SINDERLIK. Separately. (A.-S.)

SINDY. Soft in speech. Devon.

SINE. (1) Afterwards. North.

His nobille swerde he drawes syne,
And faughte with that wylde swyne.
MS. Lincoln A. i. 17, f. 141.

And syne go to the tavern house,
And buy both wine and ale.
Robin Hood, i. 102.

(2) To strain. North.

(3) To leave off milking a cow.

SIN-EATERS. It was an ancient custom at funerals to hire poor people, who were to take upon them the sins of the deceased.

Within the memory of our fathers, in Shropshire, in those villages adjoyning to Wales, when a person dyed, there was notice given to an old sire, (for so they called him,) who presently repaired to the place where the deceased lay, and stood before the door of the house, when some of the family came out and furnished him with a cricket, on which he sat down facing the door. Then they gave him a groat, which he put in his pocket ; a crust of bread, which he eat ; and a full bowle of ale, which he drank off at a draught. After this he got up from the cricket and pronounced, with a composed gesture, the ease and rest of the soul departed, for which he would pawn his own soul. This I had from the ingenious John Aubrey, Esq., who made a collection of curious observations, which I have seen, and is now remaining in the hands of Mr. Churchill, the bookseller. How can a man think otherwise of this, than that it proceeded from the ancient heathens ? Bagford, ap. Brand, ii. 152.

SINEDE. Assigned.

And on the Saturday he synede the grounde
To the chyveteynys abowte that cyté rounde.
Archæologia, xxi. 53.

SINET. The zenith. Chaucer.

SINEWAYS. Sundry ways. Cumb.

SINEWEY. Mustard seed. " As hath the corn of synewey," Gesta Rom. p. 36.

SINEY. The bladder-nut tree. It is the translation of baguenaudier in Hollyband's Dictionarie, 1593.

SINFAN. To perform a symphony.

SINGEL. Roof of a house.

Arthour smot on hem saun faile,
So on the singel do the haile.
Arthour and Merlin, p. 218.

SINGERIES. Apish tricks. Skinner.

SINGING-BREAD. The round cakes or wafers intended for the consecrated host in the eucharistic sacrament. See Davies' Rites, ed. 1672, p. 2.

Item, I bequethe to the same chirch a little round cofyn of sylver, closed in synging-bred, and not the hoste. Test. Vetust. p. 266.

SINGING-HINNY. A rich kneaded cake, a great favorite with pitmen. North. It has currants and butter in it, and is baked over the fire on a girdle.

SINGING-MEN. Choristers.

SINGLE. (1) Pure ; genuine ; disinterested ; plain ; sincere ; unreserved.

(2) Weak ; feeble ; silly. " My single state of man," Shakespeare. Single beer, week beer ; double beer, strong beer.

(3) A handful of the gleanings of corn tied up. North.

(4) An animal's tail, properly applied to that of the buck. See Hunting, sect. 12.

SINGLE-GUSS. The plant orchis. West.

SINGLE-MONEY. Small coins.

SINGLERE. A wild boar.

Boyes in the suburbis bourdene fulle heghe
At a bare synglere that to the bente rynnys.
Morte Arthure, MS. Lincoln, f. 86.

SINGLE-STICK. A well-known play with staves, which consists in attempts to bring blood from your adversary's head, when he who first effects it is pronounced victor. It is sometimes called backsword.

SINGLET. An unlined waistcoat. Derb. When double or lined it is termed a doublet.

SINGLE-TEN. A tenth card. North. A term used generally at the game of whist.

SINGLETON. A silly fellow. West.

SINGLE-WOMAN. A whore. " Syngle woman a harlot, putayn," Palsgrave.

SING-SMALL. Equivalent to must be content with less than appearances promised. Essex.

SING-SONG. A drawling song. Var. dial.

I tell the foole, whatever thou be,
That made this fyne sing-song of me,
Thou art a ryming sott ;
Thy very lynes doe the betray,
Thy barren witt makes all men say
'Tis some rebellious Scott.
Suckling's Reply to a Libel, MS.

SINGULAR. (1) Single ; lonely. Norf.

(2) Choice. Shak. " Proper or synguler, exquis," Palsgrave, adj. " Synguler or pure, absolu, exquis, singuler," ibid.

SINGULF. A sigh. Spenser.

SINGULL. A cingle, or horse-girth.

SINIFY. To signify. North.

SINISTRAL. Sinister.

They gather their sinistral opinion, as I hear say of St. Paul to the Hebrews. Becon's Workes, p. 95.

SINK. To work a mine deeper. Derb.

SINK-A-PACE. Cinque-pace, q. v. Sincopace, Gaulfrido and Barnardo, 1570.

SINK-DIRT. Gutter mud. Lanc.

SINKER. A cesspool; used in the neighbourhood of Spilsby. *Linc.*

SINK-HOLE. A hole for dirty water to run through. *South.*

SINKSANKER. A term of contempt.

SINK-STONE. A perforated hollowed stone at the top of a sink. *Var. dial.*

SINNEN. A sinew. *Sinner-grown*, having the sinews contracted. *North.*

SINNETE. A kind of cloth.

SINNOWED. Gaily ornamented. *Sinnow*, a woman very finely dressed.

> Whereas she wont in her feathered youthfulnesse to looke with amiable eye on her gray breast, and her speckled side sayles, all *sinnowed* with silver quilles, and to drive whole armies of fearfull foules b fore her to her master's table.
>
> *Nash's Pierce Pennilesse, 1592.*

SIN-SYNE. Since that time. *North.*

SINTER. " Synter of masonry," Palsgrave. It occurs in the Pr. Parv. translated by *cinctorium*, MS. Harl. 221.

SINUM. " Synum a vessell, *faiselle*," Palsgrave, 1530, subst. f. 64.

SIPE. To drain or drip, as liquor does through a cask, tap, &c. which is defective or not tight. *Linc.*

SIPPETS. Small thin pieces of bread mixed with milk or broth. *South.*

SIPPLE. To sip up; to drink. " They did but *sipple* up," Yorkshire Ale, 1697, p. 7. Brockett has *sirple*, p. 269, ed. 1829.

SIPRES. Same as *Cipress*, q. v. " Sipres or bonegraces that women use to weare one their faces or foreheads to keepe them from the the sunne," Florio, p. 590.

SI-QUIS. If any one. (*Lat.*) Advertisements or bills thus commenced formerly, and hence the name of *siquisses* was often given to them. " A siquis, or publick note, *cry public, ou cedule*," Howell.

SIR. (1) A gentleman. *Shak.*

(2) Applied to priests and curates; it was a scholastic title, the translation of *dominus*, given to a person who had taken his first degree in the university.

SIRE. A breed, or sort, as a good *sire* of pigs, or of cabbages, &c. *East.*

SIR-HARRY. A close stool. *East.*

SIR-JOHN. A priest.

> With much adoe and great difficultie obteined that a poore chapell, served with a single *Sir John*, and destitute both of font and churchyard, might remaine standing in the place.
>
> *Lambard's Perambulation, 1596, p. 317.*

SIR-JOHN-BARLEYCORN. A jocular name for ale, which is made of barley.

SIROINE. A kind of soft salve for wounds, mentioned in MS. Med. Lincoln. f. 310.

SIRPLE. The same as *Sipple*, q. v.

SIRRAH. In old plays this term is frequently addressed to women.

SIRRAP. A hard blow. *Devon.*

SIR-REVERENCE. A corruption of the phrase *save reverence*, which was said as a kind of apology before the utterance of anything that might be considered objectionable, but often simply as an apology in speaking to a superior. " Sa-reverence, *salva reverentia*, saving regard or respect; an usual word, but miscalled *sir-reverence* by the vulgar," Blount's Glossographia, ed. 1681, p. 572. Compare a curious passage in the Yorkshire Ale, 1697, p. 12. The term was also applied to human ordure, and is still used in that sense.

> A worthy knight there is of ancient fame,
> And sweet *Sir Reverence* men doe call his name;
> By whose industrious policie and wit,
> There's many things well tane were else unfit:
> If to a foule discourse thou hast pretence,
> Before thy foule words name *Sir Reverence;*
> Thy beastly tale most pleasantly will slip,
> And gaine thee praise when thou deserv'st the whip
> There's nothing vile that can be done or spoke,
> But must be covered with *Sir Reverence* cloake.
> His ancient pedigree whoever seekes,
> Shall finde he's sprung from 'mongst the gallant Greekes,
> Was Ajax squire, great champion to god Mars:
> Pray God, *Sir Reverence*, blesse your worships ( ).
>
> *Taylor's Workes, 1630, iii. 96.*

> A puppie licks Manneia's lipps, the sense
> I grant, a dog may kis.—— *sir reverence.*
>
> *Fletcher's Poems, p. 10.*

> But the old proverbe ne'r will be forgot,
> A lechers love is, like *sir reverence*, hot.
>
> *Taylor's Workes, 1630, ii. 109.*

SIRUP. A poor ha'purth of sirup, i. e. a poor weak creature. *Suffolk.*

SIS. (1) The cast of six, the highest throw upon the die. (*A.-N.*)

(2) Cicely, a common name for a girl.

> The plowman that in times past was contented in russet, must now adaies have his doublet of the fashion, with wide cuts, his garters of fine silke of Granado, to meet his *Sis* on Sunday.
>
> *Lodge's Wits Miserie, 1596.*

SISE. (1) The assizes. *Palsgrave.*

> Thes letters kepte I tyll the *sise*,
> My libertie to enterprise. *MS. Ashmole 802.*

(2) A wax-taper. " Syse waxe candell, *bougee*," Palsgrave, 1530, subst. f. 64.

(3) A lesson, or task. *North.*

SISERARA. A hard blow. *East.*

SISKIN. A greenfinch. It is the translation of *breant* in Hollyband's Dictionarie, 1593.

SISOUR. A person deputed to hold assizes.

> Now of the eytthe wyl we speke,
> That fals *sysoure* use moste to breke.
>
> *MS. Harl. 1701, f. 18.*

> What shul we sey of thys dytours,
> Thys fals men that beyn *sysours.*
>
> *MS. Harl. 1701, f. 9.*

> Ley hande on booke, the *sysour* take none hede,
> For every thing drawethe to his semblable.
>
> *MS. Ashmole 59, f. 20.*

SISS. (1) To hiss. *Linc.* Hence *sissing*, a hissing serpent. " Sibilus est genus serpentis, Anglice a syssyng," MS. Bibl. Reg. 12 B. i. f. 12, written about 1400.

(2) A huge fat woman. *Devon.*

SISSLE. A thistle. *Sussex.*

SIST. Seest. (*A.-S.*)

> For al dai thou *sist* with thin eien
> Hou this world wend, and ou men deien. *MS. Digby 86.*

SISTER. A sewster.

SISTERING. A cistern, o. reservoir.

SISTER-LAW. A sister-in-law. *West.*

SISTER-SONE. Nephew. (*A.-S.*)

> And we are *sister-sones* two,
> And aythir of us othir slo,
> He that lifes wille be fulle wo
> That ever was he made. *Perceval*, 1441.

SIT. (1) To endure.

> Was never knyghte that he fande,
> In France ne in Scotlande,
> Mighte *sitt* a strake of his hande
> One his styff stede.
> *MS. Lincoln* A. i. 17, f. 130.

(2) *To sit a woman*, to keep the night-courtship (q. v.) with a girl. *To sit eggs*, to remain a guest an unreasonable time. *To sit on*, said of milk when it burns in the pan. *To sit in*, to adhere firmly to anything.

SITE. (1) Disgrace; shame. " Sorowe and *syte*," MS. Cantab. Ff. ii. 38, f. 236.

> Now alle-weldand Gode that wyrscheppes us alle,
> Giff the sorowe and *syte*, sotte there thow lygges.
> *Morte Arthure*, MS. Lincoln, f. 64.

(2) A scythe. Nominale MS.

SIT-FAST. A kind of hard swelling on a horse's back. *Cotgrave.*

SITH. (1) Since. *North.*

> The kyng seyde, What may thys mene?
> Y trowe Syr Roger and the quene
> Be comen to thys londe,
> For nevyr *syth* they went y-wys,
> Sawe y Syr Roger hounde or thys,
> That ya wondur tythand !
> *MS. Cantab.* Ff. ii. 38, f. 74.

(2) Time. (*A.-S.*)

> Than the cokwoldes wer full blythe,
> And thankyd God a c. *syth.*
> *MS. Ashmole* 61, f. 61.

(3) Way ; journey.

SITHCUNDMAN. The head or chief of a town or parish. *Coles.* (*A.-S.*)

SITHE. (1) To sigh. *East.*

(2) To strain or purify liquor.

SITHE-CRADLE. A rack of wood fastened to a scythe for carrying the mowed barley clean into the swath. Kennett, p. 42.

SITHEN. Since. (*A.-S.*) *Sithence* is often used by later writers.

> I bade felowes to my dynere,
> And *sithen* thei wil not cum here ;
> A develle have who that reche.
> *MS. Cantab.* Ff. v. 48, f. 49.

SITHERS. Scissors. *North.*

SITHY-HANGERS. A cow's teats. *Somerset.*

SIT-STILL-NEST. Merda. *Lanc.*

SITTAND. Suitable ; becoming.

> A hundrethe pondis worthe of londe
> Of rent wele *sittande.*
> *MS. Lincoln* A. i. 17, f. 130.
> He salusede that sorowfulle with *sittande* wordez,
> And fraynes aftyre the fende fairely thereaftyre.
> *Morte Arthure*, MS. Lincoln, f. 63.

SITTEN-ON. Stunted in stature.

SITTING. A space in the pew of a church sufficient for one person.

SITTING-CLOTH. A kind of garment, the same as *strigium* in Ducange.

SITTINGS. Statute fairs for servants held in some parts of the North.

SI-VA. A cry to hounds. Maistre of the Game, MS. Bodl. 546, xv. Cent.

SIVE. (1) To follow. (*A.-N.*)

> Who that the vicis wolde eschyve,
> He mot by resone thanne *sive.*
> *Gower*, MS. Soc. Antiq. 134, f. 82.
> And bowe unto thyne heste and *sive*
> Humilité, and that y vowe.
> *Gower*, MS. Soc. Antiq. 134, f. 58.
> The forme bothe and the matere,
> As now *sivende*, thou schalt here.
> *Gower*, MS. Soc. Antiq. 134, f. 84.

(2) To sieve. Also, a sieve.

> And casting foorth silken shraps, to catch wood-
> cocks, or in *syving* of muck-hills and shop-dust,
> whereof he will boult a whole cart load to gain a
> bow'd pinne. *Nash's Pierce Pennilesse*, 1592.

(3) A scythe. *South.*

SIVEDES. Refuse of bran.

SIVELLE. Civil.

> Therin he sped hym right welle
> Of the maister of lawe *syvelle.*
> *MS. Cantab.* Ff. v. 48, f. 74.

SIX. A cup of six, i. e. a cup of beer sold at six shillings a barrel.

SIXES-AND-SEVENS. The true origin of this phrase has been given in v. *Set* (13).

SIX-LOVE. A term at whist, signifying *six to none* in scoring.

SIX-STRINGED-WHIP. A popular name for the statute of the six articles which passed in 1541. See Lingard, ed. 1844, vi. 293.

SIZE. (1) Six. *Lanc.*

(2) " A size," says Minsheu, " is a portion of bread or drinke, it is a farthing which schollers in Cambridge have at the buttery ; it is noted with the letter S." See also Ellis's Literary Letters, p. 178. The word now means anything had by the students at dinner over and above the usual commons.

(3) Assizes. Still in use.

> Our drowning scap'd, more danger was ensuing,
> 'Twas *size* time there, and hanging was a brewing.
> *Taylor's Workes*, 1630, ii. 14.

(4) One third of an inch, a term much used by shoemakers.

SIZELY. Proud ; coy. *North.*

SIZER. (1) A thin piece of brass with a round hole in it wherein they try to see whether a cast bullet is perfectly round.

(2) A student at Cambridge whose expenses for living are partially provided by the college, originally a servitor, as serving one of the fellows. Each fellow of a college had one servitor allotted to him.

SIZING. (1) Yeast. This term occurs in Lilly's Mother Bombie, ed. 1632, sig. Aa. vii.

(2) Weaver's size. *North.*

(3) A game at cards called " Jack running for mustard," is generally called " Jack running for *sizing*." The cards are placed so that by touching the first pair, all the rest must of course fall diagonally, in the form of upright wedges. *Kent.*

SIZLE. To saunter about. *North.*

SIZY. Gluey; sticky. *South.*

SIZZEN. To hiss. *North.*

SIZZLE. The half hiss, half sigh of an animal; of an owl, for instance. Also the effervescence of brisk beer, &c. through a cork; or the alarming hissing of lightning very near one. Ray says that yeast is called sizzing from the sound of the working beer. Since this was written I heard the word thus used,—" If we heen't rain in another week we shall be all *sizzled* up." This evidently meant *burnt up*, as it was spoken in a season of fearful aridity. Moor's Suffolk Words, p. 351.

SIZZUP. A hard blow. *North.*

SIƷAND. Sighing. (*A.-S.*)

> Fer in frithe as I can fare,
> Myselfe *syʒand* allone,
> I herd the mournyng of an hare;
> Thus delfully she made her mone.
> *MS. Cantab. Ff. v. 48, f. 109.*

SIƷE. Saw. (*A.-S.*)

> Thus wen sche come the lady nyʒe,
> Then toke sche better hede, and *nyʒe*
> The womman was ryʒt fayre off face,
> Allethouʒ here lackyd other grace.
> *MS. Cantab. Ff. 1. 6, f. 7.*
>
> And so bifelle, as y cam nyʒe,
> Oute of my boot whanne he me *nyʒe.*
> *Gower, MS. Soc. Antiq. 134, f. 30.*

SIƷTE. Sight. (*A.-S.*)

> The kyng comfortid the quene and other ladyes eke,
> His swete babis full tendurly he did kys:
> The yonge prynce he behelde and in his armys did bere,
> Thus his bale turnyd hym to blis:
> Aftur sorow, joy the course of the worlde is,
> The *siʒte* of his babis relesid parte of his woo,
> Thus the wille of God in every thyng is doo.
> *MS. Bibl. Reg. 17 D. xv.*

SIƷƷED. Sighed. See *Siʒand.*

> And sore *syʒʒed* that al men mythte wel se.
> *MS. Cantab. Ff. 1. 6, f. 143.*

SKAALING. A lean-to or out-office with roof asloop, appendant to a higher building. *Hant.* Kennett, MS. Lansd. 1033.

SKACHES. "*Grallator*, he that goeth on styltes or *skaches,*" Elyote's Dictionarie, 1559. "Scatches, *grallæ*," Coles' Lat. Dict.

> Away with boates and rodder,
> Farewell both bootes and *skatches.*
> *Dugdale's Imbanking, 1662, p. 391.*

SKADE. Harm; mischief. *Sussex.*

SKAFE. Awkward. *Linc.*

SKAFFAUT. A scaffold; a wooden tower; a raised stage. (*A.-N.*)

SKAG. An accidental blow, particularly of the heel of the shoe, so as to tear either the clothes or the flesh; any slight wound or rent. *Somerset.*

SKAIN. (1) A crooked sword, or scimitar, used formerly by the Irish.

> Duryng this siege arrived at Harflew the Lord of Kylmaine in Ireland, with a band of xvj. hundreth Iryshmen, armed in mayle with dartes and *skaynes*, after the maner of their countrey.
> *Hall, Henry V. f. 28.*

(2) A scarf for the head.

SKAITH. Hurt; harm. *North.*

> And as he was betwixt them past,
> They leapt upon him baith:
> The one his pyke-staff gripped fast,
> They feared for its *skaith.* Robin Hood, i.196.

SKALES. A game mentioned by Wager in his play called, "The longer thou Livest, the more Foole thou art." Some suppose it to be the same as *Skoyles*, q. v. See a mention in Clarke's Phraseologia, 1655, p. 254, and another in Florio's New World of Words, 1611, p. 19, from which latter it seems to have been a game like nine-pins, and the game of skittles is still so called in Devon.

SKALK. This word has not yet been explained. Other copies of the ballad preserved in MS. Harl. 372, f. 114, and Strype's Memorials of Cranmer, 1694, App. p. 138, agree in the reading here given.

> Its meet for every man on this matter to talk,
> And the glorious gospel ghostly to have in mind;
> It is sothe said, that sect but much unseemly *skalk*,
> As boyes babble in books, that in scripture are blind.
> *Percy's Reliques, p. 190.*

SKALLE. (1) A scald head.

(2) A drinking cup; a goblet. It is more generally written *skayle* or *skail.*

SKANSKBACK. Easily distinguishable; having some special mark. *Yorksh.*

SKARNES. Terrors.

SKASE. To run; to hurry. *Cornw.*

SKASIƷAGER. The hot seed of a wild vine. It occurs in MS. Lincoln A. i. 17, f. 280.

SKATHY. Ravenous; mischievous.

SKAVELL. A kind of spade. *Tusser.*

SKAWER. A jurat.

> Recompence of the same shall be given, and the harms amended to him that is so wronged, according to the discretion of the bayliff and the *skawer.*
> *Dugdale's History of Imbanking, 1662, p. 97.*

SKAYNEY. Long; lanky. *Dorset.*

SKEAR. Gravel; pebbles. *North.*

SKEEL. (1) A pail. *North.*

(2) To shell peas, beans, &c. *Westm.*

SKEELING. The inner part of a barn or garret, where the slope of the roof comes. *South.*

SKEEMISH. Delicate. Also, given to scheming, manœuvring, covetous. *West.*

SKEEN. A sword. (*A.-S.*)

SKEER. (1) The place where cockles are gathered. West. and Cumb. Dial. p. 386.

(2) To mow lightly over: applied to pastures which have been summer-eaten, never to meadows. In a neuter sense, to move along quickly, and slightly touching. Hence, from its mode of flight, is derived *skeer-devil.*

(3) "To *skeer* the esse" is to clear the grate, separating the ashes from the live coals. *Chesh.* See Ray's English Words, 1674, p. 17.

SKEER-DEVIL. The swift. *Somerset.*

SKEERINGS. Hay made from the bad parts of pasture land. *West.*

SKEG. (1) The stump of a branch; also, a rent in a piece of cloth, such as would be made by a skeg. *Heref.* In the following passage it means a peg of wood.

Which as the owner (for h s use) did weare,
A nayle or *sceg* by chance his breech did teare.
Taylor's Workes, 1630, ii. 119.

(2) A wild plum. *Northampt.* " A sloe, a *skeg*,
a bulleis," Florio, p. 515.

SKEGGER. A salmon.

SKEKE. A contest.
And with *skekes* and with fight,
The wayes loked wele aplight.
Arthour and Merlin, p. 167.

With I. and E. fulle sekire thou be,
That thyne executurs
Of the ne wille rekke, but skikk and *skekke*
Fulle baldely in thi boures.
MS. Lincoln A. i. 17, f. 213.

SKEKIE. Shy; frightened. *Northumb.*

SKELDER. To swindle. "If *skeldring* fall not
to decay, thou shalt flourish," Hawkins,
Origin of the English Drama, iii. 119.

SKELINGTON. A skeleton. *West.*

SKELK. To shrink. Said of wood.

SKELL. A shell. *North.*

SKELL-BOOSE. Explained by Carr, the head
of the stalls of cattle.

SKELLED. Anything twisted or warped out
of a flat or straight form into that of a curve,
skell, or shell. *North.*

SKELLERED. Warped; made crooked. *Skel-*
ler-brained, disordered in mind. *North.*

SKELLY. (1) Thin and light. *Linc.*

(2) To squint, to look awry. *North.*

SKELMS. Long poles made use of in harvest
time to carry cocks of hay on by hand, where
the distance is small and draught horses
scarce. *Glouc.*

SKELP. (1) A blow. *North.* "In payn of a
skelp," Towneley Mysteries, p. 95.

(2) To kick severely. *East.*

(3) To leap awkwardly. *Chesh.*

(4) To move rapidly. To skip or run with great
strides, or in a bounding manner. *North.*

SKELPER. Anything very large. Grose has
skelping, full, bursting, very large.

SKELT. Rumour; report. *North.*

SKELTER. *Order* as to arrangement, or *condi-*
tion as to body. *North.*

SKELTON. A skeleton. *West.* "A skelton
or a notamie," Cotgrave in v. *Eschelette.*

SKELVE. To incline; spoken of a pot or pan
that has slipped from its upright position;
thus they say, " It's all *skelved* to aside and
run over." *Linc.*

SKEMMEL. A long form or stool. *North.* It
is, of course, from the A.-S.

SKEN. To squint. *North.*

SKENSMADAM. A mock dish set upon the
table for show. *Cumb.*

SKENT. To have the diarrhœa, said only of animals. *Somerset.* Hence, perhaps, *skenter*, an
animal which will not fatten.

SKEP. A basket made of rushes or straw. A
beehive is called a bee-skep. *Var. dial.*

Sumwhat lene us bi thi *skep;*
I shal you lene, seide Josep.
Cursor Mundi, MS. Coll. Trin. Cantab. f. 30.

SKEPE. A fishing vessel. *North.*

SKER. To slide; to skate. *North.*

SKERE. (1) Clear; free. Also a verb, to escape
from, to get clear of.
And thou mightest bring me her on,
The and thine sones y schal lete gon
Fram prisoun quite and *skere.*
Gy of Warwike, p. 300.

The niytingale is on bi nome,
That wol shilden hem from shome,
Of skathe hoe wele hem *skere :*
The thresteicok hem kepeth ay,
He seith bi niyte and eke bi day
That hy beth fendes i-fere.
Reliq. Antiq. i. 241.

(2) To drive or scare away.

SKERLET. Scarlet.
In *skerlet* kyrtells over one,
The cokwoldes stodyn everychon,
Redy unto the dansyng.
MS. Ashmole 61, f. 61.

SKERRE. See *Scar* (4).

SKERRY. Slaty, as coals. *Derb.*

SKESE. To run or frisk about. *Cornw.*

SKET. (1) Part; region. (*A.-S.*)

(2) Soon; quickly; immediately.
Themperur askede him what a bet ;
Gerard, a sede, alse *sket.*
Beves of Hamtoun, p. 108.

In wiche parlement he hete
Men schuld him bring the children *skete.*
Arthour and Merlin, p. 12.

SKETCH. A latch. *North.*

SKEUL. To look askant. *Kent.*

SKEW. (1) Aslope. *Suffolk.* Also, to cast on
one side. " Skew your eie towards the margent," Stanihurst, p. 17.

(2) A cup. A cant term. Dekker's Lanthorne
and Candle-Light, 1620, sig. C. iii.

(3) The sky. MS. Cott. Vesp. D. vii.

(4) Thick drizzling rain, which lasts only for a
short time. *Cornw.*

(5) " To skue or chamfret, viz. to slope the edge
of a stone, as masons doe in windowes, &c.,
for the gaining of light," Cotgrave.

(6) The tail of a bird.

(7) A kind of rude-fashioned boat, mentioned in
Harrison's Britaine, pp. 5, 43.

(8) To shy, as a horse. *Var. dial.*

(9) To throw violently. *North.*

(10) To skewer. *Somerset.*

(11) A piebald horse. *Chesh.* Applied to a
kitten in Skelton's Works, i. 99.

(12) A projection. *Yorksh.* Also a verb, to toss
or throw up.

SKEW-BALD. Piebald. *Var. dial.*
The *skewed* horses, by myne intente,
The which into the south parte wente,
I maye well licken veramente
To Jewes and panymes eke.
Chester Plays, ii. 142.

SKEW-BOGLISH. Said, but not very commonly, of a shying horse. *Linc.*

SKEWE. To fall away; to escape.
The welkyn wanned anone and the watur *skeweth.*
MS. Cott. Culig. A. ii. f. 109.

SKEW-THE-DEW. A splayfooted person.

SKEWTING. Sloping. *East.*

SKEW-WHIFT. Aslant; slanting. *West.*

SKEWY. Askew. *Somerset.*

SKEYL. To lean to one side; to overturn a cart. *North.*

SKEYL-BEAST. The partition of cattle-stalls.

SKEYLD. Particoloured. *Yorksh.*

SKEYSE. To run away. *Cornw.*

SKIBBS. Squibs. This appears to be the meaning of the term in Brit. Bibl. i. 541.

SKICE. To play and frolic about; to run quickly and slily. *South.*

SKICER. A lamb which runs itself to death from excess of energy. *West.*

SKID. (1) To affix a hook to the wheel of a waggon to prevent it descending too rapidly down a hill. *Var. dial.* Ray says, " rotam sufflaminare, with an iron hook fastned to the axis to keep it from turning round upon the descent of a steep hill."

(2) A timber-cart; a sledge.

SKIDDBY-COCK. A water-rail. *West.*

SKIDER. A skate. *Northumb.*

SKID-PAN. The shoe with which the wheel of a carriage is locked. *Var. dial.*

SKIE. (1) A cloud. *(A.-S.)*

(2) *If the sky falls we shall catch larks*, a reply to any one who broaches a wild or improbable hypothesis.

SKIEL. A beer-cooler. *Wilts.*

SKIERETH. Escapeth. In the first of these passages, the MS. in the library of the Society of Antiquaries reads *skeereth*, f. 64.

> And thus ful oft hirself sche *skiereth*,
> And is al war of had-I-wist.
>   *Gower, MS. Bodl. 294.*
> That he the wordis lasse or more
> Of his enchauntement ne hereth,
> And in this wise himselfe he *skiereth*.
>   *Gower, MS. Soc. Antiq. 134, f. 41.*

SKIFF. (1) Distorted; awkward. *West.*

(2) To remove one's residence. *North.*

SKIFF-DISH. An instrument used for forcing down the brims of a hat.

SKIFFER. A low shallow tub. *Linc.*

SKIFF-HANDED. Inexpert in using the hands —unable to cast anything in a straight direction. *North.*

SKIFT. To shift, or remove. *North.*

SKIFTE. To appoint; to ordain. *(A.-S.)* Also, occasionally, a substantive.

> And therfore grete Godd wolde so wisely *skifte*
> alle thynges, that whenne a mane fulle of fellcitee,
> thurghe his heghe pride, wille no ţte knawe his
> makere fra the heghte of pride into the pitte of
> mekenes and lawnes he mone be plungede.
>   *MS. Lincoln A. i. 17, f. 21.*

SKILE. (1) To separate; to divide. The people are said to be *skiling* out of town when the assizes are over. *Dunelm.*

(2) An iron slice used for skimming the grease off broth. *North.*

SKILL. (1) Reason. *(A.-S.)*

> And if that thou me tellest *skil*,
> I shal don after thi will.   *MS. Digby 86.*
> When the prince hade hym beholde,
> He ţede and sate hym where he wolde,
> As *skille* and reson is.
>   *MS. Cantab. Ff. v. 48, f. 55.*

> Sche seyde, Lordynges, so God me save,
> He that me wan he schalle me have !
> Ye wot wele yowre crye was so !
> The lordys assentyd wele ther tylle,
> For sche seyde nothyng but *skylle*,
> And that sche wolde no moo.
>   *MS. Cantab. Ff. ii. 38, f. 77.*

(2) To know; to understand. Still in use in the North of England.

(3) To hull oats. *Devon.*

(4) To signify; to make a difference. " It skills not," Shakespeare.

SKILLET. A small pot of iron or copper or brass, with a long handle.

SKILLUN. An outhouse; a kind of pantry; a penthouse; a shed. *South.*

SKILLY. Water in which meat has been boiled, thickened with oatmeal. A word, I believe, of modern growth. *Linc.*

SKILTY-BOOTS. Half-boots. *Dorset.*

SKILVINGS. A wooden frame to fix on the top of a cart in order to widen and extend its size; the rails of a cart.

SKIM. (1) To mow. *Var. dial.*

(2) To make anything to fly swiftly but smoothly. *Var. dial.*

SKIMBLE-SKAMBLE. Rambling; unconnected. This phrase occurs in 1 Henry IV. iii. 1

> I meet one, thinking for my due to speake,
> He with evasions doth my purpose breake,
> And asks what newes I heare from France or Spain,
> Or where I was in the last showre of raine :
> Or when the court remooves, or what's a clocke,
> Or where's the wind, or some such windy mocke;
> With such fine *scimble-scemble*, spitter-spattar,
> As puts me cleane besides the money matter.
>   *Taylor's Workes, 1630, ii. 39.*

SKIME. (1) To look at a person in an underneath way, the head being held down. *Linc.*

(2) A ray of light. *Yorksh.*

SKIMISH. Squeamish. *Devon.*

SKIMMER. To frisk about. *East.*

SKIMMERING. Shining; an extreme degree of cleanliness. *Durham.*

SKIMMINGTON. " To ride," or " riding Skimmington," is, according to Grose, a ludicrous cavalcade in ridicule of a man beaten by his wife : it consists of a man riding behind a woman with his face to the horse's tail, holding a distaff in his hand, at which he seems to work, the woman all the while beating him with a ladle. A smock displayed on a staff is carried before them, as an emblematical standard, denoting female superiority : they are accompanied by what is called rough music, that is, frying-pans, bull's-horns, marrowbones and cleavers, &c.—a procession admirably described by Butler in his " Hudibras." According to Jennings, the custom is still in vogue in Somerset.

SKIMPING. Scanty, said of dress when cut too short or narrow for the person. *South.*

SKIMPS. The scales and refuse of flax detached in dressing it. *Somerset.*

SKINCH. To give scant measure : to nip and squeeze and pinch and pare, so as to effect a saving. *Linc.*

SKINCHING. Narrow-minded. *Linc.*

SKIN-COAT. To curry one's skin-coat, i. e. to beat him very severely.

SKIN-FLINT. A miser. *Var. dial.*

SKINGY. (1) Stingy. *Linc.*

(2) Cold, nipping, as applied to the weather. *Suffolk.*

SKINK. (1) In a family the person latest at breakfast is called the *skink*, or the *skinker*, and some domestic office is imposed or threatened for the day, such as ringing the bell, putting coal on the fire; or, in other cases, drawing the beer for the family.

(2) To fill the glass; to drink; to serve or pour out liquor. *North.* The term occurs in our old dramatists. "Shed, skinked, poured forth," Florio, p. 518, ed. 1611.

> Untill hee falls asleepe he *skinks* and drinkes,
> And then like to a bore he winkes and stinkes.
> *Taylor's Workes*, 1630, lii. 5.

(3) To spy, or peer about. *East.*

SKINKER. A tapster; a drawer. *Aquarius* is called a *skinker* in Du Bartas, p. 33.

> But no fear affrights deep drinkers,
> There I toss'd it with my *skinkers.*
> *Barnaby's Journal.*

SKINLET. Thin skin. Florio, p. 135.

SKINNER. A dealer in skins. "*Pellipius,* skynner," Nominale MS. xv. Cent.

SKINNY. (1) Lean. (2) Miserly. *South.*

SKIP. (1) The same as *Skep*, q. v.

(2) A small wooden or metal utensil used for taking up yeast. *Sussex.*

SKIP-BOY. A ship-boy; a boy who is attendant on the captain of a ship.

SKIP-JACK. (1) The merrythought of a fowl, made into a little toy by a twisted thread and small piece of stick.

(2) A dandy puppyish fellow. "A dwarfe, dandiprat, little skip-jacke," Cotgrave in v. *Nimbot.*

SKIP-KENNEL. A footboy.

SKIPPER. (1) A barn. A cant term. Dekker's Lanthorne and Candle-Light, 1620, sig. C. iii. Grose has the term.

(2) The master of a ship.

> Watt doth retourne the *skippers* tale,
> And hearb-wives courtesie,
> To him that left his sisters mayde
> About the countrie.
> *MS. Poems in Dr. Bliss's possession*, temp. James I.

SKIPPET. A small round wooden vessel with a long handle, used for lading water into troughs, &c., called in Leicestershire a ladegaun. *Linc.*

SKIR. To graze, skim, or touch lightly; to jerk. *Somerset.*

SKIRE. Loose; open; thin. *Lanc.*

SKIRGALIARD. A wild, gay, dissipated fellow? See Skelton's Works, ii. 218.

SKIRL. (1) To shrivel up. *East.*

(2) To scream; to shriek. *North.*

(3) To slide. *Yorksh.*

SKIRME. To fence; to skirmish. It occurs in Wright's Seven Sages, p. 91.

SKIRR. To scour the country. *Shak.*

SKIRRET. The water-parsnip. The following is a receipt to make *skirret-pie :*

> Take a quarter of a peck of skirrets blanched and sliced, season them with three nutmegs and an ounce of cinnamon, and three ounces of sugar, and ten quartered dates, and the marrow of three bones rouled in yolks of eggs, and one quarter of a pound of ringo roots, and preserved lettuce, sliced lemon, four blades of mace, three or four branches of preserved barberries, and half a pound of butter ; then let it stand one hour in the oven : then put a caudle made of white wine, verjuice, butter and sugar ; put it into the pie when it comes out of the oven.
> *A True Gentlewoman's Delight*, 1676, p. 124.

SCIRROCK. A scrap; a fragment; anything of very small value. *North.*

SKIRT. To throw water with a syringe : to squirt. *Somerset.*

SKIRTER. A syringe, or squirt.

SKIRTING. (1) The diaphragm of cattle. A term used by butchers. *Somerset.*

(2) A sort of half-ploughing, preparatory to beat-burning. *Devon.*

SKIRTS. To sit upon any one's skirts, i. e. to meditate revenge upon him. This phrase occurs in several old plays, but I do not recollect to have seen it anywhere explained. Tarlton, the celebrated clown, told his audience the reason why he had cut off the skirts of his mantle was that no one should be able to sit upon them. Cf. Stanihurst, p. 26.

> Crosse me not, Liza, nether be so perte,
> For if thou dost *I'll sit upon thy skirte.*
> *The Abortive of an Idle Howre*, 1620.

SKISE. To run fast. *I. Wight.*

SKISTE. To order; to arrange.

> Scathylle Scottlande by skylle he *skystys* as hym lykys,
> And Wales of were he wane at hys wille.
> *Morte Arthure, MS. Lincoln*, f. 53

SKIT. (1) To slide. *Somerset.*

(2) A scud of rain. *Devon.*

(3) The diarrhœa in animals. *Linc.* The term occurs in the Pr. Parv.

(4) A satirical reflection. *Var. dial.*

(5) Hasty; precipitate.

SKITE. Merdis aspergere. *Var. dial.* Perhaps more commonly *skitter.*

SKITLY. Small; diminutive. *West.*

SKITTER. A countryman who was leading me up a steep hill, when we came to a place which was inaccessible, said, "We had better *skitter* under here, and it won't be so steep." *Kent.*

SKITTER-BOOTS. Half boots, laced in front. Called also skittervamps. *I. of Wight.*

SKITTER-BRAINED. Giddy; thoughtless. *North.*

SKITTERING. Slight; flimsy. *Devon.*

SKITTER-WIT. A foolish, giddy, harebrained fellow. *Chesh.*

SKITTLE. To cut; to hack. *West.*

SKITTY. A moor-hen. *Somerset.*

SKIVE. (1) To pare the thicker parts of hides previously to tanning them.

(2) To turn up the eyes. *Linc.*

SKIVER. A skewer. *Skiver-wood*, dogwood, of which skewers are made. *West.*

SKIWINKIN. Awry; crooked. *East.*

SKIZZLE. A marble taw. *East.*

SKLEIRE. An iron for curling hair.

SKLEM. To steal slyly. *Heref.*

SKLISTE. A flat instrument with an upright handle, generally made of tin.

> Sprede a lyn clowte on a bord, and this plaster theron, and mak it thynne with a *skliste*, and do it on the hevede alle hate.
> *MS. Med. Rec. Lincoln.* f. 281.

SKOGGER. The leg of an old stocking, used as a kind of gaiter in snow-time. *North.*

SKOLYON. A scullion. *Palsgrave.*

SKOMFET. Discomfited. See *Scomfete.*

> If thou salle goo to batelle, saye this orysone devotely and enterely one the croys of thi swerde, and girde the therwith, and bere this orysone with the appone the, and thou salle noghte be slayne nor *skomfet.*   *MS. Lincoln A. i. 17, f. 176.*

SKOOL. The cry along the coast when the herrings appear first for the season.

SKOPPOLOIT. Play, romps, frolicking. "What ha made yeow sa long?" "Why I ha bin havin a game a *skoppoloit* along i th' man Jenkins i th' chatch yahd." This word is much used in Ipswich, and is also pronounced *skoppolot.* Whence can it have come? A schoolmistress chid a child for *skoppoloitin:* but she did not mean playing truant, or traaant, as we call it. *Scope*, to loiter, has been surmised as a possible source. *East.*

SKORCLE. To scorch. *Skorke* occurs in an early vocabulary in my possession, and also in Archæologia, xxx. 413.

SKORPHILLYS. Scrofulous.

SKOTE. A prop. *I. Wight.*

SKOTTEFERS. Shooters; archers. *(A.-S.)*

> Discoveris of schotte-mene and skyrmys a lyttille,
> Skayres thaire *skottefers*, and theire skowtte waches.
> *Morte Arthure, MS. Lincoln,* f. 79.

SKOULKERY. Skulking; lurking.

> Loke ȝe skyste it so, that us no skathe lympe,
> For na skomfitoure in *skoulkery* is skomfite ever.
> *Morte Arthure, MS. Lincoln,* f. 70.

SKOUT. The auk is so called in Northumberland. See Pennant's Tour in Scotland, ed. 1790, i. 48.

SKOVE. A sheaf of corn. *West.*

SKOWER. To be shackled.

SKOWK. To skulk. *Cotgrave.*

SKOWREGHIDE. Scourged.

> Eftirwarde thou was *skowreghide* sare.
> *MS. Lincoln A. i. 17,* f. 190.

SKOWTE.

> With me ye xall ron in rowte,
> My consell to take for a *skowte.*
> *Digby Mysteries,* p. 79.

SKOYLES. A game played with pins, alluded to in Kind Hart's Dreame, 1592.

SKOYMOSE. Squeamish.

> Thow art not *skoymose* thy fantasy for to tell.
> *Bale's Kynge Johan,* p. 11.

SKRAUM. To grope about. *Yorksh.*

SKRED. To stride. *Somerset.*

SKREEK. To creak. *North.*

> The solle of the parke was so exceeding barren

that it did beare a gray mosse, like that of an old parke pale, which *skreekes* as one walkes on it, ard putts ones teeth on edge. *Aubrey's MS. Wilts,* p. 71.

SKREENGED. Squeezed. *North.*

SKRENT. To burn; to scorch. *West.*

SKRILE. Small underwood. *South.*

SKRITHE. A shriek; a scream.

> Whenne that it was abowte mydnyghte,
> Byȝonde the water he herde a *skrythe,*
> Fulle lowde one heghte he herde it cry,
> And askede helpe over fulle rewfully.
> *MS. Lincoln A. i. 17,* f. 125

SKRUSSLE. The cracklin of pork. *East.*

SKRY. A coarse sieve for corn.

SKRYTCHE-HEULE. A screech-owl. Palsgrave, without the French synonyme.

SKUE. Same as *Skew*, q. v.

SKUFF. A precipice. *North.*

SKUT. To crouch down. *Kent.*

SKUTCHINEAL. Cochineal. *North.*

SKUTY. Smart; clean; brisk. *East.*

SKWYNECY. The quinsey.

> Som for gletony sall have emang
> The *skwynecy*, that evil swa strang.
> *John de Wageby,* p. 11

SKY. (1) To look, or peep. *Suffolk.*

(2) To shy, as horses do.

SKYBY. Shy; reluctant; averse. *Yorksh.*

SLA. To slay, or kill.

> Any conynges here to *sla,*
> And with the trespas away to ga.
> *MS. Cantab. Ff. v. 48,* f. 49.

SLAB. (1) The wryneck. *North.*

(2) A bricklayer's boy. *East.*

(3) Foot pavement. *Linc.*

(4) Slabby; adhesive. *Shak.*

(5) The outer cut of a tree when sawn up into planks. *Var. dial.*

(6) A puddle; a wet place. *North.* Perhaps, in the following passage, it may mean a slab of foot pavement.

> The Grounde of Artes who hathe well tredd,
> And noted well the slyppery *slabbes.*
> *Record's Castle of Knowledge,* 1556.

(7) In Cornwall, when the melted tin is cast into oblong square pieces in a mould made of moor-stone, the lesser pieces they call *slabs,* and the greater *blocks.* Kennett, MS.

SLABBARD. "Slabbarde, *morosus, tardus,*" Prompt. Parv. MS. Harl. 221, f. 156.

SLABBER. (1) To soil, or dirty. *West.*

> Till neere unto the haven where Sandwitch stands,
> We were enclosed with most dangerous sands.
> There were we sows'd with *slabberd,* wash'd and dash'd,
> And gravell'd, that it made us halfe abash'd.
> *Taylor's Discovery by Sea,* p. 22.

(2) To eat up greedily.

SLABBY. Sloppy; dirty.

> This threatning is to travellers that go
> Long journeys; *slabby* rain they'l have, or snow.
> *A Book for Boys and Girls,* 1686, p 13.

SLACHE. To loiter. *Yorksh.*

SLACK. (1) The low ground. *North.*

> They took the gallows from the *slack,*
> They set it in the glen,
> They hang'd the proud sheriff on that,
> Releas'd their own three men.
> *Robin Hood,* ii. 155.

(2) Coal reduced to very small pieces. The side of a mountain where the rock has crumbled and fallen down in an oblique direction is called a *slack*.

(3) Mingere. *Worc.*

(4) To cool in water. *North.*

(5) Underdone ; *slack*-baked, spoken of bread ; *slack* done, meat underdone. *Kent.* Slack-oven, an oven which bakes slowly.

(6) To put off; to procrastinate.

(7) A long pool in a streamy river.

(8) Dull ; low ; depressed ; lazy. *Slack-deed*, depression of trade. *Var. dial.*

SLACKE. Slow. (*A.-S.*)

SLACKEN. To fall in price. *Slacking*, want or deficiency of anything.

SLACKET. Slight ; slim. *Cornw.*

SLACK-TRACE. An untidy woman. *Linc.* In some places, *slackumtrans*.

SLACK-WATER. A deficiency of water, by which the machinery of mills erected on streams is deprived of its proper action.

SLADDERY. Wet and dirty. *North.*

SLADE. (1) A valley ; a ravine ; a plain. Brockett says its present meaning is " a breadth of green sward in ploughed land, or in plantations." I have heard the term in Northamptonshire applied to a flat piece of grass, and to a border of grass round a ploughed field. The first meaning (a valley) is given in the Herefordshire Gloss. p. 94 ; but Moor describes it " a small open hanging wood." See Morte d'Arthur, i. 161, 176, 192 ; British Bibl. i. 154 ; Gy of Warwike, p. 120.

> Sexty slongene in a *slade* of sleghe mene of armes.
>> *Morte Arthure, MS. Lincoln, f. 84.*

> It had bene better of William a Trent
> To have bene abed with sorrowe,
> Than to be that day in the greenwood *slade*,
> To meet with Little Johns arrowe
>> *Robin Hood, i. 118.*

> Whenne we were put fro Paradise
> Into this ilke wrecched *slade*.
>> *Cursor Mundi, MS. Coll. Trin. Cantab. f. 8.*

> And how he climbeth up the bankis,
> And falleth into *sladis* depe.
>> *Gower, MS. Soc. Antiq. 134, f. 121.*

> But when he came to Barnesdale,
> Great heaviness there hee hadd,
> For he found tow of his owne fellowès
> Were slaine both in a *slade*.
>> *Robin Hood and Guy of Gisborne.*

(2) A sled, or sledge. Also, to carry on a sledge ; to drag on the ground.

SLADE-DOWN. To draw back part of the mould into the interfurrow, with the plough dragging, or *slading* upon its side. *Norf.*

SLADERING-DRAG. A small drag, or carriage, or sledge, without wheels, and sliding on the ground, drawn by one horse. *Chesh.*

SLAG. (1) Refuse of lead, or other ores. It is sometimes applied to coal. *Slag-pigs*, small flat pigs of lead of an inferior quality. " At the silver mills in Cardiganshire the cinders or refuse of the litharge, which remain after the first boiling of the mine, are call'd *slags*, which are beat small with great stamps lifted up by a wheel moved by water; so the dross of tin in Cornwall is called the *slag ;* so likewise the slag or refuse of melted iron," Kennett, MS.

(2) The black slat, which lies commonly above the coal in sinking their pits in Flintshire, is called the *slag*. Ibid. MS.

(3) Miry and slippery. *Pr. Parv.*

SLAGER. To slacken. *West.*

SLAGHT. Hung up ; put away ?

> When we come and sitten in same,
> I shalle tech the a game,
> I can hit wel be rote ;
> Then shal thou se my slyng *slaght*,
> And of the best take us a draght,
> And drynk welle right be note.
>> *MS. Cantab. Ff. v. 48, f. 49.*

SLAGS. Sloes. *Westm.*

SLAIF. A shallow dish. *North.*

SLAIGH. The sloe. *Lanc.*

SLAIN. Smut in corn. *Cumb.*

SLAINT. To bring forth young, applied to cows and mares. *Kent.*

SLAIR. To walk slovenly. *North.*

SLAIRG. Mud. *Northumb.*

SLAISTER. (1) To beat severely. *North.*

(2) To do anything awkwardly. *Yorksh.*

SLAIT. (1) An accustomed run for sheep ; hence the place to which a person is accustomed is called slait. *West.*

(2) To slake quicklime. *Devon.*

SLAKE. (1) A deep ditch ; a ravine.

> He laf slawe in a *slak*
> fforty score on a pak,
> Wyd opene one here bake. *Sir Degrevant, MS.*

(2) To quench ; to subside. *North.*

> Whenne that here paynys *slakyd* was,
> And sche hadde passyd that hydous pas,
> Here nose barst on bloode ;
> Sche was unblemeschyd ffoot and hand,
> That sawȝ the lordys off the lande,
> And thankyd God on rode.
>> *Romance of Athelston.*

(3) To lick, e. g. plates or dishes badly washed and not well dried are said to be *slaked* over. It is also vulgarly used, I believe, in the sense of to kiss. *Linc.*

(4) To put out the tongue. *Lanc.*

(5) To fail ; to desist. (*A.-S.*)

(6) Leisure ; opportunity. *Norf.*

(7) An accumulation of mud or slime, particularly in a river. *Cumb.*

(8) A gentle light stroke. *North.*

(9) To smear ; to bedaub. *Yorksh.*

(10) Very small coals. *North.*

(11) To go silently. *Weber.*

(12) To untie ; to loosen. (*A.-S.*)

(13) Soft, as mud, dirt, &c. *Dunelm.*

SLALE. Violent ; inflamed. *North.*

SLAM. (1) To beat. *North.*

(2) A kind of game. It is also a term at whist, used when one party wins a game before the other has gained a trick.

> At post and paire, or *slam*, Tom Tuck would play
> This Christmas, but his want wherewith sayes nay.
>> *Herrick's Works, ii. 56*

(3) The side ; to go up the *slam* of the hill is to go up obliquely. *Dorset.*

(4) To throw fast, violently, as a door ; to fling down. *Var. dial.*

(5) A kind of muscle. *South.*

(6) Tall and lean. *North.*

SLAM-BANG. With great violence. *West.*

SLAMKIN. A female sloven. Perhaps *slammacks* or *slammerkin* is in more general use. Hence *slammack*, to walk slovenly, to do anything awkwardly.

SLAMMING. Large ; big. *West.*

SLAMPAMBES. To cut a person of the slampambes, or to give him the slampambes, i. e. to beat him by stratagem, to circumvent or conquer any one. It occurs in an old play quoted by Nares, who was unable to explain the phrase.

> The townesmen being pinched at the heart that one rascall in such scornefull wise should give them the *slampams*, not so much weieng the slendernesse of the losse as the shamefulnesse of the foile.
> *Stanihurst's Description of Ireland*, p. 25.

SLAMTRASH. A great sloven. *Yorksh.*

SLANE. Sloes. *Devon.*

SLANG. (1) Apparently some kind of ordnance, mentioned in Arch. xi. 439.

(2) A long narrow piece of land, sometimes called *slanket*. *West.*

SLANGAM. An awkward lout. " A tall and dull *slangam*, that hath no making to his height, nor wit to his making ; also, one that being sent on an errand is long in returning," Cotgrave, in v. *Longis.*

SLANK. (1) Slim ; slender. *North.*

(2) A slope, or declivity. *Kent.*

SLANS. Sloes. *West.*

SLANT. To exaggerate. *North.* " To mock, or lie, or dissemble," Kennett MS.

SLANT-VEIN. One vein of ore crossing another at an acute angle. *North.*

SLANY. A slattern. *West.*

SLAP. (1) Suddenly. *North.*

(2) To spill liquor. All of a slap, i. e. very sloppy. *Yorksh.*

(3) *To slap up*, to eat quickly, to lick up food. Still in use.

(4) The same as *Slab* (5).

(5) To loll out the tongue. *North.*

(6) A gap. *Somerset.*

SLAP-BANG. Violently ; headlong. *Slap-dash* is also used in the same sense.

SLAP-DASH. A cheap mode of colouring rooms by *dashing* them with a brush in imitation of paper. *North.* In masonry, rough-cast.

SLAPE. (1) Soft ; slippery ; smooth. Hence, metaphorically, crafty. *North.* Slape hawing by haw binks, i. e. slippery holding by a hall bench. Kennett, MS. Lansd. 1033.

(2) Sleep. Sevyn Sages, 929.

SLAPE-ALE. Plain ale as opposed to ale medicated with wormwood or scurvy grass, or mixed with any other liquor. Skinner says this is a Lincolnshire word.

SLAPE-FACE. A soft-spoken, mealy-mouthed hypocrite. *Linc.*

SLAPEL. A large lump. *Sussex.*

II.

SLAPER. The stump of a tree. *Norf.*

SLAPING. Walking about a house with dirty shoes and wet dripping clothes. *Oxon.*

SLAPPING. Very large. *Var. dial.*

SLAPPY. Not baked enough. *Suffolk.*

SLAP-SAUCE. A parasite. *Minsheu.*

SLAP-SHOES. Shoes with loose soles.

SLARE. (1) A hint ; an indirect reproach. *Linc.*

(2) To smear, to mark with dirt here and there; thus when a floor has been imperfectly washed it will be said, " They've *slared* it sadly."

SLART. (1) To splash with dirt. *Yorksh.* In Herefordshire, to stain.

(2) Used as a substantive, to mean a quantity ; thus one market woman will say to another, " You've got a pretty good *slart* of butter this welk." Used as a verb, to signify to taunt by insinuations, e. g. " If you've anything to say, out with it, and don't *slart* in that way." *Linc.*

SLARY. Bedaubed. *East.*

SLASH. (1) A cut, or gash. *Yorksh.*

(2) The same as *Pleach*, q. v.

SLASHING. Gay ; wild. *Var. dial.*

SLASHY. Wet and dirty. *North.*

SLAT. (1) To strike ; to slap ; to throw or cast down violently or carelessly. *Var. dial.* " Slatted his brains out," Webster, iv. 99. A slat in the face, i. e. a reproach.

(2) To split, or crack. *West.*

(3) A spot, or stain. *Yorksh.*

(4) An iron heater used for smoothing linen after washing. *Somerset.*

(5) To set on ; to incite. *North.*

(6) A share. *Bailey.*

(7) A slate. *North.* " Sklat or slat stone," Prompt. Parv. MS. Harl. 221.

SLAT-AXE. A mattock with a short axe end. *Devon.*

SLATCHIN. Untidy. *Cumb.*

SLATE. (1) A valley ?

> Certayn, tho said the knyght,
> That theffe I saw to nyght
> Here beside a *slate*.
> *Torrent of Portugal*, p. 70.

(2) To ridicule. *Var. dial.* This is probably derived from our fifth meaning.

(3) A sheet. An old cant term, occurring in Dekker's Belman of London, 1608.

(4) A woman is said to be slated, when her petticoat falls below her gown.

(5) To bait animals. " Bay of hor, of bole slatyng," Kyng Alisaunder, 200. " To slate a beast is to hound a dog at him," Yorkshire Ale, p. 115, ed. 1697.

(6) To be angry, or wroth.

> The apostille says that God thalm hatys,
> And over alle other with thaim *slatys*.
> *R. de Brunne, MS. Bowes*, p. 55.

(7) A pod or husk, of peas, &c. *Hants.*

SLATHER. To slip, or slide. *Chesh.*

SLATS. (1) Cross pieces used in the hurdles of the Midland counties.

(2) Dark blue ooze, rather hard, left dry by the ebb of the sea. *Suff.*

SLATTER. To waste ; or rather, perhaps, not to make a proper and due use of anythir

48

thus they say, " take care, or you'll *slatter* it all away ;" and when the weather is unsettled, so that the work of the farm is interrupted, the farmer will say to his men, " I fear we shall have a *slattering* time of it." Also, to be negligent and slovenly.

SLATTER-DE-POUCH.   An ancient dance, mentioned in an old play in MS. Bodl. 30. Gayton alludes to it as a boy's exercise.

SLATTERINS.   Relics.   *Lanc.*

SLATTERY.   Wet ; dirty.   *Var. dial.*

SLATY.   Miry, or muddy.

SLAUGHMESSES.   A kind of sword ?

> Beside these, we have the fierce Brabanders and strong Almaines wyth long pykes and cuttyng *slaughmesses.*   *Hall, Henry V.* f. 15.

SLAUGHTER.   A great alteration involving some destruction, e. g. applied to the thorough repair and renovation of an old mansion. *Essex.*

SLAUM.   To smear.   *Leic.*

SLAUSE.   To strain liquor.   " *Colo*, to sclause ale," MS. Gloss. xv. Cent.

SLAVEINE.   A pilgrim's mantle.   (*A.-N.*) " *Sarabarda*, Anglice a sclavene," Nominale MS. in my possession.

> He covyrde hys face wyth hys *slaveyne,*
> That Tyrrye schulde not knowe hys peyne.
>   *MS. Cantab.* Ff. ii. 38, f. 205.

> Many wente Clement agayne,
> A *sklavyn* was hys wede.
>   *MS. Cantab.* Ff. ii. 38, f. 86.

SLAVERING-CLOTH. A slobbering-bib. " Slaveryng clothe for chyldren," Palsgrave.

SLAVVEN.   A large piece.   *Sussex.*

SLAWE.   Slain.   (*A.-S.*)

> I wolde not that, sayd Robyn,
> Johan, that thou were *slawe,*
> For all the golde in mery Englond,
> Though it lay now on a rawe.
>   *Robin Hood,* i. 54.

SLAWTH.   Sloth.   *Prompt. Parv.*

SLAWTYR.   Slaughter.   *Prompt. Parv.*

SLAY. (1) Anything that moves on a pivot, as the part of the loom that is pulled by the hand among the threads.   *North.*

(2) In cutting slop, the wood is laid in regular rows, all one way, for the convenience of tying up ; these are called *slays.*

(3) As willingly.   " I would *slay* do it as not." *Somerset.*

(4) Coarse wool.   *Devon.*   Perhaps from *slay,* that part of a loom with which the work is closed.   " The slay of a weavers loome having teeth like a combe," Nomenclator, p. 253.

(5) A lane or way cut through a whin, or broom, or other cover, for the purpose of admitting a vehicle to receive and convey away the faggots or cuttings ; or for admitting a range of haynets to catch rabbits, hunted from side to side of the cover by dogs ; or for gunners to place themselves in, to shoot or *slay* them as they dart across.   *Moor.*

SLAY-WATTLE.   A kind of hurdle, made with narrow boards.   *Kent.*

SLAZY.   Of flimsy texture.   *East.*

SLE.   To kill; to slay.   (*A.-S.*)

> Gret bourde it wold be,
> Off them to *slee* twoo or thre,
> I swere the, be Seynt Gyle.
>   *MS. Cantab.* Ff. v. 48, f. 49

SLEA.   To dry or wither, spoken of corn exposed to sun or wind before it is gathered or bound.   *Chesh.*

SLEAK.   The same as *Slake*, q. v.

SLEAM.   To slumber.   *Lanc.*

SLEAVE.   To tear down.   *Heref.*

SLEAVE-SILK.   The soft floss-silk used for weaving.   " Sleave or raw silke," Florio, p. 57. See Nares, in v.

SLECK. (1) To cool.   *North.*

(2) To quench ; to assuage ; to extinguish. *North.* " Candel slekennid," Apol. Loll. p. 19.

(3) Small pit coal.   *Yorksh.*

(4) To make smooth.   *Palsgrave.*   " I slecke, I make paper smothe with a sleke stone, *je fais glissant ;* you muste slecke your paper if you wyll write Greke well," Ibid.

SLECKING.   Weak liquor.   *North.*

SLED. (1) A sledge.   *North.*   " A trucke or sled with low wheeles," Florio, p. 37. " *Traha,* a sled," Nominale MS.   " Dray or sleade whych goeth without wheles," Huloet, 1552. " Slede to drawe a thyng upon," Palsgrave.

(2) To walk awkwardly.   *Yorksh.*   Hence, an old blind person.   *Sled-hough*, one who walks badly or lamely.

(3) A sledge hammer.

SLEDE.   A valley.   *Hearne.*

SLEDGE.   To shift off.   *Dunelm.*

SLEDGER.   The lower stone in the hopper of a mill.   *Var. dial.*

SLEDIR.   Slippery.   (*A.-S.*)

> For thanne he leseth his lusty weye
> With dronkeschipe, and wot not whider
> To goo, the weyes ben so *sledir.*
>   *Gower, MS. Soc. Antiq.* 134, f. 179.

> The plank that on the brygge was,
> Was as *sledyr* as any glas.
>   *MS. Harl.* 1701, f. 35.

SLEECH. (1) To dip up water.   *North.*

(2) Mud or sea-sand used as manure. The sediment deposited by the sea in the river Rother is called sleech.   *Sussex.*   Kennett has *slitch,* " slime or mud thrown up in the cleansing of ponds or ditches," MS. Lansd. 1033.

> And I will goe gaither *slyche,*
> The shippe for to caulke and pyche.
>   *Chester Plays,* i. 47.

SLEEKED.   Smooth.   " A kind of *sleeked* pasteboord to write upon, and may bee blotted out againe," Florio, p. 86.

SLEEKER.   An iron instrument used for draining the skins that are taken from the tanpit.

SLEEP.   A limb is said to go to sleep when benumbed from being too long in one position. " My fothe ys aslepe," Nominale MS.

SLEEP-AWAY.   An idiomatic phrase signifying a gradual decay.   *Devon.*

SLEEPER. (1) A rushlight.   *East.*

(2) The stump of a tree cut off short, and left in the ground.   *Norf.*

(3) A beam of wood which supports something, as rails, &c. *Var. dial.*

(4) Grains of barley which do not vegetate when undergoing the process of malting are called *sleepers.* Salop. Antiq. p. 569.

SLEEP-WORT. Lettuce. *Gerard.*

SLEEPY. Tasteless; insipid; generally said of fruit half rotten. *Var. dial.*

SLEEPY-HEAD. An idle, sleepy person.

SLEER. One who slays. (*A.-S.*)

SLEET. (1) Cow-dung. *Yorksh.*

(2) Aslant; oblique. *Pr. Parv.*

SLEEVE. (1) A narrow channel.

(2) To split; to cleave. *North.*

SLEEVE-HAND. The cuff attached to a sleeve; the wristband of a shirt.

SLEEVELESS. Useless; unprofitable. " Syrrus, thynke not lonke, and y schall telle yow a *sleveles* reson," Reliq. Antiq. i. 83.

> If all these faile, a begger-woman may
> A sweet love letter to her hands convay;
> Or a neat laundresse or a hearbwife can
> Carry a *sleevelesse* message now and than.
> *Taylor's Workes,* 1630, ii. 111.

SLEEZY. The same as *Slazy,* q. v. " *Slesie linnen,* so calld becaus brought from the province of Silesia, or as the Germans call it *Schlesia,* wher the capital city Breslaw is maintaind by this manufacture, which is the chief if not the only merchandize of that place," Kennett, MS. Lansd. 1033.

SLEFT. Slashed. *Somerset.*

SLEIDED. Raw, untwisted, as silk.

SLEIGHLY. Cunningly. (*A.-S.*)

SLEIGHSTER. Slaughter.

> Therfor so fel ther were
> That litel was sene her *sleighster* ther.
> *Arthour and Merlin,* p. 226.

SLEIGHT. (1) Contrivance. (*A.-S.*) Still in use, signifying judgment, calculation.

(2) Smooth, as a board, &c.

SLEINT. Slipped; pushed.

SLEITH. Contrivance; cunning. Also, occasionally, stratagem, deceit. (*A.-S.*)

> What, wenest thou Him that knoweth alle
> To disseyve with thy *sleithly* wile.
> *Lydgate, MS. Soc. Antiq.* 134, f. 23.

SLEKKYN. Slacken. (*A.-S.*)

> So brennande fire that laste ay,
> That nokyn thynge it *slakkyn* may.
> *MS. Harl.* 2260, f. 71.

SLEN. To slope. *Somerset.*

SLENCH. (1) Part of a cow which lies close to the brisket. *West.*

(2) To quench one's thirst. *South.*

(3) To hunt privately, as dogs do to steal their food. *North.*

(4) To cut one side of a hedge, and leave the other untouched. *Chesh.*

SLENT. (1) To tear; to rend. *Dorset.*

(2) A deep puddle; any small pit in a common or plain. *Suffolk.*

(3) To slope; to glide. " It *slented* doune to the erthe," Morte d'Arthur, ii. 281. It is the part. pa. in Du Bartas, p. 7.

(4) A jest, or sarcasm.

SLEPE To drag. (*Flem.*)

SLEPING. A sleep, or slumber. (*A.-S.*)

SLEPIR. Slippery.

> If reches to the falle, feste noghte one thame thy herte, for thay are faylande and noghte lastande ay, and *slepir* als ane eele, that whenne mene wenys he hase hym faste, als fantome he fra hyme glyddys, and tynys hym for ay. *MS. Lincoln* A. i. 17, f. 244.

SLEPLE. To sleep gently. (*A.-S.*)

SLERRIB. A sparerib of pork. *West.*

SLETCH. To cease; to stop. *I. Wight.*

SLETE. To slete a dog, says Ray, is to set him at anything, as swine, sheep, &c. *North.*

SLETTEN. Slid; fell. *Weber.*

SLEUTH. (1) The track of any animal. Hence *sleuth-hound,* a term for the bloodhound.

> There is a law also among the borderers in time of peace, that whoso denieth entrance or sute of a *sleuthhound* in pursuit made after fellons and stolen goods, shall be holden as accessarie unto the theft, or taken for the selfe theefe.
> *Holinshed, Description of Scotland,* p. 14.
>
> The second kind is called in Scotland a *sluth-hound,* being a little greater then the hunting hound, and in colour for the most part browne, or sandy-spotted. The sence of smelling is so quicke in these that they can follow the footesteps of theevs, and pursue them with violence untill they overtake them; and if the theef take the water, they cast in themselves also, and swim to the other side, where they find out againe afresh their former labor, untill they find the thing they seeke for: for this is common in the borders of England and Scotland, where the people were wont to live much upon theft, and if the dog brought his leader unto any house, where they may not be suffred to come in, they take it for granted that there is both the stollen goods and the theef also hidden.
> *Topsell's Four-Footed Beasts,* 1607, p. 149.

(2) A herd of bears. This term occurs in the Booke of Hunting, 1586.

SLEUTHE. Sloth; idleness. (*A.-S.*)

SLEUTYNG. Shooting; letting fly. *Gawayne*

SLEVE. To cleave; to split. (*A.-S.*)

> For thaire cotis ware al to-revyne,
> And thaire lymmes in sondir *slevene.*
> *MS. Lincoln* A. i. 17, f. 190

SLEW. (1) To turn round.

(2) A kind of sieve.

(3) To get intoxicated. *Yorksh.*

SLEWER. To give way; to fall down.

SLEY. A weaver's instrument that strikes the wog close to the warp. *Kennett.*

SLE3ELY. Slily; cunningly.

> In Paradis he made him rest,
> And *slejely* slepe on him he kest.
> *Cursor Mundi, MS. Coll. Trin. Cantab.* f. 59.

SLIBBER-SLABBER. Very careless.

SLICE. (1) A fire shovel; a broad short-handled firepan for wood fires. *Dorset.* " A slice, of the shape of the ace of spades, a sort of firepan, flat and plain, without any edges turn'd up by the sides," MS. Gloss.

(2) Said of a hawk " when she mewteth a good distance from her," Gen. Rec. ii. 63.

(3) " An instrument of the kitchen to turne meate that is fried," Elyot, in v. *Spatha,* ed. 1559. It occurs in Palsgrave. The slice is still used for many purposes, particularly for taking up or turning fish in a kettle or stew-

pan. It is described in Tim Bobbin, " a thin bit of wood to stir meat in pots."

SLICH. The same as *Sleech* (2).

SLICHEN. Smooth. *Lanc.*

SLICK. (1) Smooth. *Var. dial.*

> The mole's a creature very smooth and *slick*,
> She digs i' th' dirt, but 'twill not on her stick.
> *A Book for Boys and Girls, 1686, p. 26.*

(2) Clear; entirely. *West.*

(3) To comb the hair. *Sussex.*

(4) The down of rabbits. *East.*

(5) A blow, or slap. *Oxon.*

SLICKEN. Smooth. *Derb.*

SLICKENSIDES. A species of mineral substance found in some mines, the effects of which are terrific. A blow with a hammer, a stroke or scratch with a miner's pick, are sufficient to blast asunder the massive rocks to which it is found attached.

> The mines in Eyamedge are very deep, and the New-engine mine I have heard stated as being the deepest in Derbyshire. Among the number in the edge is the Hay-cliff, a mine distinguished for having contained in great abundance of that extraordinary phenomenon in the mineral world provincially called *slickensides*. It is a species of gelena, and is well known amongst mineralogists. This mine once had it in singular quantity and quality. One writer says, " The stroke is immediately succeeded by a crackling noise, accompanied with a noise not unlike the mingled hum of a swarm of bees; shortly afterwards an explosion follows, so loud and appalling that even the miners, though a hardy race of men, and little accustomed to fear, turn pale and tremble at the shock." Of the nature of this mineral, and its terrible power, there have been a many but quite unsatisfactory solutions. Whitehurst, in his work on the formation of the earth, thus mentions its wonderful power:—" In the year 1737, an explosion took place at the Hay-cliff mine, Eyam, by the power of slickensides. Two hundred barrels of materials were blown out at one blast, each barrel containing 350 lbs. weight. During the explosion the earth shook as by an earthquake." A person of the name of Higginbotham once but narrowly escaped with life, by striking incautiously this substance in the above mine. Experienced miners can, however, work where it greatly abounds without much danger. It is also known by the name of " cracking-whole."
> *Wood's Desolation of Eyam.*

SLICKLER. An idle loiterer. *Devon.*

SLICK-STONE. " Slyckestone, *lisse a papier, lice,*" Palsgrave. Kennett mentions the slick-stone for smoothing linen cloths. *Slekystone,* Pr. Parv. MS. Harl. 221, f. 156.

SLID. A North country oath. It occurs twice in Twelfth Night, iii. 4.

SLIDDER. (1) To slide. (2) Slippery. *Sliddery* is common in the second sense. " Slyder, *glissant,*" Palsgrave. *Slidery,* MS. Arundel. 220, f. 300.

SLIDE. A sledge. *Midl. C.*

SLIDE-BUTT. A dung sledge. *Devon.*

SLIDE-GROAT. A game played with coins, the same as shove-groat. See Douce's Illust. i. 454; Brand's Pop. Antiq. ii. 259; Armin's Nest of Ninnies, 1608, ed. Collier, p. 28.

SLIDERS. Beams used for the support of shafts in mines. *North.*

SLIDING. Slippery. *Chaucer.*

SLIER. To look sly upon, but with some evil design. *Glouc.*

SLIFFE. A sleeve. *Hooper.*

SLIFT. (1) The fleshy part of the leg of beef, part of the round. *East.*

(2) A slip, or cutting. *Suffolk.*

SLIFTER. A crack, or crevice. *Lanc.* It occurs as a verb in Marston.

> The liver dryed with parsely, and three walnuts clensed from the pill and put into hony, is marvellous good for one that is liver sicke; the ashes of it mixt with oyle, taketh away wens; and the ashes of the liver, and the flesh is good against the chapping, clefts, or *slifters* in the body, which come by cold: but Dioscorides, whom I rather follow, attributeth both these vertues to the ashes of the huofe.
> *Topsell's Four-Footed Beasts, 1607, p. 96.*

SLIGHT. (1) Contrivance; artifice.

(2) A contracted form of the ancient phrase *by this light.*

(3) A trifling matter. *West.*

(4) Slighting; contemptuous.

(5) To slake lime. *Devon.*

(6) To smooth or iron linen.

(7) To throw, or cast quickly.

SLIGHTEN. To slight. *Jonson.*

SLIGHTY. Slim; weak. *East.*

SLIKE. (1) Such; such like. (*A.-S.*)

> Criste was of a maydene borne,
> And dyed for thame on *slyke* a tree,
> To brynge thame owte of my posté.
> *MS. Lincoln A. i. 17, f. 122.*

> I have herd say men suld take of twa thingcs,
> *Slik* as he fynt, or tak *slik* as he bringes;
> But specially I pray the, host ful deere,
> Get us som mete and drynk, and mak us cheere.
> *Wright's Anecdota Literaria, p. 31.*

> Whethur thy dayes, Lord, be *slyke*
> As mennes dayes that dwellen here.
> *MS. Cantab. Ff. ii. 38, f. 19.*

(2) To make sleek, or smooth. (*A.-S.*) Also an adjective, smooth, or sleek. " With bent browis both smothe and alike," Romaunt of the Rose, 542.

(3) To rend asunder; to cleave.

(4) To slide. " On the mayle slikes," Anturs of Arther, xlviii. 6.

SLIKKER. Smooth and hard. " Slykker as paper that is sleked or suche lyke, *alyse,*" Palsgrave, adject. f. 95.

SLIM. (1) Distorted, or worthless; sly. Also, a worthless fellow. *Var. dial.*

(2) To do any work in a careless or deceptive manner. *Sussex.*

(3) Slender; thin; slight. *East.* Also, a thin, tall youth.

(4) Sly; cunning; crafty. *Var. dial.*

SLIMBER. To lie at ease. *Glouc.*

SLIME. A hawk slimeth " when she mewteth without droping." Gent. Rec. ii. 63.

SLIMMY. Of slight texture. *North.* Forby has *slimslacket,* of very thin texture, loose and flaccid. East Anglia, p. 307.

SLIMSY. Idle, lazy, dawdling. *Slimsiest,* the

superlative of this word, which is in use about Woodbridge. *Moor's Suffolk MS.*

SLINCH. To sneak away. *Dunelm.*

SLING. (1) To move quickly. *Var. dial.* It has also the same meaning as *Slinch*, q. v.

(2) To cast, or throw. Also, to bring forth young prematurely. *Sussex.*

His hand sleppid and slode o-slante one the mayles,
And the tother slely *slynges* hym undire.
Morte Arthure, MS. Lincoln, f. 93.

SLINGE. (1) To sneak; to skulk about in a state of idleness. *North.*

(2) A blow. *Syr Gawayne.*

SLINGER. (1) One who steals cloth, yarn, or the like from clothiers, with a view to its being worked up or finished.

(2) A person who used a sling. *Pifundabilista,* a slynger, Nominale MS.

SLINGET. A narrow slip of ground.

SLINK. (1) To sneak off. Also, a sneaking, thievish fellow. *North.*

(2) A small piece of wet meadow land. *I. of Wight.*

(3) A calf prematurely brought forth is so termed; the leather into which the skin is made, being softer and tougher than other leather, is used by shoemakers to bind with.

(4) Slim; slender. *Suffolk.*

SLIN-POLE. A simpleton. *Devon.*

SLIP. (1) "At the potteries in Staffordshire, the earths or clays of looser and more friable texture being mixed with water, they make into a consistence thinner than syrup, so that being put into a bucket, it will run out through a quill; this they call *slip,* and is the substance wherewith they paint their wares, which from its several colours is calld the *orange slip,* the *white slip,* the *red slip,*" Kennett MS.

(2) To creep. "Why come, how you do *slip* along," applied to a person moving very slow and lazily. *Var. dial.*

(3) An outside covering, as a pillow-*slip,* for a pillow-case. Also a child's pinafore. This word was formerly used in general for a scabbard, sheath, &c. and the maker of such things was called a *slipper,* a term that has now become obsolete. In the parish register of Hexham, co. Northumberland, is this entry, "William, son of William Hutchinson, *sword sliper,* bur. Nov. 1688." Chron. Mirab. p. 156.

(4) A narrow passage between two buildings. W. Wyrc. 192. There is a passage so called on the south side of Worcester cathedral.

(5) A young pig. *Cornw.*

(6) A noose, especially applied to that by which a greyhound is kept before it is allowed to start for the game.

(7) A counterfeit coin, consisting of brass washed over with silver.

(8) Clay ready for the potter.

(9) To cast a foal prematurely.

(10) A butterfly. *Somerset.*

SLIPCOAT-CHEESE. Was thus made:

Take five quarts of new milk from the cow, and one quart of water, and one spoonful of runnet,

and stir it together, and let it stand till it doth come; then lay your cheescloth into the vate, and take up your curd as fast as you can, without breaking, and put it to your vate, and let the whey soak out itself, when you have taken it all up, lay a cloth on the top of it and one pound weight for one hour, then lay two pound weight for an hour more; then take him out of the vate, and let him lie two or three hours, and then salt him on both sides; when he is salt enough, take a clean cloth and wipe him dry, then let him lie a day or a night, then put nettles under and upon him, and change them once a day, the cheese will come to his eating in eight or nine days. *The Housewife's Oracle,* ed. 1697, p. 14.

SLIP-DOWN. Old milk slightly curdled.

SLIPE. To uncover the roof of a building; to take away the outside covering from anything. "Take the whyte of lekus, *slype* hem and shrede hem small," Forme of Cury, p. 15.

SLIP-ON. To slip on clothes, i. e. to put them on very hurriedly and loosely. *Var. dial.*

SLIPPER. (1) Slippery. *Palsgrave.*

Yf they were men, your faithfulnesse might hap to suffice, but childhod muste bee maintained by mennes autoritie, and *slipper* you the underprompted with elder counsaill. *Hall, Edward V. f. 2.*

(2) A skidpan. *Worc.*

SLIPPER-SLOPPER. Slip-shod. *Somerset.*

SLIPPERY-WHELPS. Drop dumplings. *Suff.*

SLIPPID. Slender. *Sussex.*

SLIPPY. (1) Very quick. *Var. dial.*

(2) Slippery. Still in use.

SLIP-SHAUL. Applied to nuts when so ripe, that they easily slip out of the husks.

SLIP-SHOE. A very loose shoe, so worn as to hang loosely about the foot.

He weares his apparel by leave of the peoples ignorance, for if every customer could challenge his owne remnant, hee would be stript naked. He needs not use the corn-cutter, for the *slip-shoe* favours him. *Stephens' Essayes and Characters,* 1615, p. 421.

SLIP-SLOP. Thin mud, &c. *North.*

SLIPSTRING. A knavish fellow. See Lilly, ed. 1632, sig. Aa. v; Hawkins, iii. 39. It is an adjective in the following passage:

Another should have spoke us two betweene,
But like a meacher hee's not to be seene.
Hee's runne away even in the very nick
Of this dayes businesse; such a *slippstring* trick
As never till now befell us heeretofore,
Nor shall, I hope, befall us any more.
MS. Bright 170, f. 1.

SLIR. To slip; to slide. *North.*

SLIRRUP. To lap up any liquid with a noise. *Sussex.*

SLISSE. An instrument like a large sledge, used before carts were adopted in agriculture. It is still used in turf bogs where there are few obstructions. *North.*

SLIT. (1) A crack or cleft in the breast of fat cattle. *Midl. C.*

(2) To cut through; to cleave. *(A.-S.)*

(3) The pudendum muliebre. *North.*

(4)

The king was wondred out of witt,
And toke the messanger bi the *slit.*
Arthour and Merlin, p. 54.

(5) To thrust back the lock of a door without the key. *Sussex.*

SLIT-COTE. According to Strutt, ed. Planché, ii. 260, a cote open in the front.

SLITE. The herb cidamum.

SLITHER. To slide; to slip. *Var. dial.* Jennings has *slitter*, Glossary, p. 70.

SLITHERING. Slow; indolent; procrastinating; deceitful. *Linc.*

SLITIN. Worn out; wearied.

SLITTERY. The same as *Claggum*, q. v.

SLIVE. (1) To sneak; to skulk; to proceed in a sly way; to creep; to idle away time. *North.*

(2) To cut, or slice off anything. Also, a slip or slice, a chip. (*A.-S.*)

> Sithe thai drowe brondes of stel,
> And hewe togedre hard and wel,
> And delde dentes rive,
> And laiden on with swerdes clere,
> Helm and scheld that stronge were
> Thai gonne hem al *to-schlive.*
> *Gy of Warwike*, p. 471.

(3) To slide down suddenly. "I slyve downe, I fall downe sodaynly, *je coule*," Palsgrave.

(4) To dress carelessly. *Cumb.* A garment rumpled up about any part of the person is said to be *slived.*

SLIVE-ANDREW. A good-for-nothing fellow.

SLIVEN. Slid; glided down. The term was often applied to dress. Carr has *sliving*, having the brim or edge turned down.

SLIVER. (1) A splinter; a slice; a slip; a small piece of anything. (*A.-S.*)

(2) A small wooden instrument used for spinning yarn in the West of England. Arch. xxix. 271.

(3) A short slop worn by bankers or navigators. *Linc.* It was formerly called a *sliving.* The *sliving* was exceedingly capacious and wide.

(4) A lock of combed wool.

SLIVERLY. Cunning; deceitful. *Linc.*

SLIVING. (1) See *Sliver* (3).

(2) Idle; lazy; wicked. *North.*

(3) A blow? Anturs of Arther, xlviii. 5. Perhaps from A.-S. slifan, to cleave.

SLIZE. To look sly. *Wilts.*

SLO. To slay. (*A.-S.*)

SLOACH. To drink heavily. *Northumb.*

SLOB. (1) The star fish. *North.*

(2) The same as *Slab*, q. v.

SLOBBER. (1) Untidy; wet. *West.*

> Thomas Davis used to lace them up for her. She was very untidy in her dress; all of a *slobber.*
> *The Times*, July 25th, 1843.

(2) To eat spoon meat in a filthy manner, allowing portions of it to run down over the chin.

SLOBBERER. (1) A slovenly farmer. *Norf.*

(2) A jobbing tailor. *Var. dial.*

SLOBBERING-BIB. A bib tied under a child's chin round the neck when very young to keep the pinafore clean.

SLOBBERY. Wet; sloppy. *Shak.*

SLOB-FURROWING. A particular method of ploughing. *Norf.*

SLOCK. (1) Loose. *Sussex.*

(2) To entice; to steal. *West.* "To slock, vox apud Dumnonios usitatissima, blandis et subdolis verbis servosa dominis pellicere, aut malis artibus in-fraudem dominorum allicere." MS. Devon. Glossary.

SLOCKEN. To slake; to quench. Also, to suffocate in mud, and perhaps at times to drown simply. If a person should have been suffocated by getting into a bog or marsh he would be said to have been *slockened:* and the term was applied to a drunken man, who had perished in a ditch or running stream. *Linc.*

> That bottell swet, which served at the first
> To keep the life, but not to *slocken* thirst.
> *Du Bartas*, p. 366.

SLOCKET. To convey things privately out of the house, applied to a servant. *Berks.*

SLOCKING-STONE. A rich and tempting stone of ore. *Cornw.*

SLOCKSEY. Slovenly. *Sussex.*

SLOCKSTER. (1) To waste. *Somerset.*

(2) One that slocks or enticeth away men's servants. Blount, p. 597.

SLOD. (1) A short cake baked before the bread goes into the oven. *Suffolk.*

(2) Slid. (*A.-S.*)

> Launfal dyʒte hys courser,
> Withoute knave other squyer,
> He rood with lytylle pryde:
> Hys hors *slod* and fell yn the fen,
> Wherfore hym scornede many men,
> Abowte hym fer and wyde.
> *Illustrations of Fairy Mythology*, p. 9.

(3) To wade through mire, &c. *East.*

SLODDER. Slush, or wet mud. *West.*

SLODE. (1) Slit; split; slipt.

> The Elridge knighte, he pricked his steed;
> Syr Cauline bold abode:
> Then either shooke his trustye speare,
> And the timber these two children bare
> Soe soone in sunder *slode.*
> *Sir Cauline*, ap. Percy, p. 12.

(2) The track of cart-wheels. *Lanc.*

SLOFF. To eat slovenly and greedily. *West.* It occurs in Pr. Parv. *Sloffyn.*

SLOG. To lag behind.

SLOGARDIE. Sloth. (*A.-S.*)

SLOGGER. To be slovenly or tardy. *Sloggering*, negligent in dress. *North.*

SLOGHE. A bog; a muddy pit.

> For hys company was alle gon,
> xl. he had chaunged for oon,
> Ther skaped but two away;
> The quene was aferde to be schente,
> Tyl sche sye that they were wente,
> And passyd owt of the *slogh.*
> *MS. Cantab.* Ff. ii. 38, f. 73.
> Or of the pitte, or of the *sloghe,*
> If thouʒte him thanne good y-nowe.
> *Gower, MS. Soc. Antiq.* 134, f. 58.

SLOMAX. Very untidy. *West.*

SLOMBERINGES. Slumberings. (*A.-S.*)

SLOMERANDE. Slumbering. (*A.-S.*)

> And seett thaire mynde fully in Godd withowttene cessynge, whare so thay walke or dwelle or speke. *slomerande* and slepande.
> *MS. Lincoln A.* i. 17, f. 235.

SLOMMAKIN. Slovenly; loose; untidy; dirty; unwieldy. *Var. dial.*

SLOMOWRE. Slumber. (*A.-S.*)

And fore slewthe of *slomowre* on a slepe fallis,
Bot be ane aftyre mydnyghte alle his mode changede.
Morte Arthure, MS. Lincoln, f. 87.

SLON. Sly. *Cumb.*

SLONE. (1) The sloe. *West.* Browne uses it for the plural, sloes.

(2) To slay. (*A.-S.*)

I hade catelle ; now have I non !
Thay take my beatis and don tham *slone.*
MS. Cantab. Ff. v. 48, f. 47.

SLONGENE. Flung or cast down.

He sware by mekille Goddes payne,
Bot if thou brynge the coupe agayne,
With my dart thou salle be slayne,
And *slongene* of thi mere. *Perceval, 672.*

SLONKE. To devour up. (*Flem.*)

SLOO. (1) The inner bony prominence from the quick part of a cow's horn, which bleeds when broken. *West.*

(2) To slay ; to kill. (*A.-S.*)

The douȝtur thouȝt anodur thyng,
Hir fadur for to *sloo.*
MS. Cantab. Ff. v. 48, f. 45.

(3) The same as *Sloghe,* q. v.

And moche schame we hyt do,
And caste hyt in a fowle *sloo.*
MS. Cantab. Ff. ii. 38, f. 35.

SLOOM. A gentle sleep. *Sloomy,* dull, slow, inactive. *North.*

SLOON. Slain ; killed. (*A.-S.*)

With my fadur I have done foly,
Thre childur I had hym by,
And I have hem alle *sloon.*
MS. Cantab. Ff. v. 48, f. 46.

SLOOP. To change. *Wilts.*

SLOP. (1) A smock-frock ; any kind of outer garment made of linen. " Sloppe, a night-gowne, *robe de nuit,*" Palsgrave. The term was also applied to a kind of cloak or mantle. Strutt, ii. 211, quotes a MS. which says, " a sloppe is a mourning cassocke for ladies and gentlewomen, not open before."

Ich will put on my best white *sloppe,*
And ich will weare my yellow hose.
Melismata, 1611.

(2) To wet or dirty. *West.*

(3) Underwood. *Suffolk.*

(4) A summer boot or buskin, much worn in the fifteenth century.

(5) A pocket. *Lanc.*

(6) To bend, as wood, &c. *North.*

(7) The step of a ladder or gate, &c.

SLOPE. To defraud. *North.*

SLOPED. Decayed with wet, rotten, applied to potatoes and pease. *Dorset.*

SLOP-HOSE. " Payre of sloppe hoses, *braiettes a marinier,*" Palsgrave.

SLOPPER. Loose, not fixed, applied to solid bodies. *Somerset.*

SLOPPETY. A slut. *Lanc.*

SLOPPY. Loose ; slovenly. *North.*

SLOPS. Large wide breeches.

If they can walke about their wealthy shopps
In sober gownes and very hansome *slopps.*
Stephens' Essayes and Characters, 1615, p. 6.

SLOP-SELLER. A person who sells all sorts of old clothes. *Var. dial.*

SLOP-WASH. A small intermediate washing in large families. *Var. dial.*

SLORE. (1) To grasp. *Lanc.*

(2) Dirt ; miry earth. *North.* " Sloore, *limus,*" Nominale MS. xv. Cent.

SLORP. To sob heavily ; to eat greedily and unmannerly. *North.*

SLORRIED. Bedaubed. *West.* sl*orried* with the bishop's black coal dust. *Philpot's Works, p. 233.*

SLORRY. A blind worm. *Kent.*

SLOSH. Dirty wet mud. *Var. dial.*

SLOT. (1) A young bullock. *North.*

(2) The clasp or fastening of a door. " *Vectis,* a slott," Nominale MS. " Slotte of a dore, *locquet,*" Palsgrave. Still in use in the North, applied to a bolt of almost any kind.

(3) A castle ; a fort.

Thou paydst for building of a *slot,*
That wrought thine owne decay.
Riche's Allarme to England, 1578.

(4) The print or mark of a deer's foot upon the ground. *Gent. Rec. ii. 78.*

Swiftly pursue the *slots* of this huge deer,
And rouse him from his mighty layer here.
Howard's Brittish Princes, 1669, p. 110.

(5) A hollow tuck in a cap, or other part of the dress. *Linc.*

(6) To cut, or slash. *Northumb.*

(7) A small piece. Butchers call the tongue of pork a *slot,* and a small quantity of ale is called a slot of ale. *North.*

(8) A wide ditch. *Devon.*

(9) Wet sticky clay. *Linc.*

SLOTCH. (1) A sloven. *To slotch about,* said of shoes, &c. when slovenly or slipshod.

(2) A greedy clown. *Lanc.* It is also defined, a great ugly person.

SLOTE. (1) The pit of the stomach.

Thourghe the brené and the breste, with his bryghte wapyne,
O-slante doune fro the *slote* he slyttes at ones.
Morte Arthure, MS. Lincoln, f. 77.

(2) The step of a ladder, or gate.

SLOTER. To stab. *Midx.*

SLOTES. The under pieces which keep the bottom of the cart together.

SLOTH. The same as *Sloghe,* q. v.

SLOTTEN. Divided. *Chesh.*

SLOTTER. Filth ; nastiness. Also, to dirty, to bespatter with mud, &c. *Var. dial.* " Sloturburgge, *cenulentus,*" Pr. Parv.

Than awght the sawle of synfulle withinne
Be full fowle, that es al *slotyrd* thar in synne.
Hampole, MS. Bowes, p. 76.

SLOTTISH. Bad ; wicked ; slovenly.

SLOTTIT. To walk slipshod. *West.*

SLOUCH. A lazy fellow ; a rough ungainly person. Also a verb, to walk about in an idle manner. " Slowch, a lazy lubber, who has nothing tight about him, with his stockings about his heels, his clothes unbutton'd, and his hat flapping about his ears," MS. Gloss. " Thou filthic fine slouch," Promos and Cassandra, p. 47.

SLOUCHED-HAT. Now, one that has lost its form and proper texture ; originally, a hat the roʃe of which was untied, and the brims *slouched* over the face. *Hunter.*

SLOUDRING. Clumsy; loutish. *Devon.*

SLOUGH. (1) A husk. *North.*

(2) Killed; slew. *(A.-S.)*

> How there lay the Shottyshe knyght,
> That Quene Genure with poyson *slough*.
>   *MS. Harl.* 2252, f. 96.

(3) The cast skin of a snake. Also, the skin of any animal. The slough of a snake was formerly used by labourers for a hatband.

> Take a piece of the *slough* of an adder, and tye it to the wrong side of the finger that is prickt with a thorne, it will open the orifice that you may pluck it forth.
>   *Aubrey's Wilts, Royal Soc. MS.* p. 164.
> Thenne goth this neddre and not blan,
> In this *slouʒe* Sathan thenne was.
>   *Cursor Mundi, MS. Coll. Trin. Cantab.* f. 5.
> Then shall ye slit the *slough* where the hart lieth.
> And take away the heares from it and flyeth.
>   *The Booke of Hunting,* 1586.

(4) The slime of snakes. *Lanc.*

SLOUGHER. To slide. *Devon.*

SLOUGH-SILVER. A certain rent paid to the castle of Wigmore, and is in lieu of certain days' work in harvest, heretofore reserved to the lord from his tenants. *Blount.*

SLOUM. To slumber. *Yorksh.*

SLOUNGE. An idle fellow. *North.*

SLOVEN. (1) Divided. *North.*

(2) A knave; a rascal.

SLOVEN-WOOD. Southernwood. *East.*

SLOW. (1) To make slow; to slacken. " It sloweth age," Stanihurst, p. 13.

(2) A sluggard. *(A.-S.)*

> Lothe to bedde and lothe fro bedde, men schalle know the *slow.*   *MS. Douce,* 52.

(3) Dull, as the edge of a weapon.

SLOW-BACK. A sluggard. *Devon.*

SLOWDY. A dirty sloven. *Yorksh.*

SLOWE. (1) A moth. *(A.-S.)*

(2) A sloghe, q. v. Thornton Rom. p. 246.

SLOWEN. Slew, pl. *(A.-S.)*

> That were cured in Crist, that they on crosse *slowen.*
>   *MS. Cott. Calig.* A. ii. f. 111.

SLOWNES. Sloth. *(A.-S.)*

> *Slownes* ys a cursyd thyng,
> For hyt ys ever wery of weel doyng.
>   *MS. Cantab.* Ff. ii. 38, f. 5.

SLOW-WORM. A blind-worm. *Var. dial.*

SLOX. To waste; to pilfer. *Wilts.*

SLUB. Wet and loose mud. *Sussex.* Forby says, " thick mire, in which there is some danger of sticking fast."

SLUBBER. (1) To beat up. The following passage is in the Northern dialect.

> And we will ga to the dawnes, and *slubber* up a sillibub.   *The Two Lancashire Lovers,* 1640, p. 19.

(2) To do anything slovenly. " He doth but fumble or *slubber* over the lesson he playes," Cotgrave in v. *Brouiller.*

(3) To smear; to dirty, or defile. " Sloubberde with wepyng, *esplouré*," Palsgrave.

> Detracting vassals that will vomit spight
> At what they know not, and will look asquint
> On things of worth; what ere has most worth in't

They *slubber* most with gall: in all that's evill
They'll goe as far, and be as like the devill.
       British Bibliographer, ii. 334.

(4) To dress wool. *North.*

(5) Any viscous substance. *Yorksh.*

SLUBBERDEGULLION. A paltry dirty wretch.

> Quoth she, although thou hast deserv'd,
> Base *slubberdegullion,* to be serv'd
> As thou did'st vow to deal with me,
> If thou had'st got the victory.
>   *Hudibras,* I. iii. 896.
> Who so is sped is matcht with a woman,
> He may weep without the help of an onyon.
> He's an oxe and an asse, and a *slubberdegullion.*
>   *Musarum Deliciæ,* 1656, p. 79.

SLUBBERER. A mischievous meddling person; a turbulent man. This word occurs in Hollyband's Dictionarie, 1593.

SLUCK-A-BED. A sluggard. *West.* Cotgrave has *slug-a-bed,* in v. *Dormart.*

SLUD. Wet mud. *Var. dial.*

SLUDDER. To eat slovenly. *North.*

SLUDGE. The same as *Slud,* q. v.

SLUER. To slide down. *Devon.*

SLUG. (1) To be negligent. *Yorksh.*

(2) A ship which sails badly.

(3) To lay late in bed. *Var. dial.*

SLUGGARDY-GUISE. The habit of a sluggard. *West.*

> Sluggardy-guise;
> Loth to go to bed,
> And loth to rise.

SLUGGY. Sluggish. *(A.-S.)*

SLUG-HORN. A short and ill-formed horn of an animal of the ox kind, turned downwards, and appearing to have been stunted in its growth. Perhaps it may have been contemptuously named thus, from some fancied resemblance to that common reptile called the slug, the snail without a shell. *Forby.*

SLUG-HOUNDS. A breed of dogs possessed by James I, probably bloodhounds or the Scotch wolf-dog. See Sir H. Dryden's Twici, p. 59, 4to. 1844.

SLUMBRY. Sleepy. *Palsgrave.*

SLUMP. Wet boggy earth; wet mud. Also, to slip down into slump. *Var. dial.*

SLUNK. Grose tells us, as a superstition, that " a *slunk* or abortive calf buried in the highway over which cattle frequently pass, will greatly prevent that misfortune happening to cows. This is commonly practised in Suffolk."

SLUNKEN. Lean; shrivelled. *North.*

SLUR. (1) Thin washy mud. *East.*

(2) To slip a die out of the box so as not to let it turn, a method of cheating formerly in vogue among gamblers.

SLUR-BOW. A kind of bow, probably one furnished with a barrel, through a slit in which the string slided when the trigger was pulled. Meyrick, ii. 279.

SLURRUP. To swallow greedily. *East.*

SLURRY. (1) To dirty, or smear. *North.*

(2) To do anything inefficiently.

SLUSH. (1) Wet mud; any wet dirt. Figurative'y, anything dirty. *Var. dial.*

(2) To work carelessly. *Yorksh.*

(3) Wasteful. *North.*

(4) To slop; to spill. *Var. dial.*

(5) Poor or diseased cattle. *North.*

(6) A drunken fellow. *Newc.*

SLUSH-BUCKET. A great drinker. *North.*

SLUT. An apron. *Lanc.*

SLUTTY. Dirty. *North.*

For if thou gafe a gret lorde drynke in a *slutty* coppe and foule, ware the drynke never as gude, hym wolde wiate withe alle, and byd do it awaye.
MS. Lincoln A. i. 17, f. 238.

SLWNE. Sloth; indolence.

SLY-BOOTS. A sly fellow. *Var. dial.*

The frog call'd the lazy one several times, but in vain; there was no such thing as stirring him, though the *sly-boots* heard well enough all the while.
Adventures of Abdalla, 1729, p. 32.

SLYDOM. Cunning. *Cornw.*

SLYGHE. Cunning, i. e. built with excessive ingenuity and contrivance.

And theryn was a towre fulle *slyghe,*
That was bothe stronge and hyghe.
MS. Cantab. Ff. ii. 38, f. 141.

SMACK. (1) A slap; a sounding blow; a hit with the open hand. *Var. dial.*

(2) Suddenly; sharply. *West.*

(3) To come or go against anything with great force. *Essex.*

(4) The mizen sail of a ship.

SMACKER. To kiss. Florio, p. 51.

SMACK-SMOOTH. In a reckless way; regardless of consequences. When a person acts in this way, he is said to go at a thing *smack-smooth.* *Linc.* It sometimes means, quietly; pleasantly. Carr explains it "level."

SMALE. (1) The form of a hare. *East.*

(2) Small. Still in use.

Leste to *smale* they done hyt breke,
And in here teth hyt do steke.
MS. Cott. Clawd. A. ii. f. 130.

SMALISH. Rather small. *(A.-S.)*

SMALL. (1) Low and soft, as the voice. "Speaks small like a woman," Merry Wives of Windsor, i. 1. Also, low, as the water of a river, &c.

And than the company answered all
With voices sweet entuned, and so *small.*
Chaucer's Floure and the Leafe, 180.

(2) Young. *North.*

(3) The stock of a pillar.

(4) Poor, weak, said of liquor.

SMALLAGE. Water parsley.

Smallage, balme, germander, basell, and lilly,
The pinke, the flower-de-luce, and daffadilly.
Heywood's Marriage Triumphe, 1613.

SMALLUMS. Small quantities. *North.*

SMALLY. Very small; little. *Yorksh.*

Not *smally* fortunate did he thinke himselfe to have found this unluckie receptakle, making unto himselfe a false joy of that sower subject, which was the cause of heavie sorrow unto others.
Honours Academie, 1610, p. 2.

SMARADGE. A kind of emerald.

SMARRY. A woman's smock. *Dorset.*

SMART. (1) Considerable. *Wilts.*

(2) In good health. *Heref.*

(3) To undergo; to injure. *Essex.*

(4) Quick; hasty; swift. *Leic.*

The prynce of Jerusalem and his brother,
Everiche of hem ran to other,
Smartely in the feld;
Though Antonyffygriffon yonger were,
His brother Leobertus he can down bere;
Sir Torent stode and beheld.
Torrent of Portugal, p. 104.

(5) Well or finely dressed. *Var. dial.*

SMARTISH. Considerable. *Var. dial.*

SMARTLE. To waste away. *North.* " To smartle away, *dissipo,*" Coles.

SMARTWEED. The herb arsmart. *Norf.*

SMASH. (1) To break in pieces; to crush; to shiver. Also, a blow or fall by which anything is broken. *Var. dial.*

(2) A bankruptcy. *South.*

SMASHER. (1) A pitman. *North.*

(2) Anything very large. *Var. dial.*

(3) A small gooseberry pie. *Newc.*

(4) A passer of counterfeit coin. *Var. dial.*

SMASHING. Wild; gay. *Var. dial.*

SMATCH. A taste, twang, or flavour.

SMATTER. To intermeddle. *Coles.*

SMAW. Small. *North.*

SMAWM. To smear. *Dorset.*

SMAY. To refuse. *Salop.*

SMEAGRE. Thin; lean; meagre. *East.*

SMEATH. (1) The smew, *Mergus albellus,* one of the birds of the fens.

(2) A large open level. *East.*

SMECEN. To taste; to smack. *(A.-S.)*

SMECTYMNUUS. A club of five parliamentary holders-forth, mentioned in Hudibras. See also Wright's Political Ballads, p. 230. " About the beginning of the Long Parliament, in the year 1641, five ministers wrote a book against episcopacy and the Common Prayer, in behalf of the Presbyterian government, to which they all subscribed their names, being Stephen Marshal, Edmund Calamy, Tho. Young, Matth. Newcomen, and Will. Spurstow; the first letters whereof make this word *Smectymnuus,* and from thence they and their followers were called Smectymnuans," Blount, p. 597-8, ed. 1681.

SMEDES. Flour. *(A.-S.)* The " smedes of barly" occur in a receipt in MS. Linc. Med. f. 305, xv. Cent.

SMEDME. Meal. *Dunelm.*

SMEDUM. Dust. *West.*

SMEECH. (1) A stench. *Devon.* Smych occurs in an early MS. quoted in Wright's Essay on Purgatory, p. 144. " Smeech, to make a stink with the snuff of a candle," MS. Devon Glossary in my possession.

(2) Obscurity in the air, arising from smoke, fog, or dust. *South and West.*

SMEEGY. Meat, perhaps other things, in a state between taint and sweetness. A poor sick woman said, " I sent for a bit à meat, but 'twas so *smeegy* I couldn't eat it." *Moor's Suffolk MS. Glossary.*

SMEETER. A scimetar. " Put up your smeeter," Dekker, ap. Hawkins, iii. 163.

SMEETH. To smooth. *North.*

SMEKE. To flatter. (*Flem.*)

SMEKID. Smoky. (*A.-S.*)

Swarte *smekyd* smethes smateryd with smoke
Dryve me to deth wyth den of here dyntes ;
Swech noys on nyghtes ne herd men nevere,
What knavene cry and clateryng of knockes.
Reliq. Antiq. i. 240.

SMELLERS. Cat's whiskers. *West.*

SMELL-FEAST. A parasite. *Howell.*

SMELLING-CHETE. An orchard, or garden. Dekker's Lanthorne and Candle-light, 1620, sig. C. iii. In another place, however, he explains it *a nose.*

SMELL-SMOCK. " *Mulierarius*, one given to love women, a smellsmocke," Nomenclator, 1585, p. 528. " *Brigaille*, a noteable smelsmocke, or muttonmungar, a cunning solicitor of a wench," Cotgrave.

This theame of smocke is very large and wide,
And might (in verse) be further amplifide :
But I thinke best a speedy end to make,
Lest for a *smel-smocke* some should me mistake.
Taylor's Workes, 1630, ii. 167.

SMELT. (1) The sparling. *North.*
(2) Used metaphorically by our early writers for a gull or simpleton.

SMEL3ENE. Odoriferous. (*A.-S.*)

SMERE. (1)

At the furmeste bruche that he fond,
He lep in, and over he wond.
Tho he wes inne, *smere* he lou,
And ther of he hadde gome i-nou.
Reliq. Antiq. ii. 272.

(2) Grease. (*A.-S.*)

And strong clout lether hem to clout,
And *smere* to smere hem al about.
Arthour and Merlin, p. 50.

SMEREWORTH. The round birthwort, or the herb mercury. *Phillips.*

SMERI. A woman's shift. *Beds.*

SMERM. Swarm. Hooper's Early Writings, p. 568, but probably an error.

SMERTE. (1) To smart ; to suffer pain.
(2) Quick ; fast. Sometimes the adverb, as in Syr Gowghter, 389.

The swynhorde toke owt a knyfe *smert,*
And smote the boor to the herte.
MS. Cantab. Ff. ii. 38, f. 131.

Smertly then she callis a knave,
Ful he hopeth wher I sitte ;
He cumeth stalkyng behynde me with a st:fe,
Ful wel he troweth me to hitte.
MS. Cantab. Ff. v. 48, f. 110.

SMETE. A blow. (*A.-S.*)

Then Quore felle, as ye may wete,
That was of Befyse a gode *smete.*
MS. Cantab. Ff. ii. 38, f. 123.

SMETEN. Smote ; struck. (*A.-S.*)

When Gye hym felyd *smeten* sore,
To 3ylde hyt hym he was yore.
MS. Cantab. Ff. ii. 38, f. 154.

SMETH. A medicine or physical ointment to take away hair. Blount, p. 598.

SMETHE. Smooth. (*A.-S.*)

The furthe day shal blowe a wynd so longe so hit dures,
Castles a-doun falleth, bothe halles ant bures ;
Tho hulles maketh evene *smeths* wyth the dales ;
Hym y telle a loverd that thus con bete bales.
MS. Harl. 2253, f. 57.

SMETHYMENE. Smiths. (*A.-S.*)

Bot als the knyghte went thorow a lawe,
Smethymene thore herde he blawe. *Isumbras*, 393.

SMEUSE. A hare's track. *Var. dial.*

SMICKER. Smirking ; amorous. Applied to men, finical, effeminate. " *Smikkering*, neat gay, pleasant," Kennett, MS.

The smith seeing what a *smicker* wench the coblers wife was, and what a jealous foole shee had to her husband, sorrowed at the good fortune of the cobler, that he had so faire a wife, and wished that hee could finde meanes to have such a one his friend.
Cobler of Canterburie, 1608.

SMICKET. A smock. *Var. dial.*

SMIDDY. A blacksmith's smithy. *Smiddygum*, the refuse from the smiddy. *North.*

SMID-MEAL. A coarse sort of meal. *Westm.*

SMIE. A kind of small fish. " In Essex is a fysshe called a *smie*, whyche, if he be longe kept, will turne to water," Elyot in v. *Aphya.*

SMILE. To ferment, as beer, &c. *North.*

SMILT. The spleen of an animal.

SMIRCH. To daub ; to smear. Still in use in Herefordshire.

SMIRK. (1) To smile with a self-satisfied air *Smirkle* is sometimes heard.
(2) Neat ; trim. *Oxon.*

SMIT. (1) Infection. *North.* " He provocith al to the smit of falling," Apology for the Lollards, p. 70.
(2) To mark sheep. *Yorksh.*
(3) Smiteth ; cutteth. (*A.-S.*) Also a substantive, a cut, as in this passage.

Tryamowre on the hedd he hytt,
He had gevyn hym an evylle *smytt.*
MS. Cantab. Ff. ii. 38, f. 81

(4) Marked ; adorned. *Linc.*
(5) To mar ; to destroy. *Devon.*
(6) Pleasure ; recreation.

SMITCH. Dirt, but generally applied to smoke or dust. *West.*

SMITE. A small portion ; a mite.

SMITER. (1) The assistant blacksmith who *smites* the hot iron on the stithy or anvil once with the *bout-hammer*, or heavy mall, to every two blows of the smaller hand-hammer struck by the smith. Hence applied generally to one who does anything in an energetic manner.
(2) A scimetar. " It is my simiter, which I by construction often studying to bee compendious, call my *smiter*," Lilly's Endimion, ed. 1632, sig. B. viii.

His fatal *smiter* thrice aloft he shakes,
And frowns ; the sea and ship and canvass quakes ;
Then from the hatches he descends, and stept
Into his cabin, drank again, and slept.
Legend of Captain Jones, 1659.

SMITHE. To forge, as a smith. (*A.-S.*)

SMITHEN. To scatter meal on the board before baking oat-cakes. *North.*

SMITHER. (1) Light small rain. *East.*
(2) Light ; active ?

Gavan was *smyther* and smerte,
Owte of his steroppus he sterte.
Anture of Arther, xlii. 10.

SMITHERS. Fragments ; atoms. *Linc.*

SMITHUM. The smallest sort of lead ore beaten

into dust, finely sifted, and strewed upon earthen vessels to give them a gloss, is called *smithum* in Staffordshire. Near Lawton Park they distinguish their lead ore into three kinds, round ore, small ore, and *smithum*. Kennett, MS. Lansd. 1033.

SMITS. Particles of soot. *Craven.*

SMITTLE. Infectious. Also, to infect. The adjective *smittling* is also used.

SMITY. The snuff of a candle. *Beds.*

SMOCK. A woman's shift. Also the *slop* worn by men, with this farther difference, that it is in the latter case worn over all, instead of under all, as in the former.

SMOCK-FACED. Beardless. *Var. dial.*

SMOCK-FROCK. A coarse linen shirt worn over the coat by farm-labourers.

SMOCK-MILL. A corn-mill; a windmill standing solely on a wooden basis. *East.*

SMOCK-RACE. A race run by women for the prize of a fine smock. *North.*

SMOGE. To smudge, or smear.

> Kepe thyn hondes, fayr and wel,
> From fowle *smogynge* of thy towel;
> Theron thou schalt not thy nese snyte,
> Ny at the mete thy tothe thou pyke.
>
> *Constitutions of Masonry,* 744.

SMOKE. (1) To find any one out; to discover anything meant to be kept secret.

> The two free-booters, seeing themselves *smoakd,* told their third brother he seemd to be a gentleman and a boone companion; they prayed him therefore to sit downe with silence, and sithence dinner was not yet ready, hee should heare all.
>
> *Dekker's Lanthorne and Candle-Light,* 1620, sig. F. iv.

(2) To abuse a person. *Devon.*

(3) Was formerly, and is still occasionally, applied to any steam or vapour.

(4) To beat severely. *North.*

SMOKER. (1) At Preston, before the passing of the Reform Bill in 1832, every person who had a cottage with a chimney, and used the latter, had a vote, and was called a *smoker.*

(2) An old smoker, i. e. one who is well experienced in any matters. *Var. dial.*

SMOKING-STICK. A firebrand.

SMOLDER. To suffocate. *Palsgrave.*

SMOLT. (1) The young of the salmon.

(2) Smooth and shining. *Sussex.*

(3) Mild. *Syr Gawayne.*

SMOOR. (1) To smooth; to pat. *West.*

(2) To smear, or daub. *Northumb.*

SMOOT. (1) A narrow passage. *Linc.*

(2) To enter, or pass through with some degree of difficulty. *North.*

(3) Smooth. Tim Bobbin Gl.

SMOOTH. To iron linen. *Var. dial.*

SMOOTHERY. The same as *Smeth,* q. v.

SMOOT-HOLE. A hole in a hedge made by a hare or similar animal. *North.*

SMOOTH-SHAN. The smooth blenny.

SMOPPLE. Brittle; crisp. *North.*

SMORE. (1) To abound; to swarm. Also a subst. a crowd or swarm. *East.*

(2) To smother. *North.*

> Some brains out-bet; some in the guts were gor'd;
> Some dying vomit bloud, and some were *smor'd.*
>
> *Du Bartas, History of Judith,* p. 577.
>
> So bewrapped them and entangled them, kepyng doune by force the fetherbed and pillowes harde unto their mouthes, that within a while they *smored* and styfled them. *Hall, Richard III.* f. 3.

(3) To smear, or dirty.

SMORTE. To enjoy one's self.

SMOT. Rushed; hastened. *(A.-S.)*

SMOTCH. To stain; to blot. *Norf.*

SMOTHER. To daub, or smear. *Somerset.* Hence the term in cookery, rabbits *smothered* with onions. Chaucer has *smoterlich,* smutty. dirty, Cant. T. 3961.

SMOTLEY. Pleasantly. *Ritson.*

SMOTTER.

> We wyll have cousynge Besse also,
> And two or thre proper wenchis mo,
> Ryght feyr and *smotter* of face.
>
> *Interlude of the iiij. Elements,* n. d.

SMOUCH. (1) A loud kiss. *Var. dial.* "Come smack me, I long for a smouch," Promos and Cassandra, p. 47.

(2) A low-crowned hat. *Devon.*

SMOUCHER. A kiss. *North.*

SMOULT. Hot; sultry. *Kent.*

SMOURTE. Smarted. *Hearne.*

SMOUS. A Jew. *Suffolk.*

SMOUSE. (1) To fondle. *Linc.*

(2) The same as *Muse* (2).

SMOUT. To work by-work, when out of constant employment.

SMOW. To smirk. *North.*

SMOYLE. To smile?

> Thy journey mates began to *smoyle*
> When they thy sleightes did smell.
>
> *Turbeville's Ovid,* 1567, f. 38.

SMUCKLE. To smuggle goods.

SMUDGE. (1) To stifle. *North.*

(2) To smear; to soil. *Var. dial.*

(3) To laugh. *Newc.*

SMUDGY. Hot or close, e. g. the fire is so large that it makes the room feel quite hot and *smudgy.* The same perhaps as smothery. *Linc.*

SMUG. (1) Neat; spruce. Also, to dress up with neatness, to trim. *North.*

> Thou mayst succeed Ganymede in his place,
> And unsuspected *smug* the Thund'rer's face.
> O happy she shall climbe thy tender bed,
> And make thee man first for a maiden-head!
>
> *Fletcher's Poems,* p. 74.

(2) A neat handy fellow.

> A *smug* of Vulcan's forging trade,
> Besmoak'd with sea-cole fire,
> The rarest man to helpe a horse,
> That carmen could desire.
>
> *Rowland's Knave of Clubbs,* 1611.

SMUGGING. Games had their peculiar times or seasons, and when any game was out, as it was termed, it was lawful to steal the thing played with. This was called *smugging,* and it was expressed by the boys in a doggrel, viz.

> Tops are in, spin 'em agin;
> Tops are out, *smugging* about.
>
> *Hone's Every-Day Book,* i. 253

SMULY. Demure-looking. *North.*

SMUR. Small misty rain. *East.*

SMUSH. (1) To smoulder. *Northumb.*

(2) Fine; gay; smart. *Derb.*

SMUT. Among the signs of coal above ground they look for a *smut*, i. e. a friable black earth, which they look on as a certain indication of coal beneath. *Staff.* Kennett, MS.

SMUTCH. Stain; smut; dirt.

> And when thou dost to supper come,
> Thou shall sit in a distant room,
> That my mantle take no *smutch*
> From thy coarser garments touch.
> *Fletcher's Poems*, p. 101.

SMUTCHIN. Snuff. *Howell.*

SMUTTY. Obscene; indecent.

> We may take notice that there are no *smutty* songs in their plays, in which the English are extremely scandalous.
> *Collier's Short View of the English Stage*, 1698, p. 24.

SMUYTHE. Smooth. "Smuythe, *levis*," Dict. Angl. MS. circa A. D. 1500.

SNAAR. Greedy. *Cumb.*

SNABBLE. (1) To rifle; to plunder; to kill.

(2) To eat greedily. *Dorset.*

SNACE. Snuff of a candle. *Essex.*

SNACH. (1) To pierce. (*Dut.*)

(2) A gin, snare, or trap.

SNACK. (1) A share. To go snacks, i. e. to divide anything between persons. *Var. dial.*

(2) Provisions. *South.* It is often used in the sense of a taste of provisions.

(3) To snatch. *North.* It occurs in the Dial. Creat. Moral. p. 99.

(4) A dried fungus. *Glouc.*

SNAFFLE. (1) To steal; to cheat. *Var. dial.*

(2) To speak through the nose. *Linc.*

(3) To talk nonsensically. *East.*

(4) To saunter along. *Cumb.*

SNAFFLED. Beaten down by wind or hail, applied to ripe corn. *East.*

SNAG. (1) The common snail. *Sussex.* (*A.-S.*)

(2) To trim; to cut off the twigs and small branches from a tree or pole, &c. To *snag out*, is to trim the rods, &c. after the underwood is cut, and prepare them for being made into hurdles, &c. The tool is called a *snagger*, which is a simple bill-hook without the usual edge on the back.

(3) A handle to a pot. *Derby.*

(4) A tooth standing alone. *West.*

(5) A small kind of sloe, the fruit of the black-thorn. *South.* Florio has, "*Spino*, a sloe-tree, a black-thorne, a snag-tree." Tea is called *snag-water* in the West of England.

(6) A lump on a tree where a branch has been cut off. *North.* "Knurs, knobs, *snags*, or bunches in trees," Florio, p. 162. "A snagg, vel snugg, a hard wooden ball, commonly some gnurre, knobb, or knott of a tree, which they (boys) make use of at the play of bandy instead of a ball," MS. Devon Gl.

(7) To tease incessantly. *West.*

(8) A violent scold. *Somerset.*

SNAGGLE. To nibble. *Kent.*

SNAGGLE-TOOTH. A tooth growing out irregularly from the others. *West.*

SNAG-GRET. A sort of sand that often lies in deep rivers, and is full of little shells; one load of which, for the manuring of land, is counted as good as three loads of dung. *Dict. Rust.*

SNAGGY. Full of snags, or bunches, as lopped trees. Metaphorically, snappish, cross, ill-tempered. *Linc.*

SNAICH. A thief in a candle. *Norf.*

SNAIL. (1) A slug. *Kent.*

(2) A military engine used in ancient warfare, thus described:

> They hadde also all manere gynnes and gettes that nedful is taking or seging of castel or of citee, as *snayles*, that was nou3t elles but holw pavyes and tagetis, undir the whiche, men, when thei fou3ten, were heled from schot and castynge, as the snayl is in his hous; therfore they clepid hem snayles.
> *Vegecius, MS. Douce* 291, f. 47.

SNAIL-COD. The same as *Snag-gret*, q. v.

SNAIL-HORN. A snail-shell. *North.*

SNAIL-HORNED. Having short down-hanging horns, with blunt points and somewhat bent in the usual form of the snail. Spoken of cattle. *Norf.*

SNAILS. A profane oath, corrupted from *His nails*, referring to the nails of our Saviour at the Crucifixion.

SNAIL'S-TROT. To walk a *snail's trot*, i. e. to walk slowly. Sometimes, snail's-gallop.

SNAKE. A poor wretch, a term of reproach. It occurs in early writers.

SNAKE-BIRD. The wryneck.

SNAKE-BONE-BANDSTRINGS. Bandstrings ornamented at the ends with large tassels.

SNAKE-SPIT. Cuckoo spittle. *Suff.*

SNAKES-STANG. The dragon-fly. *Var. dial.*

SNAKE-STONES. Fossil shell-fish, resembling snakes coiled up, found at Whitby.

SNAP. (1) A lad, or servant, generally used in an ironical sense. *Yorksh.*

(2) The same as *Snack*, q. v.

(3) A small round piece of gingerbread, made very crisp. *North.*

(4) To do anything hastily. *East.* To snap the eye, i. e. to wink.

(5) A small piece of anything. "A snap, *frustulum*," Coles.

SNAP-APPLE. (1) A mirth-exciting frolic, in which catching, or rather not catching, an apple in your mouth, while twirling on a stick suspended on its centre, with a candle at the other end of it, is the jet of the sport. Bob-cherry is, I believe, nearly the same. *Moor.*

(2) The long fir cone. *Oxon.*

SNAP-DRAGON. A domestic amusement among young folks in winter. Raisins are put into a large dish with brandy, which is set fire to. The party stand round the table, and boldly snap out and eat the blazing plums. This must be done quickly and boldly, leaving it optional whether you burn your fingers or your mouth. A little salt flung into the weakened flame heightens the sport, by giving a very cadaverous aspect to the countenance; and has farther the good effect of averting any risk of the liquor being drunk. Nares, under *flap-dragon*, describes the sport similarly, and gives several quotations from Shakespeare and others, showing its great antiquity. *Moor.* The original meaning of snap-dragon was a *bug-bear*. "A disguised or uglie picture to make children afraid, as wee say, a *snap-dragon*, a turke, a bug-beare," Florio, p. 298, ed. 1611.

SNAPE. (1) To pine; to wither. Leaves by a sudden blight are snaped; anything exposed too suddenly to the fire is *snaped*. A step-mother *snapes* her step-children-in-law of their meat. *North.*

(2) To check; to chide. *Linc.*

(3) A pert youth. *North.*

(4) To snub. *Linc.*

(5) A spring in arable ground. *Devon.*

(6) A woodcock. *Somerset.*

SNAPHANCE. A spring lock to a gun or pistol. It differed from the modern firelock in the hammer not forming the covering of the pan. The term was sometimes applied to the instrument itself, as in the Archæologia, xxviii. 139.

SNAPING-POLE. A strong fishing-rod, generally made of one piece of wood.

SNAPLE. To nip, as frost does. *West.*

SNAPPER. (1) A woodpecker.

(2) To stumble. *North.* "I snapper as a horse dothe that tryppeth, *je trippette*," Palsgrave.

SNAPPERS. Waspish persons that answer crossly or peevishly, &c.; also playthings for children, made of bone, or bits of board, thin, hard wood, to put between their fingers, and to make a noise like a drum. *Dyche.*

SNAPPING-TONGS. A game at forfeits. There are seats in the room for all but one, and when the tongs are snapped all run to sit down, the one that fails paying a forfeit.

SNAP-SACK. A wallet, or knapsack.

And racks the entrails, makes the belly swell,
Like Satan's *snap-sack* plund'red out of hell.
Clobery's Divine Glimpses, 1659, p. 30.

SNAPSEN. Aspen. *I. Wight.*

SNAPY. Wet; marshy. *Dorset.*

SNAR. To snarl. "I snarre as a dogge doth under a doore whan he sheweth his tethe; take hede of your dogge, alwayes as I come by he snarreth at me," Palsgrave.

SNARE. The gut or string stretched tightly across the lower head of a drum. *Somerset.*

SNARL. (1) A quarrel. *Somerset.*

(2) A snare. Also a verb, to ensnare, to entangle, to strangle. *North.* "To ruffle or snarle, as overtwisted thread," Cotgrave. *Snarl-knot*, a very intricate one.

All other things being but *snarles* to intangle honestie, and to cast us headlong into much miserie.
The Prayse of Nothing, 1585.

Lay in wait to *snarle* him in his sermons, calumniate his most godly doctrine. *Bacon's Works*, p. 52.

SNARREL. A hard knot. *Cumb.*

SNARSTED. Scorned; defied. *Suffolk.*

SNARTLY. Severely; sharply. *Gawayne.*

SNASTE. The snuff of a candle. Also a verb, to snuff a candle. *East.*

SNASTY. Cross; snappish. *Suffolk.*

SNATCH. (1) The same as *Snack*, q. v.

(2) A brief meeting. A snatch and away, i. e. gone directly. *West.*

(3) A hasp, or clasp. *Somerset.*

SNATCH-APPLE. A game similar to bob-cherry, but played with an apple.

SNATCH-HOOD. A boy's game, mentioned in a statute of Edward III.'s time.

SNATCH-PASTY. A greedy fellow.

SNATHE. To prune trees. *North.*

SNATTED. Snub-nosed.

SNATTLE. To linger; to delay. *Yorksh.*

SNATTOCKS. Scraps; fragments.

SNAUGHT. Snatched up. (*A.-S.*)

Thence to England, wheare *snaught* water of the rose,
Muske, civet, amber, also did inclose.
MS. Bibl. Reg. 17 B. xv.

Wheare Danus, like a sodaine stoopinge kite,
Up *snaught* a Venice glasse in surging flight.
Lane's Triton's Trumpet.

SNAWK. To smell. *North.*

SNAZE. To prune trees. *Yorksh.*

SNEAD. The handle of a scythe. *West.*

SNEAK. To smell. *North.*

SNEAK-BILL. "A chichiface, micher, *sneake-bill*, wretched fellow, one out of whose nose hunger drops," Cotgrave.

SNEAKER. A small bowl. *Midx.*

SNEAKSBY. A mean-spirited fellow. "A meacocke, milkesop, *sneaksbie*, worthlesse fellow," Cotgrave.

SNEAP. To snub; to browbeat; to check. Still in common use. Also to nip, as *snape*, q. v. See Ray and Nares.

SNEATH. The same as *Snead*, q. v.

SNECK. (1) That part of the iron fastening of a door which is raised by moving the latch. To *sneck* a door, is to latch it. *North.* The sneck-band is a string fastened to the latch, passing through a hole in the door for the purpose of drawing it up from the outside. "*Pessulum*, a snek; *mastiga*, a snekband," Nominale MS. "Latche or snekke, *clitorium, vel pessula*," Pr. Parv. p. 283. "*Pessulum, dicitur sera lignea qua hostium pellitur cum seratur, dicitur a pello*, a lyteke, or latche, or a snecke, or a barre of a dore," Ortus Vocab.

If I cud tell wheay's cutt our band fra'th *sneck*,
Next time they come Ise mack them jet the heck.
A Yorkshire Dialogue, 1697, p. 46.

(2) A piece of land jutting into an adjoining field, or intersecting it. *North.*

SNECK-DRAWN. Mean; stingy. *North.*

SNECKET. "*Loquet d'une huis*, the latch or *snecket* of a doore," Cotgrave.

SNECK-SNARL. To entangle. *North.*

SNED. (1) To prune; to lop. *North.*

(2) To catch. *Hartlepool.*

SNEDDER. Slender; thin. *Dunelm.*

SNEE. (1) To abound; to swarm. *North.*

(2) To sneeze. *Somerset.*

SNEERING-MATCH. A grinning match. The competition of two or more clowns endeavouring to surpass each other in making ugly faces for a prize or wager, of which matches we had many in the rural fêtes given at the close of the revolutionary war. *Forby.*

SNEEZE. Snuff. *Lanc.* Sneeze-horn, a sort of snuff-box made of an animal's horn.

SNEEZER. A severe blow. *Suffolk.*

SNEG. To push with the horns. *North.*

SNEKE. A cold in the head, "*Sneke*, pose, *rime*," Palsgrave, 1530.

SNELE. A snail. MS. Dict. c. 1500.

SNELL. (1) Quickly. Perceval, 2170.

He prekede into the feld tho full *snelle.*
Chron. Vilodun. p. 9.

(2) Sharp; keen; piercing. *Cumb.* Also a verb, to pierce as air, &c.

Teche hem alle to be war and *snel,*
That they conne sey the wordes wel.
MS. Cott. Claud. A. ii. f. 128.

(3) A short thick stick about four inches long called a *cat*, with which schoolboys play at a game termed *cat and dog.*

SNER. To snort. Still in use.

SNERE. To sneak off. *Oxon.*

SNERPLE. To shrivel up. *North.*

SNERT. To sneer; to ridicule. *Linc.*

SNEUL. A poor sneaking fellow.

SNEULS. The internal lining of a sheep's nostrils. *North.*

SNEUZE. A noose. *North.*

SNEVER. Slender; smooth. *North.*

Peepe here and peepe there, aw the wide dale is but *snever* to them.
The Two Lancashire Lovers, 1640, p. 18.

SNEVIL. A snail. *North.*

SNEVING. Sneaking. *Devon.*

SNEW. Snowed. *Var. dial.*

SNEW-SKIN. A leathern apron used by a spinner to rub the wheel with. *North.* "Snwskynne, *pellicudia, nebrida*," MS. Dict. c. 1500.

SNIB. A snub, or reproach. *Snibbe*, to reproach, occurs in old writers. *Snibbid*, rebuked; *snibbing*, blame, MS. Cotton. Vespas. D. vii.

Snybbyd of my frendys such techechys for t'amende,
Made deffe ere lyst nat to them attende.
Lydgate's Minor Poems, p. 256.

SNIBBLE-NOSE. Nasus mucosus. *Devon.* A cutted snibble-nose, i. e. a miser.

SNICK. A notch; a cut. *North.*

SNICKER. (1) A glandered horse.

(2) To laugh inwardly. *Sussex.*

(3) The low noise made by a mare to call her foal to her side. *East.*

SNICKER-SNEE. A large clasp-knife. *Norf.*

SNICKET. "One that pincheth all to nought," Hunter's Hallamsh. Gloss. p. 123.

SNICKLE. To tie a noose or running knot, generally applied to snaring hares. *Var. dial.* Marlowe uses the term in a similar manner, applied to strangling a person.

SNICK-UP. An old phrase of contempt, equivalent to *go and be hanged!* Forby says it is still in use, and explains it, *begone, away with you!*

SNICKUPS. Slight ailments. *East.*

SNICKY. A small field. *Somerset.*

SNIDDLE. Long coarse grass. *West.* According to Pegge, stubble is also so called.

SNIDGE. To hang upon a person. *Lanc.*

SNIESTY. Scornful; impudent. *North.*

SNIFFLE. To snuff up, as children do when the nose is full from a cold. *Var. dial.*

SNIFT. (1) A moment. *Lanc.*

(2) Sleet; slight snow. *North.*

(3) The same as *Sniffle*, q. v. *Snifter* is also used in the same sense.

From spyttyuge and *snyftynge* kepe the also,
By privy avoydans let hyt go.
Constitutions of Masonry, 711.

SNIFTERING. Shuffling; sneaking. *Lanc.*

SNIG. (1) A small eel. *North.*

(2) To cut, or chop off. *South.*

(3) To drag heavy substances along the ground without a sledge. *North.*

(4) Close and private. *Devon.*

SNIGGER. To jeer; to sneer. *East.*

SNIGGLE. (1) At marbles, to shuffle the hand forwards unfairly. *Devon.*

(2) To catch eels by pushing a worm with a straight needle attached to a string into any hole where they are likely to be found.

SNILE. A snail. *Yorksh.*

Tak the rede *snyle* that crepis houseles, and sethe it in water, and gedir the fatt that comes of thame.
MS. Linc. Med. f. 284.

SNIP. A small piece. *North.*

SNIPE. A low sort of a brisk unmeaning answer, implying a degree of impertinence in the question; though it mostly centres wholly in the reply. "What were you saying?" *Snipe.* The Scottish has *snipe*, a sarcasm; *snipy*, tart in speech. *Moor.*

SNIPE-KNAVE. A worthless fellow. "A snipeknave, so called because two of them are worth but one snipe," Cotgrave.

SNIPPER-SNAPPER. Small, insignificant, generally applied to a young lad.

Having ended his discourse, this seeming-gentile *snipper-snapper* vanisht, so did the rout of the nonsensicall deluding star-gazers, and I left alone.
Poor Robin's Visions, 1677, p. 12.

SNIPPET. A very small bit. *West.* Forby has *snippock*, another form of the same word.

SNIPPY. Mean; stingy. *Var. dial.*

SNIPS. Shares. *South.*

SNIRL. To shrivel up. *North.*

SNIRP. To pine; to wither. *Cumb.* This is perhaps the same word as *snurpe*, which occurs in a poem of the fourteenth century printed in Reliq. Antiq. ii. 211, "I snurpe, I snobbe, I sneipe on snoute."

SNIRRELS. The nostrils. *Northumb.*

SNIRT. A wheeze; a suppressed laugh. *North.* "In the snirt of a cat," at once.

SNISETY. Saucy. *Craven.*

SNISH. Snuff. *Glouc.*

SNITCH. (1) To twitch. *Somerset.*

(2) To confine by tying up; and hence, in allusion to the operation, to castrate. *Linc.*

SNITCHEL. The piece of wood by which the superfluous oats are swept off the measure.

SNITE. (1) To blow the nose. See MS. Sloane 1622, f. 104. "*Mouché*, snyted, wiped," Cotgrave. To snite, in falconry, to wipe the beak after feeding. It meant generally, to remove any dirty superfluity.

(2) The snipe. "*Ibis*, a snyte," Nominale MS. Still in use. "A snipe or snite, a bird lease than a woodcocke," Baret, 1580.

> Al oon to the a ffauclon and a kyghte,
> As goode an howle as a popingaye,
> A downghille doke as deynté as a *snyghte*.
> *Lydgate's Minor Poems*, p. 192.

SNITERAND. Drifting.

> For the *snyterand* snaue, that snaypely hom smellus.
> *Anturs of Arther*, vii. 4.

SNITHE. (1) Sharp, cold, cutting, applied to the wind. *North.*

> Letts spang our geates, it is varra *snithe*,
> And Ise flaid, wife, it will be frost belive.
> *A Yorkshire Dialogue*, 1697, p. 37.

(2) To abound, or swarm. *Linc.*

SNITING-IRON. A pair of snuffers.

SNIVEL. To cry, or whine. *Var. dial.* Snivel-ard, one who speaks through his nose.

SNIVEL-NOSE. A niggardly fellow.

SNIVELY-SLAVERY. Florio has, "*Bioccolóso*, snotty, snively-slavery," ed. 1611, p. 61.

SNIVY. Parsimonious. *North.*

SNIZY. Cold. *Cumb.*

SNOACH. To sniffle. *Var. dial.*

SNOB. (1) To sob violently. *Snobbinges*, violent sobbings, Wiclif, ed. Baber, gl.

(2) A journeyman shoemaker. *Suffolk.*

(3) A vulgar ignorant person. *Var. dial.*

(4) Mucus nasi. *Somerset.*

(5) The long membranous appendage to the beak of a cock turkey. *West.*

SNOCK. A hard blow. *West.*

SNOD. (1) Smooth. (2) Demure. *North.*

SNODDEN. To make smooth. *Yorksh.*

SNOFF. The eye of an apple. *West.*

SNOFFER. A sweetheart. *Somerset.*

SNOG. To shiver; to shake.

SNOGLY. Neatly; tidily. *North.*

SNOG-MALT. Malt smooth, with few combs or tails. Wheat ears are said to be *snod* when they have no beards or awns. Kennett, MS. Lansd. 1033.

SNOKE. To ferret out; to pry into. *North.* Snoke-horne, Towneley Myst. p. 68, a sneaking fellow.

SNOOD. (1) A fillet, or riband. (2) A small hair line used by fishermen. *North.*

SNOOK. (1) To lie hidden. *North.*

(2) To smell; to search out. *Linc.* It occurs in the first sense in Pr. Parv. "*Nicto*, to snoke as houndes dooth," Ortus Vocab.

(3) To lean the head forward in walking. *Var. dial.*

SNOOL. (1) A low, sneaking, dishonest fellow. *North.*

(2) To smear anything by rubbing the nose and mouth over it. *West.*

SNOOZE. A brief slumber. *Var. dial.*

SNOOZLING. Nestling. *Linc.*

SNOP. To eat off, as cattle do the young shoots of hedges, trees, &c.; a corruption perhaps of *snip* or *snap*, or of *knop*, the head of anything. Moor's Suffolk MS.

SNORSE. A small corner of land.

SNORT. To laugh loudly. *Yorksh.*

SNORTER. The wheatear. *Dorset.*

SNOT. (1) The snuff of a candle. *North.*

(2) An insignificant fellow. *Var. dial.*

(3) Neat; handsome. *North.*

SNOTCH. (1) A notch; a knot. *Suffolk.*

(2) To speak through the nose. *West.*

SNOTER-GOB. The same as *Snob* (5).

SNOTH. Mucus nasi. *Pr. Parv.*

SNOTTER. To cry; to snivel. *North.*

> And throw abroad thy spurious *snotteries*,
> Upon that puft-up lump of balmy froth.
> *Ben Jonson's Works*, ii. 818.

SNOTTER-CLOUT. A pocket-handkerchief. *North.*

SNOTTY. Mean; paltry. *Var. dial.*

SNOTTY-DOG. A blubbering lad. *Newc.*

SNOUL. A small quantity. *East and South.* Forby says "a short thick cut from the crusty part of a loaf or a cheese."

SNOUP. A blow on the head. *Glouc.*

SNOUT. To snub. *Dorset.*

SNOUTBAND. A person who rudely interrupts the conversation of a party.

SNOUTBANDS. The iron round clog soles.

SNOUT-HOLE. The same as *Muse* (2).

SNOW-BALL. The Guelder rose. *Var. dial.*

SNOW-BONES. Remnants of snow left after a thaw. *North.*

SNOWL. The head. *Somerset.*

SNOW-STORM. A continued snow, so long as it lies on the ground. *North.*

SNOWT-FAIRE. Fair in feature? The term occurs in Hall's Satires, p. 77.

> For he supposing that hungrie soldiors would be contented to accept anie courtesie, he procured a yoong harlot, who was somewhat *snowt-faire*, to go to the castell, pretending some injurie to have beene doone to hir, and to humble hirselfe to the capteins devotion. *Holinshed, Chron. Ireland*, p. 176.

SNOWT-WEARS. Great dams or wears upon a river. Kennett, MS.

SNUB. To check; to rebuke; to treat with contempt. *Var. dial.*

SNUB-NOSED. Short-nosed. *Var. dial.*

SNUCH. The same as *Snudge*, q. v.

SNUCK. To smell. *Norf.*

SNUDDLE. To nestle. *North.*

SNUDE. A fillet, or hair-lace.

> Yaw, jantlewoman, with the saffron *snude*, you shall know that 1 am Master Camillus.
> *The Two Lancashire Lovers*, 1640, p. 18.

SNUDGE. (1) To move along, being snugly wrapped up. See Forby, p. 314. It means rather to move about pensively, to sneak slily about. *Var. dial.*

(2) A mean or miserly person. Also a verb, to scrape together, to be miserly.

> The drudges and *snudges* of this world may very fitly be compared to a kings sumpter-horse.
> *Dent's Pathway*, p. 82.

Our mother Earth, possest with womans pride,
Perceiving Gerard to be beauties judge,
And that hir treasure is not unespide,
Of hir faire flowring brats she is so *snudge*.
Verses prefixed to Gerard's Herbal.

Scrapynge and *snudgynge* without ony cease,
Ever coveytynge, the mynde hath no pease.
Hye Way to the Spyttell Hous, n. d.

SNUDGE-SNOWT. A low dirty fellow.

SNUE. To sneer at any one. *North.*

SNUFF. (1) " To spite, to anger, to take a matter in *snuffe*," Hollyband's Dictionarie, 1593. We now have the phrase " up to snuff," implying great acuteness or penetration.

The broad-fac'd jests that other men put on you,
You take for favours well bestow'd upon you.
In sport they give you many a pleasant cuffe,
Yet no mans lines but mine you take in *snuffe*.
Taylor's Laugh and be Fat, p. 69.

Took *snuff* and posted up to heaven again,
As to a high court of appeal, to bee
Reveng'd on men for this indignitie.
Fletcher's Poems, p. 184.

And whereas if in *snuff* and distaste you may fling away from such *re infecta*, a little patience and good words may do your business, and send you away with what you come for.
A Cap of Gray Hairs for a Green Head, 1688, p. 112.

SNUFFERS. (1) Small open dishes for holding snuff, sometimes made of silver. They were also called snuff-dishes. The latter term was likewise applied to small receptacles for placing snuffers in.

(2) Snuffers for the nose, i. e. nostrils.

SNUFFKIN. A small muff used by ladies in cold weather. " One of their snuffkins or muffes, called so in times past when they used to play with it for feare of being out of countenance," Cotgrave in v. *Contenance*. See also in v. *Grace, Manchon.* " A snufkin that women use, *bonne grace, manchon*," Howell.

SNUFFLING. Low; mean; sneaking.

SNUFF-PEPPER. To take offence.

SNUFT. " A snuft or smoky paper, *papier bruslant, fumeux*," Howell.

SNUFTER. To snort. See *Snurt.*

SNUG. Tight; handsome. *Lanc.*

SNUGGERY. A snug little place.

SNUGGLE. To nestle. *East.*

SNURLD. Swelled; applied to the udder of a cow when swelled with milk immediately after calving. *Beds.*

SNURLE. A cold in the head. *Suffolk.*

SNURLES. Nostrils. *North.*

SNURT. To snort. Cotgrave has, " *Esbroüé*, snurted or snuftered." Also, to turn up the nose in contempt.

One *snurts* tobacco, as his nose were made
A perfum'd jakes for all scurrilities.
The Minte of Deformities, 1600.

SNUSKIN. A delicate morçeau. *East.*

SNUZZLE. To cuddle. *Var. dial.*

SNY. (1) A number, or quantity. *North.*

(2) To stow together. *North.*

(3) To scorn; to sneer at. *Lanc.*

(4) To cut. (*Hem.*)

Let falchion, polax, launce, or halbert try,
With Flemings-knives either to steake or *snye*,
I'll meet thee naked to the very skin,
And stab with pen-knives Cæsars wounds therein.
Rowland's Knave of Clubbs, 1611.

SNYT.

At the same instante time, their fell a small *snyt* or snow, which by vyolence of the wynd was driven into the faces of them which were of Kyng Henries parte, so that their sight was somwhat blemeshed and minished. *Hall, Henry VI.* f. 100.

SO. (1) A large tub, holding from twenty to thirty gallons, and carried by two men on a stang or pole is called a *so*. *Linc.* The spelling by the municipal authorities is *soa*. " Soo a vessell, *coue*," Palsgrave. " A soo, soe, sow, saw, a tub with two ears to carry on a stang or coul-staff. *Bor.* So in Bedfordshire, what we call a *coul* and a *coul-staff*, they call a *sow* and a *sow-stang*," Kennett, MS.

Hwan he havede eten inow,
He kam to the welle, water up drow,
And filde the a michel *so*.
Havelok, 933.

(2) As; so. (*A.-S.*)

Allas! thi lovesum eyghen to
Loketh *so* man doth on his fo.
Sir Orpheo, ed. Laing, 74.

(3) Pregnant. *Glouc.* She is *how come you so*, i. e. enceinte.

(4) Thereabouts. *Var. dial.*

(5) Saw. Robson, p. 77.

SOA. Be still. *Yorksh.*

SOAK. (1) A land-spring. *West.*

(2) To sit lazily over the fire. *Devon.*

(3) To bake thoroughly. *East.* In some counties, to become dry.

SOAKING-DOE. A barren doe, that going over the year is fat, when other does have fawns. *North.*

SOAKY. Effeminate. *Devon.*

SOAL. (1) A dirty pond. *Kent.*

(2) In coal pits and mines, especially in Somersetshire, the bottom of the work is called the *soal.* Kennett, MS. Lansd. 1033.

SOAM. (1) A short rope used to pull the tram in a coal mine. *North.*

(2) A horse-load. *West.*

(3) A trace used in ploughing, generally made of iron. *North.*

SOAMY. Moist and warm. *Yorksh.*

SOAP. A small taste or quantity of any liquid; a sup. *North.*

SOAP-TO. To exchange. *Craven.*

SOARE. A deer in its fourth year. See Harrison's Descr. England, p. 226.

SOB. (1) To frighten. *Linc.*

(2) To sop, or suck up. *Suffolk.* Perhaps *sob* in the old copies of the Comedy of Errors, iv. 3, means *sop.*

SOBBED. Soaked with wet. *Warw.*

SOBBLE. To beat severely. *North.*

SOBER. Was formerly applied to moderation in eating as well as drinking.

SOBERTE. Sobriety; seriousness.

For al the day than wyl they be
Before here maysters yn *soberté*.
MS. Harl. 1701, f. 48.

Also what es pacyence and clennes, rightwysnes, chastyté, and *sobirté*, and swylke other.
MS. Lincoln A. i. 17, f. 227.

SOBRESAULT. A summerset. (*Fr.*) "*Soubresault,* a sobresault," Cotgrave.

SOCAGE. An ancient tenure by which the tenants were obliged to cultivate the lands of their lord. See Lambarde's Perambulation, 1596, p. 529.

SOCCATED. Put into sockets.
Standing upon two whyte marble colums or pillers, *soccated* in two foote-stepps of black marble, well polished. *Archæologia,* x. 404.

SOCCHETRE. A woodlouse.
For the stone, take *socchetres,* that is a worme with many feete, that ben under stones on walles, that wollen whan they be touchid make hemself rounde; and wassh hem clene, &c.
MS. Med. Rec. xv. Cent.

SOCE. Friends; companions. A farmer would address his workpeople in this way. *Somerset.*

SOCIATION. Companionship. (*Lat.*)
All naked is their conversation,
And arme in arme theyr *sociation.*
Loves Owle, 1595.

SOCK. (1) The drainage of a farmyard. Hence *sock-pit,* the receptacle of such drainage.
(2) A heavy fall of rain. *East.*
(3) A ploughshare. "Socke of a plough, *soc de la cherue,*" Palsgrave, f. 65.

SOCKET-PIKLE. A kind of iron hook.

SOCKETS. Large pieces of plate armour, sometimes put on the side of the saddle at tournaments, through which the legs were thrust, that they might protect the thighs. *Meyrick.*

SOCKHEAD. A stupid fellow. *Sussex.*

SOCKIE. A sloven. *Northumb.*

SOCK-LAMB. A pet lamb. *Sussex.*

SOCKY. Moist, as ground is. *East.*

SOCOUR. Succour; help. *Socourabill,* helping, assistant. (*A-S.*)
Thane syr Percevelle the wight
Bare downe the blake knyght;
Thane was the lady so bright
His best *socour* in telde. *Perceval,* 1920.
Frendly and al passyng of franchyse,
Reiever to the pore and *socourabill*
Ben ye, and werry foo to coveytise.
MS. Fairfax, 16.

SODBANK. By this elegant expression the fishermen of Skegness and the adjoining villages on the coast, designate a species of the mirage, which in fine calm weather is seen by them in perfection. On these occasions, the sea is like glass: and the horizon is bounded, as it were, by a high dark wall, upon which may be secn, highly magnified, every object on the water. *Linc.*

SODDEN. Boiled. Sometimes *sodde.*
Also they saye that all maner flesshe and fysshe is better rosted than *soden,* and if they be *soden,* to broyle on a grydeyron, or on the coles, and they ben the more holsomer.
The Compost of Ptholomeus, n. d.

SODDEN-WHEAT. The same as *Frumenty,* q.v.

SODDER. To boil slowly. *North.*

SODDY. Heavy: sad. *North.*

II.

SODEKYN. A subdeacon. (*A.-N.*)
And also with Seynt Elmiston when he dede dwelle,
Ordour of *sodekyn* forsothe he hade.
Chron. Vilodun. p. 6.

SODENE. A subdean. (*A.-N.*)
Executours and *sodenes,*
Somonours and hir lemmannes.
Piers Ploughman, p. 303.

SODENLY. Suddenly. (*A.-S.*)
How *sodenly* that tym he was compellid to perte
To the felde of Barnet with his enmys to fyghte;
God lett never prynce be so hevy in his herte
As Kynge Edwarde was all that hole nyзte !
And aftur that shone a ster over his hede full bryзte,
The syght of the wiche made his enmys woo !
Yt was a tokyn of victory, Goddis will was soo !
MS. Bibl. Reg. 17 D. xv.
For he that casteth hym to do a dede,
More penaunce he mote have nede,
Then he that doth hyt *sodenlyche,*
And afterward hym reweth myche.
MS. Cott. Claud. A. ii. f. 146.

SODGER. (1) A soldier. *Var. dial.* "A soger of the armé," Chronicon Mirab. p. 109.
(2) The shell fish whelk. *East.*

SODS. (1) A canvas or coarse packsaddle stuffed with straw. *North.*
(2) Small nails. *Somerset.*

SOFFERE. To suffer; to permit.
Soffere hem to make no bere,
But ay to be in here prayere.
MS. Cott. Claud. A. ii. f. 130.

SOFT. (1) Silly; foolish. *Var. dial.* Its ancient meaning was *effeminate.*
(2) Moist, mild, said of the weather. *North.* In the following passage it means *warm.* The weather is said to be *soft* when likely to rain, and rain-water is called *soft-water,* whilst spring-water is distinguished as *hard.*
In a somer seson,
Whan *softe* was the sonne.
Piers Ploughman, p. 1.
(3) Gently; easily. The word is common in old plays, introduced as an ejaculation in cases of small surprise, a sudden change in the conversation, &c. "Soft, softe, the chylde is aslepe, *tout bellement, lenfant est endormy,*" Palsgrave, verb. f. 142.
Why, how now! how, what wight is this
On home we now have hit?
Softe, let me se: this same is he,
Ye, truly, this is Wit!
Mariage of Witt and Wisdome, 1579.

SOFTEN. To thaw. *North.*

SOFT-LAES. Bays formed by the waves in the softer parts of the cliffs. *Hartlepool.*

SOFTNET. A foolish fellow. *North.*

SOG. (1) A blow. *West.*
(2) A quagmire. *Devon.* Land saturated with water is said to be *sogged.*

SO-GATES. In such a manner. (*A.-S.*)

SOGER. A sea-insect that takes possession of the shell of another fish. *I. of Wight.*

SOGET. A subject. (*A.-N.*)
Kes me, leman, and love me,
And I thi *soget* wil i-be. *Sevyn Sages,* 458

SOGGIE. Full of flesh. *Northumb.*

SOGGY. Wet; moist; swampy. *West.* Jon-

49

son mentions " this green and *soggy* multitude," ii. 120.

SOGH. A slumber. *Devon.*

SOGHTE. Paid homage to. *Mason.*

SO-HOW. A cry in hunting, when the hare was found. " Sohowe, the hare ys fownde, *boema, lepus est inventus*," Pr. Parv. The phrase was also used in hawking. " A so-hoe to make a hawk stoop to the lure," Howell.

> When they loken toward me,
> I loke asyde, I lurke fulle lowe ;
> The furst man that me may see,
> Anon he cryes, so howe, so howe !
> *MS. Cantab.* Ff. v. 48, f. 109.

SOHUTE. Sought.

> The thurst him dede more wo,
> Then hevede rather his hounger do.
> Over al he ede and *sohute ;*
> On aventure his wilt him brohute
> To one putte wes water inne,
> That wes I-maked mid grete ginne.
> *Relig. Antiq.* ii. 273.

SOIGNE. Care. (*A.-N.*)

SOIL. (1) To assoil. *Palsgrave.*

(2) A rafter for a house. *North.*

(3) The fry of the coal-fish. *Cumb.*

(4) To strain liquor. *Yorksh.*

(5) To feed cattle with mown grass, or other green food. *Var. dial.* Forby says, " to fatten completely."

> In the spring time give your younger horses bullimung for many dales together, for that will not onely make them fat, but also purge their bellies ; for this purgation is most necessary for horses, which is called *soyling*, and ought to continue ten dales together, without any other meat, giving them the eleventh day a little barly, and so forward to the fourteneth ; after which day, continue them in that diet ten dales longer, and then bring them forth to exercise a little, and when as they sweat, annoint them with oyle, and if the weather bee colde, keepe a fire in the stable ; and you must remember when the horsse beginneth to purge, that he be kept from barley and drinke, and give him greene meat, or bullimung, wherof that is best that groweth neare the sea-side.
> *Topsell's Four-Footed Beasts*, 1607, p. 339.

(6) To take soil, a term in ancient hunting for taking water.

> When Remond left her, Remond then unkinde,
> Fida went downe the dale to seeke the hinde,
> And found her taking *soyle* within a flood.
> *Browne's Britannia's Pastorals*, p. 84.

(7) To explain or resolve a doubt.

SOILET. Be quiet ; go off quickly. *Yorksh.*

SOILING. " A soiling, a great opening or gaping of the earth, as it were a deepenesse without bottome," Baret, 1580.

SOILS. Window sills. *Mason.*

SOILURE. Defilement. *Shak.*

SOILYNESS. Filthiness. *Palsgrave.*

SO-INS. In such a manner. *East.*

SOITY. Dirty ; dark with dirt.

> His helme appone his heved was sett,
> And bothe fulle *soyty* were.
> *MS. Lincoln* A. I. 17, f. 104.

SOJOUR. Stay ; abode. (*A.-N.*)

SOJURNAUNT. An entertainer ; the host.

SOKE. A privilege, lordship, franchise ; land held by socage. *Phillips.* Holloway explains *soke*, an exclusive privilege claimed by millers of grinding all corn which is used within the manor or township wherein their mills stand. *North.* Originally from A.-S. *soc*, whence is derived the Law-Latin word *soca*, a liberty or franchise of holding a court, and exercising other jurisdiction over the socmen or soccage tenants within the extent of such an honor or manor. See Kennett, p. 134.

SOKELING. A suckling, as a suckling plant, a young animal, &c. *Palsgrave.*

SOKEN. (1) A toll. (*A.-S.*)

> Gret *soken* had this meller, out of doute.
> With whete and malt, of al the lond aboute.
> *Wright's Anecdota Literaria*, p. 26.

(2) A district held by tenure of socage. (*A.-S.*)

> In the country hard was we
> That in our *soken* shrews should be.
> *Blount's Law Dict.* in v. *Rime.*

SOKER. Help ; assistance. Also, to help, to succour. " *Faveo*, to sokery," MS. Vocabulary, xv. Cent.

> Meche folke of that contré
> Come hether for *soker* of me.
> *Torrent of Portugal*, p. 39.

SOKEREL. A child not weaned.

SOKET. The pointed end of a lance ?

> Gaheriet mett the douke Samiel
> With a launce, the *soket* of stiel.
> *Arthour and Merlin*, p. 206.

> With a *soket* of kene stel,
> Octiater in the scheld he gret.
> *Kyng Alisaunder*, 4415.

SOKIL-BLOME. This is translated by *locusta* in my copy of the Nominale MS.

SOKINGLY. Suckingly ; gently.

SOL. The term given by the ancient alchemists to gold. Silver was called *luna*.

SOLACE. (1) In the language of printers, a penalty or fine. *Holme.*

(2) Consolation ; recreation. (*A.-N.*) *Solacious*, affording recreation.

> Then dwellyd they bothe in fere,
> Wyth alle maner deynteys that were dere,
> Wyth alle on every syde.
> *MS. Cantab.* Ff. ii. 38, f 82.

> Gli bileft in court atte mete
> Him to play und *solauci.*
> *Gy of Warwike*, p. 131.

> Hit was a game of gret *solas*,
> Hit comford alle that ever ther was,
> Therof thai were noght sade.
> *MS. Cantab.* Ff. v. 48, f. 50.

> All that wyll of *solas* lere,
> Herkyns now, and ye schall here.
> *MS. Ashmole* 61, f. 59.

> Eke Joun Maundevyle, knyth of Ynglond, after
> his labour made a book ful *solacious* onto his nacyon.
> *MS. Bodl.* 423, f. 355.

SOLDADO. A soldier. (*Span.*)

SOLDIER. (1) To bully ; to hector. *East.*

(2) The sea-tortoise. Topsell, 1608.

SOLDIER'S-THIGH. An empty pocket.

SOLD-UP. When a man has become bankrupt or insolvent, he is said to be *sold up. Var. dial.*

SOLE. (1) A pond. *Kent.*

(2) The floor of an oven. *Linc.* In building,

the lowest part of anything. See Davies'
Rites, ed. 1672, p. 44.

(3) A collar of wood, put round the neck of
cattle to confine them to the stelch. " A
bowe about a beestes necke," Palsgrave.

(4) To handle rudely ; to haul or pull ; to pull
one's ears. *Devon.*

(5) A stake such as is driven into ground to fasten
up hurdles to. *West.*

(6) " To sole a bowl, *probe et rite emittere
globum,*" Coles' Lat. Dict.

(7) The seat or bottom of a mine, applied to
horizontal veins or lodes.

SOLEIN. (1) One ; single. (2) Sullen.
(3) A meal for one person.

SOLEMPNE. Solemn. (*A.-N.*)

> Hym that breketh *solempne* vow,
> Or chawnge hyt wole, sende hym forth now.
> *MS. Cott. Claud. A. ii. f. 148.*

SOLENT-SEA. The old name of the narrow
strait between Hampshire and Isle of Wight.

SOLER. An upper room, a loft or garret.
" *Solarium,* an upper room, chamber, or garret, which in some parts of England is still
called a sollar," Kennett, p. 134. Till within
the last few years the term was common in
leases. " Body, wher aren thy *solers,* thi
castles, ant thy toures," W. Mapes, p. 347.

> In a *soler* was in that toun
> A childe cast another doun.
> *Cursor Mundi, MS. Coll. Trin. Cantab. f. 76.*
> Hastily than went thai all,
> And soght him in the maydens hall,
> In chambers high, es noght at hide,
> And in *solers* on ilka side.
> *Ywaine and Gawin,* 897.

> In the side bynethe thou shalt make *solers,* and
> placis of thre chaumbris in the schip.
> *Wickliffe's Bible, MS. Bodl. 277.*

> Hey, ne oten, ne water clere,
> Boute be a kord of a *solere.*
> *Beves of Hamtoun,* p. 61.

SOLES. Sills of a window.

SOLE-TREE. A piece of wood belonging to
stowces, to draw ore up from the mine. *Derb.*

SOLEYNE. One left alone. (*A.-N.*)

> To muse in his philosophye,
> *Soleyne* withoute companye.
> *Gower, MS. Soc. Antiq.* 134, f. 92.

SOLFE. To call over the notes of a tune by
their proper names.

> Ya, bi God ; thu reddis. and so it is wel werre.
> I *solfe* and singge after. and is me nevere the nerre ;
> I horle at the notes. and heve hem al of herre.
> *Reliq. Antiq.* i. 292.

SOLICIT. To be solicitous.

SOLID. Grave ; serious. *Var. dial.*

SOLINGERE. Conjectured by Mr. Wright to
be an error for *losingere,* and I have scarcely
any doubt of it, but in the possibility of its
being genuine in the same sense I give it insertion. (*A.-N.*)

> But yet my witte is in a were
> Wheither ye shall fynde that *solingere.*
> *Chester Plays,* i. 180.

SOLLE. A soul. " *Anima,* Anglice a solle,"
MS. Vocabulary, xv. Cent.

SOLLERETS. Pieces of steel which formed
part of the armour for the feet.

SOLLOP. To lollop about. *East.*

SOLMAS-LOAF. Bread given away to the poor
on All Souls' Day. *North.* Mr. Hunter has
somas-cake, a sweet cake made on the second
of November, and always in a triangular form.

SOLNE. To sing by note. (*A.-N.*)

> I have be preest and parson
> Passynge thritty wynter,
> And yet can I neyther *solne* ne synge,
> Ne seintes lyves rede.
> *Piers Ploughman,* p. 109.

SOLOMONS-SEAL. A plant.

> In the woods about the Devises growes *Solomons-
> seals,* also goates-rue, as also that admirable plant
> scilicet lily-convally.
> *Aubrey's Wilts, MS. Royal Soc.* p. 121.

SOLOTACION. Solitude.

> Nowe seith I am soe solempe,
> And sett in my *solotaciun.* *Chester Plays,* i. 9.

SOLOWED. Soiled. *Prompt. Parv.*

> Heere ne nayles never grewe,
> Ne *solowed* clothes ne turned hewe.
> *MS. Harl.* 1701, f. 61.

SOLSEKILLE. The plant *solsequium.* It is
mentioned in MS. Linc. Med. f. 283.

SOLTCH. A heavy fall. *Lanc.*

SOLUBLE. " Soluble, as one that is costyfe
solluble," Palsgrave, adj. f. 96.

SOLVEGE. A term of reproach. *Devon.*

SOLWY. Sullied ; defiled. (*A.-N.*)

SOLY. Solely. *Park.*

SOMDEL. Somewhat ; in some measure. (*A.-S.*)

SOME. (1) Thus used as a termination, two-
some, threesome, &c. *North.*

(2) Applied to figures it means *about.* Some
ten, i. e. about ten. *West.*

SOMEAT. Something. *West.*

SOMEN. Samen ; together.

SOMER. A sumpter horse. (*Fr.*)

> Cartes and *somers* ous beth binome,
> And alle our folk is overcome.
> *Arthour and Merlin,* p. 181.

> Men chargyd charys and *somers,*
> Knyghtys to hors and squyers.
> *MS. Cantab. Ff.* ii. 38, f. 107.

> The monke hath fifty-two men,
> And seven *somers* full stronge,
> There rydeth no bysshop in this londe
> So ryally, I understond. *Robin Hood,* i. 39.

SOMER-CASTELLE. A temporary wooden
tower on wheels used in ancient sieges, on
board vessels of war, &c. " Sommer-castell
of a shyppe," Palsgrave, subst. f. 65.

> With *somer-castelle* and sowe appone sere halfes.
> *Morte Arthure, MS. Lincoln,* f. 85.

SOMERLAND. Ground that lies fallow all the
summer. *Kent.* The term occurs in the
Prompt. Parv. translated by *novale.*

SOMERS. The rails of a cart. " Somers or
rathes of a wayne or carte," Palsgrave.

SOMERSAULT. A summerset. " A lepe of a
tombler, *sobersault,*" Palsgrave.

> First that could make love faces, or could do
> The valters *sombersaults,* or us'd to wooe
> With hoiting gambols, his own bones to break
> *Donne's Poems,* p. 300.

SOMETOUR. A sumpter-man.

SOME-WHEN. At some time. *South.*

SOMME. Sum; amount. (*A.-N.*)

> Sexty myle on a daye, the *somme* es bott lyttille,
> Thowe moste spede at the spurs, and spare noghte
> thi fole. *Morte Arthure, MS. Lincoln, f. 58.*

SOMMERED. Tart, as ale, &c. *West.*

SOMNOUR. A summoner, apparitor.

> The thryde *somnour* to this rykynge is deeth,
> and the condicion of deth is this, &c.
> *Wimbolton's Sermon, 1388, MS. Hatton 57, p. 23.*

SOMONE. To summon. (*A.-N.*)

SOMPNOLENCE. Drowsiness.

> So that I hope in suche a wise
> To love for to ben escused
> That I no *sompnolence* have usid.
> *Gower, MS. Soc. Antiq. 134, f. 121.*

> The flemnatik is *sompnolent* and slowe,
> Withe humours groos replit ay habundaund.
> *MS. Cantab. Ff. i. 6, f. 140.*

SOMURBOYDE. A kind of insect? " *Pole-micta*, a somurboyde," Nominale MS.

SONANCE. Sound. *Heywood.*

SONAYLIE. Sounding; loud.

> And of thy love telle me playne,
> If that thy glorye hath be *sonaylie.*
> *Gower, MS. Soc. Antiq. 134, f. 56.*

SONCIE. Fortunate. It is translated by *fœlix* in Synonomorum Sylva, 1627, p. 248. It is still in use, and also used in the sense of pleasant, agreeable, plump, fat, and cunning.

SONDAY. Sunday.

> Hast thow eten any *Sonday*
> Withowte haly bred ? Sey ye or nay.
> *MS. Cott. Claud. A. ii f. 144.*

SONDE. (1) Sand. (*A.-S.*)

> A gode schypp ther they fonde,
> And sayled over bothe wawe and *sonde.*
> *MS. Cantab. Ff. ii. 38, f. 152.*

(2) A message; a sending. (*A.-S.*) "Thruw Godes sonde," MS. Harl. 2398, f. 8.

> I am thy forefader, Wylliam of Normandye,
> To see thy welefare here through Goddys *sond.*
> *MS. Lambeth 306, f. 132.*

> So befelle, thorow Goddis *sonde,*
> The bisshop that was of that londe
> Prechid in that cité.
> *MS. Cantab. Ff. v. 48, f. 45.*

> Swythe sende he hys *sonde*
> To alle men of hys londe.
> *MS. Cantab. Ff. ii. 38, f. 156.*

SONDRELY. Peculiarly. (*A.-S.*)

SONDRINESS. Diversity. *Palsgrave.*

SONE. (1) Soon. (2) A son. (*A.-S.*)

> And whenne the gospel ys i-done,
> Teche hem eft to knele downe *sone.*
> *MS. Cott. Claud. A. ii. f. 130.*

SONGEWARIE. The interpreting of dreams.

SONGLE. " A handful of leased corn after it has been tied up." Still used in Herefordshire. See a paper by Sir Edmund W. Head, Bart. in the Classical Museum, No. 4, p. 55, and Wilbraham, in v. *Songow.* " *Conspico*, to glene or els to gadyre songles," Medulla. " Songal or songle, so the poor people in Herefordshire call a handfull of corn gleaned or leazed; and probably may come from the Fr. *sengle*, a girth, because, when their hand is full, they bind or gird it about with some of the ends of

the straw, and then begin to gather a new one," Blount, p. 600.

SONIZANCE. Sounding. Peele, iii. 148.

SONKE. Sung.

> And therto of so good mesure
> He *sonke*, that he the bestes wilde
> Made of his note tame and mylde.
> *Gower, MS. Soc. Antiq. 134, f. 37.*

SONKEN. Sunk. (*A.-S.*)

SONN. To think deeply. *Cumb.*

SONNE. The sun. (*A.-S.*)

SONNISH. Like the sun. (*A.-S.*)

SONTROSS. A term of reproach. *Devon.*

SOO. The same as *So,* q. v.

SOODLE. To go unwillingly. *North.*

SOOK. A call for pigs, used when they are called to their food. *Devon.*

SOOL. Anything eaten with bread. *North.* Anything used to flavour bread, such as butter, cheese, &c. is called *sowl* in Pembrokeshire. " Tytter want ye *sowlle* then sorow," Towneley Myst. p. 87. Hence comes *soul*, q. v. " *Edulium*, Anglice sowylle," Nominale MS. xv. Cent.

> Kam he nevere hom hand bare,
> That he ne broucte bred and *sowel.*
> *Havelok, 767.*

SOOM. (1) To swim. *North.*

(2) To drink a long draught, with a sucking noise of the mouth. *Leic.*

SOON. (1) The evening. *West.*

(2) An amulet. *Cornw.*

SOOND. To swoon; to faint. *Cumb.*

SOONER. A spirit; a ghost. *Dorset.*

SOOP. A sweep. *North.*

SOOPERLOIT. Play time; any time set apart for pleasure or recreation. *South.*

SOOPLE. The heavy end of a flail, the part which strikes the corn. *North.*

SOOR. Mud; dirt; filth.

SOORD. The sword or skin of bacon.

SOORT. To punish. *Somerset.*

SOOTE. Sweet.

> And bathed hem and freisshid hem in the fresssh river,
> And drunken waters that were *soote* and clere.
> *MS. Digby 230.*

> The grete fairenesse nought appaire may
> On violettes and on herbes *soote.*
> *Lydgate, MS. Ashmole 39, f. 29.*

SOOTERING. Courting. *Devon.*

SOOTERKIN. It was fabled in ridicule of the Dutch women, that, making so great use of stoves, and often putting them under their petticoats, they engendered a kind of animal which was called a *sooterkin.*

> For knaves and fools b'ing near of kin,
> As Dutch boors are t'a *sooterkin.*
> *Hudibras, III. ii. 146.*

SOOTH. Truth. (*A.-S.*)

SOOTHFAST. Entirely true.

SOOTHLE. To walk lamely. *Midl. C.*

SOO-TRE. A stang, or cowl-staff.

SOOTY. Foul with soot. (*A.-S.*)

SOP. (1) *A sop in the pan*, a piece of bread soaked in the dripping under the meat. *Var. dial.*

(2) A hard blow. *Devon.*

(3) *Soppus of demayn*, strengthening draughts or viands. *Robson.*

SOPE. (1) A jot, or small quantity. *North.* " Never a sope," Palsgrave. A sup, or hasty repast. " A sope, a sup or supping, as a sope of milk, drink, &c." Kennett MS.

Tase a *sope* in the toure, and taryes no langere,
Bot tournes tytte to the kynge, and hym wyth tunge telles. *Morte Arthure, MS. Lincoln, f. 73.*

(2) A silly fellow. *Linc.*

SOPERE. Supper. Nominale MS.

In the way he sye come there
A pylgryme sekeynge hys *sopere.*
MS. Cantab. Ff. ii. 38, f. 156.

SOPHEME. A sophism. (*A.-N.*)

In polsie in *sopheme* reson hydes.
MS. Cantab. Ff. ii 38, f. 23.

SOPOSARE. One who guesses. *Pr. Parv.*

SOPPE. A company, or body ?

Sodanly in a *soppe* they sett in att ones,
Foynes faste att the fore breste with flawmande swerdes.
Morte Arthure, MS. Lincoln, f. 69.

SOPPER. A state of confusion. *North.*

SOPPY. As when mown grass lies in lumps upon the field. *Yorksh.*

SOPS. (1) Small detached clouds hanging about the sides of a mountain. *North.*

(2) Lumps of black-lead. *Cumb.*

(3) Tufts of green grass in the hay, not properly dried. *North.*

SOPS-AND-ALE. A curious custom prevalent at Eastbourne, Sussex, described in Hone's Every-day Book, ii. 693.

SOPS-IN-WINE. Pinks.

The pinke, the primrose, cowslip, and daffadilly,
The hare-bell blue, the crimson cullumbine,
Sage, lettis, parsley, and the milke-white lilly,
The rose and speckled flowre, cald *sops-in-wine,*
Fine pretie king-cups, and the yellow bootes,
That growes by rivers and by shallow brookes.
The Affectionate Shepheard, 1594.

SOR. (1) A wooden tub, used by brewers, or by housewives to wash their best glasses in. *Linc.*

(2) Sorrow. (*A.-S.*)

Ther was sobbing, siking, and *sor,*
Handes wringing, and drawing bi hor.
Havelok, 234.

SORANCE. Soreness.

The moist malady is that which we call the glanders : the dry maladie is an incurable consumption, which some perhaps would call the mourning of the cheine, but not rightly, as shall well appeare unto .you heereafter. The malady of the joynts comprehendeth al griefes and *sorances* that be in the joyntes. *Topsell's Four-Footed Beasts, 1607, p. 341.*

SORB. " Sorbe a kynde of frute, *sorbe,*" Palsgrave, 1530.

SORCATE. A surcoat.

To on-arme hym the knyghte goys,
In cortyls, *sorcatys,* and schorte clothys.
MS. Cantab. Ff. ii. 38, f. 70.

SORDIOUS. Filthy. (*Lat.*)

The ashes of earth-wormes duely prepared, cleanseth *sordious,* stinking and rotten ulcers, consuming and wasting away their hard lippes, or callous edges, if it be tempered with tarre and Simblian hony, as Pliny affirmeth. Dioscerides saith, that

the hony of Sicilia was taken for that *of* Simblia in his time. *Topsell's Historie of Serpents,* p. 311.

SORDS. Filth ; fluid refuse. *East.*

SORE. (1) A flock of mallards.

(2) A hawk in her first year was said to be " in her *sore* age." Spenser mentions a *soare faulcon.* The term was occasionally applied to the young of other animals.

(3) To soar. *Chaucer.*

(4) Very ; exceedingly. *Var. dial.*

(5) Vile ; worthless ; sad. *Var. dial.*

(6) Grieved. *Syr Gawayne.*

SOREGHES. Sorrows. (*A.-S.*) It occurs in MS. Cotton. Vespas. D. vii.

SORELL. A young buck. *Palsgrave.* It is properly one in its third year.

SORE-STILL. Implacable.

SORFE. A kind of wood, mentioned in Harrison's Descr. of England, p. 212.

SORFET. Surfeit.

Telle me, sone, anon ryght here,
Hast thow do *sorfet* of mete and drynke?
MS. Cott. Claud. A. ii. f. 143.

SORGARSHOT. Sacar shot. Meyrick, iii. 45.

SORGER. More sorrowful. *Linc.*

SORHET. Soreness. Arch. xxx. 413.

SOROWE. Sorry ; evil.

He wyll not come yet, sayd the justyce,
I dare well undertake.
But in *sorowe* tyme for them all
The knyght came to the gate.
Robin Hood, i. 19.

SOROWLES. Without sorrow. *Pr. Parv.*

SORPORRED. Cloyed ; surfeited.

SORREL. Chestnut-coloured, as applied to a horse, though not well described by either word. The Suffolk breed of cart-horse is uniformly *sorrel,* and some two score years ago was as uniformly so described—now chestnut is sometimes used. " The sorrel horse" is not an uncommon sign for an alehouse. In Aubrey's Lives, written about 1680, the word is used in a description of the person of Butler, author of Hudibras—" a head of sorrell haire." Moor, p. 376.

SORROPE. Syrup. " Soutteries in *sorrope*," Reliq. Antiq. i. 85, xv. Cent.

SORROW. Sorrel. *South.*

SORRY. A kind of pottage. *Holme.*

And blobsterdis in white *sorré*
Was of a nobulle curry. *Ballad of the Feest.*

SORT. (1) Set, or company. Very common in old books, but now obsolete, except in a few counties. Forby explains it " a great number."

(2) Chance ; lot ; destiny. (*A.-N.*)

(3) To approach ; to tend towards.

Doubt not Castania, I my selfe dare absolutely promise thee, that thy love shall *sort* to such happie successe, as thou thy selfe doest seeke for.
Greene's Gwydonius, 4to. Lond. 1593.

(4) Rank or degree in life. *Sortance,* suitable degree or rank.

They liv'd together in godlie *sorte,*
Fortie five years with good reporte.
Epitaph at St. Albans, A.D. 1613.

(5) *A thing of a sort,* a corresponding thing. *Words of a sort,* a quarrel.

(6) To suit; to fit; to select. *Shak.*

SORTELEGYE. Fortune-telling. (*Fr.*)

> Oft giled was this brode,
> And yerned bataill al' for wode,
> For Merlins prophe-ie,
> And oft for *sortelegye*.
> *Appendix to Walter Mapes, p. 352.*

SORT'EM-BILLYORT'EM. A Lancashire game, very similar to that known as *Hot peas and bacon.*

SORTIE. " It's *sortie* time," i. e. time for breaking up. This phrase is used by the children at High Hoyland, near Barnsley.

SORTING-CLOTHS. A kind of short cloths, with a blue selvage on both sides of the lists. made in the Eastern counties.

SORTS. A person who is not very well is said to be *out of sorts.*

SORUGHFUL. Sorrowful. (*A.-S.*)

> Synful man, loke up and see
> How reufulll I hyng on rode,
> And of my penaunce have pitee
> With *sorughful* herte and drery mode.
> *MS. Arundel 507, f. 10.*

SORWATORIE. A place of sorrow. *Sorwe,* sorrow, is very common. (*A.-S.*)

SORY. (1) Sorrowful. (*A.-S.*)

(2) Bad; very poor or moderate.

> Thaȝ me say, as they done use,
> *Sory* Laten in here wyse. *MS. Cott. Claud. A. ii. f. 134.*

SORYPPE. Syrup. *Palsgrave.*

SORZLE. Any strange mixture. *East.*

SORȜE. Sorrow. (*A.-S.*)

SO-SAY. The sake of saying a thing. *South.*
" He said it just for the *so-say.*"

SOSS. (1) A heavy fall. *North.*

(2) A mixed mess of food, a collection of scraps. *Var. dial.*

(3) To press very hard. *Yorksh.*

(4) To lap, as a dog. *North.*

(5) To fail violently. *Linc.*

(6) Anything dirty, or muddy. *North.* Also, to go about in the dirt. " Sossing and possing in the durt," Gammer Gurton's Needle. " Of any one that mixes several slops, or makes any place wet and dirty, we say in Kent, he makes a soss," Kennett MS.

(7) To pour out. *Somerset.*

(8) Direct; plump down. *Linc.*

(9) A heavy awkward fellow. " A great, unweldie, long, mishapen, ill-favoured, or ill-fashioned, man or woman; a luske, a slouch; a *sosse,*" Cotgrave.

(10) " Sosse or a rewarde for houndes whan they have taken their game, huuee," Palsgrave.

SOSS-BRANGLE. A slatternly wench. *South.*

SOSSED. Saturated. *Lanc.*

SOSSLE. To make a slop. *Sussex.*

SOST. Rendered dirty. From *Soss* (6).

SOSTREN. Sisters. (*A.-S.*)

SOT. A fool. (*A.-N.*) " Folys and sottys," Skelton, i. 183, wrongly explained.

> Of Tristem and of his lief Isot,
> How he for hire blcom a *sot ;*
> Of Odan and of Amadas,
> How Dydau diȝed for Ennyas.
> *MS. Ashmole 60, xv. Cent.*

SOTE. (1) Sweet. (*A.-S.*)

(2) Soot. *Chaucer.*

(3) Salt. *North.*

SOTED. Fooled; besotted. (*A.-N.*)

SOTH. True. (*A.-S.*)

> Then seid Adam, thou seis *soth,*
> Ȝet I have a morsel for thy toth,
> And ellis I were to blame.
> *MS. Cantab. Ff. v. 48, f. 58.*

SOTHE. Truth. (*A.-S.*)

> Gye answeryd at that case
> Not as the *sothe* was.
> *MS. Cantab. Ff. ii. 38, f. 148*

SOTHEN. Sodden; boiled.

> And all the salt sawsegis that ben *sothen* in Northefolke apon Seyturdaye, be with hus now at owre begynnyng, and helpe hus in owre endyng.
> *Reliq. Antiq. i. 82.*

SOTHER. Truer. (*A.-S.*)

> And the werkman *sother* than hee wende .
> Have of this werke seyde and prophecyed.
> *Lydgate, MS. Soc. Antiq. 134, f. 17.*
>
> For with the Lord is forȝifnesse.
>   I have suffryd, Lord, for thin lawe;
> Unryȝt schal thin lawe redresse,
>   Was nevere seyd non *sothere* sawe :
> Therfore whan thow schalt bodyes blesse,
>   And dede men out here dennys drawe ;
> Jhesu that saverist al swetnesse
>   Lete nevere the feud owre gostis gnawe.
> *Hampole's Paraphrase of the Psalms, MS.*

SOTHERNE. Southern. (*A.-S.*)

SOTHERY. Sweet; savoury.

SOTHFASTNESS. Truth. (*A.-S.*)

> For that they lovyd in *sothefastenes,*
> In grete travell, and many wysche
> Of gode menys lyvys men schulde here.
> *MS. Cantab. Ff. ii. 38, f. 147.*

SOTHNESS. Truth; reality. (*A.-S.*) It occurs in MS. Cott. Vespas. D. vii.

SOTH-SAW. Veracity; true saying.

SOTIE. Folly. (*A.-N.*)

> Bygan, as it was aftir sene,
> Of his *sotie,* and made him wene
> Hit were a womman that he syȝe.
> *Gower, MS. Soc. Antiq. 134, f. 53.*
>
> Than haddest thou the gates stoke
> Fro suche *sotye,* as cometh to wynne
> Thyne hertis wit, whiche is withinne.
> *Gower, MS. Soc. Antiq. 134, f. 41.*

SOTILE. To apply one's cunning or penetration skilfully. (*A.-N.*)

SOTILTEES. Devices made of sugar and paste, formerly much used at feasts. They generally closed every course. See an ancient bill of fare in the Reliq. Antiq. i. 88.

SOTRE. An auditor's office.

SOTTE. A stoat. *Somerset.*

SOTTEFER. A drunkard. *Devon.*

SOTTEL. Subtle; ingenious.

> O glorius God, how thou haste assigned
> Hertes disceveryd to be stablisshyd ayeue !
> In love of matrimonye thou haste them joynyd :
> Kyng Edwarde and the Duke of Claranse gret honour to attayne,
> Thay were dysceveryd be a *sottell* meane,
> Sature (?) hath compellid hem agayne together goo,
> Thus in every thyng, Lorde, thy wille be doo.
> *MS. Bibl. Reg. 17 D. xv.*

SOTTER. To boil gently. *Var. dial.*

SOTULARE. A kind of shoe. (*Lat.*)

SOT-WEED. Tobacco. *Var. dial.*

SOUCE. The head, feet, and ears of swine boiled, and pickled for eating. "I souce meate, I laye it in some tarte thynge, as they do brawne or suche lyke," Palsgrave. It was often sold at tripe-shops, and Forby says the term is applied to the paunch of an animal, usually sold for dogs' meat. "An hogshead of brawne readie *sowsed*," Harrison, p. 222.

> Ah, were we seated in a *sowce-tubs* shade,
> Over our heads of tripes a canople.
> > *A Quest of Enquirie*, 1595.
>
> A quarter of fat lambe, and three score eggs, have beene but an easie colation ; and three well larded pudding-pyes he hath at one time put to foyle, eighteene yards of blacke-puddings (London measure) have suddenly beene imprisoned in his *sowse-tub*.
> > *Taylor's Great Eater of Kent*, p. 145.

SOUCH. To sow. *Somerset.*

SOUCHE. To suspect. (*A.-N.*)

> Fulle often thynke whiche hem ne toucheth,
> But only that here herte *soucheth*
> In hindrynge of another wyȝte.
> > *Gower, MS. Soc. Antiq.* 134, f. 40.
>
> And yf so be myn herte *soucheth*,
> That ouȝte unto my lady toucheth.
> > *Gower, MS. Soc. Antiq.* 134, f. 74.

SOUDAN. A sultan. *Soudannesse*, a sultaness, the wife of a sultan.

SOUDED. Consolidated, fastened. (*A.-N.*)

SOUDES. Wages; pay. (*A.-N.*) In sowd, i. e. in hire, Maundevile's Travels, p. 155.

SOUDLETS. Small bars of iron used for holding or securing glass in windows.

SOUFRECAN. A suffragan. *Palsgrave.*

SOUGH. (1) A buzzing; a hollow murmur or roaring. A Staffordshire labourer said he heard a great *sough* in his ears or head, meaning a sound of a peculiar kind, accompanied with a rushing, buzzing, or singing-like noise. Ben Jonson uses the term, and the form *swough* is common in early English.

(2) The blade of a plough. *Chesh.*

(3) Pronounced *Suff.* An underground drain. *Warw.* The term is used in local acts of parliament; perhaps in public ones. *Soughing tiles*, draining tiles. Drayton has *saugh*, a channel of water. Kennett, p. 22, explains it a wet ditch.

(4) A brewing tub. *Linc.*

SOUGHT-TO. Solicited.

SOUKE. To suck. (*A.-N.*) Still in use in the North of England.

> Ȝef a drope of blod by any cas
> Falle upon the corporas,
> *Souke* hyt up anonryȝt,
> And be as sory as thou myȝt.
> > *MS. Cotton. Claud.* A. ii f. 150.

SOUKINGE-FERE. A foster-brother. (*A.-S.*)

SOUL. (1) To satisfy with food, no doubt derived from *sowel*, or *sool*, q. v.

(2) The black spongy part adhering to the back of a fowl. "Soule of a capon or gose, *ame*," Palsgrave, subst. f. 65.

(3) To soil, or dirty; to stain.

SOULAGE. See *Soutage.*

SOUL-CASE. The body. *North.*

SOUL-CNUL. The passing bell. *Yorksh.* Sawl-knill, MS. Lansd. 1033, f. 356.

> Ac ich am therof glad and blithe,
> That thou art nomen in clene live.
> Thi *soul-cnul* ich wile do ringe,
> And masse for thine soule singe.
> > *Reliq. Antiq.* ii. 277.

SOULDIE. Pay, or wages. (*A.-N.*)

SOULED. Endued with a soul.

SOULE-HELE. Health of the soul.

> And for *soule-hele* y wylle yow teche.
> > *MS. Cantab.* Ff. ii. 38, f. 48.

SOULES-TURNOIS. Silver coins, "whereof ten make a shilling," Harrison, p. 219.

SOULING. To go a-souling, is to go about as boys do, repeating certain rigmarole verses, and begging cakes, or money in commutation for them, the eve of All Souls' Day. These cakes are called Soul-cakes. *Wilbraham.* When the cakes were given, the person who received them said to the benefactor,

> God have your saul,
> Bones and all.
> > *Blount's Glossographia*, ed. 1681, p. 602.

SOULMAS-DAY. All Souls' Day. *Le jour des mors*, Palsgrave, 1530.

SOUL-SILVER. The whole or a part of the wages of a retainer or servant, originally paid in food, but afterwards commuted into a money payment.

SOUN. Sound; noise. (*A.-N.*)

SOUND. (1) A swoon. This word is very common in early English, and is found even as late as the last century in the Vicar of Wakefield, ch. xi.

(2) *As sound as bells*, quite sound.

> Blinde Fortune did so happily contrive,
> That we, *as sound as bells*, did safe arive
> At Dover, where a man did ready stand
> To give me entertainment by the hand.
> > *Taylor's Workes*, 1630, ii. 22.

(3) "Sounde of a fysshe, *cannon*," Palsgrave. Still in use.

(4) "I sownde I appartayne or belong, *je tens.* Thys thyng sowndeth to a good purpose, *ceste chose tent a bonne fin*," Palsgrave.

SOUNDE. To make sound; to heal.

SOUNDER. A herd of wild swine. Twelve make a sounder of wild swine, fifteen a middle sounder, and twenty a great sounder.

> That men calleth a trip of a tame swyn is called of wylde swyn a *soundre*; that is to say, ȝif ther be passyd v. or vj. togedres.
> > *MS. Bodl.* 546.

SOUNDFUL. To prosper. (*A.-S.*)

> And lef of him to-dreve noght sal,
> What swa he dos sal *soundful* al.
> > *MS. Egerton* 614, f. 1.

SOUNDLESS. Bottomless, that cannot be fathomed or sounded.

SOUNDLY. Strongly; severely.

SOUNE. Sound; noise. (*A.-S.*)

> Joly and lyght is your complexicion,
> That steryn ay and kunne nat stonde still ;
> And eke your tonge hath not forgete his *sowne*.
> Quyk, sharp, and swyft is hyt, and lowyd and shill.
> > *MS. Fairfax* 16.

SOUNSAIS.

> Ac ther was non so wise of sight
> That him ther knowe might,
> *Sounsais* he was and lene.
> *Gy of Warwike, p. 406.*

SOUP. To saturate ; to soak. *North.*

SOUPE. To sup. (*A.-N.*)

> And whanne they hadde *soupid* alle,
> The token leve and forth they goo.
> *Gower, MS. Soc. Antiq. 134, f. 52.*

SOUPINGS. Spoonmeat. *East.*

SOUPLE. Supple ; pliant. (*A.-N.*) Still in use in the North of England.

SOUPLEJACK. A cane. *North.*

SOUPY. Wet and swampy. *North.*

SOUR. (1) Coarse, said of grass. *Linc.*

(2) Dirt ; filth. *Prompt. Parv.*

SOUR-ALE. To mend like sour ale in summer, i. e. to get worse instead of getting better. *Var. dial.*

SOUR-AS-SOUR. Very sour. *North.*

SOURD. Deaf. *North.* "A sourd, or deaf emerald, which hath a deadish lustre," Howell, sect. xxvi.

SOURDE. To rise. (*A.-N.*)

SOUR-DOCK. Sorrel. *Lanc.*

SOUR-DOU. Leaven. (*A.-S.*)

SOURE. Wrongly printed and explained in Havelok, 321, "that standeth on the *sei soure*," instead of, " on the *seis ovre*," i. e. on the sea shore, A.-S. *ofer.* It is correctly written in the manuscript.

SOURING. (1) Vinegar. *West.*

(2) Dough left in the tub after the oat-cakes are baked. *North.*

(3) A kind of sour apple.

SOUR-MILK. Buttermilk. *North.*

SOUR-MOLD. The same as *Summer-voy.* q. v.

SOURMONCIE. Predominancy. (*A.-N.*)

SOURS. (1) Onions. *Derb.*

(2) A rise, a rapid ascent ; the source of a stream of water.

SOURSADEL. *Soursadel-reredos* occurs in the records of the expenses of building the royal chapel of St. Stephen's, now the House of Commons. The meaning is unknown.

SOUR-SOP. An ill-natured person. *South.*

SOURST. Soused ; drenched.

> This little barke of ours being *sourst* in cumbersome waves, which never tried the foming maine before. *Optick Glasse of Humors,* 1639, p. 161.

SOUSE. (1) A thump, or blow. *North.*

> Yf he sawe any men or women devoutlye knele
> For to serve God with theyr prayer, or stande,
> Pryvelye behynde them woulde he steale,
> And geve them a *sowce* with hys hande.
> *Roberte the Devyll, p. 11.*

(2) A dip in the water. *Var. dial.*

(3) Down flat ; straight down violently. "He fell right down souse." *Var. dial.* See the seventh meaning. "And *souse* into the foamy main," Webster, iv. 97.

(4) The ear. Still in use.

> With *souse* erect, or pendent, winks, or haws ?
> Sniveling ? or the extention of the jaws ?
> *Fletcher's Poems,* p. 203.

(5) A corbel, in architecture.

(6) To be diligent. *Somerset.*

(7) "Dead, as a fowl at souse," i. e. at the stroke of another bird descending violently on it. So explained by Mr. Dyce, Beaumont and Fletcher, vii. 278. " To leape or seaze greedily upon, to *souze* doune as a hauke," Florio, p. 48, ed. 1611.

SOUSE-CROWN. A silly fellow. *South.*

SOUSED-GURNET. That is, pickled gurnet ; an old phrase of contempt.

SOUT. Sought. (*A.-S.*)

> Dame, so have ich Wilekin *sout*,
> For nou have ich him i-brout. *MS. Digby 86.*

SOUTAGE. Bagging for hops or coarse cloth. More's MS. Additions to Ray's North Country Words. See Tusser, p. 193.

SOUTER. A cobler. (*A.-S.*)

> In a stage playe, the people knowe ryght well that he that playeth in sowdayne is percase a *souter,* yet if one of acquaintaunce perchaunce of litle nurture should call him by his name whyle he standeth in his majestie, one of his tormentours might fortune breake hys head for marryng the play.
> *Hall, Edward V. f. 24.*
> A revette boot trynkele, seyd the *souter,* when he boot of is wyfe thombe harde be the elbow, quod Jack Strawe. *Reliq. Antiq. i. 84.*

SOUTER-CROWN. A stupid person. *Linc.*

SOUTHDENE. A subdean. (*A.-N.*)

SOUTHE. Sought. (*A.-S.*)

SOUTIL. Subtle. "*Protologia,* soutil of speche," Medulla, xv. Cent.

SOVE. Seven. *Somerset.*

SOVENANCE. Remembrance. (*Fr.*)

SOVER. To suffer.

> Yit *sover* hem say and trust ryght we. this,
> A wycked tonge wol alway deme amys.
> *MS. Cantab. Ff. i. 6, f. 196.*

SOVERAINE. Excellent ; in a high degree ; noble. *Soverainly,* above all. (*A.-N.*)

SOVEREIGN. A gold coin formerly worth ten shillings. See Ben Jonson, ii. 205.

SOVEREYNE. (1) A husband.

> The prestis they gone home ajen,
> And sche goth to hire *sovereyne.*
> *Gower, MS. Soc. Antiq. 134, f. 44.*

(2) A provost, or mayor. (*A.-N.*)

> And whanne it drowe to the day of the dede doynge,
> That *sovereynes* were semblid, and the schire knyytis.
> *Deposition of Richard II. p. 28.*

SOVYSTER. " *Sophista,* a sovyster," Nominale MS. This is among the *Nomina dignitatuum clericorum.*

SOW. A head. *Lanc.*

SOWDEARS. Soldiers. Properly, hirelings, those who received pay. (*A.-N.*)

> He seyde, y have goldc y-nogh plente,
> And *sowdears* wyll come to me.
> *Le Bone Florence of Rome, 402.*

SOWDING. Soldering. Arch. xxx. 413.

> Than thay sayen at the laste,
> How the piler stode in bras,
> And with *sowdyng* sowdyt faste.
> *Wright's Sevyn Sages, p. 69.*

SOWDLE. To creep. *Devon.*

SOW-DRUNK. Beastly drunk. *Linc.*

SOWDWORT. Columbine. *Gerard.*

SOWE. (1) A blow. Jamieson, in v. *Sough.*

> Syr Egyllamowre hys swerde owt drowe,
> And to the yeant he gafe a *sowe.*
>   *MS. Cantab.* Ff. ii. 38, f. 64.

(2) To sow. (*A.-S.*) (3) To sew. (*Lat.*)

(4) A woodlouse. Still in use.

> Also geve hym of these *sowes* that crepe with many fete, and falle oute of howce rovys. Also geve hym whyte wormes that breede betwene the barke and the tre.   *MS. Lambeth* 306, f. 177.

(5) A term of reproach for a woman.

(6) An ancient warlike engine, used for battering down the walls of towns, &c.

> And he ordeynde other foure hundreth mene for to bett doune the walles with *sewes* of werre, engynes and gonnes, and other maner of instrumentes of werre.   *MS. Lincoln* A. i. 17, f. 11.

SOWEL. Same as *Sool*, q. v.

SOWENS. A Northumberland dish. The coarse seeds sifted out of oatmeal are put into a tub, and covered with water, which is allowed to stand till it turns sour. A portion of it is then taken out and boiled, and sapped with milk. It forms a jelly-like substance. Hence the proverb to express an impossibility is, " to sap *sowens* with an elsin."

SOWERS. Bucks in their fourth year.

SOWIDE. Strengthened. *Baber.*

SOWIN. A thick paste with which weavers stiffen their warps. *Lanc.*

SOW-KILNS. In the county of Durham the farmers burn *sow-kilns* upon the fields in which the lime is meant to be laid. They are conical or oblong heaps of broken lime, stone. and coal, with flues constructed through the heap, and closely thatched over with sods. A sow of hay is an oblong stack of hay in Scotland, and Sir Walter Scott supposes it is derived from the military engine called the *sow*, above mentioned.

SOWL. (1) To pull about; to pull the ears; to seize by the ears. " To sowl one by the ears," Ray, ed. 1674, p. 44. The word occurs in Shakespeare, and is still in use.

(2) To wash; to duck. *Craven.*

(3) A sull, or plough. *Somerset.*

SOWLE-GROVE. February. *Wilts.* Aubrey gives this phrase, but it does not seem to have continued in use.

SOWLERS. Wild oats.

SOWLOWS. Souls. A broad dialectic pl.

> The hydous bestys in that lake
> Drew nerre the brygge her pray to take;
> Off *sowlows* that fell of that brygge don,
> To swolow hem thei wer ay bon.
>   *Visions of Tundale*, p. 19.

SOWLY. Hot; sultry. *Oxon.*

SOWMES. (1) Traces used in ploughing, generally made of iron. *North.*

(2) Sums?

> The senatour of Sutere, wyth *sowmes* fulle huge,
> Whas assygnede to that courte be sent of his peres.
>   *Morte Arthure, MS. Lincoln,* f. 70.

SOW-MET. A young female pig. *North.*

SOW-METAL. The worst kind of iron.

SOWNYNGE. Sound. (*A.-S.*)

> This lond of Caldee is fulle gret; and the langage

of that contree is more gret in *sownynge* than it is in other parties beyonde the see.
>   *Maundevile's Travels,* 1839, p. 152.

SOWRE.

> To the *sowre* of the reke he soghte at the gayneste,
> Sayned hym sekerly with certayne wordes.
>   *Morte Arthure, MS. Lincoln,* f. 64.

SOWRED. Sourness. Arch. xxx. 413.

SOWSTER. A sempstress. *North.*

SOWT. The rot in sheep. *Westm.*

SOWTHER. To solder. *North.*

SOWTHSELERER. A subcellarer. " *Succellarius*, a sowthselerer," Nominale MS.

SOWZE. Lumps of unworked metal.

> It is the manner (right woorshipfull) of such as seeke profit by minerall, first to set men on woorke to digge and gather the owre; then by fire to trie out the metall, and to cast it into certeine rude lumpes, which they call *sowze.*
>   *Lambarde's Perambulation,* ed. 1596. Pref.

SOWȜE. Saw?

> Of that meyné lafte he noon,
> At the laste that he *sowȝe* uchon.
>   *Cursor Mundi, MS. Coll. Trin. Cantab.* f. 38.

SOYLE. To go away. *Yorksh.*

SOYNEDE. Excused. (*A.-N.*)

> Thare myghte no sydis be *soynede*
> That faghte in those feldis.
>   *MS. Lincoln* A. i. 17, f. 131.

SOYORNE. To sojourn; to remain.

> Sone on the morne, when hyt was day,
> The kyng wolde forthe on hys way
>   To the londe there God was boght;
> Than begane the quene to morne,
> For he wolde no lenger *soyorne*,
>   Prevy sche was in thoght.
>   *MS. Cantab.* Ff. ii. 38, f. 71.

SOYT. Sooth; truth.

> Be mey trowet, thow seys *soyt*, seyde Roben.
>   *Robin Hood,* i. 85.

SOYTE. Company; suite.

> And certane on owre syde, sevene score knyghtes,
> In *soyte* with theire soverayne unsownde are beleved.
>   *Morte Arthure, MS. Lincoln,* f. 94.

SOȜT. Went; departed. *Gawayne.*

SPACE. To measure by paces. *East.*

SPACEFUL. Extensive; wide.

SPACE-LEASER. A respite; a delay.

SPACK. To speak. *North.*

SPACT. Docile; ingenious. *Chesh.*

SPADE. (1) " To call a spade a spade," a phrase applied to giving a person his real character or qualities. Still in use.

> I am plaine, I must needs call *a spade a spade*, a pope a pope.   *Mar-Prelate's Epitome*, p. 2.
> I thinke it good plaine English without fraud,
> To call *a spade a spade*, a bawd a bawd.
>   *Taylor's Workes*, 1630, ii. 92.

(2) A hart in its third year.

(3) The congealed gum of the eye.

(4) To breast-plough. *Devon.*

SPADE-BIT. The quantity of soil raised by one effort of the spade. *North.*

SPADE-BONE. A blade-bone. *Var. dial.* It is called in some places the plate-bone.

SPADE-GRAFT. The depth to which a spade will dig, about a foot. *Lanc.*

SPADIARDS. The labourers or mine-workers

in the stannaries of Cornwall are so called from their *spade*. Kennett, MS. Gloss.

SPADO. A sword. (*Span.*,
SPAGIRICAL. Chemical.

SPAIE. A red deer in its third year. According to Harrison, " the yoong male is called in the first yeere a calfe, in the second a broket, the third a *spaie*, the fourth a stagon or stag, the fift a great stag, the sixt an hart, and so foorth unto his death."

SPAINING. Summer pasturage for cattle.

SPAINOLDE. A Spaniard. MS. Harl. 2270, f. 190.

SPAIRE. According to Jamieson, an opening in a gown. " Sparre of a gowne, *fente de la robe*," Palsgrave. " Speyr of a garment, *cluniculum*, *manubium*," Pr. Parv. MS. Harl. 221, f. 161.

Thane the comlyche kyng castes in fewtyre,
With a crewelle launce cowpez fulle evene
Abowne the *spayre* a spanne, emange the schortte
rybby. *Morte Arthure, MS. Lincoln*, f. 75.
He put hit efte in his *spayere*,
And out he toke hit hool and fere.
Cursor Mundi, MS. Coll. Trin. Cantab. f. 37.
His mytans hang be his *spayre*,
And alway hodit like a frere.
MS. Cantab. Ff. v. 48, f. 54.

SPAITS. Torrents of rain. *North.*

SPAK. The spoke of a wheel. Nominale MS.

SPAKE. Tame.
Seynt Benet wende he myjt hyt ha take,
For hyt sate by hym so *spake*.
MS. Harl. 1701. f. 50.

SPAKELY. Quickly; speedily.
The blode sprente owtte, and sprede as the horse
sprynges,
And he sproules fulle *spakely*, bot spekes he no more.
Morte Arthure, MS. Lincoln, f. 75.

SPAKENET. A net for catching crabs.

SPAKKY.
Seo wouw *spakky* he me spent,
Uch toth fram other is trent,
arerld is of rote. *Reliq. Antiq.* ii. 212.

SPAKLE. *Scutula*, Pr. Parv. MS. Harl. 221.

SPALDE. (1) The shoulder.
Bot thenne said Perceyvelle one bost,
Ly stille therin now and roste,
I kepe nothynge of thi coste
Ne noghte of thi *spalde*. *Perceval*, 796.

(2) To splinter, or chip.
Be thane sperls whare sproungene, *spalddyd* chippys.
Morte Arthure, MS. Lincoln, f. 92.

SPALDING-KNIFE. A knife used for the purpose of splitting fish. *North.*

SPALE. A splinter. *North.* " Splints, shivers, *spals*, rivings," Florio, p. 98. " Spalls or broken peeces of stones that come off in hewing and graving," Nomenclator, p. 411.

SPALLIARD. A sparrow. *Devon.*

SPALLIER. A labourer in tin-works.

SPALLING. In mining, breaking up into small pieces for the sake of easily separating the ore from the rock, after which it undergoes the process of cobbing.

SPALLS. See *Spale*. " To drow vore spalls, to throw one's errors and little flaws in one's teeth, quasi spalls or chips, which fly off from

the carpenter's axe or woodman's bill," Exmoor Glossary, p. 48.

SPALT. (1) Brittle; tender; liable to break or split. A carpenter in working a board with a plane, if a bit splits away or breaks off, will say that it *spalts* off. Harrison says, " of all oke growing in England, the parke oke is the softest, and far more *spalt* and brickle than the hedge oke."
(2) Heedless; careless; clumsy; pert; saucy; giddy and frail. *East.*

SPALTYRE. A psalter. " Here bygynnys Sayne Jerome *Spaltyre*," MS. Lincoln, f. 258.

SPAN. (1) To stretch asunder. *West.*
(2) To gush out?
With a roke he brac his heved than,
That the blod biforn out *span*.
Gy of Warwike, p. 296.
(3) To gripe or pinch. *Craven.*
(4) The prong of a pitchfork. *West.*
(5) To fetter a horse. *Kent.*
(6) To span a cart, to put something to stop it. *Kennett.*

SPAN-BEAM. The great beam that goes from side-wall to side-wall in a barn.

SPANCEL. " A rope to tie a cows hinder legs," Ray, ed. 1674, p. 44. This may be the same word as *spangle* in Pr. Parv. translated by *lorale*. " A spaniel, we have in these parts no other name but cow-tye," Hallamsh. Glossary, p. 123.

SPAN-COUNTER. A game thus played. One throws a counter on the ground, and another tries to hit it with his counter, or to get it near enough for him to span the space between them and touch both the counters. In either case, he wins; if not, his counter remains where it lay, and becomes a mark for the first player, and so alternately till the game be won. Strutt, p. 384. " *Jouer au tapper*, to play at spanne-counter," Cotgrave. " *Meglio al muro*, a play among boyes in Italie like our span-counter," Florio, p. 306.
He knows who hath sold his land, and now doth beg
A license, old iron, boots, shoos, and egge-
Shels to transport; shortly boyes shall not play
At *span counter*, or blow-point, but shall pay
Toll to some courtier. *Donne's Poems*, p. 131.

SPANDE. Span; small measure. *Hearne.*

SPANDREL. The triangular spaces included between the arch of a doorway, &c. and a rectangle formed by the outer mouldings over it. The term is also applied to other similar spaces included between arches, &c. and straight-sided figures surrounding them. *Oxf. Gloss. Arch.*

SPANE. (1) To wean. *North.*
(2) To germinate, as corn. *Yorksh.*

SPANES. " The prongs of a peek, a hay-fork, or dung-fork, quasi *spinæ* from their sharpness, or from their shape representing a short span, the thumb and little finger somewhat extended, or a pair of compasses opened and a little extended," MS. Devon Gloss.

SPAN-FIRE-NEW. Quite new.

SPANG. (1) To fasten. " To *spang* horses, or

fasten them to the chariot," Hollyband's Dictionarie, 1593.

(2) To throw with violence; to set forcibly in motion. *Linc.*

(3) A spangle. *Spenser.*

(4) A spring; a jump. *North.* To spang ones geates, i. e. to make haste.

(5) A span in measure. *Linc.* Brockett has *spang-and-purley-q.* a mode resorted to by boys of measuring distances, particularly at the game of marbles.

SPANGED. Variegated. *North.*

SPANGEL. A spaniel; a dog.

> I hadde a *spangel* good of plyght,
> I have hit mysde al thys seven-nyght.
> *Wright's Seven Sages,* p. 50.

SPANGER. A Spaniard. *Cornw.*

SPANGING. Rails laid across brooks to prevent cattle going from one pasture to another. *Devon.*

SPAN-GUTTER. A narrow brick drain in a coal mine. *Salop.*

SPANG-WHEW. To kill a toad by placing it on one end of a lever, and then driving it rapidly into the air by a sharp stroke on the other end. *North.*

SPANIEL. The same as *Spancel,* q. v.

SPANK. (1) A hard slap. *Var. dial.*

(2) To move energetically. *East.*

SPANKER. A man or animal very large, or excessively active. *Var. dial.*

SPANKER-EEL. The lamprey. *North.*

SPANKERS. Gold coins. *Devon.*

SPANKING. Large; lusty; sprightly; active; conspicuous; spruce, or neat.

SPANKY. Showy; smart. *Var. dial.*

SPANNER. An instrument by which the wheels of wheel-lock guns and pistols were wound up. They were at first simple levers with square holes in them. Next a turnscrew was added, and lastly, they were united to the powder-flasks for small priming. *Meyrick.* The term is still in use, applied to a wrencher, a nut screw-driver.

SPAN-NEW. Quite new. *Var. dial.* This common phrase occurs in Chaucer, and Tyrwhitt, who gives an explanation with hesitation, does not seem to be aware it is still in general use.

SPANNIMS. A game at marbles played in the eastern parts of England.

SPANNISHING. The full blow of a flower. Romaunt of the Rose, 3633.

SPANZELLE. A spaniel, or dog.

SPAR. (1) To practise boxing. Metaphorically, to disagree. *Var. dial.* "A sparring blow," a decisive hit in boxing.

2) To shut; to close; to fasten. The older form of the word is *sperre.* The bolt of a door is called the *spar.*

> Alle the jatis of Notyngham
> He made to be *sparred* everychone.
> *MS. Cantab.* Ff. v. 48, f. 127.

3) *A-spar,* in a state of opposition. *To set the legs a-spar,* to place them in the form of the rafters of a roof.

(4) The pointed stick used for fixing the thatch of a roof. *West.*

(5) *Spars,* rafters. *North.*

(6) "The coat or covering of oar or metal. In the vein of metal in silver mines there is a white fluor about the vein which they call *spar,* and a black which they call *blinds,*" Kennett, MS. Lansd. 1033, f. 388.

SPARABLES. Shoemakers' nails. *Var. dial.* Dekker spells the term *sparrowbils,* as also Wilbraham, p. 111; whence it would seem that it is derived from the nails being somewhat in the form of sparrows' bills.

SPARANDE. Sparing; niggardly. (*A.-S.*)

SPARCH. Brittle. *East.*

SPARCLE. A spark. Still in use.

> Thei shul se feades many one
> By the *sparcles* oute of fire that gone.
> *MS. Addit.* 11305, f. 98.
> Also the lanterne in the wynd that sone is aqueynt,
> Ase *sparkle* in the se that sone is adreynt,
> Ase vom in the strem that sone is to-thwith,
> Ase smoke in the lift that passet oure sith.
> *Reliq. Antiq.* ii. 229.

SPAR-DUST. The dust in wood which is produced by insects. *East.*

SPARE. (1) To refrain. (*A.-S.*)

> Than spake that byrde so bryght,
> There was bot he and his knyght,
> I spake with thame this nyghte,
> Why sold I *spare?*
> *MS. Lincoln* A. i. 17, f. 15.

(2) Slow; kept in reserve. *Devon.*

(3) Several; divers. *Gawayne.*

SPARE-BED. A bed not constantly used, kept in reserve for visitors. *Var. dial.*

SPAR-GADS. Gads or sticks to be split up into spars for thatch. *West.*

SPAR-HAWK. A sparrowhawk. (*A.-S.*)

SPAR-HOOK. A small hook used for making or cutting spars. *West.*

SPARING. The commencement of a cock-fight, by rising and striking with the heels.

SPARK. (1) A diamond. The word occurs several times in this sense in old plays.

(2) To splash with dirt. *North.*

(3) A gay dashing fellow.

> When Venus is ill placed, she inclines men to be effeminate, timerous, lustful, followers of whenches, very slugish, and addicted to idleness, an adulterer, incestuous, a fantastick *spark,* spending his moneys in ale-houses and taverns among loose lacivious people, a meer lasy companion, not careing for wife or children if marryed, coveting unlawful beds, given much to adultry, not regarding his reputation or creddit; if a woman, very impudent in all her ways; colour milky sky.
> *Bishop's Marrow of Astrology,* p. 55.

SPARKE. To glitter. (*A.-S.*)

> It *sparkede* and ful brith shon,
> So doth the gode charbucle ston,
> That men mouthe se by the lith
> A peni chesen, so was it brith.
> *Havelok,* 2144.

SPARKED. Variegated. *Var. dial.*

SPARKLE. To scatter; to disperse. Still in use in the North of England. "I sparkyll abroode, I sprede thynges asonder; I sonder or I part, whan the sowdiers of a capitayne be *sparkyllyd* abrode, what can he do in tyme of nede," Palsgrave, 1530, verb. f. 367.

SPARKLING. Claying between the spars to cover the thatch of cottages. *Norf.*

SPARKLING-HEAT. "There be several degrees of heat in a smith's forge, according to the purpose of their work, 1. A blood red heat. 2. A white flame heat. 3. A sparkling or welding heat, used to weld barrs or pieces of iron, i. e. to work them into one another," Kennett, MS. Lansd. 1033, f. 388.

SPARKY. The same as *Sparked*, q. v.

SPARKYLDE. Sprinkled.

> The chyldys clothys, ryche and gode,
> He had *sparkylde* with that blode.
> *MS. Cantab. Ff. ii. 38, f. 97.*

SPARLIE. Peevish. *Northumb.*

SPARLING. The smelt. In Wales, the samlet is called by this name.

SPARLIRE. The calf of the leg. See Beves of Hamtoun, p. 90.

> The knyght smoot with good wylle
> Strokes of thre,
> And the ape hym boot full ylle
> Thorgh the *sparlyre*. *Octovian, 330.*

SPARPIL. To disperse. See *Gerse.*

> His myʒt has made in his pouere
> Proud men to *sparpil* from his face.
> *MS. Douce 302, f. 24.*

SPARROWBLES. Same as *Sparables*, q. v.

SPARROWFART. Break of day. *Craven.*

SPARROW-TONGUE. Knot-grass. *Gerard.*

SPARSE. To disperse; to scatter.

SPART. The dwarf rush. *North.* Ground covered with sparts is said to be *sparty.*

SPARTHE. An axe, or halberd. (*A.-S.*)

> And an ax in his other, a hoge and unmete,
> A spetos *sparthe* to expoun in spelle quo so myʒt.
> *Syr Gawayn and the Grene Knyʒt, 209.*

SPARTICLES. Spectacles. *West.*

SPARTO. A kind of fish.

> Certes, such is the force of rope made of the skin of this fish, that they will hold at a plunge no lesse than the Spanish *sparto.*
> *Holinshed, Description of Scotland, p. 18.*

SPARVER. The canopy or wooden frame at the top of a bed. The term was sometimes applied to the bed itself. "*Lict de parement*, a bed of state, or a great *sparver bed*, that serves onely for shew, or to set out a roome," Cotgrave in v. *Parement.* "A canapie or sparvier for a bed," Florio, p. 349. *Sparvill tester*, the canopy of a bed, Unton Invent.

> The thrid chamber being my bedd-chamber, was apparelled with riche clothe of tyssue, raised, and a grete *sparver* and counterpointe to the same.
> *State Papers, I. 239.*

SPARWISTUNGGE. The herb sparrow's-tongue. See Archæologia, xxx. 413.

SPAT. (1) A blow. *Kent.*

(2) The cartilaginous substance by which an oyster adheres to its shell. *East.*

SPATCH-COCK. A hen just killed and quickly broiled for any sudden occasion.

SPATE. A small pond. *Dunelm.*

SPATHE. The sheath of an ear of corn.

SPATS. Gaiters. *Cumb.*

SPATTLE. (1) To spit; to slaver. "Spatyll, flame, *crachat*," Palsgrave, 1530.

> I spitte, I *spatle* in spech, I sporne,
> I werne, I lutle, ther-for I murne.
> *Reliq. Antiq. ii. 211.*

> Would to God therfore that we were come to such a detestation and loathing of lying, that we would even *spattle* at it, and cry fie upon it, and all that use it. *Dent's Pathway, p. 160.*

(2) "Spatyll an instrument," Palsgrave. A board used in turning oat cakes is so termed, but the identity is doubtful. Palsgrave perhaps meant the slice used by apothecaries for spreading their plasters or salves.

SPAUD. (1) The shoulder. *North.* "*Armus*, a spawde," Nominale MS. xv. Cent.

(2) A pen is said to have too much *spaud*, when the two members of its nib or point expand too widely when pressed upon the paper. *Yorksh.*

(3) To cut up the ground. *North.*

(4) To founder, as a ship.

SPAUL. Spittle; saliva.

> Another while the well drench'd smoky Jew,
> That stands in his own *spaul* above the shoe.
> *Hall's Poems, p. 13.*

SPAUNDRE. In architecture, a spandrel.

SPAUT. A youth. *North.*

SPAUT-BONE. The shoulder-bone. *East.* Pronounced in the North spaw-bone.

SPAVE. To castrate an animal. *North.*

SPAW. The slit of a pen. *North.*

SPAWL. (1) A splinter, as of wood, &c. *South.*

(2) To scale away, like the surface of a stone. *Somerset.*

SPAWLS. The branches of a tree; the divisions of anything. *North.*

SPAWN. A term of abuse.

SPAY. To castrate. *Var. dial.*

SPEAK. To *speak at the mouth*; that is, to speak freely and unconstrained. *North.*

SPEAK-HOUSE. The room in a convent in which the inmates were allowed to speak with their friends. Oxf. Gloss. Arch. p. 273.

SPEAKS. Same as *Skelms*, q. v.

SPEALL. A spawl or splinter. "A lath, a little boord, a splint or *speall* of wood or stone," Florio, p. 44. "*Spillo*, a pinne, a pricke, a sting, a pricking-thorne, a *spill*," ibid. p. 523, ed. 1611.

SPEANED. Newly delivered. *Northumb.*

SPEANS. Teats. *Kent.*

> His necke is short, like a tygers and a lyons, apt to bend downeward to his meat; his bellie is verie large, being uniforme, and next to it the intrals as in a wolfe: it hath also foure *speanes* to her pap.
> *Topsell's Four-Footed Beasts, 1607, p. 38.*

SPEAR. (1) Goods sold *under the spear*, that is, by public auction.

(2) A soldier who carried a spear. The *spears* were heavy armed cavalry.

(3) To inquire. See *Spere.*

> Yet saw they no man there at whom
> They might the matter *spear*.
> *Robin Hood, I. 103.*

(4) To germinate, as barley. *South.*

(5) The sting of a bee. *Var. dial.*

(6) A blade of grass; a reed. *Kent.*

SPEARE. A spire, or steeple.

The *speare* or steeple of which churche was fired by lightening, and consumed even to the stoneworke thereof. *Lambarde's Perambulation,* 1596, p. 287.

SPEAR-GRASS. Couch grass. *Suffolk.* Harrison applies the term *spearie* to coarse grass in his Description of Britaine, p. 109.

SPEAR-STAFF. *Fust de lance,* Palsgrave.

SPEAR-STICKS. Pointed sticks, doubled and twisted, used for thatching. *Devon.*

SPECES. Sorts, or kinds. (*A.-N.*)

SPECIAL. Good; excellent. *Var. dial.*

SPECIOUSLY. Especially. *North.*

SPECK. (1) The sole of a shoe. Also, the fish so called. *East.*

(2)

Adieu, good cheese and onions; stuff thy guts
With *speck* and barley-pudding for digestion.
Heywood's English Traveller.

(3) The spoke of a wheel. *North.*

SPECKINGS. Large long nails. *East.*

SPECKS. Plates of iron nailed upon a plough to keep it from wearing out. *Yorksh.*

SPECS. Spectacles. *Var. dial.*

SPECULAR-STONE. A kind of transparent stone, mentioned in Harrison's Description of England, p. 187.

SPED. (1) To speed. *North.*

(2) Went; proceeded. *Gawayne.*

(3) Versed in. *Dyce.*

SPEDE. To dispatch. (*A.-N.*)

SPEDEFUL. (1) Effectual. (2) Ready.

SPEDELYER. More quickly.

And ofte *spedelyer* speke ere I jour speche here.
MS. Cott. Calig. A. ii. f. 117.

SPEECHLESS. Using few words; concise. The term constantly occurs in this sense in early writers, distinct from the modern synonyme *dumb.* See Palsgrave.

SPEED. (1) A disease amongst young cattle common in the autumn. *North.*

(2) To destroy; to kill. *Marlowe.* Speeding-place, the place where a wound is fatal.

(3) Luck; fortune. "Spede, lucke, *encontre,*" Palsgrave. "The queen's speed," Winter's Tale, ii. 2.

SPEEKE. "A speeke, or sheathing nayle, used in shipping," Cotgrave in v. *Estoupe.*

SPEEL. (1) The same as *Speall,* q. v. "A spele, a small wand, or switch in Westmorl." Kennett, MS. Lansd. 1033, f. 388.

(2) To climb; to clamber. *North.*

SPEER. (1) The chimney-post. *Chesh.*

(2) A screen across the lower end of a hall. *Pr. Parv.* "Speere in a hall, *buffet,*" Palsgrave, 1530. "*Speer,* a shelter in a house, made between the door and fire to keep off the wind," Holloway, p. 159.

(3)

The males in this kind doe onely beare hornes, and such as do not grow out of the crownes of their head, but as it were out of the middle on either side, a little above the eies, and so bend to the sides.

They are sharp and full of bunches like harts, no where smooth but in the tops of the *speers,* and where the vaines run to carry nutriment to their whole length, which is covered with a hairye skin: they are not so rough at the beginning or at the first prosses specially in the for-part as they are in the second, for that onely is full of wrinckles; from the bottom to the middle they growe straight, but from thence they are a little recurved.
Topsell's Four-Footed Beasts, 1607, p. 327.

SPEIGHT. A kind of large woodpecker. "*Epiche,* a speight," Cotgrave.

SPEIN. A shoot.

Pride therefore may verie fitly be compared to the crab-stock *speins,* which growe out of the roote of the very best apple-tree. *Dent's Pathway,* p. 36.

SPEKABILL. Special; peculiar.

SPEKE. The spoke of a wheel. *North.*

SPEKEN. A small spike. *Suffolk.*

SPEKTAKEL. A spying-glass. (*Lat.*)

SPEL. (1) The same as *Speall,* q. v.

(2) A tale, or history. (*A.-S.*)

And thow wolt that conne wel,
Take gode hede on thys *spel.*
MS. Cott. Claud. A. ii. f. 129.

(3) Liberty. *Craven.*

SPELCH. To bruise, as in a mortar; to split, as *spelched peas,* &c. *Pegge.*

SPELDER. (1) To spell. *Yorksh.* It is an old form. "To speldyr, *syllabicare,*" MS. Dict. written about the year 1500.

(2) A splinter, or chip. "Spelder of woode, *esclat,*" Palsgrave, 1530.

The grete schafte that was longe,
Alle to *spildure* hit spronge.
Avowynge of King Arthur, xiii. 6.

SPELK. A splinter or narrow slip of wood. Hence, a very lean person. *North.* "To spelk in Yorkshire, to set a broken bone; whence the splints or splinters of wood used in binding up of broken bones are calld *spelks.* In Northumberland, a spelck is any swath, or roller, or band," Kennett MS.

SPELL. (1) The trap employed at the game of nurspell, made like that used at trap-ball. *Linc.*

(2) A piece of paper rolled up to serve for the purpose of lighting a fire, a pipe, &c. Also the transverse pieces of wood at the bottom of a chair, which strengthen and keep together the legs, are called *spells. Linc.*

(2) Pleasure; relaxation. *Somerset.*

(3) A turn; a job. *Var. dial.*

SPELL-BONE. The small bone of the leg.

SPELLE. To talk; to teach.

To lewed men Englisshe I *spelle,*
That undirstondeth what I con telle.
Cursor Mundi, MS. Coll. Trin. Cantab. f. 2.
Of an erle y wyll yow telle,
Of a better may no man *spelle:*
And of hys stewarde, bryght of hewe,
That was bothe gode and trewe.
MS. Cantab. Ff. ii. 38, f. 147.

SPELLERE. A speaker. (*A.-S.*)

Speke we of tho *spelleres* bolde,
Sith we have of this lady tolde.
Cursor Mundi, MS. Coll. Trin. Cantab. f. 127.

SPELLERS. "*Espois d'un cerf,* the top of a

red deeres head ; of a fallow, the *spellers*," Cotgrave.

SPELLYCOAT. A ghost. *North.*

SPELLYNG. A relation ; a tale. (*A.-S.*)

   As we telle yn owre *spellyng*,
   Falsenes come never to gode endyng.
         MS. Cantab. Ff. ii. 38, f. 125.

SPELONKE. A cavern. (*A.-N.*)

   Monkes and mendinaunts,
   Men by hemselve,
   In spekes and in *spelonkes*,
   Selde speken togideres.
         Piers Ploughman, p. 311.

   Than kyng Alexander and Candeobis went furthe
   alle that daye, and come tille a grete *spelunc*, and
   thare thay herberde thame.
         MS. Lincoln A. 1. 17, f. 43.

SPELT. A splinter. "Chippes or spelts of wood," Nomenclator, 1585, p. 143.

SPELT-CORN. Vetches. *Devon.*

SPENCE. (1) "Spens a buttrye, *despencier*," Palsgrave. "*Celarium*, a spens," Nominale MS. The term is still in use in the provinces, applied to a safe, a cupboard, a convenient place in a house for keeping provisions ; a pantry ; an eating-room in a farmhouse. "*Dispensorium*, a spenyse," Nominale MS.

   Yet I had lever she and I
   Where both togyther secretly
   In some corner in the *spence*.
         Interlude of the iiij. Elements, n. d.

(2) Expense. *Palsgrave.*

SPEND. (1) To consume ; to destroy. *East.*

   Than rode they two togedur a-ryght,
   Wyth scharp sperys and swerdys bryght,
    Thay smote togedur sore !
   Ther sperys they *spendyd* and brake schyldys,
   The pecys flewe into the feldys.
   Grete dyntys dud they dele thore.
         MS. Cantab. Ff. ii. 38, f. 79.

(2) To span with the fingers. *East.*

(3) Fastened. *Gawayne.*

(4) The skin of a hog. Metaphorically, any surface, as sward. *Devon.*

(5) To break ground. *Cornw.*

SPEND-ALL. A spendthrift. "*Allárga la máno*, a spend all, a wast-good," Florio.

SPENDING-CHEESE. A kind of cheese used by farmers for home consumption. *East.*

SPENDINGE. Money. (*A.-S.*)

   And gyf them some *spendynge*,
   That them owt of thy loude may bryng.
         MS. Cantab. Ff. ii. 38, f. 72.

SPENDLOW. In felling wood for hurdles, the dead wood is tied in faggots and sold for firing. These faggots are termed *spendlows.*

SPENE. (1) Block up ; stop up. *Hearne.*

(2) To spend ; to consume time.

   And *spene* that day in holynes,
   And leve alle othor bysynes.
         MS. Cott. Claud. A. ii. f. 138.

   For ful of bitternesse hit is ;
   Ful sore thou mizt ben agast,
   For after that thou *spenest* her amis,
   Leste thou be into helle i-cast.
         MS. Digby 86.

SPENGED. Pied, as cattle. *North.*

SPENISE. See *Spence* (1).

SPENSERE. A dispenser of provisions.

   The *spensere* and the botillere bothe,
   The kyng with hem was ful wrothe.
     Cursor Mundi, MS. Coll. Trin. Cantab. f. 28

   After he was kyng he wedded hure sone,
   His owne *spencere* douzter he was.
         Chron. Vilodun. p. 6.

SPENT. Exhausted. "1626, 14 Dec. Bryan Fletham, fisherman, beinge *spent*, in a cobble," Sharp's Chron. Mirab. p. 28.

SPER. (1) To prop up ; to support. Still in use, according to the Craven Gloss. ii. 158.

(2) Frail ; brittle ; fragile.

SPERAGE. Asparagus. Ray's Dict. Tril. p. 8.

   Eating of Carduus benedictus, of rue, onyons,
   anise seed, garlike, rotten cheese, stalkes of *sperage*,
   fenell.   *Fletcher's Differences*, 1623, p. 94.

SPERE. (1) To ask ; to inquire ; to seek. Still in use in the North of England. "To speer or goe a speering, to enquire and search for. *Dunelm.* And on the borders of Scotland, he that can help to cattle taken away by moss-troopers is called a *speerer*," Kennett, MS. Lansd. 1033.

   For nothyng that they cowde *spere*,
   They cowde nevyr of hur here.
         MS. Cantab. Ff. ii. 38, f. 75.

   Then was the kyng bothe blythe and gladd,
   And seyde, For Moradas y am not adrad,
    To batayle when he schalle wende
   Ofte y made men aftur yow to *spere*,
   But myght y not of yow here,
   My ryght schalle thou defende.
         MS. Cantab. Ff. ii. 38, f. 80.

   And bad them *speere* aftur a man
   That late was comyn thedur than.
         MS. Cantab. Ff. ii. 38, f. 145

   Syr, he seyde, gramercy, nay,
   Efte togedur speke we may,
    Y aske yow but a stede :
   To other londys wylle y *spere*,
   More of awnturs for to here,
    And who dothe beste yn dede.
         MS. Cantab. Ff. ii. 38, f. 79.

(2) A sphere. (*A.-S.*)

(3) A point. (*A.-S.*)

   And till the sunne was at mydday *spere*,
   On golde and sylke and on wolles softe,
   With hir hondes she wolde worche ofte.
         Lydgate, MS. Ashm. 39, f. 8.

(4) Spirit. Sharp's Cov. Myst. p. 120.

(5) To fasten ; to shut. *Palsgrave.*

(6) A spy ; one who spies.

(7) Spire ; shoot. Hence a stripling.

SPEREL. A clasp, or fastening.

SPERINGE. A fastening. "*Vulva* ys a zate or a zate with too sperynges," MS. Glouc. Cath. 19.

SPERKET. A wooden, hooked, large peg, not much curved, to hang saddles, harness, &c. on. "*Spurget*," according to Ray, "a tagge, or piece of wood to hang any thing upon ;" but we always pronounce the *k*. It is like perk, but the latter is supported at both ends, for fowls to perch on. Moor, p. 382.

SPERKLE. The collar-bone.

SPERME. Seed. (*A.-N.*)

SPERN. A buttress, or spur.

SPERR. To publish banns. *Derb.* This derived from *spere*, to ask.

SPERSE. To disperse. See *Sparse*.

> Sweete roses colour in that visage faire
> With yvorie is *sperst* and mingelled.
> > *British Bibliographer*, L. 32.

SPERT. A sudden fit or thought. *East*.

SPERTE. Spirit.

> Into thy hands, Lord, I committ
> My *sperte*, which is thy dewe. *MS. Ashmole 802*.

SPERVITER. A keeper of sparrow-hawks and musket-hawks. *Berners*.

SPETCH. To patch. *Yorksh*.

SPETCHEL-DIKE. A dike made of stones laid in horizontal rows with a bed of thin turf between each of them.

SPETOUS. Angry; spiteful. (*A.-N.*)

> Florent thanne askede his fadir Clement
> Whate alle that *spetous* noyes thanne ment?
> > *MS. Lincoln A. i. 17, f. 103*.

> Thorow my nayles, a *spetous* wounde.
> > *MS. Cantab. Ff. ii. 38, f. 42*.

SPETTACLE. A spectacle. *East*.

SPEWRING. A boarded partition. *Exmoor*.

SPEXT. Speakest.

> Mon that thuncheth he ded ys,
> Newe hous and comfort shal buen his.
> ʒef thou with dede mon *spest*,
> Muche joie the is next.
> Whose thunchest himself adreint,
> Of desturbaunce he bith ateint.
> > *Reliq. Antiq. i. 265*.

SPIAL. A spy. *Shak*.

SPICCOTY. Speckled. *Somerset*.

SPICE. (1) Sweetmeats; gingerbread; cake; any kind of dried fruit. *North*.

(2) Species; kind. (*A.-N.*) " Spyce, a kynde, *espece*," Palsgrave, 1530.

> Al that toucheth dedly synne
> In any *spyce* that we falle ynne.
> > *MS. Harl. 1701, f. 1*.

> Chydynge comys of hert hy,
> And grett pride and velany,
> And other *spice* that mekylle deres.
> > *R. de Brunne, MS. Bowes, p. 31*.

> Here aftirwarde, as undirstonde,
> Thou schalt the *spicis* as they stonde.
> > *Gower, MS. Soc. Antiq. 134, f. 61*.

(3) A slight attack of any disorder. *South*. " *Spyce of the axes*," Palsgrave, 1530.

(4) A small stick. *North*.

SPICED. Scrupulous. " Spiced conscience," Chaucer. " Under pretence of *spiced* holinesse," tract dated 1594, ap. Todd's Illustrations of Gower, p. 380.

SPICE-KYEL. Broth with raisins. *North*.

SPICE-PLATE. It was formerly the custom to take spice with wine, and the plate on which the spice was laid was termed the spice-plate.

SPICER. A grocer. See Manners and Household Expenses of England, p. 153.

SPICERY. Spices.

> He went and fett conynges thre
> Alle baken welle in a pasty,
> With wel gode *spicerye*.
> > *MS. Cantab. Ff. v. 48, f. 50*.

SPICING. In a holly rod used for the handle of a cart-whip, the great thick end is called the *stump*, and the small taper end to which the lash is tied is called the *spicing*.

SPICK. (1) A spike. Florio, p. 98.

(2) " A spycke of a bacon flycke," Skelton, I. 106. From A.-S. *spic*, bacon, *lardum*. " Spyk of flesshe, *popa*," Pr. Parv. ed. 1499.

SPICK-AND-SPAN-NEW. Quite new.

> Fortune th' audacious doth juvare,
> But lets the timidous miscarry.
> Then while the honour thou hast got
> Is *spick and span new*, piping hot,
> Strike her up bravely, thou hadst best,
> And trust thy fortune with the rest.
> > *Hudibras*, I. iii. 398.

SPICY-FIZZER. A currant cake. *Newc*.

SPIDDOCK. A spigot. *Spiddock-pot*, an earthen jar perforated to admit a spiddock. *Spiddock-pot legs*, large awkward legs.

> For whilst one drop of ale was to be had,
> They quaft and druuk it round about like mad;
> When all was off, then out they pull'd the tapps,
> And stuck the *spiddocks* finely in their hats.
> > *The Praise of Yorkshire Ale*, 1697, p. 15.

SPIDER-CATCHER. A monkey.

SPIDER-SHANKS. A lanky fellow. *North*.

SPIER. A spy; a scout. It is the translation of *explorator* in Nominale MS.

SPIFFLICATE. To dismay; to confound; to beat severely. *Var. dial*.

SPIGGOT-SUCKER. " *Pinteur*, a tippler, potcompanion, spiggot-sucker," Cotgrave.

SPIGHT. To spite. *Tusser*.

SPIKE. Lavender. *Var. dial*. " Pynte of spike water," Cunningham's Rev. Acc. p. 35. *Spik*, Barnes' Dorset Gl.

> There growes the gilliflowre, the mynt, the daysie
> Both red and white, the blue-veynd violet;
> The purple hyacynth, the *spyke* to please thee,
> The scarlet dyde carnation bleeding yet.
> > *The Affectionate Shepheard*, 1594.

SPIKE-AND-DAB. A wall of hurdle-work plastered over with mortar. *West*.

SPIKE-BIT. A spike-passer. *Heref*.

SPIKE-NAILS. Large long nails.

SPIKE-POLE. A kind of rafter. *West*.

SPIKING. A large nail. *North*. The term occurs in Palsgrave, 1530.

SPIL. The same as *Speall*, q. v.

SPILCOCK. A child's whirligig.

SPILE. (1) A peg at the end of a cask of liquor. Spile-hole, the receptacle for the same. On the top it is, as elsewhere, the vent-peg. *Spile* is also a pile, driven in wet foundations, or in embankments. *Moor*.

(2) To make a foundation in soft earth by driving in spiles or piles. *East*.

(3) To carve or cut up birds.

SPILL. (1) A trial; an attempt. *West*.

(2) The stalk of a plant. *Devon*.

(3) The spindle of a spinning-wheel.

(4) Quantity; lot. *North*.

(5) A small reward or gift. *East*.

(6) The spill of a tongue, i. e. a neat's tongue without the root. *Devon*.

SPILLE. To destroy; to mar; to perish; to waste, or throw away. (*A.-S.*)

> To a wode they wente in hye,
> There the quene schulde passe by,

And there stode they alle stylle.
There had he thoght redyly
To have do the quene a velanye,
Fayne he wolde hur *spylle.*
   MS. Cantab. Ff. ii. 38, f. 73.

And ʒef hyre herte therto grylle,
Rather thenne the chylde scholde *spyR̃e,*
Teche hyre thenne to calle a mon
That in that nede helpe hyre con.
   MS. Cotton. Claud. A. ii. t 128.

Home er nyʒt come he noʒt,
New mete with hym he broʒt,
For defaute wolde he not *spille.*
   MS. Cantab. Ff. v. 48, f. 51.

SPILLINGE. Failure.

SPILLS. Thin slips of wood or paper, used for lighting candles, &c. *Var. dial.*

SPILQUERENE. " *Giraculum, quidam ludus puerorum,* a spilquerene," Reliq. Antiq. i. 9.

SPILT. Spoiled. *Var. dial.*

SPILTE. Destroyed; undone. (*A.-S.*)

Then rose sche up and come agayne
To syr Roger, and fonde hym slayne,
 Then had sche sorow y-nogh!
Allas! sche seyde, now am y *spylte,*
Thys false thefe, withowtyn gylte,
 Why dyd he the to slon?
   MS. Cantab. Ff. ii. 38, f. 73.

When the dewke harde hym so sey,
Allas, he seyde, and wele awey!
For my men that be *spylte,*
Alle hyt ys myn owne gylte.
   MS. Cantab. Ff. ii. 38, f. 154.

SPILTERS. " The spilters of a deer's head, *in cervi cornuario apice stontes fusi, dactyli, surculi,*" Coles.

SPILTH. That which is spilt.

SPILWOOD. Refuse of wood, or wood *spilt* by the sawyers. *South.*

SPINCOPPE. A spider.

SPINDE. A pantry, or larder. (*Dut.*)

SPINDLE. (1) The piece of iron which supports the rest in a plough. *Kent.*

(2) The third swarm of bees from the same hive is so called in Warwickshire.

(3) Growing corn is said to *spindle* when it first shoots up its pointed sheath, previously to the development of the ear. *East.*

(4) " A woman that makes or spins crooked spindles, that is, maketh her husband cuckold," Florio, p. 177, ed. 1611.

(5) The same as *Newel,* q. v.

SPINDLE-RODS. Railings. *North.*

SPINE. (1) A thorn.

Thouʒ that roses at Midsomer ben fulle soote,
Yitte undernethe is hid a fulle sharp *spyne.*
   Lydgate's Bochas, MS. Hatton 2.

And oute of hem even y-like procede,
As doth a floure oute of the rouʒ *spyne.*
   Lydgate, MS. Soc. Antiq. 134, f. 17.

(2) The green sward. *West.*

(3) The hide of an animal; the fat on the surface of a joint of meat. *Devon.*

SPINEDY. Stout; muscular. *I. Wight.*

SPINET. A small wood. (*Lat.*)

Dark-shady launes agreed best with her humour,
where in some private *spinet,* conversing with her

own thoughts, she used to discourse of the effects of her love in this manner.
   The Two Lancashire Lovers, 1640, p. 79.

SPINETTED. Slit or opened. *Nares.*

SPINGARD. A kind of small cannon.

SPINGEL. Fennel. *Somerset.*

SPINK. (1) A chaffinch. *Var. dial.*

(2) A spark of fire. *North.*

(3) A chink. *Hants.*

SPINKED. Spotted. *Yorksh.*

SPINNAGE. At Norwich, children who are sickly are taken to a woman living in St. Lawrence to be cut for a supposed disease called the *spinnage.* The woman performs the operation on a Monday morning only, and charges threepence. On the first visit the woman cuts the lobe of the right ear with a pair of scissors, and with the blood makes the sign of the cross upon the child's forehead. On the second Monday she does the same with the left ear; and in some instances it is deemed necessary to subject the little sufferers to nine operations of this ridiculous ceremony.

SPINNEL. A spindle. *North.*

SPINNER. A spider. *Palsgrave.* " Eranye or spynnare," Prompt. Parv. p. 140.

SPINNEY. A thicket. A small plantation is sometimes so called. It occurs in this sense in Domesday Book. See Carlisle's Account of Charities, p. 306. In Buckinghamshire the term is applied to a brook.

At the last bi a littel dich he lepes over a *spenne,*
Steles out ful stilly by a strothe raude.
   Syr Gawayn and the Grene Knyʒt, 1709.

SPINNICK. A dwarf. *Somerset.*

SPINNING-DRONE. The cockchafer. *Cornw.*

SPINNING-MONEY. Sixpences. *Norf.*

SPINNING-TURN. A spinning-wheel. *West.*

SPINNY. Thin; small; slender. The term occurs several times in Middleton.

SPINNY-WHY. A child's game at Newcastle, nearly the same as Hide-and-seek.

SPION. A spy. *Heywood.*

SPIRACLE. " A spiracle, a loftie sentence or a quickning conceipt." List of old words prefixed to Batman uppon Bartholome, 1582.

SPIRE. (1) " Spyre of corne, *barbe du ble,*" Palsgrave. " I spyer as corne dothe whan it begynneth to waxe rype, *je espie,*" ibid.

(2) To ask; to inquire. (*A.-S.*)

When Adam dalfe and Even spane,
 Go *spire,* if thou may spede;
Whare was thanne the pride of mane,
 That nowe merres his mede.
   MS. Lincoln A. i. 17, f. 213.

In thi southe thou salle make thyne endynge, bot *spirre* me nother the tyme ne the houre whenne it schal be, for I wille on na wyse telle it to the.
   MS. Lincoln A. i. 17, f. 4.

My wille, my herte, and alle my wit
Ben fully sette to harken and *spyre*
What eny man wol speke of hire.
   Gower, MS. Soc. Antiq. 134, f. 74.

(3) A young tree. *North.*

(4) A stake. *Chaucer.*

SPIRES. Is chiefly applied to the tall species of sedge which forms elastic mounds (in some counties cut out and dried for church hassocks) in boggy places ; it is likewise used of the tall leaves of the common yellow iris, often found in wet meadows. *Isle of Wight.*

SPIRIT. The electric fluid. *East.*

SPIRIT-PLATE. In melting of iron ore the bottom of the furnace has four stones to make a perpendicular square to receive the metal, of which four stones or walls, that next the bellows is called the tuarn or tuiron wall, that against it the wind-wall or *spirit-plate.* Kennett, MS. Lansd. 1033, f. 388.

SPIRITY. Spirited. *North.*

SPIRT. Metaphorically, an interval, a brief space of time. *North.*

SPIRTLE. To sprinkle. *Drayton.*

SPIRT-NET. A kind of fishing-net, described in Blome's Gent. Rec. ii. 200.

SPISER-WIFE. A woman who sold spices, and generally grocery. Nominale MS.

SPISS. Firm ; thick. (*Lat.*) " *Condenso,* condense, thicke, spisse," Florio, p. 115.

SPIT. (1) The depth a spade goes in digging, about a foot. *Var. dial.* A spade is sometimes so called.

(2) To lay eggs, said of insects. *West.*

(3) Very slight rain. *Var. dial.*

(4) *Spit and a stride,* a phrase meaning a very short distance. *North.*

(5) A sword. A cant term.

(6) Injury. *Gawayne.*

SPITAL. See *Spittle* (4).

SPIT-BENDER. A farmer's wife-having a roasting pig to sell, will, to enhance its virtues, call it by this name, implying that it is so fat, plump, and heavy, that your spit shall scarcely preserve its straightness under the pressure of its weight. *Suffolk.*

SPIT-BOOTS. Heavy leather gaiters, covering the shoe and leg, and fastened by iron clasps and screws. *Cumb.*

SPIT-DEEP. The depth of a spade.

SPITE. " Spyte of his tethe, *maulgre quil en ayt,*" Palsgrave, 1530.

SPITEFUL. Keen ; severe. *North.*

SPITOUS. The same as *Spetous,* q. v.

SPITTARD. A two-year hart. " *Subulo,* an hart havyng hornes without tynes, called (as I suppose) a spittare," Elyot, 1559.

> Also it is not to be forgotten, that they have divers other names to dinstinguish their yeares and countries, as for example : when they begin to have hornes, which appeare in the second yeare of their age like bodkins without braunches, which are in Latine called subules, they are also called subulones for the similitude, and the Germans cal such an one spishirts, which in English is called a *spittard,* and the Italians corbiati, but the French have no proper name for this beast that I can learn until he be a three yearing.
> *Topsell's Four-Footed Beasts,* 1607, p. 122.

SPITTER. (1) Slight rain. *Var. dial.*

(2) A small tool with a long handle, used for cutting up weeds, &c. *West.*

SPITTLE. (1) A spade. *Var. dial.* " Spytyll

II.

forkys," apparently meaning pronged spades, are mentioned in Tundale's Visions, p. 24.

(2) A nasty dirty fellow. *East.*

(3) Very spiteful. *Somerset.*

(4) A hospital. The term was originally applied to a lazar-house, or receptacle for persons affected with leprosy, but afterwards to a hospital of any kind. According to Gifford, a hospital or *spital* was an almshouse, and *spittle* a lazar-house ; but this distinction seems to be an error. " A spittle, or hospitall for poore folkes diseased : a spittle, hospitall, or lazarhouse for lepres." Baret's Alvearie, 1580. *Spittle whore,* a very common whore.

> So shall you thrive by little and little,
> Scape Tyborne, counters, and the *spittle.*
> *Songs of the London Prentices,* p. 53.

SPITTLE - SERMONS. Sermons preached formerly at the Spittle, in a pulpit erected for the purpose, and afterwards at Christchurch, City, on Easter Monday and Tuesday. Ben Jonson alludes to them in his Underwoods, ap. Gifford, viii. 414.

SPITTLE-STAFF. A staff of wood four or five feet long, shod at the lower end with a wedge like a piece of iron, to *stub* thistles with. The use of this implement is much affected in small towns by the occupiers of two or three acres of pasture land. *Linc.*

SPIT-TURNER. A boy or dog employed to turn the spit for roasting.

SPLACK-NUCK. A miser. *Norf.*

SPLAIDE. Unfolded ; displayed.

> He *splayds* his baners full grete plenté,
> And herawdys unto that cete then sente he.
> *Archæologia,* xxi. 49.

SPLAIRGE. To splatter. *Northumb.*

SPLAITING. Splaiting in the shoulder of a horse is thus described by Topsell :

> This commeth by some dangerous sliding or slipping, wherby the shoulder parteth from the breast, and so leaves an open rift, not in the skin, but in the flesh and filme next under the skin, and so he halteth and is not able to goe ; you shal perceive it by trailing his legge after him in his going. The cure according to Martin is thus : First put a paire of strait pasternes on his fore-feet, keeping him stil in the stable without disquieting him. Then take of dialthea one pound, of sallet-oyle one pinte, of oyle de bayes halfe a pound, of fresh butter halfe a pound ; melt al these things together in a pipkin, and annoint the grieved place therwith, and also round about the inside of the shoulder, and within two or three dales after, both that place and all the shoulder besides wil swel. Then either prick him with a lancet or fleame in al the swelling places, or else with some other sharp hot iron, the head whereof would be an inch long, to the intent that the corruption may run out, and use to annoint it stil with the same ointment. But if you see that it wil not go away, but swel stil, and gather to a head, then lance it where the swelling doth gather most, and is soft under the finger, and then taint it with flax dipt in this ointment ; take of turpentine and of hogs grease of each two ounces, and melt them together, renewing the taint twice a day until it be whole.
> *History of Four-Footed Beasts,* 1607, p. 398.

SPLASH. (1) The same as *Plash,* q. v.

(2) Smart and gaily dressed. *East.*

SPLAT. (1) A row of pins as they are sold in the paper. *Somerset.*

> All prizes, norra blank,
> Norra blank, All prizes !
> A walter—knife—or scissis sheer—
> A *splat* o' pins—put in, my dear !—
> Whitechapel nills all sizes.
> *Ballad of Tom Gosl.*

(2) To split, or cut up.

> To *splatt* the bore they wente fulle tyte,
> Ther was no knyfe that wolde hym byte,
> So harde of hyde was hee.
> *Sir Eglamour of Artois,* 490.

(3) A large spot. *Devon.*

SPLAT-FOOTED. Splay-footed. *Devon.*

SPLAUDER. To stretch out, said generally of the arms or feet. *Yorksh.*

SPLAUTCH. To let a soft substance fall heavily, applied to its impingement with the floor. *Northumb.*

SPLAVIN. An eruptive blotch. *Heref.*

SPLAWED. Spread out. *Norf.*

SPLAYE. To spread abroad ; to unfold. (*A.-N.*) Hence the term splay-foot, splay-hand, splay-mouth, &c.

> Wonder hygh ther sate a krowe,
> His whynges *splayynge* to and ffro.
> *MS. Cott. Tiber.* A. vii. f. 42.

SPLAYED-BITCH. A castrated bitch. It is a superstition still existing in retired parts of the county, that certain persons had the power of transforming themselves into the shape of different animals, particularly hares, and that nothing could have any chance of running against them but a *splayed bitch. Linc.*

SPLAYING. Slanting. *Oxon.*

SPLEEN. Violent haste. *Shak.*

SPLEENY. Full of spleen, or anger.

SPLEET. " *Piscem exdorsuare,* to spleete out, or part alongest the ridge-bone just in the midst," Nomenclator, 1585, p. 62.

SPLENDIDIOUS. Splendid. *Drayton.*

SPLENT. (1) A lath. " Splent for an house, *laite,*" Palsgrave. The term is still in use in Suffolk. Splents are parts of sticks or poles, either whole or split, placed upright in forming walls, and supported by rizzers (qv) for receiving the clay daubing. The term seems to have been applied to any small thin piece of wood.

> Or wilt thou in a yellow boxen bole,
> Taste with a wooden *splent* the sweet lythe honey '
> *The Affectionate Shepheard,* 1594.

(2) In the following passage *splent* seems to mean a splinter, or chip, or perhaps one of the *splents,* q. v.

> On the schoulder felle the stroke,
> A grete *splente* owte hyt smote.
> *MS. Cantab.* Ff. ii. 38, f. 213.

(3) A kind of inferior coal.

SPLENTIDE.

> The spokes was *splentide* alle with speltis of silver
> The space of a spere lenghe springande fulle faire.
> *Morte Arthure, MS. Lincoln,* f. 87.

SPLENTS. In ancient armour, several little plates that run over each other, and protected

the inside of the arm. " Splent, harnesse for the arme, *garde de bras,*" Palsgrave.

> My coat of black velvet furred with martcrus, with six pair of Alman rivets complete, with *splints,* sallets, and all things thereunto belonging.
> *Test. Vetust.* p. 658

SPLETTE. To spread out flat.

SPLINTED. Supported. *Chapman.*

SPLIRT. To spurt out. *North.*

SPLIT. (1) *To make all split,* an old phrase implying great violence of action.

(2) To betray confidence. *Var. dial.*

SPLITTER-SPLATTER. Splashy dirt. *North.*

SPLOB. To split off pieces of wood.

SPLOTCH. A splash of dirt. *East.*

SPLUTTER. To talk quickly and indistinctly, as if the mouth were full. *Var. dial.*

SPOAK. The bar of a ladder.

SPOAT. Spittle. *Lanc.*

SPOCKEN. Spoken. *North.*

SPOCLE. The same as *Spole* (2).

SPOFFLE. To make one's self very busy over a matter of little consequence. *East.*

SPOIL. (1) To cut up a hen. A term in carving, given in the Booke of Hunting, 1586.

(2) To rob. This sense is still in use applied to robbing birds' nests. *East.*

SPOKE. To put a spoke in one's wheel, i. e. to say something of him which is calculated to injure or impede his success.

SPOKEN-CHAIN. An appendage of a waggon, consisting of a long strong chain, to be fixed to the spoke of the wheel, when the team is *stalled,* or set fast in a slough.

SPOKE-SHAVE. (1) A basket for bread.

(2) A narrow plane used for smoothing the inner parts of a wheel. " Spokeshave or a plane," Palsgrave, 1530.

SPOLE. (1) The shoulder. (*Fr.*)

> Sir Andrew he did swarve the tree,
> With right good will he swarved then ;
> Upon his breast did Horsley hitt,
> But the arrow bounded back agen.
> Then Horseley spyed a privye place
> With a perfect eye in a secrette part ;
> Under the *spole* of his right arme
> He smote Sir Andrew to the heart.
> *Ballad of Sir Andrew Barton.*

(2) A small wheel near the distaff in the common spinning-wheel. " Spole, a wevers instrument," Palsgrave, subst. f. 66.

SPOLETT.

> Spendis unsparely that sparede was lange,
> Spedis theme to *spolett* with speris l-newe.
> *Morte Arthure, MS. Lincoln,* f. 115.

SPOLLS. Waste wood cut off in making hurdles, &c. *East Anglia.*

SPON. A shaving of wood.

SPONDLES. The joints of the spine.

> We have, saith hee, an example of a woman, which was grievously vexed with an itch in the *spondles* or joints of the back-bone and reins, which she rubbing very vehemently, and rasing the skinne, small mammocks of stone fel from her to the number of eighteen, of the bignes of dice and colour of plaister.
> *Optick Glasse of Humors,* 1639, p. 120.

SPONE. A spoon. (*A.-S.*)

SPONENE. Spun; woven.

> Bot he has a kyrtille one kepide for hymeselvene,
> That was *sponene* in Spayne with specyalle byrdes,
> And sythyne garnesch in Grece fulle graythly togedirs.
> *Morte Arthure, MS. Lincoln, f. 64.*

SPONG. (1) An irregular, narrow, projecting part of a field, whether planted or in grass. If planted, or running to underwood, it would be called a squeech or queech. Spinny is another indefinite word applied, like dangle, reed, shaw, &c. to irregular bushy plots or pieces of land. *Moor.*

(2) To work carelessly. *Surrey.*

(3) *Hot spong,* a sudden power of heat from the sun emerging from a cloud. *East.*

(4) A boggy wet place. *Norf.*

SPONGE. One who imposes by taking more food, clothing, &c. than he is entitled to.

> Or from the wanton affection, or too profuse expence of light mistresses, who make choice of rich servants to make *sponges* of them.
> *The Two Lancashire Lovers,* 1640, p. 24.

SPONG-WATER. A small narrow stream. *East.*

SPONSIBLE. Applied to character, respectable; sometimes for responsible. *York.*

SPOOLING-WHEEL. The spole, q. v. " *Spola,* a weavers spooling-wheele or quill-turne," Florio, p. 525, ed. 1611.

SPOOM. To " go right before the wind without any sail." It was also spelt *spoon.*

> To *spoon,* or *spooning,* is putting a ship right before the wind and the sea, without any sail, which is call'd spooning afore, which is commonly done when in a great storm a ship is so weak, with age or labouring, that they dare not lay her under the sea. Sometimes, to make a ship go the steadier, they set the foresail, which is call'd *spooning with the foresail.* They must be sure of sea-room enough when they do this. *A Sea-Dictionary,* 12mo. Lond. 1708.

SPOON. The navel. *Yorksh.*

SPOON-MEAT. Broth; soup. *Var. dial.*

SPOON-PUDDINGS. Same as *Drop-dumplings,* q. v.

SPOORNE. The name of a fiend? See R. Scot's Discoverie of Witchcraft, quoted in Ritson's Essay on Fairies, p. 45.

SPORE. (1) Spur; prick. (*A.-S.*)

> He smote the stede wyth the *sporys,*
> And spared nother dyke nor forowe.
> *MS. Cantab. Ff. ii. 32, f. 159.*
> Nou thou him knowest and his bounté,
> Love him wel for charité
> Evermore to thi lyves ende,
> To joye and blisse then schalt ou wende,
> That he hath ordeyned for ure solace.
> Lord, bring us thider for thin grace!
> Thus endeth the *spore* of love,
> God grant us the blisse of hevene above.
> *The Prick of Love, Vernon MS.*

(2) A support to a post. *East.*

(3) Spared. *Cambridgesh.*

SPORGE. (1) To have a lask.

(2) To clean, or cleanse. (*A.-N.*)

SPORNE. (1) To strike the foot against anything. *Chaucer.*

(2) Shut; fastened. *Yorksh.*

SPORT. To show; to exhibit. *Var. dial.*

SPORYAR. A spurrier, or spur-maker.

SPOSAILS. Espousals; marriage.

> Hennes forward he seyd me,
> Schuld the *sposails* couthe be,
> Than schul ye acordi,
> And togider saughten wele an hi.
> *Cy of Warwike,* p. 261

SPOT. To drop; to sprinkle. *West.*

SPOTIL. Spittle.

> When thou wolt do awey the lettre, wete a pensel with *spotil* or with watur, and molst therwith the lettres that thou wolt do awey, and then cast the powder therupon, and with thi nail thou maist done awey the lettres. *Reliq. Antiq.* i. 109.

SPOTTLE. (1) A schedule. *Cumb.*

(2) To splash, or dirty. *West.*

SPOTTY. Run *spotty,* applied to hops when the crops are unequal. *Kent.*

SPOUCH. Sappy, as wood. *Suffolk.*

SPOUNCE. To splash. *Somerset.*

SPOUSE. To marry, or espouse. *Spowsyng,* marriage, espousals. (*A.-N.*)

> Yis, dame, he saide, preciouse,
> Gif thou me helpe, ich wille the *spouse.*
> *The Sevyn Sages,* 2006.
> The nyghte was gon, the day was come
> That the *spowsyng* was done.
> *MS. Cantab. Ff. ii. 38, f. 117.*

SPOUSEBRECHE. Adultery.

> And the furst day of his crownyng,
> Into *spousebreche* he feile anon.
> *Chron. Vilodun.* p. 21.
> In thys hest ys forbode alle *spousebreche* and alle fleshelyche dedys towchynge lecharye bytwene man and womman out of spowshode.
> *MS. Burney* 356, p. 96.
> For of the lest I will now speke,
> For soule-hele I wil you tech;
> Thynk on man, God wille hym wreke
> Of hym that is cause of *spouse-breke.*
> *MS. Cantab. Ff. v. 43, f. 66.*

SPOUSE-HEDE. State of marriage. See the first example quoted under *Roghte.*

SPOUT. (1) When a man is in high spirits, they say he is *in great spout. Berks.*

(2) To put anything up the spout, i. e. to place it in pawn. *Var. dial.*

SPRACK. Quick; lively; active. *West.*

SPRACKLE. To climb. *North.*

SPRADDENE. Spread out.

> Bot jit he sprange and sprente, and *spraddene* his armes,
> And one the spere lenghe spekes, he spekes thire wordes. *Morte Arthure, MS. Lincoln, f. 88.*

SPRAG. (1) The same as *Sprack,* q. v.

(2) To prop up. *Salop.*

(3) A young salmon. *North.*

SPRAGED. Spotted. *Devon.*

SPRAI. Sprigs; boughs; straw. *Hearne.*

SPRAID. (1) To sprinkle. *East.*

(2) Chopped with cold. *Devon.*

SPRAINTING. Dung of the otter.

> And of hares and of conynges he shal seye thei croteyeth, that of the fox wagyng, of the grey the warderebe, and of othere stynkyng beestys he shal clepe it dryt, and that of the otyr he shal clepe it *sprayntyng.* *MS. Bodl.* 546.

SPRALE. To sprawl about. *Devon.*

SPRALL. A carp. Holme, 1688.

SPRANGENE. Made to spring?

So they spede at the spoures, they *sprangene* theire horses,
Hyres theme hakenayes hastyly thereaftyre.
Morte Arthure, MS. Lincoln, f. 58.

SPRANK. (1) A sprinkling. *West.*
(2) Original ; clever. *I. of Wight.*
(3) A crack in wood. *Suffolk.*

SPRANKER. A watering-pot. *West.*

SPRAT-BARLEY. The species of barley with very long beards or awms, or auns. The *Hordeum vulgare* of Linn. *Moor.*

SPRAT-LOON. The small gull. *Kent.*

SPRATS. Small wood. *Kennett.*

SPRAT-WEATHER. The dark roky days of November and December are called *sprat weather*, from that being the most favorable season for catching sprats.

SPRAULEDEN. Sprawled. (*A.-S.*)
Hwan the children blth wawe
Leyen and *sprauleden* in the blod.
Havelok, 475.

SPRAWING. A sweetheart. *Wilts.*

SPRAWL. (1) Motion ; movement. *Somerset.*
2) To speak in a slow drawling tone ; to pant for want of breath.

SPRAWLS. Small branches ; twigs. *East.*

SPRAWT. To sprawl and kick. *North.*

SPRAY. (1) A twig, or sprig. (*A.-S.*) Binding sticks for thatching are called *sprays*.
(2)
The Bretans blode shalle undur falle,
The Brouttus blode shalle wyn the *spray* ;
Vij. thousynd Englisshe-men, gret and smalle,
Ther shalle be slayne that nyght and day !
MS. Cantab. Ff. v. 48, f. 121.

SPRAY-BRICKS—or SPLAY-BRICKS, are made with a bevil for reducing the thickness of a wall. They are otherwise called *set-off* bricks. I believe our names are from *display*, though that may not be deemed the most appropriate term. *Moor.*

SPREADER. A stick to keep out the traces from the horses' legs. *West.*

SPREATH. Active ; nimble. *Wilts.*

SPREATHED. Chopped with cold. *West.*

SPRECKLED. Speckled. *Var. dial.*

SPREDD.
The marynere set hur on hys bedd,
Sche hadd soone aftur a byttur *spredd.*
MS. Cantab. Ff. ii. 38, f. 238.

SPREE. (1) Spruce ; gay. *Devon.*
(2) A merry frolic. *Var. dial.*

SPREINT. Sprinkled. (*A.-S.*)
The wych was, as I understood,
Spreynt with dropys off red blood.
MS. Cott. Vitell. C. xiii. f. 97.

SPREMED. Striped. *Pegge.*

SPRENT. (1) Leapt. *Perceval, 1709.*
To the chambyr dore he *sprente,*
And claspid it with barres twoo.
MS. Harl. 2252, f. 109.

The lady ynto the schyp wente ;
xxx. fote the lyenas aftur *sprente.*
MS. Cantab. Ff. ii. 38, f. 85.

Whenne Florent sawe that swete wyghte,
He *sprent* als any fowle of flyghte,
No lenger thenne wolde he byde.
MS. Lincoln A. i. 17, f. 107.

(2) The steel spring on the back of a clasp knife *Northumb.*
(3) Sprinkled. (*A.-S.*)
(4) A spot, or stain. *Yorksh.*
(5) Sprained. *Arch. xxx. 413.*
(6) Shivered ; split. *Gawayne.*

SPRENTLENDE. Fluttering.
Sprentlende with hire wyngis twey,
As sche whiche schulde than deye.
Gower, MS. Soc. Antiq. 134, f. 103.

SPRET. (1) A boatman's pole. " Sprette for watermen, *picqz*," Palsgrave.
Some hente an oore and some a *sprytt*
The lyenas for to meete.
MS. Cantab. Ff. ii. 38, f. 85.
A lang *sprete* he bare in hande,
To strenghe hym in the water to stande.
MS. Lincoln A. i. 17, f. 125.

(2) A soul, or spirit. " *Spiritus*, a spret," Nominale MS. xv. Cent.
And wicked *spretus* so oryble and blake,
That besy bene to wayte me day and nyghte,
Let thi name dryve hem owte of syghte.
MS. Cantab. Ff. i. 6, f. 124.

SPRETCHED. Cracked ; applied only, as far as I know, to eggs, which having been set upon are said to become *spretched* a day or two before the liberation of the chicken is effected. *Linc.*

SPREY. The same as *Spree*, q. v.

SPRIG. (1) A lean lanky fellow. *North.*
(2) To turn off short. *Dorset.*
(3) A nail. *Var. dial.* Men who work in wall or mud-work, have to run barrows full of earth on planks, perhaps upwards. To prevent slips a triangular piece of iron is screwed to their shoe-heels, having three points half an inch long projecting downwards. These are called *sprigs.*

SPRIGHT. A small wooden arrow used to be discharged from a musket. " Sprights, a sort of short arrows (formerly used for sea-fight) without any other heads save wood sharpned, which were discharged out of musquets, and would pierce through the sides of ships where a bullet would not," Blount, p. 606.

SPRING. (1) Quick ; a young wood ; a young tree. Still in use in Suffolk. The term was also applied to a single rod or sprig.
(2) To dawn. Also, the dawn of day.
Be that the cok began to crow,
The day began to *spryng* ;
The scheref fond the jaylier ded,
The comyn belle made he ryng.
MS. Cantab. Ff. v. 48, f. 131.

(3) A tune.
(4) The lower part of the fore-quarter of pork, divided from the neck.
(5) To become active or sharp. *North.*
(6) To give tokens of calving. *Yorksh.*
(7) A snare for hares, birds, &c.

SPRINGAL. (1) An ancient military engine for casting stones and arrows. (*A.-N.*)
And sum thai wente to the wal
With bowes and with *springal.*
Beves of Hamtoun, p. 140.

Trybget, *spryngias*, and also engyne,
They wrouȝt owre men fulle mekyl payne.
Archæologia, xxi. 61.

(2) A youth ; a young lad.

SPRINGE. To sprinkle. (*A.-S.*) Still in use. To spring clothes is to moisten them a little previously to ironing.

SPRINGER. A lad. *East.*

SPRINGLE. (1) A rod about four feet in length, used in thatching. *Salop.*

(2) A snare for birds. *West.*

SPRINGOW. Nimble ; active. *Chesh.*

SPRING-TOOTH-COMB. A small toothed comb, one that has very fine teeth, and usually made of ivory.

SPRINGY. Elastic. *Var. dial.*

SPRINKE. (1) A crack, or flaw. *East.*

(2) To sprinkle ; to splash. *Linc.* It occurs in the Ord. and Reg. p. 469.

SPRINKLE. (1) A brush used by Roman Catholics for sprinkling the holy water. "*Ysopus*, a sprenkylle ; *aspersorium*, idem est," Nominale MS.

(2) A number, or quantity. *Var. dial.*

SPRINT. A snare for birds. *North.*

SPRIT. (1) To sprout ; to grow. *Chesh.*

(2) To split. *Devon and Cornw.*

SPRITE. The woodpecker. *East.*

SPRITTEL. A sprout, or twig.

SPROIL. Liveliness. *Devon.*

SPRONG. (1) The stump of a tree or tooth. *Sussex.* It is sometimes pronounced *spronk.*

(2) A prong of a fork, &c. *West.*

SPRONGE. Spread abroad. (*A.-S.*)
Kyng Ardus toke hys leve and wente,
And ledd with hym hys lady gente,
Home rychely conne they ryde ;
Alle hys londe was fulle fayne
That the qwene was come ageyn,
The worde *spronge* fulle wyde.
MS. Cantab. Ff. ii. 38, f. 82.

SPRONGENE. Shivered in pieces.
Whene his spere was *sprongene*, he spede hyme fulle ȝerne,
Swappede owtte with a swerde that swykede hym never. *Morte Arthure, MS. Lincoln*, f. 72.

SPROT. "Sprotte, a fysshe, *esplenc*," Palsgrave. A sprat, or smelt.

SPROTES. (1) Fragments. Small wood or sticks for firing is still called *sprote-wood.*
And thei breken here speres so rudely, that the tronchouns fleu in *sprotes* and peces alle aboute the halle. *Maundovile's Travels*, 1839, p. 238.

(2) Pimples ; eruptive spots.

SPROTTLE. To struggle. *North.*

SPROUT. To sprout potatoes is to break the young sprouts off. *North.*

SPROUZE. This strange verb is equivalent to stir or rouse up, or *uprouse* the fire. This may, probably, be its origin, with an accidental sibilant prefixed. *Moor's Suff. MS.*

SPRUCE. (1) Prussian, as Spruce-beer, &c.

(2) To make the crust of bread brown by heating the oven too much. *Beds.*

SPRUG-UP. To dress neatly. *Sussex.*

SPRUN. The fore part of a horse's hoof. Also, a sharp piece of iron to the sprun, to prevent the horse slipping on the ice.

SPRUNGE. To kick out ; to spurn. *Linc.*

SPRUNK. To crack, or split. *Essex.*

SPRUNKS.
With fryars and monks, with their fine *sprunks*,
I make my chiefest prey. *Robin Hood*, ii. 164.

SPRUNNY. (1) A sweetheart. *Var. dial.*
Where if good Satan lays her on like thee,
Whipp'd to some purpose will thy *sprunny* be.
Collins's Miscellanies, 1762, p. 111.

(2) Neat ; spruce. *Norf.*

SPRUNT. (1) A convulsive struggle. *Warw.*

(2) A steep road. *North.*

(3) Poisoned, said of cattle. *Surrey.*

SPRUNTLY. Sprucely. Ben Jonson, v. 105.

SPRUT. To jerk violently, as with a spasm. A violent jerk or sudden movement is called a sprut. *Sussex.*

SPRUTTLED. Sprinkled over. *Leic.*

SPRUZ. To keep fire at the mouth of an oven in order to preserve the heat.

SPRY. (1) Chapped with cold. *West.*

(2) Nimble ; active. *Somerset.*

SPRYNGGOLYNG. Sparkling ?
Toward the lady they come fast rennyng,
And sette this whele uppon her hede,
As eny hote yren yt was *sprynggolyng* rede.
MS. Laud. 416, f. 75.

SPRYNGYNG. *In the spryngyng of the mone*, i. e. at the time of the new moon.
A sybbe maryage thys day have we made
In the *spryngyng* of the mone.
MS. Cantab. Ff. ii. 38, f. 70.

SPRY-WOOD. Small wood, spray of the sea the foam or froth of it blown at a distance.

SPUD. (1) A spittle-staff, q. v. *Var. dial.*

(2) A baby's hand. *Somerset.*

(3) A short dwarfish person. *Essex.*

(4) A good legacy. *West.*

SPUDDLE. To move about ; to do any trifling matter with an air of business. *West.*

SPUDGEL. A small kind of trowel or knife ; also, an instrument to bale out water. *South.*

SPUDLEE. To stir or spread abroad the embers with a poker. *Exmoor.*

SPUNDGING.
On goes she with her holiday partlet, and *spundging* herself up, went with her husband to church, and came just to the service.
Tarlton's Newes out of Purgatorie, 1590.

SPUNK. (1) "*Spunk* in Herefordshire," says Urry, in his MS. notes to Ray, " is the excrescency of some tree, of which they make a sort of timber to light their pipes with."

(2) Spirit. *Var. dial.*
In that snug room where any man of *spunk*
Would find it a hard matter to get drunk.
Peter Pindar, i. 245.

(3) A spark ; a match. *North.*

SPUNKY. Very spirited. *Var. dial.*

SPUNT. Spurned. *Suffolk.*

SPUR. (1) The root of a tree. *North.*

(2) To spread manure. *West.*

(3) To prop ; to support. *South.* The spur of a post, a short buttress to support it.

(4) Time ; leisure. *West.*

SPUR-BLIND. Purblind. *Latimer.*

SPUR-GALLY. Wretched ; poor. *Dorset.*

SPURGE. (1) To ceil with a thin coat of mortar between the rafters, without laths. *East.*

(2) " I spurge, I clense as wyne or ale dothe in the vessell," Palsgrave. " I spurge, as a man dothe at the foundement after he is deed," Palsgrave, verb. f. 370.

> A mouse on a tyme felle into a barelle of newe ale, that *spourgide* ande myght not come out.
> *Gesta Romanorum,* p. 403.

> With his eyen and mouth fayre closed, withoute any staring, gapyng, or frownyng, also without any drevelyng or *spurgyng* in any place of his body.
> *Hall, Henry VIII.* f. 50.

> I have beene gathering wolves haires,
> The madd dogges foames, and adders eares ;
> The *spurging* of a deadmans eyes :
> And all since the evening starre did rise.
> *Percy's Reliques,* p. 245.

SPUR-HUNT. Or *spur-hound,* a finder, or dog that finds and puts up game.

SPURK. To rise up quickly. *East.*

SPURLING. A cart-rut. *Northumb.*

SPURN. (1) A piece of wood inserted at one end in the ground, and at the other nailed at an angle to a gatepost, for the purpose of strengthening or supporting it. *Linc.*

(2) To kick. Also, a kick.

(3) An evil spirit. *Dorset.*

SPUR-NAG.

> And like true *spur-nags,* strain hardest against the hill ; or, like thunder, tear it there most, where we meet with the sturdiest and most rugged oak.
> *A Cap of Grey Haires,* 1688, p. 52.

SPURN-POINT. An old game mentioned in a curious play called Apollo Shroving, 12mo. Lond. 1627, p. 49.

SPURRE. The same as *Spere,* q. v.

SPURRIER. A maker of spurs.

SPURRING. A smelt. *North.*

SPURRINGS. The banns of marriage.

SPURROW. To ask ; to inquire. *Westm.*

SPUR-ROYAL. A gold coin, worth about fifteen shillings. See Snelling's Coins, p. 24.

SPURS. (1) The short small twigs projecting a few inches from the trunk. *East.*

(2) When a young warrior distinguished himself by any martial act he was said *to win his spurs,* spurs being part of the regular insignia of knighthood.

SPURSHERS. Straight young fir trees.

SPURTLE. A small stick. *North.*

SPUR-WAY. A bridle-road. *East.*

SPUTE. Dispute. *Gawayne.*

SPUTHER. Squabble.

> When we know all the pretty *sputher,*
> Betwixt the one house and the other.
> *Brome's Songs,* 1661, p. 171.

SPY. The pilot of a vessel.

SQUAB. (1) An unfledged bird ; the young of an animal before the hair appears. *South.*

(2) A long seat ; a sofa. *North.* " A squob to sit on, *pulvinus mollicellus,*" Coles.

(3) To squeeze ; to knock ; to beat. *Devon.*

SQUAB-PIE. A pie made of fat mutton well peppered and salted, with layers of apple, and an onion or two. *West.*

SQUACKETT. To make any disagreeable noise with the mouth. " How Pincher *squacketis* about !" *Sussex.*

SQUAD. (1) Sloppy dirt. *Linc.*

(2) A group, or company. *Somerset.*

(3) *An awkward squad,* an awkward boy. Perhaps from *squad,* a small body of recruits learning their military exercises.

SQUAGED. Smeared ?

> For to make clens thy boke yf yt be *defowlyd* or *squaged.*—Take a schevyr of old broun bred of the crummys, and rub thy boke therwith sore up and downe, and yt shal clense yt. *Reliq. Antiq.* i. 163.

SQUAGHTE. Shook.

> The medwe *squughte* of her dentes,
> The fur flegh out so spark a flintes.
> *Beves of Hamtoun,* p. 69.

SQUAIGE. To whip, or beat. *East.*

SQUAIL. To throw sticks at cocks. *Squailer,* the stick thrown. *West.* Mr. Akerman says *squoiling* is used for *throwing,* but something more is required than merely throwing ; the thing thrown must be some material not easily managed. Jennings properly says, to fling with a stick ; and he might have added, with a stick sometimes made unequally heavy by being loaded with lead at one end. Squailing therefore is often very awkwardly performed, because the thing thrown cannot be well directed ; hence the word *squailing* is often used in ridicule, not only of what is done awkwardly, but what is untowardly or irregularly shaped. " She went up the street *squailing* her arms about, you never saw the like :" an ill shaped loaf is a *squailing* loaf ; Brentford is a long *squailing* town ; and, in Wiltshire, Smithfield Market would be called a *squailing* sort of a place.

SQUAILS. Ninepins. *Somerset.*

SQUAIMOUS. Squeamish. Perhaps as *esquaymous,* which I fear is explained wrongly.

SQUAINE. A herdsman, or servant.

> Hit is alle the kyngus waren,
> Ther is nouther knyȝt ne *swayne*
> That dar do sich a dede. *MS. Cantab.* Ff. v. 48, f. 49.

SQUALL. " *Obeseau,* a young minx or little proud squall," Cotgrave. " *Tu es un cainar,* thou art a squall," Hollyband's Dictionarie, 1593. The term was one of endearment as well as of reproach.

SQUALLEY. According to Blount, " a note of faultines in the making of cloth."

SQUALLY. A crop of turnips, or of corn, which is broken by vacant unproductive patches, is said to be squally. *Norf.*

SQUAMES. Scales. (*Lat.*)

SQUANDERED. Dispersed ; e. g. " His family are all grown up, and *squandered* about the country ;" i. e. settled in different places. *Warw.* " And other ventures he hath squandered abroad," Merch. Ven. i. 3.

SQUAP. (1) To sit down idly. *Somerset.*

(2) A blow. Also, to strike.

SQUARD. A rent in a garment. Also, to tear. *Cornw.*

SQUARE. (1) To quarrel ; to chide. *Shak.*

(2) To stand aside. *Yorksh.*

(3) To put one's self in an attitude fit for boxing. *Var. dial.*

(4) To strut; to swagger about. *Devon.*

(5) Honest; equitable. "*Square dealing.*"

SQUARE-DICE. Dice honestly made.

SQUARELY. Roundly; excessively.

SQUARES. (1) There is a common phrase, *all squares,* meaning all settled, all right. An instance of it occurs in the Pickwick Papers, p. 434. *To break squares,* means to depart from the accustomed order. See an instance of this latter phrase in Lambarde's Perambulation, 1596, p. 466. *To break no squares,* to give no offence, to make no difference. *How gang squares,* how do ye do? *How go the squares,* how goes on the game, as chess, the board being full of squares.

(2) Broad hoops of iron holding coals in the baskets while they are being drawn up from the pits. *North.*

SQUARKIN. (1) "I squarkyn, I burne the utter part of a thyng agaynst the fyer, or roste mete unkyndly, *je ars.* This mete is nat rostyd, it is squarkynnyd," Palsgrave, verb. f. 371.

(2) To suffocate. *Ibid.*

SQUARY. Short and fat. *North.*

SQUASH. (1) To splash. *East.*

(2) An unripe pod of a pea.

(3) To squeeze or crush to pieces. *West.*

SQUASHY. Soft; pulpy; watery. *Warw.*

SQUAT. (1) To bruise; to lay flat; to slap. *South.* "In our Western language *squat* is a bruise," Aubrey's Wilts, Royal Soc. MS. p. 127. "To squatte, or throwe anie thing against the ground," Baret, T. 213.

And you take me so near the net again,
I'll give you leave to *squat* me.
Middleton's Works, v. 35.

(2) To make quiet. *Var. dial.*

(3) To splash. *North.*

(4) A short stout person. *Linc.*

(5) To compress. *Devon.*

(6) A small separate vein of ore.

(7) Flat. (8) To make flat. *Kent.*

SQUAT-BAT. A piece of wood with a handle used to block the wheel while stopping on a hill. *Sussex.*

SQUATCH. A narrow cleft. *Somerset.*

SQUATMORE. The name of a plant.

Neer or at the salt-worke there growes a plant they call *squatmore,* and hath wonderfull vertue for a squatt; it hath a roote like a little carrat: I doe not heare it is taken notice of by any herballist.
Aubrey's MS. Wilts, p. 127.

SQUATTING-PILLS. Opiate pills; pills calculated to squat or quiet any one. *East.*

SQUAWK. To squeak. *Var. dial.*

SQUAWKING-THRUSH. The missel-thrush. *I. Wight.*

SQUAWP. A dirty or peevish child.

SQUEAK. To creak, as a door, &c.

SQUEAKED. Spoke. *Devon.*

SQUEAL. Infirm; weak. *Devon.*

That he was weak, and ould, and *squeal,*
And seldom made a hearty meal.
Peter Pindar, ed. 1794, 1. 286.

SQUEAN. To fret, as the hog.

SQUEECH. The same as *Queach,* q. v.

SQUEEZE. To squeeze. "Don't *squeeze me* to the wall," don't drive the bargain too close. A Gloucestershire phrase.

SQUELCH. (1) A fall. (2) To fall.

And yet was not the *squelch* so ginger,
But that I sprain'd my little finger.
Cotton's Works, 1734, p. 242.

(2) To give a blow in the stomach. *North.* See Middleton, iv. 410. "To squab, squelch, *collido,*" Coles. Also, a blow.

He was the cream of Brecknock,
And flower of all the Welsh;
But George he did the dragon fell,
And gave him a plaguy *squelch.*
St. George for England, 2d Part.

SQUELCH-BUB. An unfledged bird; used also for an ignorant youth. *Derby.*

SQUELCH-GUTTED. Very fat. *South.*

SQUELE. To squall; to shriek. *East.*

Bounden with his swatheling bonde,
There thougte him hit lay *squelunde.*
Cursor Mundi, MS. Coll. Trin. Cantab. f. 9.

SQUELSTRING. Sultry. *Devon.*

SQUELTRING. Sweltering.

The slaughter'd Trojans, *squeltring* in their blood,
Infect the air with their carcasses,
And are a prey for every rav'nous bird.
Tragedy of Locrine, p. 26.

SQUEMOUS. Saucy. *Lanc.*

SQUENCH. To quench. *Var. dial.* "Fetche pitch and flaxe, and *squench* it," First Part of the Contention, p. 59.

SQUIB. "*Connócchia,* a kinde of bushy squib," Florio, ed. 1611, p. 117.

SQUIB-CRACK. Cracking like a squib?

So your rare wit, that's ever at the full,
Lyes in the cave of your rotundious skull,
Untill your wisedomes pleasure send it forth,
From East to West, from South unto the North,
With *squib-crack* lightning, empty hogshead thundring,
To maze the world with terror and with wondring.
Taylor's Laugh and be Fat, 1630, p. 70.

SQUICHT.

But think you Basilisco *squicht* for that,
Ev'n as a cow for tickling in the horn?
Tragedy of Soliman and Perseda, p. 200.

SQUIDDLED. Cheated; wheedled. *West.*

SQUIDGE. To squeeze. *I. Wight.*

SQUIDLETS. Small pieces as of meat or cloth. "What use be sich little squidlets as that?" *Dorset.*

SQUIERIE. A company of squires.

SQUIF. A skiff, or small boat.

SQUIGGLE. To shake about. *Essex.*

SQUILLARY. A scullery. *Palsgrave.* "The pourveyours of the buttlarye and pourveyours of the squylerey," Ord. and Reg. p. 77. *Sergeaunt-squylloure,* ibid. p. 81. "All suche other as shall long unto the squyllare," Rutland Papers, p. 100. The squiller's business was to wash dishes, &c.

How the *squyler* of the kechyn,
Pers, that hath woned hereyn.
MS. Harl. 1701, f. 39.

SQUILT. A mark caused by disease. *Salop.*

SQUIMBLE-SQUAMBLE. "*Griffe graffe*, by hooke or by crooke, *squimble squamble*, scamblingly, catch that catch may," Cotgrave.

SQUINANCY. A quinsey.

> Good Lord, how many Athenian oratours have wee that counterfalte *squinancy* for a little coyne.
> *Don Simonidas*, 2d Part, 1584.
> If Jupiter be significator of the death, it denoteth that hee shall die of a plurisie, of a *squinance*, or of some hot apostumations of the liver, or of the lungs, or of other sicknesses comming of wind or of blood; and that if he be fortunate.
> *The Art of Astrologie*, 1642.

SQUINANCY-BERRIES. Black currants.

SQUINCH. (1) A quince. *Devon.*

(2) A crack in a floor. *West.*

(3) A small piece of projecting stonework at the top of the angle of a tower.

SQUINCY. A quinsey.

> Shall not we be suspected for the murder,
> And choke with a hempen *squincy.*
> *Randolph's Jealous Lovers*, 1646, p. 56.

SQUINDER. To smoulder. *East.*

SQUIN-EIES. Squinting eyes.

> Gold can make limping Vulcan walke upright,
> Make *squin-eies* looke straight.
> *How to Choose a Good Wife*, 1634.

SQUINK. To wink. *Suffolk.*

SQUINNY. (1) To squint. *Var. dial.* Shakespeare has the term, King Lear, iv. 6.

(2) Lean; slender. *East.*

(3) To fret, as a child. *Hants.*

SQUIPPAND. Sweeping. *Robson.*

SQUIR. (1) To cast away with a jerk. Boys *squir* pieces of tile or flat stones across ponds or brooks to make what are denominated *Ducks and drakes.* The term is used in the Spectator, No. 77, "I saw him squir away his watch a considerable way into the Thames."

(2) To whirl round. *Sussex.* Bailey gives *squirm* as a South country word, meaning "to move very nimbly about, spoken of an eel."

SQUIRE. (1) To wait or attend upon.

(2) *A squire of the body*, originally the attendant on a knight, but the term was afterwards applied to a pimp. *Squire of dames*, a person devoted to the fair sex; also, a pander. A pimp or procurer was also termed simply a *squire.* To squire, to pimp, as in the Citye Match, 1639, p. 35, "and spoile your *squiring* in the dark."

(3) "Squyer for a carpentar, *esquierre*," Palsgrave. "Squyer a rule, *riglet.*" *Ibid.*

(4) The neck. For *Swire.*

SQUIRILITY. Scurrility. Webster, iii. 28.

SQUIRM. To wriggle about. *South.*

SQUIRREL. A prostitute.

SQUIRREL-HUNTING. A curious Derbyshire custom. The *wakes* at Duffield are held on the first Sunday after the first of November, and on the wakes Monday the young men and boys of the village collect together, to the number of two or three hundred, and with pots and kettles, frying-pans, cows' horns, and all the discordant instruments they can pro-cure, proceed to Kedleston, about three miles distant, in search of a squirrel. They gather themselves round the fine oaks and elms in the park, and with the noise of their instruments and their loud halloos soon succeed in starting one amongst the boughs. This they chase from tree to tree, until stunned with the noise, and wearied with exertion, it falls to the ground, and is captured; it is carried back in triumph to Duffield, and not unfrequently undergoes the torment of a second hunt in a wood near the village. Whether this is the remains of a privilege of hunting in the forest of Duffield, possessed by the inhabitants or not, I know not, but many unsuccessful attempts have been made to stop it, the inhabitants always asserting their right to hunt. At the same village the old custom of wren hunting is still observed. See *Hunting-the-Wren.*

SQUIRT. "Squyrte a laxe, *foire*, Palsgrave, subst. f. 66.

SQUIRTEL. "Sqwyrtyl or swyrtyl, *sifons, sibilo*," Prompt. Parv. MS. Harl. 221, f. 162.

SQUISE. To squeeze. Baret, 1580.

SQUISH-SQUASH. The noise made by the feet in walking over a swampy piece of ground. *South.*

SQUISHY. Sloppy and dirty. *East.*

SQUIT. Small. A word confined in its use. "A little *squit* of a thing" is said disparagingly of a somewhat diminutive and not pleasing young woman.

SQUITTER. (1) To squirt. *Somerset.*

(2) Corrupt matter. Batman, 1582.

(3) A lask, or looseness. *Var. dial.*

SQUIZZEN. To crush; to rumple. *East.* Also the part. pa. of *to squeeze.*

SQULSH. The same as *Gulch*, q. v.

SQUOACE. To truck, or exchange. *Somerset.*

SQUOAVERAN-CALLAN. A jesting youth.

SQOB. (1) With a crash. "He throwed him down *squob.*" *Sussex.*

(2) *To squob a bird's nest*, to throw sticks or stones at it and break the eggs. *Oxon.*

(3) Fat and lusty; plump.

SQUOBBLE. A term among printers; when the letters fall out of a form they say it is *squobbled.* Holme, 1688.

SQUOLK. A draught of liquor. *Essex.*

SQUOLSH. The sound which is produced by the fall of soft heavy bodies. *Essex.*

SQOT. To spot with dirt. *Derb.*

SQUOURGE. To scourge. *Palsgrave.*

SQUOZZON. Squeezed. *North.*

SQUY-BOBBLES. This singular word was familiarly used by mine hostess at Felixstow. "He'd a bawt the home, but for the lawyer's *squi-bobbles*," referring to difficulties or delay about title. I know not how far the use of the word may extend. It seemed expressive and easily understood. *Moor's Suff. MS.*

SQUYWINNIKEN. Awry; askew. *East.*

SQWERYLLE. A squirrel. This form occurs in the Nominale MS. xv. Cent.

SRUD. Clothed. (*A.-S.*)

> And com into then halle,
> Ther hoe wes *srud* with palle. *MS. Digby* 86.

STA. State. *Hearne.*

STAB. A hole in the ground in which the female rabbit secures her litter while they are very young. *Sussex.*

STABBING. *Stabbing the dice,* a system of cheating by using a box so contrived that the dice would not turn in it.

STABBLE. To soil anything by walking on it with dirty shoes. *Hants.*

STABILER. "*Stabularius,* a stabyler," Nominale MS. xv. Cent.

STABLE. To make firm or stable.

> Ryʒt so the gyfte of pité festes,
> And *stables* the hert thare it restes. *MS. Harl.* 2960, f. 4.

STABLED. When a rider sinks with his horse into a deep hole or bog, he is said to be stabled. *Oxon.*

STABLISSE. To establish. (*A.-N.*)

> Til God of his goodnesse
> Gan *stablisse* and stynte,
> And garte the hevene to stekie
> And stonden in quiete. *Piers Ploughman,* p. 22.

STABLYE. Station of huntsmen. *Gawayne.*

STABULL. Stable; firm.

> Gye calde forthe the constabull,
> A nobull man, and of cowncell *stabull.* *MS. Cantab.* Ff. ii. 38, f. 167.

STACE. Statius, the Roman poet.

STACIA. A term of comparison used in Norfolk, e. g. that will do like stacia, as drunk as stacia, &c.

STACK. (1) A chimney-piece. *West.*

(2) A flight of stone steps outside a building. *Glouc. and Heref.*

STACKBARS. Large hurdles with which haystacks in the field are generally fenced. *Yorksh.*

STACKE. Stuck. (*A.-S.*)

STACKER. To reel; to stagger. *North.*

STACK-TOMB. A table monument. *East.*

STADD. Put; placed.

> Y wylle dyne for love of thee,
> Thou haste byn strongly *stadd.* *MS. Cantab.* Ff. ii. 38, f. 65.

STADDLE. (1) The stain left on metal after the rust is removed. *West.* According to Grose, "a mark or impression made on anything by something lying upon it."

(2) A support for a stack of corn, &c. *Staddling,* stuff to make a staddle.

(3) To cover. *West.*

STADDLE-ROW. A large row of dried grass ready for quiling or carrying. *Derby.*

STADDOW. An instrument used by combmakers, mentioned by Holme, iii. 383.

STADE. (1) A shore or station for ships. This word is constantly used at Hastings. "Stade and stath, a sea-bank or shore, Sax. stathe, *littus, statio navium,* whence at Hith in Kent the landing-place or sea-side to which the boats come up is now calld the *stade,* and at Hoveden in Yorkshire the like landing-places are termd *Hooden stathes,*" Kennett MS.

(2) Placed?

> When they ware *stade* on a strenghe, thou sulde hafe withstondene,
> Bot ʒif thowe wolde alle my steryne stroye fore the nonys. *Morte Arthure, MS. Lincoln* f. 73.

STADELL. The step of a ladder. *Kent.*

STADIE. A stadium.

> And with o wynde he wolde renne a *stadie.* *MS. Digby* 230.

STADLE. To cut woods in such a manner as to leave, at certain distances, young plants to replenish them. *Stadles,* young growing trees left after cutting underwood.

> It is commonlie seene that those yoong *staddles,* which we leave standing at one and twentie yeeres fall, are usuallie at the next sale cut downe without any danger of the statute, and serve for fire bote, if it please the owner to burne them. *Harrison's England,* p. 214.

STAED. A bank. *Oxon.*

STAFF. (1) Part of a knight's armour, alluded to in Warner's Albion's England, xii. 291.

(2) A measure of nine feet. *Devon.*

(3) To scoff at; to ridicule. *Devon.*

(4) A pair of fighting-cocks. *South.*

(5) *To put down his staff in a place,* to take up his residence. *To keep the staff in his hand,* to retain possession of his property; *to part with the staff,* to part with his property. *Staff hedge,* a hedge made of stakes and underwood.

(6) A stave, or stanza.

STAFF-HIRD. To have sheep under the care or a shepherd. *North.*

STAFF-HOOK. A sharp hook fastened to a long handle to cut peas and beans, and trim hedges. *I. of Wight.*

STAFFIER. A lacquey. (*Fr.*)

> Before the dame, and round about,
> March'd whifflers and *staffiers* on foot. *Hudibras,* II. ii. 650.

STAFFLE. To walk about irregularly. *North.*

STAFFORD-COURT. He has had a trial in Stafford Court, i. e. he has been beaten or illtreated. "*Il a esté au festin de Martin bastoh,* he hath had a triall in Stafford Court, or hath received Jacke Drums intertainment," Cotgrave. "*Braccésca licenza,* as we say Stafford's law," Florio, p. 66.

STAFF-RUSH. The round-headed rush.

STAFF-SLING. A kind of sling formed with a staff. "*Potraria, fustibulum,* staffslynge," Nominale MS. "Staffe slyng made of a clyfte stycke, *ruant,*" Palsgrave.

> With tarbarelle and with wilde fyre,
> With *stafslynges* and other atyre. *MS. Addit.* 10036, f. 24.

> Foremeste he sette hys arweblasteres,
> And aftyr that hys good archeres,
> And aftyr hys *staff-slyngeres,*
> And othir with scheeldes and with speres. *Richard Coer de Lion,* 4455.

STAF-FUL. Quite full.

> Now ar thay stoken of sturne werk *staf-ful* her hond. *Syr Gawayn and the Grene Knyʒt,* 494.

STAFT. Lost or wasted?

> Then take out the suet that it be not *staft,*
> For that, my freend, is good for leachcraft. *The Booke of Hunting,* 1586.

STAG. (1) A castrated bull. *Var. dial.*

(2) A hart in its fifth year. Maistre of the Game, MS. Bodl. 546.

(3) A young horse. *Cumb.*

(4) A wren. (5) A cock turkey, killed for eating in his second year. *East.*

(6) A romping girl. *Yorksh.*

(7) A gander. *North.* Aubrey gives the following Lancashire proverb :

> He that will have his fold full
> Must have an old tup, and a young bull;
> He that will have a full flock
> Must have an old *stagg* and a young cock.
> *MS. Royal Soc.* p. 298.

STAGART. A hart in its fourth year. Maistre of the Game, MS. Bodl. 546.

STAGE. A step, floor, or story. Palsgrave has, "stage, a scaffolde, *estage, beffroy.*"

> Then shall men fetch down off the stage
> All the maidens of parage,
> And bring hem into an orchard,
> The fairest of all middelard.
> *Ellis's Met. Rom.* iii. 126.

STAGGARTH. A stack-yard. *Linc.*

STAGGED. Bogged. *Devon.*

STAGGERING. "Staggeryng or leanyng of an house, *bransle,*" Palsgrave.

STAGGERING-BOB. A very young calf. *Chesh.*

STAGGERS. (1) Staggering or violent distress, metaphorically from the disease so called. *Shak.* See Nares, in v.

(2) The giddiness in sheep occasioned by a worm in its brain. *Dorset.*

(3) Old quick removed from one hedge to another. *Salop.*

STAGGERY. Liable to tremble. *Midx.*

STAGGY-WARNER. A boy's game. The boy chosen for the stag clasps his hands together, and holding them out threatens his companions as though pursuing them with horns, and a chase ensues, in which the stag endeavours to strike one of them, who then becomes stag in his turn.

STAG-HEADED. Said of a tree the upper branches of which are dead. *North.*

STAGING. (1) Scaffolding. *Norf.* The term occurs in Anecdotes and Traditions, p. 37.

(2) Standing quite upright. *Northumb.*

STAGNATE. To astonish utterly. *Var. dial.*

STAGNE. A lake. "By the *stagne* of Genazareth," Golden Legend, ed. 1483, f. 82. "Duckes meate, whiche is a kinde of weades hovering above the water in pondes or stangnes, *lens palustris,*" Huloet, 1552.

STAGON. The male of the red deer in its fourth year. See Harrison, p. 226.

STAID. Of advanced age. *Var. dial.*

STAIDLIN. A part of a corn-stack left standing. *North.*

STAIL. A handle. *Var. dial.*

STAIN. (1) To paint. *Somerset.*

(2) To outdo, or excel.

STAINCH. A root like liquorice. *North.*

STAINCHILS. Door-posts. *North.*

STAIR-FOOT. The bottom of the stairs.

STAITH. An embankment; a narrow road or lane leading over the bank of a river to the waterside; a warehouse. The same as *Stathe,* q. v.

STAK. A stake; a post. *(A.-S.)*

> He ys a lyoun in feld,
> When he ys spred undur scheld !
> Hys helme shal be wel steled,
> That stond shal as *stak*.
> *Degrevant,* 1044.

STAKE. (1) To shut; to fasten. *North.*

(2) Lot, or charge. *Devon.*

(3) To block up.

> Then caus'd his ships the river up to *stake*,
> That none with victual should the town relieve.
> *Drayton's Poems,* p. 27.

(4) In MS. Med. Rec. Lincoln, f. 294, xv. Cent. is a receipt for "the *stake* in the syde." The tightness of the chest, producing difficulty of breathing, is called *staking at the stomach.* See Salop. Antiq. p. 576. "The brest with the stak," Arch. xxx. 413.

(5) A small anvil standing on a broad iron foot, to move on the work-bench at pleasure. Holme gives the name to "a great iron for a smith to forge iron or steel-work upon."

STAKE-AND-RICE. A wattled fence.

STAKE-BEETLE. A wooden club to drive stakes in. *South.*

STAKE-HANG. Sometimes called only a *hang.* A kind of circular hedge made of stakes, forced into the sea-shore, and standing about six feet above it, for the purpose of catching salmon, and other fish. *Somerset.*

> A knaw'd all about tha *stake-hangs*
> Tha zalmon vor ta catch,
> Tha pitchin an tha dippin net,
> Tha slime an tha mud-batch.
> *Jennings' Observations,* 1825, p. 141.

STAKER. To stagger. *(A.-S.)* "*Offensator,* he that *stakereth* in redyng, as though he were not perfecte in readyng, or readeth otherwyse than it is written," Elyot, ed. 1559. "*Stakkerynge* on the ground," Morte d'Arthur, ii. 52. Still in use in Devon.

STAKING. Costiveness in cattle. *Yorksh.*

STALANE. A stallion. "*Emissarius,* a stalane," Nominale MS.

STAL-BOAT. A fishing-boat. *Blount.*

STALDER. A pile of wood. It is the translation of *chantier de bois* in Hollyband's Dictionarie, 1593. A stalder is the stool on which casks are placed.

STALE. (1) To steal. Also, stolen.

> Also if ye ever *stale* eny straynche child,
> As som women do in divers place.
> *MS. Laud.* 416, f. 62.

> Nodur no man of flesche nor felle,
> Hyt ys a fende *stale* fro helle.
> *MS. Cantab.* Ff. ii. 38, f. 118.

(2) A decoy; a snare. "Stale for foules takynge," Palsgrave. "The lyon never prayeth on the mouse, nor faulcons stoupe not to dead *stales,*" Dorastus and Fawnia, p. 38. "Laie in stale," i. e. in wait, Stanihurst's Descr. Ireland, p. 21. "A stale or pretence, a fraud or deceit," Kennett, MS. Lansd. 1033, f. 392.

> If it be a solitary beauty you court, which as yet is *intemerata virgo,* so that none beside take to the

scent, she will not long be so, for your attendance will be but like the fowlers *stale*, the appearance of which brings but others to the net.

A Cap of Gray Hairs for a Green Head, 1688, p. 96.

He ordeined certain of his men to geve assaulte to the toune of Guisnes while he stode in a *stale* to lie in waite for the relefe that might come from Callis.

Hall's Union, 1548, *Hen. IV.* f. 31.

(3) A company or band? "To keep the stale," Malory's Morte d'Arthur, i. 150.

With hys stelyne brande he strykes of hys hevede,
And sterttes owtte to hys stede, and with his *stale* wendes. *Morte Arthurs, MS. Lincoln*, f. 67.

(4) A prostitute. A cant term. Our old writers use the term in the sense of *a substitute for another in wickedness, especially in adultery*, as in Middleton, ii. 521, or sometimes as a cover for another's guilt.

And that is all I could do, for before
I could get earnest of any ones love,
To whom I made addresse, even she would say,
You have another mistresse, go to her,
I wil not be her *stale*.

The Shepheards Holyday, sig. G. 1.

Must an husband be made a *stale* to sinne, or an inlet to his owne shame?

The Two Lancashire Lovers, 1640, p. 21.

(5) Wanting freshness, formerly applied in this sense generally.

(6) Urine. Still in use. " Stale, pysse, *escloy*," Palsgrave, 1530, subst. f. 66.

(7) A stalk. *Warw.*

(8) To render stale or flat; to make cheap or common. *Shak.*

(9) A hurdle. *North.*

(10) The round of a ladder.

(11) The confederate of a thief.

Lives like a gentleman by sleight of hand,
Can play the foist, the nip, the *stale*, the stand.

Taylors Brood of Cormorants, 1630, p. 8.

(12) To hide away. *Somerset.*

(13) *A stale maid*, an old maid.

STALE-BEER. Strong beer. *I. of Wight.*

STALENGE. To compound for anything by the year or number. *North.*

STALINGE. Urine.

Summe of Alexander knyghtes lykked irene,
summe dranke oyle, and summe ware at so grete meschefe that thay dranke thaire awene *stalynge*.

MS. Lincoln A. 1. 17, f. 27.

STALK. (1) A company of foresters.

(2) To use a stalking-horse for obtaining wild-fowl and game.

(3) The. leg of a bird. " *Oiseau trop haut assis*, whose staulkes (or legs) are too long," Cotgrave, in v. *Assis.*

(4) A quill, or reed.

(5) The part of a crossbow from which the arrow is ejected. " Stalke of a shafte, *fust*," Palsgrave, 1530, subst. f. 66.

(6) The upright piece of a ladder; the principal upright in any small monumental erection.

(7) The stem of a tree. *West.*

STALKE. To step slowly. (*A.-S.*)

And to the bedde he *stalketh* stille,
Where that he wist was the wife,
And in his hande a rasour knife
He bare, with whiche hir throte he cut.

Gower, ed. 1554, f. 32

STALKER. (1) A fowler. Properly, one who used the stalking-horse. *North.*

(2) A kind of fishing net.

STALKING. Wet and miry. *Glouc.*

STALKING-COAT. A sort of coat worn in England in the reign of Henry VIII.

STALKING-HORSE. A horse real or fictitious, by which a fowler screens himself from the sight of the game.

What a slie buzzard it is! A man can scarce get a shoot at him with a *stalking-horse*. He has been scar'd sure.

Clarke's Phraseologia Puerilis, 1655, p. 126.

There is no getting at some fowl without a *stalking-horse*, which must be some old jade trained up for that purpose, who will gently, as you would have him, walk up and down in the water which way you please, flodding and eating the grass that grows therein; behind whose fore-shoulder you are to shelter yourself and gun, bending your body down low by his side, and keeping his body still full between you and the fowl. When you are within shot take your level from before the fore-part of the horse, giving fire as it were between his neck and the water, which is much better shooting than under his belly. Now to supply the defect of a real *stalking-horse*, which will take up a great deal of time to instruct and make fit for this exercise, an artificial one may be made of any piece of old canvas, which is to be shap'd in form of a horse, with the head bending downwards, as if he graz'd. It may be stuffed with any light matter, and should be painted of the colour of a horse, whereof brown is the best; in the middle let it be fixt to a staff, with a sharp iron at the end, to stick into the ground as occasion requires, standing fast while you take your level; and farther, as it must be very portable, it should also be moved, so as it may seem to graze as it goes; neither ought its stature be too high or too low, for the one will not hide the body, and the other will be apt to fright the fowl away. But when you have so beat the fowl with the *stalking-horse* that they begin to find your deceit, and will no longer endure it, you may stalk with an ox or cow made of painted canvas, till the *stalking-horse* be forgot, while others again stalk with stags, or red deer, formed out of painted canvas, with the natural horns of stags fixed thereon, and the colour so lively painted that the fowl cannot discern the fallacy. *Dictionarium Rusticum*, 1726.

STALL. (1) To forestall. *Jonson.*

(2) To tire; to satiate. *North.*

(3) To choke. *Northumb.*

(4) A temporary hut. *Northampt.*

(5) To set fast, as in mud, &c.

(6) A doorless pew in a church.

(7) A covering for a finger, used to protect it when cut or sore. *Var. dial.*

(8) A term of contempt.

So shall you meete with that *stall*,
That woulde my kingdome clayme and call.

Chester Plays, i. 178.

(9) To stall a debt, i. e. to forbear it for a time. Leycester Corresp. p. 45.

(10) Place; seat; room. *Stalle*, to sit in place, to order. (*A.-S.*)

Als he was stoken in that *stall*,
He herd byhind him, in a wall,
A dor opend fair and wele,
And tharout come a damysel.

Ywaine and Gawin, 695.

And thanke ther lord that sytteth on hye,
That formeth and *stalleth* the kyngys see.
MS. Cantab. Ff. ii. 38, f. 2.

(11) To make, or ordain. *Stalling to the rogue,*
an old method of admitting into the society
of canting rogues.

(12) To fatten. " It is tyme to stall your oxyn
that you entend to sel after Ester," *Palsgrave.*

STALLAGE. A wooden trough on which casks
are placed for working beer. *Sussex.*

STALLANT. A stallion. *Palsgrave.*

STALLING. Making, or ordaining. So explained by Dekker, in his Lanthorne and
Candle-Light, 1620, sig. C. iii.

STALLING-KEN. A house for receiving stolen
goods. *Dekker, 1612.*

STALLON. A slip from a plant.

STALUME. A stallion. *Palsgrave.*

STALWORTH. Strong; stout; brave.
We had a brodur they callyd Moradas,
Wyth the emperowre he was,
A *stalworth* man y-nogh.
MS. Cantab. Ff. ii. 38, f. 80.
And this waud noght brusell ne faldande bot *stal-
worthly* lastand. *MS. Coll. Eton. 10, f. 5.*
And scho strenyde me so *stalle-worthely*, that I
had no mouthe to speke, ne no hande to styrre.
MS. Lincoln A. i. 17, f. 193.
And *stallworthely* were so he wende,
And lastandely to hys lyves ende.
MS. Harl. 2260, f. 16.

STAM. (1) The stem of a vessel?
So stowttly the forsterne one the *stam* hyttis,
That stokkes of the stere-burde strykkys in peces.
Morte Arthure, MS. Lincoln, f. 91.

(2) To amaze ; to confound. *East.*

STAM-BANG. Plump down. *Cornw.*

STAMBER. To stammer.
Curled locks on idiots heads,
Yeallow as the amber,
Playes on thoughts as girls with beads,
When their masse they *stamber.*
Armin's Nest of Ninnies, 1608.

STAMEL. A kind of fine worsted.
Some *stamel* weaver, or some butcher's son,
That scrub'd alate within a sleeveless gown.
The Return from Parnassus, p. 248.
Shee makes request for a gowne of the new-fashion
stuffe, for a petticote of the finest *stammell,* or for a
hat of the newest fashion.
*The Arraignment of lewd, idle, froward, and
Unconstant Women, 1628, p. 12.*
But long they had not danc'd, till this yong maid,
In a fresh *stammell* petticote aray'd,
With vellure sleves, and bodies tied with points,
Began to feele a loosenesse in her joynts.
Times Curtaine Drawne, 1621, sig. D. iv.

STAMINE. (1) Linsey-woolsey cloth ; a garment
made of that material.
Oo kirtel and oo cote for somer, with a blak
habite above hem, and evereither tyme ij. *stamyns.*
MS. Bodl. 423, f. 182.

(2)
Standis styffe one the *stamyne,* steris one aftyre,
Strekyne over the streme, thare stryrynge begynnes.
Morte Arthure, MS. Lincoln, f. 91.

STAMMER. To stumble, or stagger. *North.*

STAMMERING. Doubtful. *Batman, 1582.*

STAMMIN. Wonderful ; surprising. *East.*

STAMP. (1) A halfpenny.

(2) A tune.
Songes, *stampes,* and eke daunces,
Dyvers plenté of pleasaunces,
And many unkouth notys newe
Of swich folkys as lovde trewe ;
And instrumentys that dyde excelle,
Many moo thane I kane telle. *MS. Fairfax 16.*
While Josian was in Ermonie,
She hadde lerned of minstralcie,
Upon a fithele for to play
Staumpes, notes, garibles gay.
Beves of Hamtoun, p. 143.

(3) To bruise in a mortar.
Stampe the onyone, and tempre yt with watur,
and ʒif the syke to drynk, and anoon he schal speke.
MS. in Mr. Pettigrew's Possession, xv. Cent.

(4) To thrash out the seeds of flax.

(5) Put to stampe, i. e. to press.
Wrote a greate boke of the saied false and feined
miracles and revelacions of the said Elizabeth in a
faire hand, redy to bee a copie to the printer when
the saied boke should be put to *stampe.*
Hall, Henry VIII. f. 221.

(6) Explained by Hearne, a pond.
Sir James of Beauchamp wonded and may not stand,
In a water *stampe* he was dronkled fleand.
Langtoft's Chronicle, p. 288.

STAMP-CRAB. One who treads heavily.

STAMPERS. Shoes. *Dekker.*

STAMPINGS. Holes in a horse's shoe.

STAMPS. (1) " Pounders or beating-hammers
lift up by a wheel, moved with water, and
falling by their own weight to stamp or beat
small the slags or cinders of refuse metal, are
calld *stamps,*" Kennett MS.

(2) Legs. A cant term, occurring in Dekker's
Lanthorne and Candle-Light, 1620, sig. C. iii.

STAM-WOOD. The roots of trees stubbed or
grubbed up. *South.*

STAN. (1) A stone. *Linc.*

(2) To reckon ; to count. *Newc.*

(3) A stick used by butchers for keeping the
belly and legs of a slaughtered beast stretched
out. *Holme, 1688.*

STANARD. A yard for stones. *Linc.*

STANBRODS. Slate pins, generally made of
the leg-bones of sheep.

STANCH. A lock in a river or canal, including
the masonry and gates, &c. *Linc.*

STANCHIL. (1) The stannel-hawk. *North.*

(2) A bar ; generally, the iron-bar of a window,
or a stanchion, q. v.
Round about the said tomb-stone, both at the
sides and at either end, were set up neat *stanchells*
of wood, joyned so close that one could not put in
his hand betwixt one and the other.
Davies' Ancient Rites, ed. 1672, p. 118.

STANCHION. The bar of a window. Also, a
prop or support. The term is still in use in
the first sense, generally pronounced *stansion.*
See Grose and Pegge, p. 152. " Stanchon of
a wyndowe, *croysee,*" Palsgrave. " Staunchon,
a proppe, *estancon,*" Ibid.

STANCHLESS. Insatiable. *Shak.*

STANCROPPES. The herb *crassula minor.*
See MS. Sloane 5, f. 4, xv. Cent.

STAND. (1) *To stand in hand, to stand on,* to
concern or interest. *To stand to do it,* to be

able to do it. *To stand to a child*, to be sponsor for it. *To stand to*, to maintain an assertion. *To stand upon anything*, to make it a matter of consequence. *To stand for it*, to engage to the correctness of anything. *To stand by any one*, to protect him.

(2) A stall in a stable. *North.*
(3) To put up with. *Var. dial.*
(4) The stickleback. *Suffolk.*
(5) A young unpolled tree. *East.*
(6) A beer-barrel set on one end.
(7) A building erected for spectators at a race or other amusement. ·
(8) A frame for supporting barrels, &c.
(9) To be maintained or upheld.

STANDARD. (1) A frame, or horse. Wooden frames of various kinds are so called.
(2) A large chest, generally used for carrying plate, jewels, and articles of value, but sometimes for linen.

> item, the said Anne shall have two *standard-chestes* delivered unto her for the keeping of the said diaper, the one to keep the cleane stuff, and th' other to keep the stuff that hath been occupied.
>
> *Ordinances and Regulations*, p. 215.

(3) A tree growing unsupported. *Var. dial.*
(4) One who remains long in a place.
(5) A large wax taper. "A great torch of waxe, which we call a *standard* or a quarrier," Florio, p. 161, ed. 1611.
(6) The upright bar of a window.

STANDAXE. An ox-stall. Arch. xiii. 383.

STAND-BACK-DAY. A day, among a company of sheep-shearers, in which some or all the company have no employment. *East.*

STANDELWELKS. Satyrion. *Gerard.* Standergrass is another name, ib. p. 169.

STANDERS. (1) "The trees left for encrease in the woods." This is the explanation of the word in Hollyband's Dictionarie, 1593.
(2) Iron uprights used in building? Privy Purse Expences Eliz. York, p. 25.

STANDERT. A standard. *Palsgrave.* Meyrick explains it, "a pole, on the top of which was set a mark."

STAND-FURTHER. A quarrel; a disunion. "There's quite a stand-further between them." *Wilts.*

STAND-HOLES. "*I'll stand holes*," I will hold to my bargain; sometimes thus limited, "*I'll stand holes* till next Wednesday." It seems borrowed from the game kit-kat, or bandy wicket, at which if a player indicate an intention of running indiscreetly in the opinion of another, the latter will fix him to his position by roaring out "*stand holes*."

STANDING-HOUSE. A domestic establishment. See Stanihurst, p. 21.

> The beere that is used at noble mens tables in their fixed and *standing houses*, is commonlie of a yeare old, or peradventure of two yeares tunning or more, but this is not generall.
>
> *Harrison's England*, p. 167.

STANDING-PECE. "Standyng pece, *couppe*," Palsgrave. "Standyng pece, with a cover,

couppe," ibid. "Stondyng-pece, *crathere*," MS. Arundel 249, f. 89.

STANDING-STOOL. A small wooden machine with wheels, formerly used for children.

> Thus far his infancy: his riper age
> Requires a more misterious folio page.
> Now that time speaks him perfect, and 'tis pitie
> To dandle him longer in a close committee,
> The elf dares peep abroad, the pretty foole
> Can wag without a truckling *standing-stoole*.
>
> *Fletcher's Poems*, p. 130.

STANDING-WATCH. Sentinels or scouts in an army stationed at the outer posts.

STANDISH. An inkstand.

> Pausing awhile over my *standish*, I resolved in verse to paynt forth my passion.
>
> *Pierce Pennilesse*, 1592.

STAND-STILL. A stoppage. *Var. dial.*

STANDYTH. Remaineth.

> Y tryste in God that he schalle me spede,
> He *standyth* wyth the ryght.
>
> *MS. Cantab.* Ff. ii. 38, f. 79.

STANE. A stone. *Stane-still*, still as a stone, quite still. *North.*

> When the king had said his will,
> Al the lordes sat *stane-still*;
> Of al the wise men that thar ware,
> Nane kowth gif him graith answare.
>
> *The Sevyn Sages*, 3688.

STANFRA. Backwards; unwilling. *Yorksh.*

STANG. (1) An eel-spear. *North.*
(2) To throb with pain. *Linc.*
(3) A rood of land. *North.*
(4) The bar of a door. "A bolte, a barre or stang of a dore," Florio, p. 89.
(5) A piece of wood on which the carcases of beasts are suspended. *North.*
(6) A wooden bar; the pole on which a tub is suspended. "*Tine*, a stand, open tub, or soe most in use during the time of vintage, and holding about foure or five pailefulls, and commonly borne by a *stang* betweene two," Cotgrave. "This word is still used in some colleges in the University of Cambridge: to *stang* scholars in Christmas being to cause them to ride on a coltstaff or pole for missing of chappel," Ray, ed. 1674, p. 44.

> And yet hem halches al hole the halves to-geder,
> And sythen on a stif *stange* stoutly hem henges.
>
> *Syr Gawayn and the Grene Knyзt*, 1614

(7) *Riding the stang.* This is a custom well known throughout the North, and intended for the benefit of those husbands who beat their wives. Formerly the offending party was forcibly mounted across a *stang* or pole, on which he was conveyed with a rabble at his heels through the town or village, and compelled to listen to the proclamation of his unmanly conduct, accompanied with the noise of tin cans, horns, &c. But now some one of the assembled multitude, consisting chiefly of boys, is elevated on a pole or ladder, and gives utterance to the following doggrel verses:

> Ran, Dan, Dan, the sign of our old Tin Can,
> *Taylor Wood* has been beating his good woman;

He beat her with neither stick, stone, nor stower,
But up'd with his goose and knock'd her ower.
If ever he does the like again,
As we suppose he will,
We'll mount him on a nanny goat,
And ride him down to hell.

So runs a version obtained some years ago at Louth by Mr. Adcock, and probably continues to this day. In the neighbourhood of Lincoln there is a considerable variation. The cry or proclamation is as follows:

Ran, Tan, Tan, the sign of the old Tin Can;
Stephen Smith's been paying his daughter Nan:
He paid her both behind and before,
He paid her 'cause she wouldn't be his whore.
He lick'd her neither with stake nor stower,
But up wi' his fist and knock'd her ower.
Now if Steenie Smith don't mend his manners,
The skin of his . . . shall go the tanner's:
And if the tanner don't tan it well:
Skin, tanner, and . . . shall go to hell.

(8) The shaft of a cart. *Westm.*
STANGEY. A tailor. *North.*
STANIEL. A base kind of hawk. "*Aluctus*, Anglice a staniel," Nominale MS.
STANK. (1) Stop! addressed to horses.
(2) A tank, or receptacle for water. Brockett explains it, a wet ditch. "*Stagnum*, a pounde, a stanke, a dam," MS. Harl. 2270, f. 181.

Also in that contree ther ben bestes, taughte of men to goo into watres, into ryveres, and into depe *stankes*, for to take fysche.
Maundeville's Travels, 1839, p. 209.
She doith greet harm nameliche yn pondes and in *stangkys*, for a couple of otrys withoute more shal wel destruye of fysh a greet ponde or a greet *stangks*, and therfore men huntein hem.
MS. Bodl. 546.
The fishes in *stankes* and wayters thare,
With nettes and ingynes thay tooke alwhare.
MS. Lansd. 208, f. 2.

(3) A dam. Also, to dam up.

And thane Alexander and hys oste went alle aboute that ryvere, and come tille this forsaid *stanke*, and luged thame aboute it.
MS. Lincoln A. l. 17, f. 28.
And *stanch* up the salt conducts of mine eyes
To watch thy shame, and weep mine obsequies.
Fletcher's Poems, p. 154.

(4) To tread on. *Cornw.*
(5) A disagreeable situation. *Cornw.*
(6) A pole, or stang, q. v.
(7) To sigh; to moan; to groan. *Cumb.*
(8) Weak; worn out. *Spenser.*
STANMARCHE. The herb alisaunder. Pr. Parv. MS. Harl. 221, f. 163.
STANNAGE. A stall.

In this proces of tyme, while Simon dwelte with his said master, they kepte a *stannage* at our Ladie falor. *MS. Ashmole* 208.
STANS.

The emperour seyd, that is a herd chans,
Bot what letys man to do penans?
Slauth it is withouten *stans*,
That drawys man fro hys penans.
MS. Ashmole 61, f. 86.
STANSTICKLE. The prickleback. *East.*
STAP. (1) Stay; visit. *Devon.*
(2) The stave of a tub. *North.*

STAPEL. (1) A post of the bed.

Under ech *stapel* of his bed,
That he niste, four thai hid.
The Sevyn Sages, 201.

(2) A small shaft of a coal-pit.
STAPLE. *Merchants of the staple*, a title given to an ancient company of merchants who exported the staple wares of the country.

They did prest of the *marchauntes of the staple* xviij. m. l. late before, which was a great displeasure to the kyng, and a more corasey to the quene.
Hall, Henry VI. f. 94.
STAPLER. Anything which tends to destroy the hopes or expectations of another. *Norf.*
STAP-SHARD. A stop-gap. *Somerset.*
STAR. (1) To crack glass so that it appears something like a star with many radii.
(2) A white spot on a horse's forehead.
STAR-BASON. An impudent-looking fellow.
STARCHING-BRUSH. A long square brush used by weavers for starching yarn. Holme's Academy of Armory, 1688.
STARE. (1) A starling. "Staare a byrde, *estourneaux*," Palsgrave. "*Sturnus*, a stare," MS. Arund. 249, f. 90.

Where every day the queens bird-keeper had the care of teaching me to whistle, as they doe here your *stares* or blackbirds.
A Comical History of the World in the Moon, 1659.
The *stare* wyl chatre and speke of long usage,
Though in his speche ther be no greet resoun.
Lydgate's Minor Poems, p. 150.

(2) Sedge, grass of the fens. "Bent or *starr*, on the N. W. coast of England, and especially in Lancashire, is a coarse reedy shrub—like ours perhaps—of some importance formerly, if not now, on the sandy blowing lands of those counties. Its fibrous roots give some cohesion to the siliceous soil. By the 15 and 16 G. II. c. 33, "plucking up and carrying away *starr* or bent, or having it in possession, within five miles of the sand hills, was punishable by fine, imprisonment, and whipping," Moor's Suffolk Words.
(3) Stiff; weary. *North.*
(4) To shine, or glitter. *Pr. Parv.*
(5) To swagger, or bully. A cant term.
STAREE. "To staree; can your horse staree? i. e. can your horse travel in stiff clay roads, where he must go up and down as it were over steps and stairs, which horses bred in many parts of Somersetshire can very readily do," MS. Devonshire Gloss.
STARF. (1) Died. (*A.-S.*) Hence may be derived the phrase *starved with cold*, dead or nearly dead with cold.

Merlin fram him went oway,
The king *starf* that ich day.
Arthour and Merlin, p. 103.
And he tolde oute his felonye,
And *starf* forth with his tale anone.
Gower, MS. Soc. Antiq. 134, f. 67.

(2) "*Starf take you*, a common phrase of imprecation in Kent, which signifies as much as a plague take you, Sax. steorfa, *lues, pestis*," Kennett, MS. Lansd. 1033, f. 389.
STARGAND. Starting. *Gawayne.*

STARINGS. " *Aggricciaménti*, astonishments, starings of oneshaires," Florio, p. 15, ed. 1611.

STARK. (1) Stiff. Still in use.

> Nay, gude Josephe, com nere and behold,
> This bludy lames body is *starke* and cold.
> MS. Bodl. e Mus. 160.

(2) Stout; strong. (*A.-S.*)

> And thogh Ascapart he thefe *starke*,
> 3yt many hondys make lyght warke.
> MS. Cantab. Ff. ii. 38, f. 118.

> No cunsell myght them to reformacyon call,
> In ther openyon they were so stordy and *starke*.
> Bale's Kynge Johan, p. 50.

> He had a pike-staff in his hand,
> That was both *stark* and strang. Robin Hood, i. 96.

> He was bysshope and patryarke
> Of Constatynenoble *starke*. MS. Harl. 1701, f. 45.

(3) A species of turnip. *North.*
(4) Hard; difficult. *Linc.*
(5) To walk slowly. *Dorset.*
(6) Very; exceedingly. *Var. dial.*
(7) Covetous; greedy; dear. *Yorksh.*

STARKEN. To tighten. *North.*

STARKENES. Firmness; strength.

> And bring them to the gates
> Of hell and utter derkenes,
> And all by stubborne *starkenes*.
> Doctour Doubble Ale, n. d.

STARK-GIDDY. Very angry; mad. *Lanc.*

STARKING. Quick. *North.*

STARKISH. Rather stiff, applied to land, the soil of which is principally clay. *Linc.*

STARK-STARING. Excessively. *Var. dial.*

STARKY. Stiff; dry. *West.*

STARLING. A martin. *Lanc.*

STARLINGES. Pence of sterling money.

STARN. (1) A star. *North.*
(2) A bit; a portion. *Linc.*

STAR-NAKED. Stark-naked. *Suffolk.*

STARNELL. A starling. *North.*

STAROP. A stirrup.

> Syr Befyse ynto the sadulle startyth,
> He towchyd nodur *starop* nor gyrthe.
> MS. Cantab. Ff. ii. 38, f. 101.

STARRISH. Strong, as medicine. *North.*

STARRY-GAZY-PIE. A pie made of pilchards and leeks, the heads of the pilchards appearing through the crust as if they were studying the stars. *Cornw.*

STAR-SLIME. " Sterre slyme, *lymas*," Palsgrave. Carr has *star-shubber*, star-slough, a gelatinous substance, often seen in fields after rain.

START. (1) To begin anything. *Var. dial.*
(2) The same as *Stert*, q. v.
(3) Started; moved. *Gawayne.*

START-CHAINS. Chains consisting of four or five large links attached to harrows to which the whipple-trees are hooked. *East.*

STARTHE. A handle. See *Stert.*

> Brynne it to powdere one Irene or in a pott *starthe*,
> and do a littille of that powdir to thyne eghne.
> MS. Lincoln. Med. f. 284.

STARTING-HOLE. " Stertyng hole, *ung tapynet, lieu de refuge*," Palsgrave. "A starting-hole, *subterfugium*," Coles.

STARTINGS. Openings in a coal-mine.

STARTLE. To sparkle; to shine.

STARTLER. A great drinker. *West.* "One who does not easily start from his seat and leave his pot-companions in the lurch, but maintains his part like an old soldier, unless the white sergeant makes her appearance," MS. Devonsh. Gloss.

STARTLY. Liable to startle. *Var. dial.*

START-UP. An upstart. *Shak.*

STARTUPS. A kind of rough country boots with high tops. See Nares.

> He borrowed on the working dales
> His holy russets oft,
> And of the bacon's fat, to make
> His *startops* blacke and soft.
> Percy's Reliques, p. 150.

> A payre of *startuppes* had he on his feete,
> That lased were up to the small of the legge;
> Homelie they were, and easier then meete,
> And in their soles full many a wooden pegge.
> Thynne's Debate, p. 33.

> When hee in pleasant wise
> The counterfet expreste
> Of clowne with cote of russet hew
> And *sturtups* with the reste. MS. Harl. 3885, f.19.

STARVED. Excessively cold. *Var. dial.*

STARY. To stir. *Pegge.*

STAT. Stopped. *Devon.*

STATE. (1) A canopy. Properly an eleva'td chair or throne with a canopy over it.

> From thence to the penthouse, where he breakfasted under a *state*, and from thence took horse about ten of the clock. Cartwright's Diary, p. 75.

(2) Worry; fright; fear. *Var. dial.*
(3) A personage of high rank.

STATED. Suited. *Suffolk.*

STATERY. Merchandise.

STATESMAN. One who occupies his own estate; a small landholder. *North.*

STATH. A step of a ladder. *Kent.*

STATHE. A landing-place for merchandise; a wharf. The term occurs in an old document printed in the Archæologia, xxv. 418.

> Persons desirous of contracting with the Hull corporation for the construction of a timber *landing-staith* at the Ferry-boat Dock at Hull, and other works connected therewith, and for removing the old Breakwater Jetty there, must send their tenders, marked Tender for *Landing-staith*, to the town clerk, Town-hall, Hull, on or before noon on the 6th day of July next. Newspaper Advertisement, 1846.

STATHEL. (1) To establish. (*A.-S.*)

> For thai helded in the ivels unright,
> Thai thought redes whilk *stathel* thai ne might.
> MS. Cott. Vespas. D. vii. f. 13.

(2) The same as *Staddle* (2).

STATION. (1) The act or form of standing. Also, the state of rest. *Shak.*
(2) A place of rest for pilgrims on their way to a holy seat, as the Holy Land, &c.

STATION-STAFF. A straight pole divided into feet and inches, used in measuring land.

STATIST. A statesman. Jonson, ii. 262.

STATUA. A statue. (*Lat.*) The term *statua* was sometimes applied to a picture.

STATUMINATE. To support. (*Lat.*)

STATURE. A statue. This use of the word is not uncommon in early writers.

STATUTE-CAPS. Woollen caps, enjoined to be worn by a statute dated in 1571, in behalf of the trade of cappers. See Malone's Shakespeare, iv. 419.

STATUTE-MERCHANT. Defined in the old law dictionaries, " a bond acknowledged before one of the clerks of the statutes-merchant, and mayor of the staple, or chief warden of the city of London, or two merchants of the said city for that purpose assigned, or before the chief warden or mayor of other cities or good towns, or other sufficient men for that purpose appointed."

STATUTES. Assemblages of farming servants, held possibly by statute, in the early part of May, at various places in the country, where masters and mistresses attend to hire servants for the ensuing year, commencing at Old May-day. At these statutes the groom will be distinguished by a straw or two in his hat; the carter or waggoner by a piece of whip-cord; the shepherd by a lock of wool, &c.

STAUD. Surfeited, tired; from *Stall*, q. v.

STAUGING. A custom prevalent in Cumberland on Christmas eve. The maid-servants of the substantial families, if found out of doors, are seized by the young men, placed in chairs, and borne to the nearest beer-shop, where they are detained until they buy their liberty by small sums, which are usually expended by their captors in liquor.

STAULE. A decoy; a stale, q. v.

STAULKIE. Long.

Wherefore Bacchus is pictured riding in a chariot of vine branches, Silenus ridinge beside him on an asse, and the Bacchæ or Satyres shaking togither their *staulkie* javelines and paulmers. By reason of their leaping they are caled Scirti, and the anticke or satyricall dauncing Sicinnis, and they also somtimes Sicinnistæ; somtimes Ægipanæ.

Topsell's Four-Footed Beasts, 1607, p. 13.

STAUNCHE. To stop; to satisfy.

STAUNCHES. Damps or offensive vapours arising in underground works, mines, &c.

STAUNCH-GREINE. " Staunche greyne for wrytares, *planula*," Prompt. Parv. MS. Harl. 221. f. 163.

STAUNCH-HAWK. According to Blome, " one well entred for the game." Gent. Rec. ii. 63.

STAUNDE.

Be the quartere of this yere, and hym quarte *staunde*,
He wylle wyghtlye in a qwhyle one his wayes hye.

Morte Arthure, MS. Lincoln, f. 59.

STAUP. To walk badly. *North.*

STAUPINGS. The holes made by the feet of horses and cattle in miry highways, and other places. *North.*

STAUPS. Cask-staves. *Northumb.*

STAUTER. To totter, or stagger. *Linc.*

STAVE. (1) A staff, or pole. (*A.-S.*)

Summe with arowes, summe with *staves* of engynes. The fyre also byganne for to sett in howses within the citee, and rayse a grete lowe.

MS. Lincoln A. i. 17, f. 11.

(2) In bear-baiting, to interpose with a staff to stop the bear. *Nare*

(3) The step of a ladder. *East.*

(4) To cut a hedge. *Yorksh.*

(5) A narrow bridge over a brook.

(6) To stow, knock, or force down.

STAVER. (1) A hedge-stake. *Yorksh.*

(2) To totter; to tumble. *North.*

STAVERWORT. The herb staggerwort.

STAVES-AKER. A species of larkspur.

Red leather and surflet water,
Scarlet colour or *staves-aker*.

Songs of the London Prentices, p. 153.

The small roots of ellebor which are like to onions, have power in them to purge the belly of dogs; other give them goats-milk, or salt beaten small, or sea-crabs beaten small and put into water, or *staves-acre*, and imediatly after his purgation, sweet milke.

Topsell's Four-Footed Beasts, 1607, p. 181.

STAVLAN. Lounging. *Cumb.*

STAW. (1) To stay; to hinder. *North.*

(2) To be restive, as a horse. *Lanc.*

STAWED. Set; placed. *North.*

STAW-FED. Over-fed. See *Stall.*

STAY. (1) A ladder. *Linc.*

(2) To support. *Lilly.*

(3) The stanchion of a window.

(4)

To my dear daughter Philippa, queen of Portugal, my second best *stay* of gold, and a gold cup and cover. *Test. Vetust.* p. 142.

(5) Ascended. (*A.-S.*)

How he uproos and sithen up *stay*,
Mony a mon hit herde and say.

Cursor Mundi, MS. Coll. Trin. Cantab. f. 2.

STAY-BAR. The horizontal bar of a window. See Willis's Arch. Nomen. p. 58.

STAYERS. Stairs. A very common old form of the word, most absurdly retained by Mr. Knight in the Merch. Ven. iii. 2, in a different sense. See Dyce's Remarks, p. 56. Jennings gives *stayers* as the Somersetshire pronunciation of stairs, Gloss. p. 72. Chaucer has *steyers*.

STAYKFALDHOLLIS. Holes in a wall used by workmen to erect their scaffolding.

STEAD. (1) A place; a spot; a farmhouse and offices. From the A.-S. *stede.*

(2) To aid; to assist; to support. *Shak.*

(3) To supply a place. *East.* " Stead up your appointment," Shakespeare.

STEADY. (1) A stithy. *Northampt.*

(2) Sober, attentive to work. *Var. dial.*

STEAKS. " Is that your lackey yonder in the *steaks* of velvet," Middleton, i. 336.

STEALE. (1) The handle of several agricultural implements, &c. *South.* " Steale or handell of a staffe, *manche, hantel*," Palsgrave. "Steale of a shafte, *fust*," ibid.

(2) The stalk of an apple. *Linc.* " The staulke or steale of fruits," Cotgrave.

STEALY-CLOTHES. A boys' game, thus described by Brockett.

The little party divide themselves into two bands, drawing a line as the boundary of their respective territories; and at equal distances from this line, deposit the hats, coats, or handkerchiefs of each in a heap. The game commences with a de-

ſance, and then they make mutual incursions, each trying to seize and carry away some article from the other's store ; but if they are unfortunately caught in the attempt, they must not only restore the plunder, but remain prisoners until one of their own party can make his way to them, and touch them. When all the things of the one party are transferred to the other's head quarters, the game is won. A well-contested match will sometimes last nearly a whole day.

STEAM. (1) To rise, or ascend.

The wals stand to this dale, a few streets and houses in the towne, no small parcell thereof is turned to orchards and gardens. The greater part of the towne is steepe and *steaming* upward.
Stanihurst's Description of Ireland, p. 26.

(2) To send forth dust. *South.*

STEAN. (1) A stone vessel. " A great pot or *stean*," Hollyband's Dictionarie, 1593. Spenser uses it in this sense. Palmer defines it, " a large upright jar of baked clay." *Stean* is still the pronunciation of *stone* in the North, and so it was in Elizabeth's time. See Lambarde's Perambulation, 1596, p. 205. In some places a cask or vat is so called.

(2) To mend a road with stones ; to line a well, &c. with stone or brick. *South.*

(3) A large box of stones used for pressing cheese in making it. *Dorset.*

STEANING. Any kind of path or road paved with small round stones. *West.*

STEATHING. A lath and plaster partition.

STEAVER. A collier who superintends the coal-pit ; a banksman. *North.*

STEAWK. A handle. *Lanc.*

STEAWP. All ; every part. *Lanc.*

STEAWT. Proud. *Lanc.*

STEAʒ. Ascended. (*A.-S.*) The following is written in the early Kentish dialect :

Credo. Ich leve ine God, vader almiʒti, makere of hevene and of erthe, and in Jesu Crist his zone on lepi oure Lord, thet i-kend is of the holi gost, y-bore of Marie mayde, y-pyned onder Pouns Pilate, y-nayled a rode, dyad, and be-bered, yede doun to helle, thane thridde day aros vram the dyade, *steaʒ* to hevenes, sit a the riʒt half of God the vader almiʒti, thannes to comene he is, to deme the quike and the dyade. Ich y-leve ine the holy gost, holy cherche generalliche, mennesse of halʒen, lesnesse of zennes, of vlesse arizinge, and lyf evrelestinde. Zuo by hit. *Reliq. Antiq.* i. 42.

STECHE. A stitch in the side.

A drynke for the *steche*, and narownesse of hart and other evylle. Take hartes-tonge, violet, lecorice, endyve, pelliture, fenelle, of everiche ilike miche, and of isope, a quartrone of fyges, and sethe thyce togidyr in a galon of water into a potelle. Efter powre owt the licour, and do it in a panne, and take thre rawe egges-schelles, and do therto ; and than sethe it on the fyre, and styre it fast ; efter wrynge it thurge a clothe, and than put it in a clene veselle coverd alle nyʒt, and than gyff hym to drynke that is seke tylle he be hole.
MS. Sloane 7, f. 80.

STECK. A stopping place. To take the steck, i. e. to become restive. *North.*

STEDDE. Furnished ; provided ?

I wille noghte stire with my stale halfe a stede lenghe, Bot they be *stedde* with more stuffe hane one ʒone stede hovys. *Morte Arthure, MS Lincoln*, f. 83.

IL.

STEDDLE. To support, or make steady. If a table having uneven legs does not stand steadily, it is said to be *steddled* by putting something under the deficient leg. It is also used in the participle *steddled*, when a table has been marked or stained. *Linc.*

STEDE. (1) A place ; a station. (*A.-S.*)

But she it yaff to the Scottisshe knight, For he was of an unkouth *stede*.
MS. Harl. 2252, f. 98.

And God myʒht not in no manere, Alyʒht bote in feyre *stede* and clere.
Religious Poems, xv. Cent.

Hys grete stedes schewyd me ichone, And sethyn he made me aʒene to gone Into the *sted* where he me fette, In that same *sted* ther he me sete.
MS. Ashmole 61, xv. Cent.

Joly Robyn, he seid, wel mot thou be, Be God so shuld thou to me On other *stede* than here.
MS. Cantab. Ff. v. 48, f. 52.

(2) *In hys stede*, in his place, instead of him.

Now ys he gone, my lady free, In hys *stede* ye schalle take me ; Am y not a knyght ? And we schalle do so prevely, That whethyr he leve or dye, Ther schalle wete no wyght.
MS. Cantab. Ff. ii. 38, f. 72.

(3) Set ; appointed.

That daye the tournament solde be *stede*, Thay horsede hym on ane olde crokede stede, And ʒitt for-thoghte thame alle.
Isumbras, 613.

STEDFAST. The herb palma Christi.

STEDFUL. Steadfast. *Weber.*

STEE. A ladder ; a stile. *North.*

STEE-HOPPING. Gossiping ; romping. *West.*

STEEL. (1) To iron clothes. *Devon.*

(2) *Trewe as stele*, faithful as steel, a common phrase in early romances, and found even in Shakespeare, Mids. Night's Dream, ii. 2.

He was the kynge of Arragon, A nobull man and of grete renown, Syr Ardus was hys name ; He had a quene that hyght Margaret, *Trewe as stele* y yow be-hett, That falsely was broght in blame.
MS. Cantab. Ff. ii. 38, f. 71.

(3) A stile. *North.*

(4) Courage. Kennett, MS. Lansd. 1033.

STEELY. Hard ; firm. Tusser, p. 34.

STEEM. (1) Esteem ; value.

Over gestes it has the *steem*, Over alle that is or was.
R. de Brunne, ap. Warton, i. 69.

(2) To bespeak a thing. *North.*

(3) A flame of fire. *Pr. Parv.*

STEEMING. A turn. *Devon.*

STEEN. Spite ; envy. *Norf.*

STEEP. (1) Rennet. *Lanc.*

(2) To tilt a barrel. *Devon.*

(3) To dress or trim a hedge. *West.*

(4) To finish anything off. *Oxon.*

STEEPERS. In trimming hedges, the central branches, cut half through and laid lengthwise, are so called. *West.*

STEEPING-RAIN. A soaking rain. *North.*

STEEPLE-HATS. Long hats, described by Stubbes as "pearking up like the spere or shaft of a steeple, standyng a quarter of a yarde above the croune of their heades, some more, some lesse, as please the phantasies of their inconstant mindes, 2d ed. 1585, f. 21. *Steepled hattes* are mentioned in Wright's Passions of the Minde, 1621, p. 330.

STEEPLE-HOUSE. A church.

STEER. (1) Very steep. *West.*

(2) An ox in its third year. *North.*

> Juvencus is a yonge oxe whan he is no lenger a calf, and he is then callyd a *steere* whan he begynneth to be helpfull unto the profit of man in eringe the erth. *Dialogues of Creatures Moralysed*, p. 228.

(3) To frighten. *Lanc.*

(4) To stun with noise. *North.*

(5) To stir; to move. *Palsgrave.*

STEERISH. Young, as an ox. *Glouc.*

STEERT. Acute; painful. *Somerset.* A sharp point is called a *steert.*

STEEVE. To dry; to stiffen. *West.*

STEEVING. A term used by merchants, when they stow cotton or wool by forcing it in with screws. *Dict. Rust.*

STEG. The same as *Stag*, q. v.

STEGH. Ascended. (*A.-S.*)

> And ros to lyve the thryde day,
> And *stegh* to hevene the xl. day.
> *MS. Cott. Claud.* A. ii. f. 132.

> Reke *stegh* in the ire of hym, and fire brynt of his face; coles ar kyndeled of hym.
> *MS. Coll. Eton.* 10, f. 25.

STEG-MONTH. The month of a woman's confinement. *Steg-widow*, a man whose wife is confined. *North.*

STEIER. A star. A corrupt form. The copy in MS. Bodl. 175 reads *starre.*

> A *steier* of Jacobe springe shall,
> A man of Isarell,
> That shall overcome and have in bande
> All kinges and duckes of strange lande.
> *Chester Plays*, i. 89.

STEIL. To walk very slowly. *Linc.*

STEIP. "*Steip of helms*, eighteen helms, Wilts," Holloway's Dictionary, p. 163.

STEIT. As well as. *Northumb.*

STEK. Stuck.

> Ande al graythed in grene this gome and his wedes,
> A strayt cote ful streyt, that *stek* on his sides.
> *Syr Gawayn and the Grene Knyзt*, 152.

STEKE. (1) To fasten with a stick. The following proverb is still in vogue; and Ray says *steak* is to shut a door in the North.

> When the hors is stole, *steke* the stabulle dore.
> *MS. Douce* 52.

(2) "Steke of flesshe, *charbonnee*," Palsgrave.

STEKIE. To stick fast. (*A.-S.*)

STEL. Stole; crept softly.

> And ho stepped stilly, and *stel* to his bedde,
> Kest up the cortyn, and creped withinne.
> *Syr Gawayn and the Grene Knyзt*, 1191.

STELCH. (1) Stealth. *Salop.*

(2) A stilt; a pole; a post. *West.*

STELCH-STAFF. A rod of wood which keeps asunder the traces of waggon harness. *West.*

STELE. (1) The stem of an arrow. Palsgrave,

verb. in v. *Fether.* Also, the stem or stalk of anything. "*Candelabri scapus*, the shanke or stele of the candlesticke," Nomenclator, Lond. 1585, p. 245.

(2) A handle. Still in use.

> And lerned men a ladel bugge
> With a long *stele*,
> And caste for to kepe a crokke
> To save the fatte above.
> *Piers Ploughman*, p. 412.

(3) A horse-block; a stepping-stone.

STELENDELICH. By stealth.

> Many of his men and bestes,
> Agein kyng Alisaunder hestes
> *Stelendelich* dronken of this lake.
> *Kyng Alisaunder*, 5080.

STEL-GERE. Steel clothing, i. e. armour.

> Stifest under *stel-gere* on stedes to ryde,
> The wyзtest and the worthyest of the worldes kynde.
> *Syr Gawayn and the Grene Knyзt*, 260.

STELL. (1) To stall, or fix permanently. ·

(2) A large open drain. *Cumb.*

(3) A fold for cattle. *North.*

STELLEERE. The steelyards. "A Romane beame or *stelleere*, a beame of yron or wood, full of nickes or notches, along which a certaine peize of lead playing, and at length setling towards the one end, shewes the just weight of a commoditie hanging by a hooke at the other end," Cotgrave.

STELLIFIED. "Made him stellifyed," i. e. named a constellation after him. (*Lat.*)

> And thouз Romaynis made him *stellifyed*,
> His gretheed, for alle that, dide avale.
> *Lydgate, MS. Soc. Antiq.* 134, f. 15.

STELLING. A shed for cattle. *North.*

STELLIONATE. Fraudulent dealing. (*Lat.*)

STEM. (1) The handle of a tool. *Devon.*

(2) A period of time. *Wilts.* In Cornwall, a day's work is called a *stem.*

(3) To soak a leaky vessel. *Linc.*

STEME.

> Thou shalt have garments wrought of Median silke,
> Enchast with pretious jewells fecht from far,
> By Italian marchants that with Russian *stemes*
> Plous up huge forrowes in the Terren Maine.
> *The Taming of a Shrew*, p. 22.

STEMMIN. (1) A day's work. *Cornw.*

(2) The slay of a weaver's loom.

STEMPLES. The cross pieces which are put into a frame of woodwork to cure and strengthen a shaft. See Ray's English Words, 1674, p. 118. Carr has *stemplar*, timber to support the roof of a mine. "At the silver mines in Cardiganshire, they sink a perpendicular square hole or shaft, the sides whereof they strengthen round from top to bottom with travers pieces of wood calld *stemples*, upon which, catching hold with their hands and feet, they descend without using any rope," Kennett, MS. Lansd. 1033, f. 390.

STEMPNE. Voice; command. (*A.-S.*)

> He that behynde sat to stere,
> May not the fore *stempne* here.
> *Gower, MS. Soc. Antiq.* 134, f. 91.

STENCILS. The posts of a door. *North.*

STEND. (1) A stretcher. *Lanc.*

(2) To extend; to rear, as a horse. *North.*

STENKRITH. The rush of water in a narrow channel. *Northumb.*

STENT. (1) A right of pasturage. *North.*

(2) An allotted portion. *Var. dial.* "Stent, portion, part," Palsgrave, 1530. "*Stente* or certeyne of valwe ordrede and other lyke, *taxatio*," MS. Harl. 221, f. 164.

STENTE. To cease; to desist. (*A.-S.*)

STENTINGS. Openings in a wall in a coal-mine. *North.*

STEO. To rise; to ascend. (*A.-S.*)
> Weilawei! deth the schal adun throwe,
> Ther thu wenest heȝest to *steo.*
> > *MS. Cott. Calig. A. ix. f. 243.*

STEP. (1) A walking distance. *Var. dial.*

(2) "Step, where a mast stant yn a schyppe, *parastica*," Pr. Parv. MS. Harl. 221, f. 164.

STEPE. Deep; sunk.
> Lyfte up hys hed fro the grounde,
> With *steps* eyen and roghe browe.
> > *MS. Cantab. Ff. ii. 38, f. 99.*

STEP-MOTHER. (1) A horny filament shooting up by the side of the nail. *Step-mother's blessing*, a hang-nail.

(2) The flower of the violet. *North.*

STEP-OVER-TRASH. To go beyond the bounds of propriety. *Somerset.*

STEPPING. Walking. *North.*

STEPPING-STONE. A horse-block. *West.*

STEPPLES. Short neat steps; a flight of neat steps from the parlour, &c. *Norf.*

STERCH. Hard; rough; tough. (*A.-S.*)
> Nis non so strong, ne *sterch*, ne kene,
> That mai ago deathes wither blench.
> > *MS. Cotton. Calig. A. ix. f. 243.*

STERCORY. Dung. (*Lat.*)

STERE. (1) A rudder. *Palsgrave.*
> For whanne y may my lady here,
> My wit with that hath loste his *steere.*
> > *Gower, MS. Soc. Antiq. 134, f. 42.*

(2) To guide; to direct; to rule.
> Laverd me *steres*, noght want sal me,
> In stede of fode thare me louked he.
> > *MS. Cott. Vespas. D. vii. f. 14.*

(3) To stir. *Chaucer.*
> In him thorgh the mete it sinketh,
> And *sterith* therynne out to gete.
> > *MS. Lansd. 793, f. 127.*

(4) Strong; stout.
> Then came the dewke Raynere,
> An hardy knyght and a *stere.*
> > *MS. Cantab. Ff. ii. 38, f. 151.*

STERESMAN. A pilot. (*A.-S.*)

STERE-TRE. A rudder. (*A.-S.*)
> Wife, tent the *stere-tre*, and I shalle asay
> The depnes of the see that we bere, if I may.
> > *Towneley Mysteries, p. 31.*

STERIN. Stern; cruel; fierce. (*A.-S.*)
> He herd thair strakes, that war ful *sterin*,
> And yern he waytes in ilka heryn,
> And al was made ful fast to hald.
> > *Ywaine and Gawin, 3219.*

> He was *steryne* and stowte,
> With many knyghtes hym abowte.
> > *MS. Lincoln A. i. 17, f. 130.*

STERK. Strong, or stark.

> My blod to have to this werk,
> That schuld be so strong [and] *sterk.*
> > *Arthour and Merlin, p. 47.*

STERN. (1) A helm, or rudder. (*A.-S.*)

(2) The tail of an animal. *Var. dial.*

STERNAGE. The guidance. *Shak.*

STERNE. A star. Nominale MS.
> In the mornyng to rise, the tyme at the day *sterne*,
> The emperour and hise to seke thei suld alle ȝerne.
> > *Langtoft's Chronicle, p. 161.*

> Lighte daye I wilbe called aye,
> And the *sternes* nighte, as I saie.
> > *Chester Plays, i. 20.*

STERRACLES. Performances; strange things, sights, or doings; pranks. "I take onne, as one dothe that playeth his sterakels, *je tempeste*," Palsgrave, verb. f. 384.
> Whan thou art sett upon the pynnacle,
> Thou xalt ther pleyn a qweynt *steracle*,
> Or ellys shewe a grett meracle,
> Thyself ffrom hurte thou save.
> > *Coventry Mysteries, p. 208.*

> They hem rejoise to see and to be sayne,
> And to seke soundry pilgremages,
> At grete gaderynges to walken upon the playne,
> And at *storacles* to sitte on high stages,
> If they be faire to shewe ther visages.
> > *Appendix to Walter Mapes, p. 297.*

> The dead sayntes shall shewe both visyons and myracles;
> With ymages and rellyckes he shall wurke *sterracles.*
> > *Bale's Kynge Johan, p. 30.*

> What, Pamphagus, I praye the for Goddes sake why whippest thou it about, or playest thou thy *steracles* on this faschion.
> > *Palsgrave's Acolastus, 1540.*

STERRE. A star. (*A.-S.*)
> Undirstondith, sir, truly,
> That no *sterre* falleth fro the sky,
> But I shal telle what it may be,
> That the folke so falling se.
> > *MS. Lansd. 793, f. 87.*

STERT. (1) The point of anything. *West.*

(2) A leap. *Prompt. Parv.*

(3) The tail, or handle. "Stert of a plow, *queue de lachareue*," Palsgrave.

(4) The stalk of fruit. "Stert of frute, *queue de fruit*," Palsgrave. "*Pertica*, Anglice a yerde to mete londe or a perche, a stert of an apple, *vel instrumentum quo pisces capiuntur*," Medulla MS. xv. Cent.

(5) A moment, or very short time. *At a stert*, immediately, Chaucer, Cant. T. 1707.

(6) To meet with very suddenly.

STERTLE. (1) To leap. (*A.-S.*)
> Bot I, that privaly hafe aspied thi gates, whenne thou wenes moste securely for to *stertle* abowte, I salle sterte apone the, and take the.
> > *MS. Lincoln A. i. 17, f. 7.*

(2) Hasty; in a hurry.

STERTLING-ROIL. A wanton slattern.

STERVE. To die; to perish. (*A.-S.*)
> And unrightwise samen forworth thai sal,
> And relikes of wick sal *sterve* with al.
> > *MS. Cott. Vespas. D. vii. f. 25.*

> For when he *sterves* take sal he noght alle,
> Ne with him his blis light doune salle.
> > *MS. Cott. Vespas. D. vii. f. 33.*

STERYNMESTE. Most severe. (*A.-S.*)

He was the *sterynnests* in stoure that ever stele werryde,
Vore he has stonayede oure stale and stroyede for ever.
Morte Arthure, MS. Lincoln, f. 93.

STETCH. As much land as lies between one furrow and another. *Stetched up*, laid into ridges by the plough. *East.*

STETCHELLED. Filled very full. *North.*

STETCHIL. A troublesome child. *Linc.*

STEVEL. To stagger; to stumble. *North.*

STEVEN. (1) Voice; sound; noise. *(A.-S.)*

Fader owre, that art in hevene,
Halowed be thy name with meke *stevene*.
MS. Cott. Claud. A. ii. f. 132.

Of a kyng and of a quene,
What bale and blys was them betwene,
Y schalle yow telle fulle evyn :
A gode ensaumpulle ye may lere,
Yf ye wylle thys story here
And herkyn to my *stevyne*.
MS. Cantab. Ff. ii. 38, f. 71.

When Litle John heard his master speake,
Well knewe he it was his *steven* :
Now shall I be looset, quoth Litle John,
With Christ his might in heaven.
Robin Hood and Guy of Gisborne.

(2) A time of performing any action previously fixed upon. *At unset steven*, a phrase signifying a time not previously appointed. *They setten steven*, they appointed a time. See Morte d'Arthur, i. 266. "To set the steven, is to agree upon the time and place of meeting previous to some expedition," West. and Cumb. Dial. p. 390.

For a Cristmas gestenyng, as clerkis rede,
At on-set *stevyn*, is quyt in dede.
Archæologia, xxix. 342.

Hyt ys sothe seyde, be God of heven,
Mony metyn at on-sett *stevyn* ;
And so befelle hyt there. *Eglamour*, 1283.

First let us some masterye make
Among the woods so even,
Woe may chance to meet with Robin Hood
Here att some *unsett steven*.
Robin Hood and Guy of Gisborne.

(3) To bespeak. *Yorksh.*

STEVENNED. Particoloured.

STEW. (1) A pool to preserve fish for the table to be drawn and filled again at pleasure. Ray inserts this among his South and East Country Words, ed. 1674, p. 76.

Evene anon after the owls flight,
Whan that true men shulde goo to rest,
To bribe and bere away the best,
That sojourne and kept bien in *stiewe*.
Piers of Fulham, p. 119.

(2) Fright; great suspense. *Var. dial.*

(3) A cloud of dust, or vapour.

(4) A hatter's drying room. The term was formerly applied to a small closet.

(5) A brothel. Still in use. "The stewes, or place without the wals of the citie where bawderie was kept," Baret, 1580. "Stewes, a place for commen women, *bordeau*," Palsgrave.

Venus denotes in houses, all places belonging to women, as garnished beds, *stews*, also places where gloves, rings, jewels, perfumes, the place or seat of the woman or mistress of the house, also a musick room, dancing room, bed cloaths, and where silk and other rich commodities are kept.
Bishop's Marrow of Astrology, p. 57.

(6) A stove. *Stew pot covered*, a covered pan used for heating rooms with charcoal.

STEWARDLY. Careful; managing. *Devon.*

STEWED-BROTH. Strong broth boiled up with raisins, currants, prunes, mace, &c.

STEWES. A strumpet. *Whetstone.*

STEY. A ladder; universal in Lancashire and Yorkshire, but not general in the adjoining counties. A carpenter in Todmorden said to his apprentice, "Thee a reet! theer't sa blind thagh cant see a hoile in a stey." See *Stee*.

STEYE. To ascend. *(A.-S.)*

Befyse lepe up, full lyght he was,
And up he *steyed*, y undurstonde.
MS. Cantab. Ff. ii. 38, f. 108

With laddren *steye* that couthe best,
The cité to asail have thai no rest.
Gy of Warwike, p. 85.

STEYNOUR.

And in proporcion rejoyethe the *steynour*.
MS. Ashmole 59, f. 19.

ST. HUGH'S-BONES. Shoemakers' tools.

STIBBORNE. Stubborn. *Chaucer.*

And he that holdithe a quarel agayn right,
Holdyng his purpos *stiburn* ageyn reason.
Lydgate's Minor Poems, p. 168.

STIBILLE. A carpenter's tool. "*Bipennus, bidens*, a stybylle," Nominale MS.

STICH. (1) A sheaf of corn. *Devon.*

(2) A small inclosure. *Cornw.*

(3) *Stiche* in Chester Plays, i. 47, is probably an error for *sliche*, slimy mud.

STICHALL. This term, which in some places has *Bub* prefixed to it, appears to be a word of reproach, used to children principally by their parents, when they are doing something wrong, and are in the way, or when they are heedless and inattentive to something that has been told them, e. g. "Get out of the way, you *bub-stichal*;" and, "what a young *stichall* he must be to bring such a message !" MS. Gloss. of Linc. by the Rev. J. Adcock. The term occurs in the old play of Lady Alimony, quoted by Nares.

STICHEL. To eat too much. *North.*

STICHEWORT. The herb *lingua avis*. It occurs in MS. Sloane 5, f. 5.

STICHLING. A third year perch.

STICK. (1) A term of reproach, as "you are a pretty *stick*." A clergyman is called a good or bad *stick* according as he has a good or bad delivery. *Warw.*

(2) A strike among workmen. *North.*

(3) A timber-tree. *West.*

(4) To cut a beast's throat. *Var. dial.*

(5) A lot of twenty-five eels.

(6) "Stykkyng or tukkyng up of clothys, *saffacinatio*," Pr. Parv. MS. Harl. 221, f. 164.

STICK-AND-BAIL. Trap-ball. *Oxon.*

STICK-AND-LIFT. When a person is poor and has nothing beforehand, they say such a one is at *stick and lift*, that is, lives from hand to mouth. *Linc.*

STICKER. A stick used for stopping a waggon ascending a hill. *Heref.*

STICKING-PIECE. The part of an animal's neck where the butcher sticks it. *North.*

STICKING-PLACE. A fixed place. The phrase occurs in Shakespeare, Macbeth, i. 7.

Which flower out of my hand shall never passe,
But in my harte shall have a *sticking-place*.
Proctor's Gorgious Gallery, 1578, repr. p. 182.

STICKINGS. The last of a cow's milk.

STICKLE. (1) To tickle. *Var. dial.*

(2) A shallow in a river where the water, being confined, runs with violence. *Somerset.* The term is applied to the violence and rapidity of the stream in the following passage:

When they came thither, the river of the Shenin, which invironeth and runneth round about the citie, they found the same to be so deepe and *stikle* that they could not passe over the same.
Holinshed, Conq. Ireland, p. 37.

(3) To stick firmly to anything. *Lanc.*

(4) To part combatants. " I styckyll betwene wrastellers or any folkes that prove mastries, to se that none do other wronge, or I parte folkes that be redy to fyght," Palsgrave.

(5) Haste. *Stickle busy*, very officious.

(6) Steep. *Devon.*

(7) Fright; amazement. *Cumb.*

(8) The current below a waterfall. *West.*

STICKLE-BACK. The prickleback. *Var. dial.*

Waspis and eysturis, and gret cart-sadyllys,
Moskettus in mortrous, caudrons and ladyls,
The pekerel and the perche, the mennous and the roche,
The borbottus and the *stykylbakys*, the flondyre and the loche.
Reliq. Antiq. i. 85.

STICKLE-BUTT. Headlong. *North.*

STICKLER. (1) A person who presides at back-sword or singlestick, to regulate the game; an umpire; a person who settles disputes.

Come, niver mine tha single-sticks,
Tha whoppin or tha *stickler* ;
You dwon't want now a brawken head,
Nor jitchy soort o' tickler ! *Ballad of Tom Gool.*

(2) A small officer who cut wood for the priory of Inichester within the king's parks of Clarendon. *Blount.*

STICKLING. " A sharpling, shaftling, *stickling*, bankstickle, or sticklebacke," Cotgrave in v. *Espinoche*. " *Gamerus*, a stekelyng," Nominale MS. " Stykelynge, *silurus*," Pr. Parv. " Styckelyng, a maner of fysshe," Palsgrave.

STICKLY. Rough; prickly. *North.*

STICKS. Furniture. *Cumb.*

STICKS-END. The unburnt end of a stick from the fire. *Dorset.*

STICKY-STACK. A boys' game, running up the cut part of a haystack to try who can put in a stick the highest. *North.*

STID. (1) Place. See *Stede*.

She yede into a fer cuntré,
Ther no man knew hir pryveté,
Nor fro what *stid* she come.
MS. Cantab. Ff. v. 48, f. 45.

And for that odur Edwart love,
Thou shalt sitte here above,
In *stidde* alle of the kyng.
MS. Cantab. Ff. v. 48, f. 54.

Nom wonder hafe yow therof,
My will hit wos i-wise,
For I wil kepe that like *stide*,
That in my ward now is.
MS. Cantab. Ff. v. 48, f. 78.

(2) Qu. an error for *did* ?

In Chame fair streams *stid* gently swim,
And naked bathe each curious limbs.
Randolph's Poems, 1643, p. 196.

STIDDEN. Stood. *North.*

STIDDY. An anvil. *Var. dial.*

STIE. (1) A lane. (*A.-S.*)

The scheref made to seke Notyngham
Bothe be strete and *stye*,
And Robyn was in mery Scherwode
As list as lef on lynde. *MS. Cantab.* Ff. v. 48, f. 131.

Hast thou i-come in any *sty*,
And cropped jerus of corne the by.
MS. Cott. Claud. A. ii. f. 145.

(2) To ascend. (*A.-S.*)

A shadowe of the erthe riseth sone,
And *stieth* up above the mone.
MS. Lansd. 793, f. 86.

STIFADRE. A stepfather.

I schel the telle altogadre,
Beten ichave me *stifadre*. *Beves of Hamtoun*, p. 20.

STIFE. (1) Obstinate, inflexible, stiff. " *A stife quean*, a lusty quean," Ray. Stife bread, strong bread, made with beans and peas, &c. which makes it of a strong smell and taste. *North.*

(2) Suffocating vapour. *Northumb.* Moor has the adjective *stify*, stifling.

STIFF. (1) Proud. *Var. dial.*

(2) Rich; wealthy. *North.*

(3) A ladder. *Yorksh.*

(4) Pleased; fond of. *North.*

(5) A blacksmith's anvil. *Suffolk.*

(6) Firmly; positively. *Var. dial.*

Two or three other came in and said she was by common fame accounted a witch. Wee found her guiltie, and she was condemned to prison, and to the pillorie, but stood *stiffe* in it that she was no witch.
Gifford's Dialogue on Witches, 1603.

(7) Strong; healthy; lusty. *North.* It constantly occurs in writers of the sixteenth and seventeenth centuries in the sense of *brave*.

Somtyme I was an archere good,
A *stiffe* and eke a stronge,
I was commytted the best archere,
That was in mery Englonde. *Robin Hood*, i. 77

STIFFLE. A complaint in horses.

The horse is said to be *stiffled* when the stiffling bone is removed from the place; but if it be not removed nor loosened, and yet the horse halteth by meanes of some griefe there, then we say that the horse is hurt in the stiffle, and not stiffled. The stiffle commeth by means of some blow, or some great straine, slipping or sliding. The signes be these. If he be stiffled, the one bone wil sticke out farther than the other, and is apparant to the eie. Martin woulde have you to cure the stiffle in al points like unto the shoulder-pight, saving that the pins need not bee so long, because the stifling place is not so broad as the shoulder, and standing in the stable; let him have a pasterne with a ring on his forelegge, and thereunto fasten a cord, which cord must go about his necke, and let it be so much strained as it may bring his sore legge more forward than the other to keepe the bone from starting out. But if the horse bee but hurt in the stiffle with some stripe or straine, then the bone wil not stand out, but perhaps the place may be swollen. The cure according to Martin is thus. First annoint the place with the ointment mentioned before, every day once the space of a fortnight, and if the horse amend not with this, then rowel him with a hearen rowel, or else with a quill, and let the neather hole be somewhat before the sore place, and clense the hole every daye by turning the rowel, continuing stil to annoint the place with the ointment aforesaid, and that wil make him whole.

Topsell's Four-Footed Beasts, 1607, p. 405.

STIFLE. To ruin. *Norf.*

STIFLER. (1) A busybody. *East.*

(2) A severe blow, almost sufficient to deprive one of his senses. *Norf.*

STIGH-ROPE. A rope-ladder.

STIGHTELE. To establish; to dispose.

And wele sho wend he sold be slane,
And, sertes, than war hir socor gane;
But fast he *stighteld* in that stowr,
And hastily him come socowre.

Ywaine and Gawin, 3941.

He commande Syr Cayous take kepe to thoos lordes,
To *styghtylle* tha steryne mene, as theire statte askys.

Morte Arthure, MS. Lincoln, f. 54.

STIGMATIC. Explained in the old dictionaries, " a person who has been branded with a hot iron for some crime." Metaphorically, a deformed or evil person.

For that prodigious bloody *stigmatic*
Is never call'd unto his kingly sight,
But like a comet he portendeth still
Some innovation, or some monstrous act.

Death of Robert, Earl of Huntingdon, p. 76.

STIHE. A path, or lane.

Fogheles of heven and fissches of se,
That forthgone *stihes* of the se.

MS. Cott. Vespas. D. vii. f. 4.

STIKE. (1) A verse, or stanza.

(2) To stick; to pierce. (*A.-S.*)

STIKE-PILE. The herb stork's-bill.

STIKILLICHE. Piercingly. (*A.-S.*)

Of hire faired, saun faile,
He hadde in hert gret mervaile;
On hire he lokid *stikilliche*,
And heo on him al outerliche.

Kyng Alisaunder, 219.

STIKPYLE. The herb *acus demenys*.

STILE. (1) To direct, as a gun.

(2) To iron clothes. *Exmoor.*

'3) A narrow path; a road. *Yorksh.*

The Scottes gaudes might nothing gain,
For all thai stumbilde at that *stile*.

Minot's Poems, p. 5.

(4) The upright post in a wainscot to which the panels are fixed.

STILE-BOTE. Wood claimed of the lord, by an owner of lands, for making stiles.

STILETTO-BEARD. Among the numerous fashions in beards, cultivated to excess by our ancestors, the short and pointed beard known as the *stiletto* was one of the most prominent, and is frequently referred to by our early writers. Taylor, the water-poet, in describing the beards of his time, mentions " some sharp, stiletto fashion, dagger like."

STILL. (1) A hill. *Browne.*

(2) Constant; continual. *Shak.* " By still practice," Titus And. iii. 2; " the still piercing air," All's Well that ends Well, iii. 2.

STILL-AN-END. Commonly; generally. *Shak.* This phrase is still in use.

STILLATORIE. A still. (*A.-N.*) Also, a place where distillations were performed.

STILLE. Quietly; with a low voice.

Nowt proude as Prechoures beth,
But preyen ful *stylle*. *Piers Ploughman*, p. 473.

STILLECHE. Still. (*A.-S.*)

Ac deth luteth in his scho,
Him *stilliche* to for-do.

MS. Cott. Calig. A. ix. f. 243.

Jhesu Cryste they thanked moche
And wente ageyn full *stylleche*.

MS. Cantab. Ff. ii. 38, f. 38

STILLER. (1) The inside of an oven. This word occurs in Hollyband's Dictionarie, 1593.

(2) The piece of wood carried over a milkpail to balance it. *North.*

STILLID. Distilled. *Stilling*, distillation.

For the maselles, take the *styllid* water of frumetorye. and drynke it two sponefulle therof iij. dayes togedere, and they schulle never appere more.

MS. Med. Rec. xv. Cent.

STILLING. A frame for barrels. " A gauntrie or *stilling* for hogs-heads, &c, to stand on," Cotgrave in v. *Chantier.* " A stilling for cask, subex," Coles' Lat. Dict.

STILL-ROOM. The housekeeper's room.

STILL-SOW. A sly fellow. " A close, slie, lurking knave, a *stil sow*, as we say," Florio, p. 9. " Still swine eat all the draff," Merry Wives, iv. 2. This proverb is still in use.

STILLY. Still; quiet; quietly.

Ac Arthour was wel *stilly*
With his folk neighe hem bi.

Arthour and Merlin, p. 141.

The mylners wife did rise water to make,
Stilly, for the milner should not wake,
The right way againe could she not take,
For the house was so wide.

The Milner of Abington, n. d.

STILO-NOVO. After the Roman Calendar had been reformed by Pope Gregory XIII. in 1582, English travellers writing from abroad were accustomed to date their letters *stilo novo*, and the term became a kind of cant one for anything reformed or new. " And so I leave you to your *stilo novo*," Beaumont and Fletcher.

STILT. The handle of a plough. *North.*

STILTED. Covered with dirt to a considerable height, or in a great degree. Stockings are said to be stilted, when new footings have been added to the original leggings. *Linc.*

STILTS. Crutches. *East.*

STIM. To ram down tightly. *Derb.*

STIMBLE. Mingere. *Norf.*

STIME. A particle, or ray of light.

Wherewith he blinded them so close,
A *stime* they could not see.

Robin Hood, i. 111.

They are seay gunny and furr'd up some time,
I can nut leauk at leet nor see a *stime*.

A Yorkshire Dialogue, 1697, p. 43.

STIMEY. Dim-sighted. *North.*

STIMMER. A piece of iron used to ram down powder for blasting rocks, &c.

STIN. To groan. *Yorksh.*

STINE. A sty in the eye. *Linc.*

STING. To thatch a stack. *North.*

STINGER. The sting of an insect. *West.* It is sometimes called a *stinge*.

STINGO. Strong beer or ale. The *Yorkshire Stingo* is the name of a celebrated inn in the suburbs of London.

Such *stingos*, nappy, pure ale they had found:
Lett's loo~ no time, said they, but drink a round.
The Praise of Yorkshire Ale, 1697, p. 29.

STINGUISh. To extinguish.

STINGY. (1) Ill-tempered. *Var. dial.*

(2) Piercing, as the wind. *Norf.*

STINK-A-PUSS. A term of contempt.

STINKERD. A stinking fellow. A term of reproach. "A stinkard, *homo fœtidus*," Coles.

For now the *stinkards* in their irefull wraths,
Bepelted me with lome, with stones, and laths.
Taylor's Workes, 1630, ii. 145.

He must be honyed and come over with Gentle Reader, Courteous Reader, and Learned Reader, though he have no more gentilitie in him than Adam had (that was but a gardner), no more civilitie than a tartar, and no more learning than the most errand *stinkard*. *Morgan's Phœnix Britannicus*, p. 28.

STINKERS. A sort of bad coal.

STINK-HORN. The stinking fungus.

STINK-TRAP. A small circular plate of iron, joined to a hollowed half sphere of the same material, made for covering the top of a drain to keep out any offensive smell.

STINT. A limited number of cattle gaits in common pasture. *Craven.*

STINTANCE. Stop; cessation. "Weep without any stintance," London Prodigal, p. 7.

STINTE. (1) To stop. (*A.-S.*) To blow the stint, i. e. the check or stop to the hounds. Still in use as a substantive, a limit, or quantity; a limited quantity.

And when heo *stynteth* and seyth no more,
Ȝef thou syst heo nedeth lore,
Thenne spek to hyre on thys wyse,
And say, take the gode avyse.
MS. Cott. Claud. A. ii. f. 137.

The litell boye *stint* nought
Till the horse was home brought;
Thereof wiste the clerkes nought,
For sothe as I you sale.
The Miller of Abington, n. d.

He toke hur abowte the myddelle smalle,
And layd hur downe upon the grene,
Twys or thrys he served hur soo withalle,
He wolde nat *stynt* yet as I wene.
MS. Rawl. C. 258.

Then Robin he hasted over the plain,
He did neither *stint* nor lin,
Until he came unto the church,
Where Allin should keep his wedding.
Robin Hood, ii. 49.

The byschop *stynt* in that stouude.
MS. Cantab. Ff. ii. 38, f. 47.

He drewe hys swyrde; or he *stynte*
Hys hedd he smote of at a dynte.
MS. Cantab. Ff. ii. 38, f. 173.

(2) The purr, or sea-lark. According to Moor, a species of plover. "The stint, or junco; it is a kind of a sea-lark, with a straight, long, slender bill, and black; the legs long, of a dusky or blackish colour; with a tincture of green," Holme, ii. 279.

STINTED. In foal, as a mare. *West.*

STINTLESS. Without stopping; ceaseless.

There he performd victorious conquering:
His life was nothing els but *stintlesse* passion.
Rowland's Betraying of Christ, 1598, Sig. E. iv.

STIOLING. Perishing from cold.

STIONY. The sty in the eye. *East.* "Styanye yn the eye," Prompt. Parv. f. 164.

STIPE. A steep ascent. *Heref.*

STIPONE. "A kind of sweet compound liquor drunk in some ill places in London in the summer time," Blount's Gloss. p. 612.

STIR. (1) He has plenty to stir on with, i. e. he is immensely rich. *North.*

(2) A crowd. *Norf.*

(3) Very hard wood. *Somerset.*

STIR-ABOUT. Oatmeal and dripping mixed together and *stirred about* in the frying-pan. Wilbraham, p. 80, calls it "a hasty pudding."

STIRACKES.

The Sabeans, by reason of the continuall use of mirrhe and frankinsens, grow to a loathing of that savour: for remedy of which anoyance, they perfume their houses by burning *stirackes* in goats skins. And thus much for the severall parts of a goat.
Topsell's Four-Footed Beasts, 1607, p. 239.

STIRE. (1) To stir; to move; to slip. (*A.-S.*)

If I saide *stired* mi fote be,
Thi merci, Laverd, helped me.
MS. Cott. Vespas. D. vii. f. 67.

That thorne no blaste of temptacion,
Oure hertes be *stirredde* noythere up no doun.
MS. Harl. 2260, f. 4.

(2) To steer; to direct. *Skelton.*

STIREHOUSE. A storehouse.

In rainy weather they are whiter a great deale then at other times, unlesse it be when they couple together, for then they appeare very red. I my selfe about the middest of Aprill, did once open a thicke female worme, and within the flesh I found a certain receptacle ringed round about, and filling up the whole cavity of the body, having a thinne membrance or coate enclosing it, and in this aforesaid *stirehouse* the earth which she had fed on, and wherewith she was susteyned, was held and contained. Her egges were found to bee in a safe place above the receptacle, next to the mouth, there were many of them on a heape together, being all of a whitish colour. *Topsell's Historie of Serpents*, 1608, p. 307.

STIRK. A heifer. *North.* "Hekfere, beeste, or styrke, *juvenca*," Pr. Parv. p. 234.

STIRKE. To become stiff with cold. "Clyngyne or styrkyne, *rigeo*," Pr. Parv.

STIRMAN. A steersman. "Rother or a styrman, *remex*," Nominale MS. xv. Cent.

STIROP. A stirrup.

A levedy ad my love leyt, the bole began to belle,
The cokeu ad the kite keyt, the doge is in the welle;
Stod y in my *stirop* streyt, i-schok out of the schelle.
MS. Arund. Coll. Arm. 27, f. 130.

STIRPE. A race; a family.

Of whiche maladye, because it was straung and rare to the physicians of England, he at the kynges manoure of Grenewiche desessed, levynge one sonne behynde hym to contynue his *stirpe* and familie.
Hall, Henry VII. f. 55.

STIRRIDGE. Commotion. *Devon.*

STIRRING. (1) "Amongst husbandmen, the second tilth or fallow called *stirring*," Florio, p. 273. Markham explains it "the second ploughing for barley."

(2) A bustle; a merry-making. *North.*

STIRRING-POT. "A long strong iron pot, with an handle about two yards; with it being red hot, is stirred the mettle and lead together in melting pots, till they be well incorporated," Holme, 1688.

STIRROW. A hasty-pudding. *Chesh.*

STIRRUP-CUP. A parting cup taken on horseback before leaving; a stirrup-glass.

> Boy, lead our horses out when we get up,
> Wee'l have with you a merry *stirrup-cupp*.
> *Praise of Yorkshire Ale*, 1697, p. 27.

STIRRUP-HOSE. "Stirrop-hose, *chaussettes à estrier;* the stirrop of the hose, *l'estrier de la chaussette,*" Howell, 1660, sect. 33. Holme mentions "large stirop hose, or stockings, two yards wide at the top, with points through several i-let holes, by which they were made fast to the petticoat-breeches by a single row of pointed ribbons hanging at the bottom." Grose has *stirrups*, a kind of buskins. *Stirrup-stockings*, Coles.

STIRRUP-LADDER. A thatcher's short ladder holding to the roof with spikes. *West.*

STIRRUP-OIL. A sound beating. Still in use, according to Major Moor, p. 406. "To give one some stirrup-oyl, *aliquem fustigare,*" Coles' Lat. Dict.

STIRRUPS. "Rings or iron bands that binde the shankes of the wheele, which we call the *stirrops* of a wheele," Florio, p. 68.

STIRRUP-VERSE. A verse at parting.

> Must Megg, the wife of Batt, aged eighty,
> Deceas'd November thirteenth, seventy-three,
> Be cast, like common dust, into the pit,
> Without one line of monumental wit?
> One death's head distich, or mortality-staff,
> With sense enough for church-yard epitaph?
> No *stirrup-verse* at grave before she go?
> Batt does not use to part at taverns so.
> *Batt upon Batt*, seventh ed. p. 23.

STIRT. Started. (*A.-S.*)

> And was about him to slen,
> Ac other *stirt* hem bituen.
> *Arthour and Merlin*, p. 124.

> Kay up *stirt* and King Yder,
> Afot foughten with swerdes cler.
> *Arthour and Merlin*, p. 144.

> Methought thanne I *stirte* up anone,
> And to the broke I ranne and gate a stone,
> And to the cokkowe hertly cast,
> And for drede he flyes away ful fast,
> And gladd was I whan that he was goon.
> *MS. Cantab.* Ff. i. 6, xv. Cent.

STIRTANDE. Starting; spirited. *Gawayne.*

STIRTTELYS. Quickly; immediately.

> *Stirttelys* steryne one steryne with styffe mene of armes,
> Mony lufliche launce appone lofte stondys.
> *Morte Arthure*, MS. Lincoln, f. 91.

STIR-UP-SUNDAY. The twenty-fifth Sunday after Trinity, the collect for that day beginning with the words *stir up.*

STITCH. (1) A contortion; a grimace.

(2) A narrow ridge of land. *Cumb.*

(3) A stack or bundle of ten sheaves of corn set up together in a field. *Devon.*

> I be a come whim, Thomas, an I dwon't thenk I shall goo ta school again theäse zummer. I shall

be out amangst ye. I'll goo wi' ta mawy, an ta hä makin, an ta reapy—I'll come äter, an set up tha *stitches* vor ye, Thomas. *West Country Dialogues.*

(4) A tailor. *Var. dial.*

(5) To go through stitch, i. e. to go through or accomplish completely. "Now wee are in, wee must goe through *stitch,*" Tragedy of Hoffman, 1631, sig. F. iii. "*Passe-par-tout,* a resolute fellow, one that goes *through-stitch* with every thing hee undertakes, one whose courses no danger can stop, no difficultie stay," Cotgrave. "To go thorow-stitch with the work, *opus peragere,*" Coles.

(6) *Stop stitch while I put a needle in,* a proverbial phrase applied to any one when one wishes him to do anything more slowly.

STITCHBACK. Strong ale. *South.*

STITE. As soon. *Yorksh.*

STITELERS.

> This is the watyre abowte the place, if any dyche may be mad, ther it schal be pleyed; or ellys that it be strongely barryd al abowte, and lete nowth over many *styielerys* be withinne the place.
> *Sharp's Cov. Myst.* p. 23.

STITH. (1) Ascendeth. (*A.-S.*)

> Mon that thuncheth he breketh armes,
> That y-wis bytokneth harmes.
> Mon that syth tren blowe ant bere,
> Bitokneth wynnyng, ant no lere.
> Mon that *styth* on tre an heh,
> Gode tidynge him is neh. *Reliq. Antiq.* i. 262.

(2) A blacksmith's anvil. (*A.-S.*) *Stithy* is the most general form of the word. "Stythe for a smythe, *enclume,*" Palsgrave.

> As hit were dyntes of a *stithi,*
> That smythes smyten in her smythi.
> *Cursor Mundi*, MS. Coll. Trin. Cantab. f. 136.

(3) Carbonic acid gas. *North.*

STITHE. (1) Firm; strong; stiff. "*Stithe,* strong, stiff, ab As. stidh, stiff, hard, severe, violent, great, strong; *stithe cheese,* i. e. strong cheese," Ray, p. 45. ed. 1674.

> The stremys are so styffe and *stythe,*
> That many a manne ther losses thaire lyfe.
> *MS. Lincoln* A. i. 17, f. 142.

> On stedes that were *stithe* and strong,
> Thai riden togider with schaftes long.
> *Amis and Amiloun*, 1303.

> A turnament thai ches,
> With knightes *stithe* on stede. *Sir Tristrem*, p. 142.

(2) Hot; oppressive; stifling. *East.*

(3) To ascend, or climb. Batman, 1582.

STITHOM. Confusion; bustle. *Linc.*

STIVART. Place; station.

> Love maketh moni mai with teres to wede:
> Love hath his *stivart* by sti and by strete.
> *App. to Conybeare's Octavian*, p. 59.

STIVE. (1) A kind of hive made of straw used at cock-fights for putting the birds in to keep them warm. *To be stived up,* to be stifled up in a warm place.

(2) To push with poles. *Scott.*

(3) To walk energetically. *North.* Mr. Hunter says, to walk with affected stateliness.

(4) Dust. *Var. dial.*

(5) Strong; muscular. *North. Styvest,* most strong or powerful.

And strangest upon my stede,
And styvest under gurdell,
And lovelokest to loken on,
And lykyngest a-bedde.   *Piers Ploughman*, p. 519.

(6) To shiver with cold.   *Devon.*

STIVED. Baked hard.   *Will. Werw.*

STIVEN. Sternness.   *Grose.*

STIVER. (1) To start up.   *Devon.*

(2) To exert one's self violently. " How he *stivers* through the mud."   *Sussex.* To flutter.   *Kent.*

(3) A bristling of the hair.   *West.*

(4) A small Dutch coin.

Through thy protection they are monstrous thrivers,
Not like the Dutchmen in base doyts and *stivers.*
       Taylor's Workes, ii. 3.

(5) *To stiver about*, to stagger.   *Sussex.*

STIVES. Stews, or brothels.

STIVING. Close; stifling.   *Worc.*

STIVOUR. A kind of bagpipe. Also, a player upon the stivour.   (*A.-N.*)

Ther were trumpes and fithelers,
And *stivours* and tabourers.
       Arthour and Merlin, p. 243.

Organisters and gode *stivours*,
Minstrels of mouthe, and mani dysour,
To glade tho bernes blithe.
       Gy of Warwike, p. 274.

STIVVEN. A road is said to be *stivven* up when so full of snow as to be impassable. *Norf.*

STI3T. Fixed.   *Will. Werw.*

STOACH. To make an impression on wet land, as oxen do in winter.   *Sussex.*

STOAK-HOLE. A round hole out of which the fire in the furnace proceeds.   *Holme.*

STOB. A small post. The gibbet post of the notorious Andrew Mills, in the bishopric of Durham, was called *Andrew Mills' stob.* To *stob* out, to demand or portion out land by stobs. It is also used in reference to spines or thorns that have pierced the flesh. *York.*

STOBBALL-PLAY. Aubrey, in his Nat. Hist. Wilts, Royal Soc. MS. p. 347, gives the following account of this game:—" It is peculiar to North Wilts, North Glocestershire, and a little part of Somerset, near Bath ; they strike a ball stuffed very hard with quills, and covered with soale-leather as big as a . . . . . bullet, with a staffe commonly made of withy about three and a halfe feet long. Colemdowne is the place so famous and so frequented for stobball playing. The twife is very fine, and the rock freestone is within an inch and half of the surface, which gives the ball so quick a rebound. A stobball-ball is of about four inches diameter, stuffed very hard with quills, sowed into soale leather, and as hard as a stone. I doe not heare that this game is used anywhere in England but in this part of Wiltshire, and Gloucestershire adjoyning. They strike the ball with a great turned staff of about four feet long." So far Aubrey, which I have corrected by reference to the rough draft of this work in the Ashmolean Museum. See also Stowe's Survey of London,

ed. 1720, b. i. p. 257. " A stow-ball, *pila clavata*," Coles.

STOBLE. Stubble. *Palsgrave.* " *Stipula*, a stoble and a stree," Medulla MS.

STOBWORT. The herb oxys, or sorrel. " Wood sorrell or stubwoort," Gerard, p. 1030.

STOCHE. A stab.   *Yorksh.*

STOCK. (1) The udder.   *Kent.*

(2) A root.   (3) To root up.   *West.*

(4) Strong ; muscular.   *I. of Wight.*

(5) A stocking.   *Shak.*

(6) At cards, when part of the cards only is used, the remainder was called the *stock.*

(7) The same as *Stockado*, q. v.

(8) The back of a grate.   *Var. dial.*

(9) To peck, as a bird.   *Heref.*

(10) To strike and wrench with an axe having a flat end.   *West.*

(11) Cattle.   *Var. dial.*

STOCKADO. A thrust in fencing. " *A stoccáta*, with a thrust or stoccado," Florio.

STOCK-CARD. A large wooden instrument used for carding wool.

STOCKED. Confined.   *Chaucer.*

Roges and vagabonds are often *stocked* and whipped ; scolds are ducked upon cuckingstooles in the water.   *Harrison*, p. 185.

STOCKEL. An old pollard tree.   *Heref.*

STOCKENED. Stopped in growth.   *Linc.*

STOCKERS. Persons employed to fell or grub up trees.   *West.* See *Stock* (3).

STOCKING-IRON. An implement used for grubbing weeds up.

STOCK-MILL. A fulling-mill.   *Glouc.*

STOCKPORT-COACH. A horse with two women riding sidewise upon it.   *North.*

STOCKS. (1) A wooden prison for the legs, used in villages as a punishment for petty offences. They may still be seen in many places, though generally disused. They are introduced upon the stage in the old play of Hick Scorner, and in King Lear. The Worcester Journal of Jan. 19th, 1843, informs us that this old mode of punishment was recently revived at Stratford-on-Avon for drunkenness, and a passer-by asking a fellow who was doing penance how he liked it, the reply was—" I beant the first mon as ever were in the stocks, so I don't care a fardin about it." Holme describes the stocks, " a prison or place of security to keep safe all such as the constable finds to be night-walkers, common drunkards and swearers, that have no money, and such like ; also petty thieves, strippers of hedges, robbers of hen-roosts, and light-fingered persons, who can let none of their masters or mistresses goods or cloaths lye before them ; also wandring rogues, gipsies, and such as love begging better than labour."

And twenty of thes odur ay in a pytt,
In *stokkes* and feturs for to sytt.
       MS. Cantab. Ff. ii. 38, f. 233.

And if from the *stocks* I can keep out my feet,
I fear not the Compter, King's Bench, nor the Fleet
       Academy of Compliments, 1671, p. 261.

(2) The frame of a churn or the stand upon which it is put. *West.*

STOCK-SHEARS. Shears used by needle-makers for cutting wire the required length.

STOCK-SLEEVE. "*Manche Lombarde*, a stocke sleeve, or fashion of halfe-sleeve, whose upper part is raised, and full of plaits or gathers," Cotgrave. " A stock-sleeve, or kind of half-sleeve," Howell, 1660.

STOCKY. (1) Irritable, headstrong, and contrary, combined. *Sussex.*

(2) Impudent, brassy; used on the borders of Leicestershire, to which county it perhaps more properly belongs. *Linc.*

(3) Short and thick of growth. *West.*

STODDLE. " Stodyll a toole for a wever, *lame detisserant*," Palsgrave.

STODE. Stood; remained still.

> The abbot sayd to his covent,
> There he *stode* on grounde,
> This day twelve moneth came there a knyght,
> And borowed foure hondred pounde.
> > *Robin Hood*, I. 17.

> The schylde in the schouldur wode
> Halfe a fote or hyt *stode*.
> > *MS. Cantab.* Ff. ii. 38, f. 179.

STODE-MERE. A mare in foal. (*A.-S.*)

> Bot the boye was never so blythe,
> Als whenne he herde the name kythe
> Of the *stode-mere* stythe;
> Of na thyng thanne he roghte. *Perceval*, 367.

STODGE. (1) To stuff; to fill; to distend; to squeeze tightly together. *West.*

(2) Pottage, or soft food. *Devon.* Forby has *stodge*, to stir up various ingredients into a thick mass.

(3) Thick slimy mud. *South.*

STODGE-FULL. Quite full, or unable to contain more. The ground or the road is said to be *stodgy*, or *all of a stodge*, when it is wet, deep, and miry. *Warw.*

STOFFADO. " A term for the stuffing of any joint of meat, or belly of any fowl, or the like," Holme's Academy, 1688, iii. 84.

STOGGED. Set fast in a mire. *Devon.*

STOGGEREL. An old pollard. *West.*

STOIN'D. Astounded.

> *Stoin'd* and amax'd at his own shade for dread,
> And fearing greater dangers than was need.
> > *British Bibliographer*, i. 290.

STOITH. " *Stipa*, a stoith," occurs in Nominale MS. among the *nomina vestimentorum.*

STOITING. The jumping of pilchards above the surface of the water. *East.*

STOK-DOWE. A stock-dove. " *Palumbus, palumba*, a stok dowe," Nominale MS.

STOKE. (1) A yard in length.

(2) To stir the fire. *Var. dial.*

(3) A stock. Nominale MS.

STOKEN. Shut; fastened. *North.*

> Syr, sche seyde, nothyng welle,
> For sche was *stoken* yn that castelle.
> > *MS. Cantab.* Ff. ii. 38, f. 142.

> Olimpias is now awroke,
> Ac yet heo is in prison *stoke.*
> > *Kyng Alisaunder*, 1132.

STOKER. A man employed to stir and attend to the fire in a brewery, &c. *Var. dial.*

STOKEY. Close, or sultry. *North.*

STOLDRED. Stealth. *Kent.*

> Some little corn by *stoldred* brought to town.
> > *Billingsly's Brachy-Martyrologia*, 1657, p. 107.

STOLE. (1) A stool. (*A.-S.*) There was a weaver's instrument called the *stole.*

(2) Part of the ecclesiastical habit, worn about the neck. (*A.-N.*)

> Jef the wonte *stole* or fanone,
> When thow art in the canone,
> Passe forth wythowten turne,
> But that thow moste rewe jerne.
> > *MS. Cotton. Claud.* A. ii. f. 150.

(3) Robe of royalty. *Weber.*

(4) A kind of packing-chest for robes and clothes. We still have " groom of the stole." See Privy Purse Expences of Eliz. of York, p. 45.

(5) To drink; to swallow. *Norf.*

STOLEN. " Stolen things are sweet," an old proverb still in common use.

> From busie cooks we love to steal a bit
> Behind their backs, and that in corners eat.
> Nor need we here the reason why entreat,
> All know the proverb, *stollen bread is sweet.*
> > *History of Joseph*, n. d.

STOLKY. Wet and miry. *Glouc.*

STOLNE. Stolen. (*A.-S.*)

> Than sende Joseph aftur hem men that saydon that thei were wykkyd men, that aftur that here lorde hadde made hem wel at ese, haddon *stolne* hys coupe that he lovid moste.
> > *MS. Cott. Claud.* A. ii. f. 46.

STOLPE. A post, or stulp. *North.*

> The cradle to have five *stolpes*, three at the head, and twoe at the feet, and the king's armes on the middle *stolpe*, and all the other *stulpes* with other armes, and well carpetted all about, with a pane thereon of cloth of gould furred with ermine.
> > *Ordinances and Regulations*, p. 137.

STOLSY. To walk in the dirt. *Beds.*

STOLT. Strong; stout. *Sussex.*

STOLY. Dirty; disorderly. *Suffolk.*

STOM. (1) The instrument used to keep the malt in the vat. *North.*

(2) A large branch of a tree. *Beds.*

STOMACH. (1) Pride; hauteur.

(2) To bear, or put up with. *Var. dial.*

(3) Anger. (4) To resent. *East.* Both these senses are used by early writers. To stick in the stomach, i. e. to remember with anger.

STOMACHFUL. Stubborn. Also, angry.

STOMACHY. Proud; haughty; irritable; easily offended. *Var. dial.*

STOMAGER. " Curet, breastplate, or stomager, *thorax*," Huloet, 1552.

STOMBER. To confuse; to confound. *Salop.*

STOMBLED. The same as *Poached*, q. v.

STOMELAR. A stumbler. *Pr. Parv.*

STOMPEY. To stump or walk. *Var. dial.*

STONAGE. Any heap of stones. Stonehenge is so called by the country people.

STONAS. An entire horse. *Suffolk.*

STONAYE. To confound; to astonish.

> Whenne any stirttes to stale, stuffe thame the bettere,
> Ore thei wille I e *stonayede* and stroyede in jone strayte londez. *Morte Arthure*, *MS. Lincoln*, f. 73

He was so *stonyed* of that dente,
Thi nygh he had hys lyff rente.
Richard Coer de Lion, 421.

And soche a strok to Befyse he lente,
That he was *stonyed* of that dynte.
MS. Cantab. Ff. ii. 38, f. 125.

STONCHEDE. Stopped.

And the wynde *stonchede* and blew no more,
And the meyst turnde into a bryʒt cloude.
Chron. Vilodun. p. 127.

STONCROP. The plant *crassula minor*.

STOND. "Stonde a vessell, they have none," Palsgrave, 1530, subst. f. 67:

Hwor is thi bred and thin ale,
Thi tunne and thine *stonde* ?
MS. Cott. Calig. A. ix. f. 245.

STONDAND-FIGNADE. Is thus described in an early and curious poem on cookery:

Fyrst play thy water with hony and salt,
Grynde blanchyd almondes, I wot thou shalle ;
Thurgh a streynour thou shalt hom streyne,
With the same water that is so clene:
In sum of the water stepe thou shalle
Whyte brede crustes to alye hit withalle.
Then take figgus and grynde hom wele,
Put hom in pot, so have thou cele.
Then take brede, with mylke hit streyne
Of almondes that be white and clene.
Cast in tho fyggus that ar i-grynde,
With powder of peper that is tho kynde ;
And powder of canel, in grete lordys house,
With sugur or hony thou may hit dowce.
Then take almondes cloven in twen,
That fryid ar with oyle ; and set with wyn
Thy dissh, and floryssh hit thou myʒt
Wyth powder of gynger that is so bryʒt ;
And serve hit forth, as I spake thenne,
And set hit in sale before, &c.
MS. Sloane 1986, pp. 91, 92.

STONDE. To stand ; to remain. (*A.-S.*)

No nan in chyrche *stonde* schal,
Ny lene to pyler ny to wal.
MS. Cott. Claud. A. ii. f. 130.

STONDENDE. Standing.

Thorow syʒte of hem misturnid were,
Stondende as stonis here and there.
Gower, MS. Soc. Antiq. 134, f. 41.

STOND-HORSE. "Stonde horse, *naturel*," Palsgrave, subst. f. 67.

STONDLE. A bearing-tub. *Norf.*

STONE. (1) A gun-flint.

(2) In composition, signifying *quite* ; as *stone-blind*, quite blind; *stone-cold, stone-dead, stone-still*, &c. Still in use.

Ever satt Percyvelle *stone-stille*,
And spakke nothynge hir tille,
Tille scho hade sayde alle hir wille,
And spakke lesse ne mare.   *Perceval*, 341.

STONE-AX. A stone-worker's axe.

STONE-BOW. A crossbow for shooting stones. "Stone-bowe, *arcubasta*," Pr. Parv.

STONE-BURNISHER. A stone used for polishing and making bright a piece of silver or gold. Holme, 1688.

STONE-CHAT. The wheatear. *North.*

STONE-HATCH. The ring-plover. *Norf.*

STONE-HONEY. Honey hardened and candied white like sugar. Also called corn-honey.

STONE-HORSE. A stallion. "*Cheval entier*, a stone-horse," Cotgrave in v. *Entier*.

STONE-JARS. Large jugs are so called, though composed of earthenware. *Hunter.* Forby has *stone-ware*, old-fashioned earthenware of a dusky white or grayish colour.

STONEN. Made of stone. *West.*

STONE-SPITCHIL-DIKE. A raised earthen dike, faced with stones. *North.*

STONE-WEED. Knot-grass. *Suffolk.*

STONGEN. To stab ; to pierce. (*A.-S.*)

They ben y-sewed with whight silke,
And semes ful queynte,
Y-*stongen* with stiches
That stareth as sylver.   *Piers Ploughman*, p. 483.

STONK. A shock of corn. "*Diseaux de gerbes*, sheafes of corne set tenne and tenne in a heape ; halfe-thraves of tenne sheaves apeece ; ten sheaved *stonks* or shocks of corne," Cotgrave, 1632.

STONNORD. The herb stonecrop.

STONT. Standeth. (*A.-S.*)

In the myddel the chylde *stont*,
As he ys folowed in the font.
MS. Cott. Claud. A. ii. f. 129.

Thay *stont* stilly a stownde ;
Thay putt up pavilyons ronde.
MS. Lincoln A. i. 17, f. 131.

STONY-HARD. The plant corn-gromwell.

STOO. A stool. *Lanc.*

STOOD. Cropped short. *North.*

STOOK. (1) A sort of stile beneath which water is discharged. *Somerset.*

(2) A shock of corn. *North.*

Lesly having instantly ordered to raise the countrey for the Perlam't, under the command of Col. Lawson and Col. Chomly, marched the next day towards Newcastle. The corn was then all in the *stook ;* and Lesly knew well that if he had stayed to beggar the towne, he might have taken it within a few weeks.
Tullie's Narrative of the Siege of Carlisle, p. 7.

(3) The remains of a pillar of coal after it has been riven by a board. *Newc.*

(4) To stoop the head. *North.*

STOOL. (1) To ramify, as corn. *Var. dial.*

(2) To plough ; to cultivate. *Yorksh.*

STOOL-BALL. An ancient game at ball, played by both sexes. According to Dr. Johnson, it is a play where balls are driven from stool to stool. See a further notice in Strutt, p. 97. In Lewis's English Presbyterian Eloquence, p. 17, speaking of the tenets of the Puritans, he observes that "all games where there is any hazard of loss are strictly forbidden ; not so much as a game at *stool-ball* for a Tansay, or a cross and pyle for the odd penny at a reckoning, upon pain of damnation." This quotation is given by Brand, in his Pop. Antiq. The following is from Herrick's Hesperides, 1648, p. 280 :

At *stool-ball*, Lucia, let us play
  For sugar-cakes and wine ;
Or for a tansie let us pay,
  The losse be thine or mine.
If thou, my deere, a winner be
  At trundling of the ball,
The wager thou shalt have, and me,
  And my misfortunes all.

Poor Robin, in his Almanack for 1677, in his

Observations on April, opposite the 16th and 17th, Easter Monday and Tuesday, says,—

> Young men and maids,
> Now very brisk,
> At barley-break and
> *Stool-ball* frisk.
>
> *Brand's Popular Antiquities*, i. 105.

> *Isa.* Ay, and at *stool-ball* too, sir; I've great luck at it. *Ward.* Why, can you catch a ball well? *Isa.* I have catch'd two in my lap at one game.
>
> *Middleton's Works*, iv. 597.

> When health and weather both invite,
> At *stool-ball* to play for our delight.
>
> *The Pleasant Alarum*, 1703.

STOOL-OF-OFFICE. A close-stool.

> And as of one part of a tree a chaire of state may be made, and of another part a carved image, and of a third part a *stoole of office;* so men, being compounded and composed all of one mould and mettle, are different and disconsonant in estates, conditions, and qualities. *Taylor's Workes*, i. 144.

STOOLS. The roots of copse, or hedgewood cut down nearly to the ground. *Var. dial.* "To go a stooling, signifies to be employed in woods, generally without the owner's leave, in cutting up such decayed stools, or stumps, or moots, for fuel," MS. Devon. Gl.

STOOL'S-FOOT. To lay the *stool's-foot* in water, means to make great preparation for receiving a guest. *East.*

STOOL-TERRAS. To set turfs two and two, one against the other, to be dried by the wind. *West.*

STOON. A stone. (*A.-S.*)

> Oure Lord wroot it hymselve
> In *stoon*, for it stedefast was,
> And stonde sholde evere.
>
> *Piers Ploughman*, p. 328.

STOOP. (1) To fall, or pounce upon, as a hawk on the wing does upon his prey.

(2) To steep; to macerate. *West.*

(3) A post, or stulp. *North.*

(4) A drinking cup; a pitcher. Still in use in the latter sense.

(5) A barrel; a beer-vessel. *Northumb.*

(6) To tilt a cask. *South.*

STOOR. (1) To rise up in clouds, as smoke, dust, fallen lime, &c. *Yorksh.*

(2) To stir, or move actively. *West.*

(3) A sufficient quantity of yeast for a brewing. See Forby's East Anglia, p. 329.

STOOREY. A mixture of warm beer and oatmeal stirred up with sugar. *North.*

STOOTH. To lath and plaster. *North.*

STOP. (1) To cover; to hide. "A hassocke or mat to *stop* a privy with," Florio, p. 84.

(2) A small well-bucket. *Norf.*

(3) To poke; to thrust; to place. *North.*

(4) To fasten a feather to the wing of a hawk in place of a broken one.

(5) The same as *Stab*, q. v.

STOP-DICE. A kind of false dice, mentioned in Palsgrave's Acolastus, 1540. Chapman alludes to stop-rater-trays.

STOPEN. Stopped; advanced. (*A.-S.*)

STOP-GLAT. A make-shift; a substitute.

STOPLESS. A portable wooden stopper for the mouth of an oven. *North.*

STOPPE. (1) To stuff. *Pegge.*

(2) A bucket, or milking-pail. Still in use in Norfolk. The holy-water *stoppe* was a vessel containing holy-water placed near the entrance of a church, and was sometimes made of lead.

STOPPER. A person at tennis, football, and other games, who stops the balls.

STOPPING. Honey laid so long in the cells that it has become bad and hard.

STOPPING-PAN.

> Then stop the veine with a little hogs-grease, and then tacke on the shooes, and turpentine molten together, and laid upon a little flax, and cram the place where you did let him blood hard with tow, to the intent it may be surely stopt. Then fil both his feet with hogs grease, and bran fried together in a *stopping pan*, so hot as is possible. And upon the stopping, clap a piece of leather, or else two splents to keepe the stopping.
>
> *Topsell's Four-Footed Beasts*, 1607, p. 400.

STOPPINGS. A barrier of plank, brick, or stone, filling up an excavation to give direction to a current of air in a coal mine.

STOPPLE. (1) The stopper of a bottle, &c.

> But that yt lackes a *stoppell*,
> Take thee heare my well [fayer] bottill,
> For it will houlde a good pottill,
> In faith, I can geve thee no more.
>
> *Chester Plays*, i. 142.

> Bot both your sisters and your child
> Provided well for this,
> Their tubbs can never leake,
> Because the *stopple* there is.
>
> *MS. Poems*, temp. James I.

(2) The stalk of a pipe; the tufts of straw used in thatching stacks. *West.*

(3) Stubble. *Devon.* "Halm, or stobyl, stopyll, *stipula*," Prompt. Parv. p. 223.

> And thoru haubert and ys coler, that nere nothyng souple,
> He smot of ys heved as lyȝtlyche as yt were a lute *stouple*. *Rob. Gloucester's Chronicle*, p. 223.

STOP-RODS. Are explained by Carr, "the wattling of the shafts of a mine." *North.*

STOP-SHORD. A stop-gap. *Somerset.*

STOPWOUR. The herb Alleluja.

STORBET. Disturbed. (*A.-S.*)

> Hast thou be slowe to Goddes servyse,
> Or *storbet* hyt by any wyse.
>
> *MS. Cott. Claud.* A. ii. f. 140.

STORE. (1) Strong; powerful; large. (*A.-S.*) Tyrwhitt, iv. 253, was apparently unacquainted with this meaning of the term.

> On a grene hylle he sawe a tree,
> The savyr of hyt was strong and *stora*.
>
> *MS. Cantab.* Ff. ii. 38, f. 49.

> Fra sa mekille a manne and sa *store*
> Had thay never sene byfore.
>
> *MS. Lincoln* A. i. 17, f. 126.

> For Sir Anlaf, the king of Danmark,
> With an ost *store* and stark,
> Into Inglond is come;
> With fifteen thousend knightes of prijs,
> Alle this lond thai stroyen y-wis,
> And mani a toun han nome.
>
> *Gy of Warwike*, p. 321.

> The king and his men ilkane
> Wend tharwith to have bene slane,
> So blew it *stor* with slete and rayn.
>
> *Ywaine and Gawin* 1297.

(2) Anything laid up for use. (3) *To tell no store of a thing*, to consider it of no use or importance. *Chaucer.*

(4) A receptacle for any articles.

(5) To stock, or furnish. (*A.-N.*)

(6) The plant *Libanum Olibanum*, according to MS. Sloane 5, f. 6, xv. Cent.

(7) *Store is no sore*, an old phrase meaning that things stored up cause no harm.

> Multeply thy medcyns ay more and more,
> For wyse men done sey *store ys no sore.*
> > *Ashmole's Theat. Chem. Brit.* 1652, p. 186.
> This is the cause, sir, that I judged it so vile,
> Bycause it is so common in talking every while;
> For plentie is not deintie, as the common saying is.
> No, nor *store is no sore*, perceive you this.
> > *Resorde's Grounds of Artes*, 1579.

(8) Number; quantity.

> Others were sav'd, whose crimes rose to that *store*
> As they deserv'd death twentie times before.
> > *Braithwaite's Law of Drinking*, 1617, p. 78.

(9) To move; to stir.

> Loke ye *store* not of that stedd,
> Whedur y be quyck or dedd.
> > *MS. Cantab.* Ff. ii. 38, f. 191.

STORE-PIGS. Pigs nearly full grown.

STORGIN. A sturgeon. Nominale MS.

> That made the erthe and the planettes sevyn,
> And in the see the *sturgons.*
> > *MS. Cantab.* Ff. ii. 38, f. 170.

STORIAL. Historical; true. (*A.-N.*)

STORKEN. (1) To gain strength. *Cumb.*

(2) To cool; to stiffen. *North.*

STORKING. Some kind of bird. "*Frondator*, a storkyng," Nominale MS.

STORK'S-BILL. "*Storck's bill*, to *storken*, proper to fat growing cold, and so hard," Hallamshire GL p. 124.

STORM. (1) To scold; to be angry. *East.*

(2) A shower. *Wilts.*

(3) A fall of snow. Also, a long continued frost. *North.* To be stormed, i. e. to be starved with cold.

STORM-COCK. The missel thrush. *North.*

STORMING-THE-CASTLE. A kind of sea-game mentioned in Peregrine Pickle, ch. 16.

STORM-STAID. Detained on a journey on account of a storm. *North.*

STORQUE.

> Rip up each vein and sinew of my *storque*,
> Anatomise him, searching every entraile.
> > *The Muses Looking-Glasse*, 1643, p. 48.

STORVE. To die. (*A.-S.*)

> My sone schalle not thys day *storve*,
> Be Seynt Thomas that y schalle serve.
> > *MS. Cantab.* Ff. ii. 38, f. 135.
> Ther-while Ypocras, with a knif,
> Binom that schild his swete lif;
> And let him birle sikerliche,
> Als he were *storven* sodainliche.
> > *The Sevyn Sages*, 1125.

STORVING. Slaying; killing. (*A.-S.*)

> Betwene the barons and the king
> Ought to be no *storving. MS. Cantab.* Ff. v. 48, f. 108.

STORY. A falsehood. *Var. dial.*

STORY-POSTS. The upright timbers reaching from the top to the bottom of a story in a building of carpenter's work. *Willson.*

STOT. (1) A young ox. *North.* "Stotte, *boveau*," Palsgrave. Tyrwhitt thinks Chaucer uses the term for *stod*, a stallion. "Stot hors, *caballus*," Pr. Parv. f. 165.

> And saide thaire fee was fro thame revede,
> Certis, syr, us es noghte levyde
> A *stotte* unto youre plowghe!   *Isumbras*, 22.

(2) To rebound, as a ball. *North.*

STOTAYE. To stumble; to stammer.

> Than he *stotays* for made, and alle his strenghe fayles,
> Lokes upe to the lyfte, and alle his lyre chaunges.
> > *Morte Arthure, MS. Lincoln*, f. 97.
> Un-comly in cloystre. i coure ful of care,
> I loke as a lurdeyn. and listne til my lare,
> The song of the cesolfa. dos me syken sare,
> And sitte *stotiand* on a song. a moneth and mare.
> > *Reliq. Antiq.* i. 291.

STOTCH. To poach land; "the cattle have *stotched* the field," that is, covered it with their footmarks. *Kent.*

STOTE. A kind of weasel. The polecat is called a *stote* in Somersetshire.

STOTEDE. Remained; rested?

> Anone to the forest they found,
> There they *stotede* a stound;
> They pyght pavelouns round,
> And loggede that nyght.   *Degrevant*, 226.

STOTER. To stumble. *North.*

STOTEYE. Cunning; stratagem. *Will. Werw.*

STOTHE. The slay of a weaver's loom. Also, a post or upright of a wall.

STOT-PLOUGH. A plough drawn by stots.

> Mr. Hutchinson, in his History of Northumberland, speaking of the dress of the sword-dancers at Christmas, adds: Others, in the same kind of gay attire, draw about a plough, called the *stot-plough*, and when they receive the gift make the exclamation Largess! but if not requited at any house for their appearance, they draw the plough through the pavement and raise the ground of the front in furrows. I have seen twenty men in the yoke of one plough. He concludes thus: The *stot-plough* has been conceived by some to have no other derivation than a mere rural triumph, the plough having ceased from its labour. *Brand's Popular Antiquities*, i. 280.

STOT-TUESDAY. The first Tuesday which occurs after the 27th of October.

STOTTY. Gritty, as soil is. *West.*

STOU. A place, or seat. (*A.-S.*)

> On *stou* ase thou stode,
> Thou restest the under rode.
> > *Wright's Lyric Poetry*, p. 98.

STOUD. A young colt. *West.*

STOUDE.

> Of alle oure riche clothes tid us never a shroude,
> Whose hath don for Godes love, he may be ful *stoude*.
> > *Walter Mapes, Appendix*, p. 349.

STOUK. (1) The handle of a pail. Also, a drinking-cup with a handle. *North.*

(2) To raise a steam. *North.*

(3) A stock or heap of anything.

STOUN. (1) Stolen. *North and Scot.*

(2) To smart with pain.

> Ah, Nan, steek'th winderboard and mack it dark,
> My neen are varra sair, they *stoun* and wark.
> > *A Yorkshire Dialogue*, 1697, p. 49.

STOUND. (1) To beat severely. *East.*

(2) To ache; to smart with pain. *North.*

(3) To long for; to pine for. If carrots or any

other food of which horses are very fond are given to them for a short time, and then withheld, they are said to *stownd* for them. Early in the spring cows *stownd* for grass.

(4) A wooden vessel for small beer.

(5) A moment, or short time. (*A.-S.*) Still in use, according to Forby and Moor.

> Heven blys that alle schalle wynne,
> Schylde us fro dedly synne,
> And graunte us the blys of hevyn!
> Yf ye wylle a *stounde* blynne,
> Of a story y wylle begynne,
> That gracyus ys to nevyn.
> *MS. Cantab. Ff. ii. 38, f. 71.*

> Then seyde the kyng that ylke *stounde*,
> Me thynkyth that was Sir Roger hounde,
> That wente wyth hym thoo,
> When the quene was flemed owt of my londe;
> Syr, they seyde, we undurstonde
> For sothe that hyt ys soo!
> *MS. Cantab. Ff. ii. 38, f. 74.*

> Thei shal be fedde with deth that *stounde*,
> The prophete it saith that here is founde.
> *MS. Addit. 11305, f. 96.*

> For-thi thay named [hym] that *stounde*,
> Knyghte of the table rownde.
> *MS. Lincoln A. i. 17, f. 130.*

> In what place they schal be founde,
> I schal yow telle at the *stounde*.
> *MS. Poem on Blood-letting, xv. Cent.*

(6) Stunned. *Spenser.*

(7) To astound, or astonish. *East.*

> They take also their name of the word mase and theefe, or master theefe if you will, bicause they often *stound* and put such persons to their shifts in townes and villages, and are the principall causes of their apprehension and taking.
> *Harrison's Description of England, p. 231.*

(8) To beat a drum. *North.*

STOUNDEMELE. By short spaces of time; by degrees; every moment. (*A.-S.*)

> Syn ye were first unto your make y-knyt,
> Wel han ye kept your chambre of prevetè;
> For hardely may no mane sey as yet,
> That with your bodè foleyed han ye.
> And now cometh age, foo to your beautè,
> And stelyngly it wastyth *stownde-mele*.
> *MS. Fairfax 16.*

> And every day, withoutte wordes moo,
> *Stoundemele* from the heyven aboven,
> Goddis aungels come to and froo.
> *Lydgate, MS. Ashmole 39, f. 44.*

> *Stoundemele* from the heven adoun
> Goddis aungelle cam to and fro.
> *Lydgate, MS. Soc. Antiq. 134, f. 6.*

STOUP. A post. *Linc.* "Stoulpe before a doore, *souche*," Palsgrave.

STOUPE. (1) To bend; to stoop. (*A.-S.*) Also, to stoop as a hawk does.

> For now she loves to lyve of chaunge,
> And *stowpes* to every praye;
> So he that wyll cache her
> Had neede for to wache her,
> Or els she wyll sore away. *MS. Ashmole 48.*

(2) To give up. A cant term.

STOUPINS. Steppings, or holes made by the feet of cattle. *North.*

STOUR. (1) Dust. *North.*

(2) Harsh; deep-toned. *Yorksh.*

STOURE. (1) Battle; conflict. (*A.-S.*)

> Me ys wo now for yowre sake
> Agaynste thy kynne to stonde in *stoure*.
> *MS. Harl. 2252, f. 198.*

> Tryamowre wolde nevyr have reste,
> But bare hym boldely to the beste,
> That was moost of honowre;
> To ylke a prynce he was preste,
> Hors and man downe he caste,
> So styrde he hym in that *stoure*.
> *MS. Cantab. Ff. ii. 38, f. 76.*

> He es stalworthe in *stoures*,
> By sayne Martyne of Towres.
> *MS. Lincoln A. i. 17, f. 134.*

(2) Great; severe. Arch. xxx. 413.

(3) Stiff; inflexible. *East.* "Stoure, rude as course clothe is, *gros*," Palsgrave.

(4) Palsgrave has, "Stowre of conversacyon, *estourdy*," adject. f. 96.

(5) A stake. Still in use.

> And if he wille noste do soo, I salle late hym witt that ye salle sende a grete powere to his citee, and bryne it up stikke and *stourre*.
> *MS. Lincoln A. i. 17, f. 41.*

(6) The round of a ladder; the stave in the side of a waggon.

(7) Time.

> Whilom while Venus' son did seek a bower
> To sport with Psyche, his desired dear,
> He chose her chin, and from that happy *stoure*
> He never stints in glory to appear.
> *Greene's Works, ii. 231.*

(8) Water. Kennett, MS. Lansd. 1033.

STOUT. (1) Tall. *Somerset.*

(2) The gad-fly; a gnat. *West.*

> Not all tha naisy *stouts* could wake
> En vrom is happy sleep,
> Nor emmets thick, nor vlies that buz,
> An on is hons da creep.
> *Ballad of Jerry Nutty.*

(3) Proud. Batchelor, p. 143.

STOUTE. To be disobedient to?

> For no man ful comunly
> Besecheth a wyfe of foly,
> But there the wyfe ys aboute
> The gode man for to *stoute*.
> *MS. Harl. 1701, f. 90.*

> Lewed man, thou shalt cursyng doute,
> And to thy prest thou shalt nat *stoute*.
> *MS. Harl. 1701, f. 72.*

STOUTY. Stout. *Skelton.*

STOVEN. A young shoot from the stump of a tree after it has been felled. *North.*

STOVENNED. Split; cracked. *Yorksh.*

STOVER. (1) Fodder for cattle; provisions. "Assen and muylyn with heore stoveris," Kyng Alisaunder, 1866.

> And maked hir a ful fair fer,
> And fond hire that night *stover*.
> *The Sevyn Sages, 2606.*

> Our low medowes is not onelie full of sandie cinder, which breedeth sundrie diseases in our cattell, but also more rowtie, foggie, and full of flags, and therefore not so profitable for *stover* and forrage as the higher meads be.
> *Harrison's Description of Britaine, p. 110.*

(2) To bristle up; to stiffen. *West.* The term is used by Ford, i. 402.

STOW. (1) To lop or top trees. *East.* "Stowd, cropt as horse's ears," Thoresby, 1703.

(2) To resist, hinder, or stop.

ȝiff any man *stow* me this nyth,
I xal hym ȝeve a dedly wownde.
Coventry Mysteries, p. 217.

(3) To dry in an oven. *Kent.*
(4) To silence any one. A cant term.
(5) To confine cattle. *Norf.*
(6) A place for putting things in.
(7) *Stow, stow*, a term formerly addressed to a hawk by a falconer to make it come to his fist. See Gent. Rec. ii. 58.

STOWE. (1) Stole. *Weber.*
(2) " Stowe, streyth passage betwyx ij. wallys or hedgys, *intrapedo*," Pr. Parv.
(3) To cope with an enemy.

Thay stekede stedys in stoure with stelene wapyns,
And alle *stowede* wyth strenghe that stode theme agaynes.
Morte Arthure, MS. Lincoln, f. 69.

(4) " Stowyne or waryne, or besettyne, as men done moneye or chaffer, *commuto*," Pr. Parv.

STOWER. (1) The same as *Poy*, q. v.
(2) A flock of geese. *Yorksh.*

STOWERED. Staked. *North.*

Standyng together at a comon wateryng place ther called Hedgedyke, lately *stowered* for catall to drynke at.   *Archæologia,* xxiii. 23.

STOWINGS. Loppings. *East.*
STOWLIN. A lump of meat. *Linc.*
STOW-STEDE. A narrow bank of earth laid across a ditch or stream for the passage of men and cattle. *Cambr.*

STOWTE. Strong; powerful.

The emperowre was fulle *stowte,*
And beseged the castelle abowte.
MS. Cantab. Ff. ii. 38, f. 77.

When the steward sawe Gye,
Stowtly he can hym hye.
MS. Cantab. Ff. ii. 38, f. 157.

STOWTER. To struggle; to walk clumsaily.
STRA. Straw. *East.*
STRABLET. A long narrow piece of anything. *Somerset.*
STRABRODS. The wooden pins or stobs used in fastening thatch to the roof of a building.
STRACHY. " The lady of the *Strachy* married the yeoman of the wardrobe," Twelfth Night, ii. 5. The real meaning of this word is a mystery. Mr. R. P. Knight supposes it to be a corrupt form of *stratici*, a title of magistracy in many states of Italy.
STRACK. A bar of iron.
STRACKLE-BRAINED. Dissolute; thoughtless. *Strackling*, a loose wild fellow. *North.*
STRACT. Distracted. *Var. dial.*
STRAD. A kind of leather gaiter worn as a protection against thorns. *West.*
STRADDLEBOB. A blackbeetle. *I. Wight.*
STRADDLINS. Astride. *Var. dial.*
STRADIOTES. A class of soldiers. (*Gr.*)

Among the Frenchmen were certaine light horsmen called *stradiotes*, with shorte styroppes, bever hatts, smal speres, and swerdes like semiteries of Turkay.   *Hall, Henry VIII.* f. 28.

STRAFE. To stray. *Salop.*
STRAFT. A scolding quarrel. *East.*
STRAGE. (1) Slaughter. (*Lat.*)
(2) To stray, said of cattle.
STRAGLE. To stray. *Var. dial.*

That we might not think amiss of that Almighty Being which has made us, nor of the sundry beings he has made, that we may neither dote nor dare, *stragle* nor be lost.
N. Fairfax, Bulk and Selvedge of the World, 1674.

STRAGLERS. Another name for the game of astragals, q. v. See MS. Ashmole 788, f. 162.
STRAIGHT. (1) Too tight; narrow. *North.*
(2) A narrow alley. A cant term.
(3) Straightway; immediately. *Var. dial.*
(4) *To make things straight*, to put them in order, as to balance accounts, &c.
STRAIGHTER. A smoothing iron. *North.*
STRAIGHT-NOSED-TONGS. Tongs used by smiths for holding short or flat pieces of iron in the fire.
STRAIGHTS. A kind of cloth. It is spelt *streyt* in the Exp. Elizabeth of York, p. 104. Straights were made in large quantities in Devonshire. Blount describes *straits*, " a sort of narrow, coarse cloth, or kersey."
STRAIL. " Strayle, bed cloth, *stamina, stragula*," Pr. Parv. MS. Harl. 221, f. 165.
STRAIN. (1) Lineage; descent. *Shak.*
(2) To flow, as a river. *Drayton.*
(3) *To strain courtesy*, to stand upon ceremony, to be extremely formal. " Thynke you that it is good maner to strayne courteysie on this maner," Palsgrave, verb. f. 376.
(4) To copulate, said of the cat. See Brockett and Wilbraham. Shakespeare uses the word applied to a woman, " When he *strains* that lady," Henry VIII. iv. 1.
(5) " I strayne, as a hauke doth, or any other syche lyke fowle or beest in theyr clawes, *je estraings*," Palsgrave, 1530, verb. f. 376.
STRAINE. (1) To stretch out.

Sithene was thou *straynede* one the crosse so faste.
MS. Lincoln A. i. 17, f. 190.

(2) To restrain; to curb. *Gawayne.*
STRAINGESPORTED. Transported. *East.*
STRAINT. Pressure; tension. *Spenser.*
STRAIT. To straiten; to puzzle. *East.*
STRAITE. To bind fast.

In kevil and bridel thair chekes *straite*,
That ye noght neghen ne laite.
MS. Cott. Vespas. D. vii. f. 20.

STRAKE. (1) Struck. *Hampole.*

He says, Now hase thou taughte me
How that I salle wirke with the.
Than his swerde drawes he,
And *strake* to hym thro.   *Perceval,* 1720.

(2) To go; to proceed. (*A.-S.*) " To strake about, *circumire*," MS. Devonsh. Glossary.

The stormes *straked* with the wynde,
The wawes to-bote bifore and bihynde.
Cursor Mundi, MS. Coll. Trin. Cantab. f. 12.

(3) Plighted by shaking hands.

ȝys, seyde the Erle, here myn honde,
Hys trowthe to hym he *strake*.
MS. Cantab. Ff. ii. 38, f. 64.

(4) To stretch one's self; to lie down. *East.* It is derived from the A.-S.
(5) " *Absis*, the strake of a cart whele wherin the spokes bee sette," Elyot, ed. 1559; " *vietus*, a hoope or strake of a carte," ibid. Carr has *straker*, the iron rim of a wheel.

(6) A crevice or opening in a floor, &c. A rut in a road was also so called.

(7) A slice, or narrow portion.

> Likewise another in Oxfordshire not verie farre from Burford, and the third over against Lach lade, which is parted from the main countie of Barkeshire by a little *strake* of Oxfordshire.
>
> *Harrison's Description of England, p. 155.*

(8) To blow a horn. See *Stroke* (6).

STRAKE-NAILS. " *Brócche grándi*, great headed studs called brodes or strake nailes," Florio, p. 68, ed. 1611.

STRALES. Two year old sheep. *North.*

STRAM. (1) A loud sudden noise. *West.*

(2) To beat; to spring or recoil with violence and noise; to dash down. *Devon.*

STRAMALKING. Gadding and loitering, said of a dirty slovenly female. *East.*

STRAMASH. The same as *Stram* (2).

STRAMAZOUN. A direct descending blow with the edge of a sword. " A stramasson or down-right slash," Howell.

STRAM-BANG. Violently; startlingly. *Devon.*

STRAME. A streak, mark, or trace. *West.*

STRAMMER. A great falsehood. *Var. dial.*

STRAMMERLY. Awkward; ungainly. *Kent.*

STRAMMING. Huge; great. *West.*

STRAMOTE. A stalk of grass. *Dorset.*

STRAMP. To trample upon. *North.*

STRAND. One of the twists of a line of hemp or horsehair; a withered stalk of grass. *Sussex.*

STRAND-HEADS. Arrow-heads.

STRANDY. Restive; passionate. *Strandy-mires*, children who are strandy. *North.*

STRANG. Strong. *North.*

STRANGE. (1) A strange woman, i. e. an immodest woman, a prostitute. Ben Jonson, ed. Gifford, iv. 418.

(2) Backward; retiring; shy; coy. A common use of the word in old plays.

(3) To wonder at. *North.*

(4) Foreign; uncommon. *He made it strange,* he made it a matter of difficulty or nicety. (*A.-N.*)

(5) To estrange. (*A.-N.*)

> The see his propre kynde chaungeth,
> And alle the world his forme *strangeth*.
>
> *Gower, MS. Soc. Antiq. 134, f. 191.*

STRANGER. (1) A visitor. *North.*

(2) An imperfection in the snuff of a candle, causing it to gutter.

STRANGILLION. The strangury.

STRANGLE. To tire, or weary. *Baber.*

STRAP. (1) Credit. *Yorksh.*

(2) To flog, or beat. *Var. dial.*

(3) A cluster, or bunch. *North.*

STRAP-OIL. A severe beating. It is a common joke on April 1st to send a lad for a pennyworth of strap-oil, which is generally ministered on his own person.

STRAPPADO. An ancient mode of punishment, the victim being " drawn up to his height, and then suddenly let fall half way with a jerk, which not only breaketh his arms to pieces, but also shaketh all his joints out of

joint," Holme. " The strappado, *equuleus, trochlea,*" Coles. Brathwaite wrote, " A Strappado for the Divell, epigrams and satyres alluding to the time," 1615.

> But the best is that in Spaine you shall have fellowes for a small peece of silver take the *strappado,* to endure which torture another man could not be hyrde with a kingdome.
>
> *Dekker's Knight's Conjuring, p. 6.*

STRAPPER. A strong large person. *Strapping,* large and muscular. *Var. dial.*

STRAPS. " Peeces of leather fastned to the waistband instead of eyes or holders," Holme, Academy of Armory, 1688.

STRAPULS. " Straple of a breche, *femorale, feminale,*" Pr. Parv. " *Tibiale,* a straple," MS. Harl. 2270, f. 187.

> Why hopes thu nott for sothe that ther stode wonus a coke on Seynt Pale stepull toppe, and drewe up the *strapuls* of his brech. How preves thu that? Be all the iiij. doctors of Wynberehylke, that is to saye, Vertas, Gadatryme, Trumpas, and Dadyltrymsert. *Reliq. Antiq. i. 82.*

STRASE. In MS. Med. Lincoln. f. 304, one of the tokens of approaching death is said to be if the sick person " pulle the *strase* or the clathes."

STRAT. (1) To stop; to hinder. *Devon.*

(2) To splash with mud. *Devon.*

(3) To bring forth young prematurely, applied to beasts. *Cornw.*

(4) To dash in pieces. *West.*

(5) A blow. *Somerset.*

STRATCH. To slake lime. *Somerset.*

STRATE. A street, or path. See *Martire.*

STRATH. Straight. *Ritson.*

STRAUGHNESSE. Madness. *Palsgrave.*

STRAUGHT. (1) Stretched. *West.*

> For pure joye, as in a rage,
> She *straught* to hym all at ones,
> And fill aswoune upon the stones.
>
> *Gower, ed. 1554, f. 184.*

(2) Distracted. " I am straught, *je suis enragé,*" Palsgrave, 1530.

STRAUNGID. Estranged. (*A.-N.*)

> For anone after he was changyd,
> And fram hys owne kynde *straungyd.*
>
> *Gower, MS. Cantab. Ff. i. 6, f. 2.*

STRAVAIGE. To stroll about. *North.*

STRAVE. Strove; tried. *North.*

STRAW. (1) To strew about. *North.*

(2) *Not worth a straw,* a common phrase for anything quite worthless.

> Whatesoevery he be, and yf that he
> Whante money to plede the lawe,
> Do whate he cane in ye mater than
> Shale not prove *worthe a strawe.*
>
> *Nugæ Poeticæ, p. 48.*

(3) *A man of straw,* a person who is not possessed of property.

(4) " To throw straws against the wind, *cum ventis litigare,*" Coles.

(5) *In the straw,* an accouchement.

STRAWBERRY-PREACHERS. An expression applied by Latimer to designate the non-residents of his day, who only visited their cures once a year. It afterwards became proverbial.

STRAW-CUTTER. A machine used for cutting straw into chaff. *Var. dial.*

STRAW-JOINER. A thatcher. *Devon.*

STRAW-MOTE. A straw. *Devon.*

STRAY. The right of stray, i. e. of pasturing cattle on commons.

STRAYE. The sky?

Abraham, doe as I thee saye,
Loke and tell, and yf thou maye,
Starres standinge one the *straye ;*
That unpossible were.   *Chester Plays,* i. 63.

STRA3T. Straight; directly.

Lechery, robbery, or monsla3t,
Byd hym telle even *stra3t.*
       MS. Cott. Claud. A. ii. f. 145.

STRE. A straw. (*A.-S.*)

And sayeth that suche an husbonde
Was to a wyf nou3t worth a *stre.*
       Gower, MS. Soc. Antiq. 134, f. 88.

Thei leyn upon the hors gold and silver gret quantytee, and thei putten abouten him gret plentee of *stres.*   *Maundevile's Travels,* p. 253.

STREAK. (1) To stretch. *North.* Laying out a dead body is termed *streaking.*

Goddot so I wille :
And loke that thou hire tille,
And *strek* out hire thes.   *MS. Digby* 86.

(2) The same as *Strake,* q. v.

STREAM. To pass along in a train actively; to draw out at length. *West.*

STREAMERS. (1) The Northern lights. *North.*

(2) Persons who work in search of stream tin. A mining term.

STREAM-WORKS. "In Cornwall they have two sorts of stannaries or metal works, i. e. lode-works and stream-works. The latter are in the lower places, when they trace the vein of tin by ditches, by which they carry off the water that would break in upon them," Kennett, MS. Lansd. 1033, f. 392.

STREAVE. Stray. "For some streave lordship," Hall's Satires, p. 127.

STREBERY. The strawberry tree. " *Fragum,* a strebery," Nominale MS. " *Fragum,* a streboré," MS. ibid.

STREECH. The space taken in at one striking of the rake. *Streech measure* is that in which a straight stick is struck over the top of the vessel. Barnes, p. 354.

STREEK. (1) To iron clothes. *East.*

(2) To measure corn by passing a flat piece of wood over the top of the measure. " *Hostio* is to strekyn corne," MS. Harl. 1738. *Streeked measure,* exact measure.

(3) A strata of coal. *North.*

STREELY. Long; lean. *Suffolk.*

STREET-WALKER. A common prostitute.

STREEVED. Tried; strove. *Cornw.*

STREIGHT. Stretched. (*A.-S.*)

STREINABLE. Violent.

In this Josina his daies, it chanced that a Portingale ship was driven and drowned by force of a *streinable* tempest neere unto the shore of one of the Scotish Iles. *Holinshed, Historie of Scotland,* p. 39.

He weyed up his ancors and halsed up hys sayles, havinge a prosperous and *strenable* wynd and a freshe gale sente even by God to delyver him from that perell and jeopardie. *Hall, Richard III.* f. 17.

u,

STREINE. To constrain; to press closely.

STREIT. Strict; severe.

Of his ordres he was wel *streit,* and he was in greets fere
For to ordeinl eul man bote be the betere ware.
       Life of Thomas Beket, ed. Black, p. 14.

STREIT-BRETH. Short breath.

At the hole of the throte ther be too,
That lepre and *streyt breth* wyl undo.
       MS. Poem on Blood-Letting, xv. Cent.

STREITE. (1) Straight. (*A.-S.*)

(2) Straitly; narrowly. (*A.-S.*)

STREIVES. Beasts which have strayed.

STREKE. (1) To pitch, or erect.

Furthe stepes that steryne, and *strekes* his tentis
One a strenghe by a streme in thas straytt landes.
       Morte Arthure, MS. Lincoln, f. 66.

(2) To strike ; to go rapidly.

To kepe hym thane were thay ware,
Thaire dynttis deris hym no mare,
Thenne who so hade *strekyns* sare
One a harde stone.   *Perceval,* 1371.
Bothe they *strekyn* faste,
They mett togedur at the laste.
       MS. Cantab. Ff. ii. 38, f. 157.

(3) Direct; straight. (*A.-S.*)

Girdes *streke* thourghe the stour on a stede ryche ;
Many steryne mane he steride by strenghe of hyme one.
       Morte Arthure, MS. Lincoln, f. 73.

(4) To scratch out or cancel anything.

STREMEDEN. Streamed; flowed. (*A.-S.*)

STREMERE. A flag; a banner.

Upon the hyest maste there
He set up a *stremere*
Of hys fadurs armys bryghte.
       MS. Cantab. Ff. ii. 38, f. 116.

STREMES. The rays of the sun.

STREN. Race ; progeny. (*A.-S.*)

For the misbigeten *stren,*
Quic y schal now dolven ben.
       Arthour and Merlin, p. 39.

STRENCH.

3ung and olde, brihet, and schene,
Alle he riveth in one *strench.*
       MS. Cott. Calig. A. ix. f. 243.

STRENCULT. Scattered. *Robson.*

STREND. Race ; generation. (*A.-S.*)

For he saide in his bert, noght sal I wende,
Withouten ivel, fra *strend* in *strende.*
       MS. Cotton. Vespas, D. vii. f. 5.

STRENE. (1) The shoot of a tree. *Linc.*

(2) A New-year's gift. *Dorset.*

(3) To copulate, said of a dog. *Durh.*

STRENGEST-FAITHED. Possessing the most powerful faith. *Chaucer.*

STRENGITHE. Strengthen. (*A.-S.*)

Now God, that dyed appon a rode,
Strengithe hym bothe bone and blod,
The fyld for to have !
       Torrent of Portugal, p. 6.

STRENGTH. (1) A castle ; a fortress. *Gifford.*

(2) Used in the provinces by farmers to express the number or quantity of labourers they have at their command. *Var. dial.*

(3) To strengthen. (*A.-S.*)

And more to *strength* their power, joyn'd with the Pope.
       Taylor's Workes, 1630, iii. 18

STRENGTHING. A strengthening. *Palsgrave.*

STRENKILLE. To sprinkle.

> Tak haver, and perche it wele in a panne, and *strenkille* it wele in the perchynge with water.
> *MS. Linc. Med. f. 292.*

STRENKITH. Strength.

> In hys tyme ther was no knyghte,
> Of armes, of *strenkyth* of honde,
> That bare soche pryse in all that londe.
> *MS. Cantab. Ff. ii. 38, f. 147.*

> Syr Barnard seyde, What haste thou thoght?
> Of justyng canste thou ryght noght,
> For thou art not of age.
> Syr, he seyde, what wott ye
> Of what *strenkyth* that y bee,
> Or y be provyd in felde with the sage?
> *MS. Cantab. Ff. ii. 38, f. 75.*

> And yf sche at hur day fayle,
> Ther schalle no thyng hur avayle,
> But Burlonde schalle hur wedd,
> And Tryamowre noght we kenne,
> Wherefore ther passyth here no men,
> Wyth *strenkyth* but they be kedd.
> *MS. Cantab. Ff. ii. 38, f. 80.*

STRENKLE. "Strenkyll to cast holy water, *vimpilon*," Palsgrave. It is the same as *Sprinkle*, q. v.

STRENTHE. Strength. Also, to strengthen.

> Ne the *strenthe* of hys enmys,
> Ne the sotelteys that in thaym lyes.
> *MS. Harl. 2260, f. 4.*

> To bowe hym ay into mekenes,
> And no more wery than the sone es,
> That evermore he rises in lenthe,
> Ay the more he gederis hys *strenthe.*
> *MS. Harl. 2260, f. 17.*

> The gifte of pité es swilke a grace,
> That to charité it may us purchasce,
> And oure hertys so *strenthe* faste,
> That no fondyng may us doun caste.
> *MS. Harl. 2260, f. 18.*

STRENȝERE. A strainer.

STREPE. To strip. (A.-N.)

STRESS. To confine in narrow limits.

STRESSE. A distress. A law term.

> And of this rent, yf that he doith faile,
> I gyve hym powre to akore-on the tale,
> And take an *stresse*, yf that nede be,
> Upon the grounde, one, two, or thre.
> *MS. Rawl. C. 86.*

STREST. An extremity?

> Wyndes and wedors have her drevyn,
> That in a *strest* be they revyn.
> *Torrent of Portugal, p. 73.*

STRET. (1) To stretch. *North.*

> Als fere as I may *stret* and streche,
> I wyll helpe with all my myght,
> Both by dey and by nyght,
> Fast to runne into the wode. *MS. Ashmole 61.*

(2) Strait; tight. *West.*

STRET-BODIED-COAT. "A stret-bodied coat, this is close to the body and arms, and is usually worn without a doublet, having under it a waistcote with side or deep skirts almost to the knees," Holme, 1688.

STRETCH. (1) To walk in a dignified manner. *Willan's Yorksh.*

(2) A strike to measure corn.

(3) A plot of ground on which weavers stretch their warps. *West.*

STRETCHABLE. Upright. List of old words prefixed to Batman uppon Bartholome, 1582.

STRETCHER. (1) The board in a boat against which a rower places his feet.

> He knowes, though they had an oar in every mans boat in the world, yet in his they cannot challenge so much as a *stretcher*.
> *Dekker's Knight's Conjuring, p. 39.*

(2) A falsehood. *Var., dial.*

(3) A stick to keep out the traces from the horses' legs. *Var. dial.*

STRETCHING-STICKS. Sticks used by glovers for stretching the thumbs and fingers of gloves. Holme, 1688.

STRETT. A road; a way. (A.-S.)

> Seyde Tryamowre, then wolde y fayn wytt
> Why ye two kepe thys *strett*.
> *MS. Cantab. Ff. ii. 38, f. 88.*

STREUD. Strided. *North.*

STREUT. To tear, or slit. *Dorset.*

STREVILL. A three-pronged fork for taking up barley or short hay. *Devon.*

STREWYS. Bad people? In the Latin version which accompanies the following it is *malorum.*

> And be not to moche byfore nether to fer byhynde yowre felowys for drede of *strewys.* *MS. Bodl. 565.*

STREYTHED. Straightness. (A.-S.)

STRICKE. Direct; straightway. (A.-S.)

> He sall noght eftyr hys lyfes ende
> Weende *strycke* to purgatory,
> Bot even to helle withowten mercy.
> *Hampole, MS. Bowes, p. 105.*

STRICKING-PLOUGH. A kind of plough used in some parts of the county of Kent.

STRICKLE. (1) A piece of wood used in striking off an even measure of corn. *West.*

(2) A whetstone for a scythe. *North.* It is mentioned by Holme, 1688.

(3) "A slender sparr, rabated in the ends, answerable to the breadth of the casting-frame, whereon the plummer runs his lead when it is new cast; by this he beats down the sand in the frame, and keeps it of an even height; and when the lead is cast over to run in the frame, the plummer followeth the lead with this instrument to drive it forward, and keep it that the sheet be all of a thickness," Holme, Academy of Armory, 1688.

STRICTLAND. An isthmus.

> Beyond the which I find a narrow going or *strictland* leading fro the point to Hirst Castell, which standeth into the sea as if it hoong by a thred from the maine of the iland.
> *Harrison's Description of Britaine, p. 56.*

STRIDDLE. To straddle. Also, to walk in an affected manner. *North.*

STRIDE. (1) To measure by paces.

(2) To stride a lance, i. e. to be killed by the point of a lance.

STRIDE-WIDE. A cant term for ale mentioned in Harrison's England, p. 202.

STRIDLING. Astride. "Fy on the, beest, thou standest so a *strydlyng* that a man may dryve a cart betwene thy legges," Palsgrave.

STRIE. A straw.

> Of bodi was he mayden clene,
> Nevere yete in game ne in grene,
> Thit hire ne wolde leyke ne lye,
> No more than it were a *strie.* *Havelok, 996.*

STRIG. The foot-stalk of a flower, leaf, or

fruit. *South.* " Strigges of bay leaves,"
Cunningham's Rev. Acc. p. 19.

STRIKE. (1) An iron spear or stanchel in a gate
or palisade. *Willson.*

(2) To proceed or go anywhere ; to go rapidly.
See *Streke.*

> He saide to his sone, Tak a pike,
> To-night thou schalt with me *strike.*
> *The Sevyn Sages, 1254.*

(3) To steal money. An old cant term given in
Dekker's Belman of London, 1608. " Now
we have well bousd, let us strike some chete,"
Earle's Microcosmography, p. 254.

(4) *Strike me luck,* an old phrase meaning to
conclude a bargain.

> You see what bangs it has endur'd
> That would, before new feats, be cur'd ;
> But if that's all you stand upon,
> Here, *strike me luck,* it shall be done.
> *Hudibras, II. i. 540.*

(5) A bushel. *Linc.*

> Some men and women, rich and nobly borne,
> Gave all they had for one poore *strike* of corne.
> *Taylor's Workes, 1630, i. 15.*

(6) " Stryke to gyve mesure by, *roulet a me-
surer,*" Palsgrave. See *Streek.*

(7) Flies are said to *strike* and meat to be *struck,*
when the latter is fly-blown. *Linc.*

(8) To anoint or rub gently. *Devon.*

(9) " Stryke of flaxe, *poupee de filace,*" Palsgrave.
See Chaucer, Cant. T. 678.

(10) To make a straight line by means of a
chalked piece of string. *West.*

(11) To stroke softly.

(12) To make anything smooth.

> The warderoper to delyver the second sheete unto
> two yomen, they to crosse it over theyr arme, and to
> *stryke* the bedde as the ussher shall more playnly
> shewe unto theym. *Archæologia, iv. 312.*

(13) *To strike hands,* to shake hands.

(14) To raise or rise up ? To shriek ?

> And whanne she was relevyd, she *stryked* and saide,
> My lord sire Launcelot, allas ! why be ye in this
> plyte ? and thenne she swouned ageyne.
> *Morte d'Arthur, ii. 343.*

(15) To balance accounts.

> And the said Journall, with the two other bookes,
> to lye upon the greencloth dayly, to the intent the
> accomptants, and other particular clerkes, may take
> out the solutions entred into the said bookes, where-
> by they may *strike* their lydgers, and soe to bring in
> their accompts incontinently upon the same.
> *Ordinances and Regulations, p. 229.*

(16) To rebound. *Palsgrave.*

(17) A combination among workmen to leave off
their occupations until they obtain an increase
of wages. *Var. dial.*

(18) The break of day. *North.*

(19) To tap, as a barrel, &c.

(20) To spread, or lay out flat.

(21) " I stryke, I let downe the crane, *je lache* ;
stryke lowe stryke, *lachez jusques a terre,*"
Palsgrave, 1530, verb.

STRIKE-BAULK. To plough one furrow, and
leave another. *Kent.*

STRIKE-BLOCK. A kind of plane, used by
joiners for short joints.

STRIKE IN. To begin. *Var. dial.*

STRIKER. (1) A wencher. An old cant term
occurring in Middleton, Massinger, &c.

(2) " An heavy piece of wood wherewith the
fleme is smitten or driven into the horse neck
vein when he is blooded," Holme, 1688.

STRIKILLE. It is the translation of *osorium*
in the Nominale MS. xv. Cent.

STRINDE. (1) Stride. *Linc.* Thus a hop,
strind, and jump ; a cock's *strind,* for a cock's
stride or tread, &c.

(2) Race ; progeny ; child. *(A.-S.)*

> And seyne with baptyme weschede that *strynde,*
> With synne was fylede with Adames dede.
> *MS. Lincoln A. i. 17, f. 219.*

STRINE. (1) A ditch. *Salop.*

(2) The side of a ladder. *Lanc.*

STRING. (1) *Always harping upon one string,* a
common phrase for incessant repetition.

> But her parents, ever *harping upon one string,* ex-
> pounded this averseness and declining of hers to a
> modest bashfull shame.
> *The Two Lancashire Lovers, 1640, p. 14.*

(2) I had all the world in a string, i. e. completely at my command.

(3) A narrow vein of ore. *North.*

(4) Stock ; race ; progeny. *Cumb.*

STRINGER. (1) A person who made strings for
bows. See Nares.

(2) A wencher. Beaum. and Flet. ii. 140.

STRINGY. Cold ; nipping, applied to the
weather. *Suffolk.*

STRINKLE. (1) Same as *Strenkle,* q. v. " *Aspersorium,* a strynkylle," Nominale MS.

(2) To scatter ; to sprinkle. *Var. dial.*

STRINTE. The same as *Strinde* (2).

> And leeves well, of no mans *strynte*
> Is he not gotten by lcffe of kinde.
> *Chester Plays, i. 169.*

STRINTH. Strength ; power. *(A.-S.)*

> The meke hym lawys to serve stalworthly,
> Als he that es stronge and mysty,
> That alle hys strenthe, thorue mekenes,
> To Goddes *strynth* chargettes es.
> *MS. Harl. 2260, f. 17*

STRIP. (1) To strip a cow is to milk her very
clean, so as to leave no milk in the dug. In
the dairy districts of Suffolk the greatest importance is attached to stripping the cows, as
neglect of this infallibly produces disease. It
is the same as the Norfolk *strocking.* Forby's
East Anglia, p. 330.

(2) To go very rapidly.

> The swiftest hound, when he is hallowed, *strippes*
> forth. *Gosson's Schools of Abuse, 1579.*

(3) Destruction ; mutilation. *Blount.*

STRIPE. (1) To beat. *Palsgrave.* Still in use.
Also, to beat time in music.

(2) Race ; kindred. *(Lat.)*

(3) A woodman's knife. *Linc.*

(4) A fool. *Wilts.*

(5) To thrash corn.

> Thare after it becomes cornne ripe
> Bothe for to berye and for to *strype.*
> *MS. Harl. 2260, f. 19.*

STRIPPING. " The washing and sifting of the
wast tin in order to return the rough and
course to the stamps, and the finer to the

wreck, is calld the *stripping* of tin," Kennett, MS. Lansd. 1033.

STRIPPINGS. (1) The last milk drawn from a cow in milking. *Var. dial.*

(2) Refuse ?

He is cheife under the master cooke in that place, and hath for his fee the *strippinges* of beefe.
Ordinances and Regulations, p. 288.

STRIPT. Striped. Middleton, iv. 447.

STRIT. (1) A street. *East.*

(2) Strideth ?

Mon in the mone stond and *strit,*
On his bot forke is burthen he bereth,
Hit is muche wonder that he na doun slyt,
For doute lest he valle he shoddreth ant shereth.
Introd. Mids. Night's Dream, p. 53.

STRITCH. (1) The same as *Strike* (6).

(2) To stretch. *North.*

STRITE. Straight. *North.*

STRITHE. To stride the legs.

STRIVE. (1) To take a bird's nest. *East.*

(2) Strife.

The meke hym lawes to serve symply,
Als duse the shepe es no3t wyly,
That mekely gos withouten *stryve,*
Whethere so the herde hym wille dryve.
MS. Harl. 2260, f. 17.

He lovyd ay contakt, and *stryve,*
Ther was non holdyn wors on lyf. *Tundale,* p. 2.
That made them of *stryvys* were.
MS. Cantab. Ff. ii. 38, f. 64.

STRIVELING. The town of Stirling. It occurs frequently in old documents.

STROAK. Two pecks of corn. *Yorksh.*

STROAKINGS. The same as *Strippings,* q. v. It is also called *strockings.* See Forby.

STROCAL. " A long iron instrument like a fire-shovel to carry the metall out of a broken into a whole pot, used by glass-makers," Blount's Glossographia, p. 615.

STROCKE. A kind of sweet cream.

STROD. A forked branch of a tree. *Sussex.*

STRODE. Threw. *Devon.*

STROF. Strove; contended. *(A.-N.)*

STROGGLE. To murmur; to grumble. " I strogell, I murmure with wordes secretly, *je grommelle;* he stroggleth at every thyng I do, *il grommelle a tout tant que je fays,*" Palsgrave, verb. f. 378.

STROGS. Short splatterdashes. *I. of Wight.*

STROIL. (1) Couch-grass. *West.*

(2) Strength; agility. *Devon.*

STROKE. (1) Quantity. *Var. dial.*

(2) Sway; influence; prevalence.

This house, as well for antiquitie as for the number of worshipfull gentlemen that be of the surname, beareth no small *stroke* in the English pale of Ireland. *Stanihurst's Descr. of Ireland,* p. 38.

(3) To sooth, encourage, or flatter.

(4)

So to maister the Irish that with such manner of strengths of wals and rampires had not as yet beene acquainted, for till those daies they knew no defense but woods, bogs, or *strokes.*
Holinshed, Hist. Ireland, p. 56.

(5) A game; a proceeding. *Essex.*

(6) A blast of a horn. A term formerly used by hunters. Twici, p. 45.

STROKE-BIAS. Is thus described :

The Kentish men have a peculiar exercise, especially in the eastern parts, which is nowhere else used in any other country, I believe, but their own : 'tis called *stroke-bias,* and the manner of it is thus : In the summer time one or two parishes convening make choice of twenty, and sometimes more, of the best runners which they can cull out in their precincts, who send a challenge to an equal number of racers within the liberties of two other parishes to meet them at a set day upon some neighbouring plain, which challenge, if accepted, they repair to the place appointed, whither also the country resort in great numbers to behold the match, where, having stripped themselves at the goal to their shirts and drawers, they begin the course, every one having in his eye a particular man at which he aims ; but after several traverses and courses on both sides, that side whose legs are the nimblest to gain the first seven strokes from their antagonists carry the day and win the prize. Nor is this game only appropriated to the men, but in some places the maids have their set matches too, and are as vigorous and active to obtain a victory.
Brome's Travels over England, 1700, p. 264.

STROKER. A flatterer. Jonson, vi. 84.

STROLL. A narrow slip of land. *Devon.*

STROM. (1) An instrument, according to Ray, to keep the malt in the vat. *North.*

(2) A storm, or tempest.

Al siker hii were alond to gon,
Ac swiche a *strom* hem cam upon,
That sore hem gonne drede.
Romance of Rembrun, p. 423.

STROMBOLI. A name given to pieces of bitumen, highly charged with sulphur and salt, found along the coast near Brighton. No doubt from the volcanic island so called.

STROME. To walk with long strides.

STROMMELL. Straw. A cant term, given in Dekker's Lanthorne and Candle-Light, 1620.

STROMMELLING. Awkward; unruly. *Wilts.*

STRONDE. A strand, or shore. *(A.-S.)*

We came hedur on the *stronde,*
Fro Constantyne the nobulle londe.
MS. Cantab. Ff. ii. 38, f. 164.

STRONES. Tenants who are bound to assist the lord in hunting, and turning the red deer on the tops of the mountains to the forest. *Nicolson and Burn's West. and Cumb.*

STRONG-DOCKED. Large and powerfully made about the loins. *East.*

STRONTE. Qu. *Stroute,* to contend ?

This makyth men mysdo more than ou3te ellis,
And to *stronte* and to stare, and stryve a3eyn vertu.
Deposition of Richard II. p. 21.

STROO. To strain a liquid through cloth, or to press it through a narrow passage, as through the teeth.

STROOK. Struck. *Suffolk. Strooken* occurs in Honours Academie, 1610, i. 43, 67.

'Twas profit spoyld the world. Till then, we know it,
The usurer *strook* sayles unto the poet.
Brome's Songs, 1661.

They blind his sight, whose soules more blind,
Had quite extinct the light of grace ;
They buffet him, and bid him find
Who 'twas that *strooke* him on the face.
Rowland's Betraying of Christ, 1598, sig. E. 1.

STROOP. (1) The gullet. *Norf.*

(2) To bawl out, or cry aloud; from *Stroop*, the gullet. *East.*

STROOTCH. To drag the legs in walking. *Kent.*

STROP. (1) A cord. *Devon.*

(2) To milk a cow with pressure of finger and thumb, and so to draw the last drops. In doing this cleverly consists much of the art of milking, as an unskilful hand is apt, by not attending to this part of the mystery, to dry up a cow's milk. A *stropped milk cow* is a cow about to calve, and therefore, as they express it, one not in full profit; that cannot be milked *full handed*, but must be stropped. *Linc.*

STROPE. A strap. " A thonge, or that whiche is bounden to the middes of a darte or javelyn wherwith it is throwen, a *strope* or a loupe," Elyot, 1559.

STROSSERS. Tight drawers. They were much worn by the Irish. The term is corrupted into *strouces* in Sir John Oldcastle, p. 71.

STROTHER. (1) A marsh. *North.*

(2) The rudder of a vessel.

Then Hanybald arose hym up to sese both ship and
strother.   *The History of Beryn*, 1181.

STROU. Destroy; devastate.

The king of Danmark with gret wrong,
Thurch a geaunt that is so strong,
Wil strou al our thede.   *Gy of Warwike*, p. 362.

STROUNGE. Morose; severe. *North.*

STROUPE. " Strowpe of the throte, *epiglotus*," Pr. Parv. MS. Harl. 221. The windpipe is still called the *stroupe* in Norfolk.

R. tille him ran, a stroke on him he fest,
He smote him in the helm, bakward he bare his stroupe.
       Langtoft's Chronicle, p. 190.

STROUT. (1) Same as *Astrout*, q. v.

The accidents (saith he) that doe accompany the bytings of spyders are these that follow. The wounded place waxeth red, yet doth it not swell nor grow very hot, but it is somewhat moyst. If the body become cold, there will follow trembling and shaking, the groyne and hammes doe much stroute out, and are exceeding distended, there is great provocation to make water, and striving to exonerate nature, they sweat with much difficultie, labour, and paine. Besides, the hurt persons are all of a cold sweat, and teares destill from their eyes that they grow dym-sighted therewith.
     Topsell's Historie of Serpents, 1608, p. 252.

(2) To strut. Still in use.

Shake not much thy head, nor strout it not too much out with bridling in thy chinne. for that is more comely for great horses than for thee.
     Schoole of Good Manners, 1629.

(3) A struggle; a bustle; a quarrel.

(4) To swell out. Still in use. " Bocyne owte, or strowtyne," Pr. Parv. p. 41.

STROUTE. See *Stronte* and *Strut* (3).

STROVE. (1) Argued obstinately. *Cornw.*

(2) Confusion; uproar. *West.*

STROW. (1) Confusion. *Cornw.*

(2) To strew. Still in use.

(3) Loose; scattered. See Nares.

STROYALL. A contraction of *destroy-all*, a person who delights in waste.

STROYE. To destroy. It occurs as late as 1610, in Honours Academie, p. 75.

Some they stroye and some they brenne,
They slewe my men on a day.
         MS. Cantab. Ff. ii. 38, f. 165

He sayse, his craftes are so ryfe,
Ther is no mane apone lyfe,
With swerde, spere, ne with knyfe,
May stroye hym allane.   *Percival*, 564.

Luk, my parkes are stroyed,
And my veners are drawed.
         MS. Lincoln A. i. 17, f. 132.

STROY-GOOD. A mischievous person. Forby has *stry-good*, a wasteful person.

STRUB. To rob. *Devon.*

STRUCK. (1) Stricken. *Shak.*

(2) Struck all of a heap, i. e. excessively surprised, astounded. *Var. dial.*

STRUCK-WHEEL. " The wheel of wood that is fastned at one end of the main spindle in a jack to receive the line, or chain to turn the spit, is calld the *struck-wheel*, and according to the number of grooves in them they are calld *two struck* or *three struck* wheels," Kennett, MS. Lansd. 1033, f. 392.

STRUD. Roost.

And all the cranes, because it was so early, were at strud, as their custome is generally, all stood upon one leg and held the other under their wing. Stephano, seeing the advantage, not willing to let so faire a bal fall to the ground, began himself: Now, sir, quoth he, I hope yourself and the rest of the gentlemen will confesse I have wonne the wager: for you see here is never a crane that hath more than one legge. *Tarlton's Newes out of Purgatorie*, 1590.

STRUGGED. Fat and chubby. *West.*

STRULL. Well; excellently. *Norf.*

STRUM. (1) A strumpet. *Norf.*

(2) To play music. *Var. dial.*

STRUMEL. A loose, long, and dishevelled head of hair. *Norf.*

STRUMMUCK. To stray; to wander. *Suff.*

STRUMPLES. To cock one's strumples, i. e. to utterly astonish him. *Salop.*

STRUNCHEON. A verse of a song. *Linc.*

STRUNT. (1) A bird's tail. *North.* It is sometimes used for the tail of any animal.

(2) The penis. A cant term.

Consenting she, his art'rizde strunt he drew,
And to 'es venereous game he hastily flew.
     Middleton's Epigrams and Satyres, 1608.

(3) To be sullen, or proud; to walk in an affected manner. *North.*

(4) To cut off short. *Yorksh.*

STRUNTY. Docked; short. *North.*

STRUSHINS. Orts, from *Strushion*, destruction. It lies in the way of strushion, i. e. in a likelihood of being destroyed. *North.*

STRUT. (1) To brace, in carpentry.

(2) Stubbornness; obstinacy. *North.*

(3) Dispute; contention. See *Stuntise*.

STRUYEN. To destroy. (*A.-N.*)

Thow has in thy realtee revengyde thy pople,
Thurghe helpe of thy hande thyne emmyse are
struyede.   *Morte Arthure, MS. Lincoln*, f. 66.

Hast thow i-struyed corn or gras,
Or other thynge that sowen was?
         MS. Cott. Claud. A. ii. f. 148.

STRY. (1) To spoil ; to destroy. *East.*

> Strye the rotes and bryng them to dedd,
> And set dokys and nettuls yn ther stede.
>
> *MS. Cantab.* Ff. ii. 38, f. 131.

(2) A witch. "Com hedyr, thou old stry," Towneley Mysteries, p. 148.

STRYANCE. Wastefulness. *East.*

STRYE. To stay ; to ease ; to cure.

STRY-GOODLY. Wasteful. *East.*

STUB. (1) An old root, or stump ; also, to grub such roots up. *Var. dial.*

> And badd hym take a mattok anon.
> And *stubbe* the olde rote away,
> That had stonde there many a day.
>
> *MS. Cantab.* Ff. ii. 38, f. 129.

This is a hard grisle growing upon the cronet, and sometime goeth round about the cronet, and is called in Italian *Soprosso*. Laurentius Russius saith, that it may grow in any other place of the leg, but then we cal it not a ring-bone, but a knot or knob. It commeth at the first either by some blow of another horse, or by striking his owne foote against some *stub*, or stone, or such like casualty. The paine whereof breedeth a viscous and slimy humor, which resorting to the bones, that are of their owne nature colde and dry, waxeth hard, cleaveth to some bone, and in processe of time becommeth a bone.

> *Topsell's Four-Footed Beasts*, 1611, p. 411.

(2) A considerable stock ; a good round sum. *Somerset.*

(3) A kind of short nail.

(4) A castrated bull. *Heref.*

(5) To ruin by extravagance. *North.*

(6) A prop ; a support. *East.*

STUB-APPLE. The wild apple. *East.*

STUBBERD. A kind of apple. *West.*

STUBBLE-GOOSE. A goose turned out to feed on stubble. Still in use.

> Of many a pilgrim hast thou Cristes curse,
> For of thy perselee yet fare they the werse,
> That they han eten in thy *stoble goos.*
>
> *Chaucer, Cant. T.*, 4349.

STUBBLENESS. Stubbornness ; surliness.

STUBBO. (1) Stubble. *Chesh.*

(2) Thick ; short. *Chesh.*

STUBBY. Short and thick, like the stump of a tree. *Var. dial.*

> But they were sturdy and *stubbed*,
> Myghty pestels and clubbed.
>
> *Skelton's Works*, i. 108.

STUB-FEATHERS. The short unfledged feathers on a fowl after it has been plucked.

STUB-RABBIT. One of these cunning creatures of few friends, will under alarm ensconce itself close to a *stub* whence it is difficult to dislodge it : and will then be so called. *Moor's Suffolk MS.*

STUBS. Stubble. *Northampt.*

STUCK. (1) The handle of a porcelain, or crockery vessel. *Warw.*

(2) A spike. *West.*

(3) *To stare like a stuck pig*, a metaphor borrowed from the operation of pig-killing.

(4) The same as *Stockado*, q. v.

(5) A shock of corn. *Heref.*

(6) A slough, or mire. *Norf.*

STUCKLING. (1) An apple pasty, thin, some-

what half circular in shape, and not made in a dish. *Sussex.*

(2) A small river fish. *South.*

STUCKS. Iron pins which are put into the upper part of the blocks of a drag, for the purpose of preventing the timber slipping off the side. *North.*

STUD. (1) A meditation. *West.*

(2) The upright in a lath and plaster wall. *Oxon.* "Stud and stud-breadth is in Yorkshire the way of building the walls of a house in small frames or pannels of timber filld up with brick or stones, or plaistering." Kennett, MS. Lansd. 1033, f. 392.

> For as in these our houses are commonlie strong and well timbered, so that in manie places there are not above foure, six, or nine inches betweene *stud* and *stud*. *Harrison's England*, p. 187.

STUDDERIE. A large stable.

> King Henrie the Eight erected a noble *studderie*, and for a time had verie good successe with them, till the officers, waxing wearie, procured a mixed brood of bastard races, whereby his good purpose came to little effect.
>
> *Harrison's Description of England*, p. 220.

STUDDIED. Put in a deep thought. *Yorksh.*

STUDDLES. Weavers' implements. *Westm.*

STUDDY. A smith's stithy. *North.*

STUDY. To amaze ; to astonish. *North.*

STUERDLY. Thrifty. *Devon.*

STUFF. (1) Medicine ; furniture. &c. *Var. dial.*

(2) Rubbish. (3) Nonsense ; foolish talk.

STUFFING-STICK. A stick made of iron or hard wood, used for poking the stuffing into chairs, &c. Holme, 1688.

STUFFINS. Coarse flour : used at times synonymously with *shorts* and *sharps*. The real distinction between these words is this : the first remove above bran is *shorts ;* the next above that is *sharps :* and *shorts* and *sharps* are occasionally and respectively termed coarse or fine stuffins. *North.*

STUFFURE. Stuff. *Pr. Parv.*

> And qwhen hit is braiet smal, take up the *stuffure*, and do hit in a chargeour, and putte therto pouder of pepur, and saffron, and pouder of clowes.
>
> *Ordinances and Regulations*, p. 453.

STUFFY. Very fat. *Var. dial.*

STUGGE. A hog's trough. *Pr. Parv.*

STUGGED. Healthy ; strong. *Devon.*

STUGGY. Thick and stout. *Devon.*

STUK. Short ; docked. *Pr. Parv.*

STULING-KEN. A receiving house for stolen goods. This cant term is given in Dekker's Lanthorne and Candle-Light, 1620, sig. C. iii.

STULK-HOLE. A miry puddle. *East.*

STULL. (1) A luncheon. Also, a great piece of bread, cheese, or other eatable. *Essex.*

(2) Timber placed in the backs of levels, and covered with boards or small piles to support rubbish. *Cornw.*

STULP. A short stout post, put down to mark a boundary, or driven into the ground for any purpose. See a passage in Stowe, as quoted by Nares. It is the same as *stoop*, which is still used in the North of England. See other references in Carlisle's Account of Charities,

p. 309; and Hall, Henry VI. ff. 12, 78. The reader will find this term under other forms. "Stoulpe before a doore, *souche*," Palsgrave.

STULTCH. A crutch; a stilt for boys. This is given as a Wiltshire word in MS. Lansd. 1033, f. 2. *Stelch* is still used in the same sense, and also for a post.

STUM. Strong new wine, used for strengthening weak liquor. *Stum'd*, strengthened. According to Howell, *stooming* wine was effected by putting herbs and infusions into it. "*Stum* is wine that has never fermented," Blount, p. 615.

There strength of fancy, to it sweetness joynes,
Unmixt with water, nor *stum'd* with strong lines.
Brome's Songs, 1661.

Then then to the Queen, let the next advance,
With all loyal lads of true English race;
That scorn the *stum'd* notion of Spain and France.
Songs of the London Prentices, p. 122.

STUMMATCHER-PIECE. An irregular, gored, piece of land, of no shape easily expressible, and so likened to the ancient article of dress, which becoming "fine by degrees and beautifully less," had no straight side, and affords not a very inapt description of a similar piece of land. *Moor's Suff. MS.*

STUMMER. To stumble. *North.*

STUMP. (1) To knock down the wicket by hand, a term used at cricket.
(2) The tower of Boston church is generally called Boston *Stump*. *Linc.*
(3) To step heavily. *West.*
(4) A post. *Var. dial.*
(5) A stupid heavy fellow. *North.*
(6) *To stump up*, to pay cash.
(7) To be in want of money. To be put to one's stumps, i. e. to a hard shift.
(8) To walk very heavily. *Var. dial.*
(9) *Stump and rump*, completely.

STUMPERE. Extempore.
The sed the common'st that was there
Was vrom a tub or a wicker chair,
They call'd it *stumpere*.
Wright's Political Ballads, p. 4.

STUMPFOOT. A club-foot.
And saw the net the *stumpfoot* blacksmith made,
Wherein fell Mars and Venus was betray'd.
Taylor's Workes, iii. 24.

STUMPOINTED. A hunted rabbit in its fright ran against the dogs and tumbled over was said to be *stumpointed*; whether this be of individual coinage or a current word, I now know not. A friend surmized that it be a contracted combination of stannud and disappointed. I have heard it since the preceding was written said of a rabbit also baffled by dogs in a ditch. *Moor's Suff. MS.*

STUMPS. Legs. *Var. dial. To stir one's stumps*, a common phrase, meaning to set about anything expeditiously.
His long practice of the pot has exempt him from being prest a souldier: bee has quite lost the use of his *stumps*, how should he then possibly keepe his march? *Braithwaite's Law of Drinking*, 1617, p. 70.
This makes him *stirre his stumps*, and to answer

her letter with such speedy cheerefulnesse, as Melilla can expect no lesse then all successe to her desires.
The Two Lancashire Lovers, 1640, p. 262.

STUMPY. Ready money. *Var. dial.*

STUNCH. Short and stout. *North.*

STUNDE. A short space of time.
Wellawei, sore he him biswikedh,
That for on *stunde* other two
Wurcheth him pine evermo.
MS. Cott. Calig. A. ix. f. 243.

STUNE. To empty. "The cock or spigot being laid on the hoop, and the barrel of ale *stun'd*, as they say in Staffordshire, that is, drank out without intermission," Coles' English Dictionary, in v. *Cock-on-hoop*. If from the A.-S. *Stunian*, to beat, to strike against, it may simply mean *broached*.

STUNKEY. A term applied to arable land, when it is so saturated with wet as to be unfit for ploughing or sowing. *Warw.*

STUNNED-POLL. A stupid miserable fellow; a dunce. *Somerset.*

STUNNER. A severe blow or fall which stuns a person. *Var. dial.*

STUNNISH. To stun; to sprain. *Lanc.*

STUNT. (1) Fierce and angry. *Linc.* Also sulky and obstinate. "He's as *stunt* as a *burnt wong*, there's no turning him;" how or why I know not. *Linc.*
(2) If a person's thumb is struck violently on the end against any hard substance, so as to occasion great pain at the time, and several days after, it is said to be *stunted*.
(3) To make a fool of one. *Durham.*

STUNTISE. Quarrelling?
Hil brewen strut and *stuntise* there as sholde be pes;
Hil sholde gon to the Holi Lond, and maken there her res. *Appendix to Wright's Pol. Songs*, p. 334.

STUNTISH. (1) Sullen. (2) Dumpy. *North. Stunty*, ill-tempered, obstinate.

STUPE. (1) A cloth dipped in warm medicaments, and applied to a sore.
(2) A stupid fellow. *Var. dial.*

STUPID. Obstinate. *North.*

STUPPIN. A stewpan or skillet. *Kent.*

STURBING. Disturbance; fight.
Gij werd him fast in that *sturbing*;
Now helpe him, Jhesu, heven king!
Gy of Warwike, p. 206.

STURBLE. To disturb.
Ne thou oghtes nat to be enchesun
To *sturble* mannys devocyun.
MS. Harl. 1701, f. 74.
So was he *sturbled* with the mynstral,
That he hadde no grace to sey withalle.
MS. Harl. 1701, f. 31.

STURBRIDGE-FAIR. A very celebrated fair held annually near Cambridge.
When th' fair is done, I to the Colledg come,
Or else I drink with them at Trompington,
Craving their more acquaintance with my heart
Till our next *Sturbridg faire*; and so wee part.
Braithwaite's Honest Ghost, 1658, p. 189.

STURBULING. A disturbance.
Zet the cursid Jewes kene
Made a *sturbulyng* hem betwene.
MS. Cantab. Ff. v. 48, f. 25.

Who than is thi lord,
And who is thi king,
And who the hider sent
To make me *sturbling?*
Legend of Seynt Margrete, p. 99.

STURDY. (1) The same as *Giddy* (2).

(2) Sulky and obstinate. *North.*

STURE. (1) A steer, q. v. *West.*

(2) Dust; disturbance. *Devon.*

(3) Rude; ill-looking.

STURJOUN. A sturgeon.

And in the se made the *sturjoun.*
Gy of Warwike, p. 136.

STURKEN. To grow; to thrive. *North.*

STURM. Stern; morose. *Kent.*

STURRE. To stir. (*A.-S.*)

STURRY. Inflexible; sturdy. *South.*

STURT. (1) Disturbance; annoyance. *North.* Kennett explains it, quarrel, strife. "Sturt and strive," to contend and strive, Urry's Ch.

(2) Great wages. A mining term.

STURTES. Stirrups.

And his areouns al-after, and his athel *sturtes,*
That ever glemed and glent al of grene stones.
Syr Gawayn and the Grene Knyʒt, 171.

STURTLE. To startle; to shy. *Devon.*

STUSNET. A skillet. *Sussex.*

STUT. (1) Stout; strong.

Erles myʒt and lordes *stut,*
As cherles shal yn erthe be put.
MS. Harl. 1701, f. 58.

(2) To stutter. *Palsgrave.* Still in use in the North of England. "To stut, to stagger in speaking or going," Baret, 1580.

How much better is it, then, to have an eligant lawyer to plead ones cause, than a *stutting* townsman, that loseth himselfe in his tale, and dooth nothing but make legs. *Nash's Pierce Pennilesse,*1592.

(3) A gnat. *Somerset.*

(4) Staggered. *Scott.*

STUTTLE-BACK. The prickleback. *East.*

STUWES. Stews; brothels. (*A.-S.*)

Save Jagge the jogelour,
And Jonette of the *stuwes. Piers Ploughman,* p. 121.

STY. (1) A ladder. *Yorksh.*

(2) The same as *Stie,* a lane or path. It is wrongly explained by Ritson, Weber, and some other glossarists.

(3) A small inflamed tumour on the lid of the eye is so called. *Var. dial.*

STY-BAKED. Dirty, as a pig in a sty: with the dirt adhering to or engrafted into the skin as if baked upon it. *Linc.*

STYDES. Hours? Arch. xxx. 413.

STYK. A stitch.

For the best that sewes her any *styk*
Takes bot four penys in a wik.
Ywaine and Gawin, 3053.

STYMPHALIST. From *Stymphalides,* the large birds driven away by Hercules.

This *stymphalist* is hee that with five or sixe tenements and the retinue thereunto belonging, infectes the aire with stenche, and poisons that parish.
Maroccus Extaticus, 1595.

STYWARD. A steward. (*A.-S.*)

For nyrhand every a *styward*
The dome that they ʒeve ys over hard.
MS. Harl. 1701, f. 36.

SUA. So; in like manner.

Sum in the air, sum in the lift,
Thar thai drei ful hard schrift,
Thar pin thai bere opon tham ai,
And *sua* sal do to domes-dai.
MS. Cott. Vespas. A. iii. f. 4.

SUAMONE. A kind of oil, mentioned by Chettle in his Kind Hart's Dreame, 1592.

SUART. Black; dark; swarthy.

SUBARBES. Suburbs. (*Lat.*)

SUBDUCE. To withdraw. (*Lat.*)

To *subduce* and convey themselves from the company of the worldly people. *Bacon's Works,* p. 130.

SUBDUEMENT. Defeat. *Shak.*

SUBETH. A kind of apoplexy.

SUBFUMIGATION. A species of charm by smoke. (*Lat.*)

SUBGET. Subject. *Chaucer.*

SUBLIMATORIE. A vessel used by chemists in *sublimation,* or the separation of particles in a body by means of heat.

SUBMISSE. Submissive.

Unmov'd thereto by our *submisse* intreat,
No suite of clay obtain'd it at his hands.
Rowland's Betraying of Christ, 1598.

SUBNECT. To add, or subjoin. (*Lat.*)

Why may I not here take the libertie to *subnect* to this discourse of echos some remarks of sounds.
Aubrey's Wilts, Royal Soc. MS. p. 45.

SUBPLANTARYE. Supplanting.

Whiche is conceyvid of envye,
And clepid is *subplantarye.*
Gower, MS. Soc. Antiq. 134, f. 76.

SUBPOUELLE. To support.

Tho send Hys grace to *subpouelle* and comffort,
Tho alle that ys wyth wrong repourt.
MS. Cantab. Ff. i. 6, f. 123.

SUBRUFE. Reddish. (*Lat.*) It occurs in the Dial. Creat. Moral. p. 194. *Subruphus,* Robert of Gloucester, p. 481, note.

SUBSAID. Just mentioned. *Norf.*

SUBSCRIBE. To submit. Shakespeare has also the substantive *subscription,* submission.

SUBSECUTED. Cut off. (*Lat.*)

Lord, how currioures ranne into every coast, howe lyght horsemen galloped to every streyt to folowe and deteine him, yf by any possibilité he coulde be *subsecuted* and overtaken.
Hall, Richard III. f. 22.

SUBSISTER. A poor prisoner.

Like a *subsister* in a gown of rugge, rent on the left shoulder, to sit singing the counter-tenor by the cage in Southwarke.
Kind-Hart's Dreame, 1592.

SUBSOLARY. Earthly. (*Lat.*)

Thereby the causes and effects of all
Things done upon this *subsolary* ball.
Brome's Songs, 1661, p. 198.

SUBTILITE. Subtilty.

That none his owen astate translate
Be fraude ne *subtilité.*
Gower, MS. Soc. Antiq. 134, f. 81.

SUBTLE. Smooth; fine. *Shak.*

SUBULON. A young hert.

The dung of harts cureth the dropsie, especially of a *subulon* or young hart: the urine easeth the paine in the spleene, the wind in the ventricle and bowels, and infused into the eares, healeth their ulcers. *Topsell's Four-Footed Beasts,* 1607, p. 133.

SUCCESS. That which follows. *Shak.*

SUCCESSFULLY. A common corruption of the word *successively.* Carr ii. 178.

SUCCULATION. Pruning of trees. More's MS. Additions to Ray's North Country Words.

SUCH. A country expletive. " If you don't give me my price like, I won't stay here haggling all day *and such.*" *Leic.*

SUCHE. To seek ? *Robson.*

SUCK. (1) The same as *Sock,* q. v.

(2) *To suck the monkey,* to drink at an alehouse at the cost of another person.

SUCKE. Juice; moisture.

SUCKEGGELDEST. We are happy in superlatives. The following is a genuine speech of a gamekeeper touching the magpie. " Cousim it, 'tis the most *suckeggeldest* warmant i'th' wald." *Moor's Suff. MS.*

SUCKEN. The same as *Soke,* q. v.

SUCKET. (1) A sucking-rabbit.

(2) A conserve, or sweetmeat. See Harrison's Description of England, p. 167.

> And presently after, instead of *suckets,* twelve raw puddings ; I speake not one word of drinke all this while, for indeed he is no drunkard ; hee abhorres that swinish vice.
> *Taylor's Workes,* 1630, i. 144.

SUCK-FIST. *Hume-vesne,* Cotgrave.

SUCKING-BOTTLE. A long, narrow, hollow glass, put to a sore nipple for a child to suck through. *Var. dial.*

SUCKINY. A kind of smock-frock. (*A.-N.*)

> And she had on a *suckiny,*
> That not of hempe herdis was ;
> So faire was none in all Arras.
> *Romaunt of the Rose,* 1232.

SUCKLING. (1) The honeysuckle. *East.*

(2) In Norfolk, the common purple clover. In Suffolk, the white or Dutch clover. " Suklynge herbe, *locusta,*" Pr. Parv.

SUCK-PINT. " *Humeux,* a sucke-pinte or swill-pot, a notable drunkard," Cotgrave.

SUCKREL. A sucking colt. *Suffolk.*

SUCKSTONE. " A little fishe called a *suckstone,* that staieth a ship under saile, *remora,*" Withals' Dictionarie, 1608, p. 37.

SUCRE. Sugar.

> And with the mirre taketh the *sucre.*
> *Gower, MS. Soc. Antiq.* 134, f. 49.

SUCRE-ROSETH. Sugar of roses.

SUCTION. Malt liquor. *Var. dial.*

SUD. Should. *North.*

> I *sud* hev mcaad receits for sweet pyes en rice puddins. *Westm. and Cumb. Dialects,* p. 13.

SUDARY. A napkin ; a kerchief. The kerchief mentioned in John, xx. 7, is so called in Wickcliffe's translation.

> O Jhesu, fore thi blesful face,
> Thou betoke Veroneca bi grace,
> Upon here *sudaré,*
> That face be ne consolacion,
> And to the fynd confusion,
> That day when I schal dye.
> *Poems, Douce MS.*

> His *sudary,* his wyndyng clothe,
> There were thei lafte, I say hem bothe.
> *Cursor Mundi, MS. Coll. Trin. Cantab.* f. 107.

SUDDED. Meadows are said to be *sudded*

when they are covered with drift sand left by a flood. *West.*

SUDDEN. Abrupt. *South.*

SUDDIE. Boggy ?

> Nevertheless the water of this river is for the most part sore troubled, as comming thorough a *suddie* or soddie more, so that little good fish is said to live therein.
> *Harrison's Description of Britaine,* p. 87.

SUDDLE. To soil, or tarnish. *North.*

SUDEKENE. A subdeacon. (*A.-N.*)

> Thorghe holy ordre that men tas,
> That *sudekene* or preste has.
> *MS. Harl.* 2260, f. 118.

SUDS. *To be in the suds,* to be sullen, or in a sulky peevish temper ; to be concerned in a quarrel, or other troublesome matter.

SUE. (1) To follow. (*A.-N.*)

> But by ther bonys ten thei be to you untrue,
> For homward another way thei doo *sue.*
> *Digby Mysteries,* p. 7.

(2) To issue in small quantities. *East.*

(3) To drain land. Also, a drain. *Sussex.*

SUENT. Smooth ; even ; regular ; quiet ; easy ; insinuating ; placid. *West.*

SUERES. Followers. (*A.-N.*)

> And sayde to his *sueres*
> For sothe on this wyse,
> Nought thy neighbors good
> Coveyte in no tyme.
> *Piers Ploughman,* p. 459.

SUERIE. To swear. *Hearne.*

SUERT. Sword ?

> Wend out of londe sone,
> Her nast thou nout to done.
> Wel sone bote thou flette,
> Myd *suert* y shal the sette.
> *Geste of Kyng Horn,* 714.

SUETHELBAND. A swaddling-band. (*A.-S.*)

> A new born barn lay in the croppe,
> Bondon wit a *suethelband.*
> *MS. Cotton. Vespas.* A. iii. f. 9.

SUETON. Suetonius, the historian.

SUEYNE. The same as *Swaine,* q. v.

> The ladés, that stod hyre besyde,
> Fled and durste not long abyde,
> Bot went unto the palys ayene,
> And told both knyjt and *sueyns,*
> How that the quene awey wold,
> And bad them come hyr to be-hold.
> *MS. Ashmole* 61, xv. Cent.

SUFF. (1) A sough, or drain. *North.*

(2) To sob ; to sigh ; to draw the breath in a convulsive manner. *Devon.*

SUFFER. To be punished. *Var. dial.*

SUFFETINE. " Buffetyne, or suffetyne, *alapizo, alapo,*" Prompt. Parv. p. 41.

SUFFICANT. Sufficient.

> Me thynketh that this evidence
> As to this poynte is *sufficant.*
> *Gower, MS. Soc. Antiq.* 134, f. 60.

SUFFICIENCY. Ability. *Shak.*

SUFFING. Something. *Essex.*

SUFFISANCE. Sufficiency ; satisfaction.

> What wol ye more of me but repentaunce,
> God wol Himselve have therof *suffisaunce.*
> *MS. Cantab.* Ff. l. 6, f. 116.

SUFFISANT. Sufficient. (*A.-N.*)

SUFFRAGE. " Suffrage or helpe, *suffrage,*"

Palsgrave. "Suffrage, the prayers that be in bokes, *suffrages*," Palsgrave.

SUFFRAUNT. Forbearing. (*A.-N.*)

> And, Lord, graunt me, for thy mercy digne,
> Above all thinge for to have mekenesse,
> And make me humble, *suffraunt*, and benigne.
> *Lydgate, MS. Ashmole* 39, f. 12.

SUFFRE. (1) To bear; to endure.

> And ley yt to the arme also hote as he may *suffre*,
> and whan it is colde, take yt away and ley to that
> other that is hoote. *MS. Med. Rec.* xv. Cent.

(2) To forbear. *Weber.*

SUFFRENTIE. Sovereignty.

> Or art thou aferde of thy olde name,
> That in every place is had in fame,
> And is supported in such *suffrentie*
> From the lowest unto the hyest degree.
> *Albion Knight, Shak. Soc. Pap.* i. 63.

SUFFRYNGAM. *Penitencier*, Palsgrave, f. 68.

SUFFURATE. To steal away; to withdraw.

> I could conveniently *suffurate* and steal away from
> the institution and teaching of my scholars.
> *Bacon's Works*, p. 195.

SUG. (1) A word used to call pigs to eat their wash. *Norf.*

(2) "Sugge, a byrde," Palsgrave. "Sugge, bryd, *curuca*," Pr. Parv. "*Curruca est quedam avis que alienos pullos educit vel educat, et hec litiosa se dicitur eadem avis*," MS. Harl. 2257, f. 24.

(3) To soak. *West.*

SUGAR-BARLEY. Barleysugar. *East.*

SUGAR-BREAD. A kind of sweet cake or bread mentioned in Harrison's Description of England, p. 167.

SUGAR-CANDIAN. Sugarcandy. *Hall.*

SUGAR-CUPPING. A Derbyshire custom. On Easter-day children melt sugar in a cup of water from the Dropping Tor, and drink it. *Hone.*

SUGAR-LOAF. A high-crowned hat.

SUGAR-PLATE. "*Sugar-plate* or comfettes, dragee, confite," Palsgrave, subst. f. 68. "Sukyr plate, *sucura crustalis*," Pr. Parv.

SUGAR-STONE. A name given in Cornwall to a kind of soft clayey schist.

SUGAR-TEAT. A small portion of moist sugar tied up in a rag of linen of the shape and size of a woman's nipple, given to quiet an infant when the mother is unable to attend.

SUGET. Subject. (*A.-N.*)

> To the seventhe Crist seith, Blessyd ben the
> pesible folk, in the wuche alle thinges ben wel
> ordeyned, none sturynges overcomynge resoun, bote
> al thing *suget* to the spiryt, for he is *suget* to God.
> *Reliq. Antiq.* i. 39.

SUGGE. To say?

> Ʒe, quad the vox, al thou most *sugge*,
> Other elles-wer thou most abugge.
> *Reliq. Antiq.* ii. 276.

SUGGEST. To tempt. *Shak.*

SUGGOURNE. To abide; to rest; to sojourn.

> In the vale of Viterbe vetaile my knyghttes,
> *Suggourne* there sex wokes and solace myselfene.
> *Morte Arthure, MS. Lincoln*, f. 57.

SUGRED. Sweetened, as with sugar.

> He promised to be so grateful unto them that
> they should have cause to say their great curtesies

were well bestowed upon him; but all his *sugred* sweete promises were, in the proofe, but gall and wormwood in the performance.

> *Taylor's Workes*, 1630, iii. 82.

> What swan of bright Apollo's brood doth sing,
> To vulgar love, in courtly sonneting?
> Or what immortall poets *sugred* pen
> Attends the glory of a citizen?
> *Drayton's Poems*, 1637, p. 288.

SUIFTLIKER. More swiftly.

> *Suiftliker* then hee may wink,
> Or ani mans hert mai thynk.
> *MS. Cotton. Vespas.* A. iii. f. 3.

SUILK. Such.

> Goddoth! quath Leve, y shal the fete
> Bred an chese, butere and milk,
> Pastees and flaunes, al with *suilk*.
> *Havelok*, 644.

SUIN. Sows; swine. (*A.-S.*)

> A feyre there was holdyn hende.
> This povre man had *suyn* to selle,
> And theder he wold, as I ʒu telle.
> On morwe he ros and gan hym dresse;
> Hys wyf bad hym bydyn and here messe.
> *Reliq. Antiq.* i. 62.

SUIRT. To break off the sharp edge of a hewn stone. *Northumb.*

SUIST. A person who seeks for things which merely gratify himself.

SUIT-BROKER. One who made a trade of obtaining the suits of petitioners at court. He was sometimes termed a *suit-jogger*.

> Some by their braines, as politicians, monopolists, projectmongers, *suit-joggers*, and star-gazers.
> *Taylor's Workes*, 1630, i. 143.

SUITY. Uniform; even. *Heref.*

SUKCADES. Sweetmeats; suckets. Maundevile has it *sukkarde*, Travels, p. 310.

SUKKEN. Moisture. *Cumb.*

SULE. (1) To soil. (*A.-N.*)

> And his syre a soutere
> Y-*suled* in grees.
> *Piers Ploughman*, p. 495.

(2) Soil; earth. *Prompt. Parv.*

(3) Should ye. (*A.-S.*)

> Mine knithes, hwat do ye?
> *Sule* ye thus gate fro me fle?
> *Havelok*, 2419.

SULFEROUS. Sultry. *Var. dial.*

SULING. A ploughland. *Kennett.*

SULK. To be sullen. *Var. dial.* In the sulks, i. e. sullen and peevish.

SULL. A plough. *West.*

SULLAGE. Muck, or dung. *Kent.*

SULLEN. In Cunningham's Revels Accounts, p. 189, mention is made of "ix. yardes of *sullen* cloth of gold purple." Qu. *cullen*, Cologne?

SULLENS. Sick of the sullens, i. e. very gloomy or morose. The phrase occurs in Lilly. "And let them die that age and *sullens* have," Shakespeare. See Dyce's Remarks, p. 99.

SULLEVATE. To raise into enmity.

SULLOW. A plough. *West.*

SULMARD. "*Fetruncus, pecoides*, a sulmard." Nominale MS. The MS. is distinctly *sulmard* but it may be an error for *fulmard*.

SUL-PADDLE. "Sulpaddle is used in the West for a plow-staff," Blount's Glossographia, p. 621, ed. 1681.

SULSH. To soil; to dirty. *Somerset.*

SULT. To insult. *South.*

SULTREDGE. A coarse apron worn by poor women in some parts of Wiltshire.

SULTRONG. "Sultry.

This garment is too much too warme for thee,
In the estivall of a *sultrong* heat.
Middleton's Epigrams, 1608, repr. p. 36.

SUM. (1) Some. *Sum and al,* completely.

So thow my3t knowe, *sum* and al,
Whether the synne be gret or smal.
MS. Cott. Claud. A. ii. f. 146.

(2) A question in arithmetic. *Var. dial.*

SUMA. A small cup made of blue and white stone-ware. *Somerset.*

SUMBER. Summer. *Heref.*

SUMFUN. Something. *Suffolk.*

SUMITER. A scimitar. "Sumyter, a fauchon, *sumiterre,*" Palsgrave, 1530.

SUMMED. A term in falconry. "Summed is when she is in all her plumes," Gent. Rec. ii. 63. See Dict. Rust. in v.

And when the plumes were *summ'd* with sweet desire,
To prove the pinions, it ascends the skies;
Doe what I could, it needsly would aspire
To my soules sun, those two celestiall eies:
Thus from my breast, where it was bred alone,
It after thee is like an eaglet flowne.
Drayton's Poems, 1637, p. 484.

SUMMER. (1) A sumpter-horse.

(2) The principal beam of a floor. See Thoresby's Letter to Ray, 1703, in v. *Bawks;* Harrison's England, p. 187.

(3) That part of a waggon which supports the bed or body of it. *Sussex.*

(4) To summer and winter any one, i. e. to know him thoroughly, or at all seasons.

SUMMER-BARM. To ferment. Said of malt liquor when it ferments in summer before the application of the yeast.

SUMMER-COCK. A term given to a young salmon in summer time. *North.*

SUMMERED. Agisted, as cattle; well fed on grass. *Summer-eat,* to agist. *North.*

SUMMER-FOLDS. Summer freckles. *Glouc.*

SUMMER-FRECKLED. Spots on the face caused by the heat of the sun. *South.*

SUMMER-GOOSE. Gossamer. *North.*

SUMMERINGS. (1) Country rejoicings and wakes formerly in vogue on Midsummer-day.

(2) Very early apples and pears.

(3) Riots or scolding matches. *North.*

(4) Cattle of one year old. *North.*

SUMMERLAND. To summerland a ground is to lay it fallow a year, according to Ray. *Suffolk.* Moor gives only the substantive.

SUMMER-LATEN. Summer fallowed. *Norf.*

SUMMER-RIDING-BOOTS. "*Demi-chase* (Fr.) half-chase, or half-hunting boots; so called by the French: we call them summer riding-boots," Blount's Glossographia, p. 187.

SUMMERSAULT. See *Somersault.*

SUMMER'S-DAY. As nice a person as one shall see on a summer's day, i. e. as one could

see. This vernacular phrase is not unusual in early writers. "They say hee is as goodly a youth as one shall see in a summer's day," Lilly's Mother Bombie, ed. 1632, sig. Z. x. "A proper man as one shall see in a summer's day," Mids. Night's Dream, i. 2. See Henry V. iii. 6, iv. 8. The phrase also occurs in later works. "As fine a fat thriving child as you shall see in a summer's day," Joseph Andrews, b. iv. c. 15.

SUMMER'S-RUN. Said of a horse which has been at grass during the summer.

SUMMER-TILLED. Fallowed. "That field was *summer-tilled* last year," i. e. lay fallow. *Linc.* Sometimes termed *summer-stirred.* "To summer-stir, *æstate sulcare,*" Coles. In the South of England, land is said to have a summer fallow.

SUMMER-TREE. Same as *Summer* (2).

SUMMER-VOY. Yellow freckles in the face.

SUMMING. Arithmetic. *Var. dial.*

SUMMISTER. One who abridges.

Over this, if the historian be long, he is accompted a trifler; if he be short, he is taken for a *summister.*
Holinshed, Chron. Ireland, p. 90.
And thus, though rudely, have I plaid the *summister.*
The Meanes in Spending, 1598.

SUMMITTE. To submit. *Lydgate.*

SUMMUNDER. An apparitor. "*Aparator,* a summunder," Nominale MS. Nomina dignitatum clericorum. The term occurs more usually *summoner* or *sumner.*

SUMMUT. Something. *Var. dial.*

SUMNER. See *Summunder.*

SUMNI. Summon. (*A.-S.*)

To Westmystre he let *sumni* the bischopes of his londe,
And clerkes that grettest were ek and he3ist, ich understonde. *Life of Thomas Beket, p. 19.*

SUMP. (1) According to Carr, a hole sunk below the levels or drifts of a mine at a proper distance to divide the ground, and communicate air to the different works or branches. Ray says, "a round pit of stone covered over with clay within." See his English Words, 1674, p. 114.

(2) A puddle, or dirty pond. *Cumb.*

(3) A very heavy weight. *Suffolk.* Hence, a heavy stupid fellow is so called.

SUMPH. A simpleton. *North.*

SUMP-HOLE. A cesspool. *Yorksh.*

SUMPLE. Supple; pliant. *West.*

SUMPTER. A horse which carried furniture, &c. on its back. It was more commonly termed a sumpter-horse.

But, for you have not furniture
Beseeming such a guest,
I bring his owne, and come myselfe
To see his lodging drest.
With that two *sumpters* were discharg'd,
In which were hangings brave,
Silke coverings, curtens, carpets, plate,
And al such turn should have.
Percy's Reliques, p. 78.

SUM-UP. To collect. *North.*

SUMPY. Boggy; wet. Damp, watery, as potatoes; heavy, as bread. *Var. dial.*

SUN. *In the sun,* tipsy.

SUN-AND-MOON. " Dielcystincta, a kinde of play wherein two companies of boyes holding hands all on a rowe, doe pull with hard hold one another, till one be overcome ; it is called *Sunne and Moone,*" Thomasii Dictionarium, 4to. Lond. 1644.

SUN-BEAM. Gossamer. *North.*

SUN-CATE. A dainty. *Suffolk.*

Mauther, gang the grizen into the vauncsroof, bring my hat from off the spurket, ding the door after you, nemis the cat should get in and eat the *suncate.* Girl, girl, go up stairs into the garret, and fetch my hat from off the peg; shut the door for fear the cat should get in and eat the dainty.

Grose, ed. 1839, p. 111.

SUN-DANCE. A custom was formerly in vogue of rising early on Easter-day to see the *sun dance,* the superstitious believing that the sun really did dance on that day.

SUNDAY-CLOTHES. Best clothes, kept for use on Sundays and holidays. *Var. dial.*

SUNDAY - SAINT - AND - EVERY-DAY-SIN-NER. A person who never misses church twice every Sunday, nor an opportunity of reviling or cheating his neighbours on all the rest of the week. *Moor's Suff. MS.*

SUNDAY'S-FELLOW. Monday.

One asked Tarlton why Munday was called *Sundaies fellow ?* Because he is a sausie fellow, saies Tarlton, to compare with that holy day. But it may be Munday thinkes himselfe Sundayes fellow because it followes Sunday, and is next after ; but he comes a day after the faire for that.

Tarlton's Jests, 1611.

SUNDER. To air ; to expose to the sun and wind, as hay which has been cocked, but which is still under-dry. *York.*

SUNDERLAND-FITTER. The knave of clubs.

SUNDERLY. Peculiarly ; alternately.

SUNE. Soon ?

That fur schal kumen in this world
One one *sune* nijte. *MS. Cott. Calig.* A. ix. f. 245.

SUNFEY.

Under the paine of paying the billes themselves, which they refuse eyther to file or cleare within that space, without prejudice alwaies to the complanant to use an avower if he have anie, and therby to claime his double and *sunfey.* *Egerton Papers,* p. 237.

SUNFULE. Sinful [men]. *(A.-S.)*

An the *sunfule* so ateliche heo stondeth.

MS. Cott. Calig. A. ix. f. 245.

SUN-GATE-DOWN. " Sunne settynge, or sunne gate downe, *occasus,*" Pr. Parv. " At the sonne gate downe, *sur la soleil couchant,*" Palsgrave, 1530.

SUNGILLE-STOK. See *Swingle-hand.*

SUNHOUN. A halo round the sun. *South.*

SUNK. A canvas pack-saddle stuffed with straw. *North.*

SUNKET. (1) A supper. *Cumb.*

(2) To pamper with dainties. *East.* A sunket-ting child, i. e. a delicate child.

3) A foolish fellow. *Norf.*

(4) A small quantity of food or drink, especially if given grudgingly. *Norf.*

SUNK-FENCE. A ditch cut perpendicularly on one side and obliquely on the other, com-

mon in parks, &c. affording protection without interrupting the prospect.

SUNNEN. Sins. *(A.-S.)*

Wolton, quod the vox, erift ousderfonge,
Tel thine *sunnen* on and on,
That ther bileve never on. *Reliq. Antiq.* ii. 276.

SUNNING. Basking in the sun.

So homeward bent, his eye too rude and cunning,
Spies knight and lady by a hedge a *sunning.*

Ovid de Arte Amandi, &c. 1677, p. 139.

SUNNY-SIDE. The south side of a hill.

SUN-SHINER. The dark shining beetle.

SUNTORE. Cracked by the sun. *Salop.*

SUOAK. To snuff the air. *Northumb.*

SUP. To sup sorrow, i. e. to be afflicted by anything causing sorrow.

SUPERALTARY. The slab which covered a stone altar in a church. *(Lat.)*

SUPERFICIALTIE. Superficies.

In als many jorneyes may thei gon fro Jerusalem unto other confynyes of the *superficialtie* of the erthe bejonde. *Maundevile's Travels,* p. 183.

SUPERFLUE. Superfluous. *Palsgrave.*

SUPERGRESSION. An old chemical term.

And soe with long leasure it will waste,
And not with bubling made in haste ;
For doubt of perrills many moe then one,
And for *supergression* of our stone.

Ashmole's Theat. Chem. Brit. 1652, p. 47.

SUPERNACULUM. An old drinking term, thus described by Nash, Pierce Penilesse, repr. p. 52, " a devise of drinking new come out of Fraunce, which is, after a man hath turnde up the bottom of the cup, to drop it on hys nayle, and make a pearl with that is left ; which, if it slide, and he cannot mak stand on by reason thers too much, he must drinke againe for his penance." It is supposed to be a corruption of *super ungulam.* Brathwaite mentions it in his Law of Drinking, 1617, p. 11, " they without any difficulty at all can soake and sucke it ἐν τοῦ νῦν, to a nayle." The term is still in use, and is applied, according to Grose, to " good liquor, of which there is not even a drop left sufficient to wet one's nail."

Were it a whole hogsheade, I would pledge thee.
What, if I drinke two ? fill them to the brimme ;
Wher's hee that shall marry with my sister ?
I drinke this to thee *super naculum.*

Timon, ed. Dyce, p. 38.

SUPERNE. Above ; supreme. *Lydgate.*

SUPERNODICAL. Excessive ; supreme.

O, *supernodical* foole ! wel, Ile take your
Two shillings, but Ile bar striking at legs.

Taming of a Shrew, p. 185.

SUPERTASSE. According to Stubbes, " a certaine device made of wiers, crested for the purpose, whipped over either with gold thred, silver, or silke ; this is to bee applied round about their neckes, under the ruffe, upon the outside of the bande, to beare up the whole frame and bodie of the ruffe from fallyng or hangyng doune," ed. 1585, f. 21.

SUPERVISOUR. The overlooker of a will.

And to se all thinges truly doone
After my deth, dwely and right sone,
I ordeyn to be myn executour
Of my last will, with a *supervisour,*

Aleyn Maltson, to se truly
My will performyd wele and duly,
As I have ordeynd here after myn entent,
By good avicement in my Testament.

MS. Rawl. C. 86.

SUPERVIVE. Qu. *Supervide*, to look at.

As I me lenyd unto a joyful place,
Lusty Phebus to *supervive*.

Lydgate's Minor Poems, p. 78.

SUPERVIZE. Sight; view. *Shak.*

SUPETERS. Armour for the feet.

SUPPEDITATE. To subdue, or tread under.

But oh Lorde, all thynges that I of long tyme
have in my mynde revolved and immagined, that
stelyng thief Death goeth about to subverte, and in
the moment of an houre clerely to *suppeditate.*

Hall, Edward IV. f. 60.

SUPPER. (1) *To set one his supper*, to perform
a feat impossible for another to imitate.
(2) The sucker of a pump.

SUPPINGS. (1) Spoon-meat. " Suppyyng for
a sicke man, *humaige*, *humee*," Palsgrave.
(2) The refuse milk after the cheese is made.
Chesh.

SUPPLANTARYE. Supplanting.

For in good feythe ʒit hadde I lever,
In my simpleste, for to dye,
Than werche suche *supplantarye.*

Gower, MS. Soc. Antiq. 134, f. 77.

SUPPLE. To render pliant. It is now used
only as an adjective. "To make a thing which
is hard and rough, soft ; to soften, to *supple*,"
Hollyband's Dictionarie, 1593.

Yf he be acursed than are we a mete cuppell,
For I am interdyct ; no salve that sore can *suppell.*

Bale's Kynge Johan, p. 62.

SUPPLIE. To supplicate. (*A.-N.*)

SUPPOELLE. (1) To support. (2) Support.

So that ther myghte no schippes come nere the
havene for to vetaille the citee, or *suppoelle* it with
mene, by cause of the bastelle.

MS. Lincoln A. 1. 17, f. 5.

And to live in reste and in quiete
Thoruʒ thi supporte and thi *suppowaille.*

MS. Digby 230.

And wher nede was, he made *suppowelmont.*

Hardyng's Chronicle, f. 49.

SUPPORTAILE. Support. (*A.-N.*)

And in mischef, whanne drede wolde us assayle,
Thou arte oure schilde, thou arte oure *supportayle.*

Lydgate, MS. Soc. Antiq. 134, f. 22.

SUPPORTATION. Support. (*Lat.*)

For there is no great man so weake, but hath
councell and *supportation* of inferior officers, nor
mean man so sottish, but hath friends or servants in
the dispatch of his businesse.

History of Patient Grisel, p. 33.

SUPPOSALL. A supposition.

Hee incroches often upon admittance (where
thinges be well delivered) to multiply his observation, and he will verifie things, through a scandal-
ous *supposall*, as if they were now committed.

Stephens' Essayes and Characters, 1615, p. 219.

SUPPOSE. (1) To know with certainty. A
person announcing what he knows to be a
fact will say, "I *suppose* Mr. A. is dead." *Salop.*
(2) A supposition.

To speake with him she kindly doth entreat,
Desiring him to cleare her darke *suppose.*

Taylor's Workes, 1630, iii. 22.

SUPPOSITOR. A medical term, meaning an
excitement or provocative. Ford, ii. 182.

SUPPRISSID. Oppressed.

Goddis law biddith help the *supprissid*, jugith to
the fadirles, defendith the wydow, and how tempo-
ral lordis ow to thole no wrong be don ; and maul
doctors and lawis and resoun acordyn to this.

Apology for the Lollards, p. 79

SUPPUTED. Imputed. *Drayton.*

SUP-UP. The legitimate meaning of *sup up* is
to give cattle their last meal at night, or supper. It is a rural phrase, and has extended
from the farmyard to other actions and occupations. *Var. dial.*

SURANCE. Assurance ; satisfaction.

Thus wedded he her at Yorke in all *suraunce.*

Hardyng's Chronicle, f. 86.

SUR-ANTLERS. "The sur-antlers, or bear-
antlers of a buck, but the royall of a stagg,
viz. the second branch," Howell, sect. 3.

SURBATRE. A kind of bruise. (*A.-N.*)

SURBED. "To surbed coal, to set it edge-
waies on the fire that the heat and flame may
cleare it and make it burn with greater vehe-
mence," Kennett, MS. Lansd. 1033.

SURBOTED. Grazed, as the skin is by constant rubbing or pressure ; battered. (*Fr.*)

Fresh grease is very profitable for those members
that are *surboted* or riven of their skin, and likewise
to anoint them that are weary with long journies.
The ashes of womens haire burned in a shell, and
mingled with the fat of swine, are said to ease the
paine of S. Anthonies fire, and to stanch bloud, and
to cure ring-wormes.

Topsell's Four-Footed Beasts, 1607, p. 699.

SURCARKING.

Ac in al this *surcarking*,
Merlin com to Ban the king.

Arthour and Merlin, p. 147.

SURCEASE. To stop ; to cease ; to refrain.

I shall gladly *surcease* to make any farther attempt
of the house, garden, stables, and approaches, as
falling too short of the greatness and excellency of
it. *Aubrey's Wilts, Royal Soc. MS.* p. 235.

The watchfull bird that centinels the morne,
Shrill herald to Auroraes earlie rising,
That oft proclaimes the day ere day be borne,
Distinguisher from pitch-fac'd nights disguising,
Surceas'd to heed ; why Nature taught him crow,
And did exclaime on mee for sinning so.

Rowland's Betraying of Christ, 1598.

SURCINGLE. A long upper girth which often
went over the pannel or saddle. "The pay-
trellys, *sursenglys*, and crowpers," Morte
d'Arthur, i. 211.

SURCOTE. An upper coat, or kirtle, worn over
the rest of the clothes. At a later period,
there was a mourning garment so called,
" made like a close or strayte-bodied gowne,
which is worn under the mantell."

SURCREASE. Excessive increase. *Drayton.*

SURCREW. A surplus.

It had once left me, as I thought ; but it was only
to fetch more company, returning with a *surcrew* of
those splenetick vapors that are call'd hypocon-
driacal. *Reliq. Wotton.* ed. 1651, p. 513.

SURCUDANT. Presumptuous ; arrogant.

SURDAUNT. Arising.

And ferthermore to here and determyne all man

ner causes, quarels, controversies, debates and de-
maundes, emergyng and *surdaunt* among any persons cociticins within the said citie.
Davies' York Records, p. 255.

SURDINE. " A surdine to put in a trumpet
to make it sound low," Florio, p. 514.

SURDINY. The fish sardine.

SURDOWGHT. Sour-dough ; leaven. " *Fer-
mentum*, surdowght," Nominale MS. xv. Cent.

SURE. (1) " I don't know, I am *sure*," a very
common expression, the last sentence being
merely a confirmatory tautology. *Sure and
sure*, indeed.

(2) Sour. Medulla MS.

SURE-CROP. The shrew mouse. *Dorset.*

SUREN. To assure. (*A.-N.*)

SUREPEL. A cover or case.

The sexte hade a sawtere semliche bowndene
With a *surepel* of silke sewede fulle faire.
Morte Arthure, MS. Lincoln, f. 98.

SURESBY. A person to be depended on.

SURE-TO. Assured to ; affianced.

SURETY. Defence ; safeguard. " Surety, defence, *sauve garde*," Palsgrave, 1530.

SURE-WORK. To make sure work, i. e. a certain safe conclusion to any undertaking.

Their unmannerly manner is to knocke out a
mans braines first, or else to lurke behind a tree, and
shoot a man with a peece or a pistol, and so make
sure workes with the passenger, and then search his
pockets. *Taylor's Workes*, 1630, iii. 88.

SURFANO. A plaster, or salve.

SURFEIT. A cold ; a disorder. *Craven.*

SURFEL. To wash the cheeks with mercurial
or sulphur water. See Ford, i. 405.

Having at home a well painted mannerly harlot,
as good a maid as Fletcher's mare that bare three
great foals, went in the morning to the apothecaries
for half a pint of sweet water that commonly is called
*surfulyng water. A manifest Detection of the moste
vyle and detestable Use of Dice Play*, n. d.

SURFET. Fault, offence, or trespass.

For wele, ne for worchyp, ne for the wlonk werkkes,
Bot in syngne of my *surfet* I schal se hit ofte.
Gawayn and the Grene Knijt, 2433.

SURFLE. To ornament with trimmings, edgings,
or embroidery ; to plait.

SURFOOT. Sore-footed ? See Nares.

SURGE. A quick motion. *South.*

SURGENRIE. Surgery. (*A.-N.*)

And dide hym assaie his *surgenrie*
On hem that sike were. *Piers Ploughman*, p. 336.

SURGIAN. A surgeon. *Palsgrave.*

SURHED. To surhed a stone is to set it edge-
wise, contrary to the posture it held in the
quarry. *Northumb.*

SURINGER. A surgeon. Peele, iii. 94.

SURJONER. A surgeon. Medulla MS.

SURKETE. The same as *Surcote*, q. v.

Surketes over al he con holde,
Off knyjtes and of persons bolde,
Sich hade he non sene.
MS. Cantab. Ff. v. 48, f. 54.

SURLETTES. Part of ancient armour, mentioned in Hall's Union, 1548, Hen. IV. f. 12.
See *Sollerets.*

SURMIT. To surmise.

That by the breeche of cloth were chalenged,
Nor I thinke never were, for to my wyt
They were fantasticall, imagined ;
Onely as in my dreame I dyd *surmit*.
Thynne's Debate, p. 67

SURMOUNT. To excel ; to surpass.

So as the kynge himselfe acompteth,
That he alle other men *surmounteth*.
Gower, MS. Soc. Antiq. 134, f. 233.

SURNAPPE. A napkin ; a tablecloth.

The *surnappe* must be properly layde towardes
the salt endlong the brode edge, by the handes of th'
aforenamed yeoman of the ewrie.
Warner's Antiq. Culin. p. 100.

SURPLIS. A surplice. (*A.-N.*)

SURPLUSE. Remainder ; surplus.

SURQUEDRIE. Presumption ; arrogance ; conceit. *Surquidous*, overbearing, arrogant.

O, where is alle the transitorye fame
Of pompe and pryde, and *surquidrye* in feere ?
Lydgate, MS. Soc. Antiq. 134, f. 2.

Or rebelle in any manere weye
Of *surquidrie* or pride to werreye.
MS. Digby 230.

The tother branche of pride es *surquytry*, that es,
to undirtake thyng over his powere, or wenys to be
mare wyse than he es, or better than he es, and
avauntes hym of gude that he hase of other, or of
ille that he hase of hymselfe.
MS. Lincoln A. i. 17, f. 200.

SURRE. A sore place ; a scar.

SUR-REINED. Overworked. *Shak.*

SURREPT. To invade suddenly. (*Lat.*)

But this fonde newe founde ceremony was litle regarded and lesse estemed of hym that onely studyed
and watched howe to *surrept* and steale this turtle
oute of her mewe and lodgynge.
Hall, Henry VII. f. 20.

SURREY. A corruption of *Sirrah.*

SURRY. Syria.

Nowe of the kynge of *Surry* wylle I seye more.
MS. Cott. Calig. A. ii. f. 119.

They drewe up sayle of bright hew,
The wynde them soone to *Surry* blew.
Syr Isenbras, ap. Utterson, i. 91.

SURRYALL. The second projection of the
horn on a stag's head above the sur-antler.

And fyrst whan an hert hath fourched, and then
auntelere ryall, and *surryall*, and forched one the
one syde, and troched on that other syde, than is he
an hert of .x. and of the more. *Reliq. Antiq.* i. 151.

SURS. Rising.

Att the *surs* of the sonne he sees there commande,
Raykande to Rome-warde the redyeste wayes.
Morte Arthure, MS. Lincoln, f. 89.

SURSANURE. A wound healed outwardly, but
not inwardly. (*A.-N.*)

SURSAULTED.

Returne my hart, *sursaulted* with the fill
Of thousand great unrests and thousand feares.
England's Helicon, repr. p. 162.

SURSERARA. A corruption of *certiorari ?*

With hollocke, sherant, malliga, canara,
I stuft your sides up with a *surserara*.
Taylor's Workes, 1630, iii. 126.

SURSTBYE. A courtpie ?

On morow when he shuld to court goo,
In russet clothyng he tyret hym tho,
In kyrtil and in *surstbye*.
MS. Cantab. Ff. v. 48, f. 55.

SURVEANCE. Superintendence. (*A.-N.*)

SURVEY. A species of auction, in which farms are disposed of for three lives. *Devon.*

SURVIOWRE. An overlooker.

SUSE. (1) Six. (2) She. *Lanc.*

SUSGINE. A surgeon?

A *susgyne* of Salerne enserches his wondes.
Morte Arthure, MS. Lincoln, f. 98.

SUSPECT. Suspicion.

I have been in prison thus long, only upon the occasion of the disputation made in the convocation-house, and upon *suspect* of the setting forth the report thereof. *Philpot's Works,* p. 5.

SUSPECTABLE. Liable to suspicion.

SUSPECTION. Suspicion. *Chaucer.*

SUSPENCED. Freed. "Suspenced from all their paine," Honours Academie, 1610, i. 49.

SUSPIRAL. "Suspyral of a cundyte, *spiraculum, suspiraculum,*" MS. Harl. 221, f. 168.

SUSPIRE. To respire; to sigh.

SUSPOWSE. Suspicion.'

SUSS. (1) A dog-fish. *I. of Wight.*
(2) To swill like a hog. *Suss, suss,* a call to swine to eat their suss or hog-wash. *East.*

SUSSACK. A fall; a blow. *Suffolk.*

SUSSEX-PUDDING. Boiled paste. *South.*

SUSSLE. Noise; disturbance; an impertinent meddling with the affairs of other people. *Sussex.*

SUSTER-DOUGHTERE. A niece. (*A.-S.*)

SUSTRE. A sister. (*A.-S.*)

Bycause that hurre *sustre* so besselyche of hurre souзt,
What he hadde y-don aзeyne seynt Ede.
Chron. Vilodun. p. 137.

Justice and pees, these *sustres* schal provide
Twixt reawmes tweyne stedfast love to sette.
MS. Harl. 3869, f. 2.

SUTE. (1) After. *Hearne.*
(2) Cunning; subtle. *Staff.*
(3) A sute of locks, a set of six or more locks, whereof the respective keys shall serve only for each lock, and yet one master key shall open all. Holme, 1688.
(4) A pursuit, or following. *Pr. Parv.*
(5) Soot. MS. Dictionary, c. 1500.
(6) To clothe or suit.

The moone like *suted* in a sable weed,
Mourned for sinnes outragious bloody deed.
Rowlands' Betraying of Christ, 1598.

SUTELTEE. See *Sotiltees.*

SUTELY. This word occurs in Hall, Henry IV. f. 11, but is probably a misprint for *surety,* and certainly used in the same sense.

SUTERE. A suitor, or suppliant.

Alle men may take example, lo!
Of lowly mekenes evyn ryght here,
Be oure Lorde God that comyth me to,
Hese pore servaunt and his *suters.*
Coventry Mysteries, p. 201.

SUTLER. One who sells provisions in a camp. Spelt *sutteler* by Coles.

For setting on those with the luggadge left,
A few poore *sutlers* with the campe that went.
Drayton's Poems, p. 86.

SUTTER. A cobler, or shoemaker. (*A.-S.*)

Hail be зe, *sutters,* with зour mani lestes,
With зour blote hides of selcuth bestis.
Reliq. Antiq. ii. 176.

SUTTES. Fools? (*A.-N.*)

Dyschoppes, archedekyns, and abbottes,
Wyse men of the churche and no *suttes.*
MS. Cantab. Ff. ii. 38, f. 211.

SUTTLE-BEE.

For those kind of cattle have commonly the *suttle-bee,* and are as weary of a single life as nuns of their cloisters, and therefore catch at the very appearance of match.
A Cap of Gray Hairs for a Green Head, 1688, p. 77.

SUTTLER'S-CABINE. A soldier's tent.

SUWE. To follow; to pursue. (*A.-S.*)

With his fest he me smot;
Therefore ich im *suwed,* God it wot!
And smot him so thou might se.
Gy of Warwike, p. 226.

Ful litil pris sette thei therby,
But *suwen* evere her owen foly.
MS. Ashmole 60, f. 4.

SUWELLE. To swell. (*A.-S.*)

To do that foule fleys to *suwelle,*
That foule wormes scholden ete.
Appendix to Walter Mapes, p. 334.

SUXUNDATION. Drowning. Huloet, 1552.

SWA. So. See *Sua.*

It wolde wirke me fulle wa,
So mote I one orthe ga,
It ne salle noghte be-tyde me *swa,*
If I may riзhte rede. *Perceval,* 1463.
Als werand and als dreri,
Swa rजeked I witterli.
MS. Cott. Vespas. D. vii. f. 22.

SWAB. (1) To splash over. *North.*
(2) A rough awkward fellow. *Norf.*

SWABBER. (1) A sweeper of a vessel. Also, a kind of broom for sweeping out a boat or ship. "Their ragges served to make me *swabbers,*" Dekker's Knights Conjuring, p. 65.
(2) Certain cards at whist by which the holder was entitled to a part of the stakes were termed *swabbers.*

SWABBLE. (1) To quarrel; to squabble. *East.*
(2) "Swablynge or swaggynge," Pr. Parv.

SWACHE. A tally; that which is fixed to cloth sent to dye, of which the owner keeps the other part. *North.*

SWACK. A blow, or fall. *Swacking,* huge, large. *Swacker,* anything very large.

SWAD. (1) A silly foolish fellow; a country bumpkin. "Swad, in the North, is a pescod shell; thence used for an empty shallow headed fellow," Blount, p. 627.

Let countrey swaines and silly *swads* be still;
To court, yoong wag, and wanton there thy fill.
Greene's Perimedes, 1588.

How should the reasonable soule (unlesse all his prime faculties were drowned and drenched in the lees of sense) affect such a *swad?*
The Two Lancashire Lovers, 1640, p. 22.

O, how this tickles mee, to see a *swad,*
Who ne'r so much as education had
To make him generous, advanc'd to state.
Brathwaite's Honest Ghost, 1658, p. 3.

I have opinion, and have ever had,
That when I see a stagg'ring drunken *swad,*
Then that a man worse then an asse I see.
Taylor's Motto, 1622.

(2) The pod of a pea, &c. *North.* Grose says the term is used metaphorically for one that is slender, p. 157, ed. 1839. Coles has a differ-

ent application. "A swad [of a woman], *obesula*." A handful of pease-straw is also called a *swad*.

(3) A sword. *Suffolk.*

(4) A fish-basket. *Sussex.*

SWADDER. A pedlar. Earle, p. 249. "Swadders or pedlers," Harrison's England, p. 184.

SWADDLE. To beat. "Hee bangde, belammed, thumped, *swadled* her," Cotgrave, in v. Chaperon. "Swaddled, cudgelled," Coles.

I sweare by God, and by saynt John,
Thy bones will I *swaddle*, so have I blisse.
The Wife Lapped in Morels Skin, n. d.

SWADDLE-BAND. "Swadylbande, *bande, fasse*," Palsgrave.

SWADDY. Full of husks, or pods. "*Goussu*, coddie, hullie, huskie, swaddie," Cotgrave. See *Swad* (2).

SWAFF. As much grass as a scythe cuts at one stroke. Holme, 1688.

SWAFT. Thirst. *Wilts.*

SWAG. (1) To hang loose and heavy; to sag. *Warw.* "I swagge, as a fatte persons belly swaggeth as he goth, *je assouage*," Palsgrave.

(2) To swing about. *Suffolk.*

(3) Booty; large quantity. *Leic.*

(4) "One that falls down with some violence and noise is said to come down with a swag," Kennett, MS. Lansd. 1033, f. 396.

SWAG-BELLY. A loose heavy belly.

SWAGE. (1) To assuage. *Palsgrave.* In our second example, to lessen power?

Than wil he thys war *swage*.
Guy of Warwick, Middlehill MS.

Y schall have Harrowde and Gye,
Tyll they be *swagyd* a gode partye.
MS. Cantab. Ff. ii. 38, f. 180.

(2) To move anything about. *Linc.*

(3) A notch in a blacksmith's anvil.

(4) A joiner's gauge. Holme, 1688, iii. 366.

SWAGER. A brother-in-law. *Durh.*

SWAGING. *Refrigeration*, Palsgrave.

SWAGLE. The same as *Swag* (2).

SWAIB. To swing forward and backward like a pendulum. *Somerset.*

SWAIMUS. Shy; squeamish. *Cumb.*

SWAINE. A herdsman or servant; a youth not yet an esquire. (*A.-S.*) In compositions of the fourteenth and fifteenth century, the term is not exclusively applied in the original sense. Any one not a knight seems to have been so called.

Knightes, *swaines*, levedies beld,
Maden crud hem to biheld.
Arthour and Merlin, p. 204.

Jondyr ys Gayere, an harde *swayn*,
The emperowre sone of Almayn.
MS. Cantab. Ff. ii. 38, f. 150.

SWAISE. To swing the arms in walking.

SWAITHE. (1) A row of grass cut down. *Laid o' th' swaithe bauk*, spread abroad. *North.*

(2) The ghost of a dying person. *Cumb.*

SWAKE. A pump-handle. *East.*

SWAL. Swelled. (*A.-S.*)

He *swal* so faste and wondirly,
That almest bigon he for to dy.
Cursor Mundi, MS. Coll. Trin. Cantab. f. 78.

SWALCH. A pattern. *Yorksh.*

SWALE. (1) A valley? Forby explains it, "a low place;" and Moor, "a gentle rising of the ground, but with a corresponding declivity."

Be the deth that I shalle dye,
Therto my hed then dar I ley,
Now sone in this *swale*.
MS. Cantab. Ff. v. 48, f. 48.

(2) To wither in the sun. *Warw.*

(3) A piece of wood going from an upright shaft in an oatmeal mill to one of the wheels.

(4) A gutter in a candle. Also, to sweal or gutter; to melt away. *Var. dial.* Metaphorically, to grow thin.

(5) Shade; a shady place. *East.* "Swale, *umbra*," MS. Harl. 221, f. 167.

(6) To split down or off. *Heref.*

(7) Windy; cold; bleak. *North.* To lie in the swale, i. e. in the cold air.

(8) To singe, or burn. *Grose.* "And men *swaliden* with greet heete," Wickliffe's New Testament, p. 249. Kennett explains it, "to kindle or set on fire."

SWALER. A dealer in corn, or rather one who buys corn and converts it into meal before he sells it again. *Chesh.*

SWALGE. A whirlpool.

SWALIEST. Coldest. *North.*

SWALLE. Swelled. See *Swal.*

And therfore he *swalle* for envye.
MS. Cantab. Ff. ii. 38, f. 138.

But he his ye awey ne swerveth
From hire, whiche was nakid alle,
And sche for angir therof *swalle*.
Gower, MS. Soc. Antiq. 134, f. 40.

SWALLOCKY. A term applied to the appearance of clouds in hot weather before a thunderstorm. *East.*

SWALLOP. A heavy lounging walk. *Norf.*

SWALLOW. (1) A hollow in the earth. *North.* Carr has *swallow*, a deep hollow in the ground, in which the rain is swallowed or conveyed off. It is an archaism, occurring under the form *swolowe*, a gulf or abyss, as in the Legende of Dido, 179, "the swolowe of hell." Maundevile, p. 33, mentions "a sweloghe of the gravely see." According to Kennett, "where hollow caverns remain in the earth upon mine works, if the roof or top of such caverns or hole made by such fall is calld a *swallow* and a *swallow pit*." In the Pr. Parv. occurs, "Swelwhe of a water or of a grownde, *vorago*," MS. Harl. 221, f. 167.

Howevere the sayde nowse lye or be edified with his gardeyns, wallis, gutters, *swolous*, lying or beyng upon any partye of the grownde.
Chronicon Johannis de Whethamstede, p. 546.

They schullen seke for to entre into creveys of stoonys, and into *swolowys* of the erthe, fro the dredefull face of oure Lorde.
MS. Cantab. Ff. ii. 38, f. 7

(2) *To swallow an affront*, to take an affront without any apparent retaliation.

SWALLOW-DAY. April the 15th. *Var. dial.*

SWALLOW-PEAR. The service apple.

SWALLOW'S-TAIL. "A swallowes taile in carpenters worke, which is a fastening of two pieces of timber or boards so strongly that they cannot away," Rider's Dictionarie, 1633.

SWALME. Sickness. See *Swame.* Also, to turn sick or ill, as in Ritson, iii. 33.

> That jere litulle shalbe of wyne,
> And *swalme* among fatte swyne.
> *MS. Cantab. Ff. v. 48, f. 77.*

SWALTER.

> Slippes in in the sloppes o-slaute to the girdylle,
> *Swalters* upe swyftly with his swerde drawene.
> *Morte Arthure, MS. Lincoln, f. 94.*

SWALTISH. Hot; sultry.

SWAME. An attack of sickness. In the following passage, the tokens of disease. " Sweame or swame, *subita ægrotatio,*" Rider.

> In whose bloodde bathed he should have been,
> His leprous *swames* to have weshed of clene.
> *Hardyng's Chronicle, f. 49.*

SWAMLING.

> For *swamlyng* of glet that is abowte the lyver,
> and the longus, and the mylte.
> *MS. Med. Rec. xv. Cent.*

SWAMP. Lean, as cattle. *North.*

> Our why is better tidded than this cow,
> Her ewr's but *swampe;* shee's nut for milk I trow.
> *A Yorkshire Dialogue, 1697, p. 36.*

SWAN.

> Teche hyt forthe thorow-owt thys londe,
> Oon tyll othur that thys boke have now *swan.*
> *MS. Cantab. Ff. ii. 38, f. 40.*

SWANE. To soften; to absorb, applied to a swelling. Salop. Antiq. p. 583.

SWANG. (1) A fresh piece of green swarth, lying in a bottom, among arable or barren land; a dool. *North.*

(2) A swamp, or bog. *Yorksh.*

(3) To swing with violence. *East.*

SWANGE. The groin?

> Swappes in with the swerde, that it the *swange* brystedd,
> Bothe the guttes and the gorre gusches owte at ones.
> *Morte Arthure, MS. Lincoln, f. 65.*

SWANGENE. Struck.

> Swerdes *swangene* in two swelterand knyghtes,
> Lyes wyde opyne welterande on walopande stedes.
> *Morte Arthure, MS. Lincoln, f. 76.*

SWANGWAYS. Obliquely; aside. *Norf.*

SWANK. (1) Laboured. *(A.-S.)*

> I *swank* in mi sighing stede,
> I sal wasche bi al nyghtes mi bede.
> *MS. Cott. Vespas. D. vii. f. 3.*

> I *swank* criand, haase ere made.
> Chekes mine for pine I hade.
> *MS. Cott. Vespas. D. vii. f. 46.*

(2) To abate; to shrink; to lessen. *Devon.* " When a great swelling abates, and the skin hangs loose, particularly that of the belly, it is said to swank," MS. Devon Gl.

(3) To strike with a sword ?

> He swounande diede, and on the swarthe lengede,
> Sweltes ewynne swiftly, and *swanke* he no more.
> *Morte Arthure, MS. Lincoln, f. 84.*

(4) A bog. (5) To give way, or sink.

SWANKING. Big; large. *North.*

SWANKUM. To walk to and fro in an idle and careless manner. *Somerset.*

SWANKY. (1) Boggy. *Var. dial.*

(2) Swaggering; strutting. *Wilts.*

(3) The weakest small beer. *West.*

(4) A strong strapping fellow. *North.*

SWANT. Proper; steady. *West.*

SWAN-UPPING. The taking of swans, performed annually by the swan companies, with the Lord Mayor of London at their head, for the purpose of marking them. The king's swans were marked with two *nicks* or notches, whence a double animal was invented, unknown to the Greeks, called *the swan with two necks.* A MS. of swan marks is in the library of the Royal Society, described in Arch. xvi. Upping the swans was formerly a favorite amusement, and the modern term *swan-hopping* is merely a corruption from it. The struggle of the swans when caught by their pursuers, and the duckings which the latter received in the contest, made this diversion very popular. See Kempe's Loseley Manuscripts, p. 309.

SWAP. (1) To barter; to exchange. *Var. dial.*

(2) To cut wheat in a peculiar way, to chop, not to reap it. *Sussex.*

(3) Clean; quickly; smartly. *West.*

(4) A blow. Also, to strike. In some counties, a fall is called a swap.

> With *swappes* sore thei hem swong.
> *Cursor Mundi, MS. Coll. Trin. Cantab. f. 118.*

> And on hys body so many *swappys,*
> With blody lyppys y kysse hym here.
> *MS. Cantab. Ff. ii. 38, f. 48.*

> Kastes in his clere schelde and coveres hym full faire,
> *Swappes* of the swerde hande als he by glentis.
> *Morte Arthure, MS. Lincoln, f. 97.*

SWAPE. (1) To place aslant. *North.*

(2) To sweep. *North.* *(A.-S.)*

(3) A long oar used by keelmen. *Newc.*

(4) A fork for spreading manure. *North.*

(5) The handle of a pump. *Norf.* It is also the same as *Sweep* (2).

(6) A bar for hanging kettles over the fire.

SWAPER. The same as *Sway* (1).

SWAPPER. A great falsehood. *Kent.*

SWAPPING. Large; huge; strong. *West.*

> A filch-man in his hande, a *swapping* ale dagger at his back, containing by estimation some two or three pounds of yron in the hyltes and chape.
> *A Countercuffe given to Martin Junior, 1589.*

SWAPSON. A slattern. *Warw.*

SWARBLE. The same as *Swarm* (1).

SWARD. Skin; covering. *(A.-S.)* *Swardpork,* bacon cured in large flitches. " Swarde or sworde of flesch, *coriana,*" Pr. Parv.

SWARE. (1) Sure; true. Perhaps *swete of sware,* as in l. 441, i. e. swere or neck.

> He seyde, Syrs, wendyth ovyr the see,
> And bydd the emperowre of Rome sende me
> Hys doghtur swete and *sware.*
> *Le Bone Florence of Rome, 90.*

(2) Square. *Prompt. Parv.*

(3) Painful. Conybeare's Octavian, p. 58.

(4) To answer. *Gawayne.*

SWARF. (1) The grit worn away from the grinding-stones used in grinding cutlery wet. *York.* Also called *wheel-swarf.*

(2) To swoon; to faint. *North.*

SWARFF-MONEY. " The swarff-money is one peny half-peny; it must be paid before the rising of the sun; the party most go thrice about the cross, and lay the swarff-money, and then take witness, and lay it in the hole; and when ye have so done, look well that your witness do not deceive you, for if it be not paid, ye give a great forfeiture, **xxx. s.** and a white bull," Blount.

SWARFFY. Swarthy; tawny. *Lanc.*

SWARM. (1) To climb the trunk of a tree, in which there are no side branches for one to rest the hands and feet on. *North.*

> He swarmed up into a tree,
> Whyle eyther of them might other se.
> *Syr Isenbras*, 351.

(2) The motion of the limbs in ascending the boll of a tree in contradistinction of climbing amongst the branches. *North.*

(3) To beat; to thrash. *South.*

(4) A large number of people. *Swarmen*, a great number, Tim Bobbin Gl.

> What furies guided this misguided swarms
> To bend their force against unthoughted harme?
> *Rowland's Betraying of Christ*, 1598, sig. B. iii.

SWART. (1) Black; dark; swarthy. Also, to blacken, as by burning, &c. " I swart, as a thyng dothe whan it begynneth to burne," Palsgrave, verb. f. 381.

> Foaming about the chaps like some wilde boore,
> As swart and tawnie as an India Moore.
> *Letting of Humours Blood in the Head-Vaine*, 1600.

(2) The same as *Sweard*, q. v.

> Howbeit, where the rocks and quarrie grounds are, I take the swart of the earth to be so thin, that no tree of anie greatnesse, other than shrubs and bushes, is able to grow.
> *Harrison's Description of England*, p. 212.

SWARTER. Darker; more black.

> His nek is greter than a bole,
> His bodi is swarter than ani cole.
> *Gy of Warwike*, p. 260.

SWARTH. (1) Black? (*A.-S.*)

> Watir to sle swarth lice. Take mogwort, wormewode, saveyn, the water of theis sleth the vermyn in mans eynlyddes, and in his chare benethe the navelle. *MS. Sloane* 7, f. 51.

(2) Sward; grass; any outward covering, as the rind of bacon. (*A.-S.*) " On the swarthe lengede," Morte Arthure, MS. f. 84.

(3) Grose defines *swarth*, " grass just cut to be made up into hay." A *swarth* is a row of cut grass. An anonymous correspondent has furnished me with the following observations on a passage hitherto unintelligible:

" In Mr. Wright's first volume of the Biographia Britannica Literaria (Anglo-Saxon period), there is a riddle, the seventh line of which is thus printed:

> corfen sworfen : cut and ——

leaving the second word untranslated. It strikes me that *sworfen* is the same word which is now used in Kent and elsewhere as *swarthed*, or *laid in swarth*. It is the word required in that particular part of the description to carry out the process regularly, *cut and swarthed, turned and dried, bound and twisted*, &c."

SWART-RUTTER. " A reister or swart-rutter, a German horseman," Cotgrave.

> Good thriftie men, they drawe out a dinner with

sallets, like a swart-rutter's sute, and make Madona Nature their best caterer.
> *Nash's Pierce Pennilesse*, .591.

> Next five swartrutters strangely apparelled with great hose down to the small of their legs, with strange caps agreeable, bearing on their necks long swords. *Wood's Bowmans Glory*, 1682, p. 45.

SWARVE. (1) To climb.

> Then Gordon swarved the maine-mast tree,
> He swarved it with might and maine;
> But Horseley with a bearing arrowe,
> Stroke the Gordon through the braine.
> *Percy's Reliques*, p. 136.

(2) To swerve. Morte d'Arthur, ii. 225.

> And doth hartily confesse that whosoever swerves from this patterne swarves from honesty, though hee be deepely learned.
> *Stephens' Essayes and Characters*, 1615, p. 198.

(3) To fill up; to be choked up with sediment, as the channel of a river. *South.*

SWARY. Useless; worthless. *North.*

SWASH. (1) " To fence, to swash with swords, to swagger," Florio, p. 127. " To swash, *clango, gladiis concrepo*," Coles. Forby has *swash*, to affect valour, to vapour, or swagger; but these are secondary meanings.

(2) A roaring blade; a swaggerer.

> Or score out husbands in the charcoal ashes,
> With country knights, not roaring city swashes.
> *Ovid de Arte Amandi*, &c. 1677, p. 141.

(3) A torrent of water. " A great swash of water, *magnus aquarum torrens*," Coles. The verb is still in use, to spill or splash water about.

(4) Refuse; hog-wash. *Devon.*

(5) Soft; quashy. *North.*

SWASH-BUCKET. The common receptacle of the washings of the scullery. *Devon.* A mean slatternly woman is so called. " Swash-bucket, a careless hussy that carries her bucket so that the milk or pigs wash and such like is always flapping or flashing over," MS. Devon Glossary.

SWASH-BUCKLER. Literally, one who makes a clattering noise by swashing his sword against his buckler. Hence, a swaggering ruffian, one with more show of bravery than real courage. " A bravo, a swash-buckler, one that for mony and good cheere will follow any man to defend him and fight for him, but if any danger come, he runs away the first and leaves him in the lurch," Florio, p. 74. Cotgrave translates *bravache*, " a roister, cutter, swaggerer, *swash buckler*, one thats ever vaunting of his owne valour."

> Whereby a man maie see how manie bloudie quarels a bralling swash-buckler maie picke out of a bottle of haie, namelie when his braines are forebitten with a bottle of napple ale.
> *Holinshed, Chron. Ireland*, p. 87.

> Illa ipsa, the same; I desire no more than this sheep-hook in my hand to encounter with that swash-buckler. *Heywood's Love's Mistress*, p. 25.

> A drunkard, a whore-hunter, a gamer, a swash-buckler, a ruffian to waste his money in proud apparel. *Pilkington's Works*, p. 151.

SWASHING. Slashing; dashing. *Shak.*

SWASHWAY. A deep swampy place in large sands in the sea. *Var. dial.*

SWASHY. (1) Swaggering. *East.*

(2) Watery, as vegetables are. *North.*

SWASIONS. Persuasions.

Made at his commyng into your notable presence at Wyndsore, all the *swasions* and colour, all mocions in the moste apparaunt wise that he could, to induce your highnes to your agrement.

Hall, Henry VII. f. 62.

SWASSING. Dashing; splashing.

Drench'd with the *swassing* waves and stew'd in sweat,
Scarce able with a cane our boat to set.

Taylor's Workes, 1630, lii. 74.

SWAT. (1) A quantity. *Linc.*

(2)

Of hys hele he nse ne *swat,*
Bot thow telle wo hym bygate.

Wright's Seven Sages, p. 38.

(3) Sweat. Still in use.

(4) A knock, or blow; a fall. *North.*

(5) To throw down forcibly. *North.*

(6) To squat down. *Yorksh.*

(7) To swoon. *Lanc.*

SWATCH. (1) To bind, as to swaddle, &c.

(2) A pattern, or sample; a piece or shred cut off from anything. *North.*

(3) To separate, or cut off. *Yorksh.*

(4) A row of barley, &c.

One sprendeth those bands, so in order to lie,
As barley (in *swatches*) may fill it thereby.

Tusser's Husbandry, p. 185.

SWATCHEL. (1) A fat slattern. *Warw.*

(2) To beat with a swatch or wand. *Kent.*

SWATCHELLED. Dirty; daggled; oppressed from walking or over-exertion. *Warw.*

SWATH. (1) Same as *Swarth* (3).

(2) To tie up corn in sheaves. "Swathed or made into sheaves," Cotgrave in v. *Javelé.*

SWATH-BAUKS. The edges of grass between the semicircular cuttings of the scythe. *Yorksh.* Swath-banks, rows of new-mown grass.

SWATH-BONDS. Swaddling-bands. *Nares.* "Two swathe-bands," Ord. and Reg. p. 127.

About a faint and slender body wear
A flannel *swathband* or warm stomacher.

Ovid de Arte Amandi, &c. 1677, p. 78.

SWATHE. Calm. *North.*

SWATHEL. A strong man. *Gawayne.*

SWATHELE. To swaddle. "Swathele me so that I run a-gasping," Brit. Bibl. i. 345.

SWATHER. To faint. *Somerset.*

SWATHE-RAKING. The operation of hand-raking between the swathes (or mown rows) of barley or oats, to collect on to such swathes the loose stalks or ears scattered in the mowing. From a habit of transposing harsh consonants, the word is sometimes pronounced *swake-rathing* and *rake-swathing. Moor.*

SWATHING-CLOTHES. Swaddling clothes, or bandages in which children were rolled up. *Shak.*

SWATTE. Sweated. (*A.-S.*)

SWATTER. To spill or throw about water, as geese and ducks do in drinking. *Yorksh.* Also, to scatter, to waste.

SWATTLE. (1) To waste away. *North.*

(2) To drink, as ducks do water. *North.* Hence a swattling fellow, or one that always swattles, a tippler.

SWATTOCK. A severe fall. *Norf.*

SWAUR. A swath of grass. *Devon.*

SWAVE. To pass backward and forward. *Cumb.*

SWAY. (1) A switch used by thatchers to bind their work, usually pronounced *swoy* in Suffolk. *East.*

(2) A balance, or lever. *Suffolk.*

(3) To swing. "Let us sway on," let us go on rapidly, Shak. We still use *swing* in a similar sense. "He went swinging on," i. e. at a violent pace; "he went at a swinging pace," &c.

So it happened at the last,
An halfepeny halter made hym fast,
And therin he *swayes.*

The Boke of Mayd Emlyn, p. 26.

(4) To weigh; to lean upon. *North.*

SWAYNE. Noise, or sweven.

Hys wyngges was long and wyght;
To the chyld he toke a flyght,
With an howge *swayne.*

Torrent of Portugal, p. 94.

SWAY-POLE. A long pole fixed at the top of a post as a pivot, by which water is drawn from a well. *Suffolk.* Kennett gives it as a Cheshire word, "a long pole in a pin to draw up coals from the pit, turn'd round by a horse," MS. Lansd. 1033.

SWEAK.

Or in a mystie morning if thou wilt
Make pitfalls for the larke and pheldifare,
Thy prop and *sweake* shall be both overguilt,
With Cyparissus selfe thou shalt compare
For gins and wyles, the oosels to beguile,
Whilst thou under a bush shalt sit and smile.

The Affectionate Shepheard, 1594.

SWEAKING. Squeaking.

The one in a *sweaking* treble, the other in an ale-blowen base. *Kind-Hart's Dreame, 1592.*

SWEAL. The same as *Swale*, q. v.

SWEAME. The same as *Swame*, q. v.

SWEAMISH. Squeamish; modest. *North.*

SWEAR. (1) To swear by. *Shak.*

(2) An oath. See *Swore.*

(3) To spit, said of a cat. *Var. dial.* "The dog swears when he grumbles and snarles," Kennett, MS Lansd. 1033, f. 398.

SWEARD. "Sweard, of some called Swarth, the turf or upper crust of heath ground," Holme, 1688.

SWEARLE. An eye with a peculiar cast.

SWEAT. (1) To beat; to thrash. *East.*

(2) *To sweat a person's purse,* to cause him to spend nearly all his money.

SWEAT-CLOTH. A handkerchief. *North.* "*Sudarium,* a swetyng clothe," MS. Harl. 2270, f. 183.

SWEATING. Violent perspiration was formerly considered a remedy for the *lues venerea.*

Why, sir, I thought it duty to informe you,
That you were better match a ruind bawd,
One ten times cured by *sweating* and the tub.

The Citye Match, 1639, p. 54.

SWEB. To faint; to swoon. *North.*

SWECH. Such. (*A.-S.*)

Many men in this world aftyr here pilgrimage

have left memoriales of *swech* thingis as thei have
herd and seyn. *MS. Bodl. 423, f. 355.*

SWECHT. Force, or violence. *North.*

SWEDDLE. To swell; to puff out. *North.*

SWEDE. A swarth of grass. *North.*

SWEDIRD. Jerked?

Speris to-brast and in peces flowen,
Swerdes *swedyrd* out and laid hem doun.
Roland, MS. Lansd. 388, f. 389.

SWEE. (1) A giddiness in the head. *North.*

(2) Out of the perpendicular. *Northumb.*

SWEEL. (1) A nut made to turn in the centre of
a chair, a swivel. *Northumb.*

(2) A sudden burst of laughter. *North.*

SWEEM. To swoon. *Somerset.*

SWEEMISH. Faint. *Somerset.*

SWEEP. (1) To drink up. *North.*

(2) "A great poste and high is set faste; then
over it cometh a longe beame whiche renneth
on a pynne, so that the one ende havynge
more poyse then the other, causeth the
lyghter ende to ryse; with such beere brewers in London dooe drawe up water; they call
it a *sweepe*," Elyot, ed. 1559.

(3) An instrument used by turners for making
mouldings in wood or metal.

SWEEP-CHIMNEY. A chimney-sweep. *Suff.*

SWEEPLESS. An ignoramus. *Cumb.*

SWEEP-NET. A large fishing-net. "*Esparvier*,
a great sweepe-net for fishing," Cotgrave.

SWEEPS. The arms of a mill. *Kent.*

SWEER. (1) Unwilling. *Northumb.*

(2) Sure; faithful.

Thou art a young man as I,
And seems to be as *sweer.*
Robin Hood, i. 100.

(3) A neck. (*A.-S.*)

That sche aboute hir white *sweere*
It dede, and hing hirselve there.
Gower, MS. Bodl. 294.

SWEET. (1) Perfumed. *Sweet gloves*, &c.

(2) A term of endearment applied to a woman.
Still in use. *Sweet and twenty* was also a
phrase of affection to a girl.

Say, that of all names 'tis a name of woe,
Once a kings name, but now it is not so:
And when all this is done, I know 'twill grieve thee,
And therfore (*sweet*) why should I now beleeve thee?
Drayton's Heroicall Epistles, 1637, p. 177.

In delay there lies no plenty;
Then come kiss me, *sweet-and-twenty.*
Twelfth Night, ii. 3.

SWEET-BAG. A small silk bag filled with
spices, &c. used as a cosmetic.

SWEET-BREASTED. Sweet-voiced.

SWEETFUL. Delightful; full of sweets.

SWEET-HEART. A lover. *Var. dial.* It is
also common as a verb, to court, to woo.

SWEETIES. Sweetmeats. *Var. dial.*

SWEETING. (1) A kind of sweet apple mentioned by Ascham and others, translated by
melimelum in Rider's Dictionarie, 1640. A
bitter sweeting is mentioned in Romeo and
Juliet, ii. 4. "Swetyng an apple, *pomme
doulce*," Palsgrave, 1530.

(2) A term of endearment, still in use according
to Palmer's Devon. Gl. p. 88.

By Jesu, he saide, my *sweeting*,
I have but three shylling,
That is but a lyttle thing,
But if I had more.
The Milner of Abington. n. d.

Launfal beheld that swete wyth,
Alle hys love yn her was lyth,
And keste that swete flour;
And sat adoun her bysyde,
And seyde, *swetyng*, what so betyde,
I am to thyn honure.
Illustrations of Fairy Mythology, p. 12.

SWEET-LIPS. An epicure; a glutton.

SWEET-MART. The badger. *Yorksh.*

SWEETNER. (1) A person who bids at a sale to
raise the price, not intending to purchase.

(2) A guinea-dropper; one who dropped a
guinea, and then pretending to find it when a
respectable person passed by, was liberal
enough to offer him half as a proper compliment for being present at the discovery,
treat him at a public-house, and eventually
fleece him of his money.

Guinea dropping or *sweetning* is a paultry little
cheat that was recommended to the world about
thirty years ago by a memorable gentleman that has
since had the misfortune to be taken off, I mean
hang'd, for a misdemeanour upon the highway.
The Country Gentleman's Vade Mecum, 1699, p. 97.

SWEETNINGS.

If I were to paint Sloth, (as I am not seene in the
sweetnings by Saint John the Evangelist,) I sweare
I would draw it like a stationer that I knowe.
Nash's Pierce Pennilesse, 1592.

SWEETS. The herb sweet-cicely. *North.*

SWEET-SEG. A sweet-smelling, sedge-like
plant. Acorus calamus. *East.*

SWEET-TOOTH. He has got a sweet tooth,
i. e. he is fond of sweet things.

SWEET-WORT. The decoction from malt before that of the hops is extracted. *South.*

SWEETY. Beautiful. "It's a *sweety* fine
morning." *Linc.*

SWEF. A cry to hounds to check them and
prevent their running riot. (*A.-N.*)

SWEFNE. A dream. (*A.-S.*)

His fader he tolde a *swafne* anist that him mette.
MS. Bodl. 652, f. 1.

Within on a ryche bedde rystys a littylle,
And with the swoghe of the see in *swefnyng* he felle.
Morte Arthure, MS. Lincoln, f. 61.

SWEG. To sway, or incline. *Linc.*

SWEGH. A violent motion. (*A.-S.*)

SWEIGH. To swing. See *Sway.*

SWEIGHT. Portion; greatest quantity. *North.*

SWELDERSOME. Very sultry. *East.*

SWELE. (1) To wash. *R. de Brunne.*

(2) A swelling; a tumour.

So long he pleiede with yong man,
A *swele* in his membres cam than.
The Sevyn Sages, 1366.

SWELEWE. To swallow. (*A.-S.*)

For styuche of the mowthe. Ete pillole drie and
cerfoyle, and *swelew* eysel, when thou gost to bedde,
and wasche thi mowthe with venegre.
MS. Med. Rec. xv. Cent.

That morsel *swelowe* thou good spede,
But in thin honde holde the threda.
MS. Lansd. 793, f. 126.

SWELGHE. To swallow. (*A.-S.*)

And helle salle opene than fulle wyde,
And *sweighs* that synfulle company.
Hampole, MS. Bowes, p. 1.

SWELK. The noise caused by the revolving of a barrel churn at the time of the butter separating from the milk. *East.*

SWELKING. Sultry. *Norf.*

SWELL. (1) A fop. *Var. dial.*

(2) To swallow. *Somerset.*

SWELLE. Eager; furious. (*A.-S.*)

Dewkys, erlys and barons also,
That arste were bolde and *swelle.*
MS. Cantab. Ff. ii. 38, f. 93.

SWELLED-NOSE. A person in an ill humour is said to have a *swelled nose. North.*

SWELSH. A quelsh, or fall. *West.*

SWELTE. (1) To die; to faint. (*A.-S.*) *Swelt*, died, fainted, the part. past.

Twys in a swonnyng, *swelte* as cho walde,
He pressed to his palfray in presance of lordes.
Morte Arthure, MS. Lincoln, f. 61.
And riзte as he had saide thir wordez, he *swelt* in
Alexander armes. *MS. Lincoln A. i. 17, f. 21.*
Where my payne for yhowe was maste,
And whare I *sweltte* and y-heelded the gaste.
Hampole, MS. Bowes, p. 154.

(2) To broil with heat. *North.*

The dogged dog daies now with heat doe *swelt*,
And now's the season of th' unseasn'd aire.
Taylor's Workes, ii. 256.
Soft a while, not away so fast, they melt them;
Piper, be hang'd awhile! knave, looke the dauncers
swelt them. *British Bibliographer*, i. 343.

SWELTERED. Very hot; overcome with heat; in a great perspiration. *West.* "Sweltered venom," venom moistened with the animal's sweat, Shak. "Swalterynge or swownynge, *sincopa*," Pr. Parv. MS. Harl. 221, f. 167.

SWELTH. Mud and filth. *Nares.*

SWELTING. To *swelt* rice is to soften or boil it before being baked in a pudding. *Lanc.*

SWELTRY. Overpoweringly sultry.

But as we see the sunne oft times, through over
sweltrie heate,
Changing the weather faire, great stormes and thun-
dercraks doth threat.
Honours Academie, 1610, i. 18.

SWEME. (1) Swimming; giddiness. (*A.-S.*)

Loke at thou come at that tyme,
Other swowne shal i[n] *swems*,
The lady shall i-se. *Degrevant*, 1211.

(2) Sorrow. *Swemeful*, sorrowful.

Whan this was seide, his hert began to melt
For very *swems* of this *swemeful* tale.
Lydgate's Minor Poems, p. 38.

SWENE. (1) Noise.

You wemen of Jerusalem,
Weepe not for me, ney make no *swene*,
But for your owne barne teame
You mon reme tenderlye. *Chester Plays*, ii. 53.

(2) MS. Bodl. 175 reads *swem.*

And nowe that fitte maide I not fleye,
Thinke me never so *swene.*
Chester Plays, i. 189.

SWENGINGE. (1) "Swengynge, *excussio*," Pr. Parv. "Swengyne or schakyne, as mene done clothys and other lyke," ib.

(2) Moving; stirring. *Prompt. Parv.*

SWENSIE. The quinsey in the throat.

SWEPAGE. The crop of hay in a meadow, also called the *sweps* in some parts.

SWEPE. (1) A whip. "Sweype for a top or scoorge, *flagellum*; sweype or swappe, *alapa*," Pr. Parv. MS. Harl. 221, f. 167.

Bio and blody thus am I bett,
Swongen with *sweepys* and alle to-swett.
Towneley Mysteries, p. 227.

(2) A baker's malkin. *Pr. Parv.*

(3) A crop of hay. *Blount*, p. 628.

SWEPERLYE. Swiftly; speedily. (*A.-S.*)

Swyftly with swerdes they swappene there-aftyre,
Swappes doune fulle *sweeperlye* sweltande knyghtes.
Morte Arthure, MS. Lincoln, f. 69.

SWEPING. A whip, or scourge.

Mikel *sweping* over sinful clives,
Hopand in Laverd mercy umgives.
MS. Cott. Vespas. D. vii. f. 20
And ogain me thai fained and come in ane,
Samened on me *swepinges*, and I wist nane.
MS. Cott. Vespas. D. vii. f. 22.

SWEPPENE. Laid?

In swathes *sweeppene* downe, fulle of swete floures;
Thare unbrydilles theis bolde, and baytes theire
horses. *Morte Arthure, MS. Lincoln*, f. 80.

SWEPPLE. Same as *Swipple*, q. v.

SWER. Sure.

Serche and ye shall fynd in every congregacyon
That long to the pope, for they are to me full *swer*,
And wyll be so long as they last and endwer.
Bale's Kynge Johan, p. 8.

SWERD. (1) A sword. (*A.-S.*) "*Ensis*, a swerde; *ensifer*, a swerde berer," MS. Harl. 2257, f. 38.

They schett arows heded with stele,
They faghte with scharpe *swyrdys* wele.
MS. Cantab. Ff. ii. 38, f. 168.

(2) The same as *Sward*, q. v.

SWERE. Dull; heavy. *Durh.*

SWERLE. To twist, or roll about. *North.*

SWERNE. Sworn. (*A.-S.*)

SWERNES. Sourness; sadness.

SWETE. (1) Suit. (2) Sweated. *Gawayne.*

SWETE-HOLLE. A pore in the skin; a sweathole. "*Porus*, a swete holle," Nominale MS. xv. Cent.

SWETELICHE. Sweetly. (*A.-S.*)

Heo schulen i-seon the lavedi
That Jhesu Crist of-kende:
Bi-tweonen hire armes
Swetelichs he wende.
MS. Cott. Calig. A. ix. f. 245.

SWETHENS. Swedes.

Buckling besides in many dang'rous fights,
With Norwaies, *Swethens*, and with Muscovites.
Drayton's Poems, 1637, p. 346.

SWETTER. Sweeter. (*A.-S.*)

SWEVEN. A dream; a slumber. (*A.-S.*)

As he was in sorowe and dud wepe,
Uppon hys bedd he felle on slepe;
He can mete a straunge *sweven.*
MS. Cantab. Ff. ii. 38, f. 171.
Now by my faye, sayd Jollye Robin,
A *sweaven* I had this night;
I dreamt me of two wighty yemen,
That fast with me can fight.
Percy's Reliques, p. 22

SWEVIL. The swingel of a flail.

SWEYE. 1) To fall; to descend.
> Downne he *sweys* fulle swythe, and in a swoune fallys.
>> *Morte Arthure, MS. Lincoln, f. 97.*

(2) To sound. (*A.-S.*)
SWEYN. Noise.
> The tables ther held an hond
> Bituen hem, withouten *sweyn.*
>> *Legend of Pope Gregory, p. 29.*

SWHALOUE. To swallow. MS. Gloss. xv. Cent.

SWICE. " Swyce or swycers pype, *fleuste dale-mant,*" Palsgrave, subst. f. 68.

SWICHE. Such. (*A.-S.*)
> *Swiche* schuld acomber also fele.
>> *Arthour and Merlin, p. 26.*

SWICHEN. The herb groundsel.

SWICK. Den?
> He ys black as any pyck,
> And also felle as a lyon in hys *swyck.*
>> *MS. Cantab. Ff. ii. 38, f. 195.*

SWIDDEN. To sweal, or singe. *North.*

SWIDDER. To doubt; to hesitate. *Yorksh.*

SWIDGE. (1) To smart; to ache. *North.*

(2) A puddle of water. *East.*

SWIER. (1) A squire. Nominale MS.

(2) The neck. See *Swire* (1).

SWIFT. (1) A stupid fellow. *Oxon.*

(2) A wooden revolving frame used in' the North for winding yarn, &c.

(3) A newt. " Swyfte worme, *lesarde,*" Palsgrave, subst. f. 68.
> About A.D. 1686, a boy, lying asleep in a garden, felt something dart down his throat; it killed him: 'tis probable 'twas a little newt. They are exceeding nimble; they call them *swifts* at Newmarket heath.
>> *Aubrey's MS. Wilts, p. 165.*

SWIFTER. Part of the tackling that fastens a load of wood to the waggon. *South.*

SWIG. (1) To drink; to suck. *Var. dial.* In some places, any nice liquor is called *swig.*

(2) To leak out. *Suffolk.*

(3) " A game at cardes called *swig* or new-cut," Florio, p. 580; " to put up the cardes, to swig or deale againe," ib. p. 27. " A sort of play at cards in the North, in which all the game-sters are to be silent, is calld swig," Kennett MS. Lansd. 1033, f. 398.

SWIGGLE. (1) To shake liquor violently. After linen has been washed, it is necessary to move it to and fro in clean water to get the soap out. To this operation this word is applied. " That's right, *swiggle* em right well." *Moor's Suff. MS.*

(2) To drink greedily. *Suffolk.*

SWIGMAN. " A swygman goeth with a ped-lers pack," Frat. of Vacabondes, p. 5.

SWIKE. (1) To deceive; to betray. (*A.-S.*) Also an adjective, deceitful, treacherous; and when the substantive is understood, a deceiver or betrayer.
> Swappede owtte with a swerde that *swykede* hym never,
> Wroghte wayes fulle wyde and wounded knyghttes.
>> *Morte Arthure, MS. Lincoln, f. 72.*
>
> Thanne Godard was askerlike
> Under God the moste *swike*
> That evre in erthe shaped was,
> Withuten on, the wike Judas.
>> *Havelok, 423.*

(2) To stop; to cease. (*A.-S.*)
> Sir Tirri, he seyd, forth thou go,
> Night no day thou *swike* thou no.
>> *Gy of Warwike, p. 298.*

(3) A den, or cave?
> Under that than was a *swyke,*
> That made syr Ywain to myslike.
>> *Ywaine and Gawin, 677.*

SWIKEDOME. Treachery. (*A.-S.*)
> With gyle and *swikedome*
> Thou lettust thi lorde to dethe don.
>> *MS. Cantab. Ff. v. 48, f. 106.*
>
> Of whas mallok his mouth ful is
> Of *swykedome* and of bitternes.
>> *MS. Cott. Vespas. D. vii. f. 3.*

SWIKELE. Deceitful; wicked.
> I-mette wid is soster the *swikele* wimon;
> Judas, thou were wrthe me stende the wid ston,
> For the false prophete that tou bilevest upon.
>> *Reliq. Antiq. i. 144.*
>
> Mony a *swykylle* swayne then to the swerde yode.
>> *MS. Cott. Calig. A. ii. f. 111.*
>
> Menslaers and *swykel,* Laverd, wlate sal,
> And I in mikelbede of thi mercy al.
>> *MS. Cott. Vespas. D. vii. f. 2.*

SWILE. (1) To wash. (*A.-S.*)
> The thridde day shal flowe a flod, that al this world shal hylen;
> Bothe heye ant lowe the fluule shal it *swyle.*
>> *Appendix to W. Mapes, p. 347.*

(2) Hog's-wash. " *Broda,* wash, swile or draffe for swine," Florio, p. 68.

SWILKE. Such. See *Swill.*
> But they no3t are *swylke* als they some.
>> *MS. Harl. 2260, f. 58.*
>
> And thys me made do dedys *swylke,*
> With whych my goost ys ofte unglade.
>> *MS. Cantab. Ff. ii. 38, f. 90.*
>
> A gerfawcon whyte as mylke,
> In alle thys worlde ys non *swylk.*
>> *MS. Cantab. Ff. ii. 38, f. 150.*

SWILKER. To splash about. *North.* To swilker over, i. e. to dash over. *Grose.*

SWILL. (1) Hog's-wash. This meaning of the word is given by Urry, in his MS. Additions to Ray. See *Swile* (2).

(2) A wicker basket of a round or globular form, with open top, in which red herrings and other fish and goods are carried to market for sale. "George Greeinewell, the swill maker,"Chron. Mirab. p. 33.

(3) To drink; to throw a liquid over anything. *Worc.* The first of these senses is common.

(4) To wash hastily; to rince. *Var. dial.* " I swyll, I rynce or clense any maner vessell," Palsgrave, verb. f. 381.

(5) The bladder of a fish.

(6) " A keeler to wash in, standing on three feet," Ray, ed. 1674, p. 47.

(7) A shade. *South.*

SWILL-BOWL. A drunkard. " Swilbolles, *potores bibuli,*" Baret's Alvearie, 1580.

SWILLER. A scullion; one who washed the dishes, &c. " *Lixa,* a swyllere," Nomi-nale MS. xv. Cent.

SWILLET. Growing turf set on fire for ma-nuring the land. *Devon.*

SWILLINGS. Hog's-wash. *Swilling-tub,* a tub for swillings. *Var. dial.*

SWILL-PLOUGH. "*Besot*, a dilling or a swill-plough; the last or yongest child one hath," Cotgrave.

SWILL-TUB. A drunkard; a sot.

SWILTER. To waste away slowly. *West.*

SWIM. To turn giddy. *Var. dial.*

SWIMBING. Swimming.

> Wlthynne the castell is whyte shynyng
> As is the swan when heo is *swymhyng*.
> *MS. Religious Poems,* xv. Cent.

SWIMBUL. Tyrwhitt and some manuscripts read *a romble and a swough.*

> First on the wal was peynted a foreste,
> In which ther dwelled neyther man ne beste,
> With knotty knarry barcyn trees olde
> Of stubbes scharpe and hidious to byholde;
> In which ther ran a *swymbul* in a swough,
> As it were a storme schuld berst every bough.
> *Chaucer's Cant. T.* ed. Wright, 1931.

SWIME. A swoon. (*A.-S.*)

> In tille his logge he hyede that tyme,
> And to the erthe he felle in *swyme*.
> *MS. Lincoln A. L 17, f. 125.*

> Bytwene undrone and pryme,
> Luke thou come at that tyme,
> And ane of us salle ly in *swyme*.
> *MS. Lincoln A. i. 17, f. 135.*

> Tharfore aske hyt be tyme
> For deth cumth now as yn *swyme*.
> *MS. Harl.* 1701,.f. 75.

SWIMER. A hard blow. *Devon.*

SWIMMER. A counterfeit old coin.

SWIMY. Giddy in the head; having a dimness in the sight, which causes things to turn round before you. *Sussex.* "Swymyng in the hed, *bestournement*," Palsgrave, 1530.

SWIN. To cut anything aslant. *North.*

SWINACIE. The quinsey.

SWINCHE. Labour; work.

> In strouge *swynche* nijt and dai to of-swynche here
> mete stronge:
> In such *swynch* and harde lyve hi bilevede, hem
> thojte, longe. *Life of Thomas Beket,* p. 1.

SWINDGE. The same as *Swinge*, q. v.

SWINDLE. A spindle. *North.*

SWINE-BACKED. A term in archery.

> Fourthlye in coulinge or sheeringe, whether highe
> or lowe, whether somewhat *swyne backed* (I must
> use shooters woordes) or sadle backed.
> *Ascham's Tosophilus,* 1571, f. 47.

SWINE-CARSE. The herb knotgrass. *Gerard.*

SWINE-COTE. A pig-sty. *Palsgrave.* It occurs in the Hallamshire Gl. p. 125. *Swine-crue,* Kennett's Latin Glossary, p. 115. "A swin-hull or swine-crue, a hogs-stye," Ray, p. 47.

> At the batell of Brakonwete, ther as the beyre justyd,
> Sym Saer and the *swynkots* thei wer sworne brodur.
> *Reliq. Antiq.* i. 84.

SWINE-DRONKEN. Beastly drunk.

SWINE-PIPE. The redwing. *Pegge.*

SWINE-POX. An ill sore in hogs which spreads abroad, and is a very grievous scab, proceeding sometimes from poverty, at other times from lice in the skin; so that while they have them, they'll never prosper, but will infect one another. *Dict. Rust.*

SWINE-SAME. Hog's-lard. *North.*

SWINE'S-FEATHER. A sort of small spear, about six inches long, like a bayonet, affixed to the top of the musket-rest, and which was sometimes concealed in the staff of the rest, and protruded when touched by a spring. Fairholt, p. 609.

SWINE'S-GRASS. The herb knotgrass. *Gerard.*

SWINE-STY. A pig-sty. *Palsgrave.*

SWINE-THISTLE. The herb sowthistle.

SWINFUL. Sorrowful; sad. *Suffolk.*

SWING. (1) Scope; room. *To have his own swing,* follow his own inclinations. *Var. dial.*

> If they will needs follow their lustes, their plea-
> sures, and their owne *swinge*, yet in the end, he will
> bring them to judgement. *Dent's Pathway,* p. 58.

(2) Sway, or swing.

> And there for a certayne space loytred and lurked
> with Sir Thomas Broughton knyght, whiche in those
> quarters bare great *swynge*, and was there in great
> aucthoritie. *Hall, Henry VII.* f. 5.

(3) To shake; to mix. *Pegge.*

(4) A machine on which a person stretched himself by holding a cross board, and formerly used for strengthening the limbs.

(5) The name given to the leader of ruffians who infested the country some years ago by burning stacks, &c. and which has since become proverbial.

SWING-DEVIL. The swift. *North.*

SWINGE. (1) To beat; to chastise. *North.* "To beat, swinge, lamme, bethwacke," Cotgrave in v. *Dober.*

> An ofte dede him sore *swinge*,
> And wit hondes smerte dinge;
> So that the blod ran of his fleys,
> That tendre was, and swithe neys.
> *Havelok,* 214.

> O, the passion of God! so I shalbe *swinged;*
> So, my bones shalbe bang'd!
> The poredge pot is stolne: what, Lob, I say,
> Come away, and be hangd!
> *Mariage of Witt and Wisdome,* 1579.

(2) To singe. *Var. dial.*

(3) To cut the nettles, &c. from hedges, and make them neat.

> *Swinge* brambles and brakes,
> Get forks and rakes.
> *Tusser's Husbandry,* p. 168.

(4) A leash or couple for hounds. *East.*

SWINGE-BUCKLER. A violent dashing blade.

SWINGEL. (1) That part of the flail which falls on the corn in the straw. *Var. dial.* "Fleyle swyngyl, *tribulum*," Pr. Parv.

(2) To cut weeds down. *East.*

SWINGER. Anything large or heavy.

SWINGING-STICK. A stick used for beating or opening wool or flax. *Lanc.*

SWINGLE. (1) A swing. *West.*

(2) The first operation in dressing flax, i. e. beating it to detach it from the harle or skimps.

(3) "In the wire-works at Tintern in Monmouthshire is a mill, where a wheel moves several engines like little barrles, and to each barrle is fastned a spoke of wood which they call a *swingle*, which is drawn back a good way by the calms or cogs in the axis of the wheel,

and draws back the barrle, which falls to again by its own weight," Kennett MS.

SWINGLE-HAND. "*Excudia*, a swyngelhande," Ortus Vocab. "A swingle-head, *excudia*," Coles. *Excudia*, a sungylle stok; *excudiatorium*, a sungylle hande," Nominale MS. "This is a wooden instrument made like a fauchion, with an hole cut in the top of it to hold it by : it is used for the clearing of hemp and flax from the large broken stalks or shoves by the help of the said swingle-foot which it is hung upon, which said stalks being first broken, bruised, and cut into shivers, by a brake," Holme.

SWINGLE-TREE. The same as *Heel-tree*, the bar that swings at the heels of the horse when drawing a harrow. "These are made of wood, and are fastned by iron hooks, stables, chains, and pinns to the coach-pole, to the which horses are fastned by their harnish when there is more then two to draw the coach," Holme, 1688.

SWING-SWANG. Swinging; drawling. *North.*

SWINJIN. Great; tremendous. "We shall have a *swinjin* frost to-morrow morning."

SWINKE. (1) To labour. (2) Labour. (*A.-S.*) Brockett has *swinked*, oppressed, vexed, fatigued. "One that works hard at any tasque is said to *swink* it away," Kennett MS.

Swynkyng and suetyng he muste tho,
Fore his spendyng was alle go.
    MS. Ashmole 61, f. 3.

Hast thou i-stole mete or drynke,
For thou woldest not therfore swynke,
    MS. Cott. Claud. A. ii. f. 143.

But nowe I swinke and sweate in vaine,
My labour hath no end,
And moping in my study still,
My youthfull yeares I spend.
    Mariage of Witt and Wisdome, 1579.

So bide ich evere mete other drinke,
Her thou lesest al thi swinke. *MS. Digby 86.*

SWINKY. Pliant; flexible. *Devon.*

SWINNEY. Small beer. *Newc.*

SWINNYING. A dizziness in the head, more usually termed a swimming. *North.*

SWINWROTING. A ditch, or furrow? It is the translation of *scrobs* in Nominale MS.

SWINYARD. A keeper of swine.

Porters, carmen, brick-makers, malsters, chimny-sweepers, bearers of dead corps, scavengers, hostlers, ditchers, shippards, dyers of black cloth and sad colours, chandlers, herds-men, or swinyards, coopers, black-smiths, leather-dressers, hat-makers, farmers, plough-men and the like, as collyers, &c.
    Bishop's Marrow of Astrology, p. 36.

SWIPE. (1) To drink off hastily. *Cumb.*

(2) The same as *Swape*, q. v.

SWIPES. Poor weak beer. *Var. dial.*

SWIPINGE.

But lay ther, as an hound,
Apone the bare swypinge grounde.
    MS. Addit. 10036, f. 53.

SWIPPE. To move rapidly. (*A.-S.*)

A gode man dyes to weende to rest
Whare hys lyf salle be althyrbest,
When the sawle fro the body swyppas,
Als saynt Johan says in the Apochalippes.
    Hampole, MS. Bowes, p. 71.

Tharefore thai swyppe thorow purgatory,
Als a fowyle that fleghes smartly.
    Hampole, MS. Ibid. p. 183.

SWIPPER. Nimble; quick. *North.* "Swypyr or delyvyr, *agilis*; swypyr and slydyr as a wey, *labilis*," Pr. Parv. MS. Harl. 221, f. 168.

SWIPPLE. The part of a flail which strikes the corn; the *blade* of a flail, as it were. *Warw.*

SWIPPO. (1) Supple. *Chesh.*

(2) The same as *Swipple*, q. v.

SWIR. To whirl anything about. *Devon.*

SWIRE. (1) The neck. (*A.-S.*)

For sorowe he gan hys handys wryng,
And fyl bakward of hys chayre,
And brak on two hys swyer. *MS. Harl. 1701, f. 34.*

Gye 3yt answeryd wyth grete yre,
I schall not leeve, be my swyre!
    MS. Cantab. Ff. ii. 38, f. 170.

The swyers swyre-bane he swappes in sondyre.
    Morte Arthure, MS. Lincoln, f. 84.

(2) A hollow near the top of a hill.

SWIRK. A jerk; a blow. *Suffolk.*

SWIRL. A whirling wavy motion. *East.*

SWIRREL. A squirrel. *North.*

SWIRT. (1) A squirt. *North.*

(2) To squirt, or splash with water, &c. "Bilagged wit *swirting*," MS. Arund. 220, f. 303.

SWIRTLE. To move about nimbly. *North.*

SWISE. Very. (*A.-S.*)

Tho cam ther to hem a 3unglich man, swyse fair and hende,
Fairere man ne mi3te beo, that oure Loverd hem gan sende.   *Life of St. Brandan, p. 33.*

SWISH. To dash, as water falling. *West.* To go swish, i. e. very quickly.

SWISH-SWASH. Slop.

There is a kind of swish-swash made also in Essex, and diverse other places, with honicombs and water, which the homelie countrie wives, putting some pepper and a little other spice among, call mead, verie good in mine opinion for such as love to be loose-bodied at large, or a little eased of the cough; otherwise it differeth so much from the true metheglin as chalke from cheese.
    Harrison's England, p. 170.

SWISH-TAIL. A pheasant. *Var. dial.* Also, the uncut tail of a horse.

SWISSER. The Swiss.

Leading three thousand must'red men in pay,
Of French, Scots, Alman, Swisser, and the Dutch;
Of native English, fled beyond the sea,
Whose number neere amounted to as much.
    Drayton's Poems, p. 84.

SWITCH. (1) To walk nimbly. *North.*

(2) To cut, as with a switch.

(3) To trim a hedge. *Yorksh.*

SWITCHER. A small switch. *North.*

SWITCHING. Cheating. *Linc.*

SWITE. To cut. *West.*

SWITERF. "More subtyll in craftes and swyterf than ever they were afore," Caxton's Chronicle, Notary's edition, 1515.

SWITHE. (1) Immediately; quickly. (*A.-S.*)

Forthe sche went with sorowe y-nogh,
And tyed hur hors to a bogh,
    Tylle the throwes were alle y-doo.
A feyre sone had sche borne,
When sche herde the chylde crye hur beforn,
Hyt comfortyd hur fulle swythe.
    MS. Cantab. Ff. ii. 38, f. 74.

Thider he wente him anon,
So *suithe* so he miʒtte gon.   *MS. Digby* 86.

Two servauntys Gye can calle,
And bad them hye *swythe* alle.
MS. Cantab. Ff. ii. 38, f. 151.

Tille hur felowes she seide,
To the church go we, I rede,
As *swythe* as we may.
MS. Cantab. Ff. v. 48, f. 45.

For *switheli* drie thai sal als hai,
And als wortes of grenes tite fal sal thai.
MS. Cott. Vespas. D. vii. f. 24.

(2) Very; excessively.   (*A.-S.*)

The kyng seid, Let se that drynke,
I shalle say riʒt that I thynke,
Me thirstis *swyth* sore.
MS. Cantab. Ff. v. 48, f. 49.

(3) To support?   (*A.-S.*)

In over and to the night
Swithed me mine neeres right.
MS. Cott. Vespas. D. vii. f. 8.

SWITHER. (1) To scorch; to burn.   *North.*
(2) To fear.   (3) A fright.   *North.*
(4) To throw down forcibly.   *North.*
(5) A number; a quantity.   *Warw.*
(6) A perspiration.   *Worc.*
(7) To sweal or melt away.   *Linc.*

SWITHIN (ST.)   The notion current, I believe, pretty extensively, that if we have rain on this day, not one of the next forty will be wholly without, is still in full force among us. Nares notices it as an old and often revived superstition; referring to ample illustrations thereof in Pop. Ant., where it is not, however, mentioned that Ben Jonson, in his Every Man out of his Humour, introduces it. In Alban Butler's Lives of the Saints, Swithin is recorded; but nothing is said of the rainy prodigy.   *Moor.*

SWITHINGE.

And als warme als it may be suffrede lay it on the malady, and suffre it to lygge unto the ʒokynge and *sicythynge* be alle passede awaye.
MS. Lincoln A. i. 17, f. 303.

SWITTERED.   Flooded.   *North.*
SWITTLE.   To cut; to hack.   *Wilts.*
SWITZERS.   Swiss. Nares calls them, "hired guards, attendant upon kings." *Switzer's knot*, a fashion of tying the garter. The Switzers were noted for size and fatness. " A swizzers bellie and a drunkards face are no (true) signes of penitentiall grace," Cotgrave.

SWIVE. (1) Futuo.

A! seyde the pye. by Godys wylle,
How thou art *swyved* y schalle telle.
MS. Cantab. Ff. ii. 38, f. 136.

Nor will I *swive* thee though it bee
Our very first nights jollitie.
Nor shall my couch or pallat lye
In common both to thee and I.
Fletcher's Poems, p. 101.

And now ere sary *swywers* brokyne owte of bande,
Thay fille alle fulle this Ynglande, and many other lande.
In everilk a toune ther es many one,
And everilk wyfe wenys hir selfe thar scho hafes one.
MS. Lincoln A. i. 17, f. 149.

And for to be at this fest funerall,
I will have called in generalle

Alle tho that ben very good drynkers,
And eke also alle feoble *swyvers*,
And they also that can lyft a bole. *MS. Rawl.* C. 86.

(2) To cut wheat or beans with a broad hook. *Salop.*
SWIVEL.   " Swivel is that which keepeth a hawk from twisting," Gent. Rec. ii. 63.
SWIVELLY.   Giddy.   *I. of Wight.*
SWIVET.   A deep sleep.   (*A.-S.*)
SWIZZEN.   To singe.   *North.*
SWIZZLE.   Ale and beer mixed.   *I. of Wight.* Also a verb, to drink, or swill.
SWKYR.   Sugar.   Arch. xxx. 413.
SWOB.   Same as *Swab*, q. v.
SWOBBLE.   To swagger in a low manner.
SWOB-FULL.   Brimful.   *East.*
SWOD.   A basket for measuring fish.   *Sussex.*
SWOGHE.   See *Swoughe* and *Swowe*.
SWOGHENED.   Swooned.   *Weber.*
SWOKELLI.   Deceitfully.   (*A.-S.*)

Openand thrugh es throte of tha,
With thair tunges *swokelli* dide thai swa.
MS. Cott. Vespas. D. vii. f. 7.

SWOLE.   To chain a cow in the stall.   *Lanc.*
SWOLK.   To be angry.   *Sussex.*
SWOLL.   For *swill*.   To drench with water; to cleanse by dashing down much water upon a thing.   *Linc.*
SWOLOWE.   The same as *Swallow*, q. v.
SWONGE.   Beat; chastised.
SWONGENE.   Beaten.   (*A.-S.*)

Take *swongene* eyrene in bassyne clene,
And kreme of mylke, that is so schene.
MS. Sloane 1986, p. 85.

SWONKE.   Laboured.   (*A.-S.*)

Thou haste *swonke* so sore to nyght,
That thou haste lorne thy syght.
MS. Cantab. Ff. ii. 38, f. 116.

SWOOP. (1) The sudden descent of a bird of prey upon its victim. All at one swoop, i. e. at one blow or swoop.
(2) To sweep along, as a river. Pegge has it as the pret. of *sweep*.
(3) The stroke or cut of a scythe.
SWOOP-STAKES.   Sweepstakes.   *To cry swoop-stakes*, to call the winning of the stakes.
SWOOTE.   Sweat.   (*A.-S.*)

Off the hete and of the *swoote*
Thei comen, and of grasse that is hote.
MS. Lansd. 793, f. 118.

SWOOTH.   A fright.   *Leic.*
SWOP.   The same as *Swap*, q. v.
SWOPE.   To strike off.

Let me see what ye will doe,
And laye downe selver here.
For the devell *swope* of my swire,
And I doe it without hyre,
Other for soveraigne or sire:
It is not my manere.   *Chester Plays,* ii. 16.
The syxte peyne is gret derkenesse
That is in helle, and nevere shal lesse;
So thik it is men may it grope,
But thei may not away it *swope*.
MS. Addit. 11305, f. 97.

SWORD. (1) The same as *Sward*, q. v.
(2) The sword of a dung-put is an upright bar with holes for a pin, by which the put is set to any pitch for shooting dung.

(3) *On my sword*, formerly a common oath. *Sword and buckler*, martial.

(4) " Sworde for a flaxe wyfe, *guinche*," Palsg.

SWORD-DANCING. There is a very singular custom, called *sword-dancing*, prevalent in many parts of Northumberland, and in the county of Durham, during the Christmas holidays, which seems to be peculiar to the northern part of the kingdom. The sword-dancers are men entirely or chiefly composed of miners or pitmen, and of persons engaged in the various other vocations of a colliery, who, during the week intervening between Christmas and New Year's Day, perambulate the country in parties, consisting of from twelve to twenty, partly in search of money, but much more of adventure and excitement. On these occasions they are habited in a peculiarly gaudy dress, which, with their dancing, principally attracts attention. Instead of their ordinary jackets they wear others, composed of a kind of variegated patchwork, which, with their hats, are profusely decorated with ribands of the gayest hues, prepared and wrought by their sisters or sweethearts, the sword-dancers being usually young and unmarried men. This, with slight individual variations, is the description of dress worn by all the members of a sword-dancing party, with the exception of two conspicuous characters invariably attached to the company, and denominated amongst themselves respectively the *Tommy* (or fool) and the *Bessy*. Those two personages wear the most frightfully grotesque dresses imaginable ; the former being usually clad in the skin of some wild animal, and the latter in petticoats and the costume of an old woman ; and it is the office of those two individuals, who play by far the most important part in sword-dancing excursions, to go round amongst the company which collects to see them dance, and levy contributions in money, each being furnished for this purpose with a huge tin or iron box, which they rattle in the faces of the bystanders, and perform other antics and grimaces to procure subscriptions. A fiddler also is an indispensable *attaché* to a company of sword-dancers ; and it is the business of another of the party to carry about a change of wearing apparel for his comrades, which becomes necessary when they make protracted journeys, as they sometimes do, into the country, going round amongst the towns and hamlets, and farm-steadings, and exhibiting their dance before the inhabitants. This is a peculiar kind of dance, which it would be vain to attempt to describe. It bears some resemblance to an ordinary quadrille dance, with this difference, that the sword-dancers are each furnished with long steel wands, which they call swords, and which they employ with a very peculiar and beautiful effect during the dance. The dance is sometimes accompanied with a song, and a fragment of dramatic action. The fiddler accom-

panies the song in unison with the voice, repeating at the end of each stanza the latter part of the air, forming an interlude between the verses ; during which the characters are introduced by the singer, make their bow and join the circle.

1. The first that I call in he is a squire's son ;
He's like to lose his love because he is too young.
2. Altho' he be too young, he has money for to rove
And he'll freely spénd it all before he'll lose his love.
3. The next that I call in, he is a sailor bold,
He came to poverty by the lending of his gold.
4. The next that I call in, he is a tailor fine,
What think you of his work ? he made this coat of mine.
5. The next that I call in, he is a keelman grand,
He goes both fore and aft, with his long sett in his hand.
6. Alas ! our actor's dead, and on the ground he's laid,
Some of us must suffer for't, young man, I'm sore afraid.
7. I'm sure 'twas none of me, I'm clear of the crime,
'Twas him that follows me, that drew his sword so fine.
8. I'm sure 'twas none of me, I'm clear of the fact,
'Twas him that follows me that did the bloody act.
9. Then cheer up, my bonny lads, and be of courage bold,
We'll take him to the church, and bury him in the mould.
10. Cox-Green's a pretty place, where water washes clean,
And Painshaw's on a hill, where we have merry been.
11. You've seen them all call'd in, you've seen them all go round,
Wait but a little while, some pastime shall be found.
12. Then, fiddler, change the tune, play us a merry jig,
Before I will be beat, I'll pawn both hat and wig.

In explanation of the above, it should be stated, that after the fifth verse other characters are generally introduced in a similar manner, and then the sword-dance takes place, in which one of them is killed. After the ninth verse the doctor is introduced, and a dialogue of some length takes place, which terminates in his restoring the dead man to life.

A writer in the Gent. Mag. for May, 1811, tells us that in the North Riding of Yorkshire the sword-dance is performed from St. Stephen's Day till New Year's Day. The dancers usually consist of six youths, dressed in white, with ribands, attended by a fiddler, a youth with the name of Bessy, and also by one who personates a doctor. They travel from village to village. One of the six youths acts the part of King in a kind of farce, which consists chiefly of singing and dancing, when the Bessy interferes while they are making a hexagon with their swords, and is killed. *Brand's Popular Antiquities*, i. 283.

SWORDER. A game cock that wounds its antagonist much.

SWORD-PLAYER. A juggler with swords. " *Gladiator*, a swerdplaer," Nominale MS.

SWORD-SLIPER. See *Slip* (3). The term appears to be now applied to a sword-cutler. " *Sword-sleiper*, a dresser or maker of swords ; so used in the North of England ; and a cutler with them deals onely in knives," Blount, p. 628, ed. 1681.

SWORE. An oath. (*A.-S.*)

Hast thou geten wyth fals *swore*,
Any thynge lasse or more.
MS. Cott. Claud. A. ii. f. 139.

SWORED. The neck. (*A.-S.*)
Nicolas he smot in the *swored*,
That he laide his hed in wed.
Kyng Alisaunder, 975.

SWOREN. Swore, i. e. swore to kill him.
All they chacyd me at the laste,
And my dethe they *sworen* faste.
MS. Cantab. Ff. ii. 38, f. 175.

SWORLE. To snarl, as a dog. *Sussex.*

SWORN-BROTHERS. Brothers in arms, bound by the ancient laws of chivalry. Afterwards any persons very intimate were so called. " Sworn brother and brethren in iniquity," old proverb.

SWOSE.
Ther he saw stedus and stockfesche pryckyng *swose* in the watur. Ther he saw hennus and heryngus that huntod aftur hartus in heggys. Ther hee see elys rostyng larkus. *Reliq. Antiq.* i. 83.

SWOSH. A sash. *Suffolk.*

SWOST.
Me wule swopen thin hus,
And ut mid the *swost*.
MS. Cott. Calig. A. ix.

SWOT. To throw. *Warw.*

SWOTE. Sweat. See *Swoote*.

SWOTHE.
But sche hed he deffaute off *swothe*
Towardys love, and that was rowthe.
Gower, MS. Cantab. Ff. i. 6, f. 5.

SWOTTLING. Fat and greasy. *East.*

SWOUGHE. (1) Swoon ; swooning. (*A.-S.*)
Thowe ther were no *swoghe*.
MS. Cantab. Ff. ii. 38, f. 94.
There he loste bothe mayne and myght,
And ovyr the tombe he felle in *swoughe*.
MS. Harl. 2252, f. 99.
With that worde hys body can bowe,
Downe he felle there in a *swowe*.
MS. Cantab. Ff. ii. 38, f. 148.

(2) Sound ; noise. (*A.-S.*)
A swerde lenghe within the swarthe he swappes at ones,
That nere swounes the kyng for *swoughe* of his dynttes.
Morte Arthure, MS. Lincoln, f. 65.
Into the foreste forthe he droghe,
And of the see he herde a *swoghe*.
MS. Lincoln A. i. 17, f. 140.

(3) A splinter or chip ?
Sir Eglamour his swerde owt drowthe,
And in his eghne it keste a *swoghe*,
And blynddid hym that tyde.
MS. Lincoln A. i. 17, f. 140.

(4) A sough, bog, or mire.
At a chapell with riche lyghte,
In a foreste by a *swoughe*. *MS. Harl.* 2252, f. 98.

(5) Quiet.

SWOUND. To swoon. Also, a swoon. Still in common use in East Anglia.
For grete yoye amonge them all
In a *swownde* sche dud downe falle.
MS. Cantab. Ff. ii. 38, f. 186.
Still in a *swound*, my heart revives and faints,
'Twixt hopes, despaires, 'twixt smiles and deep complaints.

As these sad accents sort in my desires,
Smooth calmes, rough stormes, sharp frosts, and raging fires,
Put on with boldnesse, and put backe with feares,
For oft thy troubles doe extort my teares.
Drayton's Heroicall Epistles, 1637, p. 174.

SWOWE. (1) To faint ; to swoon. (*A.-S.*) Also, a swoon. See *Swoughe* (1).

(2) A noise.
He come to hym wyth a *swowe*,
Hys gode stede undur hym he slowe.
MS. Cantab. Ff. ii. 38, f. 65.

(3) To make a noise, as water does in rushing down a precipice. Also, to foam or boil up. " Swowyne or sowndyn, as newe ale and other lycure," MS. Harl. 221, f. 177.
That whate *swowynges* of watyr and syngynges of byrdes,
It myghte salve hyme of sore that sounde was nevere.
Morte Arthure, MS. Lincoln, f. 63.

SWREDDEZ. Swords.
And alle done of dawes with dynttes of *swreddez*,
For thare es noghte bot dede thare the dragone es raisede.
Morte Arthure, MS. Lincoln, f. 75.

SWUGGLE. To shake liquids. *East.*

SWUKEN. Deceived; betrayed.
Unto the than cried I,
Whil that *swuken* es mi hert.
MS. Cott. Vespas. D. vii. f. 41.

SWULLOCK. To broil with heat. *East.*

SWUNNED. Swooned.
The duk lay on the ground,
In hert swyftly he *swunned*.
MS. Lincoln A. i. 17, f. 135.

SWUPPLE. The same as *Swipple*, q. v.

SWURLT. Whirled. *Cumb.*

SWY. The herb glasswort.

SYE. Saw. (*A.-S.*)
Forthe they went be day lyghte,
Tylle hyt drewe to the nyghte :
Londe they *sye* at the laste,
Thedurward they drewe faste.
MS. Cantab. Ff. ii. 38, f. 150.

SYER. Sire ; father.
And lokkethe hym in hir herte hoote as fier,
And seethe the olde, hir colde and cowherand *syer*.
Lydgate's Minor Poems, p. 35.

SYGH. An error for *Syth* ?
And sayd to the duke, my lord, *sygh* by Gods hygh provision and your incomparable wysedome and pollicie, this noble conjunction is fyrst moved.
Hall, Richard III. f. 12.

SYLES. The principal rafters of a house or building. *North.*

SYLLABE. A syllable. *Jonson.*

SYNGE. To sin. A provincial form. More usually, to sing. " *Frigilla*, a brid that *synget* for cold weder," MS. Harl. 2181, f. 46.
Thow mytte *synge* als sore in thoght
As thou that dede hadest i-wroght.
MS. Cott. Claud. A. ii. f. 139.

SYPIRS. Cloth of Cyprus.
The stowt dedis of many a knyght
With gold of *Sypirs* was dight.
MS. Lincoln A. i. 17, f. 176.

TAB   844   TAB

T (1) *Right to a T.* is a very common expression, when anything is perfectly right.

(2) Beards cut in the form of a T are often alluded to by our early writers.

TA. (1) It. *Ta dew*, it does. *East.*

(2) To take. (*A.-S.*)

> The sowdane sayse he wille her *ta ;*
> The lady wille hir-selfe sla,
> Are he that es hir maste fa
> Solde wedde hir to wyfe.   *Perceval*, 996.

TAA. (1) A toe. *North.*

> And ylke a *toa* and fynger of hand
> War a rote fro that tre growand.
>   *Hampole, MS. Bowes*, p. 63.

(2) The one.

> And whenne he was over, the lordes of Perse went
> appone the yas so grete a multitude that thay
> coverde the yss fra the *taa* banke to the tother, and
> that a grete brede, and thane onane the yss brake.
>   *MS. Lincoln* A. i. 17, f. 19.

TAANT. Tall, or too high for its breadth, or bigness ; a *Taant* mast, house, &c. *Kent.*

TAAS. Wood split thin to make baskets with. *Cumb.*

TAB. (1) The latchet of a shoe. *North.*

(2) The tag, or end of a lace. *East.*

(3) Children's hanging sleeves. *East.*

TABARD. A short coat, or mantle. " *Colobium*, a tabard," Nominale MS. Strutt describes it, ii. 29, " a species of mantle which covered the front of the body and the back, but was open at the sides from the shoulders downwards ; in the early representations of the tabard, it appears to have been of equal length before and behind, and reached a little lower than the loins." According to Nares, the name of *tabarder* is still preserved in Queen's College, Oxford, for scholars whose original dress was a tabard. " Tabard, a garment, *manteau*," Palsgrave. Verstegan says in his time, the term was confined to a herald's coat.

> Quat wylt thu ȝeve, so Cryst the save !
> And tak the qwych thu wylt have.
> The man seyde, so mote 1 the !
> A peny xal I ȝevyn the.
> He seyde, Nay, withoutyn lak,
> No lece than the *tabard* on thi bak.
>   *Reliq. Antiq.* i. 62.

TABBER.

> *Tabberys* gloson eny whare,
> And gode feyth comys all byhynde ;
> Ho shall be levyd the se the wyll spare ?
> For now the bysom ledys the bleynde.
>   *Reliq. Antiq.* ii. 240.

TABBY. A kind of cloth.

TABERING. Restless in illness. *Somerset.*

TABERN. A cellar. *North.* See Ray's English Words, 1674, p. 48. " *Taberna*, a tabyrn," a tavern or inn, Nominale MS. Hence *taberner*, a tavern-keeper. " *Tabernarius*, a taberner," Nominale MS. A person who played the tabour was also called a taberner.

TABERNACLES. Ornamental niches.

> With *tabernacles* was the halle a-bouȝte,
> With pynnacles of golde sterne and stoute.
>   *Syre Gawene and the Carle of Carelyle*, 610.

TABINE. A kind of silk. In a list of female apparel in the Egerton Papers, p. 252, mention is made of " *tabines* brauncht or wrought with sylver or gold."

TABLE. (1) To go to the table, i. e. to receive the Holy Communion. *Var. dial*

(2) In palmistry, a space between certain lines on the skin within the hand. According to our first extract, the table is a line reaching from the bottom of the little finger to the bottom of the first finger. It is incorrectly explained the " palm of the hand" in Middleton, iv. 438 ; but the term was certainly variously applied.

> Hit ys to know that the lyne that goth about the
> thombe ys cleped tho lyne of lyfe or of the hert.
> The lyne that ys betwene the medylle of the pawme
> that ys betwene the thombe and the next fynger, is
> cleped *media naturalis*. The lyne that begynnyth
> under the litille fynger and streccheth toward the
> rote of the fynger next the thombe ys cleped *men-*
> *salis*, that is, the *table ;* it ys sothely the lyne which
> is cleped the nether triangle, which is sylden
> founde, and it begynneth fro *mensali*, strecchyng
> ryȝt throw the pawme tille to the wrist. *Lina*
> *recepta* ys he that is withyn the ende of the honde,
> appon the joynt of the hond that is betwene the
> boone of the arme or of the hond. *Mons pollicis* is
> fro the lyne of the hert tille to the rote of the
> wombe, and strecchethe itselfe to the wryste. *Mons*
> *manus* or the tabulle begynnyth fro *mensali* to the
> wryste.   *Treatise on Palmistry*, MS. xv. Cent.

> Other lines also may be divided into equal sections, as the table line, the natural line, the quadrangle and triangle, which are all to be parted into equal portions, and according to proportion shall shew the time and age of life in which every accident shall happen, which the characters shall signifie, in their several natures. This space is called the *table* of the hand, which hath on the one side the mensal line, on the other the middle natural line.   *Sanders' Chiromancy*, p. 87.

(3) A tablet, or table-book ; a record of things to be remembered. *Shak.*

(4) To board ; to live at the table of another. See Autobiography of Joseph Lister, p. 48.

> All supper while, if they *table* together, he
> peereth and prieth into the platters to picke out
> dainty morsels to content her maw.
>   *The Man in the Moone*, 1609.

(5) A picture. *Shak.*

(6) In architecture, a horizontal moulding, ornamenting the face of a wall, &c.

TABLE-BOARD. A table. *Cornw.*

TABLE-BOOK. A memorandum-book ; a book with leaves of wood, slate, vellum, or asses skin, &c., for the purpose of recording observations and memoranda. It was sometimes accompanied with a calendar, &c. ; and was used on all occasions, at theatres, sermons, &c. " A reproofe or a jeer out of your table-book notes," Nabbes' Bride, 1640, sig. G. ii. A table-book of wood is in the possession of Mr. J. H. Hearn, of Newport, Isle of Wight, and is described in the Journal of the British Archæological Association, ii. 193, but very few seem to have been preserved.

> His *table-bookes* be a chiefe adjunct, and the most
> significant embleme of his owne quallity that man
> may beare about him : for the wiping out of olde

notes give way to new, and he likewise, to try a new disposition, will finally forsake an ancient friends love, because hee consists of new enterprises.
Stephens' Essayes, 1615, p. 218.

TABLE-DORMAUNT. "Tabylle dormond, *assidella, tabula fixa, stapodium*," MS. Dict. C. 1500. See *Dormant.*

TABLE-LINE. See *Table* (2).

When the *table-line* is crooked, and falls between the middle and fore finger, it signifies effusion of blood, as I said before.
Sanders' Chiromancy, p. 75.

TABLE-MAN. "A tabylle mane, *status, timpanum*," MS. Dict. c. 1500.

TABLE-MEN. Men used at the game of tables. Metaphorically, dice-players.

And knowing that your most selected gallants are the onelye *table-men* that are plaid withal at ordinaries, into an ordinary did he most gentleman-like convay himselfe in state.
Dekker's Lanthorne and Candle-Light, 1620, sig. D. iv.

TABLER. One who keeps boarders, one who *tables* people. See *Table* (4). Also, the person who tables, a boarder. "*Commensale*, a fellow border or tabler," Florio, p. 111. "*Convictor*, a tabler, boarder," Coles.

TABLERE. The game of tables.

Hauntyst taverne, or were to any pere
To pley at the ches or at the *tablere.*
MS. Harl. 1701, f. 7.

TABLES. The game of backgammon. It was anciently played in different ways, and the term appears to have been applied to any game played with the table and dice. Strutt has given a fac-simile of a backgammon-board from a MS. of the 14th century, which differs little from the form now used. See Sports and Pastimes, p. 321. "*Alea*, table," MS. Lansd. 560, f. 45.

Go we now to chaumbur same,
On some maner to make us game :
To the chesses or to the *tabels,*
Or ellys to speke of fabels.
MS. Cantab. Ff. ii. 38, f. 166.

That es, to play at *tablys* or at dyce,
Offe the wilke comes neghen manere of vice.
MS. Harl. 2260, f. 60.

An honest vicker and a kind consort
That to the ale-house friendly would resort,
To have a game at *tables* now and than,
Or drinke his pot as soone as any man.
Letting of Humours Blood in the Head-Vaine, 1600.

TABLET. Is explained in Baret's Alvearie, fol. 1580, an "ornament of gold."

TABN. Explained by Polwhele, a bit of bread and butter. *Cornw.*

TABOURE. (1) To play on the tabour. (*A.-N.*)

(2) "Tabowre for fowlares, *terrificium*," Pr. Parv. MS. Harl. 221, f. 177.

TABOURET. A pin-case. Also, a little low stool for a child to sit on. (*Fr.*)

TABOURINE. A kind of drum. (*Fr.*)

TACES. The skirts or coverings to the pockets. See Meyrick, iii. 13.

TACHE. (1) A spot, or blemish. (*Fr.*)

(2) A quality, or disposition ; a trick ; enterprise ; boldness of design. (*A.-N.*)

For south this harde I hym saye,
That he woulde rise the thirde daye ;
Nowe suerlye and he so maye,
He hath a wounderous *tache.*
Chester Plays, ii. 87.

And to his fadris maneris enclyne,
And wikkid *tacchis* and vices eschewe.
Occleve, MS. Soc. Antiq 134, f. 279.

It is a *tacche* of a devouryng hounde
To resseyve superfluyté and do excesse.
MS. Cantab. Ff. i. 6, f. 157.

(3) A clasp. Also, to clasp ; to tie. " I tache a gowne or a typpet with a tache, *je agraffe*," Palsgrave. "*Spinter*, a tache," MS. Arundel 249, f. 88.

Wylt thou have a buckle of golde or a golden pynne, suche as in olde tyme women used to *fasten* their upper garment with on the left shoulder : Stephanus calleth it a *tache* or a claspe.
Palsgrave's Acolastus, 1540.

(4) To take a thief.

(5) The piece which covered the pocket, and therefore the belly. Meyrick, ii. 251.

(6) A rest used in drilling holes. *Yorksh.*

TACHEMENTEZ. Attachments ?

I sif the for thy thysandes Tolouse the riche,
The tolle and the *tachementes*, tavernes and other.
Morte Arthure, MS. Lincoln, f. 70.

TACHING-END. The waxed thread, armed with a bristle at the end, used by shoemakers. *North.*

TACK. (1) A smack, or peculiar flavour. Drayton uses the term, and it is still in common use.

He told me that three-score pound of cherries was but a kind of washing meate, and that there was no *tacke* in them, for hee had tride it at one time.
Taylor's Workes, 1630, i. 145.

(2) A slight blow. Also, to clap with the hands, to slap. *West.*

(3) A trick at cards. *Suffolk.*

(4) To attack. *Var. dial.*

(5) The handle of a scythe. *East.*

(6) A shelf. A kind of shelf made of crossed bars of wood suspended from the ceiling, on which to put bacon, &c.

(7) To hire pasturage for cattle. *Heref.*

(8) A lease. *North.*

(9) Timber at the bottom of a river.

(10) Bad malt liquor. *North.* In some places it is applied to eatables of bad quality.

(11) Hold ; confidence ; reliance. *Chesh.*

(12) Substance ; solidity ; spoken of the food of cattle and other stock. *Norf.*

(13) A hook, or clasp. Also, to fasten to anything. "I tacke a thyng, I make it faste to a wall or suche lyke," Palsgrave. A wooden peg for hanging dresses on is sometimes called a tack.

(14) A path, or causeway. *Sussex.*

TACKELLS. "Tackells are small roapes which runne in three partes, havinge either a pendant with a block to it or a runner, and at the other end a blocke or hoke to cache houlde and heave in goodes into the shipp," MS. Harl. 6268.

TACKER. (1) The same as *Taching-end*, q. v

(2) A person who dresses cloth.

(3) A great falsehood. *Devon.*

TACKES. To mend apparel. *Essex.*

TACKET. (1) The penis. *North.*

(2) A small nail, or tack. *North.* " A takett, *claviculus*," MS. Dict. c. 1500.

TACKLE. (1) To attack. *Var. dial.*

(2) To stick to one's tackle, i. e. to be firm, not to give way in the least. " To stand to our tackling," Harrison, p. 115.

(3) Food; working implements; machinery of any kind, or of the human frame. *Var. dial.* " Tacle or wepene, *armamentum*," Pr. Parv.

(4) A horse's harness. *Var. dial.*

TACKLING. See *Tackle* (2).

TACKS. " Tacks are great ropes havinge a wale knott at one end, which is seased into the clewe of the saile, and so reeved first through the chestrees, and then comes in a hole of the shipps side," MS. Harl. 6268.

TAD. Excrement. *East.*

TADAGO-PIE. A pie made of abortive pigs from a sow that has miscarried. *Cornw.*

TADDE. A toad. Brockett has *Taed.*

> That myn herte anon ne barst,
> Whon ich was from my mooder take;
> Or ben into a put i-cast,
> Mid a *tadde* or mid a snake.
> *Appendix to W. Mapes,* p. 344.

TADE. To take. Salop. Antiq. p. 587.

TADE-PITS. Certain pits upon some of the downs of Devon where toads live dry.

TADOUS. Cross; peevish; fretful; tiresome. Applied chiefly to children. *Var. dial.*

TAFFATY-TARTS. " Are made like little pasties, round, square, or long, the paste being rolled thin, and apples in lays, strewed with sugar, fennel seeds, and limon peel cut small; then iced in the baking," Holme, Academy of Armory, 1688.

TAFFETY. (1) Dainty; nice. *West.*

(2) Taffeta, a sort of thin silk.

> When first I saw them, they appeared rash,
> And now their promises are worse then trash;
> No *taffaty* more changeable then they,
> In nothing constant but no debts to pay.
> *Taylor's Workes,* 1630, ii. 40.

TAFFLED. Entangled. *Dorset.*

TAFFY. A common coarse sweetmeat, made with treacle thickened by boiling. Almonds are often stuck into it. *Var. dial.*

TAG. (1) The common people; the rabble.

(2) A sheep of the first year. *South.*

(3) To follow closely after. *East.*

(4) To cut off the dirty locks of wool around the tail of a sheep. *South.*

(5) To understand, or comprehend.

TAGED. According to Markham, " a sheep is said to be *tag'd* or belt, when by a continual squirt running out of his ordure, he berayeth his tail in such wise that through the heat of the dung it scaldeth and breedeth the scab therein," Husbandry, ed. 1676, p. 91.

TAGGELT. A loose character. *Cumb.*

TAGILLE. To entice?

> Consaile es doynge aweye of worldes reches, and

of alle delytes of alle thynges that mane may be *tagyld* with in thoghte or dede.
> *MS. Lincoln* A. i. 17, f. 196.

> That he may hafe ryste in Goddes lufe withowttene *tagillynge* of other thynges. *MS. Ibid.* f. 196.

TAG-LOCK. An entangled lock. *Nares.*

TAGSTER. A scold; a virago. *Devon.*

TAG-WOOL. The long wool of tags or hogs not shorn while they were lambs. *Glouc.*

TAHMY. Stringy, untwisted, as tow. *Cumb.*

TAHT. (1) Given. (2) Taught. *(A.-S.)*

TAIGH. To take. *Chesh.*

TAIGLE. To linger about a place. *North.*

TAIL. (1) To turn top over tail, i. e. the head over the tail, completely over.

> Soche a strokk he gaf hym theu,
> That the dewke bothe hors and man
> Turned toppe ovyr *tayle.*
> *MS. Cantab.* Ff. ii. 38, f. 76.

(2) Slaughter. See Weber's Gloss. in v.

(3) *To keep the tail in the water,* to thrive. *To flea the tail,* to get near the conclusion of any work.

(4) To exchange animals with an even number on each side. *Var. dial.*

(5) Number?

> Cotte thow not the wordes *tayle,*
> But sey hem oute wythowte fayle.
> *MS. Cott. Claud.* A. ii. f. 158.

TAIL-BAND. A crupper. *North.* " Taylband, *subtela*," MS. Dict. c. 1500.

TAIL-BINDER. A long large piece of cut stone projecting over the corner stone of a wall to give additional firmness to it.

TAIL-CORN. The inferior portion of a dressing, not fit for market. About one in twenty, or more, according to the season, will be *tailcorn.* This, though not very much inferior, would, if left in the *boke,* injure the sale at market. By the farmer who prides himself on the goodness of his sample, this is dressed out and *spent* at home. Dross is different. This is undercorn, so light and inferior as to be given to poultry.

TAILDE. Carved.

> The wardes of the cyté of hefen bryght
> I lycken tyl wardes that stalworthly dyght,
> And clenely wroght and craftyly *taylde*
> Of clene sylver and golde, and enamaylde.
> *Hampole, MS. Bowes,* p. 232.

TAILE. (1) To cut to pieces. *(A.-N.)*

(2) A tally, or notched stick; an account scored on a piece of wood. *(A.-N.)*

> Hit is skorid here on a *tayle,*
> Have brok hit wel withowt fayle.
> *MS. Cantab.* Ff. v. 48, f. 53.

TAIL-ENDS. Inferior samples of corn, such as being hardly marketable, are usually consumed at home. See *Tail-corn.*

TAILLAGE. A tax. *(A.-N.)*

TAILLAGER. A collector of taxes. *(A.-N.)*

TAILLE. A tally. See *Tale.*

TAILLIOR. A tailor. *North.*

TAILORS. It is a very old saying that it takes three or nine tailors to make one man.

> Some foolish knave (I thinke) at first began
> The slander that three taylers are one man;

When many a taylers boy I know hath beene,
Hath made tall men much fearefull to be seene.
Taylor's Workes, 1630, iii. 73.

TAILORS-MENSE. A small portion left by way of good manners. See Brockett.

TAILOURS. A book of ancient cookery receipts thus describes the way of making *taylours* :

Take almondes, and grynde hem raw in a morter, and temper hit with wyne and a litul water, and drawe it thorgh a streynour into a goode stiff mylke into a potte, and caste thereto reysons of coraunce and grete reysons my[n]ced, dates, clowes, maces, pouder of peper, canel, saffrone a good quantité, and salt, and sette hem over the fire, and lete al boyle togidre a while, and alay hit up with floure of ryse or elles grated brede, and cast thereto sugur and salt, and serve hit forth in maner of mortrewes, and caste thereone pouder ginger in the dissh.

MS. Harl. 4016, f. 19.

TAIL-PIPING. Tying a tin can or anything to the tail of a dog, which is generally done to prevent his paying visits to the place where this punishment may be inflicted.

TAIL-ROPE. Part of a horse's harness, mentioned in MS. Coll. Jes. Oxon. 28.

TAIL-SHOTEN. A disease in the tail of cattle, in which the spinal marrow is so affected that in a short time the beast is unable to stand. Also called *tail-soke.*

TAIL-TOP. The swingle of a flail.

TAILƷOR. A tailor. Nominale MS.

TAINCT. A kind of red-coloured spider very common in the summer time.

TAINT. (1) A term at tilting, apparently meaning to injure a lance without breaking it. Gifford, Ben Jonson, ii. 55, explains it, to break a staff, but not in the most honorable or scientific manner. See, however, the second example under *Attaint.*

(2) Explained in the Booke of Hawking, "a thing that goeth overthwart the feathers of the wings and of the tail, like as it were eaten with worms."

(3) A dirty slattern. *East.*

(4) Explained by Forby, " a large protuberance at the top of a pollard tree."

(5) " A taint or overreach in the backe or shanke of a horse," Florio, p. 47.

TAINTERS.

For the outward compound remedies, a plaister made of opponax and pitch is much commended, which Menippus used, taking a pound of pitch of Brutias, and foure ounces of opponax (as Ætius and Actuarius doe prescribe) adding withall, that the opponax must be dissolved in vineger, and afterward the pitch and that vineger must be boyled together, and when the vineger is consumed, then put in the opponax, and of both together make like *taynters* or splints and thurst them into the wound, so let them remaine many dayes together, and in the meane time drinke an antidot of sea-crabs and vineger, (for vineger is always pretious in this confection).

Topsell's Four-Footed Beasts, 1607, p. 187.

TAISAND. Poising ready for throwing.

And ther biside, on o donjoun,
He kest a man of cler latoun,
And in his hond an arblast heldand,
And therinne a quarel *taisand.*

Sevyn Sages, 1978.

TAISHES. Taces, armour for the thighs. This form of the word occurs in Warner's Albion's England, xii. p. 291.

TAISTREL. A rascal ; a villain. *North.*

TAIT. (1) The top of a hill. *West.*

(2) To play at see-saw. *Dorset.*

TAKE. (1) To give ; to deliver up to. (*A.-S.*)

And alle that they aske scho wylle them *take,*
For drede of theym, swylke boste they make.

MS. Harl. 2960, f. 59.

But *take* hur an oolde stede,
And an olde knyȝt that may hur lede,
Tylle sche be paste yowre realme,
And gyf them some spendynge,
That them owt of thy londe may brynge,
Y can no bettyr deme.

MS. Cantab. Ff. ii. 38, f 72.

(2) A vulgar name for the sciatica, mentioned in Aubrey's MS. Nat. Hist. Wilts, p. 10, in the library of the Royal Society.

(3) A sudden illness. *Dorset.*

(4) A lease. *North.*

(5) " I take the wynde, as a dere dothe of a person, *je assens,*" Palsgrave.

(6) *To take up,* to reprove. " *Tanser,* to chide, rebuke, checke, taunt, reprove, take up," Cotgrave. *To take up a horse,* to make him gambol. *To take on, to take by,* to be much affected by any melancholy event. *To take in,* to capture, to subdue. *To take one along, to take one with you,* to go no faster than he can go with you, i. e. to let him understand you. *To take out,* to copy. *To take one's teeth to anything,* to set about it heartily. *To take a stick to one,* to beat him. *To take on,* to enlist for a soldier. *To take to do, to take to task, to take a talking to,* to reprove. *To take on,* to simulate. *To take after,* to resemble. *To take off,* to mimic, to ridicule. *To take to,* to capture, or seize ; to attack. Also, to marry ; to enter on a farm ; to own, or acknowledge. *To take shame,* to be ashamed. *To take up for any one,* to give surety, to protect. *To take on,* to associate with. *A take-away,* an appetite. *To take one's ease in one's inn,* to enjoy one's self, as if at home. *To take up,* to borrow money, or take commodities upon trust. *To take up a quarrel,* to settle or make it up. *To take upon,* to suspect any one of a wrong action. *To take forth,* to learn, to teach. *To take order for,* to provide for or against anything. *To take to anything,* to answer for the truth of it ; to stand to a bargain. *To take up,* to clear up, said of the weather. Also, to reform one's habits ; to commence anything. *To take clothes about one,* to wrap them well over him. *To take about the neck,* to embrace. *To take a breath,* to consider well beforehand or take advice. *To take any one forth,* to set him forwards. *To take heart,* to take courage. *To take one's part,* to defend him. *To take in worth, to take in good part,* to take anything kindly or friendly. *To take to one's legs,* to fly. *To take a horse with the spurs,* to spur him onwards. *To take on with one's*

self, to torment one's self. *To take a man's ways*, to follow his example. *To take upon*, to carry one's self proudly above one's station. *To take the air*, to go out in the fresh air. *To take any one down*, to tame him.

(7) To contain. Ben Jonson, viii. 301.

(8) To leap. *Shak.*

(9) To blast, as if by witchcraft. Shakespeare uses the term, and it is still current in the West of England. " Taken, as chyldernes lymmes be by the fayries, *faée*," Palsgrave. In an old MS. collection of receipts in my possession is one " for to make a man hole that kechith cold in his slepe that he ys ny *take* ;" and another " for a man that ys *take* in his slepe."

> A horsse which is bereft of his feeling, mooving or stirring, is said to be *taken*, and in sooth so he is, in that he is arrested by so villainous a disease, yet some farriors, not wel understanding the ground of the disease, conster the word *taken* to bee striken by some plannet or evill spirit, which is false, for it proceedeth of too great aboundance of fleme and choler, simbolis'd together. The cure is thus. Let him blood in his spur-vains, and his breast vaines, and then by foulding him in aboundant number of cloaths, drive him into an extreame sweat, during which time of his sweating, let one chafe his legs with oyle de bay, then after he hath sweat the space of two houres, abate his cloaths moderatly, and throughly after he is dry, annoint him all over with oyle petrolium, and in twice or thrice dressing him he wil be sound.
>
> *Markham, ap. Topsell's Beasts*, 1607, p. 351.

(10) To understand ; to comprehend.

(11) To begin to grow in the ground, said of young trees and herbs newly planted.

TAKE-ALL. An old game at dice, mentioned in Clarke's Phraseologia Puerilis, 1655, p. 144.

TAKEL. An arrow. (*A.-S.*)

TAKEN. (1) Took. *West.*

(2) *Taken work*, a piece of husbandry work, not done by the day. *East.*

(3) Taken by the face, i. e. put to the blush. A common Lancashire phrase.

TAKENE. (1) Given. (*A.-S.*)

> Swete modir, sayde he,
> What manere of thyng may this bee,
> That ȝe nowe hafe *takene* mee ?
> What calle ȝee this wande ?   *Perceval*, 199.

(2) To declare ; to show.

TAKER. Purveyor.

> As for capons ye can gette none,
> The kyngys *taker* toke up eche one.
>   *Interlude of the iiij. Elements*, n. d.

TAKIL. Tackle ; accoutrements.

TAKING. (1) Infectious. (2) A dilemma.

(3) Captivating ; pleasing. *Var. dial.*

(4) A sore ; an attack of sickness. *West.*

TALAGE. Appearance ?

> That passyngely was to the ye clere,
> And of *talage* inly good and fyne.
>   *Lydgate, MS. Soc. Antiq.* 134, f. 26.

TALBOTES. A receipt for " hares in *talbotes*" occurs in the Forme of Cury, p. 21.

TALC. *Oil of talc*, an ancient cosmetic very frequently alluded to. Fuller, mentioning that metal, says, " being calcined and variously

prepared, it maketh a curious white-wash, which some justify lawful, because clearing not changing the complexion." Ben Jonson, ed. Gifford, iv. 95.

TALDE. Counted. (*A.-S.*)

> The gold thane on his mantille thay *talde*,
> And tille hyme-selfene thay gane it falde.
>   *Romance of Sir Isumbras*, 306.

TALE. (1) To relate tales ; to tell. *Somerset.* Old writers term any discourse a *tale*.

> And namely whan they *talen* longe,
> My sorowis thanne ben so stronge.
>   *MS. Cantab.* Ff. ii. 38, f. 61

> Whan they this straunge vessel syȝe,
> The tone therof hath spoke and *talid*.
>   *Gower, MS. Soc. Antiq.* 134, f. 239.

(2) An account, or reckoning. (*A.-S.*) *To give no tale*, to make no account of.

> There is so muche sorowe and bale,
> And many peynes oute of *tale*,
> Though alle men that evere had witte,
> And y-lerued hadde alle holy writte,
> Thei coude not telle it in her lore
> The peynes that there ben evermore.
>   *MS. Addit.* 11305, f. 94.

> Goods in and out, which dayly ships doe fraight,
> By guesse, by *tale*, by measure and by weight.
>   *Taylor's Workes*, 1630, iii. 68.

(3) *To tell a tale*, to turn any matter to one's profit or advantage.

(4) To settle in a place ; to be reconciled to any situation. *North.*

(5) " A tale of a tub, *chose ridicule, conte, de cicogne, chanson de ricoche*," Howell.

TALENGE. A longing for anything.

TALENT. (1) A talon. An old form.

(2) Desire ; inclination ; lust ; taste. (*A.-N.*) See the example given in v. *Eyrone*.

> There he went to the kynge,
> That had grete yoye of hys comyng ;
> Sylvyr and golde be had hym sente,
> Thereof had Gye no *talente*.
>   *MS. Cantab.* Ff. ii. 38, f. 155.

> And gefe the sike theroff to ete everi day a spoo-fulle, and hit schalle do away the clett fro his herte, and make hym *talent* to ete. *MS. Med. Rec.* xv. Cent.

(3) Perhaps as *tablet*, q. v. " These talents of their hair," Collier's Shakespeare, viii. 551, where the term seems to be wrongly explained. Malone says, " lockets consisting of hair platted and set in gold."

> The *talents* of golde were on her head sette,
> Hanged low downe to her knee;
> And everye ring on her small finger
> Shone of the chrystall free. *King Estmere*, 67.

TALENTER. A hawk. Middleton, v. 165.

TALE-PIE. A tell-tale. *North.*

TALE-WIS. Wise in tales. (*A.-S.*)

TALEWORT. Wild borage. *Gerard.*

TALGHE. Fat ; grease ; tallow.

> Of thase redes garte Alexander mak bates, and anoynte thame with terre and *talghe* of bestes, and badd his knyghtis row over the water in thase bates.
>   *MS. Lincoln* A. i. 17, f. 44.

> Tak thame thane uppe, and do thame in a panne, and do to thame a gud porcyone of schepe *talghe*, and fry thame wele samene. *MS. Linc. Med.* f. 296.

TALIAGE. A tax. *Prompt. Parv.*

TALING. Relating tales. *Chaucer.*

TALISHE. Fabulous. This word occurs in Palsgrave's Acolastus, 4to. 1540.

TALL. (1) Explained by Junius, " obedient, obsequious, every way flexible." See the Glossary to Urry's Chaucer, p. 81.

(2) Valiant; bold; fine; great. This is a very common word in old plays.

> They leaping overboord amidst the billowes,
> We pluck'd her up (unsunke) like stout *tall* fellows.
> *Taylor's Workes*, 1630, ii. 23.

TALL-BOYS. High cups or glasses. Grose says, bottles or two-quart pots.

TALLE. To mock. (*A.-S.*)

> Unarmed were the paiens alle,
> Our folk hem gun to *talle*.
> *Arthour and Merlin*, p. 257

TALLEE. " When they hale aft the sheate of maine or fore-sailes, they say, *Tallee aft the sheate*," MS. Harl. 6268. *Taylia*, Reliq. Antiq. i. 2.

TALLICHE. The same as *Tally* (6).

TALLIT. A hayloft. *West*. " When the prisoner came in he was *watcherd*, which shewed he had not been all night in the *tallit*."

TALL-MEN. Dice so loaded as to come up with high numbers. A cant term.

TALLOW-CAKE. A cake of tallow; tallow made up in the form of a cake. *Var. dial.*

TALLOW-CATCH. Same as *Keech* (2).

TALLOW-CRAPS. See *Craps* (1).

TALLOW-HUED. Pale as tallow. *North*. Burton uses the phrase *tallow-faced*.

TALLOW-LAFE. *Congiarium*, MS. Dict. c. 1500.

TALL-WOOD. " Tall woode, pacte wodde to make byllettes of, *taillee*," Palsgrave. The term is still used in Kent.

TALLY. (1) A term in playing ball, when the number of aces on both sides is equal. *North*.

(2) To reckon. See Becon's Works, p. 134.

(3) In counting any articles which are sold by the hundred, one is thrown out after each hundred; that is called the *tally*. The number of tallies of course shows the number of hundreds. They are given in to the purchaser. *Hunter*.

(4) A kind of small ship.

(5) A company or division of voters at an election. *Somerset*.

(6) Stoutly; boldly.

(7) Seemly; decently; elegantly.

TALME. To become dumb?

> Hur fadur nere-hande can *talme*,
> Soche a sweme hys harte can swalme.
> *Le Bone Florence of Rome*, 769.
> I donke upon David. til mi tonge *talmes :*
> I ne rendrede nowt. sithen men beren palmes :
> Is it also mikel sorwe. in song so is in salmes ?
> *Reliq. Antiq.* i. 292.

TALSHIDES. " One pound of white lights, ten *talshides*, eight faggotts," Ord. and Reg. p. 162.

TALT. Pitched.

> There was *talt* many pavyloun
> Of riche sendel and siclatoun.
> *Kyng Alisaunder*, 5234.

TALVACE. A kind of buckler or shield, bent on each side, and rising in the middle.

> Aither broght unto the place
> A mikel rownd *talvace*.
> *Ywaine and Gawin*, 3158.
> And after mete thar it was,
> The children pleide at the *talvas*.
> *Beves of Hamtoun*, p. 145.

TALWHE. Tallow. Nominale MS.

TAM. The abbr. of pr. n. Thomasine.

TAMARA. A compound of spices.

TAME. (1) To broach or taste liquor. " To tame, tap, *dolium relinere*," Coles.

> Nowe to weete our mouthes tyme were,
> This flagette will I *tame*, yf thou reade us.
> *Chester Plays*, i. 124.

(2) To cut; to divide. *West*.

TAME-GOOSE. A foolish fellow. " I say cast away; yea, utterly cast away upon a noddy, a ninny-hammer, a *tame-goose*," The Case is Altered, 4to. Lond. 1605.

TAMER. A team of horses. *Norf*.

TAMINE. A sort of woollen cloth.

TAMLIN. A miner's tool. *Cornw.*

TAMMY. Glutinous, or sizy. *Cumb.*

TAMPIN. A long pellet.

> Make two stiffe long rowles or *tampins* of linnen clowtes, or such like stuffe, sharpe pointed like suger-loves : which *tampins* are called of the physitians in Latine *pessi*, and being annointed with the ointment aforesaid, thrust them up into the horses nostrils, and let them abide therein a pretty whilk ; then pul them out, and you shal see such abundance of matter come forth at his nose as is marvellous to behold.
> *Topsell's Four-Footed Beasts*, 1607, p. 372.

TAMPING-IRON. A tool used for beating down the earthy substance in the charge used for blasting. *Cornw.*

TAMPION. A piece of wood fitted to the mouth of a large gun. " Tampyon for a gon, *tampon*," Palsgrave, subst. f. 69.

> Unadvisedly gave fire to a peece charged with a pellet insteede of a *tampion*, the which lighting on the palaice wall, ranne through one of the privie lodgings, and did no further harme.
> *Lambarde's Perambulation*, 1596, p. 433.

TAN. (1) Taken. (*A.-S.*)

> When pese was cryed and day *tan*,
> Kyng Ardus was a yoyfulle man.
> *MS. Cantab.* Ff. ii. 38, f. 78.
> Baptem the first is holden than,
> That falleth at the fonte be *tan*.
> *MS. Sloan.* 1785, f. 34.

(2) To entice. (*A.-S.*)

> The fende of helle agayn skylle
> Put in hir a harde wille
> Hur fadur luf to wynne ;
> And also temped was that man
> His owne douyter for to *tan*,
> To do a dedly synne.
> *MS. Cantab.* Ff. v. 48, f. 43.

(3) Then. *Var. dial.*

(4) To dun. (5) To beat. *Var. dial.*

(6) A twig, or small switch. *Lanc.*

TANACLES. A kind of pincers, used formerly for torturing. " To pinch or tanacle with tongs, with pincers or tanacles," Florio, p. 552, ed. 1611.

TANBASE. To beat; to struggle. *Devon.*

TANCEL. To beat; to flog. *Derb.*

TANCRETE. A transcript, or copy. (*A.-N.*)

TAN-DAY. The second day of a fair; a day after a fair; a fair for fun. *West.*

TANE. (1) One. See *Cruke.*

(2) Taken. The same as *Tan* (1).

> And such a custome men have *tane* therein,
> That to be drunke is scarce accounted sinne.
> *Taylor's Workes*, 1630, ll. 261.

TAN-FLAWING. The taking the bark off the oak trees. *Sussex.*

TANG. (1) To sound, as a bell. Sometimes, to ring or pull a bell. *Var. dial.*

(2) A taste, or acrid twang. *Devon.*

(3) The sting of a bee, &c. *North.* "A tange of a nedyr, *acus,*" MS. Dict. c. 1500.

(4) The tongue of a buckle, &c. *East.*

(5) To tie. *Somerset.*

(6) That part of a knife or fork which passes into the haft. *West.* "A tange of a knyfe, *piramus,*" MS. Dict. c. 1500.

(7) The prong of a fork. *North.*

(8) Sea-weed. *North.*

(9) Dirt? "You are in pretty tangs," i. e. very dirty; a Norfolk expression.

> It depraves the mind, and leaves that *tang* and filth upon the intellectuals and affections as is not to be washed off without much ado by better counsels.
> *A Cap of Gray Hairs for a Green Head*, 1688, p. 66.

TANGING-NADDER. The large dragon-fly.

TANGLE. (1) Sea-weed. *North.*

(2) To entangle. *Palsgrave.*

TANGLESOME. Discontented; obstinate; fretful. "Tanggyl, or froward, and angry," Pr. Parv. MS. Harl. 221, f. 177.

TANGLING. Slatternly; slovenly. *North.*

TANK. (1) According to Willan, a piece of deep water, natural or artificial. *North.*

(2) A blow. *Warw.*

(3) An idle amusement. *West.*

(4) Wild parsnip. *Gerard.*

> Brydswete or *tank.* Hit hath leves lyke to hemlok, and a quite flower. The vertu therof is that hit [is] gud to hele the dropcy and bytynge of venemes bestus.
> *MS. Arundel 272*, f. 46.

(5) A hat round at the top, but ascending like a sugar-loaf. Holme, 1688.

TANKARD-BEARER. One who fetched water from conduits for the use of the citizens. Before the New River was brought to London, the city was chiefly supplied with water from conduits. See Ben Jonson, i. 24. "This is the manner of carrying water from the conducts in London to every particular family, and is so born both by men and women on their shoulders," Holme, 1688, iii. 259.

TANKARD-TURNIP. The long-rooted turnip.

TANKEROUS. Fretful; cross. *East.* It is sometimes pronounced *tankersome.*

TANNIKIN. A name for a Dutch woman.

> Out she would, tucks up her trinkets, like a Dutch *tannikin* sliding to market on the Ise, and away she flings. *Armin's Nest of Ninnies*, 1608.

TANQUAM. "Tanquam is a fellow's fellow in our Universities, Blount, ed. 1681, p. 638.

TANS. Pricklebacks. *Suffolk.*

TANSAY-CAKE. Was thus made:

> Breke egges in bassyn, and swynge hem sone,
> Do powder of peper therto anone.
> Then grynde tansay, tho Juse owte wrynge,
> To blynde with tho egges, withowte lesynge.
> In pan or skelet thou shalt hit frye,
> In buttur wele skymm et wyturly,
> Or white grece thou make take therto,
> Geder hit on a cake, thenne hase thou do
> With platere of tre, and frye hit browne.
> On brodeleches serve hit thou schalle,
> With fraunche-mele or other metis withalle.
> *MS. Sloane 1986*, p. 100.

TANSY. A dish very common in the seventeenth century. It was thus made:

> *How to make a very good tansie.*
> Take 15 eggs, and 6 of the whites; beat them very well; then put in some sugar, and a litle sack; beat them again, and put about a pint or a little more of cream; then beat them again; then put in the juice of spinage or of primrose leaves to make it green. Then put in some more sugar, if it be not sweet enough; then beat it again a little, and so let it stand till you fry it, when the first course is in. Then fry it with a little sweet butter. It must be stirred and fryed very tender. When it is fryed enough, then put it in a dish, and strew some sugar upon it, and serve it in.
> *A True Gentlewoman's Delight*, 1676, pp. 13-14.

TANTABLIN. Some dish or tart in cookery, mentioned in Taylor's Workes, 1630, i. 146. *Tantadlins*, apple-dumplings, Heref. Gl. 106. Forby has *tantablet*, a sort of tart in which the fruit is not covered by a crust, but fancifully tricked and flourished with slender shreds of pastry. A cow-plat, or human ordure, is called in ridicule a *tantadlin*, or *tantadlintart.*

TANTARA. A confused noise. *Var. dial.* It was formerly applied to the noise of a drum.

> There's no *tantara*, sa sa sa, or force,
> Of man to man, or warlike horse to horse.
> *Taylor's Workes*, 1630, iii. 66.

TANTARABOBS. The devil. *Devon.*

TANTER. To quarrel. *North.*

TANTICKLE. A prickleback. *Suffolk.*

TANTLE. To dawdle, or trifle; to go gently; to attend. *North.*

TANTONY-PIG. See *Anthony-pig.*

TANTONY-POUCH.

> Thou for the edge, and I the point, will make the foole bestride our mistres backes, and then have at the bagge with the dudgin hafte, that is, at the dudgen dagger, by which hangs his *tantonie pouch.*
> *Lilly*, ed. 1632, sig. Aa. iv.

TANTRELS. Idle persons. *North.*

TANTUMS. Affected airs; insolences; whims. *Var. dial.*

TAP. (1) To sole shoes. *West.*

(2) To change money. *North.*

(3) The spigot of a barrel. *Var. dial.*

(4) The hare or rabbit was said to *tap*, when making a noise at rutting time.

(5) To tap a tree at the root, i. e. to open it round about the root.

TAPART. Of the one part.

TAPE. A mole. *South.*

TAPECERY. Tapestry. "A broderer of *tapecerye,*" Ord. and Reg. p. 99.

TAPER-BIT. A joiner's tool, thus described by Holme :—" the *taper-bit* is for the making of a small hole wider and larger, being in the mouth half round, whose edges are sharp, and by reason of its being taper as it goeth into a hole with the small end, and is turned about therein, the edges cut it wide by taking shavings or pairings from the hole side."

TAPERIE. Tapers. Ord. and Reg. p. 116.

TAPER-LADDER. A kind of small rack having one end broader than the other.

TAPES. Bands of linen ; pieces of lace such as form chequer-work, &c. (*A.-S.*)

TAPET. A hanging cloth of any kind, as tapestry, the cloth for a sumpter-horse, &c. "Tappet, a clothe, *tappis*," Palsgrave. The term was applied metaphorically to the foliage of trees.

> Eke godely Flora, the goddes, ys so gay,
> Hath on her *tapites* sondré hewes sene
> Of fressh floures that so welle browded bene.
> > *MS. Cantab.* Ff. i. 6, f. 11.

> To John Vere, Earl of Oxford, seven *tappets* of counterfeit arras of the story of Solomon.
> > *Test. Vetust.* p. 674.

TAP-HOUSE. A tavern, or inn.

> Their senses are with blacke damnation drunke,
> Whose heart is Satans *tap-house* or his inne.
> > *Taylor's Workes*, 1630, i. 3.

TAPILLE. A taper.

> To signifye whoso wille be clene,
> Muste offre a *tapille* togedir made of thre.
> > *Lydgate, MS. Soc. Antiq.* 134, f. 29.

TAPINAGE. Secret skulking. (*A.-N.*)

> Ryʒt so thy newe *tapinage*
> Of Lollardye goth aboute
> To sette Cristis feythe in doute.
> > *Gower, MS. Soc. Antiq.* 134, f. 138.

TAPISED. Lurked ; lay hid. *Hearne.*

TAPISER. A maker of tapestry. (*A.-N.*) "Tappyssery worke, *tapisserie*," Palsgrave.

TAPITE. The same as *Tapet*, q. v.

TAPITER. The same as *Tapiser*, q. v. See Davies' York Records, Append. p. 235.

TAP-LASH. Bad small beer. *Var. dial.* Also, the refuse or dregs of liquor.

> His garments stunke most sweetly of his vomit,
> Fac'd with the *tap-lash* of strong ale and wine,
> Which from his slav'ring chaps doth oft decline.
> > *Taylor's Workes*, 1630, iii. 5.

TAPLEY. Early in the morning. *Exm.*

TAPLINGS. The strong double leathers made fast to the ends of each piece of a flail.

TAPPE. (1) To tap; to beat?

> And your foot ye *tappyn* and ye daunce,
> Thogh hit the fryskyst horse were in a towne.
> > *MS. Fairfax* 16.

(2)

> I crosse out all this : adewe, by Saynt Johan !
> I take my *tappe* in my lappe, and am gone.
> > *Morality of Every-Man*, p. 63.

TAPPER. An innkeeper. *North.*

TAPPIS. To lie close to the ground, said of partridges and game. *East.*

TAPPY. To hide or skulk, as a deer.

TAPPY-LAPPY. In haste, with the coat-laps flying behind through speed.

> Nanny Bell's crying out : I just gat a gliff o
> Gweorge runnin', *tappy-lappy*, for the howdey.

TAPS. The round pipes or cells in a beehive which are made for the queen-bee.

TAP-SHACKLED. Intoxicated.

TAPSTERE. A woman who had the care of the tap in a public-house, or inn. In Shakespeare's time, a man or woman who drew the beer was called the tapster.

TAPTRE. *Cervida, clipcidra*, MS. Dict. c. 1500.

TAPULL. Part of ancient armour, mentioned in Hall's Union, 1548, Hen. IV. f. 12. Meyrick conjectures it to be the projecting edge of the cuirass.

TAP-WARE. A wisp of straw or bottle of basket-work to put within side the tap-hole in a brewing or other straining vessel.

TAR. (1) There. Sevyn Sages, 207

(2) A childish word for *farewell.*

TARAGE. Appearance ?

> In every part the *tarage* is the same,
> Liche his fader of maneris and of name.
> > *MS. Digby* 232, f. 1.

TARATANTARA. The sound of trumpets.

TAR-BARELLE. A combustible missile used in ancient warfare.

> With bowes schot and with arblast,
> With *tarbarelle* and with wilde fyre.
> > *MS. Addit.* 10036, f. 34.

TARBLE. Tolerable. *West.* Also *tarblish.*

TAR-BOX. (1) A box used by shepherds for carrying tar, used for anointing sores in sheep, for marking them, and for other purposes. *Tarre boyste*, Chester Plays, i. 125.

> Sheapherds, leave singing your pastorall sonnetts,
> And to learne complements shew your endeavours :
> Cast of for ever your twoe shillings bonnetts,
> Cover your coxcombs with three pounds beavers,
> Sell carte and *tarboss* new coaches to buy,
> Then, " good your worshipp," the vulgar will cry.
> > *MS. Addit.* 5832, f. 205.

(2) A term of contempt.

TARDLE. To entangle. *Dorset.*

TARDRY. Immodest ; bawdy. *East.*

TARE. (1) Eager ; brisk. *Heref.*

(2) Torn. Vocab. MS. xv. Cent.

TAREFITCH. "Tarefytche, a corne, *lupyn*," Palsgrave, subst. f. 69.

TARGE. (1) A shield. (*A.-N.*)

> Tho that suffir so her wyfes, God let hem never thryf,
> Hyt makyth hem to ley to wed bothe bokolar and
> *targe.* *MS. Laud.* 416, f. 74.

> I wolde sey thee yit a worde of the *targe.* Ther
> is no wight weel armed ne wight defended ne kepte
> withowten *taxrge*, for the *taarge* defendethe the
> tother harneys from empeyring ; by hit is boothe the
> body and the toother herneys ekepte withouten
> enpeyring. *Romance of the Monk, Sion College MS.*

> Affter I tooke the gaynepaynes and the swerd
> with which I gurde me, and sithe whane I was thus
> armed, I putte the *targe* to my syde.
> > *Romance of the Monk, Sion College M*.

(2) To tarry; to delay. Also, delay.

> Otuwel, withoute *targing*,
> Answerede Karnlfees the king.
> > *Romance of Otuel*, p. 79.

(3) " *Targe* or chartyr, *carta*," Pr. Parv.

TAR-GRASS. Wild vetch. *Staff.*

Outward ffolkys ffor to telle
That within is wyne to selle
MS. Cotton. Tiber. A. vii. f. 72.

Mary, at the dore even hereby,
Yf we call any thynge on hye,
The *taverner* wyll answere.
Interlude of the iiij. Elements, n. d.

TAVERNGANGE. *Attabernio*, MS. Dict. c. 1500.

TAVERN-TOKEN. A token coined by a tavern-keeper. To swallow a tavern token, was a cant phrase for being tipsy. See the Honest Whore, i. 4.

TAVORT. Half a bushel. *Sussex.*

TAW. (1) To dress hemp, or leather.
And whilst that they did nimbly spin,
The hempe he needs must *taw.*
Robin Goodfellow, p. 28.

(2) To soften, or make supple.
(3) A whip. *North.*
(4) A large choice marble.
(5) To twist; to entangle. *North.*
(6) To tie; to fasten. *Somerset.*

TAW-BESS. A slatternly woman. *North.*

TAWDERIED-UP. Finely dressed. *Linc.*

TAWDRY. (1) *Tawdry lace*, a kind of fine lace alluded to by Shakespeare, Spenser, &c. "Taw-dry-lace, *fimbriæ nundinis sanctæ Etheldredæ emptæ*," Coles.

(2) A rural necklace. *Drayton*

TAWE. Tow. (*A.-S.*)

TAWER. (1) Aftergrass. *Dorset.*
(2) A leather-dresser. *Var. dial.*

TAWL. To stroke, or make smooth. *West.*

TAWLINGS. The mark from which boys shoot in playing at marbles. *South.*

TAWNY. A bullfinch. *Somerset.*

TAWNY-MEDLY. *Tanny mesley*, Palsgrave.

TAWS. A piece of tanned leather. *North.*

TAWSTOCK-GRACE. Finis. *Devon.*

TAXAGE. Taxation. MS. Dict. c. 1500.

TAXERS. Two officers yearly chosen in Cambridge to see the true gage of all weights and measures. *Blount.*

TAX-WAX. The same as *Faxwax*, q. v.

TAYE. To manure land. "Tayng of lond, *ruderacio, stercoriza*," Pr. Parv. At f. 186 it is spelt *taym*, "taym londe with schepys donge."

TAYLARD. A term of reproach.

TAYSED. Driven; harassed. *Gawayne.*

TAYTE. (1)
There he levede in a *tayte*
Bothe his modir and his gayte.
Perceval, 253.

(2) Plump; fat? Syr Gawayne, p. 52.

TAZZY. A mischievous child. *North.*

TA3TE. Taught. (*A.-S.*)
And bygynne, as I 3er *ta3te*,
At simili modo even stra3te.
MS. Cotton. Claud. A. ii. f. 150.

TE. (1) To. *Yorksh.*
(2) To go; to draw to. (*A.-S.*)
But she aunsweryd hym ay in haste,
To none bot Launcelot wold she *te*.
MS. Harl. 2252, f. 100.

The devel hevede so muche pousté,
That alle mosten to helle *te*.
Harrowing of Hell, p. 12

Never eft y nil no woman se,
Into wildernes I chil *te*,
And live ther evermore
With wylde bestes in holtes hore.
Sir Orpheo, ed. Laing, 174.

(3) To tug; to pull. (*A.-S.*)
In the toun he herd belles ring,
And loude crie and miche wepeing,
Clothes to tere, her to *te*,
More sorwe no might non be.
Gy of Warwike, p. 249.

(4) Thee. Amis and Amiloun, 1599.

TEA. (1) The one. *North.*
(2) Too; likewise. *Yorksh.*
(3) To take tea. *Var. dial.*

TEAD. A torch. This word is used several times by Spenser.
Now's the glad and cheerefull day,
Phœbus doth his beames display,
And the faire bride forth to lead
Makes his torch their nuptial *tead.*
Heywood's Marriage Triumph, 1613.

TEADY. Tired; peevish. *North.*

TEAGLE. A crane for lifting goods. *North.*

TEAGS.
All ye that love, or who pretends,
Come listen to my sonnet;
Black-baggs or vizards, who have friends,
Or English *teags* or bonnets. *Folly in Print, 1667.*

TEAK. A whitlow. *Somerset.*

TEAKERS. A running of watery matter from a sore. *Northumb.*

TEALIE. A tailor. *Lanc.*

TEAM. (1) A tandem. *Var. dial.*
(2) A litter of pigs. *Kent.* Brockett has *teem*, a brood of young ducks. A.-S. team. It is a common archaism, spelt *teme.*
(3) Empty. *Yorksh.*
(4) An ox-chain in harness. *North.*
(5) "A teame beast, everie beast that draweth or beareth burdens," Baret, 1580.

TEAM-BANDS. The same as *Start-chains*, q. v.

TEAMER. (1) A team of five horses. *Norf.*
(2) To pour out copiously. *East.*

TEAMERMAN. A waggoner, carter, or driver of a teamer. *Norf.*

TEAM-FULL. Brimful. *North.*

TEANT. It is not. *Var. dial.*

TEAP. A peak, or point. *Somerset.*

TEAR. (1) To go fast. *Var. dial.*
(2) To break, or crack. *West.*

TEAR-A-CAT. To rant violently.

TEARING. Great; rough; topping; noisy; blustering; hot-headed. *Var. dial.*

TEARN. (1) The sea-swallow. Arch. xiii. 352.
(2) They were. *Lanc.*
(3) To compare; to liken. *Yorksh.*

TEART. Sharp; severe; painful. *West.*

TEAR-THE-MOOR. "To tear the moor," says Urry, in his MS. additions to Ray, "about Hungerford signifies to gett roaringly drunk. They tore the moor bitterly."

TEARY. Weak and thin. *Dorset.* This term is generally applied to plants.

TEASER. (1) A kind of hound.

(2) Anything which causes trouble. *Var. dial.*

TEATA. Too much. *North.*

TEATH. Tithe. *North.*

Therfore, of all that I have wonne
To geve thee *teath* I wil begine.
Chester Plays, i. 58.

TEATHE. The dung of cattle. *Norf.*

TEATHY. Peevish; crabbed. *Yorksh.*

TEATISH. The same as *Teathy,* q. v.

Lightly, hee is an olde man, (for those yeares are most wayward and *teatish*) yet be he never so olde or so froward, since avarice likewise is a fellow vice of those fraile yeares, we must set one extreame to strive with another, and alay the anger of oppression by the sweet incense of a newe purse of angels.
Nash's Pierce Pennilesse, 1592.

TEATY-WAD. The same as *Sugar-teat,* q. v.

TEAUP. A tup, or ram. *North.*

TEAVE. The same as *Tave* (1).

TEAWSE. To pull, or ruffle. *Lanc.*

TEBLE. Qu. an error for *treble?*

Theophanos for God in *teble* wyse
Therinne apperid, as ȝe have herde devyse.
Lydgate, MS. Soc. Antiq. 134, f. 25.

TECHE. (1) To teach. (*A.-S.*)

(2) To intrust; to appoint to.

TECHY. Peevish; cross; touchy. *South.*

TECKEN. Taken; took. *Linc.*

TECTLY. Covertly; secretly.

TED. (1) To spread hay. "I teede hey, I tourne it afore it is made in cockes, *je fene,*" Palsgrave. Still in use.

(2) To turn flax when it has been laid on the ground to dry. *West.*

(3) To burn wood-fires. *Linc.*

(4) To be ordered to do anything. *Exm.*

(5) The nickname for *Edward.*

TEDDER. Live within thy tedder, i. e. live within thy bounds. Tusser, p. xxiii.

TEDDING-POLE. The long stick used for turning or tedding flax. *West.*

TEDDY. Edward. *Var. dial.*

TEDY. Tedious; vexatious. *North.*

TEE. (1) The same as *Te* (2).

Telle me the tyme when hyt schall bee,
When thou schall to hevene *tee.*
MS. Cantab. Ff. ii. 38, f. 33.

Of grete age schal he noȝt be
Oute of thys worlde whan he schal *tee.*
MS. Harl. 2390, f. 33.

(2) To tie. *North.*

TEE-DRAW. A place of resort. *North.*

TEE-FALL. A mode of building in the penthouse form, common in Northumberland.

TEE-HEES. Laughters. "Ye tee-heeing pixy," Exmoor Scolding, ed. 1839, p. 6.

For all the *tee-hees* that have been broke by men of droll, or dirt that has been thrown from daring spight.
Fairfax, Bulk and Selvedge of the World, 1674.

TEEHOLE. The passage in a hive through which the bees pass in and out. *East.*

TEEHT. A lock of wool, flax, &c. *Cumb.*

TEE-IRON. An instrument for drawing the lower box in the barrel of a pump.

TEEL. (1) To place anything in a leaning position against a wall, &c. *Wilts.*

(2) To give. *Devon.*

(3) To set a trap. *Devon.*

(4) To sow and harrow in seed. *West.*

TEELED. Buried. *Cornw.*

TEEM. (1) To pour out. *Var. dial.*

(2) To unload a cart. *Yorksh.*

(3) To cause? to contrive?

Ah, said he, thou hast confessed and bewrayed all - I could *teeme* it to rend thee in peeces: with that she was afraid, and wound away, and got her into companie. *Gifford's Dialogue on Witches,* 1603.

Alas, man, I could *teeme* it to go, and some counsell me to go to the man at T. B. and some to the woman at R. H. And between them both, I have lingred the time, and feare I may be spoiled before I get remedie. *Gifford's Dialogue on Witches,* 1603.

(4) To bring forth young. *Teeming-woman,* a prolific woman. *North.*

TEEMING. Overflowing.

Discard that dulness; why should soft delight
Be so oppos'd? why so should love affright
Thy tender mind, which *teeming* youth requires?
Why should dull ponderings drink up those desires?
History of Joseph, 1692.

TEEMONEER. A sea term, in common use it would appear among the Woodbridge seamen, and probably elsewhere, meaning, it is believed, the man on the look-out. *Moor's Suffolk MS.*

TEEN. (1) To light a candle. *Var. dial.* Herrick uses *teend,* to light or kindle.

(2) Angry. Also as *tene,* q. v.

(3) To shut; to close; to change. *West.* Also. to hedge or inclose a field.

(4) Taking. *Chesh.*

TEENAGE. The longer wood to make or mend hedges with. *Kennett.* In some places it is called *teenet.*

TEEN-LATHE. A tithe-barn. *North.*

TEENS. In her teens, i. e. more than twelve years old, thirteen, fourteen, &c.

That powder'd girl in blooming *teens,*
How mellow and how fine!
Caps Well Fit, Newc. 1785, p. 12.

TEENY. (1) Tiny; very small. *North.*

(2) Fretful; peevish; fractious. *Lanc.*

TEER. (1) Tar; resin; balsam. (*A.-S.*)

Men fyndeth lumpes on the sand
Of *teer,* no finer in that land.
Cursor Mundi, MS. Coll. Trin. Cantab. f. 18.

(2) "Teere of flowre, *amolum,*" Pr. Parv.

(3) To daub with clay. *North.* Hence a clay wall is sometimes called a *teer-wall.*

TE-ERE. A contraction of "this year," often used for *yet.* "I have not seen it te-ere." *Herefordsh.*

TEERE. To plaster between rafters. *Lanc.*

TEE-RING. A ring on the shaft of a waggon or cart, through which the tie of the thill-horse is put to enable him to draw.

TEERY. Full of tears? In Warwickshire, the term *teery* means smeary, moist, adhesive, as the ground is after a frost.

But these thinges overpast, if of your health and myne
You have respect, or pitty ought my *teery* weeping eyen
Romeus and Juliet, 1562.

TEERY-LERRY. The note of the lark.

The larke that many mornes herselfe makes merry
With the shrill chanting of her *toory-lorry*.
Browne's Brittannia's Pastorals, L. 140.

TEES. Iron holdfasts in the shape of the top of the letter T, pendant on short chains from the seels of a horse's collar, or from the thill-bells. They are thrust, one end first, through staples on the shafts. *Moor.*

TEEST. A vessel for refining silver.
As golde in fyre is fynid by assay,
And at the *teest* sylver is depurid.
Lydgate, MS. Soc. Antiq. 134, f. 7.

TEETHWARD. " He is clarke to the *teethward*, he hath eaten his service book ; spoken in mockage by such as maketh shew of learning and be not learned," Hollyband's Dictionarie, 1593.

TEETY. Fretful ; fractious. *North.*

TEFFIGIES. Effigies. " The teffigies and counterfait," Honours Academie, 1610, ii. 9.

TEFT. The same as *Heft*, q. v.

TEG. A sheep in its second year. *Var. dial.* " A teg or sheepe with a little head and wooll under it's belly," Florio, p. 32. Palsgrave applies the term to a young deer, " tegge or pricket, *saillant ;*" properly the doe in its second year. Skelton seems to apply the term to a woman.

TEGH. Went. (*A.-S.*)
Beves to the hors *tegh ;*
Tho the hors him knew and segh.
Beves of Hamtoun, p. 85.

TEGHELL-STANE. A tile-stone. (*A.-S.*)
If thu wenes the fever sal tak the man or the morne : tak on the even before a gude fatte ele, and do hit al qwhik in a litel pocenet ful of gude wyne, and cover hit wele with a *teghell stane* that hit gaught oute, and lat hit be swa all nyght.
Reliq. Antiq. i. 54.

TEIGHTE. Promised. See Chester Plays, i. 95. It is, perhaps, an error for *heighte.*

TEIL. To procure, or obtain. (*A.-S.*)
Go *teyl* thi mete with swynk and swoot
Into thi lyvys ende. *Coventry Mysteries*, p. 30.

TEILE. The birch tree. (*Lat.*) According to Junius, the lime tree was so called.

TEINE. Seems to signify a narrow, thin plate of metal. Tyrwhitt's Gl. p. 249.
I say, he toke out of his owen sleve
A *teine* of silver, yvel mote he cheve.
Chaucer, Cant. T. 16693.

TEINTEN. To die. (*A.-N.*)

TEISE. (1) A fathom. (*Fr.*)
In me prisoun thow schelt abide,
Under therthe twenti *teise.*
Beves of Hamtoun, p. 56.

(2) To pull to pieces with the fingers.

TEISIL. " Teysyll, *chardon*," Palsgrave.

TEITE. Quick ; speedy. (*A.-S.*)
The laddes were kaske and *teyte*,
And un-bi-yeden him ilkon. *Havelok*, 1841.

TEITHE. Tithe. Nominale MS.
Teche hem also welle and greythe
How they schule paye here *teythe.*
MS. Cotton. Claud. A. ii. f. 131.

TEJUS. Very. This word is of extensive use. *Tejus* good, *tejus* bad, *tejus* quick, *tejus* slow, &c. *Sussex.* It is sometimes used for *tedious.*

TEK. " Tek or lytylle towche, *tactulus,*" Pr. Parv. MS. Harl. 221, f. 178.

TEKE. A tick. Nominale MS.

TEKEN. To betoken ; to note ; to mark ; to observe. (*A.-S.*)

TEKYL. Ticklish.
Of hire tayle oftetyme be lyght,
And rygh *tekyl* undyr the too.
Coventry Mysteries, p. 134.

TELARY. Pertaining to weaving.

TELDE. (1) A tent ; a habitation. (*A.-S.*)
And toke ther lawneys and ther sheldes,
And leyde them upon the *teldes.*
MS. Cantab. Ff. ii. 38, f. 220.
Alle that stode on ilk a syde
Hade joye to se Clement ryde,
Byfore the sowdans *telde.*
MS. Lincoln A. i. 17, f. 107
There myght they se a wondyr thynge
Off *teldys* riche and ma[n]y a tente.
MS. Harl. 2252, f. 119.

(2) To set up ; to build ; to cover.

TELE. Deceit. (*A.-S.*)
So wyth cha[r]mes and wyth *tele*
He ys i-broste aseyn to hele.
MS. Cott. Claud. A. ii. f. 131.
Wychecrafte and *telynge*
Forbede thou hem for any thynge.
MS. Cott. Claud. A. ii. f. 131.

TELERE. A fine linen cloth, formerly worn by ladies as part of the head-dress.
That thay be trapped in gete,
Bathe *telere* and mantelete,
Ryghte of a fyne velvete,
And make we na draye.
MS. Lincoln A. i. 17, f. 134.

TELL. (1) To talk. *Somerset.*

(2) *I cannot tell*, I know not what to say or think of it. A common phrase in old plays. See Jonson, i. 125. *To hear tell*, to learn by hearsay.

TELLABILLE. Speakable.

TELLE. (1) To count ; to tell. (*A.-S.*)
(2) To recognize. (3) To remember. *Var. dial.*
(4) To proclaim a tournament ?
Now of justynges thay *telle ;*
Thay sayne that syr Percyvelle,
That he wills in the felde duelle,
Als he hase are done. *Percevall*, 113.

(5) A teal. Nominale MS.
(6) To eat hastily. *Devon.*

TELLED. Told. *Var. dial.*

TELLY. A stalk of grass, &c. *North.*

TELT. (1) Pitched ; set up. (*A.-S.*)
And swithe *telt* her paviloun
A litel withouten Cardoil toun.
Arthour and Merlin, p. 118

(2) A tent. *Prompt. Parv.*
(3) " Telte hayyr, *gauda ;* teltyd, *gaudatus,* Pr. Parv. MS. Harl. 221, f. 178.

TELWYNGE. " Telwynge or twhytynge, *scissulatus,*" Pr. Parv. MS. Harl. 221.

TEME. (1) Race ; progeny. (*A.-S.*)
Tho said the kyng of Jerusalem,
This child is come of gentille *teme.*
Torrent of Portugal, p. 81.

(2) To beget ; to propagate. (*A.-S.*)
(3) Anything following in a row, as a team of horses, &c. (*A.-S.*)

(4) To discourse?

Wan I the wolde *teme* and teche [wat] was uvel and
ȝwat was guod.　　　*Appendix to W. Mapes*, p. 335.

(5) A theme, or subject. *Palsgrave.*

(6) To emit vapour. *Somerset.*

(7) To empty; to make empty.

With swerdis swyftly thay smyte,
Thay *teme* sadlis fulle tyte.
　　　　　　　MS. Lincoln A. i. 17, f. 134.
Sire Degrevant, ar he reste,
Temede the eorl one the beste,
And hontede his forste
Wyth bernus fulle bolde.　　　*Degrevant*, 498.

TEMERATED. Violated. (*Lat.*)

Nay, they both professed that the case was so
clear and undoubted, that they both must have
sinned against their consciences, and have *temerated*
the oath they had taken when they were made
judges, if they should have argued otherwise.
　　　　　　　　　MS. Harl. 646.

TEMESE. The Thames. (*Lat.*)

And put hem in an erthen pot that be clene, and
put therto tweyne galones of clene *Temese* water that
be taken at an ebbe.　　　*MS. Sloane* 73, f. 214.

TEMNEST. Most contemned. *Shak.*

TEMOROUSLY. Rashly. (*Lat.*)

TEMPED. Intimidated; made afraid.

Thai war so temped in that tyde,
Thare thai durst no lenger bide.
　　　　　　　The Sevyn Sages, 2813.

TEMPER. Heat and moisture as productive of
vegetation. *Var. dial.*

TEMPERAL. "*Temperalium*, a temperal,"
Nominale MS. among the vestments of a
priest.

TEMPEST. A thunderstorm not necessarily
accompanied with wind. *East.*

TEMPLE-MOLD. A pattern, or mould used by
masons in fashioning their work.

TEMPLES. "The temples belong to the weavers, and are two staves with broad ends set
with sharp pins, which being laid together,
may be stretched out to any reasonable breadth
as cloth is made; and by the pins putting into
the selvage of the cloth, it is kept open while
it is in weaving," Holme. "Tempylle of a
wefer, *virguia*," MS. Dict. c. 1500.

TEMPLET. A model. *North.*

TEMPLYS. An ornament of gold set with rubies, placed upon each temple, and dependent
from the head. This fashion was prevalent
with ladies of quality, temp. Hen. VI. "Templet, a thynge made of latyn, *templete*,"
Palsgrave, subst. f. 69.

My body to be buried in the abbey of Tewks-
bury; and I desire that my great *templys*, with the
baleys, be sold to the utmost, and delivered to the
monks of that house, so that they grutched not with
my burial there.　　　*Test. Vetust.* p. 239.

TEMPRE. (1) To correct; to manage. *Tempre
thy tail*, be moderate and calm.

(2) To mix together; to mingle. Still in use,
according to Moor, p. 423.

Take warmodre, stampe it, and *temper* it with
watur, and than streyne it; and than take a sponefulle of that lekour, and putt it in his mowthe,
and he schal speke.　　　*MS. Med. Rec.* xv. Cent.

TEMPS. Time. (*A.-N.*)

TEMPT. To attempt. *South*

TEMPTATIOUS. Tempting.

TEMPTION. Temptation. *Middleton.*

TEMSE. A sieve. *North.*

Marcolphus toke a lytyll cyve or *temse* in his oon
hande, and a foot of a bere in the othre hande.
　　　　　　Salomon and Marcolphus, n. d.

TEMSING - CHAMBER. The sifting-room.
North.

TEMS-LOAF. Bread made of sifted or fine
flour. "*Miche*, a fine manchet; the countrey
people of France call so also a loafe of boulted
bread or tems bread," Cotgrave. In the notes
to Tusser, *tems loaf* is explained, "a mixture
of wheat and rye, out of which the coarser
bran only is taken."

TEMTIOUS. Tempting; inviting. *West.*

TEMZE. Thames. *Prompt. Parv.*

TEMZER. "A *temzer*, a range or coarse
searche," MS. Lansd. 1033, f. 2, an early list
of Wiltshire words.

TEN. Then. *East.*

TENANDRYE. Houses let to tenants?

His *tenandrye* was alle downe,
The beste innes in ylke towne.
　　　　　　　MS. Lincoln A. i. 17, f. 130.

TENANT-IN-TAIL. A jocular term applied to
a lady not very virtuous.

Alyed was countess would be,
For she would still be *tenaunt in taile*
To any one she could be.
　　　MS. Poems in Dr. Bliss's Possession, xvii. Cent.

TENANT-RIGHT-MEASURE.

As many use a false mile for our English mile, so
diverse use false pearches, when we have one onely
pearch allowed by Statute; for in some places in
this kingdome, notwithstanding the Statute provided for the contrarie, they use twelve foote in a
pearch, unto the great losse of the buyer, wherewith
they bee accustomed to meate medowes, calling it
tenant-right-measure; of no word of art, but onely
implying (as I take it) to be a right and proper measure belonging unto tenants; for so the word it selfe
imports. Others more proper and agreeing unto
the nature of the said measure, call it curt measure;
likewise before the said Statute (which many unto
this day use) a pearch of 18. 20. and 24. feete, called
woodland measure; all which differ from the true
and allowed measure, in such sort as ensueth.
　　　Hopton's Baculum Geodæticum, 4to. 1614.

TEN-BONES. (1) A boy's game, mentioned in
Clarke's Phraseologia Puerilis, 1655, p. 254.

(2) Fingers. A cant term.

TENCE. Cause of dispute. *Weber.*

TENCH-WEED. "A sort of pond-weed, having
a slime or mucilage about it, supposed to be
very agreeable to that fat and sleek fish. It
is *Potamogeton natans*, Lin." Forby, p. 344.

TEN-COMMANDMENTS. See *Commandments.*

TEND. (1) To watch. *North.*

(2) To wait at table. *East.*

(3) Injured; spoilt? (*A.-S.*)

Hast thow i-smelled any thynge
That hath *tend* thy lykynge?
　　　　　　MS. Cott. Claud. A. ii. f. 144

TENDABLE. Attentive. *Palsgrave.*

TENDE. (1) Tenth. Also, tithe.

The *tende* branche may men calle
Foly play, that re laste of alle.
　　　　　　　MS. Harl. 2260, f. 60.

Riʒtwis he was Goddes freude,
And trewely ʒaf to him.his *tende*.
Cursor Mundi, MS. Coll. Trin. Cantab. f. 7.

(2) To offer ; to present ; to hold out ; to stretch forth. (*A.-N.*)

TENDER. A waiter at an inn. *East.*

TENDERINGS. " *Dintiers*, the cods, dowcets, or *tenderings* of a deere," Cotgrave.

TENDER-PARNELL. A tender creature, fearful of the least puff of wind or drop of rain. As tender as Parnell, who broke her finger in a posset drink.

TENDRON. (1) A stalk of a plant. (*Fr.*)

(2) " Tendron of a wayne, *ceps*," Palsgrave.

TENE. (1) Grief ; sorrow ; anger ; hurt ; injury ; trouble. Also, to grieve, &c. (*A.-S.*)

But they wyste not what they myʒt sey,
Hur stede they fonde, sche was awey,
Then had that traytur *tene* ;
Ther jurney then they thoght evylle sett,
But they wyth the lady not mett,
They wyste not what to mene.
MS. Cantab. Ff. ii. 38, f. 73.

His gracious granseres and his grawndame,
His fader and moderis of kyngis thay came,
Was never a worthier prynce of name,
So exelent in al our day.
His fader fore love of mayd Kateryn,
In Fraunce he wroʒt turment and *tene*,
His love hee sayd hit schuld not ben,
And send him ballis him with to play.
MS. Douce 302, f. 29.

(2) Heed ; attention.

Wherby ye maye take good *toene*
That unbeleffe is a fowle syne.
Chester Plays, i. 118.

(3) To lose, or suffer loss. *Lanc.*

(4) Hard ; difficult ; perilous ; fatiguing.

TENEBLE-WEDNESDAY. *Mecredy de la semayne peneuse*, *Mecredy saint*, Palsgrave. The three nights before Easter were termed *tenebræ*. " Coles, suche as be gyven in tenebre weke," Palsgrave.

Therfore men clappes to *tenebryse*
To kyrke men for to brynge,
Bothe with claperes and with stones,
And no bellis ryng.
MS. Cantab. Ff. v. 48, f. 88.

TENEBRUS. Dark. (*Lat.*)

The radiant bryghtnes of golden Phebus
Auster gan cover with clowde *tenebrus*.
Pastime of Pleasure, p. 15.

TENEFUL. Injurious. (*A.-S.*)

TENEL. " Tenel, vessel, *tenella* ; tenel or crele, *cartallus*," Pr. Parv. f. 178.

TENENT. Opinion. The word occurs with this explanation in a table appended to the Academy of Complements, Lond. 1640.

TENGED. Stung. *Yorksh.*

TEN-GROATS. Ten groats were formerly the customary fee to priests, lawyers, &c.

TENIENTE. A lieutenant. (*Span.*)

TEN-IN-THE-HUNDRED. Was formerly the usual rate of usury, and hence the term was jocularly applied to a miser. The epitaph on Combe, attributed to Shakespeare, calls the former ten-in-the-hundred.

He that puts forth money dare not exceede the rate of 10 in the 100, but he that uttereth ware doth make his rate to his owne contentment.
The Death of Usury, 1594, sig. B. iv.

TENISLYE. Angrily. (*A.-S.*)

TENNEL. To die away, as trees. *North.*

TEN-PINS. A kind of game.

To play at loggets, nine holes, or *ten pinnes*,
To trie it out at foot-ball by the shinnes.
Letting of Humours Blood in the Head-Vaine, 1600.

Nine, a favourite and mysterious number every where, prevails in games. We have, like others, nine-pins, which we rather unaccountably call *ten-pins*, or rather *tempins*, although I never saw more than nine used in the game.
Moor's Suffolk Words, p. 249.

TEN-POUNDING. A method of punishment practised amongst harvest-men. *Suffolk.*

TEN-SIGHT. Ten times. *West.*

TENT. (1) To attend to ; to guard ; to hinder ; to prevent. *North.* To take tent, i. e. to take heed or care, Lydgate's Minor Poems, p. 34. Ray gives the following Cheshire proverb, " I'll *tent* the, quoth Wood ; if I cannot rule my daughter I'll rule my good."

He let hur have wemen at wylle
To *tent* hur, and that was skylle,
And broght hur to bede ;
What so evyr sche wolde crave,
Alle sche myght redyly hyt have,
Hur speche was sone spedd.
MS. Cantab. Ff. ii. 38, f. 74.

(2) Intent ; purpose ; design.

The feirthe es dispite off penaunce,
When a man thorue wickud comberance
Es nevere in wille ne in *tente*
Off hys syn hym to repente.
MS. Harl. 2260, f. 21.

Apon the feild his fader went,
And soght Abel wit al his *tent*.
MS. Cott. Vespas. A. iii. f. 7.

(3) A roll of lint, or other material, used in searching a wound. " Tente of a soore, *tente*," Palsgrave. To tent, to search a wound, &c.

(4) Attention ; observation. *North.*

(5) *I cannot tent*, I have no time.

(6) To scare, or frighten. *Yorksh.*

(7) A little piece of iron which kept up the cock of a gun-lock.

(8) " Tent, or tent-wine, is a kind of alicant, though not so good as pure alicant, and is a general name for all wines in Spain, except white," Blount, p. 643. " Hollock and tent would be of small repute," Taylor's Workes, 1630, iii. 65.

(9) A man's penis. *Blount.*

TENTAGE. Tent ; camp.

Upon the mount the king his *tentage* fixt,
And in the towne the barons lay in sight,
When as the Trent was risen so betwixt,
That for a while prolong'd th' unnaturall fight.
Drayton's Poems, 1637, p. 29.

TENTATION. Temptation ; trial.

Nor's any place exempted from *tentation*,
Save heaven, to ill that never had relation.
MS. Addit. 10311, f. 22.

TENT-BOB. A very small spider. See Aubrey's Miscellanies, ed. 1721, p. 145.

TENTE. To content ; to satisfy.

TENTER. (1) A person who tents cows, &c. *Linc.*

(2) A watcher; a hired collector of tolls. *North.*

(3) A stretcher or trier of cloth used by dyers and clothiers, &c. *Jacob.*

TENTERBELLY.

> Bell, the famous idoll of the Babylonians, was a meere imposture, a juggling toye, and a cheating bable, in comparison of this Nicholaitan, Kentish *tenterbelly.* *Taylor's Workes,* 1630, i. 145.

TENTER-HOOKS. He sits on tenter hooks, i. e. is very fidgety or uneasy.

TENTHEDEL. Tenth part. *Will. Werw.*

TENTYFLY. Attentively. See Maundevile's Travels, p. 299, ed. 1839.

TEONE. To injure?

> Hupe forth, Hubert, hosede pye,
> Ishot thart a-marstled into the mawe;
> Thah me *teone* with hym that myn teh mye,
> The cherld nul nout adoun er the day dawe.
> *MS. Harl.* 2253, f. 115.

TER. Anger; passion. *North.*

TERAWNTRYE. Tyranny. *Pr. Parv.*

TERCEL. The male of the gosshawk. It was called the *gentle tercel* from its tractable disposition. According to some, the term was also applied to the male eagle.

TERCEL-GENTLE. A rich man. *Grose.*

TERCIAN. Eighty-four gallons of liquor.

TERE. (1) Tedious; wearisome.

> To telle the metis were to *tere*
> That was at that sopere.
> *MS. Lincoln* A. i. 17, f. 136.

(2)

> The kyng commaundit a squyer *tere,*
> Goo telle the scheparde in his ere
> That I am the kyng.
> *MS. Cantab.* Ff. v. 48, f. 55.

(3) To hurt; to injure.

> He wenes to live and hem *tere.*
> *Arthour and Merlin,* p. 50.

(4) To cover with earth; to inter.

TEREMENT. Interment; funeral.

> Massyngers were sent to Rome
> After the Pope, and he come sone
> To here *terement.* *Syr Gowghter,* 895.

TEREPYS.

> To telle hir botonus were dure,
> Thay were anamelde with asure,
> With *terepys* and with tredoure
> Glemerand hir syde.
> *MS. Lincoln* A. i. 17, f. 133.

TEREY. Tapering. *Salop.*

TERIAR. "Teryare or ertare, *irritator;* teryar or longe lytare, *morosus,*" Pr. Parv.

TERINS. A sort of singing-bird. (*A.-N.*)

> And thrustils, *terins,* and mavise,
> That songin for to winne hem prise.
> *Romaunt of the Rose,* 665.

TERLYNCEL. The name of a devil.

> Than ye thys *terlyncels* skylle,
> Slepe thou long and y shal hele.
> *MS. Harl.* 1701, f. 29.

TERM. To call; to name.

TERMAGANT. The name of an old Saracen deity, corrupted from *Tervagant.* He was represented in our old plays as of a most violent character, and hence the term came to be applied to anything violent or fiery. A scold is still termed a termagant.

> For this teare-throat *termagant* is a fellow in folio,

a commander of such great command, and of such greatnesse to command, that I never saw any that in that respect could countermand him.
> *Taylor's Workes,* 1630, iii. 79.

TERMERS. Persons who visited the metropolis at term-time, which was formerly the fashionable season. The term is generally applied to those who came for intrigues or tricks.

TERMES. Times for work. (*A.-N.*)

TERMINED. Judged; determined. (*A.-N.*)

> Whiche to my lady stant enclyned,
> And hath his love noʒt *termined.*
> *Gower, MS. Soc. Antiq.* 134, f. 62.

And thus, with the helpe of Almighty God, the moaste glorious Virgin Mary his mothar, and of Seint George, and of (all) the Saynts of heven, was begon, finished, and *termined,* the reentrie and perfecte recover of the juste title and right of owr sayd soveraygne Lord Kynge Edward the Fowrthe, to his realme and crowne of England, within the space of xj. wekes. *Arrival of King Edward IV.* p. 39.

TERM-TROTTER. A resorter to the capital during term-time. Middleton, i. 330.

TERNE. A thrust in fencing.

TERR. To uncover. *North.*

TERRA. A turf. *Exmoor.*

TERRA-FIRMA. A name given by the Venetians to their continental possessions.

TERRAGE. Earth, or mould. (*Lat.*)

> Nor the vyne hys holsum fresche *terrage,*
> Wych gyveth comfort to all manner of age.
> *Ashmole's Theat. Chem. Brit.* 1652, p. 213.

TERRE. (1) To stir; to provoke. *Baber.*

(2) To strike to the earth. (*Lat.*)

TERREMOTE. An earthquake.

> Whereof that alle the halle quok,
> As it a *terremote* were.
> *Gower, MS. Soc. Antiq.* 134, f. 190.

TERRENE. Earthly. (*Lat.*)

> And far more lovely than the *terrene* plant,
> That blushing in the aire turnes to a stone.
> *The Taming of a Shrew,* 1607.

TERRER.

> The *terrer* of the house being master thereof, as being appointed to give entertainment to all sorts, noble, gentle, and of what degree soever, that came thither as strangers.
> *Davies' Ancient Rites,* 1672, p. 139.

TERRESTRE. Earthly. (*A.-N.*)

TERRESTRIAL-MULLET. "A kind of a stone which hath also a kind of motion with it, especially if it be put in vinegar," Holme.

TERRESTRIAL-TRIUMPHS. "*Germini,* a kind of playing-cards called terrestriall triumphs," Florio, p. 207.

TERRET. The ring on the saddle through which the gig-reins pass. *East.*

TERRIBLE. Very; excessive. *Var. dial.*

TERRICK. A trifle, or little thing. *Devon.*

TERRIER. A kind of auger. *Howell.*

TERRIFY. To tease; to torment. *Var. dial.*

TERRIT. A clump of trees. *Warw.*

TERSE. "A firkin, rundlet, or *terse,* conteining nine gallons of our measure," Higins' Nomenclator, 1585, p. 340.

TERTAGATE. A target, or buckler.

TERTIA. That portion of an army which is levied out of one particular district. (*Span.*)

TERVEE. To struggle, or kick about. *Esse.*

TERWYD. Tired; wearied. *Pr. Parv.*

TESE. To teasel wool.

TESING. A ringworm.

TESSEL. Order, condition, said of land.

TEST. To take the test, i. e. to take the Sacrament in testimony of being a member of the Church of England.

TESTE. (1) The head. (*A.-N.*)

(2) The same as *Teest*, q. v.

TESTED. Made pure as gold. *Shak.*

TESTER. (1) A sixpence. See *Testone.*

Tarlton, seeing himself so over-reacht, greatly commended the beggers wit, and withall, in recompence thereof, gave him a *teaster.* With that the begger said that hee would *most* truly pray to God for him. No, answered Tarlton, I pray thee pray for thy selfe, for I take no usury for almes-deeds.
Tarlton's Jests, 1611.

(2) The fixed top and head parts of a bedstead. *Var. dial.*

Ther was at hur *testere*
The kyngus owne banere;
Was nevere bede rychere
Of empryce ne qwene! *Degrevant,* 1485.

TESTERE. A piece of iron armour which covered the head of a horse. (*A.-N.*)

TESTIF. Headstrong. (*A.-N.*)

TESTIFICATION. Testimony.

TESTONE. The testone was in Henry VIII.'s reign applied to the English shilling, but in the time of Elizabeth the sixpence was so termed. "She restored sundrie coines of fine silver, as peeces of halfepenie farding, of a penie, of three halfe pence, peeces of two pence, of three pence, of foure pence (called the groat), of sixpence, *usuallie named the testone,* Harrison, p. 218.

TESTORN. Teaty; touchy; angred.

TESTY. A witness. *Howell.*

TETCH. (1) A spot, or blemish. (*A.-N.*)

(2) "Tetche or maner of condycion, *mos,*" Pr. Parv. MS. Harl. 221, f. 178.

TETCHY. (1) Touchy; quarrelsome. *Var. dial.*

(2) Applied to land that is difficult to work or to manage. *East.*

TETE. A woman's teat. *Palsgrave.* It also occurs in Pr. Parv. MS. Harl. f. 179.

TETER-CUM-TAWTER. A seesaw. *East.*

TETHDE. Full of tempers; ill-tempered. Towneley Mysteries, Gloss. in v.

TETHER. (1) To marry. *Warw.*

(2) The royal name Tudor. *Drayton.*

(3) A cord or chain to tie an animal at pasture. "To live within the *tether,*" to live within bounds. *Kent.*

TETHER-DEVIL. The plant woody nightshade.

TETHER-STAKE. A stake driven into the ground to which cattle are tied up. *Var. dial.*

TETHINGE. Tidings; intelligence.

So that the *tethinge* therof to the kynge com,
That a lither theof and a manquellere hadde so liзt
dom. *Life of Thomas Beket,* p. 19.

TETHTERE. The tester of a bed.

TETINE. To writhe, or turn about.

TETRICALL. Sour; sullen; gloomy.

TETRIFOL. The plant trefoil. "To the flowring tetrifol," British Bibl. ii. 283.

TETRINE. Foul; horrible? "Mystes blake and cloudes tetryne," Skelton, ii. 396.

TETSY. Elizabeth. *Linc.*

TETTA. Shall we? *Devon.*

TETTERWORT. The plant celidony.

TETTIES. Teats. *Var. dial.*

TETTY. (1) Betty. *Pegge.*

(2) Peevish; fractious.

TEUGH. Tough. *North.*

TEUK. The redshank. *Essex.*

TEW. (1) To tow along. Also, the rope by which a vessel or boat is towed.

Some on their breasts, some working on their knees,
To winne the banke whereon the Barons stood;
Which o'er the current they by strength must *tew,*
To shed that bloud which many an age shall rew.
Drayton's Poems, 1637, p. 21.

(2) To be actively employed; to labour; to work hard; to fatigue. *North.*

(3) To pull, or tear about; to tumble over; to discompose; to tease. *Var. dial.*

(4) Tender; sickly. *I. of Wight.*

(5) To mix together. *North.*

(6) A hempen string. *Somerset.*

(7) A number, or quantity. *West.*

TEWED. When applied to a muslin cover, means that it is creased and soft. *Yorksh.*

TEWEL. A tail. *Dunelm.* Kennett, MS. Lansd. 1033. It occurs in Chaucer, Cant. T. 7730, spelt *towel.* The fundament of a horse is still so called in Norfolk.

TEWELL. A pipe, or funnel; a louvre. "A tewelle of a chymney, *epicaustorium,*" MS. Dict. c. 1500. "In the back of the smith's forge, against the fire-place, is fixed a thick iron plate and a taper pipe in it about five inches long, which comes thro the back of the forge, and into which is placed the nose of the bellows; this pipe is calld a tewel, or a tewel-iron," Kennett MS. f. 411.

TEWFET. A lapwing. *North.*

TEWHE. To taw leather. *Lydgate.*

TEWKE. "Tewke to make purses of, *trelis,*" Palsgrave, subst. f. 69.

TEWLY. A word in common use in the counties of Essex and Cambridgeshire, particularly the latter, and signifying qualmish. Ex. A person feeling rather poorly in the morning, and not relishing his breakfast. "You are rather *teuly* this morning." A person in delicate health is called a *teuly* one.

TEW-TAW. To *tew-taw* hemp, i. e. to beat or dress hemp. More's MS. Additions to Ray's South and East Country Words.

TEWTER. An instrument for breaking flax, as a brake for hemp. *Chesh.*

TEXT. Truth. *Marston.*

TEXTUEL. Ready at citing texts. (*A.-N.*)

TEYE. "Teye of a cofyr or forcer, *teca, thecarium,*" Pr. Parv. f. 178.

TEYL. Scorn.

But thogh a man sey never so weyl,
Unto hys sawys men fyden *teyl.*
MS. Harl. 1701, f. 14.

TEYELLEYER. A tailor. *North.*

TEYSE. To poise it for shooting.

> And he with that an arow hath hente,
> And gan to *teyse* it in his bowe.
>
> *Gower, MS. Soc. Antiq.* 134, f. 167.

THA. (1) Then.

> That for hir sake righte *tha,*
> Sone he gane undir-ta
> The sory sowdane to sla,
> Withowttene any lett. *Percevul,* 1329.

(2) Those. Hampole, MS.

THAC. That. *Wilts.*

THACKE. (1) Thatch. "Erige, holme or thacke," Huloet, 1552. "And also for thack," Tusser, p. 164. *Thakkid,* thatched, Leland Itin. ii. 39. "Thakke, *tegmen, tectura,*" Vocab. MS. "The original meaning of this word is straw or rushes, our Saxon ancestors using no other covering for their houses. Afterwards it was extended to slate and tiles; and he who covered a building, either with these or the more antient materials, was called a thacker, or thatcher," Hallamsh. Gl. p. 162. "To thack on, to lay on or cover," Kennett, MS. Lansd. 1033, f. 412.

(2) To thump; to thwack. (*A.-S.*) "Thacked him with stones," Brit. Bibl. i. 361.

THACKER. A thatcher. *Var. dial.*

> A proud *thacker* of Thecoa would laugh them to scorn and contemn their dispiling discipline.
>
> *Pilkington's Works,* p. 381.

THACK-PRICKS. Pegs for securing thatch.

THACK-TILES. Roof-tiles. *Grose.*

THACSTARE. A thatcher. *Pr. Parv.*

THAFFER. Therefore. *Norf.*

THAGGY. Thick and misty. *Yorksh.*

THAGH. Though. (*A.-S.*)

> And *thagh* the chylde bote half be bore,
> Hed and necke and no more,
> Bydde hyre spare never the later
> To crystene hyt and caste on water.
>
> *MS. Cott. Claud.* A. ii. f. 128.

THAIRE. Their. *North.*

> That es to say, we sulde ay
> *Thairs* persones love and for thayme praye.
>
> *MS. Harl.* 2260, f. 2.

THAKNALES. The same as *Strabrods,* q. v.

THAME. A thumb. *Lanc.*

THAMPY. Damp. *Yorksh.*

THAN. (1) A common form of *then.*

(2) A den. Octovian, 553.

THANDER. Yonder. *Warw.*

THANDON. "Thandon for wylde digges, swannus, and piggus," is thus described:

> Take wasshe tho hues of swannes anon,
> And skoure tho guttus with salt ichon;
> Seth alle togedur and hew hit smalle,
> The flesshe and eke tho guttus withalle.
> Take galingale and gode gynger,
> And canel, and grynd hom al in fere;
> And mynde bred thou take therto,
> And tempur hit up with broth also:
> Colour hit with brend bred or with blode,
> Seson hit with venegur a lytelle for gode.
> Welle alle togedur in a posnet,
> In servyce forth thou schalt hit sett.
>
> *MS. Sloane* 1986, p. 56.

THANK. (1) Thankfulness; good will.

(2) *Thanks and a thousand,* a thousand thanks. *Thanks be praised,* a common exclamation of thankfulness after an unexpected blessing. *Thank God, thank you,* a reply after grace is said after dinner, and addressed to the host. *Thank you for them,* an answer to an inquiry after absent friends, meaning they are very well, I thank you for them.

THANKWORTH. Thankworthy.

> That was *thankworth* is thanne blame.
>
> *Gower, MS. Soc. Antiq.* 134, f. 54.

THANKYNGYS. Thanks.

> The vj.the tokene ys that he doythe dewe *thankyngys* to the good wylle of God.
>
> *MS. Cantab.* Ff. ii. 38, f. 8.

THANNA. Then.

> Item if any womman take any monee to lye with any man, but she ly stille with hym til it be the morwe tyme and *thanna* arise, she shal make a syn of vi. s. viij. d. *MS. Bodl.* e Mus. 229.

THANNE. Then. (*A.-S.*)

THANY. Damp. *Craven.*

THARBOROUGH. A third-borough, or constable.

THARD-CAKE. A thin circular cake of considerable size made of treacle and oatmeal. Brockett calls it, "a cake made of unfermented dough, chiefly of rye and barley, rolled very thin and baked hard." It appears to be a corruption of *tharf,* unleavened.

THARE. Behoveth; needeth. (*A.-S.*)

> Of his commyng the frere was fayne;
> The *thare* noghte be so bayne.
>
> *MS. Lincoln* A. i. 17, f. 142.

THARF. (1) Need?

> And wele y-sen, çif thai willen,
> That hem no *tharf* never spillen.
>
> *Arthour and Merlin,* p. 2

(2) Stiff; backward; shy. *North.*

THARFE. A number, or company.

THARFLY. Slowly; deliberately. *Yorksh.*

THARKY. Dark. *South.*

THARLLE. A slave or vilein.

> Lorde, sende it unto the syke *tharlle,*
> And gyff me lysens to lyve in ease.
>
> *MS. Cantab.* Ff. i. 6, f. 46.

THARMES. Entrails. *North.* "Trutum, Anglice a tharme," Nominale MS.

> Of the chylde that she bare yn here arroys,
> Al to-drawe were the *tharmys.*
>
> *MS. Harl.* 1701, f. 5.

THARN. To mock; to scorn. *Devon.*

THARNE. (1) To yearn; to need; to want.

> That es *tharnyng* for ever of the syght namely
> Of owre Loverd Godd Almyghty.
>
> *Hampole, MS. Bowes,* p. 213.

(2) To be deprived of. (*A.-S.*)

THARNEN. Made of thorn. *Wilts.*

THAROWTE. Out in the air.

THARRY. Dark. *Suffolk.*

THARST. Daring.

> What, arte thou bolde or *tharst* in eny wyse.
>
> *Lydgate, MS. Ashmole* 39, f. 26.

THART. Need. (*A.-S.*)

> He thoçt that whan Jhesu was dede,
> He *thart* have of hym no drede.
>
> *MS. Cantab.* Ff. v. 48, f. 35.

THAR-VORE. Therefore. (*A.-S.*)

Ther-sore, mon, thu the bi-thench,
Al schal falewi thi grene.
MS. Cott. Calig. A. ix. f. 243.

THARWE. Throw ; moment.

THASER. A thatcher ; a builder.

THAT. (1) It. *East.*

(2) So ; so much ; so great. *North.*

THATADONNET. See *Adonnet.*

THAT-A-WAY. That way. *Yorksh.*

THATCH'D-HEAD. One wearing the hair matted together, as the native Irish in times past. *Nares.*

THATCH-GALLOWS. A rogue.

THATENS. "A *thatens*" and a *thisens.* In that manner and this manner.

THAT-I-LEAVE. That is a point I will not determine. "So folks sah, but *that I leave*," i. e. to others to decide. *Moor's Suff. MS.*

THAT-NOT. Wherefore.

THAT-OF. Although.

THAT'S-ONCE. That is, that's once for all, that's flat. See Peele's Works, i. 129.

THAT'S-WHAT. That's what the matter is.

THAT-THERE. (1) That. *Var. dial.*

(2) A London rider. *Devon.*

THAU. Though. *Thauf*, Jennings, p. 75.
Bot *thau* he wrothe hym never so sore,
For sothe I nylle prove hym no more.
Wright's Seven Sages, p. 61.

THAVE. To give, bear, sustain. (*A.-S.*)

THAVEL. A pot-stick. *North.*

THAW. Thou. *Var. dial.*

THAYN. A nobleman. (*A.-S.*)

THE. (1) A thigh. (*A.-S.*)
If I fonde ever grace in the,
Lay thi honde undir my *the*,
And hete me truly bi covenonde,
That I not graven be in this londe.
Cursor Mundi, MS. Coll. Trin. Cantab. f. 34.
The fendys here crokys fasted yn hys knees,
And al to-drowe and rente hys *thees*.
MS. Harl. 1701, f. 10.

Beholde my shankes, behold my knees,
Beholde my hed, armes, and *thees*.
Bliss's Bibl. Miscell. p. 48.

(2) To thrive ; to prosper. (*A.-S.*)
God that sittis in trinité,
Gyffe thaym grace wel to *the*
That lystyns me a whyle.
MS. Cantab. Ff. v. 48, f. 47.

He is wys that is wood,
He is riche that hath no good ;
He is blynd that can y-see,
Wel is hym that nere may *thee*.
MS. Bodl. 100, f. 1.

(3) This. *Heref.*

(4) There ; though. (*A.-S.*)

THEABES. Gooseberries. *Norf.*

THEAD. A strainer placed at the bottom of a mash-tub in brewing. *East.* "Thede, bruares instrument, *qualus*," Pr. Parv.

THEAK. To thatch. *North.* Also, thatch. "*Tector*, a theker," Nominale MS.

THEAL. A board ; a plank ; a joist. *Leic.*

THEAN. Moist ; damp. *Westm.*

THEAT. Firm ; close ; staunch. Spoken of barrels when they do not run. *North.*

THEAVE. An ewe of the first year. Ray gives this as an Essex word, but Pegge says it is applied in the North to a sheep of three years old.

THEC. That. *I. of Wight.*

THECCHE. To thatch. (*A.-S.*)
And some he taughte to tilie,
To dyche and to *thecche*.
Piers Ploughman, p. 410.

THECHE. To teach. (*A.-S.*)
Theche hem to come and schryve hem clene,
And also hosele hem bothe at ene.
MS. Cott. Claud. A. ii. f. 128.

THE-DAY. To-day. *North.*

THEDE. (1) A brewer's instrument. *Palsgrave.*

(2) Country ; land ; kingdom. (*A.-S.*)
Scho says, blody are his wede,
And so es his riche stede,
Siche a knyght in this *thede*
Saw I never nane. *Perceval*, 1255.

THEDAM. Prosperity. (*A.-S.*)
Now thrifte and *thedam* mote thou have, my leve swete barn. *The Goode Wif*, p. 14.

THEDURWARDE. Toward that place.
He harde besyde at a place
A grete mornyng of a man ;
Thedurwarde he drew hym than.
MS. Cantab. Ff. ii. 38, f. 174.

THEE. You ; your ; thy. *West.*

THEEZAM. These. *Somerset.*

THEEFE. A term of reproach, not necessarily applied to one who thieves.
Fiftene yeres es it gane
Syne he my brodire hade slane,
Now hadde the *theefe* undirtane,
To sla us alle thenne. *Perceval*, 923.

THEER. Deer.
But sone he was besette
As *theer* ys yn a nette.
Lybeaus Disconus, 1133.

THEFELY. Like a thief. (*A.-S.*)

THEGITHER. Together. *North.*

THEI. Though ; although. (*A.-S.*)

THEINE. Thence ; therefrom.
And Alexander gert spirre thame in the langage of Inde whare thay my3te fynde any fresche water ; and thay talde whare, and schewed thame a place a littille *theine*. *MS. Lincoln* A. i. 17, f. 28.

THEINES. Servants. (*A.-S.*)
Hwer bedh thine *theines*
That the leove were.
MS. Cott. Calig. A. ix. f. 246.

THEIR. Used sometimes for *their's*.

THEIRSELS. Themselves. *North.*

THEKE. Thatch. Still in use.

THELOURE.
Gold and silver and riche stones,
That vertu bere mani for the nones ;
Gode clothes of sikelatoun and Alisaundrinis,
Theloure of Matre, and purper, and bliss.
Sir Gy of Warwike, p. 96.

THEM. Those. *Var. dial.*

THEMEL. "Save nedel and threde and *themel* of lether," Gower, MS. Soc. Antiq. 134, f. 254.

THEMMIN. Those. *Wilts.*

THEMMY. Those. *Somerset.*

THEN. That time. *Var. dial.*

THENCH. To think. (*A.-S.*)

Mon, let sunne and lustes thine ;
Wel thu do and wel thu *thench.*
MS. Cott. Calig. A. ix. f. 243.

THENE. (1) To prosper. (*A.-S.*)
Thai schal have ayrs ham betwene,
That schal have grace to thryve and *thene ;*
Thother schul have turment and tene.
MS. Douce 302, f. 1.

(2) To reach. (*A.-S.*)
Non mai longe lives *thene,*
Ac ofte him liedh the wrench.
MS. Cott. Calig. A. ix. f. 243.

THENKE. To think. (*A.-S.*)
Thus thow myʒte synge dedlyche,
ʒef thow *thenke* theron myche.
MS. Cott. Claud. A. ii. f. 139.
Upon his worde hire herte aflyʒte,
Thenkende what was best to done.
Gower, MS. Soc. Antiq. 134, f. 66.

THENNES. Thence. (*A.-S.*)
But who that cometh therein certeyn,
So lightly may he not turne ayen,
For he shal nevere *thennes* come,
These sawes hath the boke y-nome.
MS. Addit. 11305, f. 94.

THENOUTEZ. Sinews ?
Namely, of bones, of cartilages, of invictures, of grosse nerves, of *thenoutez,* and of colligaciones.
MS. Sloane 965, f. 28.

THEOFLICHE. Like a thief. (*A.-S.*) See Kyng Alisaunder, 4002.

THEOFTHE. Theft. (*A.-S.*)
And do *theofthe* and robberie in al the lond aboute.
Life of Thomas Beket, p. 19.

THEOLOGY. A theologian.

THEORBO. A kind of lute. (*Ital.*)
And wanting nothing but a song,
And a well-tun'd *theorbo* hung
Upon a bough, to ease the pain
His tugg'd ears suffer'd, with a strain.
Hudibras, I. iii. 166.

THEORIQUE. Theory. *Shak.*

THEPES. Gooseberries. An East country word, given in Sir Thomas Brown's Tracts, p. 146.

THER. (1) Those. *North.*

(2) There ; where. *Therafter,* in proportion to it. Still in use. "*Thereater,* at that rate, in proportion," Smith's I. of Wight Gloss. *Thermyd,* therewith.

THERE-A-WAY. There.

THEREAWAYS. Thereabouts. *There and thereaways,* thereabouts. *Var. dial.*

THEREFORE. Therefore I say it, i. e. that is my argument! *West.*

THERENCE. From that place. *West.*

THERE-RIGHT. (1) Straight forward. *Var. dial.*

(2) On this very spot. *West.*

THERF-BREED. Unleavened bread. (*A.-S.*)
With *therf-breed* and letus wilde,
Whiche that groweth in the filde.
Cursor Mundi, MS. Coll. Trin. Cantab. f. 38.

THERKENES. Darkness. (*A.-S.*)

THERLE. Ill-nourished ; gaunt ; delicate. *Devon.*

THERST. Durst.

That wyf *therst* not say nay,
For wordes vile,
But grauntede well that ylke day
Her lordes wylle.
Octovian, 681.

THERTHURF. There-through.
And *therthurf* me tajte hire the wei, so that heo thider com,
And jeode aboute as a best that ne couthe no wysdom.
Life of Thomas Beket, p. 4.

THERUPPE. Thereupon. (*A.-S.*)

THERWE. Through. *Will. Werw.*

THERʒEN. There-against ; against.
To hasten love is thynge in vayne,
Whan that fortune is *therʒen.*
Gower, MS. Soc. Antiq. 134, f. 95.

THESE. This. *Heref.*

THESELF. Itself. *East.*

THESTER. Dark ; obscure. (*A.-S.*) "In theater stede," Kyng Alisaunder, 4906.
For it is alle *thester* thing,
Nil ich make therof no telling.
Arthour and Merlin, p. 64.
On an *thester* stude I stod
An luitel striff to here.
MS. Digby 86, f. 195.

THETCHES. Vetches. *Oxon.*

THETHEN. Thence. (*A.-S.*)

THETHORNE. "Thethorne tre, *ramnus,*" Pr. Parv. *Ramnus* is the medlar tree.

THEUT. Giveth. See *Ungunde.*

THEVE. "Theve, brusch," Pr. Parv.

THEW. (1) Manner ; quality. (*A.-S.*)
Ful selde ys synger gode yn *thew,*
But that yn sum poynt he ys a shrew.
MS. Harl. 1701, f. 21.
His vertues and good *thewys,*
And good ensaunple that he schewys.
MS. Cotton. Tiber. A. vii. f. 72.
For wymmenes speche that ben schrewes,
Turne ofte away gode *thewes ?*
MS. Cott. Claud. A. ii. f. 127.
Also thy chyldre that were schrewes,
Hast thow i-taght hem gode *thewes ?*
MS. Cott. Claud. A. ii. f. 144.

(2) Thawed. *Var. dial.*

(3) A cucking-stool. Brand, iii. 52. "Thewe or pylory, *collistrigium,*" Pr. Parv.

THEWE. (1) Subjection. (*A.-S.*)

(2) A slave, or bondsman. (*A.-S.*)

THEWED. Towardly. *North.*

THEWES. Shakespeare seems to use this term in the sense of *sinews.* See 2 Henry IV. iii. 2. &c. Can it mean *thighs ?*

THEWID. Educated ; mannered. (*A.-S.*)
It sit a preste to be wel *thewid,*
And schame it is yf he be lewid.
Gower, MS. Soc. Antiq. 134, f. 40.

THEY. (1) Those. *Var. dial.*

(2) Thy. Skelton's Works, i. 125.

THEʒ. Though ; although.
This child, *theʒ* hit were ʒung, wel hit understod,
For seli child is sone i-lered ther he wole beo god.
Life of Thomas Beket, p. 8.

THIBEL. (1) A smooth round stick used for stirring broth, porridge, &c. *North.*

(2) A dibble, or setting-stick. *North.*

THIC. This ; that. *West.*

THICEY. That. *Cornw.*

THICK. (1) Very intimate. *Var. dial.*

(2) *To go through thick and thin*, to overcome every kind of obstacle.

(3) Frequent; plentiful. *Var. dial.*

(4) Stupid; obstinate. *South.*

(5) A thicket, or close bush. Moor has *thicks*, groves or woods with close underwood. Suffolk Words, p. 426.

THICK-BILL. The bullfinch. *Lanc.*

THICKED. Thickened.

> Thither they conveie their clothes to be *thicked* at the fulling milles, sometimes ten miles for the same. *Harrison's Britaine*, p. 52.

THICKEE. This. *Devon.*

THICKEMNY. That. *Somerset.*

THICK-END. A considerable part; as if you ask how far such a place is, the answer would probably be, " The *thick-end* of a mile." *Linc.*

THICK-HOTS. Water-porridge. *North.*

THICKLISTED. Short-winded. *Devon.*

THICK-PODDITCH. Thick water-gruel. *Lanc.*

THICK-SET. (1) Strong. (2) Closely planted.

THICK-SKINNED. Coarse; vulgar; unpolished.

THICK-SPINNING. Bad conduct. *North.*

THIDER. Thither. (*A.-S.*)

> Wher wer were aldermast,
> Thai were *thider* sent on hast.
> *Arthour and Merlin*, p. 83.

THIEF. (1) *As safe as a thief in a mill*, very secure. Still in common use.

> There she may lodge, and trade too if she will,
> As sure and safe *as theeves are in a mill*.
> *Taylor's Workes*, 1630, iii. 9.

(2) An imperfection in the wick of a candle, causing it to gutter. *Var. dial.*

THIGGE. To beg. *North.*

> Thaym were betere *thygge* thayre mete,
> Than any gode on that wyse gete. *MS. Harl.* 2960, f. 60.

THIGH. (1) To cower down.

(2) To carve a pigeon.

THIKFOLD. Very frequent.

THILKE. This same; that same. (*A.-S.*)

THILL. (1) A shaft. *Thill-horse*, a shaft-horse. " Thyll horse, *limonnier*," Palsgrave. " Thyll of a carte, *le lymon*," Ibid.

(2) In a coal mine, the surface upon which the tram runs. *Newc.*

THILLER. The same as *Filler*, q. v.

THILL-HANKS. The leather thongs fastened into the hames of the collar of the thiller.

THILTUGS. Chains attached to the collar of the shaft-horse.

THIMBLE. The boll of a gate-hook on which the gate turns. *Staff.*

THIMBLE-PIE. A fillip given with a thimble on the finger, a common term in girls' schools.

THIMMEL. A thimble. *North.*

THIN. *To run thin*, to try to get released from a disadvantageous bargain.

THINDER. Yonder. *East.*

THIN-DRINK. Small beer. *Var. dial.*

THING. (1) " The worth of a thing is what it will bring," is a common proverb, the origin of which is often erroneously attributed to Butler.

> For what is worth in any thing,
> But so much money as 'twill bring.
> *Hudibras*, II. i. 465.

(2) That's the thing, i. e. quite right.

(3) This term is constantly applied to a lady in early metrical romances.

> Seyde Organata that swete *thynge*,
> Y schalle geve the a gode golde rynge,
> Wyth a fulle ryche stone. *Eglamour*, 616.
> Gye starte to that maydyn synge,
> And seyde, Make no dole, my swete *thynge*.
> *MS. Cantab.* Ff. ii. 38, f. 176.

(4) The pudendum. *Var. dial.*

THING-DONE. An old game described in Cynthia's Revels, ed. Gifford, ii. 306.

THING-OF-NOTHING. Anything worthless.

THINGUMMITE. An unmeaning word used when the name of a person or thing is forgotten. " Hew towd ye ?" " Why, Mr. *Thingummite*." This is generally applied to a person. *Thingumbobe* and *Thingummerry* are terms about equivalent, or perhaps applied more frequently to things. I have, however, heard them all applied to persons. *Thingomy, thing-omightum*, are also used.

THINK. (1) Thing. This very common vulgarism is found in Lelandi Itin. ii. 39.

(2) *To think scorn*, to disdain. *To think shame*, to feel ashamed. *To think on*, to remember or remind.

THINKE. To seem. (*A.-S.*)

THINNE. (1) Slender; small. (*A.-S.*)

(2) To the, or prosper. See *Thene*.

> And on myne errand go thou tyte,
> Also mot thou *teynne*.
> *MS. Cantab.* Ff. v. 48, f. 12.

THINNY. To whine. *Devon.*

THIN-SKINNED. (1) A term applied to land with a thin superstratum of good soil.

(2) Easily offended. *Var. dial.*

THIN3TH. Thinketh. (*A.-S.*)

THIR. To frighten, hurt, or strike dead. *Erw.*

THIRD. For *thrid*, thread.

THIRD-BOROUGH. A constable. Lambarde says, " In some shires, where every third borow hath a constable, there the officers of the other two be called *thirdborows*."

> Hobb Andrw he was *thridborro*;
> He bad hom, Pesse! God gyff hom sorro!
> For y mey arrest yow best.
> *Huntyng of the Hare*, 199.

THIRDENDEALE. (1) A third part.

(2) A measure containing three pints. *West.* Anciently it was eighty-four gallons, according to a note in Pr. Parv. p. 117. Kennett has *thurindale*, q. v.

> Hit boldis a gode *thrydendale*,
> Ful of wyne every mele.
> *MS. Cantab.* Ff. v. 48, f. 51.

THIRD-FATHER. A great-grandfather.

THIRDING. (1) Doing a thing the third time, particularly, I think, hoeing turnips. " Ar them there tahnups done woth ?" " No, we are *thirding* 'em." *Moor's Suff. MS.*

(2) A custom practised at the universities, where two thirds of the original price is allowed by the upholsterers to the students for household goods returned to them within the year.

THIRDINGS. The Ridings. This word is given by Urry, in his MS. Additions to Ray.

THIRETELLE. The herb *apium risus*.

THIRLABILLE. Easily penetrated.

THIRLAGE. The service of certain lands, the tenants of which are bound to take their corn to grind at the lord's mill.

THIRLE. (1) To pierce through. (*A.-S.*)

And now to see tham *thyrlits* with a nayle,
How shulde my sorowfulle harte bot fayle?
Reliq. Antiq. ii. 130.

(2) Lean; thin; meagre. *Devon.*

(3) A hole. (*A.-S.*)

If thou ware in a myrke house one the daye, and alle the *thirlles*, dores and wyndows ware stokyne that na sone myght enter.
MS. Lincoln A. I. 17, f. 241.

THIRSTLE. A thrush. *Devon.*

THIRSTY. Sharp; eager; active.

THIRTEEN. *Thirteen-pence-halfpenny* was formerly the wages of a hangman, and hence the term was jocularly applied to him.

THIRTOVER. Perverse; morose. *South.*

THIRTY-ONE. See *One-and-Thirty.*

THIS. Thus.

THISAN. This. *North.*

THIS-A-WAY. This way. *Yorksh.*

THISE. These. (*A.-S.*)

THIS-HERE. This. *Var. dial.*

THISSEN. This way. *Var. dial.*

THISSUM. This. *West.*

THISTLE-CROWN. According to Snelling, p. 24, a gold coin worth about four shillings.

THISTLE-FINCH. "*Carduelis*, a linnet, a thistlefinch," Nomenclator, 8vo. 1585, p. 57.

THISTLE-HEMP. A kind of early hemp.

THISTLE-TAKE. A duty of a halfpenny, anciently paid to the lord of the manor of Halton, in the county of Chester, for every beast driven over the common, suffered to graze or eat but a thistle. *Bailey.*

THISTLE-WARP. Same as *Thistle-finch*, q. v.

THITE. Tight; close; compact. *East.* " Thyht, hool fro brekynge, not brokyne," Pr. Parv. " Thyht, not hool within, *solidus*," ib.

THITER. (1) A dung-cart. *Linc.*

(2) A foolish fellow; an idiot. *North.*

THIVEL. The same as *Thibel*, q. v.

THIXILLE. An axe, or hatchet.

THIȝANDEZ. Tidings. " I ȝif the for thy *thyȝandez*," Morte Arthure, MS. Linc. f. 70.

THO. (1) Then; when. (*A.-S.*) Still in use in the first sense in Somerset.

Tho he hadde it y-seyd,
The king sore was amayd.
Arthour and Merlin, p. 86.

(2) Those; the. (*A.-S.*)

THODDEN. Sodden; not well baked. *North.*

THODS. Gusts of wind. *North.*

THOFE. Though. Still in use in the Northern counties, pronounced *thof.*

And *thofe* the bryde blythe be
That Percyvelle hase wone the gree,
ȝete the rede knyghte es he
Hurte of his honde. *Perceval*, 81.

THOFFER. Because. *Suffolk.*

THOFT. Thought. *Devon.*

THOFT-FELLOW. A fellow oarsman.

II.

THOGFE. Though. (*A.-S.*)

Thogfe Perccvelle hase slayne the rede knyght,
ȝitt may another be als wyghte,
And in that gere be dyghte,
And takene alle hym fra I *Perceval*, 1453.

THOGHE. Though; although.

Thoghe every day a man hyt haunte,
ȝyt wyl no man be hyt agraunte.
MS. Harl. 1701, f. 23.

THOISE. The tusk of a boar.

THOKE. " Thoke, as onsadde fysch, *humorosus, insolidus*," Pr. Parv. See Blount, in v. *Thokes.*

THOKISH. Slothful; sluggish. *East.* In Lincolnshire it is usually *thoky.*

THOLD. Told. Octovian, 634.

THOLE. (1) To bear; to suffer. (*A.-S.*)

And suche a stenche is in that hole,
Noon ertly man ne myght it *thole.*
MS. Addit. 11305, f. 96.

Bad him orpedliche he schuld kethe,
For he no schuld there *tholy* dethe.
Arthour and Merlin, p. 80.

Fro Lumbardy comyn y am,
There have y *tholed* moche schame.
MS. Cantab. Ff. ii. 38, f. 155.

(2) The dome of a vaulted roof.

(3) To stay; to remain. *North.*

(4) To afford. *Yorksh.*

(5) To give freely. *North.*

THOLEMODE. Patient; forbearing. (*A.-S.*)

Be he wykked or be he gode,
Thou shalt to hym be *tholemode.*
MS. Harl. 1701, f. 72.

The fyfte es to be *tholemode* whenne mene mysdose us; the sexte es gladly to forgyffe when mene haves grevede us. *MS. Lincoln A.* i. 17, f. 217.

THOLEMODNES. Patience. (*A.-S.*)

Whenne evene commys, withe gret joye I lofe my Lorde. The ende of my lyfe I habyde in gude hope and *tholemodnes.* *MS. Lincoln A.* i. 17, f. 195.

THOLES. Are the small pins which they bear against with their oars when they row, and stand in holes on the upper side of the gunwale of the boat, being commonly made of ash, for toughness. They are also termed *thole-pins.*

THOLLE. " Tholle, a cart pynne, *cheville de charette*," Palsgrave, 1530.

THOMASING. A custom in Derbyshire, going from house to house on St. Thomas's day with a basket and can to beg milk, wheat, oatmeal, or flour.

THOMAS-OF-KENT. St. Thomas a Becket was frequently called St. Thomas of Kent.

THOME. The thumb. " *Pollex*, a thome," Nominale MS. Still in use in Linc.

THOMELLE-TAA. The great toe. *North.*

Thane blede one the fute on the same syde, and one the veyne that is bitwix the *thomelle taa* and the nexte. *MS. Lincoln. Med.* f. 301.

THONE. (1) Thawed. *Linc.*

(2) Damp; moist; limber. *Var. dial.*

(3) Then. (*A.-S.*)

Thay wolde not lett long *thone*,
Bot lavede in hir with a spone,
Then scho one slepe felle also sone,
Reght certeyne in hy. *Perceval*, 2248.

(4) A kind of stone. " *Terebentus*, Anglice a thone," Nominale MS.

THONER-FLONE. A thunderbolt. (*A.-S.*)

THONG. To rope; to stretch out into viscous threads or filaments. *Somerset.*

THONGEDOUN. Thanked. (*A.-S.*)

> They *thongedoun* God and mourendoun no more.
> *Chron. Vilodun.* p. 13.

THONGY. Ropy; viscid. *Somerset.*

THONKE. Favour. (*A.-S.*)

> This lorde whiche wolde his *thonke* purchace,
> To eche of hem yaf them a gifte.
> . *Gower, MS. Soc. Antiq.* 134, f. 43.

THONKYNG. Thanking; thanks. (*A.-S.*)

THONLY. The only. The elision of the *e* is very common in early writers.

> To intersede for me to his excellent Matie that the farme of the French wynes may retorne to hym that was the aunclent tennant and *thonly* improver of it. *Egerton Papers,* p. 460.

THONNERE. To thunder. *North.*

> Over watres that ere kalde,
> God of masthede *thonnered* he.
> *MS. Cott. Vespas.* D. vii. f. 17.

THONWANGE. The temple. (*A.-S.*)

> Stampe tham wele, and make a plaster, and lay on the forhede, and on the *thonwanges,* bot anoynte hym firste with popillone if he hafe anger in his lyver. *MS. Lincoln A. i.* 17, f. 305.
> Take puliol ryalle, and seeth it in oyle, and anoynte thi fronte and thi *thounwanges.*
> *MS. Linc. Med.* f. 280.

THONWRING. A thundering. (*A.-S.*)

THONY. Damp. *North.*

THOR. These. *North.*

THORE. There. (*A.-S.*)

> Wyth chylde waxe the lady *thore.*
> *MS. Cantab.* Ff. ii. 38, f. 82.
> They sayled forthe withowten ore,
> The syghte of Ynglonde loste they *thore.*
> *MS. Cantab.* Ff. ii. 38, f. 150.

THORES. Doors. *Ritson.*

THORH-RECHE. To reach through. (*A.-S.*)

> That londe ichulle *thorh-reche,*
> And do mi fader wreche.
> *Geste of Kyng Horn,* 1291.

THORNBUSH. A bush of thorns. "Thornbusshe, *espine noire,*" Palsgrave.

THORNE. A bush, or briar.

> Alle als nakede als thay were borne
> Stode togedir undir a *thorne,*
> Braydede owte of thaire bedd. *Isumbras,* 103.

THORN'S-BULL. The stout part of a thorn, the branches being cut off. *East.*

THORN-TREE. The medlar tree.

THOROUGH. (1) Through. *Var. dial.*

> *Thorow* the grace of God almyst,
> A worde into hir body liyt
> That the bisshop speke;
> Terys felle hir een froo,
> Down on hir brest cowth thei goo;
> Hur colars thei al to-breke.
> *MS. Cantab.* Ff. v. 48, f. 46.

(2) An interfurrow between two ridges.

(3) *Thorough go nimble,* a diarrhœa.

THOROUGH-POLE. A pole in a waggon which connects the fore axle with the hinder one.

THOROUGH-SHOT. A spavin which shows itself on both sides of a horse's hough or hock; called also Thorough-pin.

THOROW-STONE. A flat gravestone.

> Over the midst of the said vault there did lye a fair *thorow-stone,* and at either side of the stone it was open, so that when any of the monks was buried, whatsoever bones were found in his grave, they were taken out of the grave where he was buried, and thrown through the same into the said vault.
> *Davies' Ancient Rites,* 1672, p. 99.

THORP. A village. (*A.-S.*) "Thorpe, *hameu,*" Palsgrave, 1530, subst. f. 70.

> Ther been in Inglond withowt smale *thorpes* lij. ml. and iiij. townes. *MS. Cotton. Titus* D. xx. f. 90.

THORPS-MEN. Villagers. (*A.-S.*)

> Or else to call in from the fields and waters, shops and work-housen, from the inbred stock of more homely women and less filching *thorps-men.*
> *Fairfax, Bulk and Selvedge,* 1674.

THORTE. Feared. *Hearne.*

THORUE. Through. (*A.-S.*)

> For that prayer es so presyous,
> And so haly and so vertuous,
> That *thorue* vertu of and *thorue* myyt,
> Some grace sal in thare hertus lyyt.
> *MS. Harl.* 2260, f. 2.

THORUN. Thorn; bush.

> Sire Degrivaunt on the morwoun
> Com ayé to the *thurun,*
> Ther hys stede stod by-forun,
> And lenges all that day. *Degrevant,* 1332.

THORUTHLIKE. Thoroughly. (*A.-S.*)

THORZ. Through. (*A.-S.*)

> That *thorz* the myyt of the Holy Gost,
> Is in urthe of power most
> *MS. Cott. Claud.* A. ii. f. 128.

THOSTE. Dung, or ordure. It is used in Gloucestershire, according to Hole's MS. Gloss.

THOTEEN. Thirteen. *Yorksh.*

THOUCTE. Thought. (*A.-S.*)

THOUGHT. (1) The same as *Catch* (1).

(2) Opinion. *North.*

(3) A very minute difference in degree, as in Much Ado about Nothing, iii. 4.

(4) A rower's seat. *Var. dial.*

(5) Sorrow; sadness; grief. Hence *thoughtfu',* heavy, anxious, sorrowful.

THOUM. A thumb. *Craven.*

THOUNTHER. Thunder. (*A.-S.*)

> Duste drofe up on lofte dryvynge abowte,
> As *thounther* in thykke rayne persheth the skyes.
> *MS. Cott. Calig.* A. ii. f. 114.

THOUSANDEELE. A thousand times.

> For in good feythe this leveth welle,
> My wille was bettre a *thousandeelle.*
> *Gower, MS. Soc. Antiq.* 134, f. 43.

THOU'S-LIKE. You must. *Kent.*

THOUT. Thought. *North.*

THOWE. (1) Though. See Eglamour, 592.

> I drede me noghte withowt blame,
> *Thowe* thou do me peyne and schame.
> *MS. Cantab.* Ff. ii. 38, f. 57.

(2) To thaw. *Pr. Parv.* MS. f. 187.

(3) Then. *Gawayne.*

THOWGHTS. Pieces of wool matted together, and hanging down in lengths of about four inches. *Linc.*

THOWTHYSTYLLE. "Thowthystylle herbe, *rostrum porcinum,*" Pr. Parv.

THOWTS. The seat of rowers in a boat; the *thwarts* perhaps, or what go across. "The *thoughts*, the seats of rowers in a boat," Dict. ap. Moor.

THOWTYNE. "Thowtyne or seyne thow to a mane, *tuo*," Prompt. Parv.

THO3T. Thought. (*A.-S.*)

Kyng Aylbry3t gret dispyt adde in ys *tho3t*,
That the Brutons nolde Seynt Austyn abue no3t.
Robert of Gloucester's Chronicle, p. 235.

THRAA. Bold. *Thraeste*, boldest.

To forgyffe hym his werkes wylde,
That he had bene so *thraa*. MS. Lincoln A.i. 17, f. 148.
There they thronge in the thikke and thriatis to the erthe
Of the *thraeste* men thre hundrethe at ones.
Morte Arthure, MS. Lincoln, f. 92.

THRAPE. Thrived.

Thus he welke in the lande
With hys darte in his hande;
Under the wilde wodde wande
He wexe and wele *thrafe*.   *Perceval*, 212.

THRAG. To fell, or cut down.

THRAGES. Busy matters. *Speght*.

THRAIL. A flail. *Beds.*

THRALAGE. Perplexity. *Linc.*

THRALL. (1) A slave, or vilein.

This kyng, as thou herdest er this,
Hede a *thrall* that dede amys. *Religious Poems*, xv. Cent.

(2) Cruelty; severity.

Wherefore good Christian people, now
Take warning by my fall:
Live not in strife and envious hate,
To breed each other *thrall*.
Seeke not your neighbors lasting spoyle,
By greedy sute in lawe;
Live not in discord and debate,
Which doth destruction draw.
Ballad on the Burning of Beccles, 1586.

(3) Hard; cruel.

At Beverley a sudden chaunce did falle,
The parish chirch stepille it felle
At evynsonge tyme, the chaunce was *thralle*,
Ffourscore folke ther was slayn thay telle.
MS. Bodl. e Mus. 160.

(4) A stand for barrels. *Warw.*

(5) A short space of time.

THRALY. Hardly; cruelly. (*A.-S.*)

Thay toylede the bytwene thayme,
And threted the *thraly*. MS. Lincoln A. i. 17, f. 232.

THRAMP-WITH. A sliding noose of withy or rope to fasten cows in their stalls. *Chesh.*

THRANGE. (1) Thrusted; went through.

Thurch the bodi ful neythe the hert
That gode swerd thurc him *thrang*.
Gy of Warwike, p. 51.

(2) To crowd; to squeeze. *North.*

At morne when day sprange,
Gentyl men to haruds *thrange*,
Syr Degrabelle was dyght. *Eglamour*, 1109.

THRAP. (1) To crowd. A place is said to be *thrapt full* when excessively crowded. *Essex.*

(2) "As busy as Thrap's wife, who hung herself in the dishcloth." A Derbyshire proverb.

THRASHLE. A flail. Lhuyd's MS. Additions to Ray, Ashmolean Museum.

THRASTE. Thrusted out. (*A.-S.*)

THRATE. Urged; pressed. (*A.-S.*)

There as he was moste hate,
For to drynke y-nogh he *thrate*.
MS. Cantab. Ff. ii 38, f. 99.

THRATLE. To speak with a hollow rattling voice. Honours Academie, 1610, i. 80.

THRATTE. To threaten. (*A.-S.*)

THRATTLES. Sheep's dung. *East.*

THRAVE. (1) Thrived. Perceval, 226.

(2) A company, properly of threshers, but applied to any indefinite number.

Many a man wylle go bare,
And tak moche kark and care,
And hard he wylle fare
Alle the days of hys lyfe;
And after comyth a knave,
The worst of a *thrave*,
And alle he shalle have
For weddyng of hys wyffe.
MS. Lansd. 210, f. 80.

(3) Twelve fads of straw. Also, twenty-four, or twelve sheaves of wheat. *North.*

(4) To urge. *Linc.*

THRAW. (1) A twist, and v. to twist. Hence *heads and thraws*; hence, also, *thraw hook*, a rude instrument for making coarse hay ropes. *North.*

(2) To turn wood. *North.*

THRAWL. A stand for a barrel. *Linc.*

THRAWN. A scolding, or chiding. *Dunelm.*

THREAD. To spin a good thread, i. e. to succeed in any undertaking. *Thread and thrum*, the good and bad together.

THREADEN. Made of thread.

THREAD-NEEDLE. A game, in which children stand in a row joining hands, the outer one, still holding her neighbour, runs between the others, &c.

Eight people, four of each sex, who had arranged themselves together, a man and a woman alternately, and joining hands like children at *thread-needle*, form'd a straight line that reach'd across the Mall.
Adventures of Mr. George Edwards, 1751, p. 140.

THREADS. "In a skrew-plate and skrew-pin, the dents or hollows are call'd grooves, and the prominent or rising parts are the threds; the outer threds of the skrew-plate make the grooves on the skrew-pin, and the grooves in the skrew-plate make the threds on the skrew-pin," Kennett, MS. Lansd. 1033.

THREAP. (1) Obstinately to maintain or insist upon a thing in contradiction to another, e. g. "He *threaped* me down it was so." *Linc.* "I threpe a mater upon one, I beare one in hande that he hath doone or said a thing amysse," Palsgrave, verb. f. 389.

Itt's not for a man with a woman to *threape*,
Unlesse he first gave oer the plea;
As wee began wee now will leave,
And Ile take mine old cloake about mee.
Percy's Reliques, p. 52.

(2) To beat, or thrash. *North.*

(3) To urge; to press. *Linc.*

(4) To cozen, or cheat. *Lanc.*

THREAP-GROUND. Disputed land. *North.*

THREAT. To threaten. *Palsgrave.*

Which should they joyne, would be so strongly aided,
Two mighty hoasts, together safely met,
The face of warre would looke so sterne and great,
As it might *threat* to heave him from his seat.
Drayton's Poems, 1637, p. 18.

THREAVE. The same as *Thrave*, q. v.

THRECHE. To pinch. *Palsgrave.*

THREDEGAL. Unsettled, as applied to weather, and I never heard the word applied to anything else. I lately heard this speech. " The weather fare ta look thredegal, and the clumps of the evening are coming on." *Moor.*

THREDTENE. Thirteen.

THREE-COCKED-HAT. A cocked hat.

THREE-FARTHINGS. A three-farthing piece of silver current in Shakespeare's time, and frequently alluded to for its thinness, &c.

THREE-FOLD. Bog-bean; buck-bean. *Yorksh.*

THREE-HALFPENNY-HORSE-LOAF. A nickname for a very little person.

THREE-MAN. A cluster of three nuts is called a three-man cluster of nuts.

THREE-MENS-SONG. A song for three voices. " To sing rounds, catches, gigges, or *three mens songs*," Florio, p. 538. Compare pp. 59, 80, ed. 1611.

THREE-OUTS. When three persons go into a public-house, call for liquor generally considered only sufficient for two, and have a glass which will divide it into three equal portions, they are said to drink *three outs.*

> An alewife in Kesgrave neare to Ipswich, who would needs force three serving men (that had beene drinking in her house, and were taking their leaves) to stay and drinke the *three outs* first (that is, wit out of the head, money out of the purse, ale out of the pot) as shee was comming towards them with the pot in her hand was suddenly taken speechlesse and sicke, her tongue swolne in her mouth, never recovered speech, the third day after dyed.
> *Woe to Drunkards, a Sermon by Samuel Ward, Preacher of Ipswich,* 1627.

THREE-PILE. The finest kind of velvet. Hence, metaphorically, *three-piled*, refined.

> My will is that if any roaring boy springing from my race happen to be stabd, swaggering, or swearing *three-pil'd* oathes in a taverne, or to bee kild in the quarrell of his whoore, let him bee fetched hither in my own name, because heere he shall be both lookt too and provided for.
> *Dekker's Strange Horse Race,* 1613.

THREE-SHEAR. A sheep of two or three years, having been thrice shorn.

THREESOME. Treble. *North.*

THREE-SQUARE. Triangular, like a bayonet or small sword-blade. *Four-square*, die-shaped ; a cube.

THREE-SQUARE-SHEEP. A four-year sheep.

THREE-THREADS. Half common ale, mixed with stale and double beer.

THREE-THRUM. When a cat purrs she is said to sing *three-thrum.* *Linc.*

THREE-TREES. The gallows, so called from their ancient triangular form.

THREE-WAY-LEET. When three roads meet, it is called a *three-way-leet.* *Suffolk.*

THRENES. Lamentations. (*Gr.*)

THREO. Three. (*A.-S.*)

> In Noe is flood in the shippe were heo,
> Noe and hys sonys *threo.*
> *Religious Poems,* xv. Cent.

THREP. Torture ; cruelty. (*A.-S.*)

THREPE. (1) To speak ; to call ; to shout. It has likewise the same meanings as *threap*, q. v.

> 3e are sloghe and lyen to slepe
> Whan 3e agens the prochur *threpe.*
> *MS. Harl.* 1701, f. 29.

> Of the nyghtgale notes the noises was swette ;
> They *threpide* wyth the throstils thre hundreth at ones. *Morte Arthure, MS. Lincoln,* f. 63.

> Because I was arayed with some clothes of sylke of my sayde maisters, came unto me and *threpid* upon me that I should be the Duke of Clarence sonne that was before tyme at Develyn. *Hall, Henry VII.* f. 50.

THREPHEL. A flail. *Lanc.*

THREPPE. To rush ?

> Woundes those whydyrewyns, werrayede knyghttes,
> *Threppede* thorowe the thykkys thryttene sythis.
> *Morte Arthure, MS. Lincoln,* f. 76.

THREPS. Threepence. *Var. dial.*

THRESHEL. Same as *Thrashle*, q. v.

THRESHER. A duster of furniture.

THRESHFOD. A threshold. *Yorksh.*

THRESTE. To thrust. (*A.-S.*)

THRESWOLD. A threahold. (*A.-S.*)

THRET. Threatened.

> Withoute thi castel I am biset,
> Harde with thre fomen *thret.*
> *Cursor Mundi, MS. Coll. Trin. Cantab.* f. 63.

THRETE. To threaten. (*A.-S.*)

> He *thretyth* me to be slayn,
> And for to wynne hys londe agayn.
> *MS. Cantab.* Ff. ii. 38, f. 118.

THRETENETHE. The thirteenth.

> The *thretenethe* artykele, as telle I may,
> That Cryst hymself on Holy Thursday
> Stegh into hevene in flesch and blod,
> That dyede byforn on the rod.
> *MS. Cott. Claud.* A. ii. f. 133.

THRETTY. Thirty. (*A.-S.*)

> Yn the halle that he there hadd,
> V. and *thretty* knyghtys he madd,
> Be that odur day abowte none. *Eglamour,* 1004.

THREVE. The same as *Thrave*, q. v.

THRIBBLE. Treble ; threefold. *Yorksh.*

THRICHE. To thrust or press down. *Lanc.*

THRIDDE. Third. (*A.-S.*)

> The Holy Gost, persone *thrydde*,
> Leveth also I 3ow bydde.
> *MS. Cott. Claud.* A. ii. f. 133.

> The *thridde* folc ladde Bretel,
> Strong and doinde knight wel.
> *Arthour and Merlin,* p. 143.

> When hyt come to the *thrydd* day,
> That alle knyghtys went away.
> *MS. Cantab.* Ff. ii. 38, f. 151.

THRIDDE-HALF. Two and a half.

> Hard gates havy gon,
> Sorewen soffred mony on :
> Thritty wynter and *thridde-half* yer.
> Havy woned in londe her.
> *Harrowing of Hell,* p. 15.

THRIDDEN. Of thread.

> Which did reveale him then to be indeede
> A *thridden* fellow in a silken weede.
> *Stephens' Essayes and Characters,* 1615, p. 5.

THRIDDENDEL. A third part.

> And asked gif ani wer so bold ;
> *Thriddendel* his lond have he schold.
> *Gy of Warwike,* p. 239.

THRIDE. A thread. See Florio, p. 12.

And of this wolle I will spynne *thride* by *thride*,
To hill me from the coulde.   *Chester Plays*, i. 37.

THRIE. (1) Thrice.   (*A.-S.*)

> Petter, I saye thee sickerlye,
> Or the cocke have crowen *thrye*,
> Thou shalte forsake my companye,
> And take thy worde againe. *Chester Plays*, ii. 25.

(2) Trouble; affliction.   (*A.-S.*)

THRIFT. (1) Growing pains.   *Lanc.*

(2) Scurf on a horse.   *Var. dial.*

(3) The sea-pink.   *Var. dial.*

THRIFT-BOX. An earthen box for saving money in, so contrived that the coin cannot be got out without breaking it.

THRILE. To pierce through.   (*A.-S.*)

> His arowes that er scharpe sentence *thriland* mens
> hertes.   *MS. Coll. Eton.* 10.

THRILLY. Thrilling.   *North.*

THRIMMEL. To pull out; to gripe hard; to part with money reluctantly.   *North.*

THRIMMER. To handle anything.   *Lanc.*

THRIN. Three.   *Thrinfalde*, threefold.

> Selcouth thing he seide withyn
> Is closed in these gerdes *thrin*.
>   *Cursor Mundi, MS. Coll. Trin. Cantab.* f. 40.
> Cristofere in Criste I calle the here,
> In my name, by *thryne* manere.
>   *MS. Lincoln* A. i. 17, f. 125.
> Als witty men ful wele has talde,
> Schrift aw to be *thrinfulde*.
>   *MS. Galba* E. ix. f. 66.

THRINGE. (1) To thrust.   (*A.-S.*)

> Who strengths the poor, and pridful men down *thrings*,
> And wracks at once the pow'rs of puissant kings.
>   *Works of Du Bartas*, p. 369.

(2) To crowd; to press forward.   (*A.-S.*)

(3) To rumble. In MS. Med. Linc. f. 289, is a receipt for " thryngyng in the wambe."

THRINGID. Quite covered over?

> His kneys coveryd with plates many,
> His thies *thryngid* with silk, as I say.
>   *Roland, MS. Lansd.* 338, f. 388.

THRIPPA. To beat.   *Chesh.*

THRIPPLE. To labour hard.

THRIPPLES. The rails of a waggon; the moveable ladders.   *Chesh.*

THRISTY. Thirsty.   *Spenser.*

THRIVE. So mote I thrive, i. e. if I may prosper, a common expletive phrase.

> Nay, seyde Gye, *so mote y thryve*,
> Never whylle y am on lyve.
>   *MS. Cantab.* Ff. ii. 38, f. 154

THRO. (1) Eager; earnest; sharp.

> As Jewes fond he none so *thro*,
> For ofte thei souzte him to slo.
>   *Cursor Mundi, MS. Coll. Trin. Cantab.* f. 120.
> When sche come undur a wode syde,
> Sche myght no lenger abyde,
> Hur peynys were so *throo*:
> Sche lyghtyd downe, that was so mylde,
> And there sche travaylyd of a chylde,
> Hyrselfe allone, withowtyn moo.
>   *MS. Cantab.* Ff. ii. 38, f. 74.

(2) Bold.   See *Thraa*.

> Ther is no lady of flesshe ne bone,
> In this werld so thryve or *thro*.
>   *MS. Harl.* 2252, f. 94.
> Thoghe the knyzt were kene and *thro*,
> The owtlawys wanne the chylde hym fro.
>   *MS. Cantab.* Ff. ii. 38, f. 85.

THROAT. He lies in his throat, i. e. he lies flatly, a phrase implying great indignation in the person who employs it.

> And therefore, reader, understand and note,
> Whoever sayes I lye, he lies in's throat.
> *Tailor's Travels from London to the Isle of Wight,
> with his Returne and occasion of his Journey*,
> 1648, p. 14.

THROAT-BALL. " Throte gole or throte bole, *neu de la lagorge, gosier*," Palsgrave. " *Epiglotum*, a throte gole," Nomin .le MS.

> Thi mahe and thi milte, thi livre and thi lunge,
> And thi *throte bolle* that thu mide sunge.
>   *MS. Cott. Calig.* A. ix. f. 246.
> And to leave the folowyng of such a doubtful captayne which with a leaden sword would cut his owne *throte-bolle*.   *Hall's Union*, 1548.

THROAT-LATCH. (1) The narrow thong of the bridle which passes under a horse's throat. " The throat-thong or throat-band of a bridle, *sousgorge*," Sherwood. It is also called the throat-hap.

(2) The strings of a hat, cap, &c. fastened under the chin.

THROAT-PIECE. " The throat-piece (or forepart of the neck) of a hog," Sherwood.

THROAT-WORT. The giant bell-flower.

THROCK. The piece of wood on which the blade of a plough is fixed.

THROC-NEDILS. A kind of herb mentioned in MS. Lincoln A. i. 17, f. 286.

THRODDEN. To thrive; to increase.   *North.*

THROE. Eager; willing.

> There as the swift hound may no further goe
> Then the slowest of foot, be he never so *throe*.
>   *The Booke of Hunting*, 1586.

THROH. A coffin.   (*A.-S.*)

> Ase me wolde him nymen up,
> Ant leggen in a *throh* of ston.
>   *Chronicle of England*, 747.

THROLY. Earnestly; eagerly; hardly.

> In at the durres thei *throly* thrast
> With staves ful gode ilkone;
> Alas! alas! seid Robyn Hode,
> Now mysse I litulle Johne.
>   *MS. Cantab.* Ff. v. 48, f. 127.
> The theeffe at the dede thrawe so *throly* hyme thrynges,
> That three rybbys in his syde he thrystes in sundere.
>   *Morte Arthure, MS. Lincoln*, f. 65.

THROM. From.   *Salop.*

THROME. Company, or body of people.

> Whiles thou were in our *throme*,
> No were we never overcome.
>   *Arthour and Merlin*, p. 9.
> Tho thai thider weren y-come,
> Ordeind and teld her *throme*,
> Fourti thousand men thai founde.
>   *Arthour and Merlin*, p. 138.

THRONG. (1) Busy.   *North.*

> In these times, great men, yea and men of justice, are as *throng* as ever in pulling down houses, and setting up hedges. *Sanderson's Sermons*, 1689, p. 113.

(2) A press of business.   *North.*

(3) To crowd; to press.

THRONGE. Thrust down.   (*A.-S.*)

> Yn yustyng ne yn turnament,
> Ther myzt no man with-sytt hys dynte,
> But he to the erthe them *thronge*. *Eglamour*, 1023.

THROO. A slip or width of corn which a set

of reapers drive before them at once, whether it consist of one or more lands or ridges.

THROPE. A thorp, or village. (*A.-S.*)

> Naght [fer] fro that paleyse honorable,
> Where as this Mark[i]s shope his mariage,
> There stode a *thrope* of site delitable,
> In whiche that pore folke of that village
> Hadden here bestis and here herborage,
> And of her labour toke hare sustynance,
> Aftir that the erthe yeve hem habundaunce.
>> *Reliq. Antiq.* ii. 68.

THROPPLE. (1) The windpipe. *Var. dial.*

(2) To throttle, or strangle. *North.*

THROSHEL. The threshold. *Suffolk.*

THROSSEN. Thrust; pressed. *North.*

THROSTEL. A thrush. *North.* "*Merulus, merula,* Anglice a thyrstylle cok," Nominale MS. xv. Cent. "Thrusshe a byrde, *gryue*," Palsgrave. "Thrustell cocke, *maulvis*," Palsgrave, subst. f. 70.

> Gladde is the *throstel* whane the floures spring,
> The somer is to him so acceptible.
>> *MS. Ashmole* 59, f. 20.

> Or if thou wilt goe shoote at little birds,
> With bow and boult, the *thrustle-cocke* and sparrow,
> Such as our countrey hedges can afforde,
> I have a fine bowe, and an yvorie arrow.
>> *The Affectionate Shepheard,* 1594.

> The nyttyngale, the *throstylcoke*,
> The popejay, the joly laveroke.
>> *MS. Porkington* 10, f. 55.

THROUGH. (1) From. *North.*

(2) To be through with any one, i. e. to complete a bargain with him.

(3) The same as *Perpent-stone*, q. v.

(4) A flat gravestone. *North.* "Thurwhe stone of a grave, *sarcofagus*," Pr. Parv.

THROUGH-CARVED-WORK. Carved work in which spaces are cut entirely through the material.

THROUGHEN. Another copy of the Siege of Jerusalem in MS. Cott. Calig. A. ii. f. 123, reads "bounden togedur."

> xxx.ti Jewes in a thrumme, *throughen* in ropes.
>> *MS. Cott. Vespas.* E. xvi. f. 83.

THROULLID. Pierced. (*A.-S.*)

> And to be *throullid* hond and food
> With charp naylus to the rod,
> And to be lift up in the cros,
> Betwene two thevys for to hyng;
> Of aysel and gal thai propherd the drynke,
> With a spere thi hert persid was.
>> *MS. Douce* 302, xv. Cent.

THROUSHOT. The hole of a rabbit under ground through a bank. It is an expressive word, where the animal has *shot through.* It is also applied to a spendthrift, "a *through-shot* sort of a fellow." *Moor.*

THROW. (1) Time. (*A.-S.*)

> Syr, soche ys Godys myghte,
> That he make may hye lowe,
> And lowe hye in a lytylle *throwe.*
>> *MS. Cantab.* Ff. ii. 38, f. 240.

> Hayle and pulle I schall fulle faste
> To reyse housys, whyle I may laste,
> And so, within a lytell *throw*,
> My mayster gode schall not be know.
>> *MS. Ashmole* 61.

> Syr, be myn hore berd
> Thou schall se within a *throw.*
>> *MS. Ashmole* 61, f. 61

> And gadred them togyder
> In a lytell *throwe*,
> Seven score of wight yonge men
> Came redy on a rowe.
>> *Robin Hood*, i. 79.

(2) To work at the tin mines. *North.*

(3) A thoroughfare; a public road. *South.*

THROWE. To turn wood for cups, &c. A turner's lathe is still called a *throwe.*

THROWER. A sort of knife used for cleaving lath or hurdle stuff. It appears to have been formerly called *frower.* See Moor, p. 151.

THROW-IN. To pay a forfeit. *East.*

THROWING-CLAY. "At the potteries in Staffordshire they call four different sorts of clay *throwing clays*, because they are of a closer texture, and will work on the wheel," Kennett, MS. Lansd. 1033, f. 414.

THROWING-THE-STOCKING. A curious custom, thus described in a poem dated 1733:

> Then come all the younger folk in,
> With ceremony *throw the stocking;*
> Backward, o'er head, in turn they toss'd it,
> Till in sack-posset they had lost it.
> Th' intent of flinging thus the hose
> Is to hit him or her o' th' nose;
> Who hits the mark, thus, o'er left shoulder,
> Must married be ere twelve months older.
> Deucalion thus, and Pyrrha, threw
> Behind them stones, whence mankind grew.
>> *Brand's Pop. Antiq.* ii. 108.

> The first use the two lads of the castle made of their existence was to ply the bridegroom so hard with bumpers, that in less than an hour he made divers efforts to sing, and soon after was carried to bed, deprived of all manner of sensation, to the utter disappointment of the bridemen and maids, who, by this accident, were prevented from *throwing the stocking*, and performing certain other ceremonies practised on such occasions.
>> *Peregrine Pickle*, chap. 4.

> But as luck would have it ye parson said grace,
> And to frisking and dancing they shuffled apace,
> Each lad took his lass by the fist;
> And when he had squeez'd her, and gaum'd her untill
> The fat of her face ran down like a mill,
> He toll'd for the rest of the grist.
> In sweat and in dust having wasted the day,
> They enter'd upon the last act of the play,
> The bride to her bed was convey'd;
> Where knee deep each hand fell downe to the ground,
> And in seeking the garter much pleasure was found,
> 'Twould have made a man's arm have stray'd.
> This clutter ore, Clarinda lay
> Half bedded, like the peeping day
> Behind Olimpus cap;
> Whiles at her head each twittring girle
> The fatal *stocking* quick did whirle
> To know the lucky hap.
> The bridegroom in at last did rustle,
> All dissap-pointed in the bustle,
> The maidens had shav'd his breeches;
> But let him not complain, tis well,
> In such a storm, I can you tell,
> He sav'd his other stitches.
>> *Account of a Wedding,* Fletcher's Poems, p. 230.

THROWLY. Thoroughly. *North.*

THROWN. Disappointed. *Yorksh.*

THROWSTER. One that throws or winds silk or thread. "Throwstar, *devideresse de soye*," Palsgrave, 1530.

THRUBCHANDLER.

> Thén take they did that lodly boome,
> And under *thrubchandler* closed was hee.
> *Syr Gawayne*, p. 280.

THRUCK. The piece of wood that goes through the beam of a plough, at the end of which the suck or share is fastened. *Chesh.*

THRUFF. (1) Through. *North.*

(2) A table-tomb. *Cumb.*

THRULL. To piece. See *Thrile.*

THRUM. (1) Green and vigorous, usually applied to herbage. *Glouc.*

(2) The extremity of a weaver's warp, often about nine inches long, which cannot be woven. Generally, a small thread. *North.* Also, to cover with small tufts like thrums.

(3) Futuo. See Florio, pp. 5, 144.

(4) To beat. *Suffolk.*

(5) To purr, as a cat. *East.*

(6) Sullen; rough; bearish. *North.*

(7) A bundle of twigs through which the liquor percolates from a mash-tub.

THRUMBLE. To handle awkwardly. *North.* The term occurs in Howell, 1660.

THRUM-CHINNED. Rough chinned.

THRUMMED. Knitted. *Thrum-cap*, a knit cap. A thrummed hat was one made of very coarse woollen cloth. *Minsheu.*

THRUMMELD. Stunted in growth. *North.*

THRUMMY. Fat; plump. *Yorksh.*

THRUMMY-CAP. The name of a sprite who occasionally figures in the fairy tales of Northumberland. He is generally described as a "queer-looking little auld man," and the scene of his exploits frequently lies in the vaults and cellars of old castles.

THRUMP. To gossip. *North.*

THRUMS. Threepence. *Grose.*

THRUNCH. Much displeased. *North.*

THRUNK. (1) Busy. *Lanc.*

(2) Thronged; crowded. *Chesh.*

THRUNK-WIFE. A fussy, busy woman. *Lanc.*

THRUNTY. Healthy; hardy. *North.*

THRUSFIELD. A thrush. *Salop.*

THRUSHES. A disease in horses.

THRUSH-LICE. Millepes. *North.*

THRUST. "*Boute-hors*, the play called *Thrust out the harlot*, wherein the weakest ever come to the worst," Cotgrave.

THRUSTE. A thirst. (*A.-S.*)

> And suche a *thruste* was on him falle,
> They he muste other deye or drynke,
> *Gower, MS. Soc. Antiq.* 134, f. 53.

THRUSTLE-COCK. See *Throstel.*

THRUSTY. Thirsty. *North.*

THRUT. The throw of a stone; also a fall in wrestling. *Lanc.*

THRUTCH. For thrust. *Chesh.* Maxfield measure, heap and thrutch, Prov.

THRUTCHINGS. The last pressed whey in the making of cheese. *Lanc.*

THRUȝ. Through. (*A.-S.*)

> Thorow the grace of God almyȝt,
> That is mercifulle to every wyȝt,
> And *thruȝ* his modur Mary.
> *MS. Cantab.* Ff. v. 48, f. 48

THRYDDYTH. Third. (*A.-S.*)

> For hit byffell thus in the same *thryddyth* day.
> *Chron. Vilodun.* p. 61.

THRYNGE. Throng, or crowd. (*A.-S.*)

> The sowdan dud before hym brynge,
> All hys goddys in a *thrynge.*
> *MS. Cantab.* Ff. ii. 38, f. 169.

THRYȝT. (1) Threw. (2) Given. *Gawayne.*

THUCK. That. *Wilts.*

THUD. A heavy blow, or the sound which it emits. The stroke of a sledge hammer against the wall of a house is of that kind. *North.*

THUE. Slave. (*A.-S.*)

> The crie was sone wide couth, among *thue* and freo,
> That seint Thomas scholde after him archebischop beo.   *Life of Thomas Beket*, p. 11

THUELLE. The same as *Tewell*, q. v. "*Epicausterium*, a thuelle," Nominale MS.

THULGED. Endured. *Gawayne.*

THULLE. This. *Hearne.*

THUM. To beat.

> For he's such a churle waxen now of late, that and he be
> Never so little angry he *thums* me out of all cry.
> *The Taming of a Shrew*, 1607.

THUMB. To have the thumb under the girdle, i. e. to be very melancholy.

THUMB-BAND. A small band of hay, &c.

THUMB-BIT. A piece of meat eaten on bread, so called from the thumb being placed on it.

THUMBING. A Nottingham phrase, used to describe that species of intimidation practised by masters on their servants when the latter are compelled to vote as their employers please, under pain of losing their situations.

THUMB-NAIL. See *Supernaculum.*

THUMB-RING. A large ring, generally plain, formerly worn on the thumb.

THUMB-SNACK. A fastening to a door in which the latch is lifted by pressing the thumb on the broad end of a short lever which moves it.

THUMMEL-TEE. See *Thomelle-taa.*

THUMP. The same as *Bang*, q. v.

THUMPING. Large; great. *Var. dial.*

THUMPKIN. A clown, or bumpkin. *Oxon.*

THUMPLE. To fumble. *North.*

THUNCHE. To seem. (*A.-S.*)

> Of fleysh lust cometh shame,
> Thath hit *thunche* the body game,
> Hit doth the soule smerte. *Reliq. Antiq.* i. 111.

THUNDER-BOLT. (1) The corn poppy. *West.*

(2) The fossil belemnite. *North.*

THUNDER-CRACK. A clap of thunder.

THUNDER-PICK. The pyrites. *Suffolk.*

THUNDER-STONE. The water-worn gypsum is so called in the North by the vulgar.

THUNDER-THUMP. To stun with noise.

> A very clown in his own language comes off better than he that by a romantick bumbaste doth *thunderthump* his hearer into an *æquilibrium* between scorn and wonder.
> *A Cap of Gray Hairs for a Green Head*, 1688, p. 81.

THUNK. A thong. *North.*

THUNNER. Thunder. *North.*

THURCH. Through. (*A.-S.*)

> Whar *thurch* y tel moder thine
> Dingner to be ded than moder mine.
> *Arthour and Merlin*, p. 41.

> He stayred about hym with his spere,
> Many *thurgh* gane he bere.   *Perceval*, 1170.

THURF. Through. *Thurfout*, throughout.

> This child *thurf* his fader heste.
> *Life of Thomas Beket*, p. 9.

THURGHFARE. To pass through. (*A.-S.*)

> Bot in liknes *thurghfare* man,
> Bot and ydel es he droned onan.
> *MS. Cott. Vespas.* D. vii. f. 27.

THURGHOUT. Throughout; quite through.

THURH. Through. (*A.-S.*) .

> Heo brohte us blisse that is long,
> Al *thurh* hire childeringe.
> *MS. Cotton. Calig.* A. ix. f. 243.

THURIBLE. A censer. (*Lat.*)

THURIFICATION. Burning incense.

THURINDALE. A pewter flagon holding about three pints. *Wilts.* See *Thriddendel.*

THURL. A long adit in a coal-pit.

THURLES. Holes. (*A.-S.*)

> Til I se and fele his flesshe,
> The *thurles* bothe of honde and fete.
> *Cursor Mundi, MS. Coll. Trin. Cantab.* f. 114.

THURLGH. Through. (*A.-S.*)

> Mony wonders oure Lorde ther wro3t
> *Thurlgh* the cardenales rede.
> *MS. Cantab.* Ff. v. 48, f. 79.

THURLINGS. "In coal-pits there be several partitions or divisions calld wallings or stauls separated by pillars or ribs of earth and coal, with passages through them call'd *thurlings* opened for convenience of air and easier carriage of the coal," Kennett MS.

THURROK. The hold of a ship. (*A.-S.*)

THURROUGH. A furrow. *Leic.*

THURRUCK. A drain. *Kent.*

THURS-HOUSE. "A thurs-house or thursehole, a hollow vault in a rock or stony hill that serves for a dwelling-house to a poor family, of which there is one at Alveton, and another near Wettonmill, com. Staff.," Kennett.

THURSSE. A giant. (*A.-S.*)

> With schankes unschaply schowande togedyrs,
> Thykke theefe as a *thursse* and thikkere in the hanche.
> *Morte Arthure, MS. Lincoln,* f. 65.

THURSTLEW. Thirsty. (*A.-S.*)

> In reveris *thurstlew*, and moyst upon the londe ;
> Gladde in mornyng, in gladnes compleyneng.
> *Lydgate's Minor Poems*, p. 75.

THURT. (1) Across. *South.*

(2) An ill-tempered fellow. *Berks.*

THURTE. Need. (*A.-S.*)

> Als fayre a lady to wyefe had he
> Als any erthly mane *thurte* see,
> With tunge als I 3ow nevene. *Isumbras*, 26.

THURT-HANDLED. Cross-handled ; thwarthandled, having a handle standing across from side to side, as a short-handled basket.

THURTIFER. Unruly. *Wilts.*

THURTLE. To cross in discourse ; to contradict. *Somerset.*

THURT-SAW. A cross-cut saw. *Somerset.*

THUS. So ; this. *North.*

THUS-GATES. In this manner.

> Bot a mane of the citee that highte Hismonne, whene he saw his cuntree *thusgates* be destruyed, come and felle one knees before Alexander, and bigane for to synge a sange of musyke and of murnynge with an instrument of musike.
> *MS. Lincoln* A. i. 17, f. 11.

THUSSOCK. A tussock, or tuft.

THWACK. (1) To fill to overflowing.

> How deere and entier friends he and I were one to the other during his life, the letters he addressed me from time to time, to the number of six hundred, *thwackt* with love and kindnesse, doo manifestlie declare.
> *Stanihurst's Description of Ireland*, p. 42.

(2) Same as *Thwange* (2).

THWAITE. Land, which was once covered with wood, brought into pasture or tillage ; an assart. *Thwaite* enters into the name of many places in Westmoreland and Cumberland.

THWANGE. (1) The latchet of a shoe. "Thwange, *ligula*," Nominale MS.

(2) A large piece. *North.*

THWARLE. Tight ; hard. *Gawayne.*

THWARTE. To fall out, or quarrel. *To thwart the way*, to stop one in the way.

THWEYN. To prosper. (*A.-S.*)

> Addlwyst yt wylle not bee,
> I wot I mune never more *thweyn.*
> *MS. Lincoln* A. i. 17, f. 51.

THWITE. To cut ; to notch. *North.* See Stanihurst's Ireland, pp. 16, 18. "I *thwyte* a stycke, or I cutte lytell peces from a thynge," Palsgrave, verb. f. 390.

THWITEL. A knife. (*A.-S.*)

THWITTEN. Cut. *North.*

THY. (1) They.

> And of these berdede bukkes also
> Wyth hemself *thy* moche mysdo,
> That leve Crysten mennys acyse,
> And haunte al the newe gyse.
> *MS. Bodl.* 415, f. 21.

(2) Therefore. *Gawayne.*

THYRCE. A spectre. (*A.-S.*) "Thyrce, wykkyd spyryte, *ducius*," Pr. Parv. "A thurse, an apparition, a goblin, Lanc.," Kennett MS.

THYTED. Cut, as with a knife. List of old words prefixed to Batman uppon Bartholome, fol. Lond. 1582.

THYZLE. A cooper's adze. *North.*

TIAL. A tie. *Fletcher.*

TIB. (1) The anus. *North.*

(2) The ace of trumps in the game of gleek was so called. See the Compleat Gamester, ed. 1721, p. 8.

(3) A calf. A term of endearment. Tib and Tom were names for low persons.

(4) The flap of the ear. *Linc.*

(5) *Tib of the buttery*, a goose.

(6) The extreme end of a cart. *East.*

TIBBET. The overhanging peak of the bonnet. *Linc.*

TIBBY. Isabella. *North.*

TIB-CAT. A female cat. *Yorksh.*

TIBERT. A name for a cat.

TICE. To entice. *Var. dial.*

All these and more Ile give thee for thy love,
If these and more may tyce thy love away.
The Affectionate Shepheard, 1594.

TICHER. A sheaf of corn. *South.*

TICHING. Setting up turves to dry, in order to prepare them for fuel. *Devon. Cornw.*

TICHY. Fretful; touchy. *Howell.*

TICK. (1) A slight touch. A game called *tick* is mentioned by Drayton, and is still played in Warwickshire. A boy touched by one who is in the first instance fixed upon to commence the game, is in his turn obliged to overtake and touch another of the party, when he cries *tick*, and so the game proceeds.
(2) To toy. See Forby, p. 348.
　　Such *ticking*, such toving, such smiling, such winking, and such manning them home when the sports are ended, that it is a right comedie to marke their behaviour. *Gosson's Schoole of Abuse*, 1579.
(3) Loving; fond. *West.*

TICKET. A tradesman's bill, formerly written on a card or ticket. *Run o' the ticket*, run in debt, Shirley, iii. 56, since corrupted into *tick.* " Plaies upon ticket," Stephens' Characters, 1615, p. 239.

TICKETINGS. Weekly sales of ore. *Derb.*

TICKLE. (1) To excite. *Becon.*
(2) Tottering; unsteady; uncertain; inconstant. " Tyckyll, nat stedy, *inconstant*," Palsgrave. A thing is said to be *tickle* when it does not stand firmly and may easily be overturned. Sometimes, in harvest, they say, " It's very *tickle* weather," meaning thereby that it threatens rain, that it is not set fair. *Linc.*
　　Yet if she were so *tickle*, as ye would take no stand, so ramage as she would be reclaimed with no lure. *Greene's Gwydonius*, 1593.

TICKLE-BRAIN. A species of liquor.

TICKLE-ME-QUICKLY. An old game mentioned in Taylor's Motto, 1622, sig. D. iv.

TICKLE-MY-FANCY. The pansy.

TICKLE-PITCHER. A drunkard. *Var. dial.*

TICKLER. (1) Any smart animal; also a shrewd, cunning person. *I. of Wight.*
(2) Something to puzzle or perplex.
(3) An iron pin used by brewers to take a bung out of a cask. *Var. dial.*

TICKLE-TAIL. (1) A wanton. *Hall.*
(2) A schoolmaster's rod. *North.*

TICKLISH. Uncertain. *Var. dial.*

TICKLY. Ticklish. *Palsgrave.*

TICK-TACK. (1) A kind of backgammon, played both with men and pegs, and more complicated. The game is frequently alluded to, as in Apollo Shroving, 1627, p. 49; Taylor's Motto, 1622, sig. D. iv; Poems on State Affairs, ed. 1705, p. 53; Howell, 1660, sect. 28. To play at tick-tack was sometimes meant in an indelicate sense; as in Lilly, ed. 1632, sig. Dd. iii; Hawkins, i. 150.
　　In this lande I did see an ape plaie at *ticke-tacke*, and after at Irishe on the tables, with one of that lande. *Bullein's Dialogue*, 1573.
(2) A moment of time. *Yorksh.*

TID. (1) Silly; childish. *West.*
(2) Quickly; promptly; readily.
(3) A small cock of hay. *Linc.*

(4) The udder of a cow. *Yorksh.*

TIDDE. Happened. *(A.-S.)*

TIDDER. Sooner. *West.*

TIDDIDOLL. An over-dressed, affected, young woman in humble life. *Suffolk.*

TIDDLE. (1) To rear tenderly; to pet. *Tiddling*, a young pet animal. *West.*
(2) To fidget or trifle about. *South.*

TIDDLIN-TOP. The summit. *East.*

TIDDY. The four of trumps at gleek. See the Compleat Gamester, p. 8.

TIDDY-WREN. A wren. *West.*

TIDE. (1) Time; season. *(A.-S.)*
　　Oure kyng went hym in a *tyde*
　　To pley hym be a ryver side.
　　　　　MS. Cantab. Ff. v. 48, f. 47.
　　Save tho that mowe not abyde,
　　For peryle of deth, to that *tyde.*
　　　　　MS. Cott. Claud. A. ii. f. 128.
(2) The tithe. *Kent.*
(3) Tidings; news. Perceval, 1173.

TIDEFUL. Seasonable. *(A.-S.)*

TIDIFE. The titmouse. *Skinner.* Drayton mentions a singing bird called the *tidy*, perhaps the same, for Skinner's explanation appears to be doubtful.

TIDLIWINK. A beer-shop. *West.* It is called in some places *kidliwink.*

TIDN. It is not. *Somerset.*

TIDY. (1) A pinafore. *North.*
(2) A workbag. *Var. dial.*
(3) Considerable; much. *East.*
(4) Clever; ready; neat. *(A.-S.)*
(5) Honest; well-disposed. *West.*

TIE. (1) A short, thick, hair rope, with a wooden nut at one end, and an eye formed in the other, used for hoppling the hind legs of a cow while milking. *North.*
(2) To fasten, as the door, &c.
(3) A foot-race. *Kent.*
(4) The tick of a bed. *Somerset.*
(5) A casket, or box. *(A.-S.) Loken in hur tye*, a phrase sometimes meaning simply, in her possession.

TIED. Compelled. *North.*

TIE-DOG. A bandog, or mastiff.

TIED-UP. Costive, said of cattle.

TIENS. Upright poles behind the cribs in a stall for cows. *West.*

TIER. (1) A bitter drink or liquor.
(2) Moreover. *Cumb.*

TIERING. Coarse half-ceiling. *Lanc.*

TIERS. Two persons who *tie*, or count equal in a game. *Var. dial.*

TIE-TOP. A garland. *North.*

TIFE. To dress, or put in order.
　　Or 3yf thou *tyfyst* the over proudly
　　Over mesure on thy body.
　　　　　MS. Harl. 1701, f. 22.

TIFF. (1) To excite. *Somerset.*
(2) A draught of liquor. *Var. dial.*
(3) To deck out; to dress.
(4) Thin small beer. Still in use.
　　That to shall quickly follow, if
　　It can be rais'd from strong or *tiffe.*
　　　　　Brome's Songs, 1661, p. 165.

(5) To fall headlong. *Yorksh.*

TIFFANY. A portable flour sieve.

TIFFITY-TAFFETY-GIRLS. Courtesans, so called from the dress they formerly wore.

TIFFLE. To trifle. Still in use.

TIFFLES. Light downy particles.

TIFFY. Fretful; touchy. *Sussex.*

TIFFY-TAFFY. A difficult piece of work. Also, a poor silly trifler. *North.*

TIFLE. To turn, to stir, to disorder anything by tumbling in it; so standing corn, or high grass, when trodden down, is said to be tifled. *North.*

TIFLED. A tifled horse, i. e. one broken above the loins. *North.*

TIFT. (1) A small draught of liquor, or short fit of doing anything; also, condition, as to health of the body; as a verb, it means fetching of the breath quickly, as after running, &c.

(2) A tiff, or fit of anger.

(3) To irritate. *Linc.*

(4) A small boat. *North.*

(5) To adjust. *North.*

TIG. (1) A slap, as a mode of salutation.

(2) The last blow in sparring.

(3) A play among children, on separating for the night, in which every one endeavours to get the last touch. *Willan's Yorksh.*

(4) A call to pigs. *Var. dial.*

TIGGY-TOUCHWOOD. A game where children pursue each other, but are exempt from the laws of the game whilst touching wood.

TIGHT. (1) Firm; smart; thriving. Also, prompt, active, alert. *Var. dial.*

(2) Furnished; provided.

3) Promised. Chester Plays, ii. 16.

> A stiward was with king Ermin,
> That hadde *tight* to sle that swin.
> *Beves of Hamtoun*, p. 35.

(4) Begun; pitched; fixed. *Ritson.*

(5) For *tite*, soon, quickly.

TIGHTED-UP. Finely dressed. *East.*

TIGHTISH. In good health. *Var. dial.*

TIGHT-LOCK. Coarse sedge. *East.*

TIGHTLY. Smartly; quickly. *Shak.*

TIHING. Laughing?

> Li per lok and tuinkling,
> *Tihing* and tikeling,
> Opin brest and singing,
> þeise midoutin lesing
> Arin toknes of horelinge.
> *Reliq. Antiq.* ii. 14.

TIHY. To laugh. See *Tee-hees.*

TIKE. (1) A common sort of dog. *North.* Aubrey says, " The indigence of Yorkshire are strong, tall, and long legg'd; them call'em opprobriously long-legd *tyke*," *MS. Royal Soc.* p. 11. The term occurs very early as one of contempt. " ʒone heythene tykes," *MS. Morte Arthure*, f. 91.

> Tykes too they had of all sorts, bandogs,
> Curs, spaniels, water-dogs, and land-dogs.
> *Cotton's Works*, 1734, p. 77.

(2) An old horse or mare. *North.*

(3) A small bullock. *Coles.*

(4) Corn. *North.*

TIKEL. The same as *Tickle*, q. v.

TIL. (1) To. Still in use.

(2) Manure. *North.*

TILBURY. Sixpence. A cant term.

TILD. To incline, or tilt. *East.*

TILDE. Turned; moved. *Hearne.*

TILDER. A machine in a cellar, wedge-formed, for being interposed between a cask and the wall behind it, to *tild*, or *tilt* it up. The article is called *tilder*, and the operation to *tilld* or *tilt*.

TILE. (1) To set a trap; to place anything so that it may fall easily. *West.*

(2) To cure. (*A.-S.*)

> Ichave so *tyled* him for that sore,
> Schel hit never eft ake more.
> *Beves of Hamtoun*, p. 118.

TILE-KILL. A kiln for tiles.

TILESHARD. A piece of a tile. " *Chiapia*, a brick-bat, a tilesharde," Florio, p. 97.

TILE-STONE. A tile.

TILET-TREE. The linden tree.

TILIERS. Husbandmen. (*A.-S.*)

TILL. (1) Than. *West.*

(2) A drawer in a cupboard, &c. It is now only applied to the money-drawer.

(3) To prop up. *Var. dial.*

(4) Tame; gentle. *Kent.*

(5) To come; to bring. *Devon.*

TILLE. To obtain. (*A.-S.*)

TILLER. (1) To germinate. *North.*

(2) A sapling. *Kent.*

(3) The stalk of a cross-bow. Sometimes used for the bow itself. The term is applied in Suffolk to the handle of any implement.

TILLET. " *Tyllet* to wrap cloth in, *toyllette*," Palsgrave, subst. f. 70.

TILLETH. Moveth. *Hearne.*

TILLE-THAKKERS. Tilers.

TILLEUL. " *Tylleull* a kynde of frute, *tilleul*," Palsgrave, 1530, subst. f. 70.

TILLING. Crop, or produce. *West.*

TILLOR.

> I woll that the said Cecille, in full contentation of all such summes of money as I owe unto her, have my bed of arres, *tillor*, testor, and counterpane, which she late borrowed of me. *Test. Vetust.* p. 452.

TILLS. Pulse; lentils. *Var. dial.*

TILLY-VALLY. A phrase of contempt.

TILLY-WILLY. Thin and slight; unsubstantial; thus, cloth, tape, &c. are said to be poor *tilly willy* things when they are deficient in substance. *Linc.*

TILMAN. A farm-labourer. *Palsgrave.*

TILSENT. Tinsel.

TILSTERE. A magician, or charmer.

TILT. (1) Violence. *North.*

(2) On the tilt, i. e. on the saddle by the thigh. Meyrick, ii. 252.

(3) A forge. *Yorksh.*

(4) To tilt, or tournay.

> This grosse attaint so *tilteth* in my thoughts,
> Maintaining combat to abridge mine ease.
> *The Troublesome Raigne of King John*, 161.

(5) To tilt up, i. e. to canter. *Devon.*

'6) To totter. *Exmoor.*

TILTER. (1) Order. *Suffolk.* See Fairfax, Bulk and Selvedge, 12mo. 1674, p. 75.

(2) A sword. A cant term.

TILTH. (1) The produce of tilling.

> So that the *tilthe* is nyʒe forlorne,
> Whiche Criste sewe with his owen honde.
> *Gower, MS. Soc. Antiq. 134, f. 138.*

(2) A place for tilting in.

TILTISH. Apt to kick, said of a horse.

TILTURE. Cultivation. *Tusser.*

TILTY. Touchy. *West.*

TIMARRANY. Two poor things. *Norf.*

TIMBER. (1) Forty skins of fur. See a note in Harrison's England, p. 160.

(2) Strength; build; might.

> Sith thy dwelling shalle be here,
> That thou woldist my son lere,
> Hys *tymber* ffor to assay.
> *Torrent of Portugal, p. 99.*

(3) To timber a fire, i. e. to supply it with wood. To timber-cart, to go with a team for timber.

(4) A timbrel. *Palsgrave.*

(5) A kind of worm.

(6) To make a nest. *Dict. Rust.*

(7) A crest. Howell, 1660.

TIMBER-DISHES. Trenchers. *Devon.*

TIMBERED. Built. See *Timber* (2).

> Alanson, a fine *timb'red* man, and tall,
> Yet wants the shape thou art adorn'd withall :
> Vandome good carriage, and a pleasing eie,
> Yet hath not Suffolk's princely majestie.
> *Drayton's Poems, 1637, p. 299.*

TIMBER-LEAVES. Wooden shutters.

TIMBERN. Wooden. *Devon.*

TIMBERSOME. Timorous. *West.*

TIMBER-TASTER. A person in a dockyard who examines timber and pronounces it fit for use.

TIMBRE. To build. (*A.-S.*) *Timbred his tene,* occasioned his trouble.

TIMBRELL. A pillory. This word occurs in Hollyband's Dictionarie, 1593.

TIMBRES. Basins. (*A.-N.*)

TIMDOODLE. A silly fellow. *Cornw.*

TIME. (1) Tune. Jonson, v. 180.

(2) A theme, or subject. *Palsgrave.*

(3) Apprenticeship. *Var. dial.*

(4) To give one the time of the day, i. e. to salute him. This phrase is still common in the country.

(5) To summon; to call. "Whenne thus wele tymede," MS. Morte Arthure.

(6) The times. *Shak.*

TIMELESS. Untimely. *Shak.*

TIMELY. Early; recently. *Var. dial.*

TIMERSOME. Timid. *Var. dial.*

TIMES. (1) Hours. (2) *Times and often,* very frequently. *By times,* early. *Times about,* in turns. *In times,* now and then.

TIMINGS. Grounds of beer. *Kent.*

TIMMER. (1) Timber. *Var. dial.* "Tymmyr, *meremium*," Cathol. Anglic. MS.

(2) Provision; fare. *North.*

(3) To trifle, or idle.

TIMMY. Timid; fretful. *West.*

TIMOROUS. (1) Difficult to please; uncertain; fretful. Sometimes *timoursome.*

(2) Terrible. Skelton, ii. 306.

TIMOTHY. A child's penis. *South.*

TIMP. The place at the bottom of an iron furnace where the metal issues out.

TIM-SARAH. A sledge touching the ground in front, and having wheels behind.

TIM-WHISKY. A light one-horse chaise without a head. *South.*

TIN. (1) Cash; money. *Var. dial.*

(2) Till. *Chesh.*

TINCT. Tincture. *Shak.*

TIND. To kindle. *West.*

> As the seal maketh impression in the wax, and as fire conveyeth heat into iron, and as one candle *tindeth* a thousand.
> *Sanderson's Sermons, 1689, p. 55*

TINDES. Horns.

> The thrydd hownde fyghtyng he fyndys,
> The beste stroke hym wyth hys *tyndys.*
> *MS. Cantab. Ff. ii. 38, f. 78.*

TINDLES. Fires made by children in Derbyshire on the night of All Souls, Nov. 2.

TINE. (1) To lose. (*A.-S.*) It occasionally has the meaning, to perish, to cause to perish.

> Of the turtyl that *tynes* hire make,
> That nevere aftere othere wille take.
> *MS. Harl. 2260, f. 118*

> For ʒyf thou make any man falsly *tyne,*
> As for theft, thou shalt have pyne.
> *MS. Harl. 1701, f. 14.*

> For ʒyf thou doust, thou mayst hem *tyne,*
> And for that pryde go to pyne.
> *MS. Harl. 1701, f. 22.*

> He hath smetyn the dewke Segwyne,
> Hys hors he made hym for to *tyne.*
> *MS. Cantab. Ff. ii. 38, f. 161.*

> I dar saye, withouten fyne,
> That we shul so oure londes *tyne.*
> *Cursor Mundi, MS. Coll. Trin. Cantab. f. 35.*

> That ys owre God so gracyous,
> And ys so looth mannys sowle to *tyne.*
> *MS. Cantab. Ff. ii. 38, f. 17.*

> For alle if he levede als a swynne,
> He wenes God wille hym noʒt *tyne.*
> *MS. Harl. 2260, f. 20.*

(2) The prong of a fork, &c. *Var. dial.* Tined hooke, Harrison's England, p. 232.

(3) To divide a field with a hedge. Also, to mend a hedge. *West.*

(4) To light; to kindle. *Var. dial.*

(5) Wild vetch, or tare.

(6) To shut; to inclose. *North.*

(7) A forfeit, or pledge. *North.*

(8) A moment, or brief space of time.

TINESTOCKS. The short crooked handles upon the pole of a scythe. *West.*

TING. (1) The girth which secures the panniers of a packsaddle. *Devon.*

(2) To beat; to girth; to bind. *West.*

(3) To sting. (4) A sting. *North.*

(5) To ring a bell. *East.* "To ting as a bell," Cotgrave in v. *Sonner.*

(6) A prong fork. *Devon.*

(7) To chide severely. *Exmoor.*

(8) To split; to crack. *North.*

TINGE. A small red insect. *Pegge.*

TINGER. A great falsehood. *Devon.*

TINGLE-TANGLE. A small bell.

Now hang the hallowed bell about his neck,
We call it a mellisonant *tingle-tangle.*
Randolph's Amyntas, 1640.

TINGLING. Sharp. *Var. dial.*

TING-TANG. The saints-bell. *Var. dial.*

TING-WORM. A venomous worm that bites cattle under the tongue. *Glouc.*

TINING. (1) Dead wood used in tining or repairing a hedge. *Chesh.*

(2) A new inclosed ground. *Wilts.*

TINK. To tinkle, as bells.

TINKER. To mend clumsily. *West.*

TINKLE. To strike a light. *Northampt.*

TINKLER. A tinker. *North.* "A tincker, or tinkeler," Baret's Alvearie, 1580.

TINLEY. The same as *Tindles,* q. v.

TINNET. The same as *Tining,* q. v.

TINO. A contracted form of " aught I know," generally joined to a negative. *Devon.*

TINSED-BALL. A child's ball wrought with worsted of various colours. To *tinse* a ball is to work such a covering upon it. *Hunter.*

TINSEY. A water can. *Oxon.*

TINSIN. A kind of satin.

TINT. (1) Lost. *(A.-S.)*

Tille thou at helle come, thou walde noghte stynte,
And ware sesede of thas that thou hade *tynte.*
MS. Lincoln A. i. 17, f. 191.

(2) Destroyed. See *Tine* (1).

It rayned fire fra heven and brunstane,
And *tynt* al that thare was and spared nane.
MS. Cott. Galba E. ix. f. 97.

(3) *Tint for tant,* tit for tat.

(4) It is not. *West.*

(5) A goblin. *North.*

(6) Half a bushel of corn.

TINTED. Lost ; neglected. *North.*

TINTERNELL. The name of an old dance.

TINTH. The same as *Tining,* q. v.

TINTY. Tinted. *Northampt.*

TIP. (1) To overturn. *West.*

(2) To give. (3) A donation. *Var. dial.*

(4) A draught of liquor. *West.*

(5) A smart but light blow.

(6) To adjust the top of a stack.

TIP-CAT. A boy's game, fully described in Strutt, ed. 1830, p. 109.

TIP-CHEESE. A boy's game.

TIPE. (1) A ball, or globe.

(2) A trap for rabbits, &c. *Yorksh.*

(3) To empty liquor from one vessel into another. *North.*

(4) To toss with the hand. *Linc.*

TIPER-DOWN. Strong drink. *Yorksh.*

TIPE-STICK. The piece of wood which, reaching from shaft to shaft, keeps the body of a cart in its place, and prevents it from *typing* up or over. *Linc.*

TIPPED. Headed ; pointed.

TIPPERD. Badly dressed. *North.*

TIPPET. *To turn tippet,* to make a complete change. An old phrase.

TIPPLE. (1) To tumble : to turn over, as is done in tumbling.

(2) Drink. *Var. dial.*

TIPPLER. A tumbler : hence, when they talk of a tumbler pigeon, you hear them say, " What a *tippler* he is !"

TIPPLING. Haymaking. *Norf.*

TIPPLING-HOUSE. A beer-shop.

TIPPY. (1) Smart ; fine. *Var. dial.*

(2) The brim of a cap or bonnet.

TIPS. (1) Small faggots. *Suff.*

(2) Irons for the bottoms of shoes.

TIP-TEERERS. Christmas mummers. *Hants.*

TIPTOON. Tiptoes ; the extremities of the toes. Chaucer, Cant. T. 15313.

TIP-TOP. (1) Quite at the top.

(2) The best of anything. *Var. dial.*

TIRANDYE. Tyranny.

But wroujten upon *tirandye*
That no pité ne myjte hem plye.
Gower, MS. Soc. Antiq. 134, f. 91.

But now *tyrauntrye* ys holden ryjt,
And sadnesse ys turned to sotelté.
MS. Cantab. Ff. ii. 38, f. 2.

TIRANT. Special ; extraordinary. *West.*

TIRDELS. Sheep's dung. *Huloet.*

TIRE. (1) To tear ; to pluck ; to feed upon, as birds of prey. *(A.-N.)*

(2) To attire ; to dress. Also, to dress food.

Then xij. knyghtys he dud *tyre*
In palmers wede anon.
MS. Cantab. Ff. ii. 38, f. 121.

He brou3t me to a feyre palas,
Wele *tyred* and rychly in all case ;
He shewyd me hys castellus and tourys,
And hys hey haules and bourse,
Forestes, ryvers, frutes and floures
MS. Ashmole 61, xv. Cent.

Let my moyst hair grow rich with perfume sweats,
And *tyre* my brows with rose-bud coronets.
The royal tombes commands us live : since they
Teach that the very gods themselves decay.
Fletcher's Poems, p. 45.

(3) The head-dress.

Wyth wympils and *tyris* wrappid in pride,
Yelow under yelow they covyr and hyde.
MS. Laud. 416, f. 74.

In that day shall the Lord take away the ornament of the slippers, and the calles, and the round *tires,* the sweete-balles, and the bracelets.
Dent's Pathway, p. 46.

(4) Prepared ; ready ; dressed ; attired.

By that the shyppes were gon and rowed in the depe,
Trussed and *tyred* on toterynge wawes.
MS. Cott. Calig. A. ii. f. 111.

(5) A tier, row, or rank.

(6) The iron rim of a wheel.

TIREDER. More tired. *East.*

TIRELING. Worn out ; tired.

TIREMAN. A dealer in dresses, and all kinds of ornamental clothing.

TIREMENT. Interment.

TIRET. A leather strap for hawks, hounds, &c.

TIREWOMAN. A milliner.

TIRFE. The tuck of a cap, &c.

TIRING-BOY. One who stirs the colour about in printing cloth, &c. *Lanc.*

TIRING-HOUSE. An old term for the dressing-room at theatres, tennis-courts, &c.

TIRL. To put in motion. In many old ballads we read, " he *tirled* the pin at the castle gate ;" as one would say, he rang the bell. *North.*

TIRLINS. Small pebbles, coals, &c.

TIRNEDEN. Turned. (*A.-S.*)

TIRPEIL. Trouble ; broil ; villany ; base action ; vileness ; roguery. *Hearne.*

TIRSTY. Trusty. *Ritson.*

TISAN. Barley-water. (*A.-N.*)

TISCAN. A handful of corn tied up as a sheaf by a gleaner. *Cornw.*

TISE. To entice.

Lytyl or mochel synne we do,
The fend and oure fleshe *tysyn* us therto.
MS. Harl. 1701, f. 1.

Hast thow i-seyn any thynge
That *tysed* the to synnynge ?
MS. Cott. Claud. A. ii. f. 144.

Adam ansuerd with wykyd wyll,
The eddyre he *tysed* me thertyll.
MS. Ashmole 61, f. 85.

Y may evyr aftur thys
That thou woldyst *tyse* me to do amys,
No game schulde the glewe !
MS. Cantab. Ff. ii. 38, f. 72.

TISEDAY. Tuesday. " The tyseday tharaftyre," Morte Arthure, MS. Lincoln, f. 94.

TISS. To hiss. *Somerset.*

TISSICK. A tickling faint cough. *East.*

TISSUE. A riband. (*A.-N.*)

TISTY-TOSTY. (1) The blossoms of cowslips collected together, tied in a globular form, and used to toss to and fro for an amusement called *tisty-tosty.* It is sometimes called simply a *tosty.*

(2) Swaggering. The term was formerly applied to swaggering swashbucklers, &c.

TIT. (1) A horse. *Var. dial.*

This he spake to intice the minde of a lecherous young man,
But what spurres need now for an untam'd *titt* to be trotting,
Or to add old oile to the flame, new flaxe to the fier ?
Barnefield's Affectionate Shepherd, 1594.

(2) A teat. *Var. dial.*

(3) Bit ; morsel. *Somerset.*

(4) This. *Yorksh.*

(5) A nice smart girl. *Var. dial.*

(6) A dam in a river.

TIT-BIT. A delicate morsel. *Var. dial.*

TITCHED. Touched. *Var. dial.*

TITE. (1) A spring of water. *Oxon.* I believe this word is now obsolete ; but one part of Chipping Norton is, I am informed, still called *Tite-end.*

(2) For *tideth,* happeneth.

(3) To put in order. *North.*

(4) Soon. Still in use.

The steward also *tyte*
The kyng let drawe hym, with grete dyspyte,
Wyth horsys thorow the towne,
And hanged hym on the galowe tree,
That al men myght hyt see,
That he had done tresone !
MS. Cantab. Ff. ii. 38, f. 75.

(5) Weight. *Somerset.*

TITELERIS. Tattlers.

TITERING. Courtship. (*A.-S.*)

TITE-TITY. To balance on the hand ; to play at seesaw. *Somerset.*

TIT-FAGGOTS. Small short faggots.

TITH. Tight, or strong.

TITHANDE. Tidings.

Then tolde the kynge hur *tythande.*
MS. Cantab. Ff. ii. 38, f. 72

Knyghtys of dyvers londys,
When they harde of these *tythandys,*
They gysed them fulle gay ;
Of every londe the beste,
Thedur they rode withowten reste,
Fulle wele arayed and dyght.
MS. Cantab. Ff. ii. 38, f. 76.

TITHING. A company of magpies.

TITHINGE. Tidings.

There fadurs be not well lykynge,
When they harde of that *tythynge.*
MS. Cantab. Ff. ii. 38, f. 160

TITIMALE. The herb *euphorbia.*

TITIVIL. A worthless knave.

For the devill hymself, to set farther division betwene the Englishe and Frenche nacion, did apparell certain catchepoules and parasites, commonly called *titivils* and tale tellers, to sowe discord and dissencion. *Hall, Henry VI.* f. 43.

Tynckers and tabberers, typplers, taverners,
Tyttyfylles, fryfullers, turners and trumpers.
Thersytes, p. 67.

TIT-LARK. A sort of lark differing from the skylark, of a lower flight and inferior note.

TITLELES. Without title. (*A.-S.*)

TITLERES. Hounds. *Gawayne.*

TITLING. " The birde that hatcheth the cuckowes egges," Nomenclator, 1585, p. 57.

TITMOSE. The pudendum.

Hir corage was to have ado with alle ;
She had no mynd that she shuld die,
But with her prety *tytmose* to encrece and multeply.
Reliq. Antiq. ii. 22.

TITMUN. Qu. *titmuus,* a titmouse ?

That can finde a *titmuns* nest,
And keape a robin redbreste.
Misogonus, ap. Collier, ii. 479.

TITTE. (1) Soon ; quickly.

And for I may nost thys dette quyte,
Lorde, that I have done forgyve me *tytte.*
MS. Harl. 2960, f. 3.

(2) Tightened ?

And the feete uppward fast knytted,
And in strang paynes be streyned and *tytted.*
Hampole, MS. Bowes, p. 210.

TITTER. (1) Sooner ; earlier. *North.* " Titter up kå," i. e. the earliest riser call the rest. This example is taken from Urry's MS. Additions to Ray.

A I fadir, he said, takes to none ill,
For with the geaunt fighte I wille,
To luke if I dare byde ;
And bot I *titter* armede be,
I salle noghte lett, so mote I the,
That I ne salle to hyme ryde.
MS. Lincoln A. i. 17, f. 103.

(2) To tremble. *Suffolk.*

(3) To seesaw. *East.*

TITTERAVATING. Tiresome. *East.*

TITTERS. A kind of weed.

TITTER-TOTTER. The game of seesaw.

TITTIVATE. To dress neatly. *Var. dial.*

TITTLE. (1) To tickle. *East.*

(2) The mark on dice.

(3) To bring up by hand.

TITTLE-BAT. The stickleback.

TITTLE-GOOSE. A foolish blab. *West.*

TITTUP. A canter. *Var. dial.*

TITTY. (1) A cat. *North.*

(2) The breast, or milk therefrom.

(3) Sister. *Cumb.*

(4) Tiny; small. *Var. dial.*

TITTY-MOUSE. A titmouse. *Baret.*

> The mouse a *titty-mouse* was no doubt,
> A birde and generation,
> That may appeare yet more at large
> By oughten propagation.
> *MS. Poems in Dr. Bliss's Possession.*

TITTYRIES.

> No newes of navies burnt at seas;
> No noise of late spawn'd *tittyries.*
> *Herrick's Works, i. 176.*

TIV. To. *North.*

TIVER. Red ochre. *East.*

TIXHIL. A needle.

TIXTE. A text. (*A.-S.*)

TIZZY. Sixpence. A cant term.

TIʒANDIS. Tidings.

> The maydene rynnes to the haulle
> *Tyʒandis* to frayne. *MS. Lincoln A. i. 17, f. 137.*

TIʒT. (1) Position?

> The bisshop seyd anonryʒt,
> Abide, woman, in that *tiʒt*
> Tille my sermonde be done.
> *MS. Cantab. Ff. v. 48, f. 46.*

(2) Made; did.

> Stinte hit wolde he, if he myʒt,
> The foly that his bretheren *tiʒt.*
> *Cursor Mundi, MS. Coll. Trin. Cantab. f. 26*

(3) Fastened; tied. (4) Prepared.

TLICK. To click the fingers.

TO. (1) Until.

> Theys knyghtis never stynte ne blane,
> *To* thay unto the ceté wanne.
> *MS. Lincoln A. i. 17, f. 116.*

(2) In Lincolnshire, *to* is used for *of* and *for.* As "think *to* a thing," and "bread *to* breakfast." In Devonshire it often occupies the places of *at* and *with.* "When were you *to* Plymouth?"

(3) Two; twice; too. *North.*

(4) Contr. of *tobacco.*

(5) Took. Same as *Ta,* q. v.

> His panterer *to* a lofe tho y wys.
> *Chron. Vilodun, p. 15.*

Compared with. Still in use. "That man nothing to him."

To harass, or fatigue. *Yorksh.*

Thou. *North.*

Shut; put to. *Var. dial.*

) Almost. *Heref.*

1) *To and again,* from time to time.

O–. A prefix to verbs of A.-S. origin, implying destruction or deterioration.

TOAD. Like a toad under a harrow, i. e. in a state of torture. *Var. dial.*

TOAD-BIT. A disease in cattle. *North.*

TOAD-EATER. A parasite. *Var. dial.*

TOAD-IN-A-HOLE. Beefsteaks baked in batter; or, rather, a piece of beef placed in the middle of a dish of batter, and then baked.

TOAD-PADDOCK. A toadstool. *Lanc.*

TOAD-PIPES. The herb horse-tail.

TOAD'S-CAP. Toadsstool. *Todyshatte,* Pr. Parv. *East.* Called *toads-meat* in the Isle of Wight.

TOAD-SKEP. Fungus on old trees.

TOAD-SLUBBER. The mucus or jelly which incloses the eggs of a toad.

TOAD-SPIT. Cuckoo-spittle.

TOAD-STONE. A stone formerly supposed to be found in the head of a toad, and considered a sovereign remedy in many disorders.

TOADY. (1) Hateful; beastly. *West.*

(2) To flatter any one for gain.

TOAK. To soak. *Somerset.*

TOARE. Grass and rubbish on corn-land after the corn is reaped; or the long sour grass in pasture fields. *Kent.*

TOART. Towards. *West.*

TOATLY. Quiet; easily managed. - *Chesh.*

TOB. To pitch; to chuck. *Beds.*

TO-BRASTE. Burst in pieces.

> Thaire gud speris al *to-braste*
> On molde whenne thai mett.
> *MS. Lincoln A. i. 17, f. 135.*

TO-BROKE. Broken in pieces.

> The gatis that Neptunus made
> A thousande wynter thertdfore,
> They have anone *to-broke* and tore.
> *Gower, MS. Soc. Antiq. 134, f. 46.*

TOBY-TROT. A simple fellow. *Devon.*

TOCHER. A tether. *Norf.*

TO-CLATEREN. Clattered together.

> The clowdys alle *to-clateren,* as they cleve wolde.
> *MS. Cott. Calig. A. ii. f. 109.*

TOD. (1) A fox. Still in use.

(2) Two stone of wool.

(3) A bush, generally of ivy. In Suffolk, a stump at the top of a pollard.

> And, like an owle, by night to goe abroad,
> Roosted all day within an ivie *tod,*
> Among the sea-cliffes, in the dampy caves,
> In charnell-houses, fit to dwell in graves.
> *Drayton's Poems, 1637, p. 254.*

(4) A disease in rabbits. *West.*

(5) Toothed. Still in use.

(6) The upright stake of a hurdle.

TO-DAISTE. Dashed in pieces.

> And daste out the teth out of his heved,
> And *to-daiste* his bones.
> *MS. Trin. Coll. Oxon. 57.*

TO-DAY-MORNING. This morning.

TODDLE. To walk with short steps, as a child. *Toddles,* a term of endearment.

TODDY. (1) Rum and water. *Var. dial.*

(2) Very small; tiny. *North.*

TODELINGE. A little toad.

TODGE. The same as *Stodge,* q. v.

TOD-LOWREY. A bugbear, or ghost. *Linc.*

TO-DO. Fuss; ado. *Var. dial.*

TO-FALL. The same as *Tee-fall,* q. v.

TOFET. Half a bushel. *Kent.*

TOFFY. The same as *Taffy,* q. v.

TOFLIGHT. A refuge. (*A.-S.*)

TO-FORNE. Before.

> That a maide hathe a childe borne,
> The whiche thynge was not se *to-forne.*
> > *Lydgate, MS. Ashmole* 39, f. 55.

TO-FRUSCHED. Dashed to pieces.

> Downe into the dyke, and thare he felle and was
> alle *to-frusched.*   *MS. Lincoln* A. i. 17, f. 1.

TOFT. Open ground; a plain; a hill. Kennett explains it "a field where a house or building once stood."

TOG. To go, or jog along. *Glouc.*

TOGACE. The name of a cat.

TOG-BELLIED. Very fat. *Glouc.*

TOGE. A toga. *Shak.* The term is explained a *coat* in the canting dictionaries.

TOGGERY. Worn-out clothes.

TO-GIDERE. Together. (*A.-S.*)

TO-GINDE. To reduce to pieces.

TOGITHERS. Together. (*A.-S.*)

TOGMAN. A coat. A cant term.

TO-GRYNDE. Grind to pieces.

> Wylde bestys me wylle *to-grynde,*
> Or any man may me fynde.
> > *MS. Cantab.* Ff. ii. 38, f. 244.

TOIL. (1) The piece of armour which was buckled to the tasset, and hung over the cuishes. Meyrick, ii. 180.

(2) An inclosure into which game was driven.

TOILE. To tug. (*A.-S.*)

TOILOUS. Laborious. *Palsgrave.*

TOINE. (1) Shut. *Lanc.*

(2) To tune a musical instrument.

TOIT. (1) Proud; stiff. *West.*

(2) A cushion, or hassock. *Devon.*

(3) A settle. *Somerset.*

(4) To fall, or tumble over. *North.*

TOITISH. Pert; snappish. *Cornw.*

TOKE. (1) Gave; delivered up. (*A.-S.*)

(2) To glean apples. *Somerset.*

TOKEN. (1) A fool. *Wilts.*

(2) A small piece of brass or copper, generally worth about a farthing, formerly issued by tradesmen.

(3) A plague-spot on the flesh.

(4) To betroth. *Cornw.*

TOKENYNG. Intelligence.

> But forthe he went monythys three,
> But *tokenyng* of hur never harde hee.
> > *MS. Cantab.* Ff. ii. 38, f. 140.
> *Tokenynges* sone of hym he fonde,
> Slayne men on every honde.
> > *MS. Cantab.* Ff. ii. 38, f. 67.

TOKIN. An alarm-bell. (*Fr.*)

TOKNE. A token, or sign. *Pr. Parv.*

TOKYTES. Kites? The printed edition reads "gleides or puttocks."

> Theise wommen haddyn wyngges like *tokytes,* that
> with crying voyse sekyn her mete.
> > *Wimbelton's Sermon,* 1388, *MS. Hatton* 57, p. 15.

TOLD. Accounted. (*A.-S.*)

TOLDERED-UP. Dressed out. *Linc.*

TOLE. (1) To draw. Hence, to entice. It occurs in the last sense in very early writers. See Wright's Seven Sages, p. 103.

(2) A mass of large trees. *Sussex.*

(3) To tear in pieces.

(4) A weapon.

TOLEDO. A sword, or dagger, so called from the place of manufacture.

TOLERATE. To tyrannize. *East.*

TOLKE. A man; a knight.

TOLLACION. Abduction. (*A.-N.*)

> The vice of supplantacione,
> With many a fals *tollacion,*
> Whiche he conspireth alle unknowe.
> > *Gower, MS. Soc. Antiq.* 134. f. 76.

TOLL-BAR. A turnpike. *Var. dial.*

TOLL-BOOTH. A town-hall. *North.*

TOLL-BOY. Cheap goods. *Dorset.*

TOLLE. To incite one to do anything.

TOLLEN. To measure out; to count.

TOLLER. (1) Tallow. *South.*

(2) A toll-gatherer. (*A.-S.*) *Tollers,* Skelton, i. 152, erroneously explained by Mr. Dyce *tellers, speakers.*

> *Tollers* officy yit es ille,
> For they take tolle oft agayn skylle.
> > *MS. Harl.* 2260, f. 59.

TOLLETRY. Magic. This term is derived from *Tollet,* or Toledo, in Spain.

TOLL-NOOK. A corner of the market-place where the toll used to be taken. *North.*

TOL-LOL. Tolerable. *Var. dial.*

TOLMEN. Perforated stones.

TO-LOOKER. A spectator. *Devon.*

TOLPIN. A pin belonging to a cart.

TOLSERY. A penny. A cant term.

TOLSEY. The place where tolls were taken.

TOLTER. To struggle; to flounder.

TOLYONE. To plead. *Pr. Parv.*

TOM. (1) A close-stool. *Somerset.*

(2) The knave of trumps at gleek.

TOMBESTERE. A dancing woman. (*A.-S.*)

TOM-CAT. A male cat. *Var. dial.*

TOM-CONY. A simple fellow.

TOM-CULL. The fish miller's-thumb.

TOM-DRUM. "Tom Drum his interteinment, which is, to hale a man in by the head, and thrust him out by both the shoulders," Stanihurst's Ireland, p. 21.

TOME. (1) Time; leisure.

> And ye wille here and holde yow stille,
> And take yow *tome* awhile ther-tille.
> > *MS. Lincoln* A. i. 17, f. 122.
> I have no *tome* to com therto,
> I have no *tome* thider to fare.
> > *Cursor Mundi, MS. Coll. Trin. Cantab.* f. 90.
> Here may a man reede, that has *tome,*
> A lang processe of the day of dome.
> > *Hampole, MS. Bowes,* p. 184.

(2) Fanciful; light.

> It is gude powder to ete if ye thynk that thi
> hevede be *tume* abovene.
> > *MS. Lincoln* A. i. 17, f. 209.

(3) Heartburn; flushings. *North.*

(4) Empty. Wright's Pol. Songs, p. 303.

> So dud these wrecches of joye *tome,*
> Thei douted not Goddes dome.
> > *Cursor Mundi, MS. Coll. Trin. Cantab.* f. 19

(5) A hair-line for fishing. *Cumb.*

(6) To go towards. *Somerset.*

(7) To faint away. *North.*

TO-MEDIS. In the midst. (*A.-S.*)

TOMEHED.

> Schent be alle are quede doand
> Over *tomehed* in anl land.
>
> *MS. Cott. Vespas.* D. vii. f. 15.

TOMEREL. A dung-cart.

TOM-FARTHING. A silly fellow.

TOMMY. (1) Provisions. *Var. dial.*

(2) A simple fellow. *North.*

(3) A small spade for excavating the narrow bottoms of under drains. *North.*

TOMMY-BAR. The ruff fish. *North.*

TOMMY-LOACH. The loach fish.

TOM-NODDIES. Puffins are so called in Northumberland. See Pennant's Tour in Scotland, ed. 1790, i. 48.

TOM-NODDY. A fool. *Var. dial.*

TOM-NOUP. The titmouse. *Salop*

TO-MONTH. This month. *Linc.*

TOMOR. Some kind of bird.

> The pellican and the popynjay,
> The *tomor* and the turtil trw.
>
> *MS. Cantab.* Ff. v. 48, f. 68.

TO-MORROW-DAY. To-morrow. *West.*

TOM-PIN. A very large pin.

TOM-PIPER. The name of a personage in the ancient morris-dance.

TOM-POKER. A bugbear for children.

TOMRIG. A tomboy. *Glouc.*

TOMS-OF-BEDLAM. These vagabonds have already been noticed under *Abraham-men*, q. v., their other appellation. Aubrey, in his Nat. Hist. Wilts, Royal Soc. MS., p. 259, relates the following anecdote concerning Sir Thomas More:—" Where this gate now stands [at Chelsea] was, in Sir Thomas More's time, a gate-house, according to the old fashion. From the top of this gate-house was a most pleasant and delightfull prospect, as is to be seen. His lordship was wont to re-create himself in this place, to apricate and contemplate, and his little dog with him. It so happened that a Tom ô Bedlam gott up the staires when his lordship was there, and came to him, and cryed, " leap, Tom, leap," offering his lo. violence to have thrown him over the battlements. His lo. was a little old man, and in his gown, and not able to make resistance, but having presentnesse of witt, seyd, " Let's first throw this little dog over." The Tom ô Bedlam threw the dog down. " Pretty sport," sayd the Lord Chancelour, " goe down, and bring it up, and try again." Whilest the mad-man went down for the dog, his lordship made fast the dore of the staires, and called for help, otherwise he had lost his life by this unexpected danger." To this Aubrey appends the following note : " Till the breaking out of the civill warres Tom ôBedlams did travell about the countrey ; they had been poore distracted men that had been putt into Bedlam, where recovering to some sobernesse, they were licentiated to goe a begging, e. g. they had on their left arm an armilla of tinn printed in some workes, about four inches long ; they could not gett it off.

They wore about their necks a great horn of an oxe in a string or bawdrie, which when they came to an house for almes, they did wind ; and they did putt the drink given them into this horn, whereto they did putt a stopple. Since the warres I doe not remember to have seen any one of them." In a later hand is added, " I have seen them in Worcestershire within these thirty years, 1756."

TOM-TAILOR. The daddy-long-legs.

TOM-TELL-TRUTH. A true guesser.

TOM-TILER. A henpecked husband.

TOM-TIT. The wren. *Norf.*

TOM-TODDY. A tadpole. *Cornw.*

TOM-TOE. The great toe. *Var. dial.*

TOM-TOMMY. See *Double-Tom.*

TOM-TROT. A sweetmeat for children, made by melting sugar, butter, and treacle together; when it is getting cool and rather stiff, it is drawn out into pieces about four inches long, and from its adhesive nature each piece is wrapped up in a separate bit of paper.

TOM-TUMBLER. The name of a fiend ? See Scot's Discoverie of Witchcraft, 1584, as quoted in Ritson's Essay on Fairies, p. 45.

TON. (1) To mash ale.

(2) The one. (*A.-S.*)

> The erle of Lancastur is the *ton*,
> And the erle of Waryn sir Johne.
>
> *MS. Cantab.* Ff. v. 48, f. 52.

(3) Taken. Sir Tristrem, p. 214.

(4) The tunny fish ? Middleton, iv. 404.

(5) A spinning-wheel. *Exm.*

TONDER. Tinder. (*A.-S.*)

TONE. (1) Toes. (*A.-S.*)

(2) Betaken; committed. *Gawayne.*

TONEL. A kind of fowling net.

TON-END. Upright. *North.*

TONG. (1) To toll a bell. *West.*

(2) Twang, or taste. Also as *Tang*, q. v.

TONGE. Thong. Skelton, ii. 274.

TONGUE. (1) A small sole. *Suffolk.*

(2) The sting of a bee.

(3) " Tong of a balaunce, *languette*," Palsgrave.

(4) To talk immoderately. *West.*

TONGUE-BANG. To scold heartily. *South.*

TONGUE-PAD. A talkative person.

TONGUE-TREE. The pole of a waggon.

TONGUE-WALK. To abuse. *Var. dial.*

TONIKIL. Same as *Dalmatic*, q. v.

TONKEY. Stumpy and short. *Devon.*

TONMELE. A large tub, or tun.

TONNE. A barrel, or tun.

> The abot that was thider sent,
> Biheld the *tonne* was made of tre.
>
> *Legend of Pope Gregory*, p. 19.

TONNE-GRET. As large as a tun.

TONNIHOOD. The bullfinch. *North.*

TONOWRE. " Fonel or tonowre, *fusorium, infusorium*," Pr. Parv. p. 170.

TONPART. Of the one part.

TONSE. To dress, or trim. *North.*

TONSILE-HEDGE. A hedge cut neat and smooth. *North.*

TON-TOTHER. One another. *Derb.*

TONTYGH. A ton?

Item, sol. Petro sire pro iij. quarters of a *tontygh* of ffreston, vij s. vijd.

Norwich Corporation Records, temp. Hen. VI.

TONUP. A turnip. *Linc.*

TONY. A simpleton.

TOO. A toe. (*A.-S.*)

And who so on the fire goos,
He brenneth bothe foote and *toos.*

MS. Lansd. 793, f. 68.

TOODLE. A tooth. *Craven.*

TOOL. (1) It will. *Somerset.*

(2) To level the surface of a stone.

(3) A poor useless fellow. *Var. dial.*

TOOLS. Farming utensils. *West.*

TOOM. (1) Empty. *North.*

The nobleman led him through many a roome,
And through many a gallery gay.

What a deele doth the king with so many *tooms* houses,
That he gets um not fild with corne and hay?

The King and a Poore Northerne Man, 1640.

(2) To take wool off the cards.

(3) Time. See Guest, ii. 205. It also means unoccupied space or room.

Here may men rede, that have *toom,*
A longe processe of the day of doom.

MS. Addit. 11305, f 91.

TOOMING. An aching in the eyes. *North.*

TOON. (1) Too. *East.*

(2) The one; the other. *Var. dial.*

The *toon* hoved, and behelde
The strokys they gaf undur schylde,
Gret wondur had hee!

MS. Cantab. Ff. ii. 38, f. 80.

TOOR. (1) The toe. *Somerset.*

(2) Tother; the other. *Devon.*

TOORCAN. To wonder or muse on what one means to do. *North.*

TOORE. Hard; difficult.

TOOT. (1) The devil. *Linc.*

(2) To pry inquisitively. *North.* " Tooting and prying," Taylor's Workes, 1630, i. 119. Also, to gaze at eagerly.

(3) Total; the whole. *Suffolk.*

(4) To blow a horn. *Var. dial.*

(5) To whine, or cry. *West.*

(6) To shoot up, as plants. *North.*

(7) To try; to endeavour. *Devon.*

TOOTH. Keep; maintenance. *North.*

TOOTH-AND-EGG. A corruption of *tutenag,* an alloy or mixed metal. In this county spoons, &c., used by the common people are made of it, and these articles are thence vulgarly termed *tooth and egg* in this and the adjoining county of Nottingham. *Linc.*

TOOTH-AND-NAIL. To set about anything *tooth and nail,* to set about it in earnest.

TOOTH-HOD. Fine pasturage. *North.*

TOOTHING. Bricks left projecting from a party-wall ready for a house to be built next it.

TOOT-HORN. Anything long and taper, like a cornet or horn. *Somerset.*

TOOTH-SOAP. A kind of tooth-powder.

Of the heads of mice being burned is made that excellent powder, for the scowring and cleansing of the teeth, called *tooth-soape;* unto which if spikenard

II.

be added or mingled, it will take away any filthy sent or stronge savour in the mouth.

Topsell's Beasts, 1607

TOOTHSOME. Palatable.

No swagg'ring terms, no taunts; for 'tis not right
To think that onely *toothsome* which can bite.

Randolph's Jealous Lovers, 1646.

TOOTHWORT. The herb shepherd's-purse.

TOOTHY. (1) Peevish; crabbed. *South.*

(2) Having many or large teeth.

TOOTING-HOLE. A loophole in a wall, &c.

TOOTLEDUM-PATTICK. A fool. *Cornw.*

TOOTLING. The noise made with the tongue in playing on the flute. *Northamptonsh.*

TOO-TOO. Excessive; excessively; exceedingly. "*Too-too,* used absolutely for very well or good," Ray's English Words, 1674, p. 49. It is often nothing more in sense than a strengthening of the word *too,* but too-too was regarded by our early writers as a single word. See further observations in Shak. Soc. Pap. i. 39 ; Wit and Wisdom, notes, p. 72, where I have printed a very large number of quotations from early writers exhibiting the meaning of this compound word.

Who *too-too* suddenly accepting the same, hoping thereby to have upheld the Protestant party in Germany, and not being succoured out of England as the Bohemians expected, was himself the year following driven out of that his new elective kingdom.

MS. Harl. 646.

TOOZLE. To pull about roughly. *North.*

TOP. (1) To burn off the long cotton end of the wick of a candle. *Var. dial.* Also, to snuff a candle.

(2) The head. *Tail over top,* headlong. *Top over tail,* head over tail, precipitately, rashly, hastily.

But syr James had soche a chopp,
That he wyste not be my *toppe,*
Whethur hyt were day or nyght.

MS. Cantab. Ff. ii. 38, f. 76.

Thou take hym by the *toppes* and I by the tayle,
A sorowfull songe in faith he shall singe.

Chester Plays, ii. 176.

Soche a strokk he gaf hym then,
That the dewke bothe hors and man
Turned *toppe ovyr tayle!*

MS. Cantab. Ff. ii. 38, f. 76.

Wyth here kercheves the devylys sayle,
Elles shul they go to helle bothe *top and tayle.*

MS. Harl. 1701, f. 59.

(3) Good; capital. *Var. dial.*

(4) To wrestle.

(5) A pit term for coal, when quite prepared for removal by wedges or powder.

TOP-AND-SCOURGE. Whip-top.

TOPASION. The topaz stone.

TOP-CASTLES. Ledgings surrounding the mast-head. In Eglamour, 1072, it is apparently applied to the upper turrets of a castle, or perhaps to the temporary wooden fortifications built at the tops of towers in preparing for a siege. According to Mr. Hunter, Hallamshire Glossary, p. 24, " any building which overtops those around it, will be called in derision a *cob-castle.*"

TOPENS. A twopenny piece.

> Thomas Usshere de Norwico, marchaunt, indict. est coram justic. domini regis de pace in civitate Norwici observanda assign., de eo quod idem Thomas nocte diei Dominicæ in festo sancti Bartholomei apostoli, anno regni regis Henrici sexti post conquestum quinto, apud Norwicum in mansione ejusdem Thomæ solvit cuidam Thomæ atte Hirne bochere, servienti Roberti Candelere de Norwico bochere, pro bras. a dicto Thoma atte Hirne empt., x. s. in singulis denariis et in aliis denariis vocatis *pons of topens* fabricatis de ære vocatis *brasenpens*, secundum formam et similitudinem denar. vocat. *Yorkpens*, dicens et affirmans eidem Thomæ atte Hirne solutionem prædictam fore bonum argentum et abil. monetam, prædictus Thomas Usshere sciens dictam solutionem esse fals. et contrafact. eidem Thomæ atte Hirne pro bona solutione fals. et fraudulent. ibidem liberavit.
>
>   *Norwich Corporation Records*, temp. Hen. VI.

TOP-FULL. Quite full. *Var. dial.*

TOPING. Excellent; tiptop. *West.*

TOPINYERE. A paramour.

TOP-LATCH. The thong which passes through holes in the seel of a horse's collar, and serves to fasten it, or to loosen or tighten it, as may be necessary. It is also the rising and falling latch which, catching the movable part of the cow-bauk, confines her when milked. *Moor.*

TOPLESS. Supreme. *Shak.*

TOPMAN. A merchant vessel.

TOPPER. One who excels. *Var. dial.*

TOPPICE. To hide, or take shelter.

TOPPING. (1) A mode of cheating at play by holding a dice in the fingers.

(2) A curl, or tuft of hair, &c.

(3) Fine; excellent; in good health.

TOPPINGLY. In good health. *North.*

TOPPING-POT. An allowance of beer given in harvest time, when a mow was filled to the very top. *East.*

TOPPINGS. The second skimming of milk.

TOPPITS. The refuse of hemp.

TOPPLE. (1) A crest, or tuft.

(2) To fall; to tumble; to tumble in confusion. Also, to cause to fall, &c. *Topple tail over*, topsy-turvy.

> I am *topullid* in my thouȝte,
> So that of resone leveth nouȝt.
>   *Gower, MS. Soc. Antiq.* 134, f. 42.

TOPPLE-OVER. Said of sheep, beasts, or other farming live stock, when they sell for double their cost. " I jest *toppled* em over in the year."

TOP-SAWYER. A leading person.

TOPSIDE-TURVY. Topsy-turvy.

TOPS-MAN. A foreman, or bailiff.

TOP-STRING. The same as *Top-latch*, q. v.

TOP-UP. To make a finish; thus, when one has eaten largely of solid food, he is said to *top up* with pastry and lighter eatables; also, when a person has come to ruin or into distress, through any cause, he is said to be *topped up*.

TOR. A hill. *Devon.*

TORBLE. Trouble; wrangling.

TORCEYS. Torches. *(A.-N.)*

TORCH. This phrase was recently heard at Boyton, near the sea. "Law! how them clouds *torch* up, we shall ha rain." This implied a rolling upwards of heavy smoke-like clouds, as if they were the dense smoke of celestial fires.

TORE. Broke. *West.*

TORES. The ornamental wooden knobs or balls which are still to be seen on old-fashioned cradles and chairs.

TORETES. Rings. *(A.-N.)*

TORF. Chaff that is raked off the corn, after it is threshed, but before it is cleaned. *Kent.*

TORFEL. To fall; to die. *North.*

TORFITCH. Wild vetch. *West.*

TO-RIGHTS. In order. *Var. dial.*

TORKELARE. A quarrelsome person.

TORKESS. To alter a house, &c.

TORKWED. An instrument applied to the nose of a vicious horse to make it stand still during the progress of shoeing.

TORMENT. A tempest. *(A.-N.)*

TORMENTILL. The herb setfoil.

TORMENTING. Sub-ploughing, or sub-hoeing. *Devon.*

TORMIT. A turnip. *North.*

TORN. (1) Broke. *Wilts.*

(2) A spinning-wheel. *Exmoor.*

TORNAY. To tilt at a tournament.

TORNAYEEZ. Turns; wheels. *Gawayne.*

TORN-DOWN. Rough; riotous. *Linc.*

TORNE. (1) To turn. *(A.-S.)*

> But thogh a man himself be good,
> And he *torne* so his mood,
> That he haunte fooles companye,
> It shal him *torne* to grete folie.
>   *MS. Lansd.* 793, f. 68.

(2) Angry.

TO-ROBBYDD. Stolen away entirely.

> My yoye, myn herte ye all *to-robbydd*,
> The chylde ys dedd that soke my breste!
>   *MS. Cantab.* Ff. ll. 38, f 47.

TO-ROF. Crumbled to pieces.

> That he tok he al *to-rof*,
> So dust in winde, and aboute drof.
>   *Arthour and Merlin*, p. 180.
>
> Hys rakk he all *to-roof*,
> And owt of the stabull drofe.
>   *MS. Cantab.* Ff. ll. 38, f. 111.

TORPENS.

> Item, I bequeath to myne especial good Lord George Earl of Shrewsbury a cope of cloth of gold of white damasse, with *torpens* cloth of gold and velvet upon velvet.   *Test. Vetust.* p. 452.

TORPENT. Torpid. *More.*

TORREN. Torn.

> In a colde wyntur, as the kyng and Thomas ware in fere in the Chepe at London, the kyng was warre of a pore man that was sore acolde with *torren* clothys.   *MS. Cantab.* Ff. li. 38, f. ll.

TORRIDIDDLE. Bewildered. *Dorset.*

TORRIL. A worthless woman, or horse.

TORT. (1) Sparkling. *West.*

> The North Wilts horses and other stranger horses, when they come to drinke of the water of Chalke river, they will sniff and snort, it is so cold and *tort*.   *MS. Aubrey's Wilts*, p. 53.

(2) Wrong. (*A.-N.*)

(3) A wax candle.

(4) Receipt for making "torte of fysah" in MS. Cott. Julius D. viii. f. 94. [Tart ?]

(5) Large ; fat. *Glouc.*

TORTIOUS. Injurious. *Spenser.*

TORTIVE. Twisted ; turned aside.

TORTORS. Turtles. *Gawayne.*

TORTUOUS. Oblique ; winding. (*A.-N.*)

TORTYLL. Twisted. *Ritson.*

> A hundred torne y haffe schot with hem,
> Under hes *tortyll* tre.   *Robin Hood, i. 91.*

TORVED. Stern ; severe.

TORY. An Irish robber. The *tories* were noted for their ferocity and murders.

> And now I must leave the orb of Jupiter, and drop down a little lower to the sphere of Mars, who is termed a *tory* amongst the stars.
>   *Bishop's Marrow of Astrology, p. 43.*

TORY-RORY. In a wild manner.

TOS. Toes. (*A.-S.*)

> Hise *fet* he kisten an hundred sythes,
> The *tos*, the nayles, and the lithes.
>   *Havelok, 2163.*

TOSH. A projecting tooth. *Toshnail*, a nail driven in aslant like a tosh.

TOSIER. A basket-maker. *South.*

TO-SONDRE. Go to pieces ; split.

> The fyry welkne gan to thundir,
> As thouȝ the world schulde alle *to-sondre.*
>   *Gower, MS. Soc. Antiq. 134. f. 91.*

TO-SPRED. Scattered abroad. (*A.-S.*)

TOSS. The mow or bay of a barn into which the corn is put preparatory to its being threshed.

TOSSICATED. Restless ; perplexed.

TOSSING-BALL. A ball to play with.

TOSS-PLUME. A swaggering fellow.

TOSS-POT. A drunkard.

TOSSY-TAIL. Topsy-turvy. *Devon.*

TOSTICATED. (1) Tossed about. *West.*

(2) Intoxicated. *Var. dial.*

TOSTYRN. A toasting-iron.

TOT. (1) A small drinking cup, holding about half a pint. *Warw.*

(2) A tuft of grass ; a bush.

(3) A term of endearment.

(4) Anything very small. *East.*

(5) A foolish fellow.

TOTALD. Killed, or injured in an irretrievable manner. *East.*

TOTE. (1) To look, observe, or peep. (*A.-S.*)

> Devocion stondyth *fer* withowt
> At the lyppys dore, and *toteth* ynne.
>   *MS. Cantab. Ff. ii. 38, f. 25.*

(2) The whole. Still in use.

(3) To bulge out. *Somerset.*

(4) A tuft of grass, hair, &c. *Lanc.*

(5) Large ; fat. *Glouc.*

TOTEHILL. An eminence. *Chesh.* "Totehyll, montaignette," Palsgrave, 1530.

TOTELER. A whisperer. "Be no totiler," MS. Bibl. Reg. 17 B. xvii. f. 141.

TOTER. A seesaw. Nominale MS.

TOTEY. Irritable. *North.*

TO-THE-FORE. Forthcoming. *North.*

TOTHER. The other. (*A.-S.*) This is now generally considered a provincial vulgarism.

> The *tother* day on the same wyse,
> As the kynge fro the borde can ryse.
>   *MS. Cantab. Ff. ii. 38, f. 74.*

T'OTHER-DAY. The day before yesterday. *Sussex.* In some places this expression is indefinite.

TOTHEREMMY. The others. *West.*

TOTLE. A lazy person. *West.*

TOT-O'ER-SEAS. The golden-crested wren.

TO-TORN. Torn to pieces.

> Rather thanne he schulde be forlorn,
> Yit I wolde eft be al *to-torn.*
>   *MS. Coll. Caii Cantab. E. 55, f. 25.*

TOT-QUOT. A general dispensation.

TOTSANE. The herb *agnus castris.*

TOTT. To note. It is also used as a substantive.

> With letters and credence, the copy wherof, with my poore opinion upon the same, *totted* in the margyne, I sende unto your Highnes herewith.
>   *State Papers, i. 150.*

TOTTARD. The herb nascorium.

TOTTED. Excited ; elevated.

TOTTERARSE. The game of seesaw.

TOTTERED. Tattered.

TOTTER-PIE. A high-raised apple-pie.

TOTTLE. To toddle. *Var. dial.*

TOTTY. (1) Dizzy ; reeling. (*A.-S.*) This term is still used in the provinces.

> So *toty* was the brayn of his hede,
> That he desirid for to go to bede,
> And whan he was obes therin laide,
> With hymself mervaillously he fraide.
>   *MS. Rawl. C. 86.*

(2) Little. *Suffolk.*

TOTYNG-HOLE. A spy-hole.

> They within the citie perceyved well this *totyng-hole*, and layed a pece of ordynaunce directly against the wyndowe.   *Hall, Henry VI. f. 23.*

TOU. Snares for taking game. *East.*

TOUCH. (1) Time ; occasion. *West.*

(2) To bow, by touching the hat, &c. in token of respect to a superior. *North.*

(3) A cunning feat or trick. "Touche, a crafty dede, *tour,*" Palsgrave.

(4) A habit, or action.

(5) A kind of very hard black granite. See Stanihurst, p. 31. The term was also applied to marble.

(6) To infect or stain.

(7) A touchstone. *Shak.*

TOUCH-BOX. A receptacle for lighted tinder carried by soldiers for matchlocks.

> He had no sooner drawne and ventred ny her,
> Intending only but to have a bout,
> When she his flaske and *touch-boxe* set on fier,
> And till this hower the burning is not out.
>   *Letting of Humours Blood in the Head-Vaine, 1600.*

TOUCHER. A little ; a trifle. *North.*

TOUFFA. A small shed, at the end of farm-houses, to contain implements of agriculture and gardening.

TOUGH. (1) Difficult. See *Tow.*

(2) The beam of a plough.

TOUGHER. A portion, or dowry.

And she wad han you of all loves to wad me : and
you shall han me for your *tougher*.

The Two Lancashire Lovers, 1640, p. 18.

TOUGHT. Tight. Still in use.

TOUGHY. The same as *Claggum*, q. v.

TOUGINGE. Tugging.

TOUKEN. To dye. (*A.-S.*)

TOUNISCHMEN. Townsmen. *Leland*.

TOUR. A tower. (*A.-N.*)

TOURMENTES. Engines. List of old words
prefixed to Batman uppon Bartholome, 1582.

TOURN. A spinning-wheel. *Exm*.

TOURT. To decay. *Suffolk*.

TOUSE. (1) To tug, or pull about.

(2) A noise, or disturbance. *Dorset*.

(3) A slight blow. *Somerset*.

TOUSELED. Having tassels.

TOUSER. A coarse apron. *Devon*.

TOUT. (1) The backside. "Rubyng of ther
toute," MS. Ashmole 61, f. 60.

(2) A tunnel across a road. *Linc*.

(3) To solicit custom. *Var. dial*. Hence *touter*,
a person who touts for inns, &c.

(4) To follow or be followed. *North*.

TOVET. A measure of two gallons, according to
Cooper's Sussex Glossary. Kersey says, " a
measure of half a bushel or two pecks."

TOW. (1) Tough. *Var. dial*. Also, difficult.
The phrase, *to make it tow, to make it tough*,
is common in early writers in various shades
of sense, but generally, *to make it difficult*, or
take great pains with any matter ; *to treat an
insignificant task or matter with as much care
as if it were of great importance*.

Befe and moton wylle serve wele enow ;
And for to seche so ferre a lytill bakon flyk,
Which hath long hanggid, resty and *tow* ;
And the wey I telle you is comborous and thyk,
And thou might stomble, and take the cryk.

Reliq. Antiq. ii. 29.

To day thou gate no moné of me,
Made thou it never so *towȝ*.

MS. Cantab. Ff. v. 48, f. 53.

(2) Tools, or apparatus. *East*.

(3) Pleasant ; delightful. *Devon*.

TOWAIL. A towel. (*A.-N.*)

Wyth thre *towayles* and no lasse
Hule thyn auter at thy masse.

MS. Cotton. Claud. A. ii. f. 150.

TOWAN. A sand hillock. *Devon*.

TOWARD. At hand ; forthcoming.

TOWARDES. Toward. (*A.-S.*)

TOWARDLY. Prosperous ; doing well.

TOW-BLOWEN. A blown herring. *Suffolk*.

TOWD. Told. *Lanc*.

TOWEL. (1) An oaken stick. *Warw*. Also a
verb, to beat with an oaken cudgel.

(2) The anus. Reliq. Antiq. i. 192.

TOWEN. (1) To tame. *Northumb*.

(2) A town. Nominale MS.

(3) Fatigued. *Gawayne*.

TOWER. (1) A high head-dress much worn by
ladies about the year 1710.

(2) Curled hair on the forehead.

TOWER-LIGHTS. The small upper lights of a
perpendicular window in a church.

TOWGHT. A piece of rope-yarn used for tying
up sacks. *North*.

TO-WHEN. Till when ; how long.

TO-WHILS. Whilst.

TOWING-LINE. A line affixed to a barge and
a horse towing it. *Towing-path*, the path
used by horses in towing.

TOWLE. To toll, or entice.

TOWLETTS. The flaps which hung on the
thighs from the tasses. Arch. xvii. 295.

TOWLING. Whipping horses up and down at
a fair, a boy's mischievous amusement.

TOWLY. A towel. *East*.

TOWN. (1) A village. *Var. dial*. Town-gate,
the high road through a town or village.

(2) The court, or farmyard. *Devon*.

TOWN-HUSBAND. An officer of a parish who
collects the moneys from the parents of illegitimate children for the maintenance of the
latter. *East*.

TOWN-PLACE. A farmyard. *Cornw*.

TOWN-TOP. A large top whipped by several
boys at the same time. So a town-bull is a
bull kept for the use of the community.

TOWPIN. A pin belonging to a cart.

TOWRETE. To fall upon ; to attack. (*A.-S.*)

TOWRETH. "Said of a hawk when she lifteth
up her wing," Dict. Rust.

TOW-ROW. Money paid by porters to persons
who undertake to find them work. *East*.

TOWRUS. Eager. Said of the roebuck.

TOWT. To put out of order ; to entangle, or
rumple. *Var. dial*. Hence *towty*, disorderly,
ill-tempered.

TOWTE. Taught. "*Doceor*, to be towte,"
MS. Vocab. xv. Cent. in my possession.

TOXE. Tusk. Kyng Alisaunder, 6123.

TOY. Whim ; fancy ; trifle. To take a toy,
i. e. to take a fancy, to go about at random.

For these causes, I say, she ran at random and
played her pranks as the *toy* took her in the head,
sometimes publicly, sometimes privately, whereby
she both disparaged her reputation, and brought
herself into the contempt of the world.

MS. Harl. 4888.

TO-YEAR. This year. *Var. dial*. "To ȝere,
horno," Cathol. Anglic. MS. xv. Cent.

TOZE. (1) The same as *Touse*, q. v.

(2) To disentangle wool or flax.

TPROT. An exclamation of contempt. See
Wright's Political Songs, p. 381.

TRACE. (1) To walk. Still in use.

(2) A track, or path. "Trace, a streyght way,
trace," Palsgrave, 1530. Also a verb, to follow the track of an animal.

(3) A sledge, or small cart.

TRACE-SIDES. Traces separated.

TRACE-WAY. Built trace-way, i. e. stones
built longitudinally in the front of a wall.

TRACK. Right course, or track. *West*.

TRACT. (1) To trace, or track.

(2) Delay. State Papers, i. 231.

TRADE. (1) A road. *Sussex*. Metaphorically
applied to the road or path of life. Also, a rut
in a road.

(2) Stuff ; rubbish. *Devon*.

(3) Trod. (*A.-S.*)

(4) Conduct; habit; custom. *East.*

TRADERS. Tradesmen's tokens.

TRADES-AND-DUMB-MOTIONS. A country game, where one boy makes signs representing the occupation of some trade, and another boy guesses it.

TRAFER. A searcher, or hunter.

TRAFFICK. (1) Lumber; rubbish. *North.*

(2) Passage of people. *Var. dial.*

TRAFFING-DISH. A bowl through which milk is strained into the tray in which it is set to raise cream.

TRAGEDY. A tragedy, says the Prompt. Parv. is a "pley that begynnythe with myrthe and endythe with sorowe." The term was also applied to a tale.

> The last acte of a tragedie is alwaies more heavie and sorrowfull than the rest.
> *Lambarde's Perambulation*, 1596. p 329.

TRAGETTES. Juggling tricks.

> Jogulours gret avantage they getes,
> With Japes and with *tragettes.*
> *MS. Harl.* 2260, f. 58.

TRAIE. To betray. (*A.-S.*)

> And penaunce on hem layd,
> For that thai hadde God *y-trayd.*
> *Arthour and Merlin*, p. 28.
>
> For alle the golde that ever myght be,
> Fro heven unto the wordis ende,
> Thou beys never *trayed* for me,
> For with me I rede the wende.
> *MS. Cantab. Ff.* v. 48, f. 120.

TRAIK. To sicken; to die. *North.*

TRAILE. (1) A trellis work for creepers, used in an arbour. See Florio, p. 113. Drayton uses it for a creeping plant. In architecture, ornaments of leaves, &c.

(2) To loiter. *North.*

(3) To drag. Torrent, p. 56.

(4) The train of a gown.

(5) To carry hay or corn. *inc.*

(6) To hunt by the track or scent.

(7) A portion, or fragment.

(8) A kind of sledge or cart.

TRAILEBASTONS. A company of persons who bound themselves together by oath to assist one another against any one who displeased a member of the body. The Trailebastons, according to Langtoft, arose in the reign of Edward I, and judges were appointed expressly for the purpose of trying them. They are supposed to have derived their name from long staffs which they carried.

TRAILING-BEER. Beer given to mowers as a fine by persons walking over grass before it is cut. *Var. dial.*

TRAIL-TONGS. A dirty slattern. *Trail-tripes* is also used in the same sense.

TRAILY. Slovenly. *Cumb.*

TRAIN. (1) The tail of a hawk. Also, something tied to a lure to entice a hawk. A trap or lure for any animal was also called a train.

(2) Treachery; stratagem; deceit.

> Y trowe syr Marrok, be Goddes payne,
> Have slayne syr Roger be some *trayne*
> *MS. Cantab.* Ff. ii. 38, f. 75.

> At a batayle certeyne
> Of Sarsyns that have done *trayne.*
> *MS. Cantab.* Ff. ii. 38, f. 196.
>
> And now thou woldyst wondur fayne
> Be the furste to do me *trayne.*
> *MS. Cantab.* Ff. ii. 38, f. 72.

(3) Clever; apt. *Yorksh.*

(4) To harbour, said of a wolf.

TRAIS. The traces of a horse.

TRAISE. To betray. *Ritson.*

TRAISTE. (1) To trust.

(2) Dregs of wine, beer, &c.

TRAISTELY. Safely; securely. "I may traistely hym take," MS. Morte Arthure.

TRAIT. The coarser meal. *Cornw.*

TRAITERIE. Treachery. *Gower.*

TRAITHED. Trained; educated.

TRALILLY. A term of endearment.

TRALUCENT. Translucent.

TRAM. (1) A small bench for setting a tub on, used in the dairy. *Heref.*

(2) A sort of sledge running on four wheels, used in coal mines. *North.*

(3) A train or succession of things.

TRAME. (1) Deceit; treachery. *Linc.*

(2) A portion or fragment of anything.

TRAMMEL. (1) An iron hook by which kettles are hung over a fire. *Var. dial.*

(2) A contrivance used for teaching a horse to move the legs on the same side together.

(3) A kind of fowling-net.

(4) The hopper of a mill.

TRAMP. (1) To trample. *West.*

(2) A walk; a journey. *Var. dial.*

(3) A walking beggar. *Var. dial.*

TRAMPER. A travelling mechanic.

TRAMPLER. A lawyer.

TRANCE. A tedious journey. *Lanc.*

TRANCITE. A passage.

TRANE. (1) To delay, or loiter.

(2) A device; a knot. *Gawayne.*

TRANELL. To trammel for larks. (*Fr.*)

TRANLING. A perch one year old.

TRANSAM. The lintel.

TRANSCRIT. Copy; writing. (*A.-N.*)

TRANSELEMENT. To change. (*Lat.*)

> The joyfull waters did begin t'aspire,
> And would *transelement* themselves to fire.
> *Brome's Songs*, 1661, p. 116.

TRANSFISTICATED. Pierced through.

> For though your beard do stand so fine mustated,
> Perhaps your nose may be *transfisticated.*
> *Letting of Humours Blood in the Head-Vaine*, 1600.

TRANSFRET. To pass over the sea.

> Shortely after that Kyng Henry had taryed a convenient space, he *transfreted* and arryved at Dover, and so came to his maner of Grenewiche.
> *Hall, Henry VII.* f, 28.

TRANSHAPE. Transformation.

> If this displease thee, Midas, then I'll shew thee,
> Ere I proceed with Cupid and his love,
> What kind of people I commerc'd withal
> In my *transhape.* *Heywood's Love's Mistress*, p. 16.

TRANSLATOR. A cobler. *Var. dial.*

TRANSMEWE. To transform. (*A.-N.*)

TRANSMOGRIFY. To transform. *Var. dial.*

TRANSOLATE. Transferred.

The Jewes were put out of state,
And her kyngdome al *transolate*.
Cursor Mundi, MS. Coll. Trin. Cantab. f. 58.

TRANS-SHIFT. To alter; to change.

TRANSUME. To copy, or transcribe.

TRANSUMPT. (1) A copy.

(2) The lintel of a door.

TRANT. A trick, or stratagem.
Thynke no syne thus me to teyn,
And fyll with *trants*.
Craft's Excerpta Antiqua, p. 109.

TRANTER. A carrier. *Var. dial.*

TRANTERY. Money arising from fines paid by those who broke the assize of bread and ale.

TRANTY. The same as *Aud-farand*, q. v.

TRAP. (1) To pinch, or squeeze. *North.*

(2) A short hill. *Somerset.*

(3) A small cart. *Var. dial.*

(4) To tramp as with pattens. *Devon.*

(5) An old worn-out animal. *North.*

(6) *Up to trap*, very cunning.

(7) To dress up finely.
The which horse was *trapped* in a mantellet bront and backe place, al of fine golde in scifers of device, with tasselles on cordelles pendaunt.
Hall, Henry VIII. f. 76.

(8) A foot-bridge. *Beds.*

TRAP-BALL. A game played with a trap, a ball, and a small bat. The trap is of wood, made like a slipper, with a hollow at the heel end for the ball, and a kind of wooden spoon, moving on a pivot, in the bowl of which the ball is placed. By striking the end or handle of the spoon, the ball of course rises into the air, and the art of the game is to strike it as far as possible with the bat before it reaches the ground. The adversaries on the look-out, either by catching the ball, or by bowling it from the place where it falls, to hit the trap, take possession of the trap, bat, and ball, to try their own dexterity.

TRAP-BITTLE. A bat used at trap-ball.

TRAPE. (1) A pan, platter, or dish.

(2) To trail on the ground. *Var. dial.*

TRAPES. (1) A slattern. *Var. dial.*

(2) To wander about. *Var. dial.*

TRAPESING. Slow; listless. *North.*

TRAPPAN. A snare; a stratagem.

TRAPPERS. The trappings of horses.

TRAPS. Goods; furniture, &c.

TRAPSTICK. The cross-bar by which the body of a cart is confined to the shafts.

TRASE. (1) Trace; path?
Syr, that was never my purpos
For to leve oon soche a *trase*
Be nyghte nor be day.
MS. Cantab. Ff. ii. 38, f. 67.

(2) Track of game. *Gawayne.*

TRASENINGS. A term in hunting, the crossings and doublings before the hounds.

TRASH. (1) Anything worthless. It was also a cant term for money. "Pelfe, trash, *id est*, mony," Florio, p. 63. Shakespeare, however, hardly intended a pun when he wrote, "who steals my purse, steals *trash*."

(2) Nails for nailing up tapestry, &c.

(3) To harass; to fatigue. *North.*

(4) To place a collar loaded with lead, or a loose rope, round the neck of a hound, to keep him back from going before the rest of the pack. Metaphorically, to restrain, to check, to retard.

TRASH-BAG. A worthless person. *Linc.*

TRASHED. Betrayed.

TRASHES. Trifles. It is the translation of *baguenaudes* in Hollyband's Dictionarie, 1593.

TRASHMIRE. A slattern. *North.*

TRAT. (1) A tract, or treatise.

(2) An idle loitering boy. *West.*

TRATE. See *Crate.*

TRATTLE. To prattle, or talk idly.
Styll she must *trattle*: that tunge is alwayes sterynge.
Bale's Kynge Johan, p. 73.

TRATTLES. The dung of sheep, hares, &c.

TRAUNTER. A pedlar. See *Tranter.*

TRAUNWAY. A strange story. *North.*

TRAUSES. Hose, or breeches.

TRAVAILLE. To labour. (*A.-N.*)

TRAVE. (1) A frame into which farriers put unruly horses. (*A.-N.*)

(2) To stride along as if through long grass. *North.*

(3) In the trave, i. e. harnessed. *East.*

(4) To set up shocks of corn.

TRAVERS. Dispute.
And whanne they were at *travers* of thise thre,
Everiche holdynge his opinioun.
Lydgate, MS. Soc. Antiq. 134, f. 18.

TRAVERSAUNT. Unpropitious.
Thou hast a dominacioun *traversaunt*,
Wythowte numbre doyst thou greeve.
MS. Cantab. Ff. i. 6, f. 137.

TRAVERSE. (1) The place adjoining a blacksmith's shop where horses are shod. *Var. dial.*

(2) To digress in speaking.

(3) A moveable screen; a low curtain. *Traves*, State Papers, i. 257.

(4) To transgress. (*A.-N.*)

(5) Thwarting contrivance.

TRAVIST. Bewildered.

TRAWE. (1) To draw. *Hearne.*

(2) The shoeing-place of a farrier.

TRAY. (1) A hurdle. *Linc.*

(2) A mason's hood for mortar.

TRAYERES. Long boats. *Weber.*

TRAYET. Betrayed.
He seid, Jhesu, it may not be,
That thou shuldist *trayet* be.
MS. Cantab. Ff. v. 48, f. 15.

TRAYFOLES. Knots; devices. *Gawayne.*

TRAYING. Betraying.
Therfore thy sorowe schall nevyr slake,
Traytur, for thy false *traying*.
MS. Cantab. Ff. ii. 38, f. 47.

TRAYTORY. Treachery.
Owre false steward hath us schent
Wyth hys false *traytory*.
MS. Cantab. Ff. ii. 38, f. 75.

TRAY-TRIP. A game at dice. It is mentioned in Taylor's Motto, 1622, sig. D. iv.

TRE. The same as *Tree*, q. v.

TREACHER. A traitor; a deceiver.

TREACHETOUR. A traitor. *Spenser.*

TREACLE-BALL. The same as *Claggum*, q. v.

TREACLE-BUTTER-CAKE. Oat-cake spread over with treacle is so called. *North.*

TREACLE-WAG. Weak beer in which treacle is a principal ingredient. *West.*

TREACLE-WATER. A mess made with treacle, spirits of wine, &c. used for coughs.

TREADLE. The foot-board attached to a spinning-wheel, or similar machine.

TREAF. Peevish; froward. *South.*

TREAGUE. A truce. *Spenser.*

TREATABLY. Intelligibly.

TREATISE. A treaty. *Palsgrave.*

TREBGOT. According to the Pr. Parv. a "sly instrument to take brydys or beestes."

TREBUCHET. A cucking-stool.

TRECHAUNT. Pliant; yielding.

TRECHE. Track; dance. *Hearne.*

TRECHET. To cheat; to trick. *Hearne.*

TRECHOURE. (1) A cheat. (*A.-N.*)

(2) An ornament for the head, formerly worn by women. (*A.-N.*)

TREDDLE. (1) A whore. A cant term.

(2) The dung of a hare. *South.*

Tak the *triddils* of an hare; and stampe thame with wyne, and anoynte the pappes therwith.
MS. Lincoln Med. f. 291.

(3) The step of a stair, &c.

TREDE-FOULE. A cock. *Chaucer.*

TREDEN. To tread. (*A.-S.*)

TREDOURE. A caudle thus made :

Tac bred and grate hit, make a lyour of rawe eyren, do therto saffrone and poudre douce: alye hit with good broth, and mak hit as caudell, and do therto a litelle verjus.
MS. Cotton. Julius D. viii. f. 91.

TREE. (1) Wood; staff; stick. The cross is often called *tree* in early poetry.

How my sone lyeth me before
Upon my skyrte takyn fro the *tree*.
MS. Cantab. Ff. ii. 38, f. 47.

Syr, sche seyde, be Godys *tree*,
I leve hyt not tylle y hyt see.
MS. Cantab. Ff. ii. 38, f. 129.

Hyt ys Goddes body that soffered ded
Upon the holy rode *tre*,
To bye owre synnes and make us fre.
MS. Cott. Claud. A. ii. f. 130.

(2) A butcher's gambril. *Suffolk.*

(3) The handle of a spade. *West.*

TREE-GOOSE. The Solan goose.

TREEKSIN. Three weeks since. *Lanc.*

TREEN. (1) Wooden.

Plowye and harwe coude he dijt,
Treen beddes was he wont to make.
Cursor Mundi, MS. Coll. Trin. Cantab. f. 77.

(2) Trees. The A.-S. plural.

TREENWARE. Earthen vessels? *Ray.*

TREET. A kind of bran. *North.*

TREE-WORM. "*Teredo*, treworm," MS. Vocab.

TREGETOUR. This word was used in two senses : (1) A magician. (2) A cheat.

My sone, as guyle undir the hat,
With sleyytis of a *tregetoure*,
Is hid envye of suche coloure.
Gower, MS. Soc. Antiq. 134, f. 73.

Outher a *tregettour* he most be,
Or ellis God himself is he.
Cursor Mundi, MS. Coll. Trin. Cantab. f. 76.

He sall gedyr fast to hym than
Alle that of the deevels crafte kan,
Als nygromancyeres and *trygetowres*,
Wycches and fals enchawntowrs,
Hampole, MS. Bowes, p. 129.

TREIE. Vexation. (*A.-S.*)

TREJETED. Marked; adorned. *Gawayne.*

TRELAWNY. A mess, made very poor, of barley meal, water, and salt.

TRELLASDOME. A trellis work.

TREMEL. To tremble.

TRENCH. (1) A bit for a horse.

(2) To cut, or carve. (*Fr.*)

TRENCHANT. Cutting; sharp. (*A.-N.*)

TRENCHEPAINE. A person who cut bread at the royal table. (*A.-N.*)

TRENCHER. A wooden platter.

TRENCHER-CAP. The square cap worn by the collegians at Oxford and Cambridge.

TRENCHER-CLOAK. A kind of cloak worn formerly by servants and apprentices.

TRENCHERING. Eating.

TRENCHER-MAN. A good eater.

Spotted in divers places with pure fat,
Knowne for a right tall *trencher-man* by that.
Letting of Humours Blood in the Head-Vaine, 1600

TRENCHMORE. A boisterous sort of dance to a lively tune in triple time. See Stanihurst's Ireland, p. 16.

Some sweare, in a *trenchmore* I have trode a good way to winne the world.
Kemp's Nine Daies Wonder, 1600.

TREND. (1) To bend; to turn.

(2) A current, or stream. *Devon.*

TRENDLE. (1) A brewer's cooler. *West.*

(2) The turning beam of a spindle. "*Insubulus*, a webster's trendyl," MS. Harl. 1738.

(3) To roll; to trundle.

He smote the sowdan with hys sworde,
That the hedd *trendyld* on the borde.
MS. Cantab. Ff. ii. 38, f. 170.

TRENKET. A shoemaker's knife. "An instrument for a cordwayner, *batton atorner*," Palsgrave, 1530.

TRENLYNG. Twinkling.

TRENNE. Wooden.

Thenne byhulde he that body so clene,
How hit lay ther inne that *trenne* chest.
Chron. Vilodun, p. 98.

TRENNLE. A stout wooden pin driven through the outer planks of a ship's side to fasten them to the ribs. *South.*

TRENT. Handled; seized. It seems to mean *laid down* in Gy of Warwike, p. 7.

TRENTAL. Thirty masses for the dead.

Fore schryfte and fore *trental* thai scorne al this stryf,
Jif hit because of govetyse, cursud then thai be.
MS. Douce 302, f. 4.

TRENTES.

The grace of God me thynke thaim wantes,
That ledes thayre lyf with swylke *trentes*.
MS. Harl. 2260, f. 50.

TREON. Trees. (*A.-S.*)

Alle that destruyeth *treon*, other gras, growynge wythinne the cherche walles bythout leve of the person, or of the vycary, other of hem that haveth the kepynge therof. *MS. Burney 356, p. 98*

TREPEGET. A military engine used for projecting stones, arrows, &c.

> Also reparacion and amendinge of wallis, makynge and amendinge of engynes, of trepegettis, ordenaunce of stones to defende thy walles or to assaille thyn enemyes. *Vegecius, MS. Douce* 291, f. 53.

TREPETT. A stroke.

TRESAIL. A great-grandfather.

TRESAWNTE. A passage in a house.

TRES-COZES. A game mentioned by Sir J. Harrington in his Epigrams, MS. Addit. 12049.

TRESENS. "That is drawen over an estates chambre, *ciel*," Palsgrave.

TRESOURE. Treasure. (*A.-N.*)

> To gete good is my laboure,
> And to awmente my *tresoure*.
> *MS. Cott. Tiber.* A. vii. f. 40.

TRESOURYS. The tresses of the hair.

> And bad anon hys turmentours
> Do hange hur be hur *tresourys*.
> *MS. Cantab.* Ff. ii. 38, f. 38.

TRESPASET. Done wrongly.

> Therfore take hede on thy lyvynge
> Jef thou have *trespaset* in syche thynge.
> *MS. Cotton. Claud.* A. ii. f. 138.

TRESSE. (1) A clasp. (2) An artificial lock or gathering of hair. (*A.-N.*)

TRESSEL. A trestle, or support.

TRESSOUR. See *Tresourys*.

TREST. (1) Trusty?

> For he was hardi, trewe and *trest*,
> Of all this lond and yong man best.
> *Arthour and Merlin*, p. 107.

> A lok of that levedy, with lovelich lere,
> Mi gode gameliche game gurte to grounde ;
> Couthe I carpe carpying, *trestly* [crestly?] and clere,
> Of that birde bastons in bale ire bounde.
> *Reliq. Antiq.* ii. 8.

(2) A strong large stool. *Lanc.*

TRESTILLE. A trestle.

TRET.

> Hath thy herte be wroth or gret,
> When Goddes serves was drawe on *tret*.
> *MS. Cott. Claud.* A. ii. f. 140.

TRETABLE. Tractable. (*A.-N.*)

> Whate vayleth vertu wiche is not *treteabille* ?
> Recure of sykenesse is hasty medecyne.
> *MS. Cantab.* Ff. i. 6, f. 130.

TRETE. (1) To treat; to discourse. (*A.-N.*)

(2) A plaster, or salve.

(3) Row; array. *Gawayne.*

TRETEE. A treaty. *Chaucer.*

TRETIS. (1) A treaty. *Chaucer.*

(2) Long and well-proportioned. *Tyrw.*

TRETORY. Treachery. *Skelton.*

TRETOWRE. A traitor. *Pr. Parv.*

TREVED. "Trapes. treved."—MS. Lansd. 560, f. 45, co. Lanc.

TREWE. (1) A truce. (*A.-N.*)

> The emperowre was then a sory man,
> And Moradas asked *trewe*.
> *MS. Cantab.* Ff. ii. 38, f. 79.

(2) True; faithful. *Trewly*, truly.

> Seche thyn herte *trewly* ore,
> Jef thow were any tyme for-swore.
> *MS. Cott. Claud.* A. ii. f. 138.

> Hast thow be scharpe and bysy
> To serve thy mayster *trewely* ?

> Hast thow *trewely* by uche way
> Deservet thy mete and thy pay.
> *MS. Cott. Claud.* A. ii. f. 141.

TREWELUFE. (1) The herb oneberry.

(2) A true-love knot.

TREWETHE. Truth. (*A.-S.*)

TREWETS. Pattens. *Suffolk.*

TREY-ACE. Gone before you can say trey-ace, i. e. in a moment.

TREYATTE. Treaty.

TREYGOBET. An old game at dice.

TREYTE. A treatise.

> A soule that list to singe of love
> Of Crist that com tille us so lawe,
> Rede this *treyté* it may hym move,
> And may hym teche lightly with awe.
> *MS. Bodl. e Mus.* 160.

TRIACLE. A remedy; an antidote. There was, however, a particular composition in ancient medicine called *triacle*, which seems alluded to in the following passage :

> A jens venym more holsom than *tryacle*.
> *Lydgate, MS. Soc. Antiq.* 134, p. 1.

TRIBBET-DOOR. A wicket, or half-door.

TRIBET. A common children's game played in Lancashire, which perhaps may be said to be the primitive form of *trap*. It is almost impossible to describe it. It is played with a *pum*, a piece of wood about a foot long and two inches in diameter, and a *tribet*, a small piece of hard wood.

TRIBON. The desk of the officiating priest.

TRIBS. Triplets at marbles.

TRICE. (1) To thrust; to trip up. (*A.-S.*)

(2) A very small portion.

TRICELING. Tripping up.

TRICHUR. Treacherous; cunning.

> Hold man lechur,
> Jong-man *trichur*,
> Of alle mine ilve
> Ne sau I worse five.
> *Reliq. Antiq.* ii. 15.

TRICK. (1) Character; peculiarity.

(2) To dress out; to adorn.

(3) Neat; elegant.

> The ivory palace of her stately neck
> Cloth'd with majestick aw, did seem to check
> The looser pastime of her gamesome hair,
> Which in wilde rings ran *trick* about the ayre.
> *Fletcher's Poems*, p. 254.

(4) To draw arms with pen and ink.

TRICKER. The trigger of a gun.

TRICKET. (1) The game of bandy-wicket.

(2) A game at cards, somewhat like loo.

TRICKINGS. Ornaments of dress.

TRICKLE. (1) To drip. *Var. dial.*

(2) To bowl, or trundle. *East.*

TRICKLING. The small intestines.

TRICKLY. Neatly.

> Lylly whyte muskells have no peere,
> The fyshewyves fetche them quyklye ;
> So he that hathe a consciens cleere,
> May stand to hys takkell *tryklye*.
> But he that seekest to set to sale,
> Suche baggage as ys olde and stale,
> He ys lyke to tell another tale.
> *Elderton's Lenton Stuffe*, 1570.

TRICKMENTS. Decorations.

TRICKSY. (1) Neat; adroit; elegant. *Tricksie-trim*, spruce, Florio, p. 580. Goldsmith, in his Vicar of Wakefield, ch. xxvi, uses *tricksy* in the sense of *tricky*.
(2) Playful; frolicsome.
TRICK-TRACK. The same as *Tick-tack*, q. v.
TRICKY. Full of tricks. *Var. dial.*
TRICULATE. To adorn. *East.*
TRIDGE. To trudge, or labour.
TRIDLE. A weaver's treddle.
TRIDLINS. The dung of sheep. *North.*
TRIE. (1) Choice; select. (*A.-N.*)

> He wold not ete his cromys drye,
> He lovyd nothynge but it were *trie*.
> *MS. Cantab.* Ff. v. 48, f. 50.
> Claryones cryden faste and curyous pypes,
> Tymbres, tabers and trumpers fulle *trye*.
> *MS. Cott. Calig.* A. ii. f. 114.

(2) To rush in. (3) To pull out.
TRIETE. A company, or body.
TRI-FALLOW. To till ground the third time.
TRIFFE. To thrive.
TRIFLED-CORN. Corn that has fallen down in single ears mixed with standing corn.
TRIG. (1) Tight; true; faithful. *North.*
(2) Neat; trim. *Var. dial.* Also, to dress fine. *Trigged up*, smartly dressed.
(3) To fill; to stuff. (4) Full.
(5) Well in health. *West.*
(6) Sound and firm. *Dorset.*
(7) To prop or hold up. *Var. dial.*
(8) Active; clever. *Devon.*
(9) A narrow path. *Warw.*
(10) To trip and run. *East.*
(11) To stumble; to trip up.
(12) A small gutter. *Salop.*
(13) A mark at ninepins. Also, a stick across which a bowler strides when he throws the bowl away.
TRIGEN. A skidpan for a wheel.
TRIG-HALL. A hospitable house. *West.*
TRIGIMATE. An intimate friend. *Devon.*
TRIG-MEAT. Any kind of shell-fish picked up at low water. *Cornw.*
TRIGON. A triangle.
TRIKLOND. Trickling.

> He shalbe teyryd ful wondur sore,
> So away he may not fle,
> His neb shalle rife or he then fare,
> The red blode *triklond* to his knee.
> *MS. Cantab.* Ff. v. 48, f. 122.

TRILL. (1) To twirl; to throw.
(2) To roll; to trickle.
(3) The anus. A cant term.
TRILLIBUB. Anything trifling. The term is now applied only to tripe.
TRIM. (1) To beat. Still in use.
(2) Neat. (3) Neatly.
(4) To scold. *Heref.*
(5) In a correct order. *Var. dial.*
(6) To poise or make a boat even.
TRIMLE. To tremble. *North.* In MS. Sloane 7, f. 76, is a receipt "for the palsy that makyth man and woman to *trymylle*."

> The Sarazene that helde the suerde in hande,
> Fulle fast he *trymlide* fote and hande.
> *MS. Lincoln* A. i. 17, f. 129.

> Blowinge off bugles and bemes aloft,
> *Trymlinge* of tabers and tymbring soft.
> Roland, *MS. Lansd.* 388. f. 384.

TRIMMEL. A large salting tub. *Devon.*
TRIMMER. Timber that binds and supports the bricks of a hearth at some distance from the chimney.
TRIMMING. Large; huge. *West.*
TRIMPLE. To walk unsteadily. *West.*
TRIM-TRAM. A trifle, or absurdity.
TRIN. A flat tub used for receiving the cider from the press. *West.*
TRINCUMS. Jewels; trinkets.
TRINDLE. A wheel. *Derb.*
TRINDLES. (1) The dung of goats, &c.
(2) The felloes of a wheel. *North.*
TRINDLE-TAIL. A species of dog.
TRINE. (1) Triple. (*A.-N.*)
(2) To follow in a train.
(3) Thirteen fellies. Twenty-five spokes.
(4) To hang. A cant term.
TRINE-COMPAS. The Trinity.
TRINEDADO.

> I care no more to kill them in braveado,
> Then for to drinke a pipe of *Trinedado*.
> *Letting of Humours Blood in the Head-Vaine*, 1600.

TRINK. An old engine used for catching fish, mentioned in Stat. 2 Hen. VI. c. 15. See Chitty's Treatise on the Game Laws, 1812, i. 248.
TRINKET. A porringer.
TRINKLE. (1) To trickle. *Var. dial.*
(2) To endeavour to turn the opinion of another by unfair means. *East.*
TRINNEL. The same as *Trindles*, q. v.
TRIOTHT. A trout. Nominale MS.
TRIP. (1) A flock of sheep; a herd of swine, or goats. See *Sounder.*
(2) Race; family. *Craven.*
(3) New soft cheese made of milk. *East.* Chaucer mentions "a trippe of chese," but the sense appears to be doubtful.
(4) A small arch over a drain.
(5) "A hard ball with a small projecting point, made of wood, or stag's horn, or earthenware, used in the game called also *trip*. These balls are first raised from a drop, that is, a stone placed with a smooth edge at an angle towards the horizon, and then struck with a pummel placed at the end of a flexible rod called the *trip-stick*. The game is almost peculiar to the North of England," Hunter, p. 93. It is also called *trip-trap*.
(6) *To fetch trip*, to go backwards in order to jump the further.
TRIPE-CHEEK. A fat blowzy face.
TRIPLE. One of three. *Shak.*
TRIPOLY. *To come from Tripoly*, a phrase meaning to do feats of activity; to vault, or tumble.
TRIPPET. (1) The same as *Trip* (5).
(2) A quarter of a pound. *Yorksh.*
TRIP-SKIN. (1) A piece of leather, worn on the right hand side of the petticoat, by spinners with the rock, on which the spindle plays,

and the yarn is pressed by the hand of the spinner. *Forby.*

(2) The skinny part of roasted meat, which before the whole can be dressed becomes tough and dry, like a *trip* overkept, or the leather used by the old woman. *Forby.*

TRISE. To pull up.

TRISTE. (1)

> Hast thou be prowde and eke of port
> For *tryste* of lady and eke of lord.
> *MS. Cott. Claud. A. ii. f. 140.*

(2) To trust.

> I was in prison wel ye wist,
> To helpe of you ne myght I *triste.*
> *MS. Addit. 11305, f. 90.*

> My lorde, when he went to the see,
> For specyalle *tryste* he toke me to the.
> *MS. Cantab. Ff. ii. 38, f. 72.*

(3) A post or station in hunting.

> I se huntynge, I se hornes blow,
> Houndes renne, the dere drawe adowne,
> And atte her *triste* bowes set arow,
> Now in August this lusti fressh cesone.
> *MS. Cantab. Ff. i. 6, f. 13.*

(4) A trestle, or support.
(5) A windlass.
(6) A cattle-market. *North.*

TRISTER. See *Triste* (3).

TRISTESCE. Sadness.

> Save only that I crye and bidde,
> I am in *tristesce* alle amidde.
> *Gower, MS. Soc. Antiq. 134, f. 126.*

TRISTILY. Safely; securely. "Qwhenne they *tristily* had tretyd," Morte Arthure, MS. Lincoln, f. 57.

TRISTIVE. Sad. (*Lat.*)

TRISTUR. The same as *Triste* (3).

TRIUMPH. (1) A public show.

(2) A trump at cards. (*Fr.*) The game of trump was also so called.

TRIVANT. A truant; a loiterer.

TRIVET. *Right as a trivet,* perfectly right. A common phrase.

TRIVIGANT. Termagant. (*Ital.*)

TRIWEDE. Honesty. *Hearne.*

TROACHER. A dealer in smuggled goods.

TROANT. A foolish fellow. *Exm.*

TROAT. To bellow, said of the buck.

TROCHE. To branch. (*A.-N.*)

TROCHES. Were thus made:

> Take of Benjamin six ounces, wood of aloes eight ounces, styrax-calamite three ounces, musk half a dram, orrice two ounces, sugar-candy three pound; powder them, and with rose-water make *troches.*
> *Cosmeticks, 1660, p. 133.*

TROCHINGS. The cluster of small branches at the top of a stag's horn.

TROD. A footpath. *Linc.* "Ran from trod to trod," Du Bartas, p. 360.

TRODE. Track; path. (*A.-S.*)

> Yf thou ever trowyde ore undyrstode
> That thi wytt ore thi gude
> Commys of thiselfe and noʒte of Gode,
> That es grett pryde and fals *trode.*
> *R. de Brunne, MS. Bowes, p. 16.*

TRODUS. Steps.

> They nyste never wher he was a-go,
> Ne of his *trodus* no sygne ther nasse.
> *Chron. Vilodun. p. 15.*

TROEN.

> Peny rydys *troen* be *troen,*
> Ovyr all in ylke a toen,
> On land and eke on flode.
> *Rellq. Antiq. ii. 110.*

TROFELYTE. Ornamented with knots. *Gaw.*

TROGH. A tree.

TROGHTE. Belief?

> The thryde es for-thy that we have
> Alle o *troghte* that sal us save.
> *MS. Harl. 2260, f. 21.*

TROIFLARDES. Triflers; idlers.

TROITE. The cuttle-fish? "*Sepia,* Anglice a troite," Nominale MS.

TROJAN. A boon companion; a person who is fond of liquor. A cant term. According to some, a thief was so called; but it was applied somewhat indiscriminately. A rough manly boy is now termed "a fine Trojan." Grose has *trusty Trojan,* a true friend.

TROKE. (1) To barter; to truck. *North.*

(2) To fall short.

> He mone stond faste thereby,
> Or ellys hys schote wolle *troke.*
> *MS. Porkington 10, f. 56*

TROKES. Square pieces of wood at the tops of masts to put the flag-staffs in.

TROLL. To trundle. *To troll the bowl,* to pass the vessel about in drinking.

TROLLEN. To draw; to drag. (*A.-S.*)

TROLL-MADAM. A game borrowed from the French in the 16th century, now known under the name of *trunks,* q. v. Brand quotes a curious account of this game, from which it appears to have formed a favorite indoor amusement with the lady fashionables at Buxton about the year 1572, and to have been somewhat like the modern game of *bagatelle.* There is an allusion to it in the Winter's Tale, iv. 2.

TROLLOP. (1) A slattern. *Var. dial.*

(2) A string of horses. *Linc.*

TROLLOPISH. Filthy; dirty. *South.*

TROLLY. A low heavy cart. *Var. dial.*

TROLLYBAGS. Tripe. *Var. dial.*

TROLLY-LOLLY. Coarse lace.

TROLUBBER. A hedger and ditcher. *Devon.*

TROME. Band, or company. (*A.-S.*)

TROMPE. (1) A trumpet. (*A.-N.*)

(2) A shin, or shank.

TROMPOUR. A trumpeter.

TRONAGE. A toll for the weighing of wool in the market. *Coles.*

TRONCHEON. A scab.

TRONCHON. A fragment. (*A.-N.*)

> Upon a *tronchon* of a spere,
> He set the hed of the bore.
> *MS. Cantab. Ff. ii. 38, f. 106.*

TRONE. (1) A throne. (*A.-N.*) It is the verb, to enthrone, in this example.

> And ther soulys to hevyn bere,
> Before God *tronyd* they were.
> *MS. Cantab. Ff. ii. 38, f. 38.*

(2) A ridge of mown hay. *West.*

(3) A post, or log of wood.

TRONES. A steelyard. *North.*

TRONSOUN. A club, or staff.

And was bicomen a garsoun,
In hond berand a tronsoun.
Arthour and Merlin, p. 269.

TROP. An interjection used by riders to excite a dull horse. *Somerset.*

TROPE.

Ʒef he be styf and of herte heʒ,
Trope hym softe, and go hym neʒ,
And when thou herest where he wole byde,
Ʒeve hym penaunce thenne also that tyde.
MS. Cott. Claud. A. ii. f. 146.

OPERY. The first words of a psalm, &c.

TROPIE.

And aspie hem bi *tropie*,
And so fond hem to astroie.
Arthour and Merlin, p. 250.

TROROROW. The cry of hunters returning home after the hunt is over.

TROSSERS. Close drawers, or trousers.

TROSTELS. Trestles.

It. to Davy vj. peweter platters, a planke to make a table-bord, with a payer of *trostels.*
Test. Vetust. p. 786.

TROT. An old woman, in contempt.

This leare I learned of a beldame *Trot,*
(When I was yong and wylde as now thou art.)
The Affectionate Shepheard, 1594.

TROTEVALE. A trifling thing.

Yn gamys and festys and at the ale,
Love men to lestene *trotevale.*
MS. Harl. 1701, f. 1.

Ʒe wommen, thenketh on thys tale,
And taketh hyt for no *trotevale.*
MS. Harl. 1701, f. 54.

So fare men here by thys tale,
Some holde hyt but a *trotevale.*
MS. Harl. 1701, f. 61.

Or thou ledyst any man to the ale,
And madest hym drunk with *trotevale.*
MS. Harl. 1701, f. 40.

TROTH. (1) Faith; pledge; assurance.

(2) A band, or company.

TROTH-PLIGHT. The passing of a solemn vow, either of friendship or marriage.

TROTTER-PIE. Urry, in his MS. Additions to Ray, gives this as an Oxfordshire term for a round apple-pie with quinces in it. It now appears to have fallen out of use.

TROTTERS. Curds. *North.*

TROTTLES. Sheep's dung. *Linc.*

TROU. A small cart, or drag. *Chesh.*

TROUAGE. Tribute. *(A.-N.)*

TROUBLE. (1) An imperfection. *West.*

(2) Dark; gloomy. *(A.-N.)*

(3) *To be in trouble,* to be arrested for any crime. *Var. dial.*

(4) A woman's travail. *East.*

(5) To *trouble* signifies to be in *trouble.* " Don't you *trouble*" means " don't *trouble* yourself." *Herefordsh.*

TROUBLOUS. Full of troubles.

Therfor of right it must nedis be thus,
My soule to dwell in waters *troublous,*
That ben salt and bitter for to taste,
And them to take as for my repaste.
MS. Rawl. C. 86.

TROUBY. A troubling.

TROUE. A hole. *(A.-N.)*

TROUGH. A stone coffin.

TROUL. The same as *Troll,* q. v.

TROUNCE. To beat. *Var. dial.* Trouncer, one who beats, Ovid de arte Amandi, a mock poem, Lond. 1677, p. 149.

TROUNCE-HOLE. A game at ball, very like trap-ball, but more simple; a hole in the ground serving for the trap, a flat piece of bone for the trigger, and a cudgel for the bat.

TROUNCH. To tramp in the mud. *Devon.*

TROUNCHEN. To carve an eel.

TROUS. The trimmings of a hedge.

TROUT. To coagulate. See *Trouts.*

TROUTHHEDE. Truth. *(A.-S.)*

Fynde he may ynouʒe to telle
Of hir goodnesse, of hir *trouthhede.*
Cursor Mundi, MS. Coll. Trin. Cantab. f. 1.

TROUTS. Curds taken off the whey when it is boiled; a rustic word. In some places they are called trotters. *North.*

TROVEL. A mill-stream.

TROW. A trough. *Suff.* " Tyll two trowys he gan hym lede," MS. Ashm. 61.

TROWANDISE. Begging. *(A.-N.)*

TROWCAN. A little dish.

TROWE. To believe, think, suppose.

Os y nevyr syr James sloo,
He delyvyr me of woo,
And so y *trowe* he schalle !
MS. Cantab. Ff. ii. 38, f. 78.

TROWEL. To play trowel, i. e. truant.

TROWET. Truth.

Be mey *trowet,* thow seys soyt, seyde Roben.
Robin Hood, i. 85.

TROWLIS. Perfidious. *(A.-S.)*

His knyʒtehode, his power, his ordinance, his ryʒte,
Agaynst the *trowlis* tempest avaylid hym no thynge ;
What may manhode do agaynst Goddes myʒte ?
The wynde, the water spareth nodyr prynce ne kyng !
Haply that trowbill was for wickyd lyvyng,
God wolde every creature his maker shulde know,
Wherefore, good Lorde, evermore thy will be doo !
MS. Bibl. Reg. 17 D. xv.

TROW-MOTHER. A reputed mother.

TROWPES. Thorpe; villages.

The tame ruddoke and the cowarde kyte,
The coke that orlege ys of *trowpes* lyte.
Chaucer, MS. Cantab. Ff. i. 6, f. 28.

TROWS. A sort of double boat, with an open interval between, and closed at the ends ; used on the North Tyne for salmon fishing: the fisher standing across the opening, leister in hand, ready to strike any fish which may pass beneath. *Northumb.*

TROWSES. The close drawers over which the hose or slops were drawn. *Gifford.*

TROXY. Frolicsome. *Leic.*

TRUAGE. Homage ?

Hoping that, as he should stoop to doo him *truage,* he might seaze upon his throate and stifle him before he should be able to recover himselfe from his false embrace.
Nash's Pierce Pennilesse, 1592.

TRUANDISE. Idleness ?

But they me schopen that I schulde
Eschive of slep the *truandise.*
Gower, MS. Soc. Antiq. 134, f. 121.

TRUB. A slattern. *Devon.*

TRUBAGULLY. A short, dirty, ragged fellow

accustomed to perform the most menial offices.

TRUBYLYERE. More zealous?

For it may falle sumtyme that the *trubylyers* that thou hase bene owtwarde with actyfe werkes, the more brynnande desyre thou salle hafe to Godd.
MS. Lincoln A. i. 17, f. 224.

TRUCHMAN. An interpreter. *Troocheman*, Cunningham's Rev. Acc. p. 126. Sometimes printed *trounchman*, as in Peele, ii. 201.

TRUCK. (1) A cow is said to truck when her milk fails. *North.*
(2) Odds and ends; rubbish. *East.*
(3) Wicked language. *North.*
(4) A drag for timber. *Var. dial.*
(5) To bate, or diminish. *Derb.*
(6) To traffic by exchange.
(7) An old game. Holme, iii. 263.

TRUCKLE. (1) To roll. *Devon.*
(2) A pulley. Also a wheel or ball underneath anything for the purpose of moving or rolling it. Still in use.

TRUCKLE-BED. A low bed on small wheels or castors, trundled under another in the day time, and drawn out at night for a servant or other inferior person to sleep on. *Forby.*

TRUCK-SHOP. A shop at which the workmen, in some of the manufacturing districts, receive various articles of food, clothing, &c., in lieu of money, for their wages.

TRUCKY. Cheating. *Yorksh.*

TRUE. Honest.

TRUE-BLUE. The best blue colour. Metaphorically, a honest good fellow.

TRUELLE. Labour; sweat.

TRUE-PENNY. "Generally *Old-Truepenny*, as it occurs in Sh. Hamlet, where the application of it to the ghost is unseemly and incongruous, yet it has attracted no notice from any commentator. Its present meaning is, hearty old fellow; staunch and trusty; true to his purpose or pledge," Forby. This appears more to the purpose than the information given by Mr. Collier, "it is a mining term, and signifies a particular indication in the soil of the direction in which ore is to be found."

TRUFF. (1) A trough. *West.*
(2) A trout. *Cornw.*

TRUFFILLERE. A trifler.

TRUFLE. Anything worthless.

TRUG. (1) A trull. Middleton, ii. 222.
(2) A wooden basket for carrying chips or vegetables. *Sussex.* Ray says, "a tray for milk or the like."
(3) Two thirds of a bushel of wheat.

TRUGGING-PLACE. "The whore-house, which is called a *trugging-place*," The Belman of London, 1608.

TRUGH. Through.

That no man may his letters know nor se,
Allethough he looke *trugh* spectacles thre.
MS. Rawl. C. 86.

TRULL. (1) To underdrain. *Sussex.*
(2) To bowl, or trundle. *Var. dial.*

TRULL-OF-TRUST. A woman of bad character.

For to satisfye your wanton lust
I shall apoynt you a *trull-of-trust*,
Not a feyrer in this towne.
Interlude of the Four Elements.

TRUME. A company of people. (*A.-S.*)

Bisydes stondeth a feondes *trume*,
And waiteth hwenne the saules cume.
MS. Coll. Jes. Oxon. I. 29.

TRUMP. (1) A game at cards, similar to the modern game of whist.
(2) To lie; to boast. *North.*
(3) The tube of a pea-shooter.
(4) A trumpeter. (*A.-N.*)

TRUMPEN. To sound a trumpet.

The kynge, whanne it was nyʒte anone,
This man assente, and bad him gone
To *trumpen* at his brother gate.
Gower, MS. Soc. Antiq. 134, f. 52.

TRUMPET. A trumpeter.

TRUMPH. A trump at cards. *North.*

TRUMPS. Anything falling out fortunately is said *to turn up trumps.* To be put to the last trumps, i. e. to the last push.

TRUNCH. Short and thick. *East.*

TRUNCHON. A horse-worm. *Palsgrave.*

TRUNDLE. (1) Anything globular. *North.*
(2) The small entrails of a calf.

TRUNDLE-BED. Same as *Truckle-bed*, q. v.

TRUNDLE-TAIL. A curly-tailed dog.

TRUNDLING-CHEATS. Carts, or coaches.

TRUNIS. Confidence; trust. (*A.-S.*)

TRUNK. (1) A tube; a pea-shooter.
(2) A trump at cards. *North.*
(3) The same as *Trunk-hose*, q. v.
(4) A place for keeping fish in.
(5) An under-ground drain. *Sussex.*
(6) To lop off. *Howell.*
(7) A blockhead, or dunce. *Blount.*

TRUNKET. A game at ball played with short sticks, and having a hole in the ground in lieu of stumps or wicks, as in cricket; and with these exceptions, and the ball being cop'd instead of bowled or trickled on the ground, it is played in the same way; the person striking the ball must be caught out, or the ball must be deposited in the hole before the stick or cudgel can be placed there.

TRUNK-HOSE. Large breeches, which, on their first appearance, covered the greater part of the thighs, but afterwards extended below the knees. They were stuffed to an enormous size with hair, wool, &c.

An everlasting bale, hell in *trunk-hose*,
Uncased, the divel's Don Quixot in prose.
Fletcher's Poems, p. 130.

TRUNKS. (1) Same as *troll-madam*, q. v. It is still called *trunks.* Brand, ii. 215.

Yet in my opinion it were not fit for them to play at stoole-ball among wenches, nor at mum-chance or maw with idle loose companions, nor at *trunkes* in Guile-hals.
Rainoldes' Overthrow of Stage-Playes, 1599, p. 23.

(2) Iron hoops, with a bag net attached, used to catch crabs and lobsters. *Hartlepool.*

TRUNK-WAY. A watercourse through an arch of masonry, turned over a ditch before a gate

TRUNK-WEAM. A fiddle.

TRUNLIN. A large coal. *North.*

TRUNNLE. The same as *Trendle*, q. v.

TRUNTLEMENT. Trumpery. *North.*

TRUPHILLE. A trifle.

TRUSH. (1) A hassock. *Kent.*

(2) *To trush about*, to litter.

(3) To run about in the dirt. *North.*

TRUSLE. (1) Trust. *Weber.*

(2) To wrap up; to get ready.

TRUSS. (1) A padded jacket worn under the armour to protect the skin.

(2) To tie the points of hose. *To truss up*, to tuck up the gown, &c.

(3) The baggage of an army.

(4) To pack up. Hence, to make ready.

> And *trusse* al that he mithen fynde
> Of hise, in arke, or in kiste.
> *Havelok, 2018.*

(5) A boy's game, like leap-frog.

(6) *Truss up*, to hang a person.

TRUSSEL. (1) A pack, or bundle.

(2) A stand for a barrel. *Kent.*

TRUSSES. The same as *Trowses*, q. v.

TRUSSING. In falconry, is a hawk's raising any fowl or prey aloft; soaring up, and then descending with it to the ground.

TRUSSING-BASKET. A basket used for conveying large parcels of goods. Called also a trussing-coffer.

TRUSSING-BED. A travelling bed. "Trussyng bedde, *lit de champ*," Palsgrave.

> Also my large bed of black velvet, embroidered with a circle of fetter-locks, and garters, all the beds made for my body called in England *trussing-beds.*
> *Test. Vetust. p. 141.*

TRUT. (1) Stercus. *Hearne.*

(2) The cry of hunters returning home after the sport is finished.

TRUTHY. Faithful; veracious. *East.*

TRY. (1) To fare. *Somerset.*

(2) A corn screen. Also, to screen.

(3) To boil down lard. *East.*

(4) *How de try*, how do you do? *Exm.*

(5) A club tipped with iron.

TRYALYTES. Three benefices united.

TRYERS.

> And shew'd themselves as errant lyars,
> As th' were 'prentice to the *tryers.*
> *Brome's Songs, 1661. p. 167.*

TRYSTI. Trusty; secure.

> On *trysti* roche heo stoudeth fast,
> And wyth depe dyche buth all be cast.
> *Religious Poems, xv. Cent.*

TRYVE. To drive.

> In chastisynge hath made a rod
> To *tryve* awey hire wantonnesse.
> *Gower, MS. Soc. Antiq. 134, f. 111.*

TU. To work hard. *North.*

TUARN. The place in an iron furnace which receives the metal. *Staff.*

TUAY. Two.

> From amemorwe to the midday,
> He hadde strengthe of knightes *tuay.*
> *Arthour and Merlin, p. 178.*

TUB. (1) *Tale of a tub*, a stupid nonsensical story.

(2) The top of a malt-kiln. *Essex.*

(3) The gurnet. *Cornw.*

(4) One mode of curing the *lues venerea* was by the *tub*, the patient sweating for a considerable time in a heated tub. This mode is often alluded to by early writers.

TUBBAN. A clod of earth. *Cornw.*

TUBBER. A cooper. *North.*

TUBBLE. A mattock. *Devon.*

TUB-IRON. An iron placed in front of a smith's fire-place, having a hole through which the spout of the bellows is put.

TUBLE. Earthenware. *West.*

TU-BRUGGE. A drawbridge.

TUCK. (1) To eat. Also, an appetite.

(2) A short pinafore. *East.*

(3) To smart with pain. *Wilts.* In Devonshire. to pinch severely.

(4) A slap. *Devon.*

(5) A horizontal fold made in a garment to accommodate it to the height of a growing person.

(6) To touch. *Somerset.*

(7) A rapier. Still in use.

(8) To chuck. *Cornw.*

TUCKER. (1) A fuller. *West.*

(2) The same as *Pinner*, q. v.

TUCKER-IN. A chambermaid. *West.*

TUCKET. A slight flourish on a trumpet.

TUCKING. A bag used for carrying beans in when setting them. *Glouc.*

TUCKING-GIRDLE. "Tuckyng kyrdell, *saincture decourser*," Palsgrave.

TUCKS. Iron pins in the frame of a timber-tug to prevent the timber slipping off.

TUCKSHELLS. Tusks. *Sussex.*

TUE. (1) To rumple. *North.*

(2) The same as *Tew*, q. v.

TUEL. (1) A towel. *West.*

(2) The fundament. See *Tewel.*

(3) A vexatious meddling. *North.*

TUEN. To go.

> Ant alle the other that mine buen,
> Shule to blisse with me *tuen.*
> *Harrowing of Hell, p. 29.*

TUFF. (1) A Turkish turban.

(2) A tassel. Also, to ornament with tassels.

(3) A lock of wool.

(4) To spit or hiss, as a cat.

TUFFOLD. A small outhouse. *Yorksh.*

TUFT. A grove, or plantation.

TUFT-HUNTER. A hanger-on to noblemen and persons of quality.

TUFT-MOCKADO. A mixed stuff made to imitate tufted taffeta, or velvet.

TUFT-TAFFATY. A taffaty tufted, or left with a nap on it, like velvet.

> Sleeveless his jerkin was, and it had been
> Velvet, but 'twas now (so much ground was seen)
> Become *tufftaffaty*; and our children shall
> See it plain rash a while, then nought at all.
> *Donne's Poems, p. 129.*

TUG. (1) A contest. *Var. dial.*

(2) A timber-carriage. *Sussex.*

(3) To rob; to spoil. *North.*

(4) A difficult undertaking. *West.*

TUG-IRON. An iron on the shafts of a waggon to hitch the traces to.

TUGMUTTON. A great glutton.

TUGURRYSCHUDDE. A hut.

TUIGHT. Twitched; torn off.

TUINDE.

Tuynde thyn ye, that thow ne se
The cursede worldes vanyte.
MS. Cott. Claud. A. ii. f. 127.

TUKE. Gave. (*A.-S.*)

He had the letter by the noke,
To the erle he it *tuke.*
MS. Lincoln A. i. 17, f. 130.

TUL. To. *North.*

TULIEN. To labour; to till. (*A.-S.*)

TULKE. A man, or knight.

TULKY. A turkey. *Suffolk.*

TULLE. To allure. (*A.-S.*)

TULLY. A little wretch. *Yorksh.*

TULSURELIKE. Red in the face.

TULT. To it. *North.*

TULY. A kind of red or scarlet colour. Silk of this colour is often alluded to, as in Richard Coer de Lion, 67, 1516; and carpets and tapestry, Syr Gawayne, pp. 23, 33. In MS. Sloane 73, f. 214, are directions " for to make bokeram, tuly, or tuly thred, secundum Cristiane de Prake in Beme."

I schel the yeve to the wage
A mantel whit so melk,
The broider is of *tuli* selk,
Beten abouten with rede golde.
Beves of Hamtoun, p. 47.

TUM. To card wool for the first time. Ray says, to mix wool of divers colours.

After your wooll is oyl'd and anointed thus, you shall then *tum* it, which is, you shall put it forth as you did before when you mixed it, and card it over again upon your stock cards: and then those cardings which you strike off are called *tummings*, which you shall lay by till it come to a spinning.
Markham's English House-Wife, 1675, p. 126.

TUMBESTERE. A dancer.

Herodias douzter, that was a *tumbestere,* and tumblede byfore him and other grete lordes of that contre, he grantede to zeve hure whatevere he wolde bydde. *MS. Harl.* 2398, f. 8.

TUMBLE. (1) To dance.

Hyt telleth that Eroud swore
To here that *tumbled* yn the flore.
MS. Harl. 1701, f. 19.

(2) To rumple the dress. *Var. dial.*

TUMBLE-CAR. A cart drawn by a single horse; probably so named from the axle being made fast in the wheels, and turning round with them.

TUMBLER. (1) A tumbril. *East.*

(2) A dancer. See *Tumble* (1).

(3) A kind of dog formerly employed for taking rabbits. This it effected by tumbling itself about in a careless manner till within reach of the prey, and then seizing it by a sudden spring.

TUMBLING-SHAFT. A spindle rod in an oatmeal mill, lying under the floor. *East.*

TUMBREL. (1) A cucking-stool.

(2) A dung-cart. *West.*

Wherfore breake off your daunce, you fairies and elves, and come from the fieldes, with the torne carcases of your *tumbrills,* for your kingdome is expired.
Epist. prefixed to Sidney's Astrophel and Stella, 1591.

TUMMALS. A heap; a quantity. *Devon.*

TUMMLE. To tumble. *North.*

TUMMUZ. Thomas. *North.*

TUMP. A heap; a hillock. *West.*

TUMPTSNER. A settler. "That'll be a *tumptsner* for the old gentleman." *Somerset.*

TUMPY. Uneven; having tumps. *West.*

TUN. (1) A tub; a barrel. Also a verb, to put liquor into casks or barrels.

That nyze his hous he let devyse,
Endelonge upon an axeltre,
To sette a *tunne* in his degre.
Gower, MS. Soc. Antiq. 134, f. 92.

But when trouthe sette abroche here *tunne.*
Lydgate, MS. Ashmole 39, f. 45.

(2) The upper part of a chimney. Sometimes, the chimney itself. *West.*

(3) A stalking-horse for partridges.

(4) A town. Havelok, 1001.

(5) A little cup. *Kennett.*

TUNACLE. "A tunacle, *dalmatica, tunica, tunicula,*" MS. Dictionary, circa 1500.

TUNDER. Tinder. *Var. dial.*

TUN-DISH. A wooden funnel, through which liquor is poured into casks. *West.*

TUNE. (1) To the "tune" of any sum, is a phrase often used. " You look as if you were Don Diego'd to the *tune* of a thousand pounds."—*The Tatler,* No. 31.

(2) Order; temper. *Var. dial.*

TUNE-UP. To begin to sing. *South.*

TUNHOVE. Ground ivy. *Pr. Parv.*

TUNMERE. The line of procession in perambulating the bounds of a parish. *East.*

TUNNEGAR. A funnel. *West.*

TUNNEL. (1) A funnel. Still in use.

(2) An arched drain. *Yorksh.*

TUNNEL-GRUNTERS. Potatoes. *West.*

TUNNER. (1) Either. *Devon.*

(2) The same as *Tunnel,* q. v.

TUNNIF. The forget-me-not. *East.*

TUNNING. Brewing.

TUNNING-DISH. (1) A funnel. (2) A wooden dish used in dairies. *West.*

TUNWONGE. "*Tempus,* a tunwonge," Nominale MS. inter membra humani corporis. See *Thonwonge.*

TUP. (1) A ram. *Var. dial.* Turn the tup to ride, i. e. put the ram to the ewe. Also a verb, to butt. It is an archaism.

(2) To bow to a person before drinking. *Lanc.*

TUPMAN. A breeder of tups or rams.

TURBANT. A turban. Florio, p. 101.

TURBE. Squadron; troop. *Hearne.*

TURBERY. A boggy ground.

TURBOLT. A turbot.

TURCOT. The wryneck. *Howell.*

TURCULONY. An old dance.

TUREILE. A turret. *Hearne.*

TURF. (1) Cakes for firing, made by tanners from the refuse of oak bark. *Wilts.*

(2) Peat moss. *Lanc.*

(3) " Turfe of a cappe, *rebras*," Palsgrave. " Tyrf or tyrvyng upon an hoode or sleve, *resolucio*," Pr. Parv.

(4) To adjust the surface of sown turf.

TURFEGRAVER. A ploughman.

TURFING-SPADE. A spade made for undercutting turf. *Var. dial.*

TURGY. White magic ; a pretended conference with good spirits or angels. *Blount.*

TURIN. The nose of the bellows.

TURK. (1) An image made of cloth or rags, used by persons as a mark for shooting.

(2) A savage fellow. *Var. dial.*

TURKEIS. (1) Turkish. (*A.-N.*) " Turkes bowe, *arc turquoys*," Palsgrave. " Turkes sworde, *espee, esclamme*," Ibid.

(2) A precious stone, the turquoise.

TURKEY-BIRD. The wryneck. *Suffolk.*

TURLINS. Coals of a moderate size. *North.*

TURMENTILLE. The herb setfoil.

> Who so drinkyth the water of *turmentille*, it conforth mans mawe, and clensyt venym, and it abathe swellinge. *MS. Sloane 7, f. 51.*

TURMENTISE. Torment. (*A.-N.*)

TURMENTRIE. Torment ; torture.

TURMIT. A turnip. *Var. dial.*

TURN. (1) Year, or time.

(2) A spinning-wheel. *Devon.*

(3) To curdle ; to turn sour. *North.* It is used in this sense by Shakespeare.

(4) An act of industry. *West.*

(5) *To turn the head*, to tend in sickness, to attend to, to direct, to educate.

(6) The sheriff's court. *Blount.*

TURNAMENT. (1) Change.

> And all to asshis this lady was brent,
> And after arose aguyne alyve as she was,
> And oft she had this *turnament.*
> *MS. Laud. 416, f. 75.*

(2) A revolving engine.

> For thys *turnament* ys so devysyd,
> I schall be in my blode baptysyd.
> *MS. Cantab. Ff. ii. 38, f. 39.*

TURNBACK. A coward.

TURN-BROACH. Before the introduction of jacks, spits were turned either by dogs trained for the purpose, or by lads kept in the family, or hired, as occasions arose, to turn the spit, or *broach*. These boys were the turn-broaches. See Warner's Antiq. Culin. p. 97.

> A *turne-broche*, a boy for hogge at Ware.
> *Lydgate's Minor Poems, p. 52.*

TURNBULL-STREET. Formerly a noted resort for courtesans and bad characters.

> When *Turmele-street* and Clarken-well
> Have sent all bawdes and whores to hell.
> *Cobbes Prophecies, 1614.*

TURNED-CARD. A trump card.

TURNEGRECE. A spiral staircase.

TURNEPING. Collecting turnips. *West.*

TURNESOLE. A dish in ancient cookery described in Warner's Antiq. Culin. p. 84.

TURNEY. An attorney. *Var. dial.*

TURNIE. A tournament.

TURNING. (1) A plait in linen.

(2) A jest, or repartee.

(3) Tournaying. *Hall.*

TURNING-STICKS. Long crooked sticks to turn layers of corn.

TURNOVER. A sort of apple tart, where the pieces of fruit are laid upon one half of a circular piece of crust, and the uncovered part whelmed over the fruit and then baked. It also means a put off, or excuse, for not doing anything.

TURN-PAT. A crested pigeon.

TURN-PIKE. (1) A lock in a river.

(2) A turnstile, or a post with a movable cross at the top. Jonson, v. 235.

TURNSEKE. To feel giddy.

TURN-SPIT. This dog is thus described in Topsell's Four-Footed Beasts, 1607, p. 177 :

> There is comprehended, under the curres of the coursest kinde, a certaine dog in kitchen service excellent ; for when any meat is to be roasted, they go into a wheele, which they turning round about with the waight of their bodies, so dilligently looke to their businesse, that no drudge nor scullion can do the feate more cunningly. Whom the popular sort hereupon call *turnespets*, being the last of all those which wee have first mentioned.

TURN-STRING. A string made of twisted gut, much used in spinning.

TURN-TIPPET. Same as *Turn-Turk*, q. v.

TURN-TRENCHER. A Lincolnshire game.

TURN-TURK. " To turn Turk was a figurative expression for a change of condition or opinion," Gifford. The expression is still used, said when a person becomes ill-tempered on account of a joke, &c.

TURNYNG-TREE. The gallows.

> And at the last, she and her husband, as they deserved, were apprehended, arraigned, and hanged at the foresayd *turnyng-tree.*
> *Hall, Henry VIII. f. 224.*

TURPIN. A kettle. A cant term.

TURQUIS. Turkish.

> Some aftre issued oute the sameselle, and the dwarfe, and had his *turquis* bowe in his honde and the arowes. *MS. Digby, 185.*

TURR. (1) A word used in driving pigs.

(2) To butt, as a ram does.

TURRIBLE. A thurible, or censer.

TURTERS. " *Grapiller*, to gather grapes after the *turters* or first gatherers thereof," Hollyband's Dictionarie, 1593.

TURTURE. A singing shepherd. (*Lat.*)

TURVEE. To struggle. *Exm.*

TURVES. The pl. of *turf.*

TUSH. (1) A tusk ; a tooth. *North.*

(2) To draw a heavy weight. *West.*

(3) The wing of a ploughshare. *Glouc.*

TUSK. A tuft of hair. " Tuske of heer, *monceau de cheveulx*," Palsgrave. The term occurs in Ben Jonson.

TUSKIN. (1) Was thus made :

> Take raw porke and hew hit smalle,
> And grynde in a morter : temper hit thou schalle
> With swongen egges, but not to thynne ;
> In gryndynge put powder of peper within.
> Thenne this flessh take up in thy honde,
> And rolle hit on balles, I undurstonde,

In gretnes of trabbes ; I harde say
In boylande water thou kast hom may.
To harden them take hom owte to cole,
And play fressh broth fayre and wele.
Therin cast persoley, ysope, sanay, [saneray ?]
That smalle is hakked by any way.
Alye hit with floure or brede for-thy,
Coloure hit with safroun for the maystré ;
Cast powder of peper and clawes therto,
And take thy balles or thou more do,
And put therin ; boyle alle in fere,
And serve hit forth for *tuskyns* dere.
    MS. Sloane 1986, p. 93.

(2) A kind of long coloured cloth.

(3) A country carter, or ploughman.

TUSSES. Projecting stones left in the masonry to tie in the wall of a building intended to be subsequently annexed.

TUSSEY. A low drunken fellow.

TUSSICATED. Driven about ; tormented.

TUSSLE. To struggle ; to wrestle.

TUSSOCK. A tangled knot or heap. *Var. dial.* Also, a twisted lock of hair.

TUSTE. A tuft of hair.

TUT. (1) A hassock. *Cornw.*

(2) *A tut for a tusk*, equivalent in meaning to tit for tat.

(3) To pull ; to tear. *Devon.*

(4) A sort of stobball (q. v.) play.

TUT-GOT. Come upon or overtaken by a *tut*, or goblin. This spectre is recognized in and near Spilsby, but not in all parts of the county. *Linc.*

TUTHE. A tooth. Nominale MS.

TUTHERAM. The others. *West.*

TUTIVILLUS. An old name for a celebrated demon, who is said to have collected all the fragments of words which the priests had skipped over or mutilated in the performance of the service, and carried them to hell. See Piers Ploughman, p. 547 ; Townley Mysteries, pp. 310, 319 ; Reliq. Antiq. i.257 ; MS. Lansd. 762, f. 101.

TUTLESHIP. Protection ; custody.

TUT-MOUTHED. Having the lower jaw projecting further than the upper.

TUT-NOSE. A short snub-nose. *East.*

TUTS. A term at the old game of stool-ball. See Clarke's Phraseologia Puerilis, 8vo. Lond. 1655, p. 141.

TUTSON. The periwinkle. *East.*

TUT-SUB. A hassock. *Somerset.*

TUTTER. (1) To stutter. *Somerset.*

(2) Trouble ; bother. *East.*

TUTTING. (1) A tea-drinking for women, succeeded by stronger potations in company of the other sex, and ending, as might be expected, in scenes of ribaldry and debauchery. It is so called only, I believe, in Lincoln ; in other places in the county it is known by the name of a bun-feast. The custom is now obsolete, or nearly so, to the amelioration, it is hoped, of society.

(2) An inferior description of ball ; perhaps from *tuts*, a maternal term of endearment for a child's feet. *Linc.*

TUTTLE. (1) Tothill Fields.

(2) A cross-grained fellow. *Lanc.*

(3) To whisper ; to tell tales. *North.*

TUTTLE-BOX. An instrument used by ploughmen for keeping their horses a little apart, that they may see forward between them to make a straight furrow.

TUTTY. (1) A flower ; a nosegay. *West.*

(2) Ill-tempered ; sullen. *Beds.*

TUTTY-MORE. A flower-root. *Somerset.*

TUT-WORK. Work done by the piece. *West.*

TUYLES. Tools.
  And the cause hereof, as it wele semes, es for ye
  hafe na irene whareof ye myghte make yow *tuyles*
  for to wirke withalle. *MS. Lincoln* A. i. 17, f. 36.

TUYNEN. To separate.
  And as myyty, as I yow telle,
  Bothe of the yates of bevene and helle
  To *tuynen* and open at heyre byddynge,
  Wythowte yeynstondynge of any thynge.
    MS. Cott. Claud. A. ii. f. 133.

TUZ. A knot of wool or hair. *Leic.*

TUZZIMUZZY. (1) A nosegay. See Florio, p. 492 ; Nomenclator, 1585, p. 113.

(2) The female pudendum.

(3) Rough ; ragged ; dishevelled. *East.*

TWA-BLADE. A plant with two leaves.

TWACHEL. The dew-worm. *East.*

TWACHYLLE. A term applied to the female pudendum in the Reliq. Antiq. ii. 28.

TWACK. To change frequently. *East.*

TWACKT. Beaten ; knocked about.

TWAGE. To pinch ; to squeeze. *North.*

TWAILE. A towel. Also, a net, or toil.
  Hurre blessud moder, seynt Wultrud,
  Toke a *twaylle* of ryyt gode aray.
    Chron. Vilodun. p. 64.

TWAINE. Two. (*A.-S.*)

TWALE. A mattock ; an axe.

TWALL. A whim. *Suffolk.*

TWALY. Vexed ; ill-tempered. *Salop.*

TWAM. To swoon. *North.*

TWANG. (1) A sharp taste. *Var. dial.*

(2) A quick pull ; a sudden pang. *North.*

TWANGDILLOWS.
  Pleas'd with the *twangdillows* of poor Crowdero
  In a country fair. *Collins' Miscellanies*, 1762, p. viii.

TWANGEY. A tailor. *North.*

TWANGLE. To entangle ; to ruffle. *East.*

TWANGLING. (1) Small ; weak. *North.*

(2) Noisy ; jingling. *Shak.*

TWANK. (1) To let fall the carpenter's chalk-line upon the board. *East.*

(2) To give a smart slap with the flat of the hand, a stick, &c. *East.*

TWANKING. (1) Complaining. *Dorset.*

(2) Big ; unwieldy. *North.*

TWARCINGE. Crookedness.

TWARLY. Peevish ; cross. *Chesh.*

TWAT.
  Give not male names then to such things as thine,
  But think thou hast two *twats* o wife of mine.
    Fletcher's Poems, p. 104.

TWATETH. A buck or doe *twateth*, i. e. makes a noise at rutting time.

TWATTLE. (1) To tattle ; to chatter. *Twatlers*, idle talkers, Stanihurst, p. 36.

(2) To pat; to make much of. *North.*

(3) A dwarf, or diminutive person.

TWATTLE-BASKET. An idle chatterer.

TWAYE. Two.

> Dame, he seyde, how schalle we doo,
> He fayleth *twaye* tethe also.
>   *MS. Cantab. Ff. ii. 38, f. 134.*

TWEAG. Doubt; perplexity.

TWEAGERS. The same as *Plushes*, q. v.

TWEAK. A whore. Also, a whoremonger.

TWEASOME. Two in company. *North.*

TWEE. To be in a *twee* is to be sweating with fright or vexation; probably per metathesin for tew. *Linc.*

TWEEDLE. To twist. *Devon.*

TWEER. To peep; to pry. See *Twire.*

TWEERS. Bellows at an iron furnace.

TWEEZES. Tweezers. Middleton, iv. 119.

TWEIFOLD. Double. (*A.-S.*)

TWELE. The same as *Twill*, q. v.

TWELF-TYDE. Twelfth day.

> At the city of New Sarum, is a very great faire for cloath at *Twelftyde* called Twelfe market.
>   *Aubrey's Wilts, MS. Royal Soc. p. 333.*

TWELL. Twelve. Arch. xxx. 414.

TWELVE-HOLES. A game similar to nine-holes, mentioned in Florio, ed. 1611, p. 20.

TWELVE-SCORE. That is, twelve score yards, a common length for a shot in archery.

TWEY. Two. (*A.-S.*)

> *Twey* schelyng ther is more;
> Forgete hem not, be Goddis ore!
>   *MS. Cantab. Ff. v. 48, f. 53.*

TWEYANGLYS. A kind of worm.

TWEYNED. Separated.

TWIBIL. (1) A mattock; an axe. An implement like a pickaxe, but having, instead of points, flat terminations, one of which is horizontal, the other perpendicular. *Herefordsh.*

(2) An instrument used for making mortises, "Twyble an instrument for carpentars, *bernago*," Palsgrave. The two meanings of this word have been frequently confused.

> ȝe, ȝe, seyd the *twybylle*,
> Thou spekes ever ageyne skylle,
> I-wys, i-wys, it wylle not bene,
> Ne never I thinke that he wylle thene.
>   *MS. Ashmole 61.*

TWICK. A sudden jerk. *West.* It occurs as a verb in Towneley Myst. p. 220.

TWICROOKS. Little crooks bent contrary ways in order to lengthen out the trammels on which the pot-hooks are hung. *Glouc.*

TWIDDLE. (1) A pimple. *Suffolk.*

(2) To be busy about trifles. *To twiddle the fingers*, to do nothing. *Var. dial.*

TWIES. Twice. (*A.-S.*)

> The pater noster and the crede
> Preche thy paresch thou moste nede
> *Twyes* or thryes in the ȝere,
> To thy paresch hole and fere.
>   *MS. Cott. Claud. A. ii. f. 139.*

TWIFALLOW. See *Trifallow.*

TWIFILS. Two-folds.

TWIG. (1) To understand a person's motives or meaning. "I *twigged* what he'd be arter." *Var. dial.*

II.

(2) To beat. *Var. dial.*

(3) To do anything energetically.

TWIGGEN. Made of twigs.

TWIGGER. A wencher. Dido, p. 50. The term is applied to a sheep in Tusser, p. 93.

TWIGHT. (1) To twit; to reproach. The term occurs in Holinshed. Chron. Irel. p. 80.

(2) To twitch, or bind.

(3) Quickly?

> Mahoune and Margot he will forsak *twight*,
> For to be cristyned and forsak ther syne.
>   *Roland, MS. Lansd. 388, f. 384.*

(4) Pulled; snatched. (*A.-S.*)

> Bot amoong them all ryȝht,
> The quene was awey *twyȝht*,
> And with the feyry awey l-nome,
> The ne wyst wer sche was come!
>   *MS. Ashmole 61, xv. Cent.*
> Be the neck sche hym *twyȝhte*,
> And let hym hange all nyghte.
>   *MS. Cantab. Ff. ii. 38, f. 117.*

TWIGLE. (1) To wriggle. (2) Futuo.

TWIKIN. A word used in Yorkshire for two apples growing together.

TWIKLE. To walk awkwardly, as if with a twist in the legs. *Northumb.*

TWILADE. To load, unlade the load, then return for a second and take up the first load. This is done where the ground is broken or stickle. *Dorset.*

TWILL. (1) A quill; a reed. *North.*

(2) A spool to wind yarn upon.

(3) Until. *East.*

(4) A sort of coarse linen cloth.

TWILLY. To turn reversedly. *North.*

TWILT. (1) To beat. *East.*

(2) A quilt. *Var. dial.*

TWILY. Restless; wearisome. *West.*

TWIN. To divide into two parts. *Chesh.*

TWINDILLING. A twin.

TWINDLES. Twins. *Lanc.*

TWINE. (1) To entwine. *South.*

(2) To languish, or pine away. *North.*

(3) To whine, or cry. *Yorksh.*

TWINGE. (1) To afflict.

(2) An earwig. *North.*

(3) A sharp pain. *Var. dial.*

TWINK. (1) A chaffinch. *Somerset.*

(2) A moment of time; as, *in a twink*, for, in the twinkling of an eye.

TWINKLE. To tinkle.

TWINLINGES. Twin children.

> Of *twinlinges* hir thouȝte no gamen,
> That fauȝte ofte in hir wombe samen.
>   *Cursor Mundi, MS. Coll. Trin. Cantab. f. 22.*
> Se ȝe the ȝonder pore woman, how that she is pyned
> With *twynlynges* two, and that dare I my hedde wedde.
>   *Chevelere Assigne, 27.*

TWINNA. It will not. *West.*

TWINNE. To separate; to divide; to part; to depart from a place or thing.

> Thare the deth, that spares ryȝt none,
> Has *twynneds* two and hente that one.
>   *MS. Harl. 2260, f. 117.*
> That thi hous, he sendeth the word,
> Shal never *twynned* be fro sword.
>   *Cursor Mundi, MS. Coll. Trin. Cantab. f. 30.*

That never *twynneth* oute of thy presence,
But in heyven abydeth ay with the,
And in erthe mekely nowe with me.
Lydgate, MS. Ashmole 39, f. 53.

TWINNEN. To couple together. (*A.-S.*)

TWINNY. According to Forby, to rob a cask before it is broached. *East.*

TWINS. An agricultural instrument used for taking up weeds, &c. *West.*

TWINTE. A jot.

TWINTER. A beast *two winters* old.

TWINTLE. To hew, or chip. *Linc.*

TWIRE. To peep out; to pry about. Also, to twinkle, to glance, to gleam.

TWIRIN. A pair of pincers.

TWIRIPE. Imperfectly ripe. *West.*

TWIRTER. This word occurs in Grose, but seems to be an error for *twinter*, q. v.

TWISH. An interj. of contempt.

TWISSEL. A double fruit. Also, that part of a tree where the branches separate.

TWIST. (1) The fourchure. See Cotgrave.
(2) A twig. (*A.-S.*)
(3) A good appetite. *Var. dial.*
(4) To lop a tree.

TWISTE. To twitch; to pull hard. (*A.-S.*)

TWISTER. To twist, or turn. *Suffolk.*

TWISTLE. That part of a tree where the branches divide from the stock. *West.*

TWIT. (1) A fit of ill humour. *East.*
(2) The noise made by an owl.
(3) Anything entangled. *North.*
(4) An acute angle. Carr. ii. 223.
(5) *Twit com twat*, idle talk.
Heavens grant that thou wouldst speak, but bridle that,
I'me angry with thy tatling *twit com twat*.
Fletcher's Poems, p. 63.

TWITCH. (1) To tie tightly. *North.*
(2) To touch. *West.*
(3) An instrument used for holding a vicious horse. Still in use.

TWITCH-BALLOCK. The large black-beetle.

TWITCH-BELL. An earwig. *North.*

TWITCHE-BOX. The same as *Touch-box*, q. v.

TWITCHEL. (1) To castrate. *North.*
(2) A narrow passage, or alley. *North.*
(3) A childish old man. *Chesh.*
And when thou shalt grow *twychilde*, she will bee
Carefull and kinde (religiously) to thee.
Davies' Scourge of Folly, p. 218.

TWITCHER. A severe blow. *North.*

TWITCHERS. Small pincers.

TWITCH-GRASS. Couch grass. *Var. dial.*

TWITCHY. Uncertain. *East.*

TWITTEN. A narrow alley. *Sussex.*

TWITTER. (1) To tremble. *Var. dial.*
(2) A fit of laughter. *Kent.*
(3) To spin yarn or thread unevenly.
(4) The chirping of birds. *East.*
(5) The tether of cattle. *Lanc.*
(6) Uneasy. *Craven.*

TWITTER-BONE. An excrescence on a horse's hoof, owing to a contraction.

TWITTER-LIGHT. Twilight.

TWITTERS. Shreds; fragments. *North.*

TWITTLE. To tell tales; to prate.

TWITTLE-TWATTLE. Idle talk; tittle-tattle. It occurs in the True Conduct of Persons of Quality, 12mo. Lond. 1694, p. 61.

TWITTY. Cross; ill-tempered. *East.*

TWIVETE. A carpenter's tool.

TWIZZLE. To roll and twist. *Suffolk.*

TWNG. A tongue. Hampole MS.

TWO. Both. *Var. dial.*

TWO-BILL. A slat-axe, q. v. *Devon.*

TWO-BOWED-CHAIR. An armchair. *West.*

TWO-DOUBLE. Beat together; bowed in such a manner that the extremities almost meet.

TWO-FACED. Double-faced; insincere.

TWO-FURROWING. Double ploughing. *Norf.*

TWO-MEAL-CHEESE. Cheese made of equal quantities of skimmed and new milk. *Glouc.*

TWONNER. One or the other. *Linc.*

TWORE. To see. Dekker, 1620.

TWOTHREE. A large quantity. *West.*

TWYBITTLE. A very large mallet. *Herefordsh.* "Bipennis, *twybyte*"—*MS. Lansd.* 560, f. 45, co. Lanc.

TWYE. Twice. (*A.-S.*)
But folowe thow not the chylde *twye*,
Lest afterwarde hyt do the nuye.
MS. Cott. Claud. A. ii. f. 121.

TWYNNEN. Twined. *Gawayne.*

TWYVALLY. To bother, or puzzle. *Glouc.*

TYBURN-BLOSSOM. A young pickpocket.

TYBURN-CHECK. A rope.

TYBURN-TIPPET. A halter.

TYCEMENT. Enticement.
But thoghe no man have therof evyl,
3yt hyt ys the *tycement* of the devyl.
MS. Harl. 1701, f. 18.

TYD. (1) Gone. Qu. *ryd?*
The quene was greatly encouraged with the victory obtained late at Wakefeld, partly because the Duke of Yorke, her utter enemy, was *tyd* out of the worlde.
Hall, Henry VI. f. 190.
(2) A delicate morçeau. *Linc.*

TYE. (1) Tied.
Ther durste no man come hym nye,
There he stode yn hys rakke *tye*.
MS. Cantab. Ff. ii. 38, f. 107.
(2) A feather-bed. *Cornw.*
(3) An extensive common pasture.

TYKE. A sheep-tick. *West.*

TYMOR. A kind of bird.
The pellycan and the popyngay,
The *tymor* and the turtulie trewe.
MS. Cantab. Ff. ii. 38, f. 49.

TYPH-WHEAT. A kind of corn, like rye.

TYPOUN. Type; pattern. *Gawayne.*

TYRAN. A tyrant.

TYRE. A *tyre*, or as we spell it, tier or teer, of guns, is now used to signify a number of guns placed in a row, as along a ship's side. In the following passage it seems to mean the discharge of the whole row of battering ordnance. See the editor's note.
The pieces that lay upon St. Anthonie's steple were by them dismounted, and within six or seaven *tyre* after, the pieces on St. Nicholas steple were likewise cast downe. *Hayward's Qu. Eliz.*, p. 60.

TYTELET. Commencement ; chief. *Gawayne.*

TYTELID. Entitled.

> And in the boke of Elisabeth,
> That *tytelid* is of hir avisiouns.
> > *Lydgate, MS. Ashmole 39, f. 11.*

TYTER. A see-saw. *Devon*

TYTH. Quickly.

> And seyde, eteth an appel *tyth,*
> And beth as wyse as God Almyth.
> > *MS. Coll. Trin. Oxon. 57, art. 2.*

TYUP. The last basket sent out of a coal-pit at the end of the year. *North.*

U-BACK. A yule-block. *North.*

UBBERINE. To bear up ; to support.

UBBLY-BREDE. Sacramental cakes.

UBEROUS. Fruitful. (*Lat.*)

UCHE. Each ; every. (*A.-S.*)

> But bi the fruyte may men ofte se
> Of what vertu is *uche* a tre.
> > *Cursor Mundi, MS. Coll. Trin. Cantab. f. 1.*
> Owre *uche* dayes bred we the pray
> That thow ʒeve us thys same day.
> > *MS. Cott. Claud. A. ii. f. 132.*

UDE. Went. (*A.-S.*)

> As holé, as fayre, as hit upon urthe *ude.*
> > *Chron. Vilodun. p. 73.*

UFFLERS. Bargemen not in constant employ, who assist occasionally in towing. *East.*

UG. (1) A surfeit. *Northumb.*

(2) To feel a repugnance to. *North.* It has very nearly the same meaning as the old English verb *ugge,* to feel an abhorrence of, to be terrified.

> And thare was so mekille folke dede in that bataile that the sone wexe eclipte, and withdrewe his lighte, *uggande* for to see so mekille scheddynge of blude. *MS. Lincoln A. i. 17, f. 10.*
> For tha paynes ar so felle and harde,
> Als yhe sal here be redd eftyrwarde,
> That ilk man may *ugge* bothe yhowng and awlde,
> That heres thaime be rehersed and tawlde.
> > *Hampole, MS. Bowes, p. 189.*

UGHTENDITE. The morning.

UGLY. (1) Horrid ; frightful. (*A.-S.*) *Uglysome, ugsome,* horrible, frightful.

(2) An abuse ; a beating. *East.*

UINTMENT. Ointment.

ULEN-SPIEGEL. Owl-glass, pr. n. (*Germ.*)

ULLET. An owl. *Lanc.*

ULUTATION. A howling. (*Lat.*)

UM. Them. *South.*

UMAGE. Homage.

> Withouten abod wel swithe come,
> To don *umage* Arthour his sone.
> > *Arthour and Merlin, p. 127.*

UMBE-CLAPPE. To embrace. " Umbe-clappes the cors," MS. Morte Arthure, f. 72.

UMBE-GRIPPE. To seize hold of. " Umbegrippys a spere," MS. Morte Arthure, f. 92.

UMBE-LAPPE. To surround ; to wrap round.

> And he and his oste *umbylapped* alle thaire enemys, and daunge thame doune, and slewe thame like a moder sone. *MS. Lincoln A. i. 17, f. 5.*

UMBEN. About ; around. (*A.-S.*)

UMBER. (1) A sort of brown colour. Umber is a species of ochre. See Nares.

(2) The shade for the eyes placed immediately over the sight of a helmet, and sometimes attached to the vizor.

(3) Number. *Var. dial.*

(4) The grayling fish.

(5) Shade. *Chesh.* From the French. *Umbre* occurs in the Morte d'Arthur, i. 255.

UMBE-SET. To set around or about.

> The Sarasines him *umbe-set,*
> In hard shour togider thei met.
> > *Cursor Mundi, MS. Coll. Trin. Cantab. f. 49.*

UMBESTONDE. Formerly ; for a while.

UMBE-THINKE. To recollect. *North.*

> The thirde commandement es, *umbethynke* the that thow halowe thi halydaye.
> > *MS. Lincoln A. i. 17, f. 195.*
> The sevent was of clay, tille that entent that a mane that es raysed up to the dignyté of a kyng sulde alway *umbythynk* hym that he was made of erthe, and at the laste to the erthe he salle agayne.
> > *MS. Lincoln A. i. 17, f. 92.*
> Alexander thanne *umbithoghte* hym.one what wyse he myghte best come to for to destruy this citee.
> > *MS. Ibid. f. 5.*

UMBIGOON. Surrounded.

> Now have I shewed the a motley cote, a weddynge cote, a cote with golden hemmes, the whiche shuld be a maydens cote, *umbigoon* with diversitees of vertues. *MS. Bodl. 423, f. 186.*

UMBLES. The entrails of a deer.

UMBLESCE. Humility.

> It sit the welle to leve pride,
> And take *umblesce* upon thy side.
> > *Gower, MS. Soc. Antiq. 134, f. 60.*

UMBRAID. Strife ; contention.

UMBRANA. The umber, or grayling.

UMBRAS. To attain ?

> With schrifte of mouthe and penans smert,
> They wene theire blisse for to *umbras.*
> > *MS. Cantab. Ff. v. 48, f. 66.*

UMBREIDE. Upbraiding.

> Moises for this *umbreide*
> Was dredinge in his herte.
> > *Cursor Mundi, MS. Coll. Trin. Cantab. f. 36.*

UMBREL. (1) A lattice.

(2) The same as *Umber* (2). It is sometimes written *umbrere.* " Keste upe hys umbrere," MS. Morte Arthure, f. 63.

UMBREY. To censure ; to abuse.

UMBYLUKE. To look around.

> At the fyrste salle everylke gud Cristene mane *umbyluke* hyme, and ever be warre that he tyne noghte the schorte tyme, or wrange dispende it or in ydilnes late it overpasse.
> > *MS. Lincoln A. i. 17, f. 243.*

UMGANG. Round about. (*A.-S.*)

UMGIFE. To surround ; to encompass.

UMGRIPE. To seize ; to catch. (*A.-S.*)

UMLAPPE. To enfold ; to wrap around.

> Thai sal *umlappe* thaime alle abowte,
> And gnawe on ylk a lymme and sowke.
> > *Hampole, MS. Bowes, p. 203.*

UMSETTE. Surrounded ; beset.

> Thai sal be *umsette* so on ylk a syde,
> That thai may nowthyr flee, ne thaime hyde.
> > *Hampole, MS. Bowes, p. 181.*

UMSTRID. Astride. *North.*

UMSTRODE. Strided across.

> Oure swete Lorde fulle myldly
> Thk asse he *umstrode.*
> > *MS. Cantab. Ff. v. 48, f. 87.*

UMTHINES. Truth.

UMWHILE. Once; on a time; sometimes.

> Fallace ys, as who seye gyle,
> As many one aweryn *umwhyle. MS. Harl,* 1701, f. 19.
> *Umwhile* the childe sowkede hir pappe;
> *Umwhile* ganne thay kysse and clappe.
> > *MS. Lincoln A. 1. 1f, f. 101.*

UMWYLLES. Want of will; refusal. *Gaw.*

UM-YHODE. Went around. (*A.-S.*)

UN. (1) Him. (2) One. *Var. dial.*
(3) Used in composition for *in.*

UN-. In composition denotes privation or deterioration. For many words commencing with it, look under the simple forms.

UNAFFILED. Unadvised.

> No strenge of love bowe myyte
> His herte, whiche is *unaffiled.*
> > *Gower, MS. Soc. Antiq. 134, f. 53.*

UN-AVESY. Unadvised.

> I wille rathere, quod he, chese the sadnesse of an alde wyse manne, thane the *un-avesy* lightenesse of yonge menne. *MS. Lincoln A. 1. 17, f. 3.*

UNAWARES. Unaware. Still in use. It is a common metropolitan vulgarism.

UNBAIN. Inconvenient. *North.*

UNBARBED. Not trimmed; uncut.

UNBATED. Not blunted; sharp.

UNBAYNE. Disobedient. (*A.-S.*)

UNBEER. Impatient. *North.*

UNBEKNOWN. Unknown. *Var. dial.*

UNBELDE. Timid. (*A.-S.*)

UNBENE. Rugged; impassable. *Gawayne.*

UNBETHINK. To recollect. *North.* See *Umbe-thinks.* Also, to think beforehand.

UNBETIDE. To fail to happen.

UNBIDDABLE. Unadvisable. *North.*

UNBODIE. To leave the body. (*A.-S.*)

UNBOGHSOME. Disobedient. *Hampole.*

UNBOKEL. To unbuckle; to open.

UNBORELY. Weakly. (*A.-S.*)

UNBOUN. To undress. *North.*

UNBRACE. To attain?

> And with that worde, as sche dide *unbrace*
> To touche the cloth that hee lay in bounde,
> Withoute more, this Salomé hath founde
> Remedye, and was made hoolle ayen.
> > *Lydgate, MS. Soc. Antiq. 134, f. 11.*
> With schryfte of mouthe and penannce smerte,
> They were ther blys for to *unbrase.*
> > *MS. Cantab. Ff. ii. 38, f. 48.*

UNBRASE. To carve a mallard.

UNBRYCHE. Unprofitable. (*A.-S.*)

> But calleth hym yn the gospel ryche,
> As unkynde and *unbryche. MS. Harl.* 1701, f. 45.

UNBUXUM. Disobedient. (*A.-S.*)

> I usedde wronge with my body,
> And serves the *unbuxumly. MS. Harl.* 2260, f. 3.
> God put hym in odur lyknes,
> For hys grete unbuxumnes.
> > *MS. Cantab. Ff. ii. 38, f. 242.*

UNCANNY. Giddy; careless. *North.*

UNCE. (1) An ounce. (2) A claw.

UNCELY. The same as *Unsely,* q. v.

UNCERTEYNOUR. More uncertain.

> Is no thing certeynere then dede,
> Ny uncerteynour then his tide.
> > *Cursor Mundi, MS. Coll. Trin. Cantab. f. 141.*

UNCIVIL. Unacquainted with the language and manners of good society.

UNCLE. (1) Unclean.

> My lippis pollu.e, my mouth with synne foylid,
> Myn hert *uncle,* and full of cursednesse.
> > *Lydgate, MS. Ashmole 39, f. 27.*

(2) See *Aunt,* and Pegge's Gl. in v.

UNCO. Awkward; strange. *North.*

UNCOME. (1) Not come. *North.*
(2) An ulcerous swelling. This word is still used in some of the Northern counties. It occurs in Baret's Alvearie, 1580.

UNCOMMON. Very. *Var. dial.*

UNCONAND. Ignorant. (*A.-S.*)

> Bot som men has wytte to undyrstand,
> And yhit thai are fulle *unconand.*
> > *Hampole, MS. Bowes, p. 15.*

UNCONVENABLE. Inconvenient.

UNCORCED. Parted from the body.

UNCOTHS. News. *North.*

UNCOUPLE. To let or go loose.

> He *uncupplide* hys hundis
> Tille his rachis rebundys.
> > *MS. Lincoln A. 1. 17, f. 131.*

UNCOUS. Unkerd; melancholy. *Kent.*

UNCOUTH. (1) Unknown. (*A.-S.*)
(2) Uncommon; not vulgar; elegant.

UNCTURE. Greasing or oiling carts, &c.

UNCUSTOMED. (1) Smuggled. *North.*
(2) Out of use or practice.

UNDEDELY. Immortal. (*A.-S.*)

> Bot thou that arte so grete and so gloryous, and calles thiselfe *undedely,* thou salle wynne nathynge of me, if-alle thou hafe the overhande of me.
> > *MS. Lincoln A. 1. 17, f. 3.*

UNDEFOUTERE. Less devout.

UNDELICH. Manifestly. (*A.-S.*)

UNDELT. Undivided.

> Oon in Godhede *undelt* is he,
> And oon substaunce with persones thre.
> > *Cursor Mundi, MS. Coll. Trin. Cantab. f. 61.*

UNDENIABLE. Good. *Chesh.*

UNDER. (1) To subdue.
(2) An under-ground drain. *Linc.*

UNDER-ALL. In all; altogether.

UNDER-BACK. See *Under-deck.*

UNDERBEAR. To bear; to undergo.

UNDER-BRIG. An arch. *North.*

UNDER-BRIGHT. A bright light appearing under clouds when they are near the horizon. *North.*

UNDER-BUTTER. The butter which is made of the second skimmings of milk. *Suff.*

UNDERCORN. Short, weak, underling corn, overhung by the crop. *Norfolk.*

UNDERCREEPING. Mean; pitiful; in an underhand way. *Somerset.*

UNDERCUMFUN. To understand or discover a person's meaning. *Linc.* It is sometimes *undercumstand.*

UNDER-DECK. The low broad tub into which the wort runs from the mash-tub.

UNDER-DRAWING. Ceiling. *North.*

UNDER-FAVOUR. An old apologetic expression before saying anything rude.

UNDERFIND. To understand. *Derb.*

UNDERFOE. To perform, undertake.

UNDERFONG. Understood. *Havelok.*

UNDERFONGE. To undertake; to accept; to receive. Used by Spenser, to ensnare.

UNDER-FOOT. Low. To bid under-foot, i.e. to offer a low price for anything.

UNDERGA. To supplant. (*A.-S.*)

UNDERGETE. To understand. (*A.-S.*)

UNDERGROUNDS. Anemones. *Devon.*

UNDERGROWE. Of a low stature.

UNDER-GRUB. To undermine. *East.*

UNDERLAID. Trodden down. *Var. dial.*

UNDERLAY. (1) To incline from the perpendicular, said of a vein in a mine. *Derb.*

(2) To subject; to place under.

(3) To mend the sole of a shoe.

UNDERLINGE. An inferior.

> Hast thow envyet thyn *underlynge*,
> For he was gode and thryvynge.
> > *MS. Cott. Claud. A. ii. f. 141.*

> He was to alle men *undurlynge*,
> So lowe was never jyt no kynge.
> > *MS. Cantab. Ff. ii. 39, f. 241.*

UNDERLOUT. To be subject to.

UNDERLY. Poor; inferior.

UNDERMELE. The afternoon. *Chaucer.* Later writers use the term for an afternoon meal. " A middaies meale, an undermeale," Nomenclator, 1585, p. 81.

UNDERMINDING. Subornation.

UNDERMOST. The lowest. *North.*

UNDERN. Nine o'clock, a. m. (*A.-S.*)

> Bi this was *undren* of the day,
> The lijt bigan to hyde.
> > *Cursor Mundi, f. 103.*

UNDERNEAN. Beneath. *Var. dial.*

UNDERNOME. Took up; received.

> And thenne was seynt Jon in Herodes prisone,
> for he hadde *undernome* him of the fals devors, for
> that was his brothers wyf. *MS. Harl. 2398, f. 8.*

> And whan synne dothe vertu *undurnym* and myne,
> The light of grace will no lenggir shyne.
> > *MS. Laud. 416, f. 56.*

UNDER-ONE. On the same occasion.

UNDERPIGHT. Propped up. (*A.-S.*)

> And *undirpyjte* this mancyoun ryalle,
> With seven pileris, as made is memorye.
> > *Lydgate, MS. Soc. Antiq. 134, f. 3.*

UNDER-PINNING. The pediment of brick or stone on which the frame of a wooden house is placed.

UNDER-PROPPER. See *Supertasse.*

UNDERSET. To prop up. *Palsgrave.*

UNDER-SONG. The burden of a song.

UNDERSORT. The vulgar. *Yorksh.*

UNDERSPORE. To raise a thing by putting a spore or pole under it. (*A.-S.*)

UNDER-SPURLEATHER. An underling.

UNDERSTAND. To hear. *Yorksh.*

UNDERSTOD. Received. *Havelok.*

UNDERTAKE. To take in; to receive.

UNDER-THE-WIND. So situated behind a bank, house, &c. as not to feel the wind.

UNDERTIME. Evening. *Spenser.*

UNDERWROUGHT. Undermined. *Shak.*

UNDIGHT. Undressed; unprepared.

UNDIGOON. Undergone.

> Whenne Jhesus had bapteme *undigoon*,
> He lafte Jon stille bi fiom Jurdon.
> > *Cursor Mundi, MS. Coll. Trin. Cantab. f. 30.*

UNDIRSHONE. Pattens. (*A.-S.*)

UNDISPAYRID. Unimpaired.

> *Undispayrid* the heeste schalle not varye
> Of the prophecye, awhile thouj it tarye.
> > *Lydgate, MS. Soc. Antiq. 134, f. 16.*

UNDO. (1) To unfold. (*A.-S.*)

(2) To cut up game. *Gawayne.*

UNDOUBTOUS. Undoubted.

UNDREGHE. Without sorrow.

> In lufe thi hert thou heghe,
> And fyghte to felle the fende:
> Thi dayes salle be *undreghe*
> Whenne thi ded neghes neghe.
> > *MS. Lincoln A. i. 17, f. 222.*

UNDUBITATE. Undoubted. *Hall.*

UNDUR. Undern, q. v. It is spelt *undrone* in the MS. Lincoln A. i. 17, f. 135.

> The sonne schon, they had wondur,
> For hyt drewe to the *undur.*
> > *MS. Cantab. Ff. ii. 38, f. 117.*

> Hys strength shulld wex in suche a space
> From the *undyr-tyme* tylle none.
> > *MS. Harl. 2252, f. 120.*

UNDURTANE. Undertaken.

> For thy love y have *undurtane*
> Dedes of armys thre.
> > *MS. Cantab. Ff. ii. 38, f. 64.*

UNDURYEDE. Understood.

> The hors sone *undur-yede*
> That Befyse was not on hys rygge.
> > *MS. Cantab. Ff. ii. 38, f. 107.*

UNDYED. Dyed back again.

> Blakke into white may not be *undyed*,
> Ne blood infecte with corrupcioun.
> > *Lydgate, MS. Soc. Antiq. 134, f. 1.*

UNE. Even. *North.*

UNEATHILY. Unwieldy. *East.*

UNEAVE. To thaw. *Devon.*

UNEMENT. An ointment.

UNEMPT. To empty. *Heref.*

UNEQUAL. Unjust. *Jonson, iii. 233.*

UNERTE. Short.

UNESCHUABLE. Unavoidable.

UNESE. Uneasiness. (*A.-S.*)

UNEVEN. Unjust; unfair.

UNEXPRESSIVE. Inexpressible.

UNFACEABLE. Unreasonable. *East.*

UNFAINELY. Sorrowfully.

UNFAIRE. Ugly; frightful.

UNFAMOUS. Unknown.

UNFAWE. Not glad; displeased.

UNFEATHERED. Dispossessed.

UNFERE. Weak; feeble; indisposed.

> Therby lay mony *unfere.*
> > *Cursor Mundi, MS. Coll. Trin. Cantab. f. 85.*
> How he heled a mon *unfere*,
> That seke was eijte and twenty jere.
> > *Cursor Mundi, MS. Ibid. f. 2.*
> His fadir olde and *unfere*,
> Ofte he fedde with good dynere.
> > *Cursor Mundi, MS. Ibid. f. 22*

UNFEST. Weak; not firm.

UNFILED. Pure; undefiled.

UNFORBIDDEN. Disobedient. *North.*

UNFORTUNATE. In bad circumstances.

UNFREMED. Unkind. *North.*

UNGANG. Circuit?

> The whilke will noght come with me til heven bot
> thai dwell in the *ungang* of covaytise.
> 　　　　　*MS. Coll. Eton.* 10, f. 41.

VNGAYNE. (1) Inconvenience.

> There rynnes bysyde this heghe mountayne
> A water that turnes to mekille *ungayne,*
> 　　　　　*MS. Lincoln A. i.* 17, f. 142.

(2) Inconvenient; troublesome. *North.*

> Therof the pepul wold be fayne,
> Fore to cum home aȝayne,
> That hath goon gatis *ungayne.*
> 　　　　　*MS. Douce* 302, f. 2.

(3) Awkward; clumsy. *Var. dial.*

UNGEAR. To unharness. *North.*

UNGLAD. Sorry. (*A.-S.*)

> If thou my sone hast joye had.
> Whan thou another syȝe *unglad.*
> 　　　　　*Gower, MS. Soc. Antiq.* 134, f. 62.

UNGODE. Bad; evil.

UNGODLY. Squeamish; nice. *North.*

UNGONE. Not gone. *North.*

UNGRACIOUS. Unfortunate.

UNGRATHLY. Improperly; unbecomingly.

UNGREABLE. Disagreeable.

UNGUNDE. Ungrateful.

> Wit this betel be the smieth,
> And alle the worle thit wite,
> That theut the *ungunde* alle this thing,
> And goht himselve a beggyng.
> 　　　　　*MS. Bib. Reg.* 7 E. iv. f. 45.

UNHAP. Misfortune.

UNHAPPILY. Censoriously.

UNHAPPY. Mischievous; unlucky.

UNHARDELED. Dispersed. *Gawayne.*

UNHARDY. Not bold. (*A.-N.*)

UNHECKLED. Untidy; disordered.

UNHELE. (1) To uncover. See *Hele.*

(2) Misfortune. (*A.-S.*)

UNHENDE. Ungentle.

> To Sir Gawayne than sayd the kynge,
> Forsothe dethe was to *unhende.*
> 　　　　　*MS. Harl.* 2252, f. 100.

UNHEPPEN. Clumsy. *North.*

UNHERTY. Timid; cowardly.

UNHIDE. To discover.

UNHOMED. Awkward; unlikely. *Cumb.*

UNHONEST. Dishonorable. *North.*

UNION. A fine pearl. (*Lat.*)

UNITE. A gold coin worth about twenty shillings. See Snelling's Coins, p. 24.

UNJOINE. To separate; to disjoin.

UNJOINT. To carve a curlew.

UNKARD. (1) Lonely; dreary; solitary. Few provincial words are more common than this. It is derived from the A.-S. un-cwyd, quiet, solitary.

(2) Old; ugly; awkward; strange; unusual; particular; inconvenient; froward. *Var. dial.*

UNKEK. Unopened.

UNKEMBED. Uncombed.

UNKENDE. Unnatural.

> It wastes the body and forduse
> Th rue *unkende* outrage use.
> 　　　　　*MS. Harl.* 2260, f. 141.

UNKENT. Unkenned; unknown.

UNKER. Of you. (*A.-S.*)

UNKETH. Uncouth; strange.

UNKEVELEDEN. Uncovered.

UNKIND. Lonely. *North.*

UNKINDE. Unnatural. (*A.-S.*)

UNKIT. Uncut. MS. Douce 302, f. 2.

UNKNOWABLE. Incapable of being known.

UNKNOWING. Unknown. *North.*

UNKNOWN. An unknown man, one who does good secretly. *North.*

UNKUD. Unknown.

> Thou shalt have ever thi heed hud,
> Thi shame shal not be *unkud.*
> 　　　　　*Cursor Mundi, MS. Coll. Trin. Cantab.* f. 6.

UNKUNNYNGE. Ignorance.

> I am rude to reherse all
> For *unkunnynge* and for lacke of space.
> 　　　　　*Lydgate, MS. Ashm.* 39, f. 19.

UNKYNDESCHIPE. Unkindness.

> As he whiche thorow *unkyndeschipe*
> Envieth every felawschipe.
> 　　　　　*Gower, MS. Soc. Antiq.* 134, f. 81.

UNLACE. (1) To cut up. *Gawayne.*

(2) To unfasten; to unclothe. *Ib.*

UNLAWE. Injustice. (*A.-S.*)

> Cayphas herde that ilke sawe,
> He spake to Jhesu with *un-lawe.*
> 　　　　　*MS. Cantab.* Ff. v. 48, f. 18.

UNLEED. A general name for any crawling, venomous creature, as a toad, &c. It is sometimes ascribed to man, and then it denotes a sly, wicked fellow, that, in a manner, creeps to do mischief, the very pest of society.

UNLEFE. Unbeloved; loathsome.

UNLEK. Unlocked; opened.

UNLETTED. Undisturbed.

UNLICKED. Unpolished. *Var. dial.*

UNLIFTY. Unwieldy. *Devon.*

UNLIGHT. To alight. *West.*

UNLOVEN. To cease loving.

UNLUST. (1) Dislike. (2) Idleness.

UNMACKLY. Misshapen. *North.*

UNMANHODE. Cowardice.

UNMANNED. Untamed. *Shak.*

UNMATCHED. Unequally matched.

UN-MAYTE. Immense.

> Goddes grace thare he es wille noghte be *un-mayte,*
> bot ever he es wyrrkande, and he es waxeand ay
> mare and mare to mekille the mede.
> 　　　　　*MS. Lincoln A. i.* 17, f. 243.

UNMEK. Wicked. (*A.-S.*)

UNMERCIFULLY. Very. *West.*

UNMESTE.

> Heyngere of men prayse v leste,
> For that office es moste *unmeste.*
> 　　　　　*MS. Harl.* 2260, f. 59.

UNMIGHTY. Unable. *Chaucer.*

UNMYLDE. Fierce.

> Ordeyned hath by grete cruelté
> This ram to kepe boles ful *unmylde,*
> With brasen feete, ramegeous and wilde.
> 　　　　　*MS. Digby* 230.

UNNAIT. Useless; vain; unprofitable.

UNNE. To give, consent, wish well to.

UNNEATH. Beneath. *Somerset.*

UNNES. *Unnethe,* scarcely.

UNNETHE. Scarcely. (*A.-S.*)

How schulde thenne a dro[n]ken mon
Do that the sobere *unnethe* con.
MS. Cott. Claud. A. ii. f. 135.

Alle the processe in that day,
That alle this world speke of may,
Shal than so shortly ben y-do,
A moment shal *unnethe* therto.
MS. Addit. 11305, f. 91.

UNNOCK. To shoot an arrow.

UNNOTEFUL. Unprofitable.

UNNOYEAND. Agreeable.

The *unnoyeand* to sustayne us and fede,
And to helpe us and ese us in owre nede.
MS. Lincoln A. i. 17, f. 189.

UNORDAYNDE. Inordinate.

The delyte that has noghte of *unordaynde* styrrynge, and mekely has styrrynge in Criste.
MS. Lincoln A. i. 17, f. 196.

Wharefore a man that weded es,
Schulde kepe hym ay in clennes,
And no dede *unordaynly* to wyrke,
Agayn the sacrament of holy kyrke.
MS. Harl. 2260, f. 91.

UNOURNE. Old; worn out. (*A.-S.*)

Now age *unourne* putteth awey favoure,
That floury jougthe in his seson conquerid.
Occleve, MS. Soc. Antiq. 134, f. 255.

UNPATIENTNESS. Impatience.

UNPEES. Disquiet.

Thei forsoke this worldes ese,
To mon wrougte thei never *unpees.*
Cursor Mundi, MS. Coll. Trin. Cantab. f. 83.

UNPEREGAL. Unequal.

UNPERFECT. Imperfect. *North.*

UNPINNE. To unbolt. (*A.-S.*)

UNPITOUS. Cruel; not piteous.

UNPLAYNE. Obscure.

For who that is to trouthe *unplayne,*
He may not faylen of venjaunce.
Gower, MS. Soc. Antiq. 134, f. 45.

UNPLEASED. Unpaid.

UNPLITE. To unfold. *Chaucer.*

UNPLUNGE. Unexpectedly. *Linc.*

UNPLYE. Open; unfolded.

UNPOSSIBLE. Impossible. *North.*

So mighty is he evere moo,
Unpossible is not him to do.
MS. Addit. 11305, f. 92.

UNPOWER. Helplessness. *Dorset.*

UNPROPER. Not confined to one.

UNPROPICE. Unpropitious.

UNQUEMEFULLY. Unpleasantly.

Unquemefully thenne shul thei quake,
That al the erthe shal to-shake.
Cursor Mundi, MS. Coll. Trin. Cantab. f. 134.

UNQUERT. Uneasiness.

He herde her menyng and *unquert,*
And shope therfore in litil stert.
Cursor Mundi, MS. Coll. Trin. Cantab. f. 36.

UN-QUEYNTE. Unquenched.

I lycken the worlde to fyre *un-queynte.*
MS. Cantab. Ff. ii. 38, f. 26.

UNRAD. Bold; imprudent.

UNRAKE. Not stirred.

Eke as charbokylle casteth ryght bemys,
With rody lighte, as cole that is *unrake.*
MS. Cantab. Ff. i. 6, f. 12.

UNRAY. To undress. *West.*

UNREADY. Undressed.

UNREAVE. To unravel. *Spenser.*

UNRECLAIMED. Wild, as a hawk.

UNRECURING. Incurable.

UNREDE. Imprudent. (*A.-S.*)

UNREDUCT. Unreduced.

UNRESONABLE. Irrational.

Go out of the schip, thou, and thi wiif, thi sones,
and the wyves of thi sones with thee, and lede out
with thee alle livynge beestis that be at the of ech
fleish, as wel in volatils as in *unresonable* bestis.
Wickliffe, MS. Bodl. 277.

UNRESPECTIVE. Inconsiderate.

UNREST. Want of rest; uneasiness; trouble;
vexation. (*A.-S.*)

UNRID. Dirty; disorderly. *North.*

UNRIDE. Harsh; severe; large. (*A.-S.*)

And toke hys burdon yn hys honde,
Of stele that was *unryde.*
MS. Cantab. Ff. ii. 38, f. 88.

They hym assayled on every syde,
And he gave them strokys *unryde.*
MS. Cantab. Ff. ii. 38, f. 171

An iryne clube he gane hyme taa,
Was mekille and *unryde.*
MS. Lincoln A. i. 17, f. 140.

UNRIGHTE. Wrong. (*A.-S.*)

Mekille maugre hase he
That chalanges *unrighte.*
MS. Lincoln A. i. 17, f. 132.

UNRO. Vexation; trouble.

If he bigon to harpe and syng,
Of his *unro* he had restyng.
Cursor Mundi, MS. Coll. Trin. Cantab. f. 47.

UNRUDE. Civil; polished.

UNSAD. Unsteady.

UNSAUGHTE. At strife.

UNSAWNEY. Unfortunate. *Yorksh.*

UNSCAPE. To put one in mind of something
disagreeable in discoursing.

UNSCHEPELICHE. Unshapely; ugly.

UNSCIENCE. Not-science. *Tyrwhitt.*

UNSCRIFF. To put in mind of. *North.*

UNSEKE. Not sick; healthy.

UNSELE. Unhappiness. (*A.-S.*)

Lord, he selde, now se I wele,
My synne hath set me in *unsele.*
Cursor Mundi, MS. Coll. Trin. Cantab. f. 8.

Ʒa, he said, that saughe I wele;
How myghte that make so myche *unsele.*
MS. Lincoln A. i. 17, f. 123.

UNSELY. Unhappy.

Whereof the world ensample fette,
May aftir this, whanne I am goo.
Of thilke *unsely* jolyf woo.
Gower, MS. Soc. Antiq. 134, f. 38.

Galathin mett king Samgran,
An *unsely* hoge man.
Arthour and Merlin, p. 182.

Unsely ghost, hwat dostu here?
Thu were in helle mine vere.
MS. Coll. Jes. Oxon. I. 29.

UNSENE. Invisible. Hall, Henry VI. f. 63,
uses it for not previously seen.

So the soule, withouten wene,
To alle thinge hit is *unsene.*
Cursor Mundi, MS. Coll. Trin. Cantab. f. 4.

UNSENSED. Stunned; insensible. *East.*

UNSET. Not appointed. See *Steven.*

UNSETE. Unsuitable.

UNSEWYR. Insecure; unsafe.

Ful *unsewyr* atte the laste may he be,
To sette hys herte in swych abundaunce.
MS. Cantab. Ff. i. 6, f. 136.

UNSHAKEN. Perfect; in good order.
UNSHENE. Dark; not bright.
UNSHETTE. Opened.
UNSHOTE. To open a door, &c.
UNSIDED. In confusion. *North.*
UNSIGHT. Unseen. *Ritson.*
UNSITTINGE. Unsuitable.
UNSKERE. To unfold; to discover.
UNSKYLWYS. Irrational.

Bot lyfes als ane *unskylwys* best.
MS. Harl. 4196, f. 216.

UNSLEKKED. Unslacked.
UNSLEPT. Having had no sleep.
UNSLẞƷE. Unskilful; not sly.

Greet he was and also heȝe,
He semed Sathanas *unsleȝe.*
Cursor Mundi, MS. Coll. Trin. Cantab. f. 47.
A, Lord God ! that I was *unslye ;*
Alasse ! that ever he come so nye.
MS. Cantab. Ff. v. 48, f. 55.

UNSNECK. To unlatch a door. *North.*
UNSOAPED. Low; dirty. *Var. dial.*
UNSOFT. Hard. *Chaucer.*
UNSOGHT. Disturbed; disordered.
UNSOLEMPNE. Uncelebrated.
UNSOUTERLY. Unhandy. *Devon.*
UNSPARELY. Unsparingly. *Gawayne.*
UNSPERE. To unbolt. Lydgate, p. 54.
UNSPOILE. To despoil; to undress.
UNSTANCHEABLE. Inexhaustible.
UNSTANCHED. Unsatisfied.
UNSTEKE. Unfastened; not bolted.
UNSTIL. In motion. *Suffolk.*
UNSTRIKE. To draw the strings of a hawk's
hood, to be in readiness to pull off.
UNSTRONGE. Weak. (*A.-S.*)
UNSUITY. Irregular. *West.*
UNSUMED. Said of the feathers of a hawk,
when not fully grown.
UNSWADE. To take off swaddling-clothes.
UNSWARE. To answer.

Belevest thow on Fader, and Sone, and Holy Gost,
As thou art bolden, wel thow wost,
Thre persons in Trynyté,
And on God ? *Unsware* thow me.
MS. Cott. Claud. A. ii. f. 137.

UNSWEAR. To perjure. *Drayton.*
UNSWELL. To fall after swelling.
UNTALDE. Not reckoned. (*A.-S.*)
UNTANG. To untie. *Somerset.*
UNTEREST. Uttermost.
UNTERMED. Interminable.
UNTEYDE. Unabated.

In alle that·ever ȝe have seyde,
My sorow is evermore *unteyde.*
Gower, MS. Soc. Antiq. 134, f. 125.

UNTHANK. No thanks; ill-will.
UNTHAW. To thaw. *South.*
UNTHENDE. Outcast; abject.

The worldys wylys ryȝt nouȝt me payes,
For they ben false and full *unthende.*
MS. Cantab. Ff. ii. 38, f. 23.

UNTHEWID. Unmannerly.

What is to ben of pride *unthewid*
Aȝen the hyȝe Goddis lawe.
Gower, MS. Soc. Antiq. 134, f. 32.

UNTHRIFT. Prodigality.
UNTHRIVE. To be unsuccessful.

His wif made him to *unthrive.*
Cursor Mundi, MS. Coll. Trin. Cantab. f. 59.

UNTID. (1) Unseasonable. (*A.-S.*)
(2) Anointed. MS. Vocab.
UNTIDY. Dirty; slovenly; ignorant.
UNTIL. To; unto. (*A.-S.*)
UNTIME. An unseasonable time.
UNTO. Until. (*A.-S.*)
UNTOWARD. Wild; fierce.
UNTRIMMED. Being a virgin. See a note
in Dilke's Old Plays, iv. 95.
UNTRISTE. To mistrust.
UNUSAGE. Want of usage.
UNVALUED. Invaluable.
UNVAMPED. Fresh; genuine.
UNVOYANDNES.

His rightwisnes es in gude dedes and his *unvoyandnes* es that he es withouten ille.
MS. Coll. Eton. 10, f. 11.

UNWAGED. Without wages or salary.
UNWARELY. Unawares; unforeseen.

And *unwarely* affore hym on the playne
Apperid an aungell with face sterne and bright.
Lydgate, MS. Ashmole 39, f. 51.

UNWARNEDD. Without intimation.

The kyng hymselfe wolde ofte tyme come too
mete *unwarnedd,* and sytt downe, for love that he
had to Seynt Thomas.
MS. Cantab. Ff. ii. 38, f. 11.

UNWARY. Unexpected. *Spenser.*
UNWELDE. Unwieldy.

Thou shal him saye I am *unwelde*
For longe lyved am I in elde.
Cursor Mundi, MS. Coll. Trin. Cantab. f. 8.
A clobb of yron in honde hathe tan,
That was mekylle and fulle *unwelde.*
MS. Cantab. Ff. ii. 38, f. 64.

UNWEMMED. Spotless. (*A.-S.*)
UNWERNISHIT. Unexpectedly.
UNWETING. Not knowing. (*A.-S.*)
UNWEVID. Unfinished; imperfect.
UNWEXE. To decrease.
UNWINE. Want of joy. (*A.-S.*)
UNWINLY. Unjoyously. (*A.-S.*)

I sold hym *unwynly* wake
Or to morne day. MS. Lincoln A. i. 17, f. 132.

UNWISDOME. Folly. (*A.-S.*)
UNWIST. Unknown.
UNWIT. Want of wit or knowledge. *Unwit-
andnesse,* ignorance. (*A.-S.*)
UNWITONDE. Not knowing it.

And Jhesu aftir stilly stale,
Joseph and Mary *unwitonde.*
Cursor Mundi, MS. Coll. Trin. Cantab. f. 78.

UNWITTILY. Unwisely. (*A.-S.*)
UNWRAIN. To uncover; to unfold.
UNWRASTE. Wicked; base; weak.

And hys servauntes that were *unwraste,*
Fette forthe the chylde yn haste.
MS. Cantab. Ff. ii. 38, f. 140

UNWRITHLY. Unworthily.

Unwrythly art thou made gentyl,
Ȝyf thou yn wurdys and dedys be yl.
MS. Harl. 1701, f. 90.

UNWRY. Uncovered. (*A.-S.*)

> Whanne uvery racke and every cloudy skye
> Is voyde clene, so hire face uncouthe
> Schalle schewe in open and fully be *unwry*.
> *Lydgate, MS. Soc. Antiq.* 134, f. 9.

UNYED. United.

> Bowe, I beseche the, thyn heven, and come down
> to me, soo that I be knyt and *unyed* to the, and be
> made one spirite wyth the.
> *Caxton's Divers Fruytful Ghostly Maters.*

UNƷON. An onion. Nominale MS.

UON. To run. *Somerset.*

UP. (1) Upon. (*A.-S.*)

(2) To rise; to get up. *West.*

UP-A-DAISA. An expression used when dancing a child up and down.

UP-ALONG. Down along. *South.*

UPAZET. In perfection. *Exmoor.*

UP-BLOCK. A horse-block. *Glouc.*

UPBRAID. The same as *Abraid*, q. v.

UPBRAYDE. An up-stroke?

> Hys swyrde brake with the *upbrayde*,
> And therwith was Gye dysmayed.
> *MS. Cantab.* Ff. ii. 38, f. 213.

UPCAST. To reprove. *North.*

UPE. Upon. (*A.-S.*)

UPBHOVEN. Upraised. (*A.-S.*)

UPELONDERS. Country people. This word occurs in MS. Arundel. 42.

UP-FOND. To raise with effort.

UPHAF. Heaved up. (*A.-S.*)

UPHALE. To draw or pull up.

UPHAND-SLEDGE. A large iron hammer lifted up with both hands.

UPHEADED. (1) Having the horns nearly straight. (2) Ill-tempered. *North.*

UPHEPE. To heap up.

UPHEVE. To raise; to exalt.

UPHOLD. To warrant; to vouch for. *North.*

UPLAND. High land. *North.* The term occurs in Brathwait's Law of Drinking, p. 147.

UPLANDISH. Countryfied. (*A.-S.*)

UPLIFTE. Lifted up.

UP-MET. Having full measure. *North.*

UP-ON-END. Perpendicular.

UPPARD. Upwards. *Hearne.*

UPPEN. To mention; to disclose. *East.*

UPPEREST. Highest.

UPPER-HAND. To apprehend. *East.*

UPPER-HATCH. To understand. *Norf.*

UPPERLET. A shoulder-knot. *East.*

UPPER-STOCKS. Breeches.

UPPER-STORY. The head. *Var. dial.*

UPPING. Point; crisis. *North.*

UPPING-BLOCK. A horse-block. *Var. dial.*

UPPINGS. Perquisites. *Somerset.*

UPPING-STOCK. See *Upping-block.*

UPPISH. Proud; insolent. *Var. dial.*

UPRAPE. To start up.

UPRIGHT. (1) Entirely. *East.*

(2) Straight. This term was applied to persons lying down, as well as standing.

UPRIGHT-MAN. The chief of a crew of beggars. See Grose in v.

UPRISE. To church women. *Cornw.*

UPRISTE. The Resurrection.

> Jhesus seide, I am *upriste* and lif.
> *Cursor Mundi, MS. Coll. Trin. Cantab.* f. 88

UPROAR. Confusion; disorder. *West.*

UPSE-DUTCH. A heavy kind of Dutch beer, formerly much used in England. *Upse-freese*, a similar drink imported from Friesland. *Upse-English*, a strong ale made in England in imitation of these. To be *upse-Dutch*, to be tipsy, or stupified. To drink *upse-Dutch*, to drink swinishly, like a Dutchman. See Ben Jonson, iv. 150.

> Tom is no more like thee then chalks like cheese,
> To pledge a health or to drinke *up-se freese*.
> *Letting of Humours Blood in the Head-Vaine,* 1600.

UPSET. (1) A cross; an obstruction.

(2) A smith's term, when the iron at heat is driven back into the body of the work.

UPSETTING. (1) A christening. *Exmoor.* In the North, the first party after an accouchement.

(2) *Upsetting and down-throssan*, hereabouts.

(3) A disagreement; a quarrel. *South.*

UPSHOT. Result; issue. *Var. dial.*

UPSIDES. To be upsides with any one, i. e. to be even with, or a match for him.

UPSIGHTED. A defect in vision, produced by a contraction of the lower portion of the iris, thus depriving a person of the power of readily seeing objects below the level of his eyes. *Somerset.*

UPSODOUN. Upside down.

> And I kan, by collusyoun,
> Turne alle estates *up-so-doun*,
> And sette, though ffolke hadde it sworne,
> That is bakward to go by fforne.
> *MS. Cotton. Tiber.* A. vii. f. 66.
>
> Thus es this worlde torned *up-se-doun*s,
> Tyll many mans dampnacyowne.
> *Hampole, MS. Bowes,* p. 54.

UPSPRING. An upstart.

UPSTANDS. Marks for boundaries of parishes, estates, &c., being live trees or bushes cut off about breast high. *Kent.*

UPSTARING. Somewhat presuming. *Suff.*

UPSTARTS. Puddles made by the hoofs of horses in clayey ground. *East.*

UPSTIR. Disturbance. *Somerset.*

UPSTODE. Stood up. (*A.-S.*)

UPSTROKE. Conclusion. *North.*

UPTACK. (1) To understand. *North.*

(2) A person not to be equalled.

UPTAILS-ALL. Riotous confusion.

UP-TO. Equal to; upon. *Var. dial.*

UPWARD. Top, or height.

UP-WENDE. Went up.

UP-WITH. Up to or equal with.

URCHIN. (1) A hedgehog. *Var. dial.* "Urchone, a beest, *herysson*," Palsgrave.

(2) The key of the ash tree.

(3) A fairy, or spirit.

URE. (1) An hour. MS. Cott. Vesp. D. iii.

(2) An ewer, or washing-basin.

(3) Fortune; destiny. (*A.-N.*)

(4) Use. Also, to use.

(5) An udder. *North.*

(6)

Now late hire come, and liche as God ȝow ȝre,
For ȝow disposeth taketh ȝowre aventure.
Lydgate, MS. Soc. Antiq. 134, f. 7.

URED. Fortunate.

URGE. To retch. *West.*

URGEFUL. Urgent; importunate.

URINCH-MILK. Whey.

URINE. (1) A net made of fine thread, formerly used for catching hawks.

(2) Mingere. MS. Vocab.

URIST. Sunrise.

Veisith his lyȝte whanne it begynneth dawe,
At the *urist* in the morownynge.
Lydgate, MS. Soc. Antiq. 134, f. 18.

URITH. The bindings of a hedge.

URLED. (1) Starved with cold. *North.*

(2) Stunted. *Urling,* a dwarf. *North.*

URLES. Tares.

URNE. To run; to flow.

URRY. The blue clay which is often found immediately above a strata of coal.

URRYSONES. Orisons.

URTHE. Earth.

Alle thynge made wyth on spelle,
Hevene, and *urthe*, and eke helle.
MS. Cott. Claud. A. ii. f. 133.

US. We; our. *Var. dial.*

USAGE. Experience; practice.

USANT. Using; accustomed. (*A.-N.*)

USAUNCE. Usage; practice.

Brouȝte to the temple to his oblacioun,
As was the lawe, custum, and *usaunce*.
Lydgate, MS. Soc. Antiq. 134, f. 29.

And so bifelle upon a day,
As thilke tyme was *usance*.
Gower, MS. Soc. Antiq. 134, f. 51.

USCHEW. Issue, the right of a road out of a wood. *Finchale Ch.*

USE. (1) Usury; interest. *Var. dial.*

O tis a thing more than ridiculous,
To take a man's full sum, and not pay *use*.
Fletcher's Poems, p. 68.

(2) To haunt; to frequent.

USER. A profitable animal.

USERE. An usurer.

Al hys lyf, soth to say,
He wurthe to an *usere*. *MS. Harl. 2320, f. 36.*

USES. Practical inferences derived from doctrine, a term used by Puritans.

USTILMENT. Furniture; utensils.

UT. Out. Still in use.

UTAS. The eighth day, or the space of eight days, after any festival. "Utas of a feast, *octaves*," Palsgrave.

UTCHY. I. *Somerset.*

UTEN. Without; foreign. (*A.-S.*)

UTHAGE. The chaffinch. The whinchat is so termed in Shropshire.

UTRAGE. Excess. (*A.-N.*)

To bringe into that heritage
That I have lost bi myn *utrage*.
Cursor Mundi, MS. Coll. Trin. Cantab. f. 6.

UTTER. Outward; more out. *Utter-barristers*, lawyers who pleaded without the bar.

UTTERANCE. Extremity. (*A.-N.*)

UTTERESTE. Uttermost.

Telle me, ser, what thay are that base thus farene
with the, and I sewre the, als I am trew mane, I
salle venge the to the *uttereste*.
MS. Lincoln A. i. 17, f. 29.

UTTERLY. Thoroughly; entirely.

Thorowe the londe *utturly*
He dud grete chevalry.
MS. Cantab. Ff. ii. 38, f. 153.

UTTREN. To publish; to give out; to sell.

UVELE. Evil. Beket, p. 20.

UVVER. Upper; over. *North.*

UZZARD. The letter Z. *Lanc.*

UZZLE. A blackbird. *Yorksh.*

VACABONDE. A vagabond.

VACAT. Anything missing. (*Lat.*)

VACCARY. A cow-pasture. *Lanc.*

VACCHE. To fetch.

VACHERY. A dairy. *Pr. Parv.*

VADE. To fade.

All as a slope, and like the grasse,
Whose bewty sone doth *vade*. *MS. Ashmole 802.*

VADY. Damp; musty. *Devon.*

VAG. (1) To thump. *West.*

(2) Turf for fuel. *Devon.*

VAGABOND. To wander.

VAGACIONE. Wandering.

Whenne the mynde es stablede sadely withowttene changynge and *vagacyone* in Godd and gastely
thynges. *MS. Lincoln A. i. 17, f. 220.*

VAGAUNT. Vagrant; wanderer. *Baber.*

VAGE. To stroll; to wander about. Also a substantive, a voyage, a journey.

VAIL. (1) Progress. *South.*

(2) To lower; to let fall. (*Fr.*) It was used as a mark of submission or inferiority, to lower the sails of a ship, &c.

(3) Empty. *Somerset.*

VAILE. To avail.

Whate *vayleth* bewté which ys nat mercyabllle?
Whate *vayleth* a sterre when hit do nat schyne?
MS. Cantab. Ff. i. 6, f. 138.

VAILS. Gifts to servants.

VAIR. Truly. (*A.-N.*)

VAIRE. A kind of fur, supposed to be that of a species of weasel still so called.

And sythene to bedd he es broghte als it ware a
prynce, and happed with ryche robes appone hyme
ynewe, wele furrede with *vayre* and with gryse.
MS. Lincoln A. i. 17, f. 242.

VALE. Many. *Hearne.*

VALENCE. (1) To ornament with drapery. Shakespeare, in Hamlet, ii. 2, uses the word allegorically, applied to a face being *valenced* or fringed with a beard.

After folowed his three aydes, every of them
under a pavilion of crymosyn damaske, and purple
poudred with H. and K. of fyne golde, *valenced* and
frynged with golde of damaske.
Hall, Henry VIII. f. 12.

(2) Valencia in Spain.

VALENCY. Valiancy.

VALENTIA. The tin machine used for lifting beer, wine, &c., out at the bunghole of a cask, by pressing the thumb on the small hole at top. *Moor.*

VALENTINE. The custom of the different sexes choosing themselves mates on St. Valentine's Day, February 14th, the names being selected either by lots, or methods of divination, is of great antiquity in England. The name so drawn was the *valentine* of the drawer.

> Thow it be ale other wyn,
> Godys bleascyng have he and myn,
> My none gentyl *Valentyn*,
> Good Tomas the frere. *MS. Harl.* 1735, f. 48.

VALERIE. Valerius Maximus.

VALEW. Value. *Spenser.*

VALIANCE. Valour. *Spenser.*

VALIANT. Worth. Middleton, ii. 8.

VALIDITY. Value. *Shak.*

VALIDOM. Value; extent. *North.*

VALL. *To vall over the desk*, to have the banns of matrimony thrice called. *Exmoor.*

VALLEY. (1) To rock.

(2) A small hollow, or channel.

VALLIMENT. Value. *Staff.*

VALLIONS. The valance of a bed.

VALLOED. Laid in fallow.

VALLOR. A fallow. In Sussex this name is given to a large wooden dish used in dairies.

VALLOW. A press for cheese.

VALOR. Value; extent. *Becon.*

VALOUR. To esteem. *East.*

VALUATION. Quantity. *Var. dial.*

VALURE. Value; worth. (*Fr.*)

VAMBRACE. Armour for the front of the arm. See Hall, Henry IV. f. 12.

VAMP. To patch up.

VAMPER. To vapour; to swagger.

VAMPLATE. A round plate of iron fixed at the end of a tilting lance to guard the hand.

VAMPLETS. Rude gaiters to defend the legs from wet. *Wilts.*

VAMPY. The bottoms of hose, or gaiters attached to the hose, covering the foot. Grose has *vampers*, stockings. " *Pedana*, vampethe," Nominale MS.

VAMURE. The same as *Avantmure*, q. v.

VANCE-ROOF. The garret. *Norf.*

VANG. To receive; to earn; to catch; to throw. Ray says, " to answer for at the font as godfather; he *vang'd* to me at the vant."

VANISCHED. Made vain.

VANISTE. Vanished.

> And es *vanyste* to heven an hey,
> Thorue holy thou3t with gostely ey.
> *MS. Harl.* 2260, f. 18.

VANITY. Dizziness?

> For *vanité* of the hede a gude medsyn. Take the Juce of walworte, salt, hony, wex, ensence, and boyle them togyder over the fyre, and therwythe anoynt thine hede and thy templys.
> *MS. Sloane* 7, f. 79.

VANT. (1) A font. *Somerset.*

(2) The van of an army.

VANTAGE. (1) Advantage; benefit.

(2) Surplus; excess; addition.

VANTBRACE. Same as *Vambrace*, q. v.

VANT-CURRIER. Advanced guard. (*Fr.*)

VANTE. A winter trap for birds, made of willow, &c. *Somerset.*

VANTERIE. Boasting. *Daniel.*

VAPOUR. To bully; to swagger.

VAPOURED. Inclined to yawn. *East.*

VARA. Very. *Somerset.*

VARDAS. Talk; speech. *Yorksh.*

VARDET. A verdict. Still in use.

VARDLE. A common eye or thimble of a gate with a spike only. *Norf.*

VARDYKE. Verdict; judgment. *North.*

VARIAUNT. Changeable. (*A.-N.*)

VARIEN. To change; to alter. (*A.-N.*)

VARIETY. A rarity. *Chesh.*

VARLET. (1) The knave at cards.

(2) A servant. The serjeant-at-mace to the city counters was also so called.

VARMENT. Vermin. *North.*

VARMER. A large hawk. *I. of Wight.*

VARNDE. Burnt. *R. Glouc.*

VARNISH. Same as *Barnish*, q. v.

VARRAYLIER. More truly.

> And the nerrer that thai sal hym be,
> The *varraylier* thai sal hym se.
> *Hampole, MS. Bowes*, p. 235.

VARRY. To fall at variance; to contend.

VARSAL. Universal; great. *North.*

VARY. Variation; turn. *Shak.*

VASEY. To comb; to curry; to plague; to give a beating; to force away. *West.*

VASSALAGE. Valour; courage. (*A.-N.*)

VAST. (1) Waste; deserted place.

(2) A great quantity. *Var. dial.*

(3) *Vast little*, a very small portion.

VASTACIE. Waste and deserted places.

VASTURE. Great magnitude.

VASTY. Vast; immense.

VAT. The bed of a cider press.

VAULTING-HOUSE. A brothel. Florio, p. 97.

VAUMPES. Gaiters. See *Vampy.*

VAUNT. A dish made in a fryingpan with marrow, plums, and eggs.

VAUNTOUR. A boaster. (*A.-N.*)

VAUNTPERLER. A boaster. (*Fr.*)

VAUNT-WARDE. The avant-guard. (*A.-N.*)

VAUSE. According to Holme, " to make the jaumes to oversale the mullions."

VAUTER. A dancer.

VAVASOUR. A kind of inferior gentry, one who held his lands in fealty. (*A.-N.*)

> Bothe knightes and *vavasour*,
> This damisels love paramour.
> *Arthour and Merlin*, p. 320.
> And sythen he hath had grete honoure,
> That furste was a pore *vavesoure*.
> *MS. Cantab.* Ff. ii. 38, f. 202.

VAW. (1) Few. (2) Glad.

VAWARD. The vanward; the fore part.

VAWTH. A bank of dung or earth prepared for manure. *Somerset.*

VAY. To succeed; to prosper. *South.*

VAYNE. Vanity. (*A.-N.*)

VAYTE. To take. Thornton Rom. p. 308.

VAZE. To flutter about. *West.*

VAZEN. Faiths. *Somerset.*

VEAGUE. (1) A teasing child. *West.*
(2) A freak; a whim. *Somerset.*

VEAK. A gathering, or ulcer. *West.*

VEAKING. Fretful; peevish. *Devon.*

VECISE. Bladder. (*Lat.*)

VECKE. An old woman. *Chaucer.*
> Florent his wofulle heed up-lefte,
> And syye this vekke where sche sat.
>
> *Gower, MS. Soc. Antiq. 134, f. 49.*

VECTIGAL. Tithe. Leland, iv. 111.

VEDGING. Sideling. *Devon.*

VEERCE. A verse. *Pr. Parv.*

VEERING. A furrow. *Glouc.*

VEERS. Young pigs. *Cornw.*

VEGE. A run before leaping. *West.*

VEGET. Lively; brilliant. (*Lat.*)

VEGETIVE. A vegetable. *Davenant.*

VEGGE. A wedge. *Pr. Parv.*

VEILLE. An old woman. (*A.-N.*)

VEIR. Truly. See *Vair.*

VEIRE. Fair; good; beautiful.

VELANIE. Wickedness.

VELASOUR. Same as *Vavasour*, q. v.

VELATED. Vailed. Becon, p. 112.

VELE. Veil. *Spenser.*

VELL. The salted stomach of a calf, used for making cheese; a membrane.

VELLET. Velvet. *Spenser.*

VELLING. Getting turf up for burning.

VELURE. Velvet. (*Fr.*)

VELVET-GUARDS. Trimmings of velvet.

VELVET-HEAD. The incipient horns of a stag which are covered with a rough skin.

VELVET-TIPS. See *Velvet-head.*

VELYARDE. Old man; dotard.

VELYM. Vellum. *Pr. Parv.*

VEMDE. Foamed. *Hearne.*

VEMON. Venom. *North.*

VENAIG. To change; to revoke. *West.*

VENCOWSDE. Vanquished.
> He that on hys hedd hyt bare
> Schulde not be vencowsde in no warre.
>
> *MS. Cantab. Ff. ii. 38, f. 192.*

VENDABLE. To be sold. (*A.-N.*)

VENDAGE. Vintage; harvest. (*A.-N.*)

VENDS. A limited sale of coal, as arranged by the trade. *Newc.*

VENERIE. Hunting. (*A.-N.*)

VENERIEN. Venereal. *Palsgrave.*

VENETIANS. A kind of hose or breeches made to come below the garters.

VENGE. To revenge. (*A.-N.*)
> Sone, be now of comfort gode,
> And venge the, yf thou may.
>
> *MS. Cantab. Ff. ii. 38, f. 89.*
>
> For M the toone hirt the tothere sore,
> The tother ne venges hym nevere the more.
>
> *MS. Harl. 2260, f. 2.*

VENGEABLE. Revengeful; cruel.

VENGEANCE. Very.

VENGED. (1) Avenged.
> The greyhownde dyd hym sone to go,
> When hys maysyrys dethe he had venged soo.
>
> *MS. Cantab. Ff. ii. 38, f. 74.*

(2) Winged. *Chaucer, ed. Wright*, 1387.

VENICE-GLASS. A cup, goblet, or looking-glass, made of fine crystal glass.

VENIED. Musty; mouldy. *West.*

VENIME. Poison; venom. (*A.-N.*)

VENISON. Brawn of a wild boar.

VENJAWNCERE. A revenger.

VENNE. Mud; dirt. (*A.-S.*)
> Hereof mowe men so gret schewyng
> In dyvers maners of clothyng,
> Now schort, now traylyng upon the *venne*,
> Now streyt, nowe wyde as nyse menne.
>
> *MS. Laud. 486, f. 21.*

VENNEL. A gutter; a sink. *North.*

VENNY. Rather. *Heref.*

VENOM. (1) A gathering in any part of the finger but the top. *Devon.*
(2) Dry; harsh. *Warw.*

VENQUESTE. Vanquished.

VENT. (1) An inn. (*Span.*)
(2) To snuff up; to smell. (*Lat.*)
(3) To vend, or sell. Still in use.
(4) An opening in any garment.

VENTAL. See *Aventaile.*

VENTER-POYNT. A children's game.
> At shove-groate, *venter-poynt*, or crosse and pile.
>
> *Letting of Humours Blood in the Head-Vaine*, 1600.

VENT-HOLE. The button-hole at the wrist of a shirt. *Somerset.*

VENTIDUCT. A passage for air.

VENTOSE. A cupping-glass. (*A.-N.*)

VENTOSITE. The colic.

VENTOUSE. To cup. (*A.-N.*)
> Blede thane on the vayne that is bitwix the an-kille and the hele, or elles be ventoused on the thee with a boyste biside the hocche.
>
> *MS. Lincoln Med. f. 301.*

VENTOY. A fan.

VENU. A jump, or leap. (*A.-N.*)

VENUE. A bout or thrust in fencing.

VENUS. A term at the game of astragals, q. v. See MS. Ashmole 788, f. 162.

VENVIL. This word occurs in an old MS. of the rights of the parish of Mavey, quoted in Marshall's Rural Economy of the West of England, i. 326, meaning the right of pasturage and fuel. It is supposed by Marshall to be a corruption of *fen* and *field.*

VEO. Few; little. *West.*

VEOLTH. Filth. *Weber.*

VEPPE. Wept; cried.

VER. (1) The spring. (*Lat.*)
(2) Man; knight. *Gawayne.*

VERAMENT. Truly. (*A.-N.*)
> The erle off Glowsytour verament
> Toke hys leve and home he wente.
>
> *MS. Ashmole 61, f. 62.*
>
> These thre poyntes verament
> Nowther schale do but bothe assent.
>
> *MS. Catt. Cleop. A. ii. f. 131.*

VERAY. True. (*A.-N.*)

VERCLEF. Cleaved. *Hearne.*

VERD. (1) Green; greenness.
(2) Fared. Sevyn Sages, 612.

VERDE. Feared; was moved; enraged. Also, army, forces, rout. *Hearne.*

VERDED. An Italian wine.

VERDEKYN. A firkin.

VERDINGALE. A fardingale.

VERDITE. Judgment; sentence. (*A.-N.*)

VERDUGO. A hangman. (*Span.*)

VERDURE. Tapestry.

VERDUROUS. Green. *Drayton.*

VERE. Fere; companion. (*A.-S.*)

VEREL. A small iron hoop. *North.* Also, the ferule of a knife.

VERGE. Green.

VERGEOUS. Verjuice. *Palsgrave.*

VERGER. A garden; an orchard.

VERITEE. Truth.

VERLICHE. Fairly. *Hearne.*

VERLOFFE. A furlough. (*Flem.*)

VERLORE. Forlorn; lost. *Hearne.*

VERMAILE. Red. (*A.-N.*)

VERMILED. Adorned; flourished.

VERN. A partner in a mine.

VERNACLE. A miniature picture of Christ, supposed to have been miraculously imprinted upon a handkerchief preserved in St. Peter's at Rome. A diminutive of *Verony*, q. v.

> And I salle make myne avowe devotly to Criste,
> And to the haly *vernacle* vertuus and noble.
> *Morte Arthure, MS. Lincoln, f. 56.*

VERNAGE. A kind of white wine.

> A thoujt so swete in my corage,
> That never piment ne *vernage*
> Was half so swete for to drynke.
> *Gower, MS. Soc. Antiq. 134, f. 178.*

VERNISH. To varnish. (*A.-N.*)

VERNYNGE. Varnishing? "Item, fore stuffynge of a sadylle, *vernynge* and glewynge."—Manners and Household Expenses of England, p. 389.

VERONY. The cloth or napkin on which the face of Christ was depicted, that which was given by Veronica to our Saviour before his crucifixion to wipe his face, and received a striking impression of his countenance upon it.

> Like his modir was that childe,
> With faire visage and mode ful mylde;
> Sene hit is bi the *verony*,
> And bi the ymage of that lady.
> *Cursor Mundi, MS. Coll. Trin. Cantab. f. 115.*

VERQUERE. An old game on the tables, mentioned in "Games most in Use," 12mo. Lond. n. d.

VERRE. (1) Crystal glass. (*A.-N.*)

> In alle the erthe y-halowid and y-holde,
> In a closet more clere than *verre* or glas.
> *Lydgate, MS. Soc. Antiq. 134, f. 14.*

(2) Wool. (*A.-N.*)

(3) To cover over; to conceal.

(4) A fur. Same as *Vaire*, q. v.

> *Verre* and gryce we have plenté,
> Golde and sylvyr and ryche stones.
> *MS. Cantab. Ff. ii. 38, f. 164.*

VERREY. True; truly. (*A.-N.*)

> And whanne the pepull of his person had a *verrey* syjte,
> Thayre malice was quenchid, were thay never so woo.
> Wherefore, good Lorde, evet more thy wille be doo !
> *MS. Bibl. Reg. 17 D. xv.*

> Hyt ys *verré* Goddes blode
> That he schedde on the rode.
> *MS. Cott. Claud. A. ii. f. 130.*

VERSAL. Universal. *Butler.*

VERSE-COLOURED. Variegated.

VERSER. A poet; a poetaster.

VERSET. A little verse. (*A.-N.*)

VERTE. Green. (*A.-N.*)

VERTU. Power; efficacy.

> Thorugh the worshipful *vertu*,
> And the gret myght of Crist Jhesu.
> *MS. Addit. 11305, f. 91.*

VERTUES. Active; efficacious.

> Or for thow art a *vertues* mon,
> And const more then another con.
> *MS. Cott. Claud. A. ii. f. 140.*

VERVELS. The little silver rings at the ends of the jesses of a hawk.

VERVENSIE. Fervency.

VERVISES. A kind of cloth.

VERY. Really; truly; verily.

VES. Was. (*A.-S.*)

VESE. (1) To run up and down. *Glouc.*

(2) To drive away; to fly.

VESSEL. The eighth of a sheet of paper.

VESSELEMENT. Plate; furniture.

> Curteynes or outher vestyment,
> Or any outher *vesselement*.
> *MS. Harl. 1701, f. 62.*

VESSES. A sort of worsted.

VESSY. When two or more persons read verses alternately, they are said to *vessy*.

VEST. Invested; clothed.

VESTER. A fescue. *Somerset.*

VESTIARY. A wardrobe.

VESTMENT. See *Vesselement*.

VET. The feet. *West.*

VETAYLE. Provisions; victuals.

> Oxin, shepe and *vetayle*, withowtyn any dowte
> Thay stale away, and caried ever to and froo,
> God suffirs moche thyng his wille to be doo !
> *MS. Bibl. Reg. 17 D. xv.*

VETING. Courting. *Devon.*

VETOYN. The herb betony.

VETRES. Fetters. Nominale MS.

VETTY. Apposite; suitable. *Devon.*

VETUSE. Old. (*Lat.*)

VEVER. A fish-pond. (*A.-N.*)

> He drew his *vevers* of fysche,
> He slewe his fosters I-wysse.
> *MS. Lincoln A. i. 17, f. 130.*

VEWE. A yew-tree. *Chesh.*

VEWTER. A keeper of hounds.

VEY. True. (*A.-N.*)

VEYDEN. Voideth.

VEYNE. Penance.

VEYNED. Feigned.

> Sche seyde an evelle was on hur falle,
> And *veyned* hur to be dede.
> *MS. Cantab. Ff. ii. 38, f. 96.*

VEYNЗORD. A vineyard.

> Withoutyne the *veynзord* thai him cast,
> And there thai him sloзe,
> *MS. Cantab. Ff. v. 48, f. 91.*

VEZE. The same as *Pheeze*, q. v.

VI. We. *Rob. Glouc.*

VIA. An exclamation of encouragement, movement, or defiance. (*Ital.*)

VIAGE. A voyage, or journey.

VIANDRE. Feed; sustenance. (*A.-N.*)

VICARY. A vicar. (*Lat.*)

VICE. (1) Advice. Still in use.

(2) A winding or spiral stair. "Vyce, a tourn-yng stayre, *vis*," Palsgrave.

(3) The cock or tap of a vessel.

(4) The buffoon of our early dramas.

(5) Fault; crime; injury. (*A.-N.*)

(6) The fist. *Somerset.*

VICTUALLER. A tavern-keeper.

VICTUALS. For a child to be her mother's *victuals*, is to be her pet. *West.*

VIDE. To divide. *South.*

VIE. (1) To wager or put down a certain sum upon a hand of cards.

(2) The game of prisoners' base. *Devon.*

(3) To turn out well; to succeed. *West.*

(4) Life. Legendæ Cathol. p. 71.

(5) Envy.

> And afterward under Pounce Pylate
> Was i-take for *vye* and hate.
> *MS. Cott. Claud.* A. ii. f. 132.

VIERGE. A rod. (*A.-N.*)

VIES. Devizes, co. Wilts.

VIEW. (1) The footing of a beast.

(2) The discovery of an animal. An old term in hunting.

VIEWLY. Pleasing to the sight. *Viewsome* is also heard. *North.*

VIFTE. The fifth.

VIG. To rub gently. *West.*

VIGE. A voyage, or journey. *West.*

VIGILE. The eve of a festival. Also, the wake over a dead body. (*A.-N.*)

> Or any other fastynge day,
> Lentun or *vygyle*, as telle he may.
> *MS. Cott. Claud.* A. ii. f. 146.

VIGOUR. Figure. *West.*

VIKER. A vicar. (*A.-N.*)

VILANIE. Wickedness; injury.

VILARDE. An old man.

VILD. Vile. This is a very common form of the word in early writers.

VILE. A wicked fellow.

VILETE. Baseness.

> Muche dud thei me of *vileté*,
> That myne owne shuld have be.
> *Cursor Mundi, MS. Coll. Trin. Cantab.* f. 125.
> He that was hanged on a tre
> Bysyde Jhesu for *vylté*.
> *MS. Harl.* 1701, f. 35.

VILIPEND. To think ill of.

VILLIACO. A rascal; a coward. (*Ital.*)

VILOUS. Horrid.

> Then was ther a boor yn that foreste,
> That was a wondur *vylous* beste.
> *MS. Cantab.* Ff. ii. 38, f. 131.

VINE. (1) A vineyard.

(2) Any trailing plant bearing fruit.

(3) To find. *Somerset.*

VINE-GRACE. A dish in ancient cookery composed of pork, wine, &c.

VINELOME. A kind of spice.

VINE-PENCIL. A blacklead pencil.

VINEROUS. Hard to please. *North.*

VINETTES. Sprigs, or branches.

VINEWED. Mouldy. *West.*

VINID. Same as *Vinewed*, q. v.

VINNY. A scolding bout. *Exm.*

VINOLENT. Full of wine. (*Lat.*)

VINTAINE. Speedily. (*A.-N.*)

VIOL-DE-GAMBO. A six-stringed violin.

VIOLENT. To act with violence.

VIOLET-PLUM. A dark purple plum of a very sweet taste, shaped like a pear: in the eastern parts of the county it is sometimes called a Lincoln plum. *Linc.*

VIPER'S-DANCE. St. Vitus's dance.

VIPPE. The fir-tree.

> The salyng *vippe*, cypresse deth to playne.
> *MS. Cantab.* Ff. i. 6, f. 25.

VIRE. To turn about. (*Fr.*)

VIRENT. Green; unfaded.

VIRGINAL. (1) Maidenly. *Shak.*

(2) An oblong spinnet.

VIRGIN - MARY - THISTLE. The *carduus benedictus.*

VIRGIN'S-GARLANDS. Garlands carried at the funeral of virgins, and afterwards hung in the church.

VIRGIN-SWARM. A swarm of bees from a swarm in the same season.

VIRID. Green. (*Lat.*)

VIRK. To tease. *Devon.*

VIRNE. To inclose; to surround.

VIROLAI. A sort of roundelay.

> Use no tavernys where be jestis and fablis,
> Syngyng of lewde balettes, rondelettes or *virelais*.
> *MS. Laud.* 416, f. 44.

VIROLFE. The same as *Verel*, q. v.

VIROUN. A circuit. (*A.-N.*)

VIS. Countenance. (*A.-N.*)

> We may nother se hym ne here hyme, ne fele hym
> als he es, and therefore we may noghte hafe the
> *vis* of his lufe here in fulfilling.
> *MS. Lincoln* A. i. 17, f. 226.

VISAGE. To front or face a thing.

VISE. (1) Aim. (*A.-N.*)

> Thus thys worlde thow moste despyse,
> And holy vertues have in *vyse*.
> *MS. Cott. Claud.* A. ii. f. 127.

(2) The same as *Pheeze*, q. v.

VISFIGURE. To disfigure. *North.*

VISGY. A pick and hatchet in one tool, for tearing down hedges. *Cornw.*

VISIKE. Physic.

> Ther is *visike* for the seke,
> And vertuis for the vicis eke.
> *Gower, MS. Soc. Antiq.* 134, f. 82.

VISNOMY. Countenance.

VIT. To dress meat. *Devon.*

VITAILLE. Victuals. (*A.-N.*)

VITIOUS. Spiteful; revengeful. *West.*

VITLER. A tavern-keeper.

> He scornes to walke in Paules without his bootes,
> And scores his diet on the *vitlers* post.
> *Letting of Humours Blood in the Head-Vaine,* 1600.

VITTRE. A whim; a pretence. *West.*

VITTY. Decent; proper; handsome. *West.*

VIVELICHE. Lively; vividly.

VIVERS. Provisions.

VIVES. "Certaine kirnels growing under the horsses eare," Topsell, 1607, p. 360.

VIXEN. The female fox.

VLEER. A flea. *Somerset.*

VLONKE. Splendid; rich. (A.-S.)

VLOTHER. Nonsensical talk. West.

VLUEKECCHE. An imposthume in the milt.

VLY-PECKED. Low-lived. Devon.

VOAKY. Greasy; unwashed. Applied to wool as it comes from the sheep. West.

VOC. An ugly face. Rugby.

VOCABLES. Words. Palsgrave.

VOCALE. Sound.

VOCATE. To ramble about idly. West.

VOCE. Strong; nervous. Somerset.

VODE. (1) To wander. (2) To vex.

VOGUE. In vogue, i. e. en train.

VOIDE. (1) To depart; to go away.
(2) To remove; to quit; to make empty.
(3) A parting dish; the last course; a slight repast or collation.

VOIDER. A basket or tray for carrying out the relics of a dinner or other meal, or for putting bones in. Brockett says it is still in use. A clothes basket is so called in Cornwall. According to Kennett, " a wooden flasket for linnen cloaths." Dekker applies the term to a person who clears the table.

VOIDING-KNIFE. A knife used for taking off remnants of bread, &c. to put in the voider.

VOINE. To foin, in fencing.

VOISDYE. Stratagem. (A.-N.)
> Now schalt thou here a gret mervayle,
> With what voisdye that he wrouȝte.
> Gower, MS. Soc. Antiq. 134, f. 217.

VOIX. Voice.
> Kyng Edward in hys ryght hym to endowe
> The commens thirto have redy every houre :
> The voys of the peuple, the vois of Jhesu,
> Who kepe and preserve hym from all langour.
> MS. Bibl. Soc. Antiq. 101.

VOKE. (1) Folk. West.
(2) The same as Boke, q. v.

VOKET. An advocate ?
> To consente to a fals juggyng,
> Or hyredyst a voket to swyche thyng.
> MS. Harl. 1701, f. 36.

VOKY. (1) Gay; cheerful. North.
(2) Damp; moist. Var. dial.

VOL. Full. R. Glouc.

VOLAGE. Light; giddy. (A.-N.)

VOLANT-PIECE. A piece of steel on a helmet presenting an acute angle to the front.

VOLATILS. Wild fowls; game. (A.-N.)
> Make we man to oure ymage and liknesse, and be he sovereyn to the fischis of the see, and to the volatile of hevene, and to unresonable bestis of erthe.
> MS. Bodl. 277.

VOLD-SHORE. A folding stake to support hurdles. Wilts.

VOLENTE. Willing.
> For of free choice and hertely volente,
> She hathe to God avowed chastite.
> Lydgate, MS. Ashmole 39, f. 15.

VOLEY. On the voley, i. e. at random, inconsiderately, at a stroke. (Fr.)

VOLLOUTH. Wicked; unjust. (A.-S.)

VOLLOW. A fallow. Sussex.

VOLNESSE. Fulness; perfection.

> And alle thre beth oone, thawgh it be so,
> In oon volnesse and in no mo.
> Religious Poems, xv. Cent.

VOLOWTEN. Flouting. West.

VOLUNTARIE. A flourish before playing.

VOLUNTARIES. Volunteers. Shak.

VOLUNTE. Will. (A.-N.)
> To suffre deth oonly for mannis sake,
> Uncompellid, frely of volunte.
> Lydgate, MS. Soc. Antiq. 134, f. 1.

VOLUPERE. A woman's cap; a kerchief.

VOLVELLE. A contrivance found in some old astronomical works, consisting of graduated and figured circles of pasteboard or vellum made to revolve, and used for various calculations.

VOM. Foam.

VOMYSMENT. Vomiting.
> Hast thow wyth suche vomyment
> I-cast up aȝayn the sacrament ?
> MS. Cott. Claud. A. ii. f. 142.

VONDEDEN. Founded.

VONE. To take; to lead. Hearne.

VOOK. The voice. Pr. Parv.

VOOR. (1) A furrow. Sussex.
(2) To warrant. South.

VORBISEN. A parable.

VORE. Forth. To draw vore, to twit one with a fault. Exmoor.

VORE-DAYS. Late in the day. Erm. No doubt from the A.-S. forð-dæges.

VORE-RIGHT. Blunt; rude. West.

VORN. For him. West.

VORT. Till; until; for to. Hearne.

VORTHY. Forward; assuming. West.

VOUCHEN. To vouch. Vouchen safe, to vouchsafe. (A.-N.)
> To upe-ryse fra dede thou vouchede safe
> To eke the trowhe that we here hafe.
> MS. Lincoln A. i. 17, f. 191.
> Lorde, y have servyd yow many a day
> Vowche ye hur safe on mee.
> MS. Cantab. Ff. ii. 38, f. 64.

VOULTEGER. A vaulter ? Rolls House B. v. 4, temp. Hen. 8th,—" Item to Fredrego Gracian the kinges voulteger, xxxiij. s. iiij. d. per annum."

VOUR. To devour; to eat up.

VOUSE. Strong; nervous; forward. West.

VOUSSURE. A vault. (A.-N.)

VOUT. A vault. Palsgrave.

VOUTE. Mien; countenance. (A.-N.)
> Sir, sais the senatour, so Crist mott me helpe,
> The voute of thi vesage has woundyde us alle.
> Morte Arthure, MS. Lincoln, f. 54.

VOWARD. The vanguard of an army.

VOWEL. The afterbirth of a cow. West.

VOWER. (1) Devoir; duty.
(2) Four. Somerset.

VOWESS. A votaress; a nun.

VOWTES. A dish in cookery described in MS. Sloane 1201, f. 37.

VOYAGE. A journey by land. (A.-N.)

VOYDEE. The same as Voide (3).

VRAIL. A flail. South.

VRAMP-SHAKEN. Distorted. Devon.

VRAPED. Drawn tight. Devon.

VREACH. Violently. *Devon.*

VREATH. A low hedge. *Devon.*

VRITH. The bindings of hedges. *South.*

VROZZY. A nice thing. *Devon.*

VUDDICKS. A coarse fat woman. *West.*

VUDDLES. A spoilt child. *Wilts.*

VUG. To strike; to elbow. *Somerset.*

VULCH. The same as *Vug*, q. v.

VULGATE. Publicly known.

VUMP. To knock; to thump. *Devon.*

VUNG. Received. *Devon.*

VUR. (1) Far. (2) To throw. *West.*

VURE. Four? Our?

    Graunte us grace, in thyn hyȝe holde,
    Whanne we deye to holde *vure* tapris lyȝte.
        Lydgate, MS. Soc. Antiq. 134, f. 30.

VURRID-BRID. Household bread made of meal as it comes from the mill without the bran being taken from it. *Devon.*

VUR-VORE. Far-forth. *Exmoor.*

VUSTIN-FUME. A violent passion.

VUSTLED-UP. Wrapped up. *West.*

VUSTY. Fusty; mouldy. *West.*

VYCE. Countenance. (*A.-N.*)

    Gye ovyr all lovydd Felyce,
    The erlys doghtur with the feyre *vyce.*
        MS. Cantab. Ff. ii. 38, f. 148

VYLANLYCHE. Wickedly.

    Why that thou oughtiste with no righte
    To gabbe on hym so *vylanlyche.*
        MS. Harl. 2252, f. 102.

VYNCE. To conquer. (*Lat.*)

VYRE. An arrow for a crossbow. (*A.-N.*)

    That al his hert hath set a fuyre
    Of pure envye, and as a *vyre*
    Which fleeth out of a mighty bowe,
    Awey he fledde for a throwe.
        Gower, MS. Bodl. 294.

VYSERNE. A visor, or mask.

VYVERE. The same as *Vever*, q. v.

WA. Well; yea. *North.*

WAA. Woe. Still in use.

    Wyches, he said, woes mot thow be!
    Hafe ȝe fersakyne my goddis so free.
        MS. Lincoln A. i. 17, f. 128.

WAAG. A lever. *Yorksh.*

WAAST. A waste; a wilderness.

WAB. Gabble; nonsense. *Devon.*

WABBLE. (1) To tremble; to reel. *North.*

(2) To do anything awkwardly. *Var. dial.*

WABBLER. A boiled leg of mutton.

WACCHE. Watching.

    And some for *wacche* and fasting,
    That maketh her hernes to drie and cling.
        MS. Lansd. 793, f. 72.

WACCHERE. Watch.

    Duk Roland and Erle Olyver
    Thilke niȝt kepte the *wacchere.*
        MS. Ashmole 33, f. 46.

WACHE. A flock of birds.

WACHID. Weary; tired.

WACKEN. (1) Watchful. (*A.-S.*)

(2) Lively; sharp; wanton. *North.*

WACKERSOME. Wakeful. *North.*

WACNE. To awaken. (*A.-S.*)

WAD. (1) Would. *North.*

(2) Line, or rank. In land-surveying, when they are setting out their stakes they are said to *wad* in a line; hence it is taken to signify a line, and it is said of persons, they are all in the same *wad*, when connected together in any way of business, &c.

(3) A wisp of straw. Also, a bundle or quantity of anything. *West.*

(4) Blacklead. *Cumb.*

(5) Woad. (6) A forfeit. *North.*

(7) What. *Hearne.*

WADDEN. Supple. *North.*

WADDER. A grower of wad or woad.

WADDLE. (1) To roll up and down in a confused and disorderly way. *Var. dial.*

(2) The wane of the moon. *Somerset.*

(3) To fold up; to entwine. *Devon.*

(4) The wattle of a hog.

WADDOCK. A large piece. *Salop.*

WADE. (1) To go; to pass. (*A.-S.*)

(2) The sun is said to wade when covered by a dense atmosphere. *North.*

(3) A joint or tenon is said to wade when it slips too easily from any cause.

WADEABLE. Fordable. *Coles.*

WADGE. To wager; to bet. *Devon.*

WADIR. Water. *Craven.*

WADLER-WIFE. In Newcastle, the keeper of a register office for servants.

WADLING. A wattled fence. *West.*

WADMAL. A very thick coarse kind of woollen cloth. Coarse tow used by doctors for cattle is also so called.

WAE-ME. Woe is me! *North.*

WÆNE. To sneak away.

WAFERER. A person who sold wafers, a sort of cakes so called.

WAFER-PRINT. A mould for wafers.

WAFF. (1) The movement of a large flame from side to side. *Northumb.*

(2) A spirit, or ghost. *North.*

(3) A nasty faint smell. *North.*

(4) To bark. *Cumb.*

(5) To puff or boil up. *North.*

(6) A slight attack of illness.

WAFFLE. To wave; to fluctuate. *North.*

WAFFLER. (1) The green sandpiper. *North.*

(2) A person who is very weak. *Cumb.*

WAFFLES. An idle sauntering person.

WAFFY. Insipid. *Linc.*

WAFRESTERE. A maker of wafers for consecration at the sacrament. (*A.-S.*)

WAFRON. A cloud, or vapour.

WAFT. (1) A barrel. *Somerset.*

(2) A lock of hair.

(3) A puff. Also, blown, wafted.

(4) To beckon with the hand.

WAFTAGE. Passage by water.

WAFTERS. Swords having the flat part placed in the usual direction of the edge, blunted for exercises. *Meyrick.*

WAFTURE. A slight waving motion.

WAFYS. Vagabonds.

WAG. (1) The same as *Wagge*, q. v.

(2) To chatter. (3) To pass on.

WAGE. (1) To hire. Still in use.

(2) Pay; wages; reward; hire.

> For thou woldyst bryng me thys message,
> I wylle geve the thy *wage*.
> *MS. Cantab. Ff. ii. 38, f. 102.*

> Ye have a knyght at yowre *wage*,
> For yow he ys an evell page.
> *MS. Cantab. Ff. ii. 38, f. 166.*

(3) To be pledge for; to warrant. Also a substantive, a pledge.

(4) To bribe. *Var. dial.*

(5) To contend.

(6) To mould clay for pots, &c.

WAGET. Watchet colour.

WAG-FEATHER. A silly swaggerer.

WAGGE. To move; to shake.

> She had made of lethyr an howge bagge,
> By wycchecraft she cowde make it to *waggy*.
> *MS. Laud. 416, f. 1.*

> The vertu of hit is, if that a man have *waggynge*
> teth, if he ete of hit hit wulle make home fast.
> *MS. Arundel 272, f. 46.*

WAGGLE. To shake; to roll; to waddle.

WAGHE. A wall.

> So hedousely that storme ganne falle,
> That sondir it braste bothe *waghe* and walle.
> *MS. Lincoln A. i. 17, f. 125.*

WAGHT. Wage, gage, or pledge.

WAGING. The dung of the fox.

WAG-LEG. A black venomous fly.

WAGMOIRE. A quagmire. *Spenser.*

WAGSTERT. The titmouse.

WAGTAIL. A profligate woman.

WAG-WANTON. The shaking grass.

WAHAHOWE. An interj. in hallooing.

WAHAN. When. (*A.-S.*)

WAID. Weighed. *Tusser.*

WAIF. A stray cattle. *North.*

WAIFFANDE. Waving; moving.

> Schippis salle stande appone the sande
> *Wayffande* with the sees fame.
> *MS. Lincoln A. i. 17, f. 152.*

WAIFINGER. The same as *Waif*, q. v.

WAILE. (1) A veil. *Somerset.*

(2) Weal; prosperity. (*A.-S.*)

WAILY. Very sorrowful. *North.*

WAIME. A flaw, or tear. *Suffolk.*

WAIMENTE. To lament. (*A.-S.*)

> There dwelled they sore *waymentende*,
> Sixe dayes fulle to the ende.
> *MS. Trin. Coll. Oxon. 57, art. 2.*

WAIN. (1) A home, or dwelling.

(2) A waggon. Still in use.

(3) To fetch. It occurs in Tusser, p. 141, wrongly explained in glossary.

(4) To move; to go; to turn.

WAIN-MEN. Waggoners.

II.

WAINSCOTS. Boards for wainscots.

WAINT. Quaint; extraordinary. *North.*

WAINTLY. Very well. *Cumb.*

WAIR. (1) To lay out; to expend. *North.*

(2) The spring. Vocab. MS.

WAISCHE. Washed.

> The meke als wele wylle hym haste
> To serve the leste als the maste,
> Als God dyde that symply lete
> Wehn he *waysche* hys dyschyplys fete.
> *MS. Harl. 2200, f. 16.*

WAISE. A bundle or wisp of straw.

WAIST. (1) A girdle. (2) Ways.

WAISTCOATEERS. Low prostitutes.

WA-IST-HEART. An interj. of pity.

WAIT. (1) To wot, or know. *North.* "Now wayte thou wher that I was borne," MS. Cantab. Ff. v. 48, f. 48.

(2) Laid out; expended. *Cumb.*

(3) The hautboy, a musical instrument.

(4) To blame. *Yorksh.*

(5) Bold; active. Robson, Gl.

WAITE. (1) To watch. (*A.-N.*)

(2) A watchman. *Prompt. Parv.*

WAITER. (1) Water. Vocab. MS. See the third example in v. *Stank* (2).

(2) A small tray. *Var. dial.*

WAITH. An apparition of a person about to die, or recently dead. *North.*

WAITHE. Languid. *I. of Wight.*

WAIT-OF. To wait for. *Yorksh.*

WAITS. Musicians. *Var. dial.* "The waytis blew lowde," MS. Cantab. Ff. v. 48, f. 54.

> Grete lordys were at the assent,
> *Waytys* blewe, to mete they wente.
> *MS. Cantab. Ff. ii. 38, f. 60.*

WAIT-TREBLE. A sort of bagpipe.

WAIVERS. Small waving twigs. *East.*

WAK. To languish. (*A.-S.*)

WAKE. (1) To watch. (*A.-S.*)

> And anon they somonyd the knyghte,
> That he schulde *wake* the galows that nyʒt.
> *MS. Cantab. Ff. ii. 38, f. 133.*

(2) A parish festival, kept originally on the day of the dedication of the parish church. Literally a watch, a vigil.

(3) To watch the night with a corpse.

(4) To revel. Also, a revel.

(5) Hay placed in large rolls for the convenience of being carried. *West.*

WAKEMETE. Provisions for wakes.

WAKERIFE. Quite awake.

WAKES. Rows of green damp grass.

WAKKENISE. Watchful. (*A.-S.*)

WAKKER. Easily awakened. *North.*

WAKMEN. Watchmen. (*A.-S.*)

WAL. Will; pleasure.

WALAWAY. Woe! alas! *Chaucer.*

> There was rydynge and rennyng, sum cryed *wayleaway!*
> Unknowyng to many men who the bettur hadde.
> *MS. Bibl. Reg. 17 D. xv.*

WALCH. Insipid; waterish. *North.*

WALDE. (1) Power; dominion.

> For the erle hym had in *walde*,
> Of dedis of armes was he balde.
> *MS. Lincoln. A. i. 17, f. 132.*

(2) Plain; field. (*A.-S.*)

> Jhesu toke this corn in welde,
> And woodirly aboute him dalt.
> *Cursor Mundi, MS. Coll. Trin. Cantab. f. 77.*

(3) Would. Perceval, 915.

WALDING. Active; stirring. *Dunelm.*

WALE. (1) To choose; to select. *North.*

(2) Choice; good, excellent. *North.*

(3) Slaughter; carnage; death. (*A.-S.*)

(4) A whirlpool; the foaming wave.

(5) Weal; prosperity. (*A.-S.*)

(6) Will. Perceval, 1587.

(7) The ridge of threads in cloth. Hence used generally for texture.

(8) To court; to woo. *Yorksh.*

(9) A tumour, or large swelling. *Kent.*

(10) The fore-front of a horse-collar.

(11) To seek. *Gawayne.*

(12) A rod. Also, to strike.

WALEWEDE. Valued?

> An owche of sylver walewede therinne.
> *MS. Cott. Calig. A. ii. f. 113.*

WALHWE-SWETE. The herb bittersweet.

WALK. (1) To wag; to move; to work.

(2) A flock of snipes.

(3) A journey; a long absence.

(4) A plantation of willows.

(5) Uninclosed land. *East.*

(6) To depart.

(7) *To walk the round*, to go the round, said of a watchman.

WALKER. A fuller. *North.*

WALKING-SUPPER. A supper where one dish is sent round the table, every person being his own carver.

WALKLY-FIGS. Birch rods.

WALK-MILL. A fulling mill. *North.*

WALKNE. Air; sky; welkin. (*A.-S.*)

WALL. (1) *Go by the wall*, a name for strong ale. *To the wall*, in difficulties; *to go to the wall*, to be put on one side, to be slighted. *Laid by the wall*, dead but not buried. *To take the wall*, to walk nearest the wall in passing any one in the street.

(2) The stem of a rick.

(3) A wave. *North.*

(4) A spring of water. *Chesh.*

> Amyd the toure a walle dede sprynge,
> That never is drye but ernynge.
> *Religious Poems, xv. Cent.*

(5) "Wall of a shyppe," Palsgrave.

(6) "Wall of a strype, *enfleure*," ib.

(7) The side of a mine. Also, to pave the roads of a mine with stone.

WALLAGE. A confused mass. *West.*

WALL-BIRD. The spotted flycatcher.

WALLE. (1) To boil.

> Further ther is a water wallinde hot,
> That is deop, and long, and brod,
> *MS. Coll. Jes. Oxon. I. 29.*

(2)
> A wyckyd wound hath me walled,
> And traveyld me frome topp to too.
> *MS. Cantab. Ff. i. 6, f. 46.*

(3) A whale. MS. Harl. 1587, f. 43.

WALLERS. Women who rake the salt out of the leads at the salt-works at Nantwich.

WALL-EYED. Having eyes with an undue proportion of white. Any work irregularly or ill done, is called a *wall-eyed* job. It is applied also to any very irregular action.

WALLIGE. A loose bundle of anything.

WALLIS. The withers of a horse.

WALLON-TONGE. *Romant*, Palsgrave.

WALLOP. (1) To beat. *Var. dial.*

(2) To gallop. Also, a gallop. Still in use, to move quickly with great effort.

(3) To waddle. *Somerset.*

(4) To be slatternly. *Linc.*

(5) To bubble up. *North.*

(6) A thick piece of fat.

(7) To wrap up temporarily. *East.*

(8) To tumble over. *Suffolk.*

WALLOPING. Great. *Var. dial.*

WALLOW. (1) The alder tree. *Salop.*

(2) Flat; insipid. *North.*

(3) To fade away. *Somerset.*

WALLOWISH. Nauseous. *Heref.*

WALL-PLAT. (1) The flycatcher. *West.*

(2) A mantel-piece; a shelf fixed in the wall; a piece of timber lying on the top of the wall to which the timbers or spars are attached.

WALLSPRING. Wet springy land. *West.*

WALL-TILES. Bricks. *North.*

WALL-TOOTH. A large double-tooth.

WALL-UP. To spring out; to cause to spring out; to cause to swell. *West.*

WALLY. (1) To cocker; to indulge. *North.*

(2) Alas! *Yorksh.*

WALME. A bubble in boiling.

> Wyth vij. walmes that are so felle,
> Hote spryngyng out of helle.
> *MS. Cantab. Ff. ii. 38, f. 157.*

WALMYNG. Boiling. (*A.-S.*)

> Thou haste undur thy beddys hedd
> An hoot walmyng ledde.
> *MS. Cantab. Ff. ii. 38, f. 127.*

WALNOTE. A walnut. (*A.-S.*)

WALOPANDE. Galloping. "On walopande stedez," Morte Arthure, MS. Lincoln, f. 76.

WALSH. An attached lean-to building, not having a pitched roof: used in the marshes near Spilsby. *Linc.*

WALT. (1) Ruled; governed. (*A.-S.*)

(2) To totter; to overthrow. *North.*

(3) Threw; cast. *Gawayne.*

WALTED. Laid, as corn. *East.*

WALTER. To tumble; to roll about. "To turne or walter in mire," Baret, 1580.

WALTHAM'S-CALF. As wise as Waltham's calf, i. e. very foolish. Waltham's calf ran nine miles to suck a bull.

WALTYN.

> Thai waltyn at here wil to ware,
> These wodis and the wastus that ther were.
> *MS. Douce 302, f. 34.*

WALVE. To wallow, or roll about. *Devon.*

WALWORT. The herb *filipendula*.

WALY. Alas! (*A.-S.*)

WAM. Whom; which; whence. *Hearne.*

WAMBAIS. A body-garment twilled or quilted with wool, cotton, or tow. *Kennett*.

WAMBE. A bubbling up.

WAMBLE. To roll; to rumble.

WAME. The stomach. *Yorksh.* "*Venter, wame,*" Nominale MS. xv. Cent.

WAMETOWE. A belly-band, or girth.

WAMLOKES. Unwashed wool.

WAN. (1) Gained. (*A.-S.*)

(2) One. Still in use.

(3) Went. (*A.-S.*)

(4) A wand, or rod. *Var. dial.*

(5) Begot?

> He wende welle the gode man
> Were hys fadur that hym *wan.*
> *MS. Cantab. Ff. ii. 38, f. 245.*

WANBELEVE. Perfidy; treachery.

WANCE. Once. *Devon.*

WANCHANCY. Unlucky; wicked. *North.*

WAND. (1) To inclose with poles.

(2) To span. A term at marbles.

(3) Lamentation; misery.

(4) A penis. *Dunelm.*

WANDE. (1) Went.

> The aungell to hevene *wands,*
> Whan he had seyde hys errande.
> *MS. Cantab. Ff. ii. 38, f. 33.*

(2) Pole; rod; bough; club.

(3) Change?

> Sayde Tryamowre on that covenaund,
> My ryght name schalle y not *wande.*
> *MS. Cantab. Ff. ii. 38, f. 81.*

WANDED. Covered with boughs or twigs.

WANDELARD. Wandered; went. *Hearne.*

WANDLE. Supple; pliant; nimble. *North.*

WANDLY. Gently. *Cumb.*

WANDLYSAND. Mistrowing.

WANDREME. Tribulation; agony.

WANDRETHE. Trouble; sorrow.

> The sexte vertue es strenghe or stalworthnes
> noghte anely of body bot of herte and wille evynly
> to suffire the wele and the waa, welthe or *wand-*
> *rethe,* whethire so betyde. *MS. Lincoln A.i.17, f.217.*

WANE. (1) Dwelling; home.

> Than spekes that wyese in *wane,*
> Thou hase oure gude mene slane
> *MS. Lincoln A. l. 17, f. 132.*

(2) Are destroyed.

(3) To decrease. (*A.-S.*)

(4) Won. Perceval, 11.

(5) Manner. Perceval, 422, 1264.

(6) Came; arrived; went.

(7) An inequality in a board, &c.

(8) Wanting; deficient. (*A.-S.*)

WANENE. Whence. *Hearne.*

WANG. (1) A cheek-tooth. (*A.-S.*)

(2) A blow on the face. *Leic.*

WANGED. Tired. *Devon.*

WANGER. A pillow. (*A.-S.*)

WANGERY. Soft; flabby. *Devon.*

WANGHER. Large; strapping. *East.*

WANGLE. To totter; to vibrate. *Chesh.*

WANG-TOOTH. A grinder. *North.*

WANHOPE. Despair. (*A.-S.*)

> Gode men I warne alle,
> That ȝe in no *wanhope* falle.
> *MS. Cantab. Ff. v. 48, f. 47.*

WANIAND. The wane of the moon.

WANIE. To fade; to wane; to decrease.

WANION. *With a wanion,* an imprecation signifying, with a curse.

WANKE. (1) Winked.

> Oure kyng on the scheperde *wanke*
> Prively with his eye.
> *MS. Cantab. Ff. v. 48, f. 55.*

(2) Happy; prosperous.

WANKLE. (1) Ill; weak. *North.*

(2) Unstable; unsteady; uncertain.

> Thomas, truly I the say,
> This worlde is wondur *wankille;*
> Off the next batelle I wylle the say,
> That shalbe done at Spynard hille.
> *MS. Cantab. Ff. v. 48, f. 122.*

(3) Limber; flabby; ticklish.

WANKLING. Weakly. *Heref.*

WANLACE. (1)

> Where that he myghte make a *wanlace,*
> And any thyng to the kyng purchace.
> *MS. Harl. 1701, f. 29.*

(2) To drive the wanlace, i. e. to drive the deer to a stand. A hunting term.

WANNE. (1) Pale; wan. (*A.-S.*)

> The wynde owt of the havyn them blewe
> Ovyr the *wanne* streme.
> *MS. Cantab. Ff. ii. 38, f. 85.*

(2) Came; arrived.

> To Harrowde Gye sone *wanne,*
> A gode swyrde he toke hym than.
> *MS. Cantab. Ff. ii. 38, f. 180.*

WANNECLOUTE. The entrails.

WANNEL. The gait of a tired man.

WANSHONE. To want; to lack.

WANSOME. Inefficient. (*A.-S.*)

WANSONE. To wane; to decrease.

WANSY. Sickly; weak. *Suffolk.*

WANT. (1) A cross-road. *Essex.*

(2) A mole. In MS. Sloane 2584, is a receipt "for to take wontis." Still in use.

(3) I cannot want, i. e. do without, spare. A very common idiom, and still in use.

(4) A mental imbecility. *North.*

(5) Absence. Shirley, i. 277.

(6) A defect or hole in a board.

WANTERS. Unmarried persons, i. e. those who want mates. *North.*

WANTI-TUMP. A mole-hill. *Glouc.*

WANTON. A fondling; a pet.

WANTONLY. Unintentionally.

WANTOWE. Dissolute; profligate.

WANTRISTE. Mistrust.

> And for *wantriste,* hire felow Salomé,
> Opinly that alle myȝte it sev,
> Wexe in that arme deed and colde as stone.
> *Lydgate, MS. Soc. Antiq. 134, f. 10.*

WANTY. (1) A leather tie, or rope; a short waggon rope; a surcingle. *Var. dial.* Tusser uses the word in the sense of a rope by which burdens are tied to the back of a horse.

(2) Deficient; not enough. *North.*

WANWEARD. A profligate. *North.*

WANY. Spoilt by wet, said of timber.

WANZE. To waste, pine, or wither. *East.*

WAP. (1) To beat. Also, a blow.

(2) Futuo. A cant term.

> This doxy dell can cut been whids,
> And *wap* well for a win,
> And prig and cloy so beushiply
> Each deuseaville within.
> *Canting Songs*, 1725.

(3) Smartly; quickly. *Var. dial.*

(4) To yelp; to bark. *Somerset.* " Wappynge of howndes," Prompt. Parv.

(5) To flutter; to beat the wings. Generally, to move in any violent manner.

(6) A bundle of straw. *North.*

(7) To wrap or cover up.

(8) A fall. Still in use.

(9) A kind of mongrel cur.

(10) A pup. *Lanc.*

WAPE. Pale. *East.*

WAPED. Stupified. (*A.-S.*) Still in use, according to Moor's Suffolk Words, p. 467.

WAPPEN'D. Steevens seems to be correct in deriving this word from *wap*, futuo.

WAPPENG. Quaking. Batman, 1582.

WAPPER. (1) Anything large. *Var. dial.*

(2) To move tremulously. *Somerset.*

(3) A great falsehood. *Var. dial.*

WAPPERED. Restless; fatigued. *Glouc.*

WAPPER-EYED. Having eyes that move in a quick and tremulous manner, either from a natural infirmity, or from want of sleep.

WAPPER-JAW. A wry mouth. *East.*

WAPPET. A yelping cur. *East.*

WAPPING. Large. *Var. dial.*

WAPS. (1) A wasp. *Var. dial.*

(2) A large truss of straw. *North.*

WAPSE. To wash. *Sussex.*

WAPYNES. Weapons.

WAR. (1) Wary; wise; aware.

(2) Work. *North.*　(3) Was; be.

(4) Worse. Still in use.

(5) The knob of a tree.

(6) Stand aside; give way; beware.

(7) To spend; to lay out. *North.*

WARANDE. Warrant.

> Mi Fadir he is ȝe undirstande,
> Him I drawe to my *warande*.
> *Cursor Mundi, MS. Coll. Trin. Cantab. f.* 91.

WARBEETLES. The large maggots which are bred in the backs of cattle. *Norfolk.*

WARBELL. A term applied to a hawk when she makes her wings meet over her back.

WARBLES. See *Warbeetles.*

WARBOT. " A worme, *escarbot*," Palsg.

WARCH. Ache; pain. *Lanc.*

WARCK-BRATTLE. Fond of work. *Lanc.*

WARD. (1) To take care of.

(2) *Wardes*, outworks of a castle.

> And alle the towres of crystalle schene,
> And the *wardes* enamelde and overgylt clene.
> *Hampole, MS. Bowes, p.* 227.

(3) " Warde of a locke, *garde*," Palsg.

(4) Proper for keeping, as fruit, &c.

(5) World. *Chesh.*

(6) Hardness of the skin. *East.*

(7) A guard, in fencing.

(8) A prison; a gaol.

(9) A wardrobe. Skelton, ii. 184.

(10) A sort of coarse cloth.

WARDAN. Existing.

WAR-DAY. A work-day. *North.*

WARDECORPS. Body-guard. (*A.-N.*)

WARDED. Joined together. *East.*

WARDEIN. A warden; a guard; a watchman; a keeper of a gate.

WARDEMOTES. Meetings of the ward.

WARDEN. A large baking pear.

WARDER. (1) A staff; a truncheon. " Warder, a staffe, *baston*," Palsgrave.

(2) One who keeps ward.

WARDEREBE. The dung of the badger.

WARDERERE. A warder, or staff.

> Bot so it befelle apone a tyme that Alexander smate Jobas on the heved with a *warderere* for na trespasse, whare-fore Jobas was gretly angred and greved at Alexander. *MS. Lincoln* A. i. 17, f. 47

WARDICH. A bank, or ditch.

WARDROPE. (1) A house of office.

(2) An icicle; a nose-drop.

(3) A dressing-room. *Yorksh.*

WARE. (1) Aware; sensible.

> Then come syr Barnard
> Aftur a dere fulle harde,
> And of me he was *ware*.
> *MS. Cantab.* Ff. ii. 38, f. 22.

(2) Whether. *Devon.*

(3) A weir, or dam.

(4) Corn; barley; oats. *Cumb.*

(5) To lay out labour, money, &c. This term is an archaism. *North.*

(6) Goods; dairy produce. *West.*

(7) Affairs; business.

(8) Wary; cunning.

> How faryth my knyghte ser Egyllamowre,
> That doghty ys ever and *ware*.
> *MS. Cantab.* Ff. ii. 38, f. 63.

(9) Sea-weed. *Dunelm.*

WARE-HOUSE. A work-house for masons, &c.

WARELESS. Unperceived; incautious.

WARENCE. The herb madder.

WARENTMENTIS. Garments. (*Lat.*)

WARENTY. Take a warrant or bail?

> ȝys, syr, and thou wylt *warenty*,
> And geve thy sone to day respyte.
> *MS. Cantab.* Ff. ii. 38, f. 140

WARESCHE. To cure; to heal.

> Sythene aftirwarde commes the soverayne leche, and takes there medcynes, and *waresche* mane of these sevene seknes, and stabilles hym in the sevene vertuss. *MS. Lincoln* A. i. 17, f. 200.

WARESM. A gift. *Huloet.*

WARE-WASSEL. A stem of sea-weed.

WARIANGLE. A small woodpecker.

WARIE. To revile; to curse.

WARIMENT. Care; caution. *Spenser.*

WARISHED. Well stored, or furnished.

WARISON. (1) A gift. Properly, a gift or reward on completing any business, or on leaving any situation.

> He made a crye thoro owt al the tow(n),
> Whedur he be ȝoman or knave,
> That cowthe bryng hym Robyn Hode,
> His *warisons* he shuld have.
> *MS. Cantab.* Ff. v. 48, f. 131.

Boye, therefore, by my crowne,
Thou must have thee *waryson ;*
The heigh horse besides Boughton
Take thou for thie travell.
Chester Plays, 6th pag. MS. Bodl. 175.

(2) The stomach. *Cumb.*

WARIST. Cured. *Ritson.*

WARK. (1) An ache, or pain. *North.*

(2) A hard stony substance covering the veins of coal in some mines.

WARK-BRATTLE. Loving to work. *Lanc.*

WARLARE. One who stammers.

WARLAU. A wizard, or sorcerer. (*A.-S.*)
Bitulx the *warlau* and his wiif
Adam es stad in strang strilf.
MS. Cott. Vespas. A. iii. f. 5.
The foulle *warlawes* of helle,
Undir the wallys skrykked schille.
MS. Lincoln A. i. 17, f. 148.

WARLOK. (1) Mustard. (2) A fetterlock.

WARLOKER. More warily. *Gawayne.*

WARLY. (1) Warlike. (2) Warily.

WARM. (1) To beat. *Var. dial.*

(2) Rich ; in good circumstances.

WARMOT. Wormwood.

WARMSHIP. Warmth. *Heref.*

WARM-STORE. Anything laid very carefully by till it may be wanted. *North.*

WARN. To warrant. *North.*

WARNDY. To warrant. *South.*

WARNE. To deny; to forbid.
The kynges hed when hyt ys broȝt,
A kysse wylle y *warne* the noghte.
MS. Cantab. Ff. ii. 38, f. 87.

(2) To caution ; to apprise. (*A.-S.*)

WARNED. Fortified.

WARNER. (1) A boys' game. A boy with his hands closed before him, called a warner, tries to touch another, in running, and so on, till all are touched.

(2) A sort of mongrel cur.

(3) A warrener. " The warner is hardy and felle," MS. Cantab. Ff. v. 48, f. 49.

WARNESTORE. To furnish ; to store.

WARNICHED. Furnished. (*A.-N.*)

WARNING-PIECE. Anything that warns.

WARNING-STONE. " The bakers in our county take a certaine pebble, which they putt in the vaulture of their oven, which they call the *warning-stone,* for when that is white, the oven is hott," Aubrey's MS. History of Wilts, Ash. Mus. Oxon.

WARNISED. Fortified. *Hearne.*

WARNT. Was not. *Var. dial.*

WARNY. I dare say. *Devon.*

WAR-OUTE. A term used in driving.

WARP. (1) Four of fish. *East.*

(2) The deposit left by the river Trent on lands after a flood.

(3) To cast a foal. *South.*

(4) To open ; to lay eggs. *North.*

(5) In some parts, land between the sea-banks and sea is called the warp.

(6) To wrap up. *Somerset.*

(7) Uttered. Reliq. Antiq. ii. 9.

(8) To haul out a ship.

(9) To weave. Hence, to contrive.

(10) The stream of salt water that runs from the brine pits in Worcestershire.

(11) An abortive lamb. *Suffolk.*

(12) To make a waving motion.

WARPE. Cast. " And warpe of hys wedez," Morte Arthure, MS. Lincoln, f. 63.

WARPS. Distinct pieces of ploughed land separated by the furrows. *East Sussex* and *Kent.*

WARR. Worse. *North.* " Qua herd ever a warr auntur," MS. Cott. Vesp. A. iii.

WARRANT. The bottom of a coal-pit.

WARRANTIZE. A warrant, or pledge.

WARRAY. To make war on.

WARRAYNE. A warren.
His woddes and his *warrayne,*
His wylde and his tame.
MS. Lincoln A. i. 17, f. 137.

WARR'D. Spent. *North.*

WARRE. (1) Wary ; cunning.
Scho es *warre* and wysse,
Hir rod as the rose on ryse.
MS. Lincoln A. i. 17, f. 132.

(2) Aware ; conscious of.
The emperowre of this
Was *warre,* as I wysse.
MS. Lincoln A. i. 17, f. 232.

(3) Were. Still in use.

WARREN. A plot ; a deep design.

WARREN-HEAD. A dam across a river in the more northern parts of Northumberland.

WARREYDE. Made war.
When I *warreyde* in Spayne,
He mad my landis barrayne.
MS. Lincoln A. i. 17, f. 132.

WARRIABLE. Able for war.

WARRICK. To twitch a cord tight by crossing it with another. *Northumb.*

WARRIDGE. The withers of a horse.

WARRIE. To abuse ; to curse.
The fifthe es *warienge* of other men,
Offe the grace of the Holy Goste to ken.
MS. Harl. 2260, f. 90.

WARRINER. The keeper of a warren.
When the buckes take the does,
Then the *warriner* knowes,
There are rabbets in breeding ;
And when the bag showes,
Then the milke-maid knowes,
The cow hath good feeding.
Cobbes Prophecies, his Signes and Tokens, 1614.

WARROKEN. To girt. (*A.-S.*)

WARSEN. To grow worse. *North.*

WARSLE. To strive ; to wrestle. *North.*

WARSLEY. Not much. *Essex.*

WARSTEAD. A ford over a river.

WART. (1) To overturn. *Chesh.*

(2) To plough land overthwart. *East.*

(3) To work. *North.*

WARTE. Wear it ; spend it.

WARTH. A ford. *North.* In Herefordshire, a flat meadow close to a stream.

WAR-WHING. Take care ; beware. *West.*

WARY-BREED. The worms in cattle.

WAS. To wash. Robin Hood, i. 89.

WASE. (1) A bundle of straw, &c., to relieve a burthen carried on the head.

(2) Angry; ill-tempered. *West.*

(3) To breathe with difficulty. *East.*

WASELEN. To become dirty. (*A.-S.*)

WASH. (1) A narrow track through a wood; a lane through which water runs. *East.*

(2) Washy. Still in use.

(3) Ten strikes of oysters. *Blount.*

WASHAMOUTH. A blab. *Devon.*

WASHBOUGHS. The small straggling boughs of a tree. *Suffolk.*

WASHBREW. This term is still in use in Devon. It is thus described by Markham:

And lastly, from this small oat meal, by oft steeping it in water, and cleansing it, and then boyling it to a thick and stiff jelly, is made that excellent dish of meat which is so esteemed of in the west parts of this kingdome, which they call *washbrew*, and in Cheshire and Lancashire they call it flamery, or flumery.

WASH-DISH. The water-wagtail. *West.*

WASHEN. Washed. (*A.-S.*)

WASHER. (1) A sort of kersey cloth.

(2) "An iron hoope which serves to keepe the iron pin at the end of the axeltree from wearing the nave," Florio, p. 94.

WASHES. The seashore. *Norf.*

WASH-HOLE. A sink. *Var. dial.*

WASHING. To give the head for washing, i. e. to submit to insult.

WASHING-BALLS. A kind of cosmetic used in washing the face. *Markham.*

WASHMAN. A beggar who solicited charity with sham sores or fractures.

WASH-POOL. A bathing pond.

WASH-WATER. A ford.

WASK. A large wooden beetle. Also, to use a beetle. *Suffolk.*

WASPISH. Tetchy; irritable. *East.*

WASSAIL. From the A.-S. wæs hæl, be in health. It was anciently the pledge word in drinking, equivalent to the modern *your health.* See *Drinkhail.* The term in later times was applied to any festivity or intemperance; and the wassail-bowl still appears at Christmas in some parts of the country. The liquor termed *wassail* in the provinces is made of apples, sugar, and ale.

Who so drynkes furst I-wys,
Wasseyle the mare dele.
MS. Cantab. Ff. v. 48, f. 49.

WASSET-MAN. A scarecrow. *Wilts.*

WAST. (1) The belly. (*A.-S.*)

(2) Nothingness. *In wast,* in vain.

WASTE. (1) To abate. *Essex.*

(2) The body of a ship.

(3) A consumption. *North.*

(4) To bang, or cudgel. *East.*

WASTEABLE. Wasteful. *Somerset.*

WASTE-GOOD. A spendthrift.

WASTEL. A cake; fine bread. (*A.-N.*) The wastel bread was well-baked white bread, next in quality to the simnel.

WASTER. (1) A cudgel. "Wasters or cudgels used in fence-schooles," Florio, p. 95.

(2) A damaged manufactured article.

(3) A thief in a candle. *Var. dial.*

WASTERNE. A desert. "Walkede in that wasterne," MS. Morte Arthure, f. 87. (*A.-S.*)

WASTEYN. A desert. (*A.-S.*)

A gode man and ryȝt certeyn
Dwelled besyde that *wasteyn.*
MS. Harl. 1701, f. 12

An ermyte woned for over a doune,
Yn a *wasteyne* fer fro the toune.
MS. Harl. 1701, f. 41

WASTING. A consumption. *North.*

WASTLE. (1) To wander. *Heref.*

(2) A twig; a withy. *Northumb.*

WASTOUR. A destroyer. (*A.-N.*)

WASTREL. A profligate. *West.*

WASTRELS. Imperfect bricks, china, &c.

WAT. (1) Walter. It was the old name for a hare. Used metaphorically for a wily cautious person.

(2) *Thou wat,* thou knowest.

(3) Indeed; certainly. *North.*

(4) A wight; a man. *Townel. Myst.*

(5) Hot. *Var. dial.*

WATCHED. Wet shod. *Var. dial.*

WATCHET. A pale blue colour.

WATCHING. A debauch.

WATCHING-CANDLE. The candle used when a person sits the night with a corpse.

WATCH-WEBS. Same as *Stealyclothes,* q. v.

WATE. To know. (*A.-S.*)

Firste es, as clerkes *wate,*
That who so es in wedwe state
Schuld hold hym pryvly in hynne,
And use solence withoute dynne.
MS. Harl. 2260, f. 118.

His Son is wisdom that alle thinge *wate,*
For al the world he halt in state.
Cursor Mundi, MS. Coll. Trin. Cantab. f. 2.

WATER. A river. *North.*

WATER-BEWITCHED. Any very weak drink.

WATER-BLOBS. Small watery globules.

WATER-BOX. The female pudendum. This term occurs in Florio, ed. 1611, p. 185.

WATER-BRASH. Water on the stomach.

WATER-CASTER. A person who judged of diseases by the inspection of urine.

WATER-CHAINS. Small chains attached to the bits of horses. *North.*

WATER-CRAW. A water-ousel.

WATER-CROFT. A glass jug for water.

WATER-DAMAGED. See *Water-bewitched.*

WATER-DOGS. See *Mare's-Tails.* Watergalls may perhaps have the same meaning, but I am told a second rainbow above the first is called in the Isle of Wight a *watergeal.* Carr has *weather-gall,* a secondary or broken rainbow.

WATERE. Walter. *Pr. Parv.*

WATER-FURROW. A gutter, or open drain.

WATER-GATE. A floodgate. Also, a passage for water. Metaphorically, the water-box, q. v.

Fro heven oute of the *watirgatis,*
The reyny storme felle doun algatis.
Gower, MS. Soc. Antiq. 134, f. 91.

WATERHEN. The moorhen.

WATERINGS. The spot called *St. Thomas a Waterings* was situated at the second milestone on the road from London to Canterbury. It was a place of execution in Elizabeth's time, and is frequently alluded to.

WATER-LAG. See *Water-leder.*

WATER-LEDER. A water-carrier.

WATER-LOCK. A watering place fenced with walls, rails, or bars, &c. Blount, p. 702.

WATER-LYNGKE. The herb *fabria minor.*

WATER-PLOUGH. A machine formerly used for taking mud, &c. out of rivers.

WATER-POT. "Water potte for a table, *aiguiere,*" Palsgrave. "Water potte for a gardyne, *arrousouer,*" ibid.

WATER-POUKE. A water-blister.

WATER-PUDGE. A puddle. *Northampt.*

WATER-RANNY. The short-tailed field mouse.

WATERS. Watering-places. *Linc.*

WATER-SHAKEN. Saturated with water.

WATER-SHUT. A floodgate.

WATER-SLAIN. See *Water-shaken.*

WATER-SPARROW. The reed bunting.

WATER-SPRINGE. A copious flow of saliva.

WATER-SPRIZZLE. A disease in ducklings.

WATER-STEAD. The bed of a river.

WATER-SWALLOW. The water-wagtail.

WATER-SWOLLED. Completely saturated.

WATER-TABLE. A small embankment made across a road, especially on a hill, to carry off the water. *Sussex.*

WATER-TAKING. A pond from which water is taken for household purposes.

WATER-TAWV. A swooning fit. *North.*

WATER-TEEMS. Risings of the stomach when nothing but water is discharged by vomiting. *North.*

WATERWALL. A waterfall. Also, a wall to keep water within due bounds.

WATER-WHEEL. A blister.

WATER-WHELPS. Plain dumplings. *East.*

WATER-WOOD. A watered fleece of wool.

WATER-WOOSEL. The water-ouzel.

WATER-WORK. An engine for forcing water.

WATER-WORKERS. Makers of meadow-drains and wet ditches. *Norf.*

WATER-WORT. The herb maiden-hair.

WATH. A ford. *North.*

WATHE. (1) A straying. (*A.-S*)

(2) Injury; danger; evil.

> Now take hede what I the mynne,
> Ʒef a wyf have done a synne,
> Syche penaunce thou gyve hyre thenne,
> That hyre husbonde may not kenne.
> Leste for the penaunce sake,
> Wo and *waththe* bytwene hem wake.
> *MS. Cott. Claud. A. ii. f. 147.*

> I rede thou mende it with skille,
> For *wathes* walkes wyde.
> *MS. Lincoln A. i. 17, f. 131.*

(3) Game; prey. (*A.-S.*)

WATHELY. Severely.

> With fyfty speris he flede,
> And *wathely* was wondide.
> *MS. Lincoln A. i. 17, f. 131.*

WATKIN'S-ALE. A copy of this curious old tune is in Queen Elizabeth's Virginal Book. The original ballad is thus entitled,—

> A ditty delightfull of Mother *Watkin's Ale,*
> A warning wel wayed, though counted a tale.

WATLYNGE-STRETE. The milky way.

WATSTONE. A whetstone.

WATTLE. (1) To beat. *Derb.*

(2) A hurdle. *Var. dial.*

(3) To tile a roof. *North.*

WATTLE-AND-DAB. A mode of building with close hurdle-work plastered over with a mixture of clay and chopped straw. *Warw.*

WATTLE-JAWS. Long lanky jaws.

WATTLES. (1) Loose hanging flesh. *North.*

(2) A kind of hairs or small bristles near the mouth and nostrils of certain fish.

WAUDON. Supple. *Northumb.*

WAUF. Tasteless. *Yorksh.*

WAUGH. To bark. *North.* The term occurs in Bale's Kynge Johan, p. 65.

WAUGHIST. Rather faint. *North.*

WAUGH-MILL. A fulling-mill. *Yorksh.*

WAUKLING. Weak. *Linc.*

WAULCH. Insipid; tasteless. *North.*

WAUPE. The turnspit dog.

WAURE. Sea-wrack. *Kent.*

WAUVE. To cover over. *Heref.*

WAVE. (1) To hesitate. (*A.-S.*)

(2) To wander, or stray.

(3) Wove. *Chaucer.*

WAVER. (1) A common pond serving the whole village. *Suffolk.* "Wavoure, stondynge watyr," Pr. Parv.

(2) The situation of a quoit when pitched so that its rim lies on the hob. *Suffolk.*

WAVERS. Young timberlings left standing in a fallen wood. *North.*

WAW. (1) A wall. *North.*

(2) To bark. Also, to caterwaul.

WAWARDE. The vanguard.

> The kyng of Lebe before the *awarde* he ledes.
> *Morte Arthure, MS. Lincoln, f. 72.*

WAWE. (1) Woe.

> Betwene the *wawes* of wod and wroth,
> Into his douʒtris chambre he goth.
> *Gower, MS. Soc. Antiq. 134, f. 85.*

(2) A wave. (*A.-S.*)

(3) To move, wag, or shake.

WAWEYS. Waves. (*A.-S.*)

> Nothyng sawe they them aboute
> But salte water and *waweys* stowte.
> *MS. Cantab. Ff. ii. 38, f. 150.*

WAWKS. Corners of the mustachios.

WAWL. To squeak; to cry out.

WAWT. To overturn. *Lanc.*

WAXE. (1) Wood. *Leic.*

(2) To thrive; to increase. (*A.-S.*) *To was out of flesh,* to become thin.

(3) *A lad of wax,* a smart clever boy. "A man of wax," Romeo and Juliet.

WAX-END. Shoemaker's waxed thread.

WAXEN-KERNELS. Enlarged and inflamed glands in the neck. "Waxyng kyrnels, *glande, glanders,*" Palsgrave.

WAY. (1) The time in which a certain space can be passed over. *Two mile way,* the time in which two miles could be passed over, &c.

(2) A way. Still in use.

WAY-BIT. A little bit. *North.*

WAY-BREDE. The plantain tree. (*A.-S.*)

WAYE. To weigh; to press with weight.

WAY-GATE. A gate across a road. *Linc.*

WAY-GOOSE. An entertainment given by an apprentice to his fellow-workmen. *West.*

WAY-GRASS. Knot-grass.

WAYKYER. Weaker.

> There was Jollyng, there was rennyng for the sove-
> reynté,
> There was rorynge and rumbelynge, pete to here;
> Fayne was the *waykyer* away for to flee,
> That day many a stowte man was ded there.
> *MS. Bibl. Reg.* 17 D. xv.

WAYLANDE. Valiant.

WAYNE. To strike; to raise.

WAYS. *Go your ways,* get along with you. *Come your ways,* come along with me.

WAY-WARDENS. Keepers of private roads.

WAY-WORT. The herb pimpernel.

WAY-ZALTIN. A game, or exercise, in which two persons stand back to back, with their arms interlaced, and lift each other up alternately. Jennings, p. 82.

WE. (1) With. *North.*

(2) Well. In use in the North.

WEAD. Very angry. *North.*

WEAKEN. To soak in water.

WEAKLING. A weak person.

WEAKY. Moist; watery. *North.*

WEAL. (1) The same as *Wale,* q. v.

(2) A wicker basket used for catching eels.

(3) To be in woe or want.

WEALD. Forest; woody country.

WEALTHY. Well fed. *North.*

WEAMISH. Squeamish. *Devon.*

WEANELL. A young beast just weaned.

WEAR. (1) The fashion. *Shak.*

(2) To cool the pot. *North.*

WEARD. To bathe. *Beds.*

WEARIFUL. Tiresome. *Var. dial.*

WEARING. (1) A consumption. *North.*

(2) Tiresome; tedious. *Var. dial.*

WEARISH. Small; weak; shrunk. Also, unsavoury. "Werysshe as meate is that is nat well tastye, *mal savouré*," Palsgrave. Forby has *weary,* feeble, sickly, puny.

WEARY. Troublesome; vexatious.

WEASAND. The throat. (*A.-S.*)

WEAT. To search the head to find if there be lice in it. *North.*

WEATH. Pliant. *I. of Wight.*

WEATHER. (1) To dry clothes in the open air.

(2) To give hawks an airing.

WEATHER-BREEDER. A fine day.

WEATHER-CASTER. A person who computed the weather for the almanacs, &c.

WEATHERED. Experienced.

WEATHER-GAGE. To get the *weather-gage* of a person, to get the better of him. *South.*

WEATHER-GALL. See *Water-dogs.*

WEATHER-GLEAM. To see anything at a distance, the sky being bright near the horizon. *North.*

WEATHER-HEAD. The secondary rainbow.

WEATHER-LAID. Weather-bound. *East.*

WEATHER-WIND. The bindweed.

WEATIN. Urine. *Cumb.*

WEAZEL. A foolish fellow. *East.*

WEB. (1) A weaver. (*A.-S.*)

> She was the formaste *web* in kynde
> That men of that crafte dud fynde.
> *Cursor Mundi, MS. Coll. Trin. Cantab.* f. 16.
> Of carpenteres, of smythes, of *webbus,* of bakeres,
> of breweres, and of alle maner men that goeth to
> huyre by the jere, or by the wyke, or by the daye.
> *MS. Burney* 356, p. 99.

(2) The blade of a sword.

(3) A sheet or thin plate of lead.

(4) The omentum. *East.*

(5) See *Pin-and-Web,* p. 625.

WEBSTER. A weaver. *North.*

WECHE. A witch.

> Sexty geauntes before engenderide with fendes,
> With *weches* and warlaws to wacchene his tentys.
> *Morte Arthure, MS. Lincoln,* f. 89.

WED. (1) Weeded. *North.*

(2) A heap of clothes, which each party of boys put down in a game called Scotch and English.

(3) A pledge. (*A.-S.*)

> Hath any mon upon a *wedde*
> Borowet at the oght in nede.
> *MS. Cotton. Claud.* A. ii. f. 142.
> Hyddur he wolde take hys pase,
> My lyfe dar y lay to *wedd.*
> *MS. Cantab.* Ff. ii. 38, f. 80.

WEDDE. (1) Wedded. (*A.-S.*)

(2) To lay a wager; to pledge.

WEDDE-FEE. A wager. *Robson.*

WEDDE-FERE. Husband; wife. (*A.-S.*)

WEDDER. A wether sheep. *North.*

WEDDINGER. A guest at a wedding.

WEDDING-KNIVES. Knives which were formerly part of the accoutrements of a bride.

WEDE. (1) Clothing; apparel. (*A.-S.*)

> Hast thou jeve hem at here nede
> Mete and drynke, cloth or *wede.*
> *MS. Cott. Claud.* A. ii. f. 132.

(2) Madness.

> And had therof so moche drede,
> That he wende have go to *wede.*
> *MS. Harl.* 1701, f. 94.

(3) To become mad.

> To Gye he starte, as he wold *wede,*
> And smote hym downe and hys stede.
> *MS. Cantab.* Ff. ii. 38, f. 191.

WEDERINGE. Temperature.

WEDGE. A gage; a pledge.

WEDHOD. State of marriage.

> Save in here *wedhod,*
> That ys feyre to-fore God.
> *MS. Cott. Claud.* A. ii. f. 129.

WEDHOK. A weeding-hook.

WEDLAKE. Wedlock; marriage.

WEDLOCK. A wife.

WEDMAN. A husband.

WEDOWE.

> Sene alle the erthe withowttene oure lorthipe may
> be callede *wedowe.*   *MS. Lincoln* A. i. 17, f. 9.

WEDS-AND-FORFEITS. The game of forfeits is so called in Warwickshire.

WEDSETTE. Put in pledge or pawn.

WEDUR. (1) A cloud. (2) Weather.

WEDWEDE. Widowhood. (*A.-S.*)

Bot whether of thaym that lyves of the lyfe,
Be it the man, be it the wyf,
Schuld hys lif chastely lede,
Whyles he es in the state of wedwede.

MS. Harl. 2260, f. 117.

WEDYRCOKKE. A weathercock.

WEE. (1) Woe; sorrow.

(2) Very small; little. *Var. dial.*

WEEAN. (1) A quean; a jade. *North.*

(2) A child, or *wee one.* *Yorksh.*

WEED. (1) Tobacco.

(2) A heavy weight. *Devon.*

WEEDY. Sickly; ill-grown. *Var. dial.*

WEEF. "Weef or summewhat semynge to badnesse," Prompt. Parv.

WEEK. (1) The wick of a candle.

(2) To squeak; to whine. *East.*

(3) The inside of a week, i. e. from Monday till Saturday. *North.*

(4) The side of the mouth. *Lanc.*

WEEKY-DAY. A week-day. *Devon.*

WEEL. (1) Well. *North.*

(2) A whirlpool. *Lanc.*

WEEN. (1) To whimper; to cry. *Devon.*

(2) The same as *Wene,* q. v.

(3) We have. *Lanc.*

WEEPERS. Mourners.

WEEPING-CROSS. *To come home by Weeping Cross,* to repent of any undertaking.

WEEPING-RIPE. Ready for weeping.

WEEPING-TEARS. Tears. *East.*

WEEP-IRISH. To scream; to yell.

WEEPY. Moist; springy. *West.*

WEER. (1) The same as *Were,* q. v.

(2) To stop; to oppose; to keep off; to guard; to protect; to defend. *North.*

(3) Pale and ghastly. *East.*

WEES. We shall. *Cumb.*

WEESEL. The weasand, or windpipe.

WEET. (1) The same as *Wete,* q. v.

(2) Nimble; swift. *North.*

(3) Wet. Still in use.

(4) To rain rather slightly. *North.*

WEETPOT. A sausage. *Somerset.*

WEE-WOW. Wrong. *Devon.* Also, to twist about in an irregular manner.

WEEZWAI. A bridle. *Somerset.*

WEFF. (1) Taste; flavour.

(2) To snarl. *North.*

WEFFABYLLE. Able to be woven.

WEFFYNG. Weaving.

Wen sche takyth hyre werke on honde,
Off *weffyng* other enbrouderye.

Gower, MS. Cantab. Ff. 1. 6, f. 4.

WEFT. (1) Woven. *North.*

(2) A waif, or stray.

(3) Waved; put aside. *Spenser.*

(4) A loss.

(5) The ground of a wig.

WEG. A pledge. *(A.-S.)*

WEGGE. A wedge. *Pr. Parv.*

WEGHT. An article like a sieve, but without holes in the bottom, which is usually made of sheepskin.

WEGHTNES. Boldness.

WEHEE. To neigh, as a horse.

WEIEWORTH. The herb pimpernel.

WEIGH. A lever; a wedge.

WEIGH-BALK. The beam of scales.

WEIGH-BOARD. Clay intersecting a vein.

WEIGH-JOLT. A seesaw. *Wilts.*

WEIGHKEY. Soft; clammy. *Yorksh.*

WEIGHT. (1) A great number. *North.*

(2) A machine for winnowing corn.

WEIKE. Weak; slow.

WEILEWAY. Alas! See *Walaway.*

He may seye *welleway* his burth,
For wo to him is leide.

Cursor Mundi, MS. Coll. Trin. Cantab. f. 94.

WEINE. (1) A vein. Vocab. MS.

(2)

That they fynd na fawte of fude to theire horses,
Nowthire *weyne,* ne waxe, ne welthe in this erthe.

Morte Arthure, MS. Lincoln, f. 55.

WEIR. (1) A pool. (2) A dam.

WEIRD-SISTERS. The Fates.

WEIVE. To forsake; to decline; to refuse; to depart. *(A.-S.)*

WEKE. (1) The wick. *Palsgrave.*

For firste the wexe bitokeneth his manhede,
The *weke* his soule, the fire his Godhede.

Lydgate, MS. Soc. Antiq. 134, f. 29.

(2) To grow weak. *(A.-S.)*

WEKET. A wicket. Also as *Bel-chos,* q. v. "A weket of the wombe," MS. Addit. 12195.

WEKYD. Wicked; mischievous.

WEL. Well; in good condition.

WELAWILLE. Wild; dangerous. *Gaw.*

WELA-WYNNE. Well joyous. *Gaw.*

WELBODE. The insect millepes.

WELCH. A failure *Yorksh.*

WELCH-AMBASSADOR. A cuckoo.

WELCH-HOOK. A kind of bill or axe having two edges. "A Welsh hook, *rancon, un visarma,*" Howell.

WELCHMAN'S-HOSE. To turn anything to a Welchman's hose, i. e. to turn it any way to serve one's purpose.

WELCHNUT. A walnut. This is given in MS. Lansd. 1033, f. 2, as a Wiltshire word.

WELCH-PARSLEY. Hemp.

WELCOME - HOME - HUSBAND. Cypress spurge. Also called *Welcome to our house.*

WELDE. (1) To wield; to govern. *(A.-S.)*

Alle that ben of warde and elde,
That cunnen hemself kepe and *welde,*
They schulen alle to chyrche come,
And ben i-schryve alle and some.

MS. Cott. Claud. A. ii. f. 129.

And seide, Abraham, this is the land
That thou and thine shul have *woldand.*

Cursor Mundi, MS. Coll. Trin. Cantab. f. 15.

(2) A wood; a forest; a plain.

(3) To carry; to bear.

(4) To possess. Also, possession.

WELDER. An owner; a ruler.

WELDY. Active. *(A.-S.)*

WELE. (1) Well. *(A.-S.)*

(2) Wealth; prosperity; good fortune.

Wherefore lett us say in *wele* and in woo,
Good Lorde evermore thy wille be doo!

MS. Bibl. Reg. 17 D. xv. f. 22.

WELEFULNES. Happiness.

WELEWED. Dried up; decayed. (*A.-S.*)

For *welewed* in that gres grene,
That ever siththen hath ben sene.
    Cursor Mundi, MS. Coll. Trin. Cantab. f. 8.

The whiche was whilom grene gras
Is *welewed* hey, as tyme now.
    Gower, MS. Soc. Antiq. 134, f. 245.

WELKE. (1) To wither; to be musty.

The see now ebbeth, now it floweth;
The londe now *welketh*, now it groweth.
    Gower, MS. Soc. Antiq. 134, f. 36.

(2) To mark with protuberances.

(3) To wane; to decrease. *Spenser.*

(4) Walked. Perceval, 209.

Jhesus was there, he *welke* the strete,
And with this blynde gon he mete.
    Cursor Mundi, MS. Coll. Trin. Cantab. f. 84.

(5) The same as *Welte*, q. v.

WELKIN. The sky. (*A.-S.*)

WELKING. Big and awkward; thus, a great *welking* fellow; generally used in the same sense as *hulking*; though at times it seems as if it were taken to signify wallowing; for they say, "He's *welking* about with his fat sides." *Linc.*

WELKNE. The sky.

A mannis synne is for to hate,
Whiche maketh the *welkne* for to debate.
    Gower, MS. Soc. Antiq. 134, f. 36.

WELL. (1) Surface springs, used as a source of water for domestic or other special purposes, are generally termed wells. *York.*

(2) A chimney or vent-hole in a rick or mow. *Norfolk.*

(3) To bubble up. *Palsgrave.*

(4) To weld. *North.*

(5) *Well to live, well to do,* rich.

WELLADAY. Alas! *Var. dial.*

WELL-A-FINE. To a good purpose.

WELLANDE. Boiling; bubbling. Used metaphorically for furiously, madly.

Of molten leed and bras withal,
And of other *wellande* metal. *MS. Ashmole* 41, f. 127.

Who so handlyth pycche *wellyng* hote,
He shal have fylthe therof sumdeyl.
    MS. Harl. 1701, f. 44.

WELL-AN-ERE. Alas! *North.*

WELL-APAID. Satisfied. *West.*

WELL-AT-EASE. Hearty; healthy.

WELL-DOING. A benefit. *Devon.*

WELLE. (1) To boil.

Goth to the devel there shul ye go,
For to *welle* ever in wo;
Ever in his wo to *welle*,
With him and his that are in helle.
    Cursor Mundi, MS. Coll. Trin. Cantab. f. 138.

(2) To rage; to be hot.

(3) Very. (4) A wheel.

(5) To flow, as from a spring.

Mary, welle of mercy!
Wellyng ever pité.
    Cursor Mundi, MS. Coll. Trin. Cantab. f. 105.

(6) Grassy plain; sward. *Gawayne.*

WELL-HEAD. A fountain; a spring.

WELL-NIGH. Almost. *Var. dial.*

WELLS. The under parts of a waggon.

WELL-SEEN. Expert; skilful.

WELL-SOSSE. Well-a-day! *Devon.*

WELL-STREAM. A spring; a fountain.

WELLY. (1) Almost; very. *North.*

(2) Well-a-day, i. e. alas!

(3) To commiserate. *North.*

WELLYD. Coagulated, as milk.

WELME. A bubble. (*A.-S.*)

WELNE. Well-nigh; almost.

WELOGH. The willow.

WELOWE. To wither; to dry; to rot.

I am smyten downe and begynne to *welowe*,
As heye that lyeth ajeyn the sonne.
    MS. Cantab. Ff. ii. 38, f. 2.

WELSH. Insipid. *North.*

WELSOME. Wildsome.

They namyd the chylde Syr Degrabelle,
That *welsome* was of wone.
    MS. Cantab. Ff. ii. 38, f. 68.

WELT. (1) To upset. *North.*

(2) To totter. *Yorksh.*

(3) To turn down the upper leather of a shoe to which the sole is fastened.

(4) To ornament with fringe. Also, a hem or border of fur, &c.

(5) To soak. *East.*

(6) To beat severely. *Norf.*

WELTE. (1) Rolled; overturned.

Whenne the kynge hade of hym syghte,
In his chayere he *welte* up-ryghte:
And whenne thay had lyfte hym up agayne,
Thanne of Cristofer ganne he frayne.
    MS. Lincoln A. i. 17, f. 127.

(2) Wielded; governed. (*A.-S.*)

WELTER. To tumble, or roll about.

WELTHE. A welt. (*A.-S.*)

WELTHFUL. Fruitful.

WELWILLY. Favorable; propitious.

WELWYNGE. A wallowing. *Pr. Parv.*

WEM. (1) A spot; a blemish. *East.*

(2) The womb, or belly. *North.*

WEMBLE. To turn a cup upside down in token of having had enough tea. *North.*

WEMENT. To moan; to lament.

WEMLES. Without spot or stain. (*A.-S.*)

The state of maydenhed he sal spylle,
Maydenhed that es *wemles.*
    MS. Bibl. Coll. Sion. xviii. 6.

WEMMED. Corrupted. (*A.-S.*)

WENCHE. A young woman. *Wenche of the game*, a strumpet.

WENCHEN. Wenches. *Glouc.*

WENDE. (1) To change. Also, to turn, as a ship does with the tide.

(2) To go. (*A.-S.*)

Hast thow hyet hyt to the ende,
That thou my3tes hamward *wende?*
    MS. Cott. Claud. A. ii. f. 140.

For so sayeth Crist, withoute fayle,
That nyje upon the worldis ende,
Pees and accorde away schalle *wende.*
    Gower, MS. Soc. Antiq. 134, f. 57.

But whenne that I schale hennes *wende,*
Grawnte me the blysse wythowten ende.
    MS. Cott. Claud. A. ii. f. 130.

(3) To think; to conjecture. (*A.-S.*)

WENE. (1) To think; to suppose. (*A.-S.*)

No, for God, seid oure kyng,
I *wene* thou knowist me no thyng.
    MS. Cantab. Ff. v. 48, f. 48.

(2) Guess; supposition; doubt. (*A.-S.*)

WENER. Fairer. *Gawayne.*

WENGABLES. Vegetables. *East.*

WENGAND. Vengeance. *Higins.*

WENGED. Avenged. *Gawayne.*

WENIAND. See *Wanion.*

WENNEL. A calf newly weaned.

WENSDAY. Wednesday.

WENT. (1) A crossway; a passage.

(2) Went away; vanished. *West.*

(3) Gone. From *Wende*, to go.

> Of the brede, thurghe Sacrament,
> To flesshe and blode hyt ys alle *went*.
>
>   *MS. Harl.* 1701, f. 67.

(4) To turn; to turn back. Also, the turning of a stair, &c.

(5) A furlong of land.

(6) To turn sour or acid. *East.*

(7) The teasel, or fuller's thistle.

(8) Thought. (*A.-S.*)

> He *wente* that tyme haffe deyed thare,
> So that saule brynte hym thare.
>
>   *. R. de Brunne, MS. Bowes*, p. 2.

(9) Done; fulfilled.

> And badde here wyl shulde be *went*
> To Agladyous comaundement.
>
>   *MS. Harl.* 1701, f. 54.

WENTLE. To turn, or roll over.

WEODEN. Weeds. (*A.-S.*)

WEOREN. Were. (*A.-S.*)

WEORRED. Defended. (*A.-S.*)

WEP. Wept. (*A.-S.*)

WEPELY. Causing tears. (*A.-S.*)

WEPEN. (1) A weapon. (*A.-S.*)

(2) To weep. *Chaucer.*

> There the pepulle schale gedèr withinne
> To prayen and to *wepen* for here synne.
>
>   *MS. Cott. Claud.* A. ii. f. 131.

WEPENE. Membrum virile.

WEPMON. A man. (*A.-S.*)

WEPPYND. Armed. (*A.-S.*)

> Then spake Moche, the mylner sune,
> Evermore wel hym betyde,
> Take xij. of thi wyght ʒemen
> Welle *weppynd* be ther side.
>
>   *MS. Cantab.* Ff. v. 48, f. 196.

WER. Our. *North.*

WERC. Work. (*A.-S.*)

WERCE. Worse. *Pr. Parv.*

WERCHE. (1) To work. (*A.-S.*)

(2) Thin; watery; insipid. *North.*

WERCOK. A pheasant.

WERDES. Fortunes. (*A.-S.*)

WERDEZ. Are. *Gawayne.*

WERDLICHE. Worldly. (*A.-S.*)

WERDROBE. The ordure of the badger.

WERE. (1) Doubt; uncertainty; confusion.

> But we, that dwelle undir the mone,
> Stonde in this world upon a *weer*.
>
>   *Gower, MS. Soc. Antiq.* 134, f. 31.

> Ha! fadir, be nouʒt in a *weere*.
>
>   *Gower, MS. Soc. Antiq.* 134, f. 51.

> And thorowe hir merite she hathe the mouthes shit,
> And lyppes closed of hem that weren in *were*.
>
>   *Lydgate, MS. Ashmole* 39, f. 48.

> And thus he wandreth in a *weere*,
> As man blynde that may not see.
>
>   *MS. Cantab.* Ff. ii. 38, f. 20.

(2) To wear. (*A.-S.*)

> In honeste clothes thow moste gon,
> Baselard ny bawdryke *were* thow no...
>
>   *MS. Cott. Claud.* A. ii. f. 127.

(3) To defend; to protect; to save.

> ʒyf ne myʒt with noun answere
> On outher manere hymselven *were*.
>
>   *MS. Harl.* 1701, f. 25.

> That Floreus had a tame bere,
> And was an hyrde shepe to *were*.
>
>   *MS. Harl.* 1701, f. 27.

(4) War.

> And some also telles and say
> That they have loste hors and harnay,
> And theyre armoure and othere gere,
> Thorue myscheyf in londe of *were*.
>
>   *MS. Harl.* 2260, f. 58.

(5) A pool of water. *North.*

(6) A weir for catching fish.

(7) Wore. (8) Had. *Gawayne.*

WERELYE. Slily.

> As he blenchyd hym besyde,
> A lyon come toward hym *werelye*.
>
>   *MS. Cantab.* Ff. ii. 38, f. 171.

WEREMOD. Wormwood.

WERESENS. Ourselves. *Leic.*

WER-HEDLYNG. A commander in war.

WERING. (1) Growing.

(2) Bulwark; protection. (*A.-S.*)

WERKE. (1) Work. (*A.-S.*)

> Hast thou be slowe in any degré
> For to do *werke* of charyté.
>
>   *MS. Cott. Claud.* A. ii. f. 140.

(2) Ache. *Reliq. Antiq.* i. 126.

WERKE-DAY. A work-day.

> For apon the *workeday*
> Men be so bysy in uche way,
> So that for here ocupacyone
> They leve myche of here devocyone.
>
>   *MS. Cott. Claud.* A. ii. f. 138.

WERLAUGHE. A wizard. " Wreke hyme on this werlaughe," *MS. Morte Arthure*, f. 92.

WERLEDE. The world? (*A.-S.*)

> For pompe and pryde of *werlede* to se,
> And of the povre has no pyté.
>
>   *MS. Harl.* 2260, f. 70.

WERLY. Worldly. (*A.-S.*)

WERMESTORE.

> And thou sal alsua mak a boure
> For to hald in thi *wermestore*.
>
>   *MS. Cott. Vespas.* A. iii. f. 11.

WERNE. To forbid; to refuse; to hinder; to deny; to warn; to guard. (*A.-S.*)

> Joseph and Marye wolde not *werne*,
> But to the scole lad hlim ʒerne.
>
>   *Cursor Mundi, MS. Coll. Trin. Cantab.* f. 77.

> Hurtyng bothe gastly and bodely is forbed,
> And *wernyng* of mete to the pour in peril of dede.
>
>   *MS. Egerton* 927.

> Thouʒ it be nouʒt the houndis kynde
> To ete chaf, ʒit wol he *werne*
> An oxe, whiche cometh to the berne,
> Thereof to taken eny food.
>
>   *Gower, MS. Soc. Antiq.* 134, f. 61.

> And certis that may no womman *werne*,
> For love is of himselfe so derne.
>
>   *Gower, MS. Soc. Antiq.* 134, f. 52.

WERON. Were. (*A.-S.*)

WERPE. To throw; to cast.

WERRAY. Make war.

And saiden, is-not this that mon
That we say this yondir day
Aʒen Jhesu name *werray*?
Cursor Mundi, MS. Coll. Trin. Cantab. f. 120.

And alle that caste us falsly to *werray*.
Lydgate, MS. Soc. Antiq. 134, f. 22.

WERRE. (1) War. (*A.-N.*)

For pes ne bydyth in no londe
Theras *werre* is nyʒh-honde.
Religious Poems, xv. Cent.

(2) The worse.

It is to wondir of thilke werre,
In whiche none wot who hath the *werre.*
Gower, MS. Soc. Antiq. 134, f. 31.

Who may to love make a werre,
That he ne hath himselfe the *werre.*
Gower, MS. Soc. Antiq. 134, f. 95.

WERRESTE. The worst.

Sey wist y the brom,
Thwat ys me for to don?
Ich have the *werreste* bonde
That ys in oni londe. *MS. Addit.* 11579, f. 29.

WERRET. To tease; to worry. *Var. dial.*

WERRY. To bring forth young; used, however, in the case only of rabbits, rats, and mice. *Linc.*

WERRYYNGE. Making war?

And alle that specially falles
To that that men schuld hele calles,
Withoute douʒt of *weryynge,*
In the trouthe of Criste heven kynge.
MS. Harl. 2260, f. 138.

WERSE. Worse. (*A.-S.*)

WERSELLS. Ourselves. *North.*

WERSTE. Worst. (*A.-S.*)

Bakkebytynge es thys to say,
Whan a man spekys ille ay,
And tournes that he may here
Of othere men on the *werste* manere.
MS. Harl. 2260, f 19.

WERWOLVES. People who had the power of turning themselves into, or were turned into, wolves. See *A-charmed.*

WERYE. To curse.

Thai sal be fulle of hatreden thanne,
Ilkone sal othyr *werye* and banne.
Hampole, MS. Bowes, p. 216.

WESAWNT. The weasand.

WESCH. To wash.

The kyng causyd the cokwoldes ychon
To *wesch* withouten les. *MS. Ashmole* 61, f. 61.

WESE. To ooze out. (*A.-S.*)

WESELS. A dish in cookery.

Fyrst grynde porke, temper in fere
With egges and powder of peper dere,
And powder of canel thou put therto,
In chapon necke thou close hit tho,
Or elles in paunch of grys hit pyt,
And rost hit wele, and then dore hit
Withoute with batere of egges and floure,
To serve in sale or ellys in boure.
MS. Sloane 1986, p. 103.

WESH. Stale urine. *North.*

WESS. Washed. *Hearne.*

WEST. (1) To set in the West.
(2) Shows. (3) Knowest. *Weber.*
(4) A red pustule about the eye.

WESTREN. To tend to the West.

Withoute *westrynge* or drawynge to declyne.
Lydgate, MS. Soc. Antiq. 134, f. 22.

WESTRIL. A short underhand cudgel.

WESTWALE. Westphalia.

Thay were wroght in *Westwale*
With womene of lare.
MS. Lincoln A. 1. 17, f. 138

WESTWARD-HOE! To the West! It was one of the cries of the Thames' watermen.

WESTY. Dizzy; giddy. *North.*

WET. To rain. *To wet the sickle,* to drink out earnest money at harvest time. *To wet one's whistle,* to drink.

WETAND. Thinking. (*A.-S.*)

ʒyf thou ever, yn evyl *wetand,*
On fadyr or modyr leydest thyn hand.
MS. Harl. 1701, f. 8.

WETANDLY. Knowingly.

Als ofte als I hafe done dedly synne,
And thurghe malece *wetandly* fallyne thereinne.
MS. Lincoln A. 1. 17, f. 193.

WET-BOARD. A shoemaker's cutting-out board. *Var. dial.*

WET-BOARDS. Movable boards sliding in grooves in doors, &c.

WETE. (1) To know. (*A.-S.*)
(2) Wheat. Nominale MS.

The meke hym lowes to serve comonly,
Als duse ane asse that berys ofte hevy,
And berys als wel barly as *wete,*
And als faste for smale gos als for the grete.
MS. Harl. 2260, f. 17.

WETEWOLDIS. Wittol cuckolds.

WET-FINGER. To do anything with a wet finger, i. e. easily, readily.

WET-GOOSE. A poor simple fellow.

WET-HAND. A drunken fellow. *North.*

WETHE. Sweet; mild. (*A.-S.*)

WETHERBED. A feather-bed. "Cum lecto pennato, Anglice a *Wetherbed,*" Vita R. Ricardi II. ed. 1729, p. 162.

WETHERHOG. A male or heder hog. Also, a surname in the county. *Linc.*

WETHERLY. With rage and violence.

WETHEWYNDE. The plant woodbine.

WETING. Knowledge. (*A.-S.*)

WET-JACKET. A man who gets drenched in a shower is said, naturally enough, to have a *wet jacket.*

WET-SHOD. Wet in the feet.

WETTING-THE-BLOCK. A custom among shoemakers on the first Monday in March, when they cease from working by candlelight, and have a supper so called.

WEUTER. To stagger. *Lanc.*

WEVE. (1) To put off; to prevent.
(2) To lift up; to raise.

WEVED. An altar. (*A.-S.*)

WEVER. A river. *Chesh.*

WEVET. A spider's web. *Somerset.*

WEWERPOW. A dam across a ditch to keep up the water. *North.*

WEXE. To grow; to increase.

He that myghte lerne and holde faste,
He schulde *wexe* wyse at the laste.
MS. Cantab. Ff. II. 38, f. 147.

WEYBREDS. Warts. *East.*

WEYEDEN. Weighed.

WEYEY. Yes, yes. *North.*

WEYFE. A wife. Isumbras, 124.

WEYFERUS. Travellers. (*A.-S.*)

Hast thou in herte rowthe i-had
Of hem that were nede be-stad,
To seke, and sore, and prisonerus,
I-herberet alle *weyferus.*
MS. Cott. Claud. A. ii. f. 144.

WEYHEDE. Carried.

I sulde fulle foule hafe bene lettide of my passage,
whenne I solde hafe bene *weyhede* oute of thise
paynes. *MS. Lincoln A. i. 17, f. 257.*

WEYHES. Rings; bracelets.

And he broghte *weyhes* in his hand, and he was
clede alle in whitte clothes, and me thoghte this
lady was cled in white clothe of golde.
MS. Lincoln A. i. 17, f. 257.

WEYMENT. Lamentation.

Jhesus the *weyment* undirstode,
With hem to that grave he jode.
Cursor Mundi, MS. Coll. Trin. Cantab. f. 89.

And as the turtille by oontemplatyf,
For synne soroweth with greet *weymentynge.*
Lydgate, MS. Soc. Antiq. 134, p. 28.

And made more *weymentacion*
Than I can make of nominacion.
Occleve, MS. Soc. Antiq. 134, f. 271.

VEYNE. A waggon.

In *weynes* were thei put to lede,
That Joseph sent hem ful of sede.
Cursor Mundi, MS. Coll. Trin. Cantab. f. 33.

WEYNT. Done; fulfilled.

Hast thou for slowthe i-be so feynt,
That al thy wylle has be *weynt.*
MS. Cotton. Claud. A. ii. f. 141.

WEYSCHALLE. A balance.

WEYTHERNOY. The herb feverfew.

WEYVE. To wave; to forsake.

But jyf thou hope that he wul *weyve*
Hys lawe, and Crystendom receyve.
MS. Harl. 1701, f. 44.

WEYWORT. The herb *ipia major.*

WEZZLING. Giddy; thoughtless. *Linc.*

WEZZON. The weasand, or windpipe.

WHA. (1) Who. (2) Well. *North.*

WHACK. (1) Appetite. *North.*

(2) To strike; to beat. *Var. dial.*

(3) A heavy fall. Also, to fall.

WHACKER. (1) To tremble; to quake. *North.*

(2) Anything very large. *Var. dial.*

WHACKER-GERSE. The plant cow-quake.

WHACKING. Very large. *Var. dial.*

WHAD. What. *Salop.*

By whom also thow moste mynne,
And whom he gart to do that synne,
And *whad* they were that were here ferus,
Prestes or clerkus, monkes or frerus.
MS. Cott. Claud. A. ii. f. 146.

WHAINT. (1) Quaint; odd. (2) Very.

WHAINTISE. Cunning.

Pryde, and pomppe, and covatyse,
And vayne sleghtes and *whayntyse.*
Hampole, MS. Bowes, p. 47.

WHAKE. To quake; to tremble. *North.*

WHAKER. A quaker. *North.*

WHALE. To thrash; to beat. *North.*

WHALE'S-BONE. Ivory. *As white as whale s
bone,* a very common simile. Some ancient
writers imagined ivory, formerly made from
the teeth of the walrus, to be formed from
the bones of the whale.

WHALM. To cover over. *Warw.*

WHAM. (1) Home.

Than preyde the ryche man Abraham
That he wlde sende Lazare or sum other *wham.*
MS. Harl. 1701, f. 44.

(2) A bog; a morass. *North.*

WHAMIRE. A quagmire. *Yorksh.*

WHAMP. (1) A wasp. *Yorksh.*

(2) A young child. *Warw.*

WHANE. (1) To stroke down. *Cumb.*

(2) To coax; to entice. *North.*

WHANG. (1) A blow. *North.*

(2) To throw with violence. *Linc.*

(3) A thong. See Robin Hood, i. 98. Hence
the verb, to beat or flog.

(4) Anything large. *Yorksh.*

WHANGBY. Very hard cheese made of old
or skimmed milk. *North.*

WHANHOPE. Despair.

Whanhope es the secunde synne,
Wo es hym that deyes thare-inne.
MS. Harl. 2260, f. 20.

WHANNE. When.

But, Lorde, how he was in his herte amevid,
Whanne that Marye he hath with childe y-seyne.
Lydgate, MS. Soc. Antiq. 134, f. 4.

WHANTE. A long pole. *Pr. Parv.*

WHANTER. To flatter. *North.*

WHANTLE. To fondle. *Cumb.*

WHAP. (1) A blow. (2) To beat.

(3) To vanish suddenly. *North.*

WHAPPE. To wrap up. *Pr. Parv.*

WHAPPER. Anything very large.

WHAPPET. (1) The prick-eared cur.

(2) A blow on the ear. *Devon.*

WHAPPLE-WAY. A bridle-way. *South.*

WHARF-STEAD. A ford in a river.

WHARLE. "Wharle for a spyndell, *peson*,"
Palsgrave, 1530. Kennett describes it " the
piece of wood put upon the iron spindle to
receive the thread."

WHARLING. An inability in any one to pronounce the letter R.

WHARL-KNOT. A hard knot. *Lanc.*

WHARRE. Crabs, or the crab-tree. *Chesh.*
" As sowre as wharre," is the example given
by Ray.

WHARROW. The wharle of a spindle.

WHART. (1) A quart. *North.*

(2) Across. *Suffolk.*

WHARTER. A quarter. *Yorksh.*

WHARTLE. To cross; to tease. *Norf.*

WHAR-TO. Wherefore.

WHART-WHARTLE. To tease. *Forby.*

WHAT. (1) Something.

(2) Partly; in part.

(3) While; till. (4) Quickly. *Weber.*

(5) An interjection, Lo !

WHATE. (1) Quickly. (2) Hot.

WHATEKYN. What kind of

With I. and E. the dede to the
Salle come, als I the kenne,
Bot thou ne wate in *whatekyn* state,
Ne how, ne whare, ne whenne.
MS. Lincoln A. i. 17, f. 213.

Take gode hede on hys degré,
Of *whatskynnes* lyvynge that he be.
MS. Cott. Claud. A. ii. f. 146.

WHAT-FOR. For what reason. *Var. dial.*
WHAT-NOSED. Hot-nosed from drinking.
WHAT-SO. Whatsoever. *Gawayne.*
WHATSOMEVER. Whatever.
WHAT'S-WHAT. What is good.
WHATTE. Knowest.
WHATTEN. What kind of; what.
WHAT-WAY. A guide-post. *Herts.*
WHAU. Why; yes. *North.*
WHAUP. (1) The larger curlew.
(2) A knot, or twist. *North.*
WHAVE. (1) To cover, or hang over. *North.*
(2) To turn pottery when drying. *Staff.*
WHAWM. (1) To overwhelm. *Yorksh.*
(2) Warmth. *Lanc.*
WHAYLE. Whole; healed.
When hys woundys were *whayle*,
He wente to the dewke sawns fayle.
MS. Cantab. Ff. ii. 38, f. 180.
WHAY-WORMS. Whims. Carr has *whey-worms*, pimples, Craven Gloss. ii. 252.
And so marched toward London, where the Essex men, havinge wylde *whay-woormes* in their heddes, joined them with him. *Hall, Edward IV.* f. 33.
WHAZLE. To wheeze. *North.*
WHE. Who. *North.*
WHEADY. Long; tedious. *North.*
WHEAL. A blister.
WHEAM. Snug; convenient. *North.*
WHEAMLY. Slily; deceitfully. *Linc.*
WHEAMOW. Nimble; active. *Chesh.*
WHEAN. (1) To coax; to flatter. *North.*
(2) A small number or quantity.
WHEAT-EAR. The ortolan, so called in Sussex, from its coming when the wheat is in the ear.
WHEAT-PLUM. A large fleshy plum, sometimes called a bastard Orleans plum. *Linc.*
WHEAT-SHEAR. To cut wheat. *Kent.*
WHEAWTIT. Whistled. *Lanc.*
WHEAZE. A puff. *Craven.*
WHECKER. To neigh. *Somerset.*
WHEDDER. To tremble. *North.*
WHEDEN. A simple person. *West.*
WHEDER. Whether. (*A.-S.*)
WHEE. A heifer. *Yorksh.*
WHEEK. To squeak. *North.*
WHEEL. (1) A whirlpool. *Lanc.*
(2) A mill. *Yorksh.*
WHEEL-LOCK. A small machine attached to the ancient musket, used for producing sparks of fire.
WHEEL-PIT. A whirlpool. *Yorksh.*
WHEELSPUN. Strong coarse yarn.
WHEEL-SPUR. The inner high ridge on the side of a wheel-rut. *East.* "Whele spore, *orbita*," Prompt. Parv.
WHEELSWARF. Yellow sludge formed during grinding on a wet stone.

WHEEN-CAT. A queen or female cat.
WHEENE. A queen. *North.*
That es called the *wheene* of Amazonnes, Undyr whose powere that folk wonnes.
Hampole, MS. Bowes, p. 136.
WHELE. A weal, or blister.
WHELK. (1) A blow; a fall. *North.*
(2) A number, or quantity. *Yorksh.*
(3) A blister; a mark; a stripe.
WHELKER. A thump, or blow. *Cumb.*
WHELKING. Very large. *North.*
WHELL. Until. *Cumb.*
WHELME. (1) To cover over. Still in use. Also, to turn over.
Tak a bryghte bacyne, and anoynte it with mylke reme, and *whelme* it over a prene.
MS. Lincoln A. i. 17, f. 285.
(2) To sink; to depress. (*A.-S.*)
(3) Half of a hollow tree laid under a gateway for a drain. *East.*
WHELVER. A large straw hat.
WHEME. To please.
WHEMMEL. To turn over. *North.*
WHEN. An exclamation implying impatience, i. e. when will it be done, &c.
WHEN-AS. When.
WHENNES. Whence. (*A.-S.*)
WHENNY. Make haste; be nimble.
WHENNYMEGS. Trinkets. *Glouc.*
WHENSOMEVER. Whenever.
WHENT. Terrible. *North.*
WHENY. To make a bow.
WHER. (1) Whether. (2) Where.
WHERE. Whereas.
WHEREAS. Where.
WHEREBOLE. See *Quirboile.*
Whyppes of *wherebole* by-wente his whyte sythes.
MS. Cott. Calig. A. ii. f. 109.
WHEREWITH. Means; money.
WHERK. To breathe with difficulty.
WHERNE. The same as *Wharle*, q. v.
WHERR. Very sour. *Lanc.*
WHERRET. A blow on the ear.
WHERRIL. To fret; to complain. *Linc.*
WHERRY. (1) To laugh. *North.*
(2) A liquor made from the pulp of crab-apples after the verjuice is pressed out.
WHERRY-GO-NIMBLE. A looseness.
WHERT. Joy; gladness.
For thai ar so wylde when thai hafe *whert*, That thai no dreede kan halde in hert.
Hampole, MS. Bowes, p. 21.
WHERVE. A joint. *Somerset.*
WHESTIOUN. A question.
WHET. (1) To cut with a knife.
(2) To rub; to scratch. *North.*
(3) To gnash the teeth.
(4) A slight refreshment.
WHETHEN. Whence.
I caltif, *whethen* coom hit me That I Lord myn shulde baptise the.
Cursor Mundi, MS. Coll. Trin. Cantab. f. 80.
WHETHER. (1) Which of two.
(2) At all events. *North.*
(3) *Whether not*, yes, also.
WHETHERS. In doubt. *Craven.*

WHETING-CORNE. The bel-chos, q. v.

WHETKIN. The harvest supper. *North.*

WHETLEBONES. The vertebræ of the back.

WHETSTONE. An ancient reward for the person who told the greatest lie. *Lying for the whetstone* is a phrase very often met with in old works. The liar was sometimes publicly exhibited with the whetstone fastened to him.

WHETTE. Sharpened. (*A.-S.*)

WHETTLE. To cut. *North.*

WHETTYN. Wheaten?

> I clynge as dothe a *whettyn* cake.
> *MS. Porkington* 10, f. 60.

WHEUKS. Being sick. *Linc.*

WHEW. (1) To whistle. *North.*

(2) A sudden vanishing away.

WHEWER. The female widgeon.

WHEWFACED. Very pale. *Linc.*

WHEWLS. Weevils. *Linc.*

WHEWT. To whistle; to squeak.

WHEWTLE. A slight whistle. *Cumb.*

WHEWTS. Irregular tufts of grass.

WHEY-WHIG. A pleasant and sharp beverage, made by infusing mint or sage into buttermilk-whey.

WHIBIBBLE. A whim. *East.*

WHICHE. (1) A chest.

(2) Who; whom; what; what sort of. Used in Herefordshire for *when.*

WHICK. (1) Quick; lively. *North.*

(2) A quickset plant. *Chesh.*

WHICKEN. (1) Quicken; become alive.

> Yhit yf the sawle thorgh synne be slayne,
> It may thorgh grace *whycken* agayne.
> *Hampole, MS. Bowes,* p. 58.

(2) The wild ash-tree.

WHICKER. To neigh. *West.*

WHICK-FLAW. A whitlow. *North.*

WHICKS. Couch grass. *North.*

WHID. A dispute; a quarrel. *East.*

WHIDDER. To shake; to tremble. *North.*

WHIDDES. Words. *Dekker.*

WHIE. A young heifer.

WHIEW. To go very rapidly. *North.*

WHIEWER. Shrewd; sharp; violent. *Kent.*

WHIFF. A glimpse. *North.*

WHIFFING-CUP. A little cup, so called perhaps from being used by persons that smoke.

WHIFFLE. (1) To flutter. Also, to hesitate.

(2) To talk idly. *North.*

WHIFFLER. (1) A puffer of tobacco. Hence, metaphorically, a trifling fellow.

(2) The whifflers were generally pipers and horn-blowers who headed a procession, and cleared the way for it. Anti-masques were usually ushered in by whifflers.

WHIFFLE-WHAFFLE. Nonsense. *North.*

WHIFFLING. Uncertain. *Linc.*

WHIG. Buttermilk. *Linc.* According to Markham, this is merely another term for *whey.* Brockett calls it *sour whey.*

WHIK. Quick; alive.

> Thou most into the Holy Londe,
> Wher God was *whik* and dede.
> *MS. Cantab. Ff. v. 48, f. 44.*

WHIKWOD. Quick hedge.

WHILE. (1) Until. *Yorksh.*

(2) Time. (*A.-S.*) *A while's work,* work requiring a certain time. *How have you done the while,* i. e. since I saw you. *To while away the time,* to amuse one's self in an idle manner.

> Holy cherche despyse and fyle
> That wyl y blethly alle my *whyle.*
> *MS. Harl.* 1701, f. 83.

WHILERE. Some time before. (*A.-S.*)

WHILES. (1) While.

(2) Now and then. *North.*

(3) *Between whiles,* at intervals.

WHILK. (1) Who; which.

> And if I wist *whilke* thei were,
> Hit shulde come the kyng to ere.
> *MS. Cantab. Ff. v. 48, f. 48.*

(2) To complain. *Kent.*

(3) To yelp; to bark. *South.*

WHILKIN. Whether. *Yorksh.*

WHILLIMER. See *Whangby.*

WHILOM. Once; formerly. (*A.-S.*)

WHILST. Until.

WHILSUM. Doubtful.

WHILT. An idle person. *North.*

WHIM. (1) Home. *Somerset.*

(2) The brow of a hill. *Dorset.*

(3) A round table that turns round upon a screw. *Var. dial.*

WHIMBERRIES. Bilberries. *Lanc.*

WHIMLING. A childish weak person. "*Whimdlen,* small and weakly," Barnes.

WHIMLY. (1) Homely. *Somerset.*

(2) Softly; silently. *North.*

WHIMPER. To tell tales. *North.*

WHIMS. A windlass. *Yorksh.*

WHIMSY. A whim. *Devon.*

WHIM-WHAMS. Trinkets; trifles.

WHIN. Furze. *Var. dial.*

WHINACH. To cry: to sob. *West.*

WHINCOW. A bush of furze.

WHINGE. To whine; to sob. *North.*

WHINGER. A large sword. *Suffolk.*

WHINK. (1) A sharp cry. *North.*

(2) A spark of fire. *Westm.*

WHINNEL. To whine. *Glouc.*

WHINNER. To neigh. *Cumb.*

WHINNER-NEB. A meagre, thin-faced man, with a sharp nose. *North.*

WHINNOCK. (1) A milk-pail. *North.*

(2) The least pig in a litter. *South.*

WHINNY. To neigh. Also, to cry.

WHINS. Furze. *North.*

WHINSTONE. The toad-stone. *Chesh.*

WHINYARD. A sword, or hanger.

> His cloake grew large and sid,
> And a faire *whinniard* by his side.
> *Cobler of Canterburie,* 1608, sig. E. ii.

WHIP. (1) To do anything slily.

(2) *To whip the cat,* to get tipsy. Also, to be very parsimonious.

(3) The top twig of a vine.

(4) To move rapidly. *Somerset.*

WHIPARSE. A schoolmaster.

WHIP-BELLY. Thin weak liquor. *Linc.*

WHIP-CAT. Drunken. Florio, p. 358.

WHIP-CROP. The plant whitebeam.

WHIP-HER-JENNY. A game at cards, borrowed from the Welsh. It was also a term of contempt.

WHIP-JACK. A vagabond who begged for alms as a distressed seaman.

WHIPPER-SNAPPER. An insignificant person. A term of contempt.

WHIPPING. *Whipping the cat*, the custom of itinerant tailors, carpenters, &c., going from house to house to work.

WHIPPINGLY. Hastily; gorgeously.

WHIPPING-STRINGS. The reins used in guiding horses in driving.

WHIPPIT. (1) To jump about.
(2) A short light petticoat. *East.*
(3) A kind of dog, in breed between a greyhound and a spaniel.

WHIPPLE-TREE. The bar on which the traces of a dragging horse are hooked, and by which he draws his load. Pummel-tree is a longer bar, on which the *whipple-trees* are hooked when two horses draw abreast.

WHIPS. A wisp of straw. *Kent.*

WHIPS-FAGOTS. Faggots made of the tips of wood cut off in hurdle-making.

WHIPSTALK. The handle of a whip.

WHIPSTER. (1) A bleacher. *North.* (2) Grose explains it, " a sharp or subtle fellow."

From Memphis comes a *whipster* unto thee,
And a Black Indian from the Red Sea.
Fletcher's Poems, p. 64.

WHIPSTOCK. See *Whipstalk.*

WHIPSWHILE. A short time.

WHIP-THE-CAT. To *whip the cat* is a trick played in Hampshire. A bet is laid that one man shall tie a cat to another, and by whipping it shall make it draw him through a pond of water, or across a stream; the man who is foolish enough to accept the bet has a rope tied round his waist, and the other end is taken to the opposite side of the pond or stream to that on which he stands, and to this end is tied the cat, which is then whipped to make it draw the man through the water, and, of course, not being able to do so, it is assisted by men on the same side with the cat, and thus the poor simpleton is dragged through the water, to the infinite amusement of all the bystanders. *Holloway.*

WHIR. To whiz. *Var. dial.*

WHIRKEN. To suffocate. " *Noié*, drowned, whirkened," Cotgrave. *North.*

WHIRL-BONE. The kneepan. *North.*

WHIRL-BOUK. A churn which is worked by turning round. *Staffordsh.*

WHIRLE. To go about idly.

WHIRLICOTE. An open car, or chariot. According to Stow, this vehicle was used as early as 1380. See Mr. Markland's paper on coaches, in Archæologia, xx. 453.

WHIRLIGIG. A carriage. *Var. dial.*

WHIRLIGOG. A turnstile. *West.*

WHIRLPIT. A whirlpool.

WHIRLPOOL. " Whirlpole a fishe, *chaudron de mer*," Palsgrave.

WHIRL-TE-WOO. Buttermilk. *Derb.*

WHIRLY-HUFF. See *Roger's-Blast.*

WHISH. (1) Whist; silent.
(2) Sad; melancholy; pitiful. *West.*

WHISHINS. Cushions. *North.*

WHISK. (1) The game of whist. It is mentioned with other games in Taylor's Motto, 1622, sig. D. iv. It is also spelt *whisk* in the Country Gentleman's Vade-Mecum, 8vo. Lond. 1699, p. 63.
(2) To do anything hastily. *Yorksh.*
(3) To switch; to beat. *North.*
(4) A kind of winnowing machine.
(5) An impertinent fellow.
(6) A kind of tippet. *Holme.*

WHISKER. A switch, or rod.

WHISKET. (1) A basket; a straw basket in which provender is given to cattle.
(2) A small parcel. *East.*

WHISKIN. A shallow brown drinking-bowl. Ray says this is a Cheshire word.

And wee will han a *whiskin* at every rushbearing;
a wassel cup at yule; a seed-cake at fastens.
The Two Lancashire Lovers, 1640, p. 19.

WHISKING. Large; great. *North.*

WHISKISH. Frisky.

WHISK-TELT. Whorish. *Lanc.*

WHISKY. A kind of gig.

WHISP. See *Angle-berry.*

WHISS. To whistle.

WHISSONTIDE. Whitsuntide. *North.*

Byfore, after, and *whyssone tyde*,
Eghte dayes they schullen abyde.
MS. Cott. Claud. A. ii. f. 128.

WHIST. Silent; still. Also, to be silent, to make silent, to hush.

WHISTER. To whisper.

WHISTER-CLISTER. A blow. *West.* A back-handed blow is a whister-poop, a word which occurs in the London Prodigal, p. 15.

WHISTER-SNIVET. A hard blow. Jennings has *whister-twister.*

WHISTLE. (1) The throat. *Var. dial.*
(2) To try for anything uselessly.

WHISTLEJACKET. Small beer. *Linc.*

WHISTLE-OFF. A term in falconry, meaning to dismiss by a whistle.

WHIT. Quick.

WHITAKER. A species of quartz.

WHITCHEFT. Art, or cunning. *North.*

WHITE. (1) To tell; to know.

I shalle the *whyte*, be hede myne,
How hade I lever a conye.
MS. Cantab. Ff. v. 48, f. 82.

(2) Quit; free.

Bot unnethes any othyr may
Passe *whyte* thorgh purgatory away.
Hampole, MS. Bowes, p. 166

(3) A wight; a creature. (*A.-S.*)
(4) To requite. *Chesh.*
(5) A mark for an arrow, or rather the central part of a target.
(6) To cut wood. *Yorksh.*
(7) Fair specious. (*A.-S.*)

(8) An old term of endearment.

WHITE-ALE. A pale-coloured ale in great estimation in some parts of Devonshire.

WHITE-ARMOUR. Bright steel armour.

WHITE-BACK. The white poplar.

WHITE-BOTHEN. The large daisy.

WHITE-BOY. See *White* (8).

WHITECHAPEL-PLAY. See *Bungay-play*.

WHITE-FLAW. A whitlow.

WHITEFRIARS. The White-Friars near Fleet-street in London was formerly a sanctuary for offenders. See *Alsatia*.

WHITE-FROST. A hoar-frost. *Var. dial.*

WHITE-GOLDES. The large daisy.

WHITE-HEFT. Flattery; cunning.

WHITE-HERRING. A fresh herring. In the North a pickled herring is so called.

WHITE-HOUSE. A dairy-house. *Wilts.*

WHITE-LIGHT. A candle. *Linc.*

WHITE-LIVERED. Cowardly.

WHITE-MONEY. Silver.

WHITE-MOUTH. (1) A thrush. *Wilts.*
(2) A foaming mouth.

WHITE-NEB. A rook. *North.*

WHITE-PLOUGH. The fool-plough. *North.*

WHITE-POT. A dish made of cream, sugar, rice, currants, cinnamon, &c. It was formerly much eaten in Devonshire.

WHITE-POWDER. Gunpowder which exploded without noise. It was formerly believed there was such a composition.

WHITE-PUDDING. A sort of sausage made of the entrails and liver. *West.*

WHITE-RICE. The white-beam.

WHITES. White cloths.

WHITESTER. A bleacher of linen.

WHITE-STONE. Worthy of being marked with a *white stone*, i. e. very commendable.

WHITE-WOOD. The lime-tree.

WHITHER. To whiz. *North.*

WHITHERER. A strong person. *Linc.*

WHITHINE. Whence.

Whenne that thou sawe thy swete sone Jhesus
ascende into hevene, fra *whythyne* he come in the
manhede he tuke of the. ·
MS. Lincoln A. 1. 17, f. 178.

WHITIL. A blanket.

WHITING. To let leap a whiting, i. e. to miss an opportunity.

WHITINGMOP. A young whiting. Also, a young woman, a tender creature.

WHITINGS. White-puddings.

WHITLING. The young of the bull-trout in its first year. *North.*

WHITNECK. The weasel. *Cornw.*

WHITSTER. A whitesmith. *East.*

WHITSUN-ALE. A festival held at Whitsuntide, still kept up in some parts of the country. The Whitson Lord, mentioned in the following example, is one of the characters in the festival.

Ich have beene twise our *Whitson Lord*,
Ich have had ladies many vare. *Melismata*, 1611.

WHITSUN-FARTHINGS. Customary dues from parochial churches to their cathedral.

WHIT-TAWER. A collar-maker. *North.* Anciently a tanner of white leather.

WHITTEE-WHATTEE. To whisper. *North.*

WHITTEN. The wayfaring tree. *Kent.*

WHITTER. To whine; to complain. *Linc.*

WHITTERICK. A young partridge. *North.*

WHITTERY. Pale; sickly. *East.*

WHITTLE. (1) To cut; to notch. *Var. dial.*
(2) A blanket. Still in use. Kennett says, " a coarse shagged mantle." The whittle, which was worn about 1700, was a fringed mantle, almost invariably worn by country women out of doors.
(3) A knife. Still in use.
(4) To wash; to rub. *Oxon.*
(5) A knot. Also, to tie.

WHITTLED. Intoxicated.

WHITTLE-GAIT. In Cumberland, when the village schoolmaster does not receive adequate pay to support himself from his scholars' quarter-pence, he is allowed what is called a *whittle-gait*, or the privilege of using his knife, in rotation, at the tables of those who send children to his school.

WHITTLETHER. A kind of coarse cloth.

Thy gerdill made of the *whittlether* whange,
Which thow has wore God knawes howe longe,
Is turned nowe to velvet imbrethered stronge
With gould and pearle amange. *MS. Lansd.* 241.

WHITTY-TREE. The mountain ash. *West.*

WHITWITCH. A pretended conjuror, whose power depends on his learning. *Exm.*

WHIT-WOOD. The lime-tree. *Worc.*

WHITY-BROWN. A pale dusky brown.

WHIVER. To hover. *West.*

WHIVIL. To hover. *Dorset.*

WHIZ. To hiss. *Var. dial.* It occurs in Topsell's Beasts, 1607, p. 11.

WHIZZEN. To whine. *North.*

WHIZZER. A falsehood. *North.*

WHIZZLE. To obtain anything slily.

WHO. (1) How. *Kent.*
(2) Whole. (3) She. *North.*

WHOARD. A hoard; a heap.

WHOATS. Oats. *Var. dial.*

WHOAVE. To cover over. *Chesh.*

WHOCKING. Trembling; in a fluster.

WHOD. A hood.

WHOE. The same as Ho, q. v.

WHOLE-FOOTED. Very heavy footed. Also, very intimate. *East.*

WHOLESOME. Decently clean. *East.*

WHOLT. A mischievous fellow. *North.*

WHOME. Home. *North.*

And yf thou wylt not so do,
Whome with the then wyll y goo.
MS. Cantab. Ff. ii. 38, f. 213.

WHOMMLE. To turn over. *Var. dial.*

WHONE. One.

WHOO. An exclamation of surprise.

WHOOBUB. A hubbub.

WHOOK. To shake. *Chesh.*

WHOOP. To hoop, or cry out.

WHOOPER. To shout. *Dorset.*

WHOOR. Where. *Yorksh.*

WHOO-UP. The exclamation of hunters at the death of the chase.

WHOP. To put or place suddenly. *North.*

WHOPSTRAW. A country bumpkin.

WHORECOP. A bastard. See *Horcop.*

WHORE'S-BIRD. A term of reproach.

WHORLE. To rumble with noise.

WHORLE-PIT. A whirlpool.

WHORLWYL. Same as *Wharle*, q. v.

WHORRELL-WINDE. A whirlwind.

    And that Elyas was taken up
    Within a *whorrell-winde*.   *MS. Ashmole* 208.

WHORT. A small blackberry.

WHO-SAY. A dubious report. *West.*

WHOSH. To appease; to quiet.

WHOT. Hot. Still in use.

WHOTYEL. An iron auger. *Lanc.*

WHOUGH. How. (*A.-S.*)

WHOYS. Whose.

WHOZZENED. Wrinkled. *Derb.*

WHREAK. To whine. *Yorksh.*

WHRINE. Sour. *North.*

WHRIPE. To whimper; to whine. *North.*

WHULE. To whine; to howl. *Suffolk.*

WHUNE. A few. *Northumb.*

WHUNSOME. Pleasant; delightful.

WHUNT. Quaint; cunning.

WHURLE. To whine, as a cat.

WHURR. To growl, as a dog.

WHUSSEL. A whistle. *Whussel-wood*, the alder, of which whistles are made.

WHUST. To whist, or make silent.

WHUTE. To whistle.

WHUTHER. To beat; to flutter. *North.*

WHY-NOT. An arbitrary proceeding, one without any assigned reason. Also, a sudden event.

WHYTOWRE. Corrupt matter from a sore.

WHY-VORE. Wherefore. *Devon.*

WHY-WAWS. Trifles; idle talk.

WI. (1) While. *Hearne.*

(2) A man; a knight. (*A.-S.*)

(3) Sorrow; woe; trouble.

WIAN. A kind of wine.

WIBBLE. Thin weak liquor.

WIBBLE-WOBBLE. Unsteadily.

WIBLING'S-WITCH. The four of clubs.

WIBROW. The plantain. *Chesh.*

WIC. A week. *Wilts.*

WICCHE. (1) A witch. (*A.-S.*)

(2) To use witchcraft; to bewitch.

WICH. (1) Quick; alive. *North.*

(2) A salt-work. *West.*

(3) A small dairy-house. *Essex.*

WICHDOME. Witchcraft.

    So they lad hym wyth trecherye,
    Wyth *wychdome* and wyth sorcerye.
        MS. Cantab. Ff ii. 38, f. 136.

WICH-ELM. The broad-leaved elm.

WICHENE. Witches. (*A.-S.*)

    Also alle *wychene* and alle that in wychecraft by-leveth, other that doeth therafter, or by here con-sayle.   *MS. Burney* 356, p. 99.

WICH-WALLER. A salt-boiler. *Chesh.*

WICK. (1) A bay, small port, or village on the side of a river. *Yorksh.*

(2) Quick; alive. *North.*

(3) Wight; fit for war. *Scott.*

(4) A corner. *North.*

WICKE. (1) Wickedness. (2) Wicked.

    Pride is the werste of alle *wicke*,
    And costeth most and leste is worth.
        Gower, MS. Soc. Antiq. 134, f. 69.
    But a synful soule and *wicke*
    Is als blak as any picke.
        MS. Lansd. 793, f. 135.

WICKED. Dangerous. Still in use. "A wicked wounde," MS. Med. Rec. 1571.

WICKEN-TREE. The mountain-ash.

WICKER. To castrate a ram. *West.*

WICKET. The female pudendum.

WICKY. Same as *Wicken-tree*, q. v.

WIDDENT. Won't. *Westm.*

WIDDER. To wither, or dry up.

WIDDERSFUL. Earnestly striving.

WIDDERSHINS. A direction contrary to the course of the sun, from right to left.

WIDDEY. A band of osier-rods.

WIDDLE. (1) To fret. *North.*

(2) A small pustule. *East.*

WIDDLES. Very young ducks. *East.*

WIDDY. A widow. *Var. dial.*

WIDDY-WADDY. Trifling; insignificant.

WIDE. Wide of the mark.

WIDE-AWAKE. Intelligent.

WIDE-COAT. A great outer coat.

WIDE-GOBBED. Wide-mouthed. *North.*

WIDERWYNE. An enemy. (*A.-S.*)

    Whenne theise wordes was saide, the Walsche kyng hymselfene
    Was warre of this *wyderwyne* that werrayede his knyghttes.   *Morte Arthure, MS. Lincoln*, f. 75.

WIDE-WHERE. Widely; far and near.

    What woldyst thou do with soche a man
    That thou haste soght so *wyde where*,
    In dyvers londys farre and nere.
        MS. Cantab. Ff. ii. 38, f. 104.

    Beterenes es thys be skylle,
    Whan a man hires of a mans ille,
    He hekes it and i-mas it mare,
    And dous it be knowyn *wyde-ware*.
        MS. Harl. 2260, f. 15.

WIDGEON. A silly fellow.

WIDOW. Sometimes a widower.

WIDOW-BEWITCHED. A woman who is separated from her husband.

WIDOW'S-BENCH. A share of the husband's estate which widows in Sussex enjoy beside their jointures.

WIDOW'S-LUST. The horse-muscle.

WIDRED. Withered.

WIDUE. A widow. (*A.-S.*)

    And yonge wymmen queyntly dyst,
    That schewes thaym mekyl to mens syst,
    And er over mekel jangelande,
    Thys es to *wyduos* nost semande.
        MS. Harl. 2260, f. 112.

WIDVER. A widower. *West.*

WIE. With; well; yes. *North.*

WIEGH. A lever; a wedge.

WIERDE. Fate; fortune.

    And sayeth it were a wondre *wierde*
    To sen a kynge become an herde.
        Gower, MS. Soc. Antiq. 134, f. 96.

WIEST. Ugly. *West.*

WIET. To wete; to know.

WIF. (1) A woman; a wife. (*A.-S.*)

(2) The sudden turn of a hare when pursued swiftly by the hounds. *East.*

WIFE-MODIR. A mother-in-law.

WIFFLE. To be uncertain. *East.*

WIFFLER. A turncoat. *Lanc.*

WIFFS. Withies. *Kent.*

WIFHODE. The state of a wife.

   And seyde, allas ! *woyfhode* is lore
   In me, whiche whilom was honeste.
        Gower, MS. Soc. Antiq. 134, f. 44.

WIFLE. A kind of axe.

WIFLER. A huckster.

WIFLES. Unmarried. (*A.-S.*)

WIFLY. Becoming a wife. (*A.-S.*)

WIFMAN. A female. Reliq. Antiq. ii. 8.

WIG. A small cake. " *Eschaudé*, a kind of wigg or symnell," Cotgrave. *Var. dial.*

WIGGER. Strong. *North.*

WIGGIN. A mountain-ash. *Cumb.*

WIGGLE. To reel, or stagger.

WIGGLE-WAGGLE. To wriggle. *East.*

WIGHEE. An exclamation to horses.

WIGHT. (1) A person. (*A.-S.*)

   For alle this ceté wolde thou [not] habyde,
   Bot faste a waywarde wold thou ryde,
   He es so fowle a *wyghte.*
        Octavian, Lincoln MS.

   Alle thys thyng schalle be hym sent,
   And the love of that feyre *wyghte.*
        MS. Cantab. Ff. ii. 38, f. 150.

(2) Active; swift. (*A.-S.*)

   Jyt peraventure the tyme come myghte,
   That my sone may meete me *wyghte.*
        MS. Cantab. Ff. ii. 38, f. 244.

   Y schalle gyf the two greyhowndys,
   As *wyghte* as any roo.
        MS. Cantab. Ff. ii. 38, f. 64.

(2) A weight.

   Hast thou uset mesures fals,
   Or *wyghtes* that were als.
        MS. Cott. Claud. A. ii. f. 139.

   Alle that selleth by falsse mesowres, as elne, jerd,
   busshel, half busahel, other pekke, galoun, potel,
   other quart or pyntte, other by any falsse *wyjttes,*
   and alle that suche useth by here wytynge.
        MS. Burney 356, p. 98.

(3) White.

   Wyght ys *wyght,* jyf yt leyd to blake,
   And soote ys swettere aftur bytternesse.
        MS. Cantab. Ff. i. 6, f. 136.

(4) A small space of time.

(5) A witch.

WIGHTNESSE. Power; might.

   He hade weryede the worme by *wyghtnesse* of
   strenghte. *Morte Arthure, MS. Lincoln,* f. 61.

WIGHTY. Strong; active. *North.*

WIHIE. To neigh. *Lilly.*

WIK. Wicked. (*A.-S.*)

WIKE. (1) A home; a dwelling.

(2) A week. (*A.-S.*)

WIKES. (1) Temporary marks, as boughs set up to divide swaths to be mown in the common ings, &c. *Yorksh.*

(2) The corners of the mouth.

WIKET. A wicket. " *Valva*, a wyket, a double jate," MS. Harl. 2270, f. 190.

WIKHALS. A rogue. *Hearne.*

WIKKEDLOKEST. Most wickedly.

WIKNES. Wickedness. (*A.-S.*)

WILCH. Sediment of liquor. Also, a strainer used in brewing. *East.*

WILD. (1) Very anxious. *Var. dial.*

(2) A wood, or wilderness.

WILD-CAT. The polecat. *Lanc.*

WILD-DELL. A dell or girl begotten and born under a hedge.

WILDE. Wild cattle. " My wylde are awaye," MS. Lincoln A. i. 17, f. 132.

WILDECOLES. The plant colewort.

WILDERNE. Wilderness.

   Fore now I have my quene lorne,
   The best woman that ever was borne,
   To *wylderne* I wyll gone,
   Fore I wyll never woman sene,
   And lyve ther in holtys hore,
   With wyld bestes ever-more !
        MS. Ashmole 61, xv. Cent.

WILDERNESS. Wildness.

WILD-FIRE. The erysipelas.

   A medsyn for the *wyld-fyre.* Take ij. handfulle
   of letuse, ij. of planteyne, and an handfulle of syngrene, and bray this thre thynges togidyr, and when
   it is welle groundyn, take halfe a dische fulle of
   stronge vyneger and a saucer fulle of everose, and
   medyl them togidyr, and do it to the evylle.
        MS. Sloane 7, f. 79.

WILD-GOOSE-CHACE. A hunt after anything very unprofitable or absurd.

   No hints of truth on foot ? no sparks of grace ?
   No late sprung light to dance the *wild-goose chase* ?
        Fletcher's Poems, p. 202.

WILDING. The crab-apple.

WILD-MARE. The nightmare. *To ride the wild mare*, to play at see-saw. " To ride the wild-mare, as children who, sitting upon both ends of a long pole or timber-log (supported only in the middle), lift one another up and downe," Cotgrave. A game called *shooing the wild mare* is mentioned in Batt upon Batt, p. 6.

WILD-NARDUS. Asarum. *Gerard.*

WILDNESS. Cruelty.

WILD-OATS. A thoughtless person. *To sow one's wild oats*, to grow steady.

WILDRED. Bewildered.

WILD-ROGUES. Rogues brought up to stealing from their infancy.

WILD-SAVAGER. The herb cockle.

WILD-SPINNAGE. The herb goosefoot.

WILE. Deceit. *By wile*, by chance.

WILECOAT. A vest for a child. Kennett gives it as a Durham word for a waistcoat.

WILF. A willow. *North.*

WILGHE. A willow. (*A.-S.*)

   Tak the bark of *wilghe* that is bitwene the tre and
   the utter barke, and the entres of the rute; alswa do
   stamp thame wele, and sethe thame in swete mylke.
        MS. Lincoln A. i. 17, f. 295.

WILGIL. An hermaphrodite. *West.*

WILKENE.

   Than tak a hundreth *wylkene* leves, and stamp
   thame, and tak the jus, and boil al to-gedir with
   halfe a pownde of white lede, and twa unces of mercury. *MS. Lincoln* A. i. 17, f. 296.

WILKY. A frog, or toad.

WILL. (1) A sea-gull. *South.*

(2) Passion; desire. *West.* These senses of the word are used by early writers.

> Al his *wille* don him sche lete,
> And it v.as aperceived skete.
> *Arthour and Merlin*, p. 30.

(3) Is. Still in use.

WILL-A-WIX. An owl. *East.*

WILLE. *Wille of wone*, at a loss for a dwelling. *Wille of rede*, without advice.

WILLEMENT. A sickly-looking person.

WILLERN. Peevish; wilful.

WILLESAY.

> That garres thes wormes on me to byt,
> And ever ther sang ys *wyllesay*.
> *MS. Lincoln* A. 1. 17, f. 51.

WILLEY. (1) A withy. *North.*

(2) A child's nightgown. *Cumb.*

WILL-I-NILL-I. Whether I will or not; willing or unwilling.

WILLOT. Will not. *North.*

WILLOW-BENCH. A share of a husband's estate enjoyed by widows besides their jointure.

WILLY. (1) Favorable. (*A.-S.*)

(2) A large wicker basket. *South.*

(3) A bull. *Isle of Wight.*

WILLY-BEER. A plantation of willows.

WILLYLYERE. More willingly.

WILLYNGE. A supplication. *Mason.*

WILLY-WAUGHT. A full draught of ale or other strong liquor. *North.*

WILN. For *willen*, pl. of *wille.*

WILNE. To will; to desire.

> Hast thow *wylnet* by covetyse
> Worldes gode over syse?
> *MS. Cott. Claud.* A. ii. f. 142.

> Thow shalt nowзt *wylny* thy neyзborys wyf, hys hyne, hys servant, ox ne asse, hors ne beest, ne non other thyng of hys. *MS. Burney* 356, f. 96.

WILO. A willow.

> Garlandes of *wylos* schuld be fette,
> And sett upon ther hedes.
> *MS. Ashmole* 61, f. 60.

WILOCAT. A polecat. *Lanc.*

WILSOM. (1) Fat; indolent. *East.*

(2) Dreary. Torrent of Portugal, p. 86.

(3) Doubtful; uncertain; wilful.

WILT. (1) To wither. *Bucks.*

(2) A sort of rush or sedge. *East.*

WIM. (1) An engine or machine worked by horses, used for drawing ore.

(2) To winnow corn. *South.*

WIMALUE. The wild mallow. It is mentioned in MS. Lincoln, f. 302.

WIMANIS-MEDEWORT. French cress.

WIMBLE. (1) Nimble. *Spenser.*

(2) An auger. Still in use.

> Зis, зis, seyd the *wymbylle*,
> I ame als reunde as a thymbyll;
> My maysters werke I wylle remembyre,
> I schall crepe fast into the tymbyre,
> And help my mayster within a stounde
> To store his cofere with xx. pounde.
> *MS. Ashmole* 61, xv. Cent.

WIMBLE-BENT. A long tall grass.

WIMEBLING. To linger. *North.*

WIMMEY. With me. *Lanc.*

WIMMING-DUST. Chaff. *West.*

WIMMON. A woman. (*A.-S.*)

> *Wymmones* serves thow moste forsake,
> Of evele fame leste they the make.
> *MS. Cott. Claud.* A. ii. f. 127

WIMOT. The herb ibiscus.

WIMPLE. A kind of cape or tippet covering the neck and shoulders.

WIM-SHEET. A large cloth or sheet on which corn is winnowed. *West.*

WIN. (1) Will. *North.*

(2) To reach, or attain to.

(3) A friend. *Reynard the Foxe.*

(4) A vane, or narrow flag.

(5) To dry hay. *North.*

(6) Wine. (*A.-S.*)

> Teche hem thenne never the later
> That in the chalys ys but *wyn* and water.
> *MS. Cott. Claud.* A. ii. f. 138.

(7) A penny. A cant term.

WINAFLAT. Thrown on one side.

WINARD. The redwing. *Cornw.*

WINBERRIES. Whortleberries.

WINCH. To wind up anything with a windlass or crane. Palsgrave, 1530.

WINCHE. To kick.

WINCHESTER-GOOSE. "A sore in the grine or yard, which if it come by lecherie, it is called a *Winchester goose*, or a botch," Nomenclator, 1585, p. 439. Some verses on it may be seen in Taylor's Workes, 1630, i. 105. It was sometimes termed a *Winchester pigeon.*

WINCH-WELL. A whirlpool.

WIND. (1) A dotterel. *South.*

(2) A winch, or wince.

(3) *To raise the wind*, to borrow money. *To go down the wind*, to decay. *To take the wind*, to gain an advantage. *To have one in the wind*, to understand him.

(4) To winnow corn. *Devon.*

(5) To fallow land.

(6) To talk loudly. *North.*

WIND-A-BIT. Wait. *Linc.*

WINDAS. An engine used for raising stones, &c. (*A.-N.*)

WIND-BANDS. Long clouds supposed to indicate stormy weather. *North.*

WIND-BEAM. The upper cross-beam of the roof of a house. Still in use.

WIND-BIBBER. A hawk. *Kent.*

WINDE. (1) To go. (*A.-S.*)

> Syn ye wylle *wynde*,
> Ye schalle wante no wede.
> *MS. Cantab.* Ff. ii. 38, f. 73

(2) To bring.

> Fresshe watur and wyne they *wynden* in sone.
> *MS. Cott. Calig.* A. ii. f. 111.

(3) To turn round. (*A.-S.*)

WINDED. Said of meat hung up when it becomes puffed and rancid.

WIND-EGG. An egg which has a soft skin instead of a shell. Still in use.

WINDER. (1) A fan. *North.*

(2) A window. *Var. dial.*

(3) A woman who has the charge of a corpse between death and burial. *East.*

WINDER-BOARD. A shutter. *North.*

WINDERS. Fragments. *Salop.*

WINDEWE. To winnow corn.

WINDFALL. Any piece of good fortune entirely unexpected. *Var. dial.*

WIND-FANNER. The kestrel. *Sussex.*

WINDILLING. A fan for corn.

WINDING. A winding-cloth for a corpse.

WINDING-BLADE. "Payre of wynding blades, *tournettes,*" Palsgrave.

WINDING-PIECE. A piece of land which is part of a segment of a circle. *East.*

WINDING-SHEET. A collection of tallow, says Grose, rising up against the wick of a candle, is styled a winding-sheet, and deemed an omen of death in the family.

WINDING-STOLE. *Tournette,* Palsgrave.

WINDLASS. Metaphorically, art or subtlety. Also, a turn or bend.

WINDLE. (1) Drifting snow. *Linc.*

(2) The redwing. *West.*

(3) A machine or wheel on which yarn is wound. "A yarn *windle,* alabrum," Ray's Dict. Tril. p. 86.

(4) The straw of wild grass. *North.*

(5) A bushel. *North.*

(6) A basket. *Lanc.*

WIND-MOW A mow of wheatsheaves in the field. *West.*

WINDON. A window. *East.*

WINDORE. A window.

WINDOVER. According to Ray, the kestrel is so called in some places. See Ray's English Birds, p. 82.

WINDOW-CLOTHE. See *Wim-sheet.*

WINDOW-PEEPER. The district surveyor of taxes. *Var. dial.*

WINDROW. Sheaves of corn set up in a row one against another, that the wind may blow betwixt them; or a row of grass in hay-making. *Var. dial.*

WINDSHAKEN. Puny; weak. *South.* This term is used by Dekker, in his Lanthorne and Candle-Light, 4to. Lond. 1620.

WINDSHAKES. Cracks in wood.

WINDSPILL. A sort of greyhound.

WINDSUCKER. The kestrel.

WINDY. (1) To winnow corn. *West.*

(2) Talkative; noisy. *North.*

(3) Unsolid; silly; foolish.

WINDY-WALLETS. A noisy fellow; one who romances in conversation.

WINE. Wind. *Somerset.*

WINESOUR. A sort of large plum.

WINEWE. To winnow corn.

WING. To carve a quail.

WINGE. To shrivel up. *East.*

WINGER. To rumble about. *Linc.*

WINGERY. Oozing. *Cornw.*

WINGLE. To heckle hemp.

WINGS. The projections on the shoulders of a doublet. See Fairholt, p. 618.

WININ. Winding. *Somerset.*

WINK. (1) A periwinkle. *Var. dial.*

(2) A winch, or crank. *West.*

WINK-A-PIPES. A term of contempt. Palmer has *wink-a-puss,* p. 96.

WINKERS. Eyes; eyelashes. *North.*

WINKIN. *Like winkin,* very quickly.

WINKING. Dozing; slumbering. *(A.-S.)*

WINKLE. Weak; feeble. *Yorksh.*

WINLY. (1) Quietly. *North.*

(2) Pleasant; delightful.

> For some of tho *wynly* wones
> Were peynted with precyus stones.
>
> *MS. Harl.* 1701, f. 10.
>
> Wha sal stegh in hille of Laverd *winll,*
> Or wha sal stand in his stede hali.
>
> *MS. Cott. Vespas.* D. vii. f. 14.

WINNA. Will not. *North.*

WINNE. (1) Joy. *(A.-S.)*

> And the hounde wolde nevyr blynne,
> But ranne abowte faste with *wynns.*
>
> *MS. Cantab.* Ff. ii. 38, f. 74.
>
> Swete lady, full of *wynne,*
> Full of grace and gode within,
> As thou art floure of alle thi kynne,
> Do my synnes for to blynne,
> And kepe me out of dedly synne,
> That I be never takyn therin.
>
> *MS. Cantab.* Ff. v. 48, f. 74.

(2) Furze. Nominale MS.

(3) To gain; to attain. *(A.-S.)*

(4) To go; to depart.

(5) To carve, or cut up.

(6) To work. *North.*

WINNICK. To cry; to fret. *East.*

WINNOLD. St. Winwaloe. *East.* Winnold-weather, stormy March weather.

WINNOT. Will not. *Yorksh.*

WINNY. (1) To neigh. *West.*

(2) To be frightened. *Glouc.*

(3) To dry; to burn up. *Linc.*

WINSOME. Lively; gay. *(A.-S.)*

WINT. (1) Passed; went.

(2) To harrow ground twice over.

WINTE. The wind. *Lanc.*

WINTER. An implement to hang on a grate, used for warming anything on.

WINTER-CRACK. A kind of bullace.

WINTER-CRICKET. A tailor.

WINTER-DAY. The winter season. *Norf.*

WINTER-HEDGE. A clothes-horse.

WINTERIDGE. Winter eatage for cattle.

WINTER-RIG. To fallow land in the winter time. *Salop.*

WINTER-WEEDS. Those small weeds in corn, which survive and flourish during the winter; as alsine media, chickweed, veronica hederifolia, ivy-leaved veronica, &c.

WINTLE-END. The end of a shoemaker's thread. *Isle of Wight.*

WINTLING. Small. *Salop.*

WINWE. Winnowing. *(A.-S.)*

WINY-PINY. Fretful; complaining.

WIPE. (1) The lapwing.

(2) To beat, or strike. *East.*

(3) *To wipe a person's nose,* to cheat him. To

wive his ege, to kill a bird a fellow sportsman has missed.

WIPER. A hand-towel. The term is now applied to a pocket-handkerchief.

WIPES. Fence of brushwood. *Devon.*

WIPPET. A small child. *East.*

WIPPING. (1) Weeping; crying.

(2) The chirping of birds.

WIRDLE. To work slowly. *North.*

WIRE-DRAWER. A stingy grasping person.

WIRE-THORN. The yew. *North.*

WIRKE. To make; to do; to cause.

> The smyth that the made, seid Robyn,
> I pray to God *wyrke* hym woo.
> *MS. Cantab.* Ff. v. 48, f. 127.

WIRLY-BIT. A little while.

WIRLYWOO. Any revolving toy, &c.

WIRMSED. The herb *feniculus porcus.*

WIRRANGLE. The great butcher-bird is so called in the Peak of Derbyshire, according to Ray, ed. 1674, p. 83.

WIRRY. To worry. (*A.-S.*)

WIRSCHEPE. Worship; honour.

> He forges hym loos and *wirschepe,*
> Alʒif he that strykes takes no kepe.
> *MS. Harl.* 2260, f. 3.

WIRSLE. To change; to exchange. *North.*

WIRSOM. Foul pus. *Yorksh.*

WIRSTE. The wrist.

WIRTCH. To ache. *North.*

WIRT-SPRINGS. Hangnails. *Linc.*

WIS. Same as *Wisse,* q. v. *Lanc.*

WISE. (1) The stalk.

> Take the *wyse* of tormentille, and bray it, and make lee of askes, and wesche thi hevede therwith.
> *MS. Lincoln* A. i. 17, f. 280.

(2) Manner. (*A.-S.*)

(3) *To make wise,* to pretend.

(4) To show; to lead out; to let off.

WISE-MAN. A conjurer.

WISE-MORE. A wiseacre. *Devon.*

WISENED. Shrivelled.

> The tre welold and *wisened* sonc,
> And wex olde and dry;
> Nothyng therof lefte grene,
> Therof men had grete ferly.
> *MS. Cantab.* Ff. v. 48, f. 89.

WISER. And no one is the wiser, i. e. no one knows anything about it.

WISH. (1) Bad; unfit. *Devon.*

(2) To recommend; to persuade.

WISHE. Washed. Chester Plays, i. 291.

> Saber to hys ynne went,
> And *wysche* of Jocyaus oyntment.
> *MS. Cantab.* Ff. ii. 38, f. 121.

WISHED. Prayed; desired; wished for.

WISHFUL. Anxious. *North.*

WISHINET. A pincushion. *Yorksh.*

WISHLI. Wisely. (*A.-S.*)

> For as *wischli* as ever y cum too blisse,
> My wille is goode whatever y write or say.
> *MS. Cantab.* Ff. i. 6, f. 44.

WISHLY. With eager desire. *East.*

WISHNESS. Melancholy. *Devon.*

WISHT. "He's in a *wisht* state," i. e. a state in which there is much to be wished for. *Devon.*

A poor *wisht* thing, unhappy, melancholy "evil wished" or evil looked upon.

WISHY-WASHY. Pale; sickly. Also, very weak, when said of liquor.

WISIBLES. Vegetables. *East.*

WISID. Advised.

WISK. To switch; to move rapidly.

WISKET. Same as *Whisket,* q. v.

WISLOKER. More certainly. (*A.-S.*)

WISLY. Certainly. (*A.-S.*)

WISOMES. Tops of turnips, &c.

WISP. (1) A seton, in farriery.

(2) A stye in the eye. *West.*

(3) A handful of straw. *Var. dial.*

(4) To rumple. *East.*

(5) A disease in bullocks which makes them sore near the hoof. *South.*

WISS. Worse. *West.*

WISSE. (1) To teach; to direct.

> Lorde kynge, sche seyde, of hevyn blys,
> Thys day thou me rede and *wysse.*
> *MS. Cantab.* Ff. ii. 38, f. 84.
> Be thou oure helpe, be thou our socoure,
> And lyke a prophete to *wissen* us and rede.
> *Lydgate, MS. Soc. Antiq.* 134, f. 22.
> With stedfaste trouthe my wittes *wysse,*
> And defende me fra the fende.
> *MS. Lincoln* A. i. 17, f. 213.

(2) Certainly. (*A.-S.*)

(3) To suppose; to think.

WISSERE. Teacher; director.

WIST. Knew. (*A.-S.*)

> Many one, whan thay *wist,* thay were ryʒte woo,
> Hit bootid hem not to stryve, the wille of God was soo! *MS. Bibl. Reg.* 17 D. xv.
> The qwene for sorowe wolde dye,
> For sche *wyste* not wherefore nor why
> That sche was flemed soo.
> *MS. Cantab.* Ff. ii. 38, f. 73.

WISTER. A prospect, or view. *East.*

WISTEY. A large populous place. *Lanc.*

WISTLY. Earnestly; wistfully.

WIT. (1) Sense; intelligence.

(2) The yellow henbane.

WITALDRY. Folly.

WITANDLY. Knowingly. (*A.-S.*)

> As whan a man with al his myʒt,
> *Witandly* holdes ther agayne.
> *MS. Sloane* 1785, f. 50.

WITCH. (1) To bewitch. *Palsgrave.*

(2) A small candle to make up the weight of a pound. *North.*

WITCHEN. The mountain ash.

WITCH-HAZEL. The witchen, q. v.

WITCHIFY. To bewitch. *West.*

WITCH-KNOT. See *Elf* (1).

> O, that I were a witch but for her sake!
> Yfaith her Queenship little rest should take;
> I'd scratch that face, that may not feele the aire,
> And knit whole ropes of *witch-knots* in her haire.
> *Drayton's Poems,* ed. 1637, p. 253.

WITCH-RIDDEN. Having the nightmare.

WITCH-WOOD. The mountain ash.

WITCRAFT. Logic; art of wit.

WITE. (1) To know. (*A.-S.*)

> Wherfore these thynges thow moste *wyte,*
> That in thys vers nexte be wryte.
> *MS. Cott. Claud.* A. ii. f. 145.

Ac my Lord *wyteth* my soule wel,
That thou here ne spille,
For thou ne miȝt with al this myȝt,
Anuye here worth a nille.
MS. Coll. Trin. Oxon. 57.

Ȝif we be desirite,
Our coward schippe we may it *wite*.
Arthour and Merlin, p. 340.

(2) To depart; to go out.

Fra theine thay removed and come tille another felde, in the whilke ther ware growand treese of a wounderfulle heghte, and thay bigane for to sprynge up at the sone rysynge, and bi the sone settynge thay *wyted* away into the erthe agayne.
MS. Lincoln A. i. 17, f. 37.

The Russelles and the Freselles free,
Alle salle thay fade and *wyte* awaye.
MS. Lincoln A. i. 17, f. 151.

(3) To blame; to reproach. (*A.-S.*)
(4) To hinder; to keep. (*A.-S.*)
WITEL. Qu. wite it?

And *witel* wel that one of thoo
Is with tresoure so fulle begoo.
Gower, MS. Soc. Antiq. 134, f. 141.

WITEWORD. A covenant. (*A.-S.*)
WITH. (1) A twig of willow. Also, a twig or stick from any tree, a twisted flexible rod. *West.*
(2) To go with, the verb *to go* being understood. *Shak.*
(3) By. (*A.-S.*)
WITHDRADE. To withdraw.
WITHDRAWT. A chest of drawers.
WITHEN-KIBBLE. A thick willow stick.
WITHER. (1) Other. *Somerset.*
(2) To throw down forcibly. *North.*
(3) A strong fellow. *Yorksh.*
(4) Contrary; opposite to. (*A.-S.*)
WITHERGUESS. Different. *Somerset.*
WITHERING. (1) Strong; lusty. *Chesh.*
(2) The second floor of a malt-house.
WITHERLY. Hastily; violently. *Devon.*
WITHERWINS. Enemies. (*A.-S.*)

For to bring tham mightili
Als his auen kyngrik til,
His *witherwins* al for to spil.
MS. Cotton. Vespas. A. iii. f. 10.

This three princes with heore men
In the se forth i-wenden,
To fiȝten aȝein is *wytherwynes*,
Ase the aumperour heom sende.
MS. Laud. 108, f. 113.

Aboute the toun thei sette engynes
To distroie here *wytherwynes*.
MS. Addit. 10036, f. 24.

WITHERWISE. Otherwise. *West.*
WITH-HAULT. Withheld. *Spenser.*
WITHNAY. To deny; to withstand.
WITHOLDE. To stop; to retain. (*A.-S.*)
WITHOUT. (1) Unless. *Var. dial.*
(2) Without water, *water* understood.
WITHOUT-FORTH. Out of doors.
WITHOWTEN. Without. (*A.-S.*)

Me hath smetyn *withowten* deserte,
And seyth that he ys owre kynge aperte.
MS. Cantab. Ff. ii. 38, f. 241.

Preste, thyself thow moste be chast,
And say thy serves *wythowten* hast.
MS. Cott. Claud. A. ii. f. 127.

WITHSAIE. To contradict; to deny.

For thagh he fayle of hys day,
Thow schuldest not hys wed *wythsay*.
MS. Cott. Claud. A. ii. f. 142.

WITHSAT. Withstood.

It thouȝten hem alle he seyde skile,
Ther is no man *withsat* his wille.
Gower, MS. Soc. Antiq. 134, f. 96.

WITHSITTE. To withstand.

Ther myȝt no man *withsytt* hys dynte,
But he to the erthe them thronge.
MS. Cantab. Ff. ii. 38, f. 69.

WITH-SKAPID. Escaped.

To the castelle thay rade,
With-skapid nane hym fra.
MS. Lincoln A. i. 17, f. 134.

WITH-TAN. Taken from; withdrawn.

Hast thow werkemen oght *wyth-tan*
Of any thynge that they schulde han.
MS. Cott. Claud. A. ii. f. 142.

WITHTHER-HOOKED. Barbed. (*A.-S.*)

This dragoun hadde a long taile,
That was *withther-hooked* saun faile.
Arthour and Merlin, p. 210.

WITH-THI. On condition.
WITHWIND. The wild convolvulus.
WITHY. A willow. *Var. dial.*
WITHY-CRAGGED. Said of a person whose neck is loose and pliant. *North.*
WITHY-POLL. A term of endearment.
WITINFORTHE. Within.
WITING. Knowledge. *North.*

That heo avow no maner thynge,
But hyt be at hys *wytynge*.
MS. Cott. Claud. A. ii f. 131.

WITLETHER. A tough tendron in sheep.
WITNESFULLY. Evidently.
WITNESS. (1) A godmother.
(2) *With a witness*, excessively.
WITSAFE. To vouchsafe.
WIT-SHACK. A shaky bog. *North.*
WITTANDE. Knowledge; knowing.

The fyft poynte may thai noght eschape,
That commounes with hym that the pape
Cursed has at hys *wyttande*,
Or to that curssyng es assentande.
Hampole, MS. Bowes, p. 6.

WITTE. To bequeath.
WIT-TEETH. The double teeth.
WITTER. (1) To be informed.
(2) To fret one's self. *North.*
(3) A mark. Still in use.
WITTERING. A hint. *North.*
WITTERLY. Truly. (*A.-S.*)

They lokyd up toward the skye,
And they sye yn a clowde *wytterly*.
MS. Cantab. Ff. ii. 38, f. 128.

WITTERS. Fragments. *Oxon.*
WITTE-WITTE-WAY. A boy's game.
WITTOL. A contented cuckold.

Thy stars gave thee the cuckold's diadem:
If thou wert born to be a *wittol*, can
Thy wife prevent thy fortune? foolish man!
Wit's Recreations, 1641.

WITTY. (1) Knowing; wise. (*A.-S.*)

I-wysse thou art a *wytty* man,
Thou shalt wel drynk therfore.
MS. Cantab. Ff. v. 48. f. 49.

(2) The mountain ash. *Salop.*

WITY. In fault.

WIV. With. *North.*

WIVE. A wife. (*A.-S.*)
>Whenne on hath done a synne,
>Loke he lye not longe thereynne,
>But anon that he hym schryve,
>Be hyt husbande, be hyt *wyve.*
>>*MS. Cott. Claud.* A. ii f. 127.

WIVERE. A serpent. (*A.-S.*)

WIVVER. To quiver; to shake. *Kent.*

WIXTOWTYN. Without.

WIZARD. A wise man.

WIZDE. Advised; informed.

WIZEN. The gullet. *North.*

WIZLES. The tops of vegetables.

WIZZEN. To wither away; to shrivel up. *Var. dial.* Hence *wizzen-face.*

WIZZLE. To get anything slily.

WIȝT. A person. See *Lefe.*

WIȝTLY. Quickly.
>With that folke soone he met,
>And *wiȝtly* wan of hem the bet.
>>*Cursor Mundi, MS. Coll. Trin. Cantab.* f. 48.

WLAPPE. To wrap or roll up.

WLATFUL. Disgusting. (*A.-S.*)
>For-broken and *wlatful* made thai are
>In thair thoghts lesse and mare.
>>*MS. Cott. Vespas.* D. vii. f. 7.

WLATINGE. Loathing; disgust.
>Roghe thow not thenne thy thonkes,
>Ny wrynge thou not wyth thy schonkes,
>Lest heo suppose thow make that fare
>For *wlatynge* that thou herest thare.
>>*MS. Cott. Claud.* A. ii. f. 137.

WLATSOME. Loathsome. This word occurs in MS. Arundel 42, f. 82.
>For hyt schall seme nought to thy syght,
>But derke and *wlatsome,* lytull and lawe.
>>*MS. Cantab.* Ff. ii. 38, f. 29.

>Whennes thou coom bithenke also,
>Fro thi moder wombe ful riȝt,
>Out of a *wlatsome* stynkande wro,
>That was merke withouten liȝt.
>>*MS. Rawl.* A. 389, f. 101.

WLATYS. Loatheth.
>Swyche men God Almyȝty hatys,
>And with here foule synne hym *wlatys.*
>>*MS. Harl.* 1701, f. 24.

WLONKE. (1) Splendour; wealth.
(2) Fair (woman.)
>Thane I went to that *wlonke,* and winly hire gretis,
>And cho said, welcom i-wis, wele arte thow fowndene.
>>*Morte Arthure, MS. Lincoln,* f. 88.

WLTUR. A vulture.
>In the moruenynge arely ther come many fowlis
>als grete as *wlturs,* reed of colour, and thaire fete
>and thaire bekes alse blakke.
>>*MS. Lincoln* A. i. 17, f. 29.

WLUINE. A she-wolf. (*A.-S.*)

WND. A wound.

WO. (1) Sorrowful. (*A.-S.*)
(2) Stop; check. *Var. dial.*

WOARE. (1) The border or shore. Sea-weed was also so called.
(2) A whore. Nominale MS.

WOB. A sugar-teat, q. v.

WOBBLE. To reel; to totter; to roll about; to bubble up. *Var. dial.*

WOBBLE-JADE. Rickety; shaky. *South.*

WO-BEGONE. Far gone in woe.
>And there they drenchid every man,
>Save one knave that to lond cam,
>And *woo begone* is he.
>>*Torrent of Portugal.* p. 75.

WOBLET. The handle of a hay-knife.

WOC. Awoke. *Wilts.*

WOCHE. Which. See *Lasse.*

WOCKS. Oaks. *West.* The term is also applied to the clubs at cards.

WOD. An ox.

WODAKE. The woodpecker.

WODE. (1) Mad; furious. (*A.-S.*)
>Ther is no h'ert ne bucke so *wode*
>That I ne get without blode.
>>*MS. Cantab.* Ff. v. 48, f. 50.
(2) Went. Perceval, 2062.
>Hym to venge he thoght wele late,
>Hewchon on the crowne he smate,
>To the gyrdulle stede hyt *wode.*
>>*MS. Cantab.* Ff. ii. 38, f. 153
(3) A wood. Nominale MS.

WODEBRON. The herb *fraximis.*

WODEHED. Madness. (*A.-S.*)
>In *wodehed,* as hyt were yn cuntek,
>They come to a toune men calle Colbek.
>>*MS. Harl.* 1701, f. 60.

WODERE. More mad. (*A.-S.*)

WODEROVE. The herb *hastilogia.*

WODESOWR. The herb *alleluja.*

WODEWALE. The woodpecker.
>I herde the jay and the throstelle,
>The mavys mevyd in hir song,
>The *wodewale* farde as a belle,
>That the wode aboute me roug.
>>*MS. Cantab.* Ff. v. 48, f. 116.

>Ther beth briddes mani and fale,
>Throstil, thruisse, and niȝtingal,
>Chalandre and *woodwale.*   *Cocaygne,* 95.

WODEWE. A widow. (*A.-S.*)

WODEWHISTEL. Hemlock.

WODEWISE. Madly. (*A.-S.*)

WODGE. A lump; a quantity of anything stuffed together. *Warw.*

WOD-SONGS. Woodmen's songs.

WODUR. Other.
>In swownyng as the lady lay,
>Har *wodur* chylde sche bare away
>>*MS. Cantab.* Ff. ii. 38, f. 84.

WODWOS. Wild men; monsters. *Gaw.*

WOER. More sorry.
>Than began he to wepe and wrynge hys handes,
>and was so woo on eche syde that he wyste not what
>for to do, and *woer* he was fore hys wyfeys dethe.
>>*MS. Cantab.* Ff. ii. 38, f. 9.

WOESTART. An interjection of condolence or sympathy. *Linc.*

WOE-WORTH. Woe betide.
>*Woe worth* thee, Tarlton,
>That ever thou wast borne;
>Thy wife hath made thee cuckold,
>And thou must weare the horne.
>>*Tarlton's Jests,* sig. B. iv.

WOFARE. Sorrow. (*A.-S.*)
>And tolde hym of alle hys *wofare,*
>And of alle hys cumforte yn alle hys care
>>*MS. Harl.* 1701, f. 71.

WOGGIN. A narrow passage between two houses. *Yorksh.*

WOGHE. (1) A wall.

> Thys olde man was broghte so loghe,
> That he lay ful colde besyde a woghe.
> *MS. Harl.* 1701, f. 8.

(2) Harm; injustice. (*A.-S.*)

> I rede we bere hyt here besyde,
> And do we hyt no woghs.
> *MS. Cantab.* Ff. li. 38, f. 86.

(3) Crooked; bent. *Weber.*

(4) Bent, or swung? Weighed?

> And the childe swa hevy woghe,
> That ofte sythes one knees he hym droghe.
> *MS. Lincoln* A. i. 17, f. 125.

WOGHTE. Wrong. (*A.-S.*)

> As they seyd, they dyd that woghte,
> The whyche dede ful soure they boghte.
> *MS. Harl.* 1701, f. 27.

WOK. Watched.

WOKE. (1) A week.

(2) Weak. *Perceval,* 1373.

(3) To ache with pain.

WOKEN. To suffocate. *North.*

WOKEY. Moist; sappy. *Durh.*

WOL. (1) To will. (*A.-S.*)

(2) Full. Still in use.

WOLBODE. A millepedes.

WOLD. Willed; been willing.

WOLDE. (1) Old.

> And be in charyté and in acorde
> With all my neghburs wolde and syng.
> *MS. Cantab.* Ff. ii. 38, f. 18.

(2) Would. (*A.-S.*)

> They sparyd nodur for sylvyr nor golde,
> For the beste have they wolde.
> *MS. Cantab.* Ff. ii. 38, f. 118.

(3) A wood; a weald; a plain.

WOLDER. To roll up. *East.*

WOLDMAN'S-BEARD. The herb marestail.

WOLE. Same as *Wolder,* q. v.

WOLF. (1) A wooden fence placed across a ditch in the corner of a field, to prevent cattle straying into another field by means of the ditch. *East.*

(2) *To have a wolf in the stomach,* to eat ravenously. *To keep the wolf from the door,* to have food.

(3) A kind of fishing-net.

4) Some disease in the legs.

) A bit for a restive horse.

OLFETTES.

> That for every sack of woll, and the *wolfetter,* th' English shall paye after the rate of iiij. markes custume, and to cary the same to Callais.
> *Egerton Papers,* p. 12.

OLF-HEAD. An outlaw.

WOLICHE. Unjustly. (*A.-S.*)

WOLIPERE. A cap.

WOLKE. Rolled; kneaded.

WOLSTED. Worsted. *Stowe.*

WOLTHE. Willeth. (*A.-S.*)

> Another tyme, gyf hem folghthe
> As the fader and the moder wolthe.
> *MS. Cott. Claud.* A. ii. f. 128.

WOLVES-THISTLE. The plant camalion.

WOMAN-HODE. Womanhood; the virtue of a woman. (*A.-S.*)

> A goodlyer ther myght none be,
> Here womanhode in alle degré.
> *MS. Cantab.* Ff. i. 6, f. 45.

WOMBE-CLOUTES. Tripes. (*A.-S.*) It is explained by *omentum* in the Nominale.

WOMBLETY-CROPT. The indisposition of a drunkard after a debauch. *Grose.*

WOMMEL. An auger. *North.*

WON. (1) One.

> In eschewyng al maner doublenesse,
> To make too joys insted of won grevance.
> *Chaucer, MS. Cantab.* Ff. i. 6, f. 104.

(2) Will. *Somerset.*

WONDE. (1) Went. (*A.-S.*)

> He smote the dore with hys honde,
> That opyn hyt wonde. *MS. Cantab.* Ff. ii. 38, f. 117.

(2) To spare; to fear; to refrain.

> To preche hem also thou myjt not wonde,
> Bothe to wyf and eke husbonde.
> *MS. Cott. Claud.* A. ii. f. 131.
> *Wonde* thow not, for no schame:
> Paraventur I have done the same.
> *MS. Cott. Claud.* A. ii. f. 137.
> Also shal the woman wonde
> To take here godmodrys husbonde.
> *MS. Harl.* 1701, f. 12.
> Wendyth forthe for to fonde,
> For nothynge wyll we wonde.
> *MS. Cantab.* Ff. ii. 38, f. 158.

(3) Dwelled. (*A.-S.*)

WONDER. (1) Wonderful. (*A.-S.*)

> Off kyng Arthour a wonder case,
> Frendes, herkyns how it was.
> *MS. Ashmole* 61, f. 60.

(2) The afternoon. *Staff.*

WONDERCHONE. An engine or contrivance for catching fish. See Blount in v.

WONDERFUL. Very. *Var. dial.*

WONDIRLY. Wonderfully.

WONDSOME.

> And for wondsome and wille alle his wit fallede,
> That wode alles a wylde beste he wente at the gayneste.
> *Morte Arthure, MS. Lincoln,* f. 93.

WONE. (1) Manner; custom. (*A.-S.*)

(2) Quantity; plenty; a heap.

> Yea, my Lorde life and deare,
> Rosted fishe and honnye in feare,
> Theirof we have good wonne.
> *Chester Plays,* ii. 109.

(3) To dwell. Also, a dwelling.

> Lordynges, he seyde, arme yow all sone,
> Here ys no dwellyng for us to wonne.
> *MS. Cantab.* Ff. ii. 38, f. 167.

WONED. Wont; accustomed.

WONEDEN. Dwelled. (*A.-S.*)

WONET. Accustomed; used. (*A.-S.*)

> Hast thou be wonet to swere als
> By Goddes bones or herte fals.
> *MS. Cott. Claud.* A. ii. f. 138.
> Art thow i-wonet to go to the ale,
> To fulle there thy fowle male?
> *MS. Cott. Claud.* A. ii. f. 142.

WONG. (1) A cheek. (*A.-S.*)

(2) Marsh, or low land. *Linc.*

(3) A grove; a meadow; a plain.

WONIEN. To dwell. (*A.-S.*)

WONING. A dwelling. (*A.-S.*)

> Tel me, sir, what is thy name,
> And wher thy wonnyng is.
> *MS. Cantab.* Ff. v. 48, f. 48.

WONLY. Only. *Kent.*

WONMIL-CHEESE. See *Bang* (5).

WONNE. (1) One. See *Wone.*

(2) Wont ; accustomed.

> In the garden ageyne the sonne
> He laye to slepe, as he was wonne.
>   *MS. Cantab. Ff.* ii. 38, f. 173.

WONST. Once ; on purpose. *Lanc.*

WONT. To yoke animals. *Oxon.*

WONTED. (1) Turned, as milk. *Cumb.*

(2) Accustomed to a place. *North.*

WONT-HEAVE. A mole-hill. *Wont-snap*, a mole-trap. *Wont-wriggle*, the sinuous path made by moles under ground.

WOO. Wool. *North.*

WOOD. (1) Mad ; furious. Also, famished, or raging with hunger.

(2) *To go to the wood*, to be dieted for the venereal disease.

(3) A number, or quantity.

WOOD-AND-WOOD. " The strickles is a thing that goes along with the measure, which is a straight board with a staffe fixed in the side, to draw over corn in measureing, that it exceed not the height of the measure, which measureing is termed *wood and wood*," Holme's Academy, iii. 337.

WOODBOUND. Surrounded by trees.

WOODBRONEY. The herb *fraximus.*

WOODCOCK. A simpleton. This term is very common in early plays.

WOODCOCK-SOIL. Ground that hath a soil under the turf, that looks of a woodcock colour, and is not good. *South.*

WOOD-CULVER. A wood-pigeon. *West.*

WOODEN. Mad.

WOODENLY. Awkwardly. *Yorksh.*

WOODEN-RUFF. The pillory.

WOODEN-SWORD. " To wear the *wooden-sword*," to overstand the market. *Dorset.*

WOODHACK. A woodpecker.

WOOD-HACKER. A woodman. *Linc.*

WOODHEDE. Madness. (*A.-S.*)

> Jhesu schylde us fro that fal,
> That Lucifer fel for his *woodhede* ;
> And make us fre that now ben thral,
> And take us to hym to be oure mede.
>   *Hampole's Psalms, MS.*

WOOD-LAYER. Young plants of oak, or other timber laid into hedges among " white thorn layer." *Norfolk.*

WOODLICH. Madly. (*A.-S.*)

> To teche him also how he schal scheten *woodlich* or fersliche, vengyng hym on his enemyes.
>   *Vegecius, MS. Douce* 291, f. 5.

WOODMAN. (1) A carpenter. *Derb.*

(2) A wencher, or hunter after girls.

WOOD-MARCH. Sanickle. *Gerard.*

WOOD-MARE. An echo. (*A.-S.*)

WOODNEP. Ameos. *Gerard.*

WOOD-NOGGIN. A Kentish term applied to half-timbered houses.

WOOD-QUIST. The wood-pigeon.

WOOD-SERE. The month or season for felling wood. Tusser uses the term.

WOODSOAR. Cuckoo-spittle.

WOODSOWER. Wood-sorrel.

WOODSPACK. A woodpecker. *East.* Moor and Forby have *woodsprite.*

WOODWANTS. Holes in a post or piece of timber, i. e. places wanting wood.

WOODWARD. The keeper of a wood.

WOODWEX. The plant *genista tinctoria.*

WOOFET. A silly fellow. *East.*

WOOL. (1) Will. *Var. dial.*

(2) To twist a chain round a refractory horse to render him obedient. *Kent.*

WOOLFIST. A term of reproach.

WOOL-GATHERING. " Your brains are gone woolgathering," a phrase applied to a stupid or bewildered person. See Florio, p. 138.

WOOL-PACKS. A term given to light clouds in a blue sky. *Norf.*

WOOLWARD. To go woolward, or without any linen next the body, was frequently enjoined as a penance. " Wolwarde, without any lynnen nexte ones body, *sans chemyse*," Palsgrave. " Wolleward and weetshoed," Piers Ploughman, p. 369.

> Faste, and go *wolward*, and wake,
> And suffre hard for Godus sake.
>   *MS. Ashmole* 41, f. 44.

> For tha synnes that he has wroght,
> And do he penawnce with alle hys thoght,
> And be in prayers bothe day and nyght,
> And faste, and go *wolwarde*, and wake,
> And thole hardnes for Goddes sake ;
> For no man may to hefen go,
> Bot he thole here angyr and wo.
>   *Hampole, MS. Bowes*, p. 169.

WOOPES. Weeping ; sorrowful.

> All the dayes that y leve here
> In thys woofull *woopes* dale.
>   *MS. Cantab. Ff.* ii. 38, f. 21.

WOOS. Vapour. *Batman.*

WOOSH. An imperative commanding the forehorse of a team to bear to the left.

WOOSOM. An advowson.

WOOSTER. A wooer. *North.*

WOOT. Will thee. *West.*

WOP. (1) A fan for corn. *Linc.*

(2) A bundle of straw. *Var. dial.*

(3) A wasp. *Devon.*

(4) Weeping. *Hearne.*

(5) To produce an abortive lamb.

WOPNE. Urine. *Pr. Parv.*

WOR. (1) Our. (2) Were. *North.*

WORBITTEN. Said of growing timber pierced by the larvæ of beetles. *East.*

WORCESTER. " It shines like *Worcester* against Gloucester," a phrase expressing rivalry. *West.*

WORCH-BRACCO. " Work-brittle, very diligent, earnest, or intent upon one's work," Ray, ed. 1674, p. 55.

WORCHE. To work ; to cause.

> And yef thow may not come to chyrche,
> Whereever that thow do *worche*,
> When thow herest to masse knylle,
> prey to God wyth herte stylle
> To yeve the part of that servyse,
> That in chyrche i-done ys.
>   *MS. Cott. Claud.* A. ii. f. 148

And manye maneres there ben mo,
That *worcheth* to man miche woo.
    MS. Laned. 793, f. 72.
Yf we have the hylle and they the dale,
We schall them *worche* moche bale.
    MS. Cantab. Ff. ii. 38, f. 168.

WORD. (1) A motto.

(2) To take one's word again, i. e. to retract what one has said. *North.* To speak nine words at once, i. e. to talk very quickly.

(3) To dispute, or wrangle. *East.* Probably from the old English *worde*, to discourse.

(4) The world. Nominale MS.

WORDE. Talk; reputation.
    He slewe hys enemyes with grete envy,
    Grete *worde* of hym aroos.
    MS. Cantab. Ff. ii. 38, f. 72.

WORDING-HOOK. A dung-rake. *Chesh.*

WORDLE. The world. *West.*

WORDLES. Speechless. (*A.-S.*)

WORE. Were. (*A.-S.*)
    He ys woundyd swythe sore,
    Loke that he dedd *wore.*
    MS. Cantab. Ff. ii. 38, f. 153.

WORGISH. Ill tasted, as ale. *Oxon.*

WORK. (1) "To make work," i. e. to cause or make a disturbance. *Var. dial.*

(2) To suppurate. *West.*

(3) To banter. *Var. dial.*

WORKING-STOOL. "Working-stool for a silk-woman, *mettier*," Palsgrave.

WORK-WISE. In a workmanlike way.

WORLD. (1) A great quantity. *Var. dial.*

(2) *World without end*, long, tiresome. *It is a world to see*, it is a wonder or marvel. *To go to the world*, to be married. *If the world was on it*, a phrase implying utter impossibility.

WORLDES. Worldly. (*A.-S.*)

WORLING. Friday.

WORM. (1) A serpent. *North.*
    With the grace of God Almyghte,
    Wyth the *worms* jyt schalle y fyghte.
    MS. Cantab. Ff. ii. 38, f. 67.

(2) A poor creature.

(3) A corkscrew. *Kent.*

WORMIT. Wormwood. *North.*

WORM-PUTS. Worm hillocks. *East.*

WORMSTALL. An out-door shed for cattle in warm weather. *North.*

WORNIL. The larva of the gadfly growing under the skin of the back of cattle.

WOROWE. To choke. See *Worry.*

WORRA. A small round moveable nut or pinion, with grooves in it, and having a hole in its centre, through which the end of a round stick or spill may be thrust. The spill and *worra* are attached to the common spinning-wheel, which, with those and the turn-string, form the apparatus for spinning wool, &c. *Jennings.*

WORRE. Worse. (*A.-S.*)
    Hast thow baebyted thy neghbore,
    For to make hym fare the *worre* ?
    MS. Cott. Claud. A. ii. f. 141.
    They have of many a loude socowre:
    Yf we fyght we gets the *worre.*
    MS. Cantab. Ff. ii. 38, f. 190.

WORRY. To choke. *North.*

WORSEN. To grow worse. *Var. dial.*

WORSER. Worse. Still in use.

WORSET. Worsted. *North.*

WORSLE. (1) To wrestle. *North.*

(2) To clear up; to recover.

WORSTOW. Wert thou. (*A.-S.*)

WORT. A vegetable; a cabbage.

WORTESTOK. The plant colewort.

WORTHE. (1) To be; to go. (*A.-S.*)
    And lycorous folke, afture thei bene dede,
    Schuld *worth* abowte allewey ther in peyne.
    MS. Cantab. Ff. i. 6, f. 23.

(2) A nook of land, generally a nook lying between two rivers.

(3) Wrath; angry.

WORTHER. Other. *Devon.*

WORTHLIEST. Most worthy. (*A.-S.*)
    Thare myght no nother jow pay
    Bot maydene Mildor the may,
    Worthliest in wede.
    MS. Lincoln A. i. 17, f. 138.

WORTHLOKSTE. Most worthy.

WORTHY. Lucky enough. *East.*

WORTWALE. A hangnail.

WOS. A kind of corn.

WOSCHE. To wash.
    And over the chalys *wosche* hyt wel
    Twyes or thryes, as I the telle.
    MS. Cotton Claud. A. ii. f. 151.

WOSE. (1) Juice; mud; filth.
    He thrast hom in sonder as men dos
    Crapbys, thrastyng owt the *wos.*
    Tundale, p. 44.

(2) Whoso. MS. Digby 86.

WOSEN. The windpipe.

WOSERE. Whosoever.
    For *wosere* loved and worshippud Seynt Ede, y-wys,
    His travelle shalle be ryjt welle y quytte.
    Chron. Vilodun. p. 133.

WOSINGE. Oozing; running.

WOST. Knowest. (*A.-S.*)
    The fyrste artykele ys, thou *wost,*
    Leve on Fader, and Sone, and Holy Gost.
    MS. Cott. Claud. A. ii. f. 132.

WOSTUS. Oast-house, ust-house, where hops are dried. *Kent.*

WOT. Eat.
    Wot na dryng wald she nane,
    Swa mykel soru ad she tane.
    Guy of Warwick, Middlehill MS.

WOTCHAT. An orchard. *North.*

WOTE. To know. (*A.-S.*)

WOTH. Oath. *Somerset.*

WOTHE. (1) Eloquence. (*A.-S.*)

(2) Harm; injury; mischief. *Gawayne.*

WOTS. Oats. *Var. dial.*

WOU. (1) How. (2) Error; evil.

(3) Very weak liquor. *North.*

WOUCHE. Mischief; evil. *Percy.*

WOUDONE. Woven.

WOULDERS. Bandages. *East.*

WOULTERED. Fatigued; exhausted.

WOUNDER. One who wounds.

WOUNDY. Very. *Var. dial.*
    What thinkst thou of it ? *Woundy good:*
    But this is to be understood

That such an act soe jeeringly
Performed, argues certainly
A man ill nurtured, whose minde
To vertue never was inclinde.
    MS. Play, temp. Charles I.

WOUT. A vault. *Nominale MS.*

WOUTE. Without. *Hearne.*

WOUȜH. Error; mischief. (*A.-S.*)
Ther never there comyth wo ny wouȝh,
But swetnesse ther is ever i-nowgh.
    Religious Poems, xv. Cent.

But noȝt of tho, als I trowe,
That to that state are bonden, thorue wowe.
    MS. Harl. 2260, f. 118.

WOW. (1) A wall? (*A.-S.*)
So neigh togidre, as it was seene,
That ther was nothing hem bitweene,
But wow to wow and wal to wal.
    Gower, MS. Bodl. 294.

(2) Pronounced so as to rhyme to cow; to mew, as cats do. *Linc.*

WOWE. To woo. (*A.-S.*)
Hast thow wowet any wyghte,
And tempted hyre over nyghte.
    MS. Cott. Claud. A. ii. f. 143.

He wowyd the quene bothe day and nyghte,
To lye hur by he had hyt hyghte.
    MS. Cantab. Ff. ii. 38, f. 71.

WOWERIS. Wooers.
Thouȝ sche have woweris ten or twelve.
    Gower, MS. Soc. Antiq. 134, f. 61.

WOWKE. A week.

WOWL. To howl; to cry. *Var. dial.*

WOXSE. Waxed. (*A.-S.*)
And woxse into so fayre and so bryȝt a day.
    Chron. Vilodun. p. 127.

WOYSE. Juice. See *Wose* (1).

WRACK. (1) Wreck. " *Varech,* a sea-wracke or wrecke," Cotgrave.
In the eight, short life, danger of death in travell. In the ninth, in perill to be slaine by theeves. In the tenth, imprisonment, wracks, condemnation, and death by meanes of princes. In the eleventh, a thousand evills, and mischiefes for friends. In the twelfth, death in prison.   *Art of Astrology,* 1673.

(2) Brunt; consequences. *West.*

(3) The rack or torture.

WRAIE. To betray; to discover. (*A.-S.*)

WRAIN. Discovered. (*A.-S.*)

WRAITH. (1) The apparition of a person which appears before his death. *Northumb.*

(2) The shaft of a cart. *North.*

WRAKE. Destruction; mischief. *Gaw.*
Felyce, he seyde, for thy sake
To us ys comen moche wrake,
And alle for the love of the
Dedd be here knyghtys thre!
    MS. Cantab. Ff. ii. 38, f. 154.

WRALL. To cry; to wawl.

WRAMP. A sprain. *Cumb.*

WRANGDOME. Wrong.

WRANGLANDS. Dwarf trees on poor mountainous grounds. *North.*

WRANGLESOME. Cross; quarrelsome.

WRANGOUSLY. Wrongfully. *North.*

WRAPE. To ravish.

WRASE. Same as *Wase,* q. v.

WRASK. Brisk; courageous. *Hearne.*

WRASSLY. To wrestle. *Somerset.*

WRAST. (1) Worst. See *Lake* (2).

(2) A kind of cittern.

(3)
He shalbe wronge wraste,
Or I wende awaye.   *Chester Plays,* ii. 82.

(4) A shrew. *North.*

(5) Loud; stern. *Gawayne.*

WRASTELYNGE. Wrestling.
Wrastelynge, and schotynge, and suche maner game,
Thow myȝte not use wythowte blame.
    MS. Cott. Claud. A. ii. f. 127.

WRASTLE. (1) To dry; to parch. *East.*

(2) To spread with many roots, spoken of new-sown corn. *Glouc.*

WRAT. A wart. *North.*

WRATH. Severe weather.

WRATHE. To anger, or make angry. Also, to be or become angry. (*A.-S.*)
Hast thou by malys of thy doynge,
Wraththed thy neȝbore in any thynge?
    MS. Cott. Claud. A. ii. f. 141.

When he felyd hys woundys smert,
He wrathed sore yn hys herte.
    MS. Cantab. Ff. ii. 38, f. 99.

The dragon felyd strokys smerte,
And he wrathed yn hys herte.
    MS. Cantab. Ff. ii. 38, f. 114.

WRAW. Angry; peevish.
When they have one their habergon of malt,
They wene to make many a man to halt,
For they be than so angry and so wraw,
And yet they will stombile at a straw.
    MS. Rawl. C. 86.

WRAWEN. To call out. (*Dut.*)

WRAWLING. Quarrelling or contending with a loud voice. *Raising a wrow* is exciting a quarrel, and confusion in the streets, &c. *Hallan's Yorksh.*

WRAX. To stretch, or yawn. *North.*

WRAXEN. To grow out of bounds, spoken of weeds, &c. *Kent.*

WRAXLING. Wrestling. *Devon.*

WRAYWARD. Peevish; morose.

WREAK. (1) Revenge. *Shak.*

(2) To fret; to be angry. *North.*

(3) A cough. *Westm.*

WREASEL. A weasel. *North.*

WREATH. (1) A cresset-light.

(2) A swelling from a blow. *North.*

WRECHE. (1) Stranger. (*A.-S.*)

(2) Anger; wrath. Also, to anger.
Dragons galle her wyne shal be,
Of addres venym also, saith he,
That may be heled with no leche,
So violent thei are and ful of wreche.
    MS. Addit. 11305, f. 97.

And covere me atte that dredful day,
Til that thy wreche be y-passed away.
    MS. Addit. 11305, f. 75.

Men and wemen dwellyd he among,
Ȝyt wrechyd he never non with wrong.
    MS. Cantab. Ff. ii. 38, f. 75.

(3) Revenge. (*A.-S.*)

WRECK. Dead undigested roots and stems of grasses and weeds in ploughland. *Norfolk.*

WRED. Rubbish, the baring of a quarry. To wred, to clear the rubbish. To make wred, to perfo[r]m work speedily. *Northumb.*

WREE. To insinuate scandal of any one.

WREEDEN. Peevish; cross. *Cumb.*

WREEST. A piece of timber on the side of a plough made to take on and off. *Kent.*

WREINT. Awry.

WREITH. "*Destordre*, to wring or *wreith*," *Hollyband's Dictionarie*, 1593.

WREKE. (1) Sea-weed. Nominale MS.

(2) Revenged. Also, revenge.

 Of alle the Almayns they wylle be *wreke*.
    MS. Cantab. Ff. li. 38, f. 161.

WREKER. An avenger. (*A.-S.*)

WREKIN-DOVE. The turtledove.

WRENCHE. A trick; a stratagem.

 Of hys wordys he can forthenke,
 But jyt he thoght anodur *wrenche*.
    MS. Cantab. Ff. li. 38, f. 167.

WRENCKE. Same as *Wrenche*, q. v.

 Many men the worlde here fraystes,
 Bot he es noght wyse that tharein traystes,
 For it leedes a man wyth *wrenckes* and wyles,
 And at the last it hym begyles.
    Hampole, MS. Bowes, p. 52.

WRENOCK. Same as *Wretchock*, q. v.

WREST. A twist, or turn.

WRETCH. "Poor wretch" is a term of endearment in Gloucestershire.

WRETCHE. To reck, or care.

WRETCHOCK. The smallest of a brood of domestic fowls. *Gifford.*

WRETE. Written.

 Hyt ys seyde, thurghe lawe *wrete*,
 That thyn hede shulde be of smete.
    MS. Harl. 1701, f. 15.

WRETHEN. Twisted. (*A.-S.*)

WRETON. Written. (*A.-S.*)

 But men may fynde, who so wol loke,
 Som manere peyne *wreton* in boke.
    MS. Addit. 11305, f. 94.

WRETTE. The teat of a breast.

WRET-WEED. The wild euphorbia, which is sometimes used to cure warts. A wart is still called *wret* in Norfolk.

WRICHE. Wretched. (*A.-S.*)

WRICKEN. Miserable. *Linc.*

WRIDE. To spread abroad. *West.*

WRIE. (1) To betray; to discover.

 Ther is no man this place con *wrye*,
 But thyself, jif thou wilt sey,
 And than art thou unkynde.
    MS. Cantab. Ff. v. 48, f. 51.

(2) To cover. (*A.-S.*)

 Sone, me seyde, for Goddys love,
 Wrye me with sum clothe above.
    MS. Harl. 1701, f. 8.

WRIGGLE. Any narrow winding hole.

WRIGGLERS. Small wriggling animals.

WRIGHT. A workman. (*A.-S.*)

 He ded come *wrystes* for to make
 Coveryng over hem for tempest sake.
    MS. Harl. 1701, f. 61.

WRIGHTRY. The business of a wright.

WRIMPLED. Crumpled.

WRIN. To cover; to conceal.

WRINCHED. Sprained. "I have *wrinched* my foote," *Hollyband's Dictionarie*, 1593.

WRINE. A wrinkle. *Somerset.*

WRING. (1) To trouble. *Dorset.*

(2) A press for cider. *West.*

WRING-HOUSE. A house for cider-making.

WRINGLE. (1) A wrinkle. (2) To crack.

WRINGLE-GUT. A nervous fidgety man.

WRINGLE-STRAWS. Long bent, or grass.

WRINKLE. A new idea. *Var. dial.*

WRISTELE. To wrestle.

WRIT. A scroll of writing.

WRITH. The stalk of a plant.

WRITHE. (1) Anger.

 Thus thay fighte in the frythe,
 With waa wreke thay thaire *wrythe*.
    MS. Lincoln A. i. 17, f. 131

(2) To twist; to turn aside.

 The gode man to hys cage can goo,
 And *wrythed* the pyes necke yn two.
    MS. Cantab. Ff. li. 38, f. 136.

(3) Worthy.

(4) The band of a faggot. *West.*

(5) To cover anything up.

WRITHEN. Twisted. *North.*

WRITHING. A turning.

WRITHLED. Withered.

WRITINGS. Persons who quarrel are said *to burn the writings*.

WRITING-TABLE. A table-book.

WRIVED. Rubbed. (*Flem.*)

WRIZZLED. Wrinkled; shrivelled up.

WRO. A corner.

 Nere Sendyforth ther is a *wroo*,
 And nere that *wro* is a welle,
 A ston ther is the wel even fro,
 And nere the wel, truly to telle.
    MS. Cantab. Ff. v. 48, f. 124.

WROBBE.

 If I solde sytt to domesdaye,
 With my tonge to *wrobbe* and wrye,
 Certanely that lady gaye
 Never bese scho askryede for mee.
    MS. Lincoln A. i. 17, f. 149.

WROBBLE. To wrap up. *Heref.*

WROCKLED. Wrinkled. *Sussex.*

WROHTE. Worked; wrought. (*A.-S.*)

WROKE. Avenged.

 Lo! thus hath God the sclaundre *wroke*
 That thou ajens Constaunce hast spoke.
    Gower, MS. Soc. Antiq. 134, f. 67.

WROKIN. A Dutch woman.

WRONG. (1) Untrue. (2) Crooked.

(3) A large bough. *Suffolk.*

WRONGOUS. Wrong. *Palsgrave.*

 Gye seyde, thou doyst uncurteslye
 For to smyte me *wrongeuslye*.
    MS. Cantab. Ff. li 38, f. 188.

WROTE. (1) To grub, as swine, &c.

 There he wandyrde faste abowte,
 And *wrotyd* faste with hys snowte.
    MS. Cantab. Ff. i. 13, f. 108.

 Long he may dyge and *wrote*,
 Or he have hys fyll of the rote.
 In somour he lyvys be the frute,
 And berys that were full suete;
 In wynter may he no thing fynd,
 Bot levys and grasse and of the rynd.
    MS. Ashmole 61, xv. Cen.

(2) A root. *Skelton.*

WROTHELY. Angrily. (*A.-S.*)

The mayde lokyd on Gye full grymme,
And wele *wrothely* answeryd hym.
MS. Cantab. Ff. ii. 38, f. 148.

WROTHER. More wrath.

And seyd, lordynges, for your lyves,
Be never the *wrother* with your wyves.
MS. Ashmole 61, f. 60.

WROTHERHELE. Ill fate, or condition.

WROU3TE. Wrought; made.

And 3it a lechoure alle his lyf
He was, and in avoutrye
He *wrou3te* many a trecherye.
Gower, MS. Soc. Antiq. 134, f. 133.

That alle thynge has *wro3t*,
Hevene and erthe, and alle of no3t.
MS. Cott. Claud. A. ii. f. 132.

WROX. To begin to decay. *Warw.*

WRUCKED. Thrown up. *Gawayne.*

WRY. To turn aside.

But teche hyre to knele downe the by,
And sumwhat thy face from hyre thou *wry.*
MS. Cott. Claud. A. ii. f. 136.

WRYDE. Covered. *(A.-S.)*

She ran than thurghe hem and hastyly hyde,
And with here kercheves hys hepys she *wryds.*
MS. Harl. 1701, f. 88.

WRYGULDY.

Jak boy, is thy bow i-broke,
Or hath any man done the *wryguldy* wrange?
Enterlude of the Four Elementes.

WRYNCHE. On *wrynche*, across.

The vij. wyffe sat one the bynche,
And sche caste her legge one *wrynche.*
MS. Porkington 10, f. 58.

WRY-NOT. To shead wrynot, is to outdo the devil. *Lanc.*

WRYTE. A writing.

All yn yoye and delyte,
Thou muste bere hym thys *wryte.*
MS. Cantab. Ff. ii. 38, f. 103.

WUD. With. *North.*

WUDDER. To make a sullen roar.

WUDDLE. To cut. *North.*

WULB. To cry. *Sussex.*

WULLERD. An owl. *Salop.*

WULLOW. The alder. *Salop.*

WUNDERELLE. A wonder.

WURSHIPLY. Worshipfully; respectfully.

WURT. The canker-worm.

WUSK. A sudden gust. *Notts.*

WUSSET. A scarecrow. *Wilts.*

WUSTEN. Knew. *(A.-S.)*

Wel huy *wusten* in heore mod,
That it was Jhesu verred God.
MS. Laud. 108, f. 11.

WUT. Sense; knowledge.

He is ever out of *wut*, and wood;
How shul we amende his mood?
Cursor Mundi, MS. Coll. Trin. Cantab. f. 6.

WY-DRAUGHT. A sink, or drain.

WYE. A man. *(A.-S.)*

Twa thosande in tale horsede on stedys,
Of the wyghteste *wyes* in alle 3one Weste landys.
Morte Arthure, MS. Lincoln, f. 57.

WYESE. Men. *(A.-S.)*

Nowe they wende over the watyre thise *wyrchipfulle* knyghttes,
Thurghe the wode to the wone there the *wyese* rystes.
Morte Arthure, MS. Lincoln, f. 57.

WYLT. Escaped. *Gawayne.*

WYNDOWED. Blown, or winnowed.

I have one of the smale,
Was *wyndowed* away.
MS. Porkington 10, f. 58.

WYN-TRE. A vine.

Methou3te I saw a *wyn-tre*,
And a bow3e with braunches thre.
Cursor Mundi, MS. Coll. Trin. Cantab. f. 9.

WYRLYNG.

God forbede that a wylde Irish *wyrlyng*
Shoulde be chosen for to be theyr kyng.
MS. Soc. Antiq. 101, f. 6.

WYRWYNE. To choke; to suffocate.

WYTHCLEPYNE. To revoke, or recall.

WYTHENE. Whence. Perceval, 503.

WY3T. Wight, or person.

Fro the morwetyde in to the ny3t
Israel in God doth trowe,
Israel be toknith every *wy3t*
That with God schal ben and goostly knowe,
God to knowe is mannys ry3t,
That wil his wittis wel bestowe;
Therfore I hope, as he hath hy3t,
That hevyn blys is mannys owe.
Hampole's Paraphrase of the Psalms, MS.

X. Is used in some dialects for *sh*. It constantly occurs in the Coventry Mysteries, *sad*, *sal*, *suld*, *salt*, &c.

But now in the memory of my passyon,
To ben partabyl with me in my reyn above,
3e *sal* drynk myn blood with gret devocyon,
Wheche *sal* be *sad* ffor mannys love.
Coventry Mysteries, p. 275.

XENAGOGIE.

These be the things that I had to remember in Eltham; and, to make an ende of all, these be the places whereof I meant to make note in this my *xenagogie* and perambulation of Kent, the first and onely shyre that I have described.
Lambarde's Perambulation, 1596, p. 55.

XOWYNE. To shove. *Pr. Parv.*

Y Y is employed as a prefix to verbs in the
· same manner as I. See p. 472.

YA. (1) Yea. (*A.-S.*)
(2) One. (3) You. *North.*
YAAPPING. Crying in despair, lamenting;
applied to chickens lamenting the absence of
their parent hen. *North.*
YABLES. Ablins; perhaps. *North.*
YACK. To snatch. *Linc.*
YAD. Went. (*A.-S.*)

His squiers habite he had,
Whan he to the deyse *yad,*
Withoute couped shone.
Torrent of Portugal, p. 51.

YADDLE. Drainings from a dunghill.
YAF. Gave. (*A.-S.*)
YAFF. To bark. *North.*
YAFFIL. A woodpecker. *Heref.*
YAFFLE. (1) An armful. *Cornw.*
(2) To bark. Same as *Yaff,* q. v.
(3) To eat. A cant term.
(4) To snatch; to take illicitly.
YAITINGS. See *Gaitings.*
YAITS. Oats. *Cumb.*
YAK. An oak. *North.*
YAKE. To force. *Yorksh.*
YAKKER. An acorn. *West.*
YAL. (1) Whole. (2) Ale. *North.*
YALE. (1) A small quantity. *East.*
(2) To yell; to cry. *Suffolk.*
YALLOW-BEELS. Guineas. *Exmoor.*
YALOWE. Yellow. *Maundevile.*
YALT. Yielded.

He joined his honden, joe vous di,
And *yalt* hem thank and gramerci.
Arthour and Merlin, p. 219.

YALU. Yellow. *North.*

His here, that was *yalu* and bright,
Blac it bicome anonright;
Nas no man in this world so wise of sight,
That afterward him knowe might.
Gy of Warwike, p. 290.

YAM. (1) Home. (2) Aim. *Yorksh.*
(3) To eat heartily. *North.*
YAMERDE. Lamented; sorrowed.
YAMMER. (1) To yearn after. *Lanc.*
(2) To grumble; to fret. *North.* Also, to
make a loud disagreeable noise.
YAMMET. An ant, or emmet. *West.*
YAMPH. To bark continuously. *North.*
YAN. One. *North.*
YANCE. Once. *North.*
YANE. (1) To yawn. *Palsgrave.*

The bore roos and *yanyd* wyde,
Befyse let the spere to hym glyde.
MS. Cantab. Ff. ii. 38, f. 100.

(2) One ridge of corn, with the reapers employed on it.
(3) The breath. (4) One. *North.*
YANGER. Yonder. *Sussex.*
YANGLE. (1) To chatter; to wrangle.
(2) A yoke for an animal. *East.*
YANKS. Leathern or other leggings worn by
agricultural labourers, reaching from below
the knee to the top of the highlow. Sometimes they are called *Bow-Yankees.*

YANSEL. One's self. *North.*
YAP. (1) An ape. *North.*
(2) Quick; ready; apt. *North.*
(3) To bark; to yelp. Also, a cur.
YAPE. To gossip. *Sussex.*
YAPPEE. To yelp. *Devon.*
YAPPY. Cross; irritable. *North.*
YAR. (1) To snarl. *Linc.*
(2) The earth. *North.*
(3) Your. (4) Sour. *Var. dial.*
(5) Aghast; intimidated. *Sussex.*
YARBS. Herbs. *West.*
YARD. (1) Earth; land. "Myddell yarde,"
Chester Plays, i. 67. In Suffolk a garden,
especially a cottage-garden, is so termed.
(2) A rod, or staff. The term was even applied
to a long piece of timber, &c.
(3) The penis.
YARD-LAND. A quantity of land, which varies, according to the place, from 15 to 40
acres. In some places, a quarter of an acre
is called a yard of land.
YARD-MAN. The labourer who has the special
care of the farmyard.
YARE. (1) Nimble; sprightly; quick; active;
ready. Ray gives this as a Suffolk word. It
is found in Shakespeare, Decker, and contemporary writers, often as a sea term. See the
Tempest, i. 1.
(2) Ready. (*A.-S.*)

Then ij. of them made them *yare,*
And to the cyté the chylde they bare.
MS. Cantab. Ff. ii. 38, f. 86.

The erle buskyd and made hym *yare*
For to ryde ovyr the revere.
MS. Cantab. Ff. ii. 38, f. 64.

(3) A fold behind a house, &c.
(4) Brackish to the taste. *North.*
(5) A fish-lock.
YARK. (1) To strike; to beat. *North.* Also,
a stroke, a jerk, a snatch, a pluck. "A yarke
of a whip," Florio, p. 98.
(2) To take away; to take off. *Somerset.*
(3) To kick. Holme, 1688.
(4) To prepare. *North.*
(5) Sharp; acute; quick. *Devon.*
YARKE. To make ready; to prepare.
YARLY. Early. *Lanc.*

What, is he styrrynge so *yarly* this mornynge
whiche dranke so moche yesternyghte.
Palsgrave's Acolastus, 1540.

YARM. (1) To scold; to grumble. *East.*
(2) An unpleasant noise. *Linc.* Also, to make
a loud unpleasant noise.
YARMOUTH-CAPON. A red-herring.
YARN. (1) To earn. *West.*
(2) A net made of yarn.
YARN-BALL. A ball stuffed with yarn, used
by children playing at ball.
YARNE. To yearn after.
YAR-NUT. An earth-nut. *North.*
YARREL. A weed. *Suffolk.*
YARRINGLES. "An instrument of great use
among good housewifes, by means of which
yarn-slippings or hanks (after they have been
washed and whitened) are wound up into

clews or round balls; these by some are termed a pair of yarringles, or yarringle blades, which are nothing else but two sticks or pieces of wood set cross, with a hole in the middle, to turn round about a wooden or iron pin fixed in the stock; the ends are full of holes, to put the pins in, narrower or wider, according to the compass of the slipping or yarn upon it. Some have these instruments jointed with hinges, to turn treble, they being the easier for carriage; but such a.e more for curiosity than necessity. The stock is made of various shapes; some have a square on the top, with a wharl in the middle, and edged about: like the sides of a box, into which the clews are put, as they are wound, and this is set upon three or four wooden feet. Others have them in form of a pillar fixed in a square, with a three-cornered or round foot, either plain or else wrought with turned or carved work, to show the ingenuity of the artificer, or splendour of the owner," Dict. Rust. The term occurs in early vocabularies, in the Pr. Parv., &c.

YARROWAY. The common yarrow.

YARTH. The earth. *North.*

YARUM. Milk. A cant term.

YARWINGLE. See *Yarringles.*

YARY. Sharp; quick; ready. *Kent.*

YASPEN. An Essex word, according to Ray, signifying as much as can be taken up in both hands joined together. Skinner refers to Gouldman.

YAT. (1) A gate. Still in use.

> Therwhiles the king ate mete sat,
> The lyoun goth to play withouten the *yat.*
> *Gy of Warwike,* p. 151.

(2) Hot. (3) A heifer. *North.*

YATE-STOOP. A gate-post. *North.*

YATTON. The town of Ayton.

YAUD. A horse, or mare. *North.* The provincial form of *jade.*

YAUP. (1) To cry out; to shriek; to make a loud noise in talking. *North.*

(2) To be hungry. *North.*

YAVE. Gave.

> The ermyte he *yave* gode day,
> And to Pole he toke the way.
> *MS. Cantab. Ff.* ii. 38, f. 155.

YAVILL. A common; a heath. *Devon.*

YAW. (1) Yes. (2) To hew. *West.*

(3) When a ship is not steered steadily, but goes in and out with her head, they say she *yaws.* Sea-Dictionary, 12mo. 1708.

YAWLE. To cry; to howl. *East.*

> In the popes kychyne the scullyons shall not brawle,
> Nor fyght for my grese. If the priestes woulde for me *yawle.* *Bale's Kynge Johan,* p. 78.

YAWN. To howl. *Craven.*

YAWNEY. A stupid fellow. *Linc.*

YAWNEY-BOX. A donkey. *Derb.*

YAWNUPS. Same as *Yawney,* q. v.

YAWSE-BONES. Ox-bones, used by boys in a game called *yawse. Yorksh.*

Y-BLENT. Blinded.

> Others againe, too much I ween *y-blent*
> With heavenly scale and with religion.
> *Barnes's Foure Bookes of Offices,* 164.

Y-BORNE. Born; carried. *(A.-S.)*

> For the laxcre was *y-borne* up even
> With angelys to the blysse of heven.
> *MS. Harl.* 2260, f. 71.

Y-BORNID. Burnished. *(A.-S.)*

> With golde of seythe fayre and bryzte *y-bornid,*
> With charité that zeveth so clere a lyzte.
> *Lydgate, MS. Soc. Antiq.* 134, f. 15.

YCHAN. Each one. *(A.-S.)*

> I have done the grettist synne
> That any woman may be in,
> Agaynes God and his seyntes *ychan.*
> *MS. Cantab. Ff.* v. 48, f. 16.

> Into a chaumbur they be goone,
> There they schulde be dubbed *ychone.*
> *MS. Cantab. Ff.* ii. 38, f. 18.

YCHELE. An icicle.

Y-CLEDD. Clothed.

> When they were thus *y-cledd,*
> To a chaumbur the erle hym yede.
> *MS. Cantab. Ff.* ii. 38, f. 18.

Y-CORE. Chosen.

> Edgar that was Edmundys zonger sonn,
> To the kyndam of Englond was *y-core.*
> *Chron. Vilodun.* p. 5.

Y-CORN. Chosen. *(A.-S.)*

> Whare thurch we ben to heven *y-corn,*
> And the devel his might forlorn.
> *Arthour and Merlin,* p. 25.

Y-DOO. Done; finished. *(A.-S.)*

> Forthe sche went with sorowe *y-nogh,*
> And tyed hur hors to a boghe,
> Tylle the throwes were alle *y-doo.*
> *MS. Cantab. Ff.* ii. 38, f. 71.

YDUL. Idle; vain.

> I holde hyt but an *ydul* thynge
> To speke myche of teythynge.
> *MS. Cott. Claud.* A. ii. f. 131.

Y-DYT. Stopped. *(A.-S.)*

> Wyth hys tayle my knes he hath knyzt,
> And wyth hys hede my mouth *y-dyt.*
> *MS. Harl.* 1701, f. 21.

YE. (1) An eye.

> And as he louted, hys *ye* gan blenche,
> And say one sytte before the benche.
> *MS. Harl.* 1701, f. 81.

> That he make may hye lowe,
> And lowe hye in a lytylle throwe!
> God may do, withowten lye,
> Hys wylle in the twynkelyng of an *ye!*
> The kyng seyde than, with thozt unstabulle,
> Ye synge thys ofte and alle hys a fabulle!
> *MS. Cantab. Ff.* ii. 38, f. 241.

> From nyse japes and rybawdye
> Thow moste turne away thyn *ye.*
> *MS. Cott. Claud.* A. ii. f. 15.

(2) Yea; yes. *(A.-S.)*

YEAD. The head. *West.*

YEAME. Home. *North.*

YEAN. (1) To throw. *Devon.*

(2) To ean, or bring forth young.

(3) You will. *Lanc.*

YEAND-BY-TO. Before noon. *Lanc.*

YEANDER. Yonder. *Var. dial.*

YEANT. A giant.

> He come where the *yeant* was,
> And seyde, gode syr, let me passe.
> *MS. Cantab. Ff.* ii. 38, f. 64.

YEAPM. To hiccough. *North.*

YEAR-DAY. An anniversary day; a day on which prayers were said for the dead.

YEARDED. Buried.

YEARDLY. Very. *North.*

YEARLING. A beast one year old.

YEARN. To vex, or grieve.

YEARNE. To give tongue, a hunting term, applied to hounds when they open on the game.

YEARNSTFUL. Very earnest. *Lanc.*

YEASING. The eaves of a house. *Lanc.*

YEASY. Easy. *Lanc.*

YEATH. Heath; ground. *West.*

YEATHER. Same as *Ether* (3).

YEAVELING. The evening. *Devon.*

YEAVY. Wet and moist. *Exmoor.*

YEBBLE. Able. *Northumb.*

YED. (1) An aperture or way where one collier only can work at a time.

(2) Edward. *Derb.*

YEDART. Edward. *Salop.*

YEDDINGES. See *Jeddinges.*

YEDDLE. To addle, or earn. *Chesh.*

YEDE. Went. (*A.-S.*)

> Thurch the wombe and thurch the chine,
> The spere *yede* even biline.
> *Arthour and Merlin, p. 236.*

> So they waschyd and *yede* to mete,
> The byschop the grace dyd say.
> *MS. Cantab. Ff. ii. 38, f. 46.*

> But then they wente fro that stede,
> On ther way forthe they *yede*
> Ferre fro every towne,
> Into a grete wyldurnes,
> Fulle of wylde bestys hyt was,
> Be dale and eke be downe.
> *MS. Cantab. Ff. ii. 38, f. 73.*

YEDWARD. (1) Edward. *Chesh.*

(2) A dragon fly. *Grose.*

YEEKE. Itch. *Yorksh.*

YEENDER. The forenoon. *North.* This is probably a corruption of *undern,* q. v.

YEEPE. Active; alert; prompt. (*A.-S.*)

YEEPSEN. Same as *Yaspen,* q. v.

YEERY. Angry. *North.*

YEES. Eyes. *Exmoor.*

YEEVIL. A dungfork. *West.*

YEF. To give. Also, a gift.

YEFFELL. Evil.

> Y met hem bot at Wentbreg, seyde Lytyll John,
> And therfor *yeffell* mot he the,
> Seche thre strokes he me gafe,
> Yet they cleffe by my seydys.
> *Robin Hood, i. 83.*

YEFTE. A gift. (*A.-S.*)

YEGE. A wedge.

YEIFER. A heifer. *Devon.*

YEK. An oak. *North.*

YEL. An eel. *Somerset.*

YELD. Eld; age. *Skelton.*

YELD-BEASTS. Animals barren, not giving milk, or too young for giving profit.

YELDE. To yield, pay, give. (*A.-S.*)

YELDER. Better; rather. *North.*

YELD-HALL. A guild-hall.

YELDROCK. The yellow-hammer. *North.*

II.

YELE-HOUSE. A brewing-house. Brockett has *yell-house,* an alehouse.

YRLF. A dungfork. *Chesh.*

YELK. To prepare clay for the dawber by mixing straw and stubble with it.

YELLOT. The jaundice. *Heref.*

YELLOW-BELLY. A person born in the fens of Lincolnshire. *Linc.*

YELLOW-BOTTLE. Corn marigold. *Kent.*

YELLOW-BOYS. Guineas. *Var. dial.*

YELLOW-HOMBER. The chaffinch. *West.*

YELLOWNESS. Jealousy. *Shak.*

YELLOWS. (1) Jealousy.

> Thy blood is yet uncorrupted, *yellows* has not tainted it. *Two Lancashire Lovers,* 1640, p. 27.

(2) Dyers' weed. *Midl. C.*

(3) A disorder in horses.

(4) The jaundice. Still in use.

YELLOW-SLIPPERS. Very young calves.

YELLOW-STARCH. Was formerly much used for staining linen for dress, ruffs, &c. It is frequently referred to.

YELLOW-STOCKINGS. To anger the yellow stockings, i. e. to provoke jealousy.

YELLOW-TAILS. Earthworms yellow about the tail. Topsell's Serpents, p. 307.

YELLOW-YOWLEY. The yellow-hammer.

YELM. To lay straw in order fit for use by a thatcher. *East.*

YELOWSE. Jealous.

> Thou woldest be so *yelowse,*
> And of me so amerowse.
> *MS. Cantab. Ff. ii. 38, f. 152.*

YELPER. A young dog; a whelp.

YELTE. (1) Yieldeth. (*A.-S.*)

(2) A young sow. *North.*

YELVE. The same as *Yelf,* q. v.

YEM. Edmund. *Lanc.*

YEMAN. A servant of a rank next below a squire; a person of middling rank.

YEME. (1) An uncle.

> His dame nowe maye dreame,
> For her owine barne teamo,
> For nother ante nor *yeme*
> Gettes this gaye garmente.
> *Chester Plays,* ii. 55.

(2) Care; attention. Also, to take care of, to rule, guide, or govern.

> Be that hadde Beves lein in bendes
> Seve yer in peines grete,
> Lite i-dronke and lasse i-ete.
> His browe stank for defaut of *yeme,*
> That it set after ase a seme.
> *Beves of Hamtoun,* p. 62.

YEMMOUTH. Aftermath. *Glouc.*

YEN. Eyes. (*A.-S.*)

> And his felaw forthwith also
> Was blynde of bothe his *yen* two.
> *Gower, MS. Soc. Antiq. 134, f. 63.*

> The terys owte of hys *yen* yode.
> *MS. Harl. 2252, f. 133.*

YENDE. India.

> He send bysshop Swytelyn y-wys,
> Into *Yende* for hym on pilgremage.
> *Chron. Vilo dun. p. 9*

YENDEN. Ended. *West.*

YENE. (1) To yawn, or gape.

Mani mouthe the gres bot,
And griseliche *yened*, God it wot.
Arthour and Merlin, p. 263.

(2) Eyes. See *Yen*.
Sith I am wounded wyth yowre *yene* tweyne,
Lete me no lengur sighen for yowre sake.
MS. Cantab. Ff. i. 6, f. 12.

(3) To enter into. (*A.-S.*)
(4) To lay an egg. *Weber*.
(5) To give up to.

YENLET. An inlet.
I suppose that by *genlade* he meaneth a thing yet well knowne in Kent, and expressed by the word yenlade or *yenlk*, which betokeneth an indraught or inlett of water into the lande.
Lambarde's Perambulation, 1596, p. 259.

YENNED. Threw. *Devon*.

YEO. An ewe. *Exmoor*.

YEOMAN-FEWTERER. See *Fewterer*.

YEOMAN'S-BREAD. A kind of bread made for ordinary use.

YEOMATH. Aftermath. *Wilts*.

YEOVERY. Hungry. *Northumb*.

YEP. Prompt; quick. A brisk active person is said in Suffolk to be *yepper*.
The to and fourti weren *yep*,
Thai leten ther hors gode chep.
Arthour and Merlin, p. 212.
Syr Befyse that was bothe wyse and *yepe*,
He smote the hors with the spurrys of golde.
MS. Cantab. Ff. ii. 38, f. 101.

YEPPING. The chirping of birds.

YEP-SINTLE. Two handfuls. *Lanc*.

YERD. (1) A fox-earth. *Cumb*.

(2) A rod, or staff. Still in use.

YERE. (1) An heir. In a bond dated 1605, written in a copy of Hall's Union, fol. Lond. 1548, in the library of the Society of Antiquaries, the writer mentions " myne *yeres*, executors, administrators, and assignes."

(2) An ear. Nominale MS.
But sone thei cane away here hedes wrye,
And to fayre speche lyttely thaire *yeres* close.
MS. Cantab. Ff. i. 6, f. 104.

(3) A year. (*A.-S.*)

YERK. To kick, like a horse.

YERLY. Early.
Yerly when the day can sprynge,
A preest he dud a masse synge.
MS. Cantab. Ff. ii. 38, f. 83.

YERMEN. Men hired by the year.

YERNE. (1) Iron. Nominale MS. "The yern pot," Dr. Dee's Diary, p. 24.

(2) Quickly; eagerly; briskly.
For he seyd he wald as *yern*
Fight with that geaunt stern.
Gy of Warwike, p. 304.

(3) To run. Octovian, 965. See Wright's Gloss. to Piers Ploughman.

(4) To desire; to seek eagerly. (*A.-S.*)

(5) A heron. *Chesh*.

YERNFUL. Melancholy. *Nares*.

YERNIN. Rennet. *Yorksh*.

YERNING. Activity; diligence.

YERNSTFUL. Very earnest. *Lanc*.

YERRARCHY. Hierarchy.

YERRED. Swore. *Devon*.

YERRING. Noisy. *Exmoor*.

YERRIWIG. An earwig. *West*.

YERSTERNE-NIGHT. Last night.
Wel the grete that ilche knight,
That sopede with the *yerstene-night*.
Beves of Hamtoun, p. 112.

YERTH. Earth. *Var. dial*.

YERT-POINT. A game mentioned in the old play of Lady Alimony.

YES. (1) Eyes. See *Ye*.

(2) An earthworm. *Somerset*.

YESK. " I yeake, I gyve a noyse out of my stomacke, *je engloute*," Palsgrave. See *Yex*.

YEST. Froth. (*A.-S.*)

YESTE. Geat; tale.
The emperowre gaf hur xl. pownde,
In *yeste* as we rede.
MS. Cantab. Ff. ii. 38, f. 84.
Now begynnyth a *yeste* ageyn
Of Kyng Quore and Armyn.
MS. Cantab. Ff. ii. 38, f. 121.

YESTMUS. A handful. *Lanc*.

YESTREEN. Last night. *North*.

YESTY. Frothy. Hence, light.

YETE. A gate. *North*.
On ascapede and atorn
In at the castel *yete*,
Ase the king sat at the mete.
Beves of Hamptoun, p. 84.

YETEN. Gotten. *Chaucer*.

YETHARD. Edward. *Warw*.

YETH-HOUNDS. Dogs without heads, the spirits of unbaptised children, which ramble among the woods at night, making wailing noises. *Devon*.

YETLING. A small iron pan, with a bow handle and three feet. *North*.

YET-NER. Not nearly. *Sussex*.

YETS. Oats. *Var. dial*.

YETTUS. Yet. *Warw*.

YEVE. (1) To give. (*A.-S.*)
To the worlde y wylle me never *yeve*,
But serve the, Lorde, whylle y leve.
MS. Cantab. Ff. ii. 38, f. 84.

(2) Evening. Reliq. Antiq. i. 300.

YEVEN. Given. (*A.-S.*)

YEWD. Went. *North*.

YEWER. A cow's udder. *North*.

YEWERS. Embers; hot ashes. *Exm*.

YEW-GAME. A gambol, or frolic.

YEWKING. Puny; sickly.

YEWMORS. Embers. See *Yewers*.

YEWRE. A water-bearer.

YEWTHOR. A strong ill smell. This word is given by Urry, in his MS. Additions to Ray.

YEWYS. Jews.
How *Yewys* demyd my sone to dye,
Eche oon a dethe to hym they dreste.
MS. Cantab. Ff. ii. 38, f. 6.

YEX. The hiccough. It occurs as a verb, to hiccough, in Florio, p. 501.

YF. Give.
And seyde, Harrowde, what redyst thou?
Yf me thy cowncell nowe.
MS. Cantab. Ff. ii. 38, f. 16.

Y-FALLE. Fallen. (*A.-S.*)
God forgeve us owre synnes all,
That we all day beyth yn *y-falle*.
MS. Cantab. Ff. ii. 38, f. 216.

Y-FOLE. Fallen. (*A.-S.*)

But when the kyng was *y-fole* aslepe,
A wonder syȝt him thoȝt he saye.
Chron. Vilodun. p. 15.

Y-FOLUD. Fouled; defiled.

Lest that holy plase with that blod *y-folud* shuld be.
Chron. Vilodun. p. 105.

YFTLES. Giftless.

The kyng of Pervynse seyd, So mot I the!
Yftles schalle they not be.
Torrent of Portugal, p. 18.

YGNE. Eyes.

So was hyt shewyd before here *ygne*
That halvyndele she was ȝove to pyne.
MS. Harl. 1701, f. 11.

YH. Is found in some manuscripts for *y*, as *yhate*, gate, *yheme*, for *yeme*, q. v., &c.

YHE. Ye.

He says, als men *yhe* salle dye alle,
And als ane of the prynces *yhe* salle falle,
That es, *yhe* salle dye one the same manere
Als men dyes in this worlde here.
Hampole, MS. Bowes, p. 68.

YHEMING. A guard. See *Yeme* (2).

YHEN. Eyes.

Both *yhen* of myne hed were oute.
Gower, MS. Cantab. Ff. 1. 6, f. 65.

YHERDE. A yard; a rod.

In *yherde* irened salt thou stere tha,
Als lome of erthe breke tham als swa.
MS. Cott. Vespas. D. vii. f. 1.

YHERE. A year. *Ps. Cott. Antiq.*

YHERNE. To yearn; to desire.

Thal sal *yherne*, he says, to dyghe ay,
And the dede sal fleghe fro thaime away.
Hampole, MS. Bowes, p. 216.

YHIT. Yet. See *Unconand*.

Y-HOLD. Beholden. (*A.-S.*)

YHOTEN. A giant. (*A.-S.*)

YHOUGHHEDE. Youth. (*A.-S.*)

YHOWNGE. Young.

YI. Yea; yes. *Derb.*

YIELD. (1) To give; to requite.

(2) Barren, applied to cows. *North.*

(3) To give up, or relinquish. *South.*

YIFFE. To give.

And therto han ye suche benevolence
With every jantylman to speke and deylle
In honesté, and *yiffe* hem audience,
That seeke folke restoryn ye to helle.
MS. Fairfax 16.

YILD. Patience. (*A.-S.*)

YILDE. Tribute. *Weber.*

YILP. To chirp. *North.*

YILT. A female pig. *Beds.*

YINDER. Yonder. *East.*

YIP. To chirp. *East.*

YIPPER. Brisk. *East.*

YISSERDAY. Yesterday. *North.*

Y-KETE. Begotten.

Kyng Edgarus douȝter yche wene he was
Y-kete bot upon a wenche.
Chron. Vilodun. p. 94.

YKINE. To itch. *Pr. Parv.*

YLE. (1) An eel. (2) An aisle.

Y-LERD. Learned.

He seyde, y wende that ye were clerkys beste *y-lerd*,
That levyd yn thys medyllerd.
MS. Cantab. Ff. ii. 38, f. 128.

Y-LESSED. Relieved. *Chaucer.*

YLKOON. Each one.

That they schulde arme them *ylkoon*,
For to take the kyngys fone.
MS. Cantab. Ff. ii. 38, f. 194.

Y-LOGGED. Lodged. *Chaucer.*

Y-LOKE. Locked up.

And with oo worde of the mayde y-spoke,
The Holy Gost is in here breste *y-loke*.
Lydgate, MS. Soc. Antiq. 134, f. 2.

Y-LOWE. Lied.

That levedy seyd, thou misbegeten thing,
Thou hast *y-lowe* a gret lesing.
Arthour and Merlin, p. 43.

YLYCH. Alike.

And lovede well with hert trewe,
Nyght and day *ylych* newe.
Octovian, 92.

YMANGE. Among.

And as he satt at the mete *ymange* his prynces,
he was wonder mery and gladde, and jocund.
MS. Lincoln A. i. 17, f. 47.

Y-MELLE. Among. (*A.-S.*)

Whenne the leves are dryede ynowghe and bakene
y-melle the stones, take thanne and braye the leves
alle to powder.
MS. Linc. Med. f. 287.

YMENEUS. Hymenæus.

Y-MENT. Intended. (*A.-S.*)

Y-MOULID. Moulded; rusted.

And with his blood schalle wasche undefoulid
The gylte of man with ruste of synne *y-moulid*.
Lydgate, MS. Soc. Antiq. 134, f. 1.

YMPE. To engraft.

Ne hadde oure elderis cerchid out and soght
The sothfast pyth to *ympe* it in our thoght.
MS. Digby, 232.

YMPNYS. Hymns.

Thenne where they in contenuele loveynge in
ympnys and gostely sanges, when they felde his moste
helefulle comynge. *MS. Lincoln* A. i. 17, f. 186.

YND. India. *Lydgate*, p. 25.

YNENCE. Towards. See *Howgates.*

YNESCHE.

For many are that never kane halde the ordyre of
lufe *ynesche* thaire frendys, sybbe or fremmede, bot
outhire thay lufe thaym over mekille, or thay lufe
thame over lytille. *MS. Lincoln* A. i. 17, f. 194.

YNEWE. Enough.

Waynour waykly wepande hym kyssis,
Talkes to hym tenderly with teres *ynewe*.
Morte Arthure, MS. Lincoln, f. 60.

YNGYNORE. A maker of engines.

In hys court was a false traytoure,
That was a grete *yngynore*.
MS. Cantab. Ff. ii. 38, f. 39.

YNNYS. Lodgings. (*A.-S.*)

Then they departyd them in plyghte,
And to ther *ynnys* they wente.
MS. Cantab. Ff. ii. 38, f. 76.

YNWYT. Understanding; conscience.

Ymagyne no wrong nor falsenes,
Of fyne *ynwyttys* the rewle ys thys.
MS. Cantab. Ff. ii. 38, f. 5.

YO. You. *North.*

YOAK. Two pails of milk.

YOCKEN. To gargle. *North.*

YODE. Went. (*A.-S.*)

And alle the nyght ther-in he lay
Tyl on the morowe that hyt was day,
That men to mete *yode*.
Eglamour, 531.

YOGELOWRE. A juggler.

YOI. Yes. *North.*

YOKE. (1) A pair of oxen. *To yoke out*, to put a horse in a cart, gig, or other carriage.

(2) A portion of the working day; to work two *yokes*, is to work both portions, morning and afternoon. *Kent.*

(3) The hiccough. *West.*

(4) The grease of wool. *Devon.*

YOKEL. A countryman. *West.* Generally, a country bumpkin, in contempt.

YOKENS. When two trams or carriages meet, going in different directions. *Newc.*

YOKEY. Yellow; tawney. *Devon.*

YOKLE. An icicle.

YOKLET. A little farm or manor in some parts of Kent is called a yoklet. *Kennett.*

YOKLY-MOLE-KIT. A yellow, unhealthy-looking person. *Devon*

YOKY-WOOL. Unwashed wool as it comes from the sheep's back. *Devon.*

YOLDE. Yielded: delivered up.
> The chylde they to Clement *yolde*,
> xx. li he them tolde.
> *MS. Cantab. Ff. ii. 38, f. 86.*

YOLD-RING. A yellow-hammer. *North.*

YOLE. To yell; to bawl. Brockett has *youl* as still in use in the North.

YOLKINGE. Hiccupping.
> Whose ugly locks and *yolkinge* voice
> Did make all men afeard. *MS. Ashmole 208.*

YOLLER. To cry out as a dog when under chastisement. *Northumb.*

YOLT. A newt. *Glouc.*

YOLY. Handsome. (*A.-N.*)
> Wyth mony knyghtys herde of bone,
> That *yoly* colourys bare.
> *MS. Cantab. Ff. ii. 38, f. 70.*
> Toward hur come a knyghte,
> Gentylle sche thoght and a *yoly* man.
> *MS. Cantab. Ff. ii. 38, f. 244.*

YON. For *yonder*: seems to be commonly used for a thing somewhat at a distance; thus, they say, what's yon? meaning what is that over there at a distance? It is also used adjectively, as yon lass, yon house, yon country, &c. *Linc.* Skinner has *yon*, and *yonside*.

YOND. Furious; savage. *Spenser.*

YONDERLY. Reserved. *Yorksh.*

YONE. Yon; yonder.
> Jif *yone* mane one lyfe be,
> Bid hym com and speke with me,
> And pray hym als thou kanc. *Perceval, 1966.*

YONKE. Young. *Weber.*

YONT. Beyond. *North.*

YOO. An ewe. Chester Plays, i. 120.

YOON. An oven. *Var. dial.*

YOPPUL. Unnecessary talk. *South.*

YORE. (1) An ewer. It occurs in an inventory, MS. Cantab. Ff. i. 6, f. 58.

(2) A year. Sir Amadas, 655.

(3) Formerly; for a long time. (*A.-S.*)

(4) Ready. Same as *Yare*, q. v.

YORKPENCE. The name of a copper coin in the reign of Henry VI. See *Topens.*

YORKSHIRE. To put Yorkshire of a man, i. e. to cheat or deceive him. *North.*

YORKSHIRE-HUNTERS. The name of a regiment formed by the gentlemen of York-shire during the Civil Wars.

YORNANDLIKE. Desirable.

YORNE. Hastened; long. *Weber.*

YORT. A yard, or field. *Lanc.*

YOT. To unite closely. *Dorset.*

YOTE. To pour in. Grose has *yoted*, watered, a West country word.

YOTEN. Cast. *Weber.*

YOUK. To sleep. A hawking term.

YOULE. "On Malvern Hills, in Worcester-shire, when the common people fan their corn, and want wind, they crie by way of invocation, *youle, youle, youle*, which word, sais Mr. Aubrey, is no doubt a corruption of Æolus, god of winds," Kennett MS.

YOULING. A curious Kentish custom mentioned by Hasted, ap. Brand, i. 123.
> There is an odd custom used in these parts, about Keston and Wickham, in Rogation week, at which time a number of young men meet together for the purpose, and with a most hideous noise run into the orchards, and, encircling each tree, pronounce these words:
> > Stand fast root; bear well top;
> > God send us a *youling* sop;
> > Every twig apple big,
> > Every bough apple enow.
> For which incantation the confused rabble expect a gratuity in money, or drink, which is no less welcome: but if they are disappointed of both, they with great solemnity anathematize the owners and trees with altogether as insignificant a curse.

YOULRING. The yellow-hammer.

YOUNGERMER. Younger persons. *Cumb.*

YOUNKER. A young person.
> Yet such sheep he kept, and was so seemelie a shep-heard,
> Seemelie a boy, so seemelie a youth, so seemelie a *younker*,
> That on Ide was not such a boy, such a youth, such a *younker*. *Barnefield's Affectionate Shepherd, 1594.*

YOU'RE. You were.

YOURES. Of you.

YOURN. Yours. *Var. dial.*

YOUT. To cry; to yell. *Yorksh.*

YOUTHLY. Youthful.

YOVE. Given. (*A.-S.*)

YOW. (1) To reap, gathering the corn under the arm. *Devon.*

(2) An ewe. *Var. dial.*

YOWER. (1) Your. *North*

(2) An udder. *Yorksh.*

YOWFTER. To fester.

YOWL. The same as *Yole*, q. v.

YOWP. To yelp. *West.*

YOWTHE-HEDE. Youth. (*A.-S.*)
> He that may do gode dede,
> He schulde hym force in *yowthe-hede*,
> So that he may, when he ys olde,
> For a doghty man be tolde.
> *MS. Cantab. Ff. ii. 38, f. 152.*

YOYE. Joy.
> The knyyt answeryd with wordes mylde,
> Syr, yf you *yoye* of yowre chylde,
> For here may y not lende. *Eglamour, 668.*

YOYFULLE. Joyful; glad.

Hys kynne was wondur *joyfullie* than,
That he waxe so feyre a man.
MS. Cantab. Ff. ii. 38, f. 147.

YOYSTER. To frolic; to laugh. *Sussex.*

YPEQUISTO. A toadstool.

Y-REIGHT. Reached. (*A.-S.*)

YRNE. Iron.
Brenne the snayle to powdure upon a hoot *yrne,*
and put that powdur to the yjen when thou gost to
bedde.
MS. Med. Rec. in Mr. Pettigrew's Possession, xv. Cent.

YRNES. Harness, i. e. armour. *Gaw.*

YRON. A heron.
Fer out over jon mownten gray,
Thomas, a fowken makes his nest,
A fowkyn is an *yrons* pray,
For thei in place wille have no rest!
MS. Cantab. Ff. v. 48, f. 120.

YRONHARD. The herb knapweed.

YRRIGAT. Watered.
But yeer bi yeer the soil is *yrrigat,*
And ovyrflowid with the flood of Nyle.
MS. Rawl. Poet. 32.

Y-SACRYD. Consecrated. (*A.-S.*)

YS. Ice.
Se the ensaunpul that I jow schowe,
Of water, and *ys,* and eke snowe.
MS. Cott. Claud. A. ii. f. 132.

YSAIE. Isaiah.
Spake *Ysaie* and seid in wordes pleyn,
The hie hevynes doth your grace adewe.
MS. Ashmole 59, f. 174.

YSE. Ice. (*A.-S.*)
He was never wyse,
That went on the *yse.* *MS. Douce 52.*

YSELS. Ashes. (*A.-S.*)
And whenne the heved schalle be waschene, make
lce of haye *ysels,* that was mawene byfor myssomer
day. *MS. Med. Linc. f. 281.*

Y-SHROUDED. Covered; concealed.
Quod Gaubrielle, withinue thy blissid side
The Holy Goste schalle *y-shrouded* be.
Lydgate, MS. Soc. Antiq. 134, f. 2.

YSOOP. Hyssop.
Sprankle me, lord, wyth *ysoop,*
That myn herte be purged clene.
MS. Cantab. Ff. ii. 38, f. 1.

YSOPE. Æsop, the fabulist.

Y-SOYLID. Soiled. (*A.-S.*)
My lyppis polute, my mouth with synne *y-soylid.*
Lydgate, MS. Soc. Antiq. 134, f. 2.

Y-STOYNGE. Stung; pricked.

YS3. Ice. (*A.-S.*)
Whane the emperour Darius removed his oste,
and come to the revere of Graunt on the nyghte,
and went over the *ys3,* and thar he luged hym.
MS. Lincoln A. i. 17, f. 19.

YT. Yet. Arch. xxix. 135.

YTHEZ. Waves. (*A.-S.*)
Ewene walkande owte of the Weste landes,
Wanderande unworthyly overe the wale *ythes.*
Morte Arthure, MS. Lincoln. f. 61.

Y-THREVE. Thriven.
I love hym welle, for he ys welle *y-threve,*
Alle my love to hym y geve.
MS. Cantab. Ff. ii. 38, f. 128.

YU. Yule, or Christmas.

YUCK. To snatch or drag with great force.
Linc. Also a substantive, quasi *jerk,* a strong
pull.

YUCKEL. A woodpecker. *Wilts.*

YUGEMENT. Judgment.
And all they seyde with oon assente,
We graunt wele to yowre *yugement.*
MS. Cantab. Ff. ii. 38, f. 151.

YU-GOADS. Christmas playthings. *Lanc.*

YUIGTHE. Youth.
And hadde wonder of his *yuigthe,*
That ther kidde swiche strengthe.
Arthour and Merlin, p. 233.

YUKE. To itch. *North.*

YULE. (1) Christmas. (*A.-S.*) The term is
still retained in the North of England. "In
Yorkshire," says Blount, "and our other
Northern parts, they have an old custome
after sermon or service on Christmas day, the
people will, even in the churches, cry *ule, ule,*
as a token of rejoycing, and the common sort
run about the streets, singing,

Ule, ule, ule, ule,
Three puddings in a pule,
Crack nuts and cry ule."
Glossographia, ed. 1681, p. 692.

Vij. yere he levyd there,
Tylle hyt befelle agenste the *youle*
Upon the fyrste day,
The hounde, as the story says,
Ranne to the kyngys palays,
Wythowt ony more delay.
MS. Cantab. Ff. ii. 38, f. 74.

(2) To coo, said of pigeons.

YULE-CLOG. An immense piece of fire-wood,
laid on the fire on Christmas-eve.

YULE-PLOUGH. See *Fool-plough.*

YULING. Keeping Christmas. *North.*

YULK. The same as *Julk,* q. v.

YULY. Handsome. Ritson, iii. 107. So explained, but I think an error for *ynly.*

YUMMERS. Embers. *Devon.*

YURE. An udder. *North.*

YURNEY. Enterprise.

YUT. To gurgle. *North.*

YVLE. Evilly; wickedly.
Thyn host lith her ful yvele araid,
And holdeth hym ful *yvle* apaid.
MS. Ashmole 33, f. 53.

YVOR. Ivory.
And like *yvor* that cometh fro so ferre,
His teeth schalle be even, smothe and white.
Lydgate, MS. Soc. Antiq. 134, f. 14.
With golde and *yvour* that so bright shon,
That all aboute the bewté men may see.
Lydgate, MS. Ashm. 39, f. 30.

Y3E. Eye.
Whenne that traytour so hadde sayde,
Ffyve goode hors to hym were tayde,
That alle myjton see with *yje;*
They drowen hym thorwj ilke a strete,
And seththyn to the elmes, I jow hete,
And hongyd hym ful hyje.
Romance of Athelstan.

ZA. To essay; to try. *West.*

ZAHT. Soft. *Somerset.*

ZAM. (1) To parboil. *West.*

(2) Cold. *Devon.*

ZAMSAUDEN. Parboiled. Applied to anything spoilt by cooking. *West.*

ZANY. A mimic, or buffoon.

ZARUE. The plant milfoil.

ZAT. (1) Soft. (2) Salt. *West.*

ZATELY. Indolent; idle. *Dorset.*

ZATENFARE. Soft; silly. *West.*

ZAWP. A blow. *Somerset.*

ZEDLAND. The Western counties, where Z is usually substituted for S by the natives.

ZEMMIES-HAW. An interj. of surprise.

ZENZYBYR. Ginger.

Clary, pepur long, with granorum paradyse,
Zenzybyr and synamon at every tyde.
Digby Mysteries, p. 77.

ZESS. A compartment, or a threshing floor for the reception of the wheat that has been threshed, but not winnowed.

ZEWNTEEN. Seventeen. *Devon.*

ZIDLE-MOUTH. One having the mouth on one side; an ugly fellow. *West.*

ZILTER. A salting tub; a vessel for salting meat. *Somerset.*

ZIN. The sun; a son. *West.*

ZINNILA. A son-in-law. *Exm.*

ZINO. As I know. *Somerset.*

ZLEARD. Slided. *Somersetshire.*

Ice sleurd and sleurd and never gave ore,
Till ice sleurd me downe to the bellvree dore.
MS. Ashmole 36, f. 112.

ZOAT. Silly. *I. of Wight.*

ZOCK. A blow. *West.*

ZOG. To doze. *Devon.*

ZOKEY. A sawney. *Devon.*

ZOO-ZOO. A wood-pigeon. *Glouc.*

ZOTY. A fool. *South.*

ZOWL. A plough. *Exmoor.*

ZUCHES. Stumps of trees. *Kennett.*

ZUM. Some. *West.*

ZUNG. Since. *Exmoor.*

ZUO. So. Reliq. Antiq. i. 42.

ZWAIL. To swing the arms. *West.*

ZWETE. Wheat.

ZWIT-MARBRE. Explained *alabastrum*, in a list of herbs in MS. Sloane 5, f. 2.

ZWODDER. Drowsy and dull. *West.*

---

3. This character is found in early English MSS. written after the twelfth century. It is a corruption of the Anglo-Saxon letter *g*, and sometimes answers to our *g*, sometimes to *y*, sometimes to *gh*, and also to a mute consonant at the commencement of a word. In the middle of a word it occasionally stands for *i*; in the same manner the A.-S. *g* has been changed into *i*, when in a similar position. It should be remarked that the letter *z* often appears in MSS. under this character, with which, however, it has clearly no connexion. It is, therefore, incorrect to substitute it as an equivalent for *z*, or vice versa. When it occupies the place of the Anglo-Saxon letter, no other character represents its exact force.

3A. Yea; yes; truly.

And Affricane sayd 3a, withoutene drede.
MS. Cantab. Ff. i. 6, f. 22.

Whi, ame I thi sonne, thanne? quod Alexandre;
3aa, forsothe, quod Anectanabus, I gat the; and with that word he 3alde the gaste.
MS. Lincoln A. 1. 17, f. 1.

3AF. Gave.

Certeyne prestes of the Jewis lawe
Gan to grucche, as they 3af audience.
Lydgate, MS. Soc. Antiq. 134, f. 17.

Alle his ri3t tru purchase
To Dovre abbei he hit 3afe.
MS. Cantab. Ff. v. 48, f. 100.

3AL. Yelled, as a dog.

3ALDE. Yielded.

The portar 3alde hym hys travayle,
He smote hym agayne withowten fayle.
MS. Cantab. Ff. ii. 38, f. 241.

Hit 3alde, whenne hit was shorn,
As hundride fold that ilke corn.
Cursor Mundi, MS. Coll. Trin. Cantab. f. 77.

The marchande 3alde up hys goste, and yede to God fulle ryghte. *MS. Cantab. Ff. ii. 38, f. 54.*

Asswythe he deyd yn haste,
There he shuld go he 3alde the gaste.
MS. Harl. 1701, f. 37.

3ALOWE. Yellow.

Thelse cocodrilles ben serpentes, 3alowe and rayed aboven, and han four feet, and schorte thyes and grete nayles, as clees or talouns.
Maundevile's Travels, p. 198.

3ALOW-SOU3T. The jaundice.

For the 3alow sou3t, that men callin the jaundys. Take hard Speynich sope and a litille stale ale in a coppe, and rubbe the sope a3ens the coppe botum tylle the ale be qwyte. *MS. Sloane 7, f. 73.*

3ALT. Yielded; requited.

3AMYRLY. Lamentably. *Gawayne.*

3ANG. Young.

Ther may we sum 3ang man fynde,
That is both curtese and hynde.
MS. Cantab. Ff. v. 48, f. 45.

3ANYNG. Yawning; gaping.

Than come ther owt of a corner a grete dragon 3anyng on hur, so that hys mowthe was over hur hede. *MS. Cantab. Ff. ii. 38, f. 19.*

Blowyng and 3anyng too,
As he wolde hym then have sloo.
MS. Cantab. Ff. ii. 38, f. 246.

3AR. Before.

Saber was never 3ar so gladd.
MS. Cantab. Ff. ii. 38, f. 116.

3ARDE. A yard; a fore-court.

Owt of the 3arde he went aryght.
MS. Cantab. Ff. ii. 38, f. 140.

3ARE. (1) Ready.

And crossen sayle and made Kem 3are
Anon, as thou3 they wolde fare.
Gower, MS. Soc. Antiq. 134, f. 15.

His archers that ware thare,
Bathe the lesse and the mare,
Als so swythe were thay 3are.
MS. Lincoln A. 1. 17, f. 132.

(2) Quickly; readily.

> Anone that we be buskede ȝare,
> In oure journaye for to fare.
> > *MS. Lincoln A. i. 17, f. 116.*

> The birde answerde ful ȝare,
> Nevene thou it any mare,
> Thou salle rewe fulle sare,
> And lyke it fulle ille.
> > *MS. Lincoln A. i. 17, f. 136.*

ȝARLY. Early.

> Nyght and day he ys in sorowe,
> Late on evyn, ȝarly on morowe.
> > *MS. Cantab. Ff. ii. 38, f. 148.*

ȝARME. To scream.

> The fende bygane to crye and ȝarme,
> Bot he myghte do hym nankyn harme.
> > *MS. Lincoln A. i. 17, f. 123.*

ȝARNE. (1) To yearn. "Sothely he lufes, and he ȝarnes for to lufe," MS. Lincoln A. i. 17, f. 192.

(2) Yarn. *Prompt. Parv.*

> But ȝarne that ys ofte tyme evelle spon,
> Evyr hyt comyth owt at the laste.
> > *MS. Cantab. Ff. ii. 38, f. 45.*

(3) Hastily; quickly. *Pr. Parv.*

ȝARTHE. Earth. *(A.-S.)*

ȝATE. A gate. *Pr. Parv.*

> And when he to the ȝatis come,
> He askld the porter and his man
> Wher Joly Robyn was.
> > *MS. Cantab. Ff. v. 48, f. 51.*

ȝAYNED. Hallooed. *Gawayne.*

ȝE. Yes.

> He seyde nothir nay ne ȝe,
> But helde him stille and let hire chide.
> > *Gower, MS. Soc. Antiq. 134, f. 88.*

ȝEDDINGES. Tales; romances.

> As ȝeddyngis, japis and folies,
> And alle harlotries and ribaudies.
> > *MS. Ashmole 60, f. 5.*

> Songe ȝeddyngus above,
> Swyche murthus they move,
> In the chaumbur of love
> Thus thei sleye care!   *Degrevant, 1421.*

ȝEDE. Went.

> Kynge he was iij. yere and more,
> And Roberd as a fole ȝede thore.
> > *MS. Cantab. Ff. ii. 38, f. 242.*

> The man hyt toke and was ful blythe,
> He ȝede and solde hyt asswythe.
> > *MS. Harl. 1701, f. 38.*

> To the halle he went a full gode pase,
> To seke wher the stuarde was;
> The scheperde with hym ȝede.
> > *MS. Cantab. Ff. v. 48, f. 52.*

> Now he kyndils a glede,
> Amonge the buskes he ȝede,
> And gedirs fulle gude spede
> Wodde a fyre to make.   *Perceval, 758.*

ȝEDERLY. Promptly; soon. *Gawayne.*

ȝEE. Ye.

> In chambyr, thofe he nakede were,
> ȝee latto hvm gyff none ansuere.
> > *MS. Lincoln, f. 190.*

ȝEEME. To suckle; to give suck.

ȝEERLY. Early.

> Gloteny hath grete appetyte,
> To ete ȝeerly and late ys hys delyte.
> > *MS. Cantab. Ff. ii. 38, f. 5.*

ȝEESY. Easy.

> I counsel al ȝoue, al curators, that wysele ȝou wayt,
> That han the cure of mons soule in ȝoure kepyng,
> Engeyne ȝe not to ȝeesy penans, ne to strayt algat,
> Lest ȝe slene both bodé and soule with ȝour pony-
> echyng.   *Audelay's Poems, p. 47.*

ȝEF. If.

> ȝef thow be not grete clerk,
> Loke thow moste on thys werk.
> > *MS. Cott. Claud. A. ii. f. 127.*

ȝEFE. Gave.

ȝEINSEYE. To contradict; to oppose.

> For I myself shal the lede,
> That thei not ȝeinseye my sonde.
> > *Cursor Mundi, MS. Coll. Trin. Cantab. f. 36.*

ȝEKE. (1) The cuckoo. *(A.-S.)*

> Whene the ȝeke gynnys to synge,
> Thenne the schrewe begynnys to sprynge.
> > *MS. Porkington 10, f. 59.*

(2) Eke; also. See *Arrable.*

(3) To itch. MS. Vocab. xv. Cent. "*Pruritus*, a ȝekynge," Nominale MS.

ȝELDE. To yield; to give up.

> The men over al sowe feldes,
> Of corn nouȝt hit up ȝeldes.
> > *Cursor Mundi, MS. Coll. Trin. Cantab. f. 30.*

> And for suche auctoritees, thei seyn, that only to God schalle a man knouleche his defautes, ȝeldynge himself gylty, and cryenge him mercy, and beho-tynge to him to amende himself.
> > *Maundeville's Travels, 1839, p. 120.*

ȝELES.

> For mon that waleweth al in ȝeles,
> And for that joye noon angur feles.
> > *Cursor Mundi, MS. Coll. Trin. Cantab. f. 28.*

ȝELLE. To yell. Eglamour, 411.

> No have thai nouȝt sailed ariȝt
> But a day and on niȝt,
> That the se wel hard bigan
> To ȝellen and to bellen than.
> > *Legend of Marie Maudelein, p. 231.*

> I wylle hym geve, that me telles
> Why the ravens on me ȝelles.
> > *MS. Cantab. Ff. ii. 38, f. 145.*

ȝELPE. To boast, or glory. *(A.-S.)*

> For wit ne strengthe may not helpe,
> And hee which ellis wolde him ȝelpe,
> Is rathest thrown undir fote.
> > *Gower, MS. Soc. Antiq. 134, f. 38.*

> Alas, alas, and wele away, wherof may we ȝelp?
> We are shent for ever and ay, for nothing may us help.
> > *MS. Egerton 927.*

> There is no man that may ȝelpe,
> Bot he hath nede of Godes helpe.
> > *MS. Ashmole 61, f. 78.*

ȝELPYNG. Pomp; ostentation. *Gaw.*

ȝELSPE. A handful. *Pr. Parv.*

ȝELT. Yielded; requited.

ȝELUGHE. Yellow.

> Wymples, kerchyves saffrund betyde,
> ȝelughe undyr ȝelughe they hyde.
> > *MS. Harl. 1701, f.*

ȝELYE. Yellow.

> Of body, arme, and hond, and also of hir face,
> Wich that is coloured of rose and lelé ȝelye.
> > *MS. Cantab. Ff. i. 6, f. 151*

> Rotys of bothyn arn lik the applis growen on the levys as ok appul on his lef, and tho arn ȝelwe and soote.   *MS. Arundel 42, f. 32.*

ȝEME. To keep; to rule.

And oure fadrys so to queme,
That Goddys comaundement we may ӡeme.
MS. Harl. 1701, f. 9.

To be born he wol him seme
For wicked men him to ӡeme.
Cursor Mundi, MS. Coll. Trin. Cantab. f. 77.

But graunte us alle us self to ӡeme
And yn oure shryfte Jhesu to queme.
MS. Harl. 1701, f. 84.

Fulle faire salle I hym fede,
And ӡeme hym with oure awene child,
And clothe thame in one wede.
MS. Lincoln A. i. 17, f. 102.

ӡEMEN. Yeomen.
Forthe then went these ӡemen too,
Litul Johne and Moche one fere.
MS. Cantab. Ff. v. 48, f. 128.

ӡENDE. End.
And at Sir Roger ӡende we wylle dwelle,
And of the quene we wylle telle.
MS. Cantab. Ff. ii. 38, f. 75.

ӡENDIR. Yonder.
O emperoure, lyfte up anone thyn eyӡe,
And loke up ӡendir and see the sercle of golde.
Lydgate, MS. Soc. Antiq. 134, f. 16.

ӡEODE. Went. *(A.-S.)*
At his wille thei ӡeode and cam.
Cursor Mundi, MS. Coll. Trin. Cantab. f. 5.

ӡEONE. To yawn, or gape. *(A.-S.)*
ӡEOVE. To give. *(A.-S.)*
ӡEP. Prompt.
A (i in MS.) wis mon is thi son Joseph,
In al Egipte is noon so ӡep.
Cursor Mundi, MS. Coll. Trin. Cantab. f. 34.

ӡERBYS. Herbs.
A bath for that nobylle knyghte
Of ӡerbys that were fulle gode.
MS. Cantab. Ff. ii. 38, f. 66.

ӡERE. (1) An ear. (2) A year.
(3) Ere; before.
Feyre forhede end feyre here,
Soche a mayde was never ӡere.
MS. Cantab. Ff. ii. 38, f. 147.

ӡERIS. Ears of corn.
The seven ӡeris of grayne so plentevous,
This day be growe to fulle perfeccyoun,
Lydgate, MS. Soc. Antiq. 134, f. 13.

ӡERLY. Early.
He toke gode kepe to hys lore,
Late and ӡerly evyrmore.
MS. Cantab. Ff. ii. 38, f. 127.

ӡERNE. (1) To yearn; to desire.
A man hys manhede shal ӡerne
Hymself and hys meyné to governe.
MS Harl. 1701, f. 34.

Men ӡernen jestes for to here,
And romaunce rede in dyverse manere.
Cursor Mundi, MS. Coll. Trin. Cantab. f. 1.

(2) Quickly; promptly.
ӡerne thow moste thy sawtere rede,
And of the day of dome have drede.
MS. Cott. Claud. A. ii. f. 127.

(3) Yarn. *Prompt. Parv.*
(4) Earnings. Nominale MS.
ӡERNYNGE. Yearning; desire.
So mote hyt be at my ӡernynge,
On hur ys alle my thoghte.
MS. Cantab. Ff. ii. 38, f. 63.

ӡERTHF. Earth.

Hys oon brodur in ӡerthe Godes generalle vykere,
Pope of Rome as ye may here.
MS. Cantab. Ff. ii. 38, f. 940

ӡERWIGGE. An earwig.
ӡETE. To eat.
His wyves fadir and modir fre
Of this bony to ӡete ӡaf he.
Cursor Mundi, MS. Coll. Trin. Cantab. f. 45.

He sawe many dede men,
That the bore slewe yn the wode,
ӡete the flesche and dranke the blode.
MS. Cantab. Ff. ii. 38, f. 100

(2) Yet. Perceval, 83.
(3) To cast metal. *Pr. Parv.*
ӡEVE. To give. *(A.-S.)*
Then may the fader wythoute blame
Crysten the chylde, and ӡeve hyt name.
MS. Cott. Claud. A. ii. f. 128.

Prayeth for him, that lyeth now in his cheste,
To God above to ӡeve his soule good reste.
Lydgate, MS. Soc. Antiq. 134, f. 8.

ӡEVEL. Evil; harm.
When myster be, put yt in the yӡe, and it schal
do away the ӡevel, and breke that weed.
MS. in Mr. Pettigrew's Possession, f. 11.

ӡEY. An egg.
Aftur take the ӡey of an henne that is fayled when
sche hath sete, and take a lytyl flax, and dip it in
the glayre of that eye, and lay to the kancur.
MS. in Mr. Pettigrew's Possession, xv. Cent.

ӡEYNBOWGHT. Redeemed. *(A.-S.)*
And for the synne that Adam in Paradys dede,
All we that of him come shuld ha byn in sory stede,
Nere the grace of swete Jhesu,
That us ӡeynbowght thorgh gostli vertu.
Religious Poems, xv. Cent.

ӡEYNCOME. Return. *(A.-S.)*
At myn ӡeyncome bi my lif,
A son shal have Sara thi wyf.
Cursor Mundi, MS. Coll. Trin. Cantab. f. 17.

ӡEYR. Every.
ӡEӡE. (1) To jog. (2) To ask.
ӡEӡEN. Eyes.
To heven thei lifte her ӡeӡen glade,
And on her tongis thonkynge made.
Cursor Mundi, MS. Coll. Trin. Cantab. f. 110.

ӡHE. Ye.
ӡhe that welyie here of wytte,
That is wytnessyd of holy wryte.
MS. Douce 84, f. 46.

ӡIFE. If. Isumbras, 241.
ӡIFTYS. Gifts. *Pr. Parv.*
ӡIKINE. To itch. *Pr. Parv.*
ӡIPPE. To chirp, as birds do.
ӡIS. Yes.
They tolden so they hadden doo;
He seyde nay: they seyden ӡis.
Gower, MS. Soc. Antiq. 134, f. 69.

ӡISKE. To sob; to cry. *(A.-S.)*
ӡISTURDAY. Yesterday.
I hiӡt the ӡisturday seven shyllyng,
Have brok it wel to thi clothyng.
MS. Cantab. Ff. v. 48, f. 53.

Sche seyde, lordynges, where ys hee
That ӡysturday wan the gree.
MS. Cantab. Ff. ii. 38, f. 77.

ӡysturday he weddyd me with wronge,
And to nyght y have hym honge.
MS. Cantab. Ff. ii. 38, f. 113.

ʒODE. Went. (*A.-S.*)

> The kyng of Fraunce byfore hym ʒode,
> With mynstralles fulle many and gode,
> And lede hym up with pryde;
> Clement to the mynstralles gan go,
> And gafe some a stroke, and some two,
> There durste noghte one habyde!
> > *Octavian, Lincoln MS.*

> Thay sett thaire stedis ther thay stod,
> And fayrly passed the flode;
> To the chambir thay ʒode,
> Thaire gatis so gayne.
> > *MS. Lincoln A. i. 17, f. 137.*

ʒOKET. Disabled?

> Ihc ne mai no more
> Grope under gore,
>   thoʒ mi wil wold ʒete;
> Y-ʒoket ic am of ʒore,
> With last and luther lore,
>   and sunne me hath bi-set.
> > *Reliq. Antiq.* ii. 210.

ʒOKK. A yoke.

> Comforte all men in Crystys lawe,
> That they hys ʒokk love in to drawe.
> > *MS. Cantab. Ff. ii. 38, f. 5.*

ʒOKYNGE. Itching. Medulla MS.

ʒOLDE. Yielded.

> That he no myʒte with no sleyʒte
> Oute of his honde gete up on heyʒte
> Tille he was overcome and ʒolde.
> > *Gower, MS. Soc. Antiq.* 134, f. 117.

> How oure lady endede and ʒolde
> Hir semely soule, hit shal be tolde.
> > *Cursor Mundi, MS. Coll. Trin. Cantab.* f. 2.

ʒOLE. Yule; Christmas.

> Madame, appone ʒole nyghte
> My warysone ʒe me highte:
> I aske noghte bot ʒone knyghte
> To slepe be my syde.
> > *MS. Lincoln A. i. 17, f. 133.*

> Faire scho prayed hym evene thane,
> Lufamour his lemmane,
> Tille the heghe dayes of ʒole were gane
> With hir for to bee. *Perceval, 1803.*

> He made me ʒomane at ʒole, and gafe me gret gyftes,
> And c. pound and a horse, and harnayse fulle ryche.
> > *Morte Arthure, MS. Lincoln, f. 81.*

ʒOMERAND. Moaning; whining. *Gaw.*

ʒOMERLY. Lamentably; piteously. *Gaw.*

ʒOND. Yonder.

> Goo take ʒond man and pay be tyme,
> And bidde hym thonk Joly Robyne;
> We shalle sone have gamme gode.
> > *MS. Cantab. Ff. v. 48, f. 53.*

ʒONE. Yonder.

> I knowe hym by his faire face,
> That ʒone ʒong knyghte es he.
> > *MS. Lincoln A. i. 17, f. 109.*

ʒONG. Young.

> He has with hym ʒong men thre;
> Thei be archers of this contré,
> The kyng to serve at wille.
> > *MS. Cantab. Ff. v. 48. f. 49.*

> Fyrst thow moste thys mynne,
> What he ys that doth the synne;
> Whether hyt be heo or he,
> ʒonge or olde, bonde or fre.
> > *MS. Cott. Claud. A. ii. f. 145.*

ʒONGE. To go; to proceed.

> Ac weste hit houre cellerer,
> That thou were i-comen her,
> He wolde sone after the ʒonge,
> Mid pikes, and stones, and staves stronge;
> Alle thine bones he wolde to-breke,
> Then we weren wel awreke. *Reliq. Antiq.* ii. 273.

ʒONGLINGES. Youths.

> ʒonlinges of the age of on and twenty ʒer schulde
> be chosen to kniʒthode.
> > *Vegecius, MS. Douce* 291, f. 8.

ʒOODE. Went.

> When he tylle hys lord come,
> The lettre in hys hand he nome,
> He sey, Alle ʒoode to schome!
> And went one hys wey. *Degrevant, 127.*

ʒOP.

> But, confessour, be wys and ʒop,
> And sende forth these to the byschop.
> > *MS. Cott. Claud.* A. ii. f. 148.

ʒORE. Yore; formerly.

> ʒore was seid and ʒut so beth,
> Herte forʒeteth that eʒe not seth.
> > *Cursor Mundi, MS. Coll. Trin. Cantab.* f. 28.

> Thus they have do now fulle ʒore,
> And alle ys for defawte of lore.
> > *MS. Cott. Claudius* A. ii. f. 127.

(2) Mercy; pity. (*A.-S.*)

> Oftsythes scho sygkyd sore,
> And stilly scho sayed, Lord, thy ʒore!
> > *Wright's Seven Sages,* p. 51

ʒORLE. Earl.

> The ʒorle dyede that same ʒere,
> And the contasse clere;
> Bothe hore beryelus y-ffere
> Was gayly bydyʒth. *Degrevant, 1881*

ʒORN. A thorn.

ʒORNE. Quickly.

> The messengere thankyth hym ʒorne,
> And home agayne he can turne.
> > *MS. Cantab. Ff. ii. 38, f. 96*

ʒORTHE. The earth.

> Anodur he thoght to smyʒte ryght,
> Hys hedd there on the ʒorthe lyght.
> > *MS. Cantab. Ff. ii. 38, f. 170.*

> Hys oon brodur in ʒorthe Godes generalle vykere,
> Pope of Rome, as ye may here;
> Thys pope was callyd pope Urbane,
> For hym lovyd bothe God and man.
> > *MS. Cantab. Ff. ii. 38.*

ʒOUD. Went. (*A.-S.*)

> ffayir thei passed that flode,
> To tho forest thei ʒoud,
> And toke here stodus where thei stod
> Undur the hawthrone. *Degrevant, 926.*

ʒOUGTHE. Youth.

> Thorow innocence schortely to conclude,
> By engyn of fraude hire ʒougthe to delude.
> > *Lydgate, MS. Soc. Antiq.* 134, f. 5.

> Sire, yf y have in my ʒougths
> Done otherwise in other place.
> > *Gower, MS. Soc. Antiq.* 134, f. 43.

ʒOVE. Given.

> This pris was ʒove and speken oute
> Amonge the heraldis alle aboute.
> > *Gower, MS. Soc. Antiq.* 134, f. 55

> And openly hath ʒoven him a falle.
> > *Lydgate, MS. Soc. Antiq.* 134, f. 2

ʒOW. You.

> And say the wordes alle on rowe,
> As anon I wole ʒow schowe.
> > *MS. Cott. Claud.* A. ii. f. 131

ȜOWLE. (1) Yule; Christmas.

Thys ys the furste day of ȝowle,
That thy God was borne withowt dole.
MS. Cantab. Ff. ii. 38, f. 99.

2) To yell; to howl.

The kyng passed therby as the greyhound was
that kept his lord and his maystre, and the greyhound aroos agayn hem, and bygan to ȝowle upon
hem.   *MS. Bodl. 546.*

ȜOWTHEDE.   Youth.   (A.-S.)

Now, Lorde, ȝif it thi wille bee,
In ȝowthede penance send thou mee,
And welthe appone myne elde.   *Isumbras, 60.*

ȜOWULY.   Gay.

Moche of this herbe to seeth thu take
Iu water, and a bathe thow make;
Hyt schal the make lyȝt and joly,
And also lykyng and ȝowuly.   *Reliq. Antiq. i. 196.*

ȜOWYNG.   Young.

When I was ȝowyng, es now er ȝe,
Than beyd I never a fayrer lyfe.
MS. Lincoln A. i. 17, f. 51.

ȜOXE.   The hiccough.

Tak sawge, and poune hit smal, and tempre hit
with aysel, and swolue thurof ij. tymes or iij. and
that wule stanch the ȝoxe.
MS. in Mr. Pettigrew's Possession, xv. Cent.

ȜOYNG.   Yonng.   Pr. Parv. p. 268.
ȜUNCH.   Young.
ȜUNGTHE.   Youth.

Or ȝyf thou vowe yn ȝungthe or elde.
MS. Harl. 1701, f. 19.

ȜWRH.   Through.

Mi palefrey is of tre,
Wiht nayles naylede ȝwrh me,
Ne is more sorwe to se,
Certes noon more no may be.
Reliq. Antiq. ii. 119.

ȜYF.   To give.

Gyftys y hur ȝyf wolde
Of sylvyr and of ryche golde.
MS. Cantab. Ff. ii. 38, f. 27.

ȜYLDE.   To requite.   (A.-S.)

Alle that have my fadur slawe,
And broȝt hym owt of hys lyfe dawe,
I schalle them ȝylde.
MS. Cantab. Ff. ii. 38, f. 97.

ȜYNDE.   End.

And the begger at the townes ȝynde,
To hym wedlokk ys as free
As to the ryallest kyng of kynde,
For alle ys but oon dygnyté.
MS. Cantab. Ff. 38, f. 48.

ȜYNG.   Young.

Princes proude that beth in pres,
I wol ou telle thing not lees;
In Cisyle was a noble kyng,
Fair and strong, and sumdel ȝyng.
Vernon MS. Bodl. Libr. f. 300.

Than spekyth Octavyon the ȝyng
Fulle feyre to hys lorde the kyng.
MS. Cantab. Ff. ii. 38, f. 93.

ȜYNGE.   To go; to proceed.

Make thy clerk before the ȝynge
To bere lyȝt and belle rynge.
MS. Cotton. Claud. A. ii. f. 151.

ȜYS.   Yes.

Be God, seid the scheperde, ȝys;
Nay, seid oure kyng, i-wys
Noȝt for a tune of wyne !
MS. Cantab. Ff. v. 48, f. 53.

Ȝysse, quod the fyscher, y sawe hyt,
The batell to the darke nyght.
MS. Cantab. Ff. ii. 38, f. 208.

ȜYT.   Yet.   Eglamour, 76, 320.

And he schalle be thyn own fere,
Some wytt of hym ȝyt may thou lere.
MS. Cantab. Ff. ii. 38, f. 241.

Y do the wele for to wyte,
Y nel non housbond have ȝyte;
Seye the knyȝthe whan ȝe mete,
I wol hym no gude !   *Degrevant, 265.*

INDEX.

———

☞ The following list merely contains explanations of the principal Abbreviations used in the foregoing pages, with short references to those books and romances which are most frequently cited. The titles of the books from which the quotations are made have, however, been generally given with too much minuteness to require any further explanation.

SPECIMENS OF THE EARLY ENGLISH LANGUAGE,

CHRONOLOGICALLY ARRANGED.

(1) From Simon de Ghent's Rule of Nuns, of the earlier part of the thirteenth century.

Holy men ⁊ holi wummen beoð of alle von-dunges swuðest ofte i-tempted, ⁊ han to goddre heale ; vor iþe vihte ageines han, heo bigiteð þe blisfule kempene crune. Lo ! þauh hwu he meneð ham bi Jeremie : *perse-cutores nostri velociores aquilis celi, super montes persecuti sunt nos ; in deserto insidiati sunt nobis.* þet is, ure wiðerwines beoð swifture þen þe earnes ; up oðe hulles heo clumben efter us, ⁊ þer fuhten mid us, ⁊ get iðe wildernesse heo aspieden us to slean. Ure wiþerwines beoð þreo : þe veond, þe world, ⁊ ure owune vleshs, ase ich er seide. Liht-liche ne mei me nout oþerhule i-cnowen hwuc of þeos þreo weorreð him ; vor everichon helpeð oþer, þauh þe veond kundeliche eggeð us to atternesse, as to prude, to overhowe, to onde, ⁊ to wreððe, ⁊ to hore attri kundles, þet beoð her efter i-nemmed, þet flesh put propremen touward swetnesse, ⁊ touward eise, ⁊ toward softnesse, ant te world bit mon giscen wordes weole, ⁊ wunne ⁊ wurschipe, ⁊ oþer swuche ginegoven, þet bidweolieð kang men to luvien one scheadewe. þeos wiðerwines, he seið, voluwed us on hulles, ⁊ awaiteð us iðe wildernesse, hu heo us muwen hermen. Hul, þet is heih lif, þer þes deofles assauz beoð ofte strengest ; wildernesse, þet is onlich lif of ancre wuninge, vor also ase ine wildernesse beoð alle wilde bestes, ⁊ nulleð nout i-þolen monnes neihlechunge, auh fleoð hwon heo ham i-hereð oþer i-seoð, also schulen ancren over alle oþre wummen beon wilde o þisse wise, ⁊ þeonne beoð heo over alle oþre leovest to ure Loverde, ⁊ swetest him þuncheð ham ; vor of alle flesches þeonne is wilde deores fleschs leovest ⁊ swetest, I þisse wildernesse wende ure Loverdes folc, ase Exode telleð, tou-ward ted eadie londe of Jerusalem, þet he ham hefde bihoten. And ge, mine leove sustren, wendeð bi þen ilke weie toward te heie Jeru-salem, to þe kinedom ꝥ he haveð bihoten his i-corene. Goð þauh ful warliche, vor i þisse wildernesse beoð monie uvele bestes ; liun of prude, neddre of attri onde, unicorne of wreððe, beore of dead slouhðe, vox of giscunge, suwe of givernesse, scorpiun mid te teile of stin-kinde lecherie, þet is golnesse. Her beoð nu a-reawe i-told þe-seoven heaved sunnen.

(2) Hymn to the Virgin, time of Henry III.

Blessed beo thu, lavedi,
    ful of hovene blisse,
Swete flur of parais,
    moder of milternisse ;
Thu praye Jheru Crist thi sone,
    that he me i-wisse,
Thare a londe al swo ihe beo,
    that he me ne i-misse.

Of the, faire lavedi, min oreisun
    ich wile biginnen !
Thi deore swete sunnes love
    thu lere me to winnen.
Wel ofte ich sike and sorwe make,
    ne mai ich nevere blinnen,
Bote thu, thruh thin milde mod,
    bringe me out of sunne.

Ofte ihc seke merci,
    thin swete name ich calle :
Mi flehs is foul, this world is fals,
    thu loke that ich ne falle.
Lavedi freo, thu schild me
    fram the pine of helle !
And send me into that blisse
    that tunge ne mai tellen.

Mine werkes, lavedi,
    heo makieth me ful won ;
Wel ofte ich clepie and calle,
    thu i-her me for than.
Bote ic chabbe the help of the,
    other I ne kan ;
Help thu me, ful wel thu mist,
    thu helpest moni a man.

I-blessed beo thu, lavedi,
    so fair and so briht ;
Al min hope is uppon the
    bi dai and bi nicht.
Helpe, thruh thin milde mode,
    for wel wel thu mist,
That ich nevere for feondes sake
    fur-go thin eche liht.

Briht and scene quen of hovene,
    ich bidde thin sunnes hore ;
The sunnes that ich habbe i-cun,
    heo rewweth me ful sore.
Wel ofte ich chabbe the fur-saken,
    the wil ich never eft more ;
Lavedi, for thine sake,
    treuthen feondes lore.

I-blessed beo thu, lavedi,
 so fair and so hende;
Thu praie Jhesu Crist thi sone,
 that he me i-sende,
Whare a londe al swo ich beo,
 er ich honne wende,
That ich mote in parais
 wonien withuten ende.

Bricht and scene quen of storre,
 so me liht and lere,
In this false fikele world
 so me led and steore,
That ich at min ende dai
 ne habbe non feond to fere;
Jhesu, mit ti swete blod,
 thu bohtest me ful dere.

Jhesu, seinte Marie sone,
 thu i-her thin moder bone;
To the ne dar I clepien noht,
 to hire ich make min mene;
Thu do that ich for hire sake
 beo i-maked so clene,
That ich noht at dai of dome
 beo flemed of thin exsene.
  MS. Egerton 613, Reliq. Antiq. i. 102-3.

(3) *From the Harrowing of Hell, MS. Digby 86,*
 time of Edward I.
Hou Jhesu Crist herowede helle,
Of harde gates ich wille telle.
Leve frend, nou beth stille,
Lesteth that ich tellen wille.
Ou Jhesu fader him bithoute,
And Adam hout of helle broute.
In helle was Adam and Eve,
That weren Jhesu Crist wel leve;
And Seint Johan the Baptist,
That was newen Jhesu Crist;
Davit the prophete and Abraham,
For the sunnes of Adem;
And moni other holi mon,
Mo then ich ou tellen con;
Till Jhesu fader nom fles and blod
Of the maiden Marie god,
And suth then was don ful michel some,
Bonden and beten and maked ful lome,
Tilie that Gode Friday at non,
Thenne he was on rode i-don,
His honden from his body wonden,
Nit here miʒte hoe him shenden,
To helle sone he nom gate
Adam and Eve hout to take;
Tho the he to helle cam,
Suche wordes he bigan.

(4) *From 'Cokaygne,' a poem written very early*
 in the fourteenth century.
Ther is a wel fair abbei,
Of white monkes, and of grei,
Ther beth bowris and halles;
Al of pasteis beth the walles,
Of fleis, of fisse, and rich met,
The likfullist that man mai et.
Fluren cakes beth the schingles alle,
Of cherche, cloister, boure and halle.
The pinnes beth fat podinges,
Rich met to princes and kinges.
Ther is a cloister fair and liʒt,
Brod and lang, of sembli siʒt.
The pilers of that cloister alle
Beth i-turned of cristale,
With harlas and capitale
Of grene iaspe and rede corale.

In the praer is a tre
Swithe likful for to se,
The rote is gingevir and galingale,
The siouns beth al sedwale.
Trie maces beth the fiure,
The rind canel of swet odur;
The frute gilofre of gode smakke,
Of cucubes ther nis no lakke.
  MS. Harl. 913, f. 4.

(5) *From the Proverbs of Hendyng, MS. Harl.*
 2253, time of Edward II.
Mon that wol of wysdam heren,
At wyse Hendyng he may lernen,
That wes Marcolves sone;
 Gode thonkes ant monie thewes
 For te teche fele shrewes,
For that wes ever is wone.
Jhesu Crist, al folkes red,
That for us alle tholede ded
 Upon the rode tre,
Lene us alle to ben wys,
Ant to ende in his servys!
 Amen, par charité!
'God biginning maketh god endyng.'
 Quoth Hendyng.

Wyt ant wysdom lurneth ʒerne,
Ant loke that none other werne
 To be wys ant hende;
For betere were to bue wis,
Then for te where feh ant grys,
 Wher so mon shal ende.
'Wyt ant wysdom is god warysoun,'
 Quoth Hendyng.

Ne may no mon that is in londe,
For nothyng that he con fonde,
 Wonen at home ant spede;
So fele thewes for te leorne,
Ase he that hath y-sotht ʒeorne
 In wel fele theode.
'Ase fele thede, ase fele thewes;'
 Quoth Hendyng.

(6) *The Creed, from a MS. written in the reign*
 of Edward III.

I byleve in God, fader almyʒthi, maker of hevene
and of erthe, and in Jhesu Crist, the sone of hym
only oure lord, the wuche is consceyved of the holy
gost, y-boren of Marie mayden, suffrede passioun
under Pounce Pilate, y-crucified, ded, and buried,
wente doun in to helle, the thridde day he roos
from dethe, he steyet up to hevenes, he sitteth on
the riʒt syde of God the fadur almyʒti, thennes he is
to come to deme the queke and the dede. I byleve
in the holy gost, holy chirche general, the co-
munyng of halewes, the forʒefenesse of synnes, the
rysyng of flech, and the lyf whit-oute ende. Amen.

(7) *From a poem on blood-letting, written about*
 A.D. 1380.
Maystris that uthyth blode letyng,
And therwyth giteth ʒowr levyng,
Here ʒe may lere wysdom ful gode,
In what place ʒe schulle let blode
In man, woman, and in childe,
For evelys that ben wyk and wilde
Weynis ther ben .xxx.ti and two
That on a man mot ben undo;
.xvj. in the beved ful riʒt,
And .xvj. beneth in ʒow i-pyʒt.

In what place thay schal be founde,
I schal yow telle in a stounde.
Besydis the ere ther ben two,
That on a man mot ben undo
To kepe hys heved fro evyl turnyng,
And fro the scalle, wythout lesyng.
Two at the templys thay mot blede
For stoppynge of kynde, as I rode.
And on is in the mydde for-hevede,
For lepre sausfleme mot blede.
Abowe the nose thare is on,
For fuethynge mot be undon ;
And also whan eyhen ben sore,
And for resyng gout everemore.
Two they ben at the eyhen ende,
Whan they beth bleryt for to amende,
And for that cometh of smokynge,
I wol tel yow no lesynge,
At the holle of the grot ther ben two,
That for lepre and streyt breyt mot be undo.
In the lyppys .iiij. ther ben gode to bledene,
As I yow telle now bydene ;
Two by the eyhen abowen also,
I telle yow there ben two
For sor of tho mowthe to blede,
What hyt is I fynde as I rede.
Two under the tongue wythout lese
Mot blede for the squynase ;
And whan the townge is akynge
Throʒt eny maner swollynge.

(8) *From an astrological MS. written about the year* 1400.

Man born wile the sonne is in Cankyr, that is the xliij. day in Jun tyl the xiij. day in Jul, xxx. day. is whit colorid, femynin herte ; but he be born the owr of Mars or of Sol or of Jupiter, man bold and hardy, and sly inowh to falshede and tresowne, fayr spekere and evil spekere, and suptyl and wily and fals, broken in arm or in fase, desese in cheyl or nere, mekyl wytty and mikyl onwis and onkynde, and fals in fele thingis in word and dede ; shrewe to woordin wyth, hatyd of fele and of wol fewe lowyd ; a womman sehal make him to sinne ; he schal lovin a woman brown of complexown and of bettur blod than is hymself ; he schal lovin no man but for hiis owne profyt.

(9) *A song, temp. Henry VI.*

What so mene seyne,
Love is no peyne
To theme serteyne
    Butt varians ;
For they constreyne
Ther hertes to feyne,
Ther mowthis to pleyne
    Ther displesauns.
Whych is in dede
Butt feynyd drede,
So God me spede !
    And dowbilnys.
Ther othis to bede,
Ther lyvys to lede,
And proferith mede
    New-fangellenys.
For whenne they pray,
Ye shalle have nay,
What so they say,
    Beware, for shame.
For every daye
They waite ther pray,

Wher so they may,
    And make butt game.
Thenne semyth mo
Ye may welle se
They be so fre
    In evyry plase :
Hitt were peté
Butt they shold be
Bogelid, perdé,
    Withowtyne grase.

MS. Cantab. Ff. i. 6, f. 48.

(10) *Extract from the Romance of Sir Perceval, written about* 1440.

Thofe he were of no pryde,
Forthirmore ganne he glyde
Tille a chambir ther besyde,
    Moo sellys to see ;
Riche clothes fande he sprede,
A lady slepande on a bedde,
He said, " Forsothe, a tokyne to wedde
    Salle thou lefe with mee."
Ther he kyste that swete thynge,
Of hir fynger he tuke a rynge,
His awenne modir takynnynge
    He lefte with that fre.
He went forthe to his mere,
Tuke with hym his schorte spere,
Lepe one lofte as he was ere,
    His way rydes he.
Now on his way rydes he,
Moo selles to see ;
A knyghte wolde he nedis boe
    Withowttene any bade.
He come ther the kyng was
Servede of the firste mese,
To hym was the maste has
    That the childe hade ;
And thare made he no lett
At gate, dore ne wykett,
Bot in graythely he gett,
    Syche maistres he made !
At his first in comynge,
His mere withowttene faylynge
Kyste the forhevede of the kynge,
    So nerehande he rade !
The kyng had ferly thaa,
And up his hande ganne he taa,
And putt it forthir hym fraa
    The mouthe of the mere.
He saide, " Faire childe and free,
Stonde stille besyde mee,
And telle me wythene that thou bee,
    And what thou wille here."
Thanne saide the fole of the filde,
" I ame myne awnne modirs childe
Comene fro the woddes wylde
    Tille Arthure the dere ;
Jisterday saw I knyghtis three,
Siche one salle thou make mee
On this mere by-for the,
    Thi mete or thou scheret"

(11) *From MS. Porkington* 10, *written in the reign of Edward IV.*

God that dyed for us alle,
And dranke bothe eysell and galle,
    He bryng us alle oute off bale ;
And gyve hym good lyve and long,
That woll attend to my song,
    And herkyne on to my talle.

Ther dwelyd a man in my contré,
The wyche hade wyvys thre
   Yn proses of certyn tyme ;
Be hys fyrst wyffe a chyld he had,
The wyche was a propyr lad
   And ryght an happy hynd ;
And his fader lovyd hym ryght welle,
Hys steppe-dame lovyd hyme never a delle,
   I telle ȝowe as y thynke ;
She thoght hyt lost be the rode
Alle that ever dyd hyme good,
   Off mette other of drynke :
Not halfe ynowe thereof he had,
And ȝyt in faythe hit was fulle bad,
   And alle hyr thoght yt lost.
Y pray God evyll mot sche fare,
For oft sche dyde hym moche care,
   As far forthe as sche durst !
She good wyffe to hyr husbond yone say,
For to put away thys boy
   Y hold yt for the beste ;
In fayth he hys a lether lade,
Y wold som other man hym had,
   That beter myȝt hym chaste.
Than anone spake the good man,
And to hys wyff sayd he than,
   He ys but ȝong of age,
He schall be with us lenger,
Tyll that he be strenger,
   To wyn beter wage.
We have a mane a strong freke,
The wyche one fyld kypythe owr nette,
   And slepyth half the day ;
He schall come home be Mary myld,
And to the fylde schalle go the chyld,
   And kepe hem ȝyfe he may

(12) *A letter, temp. Henry VIII.*

Ryghte honorable and my syngular goode lorde and mayster, all circumstauncys and thankes sett aside, pleasithe yt youre good lordeshipe to be advertisid, that where I was constitute and made by youre honorable desire and commaundmente commissarie generall of the dyocese of Saynte Assaph, I have done my dylygens and dutie for the expulsinge and takynge awaye of certen abusions, supersticions, and ipocryses usid within the saide diocese of Saynte Assaph, acordynge to the kynges honorable actes and injunctions therin made. That notwithstondinge, there ys an image of Darvellgadarn within the saide diocese, in whome the people have so greate confidence, hope, and truste, that they cumme daylye a pillgramage unto hym, somme withe kyne, other with oxen or horsis, and the reste withe money, insomuche that there was fyve or syxe hundrethe pillgrames, to a mans estimacion, that offered to the saide image the fifte daie of this presente monethe of Aprill. The innocente people hathe ben sore aluryd and entisid to worshipe the saide image, insomuche that there is a commyn sayinge as yet amongist them that whosoever will offer anie thinge to the saide image of Davellgadarn, he hathe power to fatche hym or them that so offers oute of hell when they be dampned. Therfore, for the reformacion and amendmente of the premisses, I wolde gladlie knowe by this berer youre honorable pleasure and will, as knowithe God, who ever preserve your lordeshipe longe in welthe and honor. Writen in Northe Wales, the vj. daye of this presente Aprill.

   Youre bedman and dayelye orator by dutie,
                    ELIS PRICE.

THE END.

A
Catalogue of Books

PUBLISHED OR SOLD BY

JOHN RUSSELL SMITH,

36, SOHO SQUARE, LONDON, W.

DLARD (George).—The Sutton-Dudleys of England, and the Dudleys of Massachusetts, in New England. 8vo, *pedigrees, &c., cloth.* 15s

An interesting volume to the English genealogist, it contains a good deal of new matter relating to this old English Family and their collateral branches.

AGINCOURT.—A Contribution towards an Authentic List of the Commanders of the English Host in King Henry the Fifth's Expedition. By the Rev. JOSEPH HUNTER, post 8vo. 2s 6d

AKERMAN'S (John Yonge, *Fellow and late Secretary of the Society of Antiquaries*) Archæological Index to Remains of Antiquity of the Celtic, Romano-British, and Anglo-Saxon Periods. 8vo, *illustrated with numerous engravings, comprising upwards of five hundred objects, cloth.* 15s

This work, though intended as an introduction and a guide to the study of our early antiquities, will, it is hoped, also prove of service as a book of reference to the practised Archæologist.

" One of the first wants of an incipient Antiquary is the facility of comparison : and here it is furnished him at one glance. The plates, indeed, form the most valuable part of the book, both by their number and the judicious selection of types and examples which they contain. It is a book which we can, on this account, safely and warmly recommend to all who are interested in the antiquities of their native land."—*Literary Gazette.*

AKERMAN's (J. Y.) Introduction to the Study of Ancient and Modern Coins. Foolscap 8vo, *with numerous wood engravings from the original Coins (an excellent introductory book), cloth.* 6s 6d

CONTENTS :—SECT. 1,—Origin of Coinage—Greek Regal Coins—2. Greek Civic Coins—3. Greek Imperial Coins—4. Origin of Roman Coinage—Consular Coins —5. Roman Imperial Coins—6. Roman British Coins—7. Ancient British Coinage—8 Anglo-Saxon Coinage—9. English Coinage from the Conquest—10. Scotch Coinage—11. Coinage of Ireland—12. Anglo-Gallic Coins—13. Continental Money in the Middle Ages—14. Various Representatives of Coinage—15. Forgeries in Ancient and Modern Times—16. Table of Prices of English Coins realized at Public Sales.

AKERMAN'S (J. Y.) Remains of Pagan Saxondom, principally from Tumuli in England, drawn from the originals. Described and illustrated. One handsome volume, 4to, *illustrated with* 40 COLOURED PLATES, *half morocco.* £2. 2s (original price £3)

The plates are admirably executed by Mr. Bastre, and coloured under the direction of the author, which is not the case with a re-issue of the volume now sold bound in cloth. It is a work well worthy the notice of the Archæologist.

AKERMAN'S (J. Y.) Coins of the Romans relating to Britain. Described and Illustrated. *Second edition,* greatly enlarged, 8vo, *with plates and woodcuts, cloth.* 10s 6d

The "Prix de Numismatique" was awarded by the French Institute to the author for this work.

"Mr. Akerman's volume contains a notice of every known variety, with copious illustrations, and is published at a very moderate price; it should be consulted, not merely for these particular coins, but also for facts most valuable to all who are interested in Romano-British History."—*Archæol. Journal.*

AKERMAN'S (J. Y.) Ancient Coins of Cities and Princes, Geographically Arranged and Described—Hispania, Gallia, Britannia. 8vo, *with engravings of many hundred Coins from actual examples. Cloth.* 7s 6d (original price 18s)

AKERMAN'S (J. Y.) Tradesman's Tokens struck in London and its Vicinity, from 1648 to 1671, described from the originals in the British Museum, &c. 8vo, *with 8 plates of numerous examples. cloth,* 7s 6d (original price 15s.)—LARGE PAPER in 4to, *cloth.* 15s

This work comprises a list of nearly 3000 Tokens, and contains occasional Illustrative, topographical, and antiquarian notes on persons, places, streets, old tavern and coffee-house signs, &c., &c., with an introductory account of the causes which led to the adoption of such a currency.

AKERMAN'S (J. Y.) List of Tokens issued by Wiltshire Tradesmen in the Seventeenth Century. 8vo, *plates, sewed.* 1s 6d

AKERMAN'S (J. Y.) Wiltshire Tales, illustrative of the Manners, Customs, and Dialect of that and adjoining Counties. 12mo, *cloth.* 2s 6d

"We will conclude with a simple but hearty recommendation of a little book which is as humourous for the drolleries of the stories as it is interesting as a picture of rustic manners."—*Tallis's Weekly Paper.*

AKERMAN'S (J. Y.) Spring Tide; or, the Angler and his Friends. 12mo, *plates, cloth.* 2s 6d (original price 6s)

These Dialogues incidentally illustrate the Dialect of the West of England.

"Never in our recollection has the contemplative man's recreation been rendered more attractive, nor the delights of a country life set forth with a truer or more discriminating zest than in these pleasant pages."—*Gent.'s Mag.*

ALEXANDER (W., *late Keeper of the Prints in the British Museum*) Journey to Beresford Hall, in Derbyshire, the Seat of Charles Cotton, Esq., the celebrated Author and Angler. Crown 4to, *printed on tinted paper, with a spirited frontispiece, representing Walton and his adopted Son, Cotton, in the Fishing-house, and vignette title page. Cloth.* 5s

Dedicated to the Anglers of Great Britain and the various Walton and Cotton Clubs. *Only 100 printed.*

ALFRED'S (King) Anglo-Saxon Version of the Compendious History of the World by Orosius, with Translation, Notes, and Dissertations, by the Rev. Dr. BOSWORTH, *Professor of Anglo-Saxon at Oxford.* Royal 8vo, *map and facsimiles of the MSS., cloth.* 16s

ALFRED (King).—Memorials of King Alfred, being Essays on the History and Antiquities of England during the Ninth Century—the Age of King Alfred. BY various Authors. Edited and in part written by the Rev. Dr. GILES. Royal 8vo, pp. 400, *coloured plate of K. Alfred's Jewel, seven plates of Anglo-Saxon Coins, and views of Grimbald's Crypt, cloth,* 7s 6d

ALLIES (Jabez, *F.S.A.*) The Ancient British, Roman, and Saxon Antiquities and Folk-Lore of Worcestershire. 8vo, pp. 500, *with 6 plates and 40 woodcuts, Second Edition, cloth.* 7s 6d (original price 14s)

"The good people of Worcestershire are indebted to Mr. Jabez Allies for a very handsome volume illustrative of the history of their native county. His book, which treats *On the Ancient British, Roman, and Saxon Antiquities and Folk-lore of Worcestershire,* has now reached a second edition : and as Mr. Allies has embodied in this, not only the additions made by him to the original work, but also several separate publications on points of folk-lore and legendary interest, few counties can boast of a more industriously or carefully compiled history of what may be called its popular antiquities. The work is very handsomely illustrated."—*Notes and Queries.*

ANDERSON (Wm.) Genealogy and Surnames, with some Heraldic and Biographical Notices. 8vo, *woodcuts of Arms and Seals, cloth.* 3s 6d (original price 6s)   1865

ANGLO-SAXON Version of the Life of St. Guthlac, Hermit of Croyland. Printed, for the first time, from a MS. in the Cottonian Library, with a Translation and Notes by CHARLES WYCLIFFE GOODWIN, M.A., Fellow of Catherine Hall, Cambridge. 12mo, *cloth.* 5s

ANGLO-SAXON Version of the Hexameron of St. Basil, and the Anglo-Saxon Remains of St. Basil's Admonitio ad Filium Spiritualem. Now first printed from MSS. in the Bodleian Library, with a Translation and Notes by the Rev. H. W. NORMAN. 8vo, *second edition, enlarged, sewed.* 4s

ANGLO-SAXON.—Narratiunculæ Anglice Conscripta. De pergamenis excribebat notis illustrabat eruditis copiam, faciebat T. OSWALD COCKAYNE, M.A. 8vo. 6s

Containing Alexander the Great's Letter to Aristotle on the situation of India—Of wonderful things in the East—The Passion of St. Margaret the Virgin—Of the Generation of Man, &c.

ANGLO-SAXON.—A Fragment of Ælfric's Anglo-Saxon Grammar, Ælfric's Glossary, and a Poem on the Soul and Body, of the XIIth Century, discovered among the Archives of Worcester Cathedral, by Sir THOMAS PHILLIPPS, Bart. Folio, PRIVATELY PRINTED, *sewed.* 1s 6d

Several other Anglo-Saxon works will be found in this Catalogue.

ARCHÆOLOGIA CAMBRENSIS.—A Record of the Antiquities, Historical, Genealogical, Topographical, and Architectural, of Wales and its Marches. First Series, complete, 4 vols, 8vo, *many plates and woodcuts, cloth.* £2. 2s
Odd Parts may be had to complete Sets.

——— Second Series, 6 vols, 8vo, *cloth.* £3. 3s

——— Third Series, vol 1 to 12. £1. 10s each
Published by the Cambrian Archæological Association.

ARCHÆOLOGICAL INSTITUTE.—Report of the Transactions of the Annual Meeting of the Archæological Institute held at Chichester, July, 1853. 8vo, *many plates and woodcuts, cloth.* 7s 6d
Printed uniformly with the other Annual Congresses of the Institute.

ARCHER FAMILY.—Memorials of Families of the Surname of Archer in various Counties of England, and in Scotland, Ireland, Barbadoes, America, &c. By Capt. J. H. LAWRENCE ARCHER. 4to, *but few copies printed, cloth.* 12s 6d

ATKINSON'S (George, *Serjeant at Law*) Worthies of Westmoreland; or, Biographies of Notable Persons Born in that County since the Reformation. 2 vols, post 8vo, *cloth.* 6s (original price 16s)

AUTOBIOGRAPHY of JOSEPH LISTER (a Nonconformist), of Bradford, Yorkshire, with a contemporary account of the Defence of Bradford and Capture of Leeds, by the Parliamentarians, in 1642. Edited by THOS. WRIGHT, F.S.A. 8vo, *cloth.* 2s

AUTOBIOGRAPHY of THOMAS WRIGHT, of Birkenshaw, in the County of York, 1736-1797. Edited by his Grandson, THOMAS WRIGHT, M.A., F.S.A. Fcp. 8vo, pp. 376, *cloth.* 5s
Particularly interesting about Bradford, Leeds, Halifax, and their neighbourhoods, and a curious picture of manners and persons in the middle of the last century.

AUTOGRAPHICAL Miscellany; a Collection of Autograph Letters, Interesting Documents, &c., executed in facsimile by FREDK. NETHERCLIFT, each facsimile accompanied with a page of letter-press by R. SIMS, of the British Museum. Royal 4to, A HANDSOME VOL, *extra cloth.* £1. 1s (*original price* £1. 16s)
Containing sixty examples of hitherto unpublished Letters and Documents of Blake, Boileau, Buonaparte, Burns, Calvin, Camden, Carrier, Catherine de Medicis, Charles I., Chatterton, Congreve, Cranmer, Cromwell, Danton, D'Aubigne, Dryden, Edward VI., Elizabeth, Elizabeth (sister of Louis XVI.), Franklin, Galilei, Glover, Goethe, Goldsmith, Henry VIII., Hyde (Anne), James II., Jonson, Kepler, Kotzebue, Latimer, Loyola, Louis XIV., Louis XVI., Luther, Maintenon, Maria Antoinette, Marlborough, Marmontel, Mary Queen of Scots, Melancthon, Newton, Penn, Pompadour, Pole (Cardinal), Raleigh, Ridley, Robespierre, Rousseau, Rubens, Sand, Schiller, Spenser, Sterne, Tasso, Voltaire, Walpole (Horace), Washington, Wolfe, Wolsey, Wren, and Young.
For the interesting nature of the documents, this collection far excels all the previous ones. With two exceptions (formerly badly executed), they have never been published before.

BAIGENT (F. J., *of Winchester*) History and Antiquities of the Parish Church of Wyke, near Winchester. 8vo, *engravings.* 2s 6d

BANKS' (Sir T. C.) Baronia Anglia Concentrata, or a Concentration of all the Baronies called Baronies in Fee, deriving their Origin from Writ of Summons, and not from any Specific Limited Creation, showing the Descent and Line of Heirship, as well of those Families mentioned by Sir William Dugdale, as of those whom that celebrated Author has omitted to notice; interspersed with Interesting Notices and Explanatory Remarks. Where to is added, the Proofs of Parliamentary Sitting, from the Reign of Edward I. to Queen Anne; also, a *Glossary of Dormant English, Scotch, and Irish Peerage Titles, with reference to presumed existing Heirs.* 2 vols, 4to, *cloth.* 15s (original price £3. 3s)

―――― LARGE PAPER COPY (*very few printed*). 2 vols. £1. 1s

A book of great research, by the well-known author of the "Dormant and Extinct Peerage," and other heraldic and historical works. Those fond of genealogical pursuits ought to secure a copy while it is so cheap. It may be considered a supplement to his former works. Vol. ii. pp. 210-300. contains an Historical Account of the first Settlement of Nova Scotia, and the foundation of the Order of Nova Scotia Baronets, distinguishing those who had seizin of lands there.

BANKS' (W. Stott, *of Wakefield*) Walks in Yorkshire. I. In the North West. II. In the North East. Thick fcap. 8vo, 2 *large maps, cloth.* 5s

―――― N. E. portion separately, comprising Redcar, Saltburn, Whitby, Scarborough, and Filey, and the Moors and Dales between the Tees, &c. Fcap. 8vo, *sewed.* 1s 6d

BARBER (G. D., *commonly called Barber-Beaumont*) Suggestions on the Ancient Britons, in 3 parts. Thick 8vo, *cloth.* 7s 6d (*original price 14s*)

BARKER.—Literary Anecdotes and Contemporary Reminiscences of Professor Porson and others, from the Manuscript Papers of the late E. H. Barker, Esq., of Thetford, Norfolk, with an Original Memoir of the Author. 2 vols, 8vo, *cloth.* 12s 1852

A singular book, full of strange stories and jests.

BARKER (W. Jones) Historical and Topographical Account of Wensleydale, and the Valley of the Yore, in the North Riding of Yorkshire. 8vo, *illustrated with views, seals, arms, &c., cloth.* 4s 6d (original price 8s 6d)

"This modest and unpretending compilation is a pleasant addition to our topographical literature, and gives a good general account of a beautiful part of England comparatively little known. It is handsomely printed with a number of finely executed woodcuts by Mr. Howard Dudley . . . . No guide to the district exists applicable alike to the will-filled and scantly furnished purse—a defect which the author has endeavoured to supply by the present volume.

BARNES (Rev. W.) Tiw; or a View of the Roots and Stems of the English as a Teutonic Tongue. Fcap. 8vo, *cloth.* 5s

"I hold that my primary roots are the roots of all the Teutonic languages; and, if my view is the true one, it must ultimately be taken up by the German and other Teutonic grammarians, and applied to their languages."—*The Author.*

BARNES (Rev. William, *of Came Rectory, Dorchester*) A Philological Grammar, grounded upon English, and formed from a comparison of more than Sixty Languages. Being an Introduction to the Science of Grammars of all Languages, especially English, Latin, and Greek. 8vo (pp. 322), *cloth.* 9s

" Mr. Barnes' work is an excellent specimen of the manner in which the advancing study of Philology may be brought to illustrate and enrich a scientific exposition of English Grammar."—*Edinburgh Guardian.*

" Of the science of Grammar, by induction from the philological facts of many languages, Mr. Barnes has, in this volume, supplied a concise and comprehensive manual. Grammarians may differ as to the regularity of the principles on which nations have constructed their forms and usages of speech, but it is generally allowed that some conformity or similarity of practice may be traced, and that an attempt may be made to expound a true science of Grammar. Mr. Barnes has so far grounded his Grammar upon English as to make it an English Grammar, but he has continually referred to comparative philology, and sought to render his work illustrative of general forms, in conformity with principles common, more or less, to the language of all mankind. More than sixty languages have been compared in the course of preparing the volume ; and the general principles laid down will be found useful in the study of various tongues. It is a learned and philosophical treatise."—*Literary Gazette.*

BARNES (Rev. W.) Anglo-Saxon Delectus ; serving as a first Class-Book to the Language. 12mo, *cloth.* 2s 6d

"To those who wish to possess a critical knowledge of their own Native English, some acquaintance with Anglo-Saxon is indispensable ; and we have never seen an introduction better calculated than the present to supply the wants of a beginner in a short space of time. The declensions and conjugations are well stated, and illustrated by references to Greek, the Latin, French, and other languages. A philosophical spirit pervades every part. The Delectus consists of short pieces on various subjects, with extracts from Anglo-Saxon History and the Saxon Chronicle. There is a good Glossary at the end."—*Athenæum,* Oct. 20, 1849.

BARNES (Rev. W.) Notes on Ancient Briton and the Britons. Fcap. 8vo, *cloth.* 3s

" Mr. Barnes has given us the result of his Collections for a Course of Lectures on this subject, and has produced a series of Sketches of the Ancient Britons, their language, laws, and modes of life, and of their social state as compared with that of the Saxons, which will be read with considerable interest."—*Notes and Queries.*

" We are very glad to meet with such pleasant and readable 'Notes' as Mr. Barnes'. They are very unaffected essays, imparting much warmth to the old carcase of British lore, and evincing some real study. He has found out the value of the old Welsh laws, and has made some useful comparisons between them and those of the Saxons with much freshness if not absolute novelty."—*Guardian.*

BARNES' (Rev. W.) Views of Labour and Gold. Fcp. 8vo, *cloth.* 3s

" Mr. Barnes is a reader and a thinker. He has a third and a conspicuous merit—his style is perfectly lucid and simple. If the humblest reader of ordinary intelligence desired to follow out the process by which societies are built up and held together, he has but to betake himself to the study of Mr. Barnes's epitome. The title " Views of Labour and Gold," cannot be said to indicate the scope of the Essays, which open with pictures of primitive life, nad pass on, through an agreeably diversified range of topics, to considerations of the rights, duties, and interests of Labour and Capital, and to the enquiry, What constitutes the utility, wealth, and positive well being of a nation ? Subjects of this class are rarely handled with so firm a grasp and such light and artistic manipulation."—*Athenæum.*

" The opinion of such a Scholar and Clergyman of the Established Church on subjects of political economy cannot fail to be both interesting and instructive, and the originality of some of his views and expressions is well calculated to attract and repay the most careful attention."— *Financial Reformer.*

BARNES' (Rev. W.) Poems, partly of Rural Life, in National English. 12mo, *cloth.* 5s

BARNES' (Rev. W.) Poems of Rural Life in the DORSET DIALECT. Fcap. 8vo, *first collection, fourth edition, cloth.* 5s

———— Second Collection, *second edition,* fcap. 8vo, *cloth.* 5s

———— Third Collection, fcap. 8vo, *cloth.* 4s 6d

BATEMAN (Thos., *of Youlgrave, Derbyshire*) Vestiges of the Antiquities of Derbyshire, and the Sepulchral Usages of its Inhabitants, from the most Remote Ages to the Reformation. 8vo, *with numerous woodcuts of Tumuli and their contents, Crosses, Tombs, &c., cloth.* 15s

BATEMAN'S (Thomas) Ten Years' Diggings in Celtic and Saxon Grave Hills, in the Counties of Derby, Stafford, and York, from 1848 to 1853, with Notices of some former Discoveries hitherto unpublished, and Remarks on the Crania and Pottery from the Mounds. 8vo, *numerous woodcuts, cloth.* 10s 6d

BATTLE ABBEY.—Descriptive Catalogue of the Original Charters, Grants, Donations, etc., constituting the Muniments of Battle Abbey, also the Papers of the Montagus, Sidneys, and Websters, embodying many highly interesting and valuable Records of Lands in Sussex, Kent, and Essex, with Preliminary Memoranda of the Abbey of Battel, and Historical Particulars of the Abbots. 8vo, 234 *pages, cloth.* 1s 6d

BEDFORD'S (Rev. W. K. Riland) The Blazon of Episcopacy, being a complete List of the Archbishops and Bishops of England and Wales, and their Family Arms drawn and described, from the first introduction of Heraldry to the present time. 8vo, 144 *pages, and 62 pages of drawings of Arms, cloth.* 15s
This work depicts the arms of a great number of English Families not to be found in other works.
" There has been an amount of industry bestowed upon this curious work which is very creditable to the author, and will be found beneficial to all who care for the subject on which it has been employed."—ATHENÆUM.

BERRY'S (W.) Pedigrees and Arms of the Nobility and Gentry of Hertfordshire. Folio (only 125 printed), *bds.* £1. 10s (*original price £3. 10s*)

BIBLIOGRAPHICAL MISCELLANY, edited by JOHN PETHERAM. 8vo, Nos. 1 to 5 (all published), *with general title.* 1s
CONTENTS.—Particulars of the Voyage of Sir Thomas Button for the Discovery of a North-West Passage, A.D. 1612—Sir Dudley Digges' Of the Circumference of the Earth, or a Treatise of the North-East Passage. 1611-13—Letter of Sir Thomas Button on the North-West Passage, in the State-Paper Office—Bibliographical Notices of Old Music Books, by Dr. Rimbault—Notices of Suppressed Books—Martin Mar Prelate's Rhymes—The Hardwicke Collection of Manuscripts.

BIBLIOTHEQUE Asiatique et Africane, ou Catalogue des Ouvrages relatifs a l'Asie et a l'Afrique qui ont paru jusqu'en 1700, per H. TERNAUX-COMPANS. 8vo, *avec supplement et index, sewed.* 10s 6d

"BIBLIA PAUPERUM." One of the earliest and most curious Block Books, reproduced in facsimile from a copy in the British Museum, by J. Ph. Berjeau. Royal 4to, *half bound.* £2. 2s

The Biblia Pauperum, known also by the title of Historiæ Veteris et Novi Testamenti, is a set of woodcuts in which the Old and New Testament are both brought to memory by pictures, and some lines of text in Latin. This name, Biblia Pauperum, is derived from its use by monks of the poorer orders commonly called Pauperes Christi.

As a specimen of the earliest woodcuts and of printed block-books, destined to supersede the manuscripts anterior to the valuable invention of Guttenberg, the Biblia Pauperum is well worthy the attention of the amateur of Fine Arts as well as of the Bibliographer. It consists of 40 engravings, printed on one side only of the leaves, and disposed so as to have the figures opposite to each other.

The engravings were printed by friction, with a substance of a brownish colour instead of printing ink, which was unknown at this early period. To imitate as near as possible the original, the plates in this facsimile are disposed opposite each other, and printed in a brownish colour. Various editions of this Block-Book have been discovered, without any writer being able to say which is the first one. A review of them is given in the printed Introduction of the book.

Besides the rhymed Latin Poetry—of which part was given by Heinecken, and after him by Ottley—the Introduction gives, for the first time, the whole of the Text printed on both sides in the upper compartment, as well as an English Explanation of the subject.

Only 250 copies have been printed, uniformly with Mr. S. Leigh Sotherby's *Principia Typographica.*

BIGSBY'S (Robert, *M.A., LL.D.*) Historical and Topographical Description of Repton, in the County of Derby, with Incidental View of objects of note in its Vicinity. 4to, a handsome volume, *with* seventy *illustrations on copper, stone, and wood, cloth.* 18s (*original price* £3. 3s)

BLAKE (M.) A Brief Account of the Destructive Fire at Blandford Forum, in Dorsetshire, June 4, 1731. *Reprinted from the edition of 1735, with a plan and 2 views.* 4to, *cloth.* 2s 6d

BLAVIGNAC (J. D., *Architecte*) Histoire de l'Architecture Sacrée du quatrième au dixième siècle dans les anciens évechés de Geneve, Lausanne, et Sion. One vol, 8vo, 450 *pages,* 37 *plates,* and a 4to Atlas *of* 82 *plates of Architecture, Sculpture, Frescoes, Reliquaries, &c., &c.* £2. 10s

A very remarkable book, and worth the notice of the Architect, the Archæologist, and the Artist.

BOYNE (W., *F.S.A.*) Tokens issued in the Seventeenth Century in England, Wales, and Ireland, by Corporations, Merchants, Tradesmen, &c., described and illustrated. Thick 8vo, 42 *plates, cloth.* £1. 1s (*original price* £2. 2s)

Nearly 9500 Tokens are described in this work, arranged alphabetically under Counties and Towns. To the Numismatist, the Topographer, and Genealogist, it will be found extremely useful.

BOSWORTH (Rev. Joseph, *D.D., Anglo-Saxon Professor in the University of Oxford*) Compendious Anglo-Saxon and English Dictionary. 8vo, *closely printed in treble columns.* 12s

" This is not a mere abridgment of the large Dictionary, but almost an entirely new work. In this compendious one will be found, at a very moderate price all that is most practical and valuable in the former expensive edition, with a great accession of new words and matter."—*Author's Preface.*

BOSWORTH and WARING.—Four Versions of the Holy Gospels, viz., in Gothic, A.D. 360; Anglo-Saxon, 995; Wycliffe, 1389; and Tyndale, 1526, in parallel columns, with Preface and Notes by the Rev. Dr. BOSWORTH, Professor of Anglo-Saxon in the University of Oxford, assisted by GEORGE WARING, M.A., of Cambridge and Oxford. One vol, 8vo, *above 600 pages, cloth.* 12s 6d

A very low price has been fixed to ensure an extended sale among students and higher schools.

—— LARGE PAPER. 4to, *a handsome volume, not many printed. cloth.* £2. 2s

"The texts are printed in four parallel columns, and very great care appears to have been taken in their collation and correction."—ATHENAEUM.

"We heartily welcome this volume, brought out with so much care and ability . . . It does credit to the printers of the University. . . . The work is scholarlike, and is a valuable contribution to the materials for Biblical Criticism. . . We heartily commend it to the study of all who are interested either in the philology of the English language, or in the history and formation of our Authorized Version."—THE CHRISTIAN REMEMBRANCER, a *Quarterly Review.*

"It may almost be a question, whether the present volume phsseuses greater interest for the divine or for the philologist. To the latter it must certainly be interesting from the opportunity which it affords him of marking the gradual development of our languages. The four versions of the Gospel, . . . with a learned and instructive preface, and a few necessary notes, form a volume, the value and importance of which need scarcely be insisted upon."—NOTES AND QUERIES.

BLAKEY (Robert) Historical Sketches of the Angling Literature of all Nations, to which is added a Bibliography of English Writers on Angling, by J. R. Smith. Fcap. 8vo, *cloth.* 5s

BOWLES (Rev. W., Lisle) Hermes Britannicus, a Dissertation on the Celtic Deity Teutates, the Mercurius of Cæsar, in further proof and corroboration of the origin and designation of the Great Temple at Abury, in Wiltshire. 8vo, *bds,* 4s (*original price* 8s 6d)

BRIDGER'S (Charles) Index to the Printed Pedigrees of English Families contained in County and Local Histories, the "Herald's Visitations," and in the more important Genealogical Collections. Thick 8vo, *cloth.* 10s 6d

A similar work to Sims's "Index of Pedigrees in the MSS. in the British Museum. What that is for Manuscripts this is for Printed Books. It is the most complete Index of its kind, and contains double the matter of other hasty productions.

BROOKE (Richard, *F.S.A.*) Visits to Fields of Battle in England, of the XVth Century, with some Miscellaneous Tracts and Papers, principally upon Archæological Subjects. Royal 8vo, *plates, cloth.* 15s

The work contains a descriptive account of the scenes of most of the memorable conflicts in the Wars of York and Lancaster, comprising the celebrated battles of Shrewsbury, Blore Heath, Northampton, Wakefield, Mortimer's Cross, Towton, Barnet, Tewkesbury. Bosworth, and Stoke, and genealogical and other particulars of the powerful, warlike, and distinguished personages who were the principal actors in those stirring and eventful times, with plans of some of the fields of Battle, and an Appendix containing the principal Acts of Attainder relative to the Wars of the Roses, and Lists of the Noblemen, Knights, and other personages attainted by them.

BROOKE (Richard) A Descriptive Account of Liverpool, as it was during the last Quarter of the XVIIIth Century, 1775—1800. A handsome vol, royal 8vo, *with illustrations, cloth.* 12s 6d (*original price* £1. 5s)

In addition to information relative to the Public Buildings, Statistics, and Commerce of the Town, the work contains some curious and interesting particulars which have never been previously published, respecting the pursuits, habits, and amusements of the inhabitants of Liverpool during that period, with views of its public edifices.

BRUCE (Dr. J. Collingwood, *Author of the "Roman Wall"*) The Bayeux Tapestry Elucidated. 4to, a handsome volume. *illustrated with* 17 COLOURED *plates, representing the entire Tapestry, extra bds.* £1. 1s.

BUCHANAN (W.) Memoirs of Painting, with a Chronological History of the Importation of Pictures by the Great Masters into England since the French Revolution. 2 vols, 8vo, *bds.* 7s 6d (*original price* £1. 6s)

BUNNETT (H. Jones, *M.D.*) Genoa, with Remarks on the Climate, and its influence upon Invalids. 12mo, *cloth.* 4s

BURKE (John) Genealogical and Heraldic History of the Extinct and Dormant Baronetcies of England, Ireland, and Scotland. Medium 8vo, SECOND EDITION, 638 *closely printed pages, in double columns, with about* 1000 *Arms engraved on wood, fine port. of* JAMES I., *cloth.* 10s (*original price* £1. 8s)

This work engaged the attention of the author for several years, comprises nearly a thousand families, many of them amongst the most ancient and eminent in the kingdom, each carried down to its representative or representatives still existing, with elaborate and minute details of the alliances, achievements, and fortunes, generation after generation, from the earliest to the latest period.

CALTON'S (R. Bell) Annals and Legends of Calais, with Sketches of Emigré Notabilities, and Memoirs of Lady Hamilton. Post 8vo, *with frontispiece and vignette, cloth.* 5s

PRINCIPAL CONTENTS.—History of the Siege by Edward III in 1346-7, with a roll of the Commanders and their followers present, from a contemporary MS. in the British Museum—The Allotment of Lands and Houses to Edward's Barons—Calais as an English borough—List of the Streets and Householders of the same—Henry VIIIth's Court there—Cardinal Wolsey and his expenses—The English Pale, with the names of Roads, Farmsteads, and Villages in the English Era—The Sieges of Therouanne and Tournai—The Pier of Calais—Pros and Cons of the place—The Hotel Dessin—Sterne's Chamber—Churches of Notre Dame and St. Nicholas—The Hotel de Ville—Ancient Staple Hall—The Chateau and Murder of the Duke of Gloucester—The Courgain—The Field of the Cloth of Gold—Notice of the Town and Castle of Guisnes, and its surprise by John de Lancaster—The Town and Seigneurie of Ardres—The Sands and Duelling—Villages and Chateau of Sangatte, Coulgon, Mark, Eschalleu, and Hammes—Review of the English Occupation of Calais, and its Recapture by the Duke de Guise—The Lower Town and its Lace Trade—Our Commercial Relations with France—Emigré Notabilities—Charles and Harry Tufton, Captain Dormer and Edith Jacquemont, Beau Brummel, Jemmy Urquhart, and his friend Fauntleroy, "Nimrod," Berkeley Craven, Mytton, Duchess of Kingston—A new Memoir of Lady Hamilton, &c. Altogether an interesting volume on England's first Colony.

BURN'S (J. Southerden) The High Commission, Notices of the Court and its Proceedings. 8vo, *cloth, only* 100 *printed.* 3s

BURN's (J., Southerden) History of Parish Registers in England, and Registers of Scotland, Ireland, the Colonies, Episcopal Chapels in and about London, the Geneva Register of the Protestant Refugees, with Biographical Notes, etc. *Second edition, greatly enlarged,* 8vo, *cloth.* 10s 6d

CAMBRIDGE.—Historia Collegii Jesu Cantabrigiensis, a J. Shermanno, olim præs. ejusdem Collegii. Edita J. O. HALLIWELL. 8vo, *cloth.* 2s

CARDWELL (Rev. Dr., *Professor of Ancient History, Oxford*) Lectures on the Coinage of the Greeks and Romans, delivered in the University of Oxford. 8vo, *cloth.* 4s (*original price* 8s 6d)

A very interesting historical volume, and written in a pleasing and popular manner.

CARTWRIGHT.—Memoirs of the Life, Writings, and Mechanical Inventions of Edmund Cartwright, D.D., F.R.S., *Inventor of the Power Loom, &c.* Edited by E. H. STRICKLAND. Post 8vo, *engravings, boards.* 2s 6d (*original price* 10s 6d)

It contains some interesting literary history, Dr. Cartwright numbering among his correspondents, Sir W. Jones, Crabbe, Sir H. Davy, Fulton, Sir S. Raffles, Langhorne, and others. He was no mean Poet, as his legendary tale of "Armine and Elvira" (given in the Appendix) testifies. Sir W. Scott says it contains some excellent poetry, expressed with unusual felicity.

CATALOGUE (*Classified*) of the Library of the Royal Institution of Great Britain, with Indexes of Authors and Subjects, and a List of Historical Pamphlets, chronologically arranged. By BENJ. VINCENT, Librarian. Thick 8vo, pp. 948, *half morocco, marbled edges.* 15s

It will be found a very useful volume to book collectors, and indispensable to public librarians.

CHADWICK (William) The Life and Times of Daniel De Foe, with Remarks, Digressive and Discursive. 8vo, pp. 472, *portrait, cloth* 10s 6d.

"Daniel De Foe devoted his life and energies to the defence of free institutions and good government. He was the Radical of his day. He not only wrote, but suffered for truth and liberty. He was impoverished and persecuted for his labours in this cause; nay, he was repeatedly imprisoned for his principles, or for his unswerving attachment to them, and for his boldness and honesty in asserting them. He was the vigorous and indefatigable opponent of priestism, of ecclesiastical domination, and of the Popish tendencies of his time. We might not approve of all he wrote against the Catholics, but we should remember that he saw and *felt*, as we cannot, how inherently opposed to true freedom is the Catholic system. Although we live in very different times from those in which De Foe lived, yet his life is full of pregnant lessons for the liberals and friends of religious freedom of our day." —*Bradford Review.*

CHRONICLE of London from 1089 to 1483, written in the 15th Century, and for the first time printed from MSS. in the British Museum, with numerous Contemporary Illustrations of Royal Letters, Poems, descriptive of Public Events and Manners and Customs of the Metropolis. (Edited by SIR HARRIS NICOLAS.) 4to, *facsimile, cloth bds.* 15s

Only 250 copies printed. It forms a Supplement to the Chronicles of Harding, Rastall, Grafton, Hall, and others.

CHATTO (W. A., *Author of "Jackson's History of Wood Engraving"*) Facts and Speculations on the History of Playing Cards in Europe. 8vo, *profusely illustrated with engravings, both plain and coloured, cloth.* £1. 1s

"The inquiry into the origin and signification of the suits and their marks, and the heraldic, theological, and political emblems pictured from time to time, in their changes, opens a new field of antiquarian interest; and the perseverance with which Mr. Chatto has explored it leaves little to be gained by his successors. The plates with which the volume is enriched add considerably to its value in this point of view. It is not to be denied that, take it altogether, it contains more matter than has ever before been collected in one view upon the same subject. In spite of its faults, it is exceedingly amusing; and the most critical reader cannot fail to be entertained by the variety of curious outlying learning Mr. Chatto has somehow contrived to draw into the investigations."—*Atlas.*

"Indeed, the entire production deserves our warmest approbation."—*Literary Gazette.*

"A perfect fund of antiquarian research, and most interesting even to persons who never play at cards."—*Tait's Magazine.*

"A curious, entertaining, and really learned book."—*Rambler.*

"THE GAME OF THE CHESSE," the First Book printed in England by WILLIAM CAXTON, reproduced in facsimile from a copy in the British Museum, with a few Remarks on Caxton's Typographical Productions, by VINCENT FIGGINS. 4to, pp. 184, *with 23 curious woodcuts, half morocco, uncut.* £1. 1s—*or, in antique calf, with bevelled boards and carmine edges.* £1. 8s

Frequently, as we read of the Works of Caxton and the early English Printers, and of their Black Letter Books, very few persons ever had the opportunity of seeing any of these productions, and forming a proper estimate of the ingenuity and skill of those who first practised the "Noble Art of Printing."

THE TYPE HAS BEEN CAREFULLY IMITATED, AND THE WOODCUTS FACSIMILIED BY MISS BYFIELD. The Paper and Watermarks have also been made expressly, as near as possible, like the original; and the book is accompanied by a few remarks of a practical nature, which have been suggested during the progress of the fount, and the necessary study and comparison of Caxton's Works with those of his contemporaries in Germany, by Mr. V. FIGGINS, who spent two years' "labour of love" in cutting the matrixes for the type.

COLLECTION of Letters on Scientific Subjects, illustrative of the Progress of Science in England. Temp. Elizabeth to Charles II. Edited by J. O. HALLIWELL. 8vo, *cloth.* 3s

Comprising letters of Digges, Dee, Tycho Brahe, Lower, Hariott, Lydyatt, Sir W. Petty, Sir C. Cavendish, Brancker, Pell, &c.; also the Autobiography of Sir Samuel Morland, from a MS. in Lambeth Palace, Nat. Tarpoley's Corrector Analyticus, &c. Cost the subscribers of the Historical Society of Science £1.

COPENHAGEN.—The Traveller's Handbook to Copenhagen and its Environs. By ANGLICANUS. 12mo, *with large map of Sealand, plan of Copenhagen, and views, cloth.* 8s

COSIN's (Mr., *Secretary to the Commissioners of Forfeited Estates* Names of the Roman Catholics, Non-Jurors, and others, who Refused to Take the Oaths to King George I., together with their Titles, Additions, and Places of Abode, the Parishes and Townships where their Lands lay, the Names of the then Tenants, and the Annual Value of them as returned by themselves. *Reprinted from the Edition of* 1745. 8vo, *cloth.* 5s

A curious book for the Topographer and Genealogist.

CRAIG'S (Rev. J. Duncan) A Hand-Book to the modern Provençal Language, spoken in the South of France, Piedmont, &c., comprising a Grammar, Dialogues, Legends, Vocabularies, &c., useful for English Tourists and others. Royal 12mo, *cloth.* 3s 6d
This little book is a welcome addition to our literature of comparative philology in this country, as we have hitherto had no grammar of the sweet lyrical tongue of Southern France.

CRESWELL'S (Rev. S. F.) Collections towards the History of Printing in Nottinghamshire. Small 4to, *sewed.* 2s

DALE (Bryan, *M.A.*) Annals of Coggeshall, otherwise Sunnedon, in the County of Essex. Post 8vo, *plates, cloth.* 7s 6d

D'ALTON (John, *Barrister-of-Law, of Dublin*) Illustrations, Historical and Genealogical, of the most Ancient FAMILIES OF IRELAND (500), Members of which held Commissions in King James's Service in the War of the Revolution, wherein their respective Origins, Achievements, Forfeitures, and ultimate Destinies are set forth. 2 thick vols, 8vo, pp. 1400, *cloth.* £1. 1s

DANISH.—English-Danish Dialogues and Progressive Exercises. By E. F. ANCKER. 12mo, *cloth.* 5s 1851—Key to Ditto. 5s

DAVIES (Robt., F.S.A., *Town Clerk of York*) Extracts from the Municipal Records of the City of York during the Reigns of Edward IV., Edward V., and Richard III., with Notes, illustrative and explanatory, and an Appendix, containing some Account of the Celebration of the Corpus Christi Festival at York, in the Fifteenth and Sixteenth Centuries. 8vo, *cloth.* 4s (*original price* 10s 6d)

DAVIES (Robt.) The Fawkes's of York in the 16th Century, including Notices of Guy Fawkes, the Gunpowder Plot Conspirator. Post 8vo. 1s 6d

DE GAULLE (Chas.) The Celts of the Nineteenth Century, an Appeal to the Living Representatives of the Celtic Race. Translated, with Notes, by J. D. MASON. 8vo, *sewed.* 2s

DEVLIN (J. Dacres) Helps to Hereford History, Civil and Legendary, in an Ancient Account of the Ancient Cordwainer's Company of the City, the Mordiford Dragon, and other Subjects. 12mo (*a curious volume*), *cloth.* 3s 6d
" A series of very clever papers."—*Spectator.*
" A little work full of Antiquarian information, presented in a pleasing and popular form."—*Nonconformist*

DRUCE Family.—A Genealogical Account of the Family of Druce, of Goring, in the County of Oxford, 1735. 4to, only 50 copies PRIVATELY PRINTED, *bds.* 7s 6d

EDMONDS (Richard, *late of Penzance*) The Land's End District its Antiquities, Natural History, Natural Phenomena, and Scenery ; also a Brief Memoir of Richard Trevithick, C.E. 8vo, *maps, plates, and woodcuts, cloth.* 7s 6d

ELLIS' (W. S.) Notices of the Families of Ellis. Part I. 8vo. 2s

ELLIS (W. Smith) A Plea for the Antiquity of Heraldry, with an Attempt to Expound its Theory and Elucidate its History. 8vo, *sewed.* 1s

ELLIS' (W. S.) Hurtspierpoint (in Sussex), its Lords and Families. 8vo, *plates.* 1s 6d

ELLIOTT.—Life, Poetry, and Letters of Ebenezer Elliott, the Corn-Law Rhymer (of Sheffield). Edited by his Son-in-Law, JOHN WATKINS. Post 8vo, *cloth, (an interesting volume).* 3s (*original price 7s 6d*)

ENGLAND as seen by Foreigners in the Days of Elizabeth and James the First, comprising Translations of the Journals of the two Dukes of Wirtemberg in 1592 and 1610, both illustrative of Shakespeare. With Extracts from the Travels of Foreign Princes and others. With Copious Notes, an Introduction, and ETCHINGS. By WILLIAM BRENCHLEY RYE, *Assistant Keeper of the Department of Printed Books, British Museum.* Thick foolscap 4to, *elegantly printed by Whittingham, extra cloth.* 15s

"This curious volume has been the labours of a scholar's love, and will be read with ease by all. The idea of assembling the testimonies of foreign visitors, and showing us how we appeared to others in the days of Bess, by way of contrast and comparison to the aspect we present in the days of Victoria, was one which involved much arduous research. Mr. Rye had had no predecessor. . . . . . He has not only added an introduction to the works he assembles and translates, but has enriched them with some hundred pages of notes on all kinds of subjects, exhibiting a wide and minute research."—*Fortnightly Review.* (G. H. LEWES.)

"It contains a good deal of curious and amusing matter."—*Saturday Review.*

"Mr. Rye's work claims the credit of a valuable body of historical annotation."—*Athenæum.*

"The book is one of the most entertaining of the class we have seen for a long while. It contains a complete and lively reflex of English life and manners at the most fascinating period of our history."—*London Review.*

"A book replete both with information and amusement, furnishing a series of very curious pictures of England in the Olden Time."—*Notes and Queries.*

"It is difficult to convey a just impression of Mr. Rye's volume in a short criticism, because the really interesting feature of it is the quaintness, and, to modern eyes, the simplicity of most of the narratives, which cannot be reproduced with full effect except in quotations, for which we have no space."—*Pall Mall Gazette.*

"A handsome, well-printed, entertaining book—entertaining and something more, and comes very welcome to the time. . . . It is in such accidental notices that the chief interest and the not slight value of collections such as this consists; and when they are as well edited, they have a use on the shelves after their freshness is past: they help our familiarity with our history."—*Reader.*

EVANS (John, F.S.A., *Secretary to the Numismatic Society*) Coins of the Ancient Britons. Arranged and Described. Thick 8vo, *many plates, engraved by F. W. Fairholt, F.S.A., and cuts, cloth, a handsome volume.* £1. 1s

The "Prix de Numismatique" has been awarded by the French Academie des Inscriptions et Belles Lettres, to the author, for this book.

FOSBROKE (T. Dudley, *F.S.A.*) The Tourist's Grammar, or Rules relating to the Scenery and Antiquities incident to Travellers. including an Epitome of Gilpin's Principles of the Picturesque, Post 8vo, *bds.* 2s (*original price 7s*)

FINLAYSON (James) Surnames and Sirenames, the Origin and History of certain Family and Historical Names, and Remarks on the Ancient Right of the Crown to Sanction and Veto the Assumption of Names, and an Historical Account of the Names of Buggey anl Bugg. 8vo. 1s 6d (*original price* 2s 6d)

FRENEAU (Philip) Poems on Various Subjects, but chiefly illustrative of the Events and Actors in the American War of Independence, *reprinted from the rare edition printed at Philadelphia in 1786,* with a Preface. Thick fcap. 8vo, *elegantly printed, cloth.* 6s

Freneau enjoyed the friendship of Adams, Franklin, Jefferson, Madison, and Munroe, and the last three were his constant correspondants while they lived. His Patriotic Songs and Ballads, which were superior to any metrical compositions then written in America, were everywhere sung with enthusiasm. See Griswold's "Poets and Poetry of America," and Duyckinck's "Cyclop. of American Literature."

GILBERT (Walter B.) The Accounts of the Corpus Christi Fraternity, and Papers relating to the Antiquities of Maidstone. 12mo, *cloth, gilt leaves.* 3s 6d

GILES (Rev. Dr.) The Writings of the Christians of the Second Century, namely, Athenagoras, Tatian, Theophilus, Hermias, Papias, Aristides, Quadratus, etc., collected and first translated, complete. 8vo, *cloth.* 7s 6d

Designed as a continuation of Abp. Wake's *Apostolical Epistles,* which are those of the first century.

GILES (Rev. Dr.) Heathen Records to the Jewish Scripture History, containing all the Extracts from the Greek and Latin Writers in which the Jews and Christians are named, collected together and translated into English, with the original Text in juxtaposition. 8vo, *cloth.* 7s 6d

GILES (Rev. Dr.) Codex Apochryphus Novi Testamenti, the Uncanonical Gospels and other Writings referring to the First Ages of Christianity, in the original Languages of Arabic, Greek, and Latin, collected together from the editions of Fabricius, Thilo and others. 2 vols, 8vo, *cloth.* 14s

GILES (Rev. Dr.) History of the Parish and Town of Bampton, in Oxfordshire, with the District and Hamlets belonging to it. 8vo, *plates, second edition, cloth.* 7s 6d

GILES (Rev. Dr.) History of Witney and its Neighbouring Parishes, Oxon. 8vo, *plates, cloth.* 6s

GILES (Rev. Dr.) Passages from the Poets, chronologically arranged. Thick 12mo, nearly 700 pages, *cloth,* 7s 6d

It contains choice passages from more than 400 English Poets, in chronological order. It will be found a useful volume to candidates at competitive examinations in English Literature.

GREENHOW (Robt., *Librarian to the Dept. of State, U.S.A.*) History of Oregon and California, and the other Territories on the North-West Coast of America, accompanied by a Geographical View and Map, and a number of Proofs and Illustrations of the History. 8vo, *large map, cloth.* 7s 6d (*original price* 16s)

GILES (Rev. Dr.) Excerpta ex Scriptoribus Classicis de Britannia. A Complete Collection of those passages in the Classic Writers (124 in number), which make mention of the British Isles, Chronologically Arranged, from Ante-Christi 560 to Anno Dom. 1333. 8vo, *cloth.* 3s (*original price* 7s 6d)
An Introduction to every History of Great Britain.

GRENVILLE (Henry) Chronological Synopsis of the Four Gospels on a new plan, with Notes. 8vo, *cloth.* 1s 6d
Designed to show that on a minute critical analysis, the writings of the four Evangelists contain no contradictions within themselves, and that such passages that have appeared to many critics to raise doubt as to the consistency of these Records of our Lord's Ministry, really afford, when explained, the most satisfactory proofs that there was no COLLUSION between the several writers, and that they may therefore be thoroughly relied on as "INDEPENDENT" witnesses of the Truth of what they record.

HADFIELD (James, *Architect*) Ecclesiastical Architecture of the County of Essex, from the Norman Era to the Sixteenth Century, with Plans, Elevations, Sections, Details, &c., from a Series of Measured Drawings, and Architectural and Chronological Descriptions. Royal 4to, 80 *plates, leather back, cloth sides.* £1. 11s 6d

HAIGH'S (Daniel Henry, D.D.) The Conquest of Britain by the Saxons. A Harmony of the History of the Britons, the Works of Gildas, the "Brut," and the Saxon Chronicle, with reference to the Events of the Fifth and Sixth Centuries. 8vo, *plates of Runic Inscriptions, cloth.* 15s

HAIGH'S (Daniel Henry, D.D.) The Anglo-Saxon Sagas, an Examination of their value as aids to History, serving as a Sequel to "The Conquest of Britain by the Saxons." 8vo, *cloth.* 8s 6d
It analyses and throws new historical evidence on the origin of the Poems of Beowulf, the Lament of Deor, the Saga of Waldhere, Scyld Sceafing, the fight at Finnesham, the Story of Horn, the Lay of Hildebrand, &c.

HAKEWILL (H.) Roman Remains discovered in the Parishes of North Leigh and Stonesfield, Oxfordshire. 8vo, *map, and 2 plates.* 2s 6d

HALLIWELL'S (James Orchard, F.R.S., &c.) Dictionary of Archaic and Provincial Words, Obsolete Phrases, Proverbs, and Ancient Customs, from the Reign of Edward I. 2 vols, 8vo, containing upwards of 1,000 pages, *closely printed in double columns, cloth, a new and cheaper edition.* 15s
It contains above 50,000 words (embodying all the known scattered glossaries of the English language), forming a complete key for the reader of our old Poets, Dramatists, Theologians, and other authors, whose works abound with allusions, of which explanations are not to be found in ordinary Dictionaries and books of reference. Most of the principal Archaisms are illustrated by examples selected from early inedited MSS. and rare books, and by far the greater portion will be found to be original authorities.

HALLIWELL (J. O.) the Nursery Rhymes of England, collected chiefly from Oral Tradition. The SIXTH EDITION, enlarged, with many Designs by W. B. SCOTT, Director of the School of Design, Newcastle-on-Tyne. 12mo, *cloth, gilt leaves.* 4s 6d
The largest collection ever formed of these old ditties.

HALLIWELL'S (J. O.) Popular Rhymes and Nursery Tales, with Historical Elucidations. 12mo, *cloth.* 4s 6d

This very interesting volume on the traditional literature of England is divided into Nursery Antiquities, Fireside Nursery Stories, Game Rhymes, Alphabet Rhymes, Riddle Rhymes, Nature Songs, Proverb Rhymes, Places, and Families, Superstition Rhymes, Custom Rhymes, and Nursery Songs, a large number are here printed for the first time. It may be consinered a sequel to the preceding article.

HALLIWELL'S (J. O.) Early History of Freemasonry in England. Illustrated by an English Poem of the XIVth Century, with Notes. Post 8vo, *second edition, with a facsimile of the original MS. in the British Museum, cloth.* 2s 6d

"The interest which the curious poem, of which this publication is chiefly composed, has excited, is proved by the fact of its having been translated into German, and of its having reached a second edition, which is not common with such publications. Mr. Halliwell has carefully revised the new edition, and increased its utility by the addition of a complete and correct Glossary."—Literary Gazette.

HALLIWELL'S (J. O.) The Manuscript Rarities of the University of Cambridge. 8vo, *bds.* 3s (*original price,* 10s 6d)

A companion to Hartshorne's "Book Rarities" of the same university.

HALLIWELL'S (J. O.) A Dictionary of Old English Plays, existing either in print or in manuscript, from the earliest times to the close of the 17th century, including also Notices of Latin Plays written by English Authors during the same period, with particulars of their Authors, Plots, Characters, &c. 8vo, *cloth.* 12s

Twenty-five copies have been printed on THICK PAPER, price £1. 1s

HALLIWELL'S (J. O.) Rambles in Western Cornwall, by the Footsteps of the Giants; with Notes on the Celtic Remains of the Land's End District and the Isles of Scilly. Fcp. 4to, *elegantly printed by Whittingham, cloth.* 7s 6d

HALLIWELL (J. O.) Notes of Family Excursions in North Wales, taken chiefly from Rhyl, Abergele, Llandudno, and Bangor. Fcp. 4to, *with engravings, elegantly printed by Whittingham, cloth.* 5s

HALLIWELL'S (J. O.) Roundabout Notes, chiefly upon the Ancient Circles of Stones in the Isle of Man. Fcp. 4to, *only* 100 *printed.* 2s

HALLIWELL'S (J. O.) Introduction to the Evidences of Christianity. Fcp. 8vo, 2ND EDITION, *cloth.* 1s 6d (*original price* 3s 6d)

The only book which contains in a popular form the Ancient Heathen unconscious testimonies to the truth of Christianity.

HARROD (Henry, F.S.A.) Gleanings among the Castles and Convents of Norfolk. 8vo, *many plates and woodcuts, cloth.* 17s 6d. —LARGE PAPER, £1. 3s 6d.

"This volume is creditable to Mr. Harrod in every way, alike to his industry, aste, and his judgment. It is the result of ten years' labour. . . . . The volume is so full of interesting matter that we hardly know where to begin our extracts or more detailed notices."—GENTLEMAN'S MAGAZINE, November, 1857.

HOLLOWAY'S (W., *of Rye*) History and Antiquities of the Ancient Port and Town of Rye, in Sussex, compiled from the Original Documents. Thick 8vo (*only* 200 *printed*) *cloth.* £1. 1s

HOLLOWAY'S (W.) History of Romney Marsh, in Kent, from the time of the Romans to 1833, with a Dissertation on the Original Site of the Ancient Anderida. 8vo, *with maps and plates*, *cloth.* 12s

HARTLIB.—A Biographical Memoir of Samuel Hartlib, Milton's familiar Friend, with Bibliographical Notices of Works published by him, and a reprint of his Pamphlet entitled "An Invention of Engines of Motion." By HENRY DIRCKS, C.E., author of the Life of the Marquis of Worcester, &c. Post 8vo, *cloth.* 3s 6d

To have been the familiar friend of Milton, the correspondent of Boyle and Evelyn, Pepys and Wren, and to have had the honour of suggesting to Milton his tract on Education and of receiving his high praise in his own lofty and sonorous language, is honour enough to make Hartlib's name and life worthy of a special work.

HAWKINS (J. S., *F.S.A.*) History of the Origin and Establishment of Gothic Architecture, and an Inquiry into the mode of Painting upon and Staining Glass, as practised in the Ecclesiastical Structures of the Middle Ages. Royal 8vo, 1813, 11 *plates, bds.* 4s (original price 12s)

HERBERT'S (The Hon. Algernon) *Cyclops Christianus*, or an Argument to disprove the supposed Antiquity of the Stonehenge and other Megalithic Erections in England and Brittany. 8vo, *cloth.* 4s *(original price 6s)*

HORNE (R. H., *Author of* "*Orion*," *etc.*) Ballad Romances. 12mo, pp. 248, *cloth.* 3s (original price 6s 6d)

Containing the Noble Heart, a Bohemian Legend ; the Monk of Swinesbead Abbey, a Ballad Chronicle of the Death of King John ; The Three Knights of Camelott, a Fairy Tale ; The Ballad of Delora, or the Passion of Andrea Como : Bedd Gelert, a Welsh Legend ; Ben Capstan, a Ballad of the Night Watch ; the Elfe of the Woodlands, a Child's Story.

"Pure fancy of the most abundant and picturesque description. Mr. Horne should write us more fairy tales ; we know none to equal him since the days of Drayton and Herrick.—EXAMINER.

"The opening poem in this volume is a fine one, it is entitled the 'Noble Heart,' and not only in title but in treatment well imitates the style of Beaumont and Fletcher."—ATHENÆUM.

HUME (Rev. A., LL.D., F.S.A., &c., *of Liverpool*) Ancient Meols, or some Account of the Antiquities found near Dove Point, on the Sea Coast of Cheshire, including a Comparison of them with Relics of the same kind respectively procured elsewhere. 8vo, *full of engravings, cloth.* £1. 1s

HUNTER (Rev. Joseph, *F.S.A.*) The Pilgrim Fathers—Collections concerning the Church or Congregation of Protestant Separatists formed at Scrooby, in North Nottinghamshire, in the time of James I., the Founders of New Plymouth, the Parent Colony of New England. 8vo, *with View of the Archiepiscopal Palace at Scrooby inserted, cloth.* 8s

This work contains some very important particulars of these personages, and their connections previously to their leaving England and Holland, which were entirely unknown to former writers, and have only recently been discovered through the indefatigable exertions of the author. Prefixed to the volume are some beautiful Prefatory Stanzas by Richard Monckton Milnes, Esq., M.P. (now Lord Houghton.)

HUSSEY (Rev. Arthur) Notes on the Churches in the Counties of Kent, Sussex, and Surrey mentioned in Domesday Book, and those of more recent date ; with some Account of the Sepulchral Memorials and other Antiquities. Thick 8vo, *fine plates, cloth.* 12s (*original price* 18s)

HUTTON (W., *of Derby*) Description of Blackpool, in Lancashire. 8vo, *3rd edition.* 1s 6d

IRVING (Joseph, *of Dumbarton*) History of Dumbartonshire, with Genealogical Notices of the Principal Families in the County ; the whole based on Authentic Records, Public and Private. Thick 4to, pp. 636, *maps, plates, and portraits, cloth.* £3.

JOHNES (Arthur J.) Philological Proofs of the Original Unity and Recent Origin of the Human Race, derived from a Comparison of the Languages of Europe, Asia, Africa, and America. 8vo, *cloth.* 6s (*original price* 12s 6d)

Printed at the suggestion of Dr. Prichard, to whose works it will be found a useful supplement.

JONES' (Morris Charles) Valle Crucis Abbey, its Origin and Foundation Charter. 8vo. 1s

JORDAN (Rev. J., *the Vicar*) Parochial History of Enstone, in the County of Oxford. Post 8vo, *a closely printed volume of nearly 500 pages, cloth.* 7s

JUNIUS—The Authorship of the Letters of Junius Elucidated, including a Biographical Memoir of Lieut.-Col. Barré, M.P. By John Britton, F.S.A., &c. Royal 8vo, *with Portraits of Lord Shelburne, John Dunning, and Barré, from Sir Joshua Reynolds's picture, cloth.* 6s—LARGE PAPER, in 4to, *cloth.* 9s

An exceedingly interesting book, giving many particulars of the American War and the state of parties during that period.

KELKE (Rev. W. Hastings) Notices of Sepulchral Monuments in English Churches from the Norman Conquest to the Nineteenth Century. 8vo, *many woodcuts.* 2s (*original price* 3s 6d)

KELLY (William, *of Leicester*) Notices illustrative of the Drama, and other Popular Amusements, chiefly in the Sixteenth and Seventeenth Centuries, incidentally illustrating Shakespeare and his Contemporaries, Extracted from the Chamberlain's Accounts and other Manuscripts of the Borough of Leicester, with an Introduction and Notes by William Kelly. Post 8vo, *plates, cloth.* 9s

—— Large Paper Copies, in 4to, only 25 printed (*only 4 copies remain*), *half morocco, Roxburghe style.* £1. 5s

KENRICK (Rev. John) Roman Sepulchral Inscriptions, their Relation to Archæology, Language, and Religion. Post 8vo, *cloth.* 3s 6d

KING (Richard John) The Forest of Dartmoor and its Borders in Devonshire, an Historical Sketch. Foolscap 8vo, *cloth.* 3s

KERRY (Rev. Chas.) History and Antiquities of the Hundred of Bray, in Berkshire. 8vo, *cloth.* 7s 6d

——— The same, *with* 10 *folding pedigrees, cloth.* 10s 6d

KNOCKER'S (Edw., *Town Clerk of Dover*) Account of the Grand Court of Shepway, holden on Bredonstone Hill, at Dover, for the Installation of Viscount Palmerston as Constable of Dover and Warden of the Cinque Ports, in 1861. With Notes on the Origin and Antiquity of the Cinque Ports, Two Ancient Towns, and their Members. Foolscap 4to, *engravings, elegantly printed by Whittingham, cloth.* 15s

KYNANCE COVE ; or, The Cornish Smugglers, a Tale of the Last Century. By W. B. FORFAR, *Author of* " *Pentowan,*" " *Pengersick Castle,*" *etc., etc.* Fcap. 8vo, *boards.* 2s

LAMBARDE'S (William, *Lawyer and Antiquary*) A Perambulation of Kent, containing the Description, Hystorie, and Customs of that Shire. Written in 1576. Thick 8vo, *cloth.* 5s (*original price* 12s)
The first county history published, and one of the most amusing and *naïve* old books that can be imagined.

LANARKSHIRE—The Upper Ward of Lanarkshire Described and Delineated. The Archæological and Historical Section by G. VERE IRVING, F.S.A., Scot ; the Statistical and Topographical Section by ALEX. MURRAY. 3 vols, 8vo, *many engravings, cloth.* £3. 3s.

——— LARGE PAPER, 3 vols, 4to, *half morocco.* £5. 5s

LANGLEY'S (L.) Introduction to Anglo-Saxon Reading ; comprising Ælfric's Homily on the Birthday of St. Gregory, with a Copious Glossary, &c. 12mo, *cloth.* 2s 6d
Ælfric's Homily is remarkable for beauty of composition, and interesting as setting forth Augustine's mission to the "Land of the Angles."

LAPPENBERG'S (Dr. J. M.) History of England under the Norman Kings, with an Epitome of the Early History of Normandy. Translated, with Additions, by BENJ. THORPE. 8vo, *cloth.* 15s

LATHBURY (Rev. Thomas) History of the Nonjurors : their Controversies and Writings, with Remarks on some of the Rubrics in the Book of Common Prayer. Thick 8vo, *cloth.* 6s (*original price* 14s)

LATHBURY'S (Rev. T.) History of the Convocation of the Church of England from the Earliest Period to the Year 1742. *Second edition, with considerable additions.* Thick 8vo, *cloth.* 5s (*original price* 12s)

LAWRENCE (Sir James, *Knight of Malta*) On the Nobility of the British Gentry, or the Political Ranks and Dignities of the British Empire compared with those on the Continent. Post 8vo. 1s 6d
Useful for foreigners in Great Britain, and to Britons abroad, particularly of those who desire to be presented at Foreign Courts, to accept Foreign Military Service, to be invested with Foreign Titles, to be admitted into foreign orders, to purchase Foreign Property, or to intermarry with Foreigners.

LETTERS of the KINGS of ENGLAND—Now first collected from the Originals in Royal Archives, and from other Authentic Sources, Private as well as Public. Edited, with Historical Introduction and Notes, by J. O. HALLIWELL. *Two handsome volumes, post 8vo, with portraits of Henry VIII. and Charles I., cloth.* 8s (*original price* £1. 1s)

These volumes form a good companion to Ellis's Original Letters. The collection comprises, for the first time, the love-letters of Henry VIII. to Anne Boleyn, in a complete form, which may be regarded, perhaps, as the most singular documents of the kind that have descended to our times; the series of letters of Edward VI. will be found very interesting specimens of composition; some of the letters of James I., hitherto unpublished, throw light on the Murder of Overbury, and prove beyond a doubt the King was implicated in it in some extraordinary and unpleasant way; but his Letters to the Duke of Buchingham are of the most singular nature; only imagine a letter from a Sovereign to his Prime Minister commencing thus: "My own sweet and dear child, blessing, blessing, blessing on thy heart-roots and all thine." Prince Charles and the Duke of Buckingham's Journey into Spain has never been before so fully illustrated as it is by the documents given in this work, which also includes the very curious letters from the Duke and Duchess of Buckingham to James I.

LIBER ALBUS: the White Book of the City of London. Compiled A.D. 1419, by JOHN CARPENTER, *Common Clerk;* RICHARD WHITTINGTON, *Mayor.* Translated from the Original Latin and Anglo-Norman, by H. T. Riley, M.A. 4to, pp. 672 (*original price* 18s), *the few remaining copies offered, in cloth,* at 9s—*Half morocco (Roxburghe style),* 10s 6d—*Whole bound in vellum, carmine edges,* 12s—*Whole morocco, carmine edges,* 13s 6d

Extensively devoted to details which must of necessity interest those who care to know something more about their forefathers than the mere fact that they have existed. Many of them—until recently consigned to oblivion ever since the passing away of the remote generations to which they belonged—intimately connected with the social condition, usages, and manners of the people who—uncouth, unlearned, ill-housed, ill-fed, and comfortless though they were, still formed England's most important, most wealthy, and most influential community throughout the chequered and troublous times of the 13th and 14th centuries. During this period, in fact, there is hardly a phase or feature of English national life upon which, in a greater or less degree, from these pages of the "Liber Albus," some light is not reflected.

LIBRARY OF OLD AUTHORS.

Elegantly and uniformly printed in foolscap 8vo, in cloth. Of some there are LARGE PAPER *copies for the connoisseur of choice books.*

THE Vision and Creed of PIERS PLOUGHMAN. Edited by THOMAS WRIGHT; a new edition, revised, with additions to the Notes and Glossary. 2 vols. 10s 1856

"The Vision of Piers Ploughman' is one of the most precious and interesting monuments of the English Language and Literature, and also of the social and political condition of the country during the fourteenth century. Its author is not certainly known, but its time of composition can, by internal evidence, be fixed at about the year 1362 On this and on all matters bearing upon the origin and object of the poem, Mr. Wright's historical introduction gives ample information. . . . . In the thirteen years that have passed since the first edition of the present text was published by the late Mr. Pickering, our old literature and history has been more studied, and we trust that a large circle of readers will be prepared to welcome this cheaper and carefully revised reprint."—*Literary Gazette.*

THE Dramatic and Poetical Works of JOHN MARSTON. Now first
collected, and edited by J. O. HALLIWELL, F.R.S., &c.   3 vols.
15s   1856

"The edition deserves well of the public; it is carefully printed, and the
annotations, although neither numerous nor extensive, supply ample explanations upon a variety of interesting points. If Mr. Halliwell had done no more
than collect these plays, he would have conferred a boon upon all lovers of
our old dramatic poetry."—*Literary Gazette.*

REMARKABLE Providences of the Earlier Days of American Co-
lonisation. By INCREASE MATHER, of *Boston*, N.E. With Introductory Preface by George Offor. *Portrait.* 5s   1856

A very singular collection of remarkable sea deliverances, accidents, remarkable phenomena, witchcraft, apparitions, &c., &c., connected with inhabitants
of New England, &c., &c. A very amusing volume, conveying a faithful portrait of the state of society, when the doctrine of a peculiar providence and
personal intercourse between this world and that which is unseen was fully
believed.

THE Table Talk of JOHN SELDEN. With a Biographical Preface and
Notes by S. W. SINGER. *Third edition, portrait.* 5s   1860

——— LARGE PAPER. Post 8vo, *cloth.* 7s 6d   1860

"Nothing can be more interesting than this little book, containing a lively
picture of the opinions and conversations of one of the most eminent scholars
and most distinguished patriots England has produced. There are few volumes
of its size so pregnant with sense, combined with the most profound earning:
it is impossible to open it without finding some important fact or discussion,
something practically useful and applicable to the business of life. Coleridge
says, 'There is more weighty bullion sense in this book than I ever found in
the same number of pages in any uninspired writer.' . . . . . Its merits
had not escaped the notice of Dr. Johnson, though in politics opposed to much
it inculcates, for in reply to an observation of Boswell, in praise of the French
Ana, he said, 'A few of them are good, but we have one book of the kind better
than any of them—Selden's Table Talk.' "—*Mr. Singer's Preface.*

THE Poetical Works of WILLIAM DRUMMOND, of Hawthornden.
Now first published entire. Edited by W. B. TURNBULL. *Fine
portrait.* 5s   1856

"The sonnets of Drummond," says Mr. Hallam, "are polished and elegant,
free from conceit and bad taste, and in pure unblemished English."

ENCHIRIDION, containing Institutions—Divine, Contemplative
Practical, Moral, Ethical, Œconomical, and Political. By
FRANCIS QUARLES. *Portrait.* 3s   1856

"Had this little book been written at Athens or Rome, its author would have
been classed with the wise men of his country."—*Headley.*

THE Works in Prose and Verse of Sir THOMAS OVERBURY. Now
first collected. Edited, with Life and Notes, by E. F. RIMBAULT.
Portrait after Pass. 5s   1856

HYMNS and Songs of the Church. By GEORGE WITHER. Edited,
with Introduction, by EDWARD FARR. Also the Musical Notes,
composed by Orlando Gibbons. *With portrait after Hole.* 5s
                                                          1856

"Mr. Farr has added a very interesting biographical introduction, and we hope
to find that the public will put their seal of approbation to the present edition
of an author who may fairly take his place on the same shelf with George Herbert."—*Gent's Mag., Oct., 1856.*

HALLELUJAH; or, Britain's Second Remembrancer, in Praiseful and Penitential Hymns, Spiritual Songs, and Moral Odes. By GEORGE WITHER. With Introduction by EDWARD FARR. *Portrait.* 6s   1857

Hitherto this interesting volume has only been known to the public by extracts in various publications. So few copies of the original are known to exist, that the copy from which this reprint has been taken cost twenty-one guineas.

MISCELLANIES. By JOHN AUBREY, F.R.S., the *Wiltshire Antiquary.* FOURTH EDITION. With some Additions and an Index. *Portrait and cuts.* 4s   1857

CONTENTS:—Day Fatality, Fatalities of Families and Places, Portents, Omens, Dreams, Apparitions, Voices, Impulses, Knockings, Invisible Blows, Prophecies, Miracles, Magic, Transportation by an Invisible Power, Visions in a Crystal, Converse with Angels, Corpse Candles, Oracles, Ectasy, Second Sight, &c. : with an Appendix, containing his Introduction to the Survey of North Wiltshire.

THE Iliads of HOMER, Prince of Poets, never before in any language truly translated, with a Comment on some of his chief Places. Done according to the Greek by GEORGE CHAPMAN, with Introduction and Notes by the Rev. RICHARD HOOPER. 2 vols, sq. fcap. 8vo. SECOND AND REVISED EDITION, *with portrait of Chapman, and frontispiece.* 12s   1865

"The translation of Homer, published by George Chapman, is one of the greatest treasures the English language can boast."—*Godwin.*

"With Chapman, Pope had frequently consultations, and perhaps never translated any passage till he read his version."—*Dr. Johnson.*

"He covers his defects with a daring, fiery spirit, that animates his translation, which is something like what one might imagine Homer himself to have writ before he arrived at years of discretion."—*Pope.*

"Chapman's translation, with all its defects, is often exceedingly Homeric, which Pope himself seldom obtained."—*Hallam.*

"Chapman writes and feels as a Poet—as Homer might have written had he lived in England in the reign of Queen Elizabeth."—*Coleridge.*

"I have just finished Chapman's Homer. Did you ever read it?—it has the most continuous power of interesting you all along. . . . The earnestness and passion which he has put into every part of these poems would be incredible to a reader of mere modern translation."—*Charles Lamb.*

HOMER'S ODYSSEY. Translated according to the Greek by GEORGE CHAPMAN. With Introduction and Notes by REV. RICHARD HOOPER. 2 vols, square fcp. 8vo, *with facsimile of the rare original frontispiece.* 12s   1857

HOMER'S Battle of the Frogs and Mice ; HESIOD'S Works and Days ; MUSÆUS'S Hero and Leander ; JUVENAL'S Fifth Satire. Translated by GEORGE CHAPMAN. Edited by Rev. RICHARD HOOPER. Square fcp. 8vo, *frontispiece after Pass.* 6s 1858

"The editor of these five rare volumes has done an incalculable service to English Literature by taking George Chapman's folios out of the dust of time-honoured libraries, by collating them with loving care and patience, and, through the agency of his enterprising publisher, bringing Chapman entire and complete within the reach of those who can best appreciate and least afford to purchase the early editions."—*Athenæum.*

POETICAL Works of Robert Southwell, Canon of Loretto, now first completely edited by W. B. Turnbull. 4s. 1856

"His piety is simple and sincere—a spirit of unaffected gentleness and kindliness pervades his poems—and he is equally distinguished by weight of thought and sweetness of expression."—*Saturday Review.*

THE Dramatic Works of John Webster. Edited, with Notes, etc., by William Hazlitt. 4 vols. £1. 1857

———— Large paper, 4 vols, post 8vo, *cloth.* £1. 10s

This is the most complete edition, containing two more plays than in Dyce's edition.

THE Dramatic Works of John Lilly (the Euphuist). Now first collected, with Life and Notes by F. W. Fairholt. 2 vols. 10s. 1858

———— Large paper, 2 vols, post 8vo, *cloth.* 15s

THE Poetical Works of Richard Crashaw, Author of "Steps to the Temple," "Sacred Poems, with other Delights of the Muses," and "Poemata," now first collected. Edited by W. B. Turnbull. 5s. 1858

"He seems to have resembled Herbert in the turn of mind, but possessed more fancy and genius."—Ellis.

LA MORT d'ARTHUR. The History of King Arthur and the Knights of the Round Table. Compiled by Sir Thomas Maloby, Knight. Edited from the Edition of 1634, with Introduction and Notes, by Thomas Wright, M.A., F.S.A. 3 vols, second and revised edition. 15s. 1866

———— Large paper, 3 vols, post 8vo, *cloth.* £1. 2s 6d

ANECDOTES and Characters of Books and Men. Collected from the Conversation of Mr. Pope and other eminent Persons of his Time. By the Rev. Joseph Spence. With Notes, Life, etc., by S. W. Singer. The second edition, *portrait.* 6s. 1858

———— Large paper, post 8vo, *cloth.* 7s 6d 1858

"The 'Anecdotes' of kind-hearted Mr. Spence, the friend of Pope, is one of the best books of *ana* in the English language."—*Critic.*

Dr. COTTON MATHER'S Wonders of the Invisible World, being an account of the Trials of several Witches lately executed in New England, and of the several remarkable curiosities therein occurring. To which are added Dr. Increase Mather's Further Account of the Tryals, and Cases of Conscience concerning Witchcrafts, and Evil Spirits Personating Men. *Reprinted from the rare original editions of* 1693, with an Introductory Preface. *Portrait.* 5s. 1862

THE Dramatic and Poetical Works of Thomas Sackville, Lord Buckhurst, and Earl of Dorset. With Introduction and Life by the Hon. and Rev. R. W. Sackville West. *Fine portrait from a picture at Buckhurst, now first engraved.* 4s. 1859

REMAINS of the Early Popular Poetry of England, collected and edited by W. Carew Hazlitt. 4 vols, *with many curious woodcut facsimiles.* £1. 1864—6

———— Large paper, 4 vols, post 8vo, *cloth.* £1. 10s

LUCASTA.—The Poems of RICHARD LOVELACE, now first edited
and the Text carefully revised, with Life and Notes by W.
CAREW HAZLITT, *with 4 plates.* 5s. 1864

—————— LARGE PAPER. Post 8vo, *cloth.* 7s 6d

THE WHOLE OF THE WORKS OF ROGER ASCHAM, now first collected
and revised, with Life of the Author. By the Rev. Dr. GILES,
formerly Fellow of C. C. C., Oxford. 4 vols. £1. 1866

—————— LARGE PAPER, 4 vols, post 8vo, *cloth.* £1. 10s.

Ascham is a great name in our national literature. He was one of the first
founders of a true English style in prose composition, and of the most respectable and useful of our scholars.—*Retrospective Review.*

LONG (Henry Lawes) On the March of Hannibal from the Rhone
to the Alps. 8vo, *map.* 2s 6d

LOWER'S (Mark Antony, *M.A., F.S.A.*) Patronymica Britannica, a
Dictionary of Family Names. Royal 8vo, 500 *pages, with illustrations, cloth.* £1. 5s

This work is the result of a study of British Family Names, extending over
more than twenty years. The favourable reception which the Author's
"English Surnames" obtained in the sale of Three Editions, and the many
hundreds of communications to which that work gave rise, have convinced
him that the subject is one in which considerable interest is felt. He has
therefore been induced to devote a large amount of attention to the origin,
meaning, and history of our family designations; a subject which, when investigated in the light of ancient records and of modern philology, proves highly
illustrative of many habits and customs of our ancestors, and forms a very
curious branch of Archaeology.—*Preface.*

LOWER'S (M. A.) Curiosities of Heraldry, with Illustrations from
Old English Writers. *With illuminated Title-page, and numerous engravings from designs by the Author.* 8vo, *cloth.* 14s

"The present volume is truly a worthy sequel (to the 'SURNAMES') in the
same curious and antiquarian line, blending with remarkable facts and intelligence, such a fund of anecdote and illustration, that the reader is almost surprised to find that he has learned so much while he appeared to be pursuing
mere amusement. The text is so pleasing that we scarcely dream of its sterling value; and it seems as if, in unison with the woodcuts, which so cleverly
explain its points and adorn its various topics, the whole design were intended
for a relaxation from study, rather than an ample exposition of an extraordinary
and universal custom, which produced the most important effect upon the
minds and habits of mankind."—*Literary Gazette.*

"Mr. Lower's work is both curious and instructive, while the manner of its
treatment is so inviting and popular, that the subject to which it refers, which
many have hitherto had too good reason to consider meagre and unprofitable,
assumes, under the hands of the writer, the novelty of fiction with the importance of historical truth."—*Athenæum.*

LOWER'S (M. A.) Contributions to Literature, Historical, Antiquarian, and Metrical. Post 8vo, *woodcuts, cloth.* 7s 6d

Contents: 1. Local Nomenclature—2. The Battle of Hastings, an Historical
Essay—3. The Lord Dacre, his mournful end, a Ballad—4. Historical and Ar-
chaeological Memoir on the Iron Works of the South of England, *with numerous
illustrations*—5. Winchelsea's Deliverance, or the Stout Abbot of Battayle, in
Three Fyttes—6. The South Downs, a Sketch, Historical, Anecdotical, and
Descriptive—7. On the Yew Trees in Churchyards—8. A Lyttel Geste of a
Greate Eele, a pleasaunt Ballad—9. A Discourse of Genealogy—10. An Anti-
quarian Pilgrimage in Normandy, with woodcuts—11. Miscellanea, &c., &c.

LOWER'S (M. A.) Chronicle of Battel Abbey, in Sussex, originally compiled in Latin by a Monk of the Establishment, and now first translated, with Notes and an Abstract of the Subsequent History of the Abbey. 8vo, *with illustrations, cloth.* 9s
This volume, among other matters of local and general interest, embraces —New Facts relative to the Norman Invasion—The Foundation of the Monastery—The Names and Rentals of the Original Townsmen of Battel—Memoirs of several Abbots, and Notices of their Disputes with the Bishops of Chichester, respecting Jurisdiction—The Abbey's Possessions—A Speech of Thomas à Becket, then Chancellor of England, in favour of Abbot Walter de Luci—Several Miracles—Anecdotes of the Norman Kings—and an Historical Sketch of the Abbey, from 1176 to the present time by the Translator.

LOWER'S (M. A.) Memorials of the Town of Seaford, Sussex. 8vo, *plates.* 3s 6d

LOWER'S (M. A.) Bodiam (in Sussex), and its Lords. 8vo, *engravings.* 1s

LOWER'S (M. A.) Worthies of Sussex, Biographical Sketches of the most eminent Natives or Inhabitants of the County, from the Earliest Period to the Present Time, with Incidental Notices illustrative of Sussex History. Royal 4to, *many engravings, cloth.* £1. 16s

LOWER'S (M. A.) Sussex Martyrs, their Examinations and Cruel Burnings in the Time of Queen Mary, comprising the interesting Personal Narrative of Richard Woodman, extracted from "Foxe's Monuments." With Notes. 12mo, *sewed.* 1s

LOWER'S (M. A.) The Stranger at Rouen, a Guide for Englishmen. 12mo, *plates.* 1s

LUKIS (Rev. W. C.) Account of Church Bells, with some Notices of Wiltshire Bells and Bell-Founders, containing a copious List of Founders, a comparative Scale of Tenor Bells and Inscriptions from nearly 500 Parishes in various parts of the Kingdom. 8vo, 13 *plates, cloth.* 3s 6d (*original price* 6s)

MADDEN (Fred. W., *of the Medal Room, British Museum*) Hand-Book to Roman Coins. Fcap. 8vo, *plates of rare examples, cloth.* 5s
A very useful and trustworthy guide to Roman Coins.

MANTELL (Dr. Gideon A.) Day's Ramble in and about the Ancient Town of Lewes, Sussex. 12mo, *engravings, cloth.* 2s

MARTIN MAR-PRELATE CONTROVERSY.

AN EPISTLE to the Terrible Priests of the Convocation House. By MARTIN MAR-PRELATE. 1588. With Introduction and Notes by J. Petherham. Post 8vo. 2s

COOPER (*Bishop of Winchester*) An Admonition to the People of England against Martin Mar-Prelate, 1589, with Introduction. Post 8vo, pp. 216. 3s 6d

PAP with a Hatchet, being a Reply to Martin Mar-Prelate, 1589, with Introduction and Notes. Post 8vo. 2s

HAY any Worke for Cooper? Being a Reply to the Admonition to the People of England. By Martin Mar-Prelate, 1589, with Introduction and Notes. Post 8vo. 2s 6d

AN ALMOND for a Parrot, being a Reply to Martin Mar-Prelate, 1589, with Introduction. Post 8vo. 2s 6d

PLAINE PERCEVALL the Peace-Maker of England, being a Reply to Martin Mar-Prelate, with Introduction. Post 8vo. 2s

———

MATON'S (Dr. W. G.) Natural History of Wiltshire, as comprehended within Ten Miles round Salisbury. 8vo. *Privately printed.* 2s

MAYNARD'S (James) Parish of Waltham Abbey, in Essex, its History and Antiquities. Post 8vo, *engravings, cloth.* 2s 6d

MENZIES (Mrs. Louisa J.) Legendary Tales of the Ancient Britons, rehearsed from the Early Chronicles. Fcap. 8vo, *cloth.* 3s

Contents : 1. Esyllt and Sabrina—2. Lear and his three Daughters—3. Cynedda and Morgan—4. The Brothers Beli and Bran—5. Ellidure the Compassionate—6. Alban of Verulam—7. Vortigern—8. Cadwallon and the Final Struggle of the Britons.

MICHAEL ANGELO considered as a Philosophic Poet, with translations by JOHN EDWARD TAYLOR. Post 8vo. SECOND EDITION. *Cloth.* 2s 6d (*original price* 5s)

MILTON'S Early Reading, and the *prima stamina* of his "Paradise Lost," together with Extracts from a Poet of the XVIth Century (*Joshua Sylvester*). By CHARLES DUNSTER, *M.A.* 12mo, *cloth.* 2s 6d (*original price* 5s)

MILTON ; a Sheaf of Gleanings after his Biographers and Annotators. By the Rev. JOSEPH HUNTER. Post 8vo. 2s 6d

MOORE (Thomas) Notes from the Letters of Thomas Moore to his Music Publisher, James Power (*the publication of which was suppressed in London*), with an Introduction by Thomas Crofton Croker, *F.S.A.* Post 8vo, *cloth.* 3s 6d

The impressions on the mind of a reader of these Letters of Moore in Lord Lord Russell's edition will be not only incomplete, but erroneous, without the information to be derived from this very interesting volume.

MORLAND.—Account of the Life, Writings, and Inventions of Sir Samuel Morland, Master of Mechanics to Charles II. By J. O. HALLIWELL. 8vo, *sewed.* 1s

MUNFORD (Rev. Geo., *Vicar of East Winch, Norfolk*) Analysis of Domesday Book for the County of Norfolk. 8vo, *with pedigrees and arms, cloth.* 10s 6d

"Many extracts have been made at various times for the illustration of local descriptions, from the great national (but almost unintelligible) record known as Domesday Book : but Mr. Munford has done more in the case of his own county, for he supplies a complete epitome of the part of the survey relating to Norfolk, giving not only the topographical and statistical facts, but also a great deal that is instructive as to the manners and condition of the people, the state of the churches and other public edifices, the mode of cultivation and land tenure, together with a variety of points of interest to the ecclesiologist and antiquary."—BURY POST.

NARES' (Archdeacon) A Glossary, or Collection of Words, Phrases, Customs, Proverbs, &c., illustrating the Works of English Authors, particularly Shakespeare and his Contemporaries. A New Edition, with considerable Additions, both of Words and Examples. By JAMES O. HALLIWELL, *F.R.S.*, and THOMAS WRIGHT, *M.A., F.S.A.* 2 thick vols, 8vo, *cloth.* £1. 1s

The Glossary of Archdeacon Nares is by far the best and most useful work we possess for explaining and illustrating the obsolete language and the customs and manners of the 16th and 17th Centuries, and it is quite indispensable for the readers of the literature of the Elizabethan period. The additional words and examples are distinguished from those in the original text by a † prefixed to each. The work contains between FIVE and SIX THOUSAND additional examples, the result of original research, not merely supplementary to Nares, but to all other compilations of the kind.

NASH'S (D. W., *Member of the Royal Society of Literature*) Taliesin, or, the Bards and Druids of Britain. A Translation of the Remains of the earliest Welsh Bards, and an examination of the Bardic Mysteries. 8vo, *cloth.* 14s

NASH'S (D. W.) The Pharaoh of the Exodus. An Examination of the Modern Systems of Egyptian Chronology. 8vo, *with frontispiece of the Egyptian Calendar, from the ceiling of the Ramasseum, at Thebes, cloth.* 12s

NAVAL ARCHITECTURE, Elements of Naval Architecture, being a Translation of the Third Part of Clairbois's "Traite Elementaire de la Construction des Vaisseaux." By J. N. STRANGE, Commander, R.N. 8vo, *with five large folding plates, cloth.* 5s

———— Lectures on Naval Architecture, being the Substance of those delivered at the United Service Institution. By E. GARDINER FISHBOURNE, Commander, R. N. 8vo, *plates, cloth.* 5s 6d

Both these works are published in illustration of the "Wave System."

NETHERCLIFF'S (F. G.) Hand-Book to Autographs, being a Ready Guide to the Handwriting of Distinguished Men and Women of Every Nation, designed for the Use of Literary Men, Autograph Collectors, and others. Containing 700 Specimens, with a Biographical Index by R. Sims, of the British Museum. 8vo, *cloth extra, gilt edges.* 10s 6d (original price 15s)

———— The Same. PRINTED ONLY ON ONE SIDE. 8vo, *cloth extra.* £1. 1s

The specimens contain two or three lines each besides the signature, so that to the historian such a work will reccomend itself as enabling him to test the genuineness of the document he consults, whilst the judgment of the autograph collector may be similarly assisted, and his pecuniary resources economized by a judicious use of the Manual. To the bookworm, whose name is Legion, we would merely observe, that daily experience teaches us the great value and interest attached to books containing Marginal Notes and Memoranda, when traced to be from the pens of eminent persons.

NEWTON (William) A Display of Heraldry. 8vo, *many hundred engravings of Shields, illustrating the Arms of English Families, cloth.* 14s

NEWTON (William) London in the Olden Time, being a Topographical and Historical Memoir of London, Westminster and Southwark ; accompanying a Pictorial Map of the City and Suburbs, as they existed in the reign of Henry VIII., before the Dissolution of the Monasteries ; compiled from Authentic Documents. Folio, *with the coloured map, 4 feet 6 inches by 3 feet 3 inches, mounted on linen, and folded into the volume, leather back, cloth sides,* £1. 1s (*original price* £1. 11s 6d)

NORFOLK'S (E. E.) Gleanings in Graveyards : a Collection of Curious Epitaphs. *Third Edition, revised and enlarged,* fcap. 8vo, *cloth.* 3s

NUMISMATIC Chronicle and Journal of the Numismatic Society. NEW SERIES, Edited by W. S. W. VAUX, JOHN EVANS, and F. W. MADDEN. Nos. 1 to 24, Published Quarterly. 5s *per Number.*

This is the only repertory of Numismatic intelligence ever published in England. It contains papers on coins and medals, of all ages and countries, by the first Numismatists of the day, both English and Foreign.

Odd parts may be had to complete a few of this and the former series in 20 vols.

OLD BALLADS.—Catalogue of a unique Collection of 400 Ancient English Broadside Ballads, printed entirely in the 𝔅lack letter, lately on sale by J. RUSSELL SMITH. With Notes of their Tunes, and Imprints. Post 8vo, *a handsome volume, printed by Whittingham, in the old style, half bound.* 5s

———— A Copy on thick paper, *without the prices to each, and a different title-page, only* 10 *copies so printed.* 10s 6d

PARISH'S (Sir Woodbine, *many years Charge d'Affairs at Buenos Ayres*) Buenos Ayres, and the Provinces of the Rio de la Plata, from their Discovery and Conquest by the Spaniards to the Establishment of their Political Independence ; with some Account of their Present State, Appendix of Historical Documents, Natural History, &c. Thick 8vo, *Second Edition, plates and woodcuts, also a valuable map by Arrowsmith, cloth.* 10s 6d (original price 14s)

" Among the contributions to the geography of the South American Continent, the work of our Vice-President, Sir Woodbine Parish, holds a very important place. Professing to be a second edition of a former book, it is, in reality, almost a new work, from the great quantity of fresh matter it contains on the geography, statistics, natural history, and geology of this portion of the world." —*President of the Royal Geographical Society's Address.*

PATERSON'S (Jas.) Histories of the Counties of Ayr and Wigton. Post 8vo, vol 1. KYLE, in two parts, *cloth.* £1. 1s

———— Vol II, CARRICK, post 8vo, *cloth.* 12s

Particularly full of information about the Family History of the district.

PEDLER (E. H., *of Liskeard*) The Anglo-Saxon Episcopate of Cornwall, with some Account of the Bishops of Crediton. 8vo, *cloth.* 3s 6d (original price 7s 6d)

PETTIGREW (Thos. Jos.) On Superstitions connected with the History and Practice of Medicine and Surgery. 8vo, *frontispiece, cloth.* 4s (*original price 8s*)

PETTIGREW (Thos. Jos.) Inquiries into the Particulars connected with Death of Amy Robsart (Lady Dudley), at Cumnor Place, Berks, Sept. 8, 1560; being a refutation of the Calumnies charged against Sir Robert Dudley, Anthony Forster, and others. 8vo, 2s

PILGRIMAGES to St. Mary of Walsingham and St. Thomas of Canterbury. By DESIDERIUS ERASMUS. Newly Translated. With the Colloquy of Rash Vows, by the same Author. and his Characters of Archbishop Warham and Dean Colet, with Notes by J. GOUGH NICHOLS. Post 8vo, *engravings, cloth.* 3s 6d (*original price 6s*)

PIOZZI, Love Letters of Mrs. Piozzi (formerly Mrs. Thrale, the friend of Dr. Johnson), written when she was eighty, to the handsome actor, William Augustus Conway, aged Twenty-seven. 8vo, *sewed.* 2s

"—— written at three, four, and five o'clock (in the morning) by an octogenary pen ; a heart (as Mrs. Lee says) twenty-six years old, and as H. L. P. feels it to be, *all your own.*"—*Letter V., 3rd Feb.*, 1820.

"This is one of the most extraordinary collections of love epistles we have chanced to meet with, and the well-known literary reputation of the lady—the Mrs. Thrale, of Dr. Johnson and Miss Burney celebrity—considerably enhances their interest. The letters themselves it is not easy to characterise : nor shall we venture to decide whether they more bespeak the drivelling of dotage, or the folly of love ; in either case they present human nature to us under a new aspect, and furnish one of those riddles which nothing yet dreamt of in our philosophy can satisfactorily solve."—*Polytechnic Review.*

POPE.—Facts and Conjectures on the Descent and Family Connections of Pope, the Poet. By the REV. JOSEPH HUNTER. Post 8vo. 2s

POPE.—Additional Facts concerning the Maternal Ancestry of Pope, in a Letter to Mr. Hunter. BY ROBERT DAVIES, F.S.A. Post 8vo. 2s

POPULAR Treatises on Science, written during the Middle Ages, in Anglo-Saxon, Anglo-Norman, and English, edited by Thomas Wright, M.A. 8vo, cloth. 8s

CONTENTS :—An Anglo-Saxon Treatise on Astronomy of the Tenth Century, now first published from a MS. in the British Museum, with a translation ; Livre des Creatures, by Phillippe de Thaun, now first printed, with a translation (extremely valuable to Philologists, as being the earliest specimens of Anglo-Norman remaining, and explanatory of all the symbolical signs in early sculpture and painting) ; the Bestiary of Phillippe de Thaun, with a translation ; Fragments on Popular Science from the Early English Metrical Lives of the Saints (the earliest piece of the kind in the English Language).

POSTE (Rev. Beale) Celtic Inscriptions on Gaulish and British Coins, intended to supply materials for the Early History of Great Britain, with a Glossary of Archaic Celtic Words, and an Atlas of Coins. 8vo, *many engravings, cloth.* 10s 6d

POSTE (Beale) Vindication of the "Celtic Inscriptions on Gaulish and British Coins." 8vo, *plates, and cuts, cloth.* 1s

POSTE (Rev. Beale, M.A.) Britannic Researches ; or, New Facts and Rectifications of Ancient British History. 8vo (pp. 448), *with engravings, cloth.* 15s

"The author of this volume may justly claim credit for considerable learning, great industry, and, above all, strong faith in the interest and importance of his subject. . . . On various points he has given us additional information, and afforded us new views, for which we are bound to thank him. The body of the book is followed by a very complete index, so as to render reference to any part of it easy : this was the more necessary, on account of the multifariousness of the topics treated, the variety of persons mentioned, and the many works quoted."—*Athenaeum,* Oct. 8, 1853.

"The Rev. Beale Poste has long been known to antiquaries as one of the best read of all those who have elucidated the earliest annals of this country. He is a practical man, has investigated for himself monuments and manuscripts, and we have in the above-named volume the fruits of many years' patient study. The objects which will occupy the attention of the reader are—1. The political position of the principal British powers *before* the Roman conquest—under the Roman dominion, and struggling unsuccessfully against the Anglo-Saxon race ; 2. The Geography of Ancient Britain ; 3. An investigation of the Ancient British Historians, Gildas and Nennius, and the more obscure British chroniclers ; 4. The ancient stone monuments of the Celtic period ; and, lastly, some curious and interesting notices of the early British Church. Mr. Poste has not touched on subjects which have received much attention from others, save in cases where he had something new to offer, and the volume must be regarded therefore, as an entirely new collection of discoveries and deductions tending to throw light on the darkest, as well as the earliest, portion of our national history."—*Atlas.*

POSTE (Rev. Beale) Britannia Antiqua, or Ancient Britain brought within the Limits of Authentic History. 8vo, pp. 386, *map, cloth.* 14s

A Sequel to the foregoing work.

PUBLICATIONS OF THE ANGLIA CHRISTIANA SOCIETY.

GIRALDUS Cambrensis, De Instructione Principum, with a Preface, Chronological Abstract and Marginal Notes (in English), by the REV. J. S. BREWER. 8vo, *boards.* 5s   1846

Now first printed from the Manuscript in the Cottonian Library, particularly illustrating the Reign of Henry II. Among our earlier chroniclers, there is not a more lively writer than Giraldus de Barri.

CHRONICON Monasterii de Bello, with a Preface, Chronological Abstract, and Marginal Notes (in English), by the Editor. 8vo, *boards.* 5s   1846

A very curious History of Battle Abbey, in Sussex, by one of the Monks. Printed from a MS. in the Cottonian Library.

LIBER ELIENSIS, ad fidem Codicum Variorum. Vol 1 (all printed), with English Preface and Notes, by the Rev. D. Stewart, of the College, Ely. 8vo, *boards.* 5s   1848

An important chronicle of the early transactions connected with the Monastery of Ely, supposed to have been compiled by Richard the Monk, between 1108 and 1131.

The above three volumes are all the Society printed. They are well worthy of being placed on the same shelf with the Camden, Caxton, Surtees, and Chetham Societies' publications. From the limited number of members of the Society, the books are little known. J. R. Smith having become the proprietor of the few remaining copies, recommends an early purchase.

PROVINCIAL DIALECTS OF ENGLAND

A DICTIONARY of Archaic and Provincial Words, Obsolete Phrases, &c., by J. O. HALLIWLLI, F.R.S., &c. 2 vols, 8vo, 1000 pp., in double columns, FIFTH EDITION, *cloth.* 15s

GLOSSARY of Provincial and Local Words Used in England. By F. GROSE, F.S.A., with which is now incorporated the Supplement. By SAMUEL PEGGE, F.S.A. Post 8vo, *cloth.* 4s 6d

BROCKETT'S (J. Trotter) Glossary of North Country Words, with their Etymology and Affinity to other Languages and Occasional Notices of Local Customs and Popular Superstitions. THIRD EDITION, corrected and enlarged by W. E. BROCKETT. 2 vols, in 1, post 8vo, *cloth.* 10s 6d (*original price 21s*)

SPECIMENS of Cornish Provincial Dialect, collected and arranged by Uncle Jan Treenodle, with some Introductory Remarks and a Glossary by an Antiquarian Friend; also a Selection of Songs and other Pieces connected with Cornwall. Post 8vo, *with a curious portrait of Dolly Pentreath, cloth.* 4s

CORNISH Dialect and Poems, viz.—

1 Treagle of Dozmary Pool, and Original Cornish Ballads.
2 Cornish Thalia: Original Comic Poems illustrative of the Dialect.
3 A Companion to the Cornish Thalia. By H. J. DANIELL.
4 Mirth for "One and all." By H. J. DANIELL.
5 Humourous Cornish Legends. By H. J. DANIELL.
6 A Budget of Cornish Poems, by various Authors.
7 Dolly Pentreath, and other Humorous Cornish Tales.
8 The Great Mine Conference, and other Pieces.
9 Rustic Poems. By GEORGE HAMLYN, the "*Dartmoor Bloomfield.*"
10 Mary Anne's Experiences: her Wedding and Trip up the Tamar. By H. J. DANIELL.
11 Mary Anne's Career, and Cousin Jack's Adventures. By H. J. DANIELL.
12 A New Budget of Cornish Poems. By H. J. DANIELL.
13 Mirth for Long Evenings. By H. J. DANIELL.
14 Bobby Poldree and his Wife Sally at the Great Exhibition tion. By H. J. DANIELL. All 12mo, *Sixpence* each.

A GLOSSARY of the Words and Phrases of Cumberland. By WILLIAM DICKINSON, F.L.S. 12mo, *cloth.* 2s

JOHN NOAKES and MARY STYLES, a Poem, exhibiting some of the most striking lingual localisms peculiar to Essex, with a Glossary. By CHARLES CLARK, Esq., of Great Totham Hall, Essex. Post 8vo, *cloth.* 2s.

NATHAN HOGG'S Letters and Poems in the Devonshire Dialect. *The fifth Edition, with additions.* Post 8vo. *Coloured wrapper.* 1s.

"These letters, which have achieved considerable popularity, evince an extensive acquaintance with the vernacular of the county and its idioms and phrases, while the continuous flow of wit and humour throughout cannot fail to operate forcibly upon the risible faculties of the reader. In the Witch story Nathan has excelled himself, and it is to be hoped we have not seen his last effort in this branch of local English literature. The superstitions of Jan Vaggis and Jan Plant are most graphically and amusingly portrayed, and the various incidents whereby the influence of the 'Evil Eye' is sought to be counteracted, are at once ludicrous and irresistible."—*Plymouth Mail.*

NATHAN HOGG'S New Series of Poems in the Devonshire Dialect, including the Witch Story of Mucksy Lane, and the Kenton Ghost. *Dedicated by Permission to his Highness Prince Louis Lucien Bonaparte.* Post 8vo, 4th *edition enlarged, coloured wrapper.* 1s

A GLOSSARY of Words used in Teesdale, in the County of Durham. Post 8vo, *cloth.* 2s 6d (*original price,* 6s)

"Contains about two thousand words . . . It is believed the first and only collection of words and phrases peculiar to this district, and we hail it therefore as a valuable contribution to the history of language and literature . . . the author has evidently brought to bear an extensive personal acquaintance with the common language."—*Darlington Times.*

POEMS of Rural Life in the Dorset Dialect. By the Rev. WILLIAM BARNES, of Came Rectory, Dorchester. *First Collection.* Fcp. 8vo, FOURTH EDITION, *cloth.* 5s.

——— Second Collection. Fcap. 8vo. SECOND EDITION, *cloth.* 5s.

——— Third Collection. Fcap. 8vo, *cloth.* 4s 6d.

"The author is a genuine poet, and it is delightful to catch the pure breath of song in verses which assert themselves only as the modest vehicle of rare words and Saxon inflections. We have no intention of setting up the Dorset patois against the more extended provincialism of Scotland, still less of comparing the Dorsetshire poet with the Scotch; yet we feel sure that these poems would have delighted the heart of Burns, that many of them are not unworthy of him, and that (at any rate) his best productions cannot express a more cordial sympathy with external nature, or a more loving interest in human joys and sorrows."—*Literary Gazette.*

GRAMMAR and Glossary of the Dorset Dialect. By the Rev. W. BARNES. 8vo. 2s 6d.

DIALECT of South Lancashire, or Tim Bobbin's Tummas and Meary, revised and Corrected, with his Rhymes, and an enlarged Glossary of Words and Phrases chiefly used by the Rural Population of the Manufacturing Districts of South Lancashire. By SAMUEL BAMFORD. 12mo, *second edition, cloth.* 3s 6d.

LEICESTERSHIRE Words, Phrases, and Proverbs. By A. B. EVANS, D.D., *Head Master of Market Bosworth Grammar School.* 12mo, *cloth.* 5s.

A GLOSSARY of the Provincialisms of the County of Sussex. By W. DURRANT COOPER, F.S.A. Post 8vo, *second edition, enlarged, cloth.* 3s 6d.

A GLOSSARY of Northamptonshire Words and Phrases, with Examples of their Colloquial Use, with illustrations from various Authors, to which are added the Customs of the County. By Miss A. E. BAKER. 2 vols, post 8vo, *cloth.* 16s (*original price* £1. 4s)

"We are under great obligations to the lady, sister to the local historian of Northamptonshire, who has occupied her time in producing this very capital Glossary of Northamptonshire provincialisms."—*Examiner.*

"The provincial dialects of England contain and preserve the elements and rudiments of our compound tongue. In Miss Baker's admirable 'Northamptonshire Glossary,' we have rather a repertory of archaisms than vulgarisms. But it is much more than a vocabulary; it preserves not only dialectical peculiarities, but odd and disappearing customs; and there is hardly a page in it which does not throw light on some obscurity in our writers, or recall old habits and practices."—*Christian Remembrancer, Quarterly Review.*

WESTMORELAND and Cumberland.—Dialogues, Poems, Songs, and Ballads, by various Writers, in the Westmoreland and Cumberland Dialects, now first collected, to which is added a Copious Glossary of Words peculiar to those Counties. Post 8vo, (pp. 408), *cloth.* 9s.

A GLOSSARY of Provincial Words in use in Wiltshire, showing their Derivation in numerous instances, from the Language of the Anglo Saxons. By JOHN YONGE AKERMAN, Esq., F.S.A. 12mo, *cloth.* 3s

THE DIALECT of Leeds and its Neighbourhood, illustrated by Conversations and Tales of Common Life, etc., to which are added a Copious Glossary, Notices of the various Antiquities, Manners, and Customs, and General Folk-lore of the District. Thick 12mo, pp. 458, *cloth.* 6s

This is undoubtedly the best work hitherto published on the dialects of Yorkshire in general, and of Leeds in particular. The author, we believe one of our fellow townsmen—for his introductory remarks are dated 'Leeds, March, 1861'—has used not only great industry, but much keen observation, and has produced a book which will everywhere be received as a valuable addition to the archæological literature of England.—*Leeds Intelligencer.*

A LIST of Provincial Words in Use in Wakefield, Yorkshire, with Explanations, including a few descriptions and localities. By W. S. BANKS. 12mo. 1s 6d

THE Yorkshire Dialect, exemplified in various Dialogues, Tales, and Songs, applicable to the County, with a Glossary. Post 8vo. 1s.

A GLOSSARY of Yorkshire Words and Phrases, collected in Whitby and its Neighbourhood, with examples of their colloquial use and allusions to local Customs and Traditions. By an INHABITANT. 12mo, *cloth.* 3s 6d

A GLOSSARY, with some Pieces of Verse of the Old Dialect of the English Colony in the Baronies of Forth and Bargy, Co. Wexford, Ireland. Formerly collected by JACOB POOLE, of Growton, now edited with Notes and Introduction by the REV. W. BARNES, Author of the Dorset Poems and Glossary. Fcap. 8vo, *cloth.* 4s 6d

PUBLICATIONS OF THE CAXTON SOCIETY.

OF CHRONICLES AND OTHER WRITINGS ILLUSTRATIVE OF THE HISTORY AND MISCELLANEOUS LITERATURE OF THE MIDDLE AGES.

Uniformly printed in 8vo. with English Prefaces and Notes. Of several of the Volumes only 100 copies have been printed, and only three sets can be completed.

CHRONICON Henrici de Silgrave. Now first printed from the Cotton MS. By C. HOOK. 5s 6d

GAIMAR (Geoffrey) Anglo-Norman Metrical Chronicle of the Anglo Saxon Kings. Printed for the first time entire, with Appendix, containing the Lay of Havelok the Dane, the Legend of Ernulph, and Life of Hereward the Saxon. Edited by T. WRIGHT, Esq., F.S.A. Pp. 284 (*only to be had in a set*)
The only complete edition; that in the Monumenta Historica Britannica, printed by the Record Commission, is incomplete.

LA REVOLTE du COMTE de WARWICK contre le Roi Edouard IV., now first printed from a MS. at Ghent, to which is added a French letter, concerning Lady Jane Grey and Queen Mary, from a MS. at Bruges. Edited by Dr. GILES. 3s 6d

WALTERI Abbatis Dervensis Epistolæ, now first printed from a MS. in St. John's College, Cambridge. By C. MESSITER. 4s 6d

BENEDICTI Abbatis Petriburgensis de Vita et Miraculis St. Thomae Cantaur, now first printed from MS. at Paris and Lambeth. By Dr. GILES. 10s.

GALFRIDI le Baker de Swinbroke, Chronicon Angeliae temp. Edward II. et III., now first printed. By Dr. GILES. 10s

EPISTOLÆ Herberti de Losinga, primi Episcopi Norwicensis, et Oberti de Clara, et Elmeri Prioris Cantuariensis, now first printed. By Col. ANSTRUTHER. 8s

ANECDOTA Bedae Lanfranci, et aliorum (inedited Tracts, Letters, Poems, &c., Bede, Lanfranc, Tatwin, etc.) By Dr. GILES. 10s

RADULPHI Nigri Chronica Duo, now first printed from MSS. in the British Museum, By Lieut. Col. ANSTRUTHER. 8s

MEMORIAL of Bishop Waynflete, Founder of St. Mary Magdalene College, Oxford. By Dr. PETER HEYLYN. Now first edited from the original MS. By J. R. BLOXAM, D.D., Fellow of the same College. 5s 6d

ROBERT GROSSETETE (Bishop of Lincoln) "Chasteau d'Amour," to which is added, "La Vie de Sainte Marie Egyptienne," and an English Version (of the 13th Century) of the "Chasteau d'Amour," now first edited. By M. COOKE. 6s 6d

GALFREDI Monumentis Historia Britonum, nunc primum in Anglia novem codd. MSS. collatis. Editit J. A. GILES. 10s

ALANI Prioris Cantuariensis postea Abbatis Tewkesberiensis, Scripta quae extant. Edita J. A. GILES. 6s 6d

CHRONICON Angliæ Petriburgense Iterum post Sparkium cum ood. MSS. contulit. J. A. GILES. 6s 6d

VITA Quorandum Anglo-Saxonum, Original Lives of Anglo-Saxons and others who lived before the Conquest (*in Latin*). Edited by Dr. GILES. 10s

SCRIPTORES Rerum Gestarum Wilhelmi Conquestoris. In Unum collecti. Ab J. A. GILES. 10s.

CONTINENS:—1. Brevis relatio de Willelmo nobilissimo Comite Normannorum. 2. Protestatio Willelmi primi de primatu Cantuariensis Ecclesiæ 3. Widonis Ambrianensis Carmen de Hastingensi. 4. Charta Willelmi Bastardi. 5 Epistola Will. conquestoris ad Gregorium papam. 6. Excerpta de vita Willelmi Conquestoris. 7. De Morte Will. Conq. 8. Hymnus de Morte Will. Conq. 9. De Morte Lanfranci. 10. Gesta Will. Ducis Normannorum. 11. Excerptum ex cantatorio S. Huberti. 12. Annalis Historia brevis sive Chronica Monasterii S. Stephani Cadomensis. 13. Carmen de Morte Lanfranci. 14. Charta a rege Will. concessa Anglo-Saxonice scripta. 15. Du Roi Guillaume d'Angleterre par Chretien de Troyes. 16. Le Dit de Guillaume d'Angleterre.

QUEEN DAGMAR'S Cross, *facsimile in gold and colours* of the Enamelled Jewel in the Old Northern Museum, Copenhagen, with Introductory Remarks by Prof. GEORGE STEPHENS, F.S.A. 8vo, *sewed.* 3s

RAINE (Rev. James) History and Antiquities of North Durham, as subdivided into the Shires of Norham, Island, and Bedlington, which from the Saxon period until 1844 constituted part of the County of Durham, but are now united to Northumberland. BOTH PARTS *complete,* folio, *fine plates* (wanting 8 plates in the first part) *bds.* £1. 5s

———— Part II. (*wanting by many Subscribers*) *quite complete.* 18s. LARGE PAPER. £1. 1s

RAINE'S (Rev. Jas.) Saint Cuthbert, with an Account of the State in which his remains were found upon the opening of his Tomb in Durham Cathedral, 1827. 4to, *plates and woodcuts, bds.* (a *very interesting vol*). 10s 6d. (Original price, £1. 11s 6d)

" From the four corners of the earth they come,
To kiss this shrine—this mortal-breathing saint."

RAINE'S (Rev. Jas.) Catterick Church, Yorkshire, a correct copy of the contract for its building in 1412. Illustrated with Remarks and Notes. *With thirteen plates of views, elevations, and details, by* A. SALVIN, *Architect.* 4to, *cloth.* 6s.—Or LARGE PAPER, *cloth.* 9s

RAINE (Rev. James) Historical Account of the Episcopal Castle or Palace of Auckland. Royal 4to, *fine views, portraits, and seals, cloth.* 10s 6d (*original price,* £1. 1s)

RAINE (Rev. John, *Vicar of Blyth*) The History and Antiquities of the Parish of Blyth, in the Counties of Nottingham and York, comprising Accounts of the Monastery, Hospitals, Chapels, and Ancient Tournament Field, of the Parish of the Castle and Manor of Tickill, and of the Family Possessions of De Buiii, the First and Norman Lord thereof, together with Biographical Notices of Roger Mowbray, Philip of Olcotes, Bishop Sanderson, John Cromwell, and others, with Appendix of Documents, &c. *4to plates and pedigrees, cloth.* 15s (*original price, £1. 6s*)

—— LARGE PAPER, royal 4to. £1. 5s

These copies have an additional view of the Remains of Scrooby Palace, not issued with the early copies.

RECORDE.—The Connection of Wales with the Early Science of England, illustrated in the Memoirs of Dr. Robert Recorde, the first Writer on Arithmetic, Geometry, Astronomy, &c., in the English Language. By J. O. HALLIWELL. 8vo, *sewed.* 1s

REDFERN'S (Francis, *of Uttoxeter*), the History of Uttoxeter, in Staffordshire, with Notices of Places in the Neighbourhood. Post 8vo, *many engravings, cloth,* 7s 6d

THE RELIQUARY; a Depository for Precious Relics, Legendary, Biographical, and Historical, illustrative of the Habits, Customs, and Pursuits of our Forefathers. Edited by LLEWELLYN JEWITT, F.S.A. 8vo, Nos. 1 to 26, *illustrated with engravings, published quarterly.* 2s 6d per No.

RELIQUIÆ ANTIQUÆ; Scraps from Ancient Manuscrips, illustraing chiefly Early English Literature and the English Language. Edited by Wright and Halliwell. 8vo, Vol II., in Nos. 12s

Many subscribers want the second volume. A number of odd parts of both vols to complete copies.

RETROSPECTIVE REVIEW (New Series) consisting of Criticisms upon, Analysis of, and Extracts from, curious, useful, valuable, and scarce Old Books. 8vo, Vols I. and II., *all printed, cloth.* 10s 6d (*original price, £1. 1s*). 1853—54

These two volumes form a good companion to the old series of the *Retrospective*, in 16 vols; the articles are of the same length and character.

REYNOLDS' (Sir Joshua) Notes and Observations on Pictures chiefly of the Venetian School, being Extracts from his Italian Sketch Books; also the Rev. W. Mason's Observations on Sir Joshua's Method of Colouring, with some unpublished Letters, of Dr. Johnson, Malone, and others; with an Appendix, containing a Transcript of Sir Joshua's Account Book, showing the Paintings he executed, and the Prices he was paid for them. Edited by William Cotton, Esq. 8vo, *cloth.* 5s

"The scraps of the Critical Journal, kept by Reynolds at Rome, Florence, and Venice, will be esteemed by high-class *virtuosi.*"—*Leader.*

RIMBAULT (E. F., *LL.D.*, *F.S.A.*, &c.)—A Little Book of Songs and Ballads, gathered from Ancient Music Books, MS. and Printed. *Elegantly printed* in post 8vo., pp. 240, *hf. morocco.* 6s

"Dr. Rimbault has been at some pains to collect the words of the songs which used to delight the rustics of former times."—*Atlas.*

RIMBAULT (Dr. E. F.) Bibliotheca Madrigaliana.—A Bibliographical Account of the Musical and Poetical Works published in England during the Sixteenth and Seventeenth Centuries, under the Titles of Madrigals, Ballets, Ayres, Canzonets, &c., &c. 8vo, *cloth.* 5s

It records a class of books left undescribed by Ames, Herbert, and Dibdin, and furnishes a most valuable Catalogue of Lyrical Poetry of the age to which it refers.

ROBERTS' (George, *of Lyme Regis*)—Life, Progresses, and Rebellion of James, Duke of Monmouth, &c., to his Capture and Execution, with a full account of the " Bloody Assize," under Judge Jefferies, and Copious Biographical Notices. 2 vols, post 8vo, *plates and cuts, cloth,* 7s 6d (*original price,* £1. 4s.)

Two very interesting volumes, particularly so to those connected with the West of England. Quoted for facts by Lord Macaulay.

ROBERTS' (George) The Social History of the People of the Southern Counties of England in Past Centuries, illustrated in regard to their Habits, Municipal Bye-laws, Civil Progress, &c. Thick 8vo, *cloth.* 7s 6d (*original price,* 16s)

An interesting volume on old English manners and customs, mode of travelling, punishments, witchcraft, gipsies, pirates, stage-players, pilgrimages, prices of labour and provisions, the clothing trade of the West of England, &c., compiled chiefly from original materials, as the archives of Lyme-Regis and Weymouth, family papers, church registers, &c. Dedicated to Lord Macaulay.

ROBIN HOOD.—The Great Hero of the Ancient Minstrelsy of England, " Robin Hood," his Period, real Character, &c., investigated, and perhaps ascertained. By the Rev. JOSEPH HUNTER. Post 8vo. 2s 6d.

ROBINSON (J. B., *of Derby*)—Derbyshire Gatherings; a Fund of Delight for the Antiquary, the Historian, the Topographer, and Biographer, and General Reader. *A handsome 4to, with engravings, extra cloth, gilt edges.* £1. 5s

ROMAN COINS.—Records of Roman History, from Cnæus Pompeius to Tiberius Constantinus, as exhibited on the Roman Coins, Collected by Francis Hobler, formerly Secretary to the Numismatic Society of London. 2 vols, royal 4to, *frontispiece and numerous engravings, in cloth.* £1. 1s (*original price* £2. 2s, only 250 printed).

" A work calculated not only to interest the professed numismatist, but also to instruct the classical student and the historian. The unpublished Coins are rather numerous, especially when we consider how many works have been printed on the Roman series, and how much it has been studied. . . . . The value of the work is much enhanced by the illustrations, executed by Mr. Fairholt, with the peculiar spirit and fidelity which indicate his experienced hand."—*C. Roach Smith's Collectanea Antiqua.*

SACRED MUSIC.—By the Rev. W. Sloane Evans, M.A. Royal 8vo, third edition, *sewed.* 1s 6d (*original price,* 6s)

Consisting of Psalm Tunes, Sanctusses, Kyrie-Eleisons, &c., &c., and fifty-four Single and Double Chants (Major, Changeable, and Minor).

SALVERTE'S (Eusebius) History of the Names of Men, Nations, and Places, in their Connection with the Progress of Civilization. Translated by the Rev. L. H. Mordaque, M.A., Oxon. 2 vols, 8vo, *cloth.* £1. 4s

"Notre nom propre c'est nous-memes."
"Nomina si nescis periit cognitio rerum."

"Full of learning, well written, and well translated."—*Daily News.*

"These two volumes are filled with a minute and philosophical enquiry into the origin of names of all sorts among all nations, and show profound scholarship and patient skill in wide and elaborate research. Much of the work is, necessarily, too profound for general readers—particularly the appendices to the second volume—but the larger part of the enquiry is so curious and interesting that any ordinary reader will fully appreciate and profit by the researches."—*Birmingham Journal.*

SANDYS' (W., *F.S.A.*)—Christmastide, its History, Festivities, and Carols (*with their music*). In a handsome vol. 8vo, *illustrated with 20 engravings after the designs of F. Stephanoff, extra cloth, gilt edges.* 5s (*original price 14s*)

"Its title vouches that *Christmastide* is germane to the time. Mr. Sandys has brought together, in an octavo of some 300 pages, a great deal of often interesting information beyond the stale gossip about "Christmas in the olden time," and the threadbare make-believes of jollity and geniality which furnish forth most books on the subject. His carols, too, which include some in old French and Provençal, are selected from numerous sources, and comprise many of the less known and more worth knowing. His materials are presented with good feeling and mastery of his theme. On the whole the volume deserves, and should anticipate, a welcome."—*Spectator.*

SANDYS (W.) and S. A. FORSTER.—History of the Violin and other Instruments played on with a Bow, from the Earliest Times to the Present, also an Account of the Principal Makers, English and Foreign. Thick 8vo, pp. 408, *with many engravings, cloth.* 14s

SANDY'S (Charles, *of Canterbury*) Consuetudes Kanciæ. A History of Gavelkind, and other remarkable Customs, in the County of Kent. 8vo, *illustrated with facsimiles, a very handsome volume, cloth.* 15s.

SANDYS (Charles) Critical Dissertation on Professor Willis's "Architectural History of Canterbury Cathedral." 8vo. 2s 6d

"Written in no quarrelsome or captious spirit; the highest compliment is paid to Professor Willis where it is due. But the author has made out a clear case, in some very important instances, of inaccuracies that have led the learned Professor into the construction of serious errors throughout. It may be considered as an indispensable companion to his volume, containing a great deal of extra information of a very curious kind."—*Art-Union.*

SAULL (W. D.) On the Connection between Astronomical and Geological Phenomena, addressed to the Geologists of Europe and America. 8vo, *diagrams, sewed.* 2s

SCRASE FAMILY.—Genealogical Memoir of the Family of Scrase, of Sussex. By M. A. LOWER. 8vo. 1s 6d

SHAKESPERIANA.

A LIFE OF SHAKESPEARE, including many particulars respecting the Poet and his Family, never before published. By J. O. HALLIWELL, F.R.S., etc. 8vo, *illustrated with 75 engravings on wood, most of which are of new objects from drawings by Fairholt, cloth.* 15s.   1848

This work contains upwards of forty documents respecting Shakespeare and his family, *never before published,* besides numerous others, indirectly illustrating the Poet's biography. All the anecdotes and traditions concerning Shakespeare are here, for the first time, collected, and much new light is thrown on his personal history, by papers exhibiting him as selling Malt, Stone, &c. Of the seventy-six engravings which illustrate the volume, *more than fifty have never before been engraved.*

It is the only life of Shakespeare to be bought separately from his works.

NEW ILLUSTRATIONS of the Life, Studies, and Writings of Shakespeare. By the Rev. JOSEPH HUNTER. 2 vols, 8vo, *cloth.* 7s 6d *(original price £1. 1s).*   1845

Supplementary to all editions of the works of the Poet.

Part 2, price 8s., and Parts 3, 4, and 5 together, price 8s., may be had to complete copies.

SHAKESPEARE'S Versification, and its Apparent Irregularities Explained by Examples from Early and Late English Writers. By W. SIDNEY WALKER, Edited by WM. NANSOM LETTSOM. *Foolscap* 8vo, *cloth.* 6s.   1854

"The reader of Shakespeare would do well to make himself acquinted with this excellent little book previous to entering upon the study of the poet."— *Mr. Singer, in the Preface to his New Edition of Shakespeare.*

A CRITICAL Examination of the Text of Shakespeare; together with Notes on his Plays and Poems, by the late W. SIDNEY WALKER. Edited by W. Nanson Lettsom. 3 vols, foolscap 8vo, *cloth.* 18s.   1860

"Very often we find ourselves differing from Mr. Walker on readings and interpretations, but we seldom differ from him without respect for his scholarship and care. His are not the wild guesses at truth which neither gods nor men have stomach to endure, but the suggestions of a trained intelligence and a chastened taste. Future editors and commentators will be bound to consult these volumes, and consider their suggestions."—*Athenæum.*

"A valuable addition to our Philological Literature, the most valuable part being the remarks on contemporary literature, the mass of learning by which the exact meaning and condition of a word is sought to be established."—*Literary Gazette.*

"Mr. Walker's Works undoubtedly form altogether the most valuable body of verbal criticism that has yet appeared from an individual."—*Mr. Dyce's Preface to Vol. I. of his Shakespeare,* 1864.

NARES' (Archd.) Glossary, or Collection of Words, Phrases, Customs, Proverbs, etc., illustrating the Works of English Authors, particularly Shakespeare and his Contemporaries. A new edition, with Considerable Additions both of Words and Examples. By James O. Halliwell, F.R.S., and Thomas Wright, M.A., F.S.A. 2 thick vols, 8vo, *cloth.* £1. 1s.   1867

The Glossary of Archdeacon Nares is by far the best and most useful Work we possess for explaining and illustrating the obsolete language, and the customs and manners of the Sixteenth and Seventeenth Centuries, and it is quite indespensable for the readers of the literature of the Elizabethan period. The additional words and examples are distinguished from those of the original text by a † prefixed to each. The work contains between *five and six thousand* additional examples, the result of original research, not merely supplementary to Nares, but to all other compilations of the kind.

A LETTER to Dr. Farmer (in reply to Ritson), relative to his Edition of Shakespeare, published in 1790.   By EDMUND MALONE. 8vo, *sewed.* 1s   1792

COMPARATIVE Review of the Opinions of James Boaden in 1795 and in 1796, relative to the Shakespeare MSS. 8vo, 2s   1796

ESSAY on the Genius of Shakespeare, with Critical Remarks on the Characters of Romeo, Hamlet, Juliet, and Ophelia, by H. M. GRAVES. Post 8vo, *cloth.* 2s 6d (*original price* 5s 6d)   1826

HISTORICAL Account of the Monumental Bust of Shakespeare, in the Chancel of Stratford-upon-Avon Church, by ABR. WIVELL. 8vo, 2 *plates.* 1s 6d   1827

VORTIGERN, an Historical Play, represented at Drury Lane, April 2, 1796, as a supposed newly discovered Drama of Shakespeare, by WILLIAM HENRY IRELAND. *New Edition, with an original Preface.* 8vo, *facsimile.* 1s 6d (*original price* 3s 6d)   1832
The Preface is both interesting and curious, from the additional information it gives respecting the Shakespeare Forgeries, containing also the substance of the author's " Confessions."

SHAKESPEARE's Will, copied from the Original in the Prerogative Court, preserving the Interlineations and Facsimiles of the three Autographs of the Poet, with a few Preliminary Observations, by J. O. HALLIWELL. 4to. 1s   1838

TRADITIONARY Anecdotes of Shakespeare, collected in Warwickshire in 1693. 8vo, *sewed.* 1s   1838

OBSERVATIONS on an Autograph of Shakespeare, and the Orthography of his Name, by Sir FRED. MADDEN. 8vo, *sewed.* 1s 1838

SHAKESPEARE's Autobiographical Poems, being his Sonnets clearly developed, with his Character, drawn chiefly from his Works, by C. A. BROWN. Post 8vo, *cloth.* 4s 6d   1838

SHAKESPERIANA, a Catalogue of the Early Editions of Shakespeare's Plays, and of the Commentaries and other Publications illustrative of his works.   By J. O. HALLIWELL. 8vo, *cloth.* 3s
1841
" Indispensable to everybody who wishes to carry on any inquiries connected with Shakespeare, or who may have a fancy for Shakesperian Bibliography."— *Spectator.*

REASONS for a New Edition of Shakespeare's Works, by J. PAYNE COLLIER. 8vo. 1s   1842

ACCOUNT of the only known Manuscript of Shakespeare's Plays, comprising some important variations and corrections in the " Merry Wives of Windsor," obtained from a Playhouse Copy of that Play recently discovered.   By J. O. HALLIWELL. 8vo. 1s   1843

" WHO was 'Jack Wilson,' the Singer of Shakespeare's Stage ?" An Attempt to prove the identity of this person with John Wilson, Doctor of Music in the University of Oxford, A.D. 1644.   By E. F. RIMBAULT, LL.D. 8vo. 1s   1846

CRITICISM applied to Shakespeare. By C. BADHAM. Post 8vo. 1s
1846

CROKER (Crofton).—Remarks on an Article inserted in the Papers
of the Shakespeare Society. Small 8vo, *sewed*, 1s.   1849

THE Tempest as a Lyrical Drama. By MORRIS BARNETT. 8vo. 1s
1850

A FEW Remarks on the Emendation, "Who Smothers her with
Painting," in the Play of Cymbeline, discovered by Mr. Collier,
in a Corrected Copy of the Second Edition of Shakespeare, by
J. O. HALLIWELL, &c. 8vo. 1s   1852

CURIOSITIES of Modern Shakespeare Criticism. By J. O. HALLI-
WELL. 8vo, *with the first facsimile of the Dulwich Letter, sewed.*
1s   1853

A FEW Notes on Shakespeare, with Occasional Remarks on the
Emendations of the Manuscript-Corrector in Mr. Collier's copy
of the folio, 1632, by the REV. ALEXANDER DYCE. 8vo, *cloth.*
5s   1853
"Mr. Dyce's Notes are peculiarly delightful, from the stores of illustration
with which his extensive reading, not only among our writers, but among those
of other countries, especially of the Italian poets, has enabled him to enrich
them. All that he has recorded is valuable. We read this little volume with
pleasure, and closed it with regret."—*Literary Gazette.*

A FEW Words in Reply to the Rev. A. Dyce's "Few Notes on
Shakespeare," by the Rev. JOSEPH HUNTER. 8vo. 1s   1853

THE Grimaldi Shakespeare.—Notes and Emendations on the Plays
of Shakespeare, from a recently discovered annotated copy by
the late Joe Grimaldi, Esq., Comedian. 8vo, *woodcuts.* 1s
1853
A humourous squib on Collier's Shakespeare Emendations.

THE Moor of Venice, Cinthio's Tale, and Shakespeare's Tragedy.
By JOHN EDWARD TAYLOR. Post 8vo. 1s   1855

CURSORY Notes on Various Passages in the Text of Beaumont and
Fletcher, as edited by the Rev. Alexander Dyce, and on his
"Few Notes on Shakespeare," by the Rev. JOHN MITFORD.
8vo, *sewed.* 2s 6d   1856

BACON and Shakespeare, an Inquiry touching Players, Playhouses,
and Play-writers, in the Reign of Q. Elizabeth ; to which is appended an Abstract of a Manuscript Autobiography of Tobie
Matthews, by W. H. SMITH. Foolscap 8vo, *cloth.* 2s 6d 1857
"Lord Palmerston was tolerably well up in the chief Latin and English
Classics : but he entertained one of the most extraordinary paradoxes touching
the greatest of them that was ever broached by a man of his intellectual calibre.
He maintained that the Plays of Shakespeare were really written by Bacon,
who passed them off under the name of an actor, for fear of compromising his
professional prospects and philosophic gravity. Only last year, when this subject was discussed at Broadlands, Lord Palmerston suddenly left the room, and
speedily returned with a small volume of dramatic criticisms (*Mr. Smith's book*)
in which the same theory was supported by supposed analogies of thought and
expression. 'There,' said he, 'read that, and you will come over to my
opinion.'"—*Fraser's Mag Nov.* 1865.

HAMLET.—An Attempt to Ascertain whether the Queen were an Accessory before the Fact, in the Murder of her First Husband. 8vo, *sewed.* 2s 1856
" This pamphlet well deserves the perusal of every student of Hamlet."—Notes and Queries.

SHAKESPEARE's Story-Teller, Introductory Leaves, or Outline Sketches, with Choice Extracts in the Words of the Poet himself, with an Analysis of the Characters, by George Stephens, *Professor of the English Language and Literature in the University of Copenhagen.* 8vo, Nos. 1 to 6. 6d each. 1856

PERICLES, Prince of Tyre, a Novel, by Geo. Wilkins, printed in 1608, and founded upon Shakespeare's Play, edited by PROFESSOR MOMMSEN, with Preface and Account of some original Shakespeare editions extant in Germany and Switzerland, and Introduction by J. P. COLLIER. 8vo, *sewed.* 5s 1857

LLOYD (W. Watkiss) Essays on the Life and Plays of Shakespeare, contributed to the Edition by S. W. Singer, 1856. Thick post 8vo, *half calf gilt, marbled edges.* 9s 1858
Only 50 copies privately printed.

THE Sonnets of Shakespeare, *rearranged* and divided into Four Parts, with an Introduction and Explanatory Notes. Post 8vo, *cloth.* 3s 6d 1859

STRICTURES on Mr. Collier's New Edition of Shakespeare, published in 1858, by the Rev. ALEXANDER DYCE. 8vo, *cloth.* 5s *(original price* 7s 6d*)* 1859

THE Shakespeare Fabrications, or the MS. Notes of the Perkins folio, shown to be of recent origin; with Appendix on the Authorship of the Ireland Forgeries, by C MANSFIELD INGLEBY, LL.D. Foolscap 8vo, *with a facsimile, shewing the* pseudo *old writing and the pencilled words, cloth.* 3s 1859

STRICTURES on Mr. Hamilton's Inquiry into the Genuineness of the MS. Corrections in J. Payne Collier's Annotated Shakespeare. Folio, 1632. By SCRUTATOR. 8vo, *sewed.* 1s 1860

SHAKESPEARE and the Bible, shewing how much the great Dramatist was indebted to Holy Writ for his Profound Knowledge of Human Nature. By the Rev. T. R. EATON. Fcap. 8vo, *cloth.* 2s 6d 1860

THE Footsteps of Shakespeare, or a Ramble with the Early Dramatists, containing New and Interesting Information respecting Shakespeare, Lyly, Marlowe, Green, and others. Post 8vo, *cloth.* 5s 6d 1861

SHAKESPEARE, his Friends and Contemporaries. By G. M. Tweddell. Second Edition, 8vo, Parts I to III. 6d each.
1861—3

THE Shakespeare Cyclopœdia, or a Classified and Elucidated Summary of Shakespeare's Knowledge of the Works and Phenomena of Nature. By J. H. Fennell, 8vo, Part I., *sewed.* 1s 1862

A BRIEF Hand Book of the Records belonging to the Borough of Stratford-on-Avon; with Notes of a few of the Shakespearian Documents. Square post 8vo, *cloth (only 50 printed)*. 7s 6d
1862

SHAKESPEARE No Deerstealer ; or, a Short Account of Fulbroke Park, near Stratford-on-Avon. By C. Holte Bracebride. 8vo, *privately printed.* 1s 6d
1862

WHELER's Historical Account of the Birthplace of Shakespeare, reprinted from the edition of 1824, with a few prefatory remarks by J. O. Halliwell. 8vo, *front.* 1s 6d
1863

BRIEF Hand List of the Collections respecting the Life and Works of Shakespeare, and the History and Antiquities of Stratford-upon-Avon, formed by the late Robert Bell Wheler, and presented by his sister to that Town, to be preserved for ever in the Shakespeare Library and Museum. Small square 8vo. 7s 6d   *Chiswick Press*, 1863
Only 100 copies printed at the expense of Mr. Halliwell, not for sale.

SHAKESPEARE'S Coriolanus. Edited, with Notes and Preface, by F. A. Leo, with a quarto facsimile of the Tragedy of Coriolanus, from the folio of 1623, photolithographed by A. Burchard, and with Extracts from North's Plutarch. 4to, *elegantly printed, extra cloth.* 15s
1864

SHAKSPERE and Jonson.—Dramatic *versus* Wit-Combats —Auxiliary Forces—Beaumont and Fletcher, Marston, Decker, Chapman, and Webster. Post 8vo. 4s.
1864

REPRINTS of Scarce Pieces of Shakespearian Criticism, No. 1, "Remarks on Hamlet, 1736." Fcap. 8vo. 1s 6d
1864

THREE Notelets on Shakespeare—I. Shakespeare in Germany ; II. The Folk-lore of Shakespeare ; III. Was Shakespeare a Soldier ? By William J. Thoms, F.S.A. Post 8vo, *cloth.* 4s 6d   1865
" On this subject of Shakespeare in Germany, Mr. W. J. Thoms has reprinted a paper read some years ago before the Society of Antiquaries, together with two other 'Notelets' on the Poet—'The Folk Lore of Shakespeare,' from the ATHENÆUM, and 'Was Shakespeare a Soldier ?' from NOTES AND QUERIES. Not the least of Mr. Thoms's many services to English literature is the invention of that admirable word *folk-lore*, which appeared for the first time in these columns only a few years ago, and has already become a domestic term in every corner of the world. His illustration of Shakespeare's knowledge of this little world of fairy dreams and legends is a perfect bit of criticism. He answers the query as to Shakespeare's having seen martial service in the affirmative ; and therein we think his argument sound, his conclusion right. These 'Notelets' were very well worthy of being collected into a book."—*Athenæum.*

SHAKESPEARE's Editors and Commentators. By the Rev. W. R. Arrowsmith, Incumbent of Old St. Pancras. 8vo, *sewed.* 1s 6d
1865

NEW Readings in Shakspere, or Proposed Emendations of the Text. By Robert Cartwright, M.D. 8vo, *sewed.* 2s   1866

THE SHAKESPEARE EXPOSITOR : being Notes, and Emendations on his Works. By Thomas Keightley. Thick fcap. 8vo, *cloth.* 7s 6d
1867

SHAKESPEARE's Jest Book.—A Hundred Mery Talys, from the only perfect copy known. Edited, with Introduction and Notes, by Dr. HERMAN OESTERLEY. Fcap. 8vo, *nicely printed by Whittingham, half morocco.* 4s 6d

The only perfect copy known of the " Hundred Mery Talys " was lately discovered in the Royal Library at Gottingen. This is a verbatim reprint, supplying all the chasms and lost tales in former editions, with copious Notes by the editor, pointing out the origin of the various tales, and authors who have used them.

SHARPE's (Samuel, *author of the History of Ancient Egypt, &c.*)— The Egyptian Antiquities in the British Museum described. Post 8vo, *with many woodcuts, cloth.* 5s. 1862

" We strongly counsel every one who desires to obtain a true knowledge of the Egyptian Department of the Museum to lose no time in obtaining this cheap and excellent volume."—*Daily News.*

" Mr. Sharpe here presents the student of Egyptian antiquity and art with a very useful book. . . . . . To the accomplished student this book will be useful as a reminder of many things already known to him ; to the tyro it may serve as a guide and *aide-memoire :* to the mere visitor to the Galleries in the British Museum, this will be a handy guide book, in which an immediate answer may be sought and found for the oft-repeated questions before these wondrous remains—of what are their natures? what their meanings? what their purposes ?"—*Athenæum.*

SHARPE (Samuel) Egyptian Mythology and Egyptian Christianity, with their Influence on the Opinions of Modern Christendom. Post 8vo, *with* 100 *engravings, cloth.* 3s.

SHARPE (Samuel) History of Egypt, from the Earliest Times till the Conquest by the Arabs, A.D. 620. 2 vols, 8vo, third edition (*excepting the engravings, the same as the fourth*), *elegantly printed, cloth.* 4s 6d (*original price* 16s)

SHARPE (Samuel) Critical Notes on the Authorized English Version of the New Testament, being a Companion to the Author's "New Testament, translated from Griesbach's Text." Fcap. 8vo, SECOND EDITION, *cloth.* 2s 6d

SHEPHERD (Charles).—Historical Account of the Island of Saint Vincent, in the West Indies, with large Appendix on Population, Meteorology, Produce of Estates, Revenue, Carib Grants, etc. 8vo, *plates, cloth.* 3s (*original price* 12s)

SINDING (Professor, *of Copenhagen*) History of Scandinavia, from the early times of the Northmen, the Seakings, and Vikings, to the present day. First English Edition, thoroughly revised and augmented. 8vo, pp. 490, *large map and portrait of Q. Margaret, cloth.* 6s

SKELTON (John, *Poet Laureate to Henry VIII*) Poetical Works, the Bowge of Court, Colin Clout, Why come ye not to Court ? (his celebrated Satire on Wolsey), Phillip Sparrow, Elinour Rumming, etc., with Notes and Life. By the Rev. A. DYCE. 2 vols, 8vo, *cloth.* 16s (*original price* £1. 12s)

" The power, the strangeness, the volubility of his language, the audacity of his satire, and the perfect originality of his manner, made Skelton one of the most extraordinary writers of any age or country."—*Southey.*

SIMS (Richard, *of the Dept. of MSS. in the British Museum*) A Manual for the Genealogist, Topographer, Antiquary, and Legal Professor, consisting of Descriptions of Public Records, Parochial and other Registers, Wills, County and Family Histories, Heraldic Collections in Public Libraries, &c.   8vo, SECOND EDITION, pp. 540, *cloth.*   15s

This work will be found indispensable by those engaged in the study of Family History and Heraldry, and by the compiler of County and Local History, the Antiquary and the Lawyer. In it the Public and other Records, most likely to afford information to genealogical inquirers, are fully described, and their places of present deposit indicated. Such Records are—The Domesday Books—Monastic Records—Cartæ Antiquæ—Liber Niger—Liber Rubeus—Testa de Nevil—Placita in various Courts—Charter Rolls—Close Rolls—Coronation Rolls—Coroners' Rolls—Escheat Rolls—Fine Rolls—French, Gascon, and Norman Rolls—Hundred Rolls—Liberate Rolls—Memoranda Rolls—Oblata and other Rolls—Inquisitions Post Mortem—Inquisitions ad quod Damnum—Fines and Recoveries—Sign Manuals and Signet Bills—Privy Seals—Forfeitures, Pardons, and Attainders—Parliamentary Records—County Palatine Records—Scotch, Irish, and Welsh Records—also Wills—Parochial and other Registers—Registers of Universities and Public Schools—Heraldic Collections—Records of Clergymen, Lawyers, Surgeons, Soldiers, Sailors, &c., &c.

The whole accompanied by valuable Lists of Printed Works and Manuscripts in various Libraries, namely:—at the British Museum—The Bodleian, Ashmolean, and other Libraries at Oxford—The Public Library, and that of Caius College, Cambridge—The Colleges of Arms in London and Dublin—The Libraries of Lincoln's Inn, and of the Middle and Inner Temple—at Chetham College, Manchester; and in other repositories too numerous to mention.

The more important of these Lists are those of Monastic Cartularies—Extracts from Plea and other Rolls—Escheats—Inquisitions, &c.—Tenants in Capite—Recusants—Subsidies—Crown Lands—Wills—Parochial and other Registers—Heralds' Visitations—Royal and Noble Genealogies—Peerages, Baronetages, Knightages—Pedigrees of Gentry—County and Family Histories—Monumental Inscriptions—Coats of Arms—American Genealogies—Lists of Gentry—Members of Parliament—Freeholds—Officers of State—Justices of Peace—Mayors, Sheriffs, &c.—Collegians, Church Dignitaries—Lawyers—The Medical Profession—Soldiers—Sailors, etc.

To these is added an "Appendix," containing an Account of the Public Record Offices and Libraries mentioned in the work, the mode of obtaining admission, hours of attendance, fees for searching, copying, &c. Table of the Regnal Years of English Sovereigns; Tables of Dates used in Ancient Records, &c.

SIMS (Richard) Handbook to the Library of the British Museum, containing a brief History of its Formation, and of the various Collections of which it is composed, Descriptions of the Catalogues in present use, Classed Lists of the Manuscripts, etc., and a variety of Information indispensable for Literary Men, with some Account of the principal Public Libraries in London. Sm. 8vo (pp. 438) *with map and plan, cloth.*   2s 6d

It will be found a very useful work to every literary person or public institution in all parts of the world.

"A little Handbook of the Library has been published, which I think will be most useful to the public."—*Lord Seymour's Reply in the H. of Commons, July,* 1854.

"I am much pleased with your book, and find in it abundance of information which I wanted."—*Letter from Albert Way, Esq., F.S.A., Editor of the* "*Promptorum Parvulorum," &c.*

"I take this opportunity of telling you how much I like your nice little 'Handbook to the Library of the British Museum,' which I sincerely hope may have the success which it deserves."—*Letter from Thos. Wright, Esq., F.S.A., Author of the 'Biographia Britannica Literaria,' &c.*

"Mr. Sims's 'Handbook to the Library of the British Museum' is a very comprehensive and instructive volume. . . . . . I venture to predict for it a wide circulation."—*Mr. Bolton Corney, in "Notes and Queries," No.* 213.

SLOANE—EVANS (W. S.) Grammar of British Heraldry, consisting of Blazon and Marshalling with an Introduction on the Rise and Progress of Symbols and Ensigns. 8vo, SECOND EDITION, *many plates, cloth.* 5s (*original price* 18s)

SMITH'S (Henry Ecroyd) Reliquiae Isurianae, the Remains of the Roman Isurium, now Aldborough, near Boroughbridge, Yorkshire, illustrated and described. Royal 4to, with 37 *plates, cloth.* £1. 5s

The most highly illustrated work ever published on a Roman Station in England.

SMITH'S (Charles Roach, F.S.A.) History and Antiquities of Richborough, and Lymne, in Kent, Small 4to, *with many engravings on wood and copper, by F. W. Fairholt, cloth.* £1. 1s

"No antiquarian volume could display a trio of names more zealous, successful, and intelligent, on the subject of Romano-British remains, than the three here represented—Roach Smith, the ardent explorer; Fairholt, the excellent illustrator, and Rolfe, the indefatigable collector.—*Literary Gazette.*

SMITH (W., *jun., of Morley*) Rambles about Morley (West Riding of Yorkshire) with Descriptive and Historic Sketches, also an Account of the Rise and Progress of the Woollen Manufacture in this Place. Royal 12mo, *map and numerous engravings, cloth.* 5s

SMITH'S (Toulmin) Memorials of Old Birmingham, Men and Names, Founders, Freeholders, and Indwellers, from the 13th to the 16th Century, with particulars as to the earliest Church of the Reformation built and endowed in England, from original and unpublished documents. Royal 8vo, *plates, cloth.* 4s 6d

SMITH (John Russell) Bibliotheca Cantiana.—A Bibliographical Account of what has been published on the History, Topography, Antiquities, Customs, and Family Genealogy of the County of Kent, with Biographical Notes. 8vo (pp. 370) *with two plates of facsimiles of autographs of 33 eminent Kentish Writers.* 5s (original price 14s)

SMITH (J. R.) A Bibliographical Catalogue of English Writers on Angling and Ichthyology. Post 8vo. 1s 6d

SMITH (J. R.) A Bibliographical List of all the Works which have been published towards illustrating the Provincial Dialects of England. Post 8vo. 1s

"Very serviceable to such as prosecute the study of our provincial dialects, or are collecting works on that curious subject. . . . We very cordially recommend it to notice."—*Metropolitan.*

SPEDDING (James, *Editor of Lord Bacon*) Publishers and Authors. Post 8vo, *cloth.* 2s

Mr. Spedding wishes to expose the present mystery (?) of publishing, he thinks from a number of cases that we publishers do not act on the square. However, there are two sides to the question; but his book will be useful to the uninitiated.

STEPHENS' (Professor George, *of Copenhagen*) the Old Northern Runic Monuments of Scandinavia and England, now first Collected and Deciphered. Folio, Part 1, pp. 362, *with about* 150 *engravings.* £2. 10s

The Author promises the second and concluding Part next year.

STEPHENS' (Professor) The Ruthwell Cross (near Annan, Dumfries-shire) with its Runic Verses, by Cædmon, and Cædmon's Cross-Lay, "The Holy Rood, a Dream," from a Transcript of the 10th Century, with Translations, Notes, &c. Folio, *with two plates, sewed.* 10s

This will be included in the forthcoming second part of Professor Stephens's work, this portion is published separately to meet the wishes of a number of Archæologists.

STIRRY'S (Thos.) A Rot amongst the Bishops, or a Terible *Tempest* in the *Sea* of Canterbury, set forth in lively emblems, to please the Judicious Reader. (*A Satire on Abp. Laud*), *four very curious woodcut emblems, cloth.* 3s

A facsimile of the very rare original edition, which sold at Bindley's sale for £13.

SURREY HILLS.—A Guide to the Caterham Railway and its Vicinity. Post 8vo, 2*nd and revised edition, with a map, sewed.* 6d

Thousands of tourists and pleasure-seekers go hundreds of miles for beautiful scenery without perhaps finding a country of more varied and interesting character than that to be met with in the Caterham Valley, and within twenty miles of the metropolis.

SURTEES (Rev. Scott. F., *of Sprotburgh, Yorkshire*) Waifs and Strays of North Humber History. Post 8vo, 3 *plates, cloth.* 3s 6d

SURTEES (Rev. Scott F.) Julius Caesar, Did he Cross the Channel (into Kent)? Post 8vo, *cloth.* 1s 6d

" In giving an answer in the negative to the above question, we ask for a fair and dispassionate hearing, and in order to avoid circumlocution pass at once our Rubicon, and propound as capable of all proof the following historical heresy, viz., that Caesar never set foot at Boulogne or Calais, never crossed the Channel, or set eyes on Deal or Dover, but that he sailed from the mouths of the Rhine or Scheldt, and landed in Norfolk on both his expeditions."—AUTHOR.

TESTAMENT (The New) translated from Griesbach's Text, by SAMUEL SHARPE, Author of the History of Egypt, &c. 5th edition. 12mo, pp. 412, *cloth.* 1s 6d

The aim of the translator has been to give the meaning and idiom of the Greek as far as possible in English words. The book is printed in paragraphs (the verses of the authorised version are numbered in the margins) the speeches by inverted commas, and the quotations from the "Old Testament" in italics, those passages which seem to be poetry in a smaller type. *It is entirely free from any motive to enforce doctrinal points.* Five large impressions of the volume sufficiently test its value.

We cordially recommend this edition of the New Testament to our readers and contributors.—*British Controversialist.*

Upon the whole, we must admit that his is the most correct English Version in existence, either of the whole or of any portion of the New Testament.—*The Ecclesiastic,* and repeated by the *English Churchman.*

TESTAMENT (Old).—The Hebrew Scriptures, translated by SAMUEL SHARPE, being a revision of the authorized English Old Testament. 3 vols, fcap. 8vo, *cloth, red edges.* 7s 6d

"In the following Revision of the Authorised Version of the Old Testament, the aim of the Translator has been to shew in the Text, by greater exactness, those peculiarities which others have been content to point out in Notes and Commentaries. He has translated from Van der Hooght's edition of the Hebrew Bible, printed in Amsterdam in 1705 ; except when, in a few cases, he has followed some of the various readings so industriously collected by Dr. Kennicott."—*Preface.* ' A Prospectus may be had.

TANSWELL'S (John, *of the Inner Temple*) the History and Antiquities of Lambeth. 8vo, *with numerous illustrations, cloth.* 4s 6d (*original price* 7s 6d)

THOMPSON (James) Handbook of Leicester. 12mo, *Second Edit., woodcuts, bds.* 2s

THOMPSON (Ebenezer) A Vindication of the Hymn "Te Deum Laudamus," from the Corruptions of a Thousand Years, with Ancient Versions in Anglo Saxon, High German, Norman French, &c., and an English Paraphrase of the XVth Century, now first printed. Fcap. 8vo, *cloth.* 3s
A book well worth the notice of the Ecclesiastical Antiquary and the Philologist.

THOMPSON (Ebenezer) on the Archaic Mode of expressing Numbers in English, Anglo-Saxon, Friesic, etc. 8vo (*an ingenious and learned pamphlet, interesting to the Philologist*). 1s

TIERNEY'S (Rev. Canon) History and Antiquities of the Castle and Town of Arundel, including the Biography of its Earls. 2 vols, royal 8vo, *fine plates, cloth,* 14s (*original price,* £2. 10s.)

TITIAN.—Notices of the Life and Works of Titian the Painter. By SIR ABRAHAM HUME. Royal 8vo, *portrait, cloth.* 6s.

TONSTALL (Cuthbert, *Bishop of Durham*) Sermon preached on Palm Sunday, 1539, before Henry VIII.; *reprinted verbatim from the rare edition by Berthelet, in* 1539. 12mo. 1s 6d.
An exceedingly interesting Sermon, at the commencement of the Reformation; Strype in his "Memorials," has made large extracts from it.

TORRENT of PORTUGAL; an English Metrical Romance. Now first published, from an unique MS. of the XVth Century, preserved in the Chetham Library at Manchester. Edited by J. O. HALLIWELL, &c. Post 8vo, *cloth, uniform with Ritson, Weber, and Ellis's publications, cloth.* 5s.
"This is a valuable and interesting addition to our list of early English metrical romances, and an indispensable companion to the collections of Ritson, Weber, and Ellis."—*Literary Gazette.*

TOPOGRAPHER (The) and Genealogist. Edited by J. G. NICHOLS. 3 vols, 8vo, *cloth.* £1. 5s (pub £3. 3s)
This extremely valuable work forms a sequel to the "Collectanea Topographica Genealogica," and the intrinsic value and originality of the materials comprised therein, will entitle it not only to preservation, but to frequent reference.

TOWNEND's (William) The Descendants of the Stuarts. An Unchronicled Page in England's History. 8vo, *portraits and folding pedigrees,* SECOND EDITION, WITH ADDITIONS, *half morocco.* 5s (original price 10s)
This volume contains a most minute, precise, and valuable history of the Descendants of the Stuart Family. Neither of our Historians from Hume to Macaulay give even the more prominent facts in connection with many branches of the House of Stuart.
"This is a really interesting contribution to what we may term the private records of history. . . . . What Mr. Townend has done is full of curious information. His Genealogical tables shew all the ramifications which spring out of the matrimonial alliances of the descendants of the Stuarts, and very curious *possibilities* some of these indicate. . . . . We promise our readers that this volume contains much that is worthy of perusal and recollection, as well as much that is suggestive."—*Globe.*

TOXOPHILUS ; the School of Shooting (the first English Treatise on *Archery*. By ROGER ASCHAM, reprinted from the Rev. Dr. Giles's Edition of Ascham's Whole Works. Fcap. 8vo, *cloth.* 3s

TROLLOPE (Rev. W.) History of the Royal Foundation of Christ's Hospital, Plan of Education, Internal Economy of the Institution, and Memoirs of Eminent Blues. 4to, *plates, cloth.* 8s 6d (*original price* £3. 3s)

TUCKETT (John) Pedigrees and Arms of Devonshire Families, as recorded in the Herald's Visitation of 1620, with Additions from the Harleian MSS. and the Printed Collections of Westcote and Pole. 4to, Parts I. to XII. Each 5s

TURNER'S (Sir Gregory Page) Topographical Memorandums for the County of Oxford. 8vo, *bds.* 2s

TWEDDELL (G. M.) The Bards and Authors of Cleveland and South Durham. By G. M. TWEDDELL. 8vo, Parts I. to VI. 6d each.

TWO LEAVES of King Waldere and King Gudhere, a hitherto unknown Old English Epic of the 8th Century belonging to the Saga Cycle of King Theodoric and his Men. Now first published with a Modern English Reading, Notes, and Glossary by GEORGE STEPHENS, *English Professor in the University of Copenhagen.* Royal 8vo, *with four Photographic Facsimiles of the MS. of the 9th Century, recently discovered at Copenhagen.* 15s— *Without Facsimiles.* 7s 6d

VASEY (George) A Monograph of the Genus Bos.—The Natural History of Bulls, Bisons, and Buffaloes, exhibiting all the known Species (with an Introduction containing an Account of Experiments on Rumination from the French of M. FLOURENS). 8vo, *with 72 engravings on wood by the Author, cloth.* 6s (*original price* 10s 6d)
Written in a scientific and popular manner, and printed and illustrated uniformly with the works of Bell, Yarrell, Forbes, Johnston, &c. Dedicated to the late Mr. Yarrell, who took great interest in the progress of the work. Mr. Vasey engraved many of the beautiful woodcuts in Mr. Yarrell's works.

VASEY'S (George) Illustrations of Eating, displaying the Omnivorous Character of Man, and exhibiting the Natives of various Countries at Feeding-time. Fcap. 8vo, *with woodcuts by the Author.* 2s

VERNON'S (E. J., *B.A., Oxon*) Guide to the Anglo-Saxon Tongue, on the Basis of Professor Rask's Grammar ; to which are added Reading Lessons in Verse and Prose, with Notes, for the Use of Learners. 12mo, *cloth.* 5s
" Mr. Vernon has, we think, acted wisely in taking Rask for his model : but let no one suppose from the title that the book is merely a compilation from the work of that philologist. The accidence is abridged from Rask, with constant revision, correction, and modification ; but the syntax, a most important portion of the book, is original, and is compiled with great care and skill ; and the latter half of the volume consists of a well-chosen selection of extracts from Anglo-Saxon writers, in prose and in verse, for the practice of the student, who will find great assistance in reading them from the grammatical notes with which they are accompanied, and from the glossary which follows them. This volume, well studied, will enable anyone to read with ease the generality of Anglo-Saxon writers ; and its cheapness places it within the reach of every class. It has our hearty recommendation."—*Literary Gazette.*

VICARS' (John) England's Worthies, under whom all the Civil and
Bloody Warres, since Anno 1642 to Anno 1647, are related.
Royal 12mo, *reprinted in the old style (similar to Lady Willough-
by's Diary), with copies of the 18 rare portraits after Hollar, etc.,
half morocco.* 5s

WACE (Master, *the Anglo-Norman Poet*) His Chronicle of the Norman Conquest, from the Roman de Rou. Translated into English Prose, with Notes and Illustrations, by EDGAR TAYLOR,
F.S.A. 8vo, *many engravings from the Bayeux Tapestry, Norman
Architecture, Illuminations, etc., cloth.* 15s (*original price £1. 8s*)
Only 250 copies printed, and very few remain unsold; the remaining copies
are now in J. R. Smith's hands, and are offered at the above low price in consequence of the death of Mr. Pickering; hitherto no copies have been sold under
the published price.

WACKERBARTH (F. D.) Music and the Anglo-Saxons, being some
Account of the Anglo-Saxon Orchestra, with Remarks on the
Church Music of the 19th Century. 8vo, *2 plates, sewed.* 4s

WARNE (Charles, *F.S.A.*) The Celtic Tumuli of Dorset; an Account of Personal and other Researches in the Sepulchral
Mounds of the Durotriges. Folio, *plates and woodcuts, cloth.*
£1. 10s

WAYLEN (James, *of Devizes*) History and Antiquities of the Town
of Marlborough, and more generally of the entire Hundred of
Selkley, in Wiltshire. Thick 8vo, *woodcuts, cloth.* 14s
This volume describes a portion of Wilts not included by Sir R. C. Hoare and
other topographers.

WEST (Mrs.) A Memoir of Mrs. John West, of Chettle, Dorset.
By the Rev. JOHN WEST, A.M. A new edition, with Brief Me-
moir of the Writer. 12mo, *cloth.* 2s 6d
The fourth edition of an interesting volume of Religious Biography. The
Rev. John West was the first missionary to the Indians of Prince Rupert's
Land, the first wooden church at Red River was partly built by his own hands.

WESLEY—Narrative of a Remarkable Transaction in the Early
Life of John Wesley. Now first printed from a MS. in the
British Museum. SECOND EDITION; to which is added a Review of the Work by the late Rev. Joseph Hunter, F.S.A. 8vo,
sewed. 2s
A very curious love affair between J. W. and his housekeeper; it gives
a curious insight into the early economy of the Methodists. It is entirely
unknown to all Wesley's biographers.

WILLIAMS (John, *Archdeacon of Cardigan*) Essays, Philological,
Philosophical, Ethnological, and Archæological, connected with
the Prehistorical Records of the Civilised Nations of Ancient
Europe, especially of that Race which first occupied Great
Britain. Thick 8vo, with 7 *plates, cloth.* 16s

WINDSOR.—Annals of Windsor, being a History of the Castle and
Town, with some Account of Eton and Places Adjacent. By
R. R. TIGHE and J. E. DAVIS, Esqs. In 2 thick vols, roy. 8vo,
illustrated with many engravings, coloured and plain, extra clot
£1. 5s (*original price £4. 4s*)
An early application is necessary, as but few copies remain on sale.

WILLMOTT (Robert Aris, *some time Incumbent of Bear Wood, Berks*) A Journal of Summer Time in the Country. FOURTH EDITION; to which is added an Introductory Memoir by his Sister. Foolscap 8vo, *elegantly printed by Whittingham, extra cloth.* 5s

This 'Journal of Summer Time' is a genial gossip of literary matters under the various days of the month from May to August. It is full of anecdote, and full of interest; and is a sort of literary natural history, like that of Selbourne by good Gilbert White. The observations, the reading, the meditations of a well-trained, well-filled mind, give this volume its charm, and make it one which even the best-informed reader may wile away an hour with in recalling his own wanderings in the literary fields. The great glory of this book is that it is thoroughly natural. It does not aim at fine writing or sensational stories, but jots down from day to day such memoranda as a well-stored mind, familiar with the great treasures of our literature, would give forth in the quiet of a country parsonage, when summer smiled over the fields and woods, and a garden gave forth its pleasant sights and sounds.—*Birmingham Journal.*

WORSAAE'S (J. J. A., *of Copenhagen*) Primeval Antiquities of Denmark, translated and applied to the illustration of similar remains in England, by W. J. Thoms, F.S.A. 8vo, *many engravings, cloth.* 4s 6d (original price 10s 6d)

WRIGHT'S (Thomas, *M.A., F.S.A., Member of the Institute of France*) Essay on Archæological Subjects, and on various Questions connected with the History of Art, Science, and Literature in the Middle Ages. 2 vols, post 8vo, *printed by Whittingham, illustrated with 120 engravings, cloth.* 16s

CONTENTS :—1. On the Remains of a Primitive People in the South-East corner of Yorkshire. 2. On some ancient Barrows, or Tumuli, opened in East Yorkshire. 3. On some curious forms of Sepulchral Interment found in East Yorkshire. 4. Treago, and the large Tumulus at St. Weonard's. 5. On the Ethnology of South Britain at the period of the Extinction of the Roman Government in the Island. 6. On the Origin of the Welsh. 7. On the Anglo-Saxon Antiquities, with a particular reference to the Fausset Collection. 8. On the True Character of the Biographer Asser. 9. Anglo-Saxon Architecture, illustrated from illuminated Manuscripts. 10. On the Literary History of Geoffrey of Monmouth's History of the Britons, and of the Romantic Cycle of King Arthur. 11. On Saints' Lives and Miracles. 12. On Antiquarian Excavations and Researches in the Middle Ages. 13. On the Ancient Map of the World preserved in Hereford Cathedral, as illustrative of the History of Geography in the Middle Ages. 14. On the History of the English Language. 15. On the Abacus, or Mediæval System of Arithmetic. 16. On the Antiquity of Dates expressed in Arabic Numerals. 17. Remarks on an Ivory Casket of the beginning of the Fourteenth Century. 18. On the Carvings on the Stalls in Cathedral and Collegiate Churches. 19. Illustrations of some Questions relating to Architectural Antiquities—(a) Mediæval Architecture illustrated from Illuminated Manuscripts: (b) A Word more on Mediæval Bridge Builders: (c) On the Remains of proscribed Races in Mediæval and Modern Society, as explaining certain peculiarities in Old Churches. 20. On the Origin of Rhymes in Mediæval Poetry, and its bearing on the Authencity of the Early Welsh Poems. 21. On the History of the Drama in the Middle Ages. 22. On the Literature of the Troubadours. 23. On the History of Comic Literature during the Middle Ages. 24. On the Satirical Literature of the Reformation.

"Mr. Wright is a man who thinks for himself, and one who has evidently a title to do so. Some of the opinions published in these Essays are, he tells us, the result of his own observations or reflections, and are contrary to what have long been those of our own antiquaries and historians."—*Spectator.*

"Two volumes exceedingly valuable and important to all who are interested in the Archæology of the Middle Ages; no mere compilations, but replete with fine reasoning, new theories, and useful information, put in an intelligible manner on subjects that have been hitherto but imperfectly understood."—*London Rev.*

WRIGHT (Thomas) Essays on the Literature, Popular Superstitions, and History of England in the Middle Ages. 2 vols, post 8vo, *elegantly printed, cloth.* 16s

CONTENTS:—Essay 1. Anglo-Saxon Poetry—2. Anglo-Norman Poetry—3. Chansons de Geste, or historical romances of the Middle Ages—4. Proverbs and Popular Sayings—5. Anglo-Latin Poets of the Twelfth Century—6. Abelard and the Scholastic Philosophy—7. Dr. Grimm's German Mythology—8. National Fairy Mythology of England—9. Popular Superstitions of Modern Greece, and their connection with the English—10. Friar Rush and the Frolicsome Elves—11. Dunlop's History of Fiction—12. History and Transmission of Popular Stories—13. Poetry of History—14. Adventures of Hereward the Saxon—15. Story of Eustace the Monk—16. History of Fulke Fitzwarine—17. Popular Cycle or Robin Hood Ballads—18. Conquest of Ireland by the Anglo-Normans —19. Old English Political Songs—20. Dunbar, the Scottish Poet.

WRIGHT (Thomas) Biographia Britannica Literaria, or Biography of Literary Characters of Great Britain and Ireland. ANGLO-SAXON PERIOD. Thick 8vo, *cloth.* 6s (*original price 12s*)

—— The Anglo-Norman Period. Thick 8vo, *cloth,* 6s (*original price 12s*)

Published under the superintendence of the Council of the Royal Society of Literature.

There is no work in the English Language which gives the reader such a comprehensive and connected History of the Literature of these periods.

WRIGHT (Thomas) Wanderings of an Antiquary, chiefly upon the Traces of the Romans in Britain, *many illustrations,* post 8vo, *cloth.* 4s 6d (original price 8s 6d)

WRIGHT'S (Thomas) Saint Patrick's Purgatory, an Essay on the Legends of Hell, Purgatory, and Paradise, current during the Middle Ages. Post 8vo, *cloth.* 6s

" It must be observed that this is not a mere account of St. Patrick's Purgatory, but a complete history of the legends and superstitions relating to the subject, from the earliest times, rescued from old MSS. as well as from old printed books. Moreover, it embraces a singular chapter of literary history omitted by Warton and all former writers with whom we are acquainted : and we think we may add, that it forms the best introduction to Dante that has yet been published."—*Literary Gazette.*

" This appears to be a curious and even amusing book on the singular subject of Purgatory, in which the idle and fearful dreams of superstition are shown to be first narrated as tales, and then applied as means of deducing the moral character of the age in which they prevailed."—*Spectator.*

WRIGHT'S (Thomas) Anecdota Literaria, a Collection of Short Poems in English, Latin, and French, illustrative of the Literature and History of England in the XIIIth Century, and more especially of the Condition and Manners of the Different Classes of Society. 8vo, *cloth, only 250 copies printed.* 5s

WROXETER. The Roman City of Uriconium at Wroxeter, Salop; illustrative of the History and Social Life of our Romano-British forefathers. By J. Corbet Anderson. *A handsome volume, post 8vo, with numerous cuts drawn on wood from the actual objects by the author, extra cloth.* 12s 6d

YORKSHIRE.—The History of the Township of Meltham, near Huddersfield, by the late Rev. JOSEPH HUGHES, edited with addition by C. H. Post 8vo, *cloth.* 7s 6d

Several other books relating to Yorkshire, are interspersed through this Catalogue.

ADDENDA.

TWAMLEY'S (C.) Historical and Descriptive Account of Dudley Castle in Staffordshire. Post 8vo, *cloth.* 4s

SCOTT (Henry, *Minister of Anstruther Wester*). *Fasti-Ecclesiæ Scoticanæ*; the Succession of Ministers to the Parish Churches of Scotland, from the Reformation, A.D. 1560, to the present time. Part I. Synod of Lothian and Tweedale. 4to, pp. 400, *cl.* £1. 10s

To be completed in 3 parts—the second is now in the Printer's hands.

"The design of the present work is to present a comprehensive account of the SUCCESSION OF MINISTERS of the Church of Scotland, since the period of the Reformation. An attempt is made to give some additional interest by furnishing incidental notices of their lives, writings, and families, which may prove useful to the Biographer, the Genealogist, and the Historian.

"The sources from which the work has been compiled are the various records of Kirk Sessions, Presbyteries, Synods, and General Assemblies, together with the Books of Assignations, Presentations to Benefices, and the Commissariat Registers of Confirmed Testaments. From these authentic sources the information here collected will, it is believed, be found as accurate as the utmost care can render it. Having been commenced at an early period of life, this work has been prosecuted during all the time that could be spared from professional engagements for a period of nearly fifty years.

"Some idea of the labour and continuous research involved in preparing the work may be formed, when the Author states, that he has visited all the Presbyteries in the Church, and about seven hundred and sixty different Parishes, for the purpose of examining the existing records. In this way he has had an opportunity of searching eight hundred and sixty volumes of Presbytery, and one hundred volumes of Synod Records, besides those of the General Assembly, along with the early Registers of Assignations and Presentations to Benefices, and about four hundred and thirty volumes of the Testament Registers in the different Commissariats."—*Extract from Preface.*

RECORDS of the Convention of the Royal Burghs of Scotland, with extracts from other Records relating to the affairs of the Burghs of Scotland, 1295-1597, edited by J. D. MARWICK. 4to, pp. 600, *cloth, only* 150 *printed for sale.* £1. 10s

PASSAGES from the Autobiography of a "MAN OF KENT," together with a few rough Pen and Ink Sketches by the same hand of some of the people he has met, the changes he has seen, and the places he has visited, 1817-1865. Thick post 8vo. *Cloth.* 5s.

KENRICK (Rev. John, *Curator of Antiquities in the Museum at York, author of "Ancient Egypt under the Pharaohs," "History of Phœnicia,"* &c.) Papers on subjects of Archæology and History communicated to the Yorkshire Philosophical Society. 8vo, *cloth.* 3s 6d. (Original price 9s.)

CONTENTS.

The Rise, Extension, and Suppression of the Order of Knights Templar in Yorkshire.

Historical Traditions of Pontefract Castle, including an Enquiry into the Place and manner of Richard the Second's Death.

Relation of Coins to History, illustrated from Roman Coins found at Methal, in Yorkshire.

The Causes of the Destruction of Classical Literature.

The History of the Recovery of Classical Literature.

The Reign of Trajan, illustrated by a monument of his reign found at York.

Roman Wax Tablets found in Transylvania.

New Year's Day in Ancient Rome.

A BIBLIOGRAPHY of the Popular, Poetical, and Dramatic Literature of England, previous to 1660. By W. CAREW HAZLITT, *one thick vol,* 8vo, pp. 716, *in double columns, half morocco, Roxburghe style.* £1. 11s 6d

——— LARGE PAPER, royal 8vo, HALF MOROCCO, ROXBURGHE STYLE. £3. 3s

It will be found indispensable to Book-Collectors and Booksellers. It is far in advance of anything hitherto published on Old English Literature. A Prospectus by post on receipt of a postage label.

A MARTYR TO BIBLIOGRAPHY: A Notice of the Life and Works of JOSEPH-MARIE QUÉRARD, the French Bibliographer. By OLPHAR HAMST. 8vo, *cloth (only* 200 *printed).* 3s 6d

HANDBOOK for FICTITIOUS NAMES, being a Guide to Authors, chiefly of the Lighter Literature of the XIXth Century, who have written under assumed names; and to Literary Forgers, Impostors, Plagiarists, and Imitators. By OLPHAR HAMST, Esq., *Author of A Notice of the Life and Works of J. M. Quérard.* 8vo, *cloth.* 7s 6d

——— THICK PAPER (only 25 copies printed). *Cloth.* 15s

An exceedingly curious and interesting book on the bye ways of Literature.

A DICTIONARY of the LANGUAGE of SHAKESPEARE. By SWYFEN JERVIS, *of Darlaston Hall Staffordshire.* 4to, 378 pp., *in double columns,* 4to, *cloth (a cheap volume).* 12s

The author died while the volume was in the press, when his friend the Rev. Alex. Dyce, the Shakesperian scholar, completed it from the materials he had left.

TRANSACTIONS of the LOGGERVILLE LITERARY SOCIETY. 8vo, pp. 174, *with many humorous cuts, extra cloth gilt edges.* 7s 6d

A few copies of this privately printed volume on sale, of which the *Morning Post* says; "All the drawings are capital—full of genuine fun; and the biographical sketch of the president, Lumpkin Queer, Esq., is in the style of the introductory chapter to 'Martin Chuzzlewit,' but a much cleverer performance. Still better is the president's address, the grave and plausible absurdity of which is almost painfully laughable. A paper on 'Some Peculiarities of the French Language' is, with its delightful literal translation of 'How doth the little busy bee,' (the irrepressible insect being rendered *L'abeille peu industrieuse,*) one of the best burlesques we have ever read. A 'Retrospective Review of Juvenile Literature' is a perfect gem of fun and ingenuity. The book is a complete success."

The *Athenæum* says: "The book is not one to be read through steadily, but it will furnish a good deal of mirth if dipped into during leisure half hours. Of the papers, 'Some Observations on Ignorance,' 'A Tour in Cornwall,' and the 'Notes to Dandyndon, a Tragedy,' are the best, the notes in this case being superior to the dramatic extravaganza which they illustrate."

THE MEDIÆVAL NUNNERIES of the County of SOMERSET, with Annals of their Impropriated Benefices, by the Rev. THOMAS HUGO, F.S.A. Imp. 8vo, nearly 700 pp., *with plates, half morocco, Roxburghe style.* £1. 5s

GENEALOGY of the Family of COLE, of Devon, and of those of its Branches which settled in Suffolk, Hants, Lincoln, Surrey, and Ireland. By JAMES EDWIN-COLE. 8vo, *cloth.* 5s

PERROT NOTES: or, some Account of the various Branches of the Perrot Family. By EDW. LOWRY BARNWELL, M.A. Royal 8vo, *fine plates and pedigrees.* 12s

TEXTS from the Holy Bible explained by the Help of the Ancient Monuments. By SAMUEL SHARPE, *author of the History of Egypt, and other works.* Post 8vo, *with 160 drawings on wood, chiefly by* JAS. BONOMI, *curator of Sir John Soane's Museum.* *cloth.* 3s 6d

HAZLITT, HUNT, and LAMB. — A Chronological List of the Works of William Hazlitt and Leigh Hunt; with Notes Descriptive, Critical, and Explanatory, and Select Opinions regarding the Genius and Characteristics of these Writers, by Contemporary Critics and Friends, &c., also Notices of the Writings of Charles Lamb. Edited by ALEX. IRELAND. 8vo, pp. 260, *half morocco, Roxburghe style (only 200 printed).* 10s 6d

THE QUEST of the SANCGREALL, The Sword of Kingship, and other Poems. By THOS. WESTWOOD, author of the "Burden of the Bell," "The Chronicle of the Complete Angler," &c. Post 8vo, *cloth.* 5s

A pleasant and graceful rendering into verse of portions of the well known legend in the *Morte d'Arthur.*—*Chronicle,* Feb. 1st, 1868.

GOSSIP about PORTRAITS, chiefly of Engraved Portraits. By WALTER F. TIFFIN. Crown 8vo, *cloth.* 5s

"A capital little volume."—*Athenæum.* "Full of lively gossip, anecdotes, apt quotations, and a little sly satire."—*Morning Post.* "And very pleasant 'talk' it is. . . . Contains many valuable hints as well as some amusing histories of prints."—*Art Journal.* "A lively little book, suggested by the opening of the National Portrait Exhibition."—*Illustrated London News.* "We heartily commend the work to the notice of the public."—*Salisbury and Winchester Journal.*

A SUPPLEMENT to W. DICKINSON's "Glossary of the Words and Phrases of Cumberland." 12mo. 1s (*Vide page 32*)

THE HAMILTON MANUSCRIPTS: containing some Account of the Settlement of the Territories of the Upper Clandeboye, Great Ardes and Dufferin, in the County of Down. By JAMES HAMILTON, Knight (afterwards created Viscount Claneboye) in the Reigns of James I. and Charles I.; with Memoirs of him, and of his Son and Grandson, James and Henry, the First and Second Earl of Clanbrassil (of the first creation), and of their Families, Connexions, and Descendants. Printed from the Original MSS., and edited by T. K. LOWRY, Esq., LL.D., Q.C., with Appendixes, containing Copies of Grants from the Crown, Inquisitions of Office, Deeds, Wills, and other Original Documents, relating to the foregoing Territories. 4to, *cloth.* £1. 1s

PRINTED BY S. AND J. BRAWN, 13, PRINCES STREET, LITTLE QUEEN STREET, HOLBORN, W. C.